GREENBERG'S® LIONEL® CATALOGUES

Volume II: 1923 - 1932

Edited by Bruce C. Greenberg, Ph.D

LIONEL IS THE REGISTERED TRADEMARK OF THE LIONEL CORPORATION, NEW YORK, NY.
Lionel trains are manufactured by Lionel Trains, Inc., of Mount Clemens, Michigan, the licensee fo the Lionel Corporation.

Copyright © 1989

Greenberg Publishing Company, Inc.
7566 Main Street
Sykesville, MD 21784
(301) 795-7447

First Edition

Manufactured in the United States of America

All rights reserved. Reproduction in any form is strictly prohibited without the express written consent of the publisher, except for excerpts for review purposes.

Greenberg Publishing Company, Inc., offers the world's largest selection of Lionel, American Flyer, LGB, Ives, and other toy train publications as well as a selection of books on model and prototype railroading, dollhouse miniatures, and toys. For a copy of our current catalogue, send a stamped, self-addressed envelope to Greenberg Publishing Company, Inc. at the above address.

Greenberg Shows, Inc. sponsors the world's largest public model railroad, dollhouse, and toy shows. The shows feature extravagant operating model railroads for N, HO, O, Standard, and 1 Gauges as well as a huge marketplace for buying and selling nearly all model railroad equipment. The shows also feature a large selection of dollhouses and dollhouse furnishings. Shows are currently offered in metropolitan Baltimore, Boston, Ft. Lauderdale, Cherry Hill in New Jersey, Long Island in New York, Norfolk, Philadelphia, Pittsburgh, and Tampa. To receive our current show listing, please send a self-addressed stamped envelope marked *Train Show Schedule* to the address above.

ISBN 0-89778-121-X

INTRODUCTION

Lionel is the most important firm in the history of American toy trains. The company began manufacturing toy trains in 1901 and came to dominate the American industry in the late teens or early twenties when annual sales and production surpassed its much older rival, Ives. As the marketplace leader for almost four decades — until the late 1950s — Lionel's mechanical designs as well as its advertising style set the tone for the industry. Under its leadership model railroading became the largest category within the American toy industry, proving to be a captivating American pastime. Today, Lionel Trains, Inc., enjoys significant income from Lionel train manufacture. Fundimensions, a wholly-owned subsidiary of General Mills, was licensed from 1970 through 1986 to produce Lionel trains. Fundimensions successfully revived the line. Then General Mills divested itself of its toy divisions which it called Kenner-Parker, Inc., and Lionel became a subsidiary of Kenner-Parker. Kenner-Parker soon thereafter sold its Lionel division to Richard Kughn, a real-estate developer. Mr. Kughn named his new company Lionel Trains, Inc. Under Mr. Kughn's leadership, Lionel Trains, Inc., has enjoyed the greatest sales achieved by Lionel since 1953. A magnificent line of trains is now available.

Early-on Lionel made significant investments in its catalogues as a sales tool. Until quite recently, the first formal Lionel catalogue was believed to have been published in 1903. A recent happy discovery of a 1902 catalogue has led scholars to believe that 1902 is the initial year of formal catalogue publication. Apparently catalogues were issued annually until 1942. There is some question as to the existence of 1908 and 1907 catalogues. Lionel did not issue catalogues in 1943 or 1944. Since 1945 Lionel has issued new catalogues each year with the exception of 1967.

The earliest catalogues were printed in one color, were small in size and oriented to making sales to the dealer rather than the consumer. Sometimes multiple catalogues were issued. Lionel 1903, for example, was 6.25 inches wide and 3.5 inches high while the 1905 version was 6 inches by 6 inches. In 1910 or 1911 Lionel introduced a wrap-around full color cover in one version of the several catalogues produced at that time. The same color cover is reported to have been used in 1912. In the teens it is believed that Lionel began to issue different consumer and dealer materials.

In the entire toy field, no other area is as well documented by catalogues as that of toy trains. The usual custom for manufacturers of cars, trucks, games and other toys was to produce only dealer (wholesale) catalogues in a limited run. They tended to be single color products which lacked the interest and drama of the model railroad catalogues. And toy train catalogues were produced in large quantities. The Lionel catalogues shown in these books played an important role in reviving interest in Lionel in the late 1960s and early 1970s. Enough catalogues survived from the enormous numbers printed in the 1920s and 1930s so that a generation of adults remembered what they once had wanted and might now obtain. Surviving catalogues were eagerly sought in the late sixties and early seventies. Their appeal led to escalated values — in the $50 and $100 range! (until numerous reproductions made them affordable again).

Toy train companies, and Lionel in particular, made a significant investment in their catalogues. This allocation reflected in part the competitive quality of the industry and the desire of each competitor to gain the market edge. It also reflected the particular nature of the model train hobby. Model trains were more costly, were expected to last longer and were played with in a different manner. To run properly toy trains required additional equipment. They required track and an operating layout. They required a setting to operate in and accessories to give definition to their place in time. It was natural for the youthful builder to build or create a miniature world. Houses, stations, lamps, bells, gates and trucks and cars naturally fit into the developing miniature world. Catalogues provided the builder with a host of "add-ons" to complete his vision. The profit margin for the add-ons — the buildings, operating accessories, track and switches — was substantially higher than that for the basic train sets. Consequently, investing in catalogue advertising to build a secondary sales market was economically sound.

Our book begins in 1923. 1923 was a very important year in Lionel's history. It marked the advent of a new line of Standard Gauge equipment which would replace the well-known earlier electrics: the 42, 38, and 33 locomotives. Two years before, in 1921, Lionel's long time rival, Ives, has switched its larger line of trains from Gauge 1 to Standard Gauge. This change probably provided an incentive to Lionel to innovate. Ives' gauge change had another effect — it increased the market for

Standard Gauge by increasing both the number of buyers for it and the range of goods available. Ives' decision probably benefited both companies.

Lionel's new Standard equipment included an improved motor. It was described in typical Lionel superlatives as the "Super" motor. It was used to power two very rugged and impressive new locos -- the double-motored 402 (which eventually replaced the double-motored 42) and the 380 (which eventually replaced the 38). According to the 1923 catalogue both the 38 and the 42 continued to be available but their updated versions were also offered. The 38 was last offered in 1924. Lionel also offered a new set of large, deluxe passenger cars -- the 418, 419 and 490 to accompany the new 402. It also introduced its "automatic" coupler. Now its catalogue description would tout these new products.

The 1923 catalogue boasts a full color front cover. The 1923 catalogue shows other important innovations. For the first time since the early teens, a full color image graces the front cover. The 1923 image is quite different from the earlier color covers which showed only Lionel trains in long rows. The 1923 image is reminiscent of the 1913 and 1914 small catalogues. These showed a boy and a girl playing on the floor with their Lionel trains in a sparsely furnished setting. In 1923 the artist, Raymond Thayer, created a picturebook bordered living room scene with father in the easy chair and son on the floor with his double-tracked main line with dual crossovers.[2] Father, son and Lionel trains are a recurring theme for Lionel covers.

1923 also initiated the first of the annually changing Lionel front cover images executed by talented artists. These are exciting graphically and effective sales mechanisms. Prior to 1923, cover images were more pedestrian and were reused perfunctorily. For example, the boy with his arms spread wide over his train appeared on the 1917, 1920 and 1922 catalogues. The 1923 rear cover factory image was, however, a carryover from 1922.

[2] Although the catalogue highlighted the new 402 Standard locomotives and matching cars and devoted its centerfolds to these improvements, the front cover showed the older gray 42 with its matching 18, 19 and 190 cars.

In 1924, 1925 and 1926 Lionel continued the 1923 cover theme showing a well-dressed young man (accompanied by his dog) playing with his train on the floor. In 1927, a cover innovation occurs with the first three-quarters view of a locomotive. The new 408 locomotive completely fills the cover. This larger than life locomotive so towers over the viewer that he is in imminent danger of being run over by the train! This image, in spite of its fatal size, captures the wonderfully heady feeling that operators experience as their trains run down the mainline. This powerful image reappears once more in the prewar period when the Hudson locomotive throttles across the 1937 cover. In 1931, 1932 and 1933 Lionel covers show prototype engines and implicitly suggest that Lionel trains are close copies of the real thing. Over the twenty years covered in these two books, one can trace a consistent, romantic and strong image. One catalogue, 1930, does create a different ambiance -- called surrealistic by some and art deco by others.

Returning to our 1923 catalogue we see that although the father and son image reappeared in later Lionel advertising, it was not carried forth in the 1923 text. However Lionel directly appealed to its growing constituency -- the boys of America. The message was fun -- the catalogue starts with the marvelous phrase **"I JUMPED FOR JOY!** That's how a happy youngster expressed his feelings to us in a letter after he had run his Lionel Train" or "Imagine the delight that you will experience by turning the lever of the track switch..." or "What fun! What Excitement!..." At the same time Lionel reminds its readers of the more serious side of life -- training for adulthood. "Think boys, how useful the knowledge will be to you when you grow to manhood..." The educational message, that toys were designed to develop a child's mechanical and analytic ability, is subdued. There is a noticeable focus on the pleasures of the here and now.

One of the great treats for Lionel enthusiasts is to compare the catalogues page by page and year to year. It is fun to see which errors Lionel corrected! It is fascinating to examine Lionel patent dates, both conflicting dates and the presence and absence of dates. Compare page 3 of the 1925 catalogue (headed **"LIONEL ALWAYS LEADS"**) with page 4 of the 1926 catalogue (headed **"Lionel Always Leads."**). In the 1925 copy that we reproduced, the word **"PATENTED"** appears beneath each depicted object without any patent dates. In the 1926 copy that we reproduced, patent dates are found with each object. Why are dates absent in the earlier issue and present in the later one? Furthermore, the die-cast wheel patent date given in the 1925 text is May 17, 1925, while it is March 17, 1925 in the 1926 text! The 1926 picture shows a die-cast wheel patent date of April, 1925. When was the wheel actually patented? Obviously there was a problem. In my archives I found another original Lionel 1925 catalogue with patent dates beneath the items as in the 1926 version.

Which 1925 came first? The one with patent numbers beneath the objects or the one without the patent numbers beneath the inventions. Second, which text is correct - the 1925 or the 1926? Hopefully further research will solve these delightful puzzles.

This discussion raises another point. Lionel often issued several consumer catalogues in one year. 1925 has at least two varieties. Donald Fraley reports that there are two different 1927s, two 1933s, two 1934s, three or four 1935s, five 1936s, five 1937s, three 1938s, two 1939s, three 1940s, two 1941s and two 1942s.[3] Another catalogue expert suggests that even more editions exist.

Lionel catalogues have an unusual significance for the Lionel enthusiast. They record Lionel's production with remarkable fidelity compared to consumer catalogues issued by manufacturers in other toy fields. Because of their importance to enthusiasts, they have been reprinted on a number of other occasions. [4]

[3] **LIONEL TRAINS**: Standard of the World, 1900-1943, pages 144, 146 and 148.

[4] Les Gordon reproduced the Lionel 1929 with a full color front cover and the balance in black and white. Max Knoecklein reproduced the Lionel 1929 in full color. Richard Rex reproduced Lionel 1926 and 1930 in black and white. Greenberg Publishing Company offered inexpensive black and white reproductions of the 1923, 1924, 1925, 1926, 1931, 1932, 1933, 1934, 1935, 1936, 1937, 1938, 1939, 1940, 1941 and 1942 catalogues. Then, it offered better grade black and white reproductions with color front covers for Lionel 1923, 1924, 1925, 1926, 1927, 1928, 1930, 1931, 1932, 1933, 1934, 1935, 1936, 1937, 1938, 1939, 1940, 1941 and 1942. In addition, several people have also offered zerographic-type reproductions of various years at various times.

TECHNICAL NOTES

These two volumes represent an extraordinary publishing effort. The books provide over 900 pages in full color reproducing the entire consumer catalogue record for Lionel's grandest period -- 1923 - 1942. These catalogue books are an enormous investment for a small but devoted readership of 1,000 people. Since these books are unlikely to be reprinted for many years and because they will be intensely studied, a lengthy technical note is provided.

First, the color separations came from four different projects. Lionel 1932, 1933, 1934, 1936, 1937, 1938, 1939, 1940 and 1941 were reproduced in full color in 1975 by Greenberg Publishing Company as separate bound units with wire staples through their centerfolds. The color separations and printing were done by Barton & Cotton of Baltimore who specialize in short run color printing. These catalogues are between 98 and 99% of their original size. Some size shifting was necessary to eliminate the pre-existing original catalogue screen structure and to avoid moire, a very distracting dot pattern. Barton & Cotton achieved this goal by shooting each catalogue slightly out of focus. Also in 1975, Iron Horse Productions, founded by Frank Hare, James Burke and Steve Wolken, published full color reproductions of Lionel 1930, 1931 and 1935 in full color editions. Due to the generosity and unusual cooperation of Frank Hare, who is now sole owner of Iron Horse, the film from the previous printing was made available. Frank Hare is a man who always asks and acts on the question: How may I best serve the interests of my fellow enthusiasts?

In the 1935 reproduction, the printer went to extraordinary efforts to solve technical problems common to reproducing this type of artwork. The traditional camera-based color separation process reproduces with considerable fidelity either the objects or the background screens. Background screens are the color tint backgrounds behind objects. The 1935 background tints did not separate well. Consequently, the printer used new film screen tints of red, yellow and blue to duplicate the original backgrounds. This process required the very carefully outlining of each object which has a screen behind it. This was a very, very expensive process but the product was a delightful reproduction.

Also in 1975 Frank Heeg and Bob Schnitzer formed a partnership known as the House of Heeg to produce Lionel color reproductions. The House of Heeg produced full color reproductions of Lionel years 1923, 1924, 1925, 1926, 1927 and 1928. After initial catalogue sales the House of Heeg sold its remaining inventory and color separations to Greenberg Publishing Company. These separations were used for this book.

However, color separations for two years -- 1929 and 1942 -- were still not available. Consequently after a very thorough study of the marketplace and the new technology, Greenberg Publishing commissioned Progressive Offset, a Baltimore color separation house, to make Lionel 1929 and 1942 color separations. These separations were made by a different method. First, color transparencies of four pages at one time were made. Transparencies were made for two reasons. Most of the new color separation machines with laser computer controlled scanners require transparencies. These scanners appeared in the early 1970s and now completely dominate the production of color separations in trade houses. They provide better separations. Second, the transparencies have another advantage. Since the transparencies reduce the original image from 11 by 8.5 to about 10% of that size, the original dot structure - which caused the moire problem - is eliminated. Yet so much information is retained that the laser scanner can effectively enlarge the image ten times its original size and produce a very clean and handsome separation.

When the decision was made to offer the catalogues in a single book, other questions with important implications arose. Did the catalogues have the same general shape? Fortunately, the entire series followed a horizontal format. Lionel adopted this format in 1915 to better illustrate the very linear quality of the toy trains.[5] The centerfold, in addition, provided a magnificent panoramic space to show off the pride of the line. In 1927, Lionel extended the horizontal format concept by introducing the first three page wide centerfold (and the first in American toy train catalogues). This spread, over 34.5 inches wide, does justice to the elegant 408 set with its four passenger cars. This three page design also shows another innovation - the use of a solid black background to create a very dramatic image. Lionel continued the same image in 1928 (changing only descriptive type). In 1929, the three page centerfold appeared in a more prosaic fashion. In 1930, as business turned down, Lionel probably sought to reduce its printing costs and dropped the elaborate centerfold. We have reproduced these centerfolds as accurately as possible. The six page form adds substantially to printing costs -- as it did to Lionel's over 55 years ago. These six page sections require hand insertion in the binding process as machines could not handle them.

Since it is desirable to have a book with uniform size pages both from aesthetic and cost viewpoints, all pages would have to be large enough for the largest catalogue pages. The largest original pages are 11-3/4 by 8-3/4 inches, so the book was designed with a 12 x 9 inch trim size. However, some original pages are as small as 10 x 7 (1923). The question then is -- how to locate a 10 x 7 image on a 12 x 9 page. The logical choice from an aesthetic viewpoint is to center the image. This creates a large, even white border around the image. However, this choice creates a problem when a train image crosses the center gutter of the page as on the 1923 center spread (pages 24 and 25). Hence exceptions were made for pages where the image crossed the center gutter. These pages were centered top and bottom, but positioned so that the center image continued across the two pages.

Since this book is bound by sewing the pages in place, the holes and discoloration where the original staples were located are visible on some pages. The staples originally covered some of the image.

It seemed historically desirable to retain the original pagination of each catalogue. The location of a train set in the catalogue reflected important merchandising choices.[6] But, if we retained the original pagination, how would readers easily find the particular year for which they were looking. Inserting heavy paper dividers would be too costly and too difficult to

---

[5] Although the horizontal format is effective for presenting trains and does not generally increase printing costs, it does raise substantial binding problems. Only a few American binderies regularly handle oblong books.

[6] Until 1935, Lionel reserved the centerfold for its most important set. In 1935, Lionel located its most important sets, the Blue Comet, on page 20, and the Hiawatha sets, on page 16, in a 44 page catalogue.

bind. Our solution was to add the catalogue year to every other page. Hence, if you open the book to page 32 of the 1927 catalogue, you can turn forward or backward to find the specific page of the specific year of interest.

Lionel generally did not put the year of issue on the catalogue's front cover. For some years the copyright indicia and the year of issue are found on the rear cover. In the later years, the copyright notice and year of publication are often found on pages two or three. When we reprinted the Lionel 1932-34 and 1936-41 catalogues in 1975, we thought it helpful to add the date of issue to the front covers. Therefore, the dates appearing on these covers were added in 1975. The issue years appearing on the front covers of 1928 and 1929 were part of the original artwork.

The original catalogues chronicle the development of printing technology. For example, the 1927 and 1928 six-page centerfolds are noteworthy, not only for their dramatic black color backgrounds, but for the printing technology and quality control necessary to produce a large solid black area accompanied by sharp and clear details. The clay-coated printing paper used in these books (both in the originals and in our reproductions) is a semi-absorbent material. Images retain their sharpness and clarity because most of the ink sits on top of the paper fibers, and the small dots composing the images retain their shape. When you use heavy ink coverage to produce solid color backgrounds, the amount of ink absorbed substantially increases. Paper fibers absorbing the ink's moisture expand. With heavy ink coverage paper tends to wrinkle and press jams occur much more frequently. This increase in technical difficulties is well known by printers. Printers, then and now, charge a premium for heavy ink coverage because of the printing problems that it creates. Obviously, by 1927, technical improvements permitted the extraordinary ink coverage for the first time.

When I reviewed the catalogue film for this project, I discovered that the tape used to precisely hold the film in position had deteriorated. It had oozed and become a sticky mess. It took over 100 hours for two careful staff members to remove the old tape and its residue. Than each piece of film was repositioned since the original positioning could not be used for this volume. The original page layout was designed for a stapled catalogue and would not bind properly in our smythe sewn volumes. Since only three or four pages of color separations can be positioned in an hour, several hundred additional hours of highly skilled staff time were required.

The original pagination for the stapled 1923 catalogue, for example, is believed to have been organized as follows: page 1 through 8 were printed together with pages 41 through 48, pages 9-16 with 33-40 and pages 17-24 with 25-32. When these three units, called signatures, were asembled in 1923, they were first folded down. Then the third signature, pages 17-24/25-32, was placed inside the second signature, pages 9-16/33-40. Then the first signature, pages 1-8/41-48, was wrapped around the other two. Finally the three signatures were stapled together. This is the method for producing a stapled (or saddle wired book). However, to assemble a 480 page book using 48 catalogues as the assembly unit would be very uneconomical and very awkward. A bound book composed of 48 page units sewn together would not wear well and would be extraordinarily expensive. Rather, the usual and preferred method for so hefty a volume is to use 16 page units and to stack each unit, one on top of the other, and to sew them together as stacked with the thread going through the centerfold of each unit. Therefore in this book, pages 1-16 were printed together; then pages 17-32, 33-48, 49-64, etc. However, this means that the page relationships for the printing of the 1923 catalogue (and all others) are different from their original printing locations although the differences are not apparent to the user! Pages 1 and 16 and 2 and 15 were positioned together and printed at the same time while in the original catalogue pages 1 and 48 and 2 and 47 were, we believe, printed together! Hence, the first signature of 1923 is composed of pages 1-16 for this volume compared to 1-8/41-48 for the original catalogue.

Bruce C. Greenberg
August 24, 1982

TABLE OF CONTENTS

YEAR   **PAGES**

Lionel 1923 1-48

Lionel 1924 1-44

Lionel 1925 1-44

Lionel 1926 1-48

Lionel 1927 1-46

Lionel 1928 1-46

Lionel's Miniature Catalogues

Lionel 1929 1-46

Lionel 1930 1-48

Lionel 1931 1-52

Lionel 1932 1-52

"I Jumped for Joy"—

"I JUMPED FOR JOY'" That's how a happy youngster expressed his feelings to us in a letter after he had run his Lionel Train. Unbounded joy! That's what every boy experiences when operating a Lionel Outfit, and there are three million such happy boys; even in the farthermost corners of the world.

Just think! You can have a great railroad system in miniature under your control. You can be President, Engineer or Conductor. Dad will have lots of fun too. You can make him your assistant and bring him back to his boyhood days, although he did not have such wonderful toys to play with. Think of the days and days of fun you will have with a Lionel Train, starting and stopping it with a touch of your finger, running it at high speed, slowing it down to a crawling pace, or reversing it by just moving the controller handle.

Imagine the delight you will experience by turning the lever of the track switch, just the same as a railroad switchman does, and instantly you can run your train on to a siding to clear the track for the oncoming express. See the glaring headlight of the Lionel Limited as it comes dashing along the cleared track with its illuminated Pullman cars. Now it stops at the brilliantly lighted station. The conductor shouts, "ALL ABOARD!"—a touch of your finger on the current lever and the express is again on its way.

A grade crossing is seen in the distance. As the train approaches, the electric bell on the warning signal rings and continues to ring until the train has passed. The automatic electric crossing gates go down and remain in that position until the track is clear once more; then, up they go and traffic may cross the track.

What fun! What excitement! Your train swings around the curve and now dashes through the tunnel and out to the brightly shining signal lights along the track. Over the bridge now and down the straightaway!

Can you imagine anything more thrilling? And it is all possible with a Lionel Train and Lionel Railroad Equipment. Day after day all through the year, indoors and out, the fun will continue. New thrills will be yours by adding Lionel Accessories from time to time.

All the most up-to-date equipment, exact models of the kind that all the big railroads use, is included in the marvelous Lionel Line.

Then again, what science is more fascinating than electricity and its principles? Think boys, how useful the knowledge will be to you when you grow to manhood, the electrical and mechanical knowledge that you will gain while playing with your Lionel Outfit; the problems in transportation that you will be able to solve and the many other advantages you will have when you are ready to fight life's battle.

Only Lionel motors will stand up day after day and run with perfect ease, pulling many Pullman or freight cars around the curves and over inclines. No other trains compare with Lionel in construction, appearance, finish or durability. No other trains will provide the joy and excitement obtainable from a Lionel layout.

Boys! It's great to be able to get so much fun and knowledge for so little cost.

If Dad bought an automobile he would look at the motor first, to make sure that this vital part was all

Writes one happy boy

"STANDARD OF THE WORLD" SINCE NINETEEN HUNDRED

that it should be, to be certain that it would stand the severe usage to which it would be put. In just the same way the motors of all Lionel Locomotives are built to last and withstand even a greater strain in proportion to their size than Dad's automobile.

On the following pages we describe as fully as space will permit, the perfection of every part that enters into a Lionel Train. Read the descriptive matter, boys, and you will surely realize that Lionel Trains are built with the same care and precision as the large railroad trains which traverse the continent.

We have given much time and thought to the compilation of this beautiful book, so that you can select your Lionel Outfit, "Multivolt" Transformer and Accessories in as simple a way as possible. And please remember that Lionel products are lower priced, notwithstanding their very high quality, than any cheap grade of electric toy that may be offered to you as a substitute.

There can be no substitute for Lionel products. Go to your dealer and ask him to demonstrate a Lionel Train for you. See how easily and smoothly it runs. Examine the motor, the cars and the track. See how wonderfully well each part is made. See the infinite detail that makes every part of the equipment look as massive and realistic as the big real electric trains.

Then, insist on Lionel. Don't be satisfied with anything else. If your dealer cannot supply you please write to us, telling us of your requirements and we will see that you get what you want right from our big factory.

THE LIONEL CORPORATION

48-52 East 21st Street   New York, N. Y.

We reproduce above the beautiful and substantial box in which all Lionel outfits are packed. It is made of solid corrugated board which acts as a cushion around every part of the outfit so that the beautiful finish of the cars cannot be scratched or marred. Little nests in the box protect the locomotive, track and each car. You receive it in the same beautiful condition as it leaves the factory.

Say "LIONEL" to Your Dealer
Don't be satisfied with any other make

OPERATE YOUR LIONEL TRAIN ON ANY CURRENT

Lionel Trains can be operated on the house lighting circuit with a "Multivolt" Transformer for alternating current or a Lionel Direct Current Reducer for direct current; or from dry cells or storage batteries.

Lionel Electric Toy Trains

The Reasons for

Fig. 1—How some cars of other makes are made—in three or more pieces, rickety, put together very insecurely with little fingers that soon bend or break (see text matter).

LEADERSHIP in an industry is attained by specialization and continual effort in one direction for a number of years, and in making the product better in every way than anything similar.

For nearly twenty-five years we have devoted our entire resources and unsurpassed facilities to the manufacture of electric trains, "Multivolt" transformers and miniature railroad accessories.

Our leadership has been justly attained. Millions of Lionel Trains are in use, many of them for ten years or more.

It would take a good sized volume to print the many thousands of commendatory letters we have received since the establishment of this Corporation. Fathers have turned over to their children the outfits they used in their boyhood days, which is evidence of the long-lasting qualities of Lionel products.

An electric train is only as good as its motor. It must be electrically and mechanically perfect. If the working parts will not stand up under the severe strain they are put to, the rest of the outfit is worthless. Lionel products are sold under a broader guarantee than any similar toy in the world. If they show defects in material or construction they are replaced without charge and without question.

It is with pride that we give on these pages some of the details of manufacture, not only to show the superior and up-to-date machinery we use, but also to make clear that only the highest grade material and the most skilled work people produce the numerous items that go to make up the Lionel Line. On the next pages we show the working parts of the various types of locomotives we make.

We will now take you on a brief trip through the Lionel factory to show the most interesting processes of production of precise and important parts.

Figure No. 1 shows the ordinary lithographed car held together with easily breakable metal fingers which the public was compelled to accept before we introduced our substantial method of construction.

The superiority of Lionel cars will at once become apparent when the reader looks at Figure No. 2, which shows a "blank" of a Lionel car body made from ONE PIECE of metal.

In Figure No. 3 the next process is shown, the forming of the car body from the "blank". It will be seen that the ends of the car are open, and in Figure No. 4 the completed car body is shown with the ends soldered firmly in place, eliminating the use of fingers and making the car practically indestructible.

No lithographed metal enters into the construction of any part of Lionel trains. Our exclusive enameling and baking process, used on our entire line, is infinitely more durable and lasting than the cheaper method employed by any other manufacturer.

Figure No. 5 shows the department where the enamel is sprayed on by the most modern methods. This insures an even, highly finished surface inside and out.

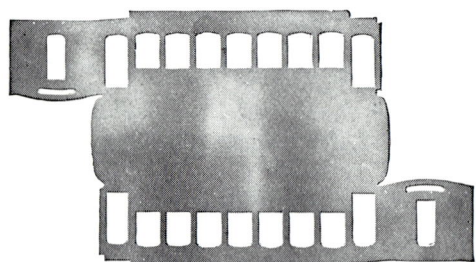

Fig. 2—Car body cut with one steel die.

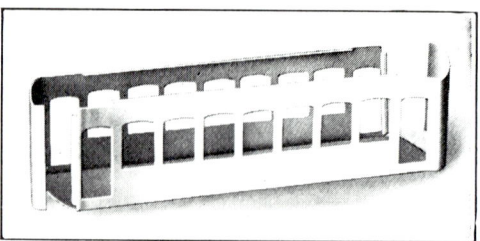

Fig. 3—Car body formed from blank in Fig. 2. Floor, sides, ends all one piece—ready to be soldered in two places—at the ends.

Then the cars and locomotive bodies are arranged on trays (See Figure No. 6) and placed in large steel ovens. These ovens are heated to a temperature of 300 degrees and the finish is baked on them for several hours. This gives a permanent lasting finish, the same as on the most expensive automobiles. You can always keep your Lionel equipment bright and new-looking by simply rubbing the surface with a cloth.

Now we will show you why Lionel Track is better. We use heavier metal and pay particular attention to the insulation to eliminate every possibility of short-circuit. Specially designed machines constructed in our own factory, turn out millions of sections a year. Our method is scientific and is patented. One reason for the strength of Lionel Track is seen in Figure No. 8. You will note that the rails are flanged outward at the base

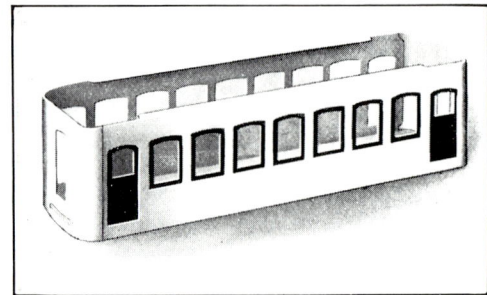

Fig. 4—Car body same as Fig. 3 with corners soldered and window frames in position.

4

LIONEL Leadership

MILLIONS OF HAPPY USERS THE WORLD OVER

Fig. 5—Spraying Enamels—Here the beautifully colored enamels are sprayed on the steel bodies to give them their permanent polished colors.

Fig. 6—Baking Ovens—Here the enamels are baked on at high temperature after spraying. The ovens are heated by electricity.

Fig. 9—Nickel Plating Dept.—Electricity flows through the nickel solution in the vats and puts a plating of nickel on many pieces, like wheels, headlights and various other parts.

instead of being turned in, the same as inferior makes of track shown in the illustration. This outward flange makes Lionel Track so rigid that it will support the weight of a full-grown man. In Figure No. 7 we show you how our track will support a suspended weight of 110 pounds against 20 pounds for the other makes of track. This was an actual test made before experts.

Fig. 8—Why Rails Are So Rigid—The base of Lionel track is flanged to a $\frac{5}{16}$-inch base with turned-over edges, instead of having a $\frac{1}{8}$-inch base as in other tracks.

Now we come to the motor—the very heart of an electric train. The length of time that an Electric Train Outfit can be used depends upon the efficiency and construction of the motor.

In Figure 10 we show you a corner of our Armature and Field Winding Departments. The battery of automatic winding machines that we use insures the correct windings which give so much power to Lionel Motors and makes them last so long. On the following pages you will see the complete descriptions of the various types of motors we manufacture.

Wherever it is possible to enhance the appearance of Lionel products we do so by nickel plating many of the parts. Figure No. 9 shows the vast department of our factory devoted to this process. Nickel plating enables you to keep the wheels, headlights, hand rails, steps and many other parts of your equipment, bright and shining for the life of the outfit.

It would take considerable space to illustrate and describe the many other wonderful departments in our big factory, which covers four acres of floor space. Hundreds of skilled men and women are employed, who work with a heartfelt interest, which is reflected by the high quality of Lionel products and which has made them

"STANDARD OF THE WORLD" SINCE 1900

Fig. 7—Other track cannot support a weight of 20 lbs. Lionel track supports 100 pounds or more.

Fig. 10—Motor Winding—This is just one corner of the motor winding department. Some wonderfully designed machines are used here.

 "O" Gauge Motor—Description of Working Parts

THE same great care in construction is used in all Lionel motors. The "O" gauge motors described on this page are constructed on new and scientific principles, unlike any toy motor on the market. The efficiency of Lionel motors has been amply demonstrated since 1900 when we first introduced them. They will haul a greater number of cars in proportion to their sizes, than any other motor now made. You will readily see the reasons when you read the following:

Driving Gears ("A" and "B")—Are made of heavy steel blanks accurately cut. They mesh without friction. These are radically different from gears with punched teeth generally used on toys.

Frame and Cowcatcher ("C")—Are made of heavy steel punchings, not cast iron. They will not break when roughly treated.

Third Rail Shoe Support ("D")—Is made of heavy fibre that supports the third rail contact rollers. The peculiar construction of the roller supports protects them from injury, for the brackets can be forced against the fibre without disturbing the arc of the spring that gives them the correct tension against the third rail. When released they will come right back to the proper position.

Wheels ("E")—These are made of die castings with a steel jacket forced over the rim. The die casting represents a perfect mechanical wheel and the steel rim is used to insure longer wear, as it is tougher than the material of which the wheel is made.

Collecting Shoes ("F")—These revolving shoes which collect the current from the third rail are made of solid brass turnings and revolve on steel shafts which pass through a phosphor-bronze support, insuring perfect contact with the third rail at all times, so that the outfits will run at a uniform speed and not work with a start and jump as is usually the case with locomotives that do not collect a continuous supply of current from the third rail.

Journals ("G")—These journals and steps are embossed on the sides of the frame at the ends of the shafts and add materially to the appearance of the structure.

Couplers ("H")—These are made of heavy steel, nickeled and polished. They are scientifically constructed so that cars do not become detached when in motion, but are easily taken apart when desired.

Brushes and Brush Holders ("J")—The brush holders to which the brushes are attached can easily be removed so that the brush may be changed when necessary in a few seconds. The brushes are made of phosphor-bronze gauze and will run for hundreds of hours if commutator is kept clean.

Commutator ("K")—The commutator is constructed of three bronze sections with insulation between them. It is perfectly turned when fastened on the shaft so that it is absolutely parallel with the brushes and the polished surface reduces friction to a minimum.

Side Plates ("L")—These are made of heavy steel and support all working parts. The alignment of the holes is absolutely perfect so that gears and motor work without friction. All holes are drilled and reamed to proper diameter. The accuracy of these plates compares with the framework of a very fine watch or clock.

Motor with Frame Attachment ("M")—Only four screws are required to support the frame to the motor.

We are the pioneers in this simple method of construction. We introduced it in 1913.

Support of Body to Frame ("N")—The simple construction of the entire motor is apparent by the method of holding the body to the frame. The letter ("N") shows a piece of the steel frame thrown up at right angles containing threaded screw hole. The hole in the body corresponds with the opening in the frame and both pieces are held together with two machine screws. These are easily removed so that working parts may be instantly released.

Transmission Cables—We use a heavy gauge copper wire with extra heavy rubber insulation so that short-circuits against the metal parts are impossible.

Field—This field is made of a number of pieces of specially prepared transformer steel. These sheets are known as laminations and produce a very much stronger field than if a single piece were used.

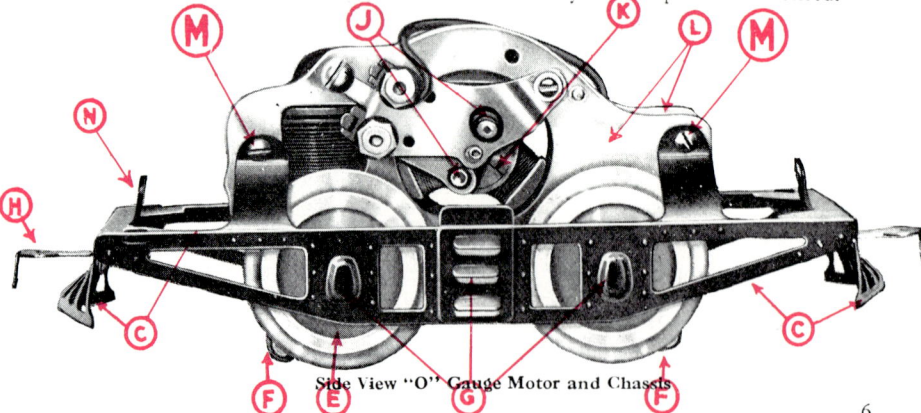
Side View "O" Gauge Motor and Chassis

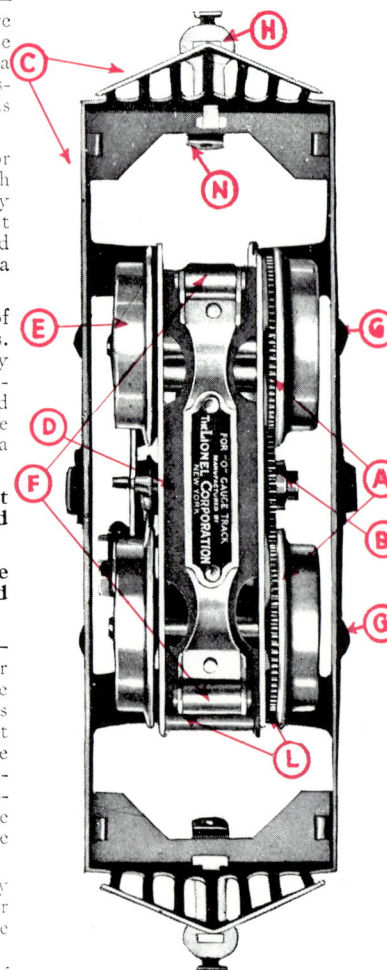
Bottom View "O" Gauge Motor and Chassis

"Standard" Gauge "Single Motors"—Description of Working Parts

STANDARD OF THE WORLD SINCE NINETEEN HUNDRED

"STANDARD" GAUGE MOTORS! What a world of meaning these words have when applied to Lionel Motors made for 2¼" gauge track. When you read the following and see how precisely and accurately these "Standard" Gauge Motors are constructed their great popularity is not to be wondered at. Many refinements incorporated in Lionel "Standard" Gauge Motors cannot be found in any other make. The bearings are reinforced; axles are made of drill rod instead of soft wire, and nuts and bolts are used instead of rivets, so that they can be replaced if necessary.

Field (1)—Made of best quality electrical steel, laminated throughout, and contains the winding properly insulated (2).

Brush Holders (3 and 4)—Made of brass, with detachable tops, so that brushes may be easily reached. Contains brass compression spring (5), which feeds brush up to the commutator. This construction prevents sparking of the brushes and prolongs the life of the commutator.

Brushes, Self-Lubricating (6)—Require no lubricating. A little cleaning of the commutator once in a while is all that is necessary. One brush is made of phosphor bronze—one of amorphous carbon. Each is made exactly true in diameter and will slip easily into the tube brush holders. They will outlast dozens of the commoner kinds.

Reversing Controller (7)—On all "Standard" gauge locomotives. Unique in construction. On its face appear two flat brass contacts on which the four spring connections slide. The tension of these brass springs against the brass cap insures perfect contact while controller is being reversed. These springs, while insuring good electrical contact, work with so little friction that controller may be easily reversed with a touch of the finger.

Armature (8)—Made of electrical steel punchings mounted on drill rod shaft, and has fibre heads. Automatically drum-wound with proper size and amount of triple covered silk magnet wire (9), then dipped in shellac and baked, so that none of the coils become loose.

The Third Rail Shoe (10)—Which collects the current from the center insulated rail, is a steel punching with spring arrangement regulating the pressure on the rail. It is case hardened so that the friction against the third rail does not wear it through.

See description of Lionel "Twin-Motor" Locomotives on page 8

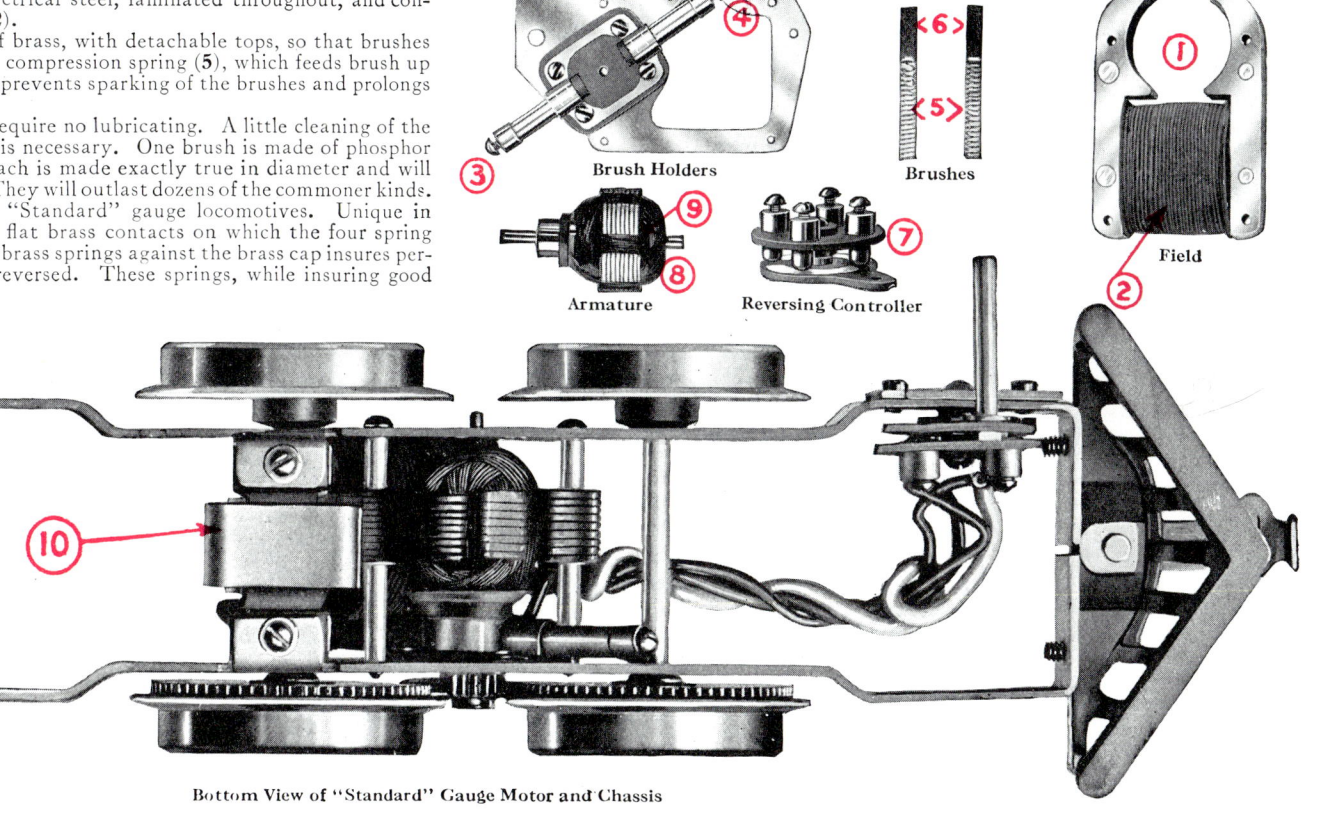

Bottom View of "Standard" Gauge Motor and Chassis

7

1923

"Standard" Gauge "Twin Motors"—Description of Working Parts

LIONEL "Twin Motor"
Locomotives will haul 20 large cars with perfect ease

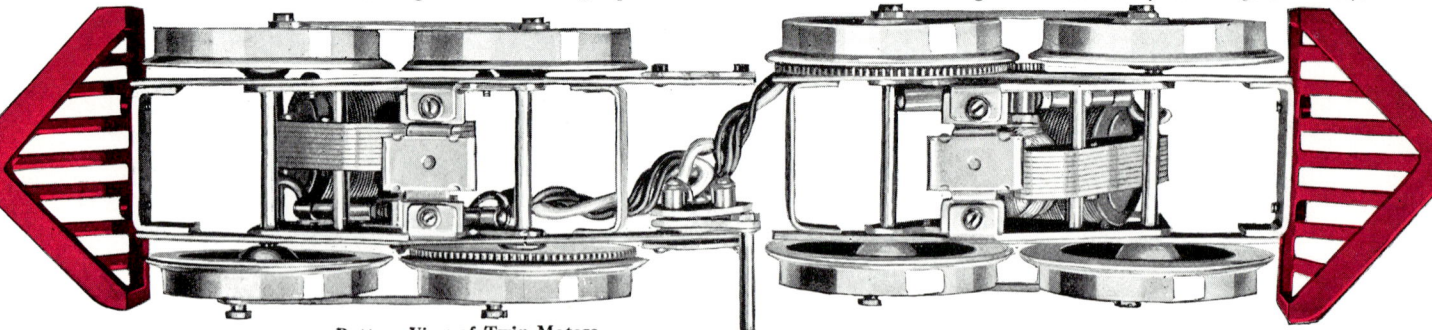

Bottom View of Twin-Motors

ON page 7 we show the working parts of our single motor locomotives for "Standard" Gauge Track. Lionel "Twin-Motors" embody the same structural features and the same materials are used in their manufacture. However, greater hauling power is obtained by doubling up these motors and making them operate in unison, yet with little extra current consumption. The power of Lionel Motors *alone* provides the traction. We do not have to resort to the unmechanical method of adding a lot of useless weight to the body of the locomotive, which soon wears down the bearings by the unnecessary strain to which the motor is subjected. Lionel Locomotives are not top-heavy. The weight is in the motors—close to the track where it belongs, according to scientific construction. They will not derail even when taking the curves at high speed.

Electrical engineers have favored the "Twin-Motor" when designing and building the great commercial electric locomotives used on many electrified railroads in this country. They have found that these locomotives have greater hauling and tractive power when equipped with two motors.

Lionel "Twin-Motor" locomotives will pull 20 of our largest freight cars or a dozen of our largest passenger cars with perfect ease around a track 12 feet in diameter.

Our single motor locomotives have greater hauling power than any other make and will haul a greater number of cars than we supply with our outfits. This statement has been proven innumerable times by the testing laboratories which have been commissioned to make tests for us.

UNIVERSAL CURRENT CONTROLLER
(Patent Applied For)

A unique device is affixed to these "Twin-Motors" so that by simply moving a lever the windings of the motors are changed to series (which is the best winding when they are operated on the reduced direct current) or to multiple (which is the best connection when operated on reduced alternating current or on dry or storage batteries).

The outfits listed below, illustrated and described on the following pages, contain Lionel "Twin-Motor" Locomotives.

Outfit No. 42
Outfit No. 54
Outfit No. 44
Outfit No. 420
Outfit No. 421
Outfit No. 422
Outfit No. 423
Outfit No. 424

The New "Super-Motor" ("Standard" Gauge)—Description of Working Parts

MILLIONS OF HAPPY USERS THE WORLD OVER

THE "SUPER-MOTOR" is so vastly superior in efficiency and design to any motor ever before offered to the public that, notwithstanding the enviable reputation we have enjoyed for more than a generation for leadership in miniature motor construction, the "Super-Motor" is supremely the finest piece of equipment our factories have ever produced.

to obtain tractive power. This unnecessary weight rapidly wears down all working parts and causes the locomotive to jump the track.

In every way we have designed these "Superior-Motors" not only to develop great power and consume a minimum amount of current, but to make it possible to operate our trains continuously for an indefinite period without the necessity of replacing any parts.

Turn to pages 24 and 25 and see Outfit No. 403, the finest train ever produced. It contains the LIONEL "SUPER-TWIN-MOTOR" Locomotive.

Minimum Current Consumption—The Lionel "Super-Motor" is not only more powerful than any motor of its size, but it consumes less than half the current of any motor developing the same power.

Re-enforced Bearings—The side plates which contain the motor are made of very heavy steel and are accurately aligned so that friction is almost entirely eliminated. All bearings are re-enforced with heavy bushings which add to the life of the motor.

Field and Armature—These parts are made of the best grade of laminated steel and are of the most improved design.

Brushes—The brushes are made of self-lubricating bronze and graphite, which insure long life to the motor.

Commutator—The commutator is made of heavy bronze, and segments are perfectly insulated.

Removable Brush-holder—This is one of the most unique features of the Lionel "Super-Motor". By simply unscrewing one screw the entire brush-holder can be removed from the motor. Change of brushes requires but an instant and the assembled part is replaced without the use of any tools. While this feature is very desirable, we are pleased to state that the user will not find it necessary to perform this operation until after the motor has been in use for a long time.

Gears—The gears used in this motor are substantially made of steel and brass. They mesh accurately and are absolutely noiseless.

Driving Wheels—Particular attention is directed to the driving wheels, which are massive in construction and are 2⅜ inches in diameter They are accurately lathe-turned. Their weight adds great tractive power to the motors. All driving wheels are directly geared to the motor, eliminating the use of connecting rods between the wheels, which insures better alignment with less friction.

Tractive Power—The tractive power of these motors is remarkable. They will haul from 12 to 20 of our largest size freight or Pullman cars with the greatest ease. The weight of the wheels and motor are close to the track, insuring low center of gravity, with the result that the locomotive is not top-heavy and slippage of the wheels is therefore unknown. This construction is infinitely superior to the method of loading down the superstructure with useless weight so as

Lionel "Super-Motor" Showing Removable Brush Plate

9

1923

Lionel Electric Toy Trains

Locomotives Only for "O" Gauge Track—1⅜ Inches Wide

OUR first thought is to give you Lionel quality even in our low priced "O" gauge locomotives. We believe they are the greatest values ever offered.

Look at the detail! Bodies are made of sheet steel and finished in a variety of durable enamels. The hand rails, bells, headlights and couplers are highly polished nickeled steel—gold lettering and decorations—heavy die-cast wheels with nickeled steel overtread, producing a steady even motion without friction. The frames, journals and cowcatchers are just like those on the big powerful electric engines.

Locomotive No. 158

Locomotive No. 158—6 inches long, 3 inches high and 2½ inches wide. Has four wheels and nickeled dummy headlight. For use with Pullman Car No. 600 or Freight Cars Nos. 800, 801, 802, 803, 804 and 901.

Code Word "GOTHAM"
Price *$4.25, †$5.00

Locomotive No. 150—6 inches long, 3 inches high, and 2½ inches wide. Has four wheels and electric headlight. For use with Pullman Cars Nos. 600, 603 and 604, or Freight Cars Nos. 800, 801, 802, 803, 804 and 901.

Code Word "GARLAND"
Price *$5.00, †$6.00

Locomotive No. 150

Locomotive No. 156

Locomotive No. 156—With electric headlight. Has twelve wheels and **reversing controller** 10 inches long, 4 inches high, and 3 inches wide. For use with Pullman Car No. 610, Observation Car No. 612, or Freight Cars Nos. 820 and 822.

Code Word "GRAMAN"
Price *$14.25, †$17.00

Locomotive No. 156X—Similar in every respect to No. 156 mentioned above, but without front and rear pilot trucks.

Code Word "GINGER"
Price *$12.95, $15.50

Locomotive No. 152

Locomotive No. 152—Has four wheels and electric headlight; 7 inches long, 3½ inches high, and 2½ inches wide. For use with Pullman Cars Nos. 601 and 603, Mail Car No. 602, Observation Car No. 604, and Freight Cars Nos. 820 and 822.

Code Word "GRAMERCY"
Price *$7.25, †$8.50

Locomotive No. 154—Has four wheels, electric headlight and **reversing controller**, 8 inches long, 3½ inches high, 2½ inches wide, as this locomotive will back up and go ahead just as you want it to. Use same cars as for No. 152.

Code Word "GARTER"
Price *$11.00, †$13.00

Locomotive No. 154

See pages 29 and 31 for the Correct Cars to use with these Locomotives

*Price, East of Missouri River. †Price, West of Missouri River.

Train Outfits for "O" Gauge Track—1⅜ Inches Wide

STANDARD OF THE WORLD SINCE NINETEEN HUNDRED

BOYS! Even if you can not buy one of the larger Lionel outfits, you can be sure of getting the very best value for your money if you buy one of the low-priced Lionel Trains listed on this page.

OUTFIT NO. 159

Outfit No. 157—Comprises one No. 158 Locomotive (with dummy headlight), two No. 600 Pullman Cars, eight sections of OC track (one with electrical connections), making a circle 30 inches in diameter. Train is 20 inches long. This is a good, low-priced passenger train.
Code Word "MODERN"   Price *$6.75, †$8.00

Outfit No. 159—Comprises one No. 158 Locomotive (with dummy headlight), eight sections of OC track (one with electrical connections), which make a circle 30 inches diameter, also two No. 901 Single Truck Gondola Cars. Train is 20 inches long. This is a well-constructed yet low-priced outfit.
Code Word "GOODLY"   Price *$5.75, †$7.00

Lionel "Multivolt" Transformers will run these trains better and more economically than by any other method. See pp. 32 and 33.

OUTFIT NO. 157

OUTFIT NO. 160

Outfit No. 160—Comprises one No. 150 Locomotive with electric headlight, two No. 600 Pullman Cars, eight sections OC curved track (one with electrical connections) and two sections OS straight track, making oval 39 x 30 inches, and one No. 88 Controlling Rheostat. Length of complete train 20 inches. The extra track provided with this outfit, and the addition of the controlling rheostat makes this outfit preferable to the two listed above.
Code Word "GRATER"   Price *$8.50, †$10.00

*Price, East of Missouri River.   †Price, West of Missouri River.

Train Outfits for "O" Gauge Track—1 3/8 Inches Wide

WHY is it possible to run Lionel trains around curves at such high speed? Because all the trucks are constructed on the Lionel patented flexible principle. All the trains shown throughout this book embody this feature. Lionel was first to introduce it.

OUTFIT NO. 155

OUTFIT NO. 162

Outfit No. 155—Comprises one No. 150 Locomotive with electric headlight, one No. 603 Pullman Car, one No. 604 Observation Car, eight sections of OC curved track (one with electrical connections), four sections of OS straight track, making an oval 49 x 30 inches. Also includes No. 88 Controlling Rheostat. Length of complete train 22 inches. Good value in this outfit. It means hours of genuine enjoyment for the boys who get it.
Code Word "PERFECT" **Price *$10.50, †$12.50**

OUTFIT NO. 164

Outfit No. 162—Comprises one No. 152 Locomotive with electric headlight, one No. 601 Pullman Car, one No. 602 Mail Car, one No. 88 Controlling Rheostat, eight sections OC curved track (one with electrical connections), and four sections OS straight track, making an oval 49 x 30 inches. Length of complete train 23 inches.
Code Word "SAMPSON"
Price *$12.95, †$15.50

Outfit No. 164—Comprises one No. 154 Reversing Locomotive with electric headlight, one No. 602 Mail Car, two No. 601 Pullman Cars, eight sections OC curved track (one with electrical connections), six sections OS straight track, making an oval 59 x 30 inches. Included is one No. 88 Controlling Rheostat. Complete length of train 31½ inches.
Code Word "SAUL" **Price *$16.75, †$19.90**

*Price, East of Missouri River. †Price, West of Missouri River.

Train Outfit for "O" Gauge Track—1⅜ Inches Wide

MILLIONS OF HAPPY USERS THE WORLD OVER

HERE you see the largest locomotives and cars made to operate on "O" gauge track. Piece for piece, the outfits shown on this page represent the greatest values in the world. Read all about the wonderful detail incorporated in these realistic trains.

OUTFIT NO 169

Outfit No. 169—Comprises one No. 156X Four-Wheel Reversible Locomotive with electric headlight, one No. 610 Pullman Car, one No. 612 Observation Car, eight sections OC curved track (one with electrical connections), four sections OS straight track, making an oval 49 x 30 inches. One No. 88 Controlling Rheostat is included. Length of complete train is 29 inches. This is a new outfit and it embodies the largest equipment we make for "O" gauge track.
Code Word "VALUE"
Price *$18.00, †$21.50

Boys! When you have selected your Lionel Train, begin to plan your complete railroad. See the many wonderful accessories you can add—Switches, Crossings, Electric Lamp Posts, Block Signals, Automatic Crossing Gates, Stations, Tunnels and a host of other realistic devices.

OUTFIT NO. 166

Outfit No. 166 De Luxe—The locomotive has 12 wheels, electric headlight, and is reversible. Attention is directed to the detail embodied in the cars included with this outfit. The die work, ornamental windows, interior seats, removable roof and lettering of the cars are especially attractive. Comprises one No. 156 Locomotive, two No. 610 Pullman Cars, one No. 612 Observation Car, eight sections OC curved track (one with electrical connections), six sections OS straight track, making an oval 30 inches wide and 59 inches long. Included is one No. 88 Controlling Rheostat. Length of train 37½ inches.   Code Word "COOKS"   Price *$22.25, †$26.50

*Price, East of Missouri River.   †Price, West of Missouri River

Lionel Electric Toy Trains

Train Outfits for "O" Gauge Track—1⅜ Inches Wide

FREIGHT trains are just as important to a railroad as passenger trains. No toy freight trains are as real looking as Lionel. The heralds of prominent railroads are reproduced on all the freight cars.

You will find all the suitable passenger cars for use with these trains, listed elsewhere in the catalogue. Great fun, boys, to make your train into a passenger or freighter by buying additional cars.

And you can be sure that the powerful Lionel locomotives will pull 'em all!

OUTFIT NO. 161

Outfit No. 163—Comprises one No. 152 Locomotive with electric headlight, one No. 820 Box Car, one No. 822 Caboose, eight sections OC curved track (one with electrical connections), four sections OS straight track, making an oval 49 x 30 inches, and one No. 88 Controlling Rheostat. Length of train 23 inches.

Code Word "HYLAND"   Price *$12.95, †$15.50

Outfit No. 161—Comprises one No. 150 Locomotive with electric headlight, one No. 800 Box Car, one No. 801 Caboose, one No. 88 Controlling Rheostat, eight sections OC curved track (one with electrical connections), and two sections OS straight track, making an oval 30 x 39 inches. The freight cars in this outfit are most realistic. Length of train 20 inches.

Code Word "HYACINTH"
Price *$8.50, †$10.00

OUTFIT NO. 163

Outfit No. 165—Comprises one No. 154 Reversing Locomotive with electric headlight, two No. 820 Box Cars, one No. 822 Caboose, eight sections OC curved track (one with electrical connections), six sections OS straight track, making an oval 30 inches wide and 59 inches long. Has one No. 88 Controlling Rheostat. Length of train 31½ inches.

Code Word "ISABEL"
Price *$16.75, †$19.90

OUTFIT NO. 165

Add to Your Track Layout, Boys! See pages 46 and 47 for a Big Variety of Track Figures which You Can Make with Straight and Curved Sections, Switches and Crossings.

*Price, East of Missouri River   †Price, West of Missouri River.

Complete Railroad Outfits for "O" Gauge Track—1⅜ Inches Wide

STANDARD OF THE WORLD SINCE NINETEEN HUNDRED

MANY boys prefer to buy a complete railroad right from the start, so we have planned the outfits shown on this and the next page. In addition to the train and track you get accessories, such as semaphores, warning signals, bridges and telegraph posts—all packed in one large attractive box.

It is remarkable how little these complete Lionel railroads cost, considering the high quality of the equipment supplied.

OUTFIT NO. 172

OUTFIT NO. 173

Outfit No. 172—This is a new outfit that we have just introduced to fill the demand for a complete railroad at very moderate cost. It comprises one No. 150 Locomotive with electric headlight, three No. 600 Pullman Cars, eight sections OC curved track (one with electrical connections), four sections OS straight track, forming an oval 30 x 49 inches. Included also are one No. 88 Controlling Rheostat, one No. 68 Warning Sign, one No. 62 Semaphore and one No. 118 Metal Tunnel.
    Code Word "QUINCY"   Price *$12.50, †$15.00

Outfit No. 173—Here is another moderate priced complete electric railroad. It comprises one No. 150 Locomotive with electric headlight, two No. 603 Pullman Cars, one No. 604 Observation Car, eight sections OC curved track (one with electrical connections), six sections OS straight track, forming an oval 30 x 59 inches. Included with this outfit are one No. 88 Controlling Rheostat, six No. 60 Telegraph Posts, one No. 106 Bridge and one No. 118 Metal Tunnel.
    Code Word "PACIFIC"   Price *$20.00, †$24.00

*Price, East of Missouri River. †Price, West of Missouri River.

All Aboard!! Over the bridge and around the curve goes your Lionel train. Loads and loads of fun for a long time after you own a Lionel outfit. Your Lionel train just runs and runs and keeps running because of its sturdy construction. All Lionel outfits, no matter what the price, are fully guaranteed.

Complete Railroad Outfits for "O" Gauge Track—1⅜ Inches Wide

THE railroads shown on this page are more complete than those previously described.

Look at the many marvelous accessories that are included with these outfits. Can any boy wish for a better present? You can set up these Lionel Railroads indoors or in your garden. You can build up a model village by adding the realistic Lionel Bungalows and Villas described in another part of this book.

Outfit No. 174—This outfit includes practically every accessory for a complete railroad. It comprises one No. 154 Reversing Locomotive with electric headlight, one No. 602 Mail Car, two No. 601 Pullman Cars, ten sections O C curved track (one with electrical connections), six sections O S straight track, one No. 88 Rheostat, two No. 022 Switches, one No. 106 Bridge, one No. 121 Station, six No. 60 Telegraph Posts, two No. 62 Semaphores, one No. 68 Railroad Crossing Sign, one No. 119 Tunnel. Size of track layout, 45 x 60 inches.

Code Word "DELAWARE"
Price *$37.50, †$45.00

OUTFIT NO. 174

Lionel "Multivolt" Transformers Operate Lionel Trains Best

Outfit No. 176—This outfit includes equipment that is larger than No. 174. Comprises one No. 156 Reversing Locomotive with electric headlight, two No. 610 Pullman Cars, one No. 612 Observation Car, ten sections OC curved track (one with electrical connections), ten sections O S straight track, one No. 88 Rheostat, one No. 109 Bridge (five sections), eight No. 60 Telegraph Posts, one No. 62 Semaphore, one No. 121 Station, one No. 119 Tunnel, two No. 022 Switches. Size of track layout, 45 x 82 inches.

Code Word "BURLINGTON"
Price *$47.50, †$57.00

*Price, East of Missouri River.
†Price, West of Missouri River.

OUTFIT NO. 176

Locomotive Outfits for "Standard" Gauge Track—2¼ Inches Wide

MILLIONS OF HAPPY USERS THE WORLD OVER

HERE they are—the big, powerful "Standard" Gauge Locomotives, every one a tremendous puller. Don't hesitate about buying several Pullman or freight cars, for these massive haulers will speed away with them like a flash. See how faithfully the detail is reproduced—the big steel bodies with their beautiful enamel finish—the handsome nickeled trimmings, heavy wheels and above all the ever-reliable Lionel mechanism.

Some boys prefer electric type engines and others the steam type. You can take your pick. They are all fully guaranteed.

Maybe you think it a good idea to start off with just a locomotive and track to lay the foundation for a wonderful Lionel Railroad; afterwards adding cars and accessories. If so, you can't go wrong by buying one of these locomotive outfits.

OUTFIT NO. 51

Outfit No. 51—Complete length of engine and tender 18 inches. The driving wheels are counter-balanced and are 2½ inches in diameter. Has electric headlight, reversing controller and connection in cab for interior lighting of passenger cars. Outfit includes 8 sections of C curved track (one with electrical connections), and 4 sections of S straight track. The track provided with this outfit makes an oval 3½ feet wide by 5 feet 9 inches long.
Code Word "OHIO"   Price *$27.50, †$33.00

OUTFIT NO. 33

Outfit No. 33—The locomotive is 11 in. long, 3 in. wide and 4½ in. above the rails. Has 4 geared driving wheels, 1¾ in. diameter, electric headlight, reversing controller and connection for interior lighting of Pullman cars. Outfit includes 8 sections of C curved track (one with electrical connections) making a circle 3½ feet diameter. Code Word "DUBUQUE"   Price *$16.25, †$19.50

OUTFIT NO. 38

Outfit No. 38—The locomotive is 12 in. long, 3½ in. wide and 5 in. above the rails. Has 4 driving wheels 2½ in. in diameter, connected with heavy steel driving rods, electric headlight, reversing controller and connection for interior lighting of Pullman cars. Outfit includes 8 sections of C curved track (one with electrical connections) making a circle 3½ feet in diameter. Code Word "AKRON"   Price *$18.50, †$22.00

OUTFIT NO. 7

Outfit No. 6—Complete length of engine and tender 22 inches. The driving wheels are counter-balanced and are 2½ inches in diameter. The four wheel pilot truck is made on the swivel principle and is perfect in its action. Has electric headlight, reversing controller and connection in cab for interior lighting of passenger cars. Outfit includes 8 sections of C curved track (one with electrical connections), and 4 sections of S straight track. The track provided with this outfit makes an oval 3½ feet wide by 5 feet 9 inches long. No. 6 Outfit is not illustrated but it is the same as No. 51 in finish and like No. 7 Outfit in construction and size.
Code Word "VICTORIA"   Price *$37.50, †$45.00

Outfit No. 7 (Illustrated above)—Dimensions of this locomotive and tender are exactly the same as No. 6 and the same track equipment is provided with it. The wonderful nickel and brass finish of this outfit makes it admirable for display purposes. It is acknowledged to be the finest steam type model ever produced.
Code Word "GEORGIA"   Price *$58.50, †$70.00

"Twin-Motor" Locomotives "Standard" Gauge Track—2¼ Inches Wide

D**ID YOU** ever see the powerful electric locomotives on the New York Central Lines pull the "Twentieth Century Limited" into Grand Central Station? The blazing headlight, the bell clanging, the hissing air brakes and the body vibrating as though with satisfaction after a successful run. Well—the Lionel reproductions of these locomotives will make you believe that the big real train is in your own home. In proportion to their size the Lionel Locomotives shown on this page are just as powerful. "Twin-Motor" Locomotives No. 42 and No. 54 have an established reputation. They are much more powerful and yet consume far less current than any other make. After you have read the details of construction on page 8 you will readily see how "wear-resisting" every part is made.

Outfit No. 54, the Locomotive de Luxe—Nothing richer or more elegant is produced by any manufacturer of electric toy trains. Search the markets of the world. To own one of these locomotives is the dream of every boy! No pictures, no words, no imagination can describe or think of the beauty of this locomotive. You *must see* it to get the shine of its splendid brass and nickel finish on body, hand-rails, ventilators, headlight and driving wheels. It is a most elaborate model. But it is not all outside show. Its powerful "twin-motors" do their wonderful work the instant the current is switched on. Dimensions and construction are same as No. 42. Has same track equipment and can be used with same cars.   Code Word "PENN"   Price *$41.75, †$50.00

OUTFIT NO. 42

Outfit No. 42—Every detail of the large, powerful electric engines is faithfully reproduced in this "Twin-Motor" locomotive. The driving wheels are 2½ inches in diameter. The trucks are swivel and flexible. Has electric headlight, reversing controller, and connection for interior lighting of Pullman cars.

Dimensions—15½ inches long, 4 inches wide, and 6 inches high. Outfit Comprises "Twin-Motor" locomotive, eight sections C curved track (one with electrical connections), and four sections of S straight track, making an oval 3½ feet wide by 5 feet 9 inches long.

Code Word "AUGUSTA"   *Price $29.25 †$35.00

OUTFIT NO. 54

See pages 29 and 31 for the Correct Cars to use with these Locomotives

---

UNIVERSAL CURRENT CONTROLLER
(Patent Applied For)

A unique device is affixed to these locomotives so that by simply moving a lever the windings of the motors are changed to series (which is the best winding when they are operated on the reduced direct current) or to multiple (which is the best connection when operated on reduced alternating current or on dry or storage batteries).

*Price, East of Missouri River.   †Price, West of Missouri River.

Train Outfits for "Standard" Gauge Track—2¼ Inches Wide

"STANDARD OF THE WORLD" SINCE NINETEEN HUNDRED

BOYS! Wouldn't you rather recommend to Dad or Mother that they buy you a toy which will be of permanent interest and give you years of honest, sensible enjoyment?

What better investment could there be for your next present than one of these powerful, long-running excellently built Lionel Trains, with either two, three or four cars as shown on this page!

Really, the number of cars makes no difference, for the ever-reliable Lionel Locomotives will pull them all with ease.

OUTFIT NO. 34

Outfit No. 34—Comprises No. 33 Reversible Locomotive with electric headlight, one No. 35 Pullman Car and one No. 36 Observation Car. This is one of our most popular numbers, and is the lowest priced outfit that can be bought anywhere, considering the quality. Includes eight sections curved C track (one with electrical connections), and two sections of S track, making an oval 3½ feet wide by 4 feet 8 inches long. The train is 34 inches long.
Code Word "AUBURN"   Price *$22.25, †$26.50

Outfit No. 40—Comprises No. 38 Reversible Locomotive with electric headlight, two No. 35 Pullman Cars and one No. 36 Observation Car, eight sections C curved track (one with electrical connections), and four sections of S straight track, making an oval 3½ feet wide by 5 feet 9 inches long. The powerful locomotive provided with this outfit will pull 8 to 12 cars with ease. The liberal amount of track supplied with it shows this set to be big value. Length of train 48 inches.   Code Word "BARROW"
Price *$29.25, †$35.00

OUTFIT NO. 40

Outfit No. 45—Comprises No. 38 Reversible Locomotive with electric headlight, one Pullman and Baggage Car No. 31, one Mail Car No. 32, one Pullman Car No. 35, one Observation Car No. 36, ten sections C curved track (one with electrical connections), four sections S straight track and one pair of No. 22 Switches. This track layout enables the user to make a figure having a circle inside the oval. Size of track 3½ feet wide by 7 feet long. The cars are enameled a rich orange and lettered in gold. The train is 60 inches long.   Code Word "SANTA"   Price *$38.50, †$46.00

OUTFIT NO. 45

*Price, East of Missouri River.   †Price, West of Missouri River.

This Illustration Shows Track Arrangement

Train Outfits for "Standard" Gauge Track—2¼ Inches Wide

LIONEL Freight Trains look just like those mighty haulers that carry merchandise across the country. The real big freight trains must be sturdily built to withstand the jolts they get on a long journey.

So it is with Lionel Trains. They are built to withstand hard usage. Pick out the freight train you like best on this page. They are all very low-priced, but of Lionel quality.

OUTFIT NO. 37

Outfit No. 37—Comprises one No. 33 Reversible Locomotive with electric headlight, one No. 112 Gondola Car, one No. 117 Caboose, and eight sections of C curved track (one with electrical connections), making a circle 3½ feet in diameter. Train is 31 inches long. A good freighter at a low price.
Code Word "CAROLINA"   Price *$18.50, †$22.00

Outfit No. 39—Comprises No. 38 Reversible Locomotive with electric headlight, one No. 116 Ballast Car, one No. 117 Caboose, eight sections of C curved track (one with electrical connections), making a circle 3½ feet in diameter. Length of train, 33 inches. Many more cars can be added to this outfit and the locomotive will speed away with them in fine shape.
Code Word "FLORIDA"   Price *$21.00, †$25.00

OUTFIT NO. 39

Outfit No. 41—This is a very low-priced outfit considering the wonderful hauling power of the locomotive and the variety of cars that are included. Outfit comprises one No. 38 Reversible Locomotive with electric headlight, one each of Nos. 112, 113, 114, 116 and 117 Freight Cars, eight sections C curved track (one with electrical connections), four sections straight track, making an oval 3½ feet wide by 5 feet 9 inches long. The train is 5 feet 3½ inches long.
Code Word "FULTON"   Price *$29.25, †$35.00

OUTFIT NO. 41

*Price, East of Missouri River   †Price, West of Missouri River

"Twin-Motor" Train Outfits for "Standard" Gauge Track—2¼ Inches Wide — MILLIONS OF HAPPY USERS THE WORLD OVER

HERE, boys, are the wonderful Lionel Trains with the famous "Twin-Motor" Locomotives. At the big Lionel display rooms in New York there are several of these "Twin-Motor" Locomotives in constant operation pulling twenty of our largest cars! Just think of the fun you will have if you get one of these real trains.

OUTFIT NO. 44

Outfit No. 44—Comprises one No. 42 "Twin-Motor" Reversible Locomotive with electric headlight, two No. 18 Pullman Cars, eight sections C curved track (one with electrical connections) and four sections of S straight track, making an oval 3½ feet wide by 5½ feet long. Complete length of train 52 inches.
Code Word "DOROTHY"
Price *$41.75, †$52.00

OUTFIT NO. 422

Outfit No. 422—Comprises No. 42 "Twin-Motor" Reversible Locomotive with electric headlight, together with one each of Freight Cars numbered 11, 12, 13, 14, 15, 16 and 17; also ten sections S straight track and eight sections C curved track (one with electrical connections) making an oval 3½ feet wide by 10 feet 5 inches long. The complete train is over 7 feet in length.
Code Word "DURABLE"
Price *$52.50, †$63.00

Outfit No. 423—Similar in every respect to Outfit No. 422, but has Locomotive No. 54, finished in nickel and brass, which is described on page 18. A perfect model of a big freight train on the New York Central Lines. Passenger Cars for this train are Nos. 18, 19 and 190.
Code Word "ELABORATE"
Price *$65.00, †$78.00

OUTFIT NO. 420

Outfit No. 421—Similar in all respects to Outfit No. 420, but No. 54 Locomotive is included which is finished in nickel and brass beautifully polished. This is one of our most elaborate Electric Trains. The cars are enameled a rich orange color to match locomotive.
Code Word "SIDONIA"
Price *$65.00, †$78.00

Outfit No. 420—Comprises No. 42 "Twin-Motor" Reversible Locomotive with electric headlight, one No. 19 Pullman Baggage Combination Car, one No. 18 Pullman and one No. 190 Observation Car, eight sections of C curved track (one with electrical connections), and eight sections of S straight track, making oval 3½ feet wide by 8 feet 4 inches long. One of our three-lamp interior lighting sets is included in the outfit. Length of train, 65 inches.
Code Word "HANDSOME"
Price *$52.50, †$63.00

*Price, East of Missouri River. †Price, West of Missouri River.

 # Train Outfits for "Standard" Gauge Track—2¼ Inches Wide

SOME of you boys possibly prefer a Steam Type Engine, electrically operated. If so, you cannot do better than select one of the trains illustrated below. The engines are true down to the minutest detail—solid steel construction in every part. And the motor?—the same electrical perfection as in every other type that bears the Lionel Name.

OUTFIT NO. 43

Outfit No. 43—Comprises No. 51 Reversible Locomotive with Tender, 2 No. 18 Pullman Cars, eight sections C curved track (one with electrical connections), and four sections of S straight track, making an oval 5 feet 9 inches long and 3½ feet wide. Complete length of train is 53 inches. The coaches in this outfit are wonderfully realistic. Every detail of the real cars is faithfully carried out. The engine is powerful enough to haul a dozen freight cars or more.
Code Word "LEEDS"   Price *$35.00, †$42.00

OUTFIT NO. 622

Outfit No. 622—A very faithful model of large freight trains seen on many prominent railroads. Outfit comprises one No. 6 Reversible Locomotive and Tender and one each of the Freight Cars numbered 11, 12, 13, 14, 15, 16 and 17, also ten sections S straight track and eight sections C curved track (one with electrical connections), making an oval 3½ feet wide by 10 feet 5 inches long. Length of complete train is nearly 8 feet.   Passenger Cars for this locomotive Nos. 18, 19, 190.
Code Word "TELFORD"   Price *$60.00, †$73.00

Outfit No. 623—Similar in every respect to Outfit No. 622, but has Locomotive and Tender No. 7, which is finished in nickel and brass.
Code Word "MONTCLAIR"   Price *$78.50, †$94.00

OUTFIT NO. 620

Outfit No. 620—For those who prefer a steam type Pullman train the above can be recommended as the finest model ever built. The outfit includes No. 6 Reversible Locomotive and Tender with electric headlight, one each of No. 18, No. 19 and No. 190 Passenger Cars, together with eight sections C curved track (one with electrical connections), and eight sections of S straight track. A lighting set for the interior illumination of Pullman Cars is also included. Track layout measures 3½ feet wide and 8 feet 4 inches long.   Code Word "WINSLOW"   Price *$60.00, †$73.00

Outfit No. 621—Similar in every respect to No. 620 described on this page, but includes Locomotive and Tender No. 7. The cars are enameled a rich orange color to harmonize with the locomotive. No finer outfit is obtainable anywhere.   Code Word "BRANCH"   Price *$78.50, †$94.00

*Price, East of Missouri River. †Price, West of Missouri River.

"Super-Motor" Locomotives for "Standard" Gauge Track—2¼ Inches Wide

STANDARD OF THE WORLD SINCE NINETEEN HUNDRED

OUTFIT NO. 402

THE very peak of perfection—that's the only way we can mention the result we have achieved after many years spent in designing and manufacturing Lionel Locomotives.

Any boy will have the ambition of a lifetime realized if he owns one of these new "Super-Motor" Locomotive Outfits.

Be sure to read all about the motor and mechanism on page 9 and about the wonderful details of construction on page 24.

Locomotive Outfit No. 402, "Twin-Super" Motor"—It is unfair to describe this beautiful model as a toy, for its appearance and efficiency represent the very highest achievement in miniature train construction.

The locomotive is 17½ inches long, 4½ inches wide and 6½ inches high.

Included are 8 sections of C curved track (one with electrical connections) and 4 sections of S straight track, making an oval 5 feet 9 inches long by 3½ feet wide.

Code Word "HAVEN"   Price *$45.00, †$55.00

For description of working parts of "Super-Motor" Locomotives see page 9. Details of construction of these new types will be found on next pages.

Locomotive Outfit No. 380, "Single-Super-Motor"—This locomotive embodies all the features enumerated in the description of the No 402 Locomotive, but it is equipped with a single "Super-Motor". It is designed to supply the demand for a low-priced locomotive of the highest efficiency. It will haul at least a dozen of the largest size freight or Pullman cars with perfect ease.

The dimensions of this locomotive are: length 15 inches, width 4 inches, height 6¼ inches above the rails.

Outfit includes 8 sections of C curved track (one with electrical connections) and 4 sections of S straight track, making an oval 5 feet 9 inches long by 3½ feet wide.

Code Word "ROCKIES"   Price *$25.00, †$30.00

See pages 29 and 31 for the Correct Cars to use with these Locomotives

OUTFIT NO. 380

*Price, East of Missouri River.   †Price, West of Missouri River.

1923

HERE IS THE WONDER TRAIN OF MODER

PASSENGER TRAIN OUTFIT No. 403 WITH "TWIN-SUPER-MOTO

THIS Train Outfit is in every respect a miniature reproduction of a de luxe express train. It is a delight to behold and operates as smoothly as though the wheels were equipped with rubber tires. Even the most superlative terms of description will not be as convincing as seeing the Outfit in operation. It is absolutely the last word in miniature train construction.

DETAILS OF LOCOMOTIVE

An exact reproduction of the most modern type of electric locomotives used on electrified systems throughout the country. It is so faithful in detail that to behold it is like seeing an actual large electric locomotive through the diminishing end of field glasses.

Body—The body is made entirely of steel. The doors, windows, ventilators, hand rails and all other fittings are made of brass highly polished.

Headlights—The headlights (one of which is placed at each end of the body) are unique in construction. Each is equipped with a switch so that one or both may be turned on at will. The headlight lamp when illuminated is visible through the green and red panels on the sides of the headlight—a touch of realism that will delight every boy.

Reversing Controller—A lever is conveniently placed on the side of the locomotive which operates simultaneously the controllers on each of the Twin-Motors. This is a great step forward in controller construction.

Frame—The frame is ma made of brass and beautifull it. Numerous rivets and oth in the frame, all of which acc locomotive.

Automatic Couplers—T automatic couplers that pro designed cowcatchers. Thes ment over any similar device other irrespective of the po conjunction with any type o ket.

Enamel Finish—The en at a high temperature, whic

TIMES—THE REAL THING—IN MINIATURE
COMOTIVE FOR "STANDARD" GAUGE TRACK—2¼ INCHES WIDE

piece of heavy steel. Journals, lated, are securely fastened to al details are heavily embossed e great detail embodied in this

tive is equipped with our new ough the centre of beautifully c couplers are a great improve- son that they engage with each e cars. They can be used in natic coupler now on the mar-

e frame and body is baked on a glasslike finish that lasts for years. It is only necessary to rub the finish with a cloth or chamois to keep the locomotive always bright and new looking.

DETAILS OF CARS

These Pullman Cars are faithful reproductions in every detail of the most modern passenger cars used on the best railroads. The bodies are made of heavy sheet steel and the parts are rigidly held together. The detail of construction is enhanced by embossed work in the nature of panels, rivets, sashes, etc. Two miniature tanks as well as nickel-plated steps and hand rails add to the great detail incorporated in these cars. The roof is removable and the interior contains individual revolving seats and two permanent electric bulbs which illuminate the car. The light coming through the glass windows adds a very realistic touch to the train.

These cars are enameled in very attractive colors baked on at a high temperature so that they always retain their fresh, glossy appearance. It is impossible to describe the beauty of these cars adequately, but suffice to say that nothing like them has ever been made before as toy railroad equipment.

The combination Pullman and Baggage Car contains a baggage compartment with sliding doors and the platform of the Observation Car is complete in detail even to the light in the ceiling.

The three new cars forming the series are listed separately on page 29.

The Locomotive Outfit is listed separately on page 23.

Outfit No. 403—Comprises No. 402 "Twin-Super-Motor" Locomotive, 1 No. 418 Pullman Car, 1 No. 419 Pullman and Baggage Car, 1 No. 490 Observation Car, all with permanent interior lighting equipment, also 8 sections of S straight track and 8 sections of C curved track (one with electrical connections), making an oval 8 feet 4 inches long by 3½ feet wide.

The complete train is 77 inches long.

Code Word "PRETTY"   Price *$75.00, †$90.00

*Price, East of Missouri River. †Price, West of Missouri River.

 "Super-Motor" Train Outfits for "Standard" Gauge Track—2¼ Inches Wide

RIGHT up to the minute! These Train Outfits include the very latest models of electric engines containing the new Lionel "Super-Motors". Year by year the great railroads of America electrify their systems, and as new types of electric engines are introduced, Lionel loses no time in reproducing them faithfully.

On page 9 you will learn all about these wonderful motors, and on page 23 the remarkable superstructure and detail are described.

Power?—no load is too great for these giant haulers.

Outfit No. 440—A beautifully proportioned, easy running, passenger train at a popular price. The Outfit comprises the new No. 380 Locomotive already described, 2 No. 18 Pullman Cars, 8 sections of C curved track (one with electrical connections), and 4 sections S straight track, making an oval 5 feet 9 inches long by 3½ feet wide. The complete train is 46 inches long.
Code Word "VERNON"
Price *$39.25, †$47.00

OUTFIT NO. 440

Outfit No. 390—A perfect reproduction of a modern freight train. The Outfit comprises No. 380 Locomotive, 1 No. 12 Gondola Car, 1 No. 14 Box Car, 1 No. 15 Oil Car, 1 No. 17 Caboose, 8 sections of C curved track (one with electrical connections), and 4 sections of S straight track, making an oval 5 feet 9 inches long by 3½ feet wide. The complete train is 65 inches long.
Code Word "PELHAM"
Price *$37.50, †$45.00

OUTFIT NO. 390

OUTFIT NO. 308

Outfit No. 308—A realistic model of a trans-continental limited train. The Outfit comprises No. 380 Locomotive, 1 No. 18 Pullman Car, 1 No. 19 Pullman and Baggage Car, 1 No. 190 Observation Car, 8 sections of C curved track (one with electrical connections) and 8 sections of S straight track, making an oval 8 feet 4 inches long by 3½ feet wide.
The complete train is 5 feet 5 inches long
Code Word "MONTY"
Price *$48.50, †$58.00

*Price, East of Missouri River.   †Price, West of Missouri River.

26

Complete Railroad Outfit for "Standard" Gauge Track—2¼ Inches Wide

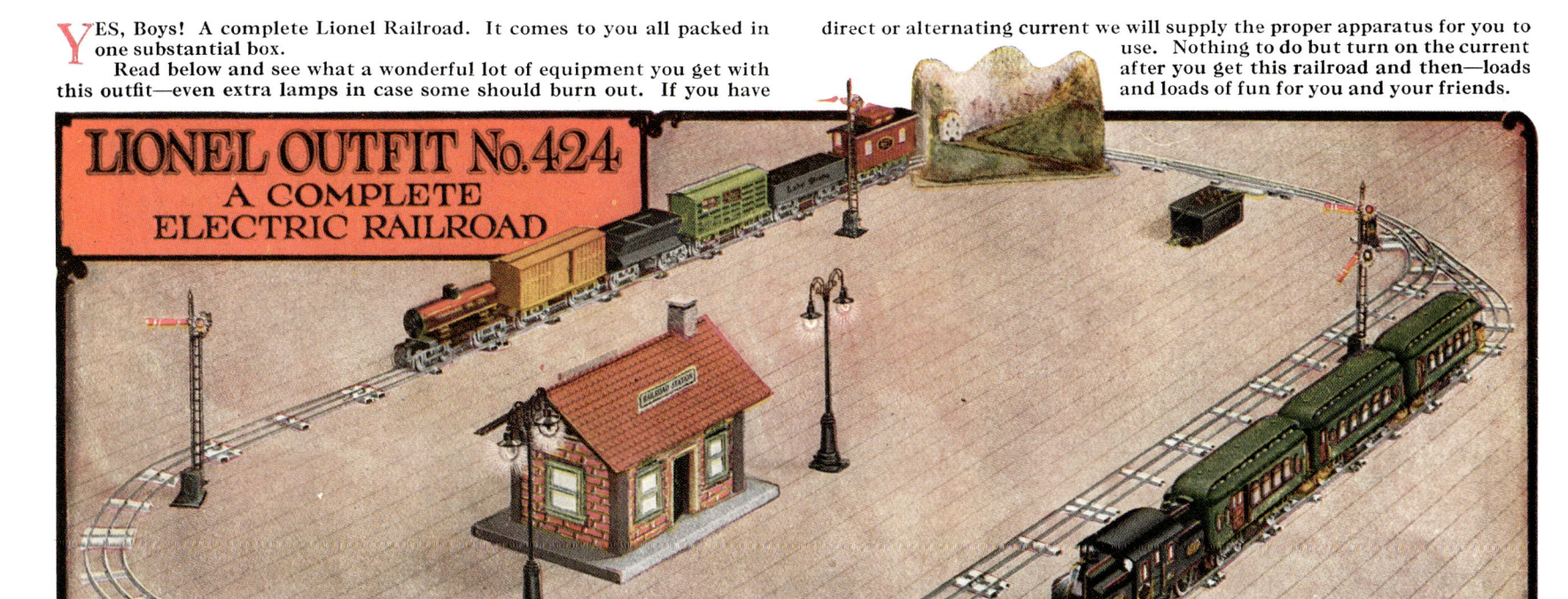

"STANDARD OF THE WORLD SINCE NINETEEN HUNDRED"

YES, Boys! A complete Lionel Railroad. It comes to you all packed in one substantial box.

Read below and see what a wonderful lot of equipment you get with this outfit—even extra lamps in case some should burn out. If you have direct or alternating current we will supply the proper apparatus for you to use. Nothing to do but turn on the current after you get this railroad and then—loads and loads of fun for you and your friends.

LIONEL OUTFIT No. 424
A COMPLETE ELECTRIC RAILROAD

EQUIPMENT WITH OUTFIT NO. 424

One No. 42 "Twin-Motor" Reversible Locomotive with electric headlight.
One No. 18 Pullman Car.
One No. 19 Pullman and Baggage Car.
One No. 190 Observation Car.
One No. 12 Gondola Car.
One No. 13 Cattle Car.
One No. 14 Box Car.
One No. 15 Oil Car.
One No. 16 Ballast Car.
One No. 17 Caboose.

Two No. 67 Lamp Posts fitted with No. 49 21-volt globe.
Two No. 65 Semaphores fitted with No. 48 21-volt lamps.
One No. 66 Semaphore fitted with No. 48 21-volt lamps.
One Pair No. 21S switches fitted with No. 48 21-volt lamps.
One No. 217 Interior Car Lighting Set fitted with No. 26 14-volt lamps.

Seven sections C curved track.
One section CC curved track, with electrical connections.
Eighteen sections S straight track.
One section ½ S straight track.
One Type K Transformer for 110 volts alternating current, or No. 107 Direct Current Reducer if desired.
One No. 121 Station.
One No. 120 Tunnel.

LAMP RENEWALS
Two No. 26 14-Volt Lamps for headlights.
Two No. 48 21-Volt Lamps for switches.
Two No. 49 21-Volt Globes for lamp posts.

Track Layout Is 11 Feet Long and 6 Feet 10 Inches Wide

Code Word "DESIRABLE"

Price *$120.00, †$144.00

*Price, East of Missouri River.
†Price, West of Missouri River.

Passenger and Mail Cars for "Standard" and "O" Gauge Track

BOYS! Don't these cars look real? No wonder, because we model them after the very latest types used by all the big railroads. You want realism in the things you play with—that's why we spare no effort to make Lionel Cars what they are—real railroad cars in miniature.

Pullman Car

Pullman and Baggage Car

U. S. Mail Car

Observation Car

WE mention with particular pride that Lionel Passenger Cars have always been faithful models of the originals, which places them far above any similar toys. All cars are constructed of sheet steel and embody the "one-piece" principle as described in the introduction. Lionel cars are not cheaply lithographed, but are hand enameled and are striped and lettered in gold. The doors are hinged, platforms are vestibuled, and colored or clear glass is inserted in the windows, doors and ventilators. These windows are inserted by a new process which insures their staying in place for the life of the car.

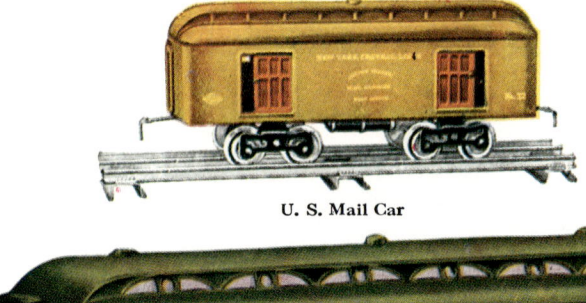

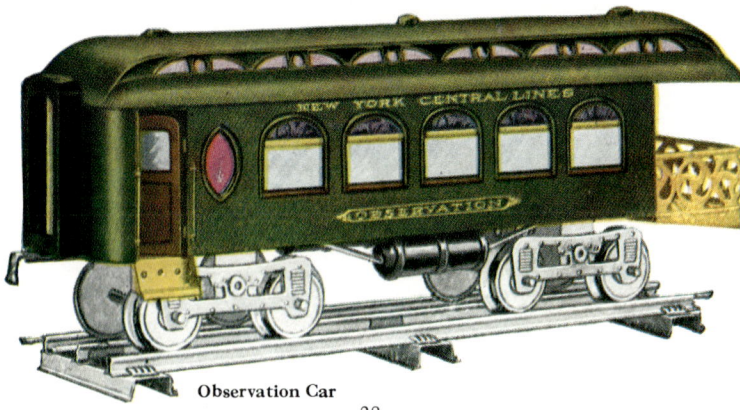

All roofs are removable and provision is made for placing a series of lights in the cars which operate on "Standard" gauge track. The lighting outfits for this purpose are described on page 43. A wonderfully realistic effect is produced by the lights shining through the colored windows. Cars are mounted on flexible trucks, which insures smooth running and staying on the track, even when rounding curves at great speed. The various sized passenger cars in conjunction with our different types of locomotives are shown throughout this catalogue.

Passenger and Mail Cars for "Standard" and "O" Gauge Track

(See Opposite Page for Illustrations)

For "O" Gauge Track—1⅜ Inches Wide

No. 600—Pullman Car, 6 inches long, 2 inches wide, 3 inches high
Code Word "HORNBY"   Price *$0.50, †$0.60

Above is for use with "O" Locomotives Nos. 150-158 and is mounted on a four-wheel truck—all other cars have two four-wheel trucks.

No. 601—Pullman Car, 7½ inches long, 2⅜ inches wide, 3½ inches high.
Code Word "HILTON"   Price *$1.25, †$1.50

No. 602—Mail Car, 7½ inches long, 2⅜ inches wide, 3½ inches high.
Code Word "LEYTON"   Price *$1.25, †$1.50

Above two cars are for use with "O" Gauge Locomotives Nos. 152-154.

No. 603—Pullman Car, 7 inches long, 2 inches wide, 3¼ inches high.
Code Word "BURTON"   Price *$1.15, †$1.40

No. 604—Observation Car, 7 inches long, 2 inches wide, 3¼ inches high.
Code Word "MONARCH"   Price *$1.15, †$1.40

Above two cars are for use with "O" Gauge Locomotives Nos. 150, 158.

No. 610—Pullman Car, 8¾ inches long, 2½ inches wide, 4 inches high.
Code Word "EALING"   Price *2.50, †$3.00

No. 612—Observation Car, 8¾ inches long, 2½ inches wide, 4 inches high.
Code Word "WALTON"   Price *$2.50, †3.00

Above two cars are for use with "O" Gauge Locomotive No. 156 and 156X.

For "Standard" Gauge Track—2¼ Inches Wide

No. 31—Pullman and Baggage Car, 11 inches long, 3 inches wide, 5 inches high.
Code Word "CAPI"   Price *$3.35, †$4.00

No. 32—Mail Car, 11 inches long, 3 inches wide, 5 inches high.
Code Word "BILL"   Price *$3.35, †$4.00

No. 35—Pullman Car, 11 inches long, 3 inches wide, 5 inches high.
Code Word "CAMDEN"   Price *$3.35, †$4.00

No. 36—Observation Car, 11 inches long, 3 inches wide, 5 inches high.
Code Word "FLINT"   Price *3.35, †$4.00

Above four cars are for use with "Standard" Gauge Locomotives Nos. 33 and 38.

No. 18—Pullman Car, 16½ inches long, 3½ inches wide, 6 inches high.
Code Word "PHILA"   Price *$6.25, †$7.50

No. 19—Pullman and Baggage Car, 16½ inches long, 3½ inches wide, 6 inches high. Code Word "TROY"   Price *$6.75, †$8.00

No. 190—Observation Car, 16½ inches long, 3½ inches wide, 6 inches high.
Code Word "VIRGINIA"   Price *$6.75, †$8.00

Above series of three cars are for use with all "Standard" Gauge Locomotives, excepting Nos. 33 and 38.

No. 418 Pullman Car, 20 inches long, 4½ inches wide and 6 inches high. Has two permanent interior lights. Code Word "COMFORT"   Price *$8.50, †$10.00

No. 419 Pullman and Baggage Car, 20 inches long, 4½ inches wide and 6 inches high. Has two permanent interior lights and baggage compartment with sliding doors. Code Word "COURT"   Price *$8.50, †$10.00

No. 490 Observation Car, 20 inches long, 4½ inches wide and 6 inches high. Has observation platform and two permanent interior lights, one of which is placed under the observation canopy.
Code Word "CABIN"   Price *$8.50, †$10.00

Above series of three cars are for use with "Super-Twin-Motor" Locomotive No. 402.

*Price, East of Missouri River. †Price, West of Missouri River.

Lionel Electric Toy Trains

Freight Cars for "Standard" and "O" Gauge Track

ALL these cars are constructed throughout of sheet steel. The individuality of each style of car has been studied and copied faithfully. They will not come apart or bend out of shape. All trucks are flexible, which means that they will not jump the track while running either forward or backward. They move so easily that one of our locomotives will haul a number of them without difficulty. The wheels are made of steel, and are reinforced at the back with heavy steel discs. They are mounted on solid Bessemer steel shafts. No wood enters the construction of these cars.

All the roofs are removable and doors slide so that the interior of the cars can be easily reached. Trucks and wheels are nickeled. The construction of all cars is similar in every respect, but vary in size in accordance with the locomotive with which they are intended to be operated. All the cars are hand enameled and trimmed and are appropriately decorated with the "heralds" of the most prominent railroads.

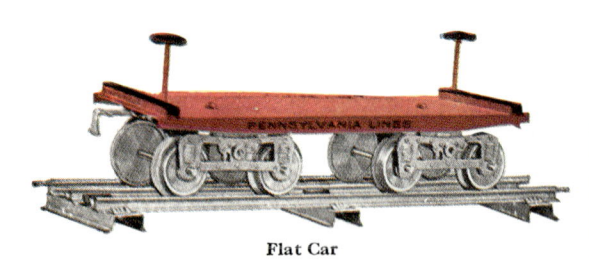

Made of Steel
These Are Real Miniature Freight Cars, Rigidly Constructed

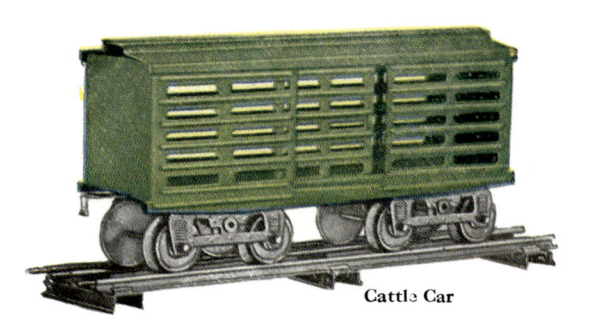

Gondola

Flat Car

Oil Car

Box Car

Ballast Car

Caboose

Cattle Car

30

Freight Cars for "Standard" and "O" Gauge Track

STANDARD OF THE WORLD SINCE NINETEEN HUNDRED

(See Opposite Page for Illustrations)

For "O" Gauge Track—1 3/8 Inches Wide

No. 800—Box Car, 6 inches long, 2 inches wide, 3 inches high.
Code Word "CHANDLER"   Price *$0.50, †$0.60

No. 801—Caboose, 6 inches long, 2 inches wide, 3 1/4 inches high.
Code Word "CONNERTON"   Price *$0.50, †$0.60

No. 802—Cattle Car, 6 inches long, 2 inches wide, 3 inches high.
Code Word "CHICKASAW"   Price *0.50, †$0.60

No. 803—Coal Car, 7 inches long, 2 inches wide, 3 inches high. Has "Hopper" bottom.
Code Word "LOAD"   Price *$0.65, †0.80

No. 804—Oil Car, 7 inches long, 2 inches wide, 3 1/2 inches high.
Code Word "FUEL"   Price *$0.60, †$0.70

No. 901—Gondola Car, 6 inches long, 2 inches wide, 2 inches high.
Code Word "CHIMES"   Price *$0.40, †$0.50

The above six cars are for use with Locomotive No. 150, No. 152 and No. 158, and are mounted on four-wheel trucks. All other freight cars have two four-wheel trucks.

No. 820—Box Car, 7 1/2 inches long, 2 3/8 inches wide, 3 1/2 inches high.
Code Word "ECOLA"   Price *$1.25, †$1.50

No. 822—Caboose, 7 1/2 inches long, 2 3/8 inches wide, 3 3/4 inches high.
Code Word "ELIXIR"   Price *$1.25, †$1.50

Above two cars for use with all "O" Gauge Locomotives, excepting Nos. 150 and 158.

For "Standard" Gauge Track—2 1/4 Inches Wide

No. 112—Gondola Car, 9 1/2 inches long, 3 inches wide, 2 1/2 inches high.
Code Word "ELMIRA"   Price *$1.50, †$1.80

No. 113—Cattle Car, 9 1/2 inches long, 3 inches wide, 4 1/2 inches high.
Code Word "SYRACUSE"   Price *$2.10, †$2.50

No. 114—Box Car, 9 1/2 inches long, 3 inches wide, 4 1/4 inches high.
Code Word "HAZLETON"   Price *$2.10, †$2.50

No. 116—Ballast Car, 9 1/2 inches long, 3 inches wide, 3 3/4 inches high.
Code Word "SCRANTON"   Price *$2.10, †$2.50

No. 117—Caboose, 9 3/4 inches long, 3 inches wide, 4 3/4 inches high.
Code Word "TOLEDO"   Price *$2.10, †$2.50

This series of five cars for use with Locomotives Nos. 33 and 38.

No. 11—Flat Car, 11 inches long, 3 1/2 inches wide, 3 1/2 inches high.
Code Word "MASS"   Price *$2.10, †$2.50

No. 12—Gondola Car, 11 inches long, 3 1/2 inches wide, 3 1/2 inches high.
Code Word "VERMONT"   Price *$2.95, †$3.50

No. 13—Cattle Car, 11 inches long, 3 1/2 inches wide, 5 1/2 inches high.
Code Word "HAMPSHIRE"   Price *$3.35, †$4.00

No. 14—Box Car, 11 inches long, 3 1/2 inches wide, 5 1/2 inches high.
Code Word "MAINE"   Price *$3.35, †$4.00

No. 15—Oil Car, 11 inches long, 3 1/2 inches wide, 5 1/4 inches high.
Code Word "QUEBEC"   Price *$3.35, †$4.00

No. 16—Ballast Car, 11 inches long, 3 1/2 inches wide, 4 3/4 inches high.
Code Word "ONTARIO"   Price *$3.35, †$4.00

No. 17—Caboose, 9 3/4 inches long, 3 1/2 inches wide, 6 1/2 inches high.
Code Word "TORONTO"   Price *$3.35, †$4.00

The above seven cars are for use with all Locomotives, excepting Nos. 33 and 38.

*Price, East of Missouri River. †Price, West of Missouri River.

Lionel "Multivolt" Transformers for Alternating Current (Approved by the National)

UNLIMITED POWER AT LITTLE COST

"Multivolt" Transformers reduce the 110 volt house lighting alternating current to the few volts necessary for operating electric toys or various other appliances. (A special transformer is made for 220 volts alternating current.)

Connect with House Circuit—A flexible lamp cord is directly connected with the transformer. The plug fits any lamp socket. If your house lighting circuit is 110 volts alternating current and you require 6 volts to operate a train set or other small electrical apparatus, this voltage can be obtained from any of our transformers by connecting the binding posts indicated on the index plate. You turn on the current and your "Multivolt" Transformer does the rest.

Useful for Many Purposes—"Multivolt" Transformers are made to operate Lionel Electric Toys, but can be used for any electrical apparatus or any other toys which demand the current within their range, such as induction coils, annunciators, bells, burglar alarms, wireless apparatus, etc., etc.

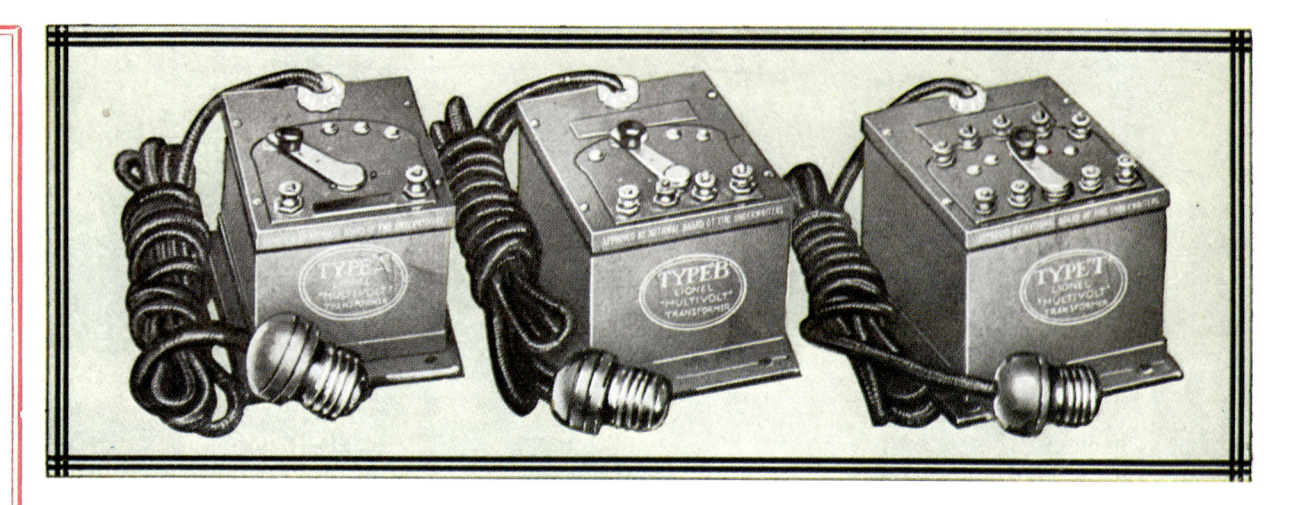

Type "A" Transformer will operate any "O" gauge outfit
For 110 volts, 60 cycles. 40 watts capacity.
Gives 15 volts in following steps: 4, 7, 10, 13, 15.
Size: 4¼ by 2¾ by 4¼ inches. Sub-base: 3¾ x 4¾ inches.
Code Word "STRONG"
Price *$3.65, †$4.30

Type "B" Transformer will operate any "O" gauge outfit, and in addition the extra binding posts enable the users to light up lamp posts, semaphores and other electrically illuminated accessories.
For 110 volts, 60 cycles. 50 watts capacity. Gives 25 volts in following steps:
Permanent: 7, 8, 15.
Variable: 2, 4, 6, 8, 9, 10, 11, 12, 13, 17, 19, 21, 23, 25.
Size: 4½ x 3¾ by 3 inches. Sub-base: 5 by 4¼ inches.
Code Word "BRADLEY"
Price *$5.00, †$6.00

Type "T" Transformer will operate any "O" gauge or "Standard" gauge outfit; also has extra binding posts for attaching illuminated electrical accessories.
For 110 volts, 60 cycles. 100 watts capacity. Gives 25 volts in following steps:
Permanent: 2, 4, 6, 7, 8, 10, 12, 14, 15, 16, 17, 18, 19, 21, 23, 25.
Variable: 2, 6, 8, 10, 12, 14, 16, 17, 18, 19, 21, 23, 25.
Size: 5 by 4 by 3¾ inches. Sub-base: 4¼ by 5½ inches.
Code Word "BIRCH"
Price *$7.50, †$9.00

Details of Construction

Sub-Base—A metal sub-base resting on four supports is attached to the bottom. The air circulating between this sub-base and the transformer case keeps it cool while in operation. Screw holes in this sub-base provide means for fastening the transformer to wall or table.

Separable Plug—All "Multivolt" Transformers are fitted with an approved, separable plug, which is a distinct advantage over the one-piece plug, because the circuit can be immediately broken when desired.

Plug Protecting Device—We have applied for a patent on a unique receptacle for protecting the plug against breakage in shipment. This device consists of a wooden container entirely covering the plug. It is sealed with a conspicuous label which draws the attention of the user to the fact that the transformer must be used **only on alternating** current of the number of cycles designated. This obviates the possibility of connecting the transformer with wrong current, which will consequently avoid mishandling and disappointment.

Double Contact Control Switch—This is new and infinitely superior to the one-piece switch, which is easily bent and does not make positive contact. Our double switch has a flexible, phosphor-bronze contact arm under the rigid switch, so that positive contact with the points is assured. This flexible contact is protected from injury by the rigid brass handle to which it is attached. This feature cannot be found on any other type of toy transformer.

Laminations—The laminations are made of the best grade of electrical sheets and the windings are perfectly insulated.

Rigid Supports for Coils—The coils and laminations of Lionel "Multivolt" Transformers are rigidly supported inside the case by means of metal bands which prevent these parts from moving and eliminate the possibility of broken lead wires. In addition to these supports the interior of the case is fitted with an insulating receptacle and the case is air cooled.

*Price, East of Missouri River. †Price, West of Missouri River.

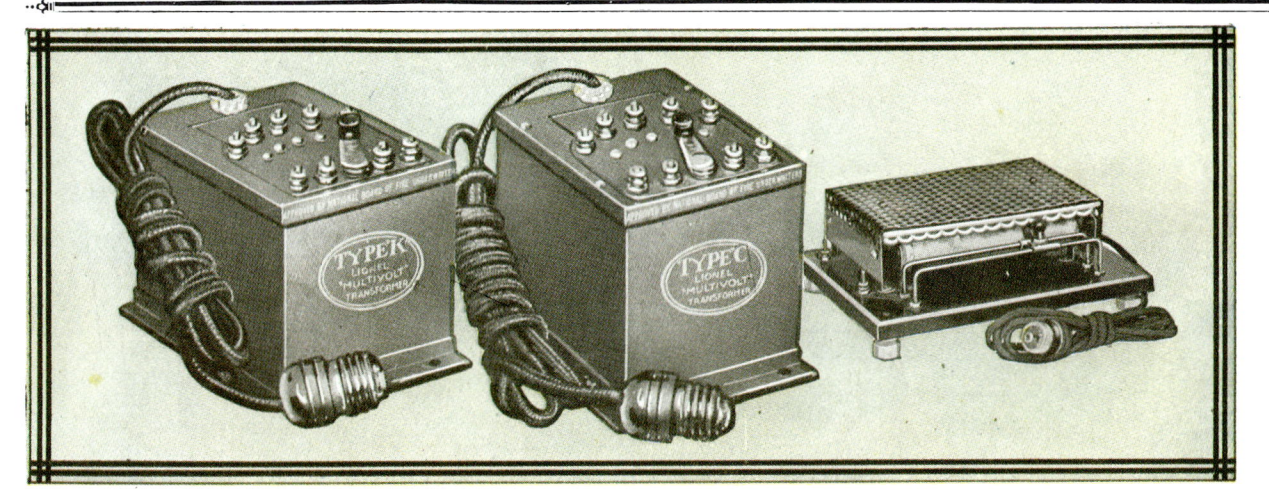

Board of Fire Underwriters) 25, 40 and 60 Cycles—110 and 220 Volts—**Lionel Direct Current Reducers—Battery Rheostat** — MILLIONS OF HAPPY USERS THE WORLD OVER

Type "K" Transformer will operate any outfit as well as illuminated accessories. This transformer has sufficient wattage capacity to operate two trains at once.
Size: 5 by 4 by 4½ inches. Sub-base: 4½ by 5½ inches.
"K"—For 110 volts, 60 cycles. 150 watts capacity. Specifications same as Type "T", but has higher wattage capacity.
Code Word (110 V.) "BINGHAM"
Price *$11.00, †$13.00
"K"—For 220 volts, 60 cycles. 150 watts capacity. Specifications same as Type "T" but is for use on 220-volt circuit.
Code Word (220 V.) "BROOK"
Price *$14.50, †$17.00

Metal Case—The case is beautiful in design and is stamped of heavier steel than is required by the National Board of Fire Underwriters.

Finish—"Multivolt" Transformer cases are covered with a rubberoid composition that is applied at 350 degrees Fahrenheit. This is much greater heat than the case is ever subjected to while in use, and the finish cannot be scratched and will not peel off, thereby insuring a beautiful finish for the entire life of the transformer.

Visible Connections—All contacts and switches are mounted on one piece of heavy insulating material and are at the top of the transformer, right under the user's eyes.

Lamp Cord—All "Multivolt" Transformers are fitted with 7 feet of flexible lamp cord which enters the transformer case through an approved porcelain bushing.

From the above specifications it will be clearly seen that we have incorporated in "Multivolt" Transformers every possible device that will increase their efficiency and safety.

Type "C" Transformer will operate any outfit and illuminated accessories on 25 or 40 cycle current.

For 110 volts, 25 to 40 cycles. 75 watts capacity. Specifications same as Type "T", but is for use on 25 or 40 cycle current.

Size: 5 by 4 by 4½ inches. Sub-base: 4½ by 5½ inches.

Code Word "LAWRENCE"
Price *$7.50, †$9.00

LIONEL DIRECT CURRENT REDUCERS
Not for Alternating Current

No. 107, Lionel Current Reducer for 110-Volt Circuit—This is constructed of four porcelain tubes wound with best quality of resistance wire. These porcelain tubes are mounted on a substantial slate base measuring 8 by 10 inches and ¾ inch thick. The porcelain tubes are protected and ventilated by a perforated steel cover lined with heavy asbestos. The sliding lever regulates the voltage so that your trains will just crawl along or shoot ahead at express speed. The reducer is connected with the house current by a screw plug with 7 feet of flexible cord. In addition, four porcelain supports or legs with long screws are supplied so that the reducer can be screwed to wall or table.
Code Word "KENTUCKY"   **Price *$10.00, †$12.00**

No. 170, Lionel Direct Current Reducer for 220-Volt Circuit—This Reducer is identical in appearance with No. 107, mentioned above, but is for use on 220 volts. Equipped with separable plug and 7 feet of flexible cord.
Code Word "ASBURY"   **Price *$14.50, †$17.00**

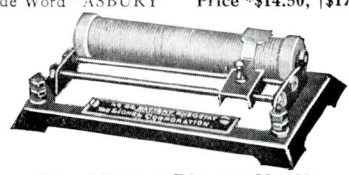

Lionel Battery Rheostat No. 88
*Price, East of Missouri River. †Price, West of Missouri River.

Don't Experiment

LIONEL "Multivolt" Transformers have been on the market for a great many years and operate all makes of Electric Trains. We justly claim that they are best. Don't experiment with other makes of doubtful value. Remember, that all transformers look alike outside, but their imperfections will only be discovered after they are in actual use for a length of time. Lionel "Multivolt" Transformers will last indefinitely and are guaranteed unconditionally as long as they are used on the current for which they are intended. They are absolutely safe and will give steady, even power.

Lionel Battery Rheostat No. 88—Use this rheostat with dry or storage batteries. It gives a gradual increase or decrease of current. A porcelain tube is wound with resistance wire of the correct gauge. This is mounted on a steel frame. A sliding finger increases or decreases the speed of the trains. All parts are of the best quality. This rheostat cannot overheat, as the coil is entirely exposed to the air—insuring free circulation, consequently rapid cooling. The steel base is beautifully enameled and other parts are nickel plated. Size 5 inches long, 2½ inches wide and 1 inch high.

Code Word "BANNER"
Price *$1.50, †$1.80

"Standard" and "O" Gauge Track—"Lockon" Track Contacts

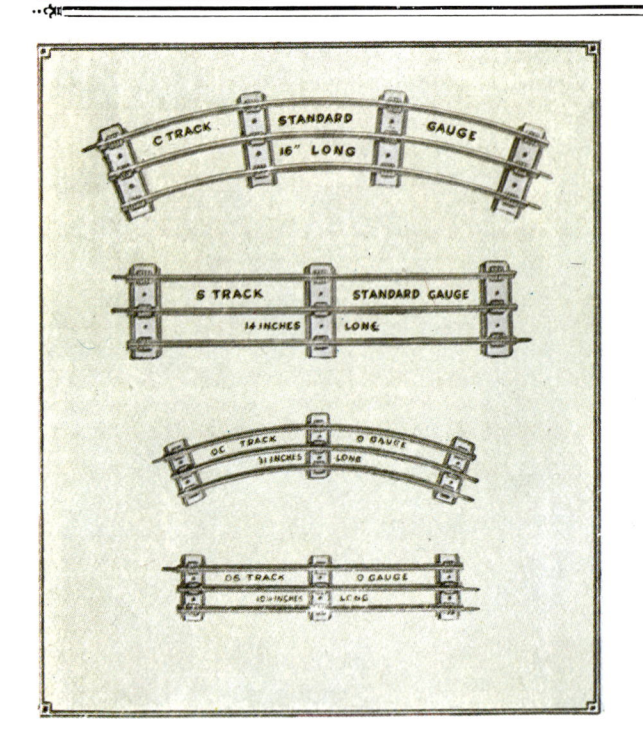

WE have described the strength and details of manufacture of this track in the introduction to this catalogue. We will merely add here the technical facts.

Tested to Carry 110 Volts—Each section of our track is tested for insulation on a circuit of 110 volts, consequently it will carry the low voltage necessary to operate our train without any chance of short-circuiting.

Sections Are Easily Connected—The ends of each section, whether curved or straight, have pin terminals which fit in openings in the adjoining sections. This allows the track to be laid and taken apart without any trouble. One section in each outfit is fitted with a "Lockon" track contact for batteries or transformer.

The track is made in straight and curved sections. Any shaped figure may be formed. The curvature of the track is mechanically correct, allowing the cars to run at very high speed without danger of derailing.

Use Right or Left—One of the greatest features of our track is that any of the curved sections may be used either right or left. This is due to the fact that the curve is not higher on the outside than on the inside. Raising the track on the outside is not necessary with our locomotives and cars because the flexible construction of the trucks prevents the cars from leaving the rails.

"STANDARD" GAUGE TRACK—2⅛ Inches Wide

C, curved track, 16 inches long.
  Code Word "BUFF"   Price per section *$0.30, †$0.40
S, straight track, 14 inches long.
  Code Word "NIAGARA"   Price per section *$0.30, †$0.40
  Eight No. C Sections make a circle 3½ feet in diameter.

"O" GAUGE TRACK—1⅜ Inches Wide

OC Curved Track, 11 inches long.
  Code Word "LEMPS"   Price per section *$0.20, †$0.26
OS Straight Track, 10¼ inches long.
  Code Word "GLENBURN"   Price per section *$0.20, †$0.25
  Eight No. OC Sections make a circle 30 inches in diameter.

Connecting Tie

We show here a cut of a hand sliding in the connecting tie. This is one of our recent improvements. It binds the ties rigidly together so that sections cannot pull apart. Yet this can be removed without difficulty—just a slight pull with the thumb and finger.

Every Lionel Train Outfit includes a sufficient number of connecting ties for the amount of track packed with the outfit.

"LOCKON" TRACK CONTACTS
(For Standard and "O" Gauge)

Lionel leadership is again evidenced in this improved device. Considering the fact that numerous electric accessories have been added to the Lionel line, which require connection with the track, these "LOCKON" contacts will readily appeal to the user, for it is no longer necessary to purchase special sections of track to which electrical contacts are affixed.

The "Lockon" contact is attached to the track by simply turning the lever at right angles. The electric connection is as perfect as though the parts were riveted or soldered to the track.

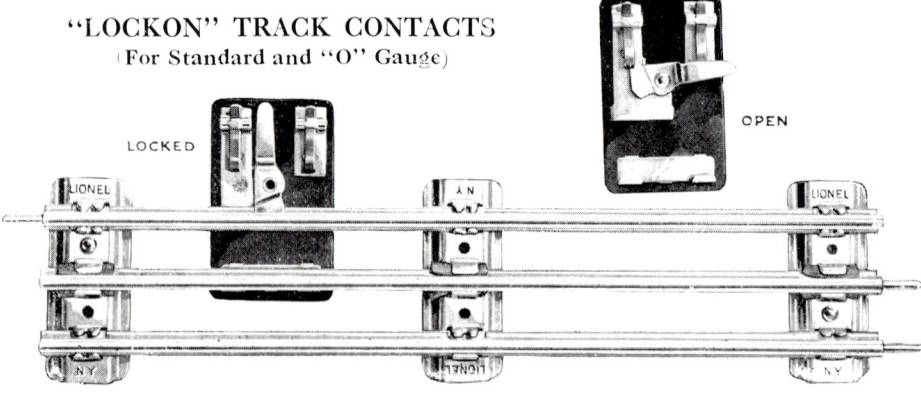

The "Lockon" contact is free from set screws and binding posts. The fingers that hold the wires in place are made of heavy tempered blue steel and are unbreakable. All parts are nickel plated and are mounted on a heavy fibre base.

No. "OTC" for "O" Gauge Track.
  Code Word "JOIN"
  Price *$0.20, †$0.24

No. "STC" for "Standard" Gauge Track.
  Code Word "JUICE"
  Price *$0.25, †$0.30

*Price, East of Missouri River.   †Price, West of Missouri River.

LIONEL Track Accessories

"STANDARD OF THE WORLD SINCE NINETEEN HUNDRED"

LOOK at these wonderful track accessories, boys! There is no part of a railroad layout that you cannot reproduce in miniature with this sturdily-built Lionel equipment. After you receive your Lionel Train Outfit be sure to get some of these "extras".

ACCESSORIES
For "Standard Gauge Track—2¼ Inches
See Track Layouts on Pages 46 and 47

Switch No. 22—(Right and Left Hand). The lever which moves the rails also sets signals and locks all mechanism. Signal lanterns have red and green discs. Length of switch, 16½ inches; width, 8 inches; height, 4½ inches. Connects with track in same manner as straight or curved sections.

Code Word "NASHVILLE"
Price per pair *$5.00, †$6.00

Electric Lighted Switch No. 21—(Right and Left Hand). This is similar in construction to No. 22 described above, but is equipped with an electric signal, having an electric bulb which can be easily removed. The light shining through the lantern shows red and green illuminated signals.

Code Word "WINTERVILLE"
Price per pair *$6.75, †$8.00

Crossing No. 20—For use in conjunction with Switches, enabling the formation of figure "8" and figure "8" loop. Measures 12 inches square. Cross rails are mounted on a solid base.

Code Word "BOSTON"
Price *$1.25, †$1.50

Bumper No. 23—An indispensable accessory for terminals or sidings. Has two spring plungers which absorb shock when car strikes it. Length, 14 inches; height, 3 inches. The Bumper frame can be removed from the track and replaced at any point desired.

Code Word "PROVIDENCE"
Price *$1.25, †$1.50

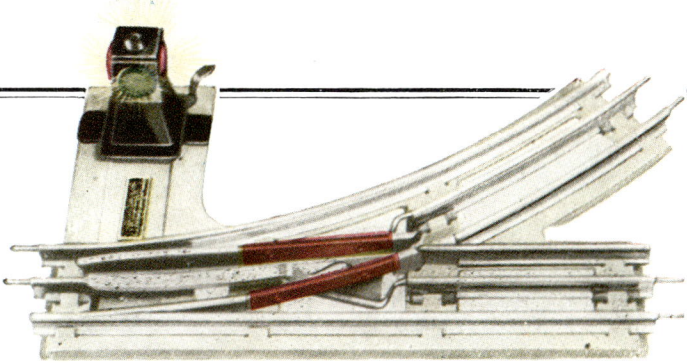

Improved Switches—Nos. 021 and 022

We are particularly desirous of drawing attention to the great improvement in the construction of our switches. Notwithstanding this improvement, prices have not been increased.

As will be seen from the illustration, the improvement consists of the insertion of two heavy fibre strips at the points where the rails cross. By the insertion of these fibre strips all danger of short-circuit is eliminated. A train passing over these points does not slow up nor does the headlight flicker or go out.

Crossing No. 020X
Crossing Nos. 20 and 020
Bumper Nos. 23 and 023

ACCESSORIES
For "O" Gauge Track—1⅜ Inches
See Track Layouts on Pages 46 and 47

Switch No. 022—(Right and Left Hand). Construction is similar to No. 22 Switch described opposite. Length, 11½ inches; width, 5½ inches; height, 3 inches.

Code Word "SPENCER"
Price per pair *$3.75, †$4.50

Electric Lighted Switch No. 021—(Right and Left Hand). Similar in construction to No. 21 Switch described opposite. Length, 11½ inches; width, 5½ inches; height, 3 inches.

Code Word "MOSHER"
Price per pair *$5.00, †$6.00

Crossing No. 020—Similar in construction to No. 20 Crossing described opposite. Measures 10¼ inches square.

Code Word "ORLAND"
Price *$1.00, †$1.20

Crossing No. 020X—This is a 45-degree crossing, forms the figure "8" when using all curved track. It occupies less space than the No. 020 Crossing.

Code Word "CROSS"
Price *$1.50, †$1.80

Bumper No. 023—Same construction as No. 23 Bumper described opposite. Length, 10¼ inches; height, 2 inches.

Code Word "DELTON"
Price *$0.80, †$1.00

*Price, East of Missouri River. †Price, West of Missouri River.

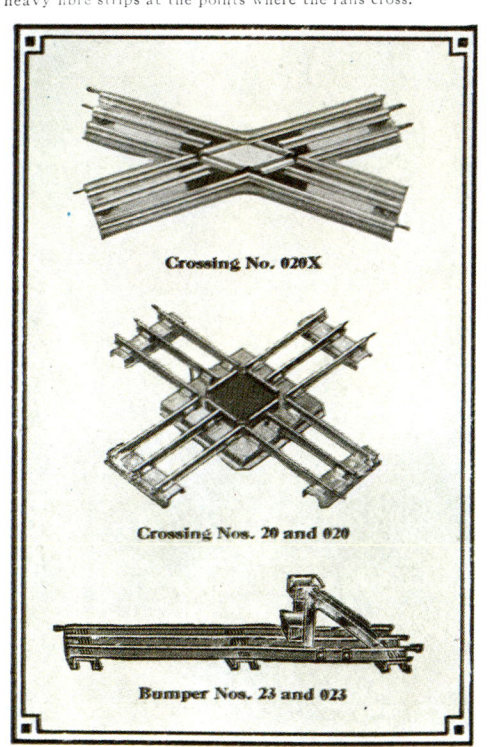

Lionel Electric Toy Trains & Multivolt Transformers

Steel Stations—Bungalows—Signal Tower

Station No. 121—Has no lighting system. Dimensions: 13½ inches long, 9 inches wide, 13 inches high.
 Code Word "UNION"   Price *$5.00, †$6.50

Station No. 122—Has inside illumination. Furnished with complete wiring circuit ready to attach to batteries, transformer, or reducer. Wires extend through wall. Complete with one 14-volt globe and nickeled center fixture. Same size as No. 121.
 Code Word "CENTRAL"   Price *$6.75, †$8.00

Station No. 123—(For 110-volt circuit.) Has inside illumination much more powerful than No. 122. This station can be lighted direct from house circuit. Is provided with nickeled center fixture, 25-watt lamp and 5 feet of cord with plug. Same size as No. 121.
 Code Word "GRAND"   Price *$8.50, †$10.00

Station No. 124, De Luxe Model—This number has two platform corner lights with reflectors, all finished in bright brass, and an inside light supported on a nickeled fixture. There is an elegance, grace and architectural dignity to this station, difficult to show in an illustration. The corner lighting brackets have specially designed supporting arms—a detail seldom attempted. For use with transformers or reducers. Equipped with three 14-volt globes. Same size as No. 121.
 Code Word "READING"   Price *$9.00, †$11.00

Station No. 125—(No interior illumination.) A beautifully proportioned model that retails at an exceedingly low price. The realistic detail must be seen to be appreciated. This station measures 10¼ inches long, 7¼ inches wide and 7 inches high.
 Code Word "ABOARD"   Price *$4.25, †$5.00

Station No. 126—Same as No. 125 described above, but has interior lighting fixture, lamp and wires ready for attaching to batteries, transformer or reducer.
 Code Word "ALIGHT"   Price *$5.00, †$6.50

Station No. 127—This can be used as a freight station for any size train outfit and will add a completing touch to a railroad layout. It is 7 in. long, 3½ inches wide and 4½ inches high. Complete with interior lighting fixture, lamp and wires ready to attach to batteries, transformer or reducer.
 Code Word "TOWNLY"   Price *$2.10, †$2.50

Station Nos. 121, 122, 123, 124

LIONEL all-steel houses and stations are substantially constructed and beautifully finished in a variety of durable enamels. They are so wonderfully proportioned that they have the appearance of real houses and stations in miniature. The die and embossing work, the inserted windows, the chimney stacks, roofs and entrances make them stand far above any similar toy ever introduced.

Interior Illumination—Some of the numbers listed on these pages have interior and outside lights complete with brackets, electric lamps and wires. This further adds to the realism and produces a wonderful effect.

Station Nos. 125, 126

Station No. 127

Bungalow Nos. 184, 185 (See opposite page for Prices)

Signal Tower No. 092 (See opposite page for Prices)

*Price, East of Missouri River. †Price, West of Missouri River.

36

Steel Bungalows and Villas—Sets of Houses

MILLIONS OF HAPPY USERS THE WORLD OVER

USE on Any Kind of Current. Lionel Stations, Bungalows and Villas can be attached to "Multi-volt" Transformers or reducers and also to dry or storage batteries.

For Model Villages. In this connection the Lionel Houses will be found invaluable. There is no limit to the wonderful effects that can be produced.

For Outdoor Railroads. Picture the fun that can be had when these houses and stations are placed around a big track layout in the garden or on any outdoor plot, and used in connection with Lionel Railroad Accessories.

Villa No. 191 (illuminated)—Size 7⅛ in. long, 5⅛ in. wide, 5¼ in. high.
Code Word "SOLID"
Price *$3.35, †$4.00

Villa No. 189 (illuminated)—Size 5½ in. long, 4⅛ in. wide, 5⅜ in. high. Code Word "MANSION"
Price *$2.95, †$3.50.

Signal Tower No. 092 (illuminated) illustrated on opposite page—Dimensions: 5 in. long, 4 in. wide, 5½ in. high. Complete with interior lighting fixture, lamp and wires for connecting to batteries, transformer or reducer.
Code Word "CYRIL"   Price *$2.10, †$2.50

Bungalow No. 184 (illuminated)—Size 4¾ in. long, 2¾ in. wide, 4 in. high.
Code Word "HOME"   Price *$1.50, †$1.80

Bungalow No. 185—Same as No. 184 but without interior illumination. *(See illustration on opposite page)*
Code Word "LEADER"   Price *$1.00, †$1.20

Bungalow Set No. 186—Comprises 5 No. 184 illuminated bungalows, assorted colors.
Code Word "HAMLET"   Price *$7.50, †$9.00

Bungalow Set No. 187—Same as above but without interior illumination.
Code Word "CITY"   Price *$5.00, †$6.00

Set No. 192—Comprises 1 No. 191 Villa, 1 No. 189 Villa and 2 No. 184 Bungalows, complete with interior lights and wires for connecting.
Code Word "VILLAGE"   Price *$7.35, †$8.80

*Price, East of Missouri River.   †Price, West of Missouri River.

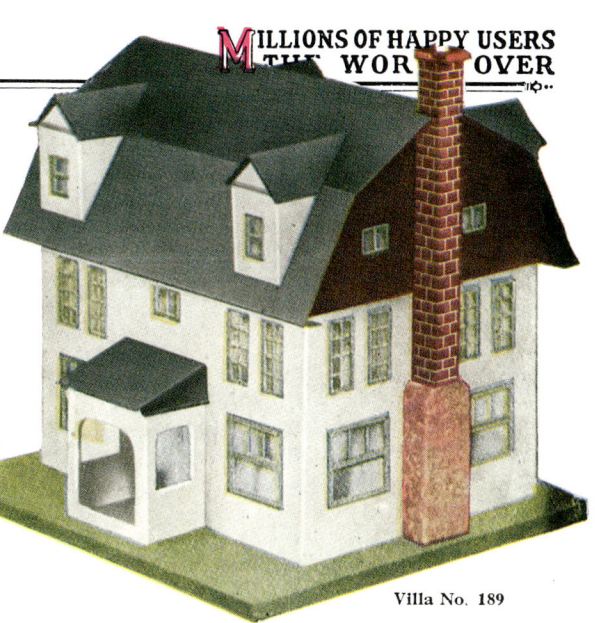

Villa No. 191

Villa No. 189

Set No. 186, 187

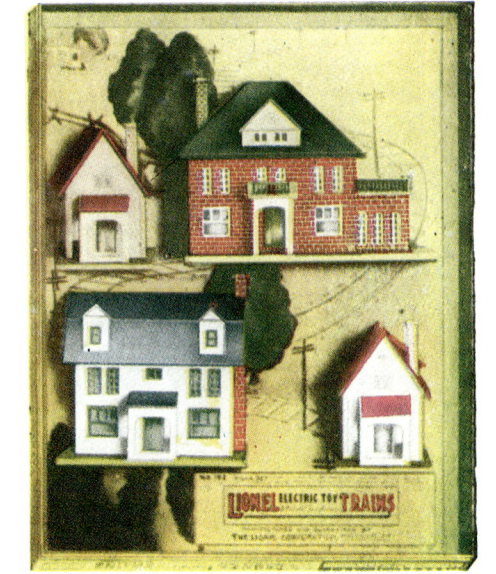

Set No. 192

37

1923

Steel Tunnels for "Standard" and "O" Gauge Track

LIONEL TRAINS are worthy of good accessories and it is therefore with great pleasure that we offer the Lionel steel tunnels, which are a wonderful improvement over the old, flimsy papier-mâché ones that users of train outfits were compelled to accept before we introduced ours.

Lionel tunnels are made of steel throughout, being accurately designed and formed in our special machinery. They stand evenly on the floor without the slightest twist. Their rigid construction does not make it necessary to have any cross-braces on the base which would interfere with the track level.

The front and rear entrances of Lionel tunnels are embossed in exact reproduction of heavy stone masonry, having a keystone at the top. The bodies of the tunnels represent mountainsides in miniature and the coloring is made to harmonize beautifully. We draw particular attention to the detail on No. 120 Tunnel, which has the mountain roadside wonderfully modelled as well as the little metal "chalet," all in perfect proportion to the size of the tunnel.

All Lionel tunnels are practically indestructible and are very low priced considering the workmanship in them.

No. 120

No. 119

No. 118

Your "Power-Plant" Should Be a LIONEL "Multivolt" Transformer. See pages 32 and 33.

Tunnel No. 118, for "O" Gauge Only—Will allow passage of any "O" gauge train. Is 8 inches long, 7 inches wide and 7½ inches extreme height. Portals are 4 inches wide and 5⅓ inches high inside.
Code Word "SIMPLON"   Price *$2.10, †$2.50

*Price, East of Missouri River.   †Price, West of Missouri River.

Tunnel No. 119, for "O" Gauge and Some "Standard" Gauge Trains—For use with all "O" gauge trains and "Standard" gauge trains Nos. 34, 37, 39, 40 and 41. Is 12 inches long, 9 inches wide and 10 inches extreme height. Portals are 5 inches wide and 6½ inches high inside.
Code Word "HOOSAC"   Price *$3.35, †$4.00

Tunnel No. 120, for All Lionel Trains—This splendid model is the very best produced for beauty, grace of design and substantial construction. Is 17 inches long, 12 inches wide and 11 inches extreme height. Inside dimensions of portals are 6½ inches wide and 8 inches high.
Code Word "HUDSON"   Price *$5.85, †$7.00

Steel Bridges for "Standard" and "O" Gauge Track

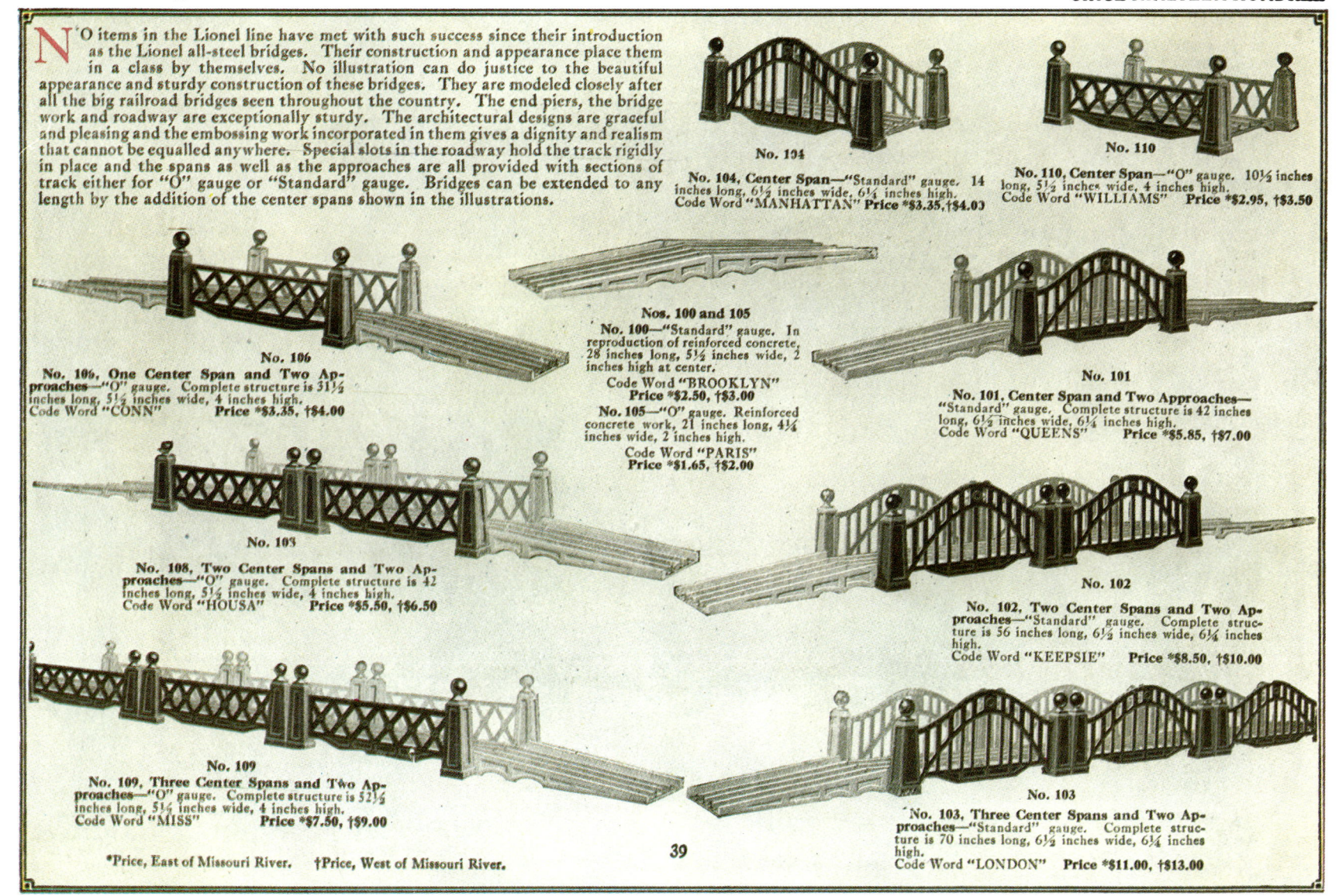

"TANDARD OF THE WORLD SINCE NINETEEN HUNDRED

NO items in the Lionel line have met with such success since their introduction as the Lionel all-steel bridges. Their construction and appearance place them in a class by themselves. No illustration can do justice to the beautiful appearance and sturdy construction of these bridges. They are modeled closely after all the big railroad bridges seen throughout the country. The end piers, the bridge work and roadway are exceptionally sturdy. The architectural designs are graceful and pleasing and the embossing work incorporated in them gives a dignity and realism that cannot be equalled anywhere. Special slots in the roadway hold the track rigidly in place and the spans as well as the approaches are all provided with sections of track either for "O" gauge or "Standard" gauge. Bridges can be extended to any length by the addition of the center spans shown in the illustrations.

No. 104
No. 104, Center Span—"Standard" gauge. 14 inches long, 6½ inches wide, 6¼ inches high.
Code Word "MANHATTAN" Price *$3.35, †$4.00

No. 110
No. 110, Center Span—"O" gauge. 10½ inches long, 5½ inches wide, 4 inches high.
Code Word "WILLIAMS" Price *$2.95, †$3.50

No. 106
No. 106, One Center Span and Two Approaches—"O" gauge. Complete structure is 31½ inches long, 5½ inches wide, 4 inches high.
Code Word "CONN" Price *$3.35, †$4.00

Nos. 100 and 105
No. 100—"Standard" gauge. In reproduction of reinforced concrete, 28 inches long, 5½ inches wide, 2 inches high at center.
Code Word "BROOKLYN" Price *$2.50, †$3.00
No. 105—"O" gauge. Reinforced concrete work, 21 inches long, 4¼ inches wide, 2 inches high.
Code Word "PARIS" Price *$1.65, †$2.00

No. 101
No. 101, Center Span and Two Approaches—"Standard" gauge. Complete structure is 42 inches long, 6½ inches wide, 6¼ inches high.
Code Word "QUEENS" Price *$5.85, †$7.00

No. 108
No. 108, Two Center Spans and Two Approaches—"O" gauge. Complete structure is 42 inches long, 5½ inches wide, 4 inches high.
Code Word "HOUSA" Price *$5.50, †$6.50

No. 102
No. 102, Two Center Spans and Two Approaches—"Standard" gauge. Complete structure is 56 inches long, 6½ inches wide, 6¼ inches high.
Code Word "KEEPSIE" Price *$8.50, †$10.00

No. 109
No. 109, Three Center Spans and Two Approaches—"O" gauge. Complete structure is 52½ inches long, 5½ inches wide, 4 inches high.
Code Word "MISS" Price *$7.50, †$9.00

No. 103
No. 103, Three Center Spans and Two Approaches—"Standard" gauge. Complete structure is 70 inches long, 6½ inches wide, 6¼ inches high.
Code Word "LONDON" Price *$11.00, †$13.00

*Price, East of Missouri River. †Price, West of Missouri River.

Lionel Electric Toy Trains — Accessories—Electrically Illuminated and Operated

BOYS! Read all about these wonderful "live" accessories. They are built just like the real equipment seen on the big railroads. The mechanism is perfect, they are all "sure" in their action and are built of steel all through.

No. 65 and 66 Semaphores—The base is made of heavy sheet steel. The post, semaphore arms and ladder are also constructed of steel. The transparent colored discs which are securely fastened to the semaphore arms show "Danger", "Clear" or "Caution" signals. The electric lamps are enclosed in beautifully enameled steel lanterns which are removable so that lamps can be easily renewed. A metal finger holds these lantern caps in place. The levers which operate the signal arms are fastened to the base and are connected to rods running up beneath the ladder. The wiring and insulation are inside the post and short circuits are impossible. The electric lamps shining through the colored discs present a wonderfully realistic effect.

No. 69 and 069 Warning Signals—A substantially constructed fully nickeled bell is mounted on an ornamental post bearing a heavy brass warning sign. A specially constructed section of track is supplied to which the warning signal is connected, wires being also provided for the purpose. The electric bell rings as long as the locomotive and cars pass over the special section of track, and the bell automatically stops ringing when the train has passed. The signal post is made of steel and the heavy base has holes so that the warning signal can be fastened near the railroad crossing.

No. 77 and 077 Crossing Gates—These can be used singly or in pairs, with the special sections of track supplied with them and which are attached to the rest of the layout in the usual manner. When the train approaches and passes over the special section, the gates close and they open as soon as the train has gone by.

Lionel Crossing Gates are exact reproductions of the real ones. Be sure to add them to your train layout if you want the finishing touch.

No. 76 and 076 Block Signals—This new Lionel accessory will add life and realism to any train outfit. It consists of a steel standard to which are attached two electric illuminated lanterns showing red and green signals.

When the train passes over the special sections of track supplied with the signal, the green lantern lights up, indicating "Track clear", and after it leaves the first section of special track the red light shows, indicating "Stop" to the train following. This red light goes out as soon as the train leaves the second special section of track, the same as the block signals operating on real railroads.

No. 65—One signal arm. Complete with electric bulb; 14 inches high.
Code Word "TOWER"
Price *$2.50, †$3.00

No. 069—For "O" gauge track. Complete with special section of track and wires for connecting.
Code Word "RINGER"
Price *$3.15, †$3.70
No. 69—For "Standard" gauge track. Complete with special section of track and wires for connecting.
Code Word "BEWARE"
Price *$3.35, †$4.00
Dimensions: 8¾ inches high, base 2½ inches square, sign 2½ inches square.

No. 77 Crossing Gate for "Standard" Gauge Track—Complete with one special section of track and wires for connecting.
Code Word "TARRY"
Price *$4.25, †$5.00
No. 077 Crossing Gate for "O" Gauge Track—Complete with one special section of track and wires for connecting.
*Price $4.00, †$4.80
Code Word "ADVANCE"
Dimensions: 11 inches long, base is 4¾ inches long, 2½ inches wide.

No. 66—Two signal arms. Complete with two electric bulbs; 14 inches high.
Code Word "LEMPSTER"
Price *$3.75, †$4.50

No. 65 Semaphore

No. 076 for "O" Gauge Track—Complete with wires and two special sections of track. Code Word "FORWARD"
Price *$3.15, †$3.70
No. 76 for "Standard" Gauge Track—Complete with wires and two special sections of track.
Dimensions: 8¾ inches high, base 2¾ inches square
Code Word "ONWARD" Price *$3.35, †$4.00

No. 69 and 069 Warning Signals

No. 76 and 076 Block Signals

No. 77 and 077 Crossing Gates

Special Track for Warning Signals, Crossing Gates and Block Signals
—OSS ("O" gauge), per section, Code Word "RELAY" Price *$0.40, †$0.50
—SS ("Standard" Gauge), per section, Code Word "BURT" Price *$0.60, †$0.70.

No. 66 Semaphore

*Price, East of Missouri River. †Price, West of Missouri River.

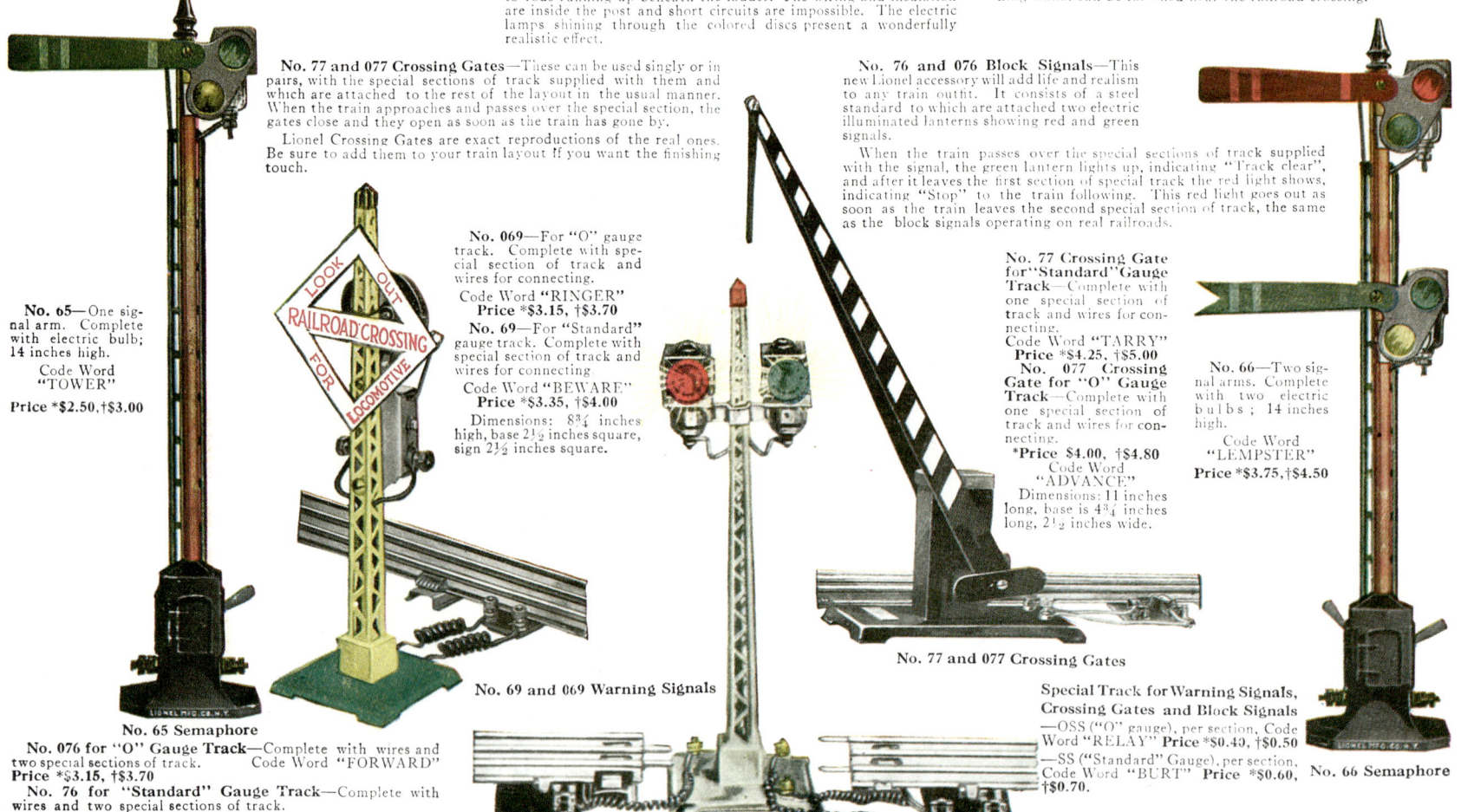

40

Accessories—Accessory Sets

MILLIONS OF HAPPY USERS THE WORLD OVER

LIONEL accessory sets are unquestionably the best constructed as well as the most popular on the market. This is not to be wondered at considering the fact that they are so durable and attractive in design. A miniature railroad layout is considerably enhanced by the addition of a set of telegraph posts placed at regular intervals around the track. Copper wire can be strung from the insulators, producing an effect of great realism.

If the semaphores, lamp post and warning signal which form No. 70 set are added to your train layout the finishing touches are provided. All Lionel accessories are constructed of steel throughout and are beautifully finished.

Outfit No. 70—Comprises two No. 62 Semaphores, one No. 59 Lamp Post, one No. 68 Warning Signal and two globes for the lamp post. Attractively packed.
Code Word "HOBART"
Price *$4.25, †$5.00

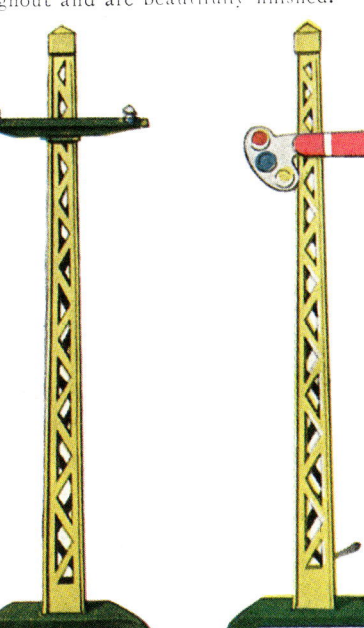

No. 60 Telegraph Post—A companion to No. 62 Semaphore and No. 68 Warning Signal. The arm is equipped with real glass insulators. Height 8¾ inches, base 2½ inches square.
Code Word "WIRE"
Price *$0.65, †$0.80

No. 62 Semaphore—The semaphore arm has three discs—red, green and yellow—and the arm is operated by a lever near the base. Steel construction throughout. Height 8¾ ins, base 2½ inches square.
Code Word "CAUTION"
Price *$0.80, †$1.00

Outfit No. 71—Comprises six No. 60 Steel Telegraph Posts as described on this page. Packed in a very attractive box.
Code Word "USEFUL"
Price *$3.75, †$4.50

No. 68 Warning Signal—This conforms in size with No. 62 Semaphore and No. 60 Telegraph Post, and the construction and size are similar to No. 69 and No. 069 described on the opposite page. These should be placed at every railroad crossing.
Code Word "STOP"
Price *$0.90, †$1.10

No. 89 Flag Staff—This is substantially constructed of steel and is 14 inches high. The base is 2½ inches square. It is beautifully finished in white enamel and the spire is finished in a rich black. The silk flag supplied with it can be raised or lowered by means of a cord to which it is attached and which is fastened on a hook near the base.

Boys! Place it in front of a station or in the centre of a grass plot that may be laid out in connection with a model village or railroad. Let it wave proudly.
Code Word "ARTHUR"
Price *$0.75, †$0.90

*Price, East of Missouri River. †Price, West of Missouri River.

41

1923

Lionel Electric Toy Trains — Steel Lamp Posts

No miniature railroad is complete without the addition of Lionel lamp posts, which are faithful reproductions of boulevard and street lamp posts seen everywhere. All Lionel lamp posts are substantially constructed of steel throughout—they won't bend or break. The binding posts to which electrical connections are made are conveniently situated and are securely fastened and perfectly insulated. There is no chance of short circuit with Lionel lamp posts, for great care is used in their construction and every one is thoroughly tested before leaving the factory. The globes supplied with all lamp posts are in exact proportion to the size of the posts. It is impossible to secure any other make of lamp post that has the dignity and grace of design to be found in the Lionel lamp posts illustrated below.

Lamp Post No. 61—13 inches high. Complete with electric globe.
Code Word "INDIANA"
Price *$2.10, †$2.50

No. 61

No. 58
Lamp Post No. 58—Another new addition. This lamp post is graceful in design and is 7⅜ inches high. Complete with globe.
Code Word "JENNY"
Price *$1.25, †$1.50

No. 57
Lamp Post No. 57—This is a new addition to the Lionel family and is a wonderful reproduction of the street lamp posts seen in many cities. It is 7½ inches high. The top is easily removable so that the lamp can be renewed when necessary. Complete with lamp.
Code Word "CHEERY"
Price *$1.65, †$2.00

No. 59
Lamp Post No. 59—Similar in design to No. 61, but is 8¾ inches high. Complete with globe.
Code Word "BRIGHT"
Price *$1.50, †$1.80

Lamp Post No. 67—13 inches high. Complete with two electric globes.
Code Word "EDMUNDS"
Price *$2.95, †$3.50

No. 67

*Price, East of Missouri River. †Price, West of Missouri River.

42

Interior Lighting Outfits—Lamp Renewals

"STANDARD OF THE WORLD" SINCE NINETEEN HUNDRED

Pullman Illuminating Outfits for "Standard" Gauge Trains

THESE outfits consist of flexible cords, equipped with lamp sockets and bulbs, so arranged that they fit to the terminals with which all locomotives operating on "Standard" gauge track are equipped. The connections are permanent and lamps can be arranged in any manner desired by the user. A set of two or three lamps can be strung through one or more cars. The effect of the Pullman cars illuminated by these lamps is very realistic and materially adds to the appearance of the train. Lamps screw into sockets the same as large ones and can be renewed at will. A steel clip is fastened to each lamp socket. The clip clamps onto the crossbar in the center of the roof of each car. Both ends of the cord have brass terminals; one of which connects to binding post on locomotive and the other fastens to connection in rear car.

We make outfits to be used on direct or alternating current when properly reduced with "Multivolt" transformers; also for dry and storage batteries. Be sure to specify the current you use when ordering.

Outfit No. 27—A three-car lighting set. Consists of three 8-volt bulbs with 5 feet of flexible cord and sockets. To be used on **batteries** or **reduced direct current**. Complete with directions for connecting.
Code Word "ANDERSON"   Price *$2.95, †$3.50

Outfit No. 217—A three-car lighting set. Same as above, but equipped with three 14-volt bulbs to be used on **reduced alternating current**. Complete with directions for connecting.
Code Word "STEPNEY"   Price *$2.95, †$3.50

Outfit No. 270—A two-car lighting set. Consists of two 8-volt bulbs with 3 feet of flexible cord and sockets. To be used on **batteries** or **reduced direct current**. Complete with directions for connecting.
Code Word "PARSLEY"   Price *$2.10, †$2.50

Outfit No. 271—A two-car lighting set. Same as above, but equipped with two 14-volt bulbs to be used on **reduced alternating current**. Complete with directions for connecting.
Code Word "BALLARD"   Price *$2.10, †$2.50

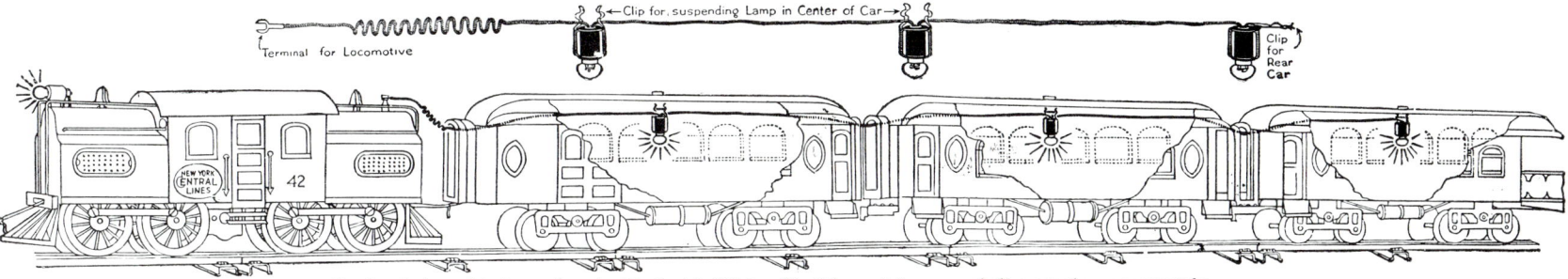

Sectional view of train equipped with electric lights. Flexible cord, lamps and clips are shown separately.

Lamp Assortment No. 111

We supply Lionel dealers with a handsome cabinet of renewal lamps for use in headlights and all electrically illuminated accessories. These lamps are of the finest quality and are supplied in 8, 14 and 21 volts, either ½ inch round or 1 inch round, as described opposite. Fifty assorted lamps are packed in each cabinet. The chart on the inside cover gives valuable information as to the uses of the various lamps. Each lamp is packed in a wooden container.

No. 111 Lamp Assortment.
Code Word "LUX."
Price *$15.00, †$20.00

*Price, East of Missouri River.   †Price, West of Missouri River.

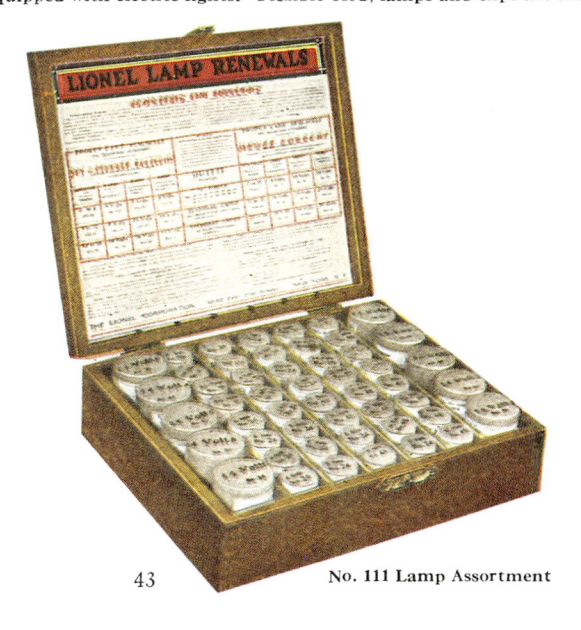

No. 111 Lamp Assortment

Lamp Renewals

Lamp No 24, ½ inch round, 8 volts.
Code Word "CAMBRIDGE"
Price *$0.30, †$0.40

Lamp No. 26, ½ inch round, 14 volts.
Code Word "OXFORD"
Price *$0.30, †$0.40

Lamp No. 48, ½ inch round, 21 volts.
Code Word "MILTON"
Price *$0.30, †$0.40

Globe No. 46, 1 inch round, 8 volts.
Code Word "ETON"
Price *$0.30, †$0.40

Globe No. 30, 1 inch round, 14 volts.
Code Word "KINGS"
Price *$0.30, †$0.40

Globe No 49, 1 inch round, 21 volts.
Code Word "HUNTERS"
Price *$0.30, †0.40

LIONEL ELECTRIC TOY TRAINS | LIONEL Scenic

WHAT a fascinating outfit to put in a boy's playroom! Hours and hours of good honest fun will be had by the lucky owner of one of these wonderful Lionel Scenic Railways. They are practically indestructible and are easily attached to the house current either with a "Multivolt" Transformer or Direct Current Reducer. The liberal amount of equipment provided with these Scenic Railways as well as the detail embodied in their construction makes them worth far more than the prices at which they sell. Read all about the various sizes we make and place your order for them early as we only make a limited quantity each year.

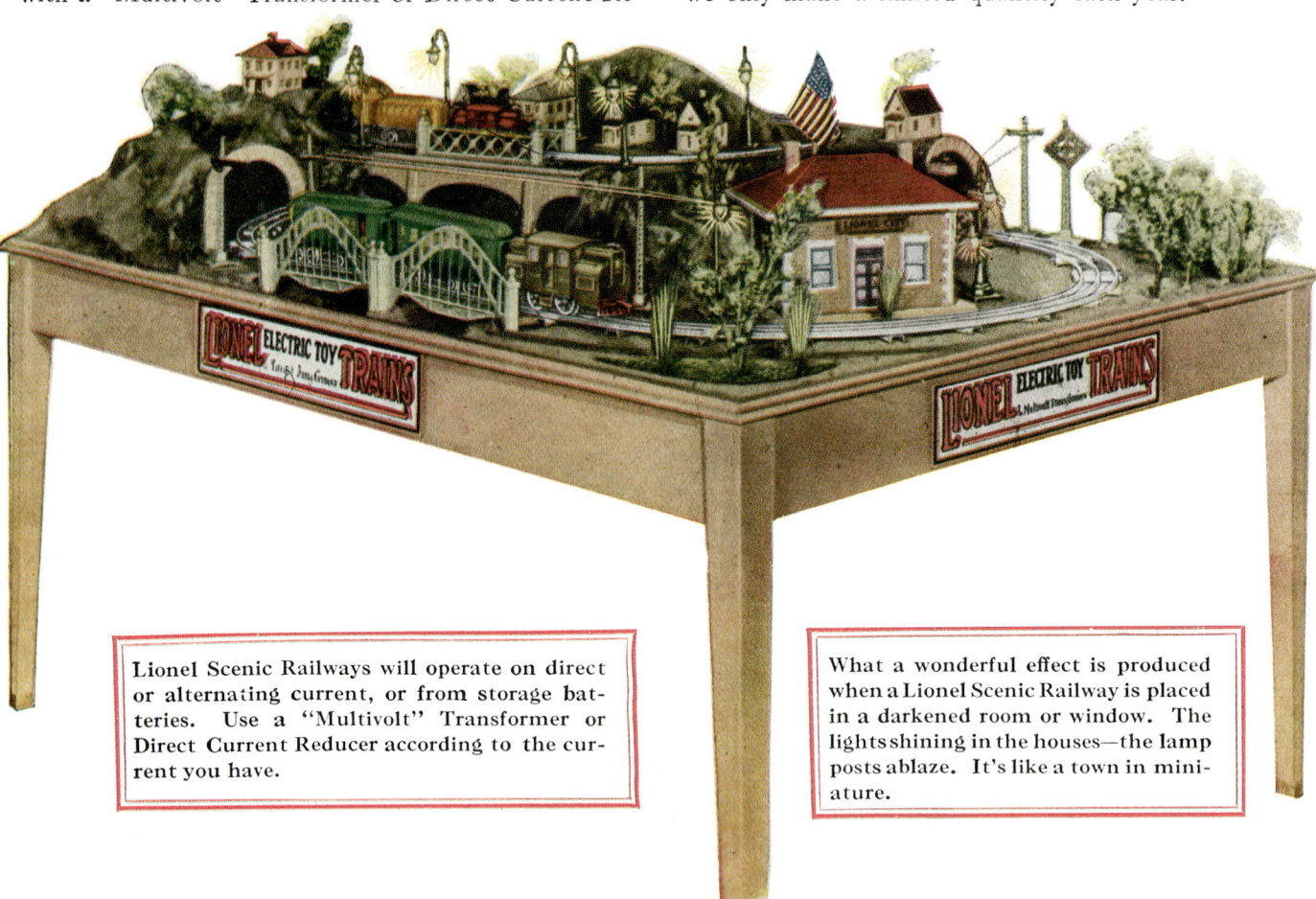

Lionel Scenic Railways will operate on direct or alternating current, or from storage batteries. Use a "Multivolt" Transformer or Direct Current Reducer according to the current you have.

What a wonderful effect is produced when a Lionel Scenic Railway is placed in a darkened room or window. The lights shining in the houses—the lamp posts ablaze. It's like a town in miniature.

TO DEALERS

THE Lionel Corporation originated and developed these wonderfully attractive Scenic Railway Displays last year and are now introducing greatly improved models.

These Scenic Railways not only increase the sale of Lionel Trains but draw attention to all other toys carried by the dealer. The tables are made with removable legs and the entire scenic effect is constructed of indestructible sheet steel. No detail is omitted to make them as complete and realistic as possible. The mountains, trees, bridges and other details combine to make an exceptionally beautiful display. Water can be placed in the metal-lined tank which forms the brook and in which gold fish can be placed. The station, lamp posts and houses are illuminated and the table is wired ready for use on the house current, either with a "Multivolt" Transformer for alternating current or a direct current reducer for direct current. Dry cells or storage batteries can be used where no house current is available.

Railways

MILLIONS OF HAPPY USERS THE WORLD OVER

PRICES AND SPECIFICATIONS

No. 177 Scenic Railway—(Illustrated on opposite page). Size of table, 6 feet 6 inches long by 4 feet 9 inches wide. Table has removable legs. Two track layouts are incorporated in this display; one "O" Gauge and one "Standard" Gauge, together with the following equipment:

1 No. 34 Train	2 No. 104 Spans	1 No. 57 Lamp Post
1 No. 155 Train	1 No. 110 Span	1 No. 62 Semaphore
1 No. 191 Villa	1 No. 124 Station	1 No. 69 Warning Signal
1 No. 189 Villa	2 No. 59 Lamp Posts	3 No. 60 Telegraph Posts
5 No. 184 Bungalows	5 No. 58 Lamp Posts	1 No. 89 Flagstaff

The station, houses and accessories are all illuminated and wired as well as the track for train outfits, ready to attach to transformer or reducer.

We guarantee these Scenic Railway Displays to reach any part of the country in perfect condition, due to the extra care we use in packing.

Code Word "ATTRACT"   Price *$200.00, †$250.00

No. 178 Scenic Railway—This is similar in appearance to the No. 177 and is constructed in just the same manner, but has one "O" Gauge Track layout. The table measures 5 feet long by 3 feet wide. The following equipment is supplied with it:

1 No. 57 Lamp Post	1 No. 155 Train	5 No. 184 Bungalows
1 No. 62 Semaphore	2 No. 110 Spans	1 No. 89 Flagstaff
1 No. 118 Tunnel	1 No. 124 Station	1 No. 069 Warning Signal
4 No. 58 Lamp Posts		5 No. 60 Telegraph Posts

The station, houses and accessories are all illuminated and wired as well as the track for train outfit, ready to attach to transformer or reducer.

Code Word "ALBERT"   Price *$150.00, †$180.00

No. 180 Scenic Railway (Platform Only)—Size of platform 3 feet by 3 feet. The following equipment is supplied with it:

1 No. 160 Train	2 No. 58 Lamp Posts	1 No. 62 Semaphore
1 No. 127 Station	3 No. 184 Bungalows	1 No. 89 Flagstaff
	2 No. 60 Telegraph Posts	

The station, houses and accessories are all illuminated and wired as well as the track for train outfit, ready to attach to transformer or reducer.

Code Word "PEARL"   Price *$50.00, †$60.00

The New Small Size Lionel Scenic Railway

(Illustrated below)

Many Lionel enthusiasts who saw our Scenic Railways in windows and stores last year purchased them after they had served the dealer's purpose as display pieces.

Many others who wanted them but who could not pay the price have asked us to bring out a smaller one at less cost.

We now present Lionel Scenic Railway No. 180—built just as beautifully and substantially as our larger sizes.

The mountain scenery, illuminated houses, tunnel, shrubbery and all the equipment, are on the same scale of excellence as those incorporated in our larger numbers. Being smaller, they are sold at a very reasonable price.

No finer toy will ever be produced.

*Price, East of Missouri River.   †Price, West of Missouri River.

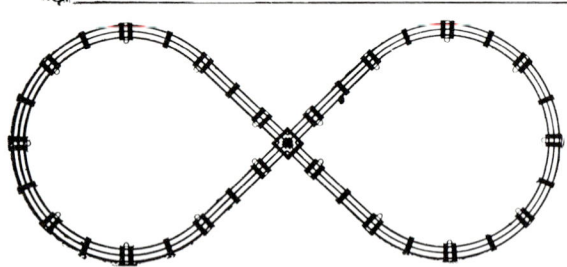

Layouts Constructed With Lionel

Track Layout OA—"O" Gauge Track Used—One No. 020 Crossing, four sections OS straight track, twelve sections OC curved track. Outside dimensions, 72 inches long and 30 inches wide.
Track Layout SA—"Standard" Gauge Track Used—One No. 20 Crossing, four sections S straight track, twelve sections C curved track. Outside dimensions 100 inches long and 42 inches wide.

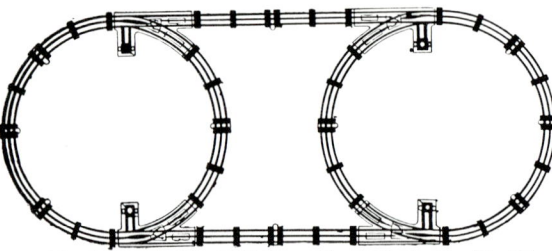

Track Layout OB—"O" Gauge Track Used—Two No. 021 or No. 022 Left Hand Switches, two No. 021 or No. 022 Right Hand Switches, four sections OS straight track, twelve sections OC curved track. Outside dimensions, 72 inches long, 30 inches wide.
Track Layout SB—"Standard" Gauge Track Used—Two No. 21 or No. 22 Left Hand Switches, two No. 21 or No. 22 Right Hand Switches, four sections S straight track, twelve sections C curved track. Outside dimensions, 100 inches long and 42 inches wide.

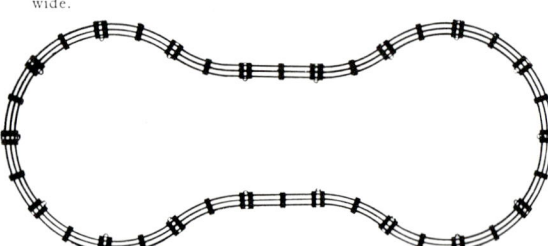

Track Layout OD—"O" Gauge Track Used—Sixteen sections OC curved track, two sections OS straight track. Outside dimensions, 74 inches long and 30 inches wide.
Track Layout SD—"Standard" Gauge Track Used—Sixteen sections C curved track, two sections S straight track. Outside dimensions, 117 inches long and 42 inches wide.

HERE'S loads of fun for everybody—making various track figures with Lionel "O" gauge or Standard gauge track. The very foundation of your railroad must be strong. Therefore, use Lionel Track.

Look at the number of figures you can construct—and hundreds more by using straight and curved sections, switches, crossings and bumpers.

Isn't it great to watch your train go over the crossing—then you turn the switch and send it over to the siding—back again at full speed down the straightaway.

Your train will always operate better if you make the curves large in diameter. Always break up the circles as much as possible by inserting straight sections.

See pages 34 and 35 for Prices of Track, Switches and other Accessories.

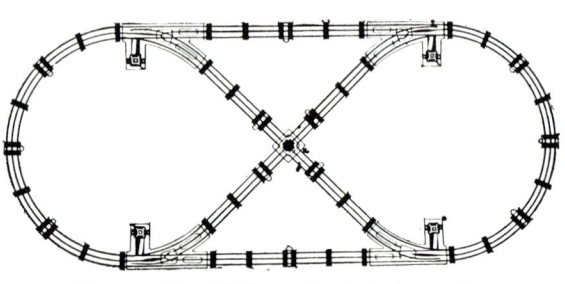

Track Layout OE—"O" Gauge Track Used—Two No. 021 or No. 022 Left Hand Switches, two No. 021 or No. 022 Right Hand Switches, one No. 020 Crossing, eight sections OC curved track, eight sections OS straight track. Outside dimensions, 72 inches long and 30 inches wide.
Track Layout SE—"Standard" Gauge Track Used—Two No. 21 or No. 22 Left Hand Switches, two No. 21 or No. 22 Right Hand Switches, one No. 20 Crossing, eight sections C curved track, eight sections S straight track. Outside dimensions, 100 inches long and 42 inches wide.

Track Layout OF—"O" Gauge Track Used—One No. 020X Crossing, fourteen sections OC curved track. Outside dimensions, 60 inches long and 30 inches wide.

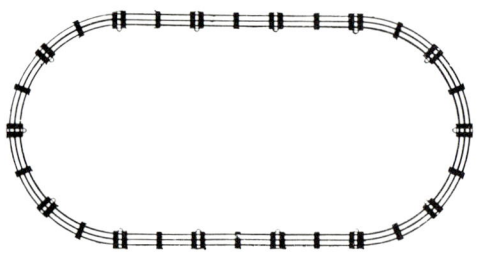

Track Layout OG—"O" Gauge Track Used—Eight sections OC curved track, six sections OS straight track. Outside dimensions, 60 inches long and 30 inches wide.
Track Layout SG—"Standard" Gauge Track Used—Eight sections C curved track, 6 sections S straight track. Outside dimensions, 87 inches long and 42 inches wide.

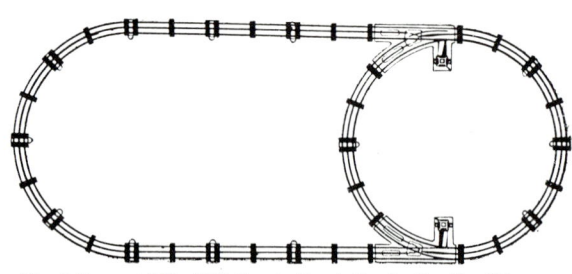

Track Layout OH—"O" Gauge Track Used—One No. 021 or No. 022 Left Hand Switch, one No. 021 or No. 022 Right Hand Switch, ten sections OC curved track, six sections OS straight track. Outside dimensions, 72 inches long and 30 inches wide.
Track Layout SH—"Standard" Gauge Track Used—One No. 21 or No. 22 Left Hand Switch, one No. 21 or No. 22 Right Hand Switch, ten sections C curved track, six sections S straight track. Outside dimensions, 100 inches long and 42 inches wide.

"O" Gauge and "Standard" Gauge Track

"STANDARD OF THE WORLD" SINCE NINETEEN HUNDRED

Track Layout OJ—"O" Gauge Track Used—Two No. 021 or No. 022 Right Hand Switches, two No. 021 or No. 022 Left Hand Switches, one No. 020 Crossing, sixteen sections OC curved track, four sections OS straight track. Outside dimensions, 92 inches long and 30 inches wide.

Track Layout SJ—"Standard" Gauge Track Used—Two No. 21 or No. 22 Right Hand Switches, two No. 21 or No. 22 Left Hand Switches, one No. 20 Crossing, sixteen sections C curved track, four sections S straight track. Outside dimensions 132 inches long and 42 inches wide.

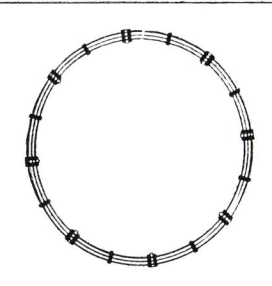

Track Layout OM—"O" Gauge Track Used—Eight sections OC curved track. Outside dimensions, 30 inches in diameter.

Track Layout SM—"Standard" Gauge Track Used—Eight sections C curved track. Outside dimensions, 42 inches in diameter.

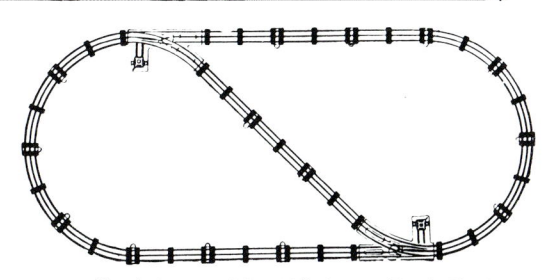

Track Layout ON—"O" Gauge Track Used—Two No. 021 or No. 022 Right Hand Switches, 8 sections OC curved track, nine sections OS straight track. Outside dimensions, 66 inches long and 30 inches wide.

Track Layout SN—"Standard" Gauge Track Used—Two No. 21 or No. 22 Right Hand Switches, 8 sections C curved track, nine sections S straight track. Outside dimensions, 100 inches long and 42 inches wide.

See pages 34 and 35 for Prices of Track, Switches and other Accessories.

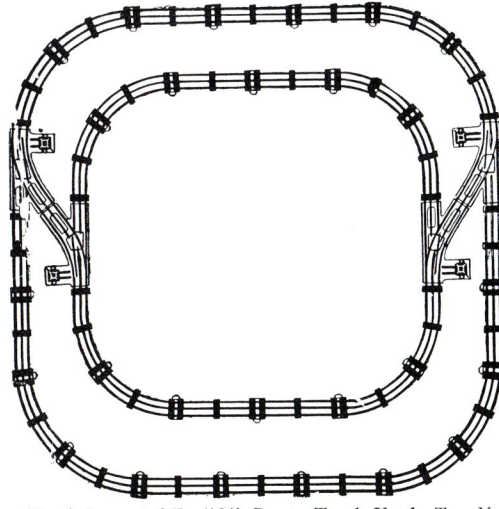

Track Layout OK—"O" Gauge Track Used—Two No. 021 or No. 022 Right Hand Switches, two No. 021 or No. 022 Left Hand Switches, sixteen sections OC curved track, fourteen sections OS straight track. Outside dimensions, 64 inches long and 64 inches wide.

Track Layout SK—"Standard" Gauge Track Used—Two No. 21 or No. 22 Right Hand Switches, two No. 21 or No. 22 Left Hand Switches, sixteen sections C curved track, fourteen sections S straight track. Outside dimensions, 85 inches long and 85 inches wide.

Isaac Goldmann Company, Printers, New York

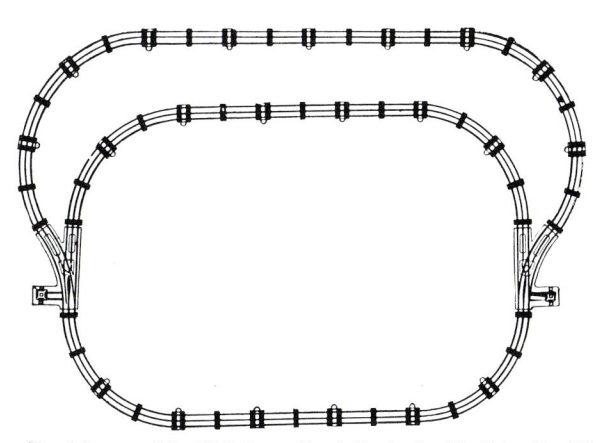

Track Layout OO—"O" Gauge Track Used—One No. 021 or No. 022 Right Hand Switch, one No. 021 or No. 022 Left Hand Switch, fourteen sections OC curved track, ten sections OS straight track. Outside dimensions, 75 inches long and 50 inches wide.

Track Layout SO—"Standard" Gauge Track Used—One No. 21 or No. 22 Right Hand Switch, one No. 21 or No. 22 Left Hand Switch, fourteen sections C curved track, ten sections S straight track. Outside dimensions, 100 inches long and 75 inches wide.

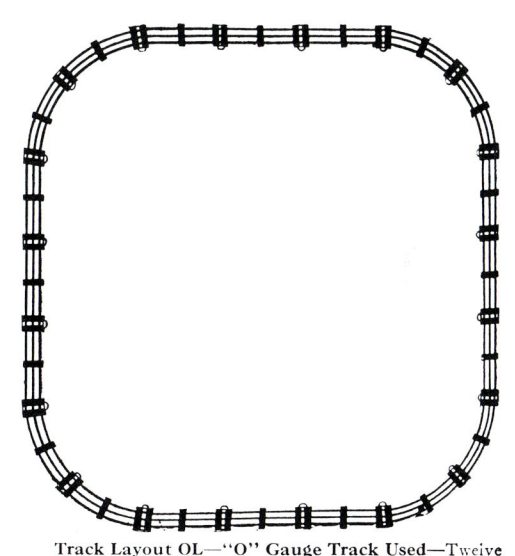

Track Layout OL—"O" Gauge Track Used—Twelve sections OS straight track, eight sections OC curved track. Outside dimensions, 64 inches long and 64 inches wide.

Track Layout SL—"Standard" Gauge Track Used—Twelve sections S straight track, eight sections C curved track. Outside dimensions, 85 inches long and 85 inches wide.

THE FACTORY THAT HAS MADE
MILLIONS OF BOYS HAPPY

THE LIONEL BUILDINGS COVER
FOUR ACRES OF FLOOR SPACE

Factory and Service Department
605-619 SOUTH TWENTY-FIRST STREET
IRVINGTON, NEW JERSEY

Offices and Display Rooms
48-52 EAST TWENTY-FIRST STREET
NEW YORK, N. Y.

LIONEL ELECTRIC TOY TRAINS
1924 & "Multivolt" Transformers

REG. U.S. PAT. OFF.

The Fascinating Sport of Lionel Railroading

BOYS, the world's finest miniature railroads are waiting for you—electric railroads that are more than toys—that can be bought at prices you can afford to pay and of a quality that is summed up in one word—SUPREME.

Go through this book now with Dad and plan your Lionel Railroad—make him your assistant—he'll have just as much fun as you do. He'll be a boy again—chances are he played with a Lionel Train himself long ago, for Lionel has been building Miniature Electric Trains and Accessories for twenty-five years.

Lionel equipment includes massive locomotives with all-steel bodies and motors of tremendous hauling power, passenger and freight cars of many sizes and types, all modeled after the latest steel equipment used on America's greatest railroads—and accessories that are wonders of realism and sturdiness.

The beauty of it is that you can add to your Lionel Railroad all the time. Even if you start with only a locomotive and track you can have loads of fun, which increases every time you add to your layout. Then picture what it means to own and control a complete Lionel Railroad—everything that makes for good, wholesome enjoyment—equipment that will give you a knowledge of the principles of electricity—that will help you solve problems in traction and transportation—knowledge that will be of inestimable value to you when you grow to manhood.

ALL ABOARD!!! A touch of your finger on the "Multivolt" Transformer and away goes the Lionel Limited. She glides down the straightaway as smoothly as a sled, hauling the illuminated passenger coaches with the greatest ease, past the steel telegraph posts. The warning signal bell rings out as the train approaches the grade crossing—the automatic crossing gates go down as the express flashes past—up go the gates again when the crossing's clear.

Steady there, engineer—there's a semaphore, and the light says, "Caution!"—you slow up and then, around the curve carefully and into the tunnel. Another stretch of straightaway and the brightly illuminated station of "Lionel City" is seen. Again you touch the transformer lever and the train comes to a full stop. The conductor signals, "All Aboard!"—the Lionel Express is on its way again, past the illuminated villas and bungalows in the Lionel village and over the steel bridge.

Red light ahead! A dead stop! Say, boy, but your Lionel Railroad is certainly up to the minute. That Automatic Train Control stopped the train without your hand touching it—it won't move until the red light changes to green. There it goes now! Line's clear—you're off once more.

Why—the fun is only just beginning. Look through this book with Dad and Mother and you will find hundreds of other realistic accessories to add to your Lionel Railroad.

Despite the built-in quality of Lionel products prices are remarkably low. Go to your dealer and ask him to demonstrate a Lionel Train. He'll take it out of the handsome box shown below. Look at the beautiful enamel finish—see how easily and smoothly the Lionel Train runs. Examine the motor, the cars and the track—see how wonderfully well each part is made. See the infinite detail that makes the equipment look as massive and realistic as the real big electric trains. Don't be satisfied with anything but Lionel products. If your dealer cannot supply you, please let us know and we will see that you get exactly what you want right from our big factories—and don't forget while Lionel Electric Toy Trains and "Multivolt" Transformers have been "Standard of the World since 1900" they are the cheapest in cost consistent with their design, detail and manufacture.

THE LIONEL CORPORATION

48-52 EAST 21ST STREET   NEW YORK, N. Y.

LOOK FOR THIS PACKAGE—IT IS YOUR GUARANTEE OF QUALITY

You Can Operate Your Lionel Train on Reduced Alternating or Direct Current—or on Dry Cells or Storage Batteries

The Reason Why Lionel Trains Are Supreme

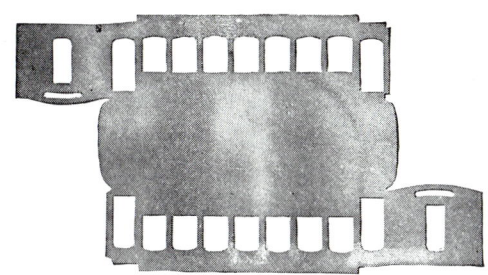

Fig. 1—Car body cut with one steel die.

LIONEL leadership has been attained by specialization in the manufacture of one product for a quarter of a century. Our entire resources and unsurpassed facilities have been exclusively devoted to the manufacture of Electric Trains, "Multivolt" Transformers and Miniature Railroad Accessories.

For twenty-four years Lionel products have been recognized as the world's standard. Millions of Lionel Outfits are in use, many of them for a decade or more. The following descriptive matter and illustrations will show why the Lionel Line is of such supremely high quality. The materials used and the scientific methods of production employed by us combine to make all Lionel products handsome in appearance, wear-resisting in construction and realistic in design and detail. Space only permits us to dwell upon some of the most important parts of the Lionel Line, so we will be brief in describing how quality is built in from the very foundation.

The Motors. In Figure 5 we show a corner of our armature and field winding departments. The battery of automatic winding machines we use insures absolutely correct windings which give so much power to Lionel Motors with a minimum current consumption. On the following pages will be found complete specifications of the various types of Lionel Motors.

The Cars. The unique method of construction employed exclusively by us is the reason why the all-steel Lionel Cars far outlast every other kind. Figure 1 shows a "blank" of a Lionel car body stamped from one piece of steel. Figure 2 shows the completely formed body firmly soldered at the corners. Window frames and doors, all in one piece, are then placed in position, making the walls of the car doubly strong.

Fig. 2—Car body same as Fig. 1 with corners soldered and window frames in position.

Fig. 3—Why Rails Are So Rigid—The base of Lionel track is flanged to a 5/16-inch base with turned-over edges, instead of having a 1/8-inch base as in other tracks.

The Enamel Finish. All Lionel car and locomotive bodies are enameled, not lithographed. The Lionel enameled finish is applied by a modern spraying process and baked at high temperature in specially designed ovens as shown in Figure 4. This process insures a permanent finish that can always be kept bright by any ordinary cleaning process.

The Track. Lionel Steel Track is made of a heavier gauge of metal than that used by any other manufacturer. We pay great attention to the insulation of the rails to guard against any possibility of short-circuit. Figure 3 shows one of the reasons for the strength of Lionel Track. It

Fig. 4—Baking Ovens—Here the enamels are baked on at high temperature after spraying. The ovens are heated by electricity.

will be seen that the rails are flanged outward at the base instead of being turned in as is the case with ordinary track. This outward flange is made possible by a patented process used exclusively by us and makes Lionel Track so rigid that it will support the weight of a full grown man.

In other parts of this book we show the quality and perfection of every piece that forms part of a Lionel Outfit.

Hundreds of skilled operatives employed in our factory shown on the back cover of this book contribute to the quality that has made Lionel Electric Trains

"STANDARD OF THE WORLD SINCE 1900"

Fig. 5—Motor Winding—This is just one corner of the motor winding department. Some wonderfully designed machines are used here.

Every Number in the Lionel Line Reflects High Quality Because of the Excellent Grade of Materials Used

"O" Gauge Single and Twin-Motor Specifications

DRIVING Gears ("A" and "B")—Are made of heavy steel blanks accurately cut. They mesh without friction. These are radically different from gears with punched teeth generally used on toys.

Frame and Cowcatcher ("C")—Are made of heavy steel punchings, not cast iron. They will not break when roughly treated.

Third Rail Shoe Support ("D")—Is made of heavy fibre that supports the third rail contact rollers. The peculiar construction of the roller supports protects them from injury, for the brackets can be forced against the fibre without disturbing the arc of the spring that gives them the correct tension against the third rail. When released they will come right back to the proper position.

Wheels ("E")—These are made of die castings with a steel jacket forced over the rim. The die casting represents a perfect mechanical wheel and the steel rim is used to insure longer wear, as it is tougher than the material of which the wheel is made.

Collecting Shoes ("F")—These revolving shoes which collect the current from the third rail are made of solid brass turnings and revolve on steel shafts which pass through a phosphor-bronze support, insuring perfect contact with the third rail at all times, so that the outfits will run at a uniform speed and not work with a start and jump as is usually the case with locomotives that do not collect a continuous supply of current from the third rail.

Journals ("G")—These journals and steps are embossed on the sides of the frame at the ends of the shafts and add materially to the appearance of the structure.

Couplers ("H")—These are made of heavy steel, nickeled and polished. They are scientifically constructed so that cars do not become detached when in motion, but are easily taken apart when desired. Several of the new "O" Gauge Locomotives illustrated on the following pages are equipped with the new Lionel patented Automatic Coupler, a great advance over any similar device ever made. This Coupler is seen in the illustration of the "O" Gauge Twin-Motor shown on this page. Lionel Automatic Couplers will connect with the ordinary couplers by means of the slotted attachment welded on to it.

Brushes and Brush Holders ("J")—The brush holders to which the brushes are attached can easily be removed so that the brush may be changed when necessary in a few seconds. The brushes are made of phosphor-bronze gauze and will run for hundreds of hours if commutator is kept clean.

Commutator ("K")—The commutator is constructed of three bronze sections with insulation between them. It is perfectly turned when fastened on the shaft so that it is absolutely parallel with the brushes and the polished surface reduces friction to a minimum.

Side Plates ("L")—These are made of heavy steel and support all working parts. The alignment of the holes is absolutely perfect so that gears and motor work without friction. All holes are drilled and reamed to proper diameter. The accuracy of these plates compares with the framework of a very fine watch or clock.

Motor with Frame Attachment ("M")—Only four screws are required to support the frame to the motor.

We are the pioneers in this simple method of construction. We introduced it in 1913.

Support of Body to Frame ("N")—The simple construction of the entire motor is apparent by the method of holding the body to the frame. The letter ("N") shows a piece of the steel frame thrown up at right angles containing threaded screw hole. The hole in the body corresponds with the opening in the frame and both pieces are held together with two machine screws. These are easily removed so that working parts may be instantly released.

Transmission Cables—We use a heavy gauge copper wire with extra heavy rubber insulation so that short-circuits against the metal parts are impossible.

Field—This field is made of a number of pieces of specially prepared transformer steel. These sheets are known as laminations and produce a very much stronger field than if a single piece were used.

The "O" Gauge Twin-Motor Chassis here illustrated incorporates Twin-Motors similar in construction to the single "O" Gauge Motors shown on this page. These Twin-Motors are built to give great hauling power and are contained in Locomotive No. 256 described on page 11. Both motors are reversed simultaneously by one controller and operate absolutely in unison. Despite their great hauling power they consume a minimum amount of current.

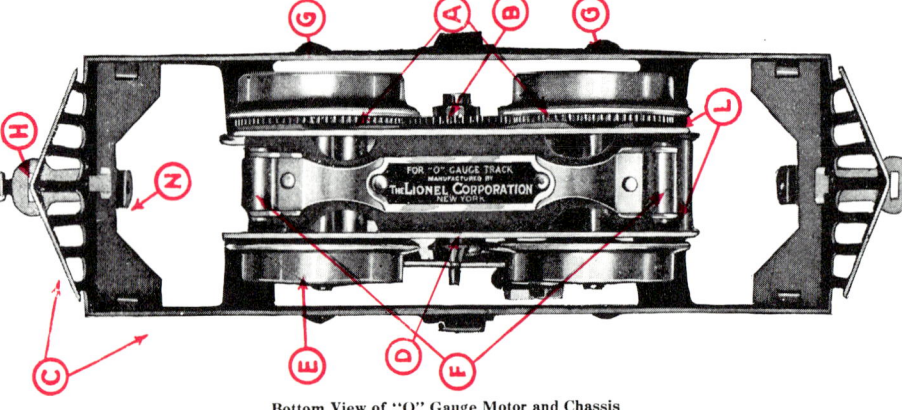

Bottom View of "O" Gauge Motor and Chassis

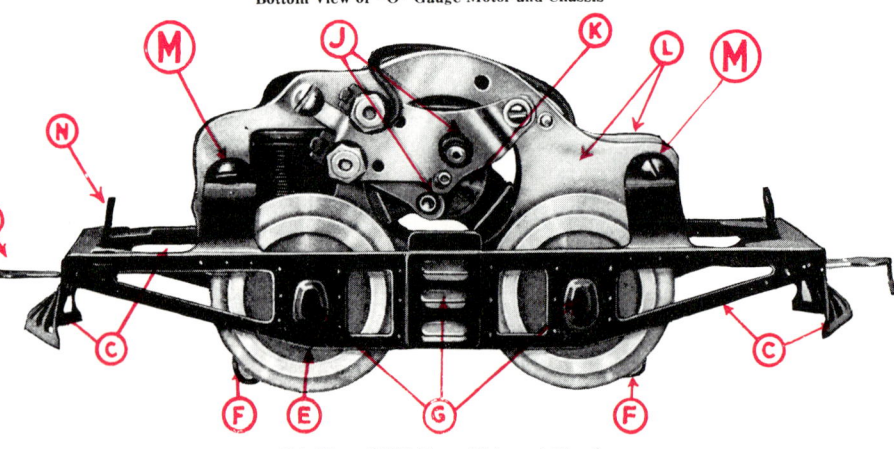

Side View of "O" Gauge Motor and Chassis

Bottom View of Twin-Motor "O" Gauge Chassis

An Electric Train Is Only as Good as Its Motor—All Lionel Motors Are Electrically and Mechanically Perfect

Reg. U. S. Pat. Office
"Lionel Standard" Motor Specifications

"LIONEL Standard" Locomotives contain motors of tremendous hauling power. The specifications on this page cover the motors used in Locomotives Nos. 33 and 38. The method of construction, as the following paragraphs show, clearly proves that they are built with the utmost care, of materials that will resist hard usage and which insure long wear. The Lionel Corporation are pioneers in the manufacture of track measuring 2¼ inches between centers of rails, upon which the above motors operate.

Field (1)—Made of best quality electrical steel, laminated throughout, and contains the winding properly insulated (2).

Brush Holders (3 and 4)—Made of brass, with detachable tops, so that brushes may be easily reached. Contain brass compression spring (5), which feeds brush up to the commutator. This construction prevents sparking of the brushes and prolongs the life of the commutator.

Brushes, Self-Lubricating (6)—Require no lubricating. A little cleaning of the commutator once in a while is all that is necessary. One brush is made of phosphor bronze—one of amorphous carbon. Each is made exactly true in diameter and will slip easily into the tube brush holders. They will outlast dozens of the commoner kinds.

Reversing Controller (7)—On all "Lionel Standard" locomotives. Unique in construction. On its face appear two flat brass contacts on which the four spring connections slide. The tension of these brass springs against the brass cap insures perfect contact while controller is being reversed. These springs, while insuring good electrical contact, work with so little friction that controller may be easily reversed with a touch of the finger.

Armature (8)—Made of electrical steel punchings mounted on drill rod shaft, and has fibre heads. Automatically drum-wound with proper size and amount of triple covered silk magnet wire (9), then dipped in shellac and baked, so that none of the coils become loose.

The Third Rail Shoe (10)—Which collects the current from the center insulated rail, is a steel punching with spring arrangement regulating the pressure on the rail. It is case hardened so that the friction against the third rail does not wear it through.

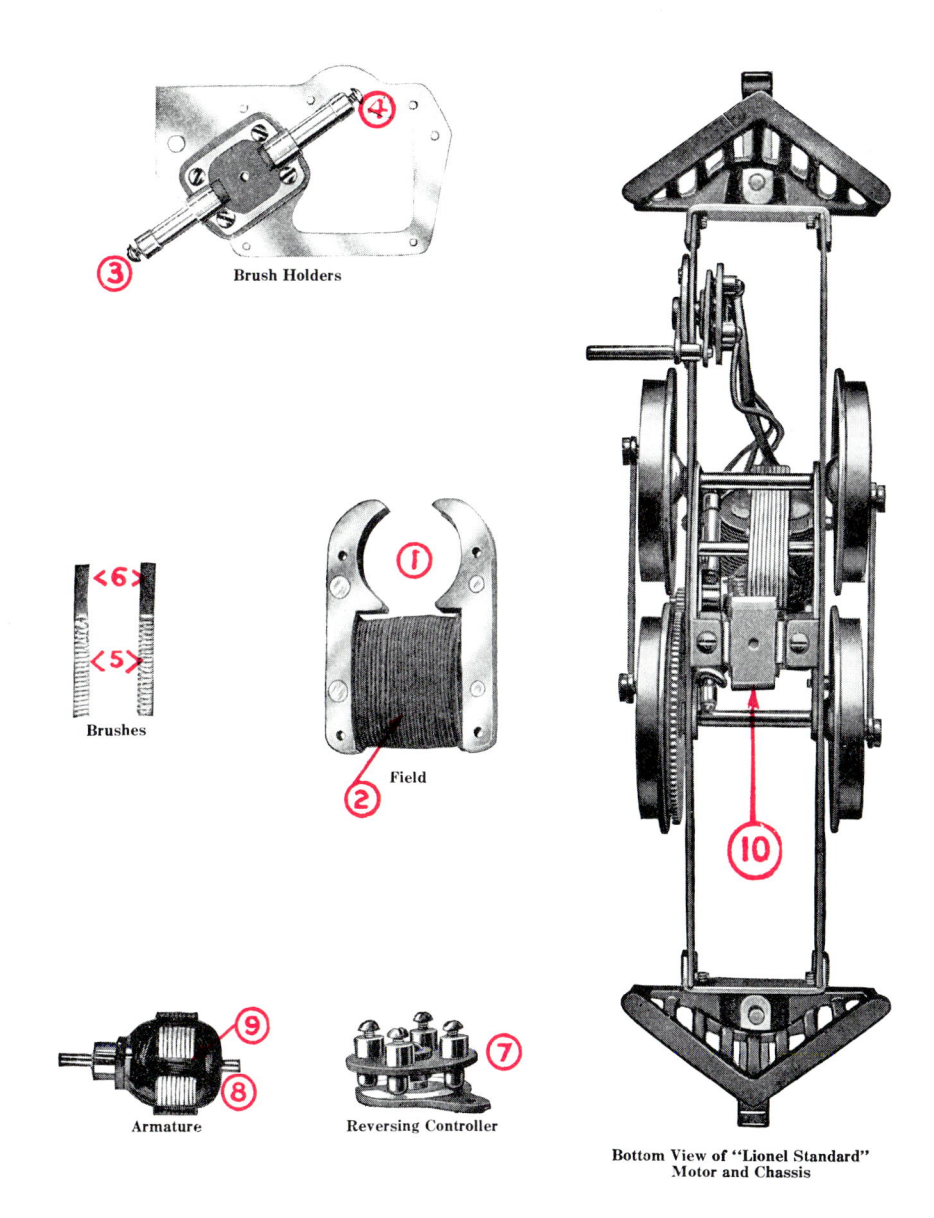

Brush Holders

Brushes

Field

Armature

Reversing Controller

Bottom View of "Lionel Standard" Motor and Chassis

The Original "Standard" Track—2¼ Inches Wide—Was Introduced by Lionel More Than Twenty Years Ago

Reg. U. S. Pat. Office
Specifications of "Lionel Standard" Super-Motor

THE Lionel "Super-Motor" is so vastly superior in efficiency and design to any motor ever before offered to the public that notwithstanding our enviable reputation as leaders in miniature motor construction, the Super-Motor is supremely the finest piece of electrical mechanism our factories have ever produced. It is quite fitting that we, as pioneer builders of miniature locomotives to operate on "Lionel Standard" Track, should retain our leadership with the new Super-Motor which is the acme of perfection.

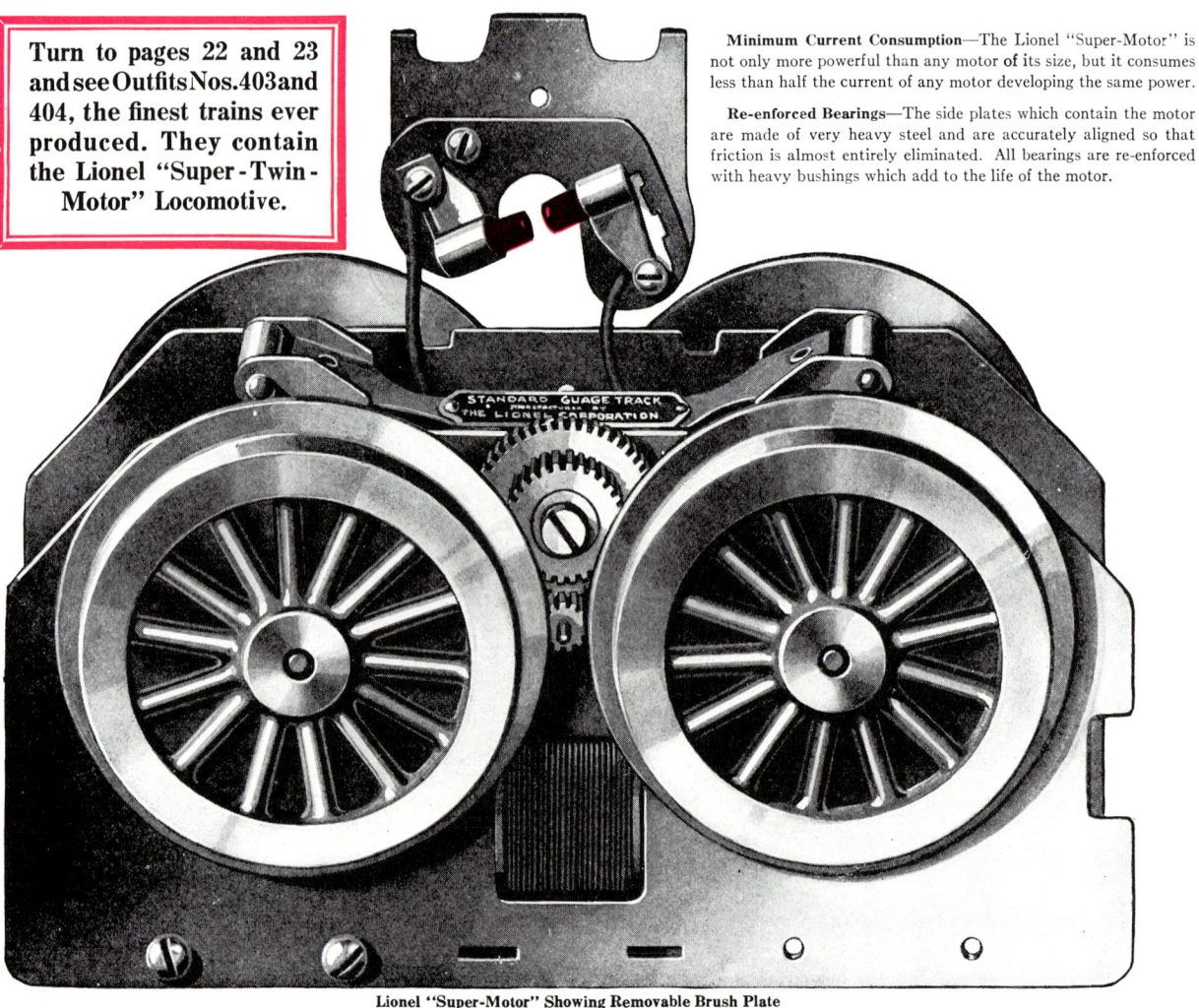

Turn to pages 22 and 23 and see Outfits Nos. 403 and 404, the finest trains ever produced. They contain the Lionel "Super-Twin-Motor" Locomotive.

Minimum Current Consumption—The Lionel "Super-Motor" is not only more powerful than any motor of its size, but it consumes less than half the current of any motor developing the same power.

Re-enforced Bearings—The side plates which contain the motor are made of very heavy steel and are accurately aligned so that friction is almost entirely eliminated. All bearings are re-enforced with heavy bushings which add to the life of the motor.

Field and Armature—These parts are made of the best grade of laminated steel and are of the most improved design.

Brushes—The brushes are made of self-lubricating bronze and graphite, which insure long life to the motor.

Commutator—The commutator is made of heavy bronze, and segments are perfectly insulated.

Removable Brush Holder—This is one of the most unique features of the Lionel "Super-Motor". By simply unscrewing one screw the entire brush holder can be removed from the motor. Change of brushes requires but an instant and the assembled part is replaced without the use of any tools. While this feature is very desirable, we are pleased to state that the user will not find it necessary to perform this operation until after the motor has been in use for a long time.

Revolving Double Contact Shoes—This method of collecting current from the third rail, so successfully used for many years past in our "O" Gauge Locomotives, has been applied with equal success to the new Super-Motors. The shoes are heavy bronze rollers, securely affixed to the flexible phosphor bronze plate, which insures the proper tension on the third rail and gives a steady flow of current to the motors. This complete shoe assembly is mounted on a heavy fibre plate and is rigidly attached to the motor frame.

Gears—The gears used in this motor are substantially made of steel and brass. They mesh accurately and are absolutely noiseless.

Driving Wheels—Particular attention is directed to the driving wheels, which are massive in construction and are $2\frac{1}{8}$ inches in diameter. They are accurately lathe-turned. Their weight adds great tractive power to the motors. All driving wheels are directly geared to the motor, eliminating the use of connecting rods between the wheels, which insures better alignment with less friction.

Tractive Power—The tractive power of these motors is remarkable. They will haul from 12 to 20 of our largest size freight or Pullman cars with the greatest ease. The weight of the wheels and motor is close to the track, insuring low center of gravity, with the result that the locomotive is not top-heavy and slippage of the wheels is therefore unknown. This construction is infinitely superior to the method of loading down the superstructure with useless weight so as to obtain tractive power. This unnecessary weight rapidly wears down all working parts and causes the locomotive to jump the track.

In every way we have designed these "Super-Motors" not only to develop great power and consume a minimum amount of current, but to make it possible to operate our trains continuously for an indefinite period without the necessity of replacing any parts.

Lionel "Super-Motor" Showing Removable Brush Plate

Lionel Super-Motors Combine the Greatest Hauling Power with Minimum Current Consumption

Reg. U. S. Pat. Office
Specifications of "Lionel Standard" Twin-Super-Motors

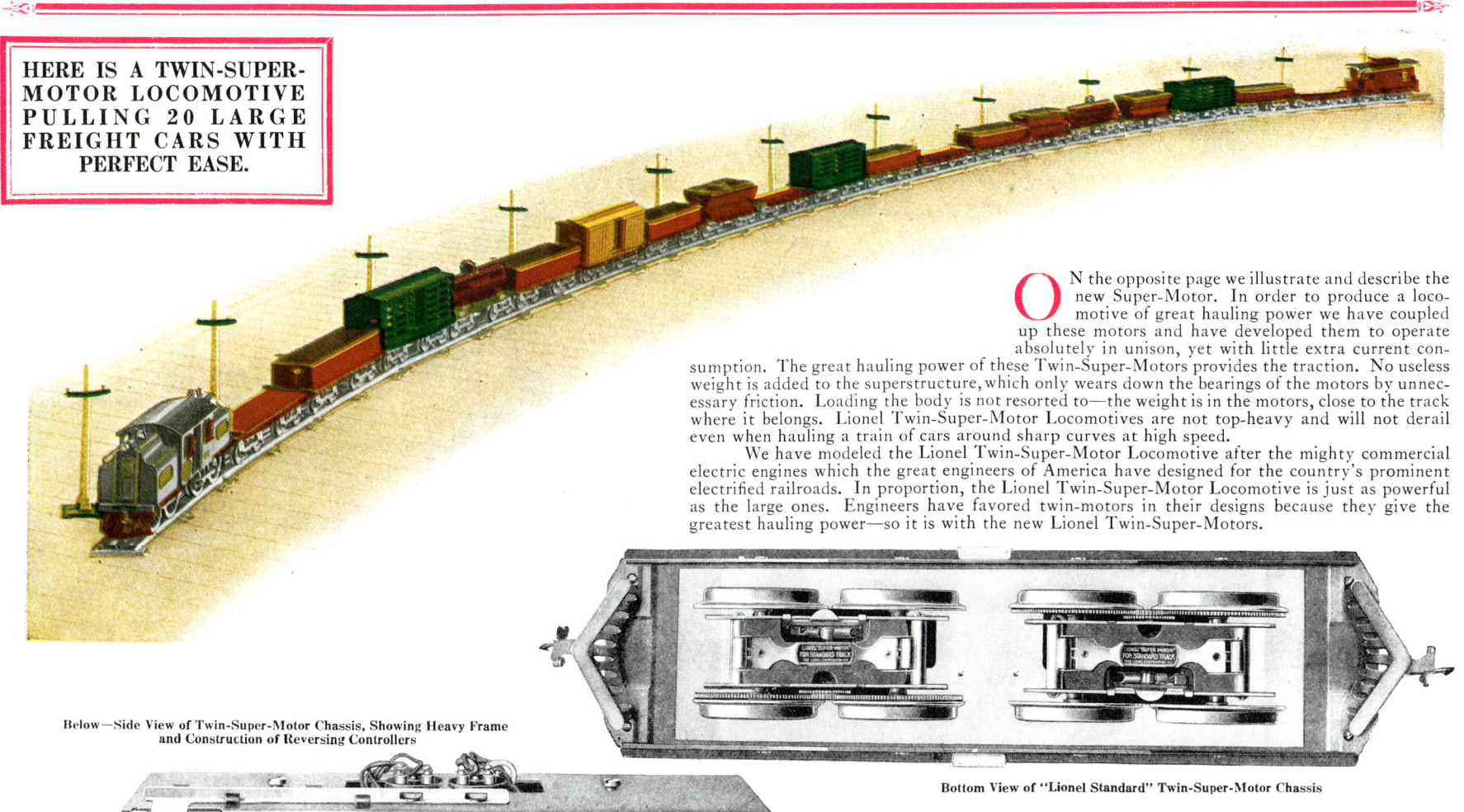

HERE IS A TWIN-SUPER-MOTOR LOCOMOTIVE PULLING 20 LARGE FREIGHT CARS WITH PERFECT EASE.

ON the opposite page we illustrate and describe the new Super-Motor. In order to produce a locomotive of great hauling power we have coupled up these motors and have developed them to operate absolutely in unison, yet with little extra current consumption. The great hauling power of these Twin-Super-Motors provides the traction. No useless weight is added to the superstructure, which only wears down the bearings of the motors by unnecessary friction. Loading the body is not resorted to—the weight is in the motors, close to the track where it belongs. Lionel Twin-Super-Motor Locomotives are not top-heavy and will not derail even when hauling a train of cars around sharp curves at high speed.

We have modeled the Lionel Twin-Super-Motor Locomotive after the mighty commercial electric engines which the great engineers of America have designed for the country's prominent electrified railroads. In proportion, the Lionel Twin-Super-Motor Locomotive is just as powerful as the large ones. Engineers have favored twin-motors in their designs because they give the greatest hauling power—so it is with the new Lionel Twin-Super-Motors.

Below—Side View of Twin-Super-Motor Chassis, Showing Heavy Frame and Construction of Reversing Controllers

Bottom View of "Lionel Standard" Twin-Super-Motor Chassis

Reversing Controllers and Motor Frame—The illustration to the left shows the unique construction of the reversing controllers which operate the twin-super-motors. Both controllers function simultaneously by means of a lever conveniently placed on the side of the locomotive body. The slightest touch of the finger sends the locomotive forward or backward or causes it to stop when the lever is placed at "OFF". Accuracy of construction insures positive action of the reversing controller at all times. Our reversing controllers are absolutely dependable—they are free from complicated mechanism.

Attention is directed to the heavy steel one-piece frame to which the motors are attached. Great detail is embodied in this frame. The springs and journals are separate brass pieces, heavily nickeled, and are securely fastened to it. Brass steps and flag supports are also attached, while the heavy steel cow-catchers are riveted to both ends, from which protrude the patented Lionel Automatic Couplers. The whole chassis represents a power unit that will give years of service.

Accuracy of Design, Sturdy Construction and Beautiful Finish Are Leading Characteristics of All Lionel Motors

[7]

1924

Specifications of Lionel Locomotive Bodies

THE details of the construction of Lionel Locomotive Bodies given below are typical of Lionel supreme quality throughout the entire line. Even the lowest priced Lionel Locomotives incorporate many of these features.

Of utmost importance is the fact that cast iron does not enter into the manufacture of any of these bodies—heavy sheet steel is used for every model; therefore Lionel Locomotives are practically indestructible. All parts of the bodies are re-enforced and are firmly soldered. They are not held together only by slots and fingers.

Lionel Locomotive Bodies are enameled, not lithographed —a beautiful and lasting lustre is obtained by finishing all Lionel Locomotive Bodies in rich enamel, baked on at high temperature as described in the introduction to this book.

Brass and nickeled fittings add further charm to the general appearance of Lionel Locomotives. These fittings are secured to the bodies by a process employed exclusively by us.

In all ways Lionel Locomotive Bodies combine sturdy construction, wonderful design and graceful appearance, as the indications below clearly show.

The High-Grade Construction of Lionel Locomotive Bodies Is in Keeping with the Excellence of Lionel Motors

Specifications of Lionel Passenger Coaches

ALL Lionel Passenger Coaches, irrespective of price, are made entirely of sheet steel. Not only are the cars modeled after the new style coaches used on the principal railroads of the country, but they are built to scale. An enormous amount of detail is incorporated in them such as hinged doors, inserted window frames and seats. Transparencies are placed in the windows and transoms of almost every car. The roofs are easily removable so that the interior electric lamp can be reached. Every car is finished with lasting, glossy enamel baked on at high temperature, insuring a permanent lustre. A revolving shoe, affixed to one of the trucks, collects current for the interior illumination of the car. Many of the trucks are fitted with nickeled journals. The heavy steel axles and wheels are nickeled and polished and are so perfectly made that they operate with a minimum amount of friction. We are proud to draw attention to the many desirable features contained in these coaches as indicated below.

Window frames and seats made of one piece of heavy metal securely fastened inside the car body.

Rear view of car, showing interior light and construction of the observation platform, made of sheet brass.

The patented revolving shoe which collects current from the third rail. It is built into the car truck.

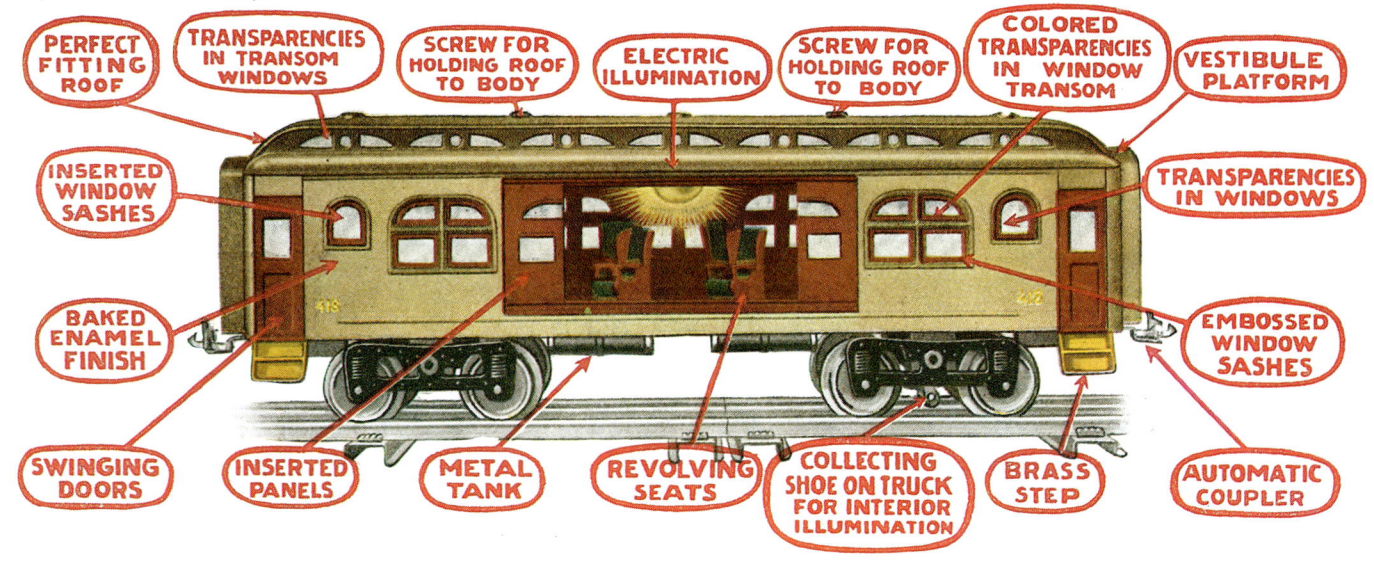

Features labeled on coach diagram:
- PERFECT FITTING ROOF
- TRANSPARENCIES IN TRANSOM WINDOWS
- SCREW FOR HOLDING ROOF TO BODY
- ELECTRIC ILLUMINATION
- SCREW FOR HOLDING ROOF TO BODY
- COLORED TRANSPARENCIES IN WINDOW TRANSOM
- VESTIBULE PLATFORM
- INSERTED WINDOW SASHES
- TRANSPARENCIES IN WINDOWS
- BAKED ENAMEL FINISH
- EMBOSSED WINDOW SASHES
- SWINGING DOORS
- INSERTED PANELS
- METAL TANK
- REVOLVING SEATS
- COLLECTING SHOE ON TRUCK FOR INTERIOR ILLUMINATION
- BRASS STEP
- AUTOMATIC COUPLER

The Most Modern Types of "All-Steel" Passenger Coaches Are Faithfully Reproduced by Lionel

Locomotives for Lionel "O" Gauge Track—1⅜ Inches Wide

WE show on this page three types of locomotives in the Lionel "O" Gauge Line. They are reproductions of the powerful New York Central type of electric engines which haul the big express trains.

The motors are fully described on page 4. They are powerful enough to haul four or more "O" Gauge Passenger or Freight Cars, according to their size. The bodies incorporate many of the structural details shown on page 8.

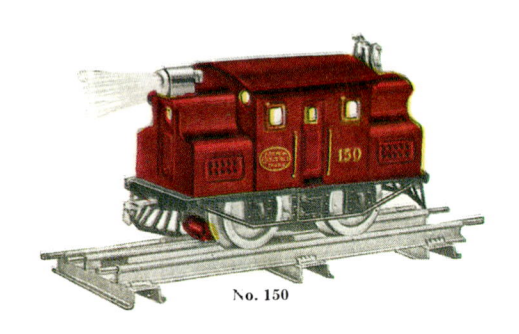

Locomotive No. 152—With electric headlight. This locomotive is 7 inches long and stands 3½ inches above the rails. Sturdily built and of proven strength. Price, complete with electric lamp for headlight and directions for operating **$6.50**
Western Price $8.00
Code Word "GRAMERCY"

THESE LOCOMOTIVES WILL ENABLE YOU TO BUILD UP A COMPLETE LIONEL RAILROAD AT VERY MODERATE COST

No. 150

Nos. 152 and 153

Locomotive No. 150—With electric headlight. This locomotive is 6 inches long and stands 3 inches above the rails. It is a good, low priced locomotive. Price, complete with electric lamp for headlight and directions for operating **$5.00**
Western Price $6.00
Code Word "GARLAND"

Locomotive No. 153—With electric headlight and reversing controller. Same dimensions and design as the No. 152, but has new type reversing controller conveniently placed on rear end of locomotive. This is the lowest priced, high-grade reversible locomotive obtainable anywhere. Price, complete with electric lamp for headlight and directions for operating **$7.85**
Western Price $9.50
Code Word "GAME"

Locomotive No. 156X—With electric headlight and reversing controller. This locomotive is 10 inches long and stands 4 inches above the rails. It is the largest of the New York Central type locomotives to operate on "O" gauge track and will easily haul 6 or more cars. Price, complete with electric lamp for headlight and directions for operating **$12.75**
Western Price $15.50
Code Word "GINGER"

PAGES 29 AND 31 DESCRIBE AND ILLUSTRATE THE PASSENGER COACHES AND FREIGHT CARS TO BE USED WITH THESE LOCOMOTIVES

No. 156X

A Lionel Locomotive Will Help You to Obtain a Knowledge of Electricity and Mechanical Traction Principles

[10]

Locomotives for Lionel "O" Gauge Track—1⅜ Inches Wide

LIONEL supremacy is again proven by the introduction of the new types of "O" Gauge Locomotives shown on this page. They are real electric engines in miniature. The new body designs suggest in a remarkable manner the massive outlines of the enormous electric locomotives seen on prominent electrified railroads like the C. M. and St. P., and the New York and New Haven. All the wonderful features described on page 8 are incorporated in these new models, including two electric headlights and reversing controllers. They are also equipped with the new patented Lionel Automatic Couplers. The motors have great hauling power, consume very little current, and will last for years with ordinary care.

Locomotive No. 254—With two electric headlights and reversing controller. This locomotive is 10 inches long and stands 4 inches above the rails. Smooth and silent in operation, beautiful in appearance. Price, complete with two electric lamps for headlights and directions for operating, **$13.25**

Code Word "MANY" Western Price $16.00

No. 254

No. 253

Locomotive No. 253—With two electric headlights and reversing controller. This locomotive is 9¾ inches long and stands 2¾ inches above the rails. An attractive model of great power. Price, complete with two electric lamps for headlights and directions for operating **$10.50**

Code Word "FINE" Western Price $12.50

Twin-Motor Locomotive No. 256—With two electric headlights and reversing controller. This locomotive is 13½ inches long and stands 5½ inches above the rails. The headlights have individual switches so that one or both can be used as desired. The reversing controller operates both motors simultaneously. This is the only twin-motor locomotive ever made to operate on "O" Gauge Track. It will haul a great number of passenger or freight cars. A wonderful model replete with many realistic features. Price, complete with two electric lamps for headlights and directions for operating **$20.00**

Code Word "CHAIN" Western Price $24.00

No. 256

Lionel Products Are More Than Toys—They Are Triumphs of Model Railroad Engineering

Train Outfits for Lionel "O" Gauge Track—1⅜ Inches Wide

HERE are three very low priced train outfits that prove Lionel values. Every locomotive is equipped with an electric headlight. The cars and in fact every piece of Lionel equipment that forms part of the outfit is typical of Lionel quality, which means the best obtainable, notwithstanding their moderate cost.

Outfit No. 260—Comprises one No. 152 locomotive (7 inches long) with electric headlight, one No. 629 pullman car (7¾ inches long), one No. 630 observation car (7¾ inches long), eight sections OC track, two sections OS track, one OTC "Lockon" connection and one No. 88 rheostat. Track forms an oval 39 by 30 inches. Train is 22½ inches long. The new cars included with this outfit are attractive in design and have inserted doors and panels as well as interior seats. The observation platform is made of brass. Price, complete with electric lamp for headlight, connecting ties for joining sections of track, wires for transformer or battery connections and directions for operating . . . **$8.50**
Code Word "REAL"   Western Price $10.00

No. 260

Outfit No. 259—Comprises one No. 150 locomotive (6 inches long) with electric headlight, one No. 901 gondola car (7 inches long), one No. 801 caboose (7 inches long), eight sections OC track and one OTC "Lockon" connection. Track forms a circle 30 inches in diameter. Train is 20 inches long. This is the lowest priced outfit in the Lionel Line. Every part that enters into it is well built and durable.
Price, complete with electric lamp for headlight, connecting ties for joining sections of track, wires for transformer or battery connections and directions for operating **$5.75**
Code Word "RUN"   Western Price $7.00

No. 259

Outfit No. 257—Comprises one No. 150 locomotive (6 inches long) with electric headlight, two No. 600 pullman cars (7 inches long), eight sections OC track and one OTC "Lockon" connection. Track forms a circle 30 inches in diameter. Train is 20 inches long. This outfit represents very great value.
Price, complete with electric lamp for headlight, connecting ties for joining sections of track, wires for transformer or battery connections and directions for operating **$6.75**
Code Word "HIGH"   Western Price $8.00

No. 257

Use a Lionel "Multivolt" Transformer for Operating All Trains—An Ever Reliable Power Plant

Train Outfits for Lionel "O" Gauge Track—1⅜ Inches Wide

EVERY outfit in the Lionel "O" Gauge Line is replete with desirable features. On this and the following pages we show new and improved types of locomotives, improved cars and many other interesting new features.

No. 261

Outfit No. 261—Comprises one No. 152 locomotive (7 inches long) with electric headlight, one No. 800 box car (7 inches long), one No. 801 caboose (7 inches long), eight sections OC track, two sections OS track, one OTC "Lockon" connection and one No. 88 rheostat. Track forms an oval 39 by 30 inches. Train is 21 inches long. This is a popular freight that has a powerful locomotive included with it. Many cars can be coupled to it with the assurance that it will easily haul them.
Price, complete with electric lamp for headlight, connecting ties for joining sections of track, wires for transformer or battery connections and directions for operating **$8.50**
Western Price **$10.00**
Code Word "COB"

No. 255

Outfit No. 255—Comprises one No. 153 reversible locomotive (7 inches long) with electric headlight, one No. 603 pullman car (8 inches long), one No. 604 observation car (8 inches long), both equipped with automatic couplers and permanent interior lights, eight sections OC track, four sections OS track, one OTC "Lockon" connection and one No. 88 rheostat. Track forms an oval 49 by 30 inches. The complete train is 23 inches long. The new reversible locomotive included with this outfit is a great improvement over the former type which only ran one way. The permanently illuminated cars are another added new feature, making the entire outfit particularly attractive.
Price, complete with electric lamps for headlight and interior of cars, connecting ties for joining sections of track, wires for transformer or battery connections and directions for operating **$10.00**
Code Word "RIDE"
Western Price **$12.00**

No. 265

Outfit No. 265—Comprises one No. 253 new model reversible locomotive (9¾ inches long) with two electric headlights, two No. 820 box cars, one No. 822 caboose (each 8¼ inches long), eight sections OC track, six sections OS track, one OTC "Lockon" connection and one No. 88 rheostat. Track forms an oval 59 by 30 inches. Train is 34½ inches long. The new type reversible engine with this outfit (described on page 11) combined with the attractive double-truck freight cars, forms an outfit of extreme beauty.
Price, complete with electric lamps for headlights, connecting ties for joining sections of track, wires for transformer or battery connections and directions for operating **$15.00**
Code Word "THORO"
Western Price **$18.00**

Outfits on This Page Having Double-Truck Cars Are Equipped with the Patented Lionel Automatic Couplers

[13]

1924

Train Outfits for Lionel "O" Gauge Track—1⅜ Inches Wide

NOW we come to the big, sturdy outfits of the Lionel "O" Gauge Line—brimming with improvements and handsomely finished. Any one of these outfits is good for years of wholesome enjoyment for the lucky owner. You pay no more for these durable, long-wearing train outfits than for the inferior kind. Therefore, always look for the name "Lionel" when buying miniature electric railroad equipment.

Outfit No. 169—Comprises one No. 156X reversible locomotive (10 inches long) with electric headlight, one No. 610 pullman car, one No. 612 observation car (each 9 inches long), eight sections OC track, four sections OS track, one OTC "Lockon" connection and one No. 88 rheostat. Track forms an oval 49 by 30 inches. Complete train is 28 inches long. This number has long been a favorite in the Lionel Line and its popularity will now be increased due to the reduction in price.

Price, complete with electric lamp for headlight, connecting ties for joining sections of track, wires for transformer or battery connections and directions for operating $15.00

Code Word "VALUE"   Western Price $20.00

No. 169

ON THIS AND THE NEXT PAGE WE SHOW FOUR OF THE FINEST "O" GAUGE PASSENGER TRAINS EVER PRODUCED.

THE UP-TO-DATE ACCESSORIES ILLUSTRATED ON THE FOLLOWING PAGES WILL ENABLE YOU TO BUILD A COMPLETE LIONEL RAILROAD—DUPLICATING IN MINIATURE ALL THE MODERN EQUIPMENT OF AMERICA'S BIG ELECTRIFIED SYSTEMS.

No. 264

Outfit No. 264—Comprises one No. 253 new model reversible locomotive (9¾ inches long) with two electric headlights, two No. 603 illuminated pullman cars, one No. 604 illuminated observation car (each 8 inches long and equipped with automatic couplers), eight sections OC track, six sections OS track, one OTC "Lockon" connection and one No. 88 rheostat. Track forms an oval 59 by 30 inches. Complete train is 33¾ inches long. Every detail of a modern passenger train is faithfully carried out in this model. It is indeed a wonderful sight to see this train with its brilliantly illuminated cars go dashing down the track.

Price, complete with electric lamps for headlights and interior of cars, connecting ties for joining sections of track, wires for transformer or battery connections and directions for operating $15.00

Code Word "FLY"   Western Price $18.00

Permanently Illuminated Cars—An Attractive Feature of the New No. 264 Train Outfit

Train Outfits For Lionel "O" Gauge Track—1⅜ Inches Wide

ANY boy will be proud to own either of the remarkable train outfits illustrated below. Is there anything more to be desired than these supremely fine Lionel products? The single and twin-motor locomotives that form part of these outfits have already been described on page 11. These trains are equipped with the Lionel Automatic Couplers—the cars have permanent interior lights and many other realistic details that place them far and away above anything similar ever made.

No. 266

Outfit No. 266—Comprises one new model No. 254 reversible locomotive (10 inches long) with two electric headlights and automatic couplers, two No. 610 illuminated pullman cars (9 inches long), one No. 612 illuminated observation car (9 inches long), all with automatic couplers, eight sections OC track, six sections OS track, one OTC "Lockon" connection and one No. 88 rheostat. Track forms an oval 59 by 30 inches. Train is 37 inches long. The bright, rich enameled finish of this splendid train will appeal instantly. The powerful locomotive and all-steel cars together with the liberal track layout, stamp it as tremendous value for the price.

Price, complete with electric lamps for headlights and interior of cars, connecting ties for joining sections of track, wires for transformer or battery connections and directions for operating **$20.75**

Code Word "HEAD"   Western Price $25.00

No. 268

Outfit No. 268—Comprises one new model No. 256 twin-motor reversible locomotive (13½ inches long) with two electric headlights and automatic couplers, two No. 710 illuminated pullman cars (12½ inches long), one No. 712 illuminated observation car (12½ inches long), all with automatic couplers, eight sections OC track, eight sections OS track, one OTC "Lockon" connection and one No. 88 rheostat. Track forms an oval 79 by 30 inches. Train is 51 inches long. This is the largest train ever made to operate on "O" Gauge Track. The locomotive with its marvelous twin-motors will haul an unlimited number of cars. Every part that enters into this outfit bears the mark of Lionel quality.

Price, complete with electric lamps for headlights and interior of cars, connecting ties for joining sections of track, wires for transformer or battery connections and directions for operating **$33.00**

Code Word "TAKE"   Western Price $40.00

Look Closely at the Above Illustrations—See the Many Wonderful Details Incorporated in Lionel Trains

Complete Lionel Railroads for "O" Gauge Track—1⅜ Inches Wide

MANY boys prefer to buy a Lionel Train Set with a variety of accessories right from the start, so we have made up the outfits illustrated on this page. It will be seen that many wonderful accessories are provided in addition to the train and track layout. Every piece is of steel construction throughout with the famous Lionel enameled finish. It is only necessary to get one of the low priced "Multivolt" Transformers and the railroad can be operated instantly, or if no house current is available dry or storage batteries can be used.

Outfit No. 174—Comprises one complete No. 264 train described on page 14 together with ten sections OC track, six sections OS track, one OTC "Lockon" connection, one No. 88 rheostat, one pair No. 022 switches (one right and one left), one No. 106 bridge (three sections), one No. 121 station, six No. 60 telegraph posts, two No. 62 semaphores, one No. 68 crossing sign and one No. 119 tunnel. Size of track layout 45 by 60 inches. The complete train is 33¾ inches long. The appearance of this railroad can be enhanced by adding the illuminated bungalows and villas described on pages 34 and 35.

Price, complete with electric lamps for headlights and interior of cars, connecting ties for joining sections of track, wires for transformer or battery connections and directions for operating . . . **$35.00**

Code Word "DELAWARE"　　　　Western Price $42.00

No. 174

Outfit No. 176—Comprises one complete No. 266 train described on page 15 together with ten sections OC track, ten sections OS track, one OTC "Lockon" connection, one No. 88 rheostat, one pair No. 022 switches (one right and one left), one No. 109 bridge (5 sections), one No. 121 station, eight No. 60 telegraph posts, one No. 62 semaphore, one No. 68 crossing sign and one No. 119 tunnel. Size of track layout 45 by 82 inches. The complete train is 37 inches long. The new automatic accessories described on pages 38 and 39 will make welcome additions to this railroad.

Price, complete with electric lamps for headlights and interior of cars, connecting ties for joining sections of track, wires for transformer or battery connections and directions for operating. **$44.00**
　　　　Western Price $53.00

Code Word "BURLINGTON"

No. 176

A Complete Model Village Can Be Built with the Aid of Lionel Steel Bungalows and Villas—See Pages 34 and 35

Reg. U. S. Pat. Office
Locomotive Outfits for "Lionel Standard" Track—2¼ Inches Wide

THE mechanism and motors of these mighty locomotives have already been described on pages 5 and 6, while details of the body construction are given on page 8. Because of their larger size we are able to incorporate more powerful motors in "Lionel Standard" locomotives than in the "O" Gauge.

An extra locomotive adds greater variety to your train layout—switching engines from track to track is great sport and is real railroad practice.

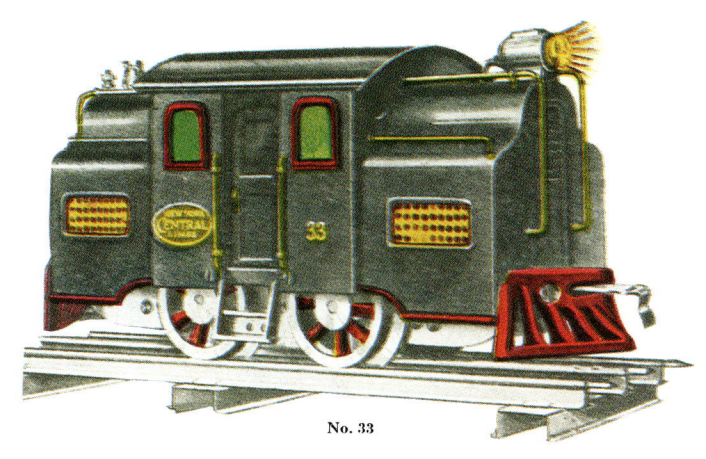

No. 33

Outfit No. 33—Comprises one No. 33 reversible locomotive with electric headlight and automatic couplers, eight sections C track, and one STC "Lockon" connection. Track forms a circle 42 inches in diameter. This locomotive is 11 inches long and stands 4½ inches above the rails. All four 1¾-inch wheels are geared to the motor, insuring great tractive power.
Price, complete with electric lamp for headlight, connecting ties for joining sections of track, wires for transformer or battery connections and directions for operating $16.25
Code Word "DUBUQUE"   Western Price $19.50

No. 38

Outfit No. 38—Comprises one No. 38 reversible locomotive with electric headlight and automatic couplers, eight sections C track, and one STC "Lockon" connection. Track forms a circle 42 inches in diameter. This locomotive is 12 inches long and stands 5 inches above the rails. The driving wheels are larger than in locomotive No. 33, being 2½ inches in diameter. They are made of heavy steel, nickeled and polished, and provide great hauling power for the locomotive.
Price, complete with electric lamp for headlight, connecting ties for joining sections of track, wires for transformer or battery connections and directions for operating $18.50
Code Word "AKRON"   Western Price $22.00

Outfit No. 50—Comprises one No. 50 reversible super-motor locomotive with two electric headlights and automatic couplers, eight sections C track and one STC "Lockon" connection. Track forms a circle 42 inches in diameter. This locomotive is 12 inches long and stands 5 inches above the rails. It is the lowest priced new super-motor locomotive and is extremely powerful. The driving wheels are of the latest Lionel type—2⅛ inches in diameter. Complete specifications of the new super-motor will be found on page 6.
Price, complete with electric lamps for headlights, connecting ties for joining sections of track, wires for transformer or battery connections and full directions for operating $20.00
Western Price $24.00
Code Word "IOWA"

No. 50

"Lionel Standard" Track—2¼ Inches Wide—Was Originated and Developed by Lionel More Than 20 Years Ago

[17]

1924

Super-Motor Locomotive Outfits for "Lionel Standard" Track—2¼ Inches Wide

IT is only natural that this Corporation, the originators of "Lionel Standard" equipment, should develop and perfect what are universally acknowledged to be the best and most efficient locomotives to operate on "Lionel Standard" Track.

We illustrate here three Super-Motor Locomotives that far surpass any of our previous models. If you have not already read the details of construction please turn to page 6 for specifications of the Super-Motor, page 7 for the Twin-Super-Motor, and page 8 for details of body construction. You will immediately recognize the superiority of the many desirable features incorporated in these models.

No. 318

No. 380

No. 402

Outfit No. 318—Comprises one No. 318 reversible super-motor locomotive with two electric headlights and automatic couplers, eight sections C track and one STC "Lockon" connection. Track makes an oval 42 inches in diameter. This locomotive is 14½ inches long and stands 6 inches above the rails. It is introduced in response to a great demand for a single-super-motor locomotive built on the lines of our No. 402, but smaller and contains many of the structural features of the larger engine. It will be favored by many Lionel enthusiasts who already have "Lionel Standard" outfits which they wish to enlarge.

Price, complete with electric lamps for headlights, connecting ties for joining sections of track, wires for transformer or battery connections and directions for operating $22.50
Western Price $27.00
Code Word "VERB"

Outfit No. 380—Comprises one No. 380 reversible super-motor locomotive with two electric headlights and automatic couplers, eight sections C track, four sections S track and one STC "Lockon" connection. Track forms an oval 69 by 42 inches. This locomotive is 15 inches long and stands 6¼ inches above the rails. It met with instant success when we added it to the Lionel Line last year. In appearance it is exactly like the new monster locomotives which haul the C. M. and St. P. trains over the electrified stretch of the railroad through the Rocky Mountains. The wonderful Super-Motor and the characteristics of body construction have already been described. The headlights have individual switches so that they can be turned on or off at will. Red and green transparent discs are placed on the sides of the headlight lantern, presenting a dazzlingly beautiful effect.

Price, complete with electric lamps for headlights, connecting ties for joining sections of track, wires for transformer or battery connections and directions for operating $25.00
Western Price $30.00
Code Word "ROCKIES"

Outfit No. 402—Comprises one No. 402 Twin-Super-Motor Locomotive with two electric headlights and automatic couplers, eight sections C track, four sections S track and one STC "Lockon" connection. Track forms an oval 69 by 42 inches. Describing this beautiful model as a toy does not do it justice—it is the very peak of perfection, the result of many years of diligent research and development in miniature motor construction. The locomotive is 17½ inches long and stands 6½ inches above the rails. Pages 6, 7 and 8 show you the high grade details of motor, chassis and body. On pages 22 and 23 you will see this massive engine coupled with our largest passenger and freight cars—really magnificent trains. The unique headlights placed on this locomotive have already been described on this page. Truly, No. 402 is a locomotive that will realize any boy's lifelong ambition.

Price, complete with electric lamps for headlights, connecting ties for joining sections of track, wires for transformer or battery connections and directions for operating $37.50
Code Word "HAVEN"   Western Price $45.00

The Foundation for a Wonderful Miniature Railroad—Any of the Locomotives on this page

[18]

Reg. U. S. Pat. Office
Train Outfits for "Lionel Standard" Track—2¼ Inches Wide

THIS and the following pages are devoted to the "Lionel Standard" Line of Passenger and Freight Trains of which we are the originators. Manufacturing experience extending over a period of twenty-five years has enabled us to produce a line as near perfection as human ingenuity can attain. There is not a number in the entire "Lionel Standard" Line that does not show remarkable improvements and greater values than ever before. On previous pages we have described the locomotives to operate on "Lionel Standard" Track. These locomotives in conjunction with the large variety of up-to-date passenger coaches and freight cars combine to form the best miniature electric trains in the world.

Typical instances are shown on this page—read the specifications and you have proof that any train in the "Lionel Standard" Line offers everything desirable in quality and price.

No. 34

Outfit No. 34—Comprises one No. 33 reversible locomotive (11 inches long) with electric headlight and automatic couplers, one No. 35 illuminated pullman car (11½ inches long), one No. 36 illuminated observation car (11½ inches long), both with automatic couplers, eight sections C track, two sections S track and one STC "Lockon" connection. Track forms an oval 56 by 42 inches. Complete train is 34 inches long. The famous No. 33 locomotive included with this outfit leaves nothing to be desired in a low priced "Lionel Standard" locomotive of great hauling power. The cars are permanently illuminated by means of a collecting shoe placed on one of the trucks.

Price complete with electric lamps for headlight and interior of cars, connecting ties for joining sections of track, wires for transformer or battery connections and directions for operating $16.50

Code Word "AUBURN"   Western Price $21.00

No. 370

Outfit No. 370—Comprises one No. 33 reversible locomotive (11 inches long) with electric headlight, one No. 112 gondola car, one No. 114 box car, one No. 117 caboose (each 9¾ inches long), eight sections C track, two sections S track and one STC "Lockon" connection. Track forms an oval 56 by 42 inches. Complete train is 40¼ inches long. No better freight train has ever been produced to retail at the price of this new No. 370 outfit. The well known No. 33 locomotive will easily haul many more passenger or freight cars than are included with the outfit.

Price complete with electric lamp for headlight, connecting ties for joining sections of track, wires for transformer or battery connections and directions for operating, $20.75

Code Word "MINE"   Western Price $25.00

Two Famous Trains in the "Lionel Standard" Line—Perfect Construction and Wonderful Values

Reg. U. S. Pat. Office
Train Outfits for "Lionel Standard" Track—2¼ Inches Wide

TWO new passenger trains have been added to the "Lionel Standard" Line this year as shown on this page, in addition to a very popular freight number. Special attention is directed to the new passenger cars included with the outfit illustrated at the bottom of this page. These cars embody all the desirable features described on page 9.

No. 340

Outfit No. 340—Comprises one new model No. 50 reversible locomotive (12 inches long) with two electric headlights, one No. 31 illuminated pullman and baggage car, one No. 35 illuminated pullman car, one No. 36 illuminated observation car (each 11½ inches long), eight sections C track, four sections S track and one STC "Lockon" connection. Track forms an oval 69 by 42 inches. Complete train is 46½ inches long. The locomotive included with this outfit contains the famous Lionel Super-Motor. Its great hauling power is truly remarkable. The superstructure has been greatly enhanced by the addition of an extra headlight, one being placed at each end of the cab. The locomotive is also equipped with our patented Automatic Couplers. The cars supplied with this outfit are complete with Automatic Couplers and permanent interior illuminating fixture. Nickel plated journals are rigidly attached to the trucks. This feature is faithful in construction and adds greatly to the appearance of the passenger coaches.
Price, complete with electric lamps for headlights and interior of cars, connecting ties for joining sections of track, wires for transformer or battery connections and directions for operating $25.00
Code Word "IVOR"   Western Price $30.00

No. 41

Outfit No. 41—Comprises one No. 38 reversible locomotive (12 inches long) with electric headlight, one No. 112 gondola car, one No. 113 cattle car, one No. 114 box car, one No. 116 coal car, one No. 117 caboose (each 9¾ inches long), eight sections C track, four sections S track and one STC "Lockon" connection. Track forms an oval 69 by 42 inches. Complete train is 60¾ inches long. Lionel freight trains have always been known for their great value. The No. 38 locomotive included with this outfit is famous for its rigid construction and great hauling power, while the cars are of Lionel quality throughout. These cars are faithful models of the latest types of steel freight cars used on all the large railroads.
Price, complete with electric lamp for headlight, connecting ties for joining sections of track, wires for transformer or battery connections and directions for operating, $29.25
Code Word "FULTON"   Western Price $35.00

No. 342

Outfit No. 342—Comprises one new No. 318 reversible super-motor locomotive (14½ inches long) with two electric headlights and automatic couplers, two No. 319 illuminated pullman cars, one No. 322 illuminated observation car (each 15 inches long), all with automatic couplers, eight sections C track, six sections S track, one STC "Lockon" connection. Track forms an oval 88 by 42 inches. Complete train is 59½ inches long. This handsome new train outfit is in every respect a faithful reproduction of the most up-to-date pullman trains. The new No. 318 locomotive included with it has already been described. The richly enameled cars embody great detail. Their graceful proportions are immediately apparent. The inserted windows, doors and panels exemplify to the highest degree the new method of Lionel car construction. These are separable parts securely fastened to the body and add materially to the realistic appearance of the cars. Nickel plated journals are mounted on the trucks and miniature metal tanks are securely held to the bottom of the car. Each car is equipped with automatic couplers as well as a fixture for interior illumination. The observation platform on the rear car is made of brass and is an exact reproduction of those used on the large cars.
Price, complete with electric lamps for headlights and interior of cars, connecting ties for joining sections of track, wires for transformer or battery connections and directions for operating $33.00
Code Word "VIEW"   Western Price $40.00

Many More Cars Can Be Added to These Trains—The Powerful Lionel Locomotives Will Easily Haul Them

Super-Motor Train Outfits for "Lionel Standard" Track—2¼ Inches Wide

THESE trains are established favorites in the "Lionel Standard" Line and are offered this year in a much improved form. Permanently lighted cars and automatic couplers are just two of the many interesting refinements incorporated in the passenger trains. Yet—prices have been materially reduced.

Outfit No. 344—Comprises one No. 380 reversible super-motor locomotive (15 inches long) with two electric headlights, one No. 18 illuminated pullman car, one No. 190 illuminated observation car (each 16½ inches long), eight sections C track, four sections S track and one STC "Lockon" connection. Track forms an oval 69 by 42 inches. Complete train is 48 inches long. Here is another perfectly built passenger train that is exceptionally popular. Its great value is further enhanced by the addition of an observation car in place of one of the pullman coaches that was formerly included with it.

Price, complete with electric lamps for headlights and interior of cars, connecting ties for joining sections of track, wires for transformer or battery connections and directions for operating, **$35.00**
Western Price $42.00
Code Word "VERNON"

No. 344

No. 345

Outfit No. 345—Comprises one No. 380 reversible super-motor locomotive (15 inches long) with two electric headlights, one No. 12 gondola car, one No. 14 box car, one No. 15 oil car, one No. 17 caboose (each 11 inches long), eight sections C track, four sections S track, one STC "Lockon" connection. Track forms an oval 66 by 42 inches. Complete train is 59 inches long. The No. 380 locomotive included with this outfit needs no further introduction.

The freight cars are large and well proportioned and the entire outfit stands out as a realistic model of an up-to-date freight train.
Price, complete with electric lamps for headlights, connecting ties for joining sections of track, wires for transformer or battery connections and directions for operating **$35.75**
Code Word "PELHAM"   **Western Price $43.00**

No. 346

Outfit No. 346—Comprises one No. 380 reversible super-motor locomotive (15 inches long) with two electric headlights, one No. 18 illuminated pullman car, one No. 19 illuminated pullman and baggage car, one No. 190 illuminated observation car (each 16½ inches long), eight sections C track, eight sections S track, and one STC "Lockon" connection. Track forms an oval 102 by 42 inches. Complete train is 64½ inches long. The cars included with this outfit are the well known passenger coaches Nos. 18, 19 and 190, which have been greatly improved by having permanent interior illumination equipment, the current for which is obtained directly from the track by use of our patented collecting shoe built into one of the trucks. Locomotive and cars are also equipped with our new patented universal automatic couplers.

Price, complete with electric lamps for headlights and interior of cars, connecting ties for joining sections of track, wires for transformer or battery connections and directions for operating **$44.50**
Code Word "MONTY"   **Western Price $53.50**

Read About the New Locomotives Included with These Train Outfits, on Page 18—Electrically Perfect

Twin-Super-Motor Train Outfits

TRAIN Outfit No. 403 is in every respect a miniature reproduction of a de luxe express train. It is a delight to behold and operates as smoothly as though the wheels were equipped with rubber tires. Even the most superlative terms of description will not be as convincing as seeing the outfit in operation. It is absolutely the last word in miniature train construction.

A companion number quite in keeping with the handsome

No. 403

Details of Locomotive—An exact reproduction of the most modern type of electric locomotives used on electrified systems throughout the country. It is so faithful in detail that to behold it is like seeing an actual large electric locomotive through the diminishing end of field glasses.

Body—The body is made entirely of steel. The doors, windows, ventilators, hand rails and all other fittings are made of polished brass and are securely fastened by our patented nickeled stanchions.

Headlights—The headlights (one of which is placed at each end of the body) are unique in construction. Each is equipped with a switch so that one or both may be turned on at will. The headlight lamp when illuminated is visible through the green and red panels on the sides of the headlight—a touch of realism that will delight every boy.

Reversing Controller—A lever is conveniently placed on the side of the locomotive which operates simultaneously the controllers on each of the twin-motors. This is a great step forward in controller construction.

Frame—The frame is made of one piece of heavy steel. Journals, made of brass and beautifully nickel plated, are securely fastened to it. Numerous rivets and other structural details are heavily embossed in the frame, all of which accentuate the great detail embodied in this locomotive.

Automatic Couplers—This locomotive is equipped with our new automatic couplers which protrude through the centre of beautifully designed cow-catchers. These automatic couplers are a great improvement over any similar device, for the reason that they engage with each other irrespective of the position of the cars. They can be used in conjunction with any type of non-automatic coupler now on the market.

Enamel Finish—The enamel on the frame and body is baked on at a high temperature, which insures a glasslike finish that lasts for years. It is only necessary to rub the surface with a cloth or chamois to keep the locomotive always bright and new looking.

Details of Cars—These pullman cars are faithful reproductions in every detail of the most modern passenger cars used on the best railroads. The bodies are made of heavy sheet steel and the parts are rigidly held together. The detail of construction is enhanced by embossed work in the nature of panels, rivets, sashes, etc. Two miniature tanks as well as nickel plated steps and hand rails add to the great detail incorporated in these cars. The roof is removable and the interior contains individual revolving seats and permanent electric fixtures for illuminating the cars. Current is obtained from our patented collecting shoe built into one of the trucks. The light shining through the colored glass windows produces a very realistic effect. These cars are enameled in very attractive colors baked on at a high temperature so that they always retain their fresh, glossy appearance. It is impossible to describe the beauty of these cars adequately, but

The Culmination of 25 Years of Specialization in Miniature Train Building—These Marvelous Outfits

[22]

Reg. U. S. Pat. Office
For "Lionel Standard" Track—2¼ Inches Wide

No. 403 is the new freight train outfit No. 404 illustrated at the bottom of this page. Every style of modern freight car is included with it, but many more can be added with the full assurance that the powerful twin-super-motor locomotive will haul them without difficulty.

Liberal track layouts are included with these outfits.

Outfit No. 403—Comprises one No. 402 twin-super-motor reversible locomotive (17½ inches long), one No. 418 illuminated pullman car, one No. 419 illuminated pullman and baggage car, one No. 490 illuminated observation car (each 20 inches long), eight sections S track, eight sections C track and one STC "Lockon" connection. Track forms an oval 102 by 42 inches. Complete train is 77½ inches long.

Price, complete with electric lamps for headlights and interior of cars, connecting ties for joining sections of track, wires for transformer or battery connections and directions for operating **$62.50**

Code Word "PRETTY"   Western Price $75.00

suffice to say that nothing like them has ever been made before as miniature toy railroad equipment. The combination pullman and baggage car contains a baggage compartment with sliding doors and the platform of the observation car is made of brass and is complete in every detail.

No. 404

Outfit No. 404—Comprises one No. 402 twin-super-motor reversible locomotive (17½ inches long) with two electric headlights, one No. 11 flat car, one No. 12 gondola car, one No. 13 cattle car, one No. 14 box car, one No. 15 oil car, one No. 16 coal car, one No. 17 caboose (each 11 inches long), eight sections C track, ten sections S track, and one STC "Lockon" connection. Track forms an oval 116 by 42 inches. Complete train is 94½ inches long. The locomotive is the same as included with outfit No. 403, while the freight cars are of steel construction all through, richly enameled, with nickeled trucks and wheels. The complete train presents a beautiful appearance and is in all respects a perfect miniature replica of a transcontinental heavy freighter.

Price, complete with electric lamps for headlights, connecting ties for joining sections of track, wires for transformer or battery connections and directions for operating **$60.00**

Code Word "ELITE"   Western Price $72.00

The Type K "Multivolt" Transformer Listed with Others on Page 27 Will Operate These Trains Perfectly

Complete Railroad for "Lionel Standard" Track—2¼ Inches Wide

Reg. U. S. Pat. Office

HERE is a lavishly planned complete railroad that reflects to the highest degree a perfect layout of equipment and miniature village. A "Multivolt" Transformer is included with this beautiful outfit for operating it from the Alternating House Current, or a Lionel Current Reducer will be supplied if your current is "Direct". Please be sure to specify which one is required.

This complete railroad comes to you securely packed.

OUTFIT No. 405

EQUIPMENT WITH OUTFIT No. 405

LOCOMOTIVES
1 No. 402 Twin-Super-Motor
1 No. 5 Switching Engine

PASSENGER CARS
1 No. 418 Illuminated Pullman
1 No. 419 Illuminated Pullman and Baggage
1 No. 490 Illuminated Observation

FREIGHT CARS
1 No. 11 Flat Car
1 No. 12 Gondola Car
1 No. 13 Cattle Car
1 No. 14 Box Car

1 No. 15 Oil Car
1 No. 16 Coal Car
1 No. 17 Caboose

TRACK
38 sections S straight track
18 sections C curved track
4 sections ½S straight track

TRACK ACCESSORIES
3 pairs No. 22 Switches (right and left)
2 No. 23 Bumpers
6 No. STC "Lockon" Connectors

STATIONS AND HOUSES
1 No. 121 Station
1 No. 191 Villa
1 No. 189 Villa
4 No. 184 Bungalows

ACCESSORIES
1 Type K Transformer (or No. 107 Direct Current Reducer if desired)
1 No. 69 Warning Signal
2 No. 77 Crossing Gates
8 No. 60 Telegraph Posts
1 No. 89 Flag Staff
1 No. 65 Semaphore

1 No. 66 Semaphore
1 No. 120 Tunnel
1 No. 101 Bridge (3 sections)
2 No. 59 Lamp Posts
4 No. 57 Lamp Posts

The complete dimensions of the entire track layout are 11 feet 8 inches long and 9 feet 2 inches wide.

Price, complete with electric lamps for locomotives, cars and all accessories, connecting ties for joining sections of track, connecting wires for transformer or reducer and directions for operating **$200.00**
Western Price $250.00
Code Word "MARK"

The Finishing Touch to This Complete Railroad Is Provided by the New Automatic Train Control—See Page 38

[24]

Lionel "All-Steel" Tunnels

LIONEL TRAINS are worthy of good accessories and it is therefore with great pleasure that we offer the Lionel steel tunnels, which are a wonderful improvement over the old, flimsy, papier-mâché ones that users of train outfits were compelled to accept before we introduced ours.

Lionel tunnels are made of steel throughout, being accurately designed and formed in our special machinery. They stand evenly on the floor without the slightest twist. Their rigid construction does not make it necessary to have any cross-braces on the base which would interfere with the track level.

The front and rear entrances of Lionel tunnels are embossed in exact reproduction of heavy stone masonry, having a keystone at the top. The bodies of the tunnels represent mountainsides in miniature and the coloring is made to harmonize beautifully. We draw particular attention to the detail on No. 120 Tunnel, which has the mountain roadside wonderfully modelled as well as the little metal "chalet", all in perfect proportion to the size of the tunnel.

All Lionel tunnels are practically indestructible and are very low priced considering the workmanship in them.

No. 120

No. 119

No. 118

Your "Power-Plant" Should Be a LIONEL "Multivolt" Transformer or a Lionel Direct Current Reducer. See pages 26 and 27.

Tunnel No. 118, for "O" Gauge Only—Will allow passage of any "O" gauge train. Is 8 inches long, 7 inches wide and 7½ inches extreme height. Portals are 4 inches wide and 5½ inches high inside.
Price $2.10
Code Word "SIMPLON"   Western Price $2.50

Tunnel No. 119, for "O" Gauge and Some "Lionel Standard" Trains—For use with all "O" gauge trains and "Lionel Standard" trains Nos. 34, 370, 340 and 41. Is 12 inches long, 9 inches wide and 10 inches extreme height. Portals are 5 inches wide and 6½ inches high inside.
Price $3.35
Code Word "HOOSAC"   Western Price $4.00

Tunnel No. 120, for All Lionel Trains—This splendid model is the very best produced for beauty, grace of design and substantial construction. Is 17 inches long, 12 inches wide and 11 inches extreme height. Inside dimensions of portals are 6½ inches wide and 8 inches high.
Price $5.85
Code Word "HUDSON"   Western Price $7.00

All Lionel Accessories Are Faithful Models of the Originals—Many New Devices Are Shown Throughout This Book

Lionel "Multivolt" Transformers—Specifications

LIONEL DIRECT CURRENT REDUCERS
Not for Alternating Current

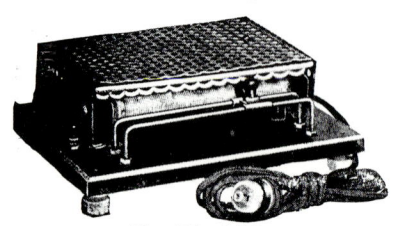

Nos. 107 and 170

No. 107, Lionel Current Reducer for 110-Volt Circuit—This is constructed of four porcelain tubes wound with best quality of resistance wire. These porcelain tubes are mounted on a substantial slate base measuring 8 by 10 inches and ¾ inch thick. The porcelain tubes are protected and ventilated by a perforated steel cover lined with heavy asbestos. The sliding lever regulates the voltage so that your trains will just crawl along or shoot ahead at express speed. The reducer is connected with the house current by a screw plug with 7 feet of flexible cord. In addition, four porcelain supports or legs with long screws are supplied so that the reducer can be screwed to wall or table.

Price $10.00
Western Price $12.00
Code Word "KENTUCKY"

No. 170, Lionel Direct Current Reducer for 220-Volt Circuit—This Reducer is identical in appearance with No. 107, mentioned above, but is for use on 220 volts. Equipped with separable plug and 7 feet of flexible cord.

Price $14.50
Western Price $17.00
Code Word "ASBURY"

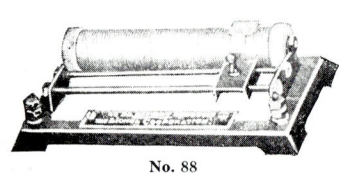

No. 88

Lionel Battery Rheostat No. 88—Use this rheostat with dry or storage batteries. It gives a gradual increase or decrease of current. A porcelain tube is wound with resistance wire of the correct gauge. This is mounted on a steel frame. A sliding finger increases or decreases the speed of the trains. All parts are of the best quality. This rheostat cannot overheat, as the coil is entirely exposed to the air—insuring free circulation, consequently rapid cooling. The steel base is beautifully enameled and other parts are nickel plated. Size 5 inches long, 2½ inches wide and 1 inch high.

Price $1.50
Western Price $1.80
Code Word "BANNER"

Details of Transformer Construction

Sub-Base—A metal sub-base resting on four supports is attached to the bottom. The air circulating between this sub-base and the transformer case keeps it cool while in operation. Screw holes in this sub-base provide means for fastening the transformer to wall or table.

Separable Plug—All "Multivolt" Transformers are fitted with an approved, separable plug, which is a distinct advantage over the one-piece plug, because the circuit can be immediately broken when desired.

Plug Protecting Device—We have applied for a patent on a unique receptacle for protecting the plug against breakage in shipment. This device consists of a wooden container entirely covering the plug. It is sealed with a conspicuous label which draws the attention of the user to the fact that the transformer must be used **only** on **alternating** current of the number of cycles designated. This obviates the possibility of connecting the transformer with wrong current, which will consequently avoid mishandling and disappointment.

Double Contact Control Switch—This is new and infinitely superior to the one-piece switch, which is easily bent and does not make positive contact. Our double switch has a flexible, phosphor-bronze contact arm under the rigid switch, so that positive contact with the points is assured. This flexible contact is protected from injury by the rigid brass handle to which it is attached. This feature cannot be found on any other type of toy transformer.

Laminations—The laminations are made of the best grade of electrical sheets and the windings are perfectly insulated.

Rigid Supports for Coils—The coils and laminations of Lionel "Multivolt" Transformers are rigidly supported inside the case by means of metal bands which prevent these parts from moving and eliminate the possibility of broken lead wires. In addition to these supports, the interior of the case is fitted with an insulating receptacle and the case is air cooled.

Metal Case—The case is beautiful in design and is stamped of heavier steel than is required by the National Board of Fire Underwriters.

Finish—"Multivolt" Transformer cases are covered with a rubberoid composition that is applied at 350 degrees Fahrenheit. This is much greater heat than the case is ever subjected to while in use, and the finish cannot be scratched and will not peel off, thereby insuring a beautiful finish for the entire life of the transformer.

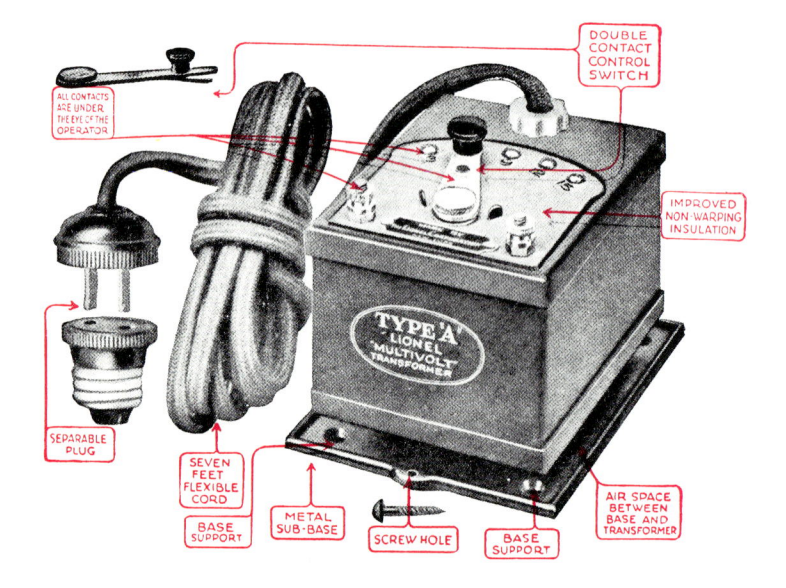

Visible Connections—All contacts and switches are mounted on one piece of heavy insulating material and are at the top of the transformer, right under the user's eyes.

Lamp Cord—All "Multivolt" Transformers are fitted with 7 feet of flexible lamp cord which enters the transformer case through an approved porcelain bushing.

From the above specifications it will be clearly seen that we have incorporated in "Multivolt" Transformers every possible device that will increase their efficiency and safety.

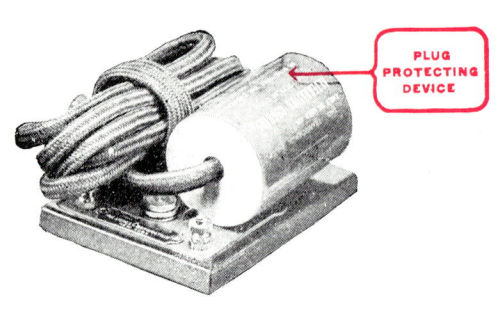

Lionel "Multivolt" Transformers Are Approved by the National Board of Fire Underwriters

Lionel "Multivolt" Transformers for 110 and 220 Volts, 60, 40 or 25 Cycles

LIONEL "Multivolt" Transformers have been on the market for a great many years and operate all makes of Electric Trains. We justly claim that they are best. Don't experiment with other makes of doubtful value. Remember, that all transformers look alike outside, but their imperfections will only be discovered after they are in actual use for a length of time. Lionel "Multivolt" Transformers will last indefinitely and are guaranteed unconditionally as long as they are used on the current for which they are intended. They are absolutely safe and will give steady, even power.

THESE TRANSFORMERS ARE FOR USE ONLY ON "ALTERNATING" CURRENT—DO NOT USE THEM ON "DIRECT" CURRENT

Type "A" Transformer will operate any "O" gauge outfit.

For 110 volts, 60 cycles. 40 watts capacity.

Gives 15 volts in following steps: 4, 7, 10, 13, 15.

Size: 4¼ by 2¾ by 4¼ inches. Sub-base: 3¾ by 4¾ inches.

Price $3.75
Western Price $4.50
Code Word "STRONG"

Type "B" Transformer will operate any "O" gauge outfit, and in addition the extra binding posts enable the users to light up lamp posts, semaphores and other electrically illuminated accessories.

For 110 volts, 60 cycles. 50 watts capacity.

Gives 25 volts in following steps: Permanent: 7, 8, 15. Variable: 2, 4, 6, 8, 9, 10, 11, 12, 13, 17, 19, 21, 23, 25.

Size: 4½ by 3¾ by 5 inches. Sub-base: 5 by 4¼ inches.

Price $5.00
Western Price $6.00
Code Word "BRADLEY"

Type "T" Transformer will operate any "O" gauge or "Lionel Standard" outfit; also has extra binding posts for attaching illuminated electrical accessories.

For 110 volts, 60 cycles. 100 watts capacity.

Gives 25 volts in following steps: Permanent: 2, 4, 6, 7, 8, 10, 12, 14, 15, 16, 17, 18, 19, 21, 23, 25. Variable: 2, 6, 8, 10, 12, 14, 16, 17, 18, 19, 21, 23, 25.

Size: 5 by 4 by 3¾ inches. Sub-base: 4½ by 5½ inches.

Price $7.50
Western Price $9.00
Code Word "BIRCH"

Type "K" Transformer will operate any outfit as well as illuminated accessories. This transformer has sufficient wattage capacity to operate two trains at once.

Size: 5 by 4 by 4½ inches. Sub-base: 4½ by 5½ inches.

"K"—For 110 volts, 60 cycles. 150 watts capacity. Specifications same as Type "T", but has higher wattage capacity. **Price $11.00**
Western Price $13.00
Code Word (110 V.) "BINGHAM"

"K"—For 220 volts, 60 cycles. 150 watts capacity. Specifications same as Type "T", but is for use on 220-volt circuit. **Price $14.50**
Western Price $17.00
Code Word (220 V.) "BROOK"

Type "C" Transformer will operate any outfit and illuminated accessories on 25 or 40 cycle current.

For 110 volts, 25 to 40 cycles. 75 watts capacity. Specifications same as Type "T", but is for use on 25 or 40 cycle current.

Size: 5 by 4 by 4½ inches. Sub-base: 4½ by 5½ inches.

Price $7.50
Western Price $9.00
Code Word "LAWRENCE"

Lionel "Multivolt" Transformers Are Efficient—Economical—Easily Operated

[27]

1924

Lionel "All-Steel" Passenger and Mail Cars

THE construction of all Lionel Pullman Coaches is worthy of special notice, as it represents the highest form of miniature car manufacture. Not only are all bodies made of heavy steel and beautifully embossed with panels, rivets, etc., but many types are made of one single piece formed and soldered at the ends, and the cars of the larger type are rigidly held together by mechanical means and soldered. Cross braces and partitions placed inside the cars not only add to the detail but make them rigid and almost indestructible. Some outstanding features of Lionel Coaches are hinged doors, inserted window frames and sashes and interior seats. These separable pieces are enameled in various colors to harmonize with the body of the car and accentuate the great detail that is incorporated in them. All cars, even the lowest priced ones, are finished in enamel baked on at high temperature so that the finish is everlasting and can always be kept bright and clean.

No. 490 Observation Car—Same size as No. 418 Pullman and No. 419 Pullman and Baggage Car.

No. 19 Pullman and Baggage Car—Same size as No. 18 Pullman and No. 190 Observation Car.

In almost every car clear transparencies are placed in the windows and leaded glass effects will be found at the upper parts of the windows and in the transoms. The light shining through these transparencies produces a most realistic effect. The roofs are firmly held in place with an ornamental screw—easily removable so that the electric lamp in the interior can be reached.

Many of the models have miniature tanks affixed to the bottom as well as brass steps and hand rails and with the exception of a few of the lowest priced "O" Gauge cars, are all equipped with the new Lionel Automatic Coupler. The rear platforms of observation cars are made of ornamental sheet brass, highly polished.

All cars are mounted on scientifically designed trucks with perfectly aligned nickeled wheels and axles. They operate without friction and are so absolutely true that they will not derail even when travelling at a high rate of speed. All the desirable features mentioned above will be apparent by referring to the illustration and indications on page 9.

No. 319 Pullman Car—Same size as No. 322 Observation Car.

No. 610 Pullman Car—Same size as No. 612 Observation Car.

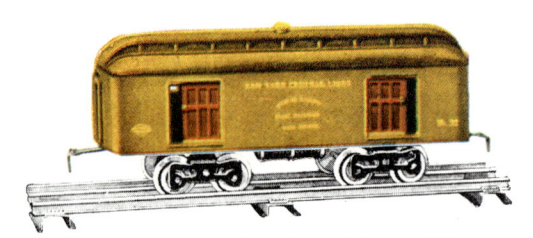

No. 32 Mail Car—Same size as No. 31 Pullman and Baggage Car, No. 35 Pullman and No. 36 Observation Car.

These Are Real Passenger Cars in Miniature—Replete with Realistic Features

Prices of Lionel "All-Steel" Passenger and Mail Cars

(See Opposite Page for Illustrations)

For Lionel "O" Gauge Track — 1⅜ Inches Wide

No. 600 Pullman Car—7 inches long, 3 inches high . . . . **Price $ .50**
Code Word "HORNBY"   Western Price $ .60

No. 629 Pullman Car—7¾ inches long, 3½ inches high . . **Price $ .60**
Code Word "FAME"   Western Price $ .70

No. 630 Observation Car—7¾ inches long, 3½ inches high . **Price $ .60**
Code Word "IDEAL"   Western Price $ .70

Above three cars are mounted on a four-wheel truck and are for use with Locomotives Nos. 150, 152 and 153.

No. 603 Illuminated Pullman Car—complete with electric lamp. Car is 8 inches long, 3⅜ inches high . . . . **Price $1.35**
Code Word "BURTON"   Western Price $1.70

No. 604 Illuminated Observation Car—complete with electric lamp. Car is 8 inches long, 3⅜ inches high . . . . **Price $1.50**
Code Word "MONARCH"   Western Price $1.80

Above two cars are mounted on double four-wheel trucks and are for use with Locomotives Nos. 150, 152, 153 and 253.

No. 610 Illuminated Pullman Car—complete with electric lamp. Car is 9 inches long, 4 inches high . . . . **Price $2.95**
Code Word "EALING"   Western Price $3.50

No. 612 Illuminated Observation Car—complete with electric lamp. Car is 9 inches long, 4 inches high . . . . **Price $3.15**
Code Word "WALTON"   Western Price $3.70

Above two cars are mounted on double four-wheel trucks and are for use with Locomotives Nos. 156X, 253, 254 and 256.

No. 710 Illuminated Pullman Car—complete with electric lamp. Car is 12½ inches long, 4¾ inches high . . . . **Price $3.75**
Code Word "HOLLY"   Western Price $4.50

No. 712 Illuminated Observation Car—complete with electric lamp. Car is 12½ inches long, 4¾ inches high . . . . **Price $3.85**
Code Word "RISE"   Western Price $4.70

Above two cars are mounted on double four-wheel trucks and are for use with Locomotives Nos. 254 and 256.

For "Lionel Standard" Gauge Track — 2¼ Inches Wide
Reg. U. S. Pat. Office

No. 31 Illuminated Pullman and Baggage Car—complete with electric lamp. Car is 11½ inches long, 5 inches high . . . . **Price $3.75**
Code Word "CAPI"   Western Price $4.50

No. 32 Mail Car. Car is 11½ inches long, 5 inches high . . **Price $3.35**
Code Word "BILL"   Western Price $4.00

No. 35 Illuminated Pullman Car—complete with electric lamp. Car is 11½ inches long, 5 inches high . . . . **Price $3.75**
Code Word "CAMDEN"   Western Price $4.50

No. 36 Illuminated Observation Car—complete with electric lamp. Car is 11½ inches long, 5 inches high . . . . **Price $3.85**
Code Word "FLINT"   Western Price $4.70

Above four cars are mounted on double four-wheel trucks and are for use with Locomotives Nos. 33, 38, 50, 318 and 380.

No. 319 Illuminated Pullman Car—complete with electric lamp. Car is 15 inches long, 5½ inches high . . . . **Price $5.00**
Code Word "COTT"   Western Price $6.50

No. 322 Illuminated Observation Car—complete with electric lamp. Car is 15 inches long, 5½ inches high . . . . **Price $5.85**
Code Word "JANE"   Western Price $7.00

Above two cars are mounted on double four-wheel trucks and are for use with Locomotives Nos. 38, 50, 318 and 380.

No. 18 Illuminated Pullman Car—complete with electric lamp. Car is 16½ inches long, 6 inches high . . . . **Price $6.75**
Code Word "PHILA"   Western Price $8.00

No. 19 Illuminated Pullman and Baggage Car—complete with electric lamp. Car is 16½ inches long, 6 inches high . . . . **Price $7.00**
Code Word "TROY"   Western Price $8.50

No. 190 Illuminated Observation Car—complete with electric lamp. Car is 16½ inches long, 6 inches high . . . . **Price $7.50**
Code Word "VIRGINIA"   Western Price $9.00

Above three cars are mounted on double four-wheel trucks and are for use with Locomotives Nos. 380 and 402.

No. 418 Illuminated Pullman Car—complete with electric lamp. Car is 20 inches long, 6¼ inches high . . . . **Price $8.50**
Code Word "COMFORT"   Western Price $10.00

No. 419 Illuminated Pullman and Baggage Car—complete with electric lamp. Car is 20 inches long, 6¼ inches high . . . . **Price $8.50**
Code Word "COURT"   Western Price $10.00

No. 490 Illuminated Observation Car—complete with electric lamp. Car is 20 inches long, 6¼ inches high . . . . **Price $8.50**
Code Word "CABIN"   Western Price $10.00

Above three cars are mounted on double four-wheel trucks and are for use with Locomotive No. 402.

All Cars Listed Above Are Shown Throughout This Catalog in Conjunction with the Various Train Outfits

Lionel "All-Steel" Freight Cars

EXPRESSING the individuality of every style of real commercial freight car has been our aim, and in designing Lionel Freight Cars we have embodied in them the utmost realism. They are constructed entirely of steel and beautifully finished in rich, lasting enamels—not lithographed on flimsy tin. All trucks are flexible, which means that they will not jump the track while running either forward or backward. They move so easily that one of our locomotives will haul a number of them without difficulty. The wheels are made of steel, and are reinforced at the back with heavy steel discs. They are mounted on solid Bessemer steel shafts. No wood enters the construction of these cars. All the roofs are removable and doors slide so that the interior of the cars can be easily reached. Trucks and wheels are nickeled. The construction of all cars is similar in every respect, but vary in size in accordance with the locomotive with which they are intended to be operated. All the cars are hand enameled and trimmed and are appropriately decorated with the "heralds" of the most prominent railroads.

Oil Car—Made in one size for "Lionel Standard" track.

Ballast Car—Made in two sizes for "Lionel Standard" track.

Gondola Car—Made in three sizes. For "Lionel Standard" and "O" Gauge tracks.

Cattle Car—Made in three sizes. For "Lionel Standard" and "O" Gauge tracks.

Flat Car—Made in one size for "Lionel Standard" track.

Box Car—Made in four sizes. For "Lionel Standard" and "O" Gauge tracks.

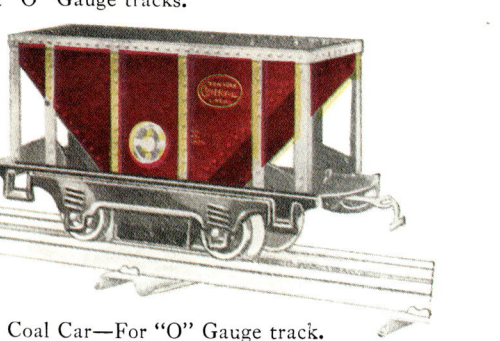

Coal Car—For "O" Gauge track.

Caboose—Made in four sizes. For "Lionel Standard" and "O" Gauge tracks.

Oil Car—For "O" Gauge track.

A Combination of These Freight Cars Behind a Lionel Locomotive Makes an Extremely Realistic Train

Prices of Lionel "All-Steel" Freight Cars

(See Opposite Page for Illustrations)

Reg. U. S. Pat. Office

For Lionel "O" Gauge Track—1⅜ Inches Wide

No. 800 Box Car—7 inches long, 3 inches high . . . . . Price $ .50
Code Word "CHANDLER"   Western Price $ .60

No. 801 Caboose—7 inches long, 3¼ inches high . . . . Price $ .50
Code Word "CONNERTON"   Western Price $ .60

No. 802 Cattle Car—7 inches long, 3 inches high . . . . Price $ .50
Code Word "CHICKASAW"   Western Price $ .60

No. 803 Coal Car—7 inches long, 3 inches high . . . . . Price $ .65
Code Word "LOAD"   Western Price $ .80

No. 804 Oil Car—7 inches long, 3½ inches high . . . . Price $ .60
Code Word "FUEL"   Western Price $ .70

No. 901 Gondola Car—7 inches long, 2 inches high . . . . Price $ .40
Code Word "CHIMES"   Western Price $ .50

Above six cars mounted on a four-wheel truck are for use with Locomotives Nos. 150, 152, 153 and 253.

No. 820 Box Car—8¼ inches long, 3½ inches high . . . . Price $1.25
Code Word "ECOLA"   Western Price $1.50

No. 822 Caboose—8¼ inches long, 3¾ inches high . . . Price $1.25
Code Word "ELIXIR"   Western Price $1.50

Above two cars are mounted on double four-wheel trucks and are for use with Locomotives Nos. 152, 153, 156X, 253 and 254.

For "Lionel Standard" Track—2¼ Inches Wide

No. 112 Gondola Car—9¾ inches long, 2½ inches high . . Price $1.50
Code Word "ELMIRA"   Western Price $1.80

No. 113 Cattle Car—9¾ inches long, 4½ inches high . . Price $2.10
Code Word "SYRACUSE"   Western Price $2.50

No. 114 Box Car—9¾ inches long, 4½ inches high . . Price $2.10
Code Word "HAZLETON"   Western Price $2.50

No. 116 Ballast Car—9¾ inches long, 3¾ inches high . . . Price $2.10
Code Word "SCRANTON"   Western Price $2.50

No. 117 Caboose—9¾ inches long, 4¾ inches high . . . . Price $2.10
Code Word "TOLEDO"   Western Price $2.50

Above five cars are mounted on double four-wheel trucks and are for use with Locomotives Nos. 33, 38, 50 and 318.

No. 11 Flat Car—11 inches long, 3½ inches high . . . . . Price $2.10
Code Word "MASS"   Western Price $2.50

No. 12 Gondola Car—11 inches long, 3½ inches high . . . Price $2.95
Code Word "VERMONT"   Western Price $3.50

No. 13 Cattle Car—11 inches long, 5½ inches high . . . . Price $3.35
Code Word "HAMPSHIRE"   Western Price $4.00

No. 14 Box Car—11 inches long, 5½ inches high . . . . . Price $3.35
Code Word "MAINE"   Western Price $4.00

No. 15 Oil Car—11 inches long, 5¼ inches high . . . . . Price $3.35
Code Word "QUEBEC"   Western Price $4.00

No. 16 Ballast Car—11 inches long, 4¾ inches high . . . . Price $3.35
Code Word "ONTARIO"   Western Price $4.00

No. 17 Caboose—11 inches long, 6½ inches high . . . . . Price $3.35
Code Word "TORONTO"   Western Price $4.00

Above seven cars are mounted on double four-wheel trucks and are for use with Locomotives Nos. 318, 380 and 402.

The Freight Cars Listed Here Are Shown Made Up Into Various Train Outfits Throughout This Catalog

Lionel "All-Steel" Lamp Posts—Lamp Assortment—Renewal Lamps

NO miniature railroad is complete without the addition of Lionel lamp posts, which are faithful reproductions of boulevard and street lamp posts seen everywhere. All Lionel lamp posts are substantially constructed of steel throughout—they won't bend or break. The binding posts to which electrical connections are made are conveniently situated and are securely fastened and perfectly insulated.

LAMP ASSORTMENT No. 111
We supply Lionel dealers with a handsome cabinet of renewal lamps for use in headlights and all electrically illuminated accessories. These lamps are of the finest quality and are supplied in 8, 14 and 21 volts.
Fifty assorted lamps are packed in each cabinet. The chart on the inside cover gives valuable information as to the uses of the various lamps. Each lamp is packed in a wooden container.

No. 111 LAMP ASSORTMENT
Code Word "LUX"
PRICE $15.00
Western Price $20.00

THERE is no chance of short circuit with Lionel lamp posts, for great care is used in their construction and every one is thoroughly tested before leaving the factory. The globes supplied with all lamp posts are in exact proportion to the size of the posts. It is impossible to secure any other make of lamp post that has the dignity and grace of design to be found in the Lionel lamp posts illustrated below.

SEPARATE RENEWAL LAMPS
(Each Lamp Packed in Wooden Container)

No. 24—Round lamp, clear glass, half inch diameter, 8 volts.
Price . . . . $ .30
Code Word "CAMBRIDGE"   Western Price $ .40

No. 26—Round lamp, clear glass, half inch diameter, 14 volts.
Price . . . . $ .30
Code Word "OXFORD"   Western Price $ .40

No. 48—Round lamp, clear glass, half inch diameter, 21 volts.
Price . . . . $ .30
Code Word "MILTON"   Western Price $ .40

Above three lamps are for use in headlights and all electrically illuminated accessories.

No. 25—Pear-shaped lamp, frosted, three-quarter inch diameter.
8 volts. Price . . . . $ .30
Code Word "LUME"   Western Price $ .40

No. 55—Pear-shaped lamp, frosted, three-quarter inch diameter, 14 volts. Price . . . . $ .30
Code Word "LIT"   Western Price $ .40

No. 75—Pear-shaped lamp, frosted, three-quarter inch diameter, 21 volts. Price . . . . $ .30
Code Word "BLAZE"   Western Price $ .40

Above three lamps are for use in lamp posts Nos. 58 and 59.

No. 46—Pear-shaped lamp, frosted, one inch diameter, 8 volts.
Price . . . . $ .30
Code Word "ETON"   Western Price $ .40

No. 30—Pear-shaped lamp, frosted, one inch diameter, 14 volts.
Price . . . . $ .30
Code Word "KINGS"   Western Price $ .40

No. 49—Pear-shaped lamp, frosted, one inch diameter, 21 volts.
Price . . . . $ .30
Code Word "HUNTERS"   Western Price $ .40

Above three lamps are for use in lamp posts Nos. 61 and 67, also for outside light brackets of Station No. 124.

Lamp Post No. 67—13 inches high. Complete with two electric globes.
Price $2.95
Western Price $3.50
Code Word "EDMUNDS"

Lamp Post No. 58—7⅜ inches high. Complete with globe.
Price $1.25
Western Price $1.50
Code Word "JENNY"

Lamp Post No. 56—8¾ inches high. The top is easily removable so that the lamp can be renewed when necessary. Complete with lamp.
Price $1.65
Western Price $2.00
Code Word "SHINE"

Lamp Post No. 57—7½ inches high. The top is easily removable so that the lamp can be renewed when necessary. Complete with lamp.
Price $1.65
Western Price $2.00
Code Word "CHEERY"

Lamp Post No. 59—Similar in design to No. 61, but is 8¾ inches high. Complete with globe.
Price $1.50
Western Price $1.80
Code Word "BRIGHT"

Lamp Post No. 61—13 inches high. Complete with electric globe.
Price $2.10
Western Price $2.50
Code Word "INDIANA"

Every Lionel Lamp Post Conforms in Size to the Various Train Outfits Shown in This Book

"All-Steel" Bridges for "Lionel Standard" and "O" Gauge Track
Reg. U. S. Pat. Office

NO items in the Lionel Line have met with such success since their introduction as the Lionel all-steel bridges. The construction and appearance place them in a class by themselves. No illustration can do justice to the beautiful appearance and sturdy construction of these bridges. They are modeled closely after all the big railroad bridges seen throughout the country. The end piers, the bridge work and roadway are exceptionally sturdy. The architectural designs are graceful and pleasing and the embossing work incorporated in them gives a dignity and realism that cannot be equalled anywhere. Special slots in the roadway hold the track rigidly in place and the spans as well as the approaches are all provided with sections of track either for "O" gauge or "Lionel Standard" track. Bridges can be extended to any length by the addition of the spans shown in the illustration.

No. 101
No. 101, Center Span and Two Approaches—"Lionel Standard" track. Complete structure is 42 inches long, 6½ inches wide, 6¼ inches high.
Price $5.85
Code Word "QUEENS"   Western Price $7.00

No. 102
No. 102, Two Center Spans and Two Approaches—"Lionel Standard" track. Complete structure is 56 inches long, 6½ inches wide, 6¼ inches high . . . . **Price $8.50**
Code Word "KEEPSIE"   Western Price $10.00

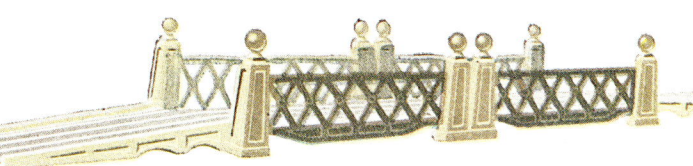

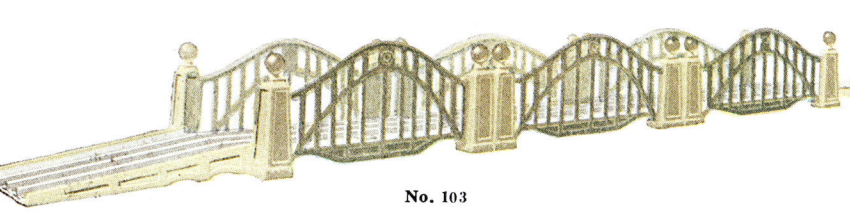

No. 103
No. 103, Three Center Spans and Two Approaches—"Lionel Standard" track. Complete structure is 70 inches long, 6½ inches wide, 6¼ inches high . . . . **Price $11.00**
Code Word "LONDON"   Western Price $13.00

No. 104
No. 104, Center Span—"Lionel Standard" track. 14 inches long, 6½ inches wide, 6¼ inches high.
Price $3.35
Western Price $4.00
Code Word "MANHATTAN"

Nos. 100 and 105
No. 100—"Lionel Standard" track. In reproduction of reinforced concrete, 28 inches long, 5½ inches wide, 2 inches high at center . . . . . **Price $2.50**
Western Price $3.00
Code Word "BROOKLYN"

No. 105—"O" gauge. Reinforced concrete work, 21 inches long, 4¼ inches wide, 2 inches high . **Price $1.65**
Western Price $2.00
Code Word "PARIS"

No. 106
No. 106, One Center Span and Two Approaches—"O" gauge. Complete structure is 31½ inches long, 5½ inches wide, 4 inches high. . **Price $3.35**
Western Price $4.00
Code Word "CONN"

No. 108
No. 108, Two Center Spans and Two Approaches—"O" gauge. Complete structure is 42 inches long, 5½ inches wide, 4 inches high . . **Price $5.50**
Western Price $6.50
Code Word "HOUSA"

No. 109
No. 109, Three Center Spans and Two Approaches—"O" gauge. Complete structure is 52½ inches long, 5½ inches wide, 4 inches high. **Price $7.50**
Western Price $9.00
Code Word "MISS"

No. 110
No. 110, Center Span—"O" gauge. 10½ inches long, 5½ inches wide, 4 inches high. **Price $2.50**
Code Word "WILLIAMS"   Western Price $3.00

Lionel Trains Look Extremely Realistic Gliding Over These Sturdy, Well-Designed Bridges

Lionel "All-Steel" Stations—Bungalows—Villas—Signal Tower

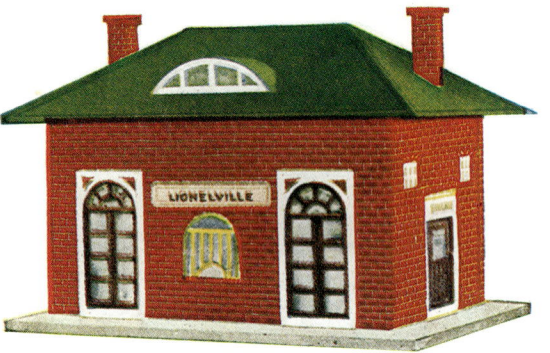

LIONEL all-steel houses and stations are substantially constructed and beautifully finished in a variety of durable enamels. They are so wonderfully proportioned that they have the appearance of real houses and stations in miniature. The die and embossing work, the inserted windows, the chimney stacks, roofs and entrances make them stand far above any similar toy ever introduced.

Interior Illumination—Some of the numbers listed on these pages have interior and outside lights complete with brackets, electric lamps and wires. This further adds to the realism and produces a wonderful effect.

Station No. 121—Has no lighting system. Dimensions: 13½ inches long, 9 inches wide, 13 inches high.
        Price $5.00
        Western Price $6.50
    Code Word "UNION"

Station No. 122—Has inside illumination. Furnished with complete wiring circuit ready to attach to batteries, transformer, or reducer. Wires extend through wall. Complete with one 14-volt globe and nickeled center fixture. Same size as No. 121 . . . . **Price $6.75**
        Western Price $8.00
    Code Word "CENTRAL"

Station No. 124, De Luxe Model—This number has two platform corner lights with reflectors, all finished in bright brass; and an inside light supported on a nickeled fixture. There is an elegance, grace and architectural dignity to this station difficult to show in an illustration. The corner lighting brackets have specially designed supporting arms—a detail seldom attempted. For use with batteries, transformers or reducers. Equipped with three 14-volt globes. Same size as No. 121 . . . . **Price $9.00**
        Western Price $11.00
    Code Word "READING"

Station No. 125—(No interior illumination.) A beautifully proportioned model that retails at an exceedingly low price. The realistic detail must be seen to be appreciated. This station measures 10¼ inches long, 7¼ inches wide and 7 inches high . . . . **Price $4.25**
        Western Price $5.00
    Code Word "ABOARD"

Station No. 126—Same as No. 125 described above, but has interior lighting fixture, lamp and wires ready for attaching to batteries, transformer or reducer . . . **Price $5.00**
        Western Price $6.50
    Code Word "ALIGHT"

Station No. 127—This can be used as a freight station for any size train outfit and will add a completing touch to a railroad layout. It is 7 inches long, 3½ inches wide and 4½ inches high. Complete with interior lighting fixture, lamp and wires ready to attach to batteries, transformer or reducer . . . . **Price $2.10**
        Western Price $2.50
    Code Word "TOWNLY"

Villa No. 189 (illuminated)—Size 5½ inches long, 4⅞ inches wide, 5⅜ inches high. Complete with interior lighting fixture, lamp and wires for connecting to batteries, transformer or reducer . . . . **Price $2.95**
        Western Price $3.50
    Code Word "MANSION"

Signal Tower No. 092 (illuminated)—Dimensions: 5 inches long, 4 inches wide, 5½ inches high. Complete with interior lighting fixture, lamp and wires for connecting to batteries, transformer or reducer . . . . . . **Price $2.10**
        Western Price $2.50
    Code Word "CYRIL"

Nos. 121, 122, 124

Nos. 125, 126

No. 127

No. 092

No. 189

Add These Interesting Accessories to Your Train Layout—They Provide a Completing Touch

Lionel "All-Steel" Villas—Sets of Assorted Houses

FOR Outdoor Railroads. Picture the fun that can be had when these houses and stations are placed around a big track-layout in the garden or on any outdoor plot, and used in connection with Lionel Railroad Accessories.

For Model Villages. In this connection the Lionel Houses will be found invaluable. There is no limit to the wonderful effects that can be produced.

Use on Any Kind of Current. Lionel Stations, Bungalows and Villas can be attached to "Multivolt" Transformers for "Alternating" Current or to Lionel Reducers for "Direct" Current and also to dry or storage batteries.

Villa No. 191 (illuminated)—Size 7⅛ in. long, 5⅛ in. wide, 5¼ in. high.
Complete with interior lighting fixture, lamp and wires for connecting to batteries, transformer or reducer.

Code Word "SOLID" — Price $3.35 — Western Price $4.00

Bungalow No. 184 (illuminated)—Size 4¾ in. long, 2¾ in. wide, 4 in. high. Complete with lamp and wires for connecting.

Code Word "HOME" — Price $1.50 — Western Price $1.80

Bungalow No. 185—Same as No. 184 but without interior illumination.

Code Word "LEADER" — Price $1.00 — Western Price $1.20

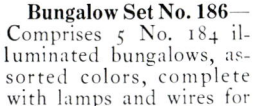

Bungalow Set No. 186—Comprises 5 No. 184 illuminated bungalows, assorted colors, complete with lamps and wires for connecting.

Price $7.50 — Western Price $9.00
Code Word "HAMLET"

Bungalow Set No. 187—Same as above but without interior illumination.

Price $5.00 — Western Price $6.00
Code Word "CITY"

Set No. 192—Comprises 1 No. 191 Villa, 1 No. 189 Villa and 2 No. 184 Bungalows, complete with interior lights and wires for connecting.

Price $7.35 — Western Price $8.80
Code Word "VILLAGE"

Nos. 184, 185

No. 191

No. 192

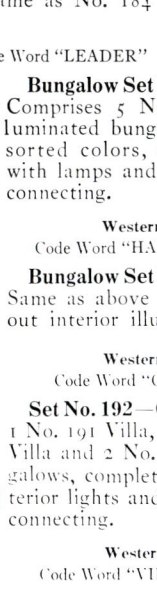

Nos. 186, 187

You Can Build a Complete, Illuminated Village with These Real Miniature Houses

[35]

1924

Reg. U. S. Pat. Office
"Lionel Standard" and "O" Gauge Track—"Lockon" Track Contacts

WE have described the strength and details of manufacture of Lionel Track in the introduction to this catalog. We will merely add here the technical facts.
Tested to Carry 110 Volts—Each section of track is tested for insulation on a circuit of 110 volts, consequently it will carry the low voltage necessary to operate our trains without any chance of short-circuiting.
Sections Are Easily Connected—The ends of each section have pin terminals which fit in openings in the adjoining sections. This allows the track to be laid and taken apart without any trouble. One section in each outfit is fitted with a "Lockon" track contact for batteries, "Multivolt" Transformer or Reducer.

The track is made in straight and curved sections. Any shaped figure may be formed. The curvature of the track is mechanically correct, allowing the cars to run at very high speed without danger of derailing.

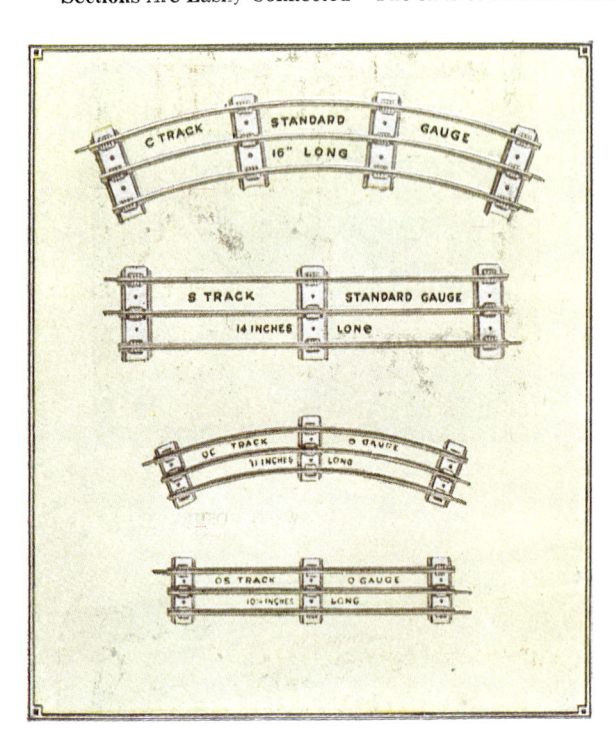

"LIONEL STANDARD" TRACK—2¼ Inches Wide
C, curved track, 16 inches long.
Code Word "BUFF"
Price per Section $ .30
Western Price $ .40

S, straight track, 14 inches long.
Code Word "NIAGARA"
Price per Section $ .30
Western Price $ .40

Eight No. C Sections make a circle 42 inches in diameter

LIONEL "O" GAUGE TRACK—1⅜ Inches Wide
OC, curved track, 11 inches long.
Code Word "LEMPS"
Price per Section $ .20
Western Price $ .26

OS, straight track, 10¼ inches long.
Code Word "GLENBURN"
Price per Section $ .20
Western Price $ .26

Eight No. OC Sections make a circle 30 inches in diameter

"LOCKON" TRACK CONTACTS For "Lionel Standard" and "O" Gauge

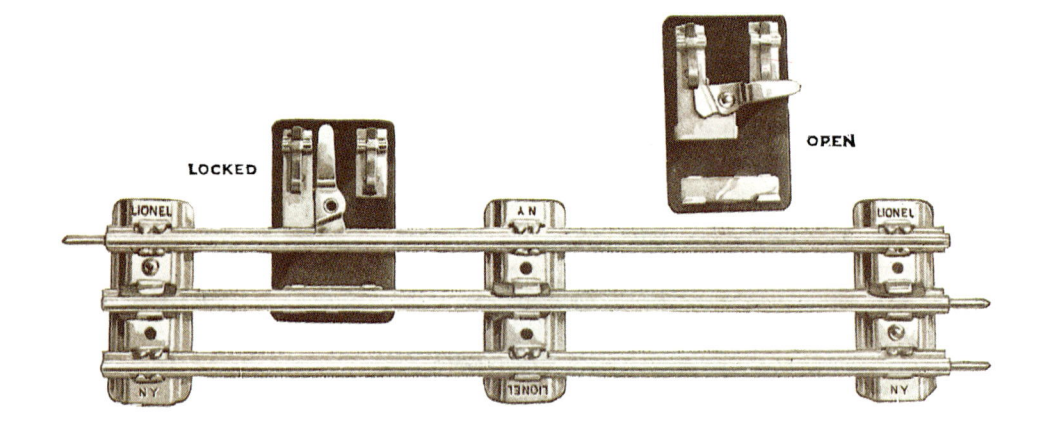

CONNECTING TIE
We show here the method of sliding in the connecting tie. This is one of our recent improvements. It binds the ties rigidly together so that sections cannot pull apart. Yet this can be removed without difficulty—just a slight pull with the thumb and finger.

Every Lionel Train Outfit includes a sufficient number of connecting ties for the amount of track packed with the outfit.

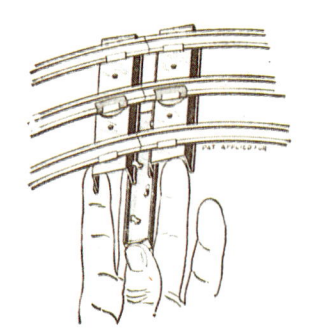

Lionel leadership is again evidenced in this improved device. Considering the fact that numerous electric accessories have been added to the Lionel line, which require connection with the track, these "LOCKON" contacts will readily appeal to the user, for it is no longer necessary to purchase special sections of track to which electrical contacts are affixed.

The "Lockon" contact is attached to the track by simply turning the lever at right angles. The electric connection is as perfect as though the parts were riveted or soldered to the track.

The "Lockon" contact is free from set screws and binding posts. The fingers that hold the wires in place are made of heavy tempered blue steel and are unbreakable. All parts are nickel plated and are mounted on a heavy fibre base.

No. "STC" for "Lionel Standard" Track

Code Word "JUICE"
Price $ .25
Western Price $ .30

No. "OTC" for Lionel "O" Gauge Track

Code Word "JOIN"
Price $ .20
Western Price $ .24

Build Your Miniature Railroad on a Good, Solid Foundation—Lionel Track

Lionel Track Accessories

ALL Lionel track accessories are perfectly insulated and are mounted on a heavy steel base which gives them great strength and will enable them to withstand hard usage.

ACCESSORIES
For "Lionel Standard" Track—2¼ Inches

Switch No. 22—(Right and Left Hand). The lever which moves the rails also sets signals and locks all mechanism. Signal lanterns have red and green discs. Length of switch, 16½ inches; width, 8 inches; height, 4½ inches. Connects with track in same manner as straight or curved sections.
Price per Pair, $5.00
Western Price $6.00
Code Word "NASHVILLE"

Electric Lighted Switch No. 21—(Right and Left Hand). This is similar in construction to No. 22 described above, but is equipped with an electric signal, having an electric bulb which can be easily removed. The light shining through the lantern shows red and green illuminated signals.
Price per Pair, $6.75
Western Price $8.00
Code Word "WINTERVILLE"

Crossing No. 20—For use in conjunction with Switches, enabling the formation of figure "8" and figure "8" loop. Measures 12 inches square. Cross rails are mounted on a solid base.
Price $1.25
Western Price $1.50
Code Word "BOSTON"

Bumper No. 23—An indispensable accessory for terminals or sidings. Has two spring plungers which absorb shock when car strikes it. Length, 14 inches; height, 3 inches. The Bumper frame can be removed from the track and replaced at any point desired.
Price $1.25
Western Price $1.50
Code Word "PROVIDENCE"

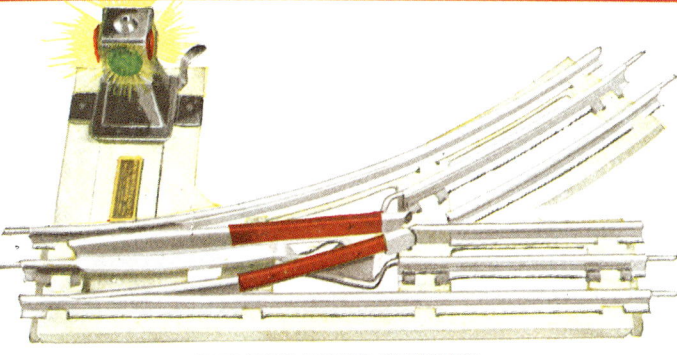

IMPROVED LIONEL SWITCHES

We are particularly desirous of drawing attention to the great improvement in the construction of our switches. Notwithstanding this improvement, prices have not been increased.

As will be seen from the illustration, the improvement consists of the insertion of two heavy fibre strips at the points where the rails cross.

By the insertion of these fibre strips all danger of short-circuit is eliminated. A train passing over these points does not slow up nor does the headlight flicker or go out.

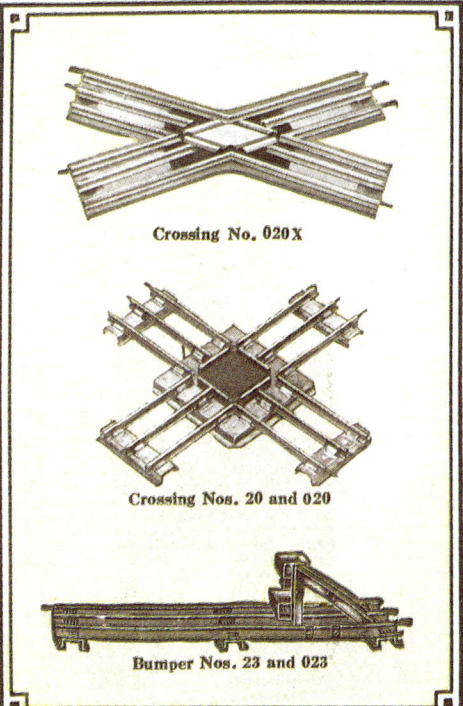

Crossing No. 020X

Crossing Nos. 20 and 020

Bumper Nos. 23 and 023

Every conceivable shape or figure can be made with the scientifically planned Lionel Track accessories illustrated on this page. It is always great fun to add to your railroad equipment.

ACCESSORIES
For Lionel "O" Gauge Track—1⅜ Inches

Switch No. 022—(Right and Left Hand). Construction is similar to No. 22 Switch described opposite. Length, 11½ inches; width, 5½ inches; height, 3 inches.
Price per Pair, $3.75
Western Price $4.50
Code Word "SPENCER"

Electric Lighted Switch No. 021—(Right and Left Hand). Similar construction to No. 21 Switch described opposite. Length, 11½ inches; width, 5½ inches; height, 3 inches.
Price per Pair, $5.00
Western Price $6.00
Code Word "MOSHER"

Crossing No. 020—Similar in construction to No. 20 Crossing described opposite. Measures 10¼ inches square.
Price $1.00
Western Price $1.20
Code Word "ORLAND"

Crossing No. 020X—This is a 45-degree crossing; forms the figure "8" when using all curved track. It occupies less space than the No. 020 Crossing.
Price $1.50
Western Price $1.80
Code Word "CROSS"

Bumper No. 023—Same construction as No. 23 Bumper described opposite. Length, 10¼ inches; height, 2 inches.
Price $ .80
Western Price $1.00
Code Word "DELTON"

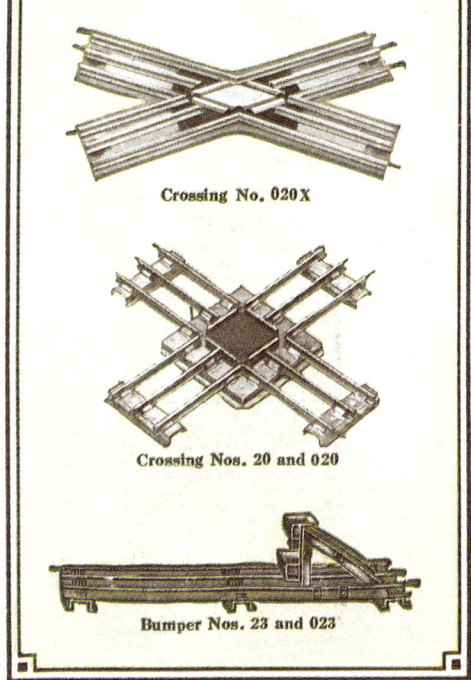

See Page 41 for the Great Variety of Figures Which Can Be Formed with These Accessories

Lionel Automatic Train Control—Electric Block Signal

The Greatest Achievement in Miniature Electric Train Engineering
The Lionel Automatic Train Control

THE simplest and most amazing accessory ever invented.

Place it at any desired spot in the track formation. The train approaches! The red signal light shows vividly! The train stops! It's absolutely automatic. After an interval of from 2 to 30 seconds the red signal light turns to green. Line's clear! All aboard! The train is on its way again.

Can you imagine anything more realistic? Is there anything in the world that will increase your sales of Electric Trains more than this marvelous accessory? The Lionel Automatic Train Control will delight the heart of every boy.

Its action is absolutely automatic and positive—the length of the interval between stopping and starting is fixed before the train is set in motion—after that it functions continuously and does not require any attention on the part of the operator.

The Lionel Automatic Train Control is substantially constructed of metal on the lines of the most modern electric signals used on standard railroads. It is 10½ inches high. Great detail is incorporated in the design as the illustration shows. The lantern case is easily removable so that the two interior lamps can be readily replaced. Green and red discs are permanently affixed in the openings so that our standard clear bulbs can be used for replacement. A metal ladder joins the upper and lower portions of the superstructure and faithfully carries out the true details of these signals. The mechanism is mounted on a solid piece of insulating material and is entirely concealed in the base of the signal. Posts for connecting to the track are plainly marked so that no difficulty is experienced in making the proper connections. A small fibre knob on the rear of the base is used for regulating the length of time the train stops at any given point. Necessary "Lockon" connections, wire and fibre insulating pins are furnished with each Automatic Train Control.

The Lionel Automatic Train Control can be used either on "O" Gauge or "Lionel Standard" track and will operate on dry or storage batteries, reduced direct, or reduced alternating current.

Lionel Automatic Train Control No. 078 for "O" Gauge Track—Complete with OTC "Lockon" contact and connecting wires. Attractively packed with directions for operating . . . . **Price $5.00**
Code Word "HEAVE"   Western Price $6.00

Lionel Automatic Train Control No. 78 for "Lionel Standard" Track—Complete with STC "Lockon" contact and connecting wires. Attractively packed with directions for operating . . . . **Price $5.00**
Code Word "WEAVE"   Western Price $6.00

Nos. 78, 078

Nos. 76 and 076 Block Signals

THIS new Lionel accessory will add life and realism to any train outfit. It consists of a steel standard (8¾ inches high) to which are attached two electric illuminated lanterns showing red and green signals.

When the train passes over the special sections of track supplied with the signal, the green lantern lights up, indicating "Track Clear", and after it leaves the first section of special track the red light shows, indicating "Stop" to the train following. This red light goes out as soon as the train leaves the second special section of track, the same as the block signals operating on real railroads.

In order to carry out true detail several of these block signals can be used at different points of the track formation.

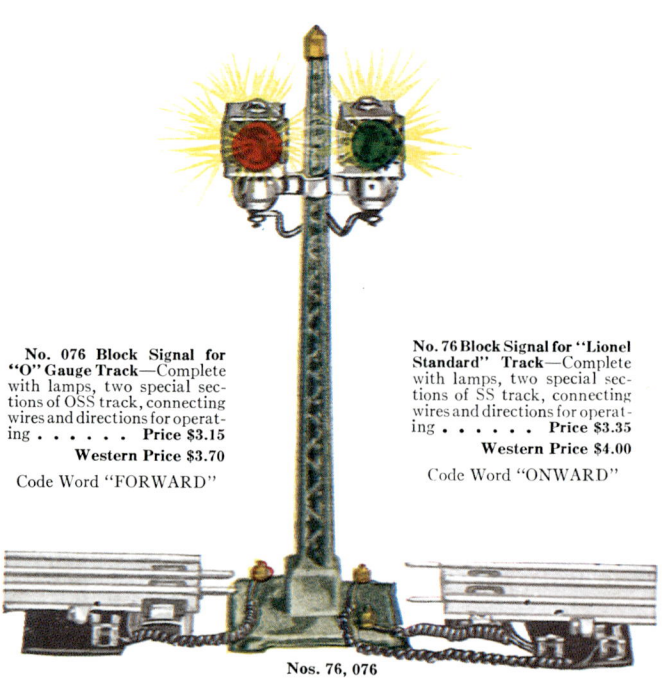

No. 076 Block Signal for "O" Gauge Track—Complete with lamps, two special sections of OSS track, connecting wires and directions for operating . . . . . . **Price $3.15**
Western Price $3.70
Code Word "FORWARD"

No. 76 Block Signal for "Lionel Standard" Track—Complete with lamps, two special sections of SS track, connecting wires and directions for operating . . . . . . **Price $3.35**
Western Price $4.00
Code Word "ONWARD"

Nos. 76, 076

The Only Miniature Railroad Accessories That Are Positively Automatic in Action

[38]

Lionel Accessories—Electrically Operated and Electrically Illuminated

NOS. 65 and 66 Semaphores—The base is made of heavy sheet steel. The post, semaphore arms and ladder are also constructed of steel. The colored discs which are securely fastened to the semaphore arms show "Danger," "Clear" or "Caution" signals. The electric lamps are enclosed in beautifully enameled steel lanterns, which are removable so that lamps can be easily renewed. A metal finger holds these lantern caps in place. The levers which operate the signal arms are fastened to the base and are connected to rods running up beneath the ladder. The wiring and insulation are inside the post and short circuits are impossible. The electric lamps shining through the colored discs present a wonderfully realistic effect.

Nos. 69 and 069 Warning Signals—A substantially constructed, fully nickeled bell is mounted on an ornamental post bearing a heavy brass warning sign. A specially constructed section of track is supplied to which the warning signal is connected, wires being also provided for the purpose. The electric bell rings as long as the locomotive and cars pass over the special section of track, and the bell automatically stops ringing when the train has passed. The signal post is made of steel and is fastened to a heavy steel base which has holes for fastening to floor or platform.

Nos. 77 and 077 Crossing Gates—These are exact reproductions of the real ones used at all grade crossings. They are of steel construction throughout, finished in handsome black enamel with nickeled top on the case that contains the mechanism. The special section of track provided with the crossing gates is connected with the track layout in the usual manner. While the train is on this section the gates close and they automatically open again as soon as the train has passed. These gates can be used singly or in pairs. The special track can be placed a few sections away from the gates so that they will operate some time before the train approaches. The raising and lowering of these gates in connection with the operation of the train produces an effect of great realism.

Special Track for Warning Signals, Crossing Gates and Block Signals

No. OSS Track—"O" Gauge, 10¼ inches long. Complete with OTC "Lockon" Contact and connecting wires.
Price per Section $ .40
Western Price $ .50
Code Word "RELAY"

No. SS Track—"Lionel Standard", 14 inches long. Complete with STC "Lockon" Contact and connecting wires.
Price per Section $ .60
Western Price $ .70
Code Word "BURT"

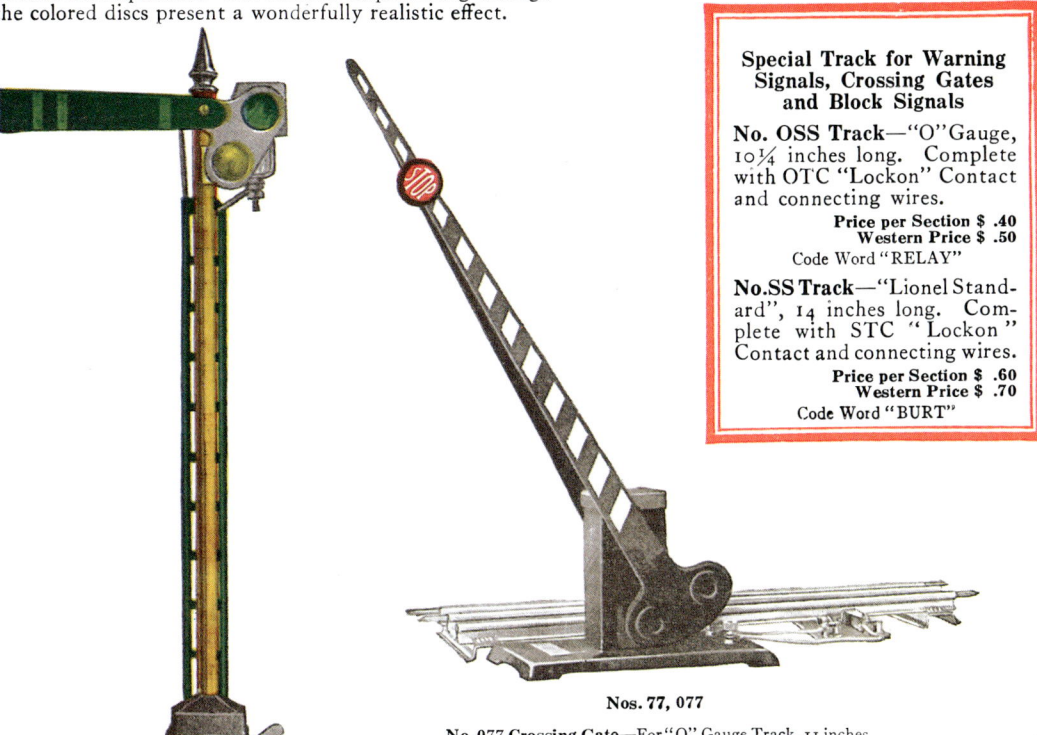

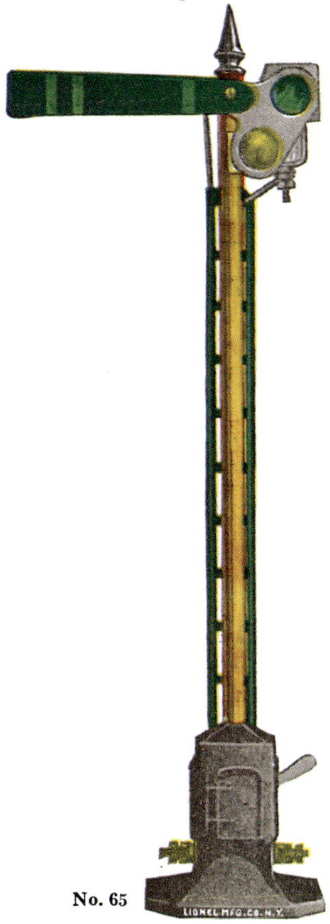

Nos. 77, 077

No. 077 Crossing Gate—For "O" Gauge Track, 11 inches long. Complete with one section of OSS track, OTC "Lockon" Contact, connecting wires and directions for operating.
Price $4.00
Western Price $4.80
Code Word "ADVANCE"

No. 77 Crossing Gate—For "Lionel Standard" Track, 11 inches long. Complete with one section of SS track, STC "Lockon" Contact, connecting wires and directions for operating.
Price $4.25
Western Price $5.00
Code Word "TARRY"

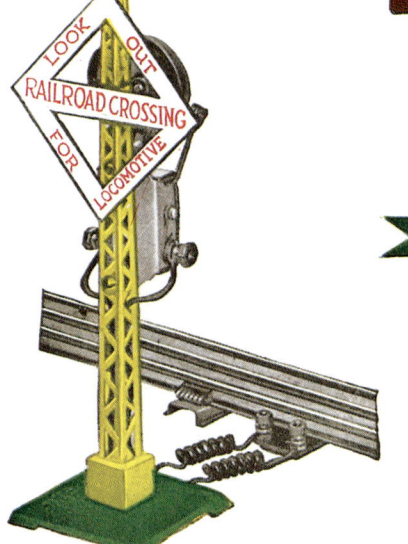

No. 69, 069

No. 069 Warning Signal—for "O" Gauge Track, 8¾ inches high. Complete with one section of OSS track, OTC "Lockon" Contact, connecting wires and directions for operating.
Price $3.15
Western Price $3.70
Code Word "RINGER"

No. 69 Warning Signal—For "Lionel Standard" Track, 8¾ inches high. Complete with one section of SS track, STC "Lockon" Contact, connecting wires and directions for operating.
Price $3.35
Western Price $4.00
Code Word "BEWARE"

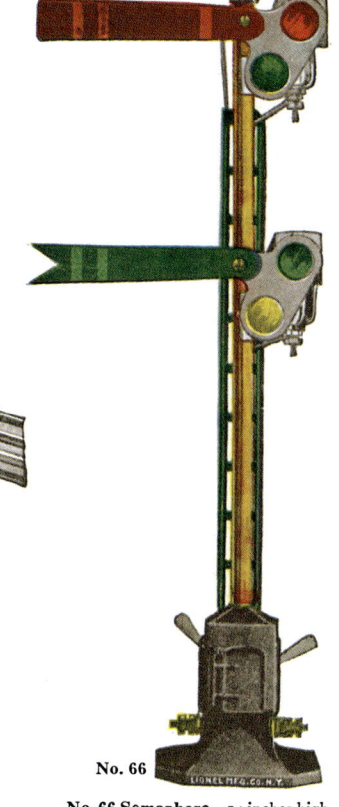

No. 65

No. 65 Semaphore—14 inches high. Has one signal arm. Complete with electric lamp.
Price $2.50
Western Price $3.00
Code Word "TOWER"

No. 66

No. 66 Semaphore—14 inches high. Has two signal arms. Complete with electric lamps.
Price $3.75
Western Price $4.50
Code Word "LEMPSTER"

A Completing Touch for Any Miniature Railroad—the Wonderful Lionel Accessories Shown Here

Lionel Accessories—Accessory Sets

LIONEL accessory sets are unquestionably the best constructed as well as the most popular on the market. This is not to be wondered at considering the fact that they are so durable and attractive in design. A miniature railroad layout is considerably enhanced by the addition of a set of telegraph posts placed at regular intervals around the track. Copper wire can be strung from the insulators, producing an effect of great realism.

If the semaphores, lamp post and warning signal which form No. 70 set are added to the train layout the finishing touches are provided. All Lionel accessories are constructed of steel throughout and are beautifully finished.

Outfit No. 70—Comprises two No. 62 Semaphores, one No. 59 Lamp Post, one No. 68 Warning Signal and two globes for the lamp post. Attractively packed.
Price $4.25
Code Word "HOBART"   Western Price $5.00

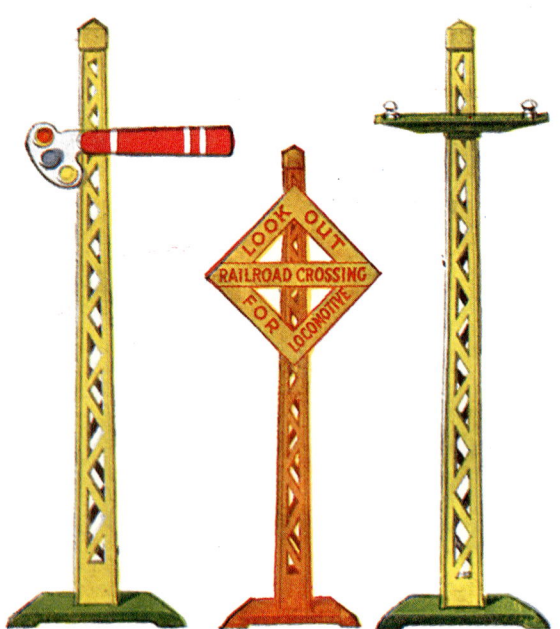

No. 62 Semaphore—The semaphore arm has three discs—red, green and yellow—and the arm is operated by a lever near the base. Steel construction throughout. Height 8¾ inches, base 2½ inches square.
Price $ .80
Western Price $1.00
Code Word "CAUTION"

No. 068 Warning Signal—A new accessory designed for use with "O" Guage Trains. Made of steel throughout and similar in construction to the other Warning Signals listed by us. Height 6¾ inches, base 2 inches square.
Price $ .50
Western Price $ .60
Code Word "LOOK"

No. 60 Telegraph Post—A companion to No 62 Semaphore and No. 68 Warning Signal. The arm is equipped with real glass insulators. Height 8¾ inches, base 2½ inches square.
Price $ .65
Western Price $ .80
Code Word "WIRE"

Outfit No. 71—Comprises six No. 60 Steel Telegraph Posts as described on this page. Packed in a very attractive box.
Price $3.75
Code Word "USEFUL"   Western Price $4.50

No. 68 Warning Signal—This conforms in size with No. 62 Semaphore and No. 60 Telegraph Post, and the construction and size are similar to No. 69 and No. 069 described on the opposite page. These should be placed at every railroad crossing.
Price $ .90
Western Price $1.10
Code Word "STOP"

No. 89 Flag Staff—This is substantially constructed of steel and is 14 inches high. The base is 2½ inches square. It is beautifully finished in white enamel and the spire is finished in a rich black. The silk flag supplied with it can be raised or lowered by means of a cord to which it is attached and which is fastened on a hook near the base.
Boys! Place it in front of station or in the centre of a grass plot that may be laid out in connection with a model village or railroad. Let it wave proudly.
Price $ .75
Western Price $ .90
Code Word "ARTHUR"

See How Faithfully Lionel Accessories Are Modeled from Real Railroad Equipment

"Lionel Standard" and "O" Gauge Track Formations

Reg. U. S. Pat. Office

HERE'S loads of fun for everybody—making various track figures with "Lionel Standard" or "O" gauge track. The very foundation of your railroad must be strong. Therefore, use Lionel Track.

Look at the number of figures you can construct—and hundreds more by using straight and curved sections, switches, crossings and bumpers.

Isn't it great to watch your train go over the crossing—then you turn the switch and send it over to the siding—back again at full speed down the straightaway.

Your train will always operate better if you make the curves large in diameter. Always break up the circles as much as possible by inserting straight sections.

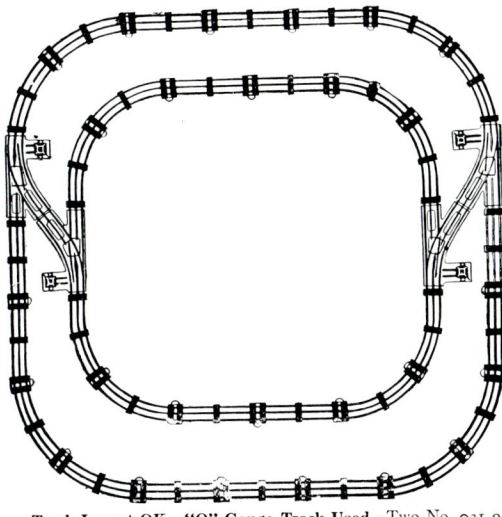

Track Layout OK—"O" Gauge Track Used—Two No. 021 or No. 022 Right Hand Switches, two No. 021 or No. 022 Left Hand Switches, sixteen sections OC curved track, fourteen sections OS straight track. Outside dimensions, 64 inches long and 64 inches wide.

Track Layout SK—"Lionel Standard" Track Used—Two No. 21 or No. 22 Right Hand Switches, two No. 21 or No. 22 Left Hand Switches, sixteen sections C curved track, fourteen sections S straight track. Outside dimensions, 85 inches long and 85 inches wide.

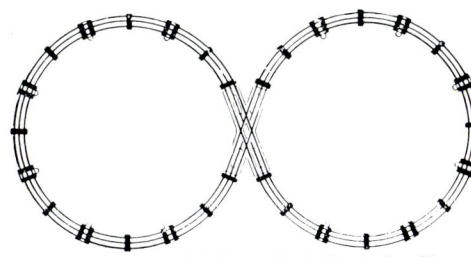

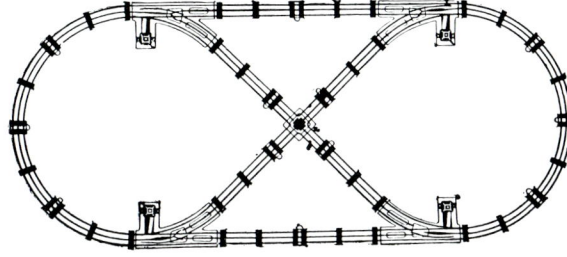

Track Layout OE—"O" Gauge Track Used—Two No. 021 or No. 022 Left Hand Switches, two No. 021 or No. 022 Right Hand Switches, one No. 020 Crossing, eight sections OC curved track, eight sections OS straight track. Outside dimensions, 72 inches long and 30 inches wide.

Track Layout SE—"Lionel Standard" Track Used—Two No. 21 or No. 22 Left Hand Switches, two No. 21 or No. 22 Right Hand Switches, one No. 20 Crossing, eight sections C curved track, eight sections S straight track. Outside dimensions, 100 inches long and 42 inches wide.

WHAT A THRILLING SIGHT IT IS TO SEE YOUR TRAIN GLIDING DOWN THE STRAIGHT STRETCH, OVER THE SWITCHES AND AROUND THE CURVES—IT'S GREAT FUN!

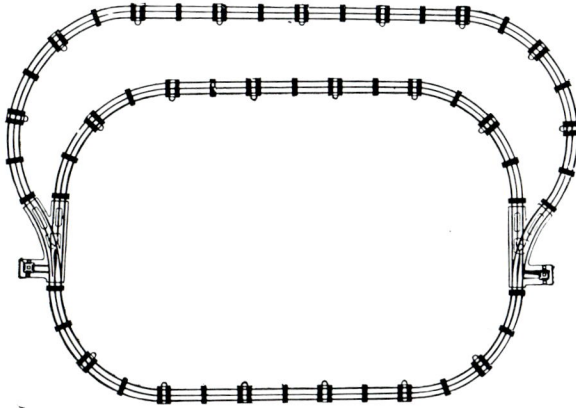

Track Layout OO—"O" Gauge Track Used—One No. 021 or No. 022 Right Hand Switch, one No. 021 or No. 022 Left Hand Switch, fourteen sections OC curved track, ten sections OS straight track. Outside dimensions, 75 inches long and 50 inches wide.

Track Layout SO—"Lionel Standard" Track Used—One No. 21 or No. 22 Right Hand Switch, one No. 21 or No. 22 Left Hand Switch, fourteen sections C curved track, ten sections S straight track. Outside dimensions, 100 inches long and 75 inches wide.

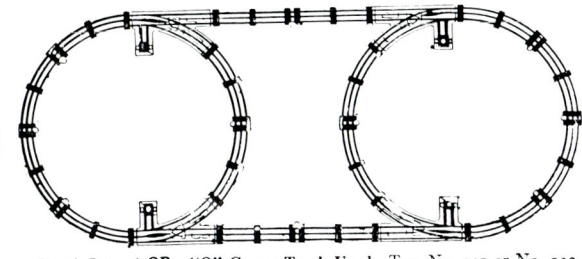

Track Layout OF—"O" Gauge Track Used—One No. 020X Crossing, fourteen sections OC curved track. Outside dimensions, 60 inches long and 30 inches wide.

Track Layout OJ—"O" Gauge Track Used—Two No. 021 or No. 022 Right Hand Switches, two No. 021 or No. 022 Left Hand Switches, one No. 020 Crossing, sixteen sections OC curved track, four sections OS straight track. Outside dimensions, 92 inches long and 30 inches wide.

Track Layout SJ—"Lionel Standard" Track Used—Two No. 21 or No. 22 Right Hand Switches, two No. 21 or No. 22 Left Hand Switches, one No. 20 Crossing, sixteen sections C curved track, four sections S straight track. Outside dimensions, 132 inches long and 42 inches wide.

Track Layout OB—"O" Gauge Track Used—Two No. 021 or No. 022 Left Hand Switches, two No. 021 or No. 022 Right Hand Switches, four sections OS straight track, twelve sections OC curved track. Outside dimensions, 72 inches long and 30 inches wide.

Track Layout SB—"Lionel Standard" Track Used—Two No. 21 or No. 22 Left Hand Switches, two No. 21 or No. 22 Right Hand Switches, four sections S straight track, twelve sections C curved track. Outside dimensions, 100 inches long and 42 inches wide.

See Pages 36 and 37 for Prices of Track and All Track Accessories

The New Lionel Scenic Railway—"O" Gauge

THE Lionel Scenic Railway Tables originated by this Corporation several years ago were the best of their kind ever devised. While they were primarily intended for display purposes, they were also in great demand by users of miniature electric railroads who desired complete scenic effects in addition to the train layout. However, price and the cost of shipping prevented their being purchased by all who desired them; therefore we present with great pleasure the new Lionel Scenic Railways—made in sections, that are light in weight, portable and at prices within the reach of all. As the specifications show, we do not charge for the scenic effects such as the base and wiring, mountains and sky background. All the rest of the equipment is listed at our regular catalog prices and these items are the only ones charged for.

No. 198 "O" Gauge Scenic Railway—Details of Construction

The platform or base is made of composition board in two sections, each mounted in a rigid wooden frame. The dimensions over all are 60 inches long and 42 inches deep. The top of the platform is beautifully decorated in colors representing grass plots, roads, etc. Indicating marks show the proper points at which the various accessories are to be placed. The platform is electrically wired so that the illuminated accessories and track can be connected in a few moments. Special large metal tunnels are supplied, realistically painted and embellished with miniature houses and trees as well as mountainous sections, flower beds and grass plots, all made of indestructible sheet steel. Many shrubs, bushes and miniature trees are also furnished, all of which greatly enhance the appearance and detail of these beautiful displays. Three large reproductions of mountains, beautifully decorated, each measuring 36 by 18 inches, form the background of the display and two additional large panels representing the skyline, measuring 72 by 28 inches, complete the scenic effect.

The entire display is very light in weight and can be easily moved from place to place. The background scenic effects are so placed that the display can either be condensed in size or extended to fit the space in which it is to be used.

SPECIFICATIONS OF SCENIC RAILWAY NO. 198 FOR "O" GAUGE TRACK

ACCESSORIES

1 No. 076 Block Signal	$3.15
1 No. 077 Crossing Gate	4.00
1 No. 069 Warning Signal	3.15
1 No. 56 Lamp Post	1.65
1 No. 58 Lamp Post	1.25
1 No. 89 Flag Staff	.75
1 No. 184 Bungalow	1.50
1 No. 191 Villa	3.35
1 No. 189 Villa	$2.95
1 No. 092 Signal Tower	2.10

ALL STEEL DISPLAY PIECES

1 No. 130 Tunnel	$15.00
1 No. 131 Corner Elevation	4.50
1 No. 132 Corner Grass Plot	2.50
2 No. 133 Heartshape Grass Plots, $1.50 each	3.00
1 No. 134 Oval Grass Plot	1.25

SCENIC EFFECTS SUPPLIED FREE

1 Compo board painted platform, completely wired.
3 Compo board mountains.
1 Compo board sky background.
3 No. 505 Trees.
2 No. 504 Bushes.

Price Complete, $50.00
Western Price $60.00

Code Word "BEAUTY"

Any Lionel "O" Gauge Train Outfit May Be Used With This Scenic Display

[42]

Reg. U. S. Pat. Office
The New Scenic Railway for "Lionel Standard" Track

No. 199 Scenic Railway—Details of Construction

ON account of its larger size we have been able to incorporate many more scenic details, and to supply a larger amount of accessories in this scenic railway for "Lionel Standard" Track. The general construction and appearance are similar to the "O" Gauge Scenic Railway described on the opposite page.

The platform of the "Lionel Standard" Scenic Railway is made in three sections and measures 90 inches long by 60 inches deep. The dimensions of the three mountains and the skyline background are the same as those supplied with "O" Gauge Scenic Railway No. 198.

By referring to the specifications it will be seen that in this case also the scenic effects are supplied free, the complete price taking in only the accessories supplied.

No amount of description can do adequate justice to the beauty of the new Lionel Scenic Displays. They are decorated in brilliant and harmonizing colors, while the art work is of the highest possible character.

IMPORTANT TO THE TRADE

DEALERS—no greater aid to increasing your toy sales has ever been offered. The flexibility of the new Lionel Scenic Railways makes them particularly adaptable to any size show window or store fixture, while their low price means but a small investment when compared with their sales promoting possibilities. The demand is already tremendous—place your order at once so that you will be sure to obtain them in ample time for holiday needs.

SPECIFICATIONS OF SCENIC RAILWAY NO. 199 FOR "LIONEL STANDARD" TRACK

ACCESSORIES

1 No. 124 Station	$9.00
1 No. 189 Villa	2.95
1 No. 191 Villa	3.35
3 No. 184 Bungalows, $1.50	4.50
1 No. 092 Signal Tower	2.10
5 No. 60 Telegraph Posts, $0.65	3.25
2 No. 61 Lamp Posts, $2.10	4.20
3 No. 58 Lamp Posts, $1.25	3.75
1 No. 57 Lamp Post	1.65
1 No. 89 Flag Staff	.75
1 No. 66 Semaphore	$3.75
1 No. 78 Automatic Control	5.00
1 No. 77 Crossing Gate	4.25
1 No. 69 Warning Signal	3.35
1 No. 120 Tunnel	5.85

ALL STEEL DISPLAY PIECES

1 No. 136 Elevation (large)	$10.00
1 No. 131 Corner Elevation	4.50
1 No. 132 Corner Grass Plot	2.50
2 No. 133 Heartshape Grass Plots, $1.50	3.00
2 No. 134 Oval Grass Plots, $1.25	$2.50
1 No. 135 Circular Grass Plot	1.00

SCENIC EFFECTS SUPPLIED FREE

1 Compo board sky background.
1 Compo board painted platform, completely wired.
3 Compo board mountains.
16 No. 505 Trees.
8 No. 504 Bushes.

Code Word "NATURE"

Price Complete $80.00
Western Price $100.00

Any "Lionel Standard" Train May Be Used With This Scenic Display

[43]

1924

THE LIONEL CORPORATION
Offices and Display Rooms
48-52 EAST TWENTY-FIRST STREET
NEW YORK, N. Y.

The Home of
LIONEL ELECTRIC TOY **TRAINS**
& Multivolt Transformers

THE LIONEL CORPORATION
Factories and Service Departments
SOUTH TWENTY-FIRST STREET
IRVINGTON, N. J.

House of Heeg is not affiliated in any way with the Lionel Toy Corp., or the Lionel Fundimensions Division of General Mills Fun Group, Inc.

1924 Lionel Catalog
Reproduction
House of Heeg 1975

THE FACTORIES THAT BRING JOY TO MILLIONS OF BOYS

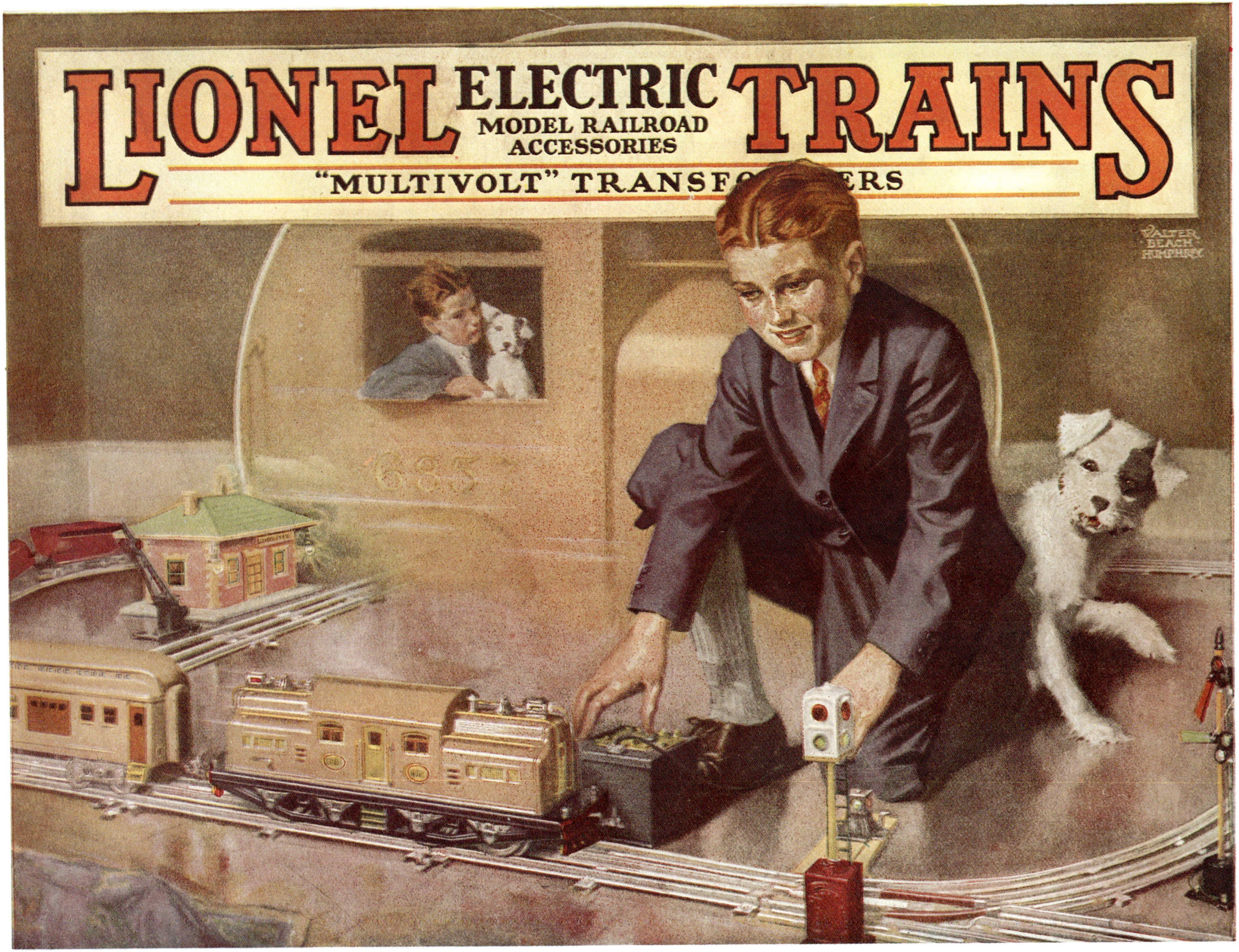
LIONEL ELECTRIC TRAINS
MODEL RAILROAD ACCESSORIES
"MULTIVOLT" TRANSFO ERS
WALTER BEACH HUMPHREY
685

LIONEL ELECTRIC TRAINS
MODEL RAILROAD ACCESSORIES
"MULTIVOLT" TRANSFORMERS

The Fascination of Lionel Railroading

BRINGING joy to the youth of America has been the good fortune of Lionel for twenty-five years. Our products have helped them to keep pace with the development of electric traction while providing healthful fun and education.

The day of "toy" trains is past—Lionel Model Electric Trains, faithful reproductions of the massive locomotives and cars used on America's great electrified systems, have replaced them.

Every automatic device known to modern electric railroading—all triumphs of engineering skill, all perfect in construction, built to last and with a view to providing unlimited joy to the user for many years, have also been perfected by Lionel.

Boys—a Lionel Model Train and Miniature Railroad Equipment will aid you to obtain a valuable technical knowledge of electricity and its relation to the principles of modern railroading. Who knows but what it may be your destiny to go into fields as yet untouched and pioneer big engineering projects, like Hill, Harriman and others whose names will always be identified with the railroad history and development of our great land.

A prominent railroad president in a recent letter received by us wrote, "The boy who owns a Lionel must get all the thrill of operating a real railroad."

Boys, you will get a real thrill when you see your Lionel laid out before you complete in every detail—and you play the part of railroad director.

All aboard! You switch on the current from your "Multivolt" Transformer—the Lionel Limited, with its powerful headlights shining and cars brilliantly illuminated, gracefully glides away—smooth and silent, just like a big all-steel pullman train. You advance the transformer switch and immediately the massive motor increases speed, hauling the big train with perfect ease—past the steel telegraph posts, semaphores and over the famous Lionel bridge.

As you approach the illuminated village built with Lionel Villas and Bungalows the bell on the warning signal rings out at the grade crossing. The automatic gates go down—your train speeds by and up go the gates again.

Now your Lionel speeds down the straightaway stretch. The green semaphore lights show "Line Clear"—now comes the curve and you reduce speed; into the approaching tunnel goes the express.

Your block signals all along the line show green lights as the train approaches— as soon as it leaves the block section the lights change to red, to prevent rear end collisions.

The brilliantly illuminated station at "Lionel City" is seen in the distance—a touch of the transformer lever and your Lionel reduces speed and then majestically stops—the body of the engine quivering like a living thing as though satisfied with a glorious run. Passengers rush aboard—a signal from the conductor—we are on our way again.

Steady there! A red light shows ahead!! It is the signal on the Automatic Train Control. We haven't time to reduce speed from the transformer, but just the same our train comes to a dead stop!!! Why? The Automatic Control stops it alone. Soon the track ahead is clear, the red light changes to green and away we dart once more. Boys, do you know that the Lionel Train Control is the only perfected device that automatically starts and stops the train and changes the color of the controlling lights?

Can you think of anything that will hold your interest as intensely as a Lionel Model Railroad? You cannot find anything more real.

Refuse to purchase a cheap "toy" train. Ask your dealer to show you "Lionel" —examine the locomotive, the motor, cars and track—look at the design, construction and finish—see the infinite detail that makes the equipment massive, durable and as real as actual big trains.

If your dealer cannot supply you, please write to us and we will see that you get what you want right from our big factories. Always remember that Lionel prices are lowest consistent with quality— Lionel always originates, never imitates — Lionel has never marketed a mechanical failure.

THE LIONEL CORPORATION

48-52 EAST TWENTY-FIRST STREET
NEW YORK, N.Y.

LOOK FOR THIS PACKAGE ~ IT IS YOUR GUARANTEE OF QUALITY

LIONEL ALWAYS LEADS

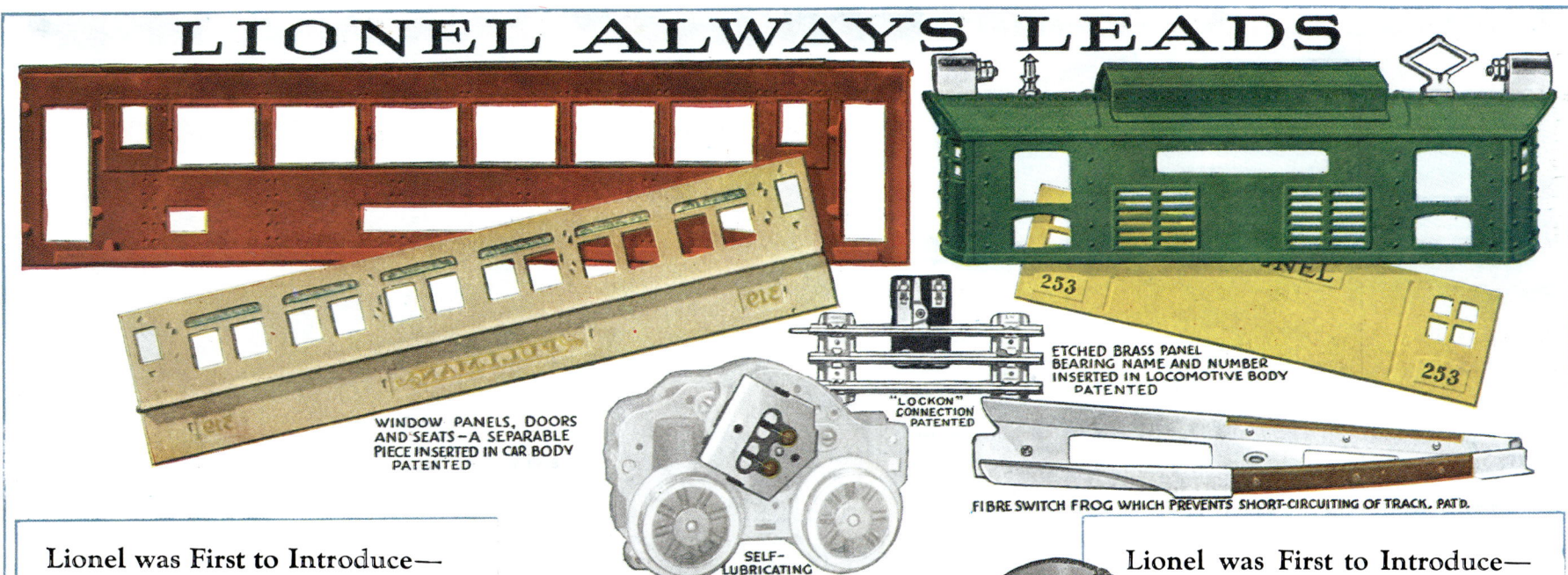

Labels on illustrations:
- WINDOW PANELS, DOORS AND SEATS—A SEPARABLE PIECE INSERTED IN CAR BODY. PATENTED
- ETCHED BRASS PANEL BEARING NAME AND NUMBER INSERTED IN LOCOMOTIVE BODY. PATENTED
- "LOCKON" CONNECTION PATENTED
- FIBRE SWITCH FROG WHICH PREVENTS SHORT-CIRCUITING OF TRACK. PAT'D.
- SELF-LUBRICATING AUTOMATIC-FEEDING BRUSHES IN "O" GAUGE MOTOR. PAT'D.
- DIE-CAST WHEEL WITH NICKEL POLISHED STEEL RIM. PATENTED
- MACHINE-CUT, HEAVY STEEL GEARS—NOT PUNCHED
- REMOVABLE BRUSH-HOLDER CONTAINING SELF-LUBRICATING AUTOMATIC-FEEDING BRUSHES. PAT'D.
- LOCOMOTIVE HEADLIGHT WITH RED AND GREEN LIGHTS IN SIDES. PATENTED
- REAR VIEW OF HEADLIGHT, SHOWING SWITCH. PATENTED
- SIX WHEEL TRUCK WITH NICKELED JOURNALS

Lionel was First to Introduce—

Inserted panels in doors and windows of cars and locomotive bodies, which give great strength and add real detail to construction. Far superior to representing these details by lithographed process on tin. Patented July 16, 1918.

Inserted etched brass plates in locomotive bodies. Patented July 16, 1918.

A perfect die-cast wheel with nickeled steel rim over the tread—insuring accuracy and long use. Pat'd May 17, 1925.

Removable motor brush holder. Patented May 5, 1925.

Self-feeding brushes. Pat'd Feb. 7, 1922.

Insulated fibre frogs on switches. Patented April 21, 1925.

"Lockon" Track Connections. Patented June 16, 1925.

Headlights with individual switches and green and red transparent side panels. Patented June 2, 1925.

Automatic Train Control—the only device that automatically controls the operation of the train. Pat'd August 21, 1917.

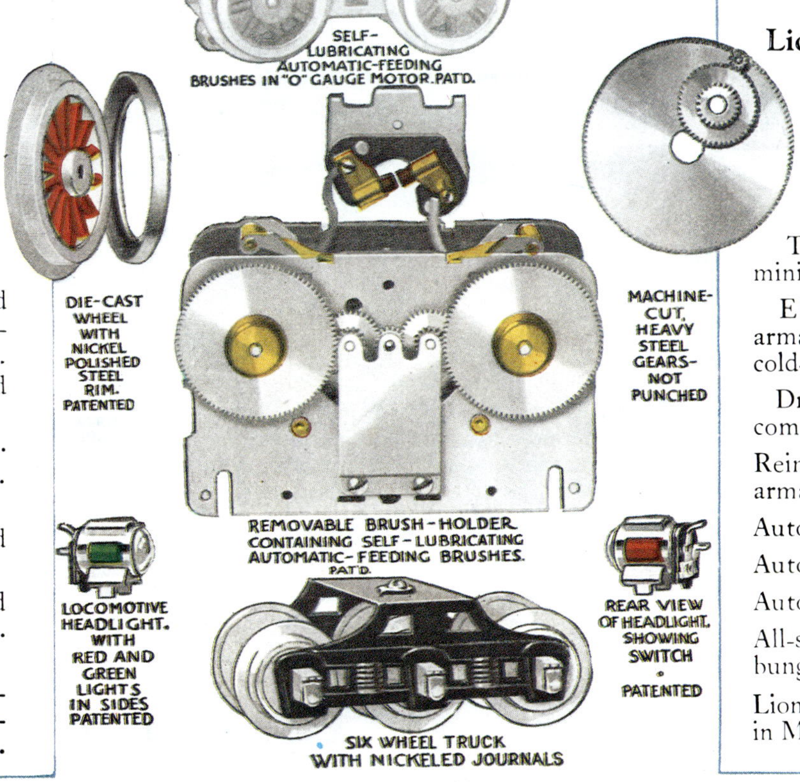

Lionel was First to Introduce—

All-steel car and locomotive bodies, hand enameled and rigidly assembled, instead of flimsy lithographed tin.

Trucks with nickeled journals.

Roller contact shoes on locomotives.

Three-bearing armature shafts on miniature motors.

Electrical sheets for motor and armature construction instead of cheap cold-rolled steel.

Drill rod shaft for armature, instead of commercial iron wire.

Reinforced phosphor-bronze bearings for armature shaft and wheel axles.

Automatic Crossing Gates.

Automatic Warning Signals.

Automatic Block Signals.

All-steel electric lighted miniature bungalows and villas.

Lionel originated every desirable detail in Model Electric Trains and Accessories.

Why Lionel Leads

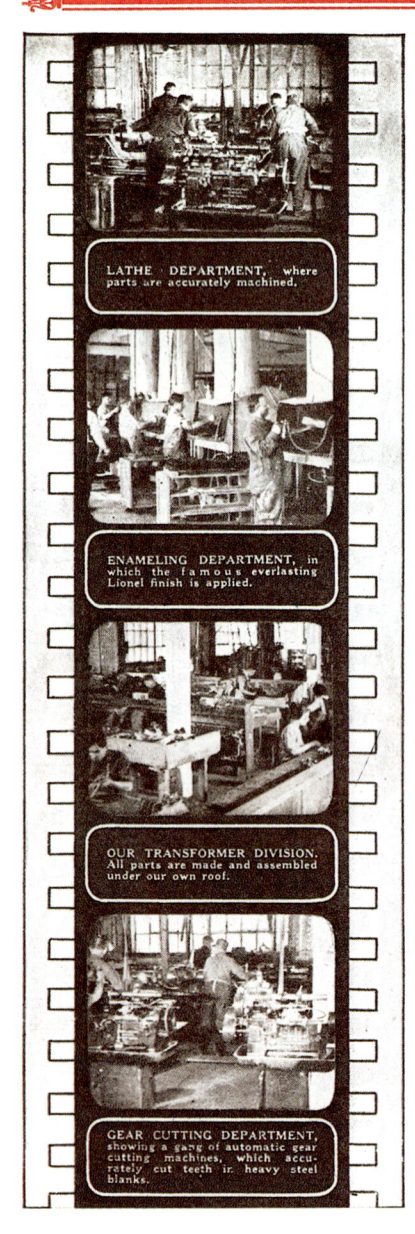

LIONEL leadership has been attained by specialization in the manufacture of one product for 25 years. Our entire resources and unsurpassed manufacturing facilities are exclusively devoted to the production of Model Electric Trains, Railroad Accessories and "Multivolt" Transformers.

Millions of Lionel Outfits are in use, many of them for a decade or more. Reference to the descriptive matter and illustrations on the following pages will show why the Lionel Line is of such supremely high quality. Not only are the raw materials used the best obtainable, but all Locomotives, Pullman and Freight Cars, as well as Railroad Accessories, are actually built to scale. Every detail found in real railroad equipment is faithfully reproduced in our models. Space does not permit us to dwell at length on the many improvements incorporated in our goods, but on page 3 we take great pleasure in mentioning only a few of the improvements introduced and patented by us.

Enamel Finish—All Lionel Cars and Locomotive Bodies are enameled and baked at high temperature, which insures a permanent lasting finish that can always be kept bright by any ordinary cleaning process. Special attention is directed to the fact that our products are not made of flimsy lithographed tin.

Lionel Track (both "O" Gauge and "Lionel Standard") is made of heavier metal than that used by any other manufacturer. Great attention is given to the insulation of the third rail, which absolutely eliminates short circuits. The illustration on this page shows one of the reasons for the rigidity and strength of Lionel rails. It will be readily noted that the base of the rails is formed outward instead of being turned in, as is the case with ordinary track. This outward flange increases the strength of the track more than 300%, and is only made possible by our process (patented October, 1909). Lionel Track, without bending, will support the weight of a full-grown person.

Note that the base of Lionel Track is bent outward, making it rigid and strong. Pat., Oct., 1909

In every part of this catalogue we show the quality and perfection of every piece that forms part of Lionel Outfits, but it is impossible to convey to the mind of the reader, through this medium, the high quality of our goods. They must be seen to be appreciated. Insist that your dealer demonstrates them for you. You will then realize that Lionel is the lowest priced line obtainable, consistent with quality.

Hundreds of skilled operatives employed in our factories, shown on the back cover of this book, contribute to the perfection of Lionel Model Electric Trains, Accessories and "Multivolt" Transformers.

We are proud of our achievement in developing and perfecting the line which is recognized as

"STANDARD OF THE WORLD"

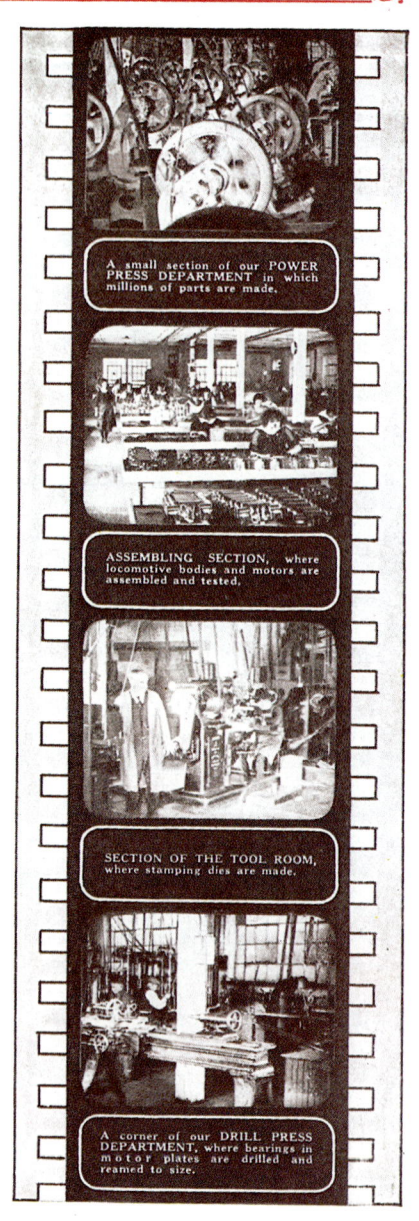

LATHE DEPARTMENT, where parts are accurately machined.

ENAMELING DEPARTMENT, in which the famous everlasting Lionel finish is applied.

OUR TRANSFORMER DIVISION. All parts are made and assembled under our own roof.

GEAR CUTTING DEPARTMENT, showing a gang of automatic gear cutting machines, which accurately cut teeth in heavy steel blanks.

A small section of our POWER PRESS DEPARTMENT in which millions of parts are made.

ASSEMBLING SECTION, where locomotive bodies and motors are assembled and tested.

SECTION OF THE TOOL ROOM, where stamping dies are made.

A corner of our DRILL PRESS DEPARTMENT, where bearings in motor plates are drilled and reamed to size.

The Above "Stills" Are Part of the 5,000 Foot Lionel Industrial Film

"O" Gauge Single and Twin-Motor Specifications

DRIVING Gears ("A")—They are made of heavy steel blanks, machine cut. They mesh without friction, and are radically different from gears with punched teeth generally used on "toy" trains.

Field ("B")—The field is made of a number of specially prepared transformer steel laminations. This construction represents a much stronger field than if a single piece of steel were used.

Third Rail Shoe Support ("C")—This part is made of heavy fibre to which the third rail contact rollers are attached. The peculiar construction of this device protects rollers from injury, for the brackets can be bent against the fibre without disturbing the arc of the spring that gives them the correct tension against the third rail.

Wheels ("D")—Lionel was first to introduce die-cast wheels. They are absolutely balanced and run true on the axle. A nickel-plated steel rim is forced over the wearing surface of the wheel to insure long wear.

Collecting Shoes ("E")—These revolving shoes collect current from the third rail. They are made of solid brass turnings and revolve on steel shafts which pass through phosphor bronze supports. They insure perfect contact with the third rail at all times so that locomotives will run at uniform speed and not operate in a jerky manner.

Frame ("F")—The frames are made of very heavy steel punchings, not cast iron. They embody great detail and will withstand more than the ordinary amount of wear and tear.

Journals ("G")—These journals are made of heavy brass, nickel-plated, and are attached to the frames by mechanical means. They add greatly to the appearance of the structure.

Cowcatchers ("H")—The construction of the cowcatchers varies with the type of locomotive on which they are used. Many of them are part of the steel frame which is made in one piece, and others are heavy castings rigidly attached to the frame.

Flag Posts ("J")—All our locomotives, except Nos. 150, 152 and 153, are equipped with four flag posts, two at each end of the frame; a very realistic detail.

Tanks ("K")—These tanks are made of brass, nickel-plated, and are separable pieces attached to the frame, which further accentuates the great detail incorporated in the locomotives.

Lionel Automatic Couplers ("L")—Lionel Couplers are made of heavy steel, nickel-plated and polished. They are scientifically constructed so that cars cannot become detached when in motion, but are easily taken apart when desired. The new improved Lionel Coupler with invisible spring arrangement is a great improvement over our original model, and is a great advance over any similar device ever made.

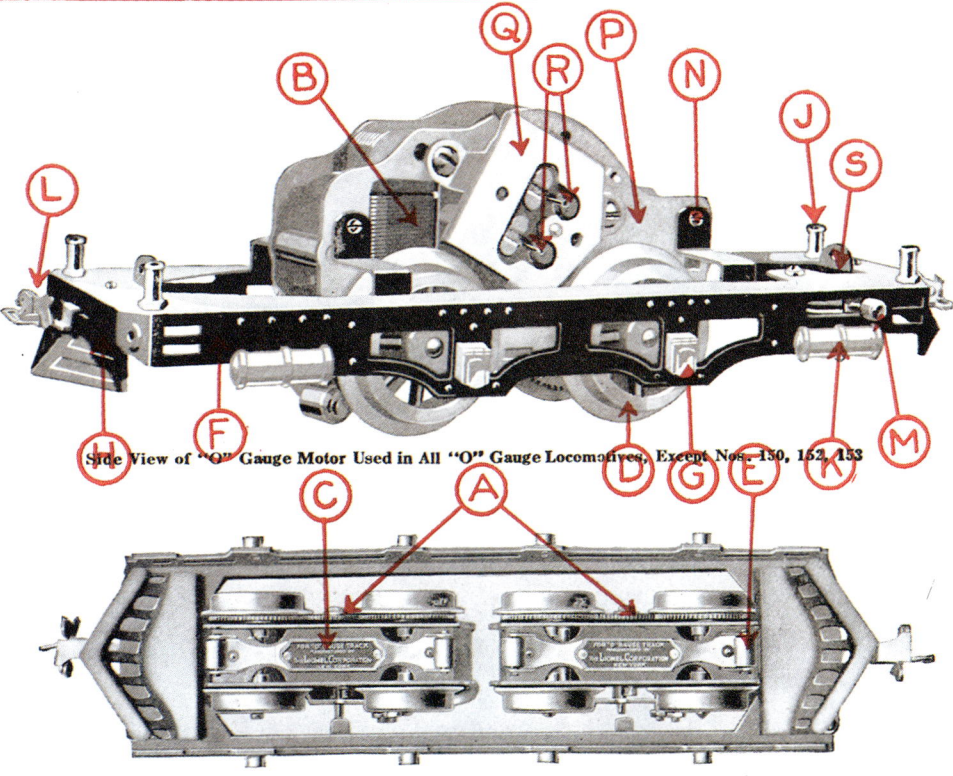

Side View of "O" Gauge Motor Used in All "O" Gauge Locomotives, Except Nos. 150, 152, 153

Bottom View of "O" Gauge Twin-Motor Used in Locomotive No. 256

Side View of "O" Gauge Motor Used in Locomotives Nos. 150, 152 and 153

Reversing Controllers ("M")—Lionel Reversing Controllers have been in use for many years during which time they have given thorough satisfaction. They are the only controllers in use on model trains that cannot get out of order. They operate very easily and due to the brass cups and spring tension, the electrical contact is always permanent.

Frame Support ("N")—The frame is supported to the motor with only four screws. This simple method of construction was originally introduced by us in 1913. It is typical of Lionel construction. All parts of Lionel Locomotives can be easily reached for cleaning or replacement.

Side Plates ("P")—Lionel Motor Side Plates are made of heavy gauge steel and support all working parts. All bearing holes are reinforced with phosphor bronze bushings. The alignment of these holes is absolutely perfect so that gears work with a minimum amount of friction. All holes are drilled and reamed to proper diameter. The accuracy of these plates compares with the frame work of a very fine clock.

Brush Plate ("Q")—The unique construction of this brush plate permits rapid change of brushes after motor has been in use for a considerable period. The brushes fit in brass cups and two properly tempered steel springs give the correct pressure of the brush on the commutator until brushes are worn down to the end. Brushes are replaced by simply raising the springs, lifting up worn out brushes and dropping new ones in their place.

Brushes ("R")—We were the first manufacturers of model trains to equip our motors with combination gauze and graphite brushes that wear long and are self-lubricating.

Removable Locomotive Body ("S")—The bodies of all Lionel Locomotives are held in place on the frame with only two screws, one at each end of the locomotive. Supporting members are placed at several points of the frame that rigidly hold the body in place.

Commutator—The commutator is made of bronze. It is perfectly turned when connected to the armature so that it is absolutely parallel with the brushes. The commutator surface is polished so as to reduce all friction when in contact with the brushes.

Armature—The armature is made of specially prepared electrical sheets mounted on a drill rod shaft. It is perfectly insulated and wound with the correct amount of triple insulated wire.

"O" Gauge Twin-Motor—The chassis illustrated contains two "O" Gauge Motors which give great hauling power to Locomotive No. 256 described on Page 11. Both motors reverse simultaneously from one controller. Despite the great hauling power of this locomotive, it consumes a minimum amount of current.

An Electric Train Is Only as Good as Its Motor—All Lionel Motors Are Electrically and Mechanically Perfect

Reg. U. S. Pat. Office

Specifications of "Lionel Standard" Three-Point-Bearing Super-Motor

THE New Lionel "Super-Motor" is so vastly superior in efficiency and design to any motor ever before offered to the public that notwithstanding our enviable reputation as leaders in miniature motor construction, the new and improved Super-Motor is supremely the finest piece of electrical mechanism our factories have ever produced. It is quite fitting that we, as pioneer builders of model locomotives to operate on "Lionel Standard" Track, should retain our leadership with the new Super-Motor which is the acme of perfection.

The Super-Motor shown here is made expressly for No. 8 locomotive which is our smallest model for "Lionel Standard" Track. The wheel base of the motor is a trifle shorter, which necessitates different speed reduction gearing. In every other detail it is absolutely similar to super-motor described below.

Removable Brush Holder (1)—This is one of the most unique features of the Lionel "Super-Motor." By simply unscrewing one screw the entire brush holder can be removed from the motor. Change of brushes requires but an instant and the assembled part is replaced without the use of any tools.

Brushes (2)—The brushes are made of bronze and graphite which are self-lubricating. They insure long life to the commutator. They are contained in brass tubes and held in place by a simple spring arrangement which feeds brushes to commutator at the same pressure until the brush is entirely used up. Replacement of brushes is a very simple operation.

Field—Made of the highest grade electrical steel correctly wound and scientifically designed.

Commutator—Made of heavy copper. The segments are perfectly insulated, making short-circuits impossible.

Revolving Double Contact Shoes (3)—This method of collecting current from the third rail, so successfully used for many years past on our "O" Gauge Locomotives, has been applied with equal success to the new Super-Motors. The shoes are heavy bronze rollers, securely affixed to the flexible phosphor bronze plate, which insures the proper tension on the third rail and gives a steady flow of current to the motors. This complete shoe assembly is mounted on a heavy fibre plate and is rigidly attached to the motor frame.

New Gear Arrangement (4)—This new method of gearing is embodied only in Lionel Super-Motors. The seven gears in this new layout give the motor greater tractive power, and are almost frictionless. The gears are made of very heavy steel and teeth are machine cut, not stamped. Special attention is directed to the plate supporting the gear studs, which also acts as an additional bearing for the armature shaft, as described in the following paragraph.

Three-Point-Bearing Armature Shaft (5)—For the first time in the development of miniature motors it has been possible to perfect an arrangement whereby the armature shaft revolves in three bearings—two of them are contained in the side plates of the motor and the third one in the plate that holds the gearing studs.

This three-point-bearing eliminates all vibration of the armature shaft, with the result that the commutator and brushes wear long and evenly. Considering the fact that the commutator and brushes are the life of the motor, this improvement is of great importance.

Driving Wheels (6)—Particular attention is directed to the driving wheels, which are massive in construction and are accurately die-cast. Their weight adds great tractive power to the motors. All driving wheels are directly geared to the motor, eliminating the use of connecting rods between the wheels, which insures better alignment with less friction.

Steel Tread on Wheels (7)—A steel tread beautifully nickel plated and polished is forced over the rim, insuring longer wear and a smooth, even riding surface. Lionel originated this method of wheel construction. See illustration on Page 3.

Reinforced Bearings (8)—Six phosphor bronze bearings are contained in the side plates of the motor. They add to the life of the motor and insure accurate alignment of the armature shaft and axles.

Armature—The armature is made of laminated electrical steel punchings. It is automatically drum wound with triple-covered magnet wire, dipped in shellac and baked. The armature shaft (9) is made of the best quality drill rod.

Side Plates (10)—Made of heavy steel, with bronze bushings inserted for shaft and axles.

Tractive Power—The tractive power of these motors is remarkable. They will haul from 12 to 20 of our largest size freight or pullman cars with the greatest ease. The weight of the wheels and motor is close to the track, insuring low center of gravity, with the result that the locomotive is not top-heavy and slippage of the wheels is therefore unknown. This construction is infinitely superior to the method of loading down the superstructure with useless weight so as to obtain tractive power. This unnecessary weight rapidly wears down all working parts and causes the locomotive to jump the track.

Minimum Current Consumption—The new Lionel "Super-Motor" is not only more powerful than any motor of its size, but it consumes less than half the current of any motor developing the same power.

Side View of Super-Motor Showing Removable Brush Plate and Extra Armature Shaft Bearing

Lionel Super-Motors Combine the Greatest Hauling Power with Minimum Current Consumption

Reg. U. S. Pat. Office
Specifications of "Lionel Standard" Twin-Super-Motors

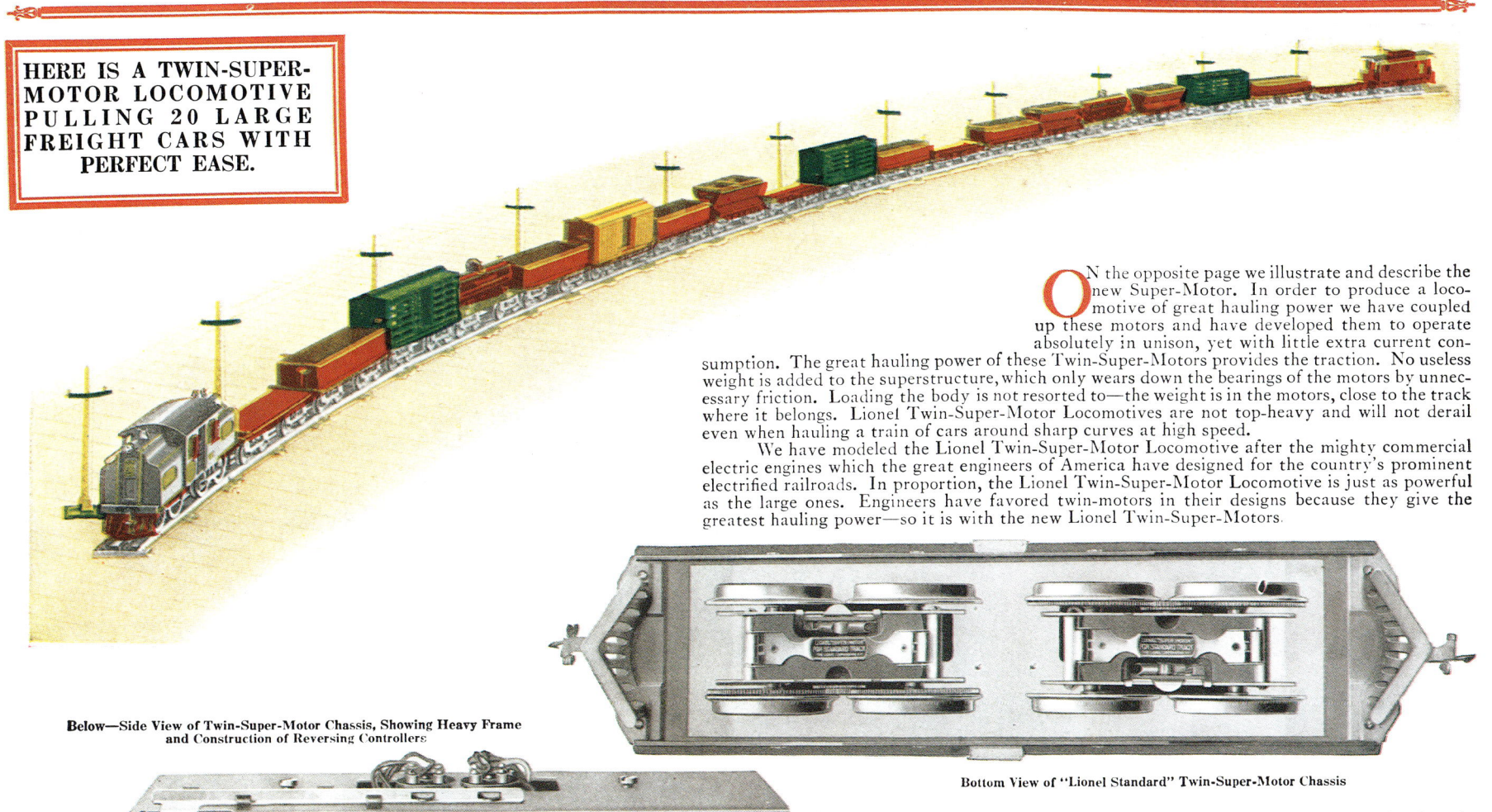

HERE IS A TWIN-SUPER-MOTOR LOCOMOTIVE PULLING 20 LARGE FREIGHT CARS WITH PERFECT EASE.

ON the opposite page we illustrate and describe the new Super-Motor. In order to produce a locomotive of great hauling power we have coupled up these motors and have developed them to operate absolutely in unison, yet with little extra current consumption. The great hauling power of these Twin-Super-Motors provides the traction. No useless weight is added to the superstructure, which only wears down the bearings of the motors by unnecessary friction. Loading the body is not resorted to—the weight is in the motors, close to the track where it belongs. Lionel Twin-Super-Motor Locomotives are not top-heavy and will not derail even when hauling a train of cars around sharp curves at high speed.

We have modeled the Lionel Twin-Super-Motor Locomotive after the mighty commercial electric engines which the great engineers of America have designed for the country's prominent electrified railroads. In proportion, the Lionel Twin-Super-Motor Locomotive is just as powerful as the large ones. Engineers have favored twin-motors in their designs because they give the greatest hauling power—so it is with the new Lionel Twin-Super-Motors.

Below—Side View of Twin-Super-Motor Chassis, Showing Heavy Frame and Construction of Reversing Controllers

Bottom View of "Lionel Standard" Twin-Super-Motor Chassis

Reversing Controllers and Motor Frame—The illustration to the left shows the unique construction of the reversing controllers which operate the twin-super-motors. Both controllers function simultaneously by means of a lever conveniently placed on the side of the locomotive body. The slightest touch of the finger sends the locomotive forward or backward or causes it to stop when the lever is placed at "OFF". Accuracy of construction insures positive action of the reversing controller at all times. Our reversing controllers are absolutely dependable—they are free from complicated mechanism.

Attention is directed to the heavy steel one-piece frame to which the motors are attached. Great detail is embodied in this frame. The springs and journals are separate brass pieces, heavily nickeled, and are securely fastened to it. Brass steps and flag supports are also attached, while the heavy steel cow-catchers are riveted to both ends, from which protrude the patented Lionel Automatic Couplers. The whole chassis represents a power unit that will give years of service.

Accuracy of Design, Sturdy Construction and Beautiful Finish Are Leading Characteristics of All Lionel Motors

Specifications of Lionel Locomotive Bodies

THE details of the construction of Lionel Locomotive Bodies given below are typical of Lionel supreme quality throughout the entire line. Even the lowest priced Lionel Locomotives incorporate many of these features.

Of utmost importance is the fact that cast iron does not enter into the manufacture of any of these bodies—heavy sheet steel is used for every model; therefore Lionel Locomotives are practically indestructible. All parts of the bodies are re-enforced and are firmly soldered. They are not held together only by slots and fingers.

Lionel Locomotive Bodies are enameled, not lithographed—a beautiful and lasting lustre is obtained by finishing all Lionel Locomotive Bodies in rich enamel, baked on at high temperature as described in the introduction to this book.

Brass and nickeled fittings add further charm to the general appearance of Lionel Locomotives. These fittings are secured to the bodies by a process employed exclusively by us.

In all ways Lionel Locomotive Bodies combine sturdy construction, wonderful design and graceful appearance, as the indications below clearly show.

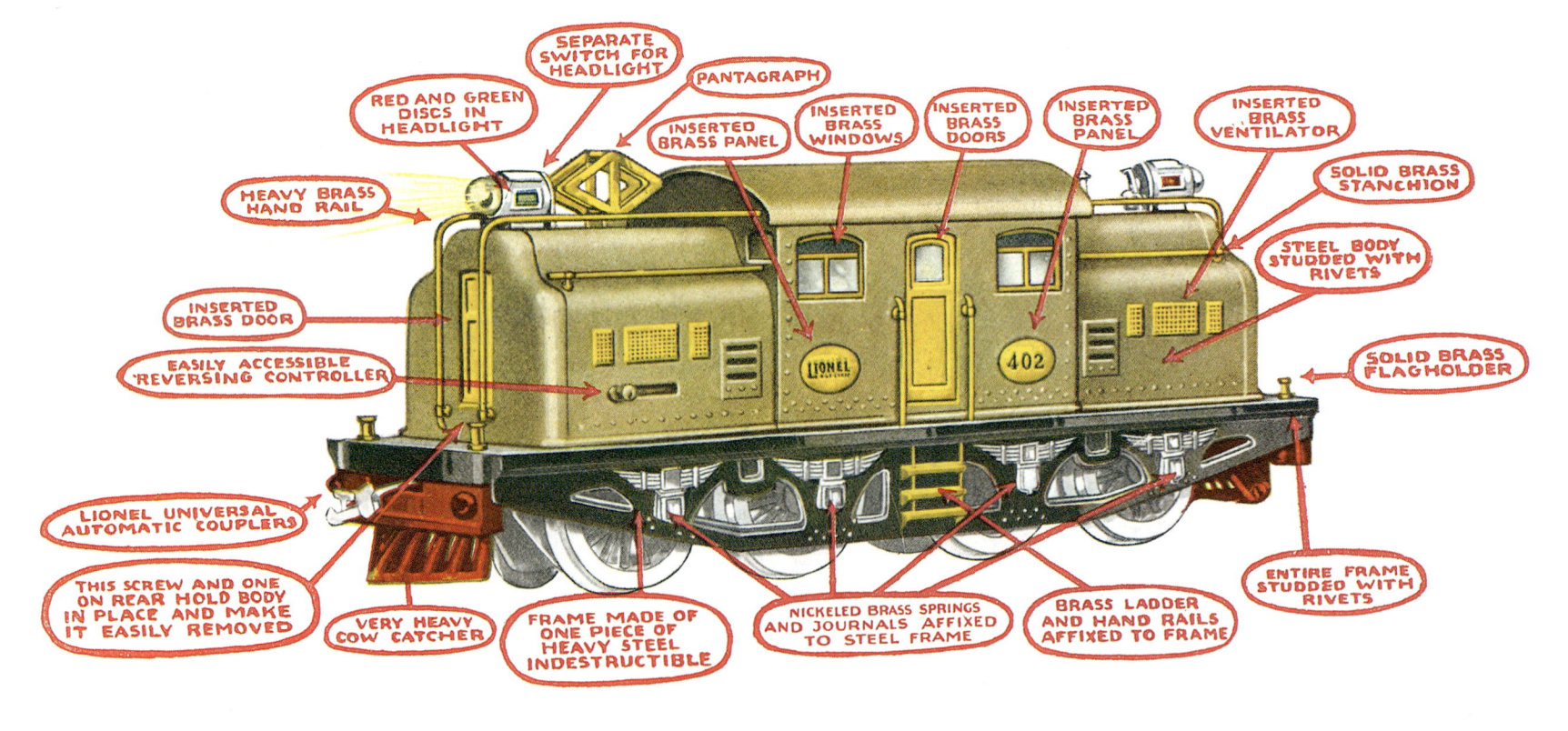

The High-Grade Construction of Lionel Locomotive Bodies Is in Keeping with the Excellence of Lionel Motors

Specifications of Lionel Passenger Coaches

ALL Lionel Passenger Coaches, irrespective of price, are made entirely of sheet steel. Not only are the cars modeled after the new style coaches used on the principal railroads of the country, but they are built to scale. An enormous amount of detail is incorporated in them such as hinged doors, inserted window frames and seats. Transparencies are placed in the windows and transoms of almost every car. The roofs are easily removable so that the interior electric lamp can be reached. Every car is finished with lasting, glossy enamel baked on at high temperature, insuring a permanent lustre. A revolving shoe, affixed to one of the trucks, collects current for the interior illumination of the car. Many of the trucks are fitted with nickeled journals. The heavy steel axles and wheels are nickeled and polished and are so perfectly made that they operate with a minimum amount of friction. We are proud to draw attention to the many desirable features contained in these coaches as indicated below.

Window frames and seats made of one piece of heavy metal securely fastened inside the car body.

Rear view of car, showing interior light and construction of the observation platform, made of sheet brass.

The patented revolving shoe which collects current from the third rail. It is built into the car truck.

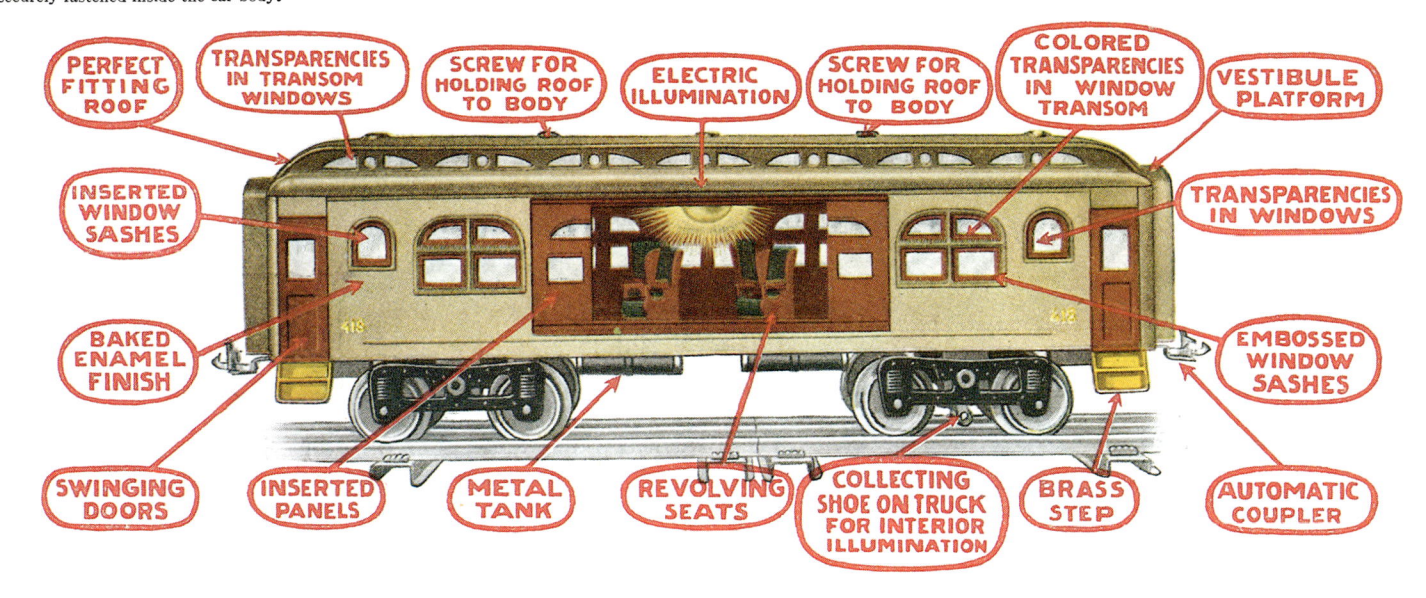

The Most Modern Types of "All-Steel" Passenger Coaches Are Faithfully Reproduced by Lionel

Locomotives for Lionel "O" Gauge Track—1⅜ Inches Wide

WE show on this page three types of locomotives in the Lionel "O" Gauge Line. They are reproductions of the powerful electric engines which haul the big express trains into the great railroad terminals.

The motors are fully described on page 5. They are powerful enough to haul four or more "O" Gauge Passenger or Freight Cars, according to their size. The bodies incorporate many of the structural details shown on page 8.

Locomotive No. 152—With electric headlight. This locomotive is 7 inches long and stands 3½ inches above the rails. Sturdily built and of proven strength. Price, complete with electric lamp for headlight and directions for operating **$5.75**
Western Price $6.75
Code Word "GRAMERCY"

THESE LOCOMOTIVES WILL ENABLE YOU TO BUILD UP A COMPLETE LIONEL RAILROAD AT VERY MODERATE COST

No. 150

Nos. 152 and 153

Locomotive No. 150—With electric headlight. This locomotive is 6 inches long and stands 3 inches above the rails. It is a good, low priced locomotive. Price, complete with electric lamp for headlight and directions for operating **$4.50**
Western Price $5.50
Code Word "GARLAND"

Locomotive No. 153—With electric headlight and reversing controller. Same dimensions and design as the No. 152, but has new type reversing controller conveniently placed on rear end of locomotive. This is the lowest priced, high-grade reversible locomotive obtainable anywhere. Price, complete with electric lamp for headlight and directions for operating **$7.25**
Western Price $8.50
Code Word "GAME"

Locomotive No. 253—With two electric headlights and reversing controller. This locomotive is 9¾ inches long and stands 3¾ inches above the rails. An attractive model of great power. Price, complete with two electric lamps for headlights and directions for operating **$9.50**
Western Price $11.25
Code Word "FINE"

PAGES 29 AND 31 DESCRIBE AND ILLUSTRATE THE PASSENGER COACHES AND FREIGHT CARS TO BE USED WITH THESE LOCOMOTIVES

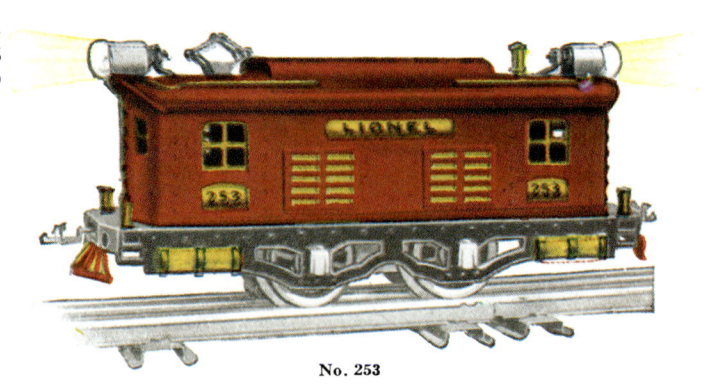

No. 253

A Lionel Locomotive Will Help You to Obtain a Knowledge of Electricity and Mechanical Traction Principles

Locomotives for Lionel "O" Gauge Track—1⅜ Inches Wide

LIONEL supremacy is again proven by the introduction of the new types of "O" Gauge Locomotives shown on this page. They are real electric engines in miniature. The new body designs suggest in a remarkable manner the massive outlines of the enormous electric locomotives seen on prominent electrified railroads like the C. M. and St. P., and the New York and New Haven. All the wonderful features described on page 8 are incorporated in these new models, including two electric headlights and reversing controllers. They are also equipped with the new patented Lionel Automatic Couplers. The motors have great hauling power, consume very little current, and will last for years with ordinary care.

Locomotive No. 251—With two electric headlights and reversing controller. This locomotive is 11¾ inches long and stands 5¼ inches above the rails. It is the latest addition to the Lionel "O" Gauge Line. The body design is entirely new and closely resembles the most modern types of electric engines. The method of construction, originated by Lionel and described on page 8, is fully exemplified in this beautiful model. Price, complete with electric lamps for headlight and directions for operating . . . **$15.00**

Code Word "ACME"   Western Price $17.50

Locomotive No. 254—With two electric headlights and reversing controller. This locomotive is 10 inches long and stands 4 inches above the rails. Smooth and silent in operation, beautiful in appearance. Price, complete with two electric lamps for headlights and directions for operating, **$12.25**

Code Word "MANY"   Western Price $14.50

Twin-Motor Locomotive No. 256—With two electric headlights and reversing controller. This Locomotive is 13½ inches long and stands 5½ inches above the rails. The headlights have individual switches so that one or both can be used as desired. The reversing controller operates both motors simultaneously. This is the only twin-motor locomotive ever made to operate on "O" Gauge Track. It will haul a great number of passenger or freight cars. A wonderful model replete with many realistic features. Price, complete with two electric lamps for headlights and directions for operating **$18.25**

Code Word "CHAIN"   Western Price $21.50

Lionel Products Are More Than Toys—They Are Triumphs of Model Railroad Engineering

Train Outfits for Lionel "O" Gauge Track—1⅜ Inches Wide

HERE are three very low priced train outfits that prove Lionel values. Every locomotive is equipped with an electric headlight. The cars and in fact every piece of Lionel equipment that forms part of the outfit is typical of Lionel quality, which means the best obtainable, notwithstanding the low cost.

Outfit No. 257—Comprises one No. 150 locomotive (6 inches long) with electric headlight, two No. 600 pullman cars (7 inches long), eight sections OC track and one OTC "Lockon" connection. Track forms a circle 30 inches in diameter. Train is 20 inches long. This outfit represents very great value.
Price, complete with electric lamp for headlight, connecting ties for joining sections of track, wires for transformer or battery connections and directions for operating $5.75

Code Word "HIGH"   Western Price $7.00

Outfit No. 92—Comprises one No. 152 locomotive (7 inches long) with electric headlight, one No. 629 pullman car (7¾ inches long), one No. 630 observation car (7¾ inches long), eight sections OC track and one OTC "Lockon" connection. Track forms a circle 30 inches in diameter. Train is 22½ inches long. The new cars included with this outfit are attractive in design and have inserted doors and panels as well as interior seats. The observation platform is made of brass.
Price, complete with electric lamp for headlight, connecting ties for joining sections of track, wires for transformer or battery connections and directions for operating $6.50

Code Word "REAL"   Western Price $7.75

Outfit No. 94—Comprises one No. 153 reversible locomotive (7 inches long) with electric headlight, two No. 629 pullman cars, one No. 630 observation car (each 7¾ inches long), eight sections OC track, two sections OS track, one OTC "Lockon" connection and one No. 88 rheostat. Track forms an oval 39 by 30 inches. Train is 30¼ inches long. We are proud of our achievement in being able to produce this high grade moderate priced complete outfit with a reversible locomotive.
Price, complete with electric lamp for headlight, connecting ties for joining sections of track, wires for transformer or battery connections and directions for operating $8.50
Western Price $10.00
Code Word "TRIO"

Use a Lionel "Multivolt" Transformer for Operating All Trains—An Ever Reliable Power Plant

Train Outfits for Lionel "O" Gauge Track—1⅜ Inches Wide

EVERY outfit in the Lionel "O" Gauge Line is replete with desirable features. On this and the following pages we show new and improved types of locomotives, improved cars and many other interesting innovations.

No. 91

Outfit No. 91—Comprises one No. 153 reversible locomotive (7 inches long) with electric headlight, one No. 800 box car, one No. 804 oil car, one No. 801 caboose (each 7 inches long), eight sections OC track, two sections OS track, one OTC "Lockon" connection and one No. 88 rheostat. Track forms an oval 39 by 30 inches. Train is 28 inches long. This well-built freight outfit also includes a reversible locomotive and is a companion number to Outfit No. 94 described on opposite page.

Price, complete with electric lamp for headlight, connecting ties for joining sections of track, wires for transformer or battery connections and directions for operating **$8.50**
Code Word "MIGHTY"   **Western Price $10.00**

No. 96

Outfit No. 96—Comprises one No. 153 reversible locomotive (7 inches long) with electric headlight, two No. 603 illuminated pullman cars, one No. 604 illuminated observation car (each 8 inches long), eight sections OC track, two sections OS track, one OTC "Lockon" connection and one No. 88 Rheostat. Track forms an oval 39 by 30 inches. Train is 31 inches long. The cars included with this train are equipped with two 4 wheel trucks and automatic couplers. Considering all the important details such as the reversible locomotive and the illuminated cars, this train represents the greatest possible value.

Price, complete with electric lamps for headlight and cars, connecting ties for joining the sections of track, wires for transformer or battery connections and directions for operating **$10.75**
Code Word "GIANT"   **Western Price $12.50**

No. 95

Outfit No. 95—Comprises one No. 253 reversible locomotive (9¾ inches long), with two electric headlights and automatic couplers, two No. 820 box cars, one No. 821 cattle car, one No. 822 caboose (each 8¼ inches long), eight sections OC track, six sections OS track, one OTC "Lockon" connection and one No. 88 rheostat. Track forms an oval 59 by 30 inches. Train is 42¾ inches long. Attention is directed to the new double-truck cattle car included with this splendid four car train, which is a faithful model of a big transcontinental freight train.

Price, complete with electric lamps for headlights, connecting ties for joining sections of track, wires for transformer or battery connections and directions for operating **$14.00**
Code Word "SPEEDY"   **Western Price $16.50**

The Only Difference Between Lionel Trains and Real Trains Is the Size

Train Outfits for Lionel "O" Gauge Track—1⅜ Inches Wide

NOW we come to the big, sturdy outfits of the Lionel "O" Gauge Line—brimming with improvements and handsomely finished. Any one of these outfits is good for years of wholesome enjoyment for the lucky owner. You pay no more for these durable, long-wearing train outfits than for the inferior kind. Therefore, always look for the name "Lionel" when buying miniature electric railroad equipment. Quality is built right in from the very foundation.

No. 98

Outfit No. 98—Comprises one No. 253 Reversible Locomotive (9¾ inches long) with two electric headlights, two No. 610 illuminated pullman cars, one No. 612 illuminated observation car (each 9 inches long), eight sections OC track, six sections OS track, one OTC "Lockon" connection and one No. 88 rheostat. Track forms an oval 59 by 30 inches. Train is 36¾ inches long. The entire train is equipped with automatic couplers.

This new outfit replaces the No. 264 listed last year and although the equipment it incorporates is larger than in the train formerly made by us, the price has not been increased.

Price, complete with electric lamps for headlights and cars, connecting ties for joining sections of track, wires for transformer or battery connections and directions for operating $15.00

Code Word "GOLD" Western Price $18.00

No. 266

Outfit No. 266—Comprises one new model No. 254 reversible locomotive (10 inches long) with two electric headlights and automatic couplers, two No. 610 illuminated pullman cars (9 inches long), one No. 612 illuminated observation car (9 inches long), all with automatic couplers, eight sections OC track, six sections OS track, one OTC "Lockon" connection and one No. 88 rheostat. Track forms an oval 59 by 30 inches. Train is 37 inches long. The bright, rich enameled finish of this splendid train will appeal instantly. The powerful locomotive and all-steel cars together with the liberal track layout, stamp it as tremendous value for the price.

Price, complete with electric lamps for headlights and interior of cars, connecting ties for joining sections of track, wires for transformer or battery connections and directions for operating $18.00

Code Word "HEAD" Western Price $21.50

Permanently Illuminated Cars—An Attractive Feature of these New Passenger Trains

Train Outfits for Lionel "O" Gauge Track—1⅜ Inches Wide

ANY boy will be proud to own either of the remarkable train outfits illustrated below. Is there anything more to be desired than these supremely fine Lionel products? The single and twin-motor locomotives that form part of these outfits have already been described on page 11.

These trains are equipped with the Lionel Automatic Couplers—the cars have permanent interior lights and many other realistic details that place them far and away above anything similar ever made. They are in every respect real models of all-steel pullman trains.

No. 97

Outfit No. 97—Comprises one No. 251 reversible locomotive (11¾ inches long) with two electric headlights, two No. 605 illuminated pullman cars, one No. 606 illuminated observation car (each 10½ inches long), eight sections OC track, eight sections OS track, one OTC "Lockon" connection and one No. 88 rheostat. Track forms an oval 79 by 30 inches. Train is 43¼ inches long. This train is completely equipped with automatic couplers and is a well-designed model. It stands far above anything similar ever made, and is truly a de luxe model or a modern passenger train. It embodies all the excellent features of Lionel construction as described on pages 8 and 9.

Price, complete with electric lamps for headlights and cars, connecting ties for joining sections of track, wires for transformer or battery connections and directions for operating **$22.50**

Code Word "EXCEL"   Western Price $26.00

No. 268

Outfit No. 268—Comprises one new model No. 256 twin-motor reversible locomotive (13½ inches long) with two electric headlights and automatic couplers, two No. 710 illuminated pullman cars (12½ inches long), one No. 712 illuminated observation car (12½ inches long), all with automatic couplers, eight sections OC track, eight sections OS track, one OTC "Lockon" connection and one No. 88 rheostat. Track forms an oval 79 by 30 inches. Train is 51 inches long. This is the largest train ever made to operate on "O" Gauge Track. The locomotive with its marvelous twin-motors will haul an unlimited number of cars. Every part that enters into this outfit bears the mark of Lionel quality.

Price, complete with electric lamps for headlights and interior of cars, connecting ties for joining sections of track, wires for transformer or battery connections and directions for operating **$33.00**

Code Word "TAKE"   Western Price $38.75

Look Closely at the Above Illustrations—See the Many Wonderful Details Incorporated in Lionel Trains

Complete Lionel Railroads for "O" Gauge Track—1⅜ Inches Wide

MANY boys prefer to buy Lionel Train Set with a variety of accessories right from the start, so we have made up the outfits illustrated on this page. It will be seen that many wonderful accessories are provided in addition to the train and track layout. Every piece is of steel construction throughout with the famous Lionel enameled finish. It is only necessary to get one of the low priced "Multivolt" Transformers and the railroad can be operated instantly, or if no house current is available dry or storage batteries can be used. The track layout can always be extended.

Outfit No. 174—Comprises one complete No. 96 train described on page 13 together with ten sections OC track, six sections OS track, one OTC "Lockon" connection, one No. 88 rheostat, one pair No. 022 switches (one right and one left), one No. 106 bridge (three sections), one No. 121 station, six No. 60 telegraph posts, two No. 62 semaphores, one No. 68 crossing sign and one No. 119 tunnel. Size of track layout 45 by 60 inches. The complete train is 31 inches long. The appearance of this railroad can be enhanced by adding the illuminated bungalows and villas described on pages 34 and 35.

Price, complete with electric lamps for headlights and interior of cars, connecting ties for joining sections of track, wires for transformer or battery connections and directions for operating . . . **$35.00**
Western Price $40.00

Code Word "DELAWARE"

No. 174

No. 176

Outfit No. 176—Comprises one complete No. 98 train described on page 14 together with ten sections OC track, ten sections OS track, one OTC "Lockon" connection, one No. 88 rheostat, one pair No. 022 switches (one right and one left), one No. 109 bridge (5 sections), one No. 121 station, eight No. 60 telegraph posts, one No. 62 semaphore, one No. 68 crossing sign and one No. 119 tunnel. Size of track layout 45 by 82 inches. The complete train is 35½ inches long. The new automatic accessories described on pages 38 and 39 will make welcome additions to this railroad.

Price, complete with electric lamps for headlights and interior of cars, connecting ties for joining sections of track, wires for transformer or battery connections and directions for operating **$43.75**
Western Price $50.00

Code Word "BURLINGTON"

A Complete Model Village Can Be Built with the Aid of Lionel Steel Bungalows and Villas—See Pages 34 and 35

Super-Motor Locomotives for "Lionel Standard" Track—2¼ Inches Wide

IT IS only natural that this Corporation, the originators of "Lionel Standard" equipment, should develop and perfect what are universally acknowledged to be the best designed and most efficient locomotives to operate on "Lionel Standard" track. We illustrate on this and the following pages five improved Super-Motor Locomotives with new three-point-bearing armature shafts that far surpass any of our previous models. If you have not already read the details of construction, please turn to page 6 for specifications of the Super-Motor, page 7 for the Twin-Super-Motor and page 8 for details of body construction. You will immediately recognize the superiority of the many desirable features incorporated in these models. Always remember that Lionel was first to develop a complete "Lionel Standard" line of Locomotives, Cars and Model Railroad Accessories.

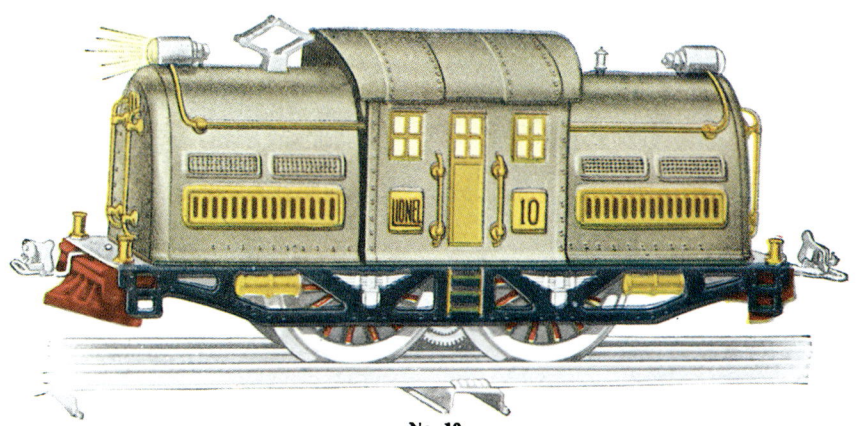

No. 8

Locomotive No. 8—With electric headlight, reversing controller and automatic couplers. This locomotive is 13 inches long and stands 5¼ inches above the rails. It contains the improved Super-Motor and is one of the very latest types of electric locomotives now being used on big electrified railroads.

Price, complete with electric lamp for headlight and directions for operating $11.50
Code Word "POWER"   Western Price $13.25

No. 318

Locomotive No. 318—With two electric headlights, reversing controller and automatic couplers. This locomotive is 14½ inches long and stands 6 inches above the rails. It is introduced in response to a great demand for a single-super-motor locomotive built on the lines of our No. 402, but smaller, and contains many of the constructional features of the larger engine. It will be favored by many Lionel enthusiasts who already have "Lionel Standard" Outfits that they wish to enlarge.

Price, complete with electric lamps for headlights and directions for operating, $16.50
Code Word "VERB"   Western Price $19.00

No. 10

Locomotive No. 10—With two electric headlights, reversing controller and automatic couplers. This locomotive is 14 inches long and stands 5½ inches above the rails. Here is another new type of electric engine of superior construction. Examine the many fine features and graceful outlines of the body. No load is too great for this powerful hauler. It will easily pull a large number of the passenger or freight cars designed for use with it.

Price, complete with electric lamps for headlights and directions for operating . . . $13.75
Code Word "PULL"   Western Price $15.85

"Lionel Standard" Track—2¼ Inches Wide—Was Originated and Developed by Lionel More Than 21 Years Ago

Super-Motor Locomotives for "Lionel Standard" Track—2¼ Inches Wide

THE mechanism and motors of these mighty locomotives have already been described on pages 6 and 7, while details of the body construction are given on page 8. Because of their larger size we are able to incorporate more powerful motors in "Lionel Standard" locomotives than in the "O" Gauge.

An extra locomotive adds greater variety to your train layout—switching engines from track to track is great sport and is real railroad practice.

Locomotive No. 380—With two electric headlights, reversing controller and automatic couplers. This locomotive is 15 inches long and stands 6¼ inches above the rails. It met with instant success when we added it to the Lionel Line. In appearance it is exactly like the new monster locomotives which haul the C. M. and St. P. trains over the electrified stretch of the railroad through the Rocky Mountains. The improved Super-Motor and the characteristics of body construction have already been described. Red and green transparent discs are placed on the sides of the headlight lantern, presenting a dazzlingly beautiful effect. These headlights have individual switches so that one or both may be turned on at will.

Price, complete with electric lamps for headlights and directions for operating $18.75

Code Word "ROCKIES" Western Price $21.65

No. 380

Twin-Super-Motor Locomotive No. 402—With two electric headlights, reversing controller and automatic couplers. This locomotive is 17½ inches long and stands 6½ inches above the rails. It is far above the "toy" class, and is the very peak of perfection, the result of many years of diligent research and development in Model Railroad Engineering. Pages 6, 7 and 8 show you the high grade details of motor, chassis and body. On pages 22 and 23 you will see this massive engine coupled to our largest passenger and freight cars—really magnificent trains. The unique headlights placed on this locomotive have already been described on this page. Truly, No. 402 is a locomotive that will realize any boy's life long ambition.

Price, complete with electric lamps for headlights and directions for operating $32.25

Code Word "HAVEN" Western Price $37.00

No. 402

The Foundation for a Wonderful Miniature Railroad—Any of the Locomotives on this page

Super-Motor Train Outfits for "Lionel Standard" Track—2¼ Inches Wide

THIS and the following pages are devoted to the "Lionel Standard" Line of Passenger and Freight Trains of which we are the originators. Manufacturing experience extending over a period of twenty-five years has enabled us to produce a line as near perfection as human ingenuity can attain. There is not a number in the entire "Lionel Standard" Line that does not show remarkable improvements and greater values than ever before. On previous pages we have described the locomotives to operate on "Lionel Standard" Track. These locomotives in conjunction with the large variety of up-to-date passenger coaches and freight cars combine to form the best miniature electric trains in the world.

Typical instances are shown on this page—read the specifications and you have proof that any train in the "Lionel Standard" Line offers everything desirable in quality and price.

No. 350

Outfit No. 350—Comprises one No. 8 Locomotive (13 inches long) with electric headlight and reversing controller, one No. 35 illuminated pullman car, one No. 36 illuminated observation car (each 11½ inches long), eight sections C track, two sections S track, and one STC "Lockon" connection. Track forms an oval 56 by 42 inches. Train is 36 inches long. The entire train is equipped with automatic couplers. An entirely new locomotive is introduced with this outfit. It contains the improved Super-Motor. Because of the strikingly beautiful superstructure of the locomotive and the improvements in the passenger cars that go with it, this new train represents the greatest possible value. Not only is the locomotive far superior to anything of its kind, but the cars are replete with new features, including newly designed trucks with nickeled journals, and heavy brass steps. No finer model train will ever be made at this price.

Price, complete with electric lamps for headlight and cars, connecting ties for joining sections of track, wires for transformer or battery connections and directions for operating **$17.50**

Code Word "PROOF"   Western Price $21.00

No. 351

Outfit No. 351—Comprises one No. 8 locomotive (13 inches long) with electric headlight, reversing controller and automatic couplers, one No. 112 gondola car, one No. 114 box car, one No. 117 caboose (each 9¾ inches long), eight sections C track, two sections S track, and one STC "Lockon" connection. Track forms an oval 56 by 42 inches. Train is 42¼ inches long. This new freight outfit also contains the improved Super-Motor Locomotive mentioned above. If a freight train is your choice, you are sure to obtain a superior outfit when you select this one. Considering the low price there is nothing more desirable in the way of a durable, long-wearing, perfect model of a modern freight train.

Price, complete with electric lamp for headlight, connecting ties for joining sections of track, wires for transformer or battery connections and directions for operating, **$17.50**

Code Word "LION"   Western Price $21.00

Two New Trains in the "Lionel Standard" Line—Perfect Construction and Wonderful Values

Reg. U. S. Pat. Office

Super-Motor Train Outfits for "Lionel Standard" Track—2¼ Inches Wide

WITH justifiable pride we direct attention to the new Lionel Models illustrated on this page. New and improved locomotives and cars are included with these outfits, all of supremely high quality, richly finished, and of great durability. Every modern detail of real trains has been incorporated in them. Lionel values have never been greater.

No. 352

Outfit No. 352—Comprises one No. 10 reversible locomotive (14 inches long) with two electric headlights and automatic couplers, two No. 337 illuminated pullman cars, one No. 338 illuminated observation car (each 14 inches long), all with automatic couplers, eight sections of C track, four sections of S track and one STC "Lockon" connection. Track forms an oval 69 x 42 inches. Train is 56 inches long. Another great Lionel achievement is exemplified in this new train. All the prominent features of our new locomotives and passenger cars, as described on pages 8 and 9 of this catalogue, are embodied in it. The built-in excellence of every piece, and the low price of this splendid model make it particularly desirable.

Price, complete with electric lamps for headlights and cars, connecting ties for joining sections of track, wires for transformer or battery connections and directions for operating $25.00
Code Word "PRINCE"   Western Price $30.00

No. 41

Outfit No. 41—Comprises one No. 318 reversible locomotive (14½ inches long) with two electric headlights and automatic couplers, one No. 112 gondola car, one No. 113 cattle car, one No. 114 box car, one No. 116 coal car, one No. 117 caboose (each 9¾ inches long), eight sections of C track, four sections S track and one STC "Lockon" connection. Track forms an oval 69 by 42 inches. Complete train is 63¾ inches long. Lionel freight trains have always been known for their great value. The No. 318 locomotive included with this outfit is famous for its rigid construction and great hauling power, while the cars are of Lionel quality throughout. These cars are faithful models of the latest types of steel freight cars used on all the large railroads.

Price, complete with electric lamps for headlights, connecting ties for joining sections of track, wires for transformer or battery connections and directions for operating $26.75
Code Word "FULTON"   Western Price $31.50

No. 342

Outfit No. 342—Comprises one new No. 318 reversible super-motor locomotive (14½ inches long) with two electric headlights and automatic couplers, two No. 339 illuminated pullman cars, one No. 341 illuminated observation car (each 14 inches long), all with automatic couplers, eight sections of C track, six sections of S track, one STC "Lockon" connection. Track forms an oval 88 by 42 inches. Complete train is 56½ inches long. This handsome new train outfit is in every respect a faithful reproduction of the most up-to-date pullman trains. The new No. 318 locomotive included with it has already been described. The richly enameled cars embody great detail. Their graceful proportions are immediately apparent. The inserted windows, doors and panels exemplify to the highest degree the new method of Lionel car construction. These are separable parts securely fastened to the body and add materially to the realistic appearance of the cars. Nickel plated journals are mounted on the trucks and miniature metal tanks are securely held to the bottom of the car. Each car is equipped with automatic couplers as well as a fixture for interior illumination. The observation platform on the rear car is made of brass and is an exact reproduction of those used on the large cars.

Price, complete with electric lamps for headlights and interior of cars, connecting ties for joining sections of track, wires for transformer or battery connections and directions for operating $29.50
Code Word "VIEW"   Western Price $35.00

Many More Cars Can Be Added to These Trains—The Powerful Lionel Locomotives Will Easily Haul Them

Super-Motor Train Outfits for "Lionel Standard" Track—2¼ Inches Wide

THE locomotives included with the outfits listed below are firmly established favorites in the "Lionel Standard" Line and are offered this year in a much improved form. The high grade cars shown in conjunction with them combine to make Model Trains which differ from real ones only in size. Many interesting refinements have been incorporated—yet prices have been materially reduced.

No. 344

Outfit No. 344—Comprises one No. 380 reversible super-motor locomotive (15 inches long) with two electric headlights, one No. 18 illuminated pullman car, one No. 190 illuminated observation car (each 16½ inches long), eight sections C track, four sections S track and one STC "Lockon" connection. Entire train is equipped with automatic couplers. Track forms an oval 69 by 42 inches. Complete train is 48 inches long. Here is another perfectly built passenger train that is exceptionally popular. Its great value is further enhanced by the addition of an observation car in place of one of the pullman coaches that was formerly included with it.

Price, complete with electric lamps for headlights and interior of cars, connecting ties for joining sections of track, wires for transformer or battery connections and directions for operating, **$34.50**
Western Price $41.00
Code Word "VERNON"

No. 345

Outfit No. 345—Comprises one No. 380 reversible super-motor locomotive (15 inches long) with two electric headlights and automatic couplers, one No. 12 gondola car, one No. 14 box car, one No. 15 oil car, one No. 17 caboose (each 11 inches long), eight sections C track, four sections S track, one STC "Lockon" connection. Track forms an oval 69 by 42 inches. Complete train is 59 inches long. The No. 380 locomotive included with this outfit needs no further introduction. The freight cars are large and well proportioned and the entire outfit stands out as a realistic model of an up-to-date freight train.

Price, complete with electric lamps for headlights, connecting ties for joining sections of track, wires for transformer or battery connections and directions for operating **$34.50**
Code Word "PELHAM" **Western Price $41.00**

No. 343

Outfit No. 343—Comprises one No. 380 reversible super-motor locomotive (15 inches long) with two electric headlights, two No. 319 illuminated pullman cars, one No. 320 illuminated mail and baggage car, one No. 322 illuminated observation car (each 15 inches long), eight sections C track, eight sections S track and one STC "Lockon" connection. Entire train is equipped with automatic couplers. Track forms an oval 102 x 42 inches. The train is 75 inches long. The powerful No. 380 locomotive will easily haul with great speed the four cars supplied with it, and many others in addition.

Price, complete with electric lamps for headlights and cars, connecting ties for joining sections of track, wires for transformer or battery connections and directions for operating **$42.25**
Code Word "TIME" **Western Price $50.00**

Read About the New Locomotives Included with These Train Outfits, on Page 18—Electrically Perfect

Twin-Super-Motor Train Outfits

TRAIN Outfit No. 403 is in every respect a miniature reproduction of a de luxe express train. It is a delight to behold and operates as smoothly as though the wheels were equipped with rubber tires. Even the most superlative terms of description will not be as convincing as seeing the outfit in operation. It is absolutely the last word in miniature train construction.

A companion number quite in keeping with the handsome

No. 403

Details of Locomotive—An exact reproduction of the most modern type of electric locomotives used on electrified systems throughout the country. It is so faithful in detail that to behold it is like seeing an actual large electric locomotive through the diminishing end of field glasses.

Body—The body is made entirely of steel. The doors, windows, ventilators, hand rails and all other fittings are made of polished brass and are securely fastened by our patented nickeled stanchions.

Headlights—The headlights (one of which is placed at each end of the body) are unique in construction. Each is equipped with a switch so that one or both may be turned on at will. The headlight lamp when illuminated is visible through the green and red panels on the sides of the headlight—a touch of realism that will delight every boy.

Reversing Controller—A lever is conveniently placed on the side of the locomotive which operates simultaneously the controllers on each of the twin-motors. This is a great step forward in controller construction.

Frame—The frame is made of one piece of heavy steel. Journals, made of brass and beautifully nickel plated, are securely fastened to it. Numerous rivets and other structural details are heavily embossed in the frame, all of which accentuate the great detail embodied in this locomotive.

Automatic Couplers—This locomotive is equipped with our new automatic couplers which protrude through the centre of beautifully designed cow-catchers. These automatic couplers are a great improvement over any similar device, for the reason that they engage with each other irrespective of the position of the cars. They can be used in conjunction with any type of non-automatic coupler now on the market.

Enamel Finish—The enamel on the frame and body is baked on at a high temperature, which insures a glasslike finish that lasts for years. It is only necessary to rub the surface with a cloth or chamois to keep the locomotive always bright and new looking.

Details of Cars—These pullman cars are faithful reproductions in every detail of the most modern passenger cars used on the best railroads. The bodies are made of heavy sheet steel and the parts are rigidly held together. The detail of construction is enhanced by embossed work in the nature of panels, rivets, sashes, etc. Two miniature tanks as well as nickel plated steps and hand rails add to the great detail incorporated in these cars. The roof is removable and the interior contains individual revolving seats and permanent electric fixtures for illuminating the cars. Current is obtained from our patented collecting shoe built into one of the trucks. The light shining through the colored glass windows produces a very realistic effect. These cars are enameled in very attractive colors baked on at a high temperature so that they always retain their fresh, glossy appearance. It is impossible to describe the beauty of these cars adequately, but suffice to say that nothing like them has ever been made before as miniature toy railroad equipment. The combination pullman and baggage car contains a baggage compartment

The Culmination of 25 Years of Specialization in Miniature Train Building—These Marvelous Outfits

For "Lionel Standard" Track—2¼ Inches Wide
Reg. U. S. Pat. Office

No. 403 is the new freight train outfit No. 404 illustrated at the bottom of this page. Every style of modern freight car is included with it, but many more can be added with the full assurance that the powerful twin-super-motor locomotive will haul them without difficulty.

Liberal track layouts are included with these outfits.

with sliding doors and the platform of the observation car is made of brass and is complete in every detail.

Improved Car Trucks—It is with great pleasure that we draw attention to the new six-wheel car trucks with which all cars in the new No. 403 train are equipped. This new truck is the latest Lionel development, and it adds realism to an already beautiful model. Made in exact reproduction of the style used on modern all-steel pullmans, these trucks are assembled on a heavy steel frame, richly enameled in black and embossed with springs and numerous rivets. The wheels and axles are made of heavy steel, nickel plated. The journals in which the axles revolve, are also of steel and are faithfully designed.

Outfit No. 403—Comprises one No. 402 twin-super-motor reversible locomotive (17½ inches long), one No. 418 illuminated pullman car, one No. 419 illuminated pullman and baggage car, one No. 490 illuminated observation car (each 20 inches long), eight sections S track, eight sections C track and one STC "Lockon" connection. Track forms an oval 102 by 42 inches. Complete train is 77½ inches long.

Price, complete with electric lamps for headlights and interior of cars, connecting ties for joining sections of track, wires for transformer or battery connections and directions for operating. $60.75

Code Word "PRETTY"   Western Price $71.50

No. 404

Outfit No. 404—Comprises one No. 402 twin-super-motor reversible locomotive (17½ inches long) with two electric headlights, one No. 11 flat car, one No. 12 gondola car, one No. 13 cattle car, one No. 14 box car, one No. 15 oil car, one No. 16 coal car, one No. 17 caboose (each 11 inches long), eight sections C track, ten sections S track, and one STC "Lockon" connection. Track forms an oval 116 by 42 inches. Complete train is 94½ inches long. The locomotive is the same as included with outfit No. 403, while the freight cars are of steel construction all through, richly enameled, with nickeled trucks and wheels. The complete train presents a beautiful appearance and is in all respects a perfect miniature replica of a transcontinental heavy freighter.

Price, complete with electric lamps for headlights, connecting ties for joining sections of tracks, wires for transformer or battery connections and directions for operating $57.75

Code Word "ELITE"   Western Price $67.50

The Type K "Multivolt" Transformer Listed with Others on Page 27 Will Operate These Trains Perfectly

Reg. U. S. Pat. Office
Complete Railroad for "Lionel Standard" Track—2¼ Inches Wide

HERE is a lavishly planned complete railroad that reflects to the highest degree a perfect layout of equipment and miniature village. A "Multivolt" Transformer is included with this beautiful outfit for operating it from the Alternating House Current, or a Lionel Current Reducer will be supplied if your current is "Direct". Please be sure to specify which one is required.

This complete railroad comes to you securely packed.

Outfit No. 405

EQUIPMENT WITH OUTFIT No. 405

LOCOMOTIVES
1 No. 402 Twin-Super-Motor
1 No. 5 Switching Engine

PASSENGER CARS
1 No. 418 Illuminated Pullman
1 No. 419 Illuminated Pullman and Baggage
1 No. 490 Illuminated Observation

FREIGHT CARS
1 No. 11 Flat Car
1 No. 12 Gondola Car
1 No. 13 Cattle Car
1 No. 14 Box Car

1 No. 15 Oil Car
1 No. 16 Coal Car
1 No. 17 Caboose

TRACK
38 sections S straight track
18 sections C curved track
4 sections ½S straight track

TRACK ACCESSORIES
3 pairs No. 22 Switches (right and left)
2 No. 23 Bumpers
6 No. STC "Lockon" Connectors

STATIONS AND HOUSES
1 No. 121 Station
1 No. 191 Villa
1 No. 189 Villa
4 No. 184 Bungalows

ACCESSORIES
1 Type K Transformer (or No. 107 Direct Current Reducer if desired)
1 No. 69 Warning Signal
2 No. 77 Crossing Gates
8 No. 60 Telegraph Posts
1 No. 89 Flag Staff
1 No. 65 Semaphore

1 No. 66 Semaphore
1 No. 120 Tunnel
1 No. 101 Bridge (3 sections)
2 No. 59 Lamp Posts
4 No. 57 Lamp Posts

The complete dimensions of the entire track layout are 11 feet 8 inches long and 9 feet 2 inches wide.

Price, complete with electric lamps for locomotives, cars and all accessories, connecting ties for joining sections of track, connecting wires for transformer or reducer and directions for operating $200.00

Western Price $230.00

Code Word "MARK"

A Desirable Accessory for This Railroad Is the New Automatic Train Control—See Page 38

Lionel "All-Steel" Tunnels

LIONEL TRAINS are worthy of good accessories and it is therefore with great pleasure that we offer the Lionel steel tunnels, which are a wonderful improvement over the old, flimsy, papier-mâché ones that users of train outfits were compelled to accept before we introduced ours.

Lionel tunnels are made of steel throughout, being accurately designed and formed in our special machinery. They stand evenly on the floor without the slightest twist. Their rigid construction does not make it necessary to have any cross-braces on the base which would interfere with the track level.

The front and rear entrances of Lionel tunnels are embossed in exact reproduction of heavy stone masonry, having a keystone at the top. The bodies of the tunnels represent mountainsides in miniature and the coloring is made to harmonize beautifully. We draw particular attention to the detail on No. 120 Tunnel, which has the mountain roadside wonderfully modelled as well as the little metal "chalet", all in perfect proportion to the size of the tunnel.

All Lionel tunnels are practically indestructible and are very low priced considering the workmanship in them.

No. 120

No. 119

No. 118

Your "Power-Plant" Should Be a Lionel "Multivolt" Transformer or a Lionel Direct Current Reducer. See pages 26 and 27.

Tunnel No. 118, for "O" Gauge Only—Will allow passage of any "O" gauge train. Is 8 inches long, 7 inches wide and 7½ inches extreme height. Portals are 4 inches wide and 5½ inches high inside.
Price $2.10
Code Word "SIMPLON" Western Price $2.50

Tunnel No. 119, for "O" Gauge and Some "Lionel Standard" Trains—For use with all "O" gauge trains and "Lionel Standard" trains Nos. 350, 351, 352 and 41. Is 12 inches long, 9 inches wide and 10 inches extreme height. Portals are 5 inches wide and 6½ inches high inside.
Price $3.35
Code Word "HOOSAC" Western Price $4.00

Tunnel No. 120, for All Lionel Trains—This splendid model is the very best produced for beauty, grace of design and substantial construction. Is 17 inches long, 12 inches wide and 11 inches extreme height. Inside dimensions of portals are 6½ inches wide and 8 inches high.
Price $5.85
Code Word "HUDSON" Western Price $7.00

All Lionel Accessories Are Faithful Models of the Originals—Many New Devices Are Shown Throughout This Book

Lionel "Multivolt" Transformers—Specifications

LIONEL DIRECT CURRENT REDUCERS
Not for Alternating Current

Nos. 107 and 170

No. 107, Lionel Current Reducer for 110-Volt Circuit—This is constructed of four porcelain tubes wound with best quality of resistance wire. These porcelain tubes are mounted on a substantial slate base measuring 8 by 10 inches and ¾ inch thick. The porcelain tubes are protected and ventilated by a perforated steel cover lined with heavy asbestos. The sliding lever regulates the voltage so that your trains will just crawl along or shoot ahead at express speed. The reducer is connected with the house current by a screw plug with 7 feet of flexible cord. In addition, four porcelain supports or legs with long screws are supplied so that the reducer can be screwed to wall or table.
Price $10.00
Western Price $12.00
Code Word "KENTUCKY"

No. 170, Lionel Direct Current Reducer for 220-Volt Circuit—This Reducer is identical in appearance with No. 107, mentioned above, but is for use on 220 volts. Equipped with separable plug and 7 feet of flexible cord.
Price $14.50
Western Price $17.00
Code Word "ASBURY"

No. 88

Lionel Battery Rheostat No. 88—Use this rheostat with dry or storage batteries. It gives a gradual increase or decrease of current. A porcelain tube is wound with resistance wire of the correct gauge. This is mounted on a steel frame. A sliding finger increases or decreases the speed of the trains. All parts are of the best quality. This rheostat cannot overheat, as the coil is entirely exposed to the air—insuring free circulation, consequently rapid cooling. The steel base is beautifully enameled and other parts are nickel plated. Size 5 inches long, 2½ inches wide and 1 inch high.
Price $1.50
Western Price $1.80
Code Word "BANNER"

Details of Transformer Construction

Sub-Base—A metal sub-base resting on four supports is attached to the bottom. The air circulating between this sub-base and the transformer case keeps it cool while in operation. Holes in this sub-base provide means for fastening the transformer to wall or table.

Separable Plug—All "Multivolt" Transformers are fitted with an approved, separable plug, which is a distinct advantage over the one-piece plug, because the circuit can be immediately broken when desired.

Plug Protecting Device—We have applied for a patent on a unique receptacle for protecting the plug against breakage in shipment. This device consists of a wooden container entirely covering the plug. It is sealed with a conspicuous label which draws the attention of the user to the fact that the transformer must be used **only** on **alternating** current of the number of cycles designated. This obviates the possibility of connecting the transformer with wrong current, which will consequently avoid mishandling and disappointment.

Double Contact Control Switch—This is infinitely superior to the one-piece switch, which is easily bent and does not make positive contact. Our double switch has a flexible, phosphor-bronze contact arm under the rigid switch, so that positive contact with the points is assured. This flexible contact is protected from injury by the rigid brass handle to which it is attached. This is an exclusive feature of "Multivolt" Transformers.

Laminations—The laminations are made of the best grade of electrical sheets and the windings are perfectly insulated.

Rigid Supports for Coils—The coils and laminations of Lionel "Multivolt" Transformers are rigidly supported inside the case by means of metal bands which prevent these parts from moving and eliminate the possibility of broken lead wires. In addition to these supports, the interior of the case is fitted with an insulating receptacle and the case is air cooled.

Metal Case—The case is beautiful in design and is stamped of heavier steel than is required by the National Board of Fire Underwriters.

Finish—"Multivolt" Transformer cases are covered with a rubberoid composition that is applied at 350 degrees Fahrenheit. This is much greater heat than the case is ever subjected to, and the finish cannot be scratched and will not peel off, thereby insuring a beautiful finish for the entire life of the transformer.

Visible Connections—All contacts and switches are mounted on one piece of heavy insulating material and are at the top of the transformer, right before the user.

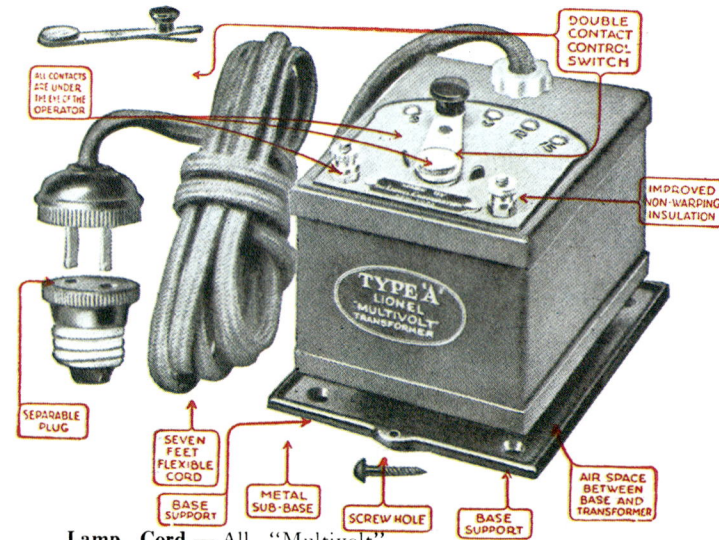

Lamp Cord—All "Multivolt" Transformers are fitted with 7 feet of flexible lamp cord which enters the transformer case through an approved porcelain bushing.

From the above specifications it will be clearly seen that we have incorporated in "Multivolt" Transformers every possible device that will increase their efficiency.

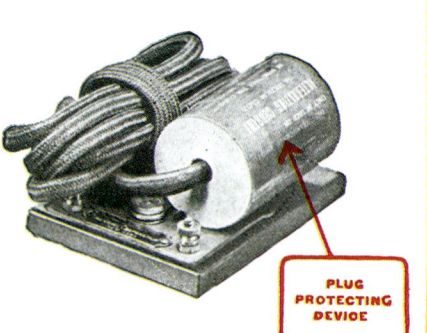

IMPORTANT

Lionel "Multivolt" Transformers are made completely at our own factories. The department in which they are made is the largest of its kind devoted exclusively to the manufacture of low-voltage transformers.

The only parts purchased are the raw materials. We correctly wind and insulate the coils, make the cases, laminations, switch handles, and in fact do every operation. That is why Lionel "Multivolt" Transformers are the best designed, best constructed, and are approved by the Underwriters' Laboratories.

Be sure to use only Lionel "Multivolt" Transformers with Lionel Model Trains. They are the cheapest and best in the long run.

Lionel "Multivolt" Transformers Are Approved by the Underwriters' Laboratories

Lionel "Multivolt" Transformers for 110 and 220 Volts, 60, 40 or 25 Cycles

LIONEL "Multivolt" Transformers have been on the market for a great many years and operate all makes of Electric Trains. We justly claim that they are best. Don't experiment with other makes of doubtful value. Remember, that all transformers look alike outside, but their imperfections will only be discovered after they are in actual use for a length of time. Lionel "Multivolt" Transformers will last indefinitely and are guaranteed unconditionally as long as they are used on the current for which they are intended. They are absolutely safe and will give steady, even power.

THESE TRANSFORMERS ARE FOR USE ONLY ON "ALTERNATING" CURRENT—DO NOT USE THEM ON "DIRECT" CURRENT

Type "A" Transformer will operate any "O" gauge outfit.
For 110 volts, 60 cycles. 40 watts capacity.
Gives 15 volts in following steps: 4, 7, 10, 13, 15.
Size: 4¼ by 2¾ by 4¼ inches.
Sub-base: 3¾ by 4¾ inches.
Price $3.75
Western Price $4.50
Code Word "STRONG"

Type "B" Transformer will operate any "O" gauge outfit, and in addition the extra binding posts enable the users to light up lamp posts, semaphores and other electrically illuminated accessories.
For 110 volts, 60 cycles. 50 watts capacity.
Gives 25 volts in following steps.
Permanent: 7, 8, 15.
Variable: 2, 4, 6, 8, 9, 10, 11, 12, 13, 17, 19, 21, 23, 25.
Size: 4½ by 3¾ by 3 inches.
Sub-base: 5 by 4¼ inches.
Price $5.00
Western Price $6.00
Code Word "BRADLEY"

Type "T" Transformer will operate any "O" gauge or "Lionel Standard" outfit; also has extra binding posts for attaching illuminated electrical accessories.
For 110 volts, 60 cycles. 100 watts capacity.
Gives 25 volts in following steps:
Permanent: 2, 4, 6, 7, 8, 10, 12, 14, 15, 16, 17, 18, 19, 21, 23, 25.
Variable: 2, 6, 8, 10, 12, 14, 16, 17, 18, 19, 21, 23, 25.
Size: 5 by 4 by 3¾ inches.
Sub-base: 4½ by 5½ inches.
Price $7.50
Western Price $9.00
Code Word "BIRCH"

Type "K" Transformer will operate any outfit as well as illuminated accessories. This transformer has sufficient wattage capacity to operate two trains at once.
Size: 5 by 4 by 4½ inches. Sub-base: 4½ by 5½ inches.
"K"—For 110 volts, 60 cycles. 150 watts capacity. Specifications same as Type "T," but has higher wattage capacity. **Price $11.00**
Western Price $13.00
Code Word (110V.) "BINGHAM"
"K"—For 220 volts, 60 cycles. 150 watts capacity. Specifications same as Type "T," but is for use on 220-volt circuit. **Price $14.50**
Western Price $17.00
Code Word (220 V.) "BROOK"

Type "C" Transformer will operate any outfit and illuminated accessories on 25 or 40 cycle current.
For 110 volts, 25 to 40 cycles. 75 watts capacity. Specifications same as Type "T," but is for use on 25 or 40 cycle current.
Size: 5 by 4 by 4½ inches. Sub-base: 4½ by 5½ inches.
Price $7.50
Western Price $9.00
Code Word "LAWRENCE"

Lionel "Multivolt" Transformers Are Efficient—Economical—Easily Operated

[27]

Lionel "All-Steel" Passenger and Mail Cars

THE construction of all Lionel Pullman Coaches is worthy of special notice, as it represents the highest form of miniature car manufacture. Not only are all bodies made of heavy steel and beautifully embossed with panels, rivets, etc., but many types are made of one single piece formed and soldered at the ends, and the cars of the larger type are rigidly held together by mechanical means and soldered. Cross braces and partitions placed inside the cars not only add to the detail but make them rigid and almost indestructible. Some outstanding features of Lionel Coaches are hinged doors, inserted window frames and sashes and interior seats. These separable pieces are enameled in various colors to harmonize with the body of the car and accentuate the great detail that is incorporated in them. All cars, even the lowest priced ones, are finished in enamel baked on at high temperature so that the finish is everlasting and can always be kept bright and clean.

No. 490 Observation Car—Same size as No. 418 Pullman and No. 419 Pullman and Baggage Car.

No. 19 Pullman and Baggage Car—Same size as No. 18 Pullman and No. 190 Observation Car.

In almost every car clear transparencies are placed in the windows and leaded glass effects will be found at the upper parts of the windows and in the transoms. The light shining through these transparencies produces a most realistic effect. The roofs are firmly held in place with an ornamental screw—easily removable so that the electric lamp in the interior can be reached.

Many of the models have miniature tanks affixed to the bottom as well as brass steps and hand rails and with the exception of a few of the lowest priced "O" Gauge cars, are all equipped with the new Lionel Automatic Coupler. The rear platforms of observation cars are made of ornamental sheet brass, highly polished.

All cars are mounted on scientifically designed trucks with perfectly aligned nickeled wheels and axles. They operate without friction and are so absolutely true that they will not derail even when travelling at a high rate of speed. All the desirable features mentioned above will be seen by referring to the illustration and indications on page 9.

Six-Wheel Trucks and Nickeled Journals are Features of some of Our New Passenger Cars.

No. 319 Pullman Car—Same size as No. 320 Mail and Baggage Car and No. 322 Observation Car

Above cars are similar in construction to pullman and observation cars Nos. 337, 338, 339 and 341 listed on page 29.

No. 610 Pullman Car—Same size as No. 612 Observation Car.

No. 32 Mail Car—Same size as No. 31 Pullman and Baggage Car, No. 35 Pullman and No. 36 Observation Car.

These Are Real Passenger Cars in Miniature—Replete with Realistic Details

Prices of Lionel "All-Steel" Passenger and Mail Cars

(See Opposite Page for Illustrations)

Reg. U. S. Pat. Office

For Lionel "O" Gauge Track 1⅜ Inches Wide

No. 600 Pullman Car
7 inches long, 3 inches high . . . . . . Price $ .50
Code word "HORNBY"   Western Price $ .60

No. 629 Pullman Car
7¾ inches long, 3½ inches high . . . Price $ .60
Code Word "FAME"   Western Price $ .70

No. 630 Observation Car
7¾ inches long, 3½ inches high . . . Price $ .60
Code Word "IDEAL"   Western Price $ .70
Above three cars are mounted on a four-wheel truck and are for use with Locomotives Nos. 150, 152 and 153.

No. 603 Illuminated Pullman Car
Complete with electric lamp. Car is 8 inches long, 3⅜ inches high . . . . Price $1.35
Code Word "BURTON"   Western Price $1.70

No. 604 Illuminated Observation Car
Complete with electric lamp. Car is 8 inches long, 3⅜ inches high . . . . Price $1.50
Code Word "MONARCH"   Western Price $1.80
Above two cars are mounted on double four-wheel trucks and are for use with Locomotives Nos. 150, 152, 153 and 253.

No. 610 Illuminated Pullman Car
Complete with electric lamp. Car is 9 inches long, 4 inches high . . . . Price $2.95
Code Word "EALING"   Western Price $3.50

No. 612 Illuminated Observation Car
Complete with electric lamp. Car is 9 inches long, 4 inches high . . . . Price $3.15
Code Word "WALTON"   Western Price $3.70
Above two cars are mounted on double four-wheel trucks and are for use with Locomotives Nos. 251, 253, 254 and 256.

No. 605 Illuminated Pullman Car
Complete with electric lamp. Car is 10½ inches long, 4½ inches high . . . . Price $3.25
Code Word "NOVA"   Western Price $4.00

No. 606 Illuminated Observation Car
Complete with electric lamp. Car is 10½ inches long, 4½ inches high . . . . Price $3.50
Code Word "MODE"   Western Price $4.25
Above two cars are mounted on double four-wheel trucks and are for use with Locomotives Nos. 251, 254 and 256.

No. 710 Illuminated Pullman Car
Complete with electric lamp. Car is 12½ inches long, 4¾ inches high . . . . Price $3.75
Code Word "HOLLY"   Western Price $4.50

No. 712 Illuminated Observation Car
Complete with electric lamp. Car is 12½ inches long, 4¾ inches high . . . . Price $3.85
Code Word "RISE"   Western Price $4.70
Above two cars are mounted on double four-wheel trucks and are for use with Locomotives Nos. 251, 254 and 256.

For "Lionel Standard" Track 2¼ Inches Wide

No. 31 Illuminated Pullman and Baggage Car
Complete with electric lamp. Car is 11½ inches long, 5 inches high . . . . Price $3.75
Code Word "CAPI"   Western Price $4.50

No. 32 Mail Car
Car is 11½ inches long, 5 inches high . . Price $3.35
Code Word "BILL"   Western Price $4.00

No. 35 Illuminated Pullman Car
Complete with electric lamp. Car is 11½ inches long, 5 inches high . . . . Price $3.75
Code Word "CAMDEN"   Western Price $4.50

No. 36 Illuminated Observation Car
Complete with electric lamp. Car is 11½ inches long, 5 inches high . . . . Price $3.85
Code Word "FLINT"   Western Price $4.70
Above four cars are mounted on double four-wheel trucks and are for use with Locomotives Nos. 8, 10, 318 and 380.

No. 337 Illuminated Pullman Car
Complete with electric lamp. Car is 14 inches long, 5¼ inches high . . . . Price $4.25
Code Word "PASS"   Western Price $5.00

No. 338 Illuminated Observation Car
Complete with electric lamp. Car is 14 inches long, 5¼ inches high . . . . Price $4.50
Code Word "ORBIT"   Western Price $5.50

No. 339 Illuminated Pullman Car
Complete with electric lamp. Car is 14 inches long, 5¼ inches high . . . . Price $4.50
Code Word "STAR"   Western Price $5.50

No. 341 Illuminated Observation Car
Complete with electric lamp. Car is 14 inches long, 5¼ inches high . . . . Price $5.00
Code Word "LEO"   Western Price $6.00
Above four cars are mounted on double four-wheel trucks and are for use with Locomotives Nos. 8, 10, 318 and 380.

No. 319 Illuminated Pullman Car
Complete with electric lamp. Car is 15 inches long, 5½ inches high . . . . Price $5.00
Code Word "COTT"   Western Price $6.00

No. 320 Illuminated Mail and Baggage Car
Complete with electric headlight. Car is 15 inches long, 5½ inches high . . . . . Price $5.85
Code Word "TALL"   Western Price $7.00

No. 322 Illuminated Observation Car
Complete with electric lamp. Car is 15 inches long, 5½ inches high . . . . Price $5.85
Code Word "JANE"   Western Price $7.00
Above three cars are mounted on double four-wheel trucks and are for use with Locomotives Nos. 10, 318 and 380.

No. 18 Illuminated Pullman Car
Complete with electric lamp. Car is 16½ inches long, 6 inches high . . . . Price $6.75
Code Word "PHILA"   Western Price $8.00

No. 19 Illuminated Pullman and Baggage Car
Complete with electric lamp. Car is 16½ inches long, 6 inches high . . . . Price $7.50
Code Word "TROY"   Western Price $9.00

No. 190 Illuminated Observation Car
Complete with electric lamp. Car is 16½ inches long, 6 inches high . . . . Price $7.50
Code Word "VIRGINIA"   Western Price $9.00
Above three cars are mounted on double four-wheel trucks and are for use with Locomotives Nos. 380 and 402.

No. 418 Illuminated Pullman Car
Complete with electric lamp. Car is 20 inches long, 6¼ inches high . . . . Price $8.50
Code Word "COMFORT"   Western Price $10.00

No. 419 Illuminated Pullman and Baggage Car
Complete with electric lamp. Car is 20 inches long, 6¼ inches high . . . . Price $8.75
Code Word "COURT"   Western Price $10.50

No. 490 Illuminated Observation Car
Complete with electric lamp. Car is 20 inches long, 6¼ inches high . . . . Price $8.75
Code Word "CABIN"   Western Price $10.50
Above three cars are mounted on double six-wheel trucks and are for use with Locomotive No. 402.

All Cars Listed Above Are Shown Throughout This Catalog in Conjunction with the Various Train Outfits

Lionel "All-Steel" Freight Cars

EXPRESSING the individuality of every style of real commercial freight car has been our aim, and in designing Lionel Freight Cars we have embodied in them the utmost realism. They are constructed entirely of steel and beautifully finished in rich, lasting enamels—not lithographed on flimsy tin. All trucks are flexible, which means that they will not jump the track while running either forward or backward. They move so easily that one of our locomotives will haul a number of them without difficulty. The wheels are made of steel, and are reinforced at the back with heavy steel discs. They are mounted on solid Bessemer steel shafts. No wood enters the construction of these cars. All the roofs are removable and doors slide so that the interior of the cars can be easily reached. Trucks and wheels are nickeled. The construction of all cars is similar in every respect, but vary in size in accordance with the locomotive with which they are intended to be operated. All the cars are hand enameled and trimmed and are appropriately decorated with the "heralds" of the most prominent railroads.

Ballast Car in two sizes for "Lionel Standard" track.

Cattle Car in four sizes. For "Lionel Standard" and "O" Gauge tracks.

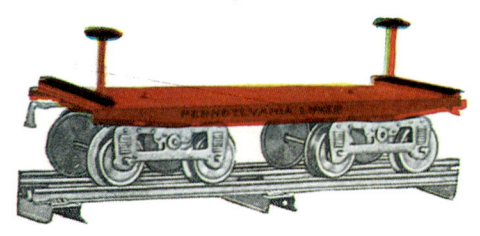

Flat Car in one size for "Lionel Standard" track.

Box Car in four sizes. For "Lionel Standard" and "O" Gauge tracks.

Oil Car in one size for "Lionel Standard" track.

Caboose in four sizes. For "Lionel Standard" and "O" Gauge tracks.

Gondola Car in three sizes. For "Lionel Standard" and "O" Gauge tracks.

Coal Car—For "O" Gauge track.

Oil Car—For "O" Gauge track.

A Combination of These Freight Cars Behind a Lionel Locomotive Makes an Extremely Realistic Train

Prices of Lionel "All-Steel" Freight Cars

(See Opposite Page for Illustrations)

Reg. U. S. Pat. Office

For Lionel "O" Gauge Track 1⅜ Inches Wide

For "Lionel Standard" Track 2¼ Inches Wide

No. 800 Box Car
7 inches long, 3 inches high . . . . Price $ .50
Code Word "CHANDLER"   Western Price $ .60

No. 801 Caboose
7 inches long, 3¼ inches high . . . . Price $ .50
Code Word "CONNERTON"   Western Price $ .60

No. 802 Cattle Car
7 inches long, 3 inches high . . . . Price $ .50
Code Word "CHICKASAW"   Western Price $ .60

No. 803 Coal Car
7 inches long, 3 inches high . . . . Price $ .65
Code Word "LOAD"   Western Price $ .80

No. 804 Oil Car
7 inches long, 3½ inches high . . . . Price $ .60
Code Word "FUEL"   Western Price $ .70

No. 901 Gondola Car
7 inches long, 2 inches high . . . . Price $ .40
Code Word "CHIMES"   Western Price $ .50

Above six cars mounted on a four-wheel truck are for use with Locomotives Nos. 150, 152, 153 and 253

No. 820 Box Car
8¼ inches long, 3½ inches high . . . . Price $1.25
Code Word "ECOLA"   Western Price $1.50

No. 821 Cattle Car
8¼ inches long, 3½ inches high . . . . Price $1.25
Code Word "STEER"   Western Price $1.50

No. 822 Caboose
8¼ inches long, 3¾ inches high . . . . Price $1.25
Code Word "ELIXIR"   Western Price $1.50

Above three cars are mounted on double four-wheel trucks and are for use with Locomotives Nos. 152, 153, 251, 253 and 254.

No. 112 Gondola Car
9¾ inches long, 2½ inches high . . . . Price $1.50
Code Word "ELMIRA"   Western Price $1.80

No. 113 Cattle Car
9¾ inches long, 4½ inches high . . . . Price $2.10
Code Word "SYRACUSE"   Western Price $2.50

No. 114 Box Car
9¾ inches long, 4½ inches high . . . . Price $2.10
Code Word "HAZLETON"   Western Price $2.50

No. 116 Ballast Car
9¾ inches long, 3¾ inches high . . . . Price $2.10
Code Word "SCRANTON"   Western Price $2.50

No. 117 Caboose
9¾ inches long, 4¾ inches high . . . . Price $2.10
Code Word "TOLEDO"   Western Price $2.50

Above five cars are mounted on double four-wheel trucks and are for use with Locomotives Nos. 8, 10, 318 and 380.

No. 11 Flat Car
11 inches long, 3½ inches high . . . Price $2.10
Code Word "MASS"   Western Price $2.50

No. 12 Gondola Car
11 inches long, 3½ inches high . . . Price $2.95
Code Word "VERMONT"   Western Price $3.50

No. 13 Cattle Car
11 inches long, 5½ inches high . . . Price $3.35
Code Word "HAMPSHIRE"   Western Price $4.00

No. 14 Box Car
11 inches long, 5½ inches high . . . Price $3.35
Code Word "MAINE"   Western Price $4.00

No. 15 Oil Car
11 inches long, 5¼ inches high . . . Price $3.35
Code Word "QUEBEC"   Western Price $4.00

No. 16 Ballast Car
11 inches long, 4¾ inches high . . . Price $3.35
Code Word "ONTARIO"   Western Price $4.00

No. 17 Caboose
11 inches long, 6½ inches high . . . . Price $3.35
Code Word "TORONTO"   Western Price $4.00

Above seven cars are mounted on double four-wheel trucks and are for use with Locomotives Nos. 318, 380 and 402.

The Freight Cars Listed Here Are Shown Made Up Into Various Train Outfits Throughout This Catalog

Lionel "All-Steel" Lamp Posts—Lamp Assortment—Renewal Lamps

NO miniature railroad is complete without the addition of Lionel lamp posts, which are faithful reproductions of boulevard and street lamp posts seen everywhere. All Lionel lamp posts are substantially constructed of steel throughout—they won't bend or break. The binding posts to which electrical connections are made are conveniently situated and are securely fastened and perfectly insulated.

LAMP ASSORTMENT No. 111
We supply Lionel dealers with a handsome cabinet of renewal lamps for use in headlight and all electrically illuminated accessories. These lamps are of the finest quality and are supplied in 8 and 14 volts.
Fifty assorted lamps are packed in each cabinet. The chart on the inside cover gives valuable information as to the uses f the various lamps. Each lamp is packed in a wooden container.

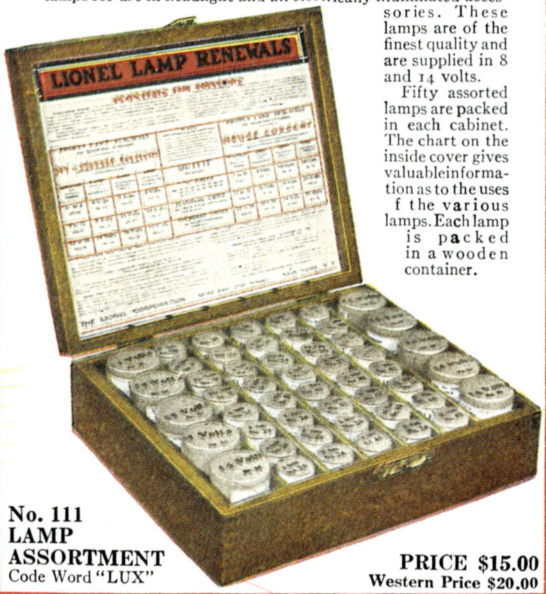

No. 111 LAMP ASSORTMENT
Code Word "LUX"
PRICE $15.00
Western Price $20.00

THERE is no chance of short circuit with Lionel lamp posts, for great care is used in their construction and every one is thoroughly tested before leaving the factory. The globes supplied with all lamp posts are in exact proportion to the size of the posts. It is impossible to secure any other make of lamp post that has the dignity and grace of design to be found in the Lionel lamp posts illustrated below.

SEPARATE RENEWAL LAMPS
(Each Lamp Packed in Wooden Container)

No. 24—Round lamp, clear glass, half inch diameter, 8 volts.
Price .... $ .30
Code Word "CAMBRIDGE"   Western Price $ .40

No. 26—Round lamp, clear glass, half inch diameter, 14 volts.
Price .... $ .30
Code Word "OXFORD"   Western Price $ .40

Above two lamps are for use in headlights and all electrically illuminated accessories.

No. 55—Pear-shaped lamp, frosted, three-quarter inch diameter, 14 volts. Price .... $ .30
Code Word "LIT"   Western Price $ .40

Above lamp is for use in lamp posts Nos. 58 and 59.

No. 30—Pear-shaped lamp, frosted, one inch diamter, 14 volts.
Price .... $ .30
Code Word "KINGS"   Western Price $ .40

Above lamp is for use in lamp posts Nos. 61 and 67, also for outside light brackets of Station No. 124

Lamp Post No. 67—13 inches high. Complete with two electric globes.
Price $2.95
Western Price $3.50
Code Word "EDMUNDS"

Lamp Post No. 58—7⅜ inches high. Complete with globe.
Price $1.25
Western Price $1.50
Code Word "JENNY"

Lamp Post No. 56—8¾ inches high. The top is easily removable so that the lamp can be renewed when necessary. Complete with lamp.
Price $1.65
Western Price $2.00
Code Word "SHINE"

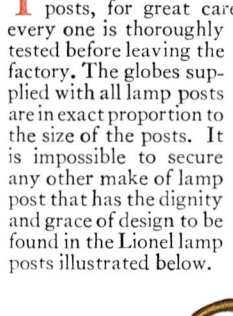

Lamp Post No. 57—7½ inches high. The top is easily removable so that the lamp can be renewed when necessary. Complete with lamp.
Price $1.65
Western Price $2.00
Code Word "CHEERY"

Lamp Post No. 59—Similar in design to No. 61, but is 8¾ inches high. Complete with globe.
Price $1.50
Western Price $1.80
Code Word "BRIGHT"

Lamp Post No. 61—13 inches high. Complete with electric globe.
Price $2.10
Western Price $2.50
Code Word "INDIANA"

Every Lionel Lamp Post Conforms in Size to the Various Train Outfits Shown in This Book

"All-Steel" Bridges for "Lionel Standard" and "O" Gauge Track

Reg. U. S. Pat. Office

O items in the Lionel Line have met with such success since their introduction as the Lionel all-steel bridges. The construction and appearance place them in a class by themselves. No illustration can do justice to the beautiful appearance and sturdy construction of these bridges. They are modeled closely after all the big railroad bridges seen throughout the country. The end piers, the bridge work and roadway are exceptionally sturdy. The architectural designs are graceful and pleasing and the embossing work incorporated in them gives a dignity and realism that cannot be equalled anywhere. Special slots in the roadway hold the track rigidly in place and the spans as well as the approaches are all provided with sections of track either for "O" gauge or "Lionel Standard" track. Bridges can be extended to any length by the addition of the spans shown in the illustrations.

No. 101
No. 101, Center Span and Two Approaches—"Lionel Standard" track. Complete structure is 42 inches long, 6½ inches wide, 6¼ inches high. **Price $5.85**
Code Word "QUEENS" Western Price $7.00

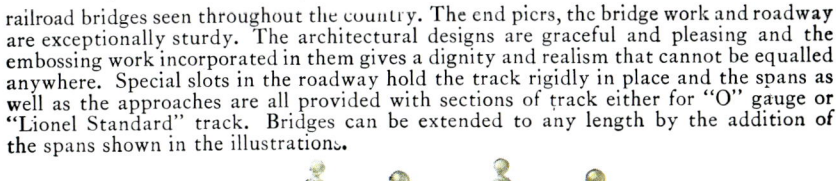

No. 102
No. 102, Two Center Spans and Two Approaches—"Lionel Standard" track. Complete structure is 56 inches long, 6½ inches wide, 6¼ inches high. **Price $8.50**
Code Word "KEEPSIE" Western Price $10.00

No. 103
No. 103, Three Center Spans and Two Approaches—"Lionel Standard" track. Complete structure is 70 inches long, 6½ inches wide, 6¼ inches high. **Price $11.00**
Code Word "LONDON" Western Price $13.00

No. 104
No. 104, Center Span—"Lionel Standard" track. 14 inches long, 6½ inches wide, 6¼ inches high. **Price $3.35**
Western Price $4.00
Code Word "MANHATTAN"

Nos. 100 and 105
No. 100—"Lionel Standard" track. In reproduction of reinforced concrete, 28 inches long, 5½ inches wide, 2 inches high at center . . . . . **Price $2.50**
Western Price $3.00
Code Word "BROOKLYN"

No. 105—"O" gauge. Reinforced concrete work, 21 inches long, 4¼ inches wide, 2 inches high. **Price $1.65**
Western Price $2.00
Code Word "PARIS"

No. 106
No. 106, One Center Span and Two Approaches—"O" gauge. Complete structure is 31½ inches long, 5½ inches wide, 4 inches high. **Price $3.15**
Western Price $4.00
Code Word "CONN"

No. 108
No. 108, Two Center Spans and Two Approaches—"O" gauge. Complete structure is 42 inches long, 5½ inches wide, 4 inches high. **Price $5.50**
Western Price $6.50
Code Word "HOUSA"

No. 109
No. 109, Three Center Spans and Two Approaches—"O" gauge. Complete structure is 52½ inches long, 5½ inches wide, 4 inches high. **Price $7.50**
Western Price $9.00
Code Word "MISS"

No. 110
No. 110, Center Span—"O" gauge. 10½ inches long, 5½ inches wide, 4 inches high. **Price $2.50**
Code Word "WILLIAMS" Western Price $3.00

Lionel Trains Look Extremely Realistic Gliding Over These Sturdy, Well-Designed Bridges

Lionel "All-Steel" Stations—Bungalows—Villas—Signal Tower

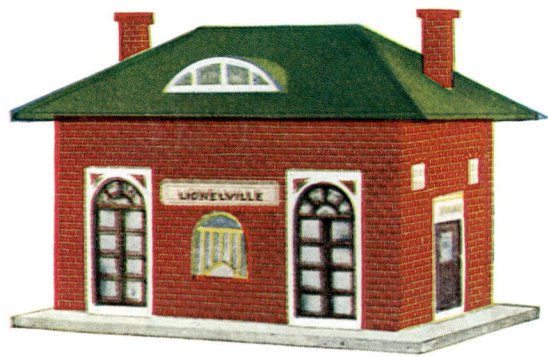

LIONEL all-steel houses and stations are substantially constructed and beautifully finished in a variety of durable enamels. They are so wonderfully proportioned that they have the appearance of real houses and stations in miniature. The die and embossing work, the inserted windows, the chimney stacks, roofs and entrances make them stand far above any similar toy ever introduced.

Interior Illumination—Some of the numbers listed on these pages have interior and outside lights complete with brackets, electric lamps and wires. This further adds to the realism and produces a wonderful effect.

Station No. 121—Has no lighting system. Dimensions: 13½ inches long, 9 inches wide, 13 inches high.
          Price $5.00
        Western Price $6.50
    Code Word "UNION"

Station No. 122—Has inside illumination. Furnished with complete wiring circuit ready to attach to batteries, transformer, or reducer. Wires extend through wall. Complete with one 14-volt globe and nickeled center fixture. Same size as No. 121 . . . . **Price $6.75**
        Western Price $8.00
    Code Word "CENTRAL"

Station No. 124, De Luxe Model—This number has two platform corner lights with reflectors, all finished in bright brass; and an inside light supported on a nickeled fixture. There is an elegance, grace and architectural dignity to this station difficult to show in an illustration. The corner lighting brackets have specially designed supporting arms—a detail seldom attempted. For use with batteries, transformers or reducers. Equipped with three 14-volt globes. Same size as No. 121 . . . . . . **Price $9.00**
        Western Price $11.00
    Code Word "READING"

Station No. 125—(No interior illumination.) A beautifully proportioned model that retails at an exceedingly low price. The realistic detail must be seen to be appreciated. This station measures 10¼ inches long, 7¼ inches wide and 7 inches high . . . . **Price $4.25**
        Western Price $5.00
    Code Word "ABOARD"

Station No. 126—Same as No. 125 described above, but has interior lighting fixture, lamp and wires ready for attaching to batteries, transformer or reducer . . . **Price $5.00**
        Western Price $6.50
    Code Word "ALIGHT"

Station No. 127—This can be used as a freight station for any size train outfit and will add a completing touch to a railroad layout. It is 7 inches long, 3½ inches wide and 4½ inches high. Complete with interior lighting fixture, lamp and wires ready to attach to batteries, transformer or reducer . . . . **Price $2.95**
        Western Price $3.50
    Code Word "TOWNLY"

Villa No. 189 (illuminated)—Size 5½ inches long, 4⅜ inches wide, 5¾ inches high. Complete with interior lighting fixture, lamp and wires for connecting to batteries, transformer or reducer . . . . **Price $2.95**
        Western Price $3.50
    Code Word "MANSION"

Signal Tower No. 092 (illuminated)—Dimensions: 5 inches long, 4 inches wide, 5½ inches high. Complete with interior lighting fixture, lamp and wires for connecting to batteries, transformer or reducer . . . . **Price $2.10**
        Western Price $2.50
    Code Word "CYRIL"

Nos. 121, 122, 124

Nos. 125, 126

No. 127

No. 092

No. 189

Add These Interesting Accessories to Your Train Layout—They Provide a Completing Touch

Lionel "All-Steel" Villas—Sets of Assorted Houses

FOR **Outdoor Railroads.** Picture the fun that can be had when Lionel houses and stations are placed around a big track-layout in the garden or on any outdoor plot, and used in connection with Lionel Railroad Accessories.

For Model Villages. In this connection the Lionel Houses will be found invaluable. There is no limit to the wonderful effects that can be produced.

Use on Any Kind of Current. Lionel Stations, Bungalows and Villas can be attached to "Multivolt" Transformers for "Alternating" Current or to Lionel Reducers for "Direct" Current and also to dry or storage batteries.

Villa No. 191 (illuminated)—Size 7⅛ in. long, 5⅛ in. wide, 5¼ in. high.
Complete with interior lighting fixture, lamp and wires for connecting to batteries, transformer or reducer.
Price $3.35
Code Word "SOLID"   Western Price $4.00

Bungalow No. 184 (illuminated)—Size 4¾ in. long, 2¾ in. wide, 4 in. high. Complete with lamp and wires for connecting.
Price $1.50
Code Word "HOME"   Western Price $1.80

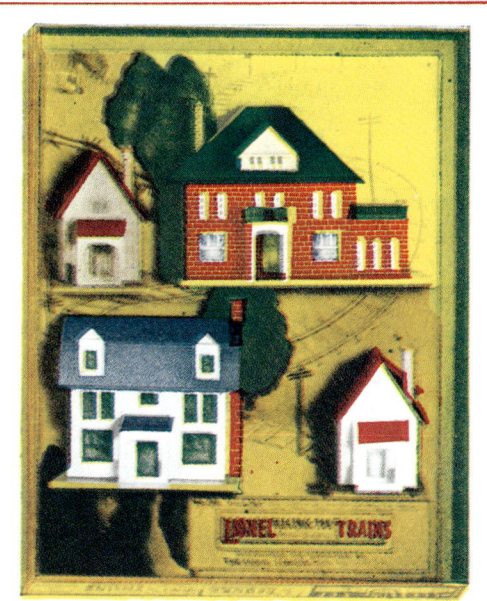

Bungalow Set No. 186—Comprises 5 No. 184 illuminated bungalows, assorted colors, complete with lamps and wires for connecting.
Price $7.50
Western Price $9.00
Code Word "HAMLET"

Set No. 192—Comprises 1 No. 191 Villa, 1 No. 189 Villa and 2 No. 184 Bungalows, complete with interior lights and wires for connecting.
Price $8.75
Western Price $10.50
Code Word "VILLAGE"

No. 184

No. 192

No. 191

No. 186

You Can Build a Complete, Illuminated Village with These Real Miniature Houses

Reg. U. S. Pat. Office

"Lionel Standard" and "O" Gauge Track—"Lockon" Track Contacts

WE have described the strength and details of manufacture of Lionel Track in the introduction to this catalog. We will merely add here the technical facts.

Tested to Carry 110 Volts—Each section of track is tested for insulation on a circuit of 110 volts, consequently it will carry the low voltage necessary to operate our trains without any chance of short-circuiting.

Sections Are Easily Connected—The ends of each section have pin terminals which fit in openings in the adjoining sections. This allows the track to be laid and taken apart without any trouble. One section in each outfit is fitted with a "Lockon" tract contact for batteries, "Multivolt" Transformer or Reducer.

The track is made in straight and curved sections. Any shaped figure may be formed. The curvature of the track is mechanically correct, allowing the cars to run at very high speed without danger of derailing.

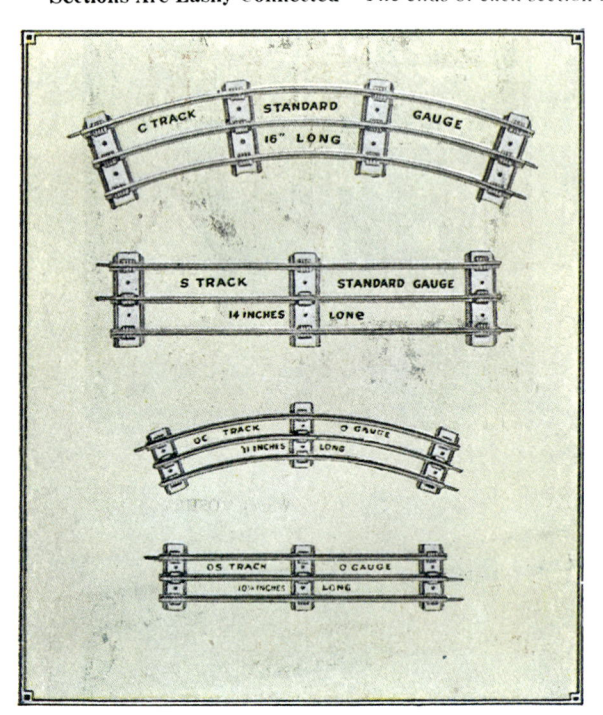

"LIONEL STANDARD" TRACK—2¼ Inches Wide

C, curved track, 16 inches long.
Code Word "BUFF"
Price per section $ .30
Western Price $ .40

S, straight track, 14 inches long.
Code Word "NIAGARA"
Price per section $ .30
Western Price $ .40

Eight No. C Sections make a circle 42 inches in diameter.

LIONEL "O" GAUGE TRACK—1⅜ Inches Wide

OC, curved track, 11 inches long.
Code Word "LEMPS"
Price per section $ .20
Western Price $ .26

OS, straight track, 10¼ inches long.
Code Word "GLENBURN"
Price per section $ .20
Western Price $ .26

Eight No. OC Sections make a circle 30 inches in diameter.

"LOCKON" TRACK CONTACTS For "Lionel Standard" and "O" Gauge

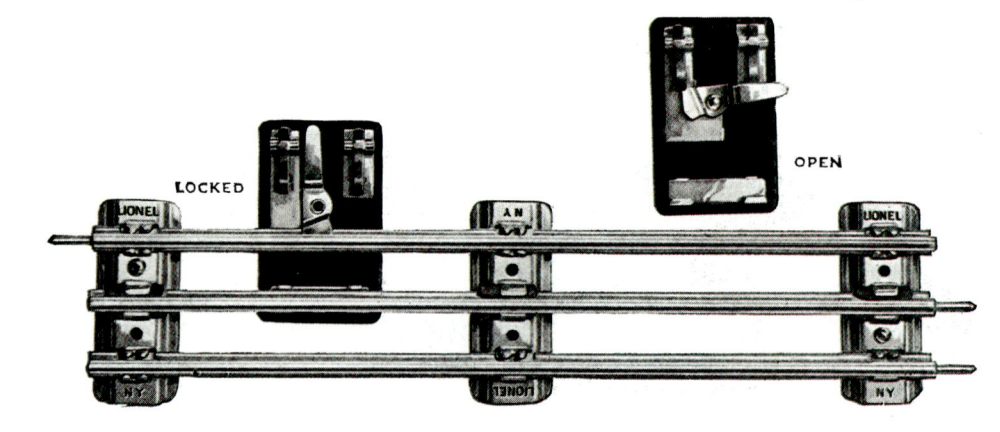

CONNECTING TIE

We show here the method of sliding in the connecting tie. This is one of our recent improvements. It binds the ties rigidly together so that sections cannot pull apart. Yet this can be removed without difficulty—just a slight pull with the thumb and finger.

Every Lionel Train Outfit includes a sufficient number of connecting ties for the amount of track packed with the outfit.

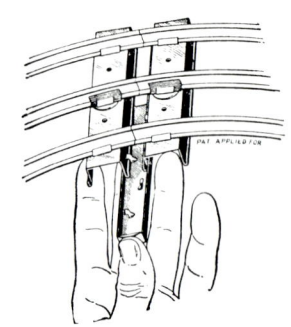

Lionel leadership is again evidenced in this improved device. Considering the fact that numerous electric accessories have been added to the Lionel line, which require connection with the track, these "LOCKON" contacts will readily appeal to the user, for it is no longer necessary to purchase special sections of track to which electrical contacts are affixed.

The "Lockon" contact is attached to the track by simply turning the lever at right angles. The electric connection is as perfect as though the parts were riveted or soldered to the track.

The "Lockon" contact is free from set screws and binding posts. The fingers that hold the wires in place are made of heavy tempered blue steel and are unbreakable. All parts are nickel plated and are mounted on a heavy fibre base.

No. "STC" for "Lionel Standard" Track

Code Word "JUICE"
Price $ .25
Western Price $ .30

No. "OTC" for Lionel "O" Gauge Track

Code Word "JOIN"
Price $ .20
Western Price $ .24

Build Your Miniature Railroad on a Good, Solid Foundation—Lionel Track

[36]

Lionel Track Accessories

ALL Lionel track accessories are perfectly insulated and are mounted on a heavy steel base which gives them great strength and will enable them to withstand hard usage.

ACCESSORIES
For "Lionel Standard" Track—2¼ Inches

Switch No. 22—(Right and Left Hand). The lever which moves the rails also sets signals and locks all mechanism. Signal lanterns have red and green discs. Length of switch, 16½ inches; width, 8 inches; height, 4½ inches. Connects with track in same manner as straight or curved sections.
Price per Pair, $5.00
Western Price $6.00
Code Word "NASHVILLE"

Electric Lighted Switch No. 21—(Right and Left Hand). This is similar in construction to No. 22 described above, but is equipped with an electric signal, having an electric bulb which can be easily removed. The light shining through the lantern shows red and green illuminated signals.
Price per Pair, $6.75
Western Price $8.00
Code Word "WINTERVILLE"

Crossing No. 20—For use in conjunction with Switches, enabling the formation of figure "8" and figure "8" loop. Measures 12 inches square. Cross rails are mounted on a solid base.
Price $1.25
Western Price $1.50
Code Word "BOSTON"

Bumper No. 23—An indispensable accessory for terminals or sidings. Has two spring plungers which absorb shock when car strikes it. Length, 14 inches; height, 3 inches. The Bumper frame can be removed from the track and replaced at any point desired.
Price $1.25
Western Price $1.50
Code Word "PROVIDENCE"

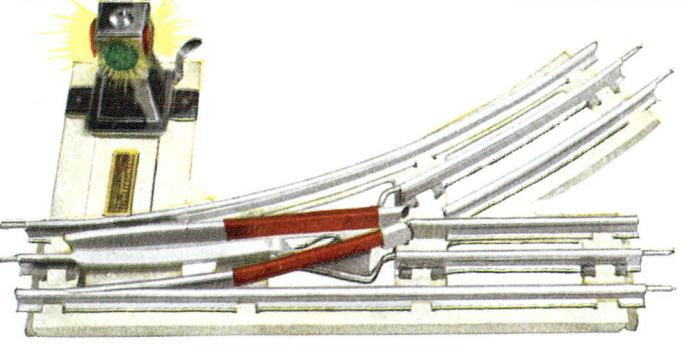

IMPROVED LIONEL SWITCHES

We are particularly desirous of drawing attention to the great improvement in the construction of our switches. Notwithstanding this improvement, prices have not been increased.

As will be seen from the illustration, the improvement consists of the insertion of two heavy fibre strips at the points where the rails cross.

By the insertion of these fibre strips all danger of short-circuit is eliminated. A train passing over these points does not slow up nor does the headlight flicker or go out.

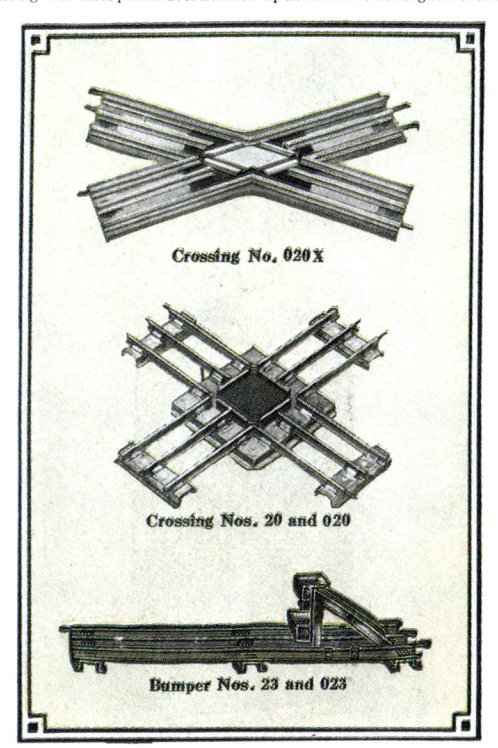

Crossing No. 020X
Crossing Nos. 20 and 020
Bumper Nos. 23 and 023

Every conceivable shape or figure can be made with the scientifically planned Lionel Track accessories illustrated on this page. It is always great fun to add to your railroad equipment.

ACCESSORIES
For Lionel "O" Gauge Track—1⅜ Inches

Switch No. 022—(Right and Left Hand). Construction is similar to No. 22 Switch described opposite. Length, 11½ inches; width, 5½ inches; height, 3 inches.
Price per Pair, $3.75
Western Price $4.50
Code Word "SPENCER"

Electric Lighted Switch No. 021—(Right and Left Hand). Similar in construction to No. 21 Switch described opposite. Length, 11½ inches; width, 5½ inches; height, 3 inches.
Price per Pair, $5.00
Western Price $6.00
Code Word "MOSHER"

Crossing No. 020—Similar in construction to No. 20 Crossing described opposite. Measures 10¼ inches square.
Price $1.00
Western Price $1.20
Code Word "ORLAND"

Crossing No. 020X—This is a 45-degree crossing; forms the figure "8" when using all curved track. It occupies less space than the No. 020 Crossing.
Price $1.50
Western Price $1.80
Code Word "CROSS"

Bumper No. 023—Same construction as No. 23 Bumper described opposite. Length, 10¼ inches; height, 2 inches.
Price $ .80
Western Price $1.00
Code Word "DELTON"

See Page 41 for the Great Variety of Figures Which Can Be Formed with These Accessories

Lionel Automatic Train Control—Electric Block Signal

The Greatest Achievement in Miniature Electric Train Engineering

The Lionel Automatic Train Control

THE simplest and most amazing accessory ever invented.

Place it at any desired spot in the track formation. The train approaches! The red signal light shows vividly! The train stops! It's absolutely automatic. After an interval of from 2 to 30 seconds the red signal light turns to green. Line's clear! All aboard! The train is on its way again.

Can you imagine anything more realistic? Is there anything in the world that will increase your fun with Electric Trains more than this marvelous accessory? The Lionel Automatic Train Control will delight the heart of every boy.

Its action is absolutely automatic and positive—the length of the interval between stopping and starting is fixed before the train is set in motion—after that it functions continuously and does not require any attention on the part of the operator.

The Lionel Automatic Train Control is substantially constructed of metal on the lines of the most modern electric signals used on standard railroads. It is 10½ inches high. Great detail is incorporated in the design as the illustration shows. The lantern case is easily removable so that the two interior lamps can be readily replaced. Green and red discs are permanently affixed in the openings so that our standard clear bulbs can be used for replacement. A metal ladder joins the upper and lower portions of the superstructure and faithfully carries out the true details of these signals. The mechanism is mounted on a solid piece of insulating material and is entirely concealed in the base of the signal. Posts for connecting to the track are plainly marked so that no difficulty is experienced in making the proper connections. A small fibre knob on the rear of the base is used for regulating the length of time the train stops at any given point. Necessary "Lockon" connections, wire and fibre insulating pins are furnished with each Automatic Train Control.

The Lionel Automatic Train Control can be used either on "O" Gauge or "Lionel Standard" track and will operate on dry or storage batteries, reduced direct, or reduced alternating current.

Lionel Automatic Train Control No. 078 for "O" Gauge Track—Complete with OTC "Lockon" contacts and connecting wires. Attractively packed with directions for operating . . . . Price $5.00
Code Word "HEAVE" Western Price $6.00

Lionel Automatic Train Control No. 78 for "Lionel Standard" Track—Complete with STC "Lockon" contacts and connecting wires. Attractively packed with directions for operating . . . . Price $5.00
Code Word "WEAVE" Western Price $6.00

Nos. 78, 078

Nos. 76 and 076 Block Signals

THIS new Lionel accessory will add life and realism to any train outfit. It consists of a steel standard (8¾ inches high) to which are attached two electric illuminated lanterns showing red and green signals.

When the train passes over the special sections of track supplied with the signal, the green lantern lights up, indicating "Track Clear", and after it leaves the first section of special track the red light shows, indicating "Stop" to the train following. This red light goes out as soon as the train leaves the second special section of track, the same as the block signals operating on real railroads.

In order to carry out true detail several of these block signals can be used at different points of the track formation.

No. 076 Block Signal for "O" Gauge Track—Complete with lamps, two special sections of OSS track, connecting wires and directions for operating . . . . . Price $3.15
Western Price $3.70
Code Word "FORWARD"

No. 76 Block Signal for "Lionel Standard" Track—Complete with lamps, two special sections of SS track, connecting wires and directions for operating . . . . Price $3.35
Western Price $4.00
Code Word "ONWARD"

Nos. 76, 076

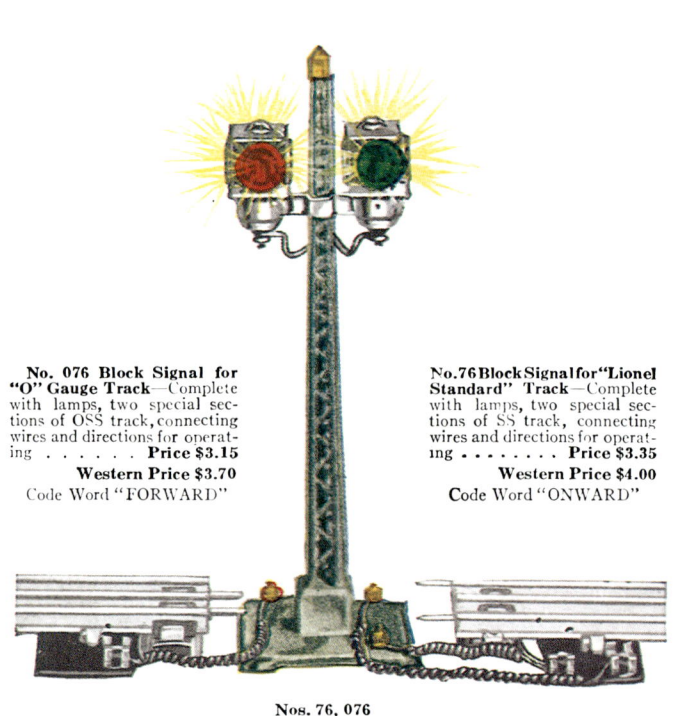

The Only Miniature Railroad Accessories That Are Positively Automatic in Action

Lionel Accessories—Electrically Operated and Electrically Illuminated

Nos. 65 and 66 Semaphores—The base is made of heavy sheet steel. The post, semaphore arms and ladder are also constructed of steel. The colored discs which are securely fastened to the semaphore arms show "Danger", "Clear" or "Caution" signals. The electric lamps are enclosed in beautifully enameled steel lanterns, which are removable so that lamps can be easily renewed. A metal finger holds these lantern caps in place. The levers which operate the signal arms are fastened to the base and are connected to rods running up beneath the ladder. The wiring and insulation are inside the post and short circuits are impossible. The electric lamps shining through the colored discs present a wonderfully realistic effect.

Nos. 69 and 069 Warning Signals—A substantially constructed, fully nickeled bell is mounted on an ornamental post bearing a heavy brass warning sign. A specially constructed section of track is supplied to which the warning signal is connected, wires being also provided for the purpose. The electric bell rings as long as the locomotive and cars pass over the special section of track, and the bell automatically stops ringing when the train has passed. The signal post is made of steel and is fastened to a heavy steel base which has holes for fastening to floor or platform.

Nos. 77 and 077 Crossing Gates—These are exact reproductions of the real ones used at all grade crossings. They are of steel construction throughout, finished in handsome black enamel with nickeled top on the case that contains the mechanism. The special section of track provided with the crossing gates is connected with the track layout in the usual manner. While the train is on this section the gates close and they automatically open again as soon as the train has passed. These gates can be used singly or in pairs. The special track can be placed a few sections away from the gates so that they will operate some time before the train approaches. The raising and lowering of these gates in connection with the operation of the train produces an effect of great realism.

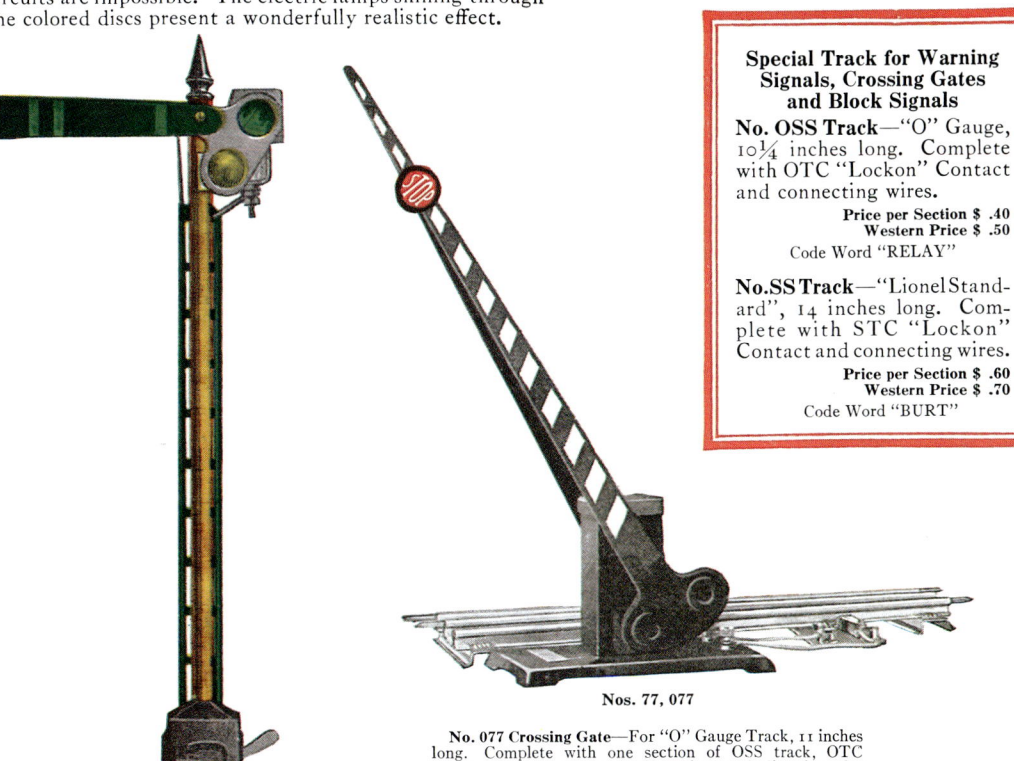

Special Track for Warning Signals, Crossing Gates and Block Signals

No. OSS Track—"O" Gauge, 10¼ inches long. Complete with OTC "Lockon" Contact and connecting wires.
Price per Section $ .40
Western Price $ .50
Code Word "RELAY"

No. SS Track—"Lionel Standard", 14 inches long. Complete with STC "Lockon" Contact and connecting wires.
Price per Section $ .60
Western Price $ .70
Code Word "BURT"

No. 65

No. 65 Semaphore—14 inches high. Has one signal arm. Complete with electric lamp. **Price $2.50**
Western Price $3.00
Code Word "TOWER"

Nos. 77, 077

No. 077 Crossing Gate—For "O" Gauge Track, 11 inches long. Complete with one section of OSS track, OTC "Lockon" Contact, connecting wires and directions for operating.
Price $4.00
Western Price $4.80
Code Word "ADVANCE"

No. 77 Crossing Gate—For "Lionel Standard" Track, 11 inches long. Complete with one section of SS track, STC "Lockon" Contact, connecting wires and directions for operating.
Price $4.25
Western Price $5.00
Code Word "TARRY"

No. 69, 069

No. 069 Warning Signal—for "O" Gauge Track, 8¾ inches high. Complete with one section of OSS track, OTC "Lockon" Contact, connecting wires and directions for operating.
Price $3.15
Western Price $3.70
Code Word "RINGER"

No. 69 Warning Signal—For "Lionel Standard" Track, 8¾ inches high. Complete with one section of SS track, STC "Lockon" Contact, connecting wires and directions for operating.
Price $3.35
Western Price $4.00
Code Word "BEWARE"

No. 66

No. 66 Semaphore—14 inches high. Has two signal arms. Complete with electric lamps. **Price $3.75**
Western Price $4.50
Code Word "LEMPSTER"

A Completing Touch for Any Miniature Railroad—the Wonderful Lionel Accessories Shown Here

Lionel Accessories—Accessory Sets

LIONEL accessory sets are unquestionably the best constructed as well as the most popular on the market. This is not to be wondered at considering the fact that they are so durable and attractive in design. A miniature railroad layout is considerably enhanced by the addition of a set of telegraph posts placed at regular intervals around the track. Copper wire can be strung from the insulators, producing an effect of great realism.

If the semaphores, lamp post and warning signal which form No. 70 set are added to the train layout the finishing touches are provided. All Lionel accessories are constructed of steel throughout and are beautifully finished.

Outfit No. 70—Comprises two No. 62 Semaphores, one No. 59 Lamp Post, one No. 68 Warning Signal and two globes for the lamp post. Attractively packed.
Price $4.25
Code Word "HOBART"   Western Price $5.00

No. 62 Semaphore—The semaphore arm has three discs—red, green and yellow—and the arm is operated by a lever near the base. Steel construction throughout. Height 8¾ inches, base 2½ inches square.
Price $ .80
Western Price $1.00
Code Word "CAUTION"

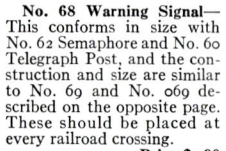

No. 68 Warning Signal—This conforms in size with No. 62 Semaphore and No. 60 Telegraph Post, and the construction and size are similar to No. 69 and No. 069 described on the opposite page. These should be placed at every railroad crossing.
Price $ .90
Western Price $1.10
Code Word "STOP"

Outfit No. 71—Comprises six No. 60 Steel Telegraph Posts as described on this page. Packed in a very attractive box.
Price $3.75
Code Word "USEFUL"   Western Price $4.50

No. 60 Telegraph Post—A companion to No. 62 Semaphore and No. 68 Warning Signal. The arm is equipped with real glass insulators. Height 8¾ inches, base 2½ inches square.
Price $ .65
Western Price $ .80
Code Word "WIRE"

No. 89 Flag Staff—This is substantially constructed of steel and is 14 inches high. The base is 2½ inches square. It is beautifully finished in white enamel and the spire is finished in a rich black. The silk flag supplied with it can be raised or lowered by means of a cord to which it is attached and which is fastened on a hook near the base.
Boys! Place it in front of station or in the centre of a grass plot that may be laid out in connection with a model village or railroad. Let it wave proudly.
Price $ .75
Western Price $ .90
Code Word "ARTHUR"

See How Faithfully Lionel Accessories Are Modeled from Real Railroad Equipment

Reg. U. S. Pat. Office
"Lionel Standard" and "O" Gauge Track Formations

HERE'S loads of fun for everybody—making various track figures with "Lionel Standard" or "O" gauge track. The very foundation of your railroad must be strong. Therefore, use Lionel Track.

Look at the number of figures you can construct—and hundreds more by using straight and curved sections, switches, crossings and bumpers.

Isn't it great to watch your train go over the crossing—then you turn the switch and send it over to the siding—back again at full speed down the straightaway.

Your train will always operate better if you make the curves large in diameter. Always break up the circles as much as possible by inserting straight sections.

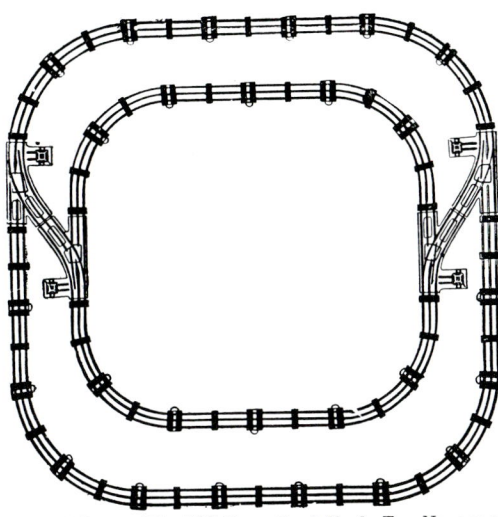

Track Layout OK—"O" Gauge Track Used—Two No. 021 or No. 022 Right Hand Switches, two No. 021 or No. 022 Left Hand Switches, sixteen sections OC curved track, fourteen sections OS straight track. Outside dimensions, 64 inches long and 64 inches wide.

Track Layout SK—"Lionel Standard" Track Used—Two No. 21 or No. 22 Right Hand Switches, two No. 21 or No. 22 Left Hand Switches, sixteen sections C curved track, fourteen sections S straight track. Outside dimensions, 85 inches long and 85 inches wide.

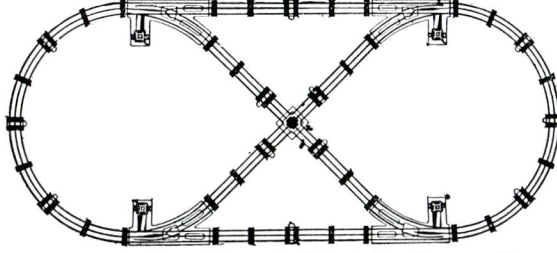

Track Layout OE—"O" Gauge Track Used—Two No. 021 or No. 022 Left Hand Switches, two No. 021 or No. 022 Right Hand Switches, one No. 020 Crossing, eight sections OC curved track, eight sections OS straight track. Outside dimensions, 72 inches long and 30 inches wide.

Track Layout SE—"Lionel Standard" Track Used—Two No. 21 or No. 22 Left Hand Switches, two No. 21 or No. 22 Right Hand Switches, one No. 20 Crossing, eight sections C curved track, eight sections S straight track. Outside dimensions, 100 inches long and 42 inches wide.

WHAT A THRILLING SIGHT IT IS TO SEE YOUR TRAIN GLIDING DOWN THE STRAIGHT STRETCH, OVER THE SWITCHES AND AROUND THE CURVES—IT'S GREAT FUN!

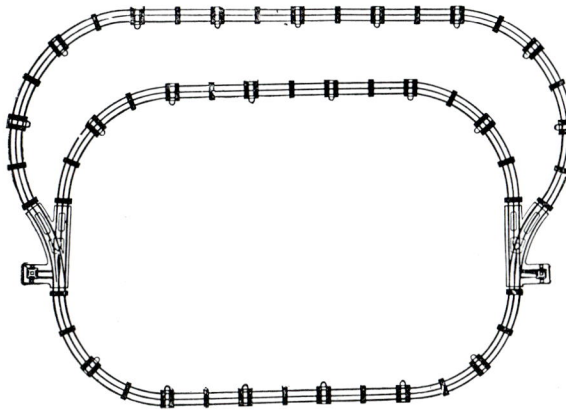

Track Layout OO—"O" Gauge Track Used—One No. 021 or No. 022 Right Hand Switch, one No. 021 or No. 022 Left Hand Switch, fourteen sections OC curved track, ten sections OS straight track. Outside dimensions, 75 inches long and 50 inches wide.

Track Layout SO—"Lionel Standard" Track Used—One No. 21 or No. 22 Right Hand Switch, one No. 21 or No. 22 Left Hand Switch, fourteen sections C curved track, ten sections S straight track. Outside dimensions, 100 inches long and 75 inches wide.

Track Layout OF—"O" Gauge Track Used—One No. 020X Crossing, fourteen sections OC curved track. Outside dimensions, 60 inches long and 30 inches wide.

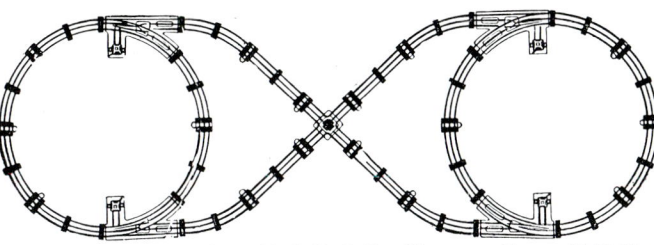

Track Layout OJ—"O" Gauge Track Used—Two No. 021 or No. 022 Right Hand Switches, two No. 021 or No. 022 Left Hand Switches, one No. 020 Crossing, sixteen sections OC curved track, four sections OS straight track. Outside dimensions, 92 inches long and 30 inches wide.

Track Layout SJ—"Lionel Standard" Track Used—Two No. 21 or No. 22 Right Hand Switches, two No. 21 or No. 22 Left Hand Switches, one No. 20 Crossing, sixteen sections C curved track, four sections S straight track. Outside dimensions, 132 inches long and 42 inches wide.

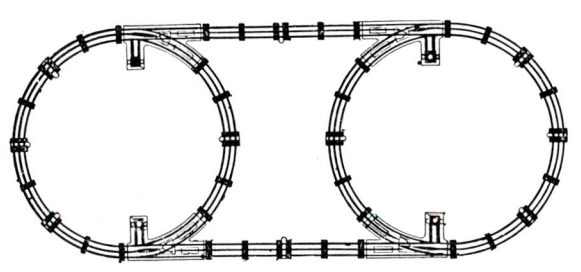

Track Layout OB—"O" Gauge Track Used—Two No. 021 or No. 022 Left Hand Switches, two No. 021 or No. 022 Right Hand Switches, four sections OS straight track, twelve sections OC curved track. Outside dimensions, 72 inches long, 30 inches wide.

Track Layout SB—"Lionel Standard" Track Used—Two No. 21 or No. 22 Left Hand Switches, two No. 21 or No. 22 Right Hand Switches, four sections S straight track, twelve sections C curved track. Outside dimensions, 100 inches long and 42 inches wide.

See Pages 36 and 37 for Prices of Track and All Track Accessories

The New Lionel Scenic Railway—"O" Gauge

THE Lionel Scenic Railway Tables originated by this Corporation several years ago were the best of their kind ever devised. While they were primarily intended for display purposes, they were also in great demand by users of miniature electric railroads who desired complete scenic effects in addition to the train layout. However, price and the cost of shipping prevented their being purchased by all who desired them; therefore we present with great pleasure the new Lionel Scenic Railways—made in sections, that are light in weight, portable and at prices within the reach of all. As the specifications show, we do not charge for the scenic effects such as the base and wiring, mountains and sky background. All the rest of the equipment is listed at our regular catalog prices and these items are the only ones charged for.

No. 198 "O" Gauge Scenic Railway—Details of Construction

The platform or base is made of composition board in two sections, each mounted in a rigid wooden frame. The dimensions over all are 60 inches long and 42 inches deep. The top of the platform is beautifully decorated in colors representing grass plots, roads, etc. Indicating marks show the proper points at which the various accessories are to be placed. The platform is electrically wired so that the illuminated accessories and track can be connected in a few moments. Special large metal tunnels are supplied, realistically painted and embellished with miniature houses and trees as well as mountainous sections, flower beds and grass plots, all made of indestructible sheet steel. Many shrubs, bushes and miniature trees are also furnished, all of which greatly enhance the appearance and detail of these beautiful displays. Three large reproductions of mountains, beautifully decorated, each measuring 36 by 18 inches, form the background of the display, and two additional large panels representing the skyline, measuring 72 by 28 inches, complete the scenic effect.

The entire display is very light in weight and can be easily moved from place to place. The background scenic effects are so placed that the display can either be condensed in size or extended to fit the space in which it is to be used.

SPECIFICATIONS OF SCENIC RAILWAY NO. 198 FOR "O" GAUGE TRACK

ACCESSORIES

1 No. 076 Block Signal	$3.15
1 No. 077 Crossing Gate	4.00
1 No. 069 Warning Signal	3.15
1 No. 56 Lamp Post	1.65
1 No. 57 Lamp Post	1.65
1 No. 58 Lamp Post	1.25
1 No. 89 Flag Staff	.75
1 No. 184 Bungalow	1.50
1 No. 191 Villa	3.35
1 No. 189 Villa	$2.95
1 No. 092 Signal Tower	2.10

ALL STEEL DISPLAY PIECES

1 No. 130 Tunnel	$15.00
1 No. 131 Corner Elevation	4.50
1 No. 132 Corner Grass Plot	2.50
2 No. 133 Heartshape Grass Plots, $1.50 each	3.00
1 No. 135 Circular Grass Plot	1.00

SCENIC EFFECTS SUPPLIED FREE

1 No. 506 Compo board painted platform, completely wired. (2 sections.)
3 No. 509 Compo board mountains.
1 No. 508 Compo board sky background. (2 sections.)
3 No. 505 Trees.
2 No. 504 Bushes.

Price Complete $50.00
Code Word "BEAUTY" Western Price $60.00
Train and Track Are Not Included

Any Lionel "O" Gauge Train Outfit May Be Used With This Scenic Display

The New Scenic Railway for "Lionel Standard" Track

Reg. U. S. Pat. Office

No. 199 Scenic Railway; Details of Construction

ON account of its larger size we have been able to incorporate many more scenic details, and to supply a larger amount of accessories in this scenic railway for "Lionel Standard" Track. The general construction and appearance are similar to the "O" Gauge Scenic Railway described on the opposite page.

The platform of the "Lionel Standard" Scenic Railway is made in three sections and measures 90 inches long by 60 inches deep. The dimensions of the three mountains and the skyline background are the same as those supplied with "O" Gauge Scenic Railway No. 198.

By referring to the specifications it will be seen that in this case also the scenic effects are supplied free, the complete price taking in only the accessories supplied.

No amount of description can do adequate justice to the beauty of the new Lionel Scenic Displays. They are decorated in brilliant and harmonizing colors, while the art work is of the highest possible character.

DEALERS—No greater aid to increasing your toy sales has ever been offered. The flexibility of the new Lionel Scenic Railways makes them particularly adaptable to any size show window or store fixture, while their low price means but a small investment when compared with their sales promoting possibilities. The demand is already tremendous—place your order at once so that you will be sure to obtain them in ample time for holiday needs.

SPECIFICATIONS OF SCENIC RAILWAY NO. 199 FOR "LIONEL STANDARD" TRACK

ACCESSORIES
1 No. 124 Station	$9.00
1 No. 189 Villa	2.95
3 No. 191 Villas, $3.35	10.05
3 No. 184 Bungalows, $1.50	4.50
1 No. 092 Signal Tower	2.10
5 No. 60 Telegraph Posts, $0.65	3.25
2 No. 59 Lamp Posts, $1.50	3.00
3 No. 58 Lamp Posts, $1.25	3.75
1 No. 57 Lamp Post	1.65
1 No. 89 Flag Staff	.75
1 No. 66 Semaphore	$3.75
1 No. 78 Automatic Control	5.00
1 No. 77 Crossing Gate	4.25
1 No. 69 Warning Signal	3.35
1 No. 120 Tunnel	5.85

ALL STEEL DISPLAY PIECES
1 No. 136 Elevation (large)	$10.00
1 No. 131 Corner Elevation	4.50
1 No. 132 Corner Grass Plot	2.50

Train and Track Are Not Included

2 No. 133 Heartshape Grass Plots, $1.50	$3.00
2 No. 135 Circular Grass Plots, $1.00	2.00

SCENIC EFFECTS SUPPLIED FREE
1 No. 507 Compo board painted platform, completely wired. (3 sections.)
3 No. 509 Compo board mountains.
1 No. 508 Compo board sky background. (2 sections.)
16 No. 505 Trees.
8 No. 504 Bushes.

Code Word "NATURE"

Price Complete $80.00
Western Price $100.00

Any "Lionel Standard" Train May Be Used With This Scenic Display

[43]

1925

THE LIONEL CORPORATION

THE HOME OF

Offices and Display Rooms
48-52 EAST TWENTY-FIRST STREET
NEW YORK, N. Y.

LIONEL ELECTRIC TRAINS
MODEL RAILROAD ACCESSORIES
"MULTIVOLT" TRANSFORMERS

Factories and Service Departments
SOUTH TWENTY-FIRST STREET
IRVINGTON, N. J.

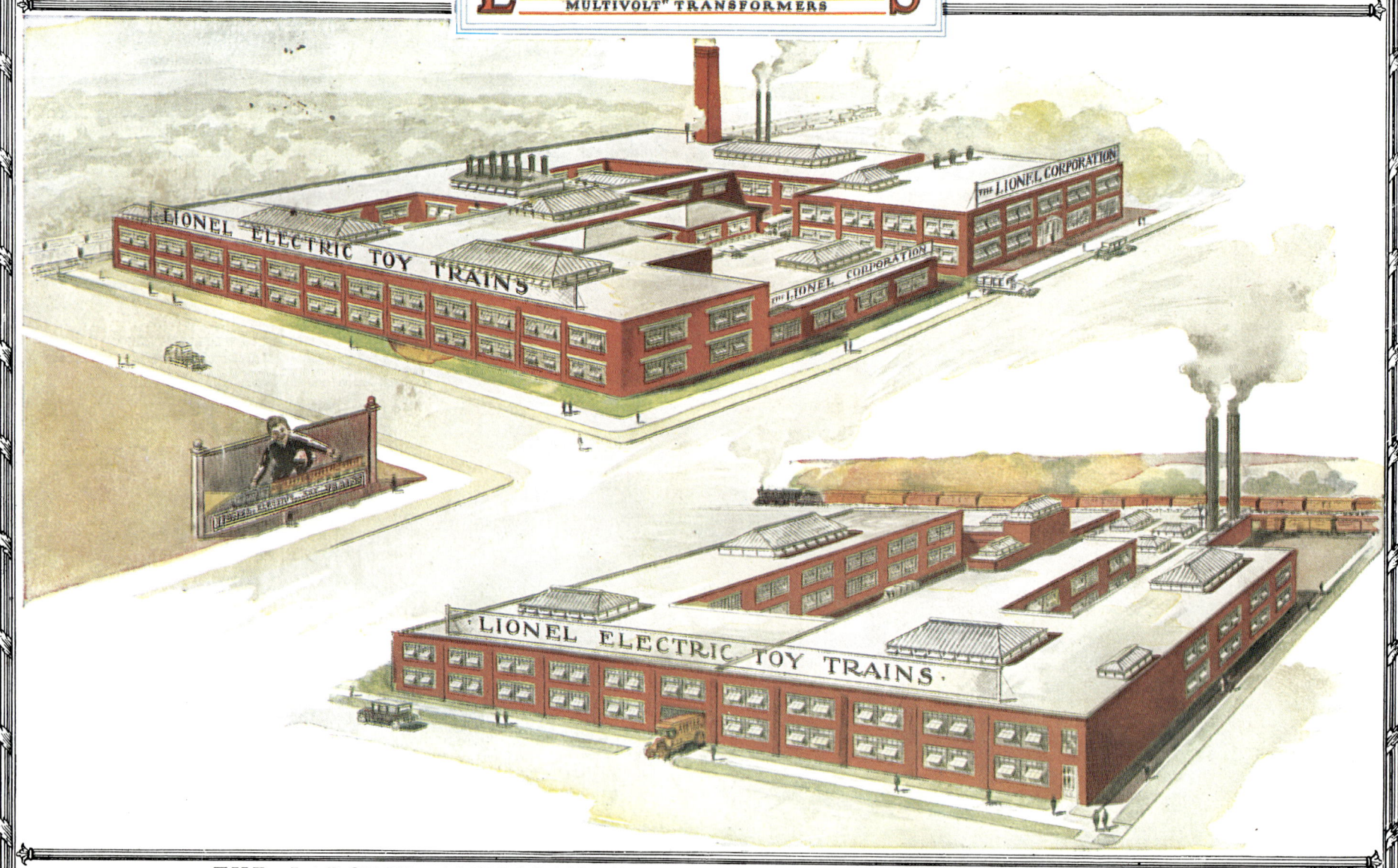

THE LARGEST AMERICAN FACTORIES EXCLUSIVELY PRODUCING MODEL ELECTRIC TRAINS AND RAILROAD EQUIPMENT

The entire contents of this catalog copyrighted 1925 by The Lionel Corporation, New York, N. Y.

LIONEL ELECTRIC TRAINS
MODEL RAILROAD
ACCESSORIES
"MULTIVOLT" TRANSFORMERS
LIONEL CITY
WALTER BEACH HUMPHREY

1926

LIONEL ELECTRIC TRAINS
MODEL RAILROAD ACCESSORIES
"MULTIVOLT" TRANSFORMERS

The Thrill of Lionel Railroading

BRINGING joy to the youth of America has been the good fortune of Lionel for twenty-six years. Our products have helped them to keep pace with the development of electric traction while providing healthful fun and education.

The day of "toy" trains is past—Lionel Model Electric Trains, faithful reproductions of the equipment used on America's great electrified systems, have replaced them. The only difference between Lionel Trains and real trains is the size. The high quality of Lionel Products does not make them high in price—complete outfits can be bought for as little as $5.75.

Every automatic device known to modern railroading—all triumphs of engineering skill, perfect in construction, built to last, and to provide unlimited joy to the user for many years, have been perfected by Lionel.

The new 100% Lionel Electrically Controlled Railroad—the supreme achievement in model railroad construction, is described on the following page.

Boys—Lionel will aid you to obtain a valuable technical knowledge of electricity and the principles of modern railroading. Who knows but what it may be your destiny to go into fields as yet untouched and pioneer big engineering projects, like Hill, Harriman and others whose names will always be identified with the railroad history of our great land.

A prominent railroad president recently wrote: "The boy who owns a Lionel must get all the thrill of operating a real railroad."

Boys, you will get a real thrill when you behold your Lionel Train complete in every detail—and you play the part of railroad director.

All aboard! You switch on the current from your "Multivolt" Transformer—the Lionel Limited, with its powerful headlights shining and cars brilliantly illuminated, gracefully glides away—smooth and silent, just like a big all-steel Pullman train. You advance the transformer switch and immediately the massive motor increases speed, hauling the big train with perfect ease—past the steel telegraph posts, semaphores and over the famous Lionel bridge.

As you approach the illuminated village built with Lionel Villas and Bungalows, the bell on the Warning Signal rings out at the grade crossing. The Automatic Gates go down—your train speeds by and up go the Gates again.

Now your Lionel speeds down the straightaway stretch. The green Semaphore lights show "Line Clear"—now comes the curve and you reduce speed; into the approaching Tunnel goes the Express. Your Block Signals all along the line show green lights as the Train approaches—as soon as it leaves the block section the lights change to red, to prevent rear end collisions.

The brilliantly illuminated Station at "Lionel City" is seen in the distance—a touch of the transformer lever and your Lionel reduces speed and then majestically stops—the body of the engine quivering like a living thing as though satisfied with a glorious run. Passengers rush aboard,—a signal from the conductor—we are on our way again.

Steady there! A red light shows ahead!! It is the stop signal on the Automatic Train Control. You've been negligent in not heeding that signal, but just the same your train comes to a dead stop!!! Why? The Train Control stops it automatically.

Now the track ahead is clear, the red light changes to green, the current is automatically carried to the locomotive, and away we dart once more. Boys, do you know that the Lionel Train Control is the only device that is positively automatic in operation.

Can you think of anything that will hold your interest as intensely as a Lionel Model Railroad? You cannot find anything more real.

Ask your dealer to show you "Lionel"—examine the locomotive, the motor, cars and track—look at the design, construction and finish—see the infinite detail that makes the equipment massive, durable and as real as actual big trains.

If your dealer cannot supply you, please write to us and we will see that you get what you want right from our big factories. Always remember that Lionel prices are lowest consistent with quality.

This year, Lionel's previous achievements have been surpassed—by Lionel.

THE LIONEL CORPORATION
15-17-19 East 26th Street
(Madison Square North)
New York City

The entire contents of this catalog copyrighted 1926 by The Lionel Corporation, New York, N. Y. Printed in U. S. A.

The New Lionel 100% Electrically Controlled Railroad

BOYS—*The Thrill of Your Life Awaits You!*

After reading the previous page you must be all excited about Lionel Model Trains, but we didn't tell you all about the New 100% Electrically Controlled Locomotives to operate on "Lionel Standard" Track.

Heretofore, you had to reverse your locomotive by hand, or affix a mechanical appliance on the track that would reverse the locomotive at only one spot, but Lionel Electrically Controlled Locomotives can be operated at various speeds, stopped and reversed at any distance from the track and at every spot of the track.

Lionel Model Trains differ from real ones only in size. They are not large enough to permit you to ride in the cab, but you can operate them like real trains at any distance from the track. Now this seems uncanny, but it is a fact nevertheless.

The illustration shows one of the many thousands of Lionel boys operating his Electrically Controlled "Lionel Standard" Train. You will notice that his hand is on a little lever. When this lever is moved from side to side it increases or reduces the speed of the train. When the lever is lowered his train comes to a stop. When it is raised the train starts off again in the opposite direction, but, boys—the mechanism is so perfect that when the lever is rapidly raised and lowered twice the train will resume speed in the direction in which it was going before being stopped.

Picture the fun of bringing your train to a stop at a Railroad Crossing or Station, or when the Semaphore or Block Signal shows "Danger Ahead," without even touching it. There's a real thrill for you!

At times, Mr. Engineer, you must reverse your train to couple on another Pullman or Freight Car. Just think how simply this is done. By one slight movement of the lever, as if by magic, your locomotive will reverse itself.

By sliding the lever to one side the train will gradually reduce speed, and by lowering the same lever the train will stop right up against the car that is to be coupled to it.

Then again, as a real railroad engineer following instructions, you must switch your train from one track to another. This operation is decidedly interesting and clearly exemplifies the realism of Lionel Electrically Controlled Railroads. Not only do you reverse the train by manipulating a lever, but you also set your switches in their proper position by operating another lever—and let us repeat that all these operations are performed at any distance from the track—yes, either a few feet or hundreds of feet away.

All the other Electrically Controlled Lionel Railroad Accessories such as Semaphores, Crossing Gates, Block Signals, Warnings Bells and the famous Lionel Train Control are automatically operated, either by the movement of the train, or they can all be controlled at any distance from the track by connecting them to the series of switch levers that are contained in the new Lionel No. 437 Switch Tower shown in the accompanying illustration.

So you see, boys, that Lionel has perfected a distant-control that marks a new epoch in Model Railroading. It is the culmination of twenty-six years devoted exclusively to the manufacture of Lionel Electric Trains and Model Railroad Accessories—all fully guaranteed. That's why Lionel has been "Standard of the World Since 1900."

Lionel Always Leads

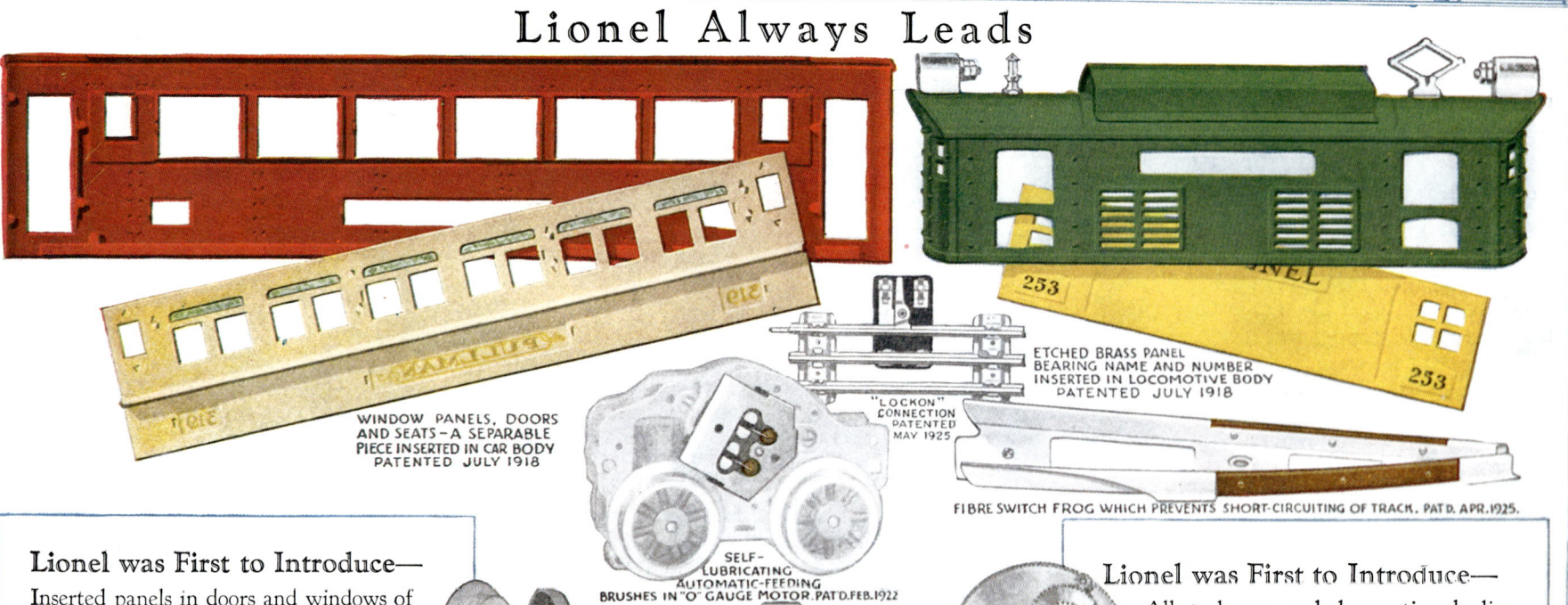

WINDOW PANELS, DOORS AND SEATS—A SEPARABLE PIECE INSERTED IN CAR BODY PATENTED JULY 1918

ETCHED BRASS PANEL BEARING NAME AND NUMBER INSERTED IN LOCOMOTIVE BODY PATENTED JULY 1918

"LOCKON" CONNECTION PATENTED MAY 1925

FIBRE SWITCH FROG WHICH PREVENTS SHORT-CIRCUITING OF TRACK. PAT'D. APR. 1925.

SELF-LUBRICATING AUTOMATIC-FEEDING BRUSHES IN "O" GAUGE MOTOR. PAT'D. FEB. 1922

DIE-CAST WHEEL WITH NICKEL POLISHED STEEL RIM. PATENTED APRIL, 1923.

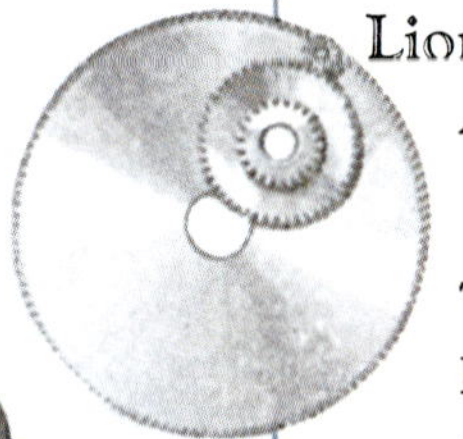

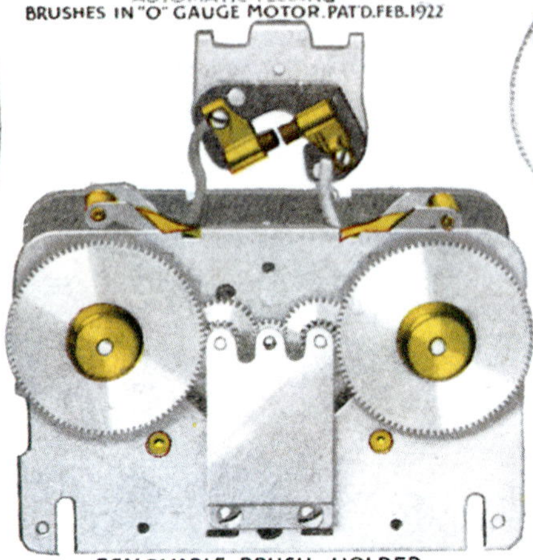

MACHINE-CUT, HEAVY STEEL GEARS—NOT PUNCHED

REMOVABLE BRUSH-HOLDER CONTAINING SELF-LUBRICATING AUTOMATIC-FEEDING BRUSHES. PAT'D. MAY 1925

LOCOMOTIVE HEADLIGHT. WITH RED AND GREEN LIGHTS IN SIDES PATENTED APRIL 1925

REAR VIEW OF HEADLIGHT, SHOWING SWITCH PATENTED APRIL 1925

SIX WHEEL TRUCK WITH NICKELED JOURNALS

Lionel was First to Introduce—

Inserted panels in doors and windows of cars and locomotive bodies. Patented July 16, 1918.

Inserted etched brass plates in locomotive bodies. Patented July 16, 1918.

Die-cast wheel with nickeled steel rim over tread. Patented March 17, 1925.

Removable motor brush holder. Patented May 5, 1925.

Self-feeding brushes. Patented February 7, 1922.

Insulated fibre frogs on switches. Patented April 21, 1925.

"Lockon" Track Connections. Patented June 16, 1925.

Headlights with individual switches and green and red transparent side panels. Patented June 2, 1925.

Automatic Train Control—the only device that automatically stops and starts the train. Patented August 21, 1917.

Electrically Controlled Track Switches. Patented August 11, 1925.

Automatic Crossing Gates. Patented September 21, 1925.

Lionel was First to Introduce—

All-steel car and locomotive bodies, hand enameled and rigidly assembled, instead of flimsy lithographed tin.

Trucks with nickeled journals.

Roller contact shoes on locomotives.

Three-point armature shaft bearings on miniature motors.

Electrical sheets for motor and armature construction instead of cheap cold-rolled steel.

Drill rod shaft for armature, instead of commercial iron wire.

Reinforced phosphor-bronze bearings for armature shaft and wheel axles.

Automatic Warning Signals.

Automatic Block Signals.

All-steel electric lighted miniature bungalows and villas,

AND

Every desirable detail in Model Electric Trains and Accessories.

"O" Gauge Single and Twin-Motor Specifications

Driving Gears ("A")—They are made of heavy steel blanks, machine-cut. They mesh without friction and are far superior to gears with punched teeth.

Field ("B")—The field is made of a number of specially prepared transformer steel laminations. This construction represents a much stronger field than if a single piece of steel were used.

Third Rail Shoe Support ("C")—Made of heavy fibre to which the third rail contact rollers are attached. Our construction protects rollers from injury, for the brackets can be bent against the fibre without disturbing the arc of the spring that gives them the correct tension against the third rail.

Wheels ("D")—Lionel was first to introduce die-cast wheels. They are absolutely balanced. A nickel-plated steel rim is forced over the tread of the wheel to insure long wear.

Collecting Shoes ("E")—They collect current from the third rail. Made of solid brass turnings and revolve on steel shafts which pass through phosphor bronze supports. They insure perfect contact with the third rail at all times so that locomotives will run at uniform speed.

Frame ("F")—Made of very heavy steel punchings, embodying great detail. Will withstand more than the ordinary amount of wear and tear.

Journals ("G")—Made of heavy brass, nickel-plated. Attached to the frames by mechanical means. They add greatly to the appearance of the structure.

Cowcatchers ("H")—The construction of the cowcatchers varies with the type of locomotive on which they are used. Many of them are part of the steel frame which is made in one piece, and others are heavy castings rigidly attached to the frame.

Flag Posts ("J")—All our locomotives, except No. 152, are equipped with four flag posts, two at each end of the frame; a very realistic detail.

Tanks ("K")—These tanks are made of brass, nickel-plated, and are separable pieces attached to the frame, which further accentuates the great detail.

Lionel Automatic Couplers ("L")—Made of heavy steel, nickel-plated and polished. They are scientifically constructed so that cars cannot become detached when in motion, but are easily taken apart when desired. The new improved Lionel Coupler with invisible spring arrangement is a great advance over any similar device ever made.

Reversing Controllers ("M")—Lionel Reversing Controllers have been in use for many years during which time they have given thorough satisfaction. They are the only controllers in use that cannot get out of order. They operate very easily and due to the brass cups and spring tension, the electrical contact is always permanent.

Frame Support ("N")—The frame is supported to the motor with only four screws. This simple method of construction was originally introduced by us in 1913. All parts of Lionel Locomotives can be easily reached for cleaning.

Side Plates ("P")—Made of heavy gauge steel and support all working parts. All bearing holes are reinforced with phosphor bronze bushings. The alignment of these holes is absolutely perfect so that gears work with minimum friction. All holes are drilled and reamed to proper diameter. The accuracy of these plates compares with the frame work of a very fine clock.

Brush Plate ("Q")—The unique construction permits rapid change of brushes after motor has been in use for a considerable period. The brushes fit in brass cups. Two properly tempered steel springs give the correct pressure of the brush on the commutator until brushes are worn down to the end. Brushes are replaced by simply raising the springs, lifting up worn out brushes and dropping in new ones.

Brushes ("R")—We were the first manufacturers of model trains to equip our motors with combination gauze and graphite brushes that wear long and are self-lubricating.

Removable Locomotive Body ("S")—The bodies of all Lionel Locomotives are held in place on the frame with only two screws, one at each end of the locomotive. Supporting members are placed at several points of the frame that rigidly hold the body in place.

Commutator—Made of bronze, and perfectly turned when connected to armature so that it is absolutely parallel with brushes. Commutator surface is polished so as to reduce all friction when in contact with brushes.

Armature—Made of specially prepared electrical sheets mounted on a drill rod shaft. It is perfectly insulated and wound with the correct amount of triple insulated wire.

"O" Gauge Twin-Motor—The chassis illustrated contains two "O" Gauge Motors which give great hauling power to Locomotive No. 256 described on Page 11. Both motors reverse simultaneously from one controller. Despite the great hauling power of this locomotive, it consumes a minimum amount of current.

Side View of "O" Gauge Motor Used in All Our "O" Gauge Locomotives.

Bottom View of "O" Gauge Twin-Motor Used in Locomotive No. 256

1926

Specifications of "Lionel Standard" Super-Motor
Reg. U. S. Pat. Office

THE New Lionel "Super-Motor" is so vastly superior in efficiency and design to any motor ever before offered to the public that notwithstanding our enviable reputation as leaders in miniature motor construction, the new and improved Super-Motor is supremely the finest piece of electrical mechanism our factories have ever produced. It is quite fitting that we, as pioneer builders of model locomotives to operate on "Lionel Standard" track, should retain our leadership with the Super-Motor which is the acme of perfection.

Removable Brush Holder (1)—This is one of the most unique features of the Lionel "Super-Motor." By simply unscrewing one screw the entire brush holder can be removed from the motor. Change of brushes requires but an instant and the assembled part is replaced without the use of any tools.

Brushes (2)—The brushes are made of bronze and graphite which are self-lubricating. They insure long life to the commutator. They are contained in brass tubes and held in place by a simple spring arrangement which feeds brushes to commutator at the same pressure until the brush is entirely used up. Replacement of brushes is a very simple operation.

Field—Made of the highest grade electrical steel correctly wound and scientifically designed.

Commutator—Made of heavy copper. The segments are perfectly insulated, making short-circuits impossible.

Revolving Double Contact Shoes (3)—This method of collecting current from the third rail, so successfully used for many years past on our "O" Gauge Locomotives, has been applied with equal success to the new Super-Motors. The shoes are heavy bronze rollers, securely affixed to the flexible phosphor bronze plate, which insures the proper tension on the third rail and gives a steady flow of current to the motors. This complete shoe assembly is mounted on a heavy fibre plate and is rigidly attached to the motor frame.

New Gear Arrangement (4)—This new method of gearing is embodied only in Lionel Super-Motors. The seven gears in this new layout give the motor greater tractive power, and are almost frictionless. The gears are made of very heavy steel and teeth are machine cut, not stamped. Special attention is directed to the plate supporting the gear studs, which also acts as an additional bearing for the armature shaft, as described in the following paragraph.

Side View of Super-Motor Showing Removable Brush Plate and Extra Armature Shaft Bearing

Three-Point Armature Shaft Bearing (5)—For the first time in the development of miniature motors it has been possible to perfect an arrangement whereby the armature shaft revolves in three bearings—two of them are contained in the side plates of the motor and the third one in the plate that holds the gearing studs. This three-point-bearing eliminates all vibration of the armature shaft, with the result that the commutator and brushes wear long and evenly. Considering the fact that the commutator and brushes are the life of the motor, this improvement is of great importance.

Driving Wheels (6)—Particular attention is directed to the driving wheels, which are massive in construction and are accurately die-cast. Their weight adds great tractive power to the motors. All driving wheels are directly geared to the motor, eliminating the use of connecting rods between the wheels, which insures better alignment with less friction.

Steel Tread on Wheels (7)—A steel tread beautifully nickel plated and polished is forced over the rim, insuring longer wear and a smooth, even riding surface. Lionel originated this method of wheel construction. See illustration on Page 4.

Reinforced Bearings (8)—Six phosphor bronze bearings are contained in the side plates of the motor. They add to the life of the motor and insure accurate alignment of the armature shaft and axles.

Armature—The armature is made of laminated electrical steel punchings. It is automatically drum wound with triple-covered magnet wire, dipped in shellac and baked. The armature shaft (9) is made of the best quality drill rod.

Side Plates (10)—Made of heavy steel, with bronze bushings inserted for shaft and axles.

Tractive Power—The tractive power of these motors is remarkable. They will haul from 12 to 20 of our largest size freight or Pullman cars with the greatest ease. The weight of the wheels and motor is close to the track, insuring low center of gravity, with the result that the locomotive is not top-heavy and slippage of the wheels is therefore unknown. This construction is infinitely superior to the method of loading down the superstructure with useless weight so as to obtain tractive power. This unnecessary weight rapidly wears down all working parts and causes the locomotive to jump the track.

Minimum Current Consumption—The new Lionel "Super-Motor" is not only more powerful than any motor of its size, but it consumes less than half the current of any motor developing the same power.

{ 6 }

Reg. U. S. Pat. Office
Specifications of "Lionel Standard" Twin-Super-Motors

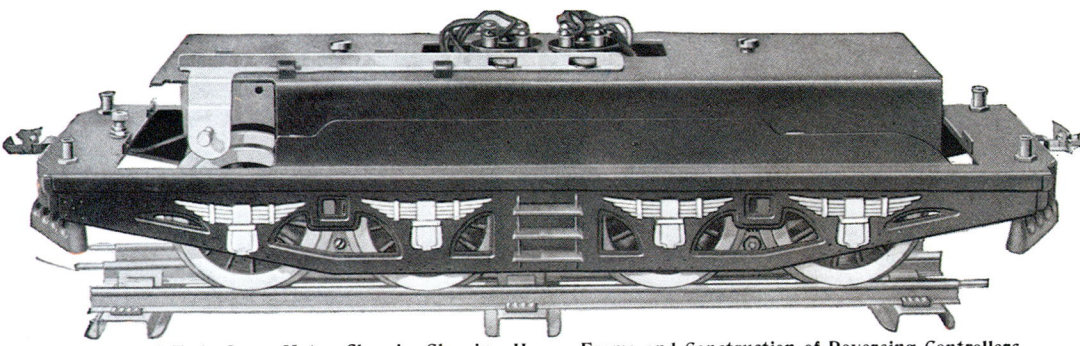

Side View of Twin-Super-Motor Chassis, Showing Heavy Frame and Construction of Reversing Controllers

ON the opposite page we illustrate and describe the new Super-Motor. In order to produce a locomotive of great hauling power we have coupled up these motors and have developed them to operate absolutely in unison, yet with little extra current consumption. The great hauling power of these Twin-Super-Motors provides the traction. No useless weight is added to the superstructure, which only wears down the bearings of the motors by unnecessary friction. Loading the body is not resorted to—the weight is in the motors, close to the track where it belongs. Lionel Twin-Super-Motor Locomotives are not top-heavy and will not derail even when hauling a train of cars around sharp curves at high speed.

WE have modeled the Lionel Twin-Super-Motor Locomotive after the mighty commercial electric engines which the great engineers of America have designed for the country's prominent electrified railroads. In proportion, the Lionel Twin-Super-Motor Locomotive is just as powerful as the large ones. Engineers have favored twin-motors in their designs because they give the greatest hauling power—so it is with the new Lionel Twin-Super-Motors.

Reversing Controllers and Motor Frame—
The illustration above shows the unique construction of the reversing controllers which operate the twin-super-motors. Both controllers function simultaneously by means of a lever conveniently placed on the side of the locomotive body. The slightest touch of the finger sends the locomotive forward or backward or causes it to stop when the lever is placed at "OFF." Accuracy of construction insures positive action of the reversing controller at all times. Our reversing controllers are absolutely dependable—they are free from complicated mechanism.

Attention is directed to the heavy steel one-piece frame to which the motors are attached. Great detail is embodied in this frame. The springs and journals are separate brass pieces, heavily nickeled, and are securely fastened to it. Brass steps and flag supports are also attached, while the heavy steel cow-catchers are riveted to both ends, from which protrude the patented Lionel Automatic Couplers. The whole chassis represents a power unit that will give years of service.

THE LIONEL TWIN-SUPER-MOTOR LOCOMOTIVE WILL HAUL 20 LARGE FREIGHT CARS WITH PERFECT EASE.

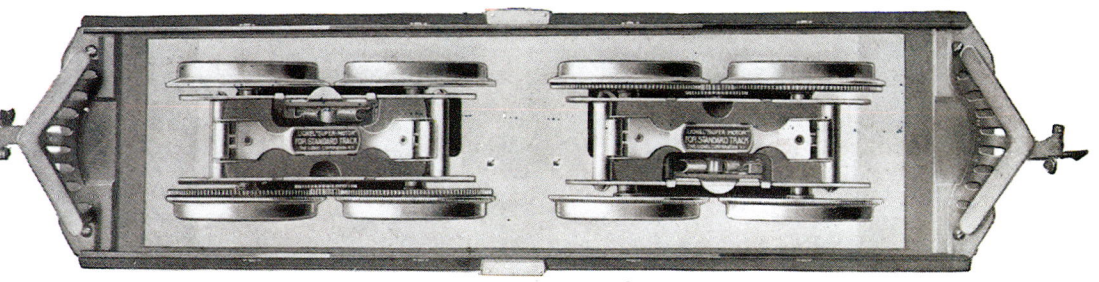

Bottom View of "Lionel Standard" Twin-Super-Motor Chassis

Construction of Lionel Locomotives

LIONEL leadership has been attained by specialization in the manufacture of one product for 26 years. Our entire resources and unsurpassed manufacturing facilities are exclusively devoted to the production of Model Electric Trains, Railroad Accessories and "Multivolt" Transformers.

Millions of Lionel Outfits are in use, many of them for a decade or more. Reference to the descriptive matter and illustrations on these pages will show why the Lionel Line is of such supremely high quality. Not only are the raw materials used the best obtainable, but all Locomotives, Pullman and Freight Cars, as well as Railroad Accessories, are actually built to scale. Every detail found in real railroad equipment is faithfully reproduced in our models. Space does not permit us to dwell at length on the many improvements incorporated in our goods, but on page 4 we take great pleasure in mentioning only a few of the improvements introduced during the past few years and patented by us.

All Lionel Cars and Locomotive Bodies are enameled and baked at high temperature, which insures a permanent finish that can always be kept bright by any ordinary cleaning process.

Lionel Locomotives, Cars and Accessories are finished in a variety of attractive colors.

The details of the construction of Lionel Locomotive Bodies given on this page are typical of Lionel supreme quality throughout the entire line. Even the lowest priced Lionel Locomotives incorporate many of these features.

Of utmost importance is the fact that cast iron does not enter into the manufacture of any of these bodies—heavy sheet steel is used for every model; therefore Lionel Locomotives are practically indestructible. All parts of the bodies are re-enforced and are firmly soldered. They are not held together only by slots and fingers.

Brass and nickeled fittings add further charm to the general appearance of Lionel Locomotives. These fittings are secured to the bodies by a process employed exclusively by us.

In all ways Lionel Locomotive Bodies combine sturdy construction, wonderful design and graceful appearance, as the indications below clearly show.

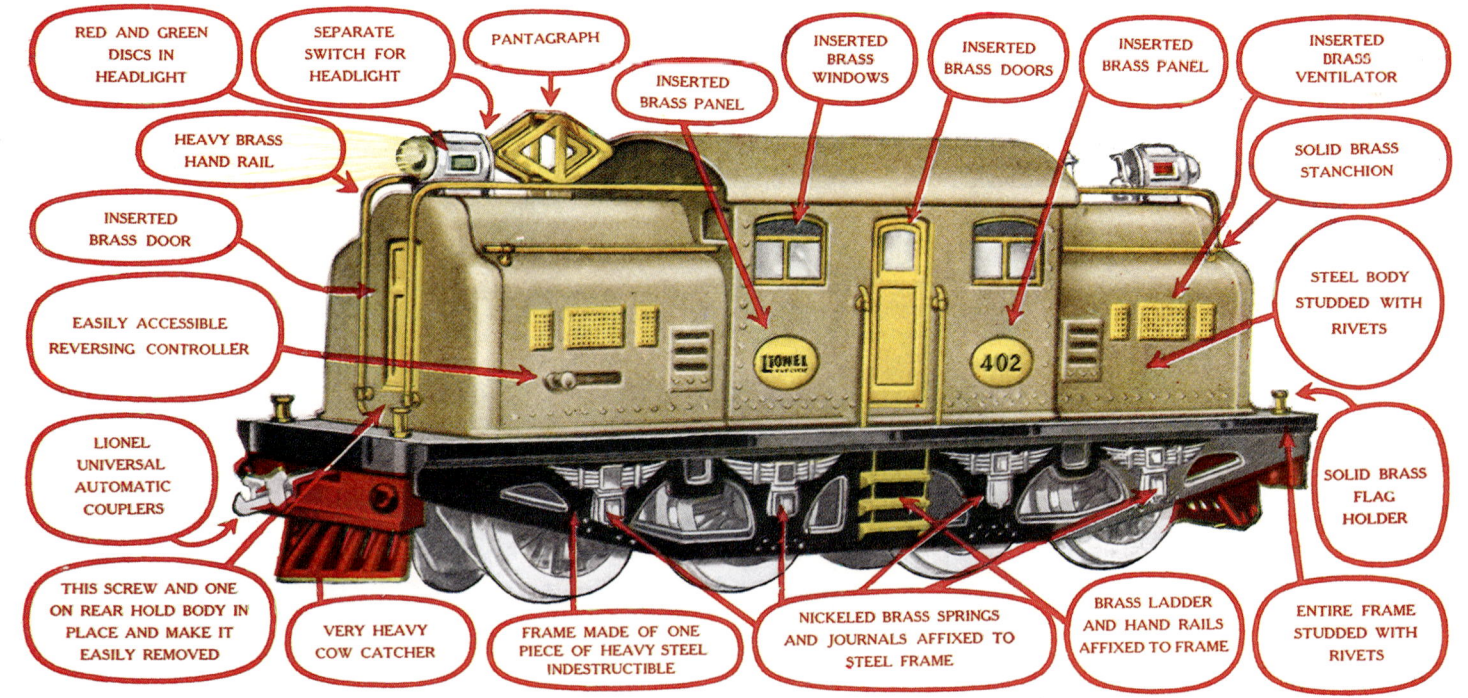

Construction of Lionel Passenger Coaches

IN every part of this catalog we show the quality and perfection of every piece that forms part of Lionel Outfits, but it is impossible to convey to the mind of the reader through this medium, the high quality of our goods. They must be seen to be appreciated. Insist that your dealer demonstrates them for you. You will then realize that Lionel is the lowest priced line obtainable, consistent with quality.

All Lionel Passenger Coaches, irrespective of price, are made entirely of sheet steel. Not only are the cars modeled after the newest coaches used on the principal railroads of the country, but they are built to scale. An enormous amount of detail is incorporated in them, such as hinged doors, inserted window frames and seats, metal tanks, etc. Transparencies are placed in the windows and transoms of almost every car. The roofs are easily removable so that the interior electric lamp can be reached.

Particular attention is drawn to the new Observation Cars for "Lionel Standard" Track, which have a dome light over the observation platform, in addition to the light in the centre of the car. They also are fitted with red transparent discs that are illuminated by the lamp in the dome, producing a dazzlingly beautiful effect. The transparent "Lionel Limited" sign, affixed to the observation rail-

ing, is another touch of realism in which every boy will delight. See Page 31 for illustration of these interesting new details.

Every car is finished with lasting, glossy enamel baked on at high temperature, insuring a permanent lustre. A revolving shoe, affixed to one of the trucks, collects current for the interior illumination of the car.

This desirable feature is also illustrated on Page 31, on which page, as well as on Page 30, the full line of Passenger and Observation Coaches for "Lionel Standard" and "O" Gauge Tracks is described. Many of the trucks on Lionel Passenger Coaches are fitted with nickeled journals. The heavy steel axles and wheels are nickeled and polished and are so perfectly made that they operate with a minimum amount of friction.

Attention is invited to the indications below which clearly show the superior construction incorporated in all parts of Lionel Passenger Coaches.

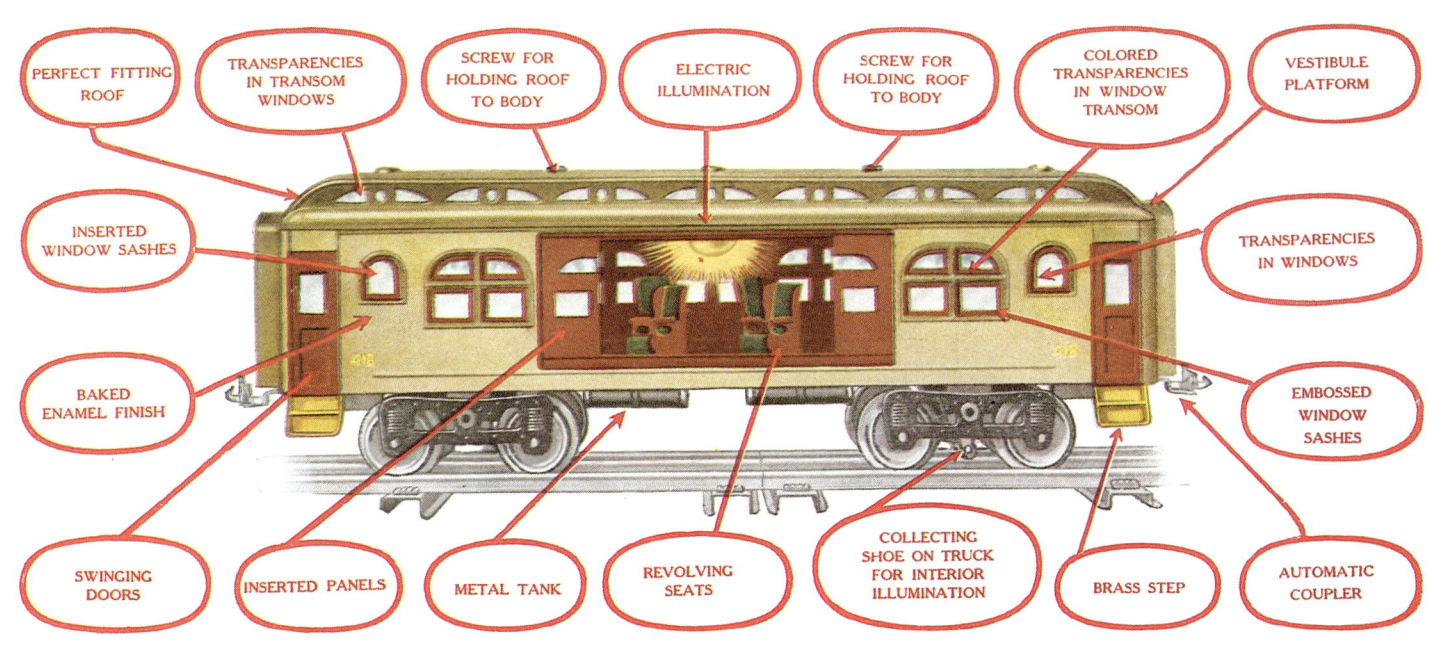

1926

Locomotives for Lionel "O" Gauge Track—1⅜ Inches Wide

Locomotive No. 152— With electric headlight. This locomotive is 7 inches long and 3½ inches high. Sturdily built and of proven strength. Price, complete with electric lamp for headlight and directions for operating . **$5.75**
Western Price $6.75
Code Word "GRAMERCY"

LIONEL supremacy is again proven by the introduction of the new types of "O" Gauge Locomotives shown on these pages. They are real electric engines in miniature. The new body designs suggest in a remarkable manner the massive outlines of the enormous electric locomotives seen on prominent electrified railroads like the New York Central, C. M. and St. P., and the New York and New Haven. All the wonderful features described on Page 8 are incorporated in these new models, including two electric headlights and reversing controllers (excepting Nos. 152 and 250). They are also equipped with the new patented Lionel Automatic Couplers. The motors have great hauling power, consume very little current, and will last for years with ordinary care.

YOU WILL BE INTERESTED IN READING THE SPECIFICATIONS OF THESE POWERFUL MOTORS ON PAGE FIVE

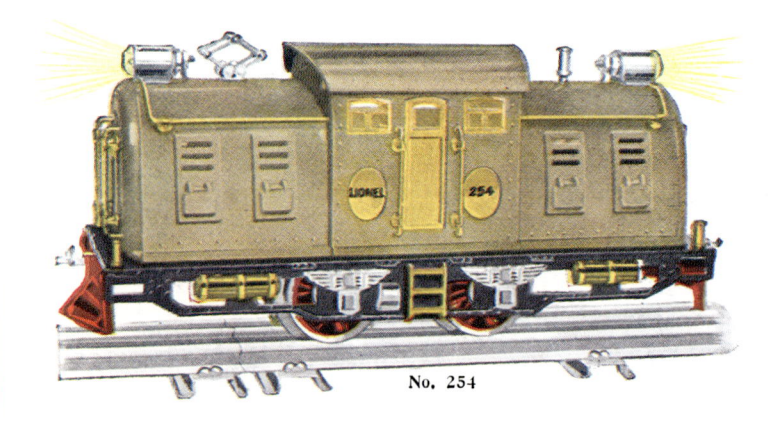

Locomotive No. 253— With two electric headlights and reversing controller. This locomotive is 9 inches long and 4 inches high. An attractive model of great power. Price, complete with two electric lamps for headlights and directions for operating **$9.75**
Western Price $11.25
Code Word "FINE"

Locomotive No. 254— With two electric headlights and reversing controller. This locomotive is 10 inches long and 4¼ inches high. Smooth and silent in operation, beautiful in appearance. Price, complete with two electric lamps for headlights and directions for operating, **$12.25**
Western Price $14.50
Code Word "MANY"

Locomotives for Lionel "O" Gauge Track—1⅜ Inches Wide

THE scientific construction and unique features of the powerful motors contained in all the Lionel "O" Gauge Locomotives illustrated here are fully described on Page 5.

All Lionel Motors are mechanically and electrically perfect and the superstructures embody a wealth of detail developed as a result of Lionel's specialization in one product for 26 years.

Particular attention is directed to the Twin-Motor Locomotive No. 256—a mighty hauler that cannot be equalled in design and efficiency.

All Lionel "O" Gauge Locomotives—no matter how low in price, represent the greatest achievement in Model Railroad Engineering.

Locomotive No. 252—With electric headlight and reversing controller. This locomotive is 8 inches long and 3¾ inches high. Note that the reversing controller is conveniently placed at the top of the body, within easy reach. A new and exclusive design.
Price, complete with electric lamp for headlight and directions for operating **$8.00**
Western Price $9.50
Code Word "LAND"

Nos. 250 and 252

Locomotive No. 250—Similar in every way to Locomotive 252 described above, but without reversing controller. Price, complete with electric lamp for headlight and directions for operating **$6.50**
Code Word "AMBER"   Western Price $7.75

No. 251

Locomotive No. 251—With two electric headlights and reversing controller. This locomotive is 10¼ inches long and 5 inches high. A recent addition to the Lionel "O" Gauge Line. The body design is entirely new and closely resembles the most modern types of electric engines. The method of construction, originated by Lionel and described on Page 8, is fully exemplified in this beautiful model. Price, complete with electric lamps for headlights and directions for operating **$15.00**
Code Word "ACME"   Western Price $17.50

No. 256

Twin-Motor Locomotive No. 256—With two electric headlights and reversing controller. This Locomotive is 11½ inches long and 5¼ inches high. The headlights have individual switches so that one or both can be used as desired. The reversing controller operates both motors simultaneously. This is the only twin-motor locomotive ever made to operate on "O" Gauge Track. It will haul a great number of passenger or freight cars. A wonderful model replete with many realistic features. Price, complete with two electric lamps for headlights and directions for operating **$18.25**
Code Word "CHAIN"   Western Price $21.50

Train Outfits for Lionel "O" Gauge Track—1⅜ Inches Wide

THIS WARNING SIGNAL INCLUDED IN ALL "O" GAUGE OUTFITS WITHOUT CHARGE

No. 290

Outfit No. 290—Comprises No. 152 locomotive with electric headlight, 1 No. 901 gondola car, 1 No. 801 caboose, 8 sections No. OC curved track, 1 No. OTC "Lockon" connection and 1 No. 068 warning signal. Track forms a circle 30 inches in diameter. Complete train is 20½ inches long. Outfit includes electric lamp for headlight, wires for transformer or battery connection, connecting ties for joining sections of track and directions for operating.

This is a low priced train outfit that represents great value. Price complete $5.75

Code Word "RECENT"   Western Price $6.75

No. 92

Outfit No. 92—Comprises No. 152 locomotive with electric headlight, 1 No. 629 pullman car, 1 No. 630 observation car, 8 sections No. OC curved track, 1 No. OTC "Lockon" connection and 1 No. 068 warning signal. Track forms a circle 30 inches in diameter. Train is 22½ inches long. Outfit includes electric lamp for headlight, wires for transformer or battery connection, connecting ties for joining sections of track and directions for operating.

The cars in this outfit have inserted doors and panels, as well as interior seats. The observation car has an ornamental brass platform. Price complete .. $6.50

Code Word "REAL"   Western Price $7.75

LIONEL "MULTIVOLT" TRANSFORMERS ARE BEST FOR OPERATING ALL TRAINS. THEY ARE FULLY GUARANTEED. APPROVED BY THE UNDERWRITERS LABORATORIES.

No. 93

Outfit No. 93—Comprises No. 250 locomotive with electric headlight, 1 No. 629 pullman car, 1 No. 630 observation car, 8 sections No. OC curved track, 1 No. OTC "Lockon" connection and 1 No. 068 warning signal. Track forms a circle 30 inches in diameter. Train is 24¾ inches long. Outfit includes electric lamp for headlight, wires for transformer or battery connection, connecting ties for joining sections of track and directions for operating.

This outfit is handsomely enameled in rich colors. When you are ready to add more freight or passenger cars to the outfit you can be sure that the powerful locomotive will easily haul them. Price, complete $7.75

Code Word "RUTH"   Western Price $9.00

{ 12 }

Train Outfits for Lionel "O" Gauge Track—1⅜ Inches Wide

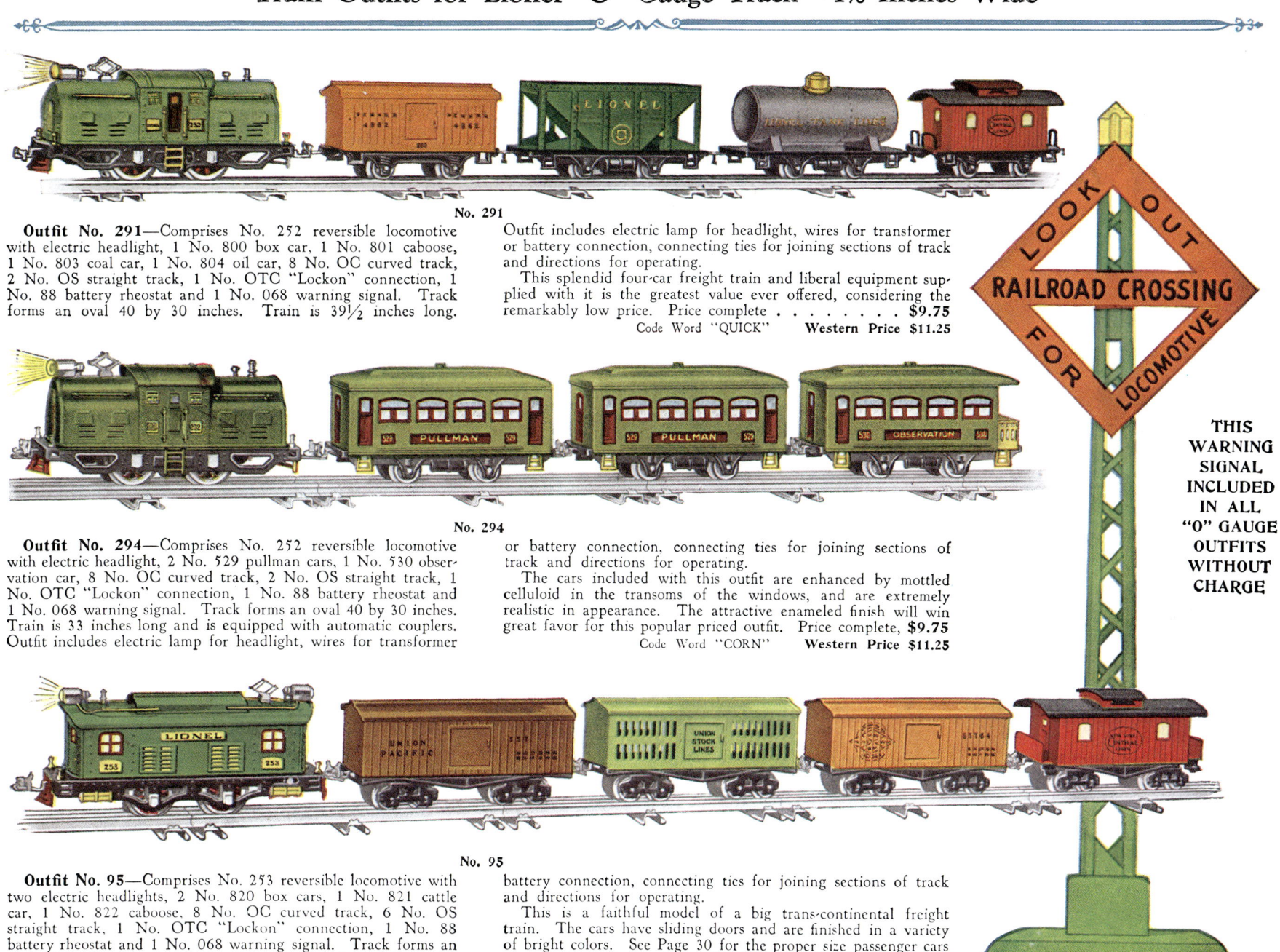

No. 291

Outfit No. 291—Comprises No. 252 reversible locomotive with electric headlight, 1 No. 800 box car, 1 No. 801 caboose, 1 No. 803 coal car, 1 No. 804 oil car, 8 No. OC curved track, 2 No. OS straight track, 1 No. OTC "Lockon" connection, 1 No. 88 battery rheostat and 1 No. 068 warning signal. Track forms an oval 40 by 30 inches. Train is 39½ inches long. Outfit includes electric lamp for headlight, wires for transformer or battery connection, connecting ties for joining sections of track and directions for operating.

This splendid four-car freight train and liberal equipment supplied with it is the greatest value ever offered, considering the remarkably low price. Price complete $9.75
Code Word "QUICK"   Western Price $11.25

No. 294

Outfit No. 294—Comprises No. 252 reversible locomotive with electric headlight, 2 No. 529 pullman cars, 1 No. 530 observation car, 8 No. OC curved track, 2 No. OS straight track, 1 No. OTC "Lockon" connection, 1 No. 88 battery rheostat and 1 No. 068 warning signal. Track forms an oval 40 by 30 inches. Train is 33 inches long and is equipped with automatic couplers. Outfit includes electric lamp for headlight, wires for transformer or battery connection, connecting ties for joining sections of track and directions for operating.

The cars included with this outfit are enhanced by mottled celluloid in the transoms of the windows, and are extremely realistic in appearance. The attractive enameled finish will win great favor for this popular priced outfit. Price complete, $9.75
Code Word "CORN"   Western Price $11.25

No. 95

Outfit No. 95—Comprises No. 253 reversible locomotive with two electric headlights, 2 No. 820 box cars, 1 No. 821 cattle car, 1 No. 822 caboose, 8 No. OC curved track, 6 No. OS straight track, 1 No. OTC "Lockon" connection, 1 No. 88 battery rheostat and 1 No. 068 warning signal. Track forms an oval 60 by 30 inches. Train is 42¾ inches long. Outfit includes electric lamps for headlights, wires for transformer or battery connection, connecting ties for joining sections of track and directions for operating.

This is a faithful model of a big trans-continental freight train. The cars have sliding doors and are finished in a variety of bright colors. See Page 30 for the proper size passenger cars that can be used with this outfit. Price complete . . . $14.00
Code Word "SPEEDY"   Western Price $16.25

LOOK OUT FOR RAILROAD CROSSING LOCOMOTIVE

THIS WARNING SIGNAL INCLUDED IN ALL "O" GAUGE OUTFITS WITHOUT CHARGE

Train Outfits for Lionel "O" Gauge Track—1⅜ Inches Wide

No. 296

Outfit No. 296—Comprises No. 252 reversible locomotive with electric headlight, 2 No. 607 illuminated pullman cars, 1 No. 608 illuminated observation car, 8 sections No. OC curved track, 4 sections No. OS straight track, 1 No. OTC "Lockon" connection, 1 No. 88 battery rheostat and 1 No. 068 warning signal. Track forms an oval 50 by 30 inches. Train is 35½ inches long and is equipped with automatic couplers. Outfit includes electric lamps for headlight and interior of cars, wires for transformer or battery connection, connecting ties for joining sections of track and directions for operating.

Note the nickeled journals on the car trucks and the tanks fitted to the car body. This beautiful new passenger train, one of the latest additions to the Lionel "O" Gauge Line, incorporates all the exclusive Lionel features of locomotive and car construction as described on Pages 8 and 9.
Price complete $11.75
Code Word "DART"   Western Price $14.00

No. 98

Outfit No. 98—Comprises No. 253 reversible locomotive with two electric headlights, 2 No. 610 illuminated pullman cars, 1 No. 612 illuminated observation car, 8 sections No. OC curved track, 6 sections No. OS straight track, 1 No. OTC "Lockon" connection, 1 No. 88 battery rheostat and 1 No. 068 warning signal. Track forms an oval 60 by 30 inches. Train is 39½ inches long and is equipped with automatic couplers. Outfit includes electric lamps for headlights and interior of cars, wires for transformer or battery connection, connecting ties for joining sections of track and directions for operating.

The new passenger cars now included with this outfit are larger and are a great improvement over our former models. You will note from the illustration that the roofs fit perfectly. Also note the real pullman car windows, journals on trucks, tanks attached to car body, and other realistic details. Price complete $15.00
Code Word "GOLD"   Western Price $17.50

No. 266

Outfit No. 266—Comprises No. 254 reversible locomotive with two electric headlights, 2 No. 610 illuminated pullman cars, 1 No. 612 illuminated observation car, 8 sections No. OC curved track, 6 sections No. OS straight track, 1 No. OTC "Lockon" connection, 1 No. 88 battery rheostat and 1 No. 068 warning signal. Track forms an oval 60 by 30 inches. Train is 40¼ inches long and is equipped with automatic couplers. Outfit includes electric lamps for headlights and interior of cars, wires for transformer or battery connection, connecting ties for joining sections of track and directions for operating.

The new passenger cars described in Outfit No. 98 above are also included with this greatly improved train outfit. This is an exact replica of the Limited Trains you see on the C. M. and St. Paul Railroad. Price complete $18.00
Code Word "HEAD"   Western Price $21.25

THIS WARNING SIGNAL INCLUDED IN ALL "O" GAUGE OUTFITS WITHOUT CHARGE

Train Outfits for Lionel "O" Gauge Track—1⅜ Inches Wide

No. 97

Outfit No. 97—Comprises No. 251 reversible locomotive with two electric headlights, 2 No. 605 illuminated pullman cars, 1 No. 606 illuminated observation car, 8 sections No. OC curved track, 8 sections No. OS straight track, 1 No. OTC "Lockon" connection, 1 No. 88 battery rheostat and 1 No. 068 warning signal. Track forms an oval 70 by 30 inches. Train is 43¼ inches long, and is equipped with automatic couplers. Outfit includes electric lamps for headlights and interior of cars, wires for transformer or battery connection, connecting ties for joining sections of track and directions for operating.

This well-designed model train stands far above anything similar ever made. Every desirable feature that has been developed and patented by Lionel has been embodied in this De Luxe model. Price complete $22.50
Code Word "EXCEL" Western Price $26.25

No. 299

Outfit No. 299—Comprises No. 254 reversible locomotive with two electric headlights, 1 No. 813 cattle car, 1 No. 814 box car, 1 No. 817 caboose, 8 sections No. OC curved track, 6 sections No. OS straight track, 1 No. OTC "Lockon" connection, 1 No. 88 battery rheostat and 1 No. 068 warning signal. Track forms an oval 60 by 30 inches. Train is 40¼ inches long, and is equipped with automatic couplers. Outfit includes electric lamps for headlights, wires for transformer or battery connections, connecting ties for joining sections of track and directions for operating.

To form this outfit we have taken one of the best types of our "O" Gauge locomotives, as well as several of the new series of Lionel Freight Cars described on Page 33. There are six cars in this new series made in various styles in accordance with the latest all-steel freight cars seen on the big railroads. You can be sure that the locomotive included with this outfit will haul all these cars if you desire to add them. Price complete $17.00
Code Word "FLORA" Western Price $19.75

No. 268

Outfit No. 268—Comprises No. 256 twin-motor reversible locomotive with two electric headlights (equipped with individual switches), 2 No. 710 illuminated pullman cars, 1 No. 712 illuminated observation car, 8 sections No. OC curved track, 8 sections No. OS straight track, 1 No. OTC "Lockon" connection, 1 No. 88 battery rheostat and 1 No. 068 warning signal. Track forms an oval 70 by 30 inches. Train is 51 inches long, and is equipped with automatic couplers. Outfit includes electric lamps for headlights, wires for transformer or battery connection, connecting ties for joining sections of track and directions for operating.

This is the largest train ever made to operate on "O" Gauge Track and includes the famous No. 256 twin-motor reversible locomotive which develops sufficient power to haul a large number of freight or passenger cars. The new series of Lionel Freight Cars described on Page 33 can be used with this outfit. Every part that enters into it bears the mark of Lionel quality. Price complete $33.00
Code Word "TAKE" Western Price $38.75

Complete Lionel Railroad for "O" Gauge Track—1⅜ Inches Wide

MANY boys prefer to buy Lionel Train Sets with a variety of accessories right from the start, so we have made up the outfit illustrated on this page. It will be seen that many wonderful accessories are provided in addition to the train and track layout. Every piece is of steel construction throughout with the famous Lionel enameled finish. It is only necessary to get one of the low priced "Multivolt" Transformers and the railroad can be operated instantly, or if no house current is available dry or storage batteries can be used. The track layout can always be extended.

No. 174

Outfit No. 174—Comprises one No. 296 train described on Page 14, together with ten sections OC track, six sections OS track, one OTC "Lockon" connection, one No. 88 rheostat, one pair No. 022 switches (one right and one left), one No. 106 bridge (three sections), one No. 121 station, six No. 60 telegraph posts, two No. 62 semaphores, one No. 068 warning signal and one No. 119 tunnel. Size of track layout 45 by 60 inches. The complete train is 35½ inches long, is equipped with automatic couplers, and cars have interior illumination. The outfit also includes lamps for headlight and interior of cars, wires for transformer or battery connection, connecting ties for joining sections of track, and directions for operating. Price complete . . . $35.00

Code Word "DELAWARE" Western Price $41.00

The New Electrically Controlled Locomotives

FOR "LIONEL STANDARD" TRACK—2¼ INCHES WIDE
Reg. U. S. Pat. Office

LIONEL engineers after many years of research have developed Electrically Controlled Locomotives that are in keeping with the other high grade features of Lionel Equipment, which means 100% perfection in operation, design, workmanship and efficiency.

Lionel Electrically Controlled Locomotives shown on the following pages are made in great variety and have withstood the severest tests. They carry the usual liberal Lionel guarantee.

One of the outstanding features of Lionel Electrically Controlled Locomotives is the simplicity of operation. By manipulating a small lever on the controlling rheostat (supplied with each Electrically Controlled Locomotive and Train Outfit) they may be started, stopped, reversed and operated at various speeds from any distance.

The lever on the controlling rheostat when moved from side to side reduces or increases the speed, and when lowered, stops the train. When the lever is raised the train starts in the opposite direction. The mechanism is so perfect that when the lever is quickly lowered and raised *twice* the train will continue in the direction in which it ran before being stopped.

Another desirable feature of Lionel Electrically Controlled Locomotives is the fact that they can also be reversed by hand.

Two headlights are mounted on the superstructure and are so connected that when the locomotive is moving forward the front headlight is illuminated, and when the locomotive is reversed the rear headlight shines, while the other is automatically disconnected.

The Lionel Electric Controlling Mechanism is built into the motor. It does not require any adjustment or repairs, nor does it consume any extra amount, and operates perfectly on reduced direct or alternating current, dry or storage batteries.

Patents are now pending covering the unique construction of the controlling mechanism, as well as the principle that makes it possible to operate Lionel Electrically Controlled Locomotives without using extra current.

The construction throughout is dependable, and must not be confused with so-called "Automatic Reversing Locomotives."

Lionel Electrically Controlled Locomotives are the greatest improvement ever made in model train construction and are worth considerably more than we charge for this very desirable feature.

The Electrically Controlled Locomotives and Train Outfits are distinguished by the letter "E" after the catalog number. They are fully described on the following pages.

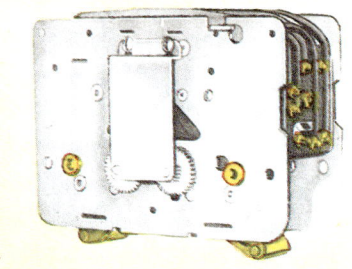

Illustration shows the simplicity and compactness of Lionel Electrically Controlled Super-Motors. All working parts are mounted between two heavy steel plates. All shaft bearings are reinforced with bronze bushings. All parts are easily accessible, including the removable brush holder, the lever for reversing locomotive by hand and an additional lever for disconnecting the electric-controlling mechanism.

Electrically Controlled and Hand Reversing "Super-Motor" Locomotives

Reg. U. S. Pat. Office
FOR "LIONEL STANDARD" TRACK—2¼ INCHES WIDE

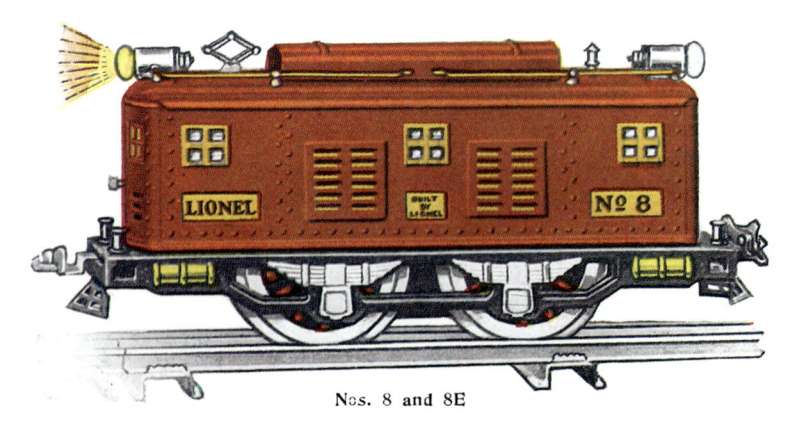

Electrically Controlled Locomotive No. 10E—With two electric headlights and automatic couplers. This locomotive is 11½ inches long and 5¼ inches high. Its powerful Super-Motor and graceful lines of the body stamp it as a locomotive of superior construction throughout. The electric controlling mechanism built into the locomotive, starts, stops and reverses it at any distance from the track by means of the controlling rheostat supplied with it.
Price complete, with electric lamps for headlights, controlling rheostat, wires and directions for operating $18.75
Code Word "SELF"   Western Price $22.00

Locomotive No. 10—Similar in every way to No. 10E described above, but is equipped with hand reversing controller.
Price complete, with electric lamps for headlights and directions for operating,
$13.75
Code Word "PULL"   Western Price $16.25

Nos. 8 and 8E

Electrically Controlled Locomotive No. 8E—With two electric headlights and automatic couplers. This locomotive is 11 inches long and 4½ inches high. It contains the powerful Lionel Super-Motor, and is similar to the very latest type of electric locomotives now being used on the big electrified railroad systems. The electric controlling mechanism built into the locomotive, starts, stops and reverses it at any distance from the track by means of the controlling rheostat supplied with it.
Price complete, with lamps for headlights, controlling rheostat, wires and directions for operating $16.50
Code Word "PEPPY"   Western Price $19.25

Locomotive No. 8—Similar in every way to No. 8E described above, but is equipped with hand reversing controller.
Price complete, with electric lamps for headlights and directions for operating $11.50
Code Word "POWER"   Western Price $13.50

Electrically Controlled Locomotive No. 318E—With two electric headlights and automatic couplers. This locomotive is 12½ inches long and 5⅜ inches high. It is introduced in response to a great demand for a single Super-Motor Locomotive built on the lines of our No. 402 Locomotive, but smaller, and contains all the structural features of the larger engine. The electric controlling mechanism built into the locomotive, starts, stops and reverses it at any distance from the track by means of the controlling rheostat supplied with it.
Price complete, with electric lamps for headlights, controlling rheostat, wires and directions for operating $21.50
Code Word "MOVE"   Western Price $25.00

Locomotive No. 318—Similar in every way to No. 318E described above, but is equipped with hand reversing controller.
Price complete, with electric lamps for headlights and directions for operating,
$16.50
Code Word "VERB"   Western Price $19.25

Nos. 10 and 10E

Nos. 318 and 318E

LENGTH OF LOCOMOTIVES DOES NOT INCLUDE COUPLERS

Electrically Controlled and Hand Reversing "Super-Motor" Locomotives

Reg. U. S. Pat. Office
FOR "LIONEL STANDARD" TRACK—2¼ INCHES WIDE

As the American boy expects Lionel to introduce everything in model railroad equipment that is in keeping with electric railroad development, we offer the new Electrically Controlled Locomotives, made in five different types as illustrated on these pages. They are the result of years of experiment and research by Lionel engineers.

The new Electrically Controlled Locomotives will operate on direct current, alternating current, dry batteries or storage batteries. They do not consume any extra current and are included in the Lionel Line with the fullest guarantee.

When the Electrically Controlled Locomotive is running forward, front headlight is illuminated—when it is reversed, rear one shines brilliantly and forward one is automatically disconnected.

All the "Lionel Standard" Locomotives are made with hand reversing controller, as well as with electrically controlled mechanism.

Nos. 380 and 380E

Electrically Controlled Locomotive No. 380E—With two electric headlights and automatic couplers. This locomotive is 13½ inches long and 5½ inches high. In appearance it is exactly like the new large locomotives used on the C. M. and St. Paul Railroad. The improved Super-Motor and the details of body construction have already been described. The electric controlling mechanism built into the locomotive, starts, stops and reverses it at any distance from the track by means of the controlling rheostat supplied with it.
Price complete, with electric lamps for headlights, controlling rheostat, wires and directions for operating **$24.50**
Code Word "SAINT"   Western Price $28.75

Locomotive No. 380—Similar in every way to No. 380E described above, but is equipped with hand reversing controller.
Price complete, with electric lamps for headlights and directions for operating **$18.75**
Code Word "ROCKIES"   Western Price $22.00

Electrically Controlled Twin-Super-Motor Locomotive No. 402E—With two electric headlights and automatic couplers. This locomotive is 17 inches long and 6½ inches high. The unique headlights, an exclusive patented Lionel feature, have already been described on this page. You will be amazed at the large number of passenger and freight cars this locomotive will pull. The electric controlling mechanism starts, stops and reverses this locomotive at any distance from the track by means of the controlling rheostat supplied with it.
Price complete, with electric lamps for headlights, controlling rheostat, wires and directions for operating **$38.75**
Code Word "YORK"   Western Price $45.50

Nos. 402 and 402E

Locomotive No. 402—Similar to No. 402E described here, but is equipped with hand reversing controller.
Price complete, with electric lamps for headlights and directions for operating **$32.25**
Code Word "HAVEN"   Western Price $37.75

LENGTH OF LOCOMOTIVES DOES NOT INCLUDE COUPLERS

Electrically Controlled and Hand Reversing "Super-Motor" Train Outfits

Reg. U. S. Pat. Office
FOR "LIONEL STANDARD" TRACK—2¼ INCHES WIDE

No. 350

Outfit No. 350—Comprises No. 8 Super-Motor Reversible Locomotive with two electric headlights, 1 No. 35 illuminated pullman car, 1 No. 36 illuminated observation car, 8 sections No. C curved track, 2 sections No. S straight track and 1 No. STC "Lockon" connection. Track forms an oval 56 by 42 inches. Train is 36 inches long, and is equipped with automatic couplers. Outfit also includes lamps for headlights and interior of cars, wires for transformer or battery connection, connecting ties for joining sections of track, and directions for operating.

This is a popular priced "Lionel Standard" Outfit.

Price complete $18.00
Code Word "PROOF"   Western Price $21.25

Note: The complete No. 350 Train is only sold with the hand reversing locomotive. Electrically Controlled Locomotive No. 8E can be purchased separately. (See Page 18.)

Nos. 347 and 347E

Outfit No. 347—Comprises No. 8 Super-Motor Reversible Locomotive with two electric headlights, 1 No. 337 illuminated pullman car, 1 No. 338 illuminated observation car, 8 sections No. C curved track, 2 sections No. S straight track and 1 No. STC "Lockon" connection. Track forms an oval 56 by 42 inches. Train is 38½ inches long, and is equipped with automatic couplers. Outfit also includes lamps for headlights and interior of cars, wires for transformer or battery connection, connecting ties for joining sections of track, and directions for operating.

Nothing finer in a moderately priced passenger train has ever been produced. The coaches included with this outfit are replete with new features, including trucks with nickeled journals, heavy brass steps, hinged doors and many other exclusive Lionel patented features as described on Page 9. The new observation car has in addition to the center light, a dome light over the observation platform. This observation platform, made of heavy ornamental brass, is fitted with red transparent lanterns that are illuminated by the lamp in the dome. Another attractive feature is the transparent "Lionel Limited" sign affixed to the observation railing.

Price complete $20.00
Code Word "ZENA"   Western Price $23.50

Outfit No. 347E—This is in every way similar to Outfit No. 347 described above, but includes Electrically Controlled Super-Motor Locomotive No. 8E, together with controlling rheostat which starts, stops and reverses the train at any distance from the track.

Price complete $24.50
Code Word "GLIDE"   Western Price $28.75

Electrically Controlled and Hand Reversing "Super-Motor" Train Outfits

Reg. U. S. Pat. Office
FOR "LIONEL STANDARD" TRACK—2¼ INCHES WIDE

Nos. 351 and 351E

Outfit No. 351—Comprises No. 8 Super-Motor Reversible Locomotive with two electric headlights, 1 No. 112 gondola car, 1 No. 114 box car, 1 No. 117 caboose, 8 sections No. C curved track, 2 sections No. S straight track and 1 No. STC "Lockon" connection. Track forms an oval 56 by 42 inches. Train is 44 inches long. Outfit also includes lamps for headlights, wires for transformer or battery connection, connecting ties for joining sections of track and directions for operating.

This freight train offers great value at a low price. There is nothing more desirable in the way of a durable, long-wearing, perfect model of a modern freight train.
Price complete $18.00
Code Word "LION"   Western Price $21.25

Outfit No. 351E—This is in every way similar to Outfit No. 351 described above, but includes Electrically Controlled Super-Motor Locomotive No. 8E, together with controlling rheostat which starts, stops and reverses the train at any distance from the track.
Price complete $22.75
Code Word "MARCH"   Western Price $26.50

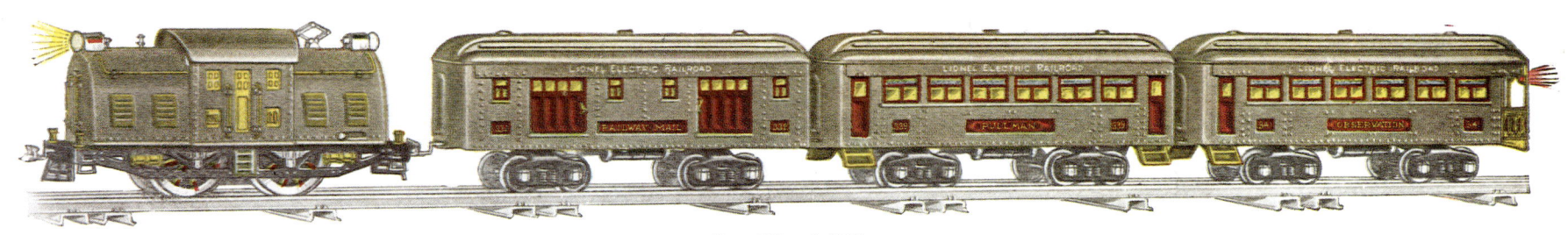

Nos. 352 and 352E

Outfit No. 352—Comprises No. 10 Super-Motor Reversible Locomotive with two electric headlights, 1 No. 332 illuminated combination mail and baggage car, 1 No. 339 illuminated pullman car, 1 No. 341 illuminated observation car, 8 sections No. C curved track, 4 sections No. S straight track and 1 No. STC "Lockon" connection. Track forms an oval 69 by 42 inches. Train is 52 inches long, and is equipped with automatic couplers. Outfit also includes lamps for headlights and interior of cars, wires for transformer or battery connection, connecting ties for joining sections of track, and directions for operating.

All the features of our new locomotives and passenger cars as described on Pages 8 and 9 are embodied in this desirable outfit. The built-in excellence of every piece and the low price of this sturdy model make it particularly attractive.
Price complete $25.00
Code Word "PRINCE"   Western Price $29.25

Outfit No. 352E—This is in every way similar to Outfit No. 352 described above, but includes Electrically Controlled Super-Motor Locomotive No. 10E, together with controlling rheostat which starts, stops and reverses the train at any distance from the track.
Price complete $29.75
Code Word "WIN"   Western Price $34.75

Electrically Controlled and Hand Reversing "Super-Motor" Train Outfits

Reg. U. S. Pat. Office
FOR "LIONEL STANDARD" TRACK—2¼ INCHES WIDE

Nos. 342 and 342E

Outfit No. 342—Comprises No. 318 Super-Motor Reversible Locomotive with two electric headlights, 1 No. 310 illuminated combination mail and baggage car, 1 No. 309 illuminated pullman car, 1 No. 312 illuminated observation car, 8 sections No. C curved track, 6 sections No. S straight track and 1 No. STC "Lockon" connection. Track forms an oval 88 by 42 inches. Complete train is 56½ inches long, and is equipped with automatic couplers. Outfit also includes lamps for headlights and interior of cars, wires for transformer or battery connection, connecting ties for joining sections of track, and directions for operating.

This handsome outfit is in every respect a faithful reproduction of the most up-to-date pullman trains. A few of the new features are nickel-plated journals on trucks, metal tanks securely held to the bottom of cars, dome light and red transparent lanterns on the observation platform and many other unique and realistic details as described on Page 9.

Price complete $30.75
Code Word "VIEW"   Western Price $36.00

Outfit No. 342E—This is in every way similar to Outfit No. 342 described above, but includes Electrically Controlled Super-Motor Locomotive No. 318E, together with controlling rheostat which starts, stops and reverses the train at any distance from the track.

Price complete $35.75
Code Word "FORUM"   Western Price $41.75

Nos. 41 and 41E

Outfit No. 41—Comprises No. 318 Super-Motor Reversible Locomotive with two electric headlights, 1 No. 112 gondola car, 1 No. 113 cattle car, 1 No. 114 box car, 1 No. 116 coal car, 1 No. 117 caboose, 8 sections No. C curved track, 4 sections No. S straight track and 1 No. STC "Lockon" connection. Track forms an oval 69 by 42 inches. Complete train is 65 inches long. Outfit also includes lamps for headlights, wires for transformer or battery connection, connecting ties for joining sections of track and directions for operating.

Lionel Freight Trains have always been famous for their great value. The locomotive and cars included with this outfit are of Lionel quality throughout. This type of freight train is found on all the large railroads. See Page 31 for the correct passenger cars that can be used with this outfit.

Price complete $26.75
Code Word "FULTON"   Western Price $31.50

Outfit No. 41E—This is in every way similar to Outfit No. 41 described above, but includes Electrically Controlled Super-Motor Locomotive No. 318E, together with controlling rheostat which starts, stops and reverses the train at any distance from the track.

Price complete $32.00
Code Word "YALE"   Western Price $37.25

Electrically Controlled and Hand Reversing "Super-Motor" Train Outfits

Reg. U. S. Pat. Office
FOR "LIONEL STANDARD" TRACK—2¼ INCHES WIDE

Nos. 348 and 348E

Outfit No. 348—Comprises No. 380 Super-Motor Reversible Locomotive with two electric headlights, 1 No. 428 illuminated pullman car, 1 No. 429 illuminated pullman and baggage car, 1 No. 430 illuminated observation car, 8 sections No. C curved track, 8 sections No. S straight track and 1 No. STC "Lockon" connection. Track forms an oval 102 by 42 inches. Complete train is 70½ inches long, and is equipped with automatic couplers. The headlights on the locomotive are equipped with individual switches so that one or both may be turned on at will. Outfit also includes lamps for headlights and interior of cars, wires for transformer or battery connection, connecting ties for joining sections of track, and directions for operating.

The cars included with this outfit are the largest manufactured by us and are similar in size to those included with Outfit No. 403 shown on the following page. A great wealth of detail, including revolving arm chairs, as shown in the illustration on Page 9, is incorporated in these cars. The powerful locomotive is capable of hauling them without difficulty. The new observation car with extra dome light and red transparent lanterns affixed to the observation platform is included with this wonderful new outfit. Price complete..$42.25
Code Word "YARD"   Western Price $49.50

Outfit No. 348E—This is in every way similar to Outfit No. 348 described above, but includes Electrically Controlled Super-Motor Locomotive No. 380E, together with controlling rheostat which starts, stops and reverses the train at any distance from the track. Price complete..$48.00
Code Word "ONYX"   Western Price $56.25

Nos. 343 and 343E

Outfit No. 343—Comprises No. 380 Super-Motor Reversible Locomotive with two electric headlights, 2 No. 319 illuminated pullman cars, 1 No. 320 illuminated combination mail and baggage car, 1 No. 322 illuminated observation car, 8 sections No. C curved track, 8 sections No. S straight track and 1 No. STC "Lockon" connection. Track forms an oval 102 by 42 inches. Complete train is 73 inches long, and is equipped with automatic couplers. The headlights on the locomotive are equipped with individual switches so that one or both may be turned on at will. Outfit also includes lamps for headlights and interior of cars, wires for transformer or battery connection, connecting ties for joining sections of track, and directions for operating.

This splendid four-car train represents great value. Every piece of equipment is replete with Lionel exclusive patented features, combining to make a model electric train that differs from a real one only in size. The powerful No. 380 locomotive will haul a surprisingly large number of passenger or freight cars designed for use with it. Price complete $42.25
Code Word "TIME"   Western Price $49.50

Outfit No. 343E—This is in every way similar to Outfit No. 343 described above, but includes Electrically Controlled Super-Motor Locomotive No. 380E, together with controlling rheostat which starts, stops and reverses the train at any distance from the track. Price complete..$48.00
Code Word "QUIRE"   Western Price $56.25

Electrically Controlled and Hand Reversing "Twin-Super-Moto

Nos. 403

TRAIN OUTFIT No. 403 is in every respect a De Luxe Model Express Train. It is a delight to behold, and operates as smoothly as though the wheels were equipped with rubber tires. Even the most superlative terms of description would not be as convincing as seeing the outfit in operation.

The locomotive is an exact reproduction of the modern types used on the big electrified systems, and its many remarkable features are indicated on Page 8.

The construction of the twin-motors is fully described on Page 7.

The pullman coaches are in every detail similar to the most modern passenger cars. See Page 9 for complete description of the many wonderful features incorporated in these cars, the interiors of which contain individual

Nos.

A companion number, quite in keeping with the De Luxe No. 403 Outfit described above, is the new Freight Train Outfit No. 406. It is the acme of perfection.

Lionel engineers and car designers have spent considerable time in diligent research in order to produce the new all-steel freight cars. On Page 35 you will find large illustrations of these cars which will enable you to get a clearer idea of the wonderful detail they embody.

Not only are these new cars patterned after the big all-steel cars that carry freight across the country, but they incorporate many original and

exclusive features of design that only Lionel can carry out to such perfection.

Attention is drawn to the heavy steel frames upon which the superstructure is mounted, the new steel trucks with nickeled journals, automatic couplers and the rivets and other structural details that are so perfectly designed. The car bodies also show a wealth of detail.

The Cattle Car and Box Car have sliding doors. The Flat Car has removable supports inserted in sockets in the platform. The Coal Car has a "Hopper" bottom which operates by turning a wheel on the side. The Caboose is equipped with illuminated lanterns on the rear platform.

Train Outfits for "Lionel Standard" Track—2¼ Inches Wide

revolving seats and permanent electric illuminating fixtures. Current is obtained through our patented collecting shoe built into one of the six-wheel trucks on each car. The light shining through the colored glass windows produces a very realistic effect.

A feature of the observation car is the dome light over the observation platform in addition to the light in the center of the car. Red transparent lanterns are illuminated by the lamp on the rear platform dome. The transparent "Lionel Limited" sign affixed to the observation railing is another new detail.

Outfit No. 403—Comprises No. 402 Twin-Super-Motor Reversible Locomotive with two electric headlights, 1 No. 418 illuminated pullman car, 1 No. 419 illuminated pullman and baggage car, 1 No. 490 illuminated observation car, 8 sections No. S straight track, 8 sections No. C curved track and 1 No. STC "Lockon" connection. Track makes an oval 102 by 42 inches. Train is 74½ inches long and is equipped with automatic couplers. Outfit also includes lamps for headlights and interior of cars, wires for transformer or battery connection, connecting ties for joining sections of track and directions for operating. Price complete $60.75
Code Word "PRETTY"   Western Price $71.00

Outfit No. 403E—This is in every way similar to Outfit No. 403 described above, but includes Electrically Controlled Twin-Super-Motor Locomotive No. 402E, together with controlling rheostat which starts, stops and reverses the train at any distance from the track. Price complete $66.50
Code Word "DEMY"   Western Price $77.75

The powerful Twin-Super-Motor Locomotive No. 402 already described, will haul this train with the greatest ease, and you can add the new No. 218 Operating Dump Car and No. 219 Operating Derrick Car illustrated on Page 35, with full assurance that you will not be overtaxing this sturdy locomotive.

This outfit is truly a remarkable model and one that any boy would be proud to own.

Outfit No. 406—Comprises No. 402 Twin-Super-Motor Reversible Locomotive with two electric headlights, 1 No. 211 flat car, 1 No. 212 gondola car, 1 No. 213 cattle car, 1 No. 214 box car, 1 No. 215 oil car, 1 No. 216 coal car, 1 No. 217 caboose, 8 sections No. C curved track, 10 sections No. S straight track and 1 No. STC "Lockon" connection. Track forms an oval 116 by 42 inches. Complete train is 109¾ inches long and is equipped with automatic couplers. Outfit also includes lamps for headlights and caboose, wires for transformer or battery connection, connecting ties for joining sections of track and directions for operating. Price complete . . $65.50
Code Word "KIRK"   Western Price $76.50

Outfit No. 406E—This is in every way similar to Outfit No. 406 described above, but includes Electrically Controlled Twin-Super-Motor Locomotive No. 402E, together with controlling rheostat which starts, stops and reverses the train at any distance from the track. Price complete $71.25
Code Word "DIAL"   Western Price $83.25

Electrically Controlled and Hand Reversing "Super-Motor" Train Outfits

Reg. U. S. Pat. Office
FOR "LIONEL STANDARD" TRACK—2¼ INCHES WIDE

Nos. 344 and 344E

Outfit No. 344—Comprises No. 380 Super-Motor Reversible Locomotive with two electric headlights, 1 No. 18 illuminated pullman car, 1 No. 190 illuminated observation car, 8 sections No. C curved track, 4 sections No. S straight track and 1 No. STC "Lockon" connection. Track forms an oval 69 by 42 inches. The complete train is 48 inches long, and is equipped with automatic couplers. The locomotive headlights are equipped with individual switches so that one or both may be illuminated at will. The outfit also includes lamps for headlights and interior of cars, wires for transformer or battery connection, connecting ties for joining sections of track, and directions for operating.

The passenger cars included with this outfit are of steel construction throughout and have hinged doors and interior seats. Price complete **$34.50**
Code Word "VERNON"   Western Price $40.50

Outfit No. 344E—This is in every way similar to outfit No. 344 described above, but it includes Super-Motor Locomotive No. 380E, electrically controlled, together with controlling rheostat which starts, stops and reverses the train at any distance from the track.   Price complete **$40.25**
Code Word "LEVER"   Western Price $47.25

Nos. 345 and 345E

Outfit No. 345—Comprises No. 380 Super-Motor Reversible Locomotive with two electric headlights, one No. 12 gondola car, one No. 14 box car, one No. 15 oil car, one No. 17 caboose, 8 sections No. C curved track, 4 sections No. S straight track and one No. STC "Lockon" connection. Track forms an oval 69 by 42 inches. Train is 59 inches long. The locomotive headlights are equipped with individual switches so that one or both may be illuminated at will. The outfit also includes lamps for headlights, wires for transformer or battery connection, connecting ties for joining sections of track, and directions for operating.

This outfit includes several of our large size freight cars which are of steel construction throughout. On Page 34 we show many additional types of freight cars that can be added to this outfit.   Price complete **$34.50**
Code Word "PELHAM"   Western Price $40.50

Outfit No. 345E—This is in every way similar to Outfit No. 345 described above, but it includes Super-Motor Locomotive No. 380E, electrically controlled, together with controlling rheostat which starts, stops and reverses the train at any distance from the track.   Price complete **$40.25**
Code Word "BRONX"   Western Price $47.25

{ 26 }

Complete Railroads for "Lionel Standard" Track—2¼ Inches Wide

Reg. U. S. Pat. Office

HERE are lavishly planned complete railroads that reflect to the highest degree perfect layouts of equipment and miniature villages. A "Multivolt" Transformer is included with these beautiful outfits for operating them from the Alternating House Current, or a Lionel Current Reducer will be supplied if your current is "Direct." Please be sure to specify which one is required.

These complete railroads come to you securely packed and ready for operating.

Nos. 405 and 405E

EQUIPMENT WITH OUTFIT No. 405

LOCOMOTIVES
1 No. 402 Twin-Super-Motor
1 No. 5 Switching Engine

PASSENGER CARS
1 No. 418 Illuminated Pullman
1 No. 419 Illuminated Pullman and Baggage
1 No. 490 Illuminated Observation

FREIGHT CARS
1 No. 11 Flat Car
1 No. 12 Gondola Car
1 No. 13 Cattle Car
1 No. 14 Box Car
1 No. 15 Oil Car
1 No. 16 Coal Car
1 No. 17 Caboose

TRACK
38 sections S straight track
18 sections C curved track
4 sections ½S straight track

TRACK ACCESSORIES
3 pairs No. 220 Switches (right and left)
2 No. 23 Bumpers
6 No. STC "Lockon" Connections

STATIONS AND HOUSES
1 No. 121 Station
1 No. 191 Villa
1 No. 189 Villa
4 No. 184 Bungalows

ACCESSORIES
1 Type K Transformer (or No. 107 Direct Current Reducer if desired)
1 No. 69 Warning Signal
2 No. 77 Crossing Gates
8 No. 60 Telegraph Posts
1 No. 89 Flag Staff
1 No. 65 Semaphore
1 No. 66 Semaphore
1 No. 120 Tunnel
1 No. 101 Bridge (3 sections)
2 No. 59 Lamp Posts
4 No. 57 Lamp Posts

The complete dimensions of the entire track layout are 11 feet 8 inches long and 9 feet 2 inches wide.

Price, complete with electric lamps for locomotives, cars and all accessories, connecting ties for joining sections of track, connecting wires for transformer or reducer and directions for operating, **$200.00**
Code Word "MARK"
Western Price $234.00

Outfit No. 405E—This is in every way similar to Outfit No. 405 described above, but it includes twin-super-motor locomotive No. 402E, electrically controlled, together with controlling rheostat which starts, stops and reverses the train at any distance from the track. All the accessories as described above are also included. Price complete **$205.75**
Code Word "HONOR"   Western Price $240.75

1926

Specifications of Lionel "Multivolt" Transformers

LIONEL DIRECT CURRENT REDUCERS
Not for Alternating Current

Nos. 107 and 170

No. 107, Lionel Current Reducer for 110-Volt Circuit—This is constructed of four porcelain tubes wound with best quality of resistance wire. These porcelain tubes are mounted on a substantial base measuring 8 by 10 inches and 3/4 inch thick. The porcelain tubes are protected and ventilated by a perforated steel cover lined with heavy asbestos. The sliding lever regulates the voltage so that train will just crawl along or go ahead at express speed. The reducer is connected with the house current by a screw plug with 7 feet of flexible cord. Four porcelain supports with screws are supplied so that the reducer can be screwed to wall or table.

Price **$10.00**
Western Price **$11.00**
Code Word "KENTUCKY"

No. 170, Lionel Direct Current Reducer for 220-Volt Circuit—This reducer is identical in appearance with No. 107, mentioned above, but is for use on 220 volts. Equipped with separable plug and 7 feet of flexible cord.

Price **$14.50**
Western Price **$15.25**
Code Word "ASBURY"

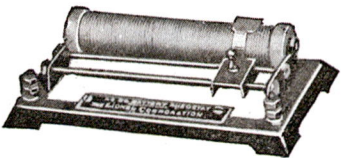

No. 88

Lionel Battery Rheostat No. 88—For dry or storage batteries. It gives a gradual increase or decrease of current. A porcelain tube is wound with resistance wire of the correct gauge. This is mounted on a steel frame. A sliding finger increases or decreases the speed of the trains. All parts are of the best quality. This rheostat cannot overheat, as the coil is entirely exposed to the air—insuring free circulation, consequently rapid cooling. The steel base is beautifully enameled and other parts are nickel plated. Size 5 inches long, 2½ inches wide and 1 inch high.

Price **$1.50**
Western Price **$1.65**
Code Word "BANNER"

LIONEL "Multivolt" Transformers are made completely at our own factories. The department in which they are made is the largest of its kind devoted exclusively to the manufacture of low-voltage transformers. The only parts purchased are the raw materials. We correctly wind and insulate the coils, make the cases, laminations, switch handles, and in fact do every operation. That is why Lionel "Multivolt" Transformers are the best designed, best constructed, and are approved by the Underwriters' Laboratories.

Details of Transformer Construction

Sub-Base—A metal sub-base resting on four supports is attached to the bottom. The air circulating between this sub-base and the transformer case keeps it cool while in operation. Holes in this sub-base provide means for fastening to wall or table.

Separable Plug—All "Multivolt" Transformers are fitted with an approved, separable plug, which is a distinct advantage over the one-piece plug, because the circuit can be immediately broken.

Plug Protecting Device—A unique receptacle for protecting the plug against breakage in shipment. This device consists of a wooden container entirely covering the plug. It is sealed with a conspicuous label which draws the attention to the fact that the transformer must be used **only** on **alternating** current of the number of cycles designated. This obviates the possibility of connecting the transformer with wrong current and avoids mishandling.

Double Contact Control Switch—This is infinitely superior to the one-piece switch, which is easily bent and does not make positive contact. Our double switch has a flexible, phosphor-bronze contact arm under the rigid switch, so that positive contact with the points is assured. This flexible contact is protected from injury by the rigid brass handle to which it is attached. An exclusive feature of "Multivolt" Transformers.

Laminations—The laminations are made of the best grade of electrical sheets and the windings are perfectly insulated.

Rigid Supports for Coils—The coils and laminations of Lionel "Multivolt" Transformers are rigidly supported inside the case by means of metal bands which prevent these parts from moving and eliminate the possibility of broken lead wires. In addition to these supports, the interior of the case is fitted with an insulating receptacle and the case is air cooled.

Metal Case—The case is beautiful in design and is stamped of heavier steel than is required by the Underwriters' Laboratories.

Finish—"Multivolt" Transformer cases are covered with a rubberoid composition that is applied at 350 degrees Fahrenheit. This is much greater heat than the case is ever subjected to, and the finish cannot be scratched and will not peel off during the entire life of the transformer.

Visible Connections—All contacts and switches are mounted on one piece of heavy insulating material and are at the top of the transformer, right before the user.

Lamp Cord—All "Multivolt" Transformers are fitted with 7 feet of flexible lamp cord which enters the transformer case through an approved porcelain bushing.

It will be seen that "Multivolt" Transformers incorporate every device that will increase their efficiency.

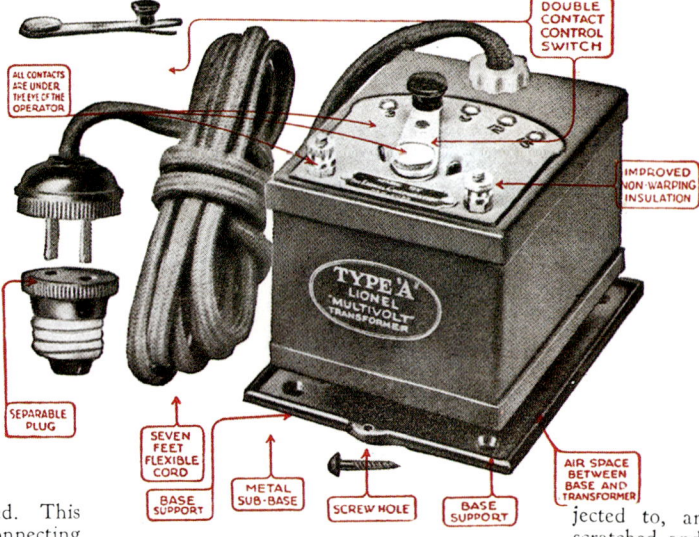

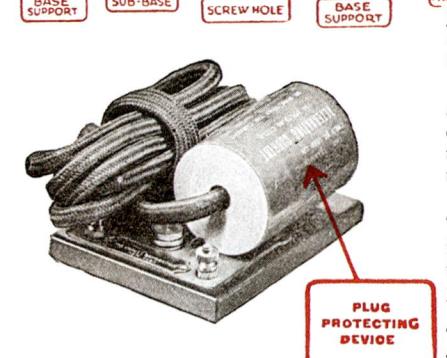

{ 28 }

Lionel "Multivolt" Transformers—for 110 and 220 Volts, 60, 40, or 25 Cycles

This illustration shows transformer contained within the new Lionel Power Station. They are made in two sizes to accommodate every type of Lionel "Multivolt" Transformer. Full description of this desirable new accessory will be found on Page 43.

The Lionel Power Station is placed over the transformer and you can manipulate the controlling switch by simply raising the grating on the roof.

LIONEL "Multivolt" Transformers have been on the market for a great many years and operate all makes of Electric Trains. We justly claim they are best. Don't experiment with other makes of doubtful value. Remember, that all transformers look alike outside, but their imperfections will only be discovered after they are in actual use for a length of time. Lionel "Multivolt" Transformers will last indefinitely and are guaranteed unconditionally as long as they are used on the current for which they are intended. They are absolutely safe and will give steady, even power.

THESE TRANSFORMERS ARE FOR USE ONLY ON "ALTERNATING" CURRENT—DO NOT USE THEM ON "DIRECT" CURRENT

Type "A" Transformer will operate any "O" gauge outfit.

For 110 volts, 60 cycles. 40 watts capacity.

Gives 15 volts in following steps: 4, 7, 10, 13, 15.

Size: 4¼ by 2¾ by 4¼ inches. Sub-base: 3¾ by 4¾ inches.

Price $3.75
Western Price $4.00
Code Word "STRONG"

Type "B" Transformer will operate any "O" gauge outfit, and in addition the extra binding posts enable the user to light up lamp posts, semaphores and other electrically illuminated accessories.

For 110 volts, 60 cycles. 50 watts capacity.

Gives 25 volts in following steps:
Permanent: 7, 8, 15.
Variable: 2, 4, 6, 8, 9, 10, 11, 12, 13, 17, 19, 21, 23, 25.

Size 4½ by 3¾ by 3 inches. Sub-base: 5 by 4¼ inches.

Price $5.00
Western Price $5.50
Code Word "BRADLEY"

Type "T" Transformer will operate any "O" gauge or "Lionel Standard" outfit; also has extra binding posts for attaching illuminated electrical accessories.

For 110 volts, 60 cycles. 100 watts capacity.

Gives 25 volts in following steps:
Permanent: 2, 4, 6, 7, 8, 10, 12, 14, 15, 16, 17, 18, 19, 21, 23, 25.
Variable: 2, 6, 8, 10, 12, 14, 16, 17, 18, 19, 21, 23, 25.

Size: 5 by 4 by 3¾ inches. Sub-base 4½ by 5½ inches.

Price $7.50
Western Price $8.00
Code Word "BIRCH"

Type "K" Transformer will operate any outfit as well as illuminated accessories. This transformer has sufficient wattage capacity to operate two trains at once.

Size: 5 by 4 by 4½ inches. Sub-base: 4½ by 5½ inches.

"K"—For 110 volts, 60 cycles. 150 watts capacity. Specifications same as Type "T," but has higher wattage capacity. **Price $11.00**
Western Price $11.75
Code Word (110V.) "BINGHAM"

"K"—For 220 volts, 60 cycles. 150 watts capacity. Specifications same as Type "T," but is for use on 220-volt circuit. **Price $14.50**
Western Price $15.25
Code Word (220 V.) "BROOK"

Type "C" Transformer will operate any outfit and illuminated accessories on 25 or 40 cycle current.

For 110 volts, 25 to 40 cycles. 75 watts capacity. Specifications same as Type "T," but is for use on 25 or 40 cycle current.

Size: 5 by 4 by 4½ inches. Sub-base: 4½ by 5½ inches.

Price $7.50
Western Price $8.00
Code Word "LAWRENCE"

Pullman and Observation Cars for Lionel "O" Gauge Track—1⅜ Inches Wide

THE construction of all Lionel Pullman Coaches is worthy of special notice, as it represents the highest form of miniature car manufacture. Not only are all bodies made of heavy steel and beautifully embossed with panels, rivets, etc., but they are rigidly held together by mechanical means and soldered. Cross braces and partitions placed inside the cars add to the detail and make them rigid and almost indestructible. Some outstanding features of Lionel Coaches are hinged doors, inserted window frames and sashes and interior seats. These separable pieces are enameled in various colors to harmonize with the body of the car and accentuate the great detail that is incorporated in them. All Lionel Cars are finished in enamel baked on at high temperature. The finish is everlasting and can always be kept bright and clean.

In almost every car clear transparencies are placed in the windows and leaded glass effects will be found at the upper parts of the windows and in the transoms. The light shining through these transparencies produces a most realistic effect. The roofs are firmly held in place with an ornamental screw—easily removable so that lamp in the interior can be reached.

Many of the models have miniature tanks affixed to the bottom as well as brass steps and hand rails, and with the exception of two of the lowest priced "O" Gauge Cars, are all equipped with the new Lionel Automatic Coupler. The rear platforms of observation cars are made of ornamental sheet brass, highly polished.

All cars are mounted on scientifically designed trucks with perfectly aligned nickeled wheels and axles. They operate without friction and are so absolutely true that they will not derail even when traveling at a high rate of speed. All the desirable features mentioned here will be seen by referring to the indications on Page 9.

We have incorporated all these features in the "Lionel Standard" Passenger Cars illustrated on the opposite page.

No. 710
No. 710 Illuminated Pullman Car—With automatic couplers. 11½ inches long, 4½ inches high. Mounted on two 4-wheel trucks. Complete with electric lamp. For use with Locomotive No. 256.
Price $3.75
Code Word "HOLLY" Western Price $4.00

No. 605
No. 605 Illuminated Pullman Car—With automatic couplers. 10⅝ inches long, 4¼ inches high. Mounted on two 4-wheel trucks. Complete with electric lamp. For use with Locomotives No. 251 or 254.
Price $3.25
Code Word "NOVA" Western Price $3.65

No. 610
No. 610 Illuminated Pullman Car—With automatic couplers. 9 inches long, 3¾ inches high. Mounted on two 4-wheel trucks. Complete with electric lamp. For use with Locomotives No. 253 or 254.
Price $2.95
Code Word "EALING" Western Price $3.25

No. 607
No. 607 Illuminated Pullman Car—With automatic couplers. 7½ inches long, 3⅜ inches high. Mounted on two 4-wheel trucks. Complete with electric lamp. For use with Locomotives No. 250, 252 or 253.
Price $1.65
Code Word "BRAND" Western Price $1.85

Nos. 529 and 629
No. 529 Pullman Car—Automatic couplers, mottled celluloid in windows, 6¾ inches long, 3¼ inches high. For use with Locomotives No. 152, 250 or 252.
Price $ .75
Code Word "IMPY" Western Price $ .80
No. 629 Pullman Car—Similar to No. 529, no mottled celluloid in windows. Price $ .60
Code Word "FAME" Western Price $ .65

No. 712
No. 712 Illuminated Observation Car—With automatic couplers. 11½ inches long, 4½ inches high. Mounted on two 4-wheel trucks. Similar in every way to No. 710 Car illustrated above, but has ornamental brass observation platform. Complete with electric lamp. For use with Locomotive No. 256.
Price $3.85
Code Word "RISE" Western Price $4.25

No. 606
No. 606 Illuminated Observation Car—With automatic couplers. 10⅜ inches long, 4¼ inches high. Mounted on two 4-wheel trucks. Similar in every way to No. 605 Car illustrated above, but has ornamental brass observation platform. Complete with electric lamp. For use with Locomotives No. 251 or 254.
Price $3.50
Code Word "MODE" Western Price $3.75

No. 612
No. 612 Illuminated Observation Car—With automatic couplers. 9 inches long, 3¾ inches high. Mounted on two 4-wheel trucks. Similar in every way to No. 610 Car illustrated above, but has ornamental brass observation platform. Complete with electric lamp. For use with Locomotives No. 253 or 254.
Price $3.15
Code Word "WALTON" Western Price $3.35

No. 608
No. 608 Illuminated Observation Car—With automatic couplers. 7½ inches long, 3⅜ inches high. Mounted on two 4-wheel trucks. Similar in every way to No. 607 Car illustrated above, but has ornamental brass observation platform. Complete with electric lamp. For use with Locomotives No. 250, 252 or 253.
Price $1.75
Code Word "TWIG" Western Price $2.00

Nos. 530 and 630
No. 530 Observation Car—Automatic Couplers, mottled celluloid in windows. 6¾ inches long, 3¼ inches high. Mounted on 4-wheel truck. For use with Locomotives No. 152, 250 or 252.
Price $ .80
Code Word "IONA" Western Price $ .90
No. 630 Observation Car—Similar to No. 530, no mottled celluloid in windows.
Price $ .65
Code Word "IDEAL" Western Price $ .75

LENGTH OF CARS DOES NOT INCLUDE COUPLERS

Pullman, Combination, Observation, Mail and Baggage Cars for "Lionel Standard Track—2¼ In. Wide

Reg. U. S. Pat. Office

ALL CARS LISTED ON THIS PAGE ARE EQUIPPED WITH AUTOMATIC COUPLERS
Length of cars does not include couplers.

No. 338 Illuminated Observation Car—12 inches long, 4¾ inches high. Observation platform made of ornamental brass. Has center light and dome light over observation platform. Complete with two electric lamps. **Price $5.00**
Code Word "ORBIT"   Western Price $5.50

No. 337 Illuminated Pullman Car—12 inches long, 4¾ inches high. Complete with electric lamp. **Price $4.25**
Code Word "PASS"   Western Price $4.50

No. 332 Illuminated Mail and Baggage Car—12 inches long, 4¾ inches high. Has two baggage compartments with sliding doors. Complete with electric lamp. **Price $4.50**
Code Word "WILE"   Western Price $5.00

Above cars are mounted on two 4-wheel trucks and are for use with Locomotives No. 8 or 10.

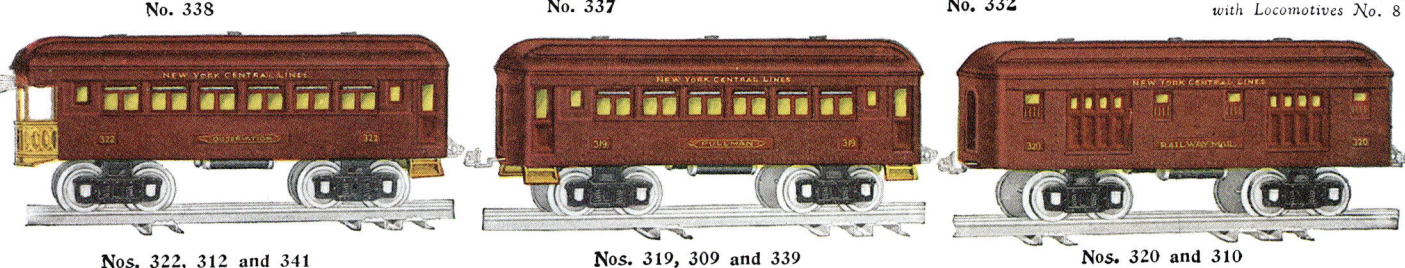

No. 338   No. 337   No. 332

Nos. 322, 312 and 341   Nos. 319, 309 and 339   Nos. 320 and 310

Illustration shows the patented revolving shoe. It collects current from the third rail for lighting interior of passenger coaches.

Nos. 490 and 430   Nos. 418 and 428   Nos. 419 and 429

Illustration shows dome light over platform on "Lionel Standard" Observation Cars—also red transparent lanterns which are illuminated by the dome light.

No. 322 Illuminated Observation Car—13¼ inches long, 5½ inches high. Observation platform made of ornamental brass. Has center light and dome light over observation platform. Complete with two electric lamps. **Price $6.35**
Code Word "JANE"   Western Price $6.95

No. 319 Illuminated Pullman Car—13¼ inches long, 5½ inches high. Complete with electric lamp. **Price $5.35**
Code Word "COTT"   Western Price $5.85

No. 320 Illuminated Mail and Baggage Car—13¼ inches long, 5½ inches high. Has two baggage compartments with sliding doors. Complete with electric lamp. **Price $5.85**
Code Word "TALL"   Western Price $5.85

Above cars are mounted on two 4-wheel trucks and are for use with Locomotives No. 380 or 402.

No. 312 Illuminated Observation Car—13¼ inches long, 5⅛ inches high. Complete with two electric lamps. **Price $5.85**
Code Word "DOMO"   Western Price $6.50

No. 309 Illuminated Pullman Car—13¼ inches long, 5⅛ inches high. Complete with electric lamp. **Price $5.00**
Code Word "ROAD"   Western Price $5.50

No. 310 Illuminated Mail and Baggage Car—13¼ inches long, 5⅛ inches high. Complete with electric lamp. **Price $5.35**
Code Word "WEC"   Western Price $5.85

Above cars are similar in size and construction to No. 322, 319 and 320 described above, but have smaller wheels. For use with Locomotives No. 318 or 380.

No. 341 Illuminated Observation Car—12 inches long, 4¾ inches high. Complete with two electric lamps. **Price $5.50**
Code Word "LEO"   Western Price $6.00

No. 339 Illuminated Pullman Car—12 inches long, 4¾ inches high. Complete with electric lamp. **Price $4.50**
Code Word "STAR"   Western Price $5.00

Cars No. 339 and 341 are similar in construction to No. 312 and 309, but are smaller in size. For use with Locomotives No. 8 or 10.

No. 490 Illuminated Observation Car—17½ inches long, 6 inches high. Observation platform is made of ornamental brass. Equipped with center light and dome light over observation platform. Car is fitted with revolving arm chairs, exact replicas of parlor car chairs. Complete with two electric lamps. **Price $9.50**
Code Word "CABIN"   Western Price $10.50

No. 419 Illuminated Pullman and Baggage Car—17½ inches long, 6 inches high. Has baggage compartment with sliding doors. Car is fitted with revolving arm chairs. Complete with electric lamp. **Price $8.75**
Code Word "COURT"   Western Price $9.50

No. 418 Illuminated Pullman Car—17½ inches long, 6 inches high. Complete with electric lamp. Fitted with revolving arm chairs. **Price $8.50**
Code Word "COMFORT"   Western Price $9.00

Above cars are mounted on two 6-wheel trucks and are for use with Locomotives No. 380 or 402.

No. 430 Illuminated Observation Car—Complete with two electric lamps. **Price $8.50**
Code Word "NERO"   Western Price $9.00

No. 429 Illuminated Pullman and Baggage Car—Complete with electric lamp. **Price $7.85**
Code Word "DORA"   Western Price $8.50

No. 428 Illuminated Pullman Car—17½ inches long, 5¾ inches high. Complete with electric lamp. **Price $7.50**
Code Word "IRIS"   Western Price $8.00

Above cars are similar in construction to No. 490, 419 and 418 described above, but are mounted on two 4-wheel trucks. For use with Locomotives No. 380 or 402.

{ 31 }

1926

Freight Cars for Lionel "O" Gauge Track—1⅛ Inches Wide

THE series of Lionel "O" Gauge Freight Cars listed on this page, while remarkably low in price are of Lionel quality throughout. They are constructed entirely of sheet steel and are enameled (not lithographed) by the Lionel Process, which imparts a handsome glossy appearance that lasts for the life of the cars. In appearance Lionel "O" Gauge Freight Cars are exactly like real massive all-steel cars seen in the big freight yards. Appropriate railroad "heralds" and trimmings on the various types of cars greatly add to their realism.

No. 803 Coal Car—6⅞ inches long, 3⅛ inches high. Mounted on a four-wheel truck. Has "Hopper" bottom operated by wheel on the side of the car. For use with Locomotives No. 152, No. 250 and No. 252.
Price $ .65
Code Word "LOAD"   Western Price $ .75

No. 801 Caboose—5¾ inches long, 3½ inches high. Mounted on a 4-wheel truck. For use with Locomotives No. 152, No. 250 and No. 252.
Price $ .50
Code Word "CONNERTON"   Western Price $ .55

No. 804 Oil Car—6¾ inches long, 3¾ inches high. Mounted on a 4-wheel truck. For use with Locomotives No. 152, No. 250 and No. 252.
Price $ .60
Code Word "FUEL"   Western Price $ .65

No. 800 Box Car—5¾ inches long, 3¼ inches high. Mounted on a 4-wheel truck. Has sliding doors. For use with Locomotives No. 152, No. 250 and No. 252.
Price $ .50
Code Word "CHANDLER"   Western Price $ .55

No. 901 Gondola Car—5¾ inches long, 2 inches high. Mounted on a 4-wheel truck. For use with Locomotives No. 152, No. 250 and No. 252.
Price $ .40
Code Word "CHIMES"   Western Price $ .45

No. 802 Cattle Car—5¾ inches long, 3¼ inches high. Mounted on a 4-wheel truck. Has sliding doors. For use with Locomotives No. 152, No. 250 and No. 252.
Price $ .50
Code Word "CHICKASAW"   Western Price $ .55

No. 820 Box Car—7¼ inches long, 3⅛ inches high. Mounted on two 4-wheel trucks. Has sliding doors. For use with Locomotives No. 253 or No. 254.
Price $1.25
Code Word "ECOLA"   Western Price $1.35

No. 822 Caboose—7¼ inches long, 3½ inches high. Mounted on two 4-wheel Locomotives No. 253 or No. 254.
Price $1.25
Code Word "ELIXIR"   Western Price $1.35

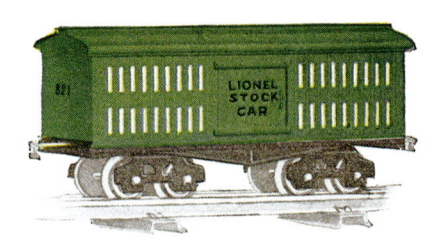

No. 821 Cattle Car—7¼ inches long, 3⅛ inches high. Mounted on two 4-wheel trucks. Has sliding doors. For use with Locomotives No. 253 or No. 254.
Price $1.25
Code Word "STEER"   Western Price $1.35

LENGTH OF CARS DOES NOT INCLUDE COUPLERS

New Line of Freight Cars for Lionel "O" Gauge Track—1⅜ Inches Wide

IN designing this marvelous new series of Lionel "O" Gauge Freight Cars, our aim has been to express the individuality of every type of commercial freight car used on all railroads. Many new features never before carried out to such perfection are apparent in these cars.

The cars are of all-steel construction—trucks are of a new design and are fitted with nickeled journals—cars have automatic couplers and the bodies of some types have inserted brass panels, highly polished, upon which the name and number are etched. This exclusive Lionel method of manufacture not only adds to the appearance of the cars, but greatly strengthens them. The cars are enamel finished in attractive colors.

All the skill of Lionel designers and engineers plus the manufacturing experience of twenty-six years has been brought to bear in the production of these new cars.

No. 814 Box Car—With automatic couplers. 8¾ inches long, 4⅜ inches high. Mounted on two 4-wheel trucks, which are fitted with nickeled journals. Car has sliding doors and is equipped with ladder and hand brake. This car is for use with Locomotives No. 253, No. 254 and No. 256.
Price $2.10
Code Word "YOKE"   Western Price $2.25

No. 815 Oil Car—With automatic couplers. 8¾ inches long, 4½ inches high. Mounted on two 4-wheel trucks, which are fitted with nickeled journals. Tank is rigidly fastened to car platform and is surrounded by hand rails to which ladders are attached. This car is for use with Locomotives No. 253, No. 254 and No. 256.
Price $2.10
Code Word "YAM"   Western Price $2.25

No. 813 Cattle Car—With automatic couplers. 8¾ inches long, 4⅜ inches high. Mounted on two 4-wheel trucks, which are fitted with nickeled journals. Car has sliding doors and is equipped with ladder and hand brake. This car is for use with Locomotives No. 253, No. 254 and No. 256.
Price $2.10
Code Word "YAWL"   Western Price $2.25

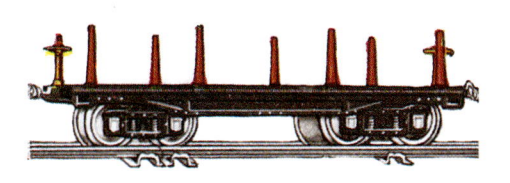

No. 811 Flat Car—With automatic couplers. 8¾ inches long, 3½ inches high. Mounted on two 4-wheel trucks, which are fitted with nickeled journals. Removable supports are inserted in sockets in the platform. Hand brake is fitted to the car platform. This car is for use with Locomotives No. 253, No. 254 and No. 256.
Price $2.10
Code Word "DRUM"   Western Price $2.25

No. 817 Caboose—With automatic couplers. 8¾ inches long, 4⅜ inches high. Mounted on two 4-wheel trucks, which are fitted with nickeled journals. Front and rear platforms have a ladder running to the roof of the car. This car is for use with Locomotives No. 253, No. 254 and No. 256.
Price $2.95
Code Word "DEFT"   Western Price $3.25

No. 812 Gondola Car—With automatic couplers. 8¾ inches long, 3¼ inches high. Mounted on two 4-wheel trucks, which are fitted with nickeled journals. Car is equipped with hand brake which is rigidly fastened to the platform. This car is for use with Locomotives No. 253, No. 254 and No. 256.
Price $2.10
Code Word "DALE"   Western Price $2.25

LENGTH OF CARS DOES NOT INCLUDE COUPLERS

Freight Cars for "Lionel Standard" Track—2¼ Inches Wide

Reg. U. S. Pat. Office

THE popular priced line of "Lionel Standard" Freight Cars listed here have been Lionel favorites for many years past, and are always welcome additions to a model railroad.

They are constructed of sheet steel, beautifully finished in rich lasting enamel, and are appropriately decorated with "heralds" of the most prominent railroads. Trucks are flexible and will not jump the track, even while running at high speed.

These freight cars run so easily that any "Lionel Standard" Locomotive will haul a number of them. The construction of all cars is similar, but they vary in size according to the locomotive with which they are operated.

No. 13 Cattle Car—11¼ inches long, 5¾ inches high. Mounted on two 4-wheel trucks. Has sliding doors. For use with Locomotives No. 380 and 402. **Price $3.35**
Code Word "HAMPSHIRE" Western Price $3.50

No. 113 Cattle Car—9½ inches long, 4½ inches high. Mounted on two 4-wheel trucks. Similar to No. 13 Car described above. For use with Locomotives No. 8, 10 and 318. **Price $2.10**
Code Word "SYRACUSE" Western Price $2.50

No. 17 Caboose—11 inches long, 6½ inches high. Mounted on two 4-wheel trucks. For use with Locomotives No. 380 and 402. **Price $3.35**
Code Word "TORONTO" Western Price $3.50

No. 117 Caboose—9¾ inches long, 5 inches high. Mounted on two 4-wheel trucks. Similar to No. 17 Car described above. For use with Locomotives No. 8, 10 and 318. **Price $2.10**
Code Word "TOLEDO" Western Price $2.50

No. 14 Box Car—11¼ inches long, 5¾ inches high. Mounted on two 4-wheel trucks. Has sliding doors. For use with Locomotives No. 380 and 402. **Price $3.35**
Code Word "MAINE" Western Price $3.50

No. 114 Box Car—9½ inches long, 4½ inches high. Mounted on two 4-wheel trucks. Similar to No. 14 Car described above. For use with Locomotives No. 8, 10 and 318. **Price $2.10**
Code Word "HAZELTON" Western Price $2.50

No. 16 Ballast Car—10½ inches long, 4½ inches high. Mounted on two 4-wheel trucks. Car has hinged sides operated by levers at end. For use with Locomotives No. 380 and 402. **Price $3.35**
Code Word "ONTARIO" Western Price $3.50

No. 116 Coal Car—8¾ inches long, 3½ inches high. Mounted on two 4-wheel trucks. This car is illustrated with Outfit No. 41 on Page 22. For use with Locomotives No. 8, 10 and 318. **Price $2.10**
Code Word "SCRANTON" Western Price $2.50

No. 12 Gondola Car—11¼ inches long 4⅜ inches high. Mounted on two 4-wheel trucks. For use with Locomotives No. 380 and 402. **Price $2.95**
Code Word "VERMONT" Western Price $3.25

No. 112 Gondola Car—9½ inches long, 3 inches high. Mounted on two 4-wheel trucks. Similar to No. 12 Car described above. For use with Locomotives No. 8, 10 and 318. **Price $1.50**
Code Word "ELMIRA" Western Price $1.60

No. 11 Flat Car—11½ inches long, 3¾ inches high. Mounted on two 4-wheel trucks. For use with Locomotives No. 318. **Price $2.10**
Code Word "MASS" Western Price $2.50

No. 15 Oil Car—10¾ inches long, 5¼ inches high. Mounted on two 4-wheel trucks. For use with Locomotives No. 380 and 402. **Price $3.35**
Code Word "QUEBEC" Western Price $3.50

LOCOMOTIVES FOR "LIONEL STANDARD" TRACK ARE ILLUSTRATED ON PAGES 18 AND 19

LENGTH OF CARS DOES NOT INCLUDE COUPLERS

New Line of Freight Cars for "Lionel Standard" Track—2¼ Inches Wide

Reg. U. S. Pat. Office

STILL another remarkable Lionel achievement—this wonderful new line of "Lionel Standard" all-steel freight cars, introducing every known type of modern car that will be eagerly welcomed by all who desire to add real railroad equipment in miniature to their layouts.

Words are inadequate to describe the great detail and many realistic features built into these cars—the illustrations in some measure will enable you to judge; but this new series of cars must be actually seen to be fully appreciated.

No. 213 Cattle Car—With automatic couplers. 11¾ inches long, 5¾ inches high. Mounted on two 4-wheel trucks which are fitted with nickeled journals. Car has sliding doors and is equipped with ladders and hand brakes. This car is for use with Locomotives No. 380 and No. 402. **Price $5.00**
Code Word "WAKE" **Western Price $5.50**

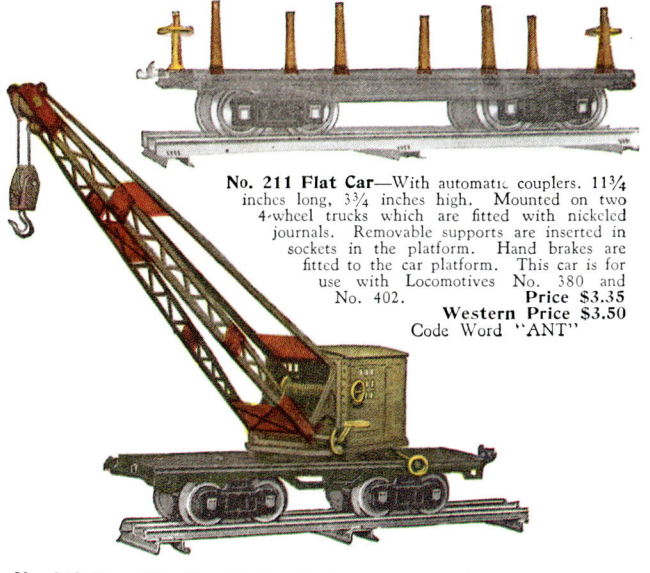

No. 211 Flat Car—With automatic couplers. 11¾ inches long, 3¾ inches high. Mounted on two 4-wheel trucks which are fitted with nickeled journals. Removable supports are inserted in sockets in the platform. Hand brakes are fitted to the car platform. This car is for use with Locomotives No. 380 and No. 402. **Price $3.35**
Code Word "ANT" **Western Price $3.50**

No. 214 Box Car—With automatic couplers. 11¾ inches long, 5¾ inches high. Mounted on two 4-wheel trucks which are fitted with nickeled journals. Car has sliding doors and is equipped with ladders and hand brakes. This car is for use with Locomotives No. 380 and No. 402. **Price $5.00**
Code Word "WOOL" **Western Price $5.50**

No. 216 Coal Car—With automatic couplers. 11¾ inches long, 4⅞ inches high. Mounted on two 4-wheel trucks which are fitted with nickeled journals. Car has "Hopper" bottom operated by wheel on the side of the car. Equipped with hand brakes. This car is for use with Locomotives No. 380 and No. 402. **Price $5.00**
Code Word "ALAMA" **Western Price $5.50**

No. 219 Operating Derrick Car—With automatic couplers. 11¾ inches long and 5⅝ inches high. The "boom" is 16 inches long. Mounted on two 4-wheel trucks which are fitted with nickeled journals. Equipped with levers and wheels for operating the pulley and tackle, raising and lowering the "boom," and for revolving the entire housing. It works just like a real railroad crane. This car can be used with any "Lionel Standard" Locomotive. **Price $8.50**
Code Word "ALUM" **Western Price $9.00**

No. 218 Operating Dump Car—With automatic couplers. 11¾ inches long, 4½ inches high. Mounted on two 4-wheel trucks which are fitted with nickeled journals. Body of the car can be tilted by means of the levers placed at each end. As car tilts, sides automatically open. This car can be used with any "Lionel Standard" Locomotive. **Price $5.85**
Code Word "DEPEW" **Western Price $6.50**

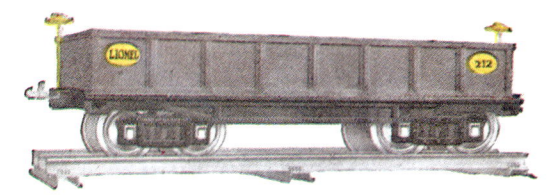

No. 215 Oil Car—With automatic couplers. 11¾ inches long, 6 inches high. Mounted on two 4-wheel trucks which are fitted with nickeled journals. Tank is rigidly fastened to the car platform and is surrounded by hand rails to which ladders are attached. Equipped with hand brakes. This car is for use with Locomotives No. 380 and No. 402. **Price $5.00**
Code Word "DICE" **Western Price $5.50**

No. 217 Caboose—With automatic couplers. 11¾ inches long, 6 inches high. Mounted on two 4-wheel trucks which are fitted with nickeled journals. Front and rear platforms are equipped with ladders running to the roof of the car. Tail light is mounted on rear platform. This car is for use with Locomotives No. 380 and No. 402. **Price $5.85**
Code Word "RAFT" **Western Price $6.50**

No. 212 Gondola Car—With automatic couplers. 11¾ inches long, 3½ inches high. Mounted on two 4-wheel trucks which are fitted with nickeled journals. Equipped with hand brakes. This car is for use with Locomotives No. 380 and No. 402. **Price $3.35**
Code Word "ROY" **Western Price $3.50**

LENGTH OF CARS DOES NOT INCLUDE COUPLERS

{ 35 }

1926

Lionel "All-Steel" Lamp Posts—Lamp Assortment—Renewal Lamps

NO miniature railroad is complete without the addition of Lionel lamp posts, which are faithful reproductions of boulevard and street lamp posts seen everywhere. All Lionel lamp posts are substantially constructed of steel throughout — they won't bend or break. The binding posts to which electrical connections are made are conveniently situated and are securely fastened and perfectly insulated.

LAMP ASSORTMENT No. 111

We supply Lionel dealers with a handsome cabinet of renewal lamps for use in headlights and all electrically illuminated accessories. These lamps are of the finest quality and are supplied in 8, 14 and 21 volts. Fifty assorted lamps are packed in each cabinet. The chart on the inside cover gives valuable information as to the uses of the various lamps. Each lamp is packed in a wooden container.

No. 111 LAMP ASSORTMENT
Code Word "LUX"

PRICE $15.00
Western Price $18.00

THERE is no chance of short circuit with Lionel lamp posts, for great care is used in their construction and every one is thoroughly tested before leaving the factory. The globes supplied with all lamp posts are in exact proportion to the size of the posts. It is impossible to secure any other make of lamp post that has the dignity and grace of design to be found in the Lionel lamp posts illustrated below.

SEPARATE RENEWAL LAMPS
(Each Lamp Packed in Wooden Container)

No. 24—Round lamp, clear glass, half inch diameter, 8 volts.
Price . . . . $ .30
Code Word "CAMBRIDGE"   Western Price $ .35

No. 26—Round lamp, clear glass, half inch diameter, 14 volts.
Price . . . . $ .30
Code Word "OXFORD"   Western Price $ .35

No. 48—Round lamp, clear glass, half inch diameter, 21 volts.
Price . . . . $ .30
Code Word "MILTON"   Western Price $ .35

Above lamps are for use in headlights and all electrically illuminated accessories

No. 55—Pear-shaped lamp, frosted, three-quarter inch diameter, 14 volts. Price . . . . $ .30
Code Word "LIT"   Western Price $ .35

Above lamp is for use in lamp posts Nos. 58 and 59

No. 30—Pear-shaped lamp, frosted, one inch diameter, 14 volts. Price . . . . $ .30
Code Word "KINGS"   Western Price $ .35

Above lamp is for use in lamp posts Nos. 61 and 67, also for outside light brackets of Station No. 124

Lamp Post No. 67—13 inches high. Complete with two electric globes.
Price $2.95
Western Price $3.25
Code Word "EDMUNDS"

Lamp Post No. 58—7 3/8 inches high. Complete with globe.
Price $1.25
Western Price $1.35
Code Word "JENNY"

Lamp Post No. 56—8 3/4 inches high. The top is easily removable so that the lamp can be renewed. Complete with lamp.
Price $1.65
Western Price $1.75
Code Word "SHINE"

Lamp Post No. 57—7 1/2 inches high. The top is removable so that the lamp can be renewed. Complete with lamp.
Price $1.65
Western Price $1.75
Code Word "CHEERY"

Lamp Post No. 59—Similar in design to No. 61, but is 8 3/4 inches high. Complete with globe.
Price $1.50
Western Price $1.65
Code Word "RIGHT"

Lamp Post No. 61—13 inches high. Complete with electric globe.
Price $2.10
Western Price $2.25
Code Word "INDIANA"

Reg. U. S. Pat. Office

"Lionel Standard" and "O" Gauge Track—"Lockon" Track Contacts

LIONEL Track is made of heavier metal than that used by any other manufacturer. The illustration on this page shows one of the reasons for the rigidity and strength of Lionel rails. It will be readily noted that the base of the rails is formed outward instead of being turned in, as is the case with ordinary track. This outward flange increases the strength of the track more than 300%, and is only made possible by our process (patented October, 1909). Lionel Track, without bending, will support the weight of a full-grown person.

Each section of track is tested for insulation on 110 volts, consequently it will carry the low voltage necessary to operate Lionel trains without any chance of short-circuiting. The ends of each section have pin terminals which fit in openings in the adjoining sections. This allows the track to be laid and taken apart without any trouble. One section in each outfit is fitted with a "Lockon" track contact for batteries, "Multivolt" Transformer or Reducer.

The track is made in straight and curved sections. The curvature of the track is mechanically correct, allowing trains to run at very high speed without derailing.

LIONEL TRACK

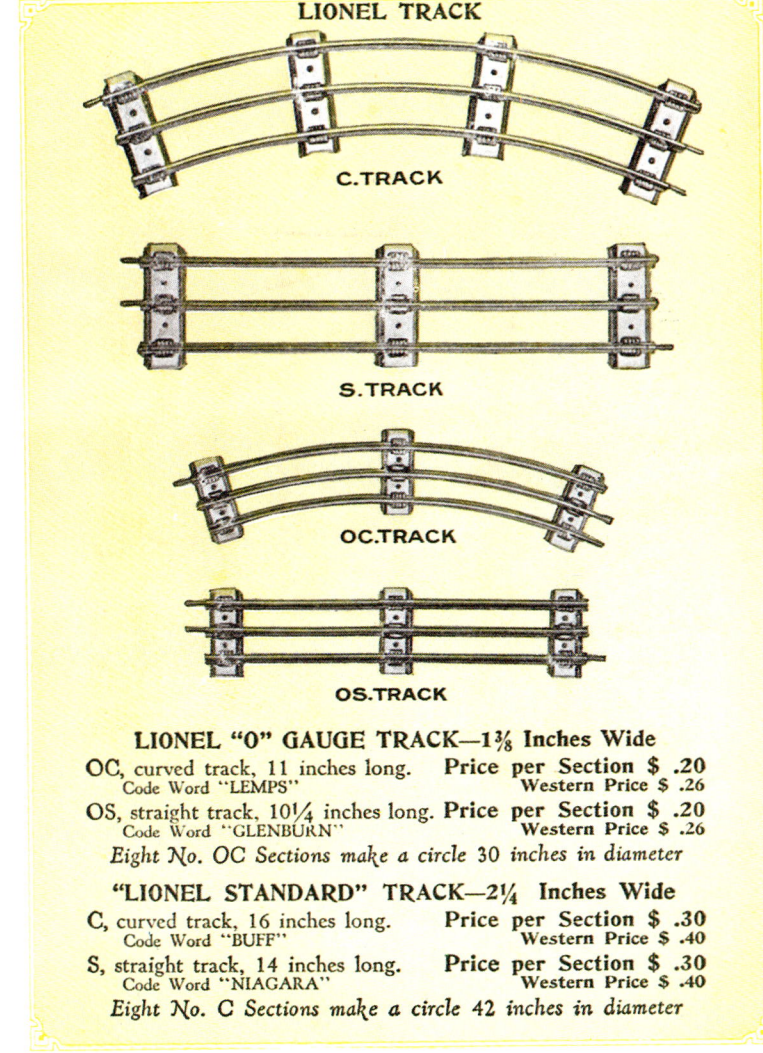

C. TRACK

S. TRACK

OC. TRACK

OS. TRACK

LIONEL "O" GAUGE TRACK—1⅜ Inches Wide

OC, curved track, 11 inches long.   Price per Section $ .20
  Code Word "LEMPS"   Western Price $ .26

OS, straight track, 10¼ inches long. Price per Section $ .20
  Code Word "GLENBURN"   Western Price $ .26

Eight No. OC Sections make a circle 30 inches in diameter

"LIONEL STANDARD" TRACK—2¼ Inches Wide

C, curved track, 16 inches long.   Price per Section $ .30
  Code Word "BUFF"   Western Price $ .40

S, straight track, 14 inches long.   Price per Section $ .30
  Code Word "NIAGARA"   Western Price $ .40

Eight No. C Sections make a circle 42 inches in diameter

Note that the base of Lionel Track is bent outward, making it rigid and strong.
Pat., Oct., 1909

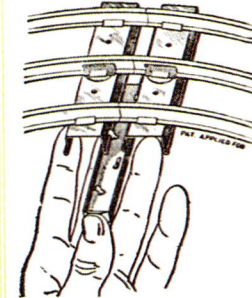

CONNECTING TIE

We show here the method of sliding in the connecting tie. This is one of our recent improvements. It binds the ties rigidly together so that sections cannot pull apart. Can be removed by a slight pull with thumb and finger. Every Lionel Train Outfit includes a sufficient number of connecting ties for the amount of track packed with the outfit.

Special Track for Warning Signals, Crossing Gates and Block Signals

No. OSS Track—"O" Gauge, 10¼ inches long. Complete with OTC "Lockon" Contact and connecting wires.
  Price per Section $ .40
    Western Price $ .50
  Code Word "RELAY"

No. SS Track—"Lionel Standard," 14 inches long. Complete with "Lockon" Contact and connecting wires.
  Price per Section $ .60
    Western Price $ .70
  Code Word "BURT"

"LOCKON" TRACK CONTACTS
Pat. June 16, 1925

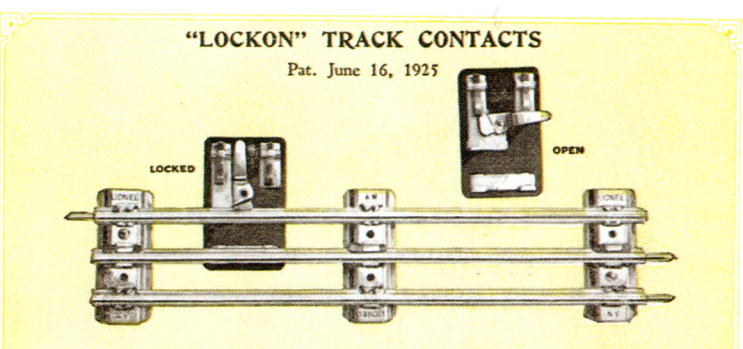

LOCKED   OPEN

Lionel leadership is again evidenced in this improved device. Considering the fact that numerous electric accessories have been added to the Lionel line, which require connection with the track, these "LOCKON" contacts will readily appeal to the user, for it is no longer necessary to purchase special sections of track to which electrical contacts are affixed.

The "Lockon" contact is attached to the track by simply turning the lever at right angles. The electric connection is as perfect as though the parts were riveted or soldered to the track.

The "Lockon" contact is free from set screws and binding posts. The fingers that hold the wires in place are made of heavy tempered blue steel and are unbreakable. All parts are nickel plated and are mounted on a heavy fibre base.

No. "OTC" for Lionel "O" Gauge Track   Price $ .20
                                       Western Price $ .26
  Code Word "JOIN"

No. "STC" for "Lionel Standard" Track   Price $ .25
                                         Western Price $ .30
  Code Word "JUICE"

Reg. U. S. Pat. Office

"Lionel Standard" and "O" Gauge Switches, Crossings and Bumpers

LIONEL Track Accessories are perfectly insulated and are mounted on a steel base which gives them great strength and enables them to withstand hard usage. Every shape or figure can be formed with the scientifically constructed accessories shown on this page.

Improved Lionel Switches—We are particularly desirous of drawing attention to the improved construction of our switches, patented April 21st, 1925. As will be seen from the illustrations, the improvement consists of the insertion of two heavy fibre strips in the "frog," at the points where the rails cross. By the insertion of these fibre strips all possibility of short-circuit is eliminated. A train passing over these points does not slow up, nor does the headlight flicker or go out. The No. 210 and No. 220 "Lionel Standard" Switches listed on this page are of the same improved construction as the Electrically Controlled Switches described on the opposite page, but are equipped with a lever which throws the switch by hand.

Nos. 021 and 022

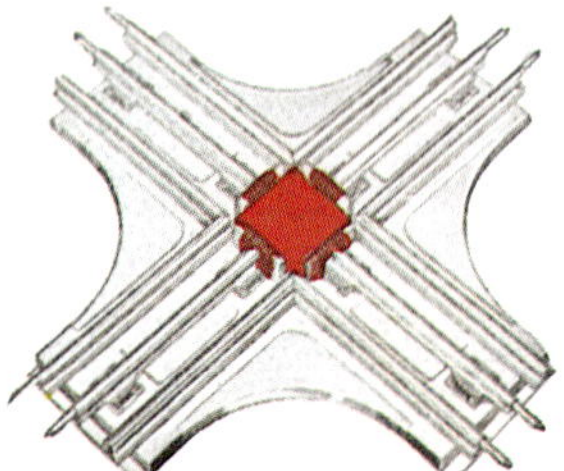

No. 020

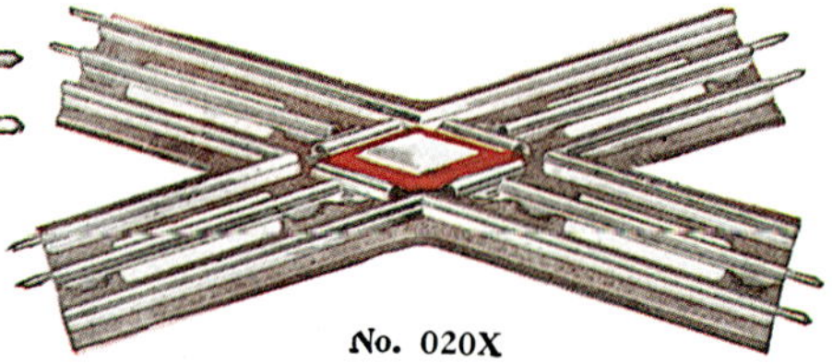

No. 020X

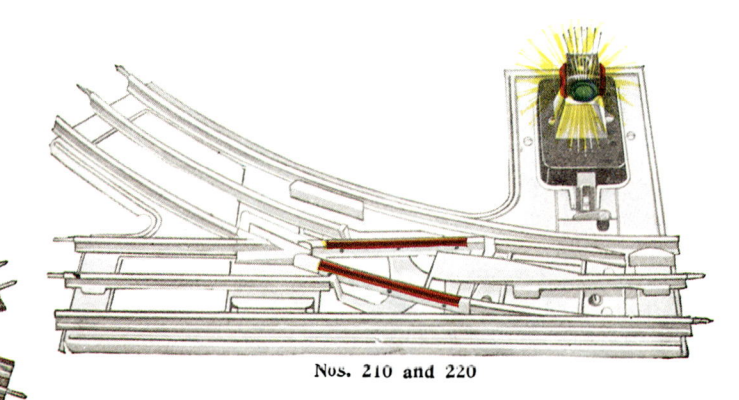

No. 20

No. 023

No. 23

Nos. 210 and 220

FOR LIONEL "O" GAUGE TRACK
1⅜ INCHES WIDE

No. 021 Electric Lighted Switch—(right and left hand). Hand lever moves rails, sets signals and locks all mechanism. Signal has electric lamp which can be easily renewed. Light shining through the lantern shows red and green signals. Switch is 11¼ inches long, 6 inches wide, 2½ inches high. Price per pair, complete with lamps . . $5.00
    Code Word "MOSHER"   **Western Price $5.50**

No. 022 Switch—(right and left hand). Similar to No. 021 Switch described above, but without electric light. Price per pair $3.75
    Code Word "SPENCER"   **Western Price $4.00**

No. 020 Crossing—90 degree. For making figure "8" with switches and track. Fibre strips in cross rails prevent short-circuit. Mounted on a solid base. Size 10¼ inches square. Price $1.00
    Code Word "ORLAND"   **Western Price $1.10**

No. 020X Crossing—45 degree. Makes figure "8" when using only curved track. Rails are perfectly insulated. Base represents ballasted roadbed. Size 11¼ inches long, 6 inches wide. Price $1.50
    Code Word "CROSS"   **Western Price $1.65**

No. 023 Bumper—Spring plunger absorbs shock of car. Bumper frame is removable. Used when railroad layout requires a siding. Length 10¼ inches, height 2 inches. Price . . . . $ .80
    Code Word "DELTON"   **Western Price $ .90**

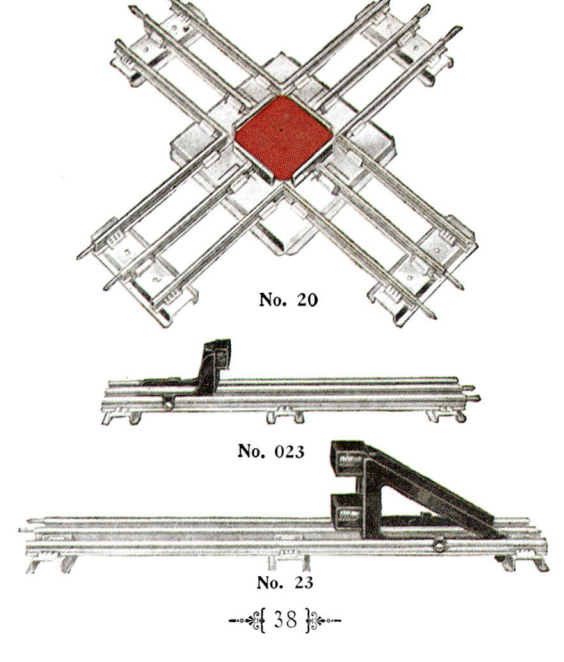

FOR "LIONEL STANDARD" TRACK
2¼ INCHES WIDE

No. 210 Electric Lighted Switch—(right and left hand). Equipped with hand lever which moves the rails, sets the signals and locks all mechanism. Fitted with electric signal having an electric lamp which can be easily renewed. Light shining through the lantern shows red and green illuminated signals. The construction of this switch is similiar to No. 222 Switch fully described on the opposite page. Switch is 15 inches long, 8½ inches wide, 3 inches high.
    Price per pair, complete with lamps $6.75
    Code Word "NASH"   **Western Price $7.25**

No. 220 Switch—(right and left hand). Similar in construction and appearance to No. 210 Switch described above, but without electric light.
    Price per pair $5.00
    Code Word "NOME"   **Western Price $5.50**

No. 20 Crossing—A 90 degree crossing largely used for making figure "8" in conjunction with switches and track. Cross rails are mounted on a solid base. Size 12 inches square. Price $1.25
    Code Word "BOSTON"   **Western Price $1.35**

No. 23 Bumper—Indispensable for terminals or sidings. Fitted with two spring plungers which absorb shock when car strikes it. Length 14 inches, height 3 inches.
    Price $1.25
    Code Word "PROVIDENCE"   **Western Price $1.35**

The New Electrically Controlled Switches

FOR "LIONEL STANDARD" TRACK—2¼ INCHES WIDE

THESE new Electrically Controlled Switches (Patented August 11, 1925) add immeasurably to the realism of Lionel Model Trains, and in conjunction with our Electrically Controlled Locomotives and Automatic Accessories form a model railroad that is 100% Electrically Controlled.

With the introduction of this wonderful new accessory it is no longer necessary to operate switches by hand. Lionel Electrically Controlled Switches can be operated at any distance from the track by means of a controlling lever, in every way similar to the real large ones used by switchmen. By manipulating this lever, the same as the switchman does, the position of the switch instantly changes and the red and green lights in the switch lantern change with the movement of the switch. The controlling lever is permanently connected with the switch by means of flexible wires so that no additional wiring is required.

The mechanism of Lionel Electrically Controlled Switches is extremely simple. There is nothing to get out of order. They are scientifically constructed. Several guide rails are used to eliminate the possibility of the train leaving the track even when operating at high speed.

The patented Lionel fibre frog rails are embodied in the construction of these switches. This exclusive feature prevents the possibility of a short-circuit, when the train is passing over the switch.

The manipulating lever for Lionel Electrically Controlled Switches can be placed in the new Lionel Switch Signal Tower illustrated above and fully described on Page 43, and this structure can also be placed at any distance from the track. It adds considerably to the realism of a Lionel Electrical Railroad.

No. 222 Electrically Controlled Switch—Length 15 inches, width 8½ inches, height 3 inches. Complete, attached to wires and controlling lever.
Price per pair (one right—one left) $10.00
Western Price $11.00
Code Word "AFAR"

Lionel Electrically Controlled Automatic Accessories

THE Lionel Automatic Train Control can be placed at any spot in the track formation. The train approaches —the red signal light shows vividly. The train stops —it is absolutely automatic. After an interval, the red signal light turns to green. "Line's Clear"— All aboard!—the train starts again. Can you imagine anything more realistic?

Its action is positive—does not require any attention.

The Lionel Automatic Train Control is 10½ inches high, is constructed on the lines of the most modern electric signals, and incorporates great detail. Lantern case is easily removable and lamps can be readily replaced. Green and red discs are permanently affixed in the openings so that our standard clear bulbs can be used for replacement. A metal ladder joins the upper and lower parts of the superstructure, faithfully carrying out the true details of these signals. Mechanism is mounted on solid piece of insulating material and is entirely concealed in the base of the signal. Special "Lockon" connection, wires and fibre insulating pins are included.

Operates on dry or storage batteries, reduced direct, or reduced alternating current.

No. 078 for "O" Gauge Track. Complete with lamps, special "Lockon" Contact, connecting wires, fibre insulating pins and directions for operating $5.00
Code Word "HEAVE"   Western Price $5.50

No. 78 for "Lionel Standard" Track. Same as above, but with special "Lionel Standard" "Lockon" Contact $5.00
Code Word "WEAVE"   Western Price $5.50

Lionel Electric Block Signals—Two electric illuminated lanterns showing red and green signals are attached to a steel standard, 8⅝ inches high. When train passes over special sections of track supplied with the signal, green lantern lights up, and after it leaves the first section of special track, the red light shows. This red light goes out as soon as train leaves the second special section of track. To carry out true detail, several block signals can be used at different points of the track formation.

Lionel Electric Warning Signals—A nickeled double bell is mounted on an ornamental steel standard (8¾ inches high), bearing a heavy brass warning sign. Special section of track is supplied to which warning signal is connected. Electric bell rings while train passes over special section of track. Bell automatically stops when train has passed.

Lionel Automatic Crossing Gates—These are exact reproductions of the real ones used at grade crossings. They are of steel construction throughout, finished in handsome black enamel with nickeled top on the case that contains the mechanism. The special section of track provided with the crossing gates is connected with the track layout in the usual manner. While the train is on this section the gates close. They automatically open as soon as the train has passed. These gates can be used singly or in pairs. The special track can be placed a few sections away from the gates so that they will operate some time before the train approaches. The raising and lowering of these gates with the operation of the train produces an effect of great realism.

No. 069 Warning Signal—For "O" Gauge Track. Complete with one section of OSS track, OTC "Lockon" Contact, connecting wires and directions for operating.   Price $3.15
Western Price $3.35
Code Word "RINGER"

No. 69 Warning Signal—For "Lionel Standard" Track. Complete with one section of SS track, STC "Lockon" Contact, connecting wires and directions for operating.
Price $3.35
Western Price $3.50
Code Word "BEWARE"

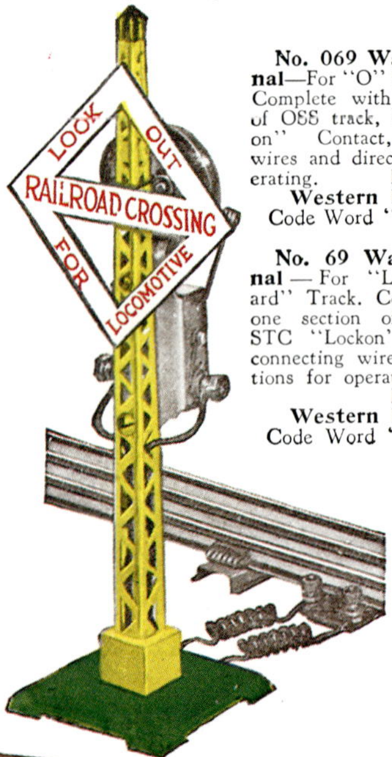

No. 076 Block Signal for "O" Gauge Track—Complete with lamps, two special sections of OSS track, connecting wires and directions for operating.
Price $3.15
Western Price $3.35
Code Word "FORWARD"

No. 76 Block Signal for "Lionel Standard" Track—Complete with lamps, two special sections of SS track, connecting wires and directions for operating.
Price $3.35
Western Price $3.50
Code Word "ONWARD"

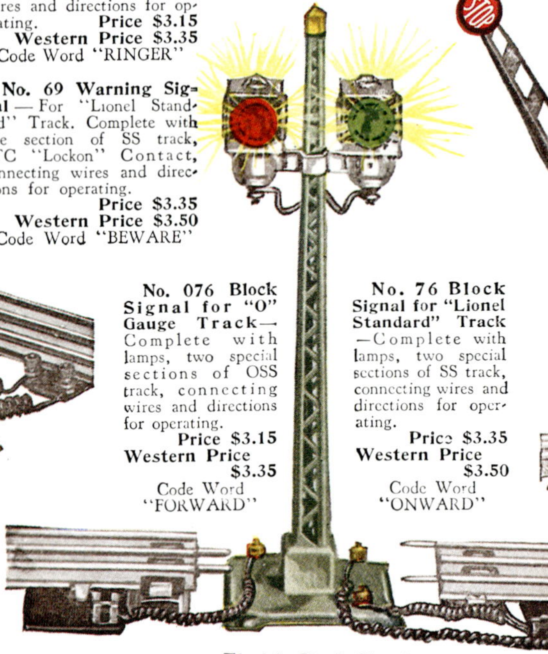

No. 077 Crossing Gate—For "O" Gauge Track, 11 inches long. Complete with one section of OSS track, OTC "Lockon" Contact, connecting wires and directions for operating.
Price $4.00   Western Price $4.35
Code Word "ADVANCE"

No. 77 Crossing Gate—For "Lionel Standard" Track, 11 inches long. Complete with one section of SS track, STC "Lockon" Contact, connecting wires and directions for operating.
Price $4.25   Western Price $4.50
Code Word "TARRY"

No. 080 Electrically Controlled Semaphore for Lionel "O" Gauge Track $4.50
Western Price $5.00
Code Word "DROP"

No. 80 Electrically Controlled Semaphore for "Lionel Standard" Track . . $4.50
Western Price $5.00
Code Word "DRAW"

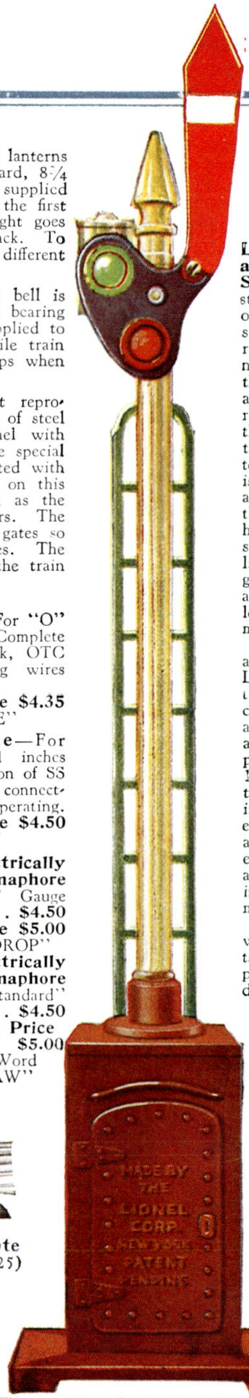

Lionel Electrically Controlled Semaphore—A striking reproduction of the latest type of signal used on all railroads. It requires no manipulation — the arm automatically assumes an upright position when the train approaches the section of track to which semaphore is attached. As soon as train has passed, the arm falls to horizontal; at the same time signal light changes from green to red. This action continues as long as train is in motion.

The construction and finish are of Lionel quality throughout. Lantern case is removable and lamp is easily accessible. Semaphore standard is 12¾ inches high, the arm is 3¾ inches long, and is equipped with red and green transparent discs. It can be attached to the track in a very simple manner.

Supplied complete with "Lockon" Contact, fibre insulating pins, wires and directions for operating.

THE MOST AMAZING RAILROAD ACCESSORY EVER INVENTED

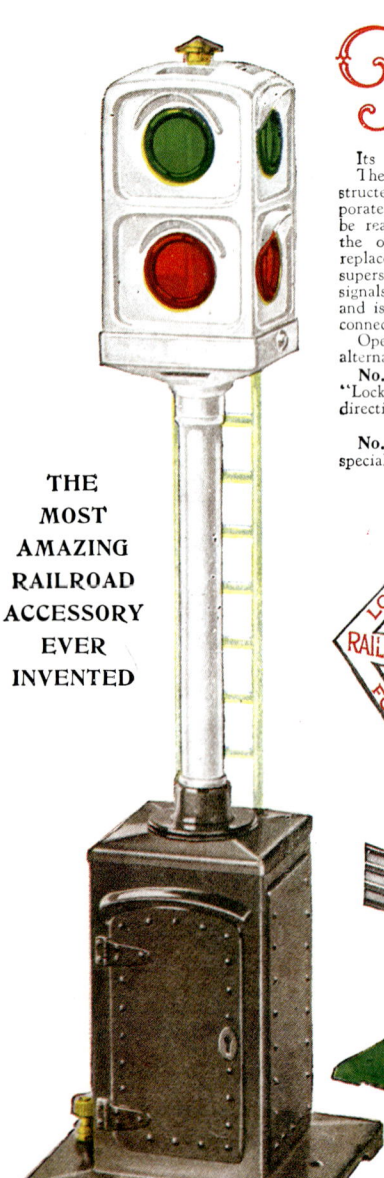

Automatic Train Control
(Pat. Aug. 21, 1917)

Electric Warning Signal

Electric Block Signal

Automatic Crossing Gate
(Pat. Sept. 21, 1925)

Electrically Controlled Semaphore

Lionel Accessories and Accessory Sets

LIONEL accessory sets are unquestionably the best constructed as well as the most popular on the market. This is not to be wondered at considering the fact that they are so durable and attractive in design. A miniature railroad layout is considerably enhanced by the addition of a set of telegraph posts placed at regular intervals around the track. Copper wire can be strung from the insulators, producing an effect of great realism.

If the semaphores, lamp post and warning signal, which form No. 70 set, are added to the train layout the finishing touches are provided. All Lionel accessories are constructed of steel throughout and are beautifully finished.

65 and 66 Semaphores—Constructed of steel. The colored discs which are securely fastened to the semaphore arms show "Danger," "Clear" or "Caution" signals. The electric lamps are enclosed in beautifully enameled steel lanterns, which are removable so that lamps can be easily renewed. A metal finger holds these lantern caps in place. The levers which operate the signal arms are fastened to the base and are connected to the rods running up beneath the ladder. The wiring and insulation are inside the post and short-circuits are impossible.

No. 70

Outfit No. 70—Comprises two No. 62 Semaphores, one No. 59 Lamp Post, one No. 68 Warning Signal and two globes for the lamp post. Attractively packed.
Price $4.25
Western Price $4.50
Code Word "HOBART"

No. 66 Semaphore—14 inches high. Has two signal arms. Complete with electric lamps.
Price $3.75
Western Price $4.00
Code Word "LEMPSTER"

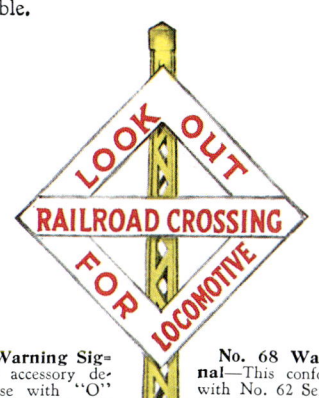

No. 60 Telegraph Post—A companion to No. 62 Semaphore and No. 68 Warning Signal. The arm is equipped with real glass insulators. Height 8¾ inches, base 2½ inches square.
Price $ .65
Western Price $ .75
Code word "WIRE"

No. 068 Warning Signal—A new accessory designed for use with "O" Gauge Trains. Made of steel throughout and similar in construction to the other Warning Signals listed by us. Height 6¾ inches, base 2 inches square.
Price $ .50
Western Price $ .55
Code Word "LOOK"

No. 68 Warning Signal—This conforms in size with No. 62 Semaphore and No. 60 Telegraph Post, and the construction is similar to No. 69 described on page 40. These should be placed at every railroad crossing.
Price $ .90
Western Price $1.00
Code Word "STOP"

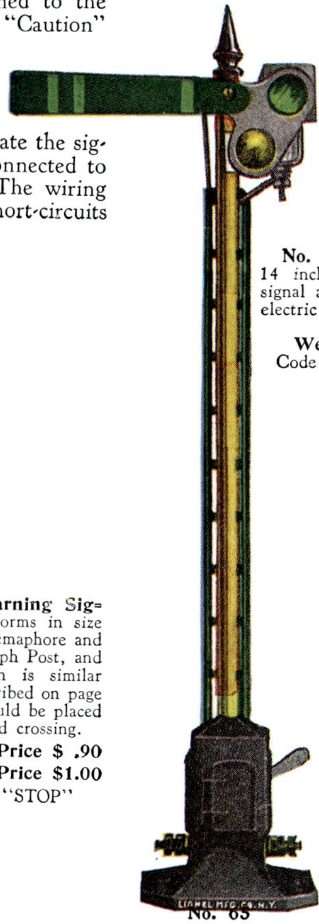

No. 71

Outfit No. 71—Comprises six No. 60 Steel Telegraph Posts as described on this page. Packed in a very attractive box.
Price $3.75
Western Price $4.00
Code Word "USEFUL"

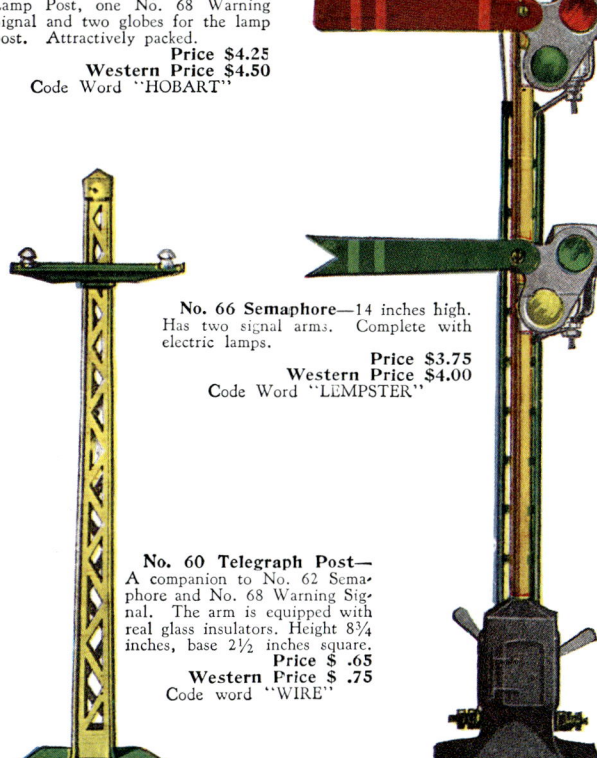

No. 65 Semaphore—14 inches high. Has one signal arm. Complete with electric lamp.
Price $2.50
Western Price $2.75
Code Word "TOWER"

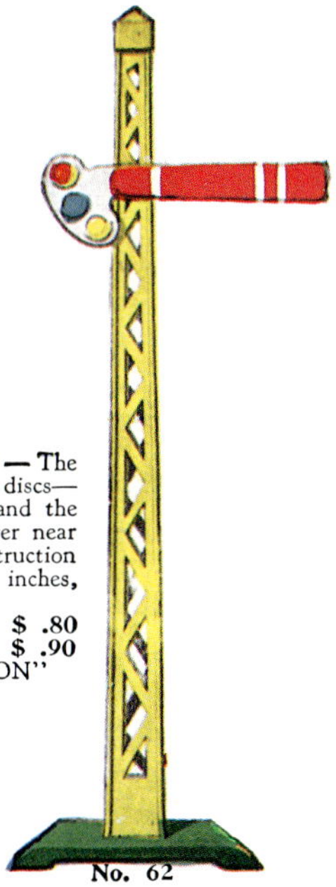

No. 62 Semaphore—The semaphore arm has three discs—red, green and yellow—and the arm is operated by a lever near the base. Steel construction throughout. Height 8¾ inches, base 2½ inches square.
Price $ .80
Western Price $ .90
Code Word "CAUTION"

1926

Lionel "All-Steel" Illuminated Stations

No. 124, 122 and 121   No. 126   No. 127

No. 124 Illuminated Station—De Luxe Model. There is elegance, grace and architectural dignity to this all-steel station difficult to show in an illustration. It is an exact reproduction of stations seen in most suburban towns. It is equipped with two corner platform lights and reflectors, all finished in polished nickel. These corner lighting brackets have beautifully designed supporting arms. This station is also fitted with inside light supported on a nickeled fixture. Roof is removable so that interior lamp can be easily reached. A most essential accessory to complete your model railroad. 13½ inches long, 9 inches wide and 13 inches high.

Price complete, with lamps and wires for connecting to transformer, reducer or batteries . . . **$9.00**
Code Word "READING"   Western Price $10.00

No. 122 Illuminated Station—This is in every way similar to No. 124 Station described above, but has one inside electric light supported on a nickeled fixture.

Price complete, with lamps and wires for connecting to transformer, reducer or batteries . . . **$6.75**
Code Word "CENTRAL"   Western Price $7.25

No. 121 Illuminated Station—Similar to No. 122 and No. 124 Stations described above, but without illumination. Price **$5.00**
Code Word "UNION"   Western Price $5.85

No. 126 Illuminated Station—This station has been specially designed for use with our smaller train outfits and has many of the architectural and structural features of our larger models. The interior light is supported on a fixture placed beneath the removable roof. A beautifully proportioned model that retails at a low price. 10¼ inches long, 7¼ inches wide and 7 inches high.

Price complete, with lamp and wires for connecting to transformer, reducer or batteries **$4.50**
Code Word "ALIGHT"   Western Price $5.00

No. 127 Illuminated Station—This is particularly adaptable for use with any of our "O" Gauge Trains. Interior light is rigidly fastened to a supporting fixture. Roof is removable so that interior lamp can be easily reached. A better built or lower priced miniature station has never before been offered. 8½ inches long, 4¼ inches wide and 5 inches high.

Price complete, with lamp and wires for connecting to transformer, reducer or batteries, **$2.95**
Western Price $3.25
Code Word "TOWNLY"

THE NEW LIONEL SWITCH-SIGNAL TOWER — (Illustrated on Next Page)

No. 437 Illuminated Switch-Signal Tower—In keeping with our policy to introduce everything new in model railroading, we are proud to present our new Switch-Signal Tower, which every boy will want to add to his model railroad layout.

It is built absolutely to scale and has a panel board on the rear (see illustration on next page) with six knife-switches which may be used for operating illuminated accessories, such as Stations, Lamp Posts, Bungalows and Villas. The lights in these accessories can be turned on and off by means of these switches, so that it is not necessary to have them illuminated all the time the train is in operation.

One or more controlling levers for our No. 222 Electrically Controlled Switches can be accommodated in the upper part.

The interior of the switch-signal tower is fitted with an electric lamp. The illumination adds realism to this very desirable accessory.

The Signal Tower is made of very heavy steel, beautifully enameled in various colors. The windows, doors, sashes and other parts are separable pieces inserted in the main body. The roof is removable so that the interior can easily be reached.

In every way this Switch-Signal Tower is typical of Lionel quality and perfection in model railroad accessories. No railroad layout is complete without one. 10¼ inches long, 9½ inches high, 7¼ inches wide.

Price complete, with lamp and wires for connecting to transformer, reducer or batteries, **$8.50**
Code Word "ZEV"   Western Price $9.00

"All-Steel" Illuminated Switch-Signal Towers and Power Stations

No. 437   No. 436   No. 435   No. 092

The New Lionel Power Stations—Boys, you see them in every town and on all electrified railroads. Lionel, as usual, is first to reproduce them.

The illustration below shows how simple it is to house a Lionel "Multivolt" Transformer (illustrated and described on Pages 28 and 29) within the Power Station. Transformer is operated by raising the grid in the roof. Lionel Power Stations are made in two sizes to accommodate all types of Lionel "Multivolt" Transformers. In appearance they suggest the massive concrete buildings in which electric current is generated. Notice the beautiful embossing and die work, inserted windows and doors—see how the great chimney stack is reproduced in true proportion.

No. 435 Power Station—For use with Type "A" or "B" Transformers. 5¾ inches long, 4½ inches wide, 5⅜ inches high to the roof. Chimney stack rises 4⅜ inches above the roof. Base, which measures 8⅝ inches by 6 inches, is hollow so that Power Station can be easily placed over transformer. Grid in roof is removable.
Price $2.50
Code Word "JENA"   Western Price $2.75

No. 436 Power Station—For use with Type "T," "C" or "K" Transformers. Similar in construction to No. 435 Power Station described above. Dimensions 7½ inches long, 6 inches wide, 6½ inches high. Chimney stack rises 4½ inches above the roof. Base measure 9¼ inches by 7¼ inches. Price . . . $3.35
Code Word "WATTS"   Western Price $3.50

No. 092 Illuminated Signal Tower—A desirable accessory for "O" Gauge Railroads. Dimensions 5 inches long, 4 inches wide, 5½ inches high. Roof is removable. Price complete, with lamp and wires for connecting to transformer, reducer or batteries . . . $2.10
Western Price $2.25
Code Word "CYRIL"

No. 89 Flag Staff—Can be placed near any of the Lionel buildings shown on these pages. Also for use with model villages built with Lionel Bungalows and Villas. Base is 2½ inches square, standard is 14 inches high. Beautifully finished in white enamel—spire finished in rich black. Silk flag may be lowered by cord which is attached. Can be fastened on hook near base.
Price . . . $ .75
Western Price $.80
Code Word "ARTHUR"

Illustration above is a rear view of No. 437 Switch-Signal Tower showing panel board equipped with six knife-switches.

Illustration above shows transformer housed within the new Lionel Power Station.

—{ 43 }—

1926

Lionel "All-Steel" Bungalows, Villas and Sets

For Outdoor Railroads. Picture the fun you can have when Lionel houses are placed around a big track-layout in the garden or on any outdoor plot, and used in connection with Lionel Railroad Accessories. For Model Villages the Lionel Houses will be found invaluable. There is no limit to the wonderful effects that can be produced.

Villa No. 191 (illuminated)—Size 7⅛ inches long, 5⅛ inches wide, 5¼ inches high. Complete with interior lighting fixture, lamp and wires for connecting to batteries, transformer or reducer. **Price $3.35**
Code Word "SOLID" **Western Price $3.50**

Villa No. 189 (illuminated)—Size 5½ inches long, 4⅞ inches wide, 5⅜ inches high. Complete with interior lighting fixture, lamp and wires for connecting to batteries, transformer or reducer.
Price $2.95
Western Price $3.25
Code Word "MANSION"

No. 191

No. 189

Set No. 192—Comprises 1 No. 191 Villa, 1 No. 189 Villa and 2 No. 184 Bungalows, complete with interior lights and wires for connecting. **Price $8.75**
Code Word "VILLAGE" **Western Price $9.50**

Bungalow Set No. 186—Comprises 5 No. 184 illuminated bungalows, assorted colors, complete with lamps and wires for connecting. **Price $7.50**
Code Word "HAMLET" **Western Price $8.00**

Bungalow No. 184 (illuminated)—Size 4¾ inches wide, 4 inches high. Complete with lamps and wires for connecting. **Price $1.50**
Western Price $1.65
Code Word "HOME"

No. 186

No. 184

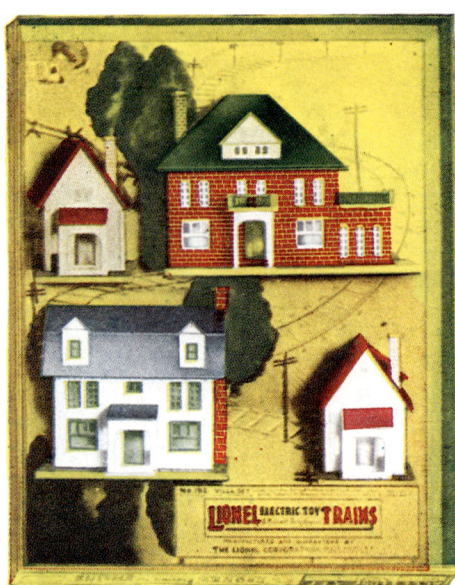

No. 192

— 44 —

Reg. U. S. Pat. Office
"All-Steel" Bridges for "Lionel Standard" and "O" Gauge Track

NO accessories in the Lionel Line have met with so much success since their introduction as the Lionel all-steel bridges. The construction and appearance place them in a class by themselves. No illustration can do justice to the beautiful appearance and rigid construction of these bridges. They are modeled closely after all the big railroad bridges seen throughout the country. The end piers, the bridge work and roadway are exceptionally sturdy. The architectural designs are graceful and pleasing and the embossing work incorporated in them gives a dignity and realism that cannot be equalled. Special slots in the roadway hold the track in place and the spans as well as the approaches are all provided with sections of track either "O" gauge or "Lionel Standard." Bridges can be extended to any length by the addition of the spans shown in the illustrations.

No. 101
No. 101, Bridge (three sections)—For "Lionel Standard" track. Complete structure is 42 inches long, 6½ inches wide, 6¼ inches high.
Price complete, with track $5.85
Code Word "QUEENS"   **Western Price $6.50**

No. 102
No. 102, Bridge (four sections)—For "Lionel Standard" track. Complete structure is 56 inches long, 6½ inches wide, 6¼ inches high.
Price complete, with track $8.50
Code Word "KEEPSIE"   **Western Price $9.00**

No. 103
No. 103, Bridge (five sections)—For "Lionel Standard" track. Complete structure is 70 inches long, 6½ inches wide, 6¼ inches high.
Price complete, with track $11.00
Code Word "LONDON"   **Western Price $12.00**

No. 104
No. 104, Span—For "Lionel Standard" track. 14 inches long, 6½ inches wide, 6¼ inches high.
Price complete, with track $3.35
Western Price $3.50
Code Word "MANHATTAN"

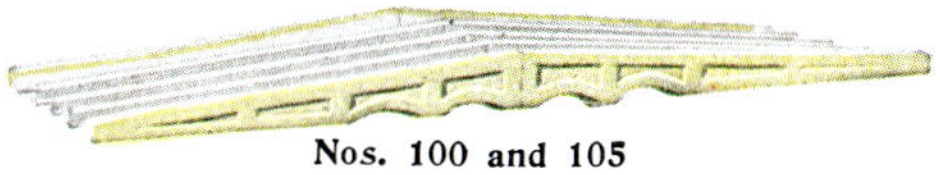

Nos. 100 and 105
No. 100, Bridge (two sections)—For "Lionel Standard" track. In reproduction of reinforced concrete, 28 inches long, 5½ inches wide, 2 inches high at center.
Price, complete with track, $2.50
Western Price $2.75
Code Word "BROOKLYN"

No. 105, Bridge (two sections)—Reinforced concrete work, 21 inches long, 4¼ inches wide, 2 inches high.
Price complete, with track, $1.65
Western Price $1.75
Code Word "PARIS"

No. 106
No. 106, Bridge (three sections)—For "O" Gauge track. Complete structure is 31½ inches long, 5½ inches wide, 4 inches high.
Price complete, with track $3.35
Code Word "CONN"   **Western Price $3.50**

No. 108
No. 108, Bridge (four sections)—For "O" gauge track. Complete structure is 42 inches long, 5½ inches wide, 4 inches high.
Price complete, with track $5.50
Code Word "HOUSA"   **Western Price $5.85**

No. 109
No. 109, Bridge (five sections)—For "O" gauge track. Complete structure is 52½ inches long, 5½ inches wide, 4 inches high.
Price complete, with track $7.50
Code Word "MISS"   **Western Price $8.00**

No. 110
No. 110, Span—For "O" gauge track. 10½ inches long, 5½ inches wide, 4 inches high.
Price complete, with track $2.50
Western Price $2.75
Code Word "WILLIAMS"

1926

"All-Steel" Tunnels for "Lionel Standard" and "O" Gauge Track

Reg. U. S. Pat. Office

LIONEL TRAINS are worthy of good accessories and it is therefore with great pleasure that we offer the Lionel steel tunnels, which are a wonderful improvement over the old, flimsy, papier-mâché ones that users of train outfits were compelled to accept before we introduced ours.

Lionel tunnels are made of steel throughout, being accurately designed and formed in our special machinery. They stand evenly on the floor without the slightest twist. Their rigid construction does not make it necessary to have any cross-braces on the base which would interfere with the track level.

The front and rear entrances of Lionel tunnels are embossed in exact reproduction of heavy stone masonry, having a keystone at the top. The bodies of the tunnels represent mountainsides in miniature and the coloring is made to harmonize beautifully. We draw particular attention to the details on the large size tunnels, which have the mountain roadsides wonderfully reproduced, as well as the little metal "chalets," all in perfect proportion to the size of the tunnel.

All Lionel tunnels are practically indestructible and are very low priced considering the workmanship in them.

No. 130 Tunnel—for "O" Gauge Trains only. In response to numerous requests we have added this new number to our line of tunnels, as it is greatly in demand to provide the finishing touch for very elaborate "O" Gauge Railroads built by Lionel enthusiasts.

As will be seen from the illustration, it contains a wealth of detail. It sets on the curve of the track layout and is embellished by numerous houses and "chalets." The snow-capped peak and mountain roadways so beautifully brought out, make this tunnel strikingly realistic. Length 26 inches, width 23 inches, height 14½ inches. The portals are 4½ inches wide and 5½ inches high . . **Price $12.50**
Western Price $13.50
Code Word "OPUS"

No. 120 Tunnel—for all Lionel Trains—This splendid model is the very best produced for beauty, grace of design and substantial construction. All Lionel tunnels are hand-painted in attractive, durable colors. They can be easily cleaned with a damp cloth or chamois. Is 17 inches long, 12 inches wide and 11 inches extreme height. Inside dimensions of portals are 6½ inches wide and 8 inches high.
Price $5.85
Western Price $6.50
Code Word "HUDSON"

No. 119 Tunnel—For use with all "O" gauge trains and "Lionel Standard" trains Nos. 347, 350, 351, 352 and 41. Is 12 inches long, 9 inches wide and 10 inches extreme height. Portals are 5 inches wide and 6½ inches high inside.
Price $3.35
Western Price $3.50
Code Word "HOOSAC"

No. 118 Tunnel—For any size "O" gauge train. Is 8 inches long, 7 inches wide and 7½ inches extreme height. Portals are 4 inches wide and 5½ inches high inside . **Price $2.10**
Western Price $2.25
Code Word "SIMPLON"

Scenic Railways for "Lionel Standard" and "O" Gauge Track

Reg. U. S. Pat. Office

NO. 198—FOR "O" GAUGE TRACK

THE platform is made of composition board in two sections, mounted in a rigid wooden frame. The dimensions are 60 by 42 inches. The top of the platform is decorated in colors representing grass plots, roads, etc. Indicating marks show the points at which the accessories are to be placed. The platform is electrically wired so that accessories and track can be connected in a few moments. A large metal tunnel is supplied, realistically painted and embellished with miniature houses. Mountainous sections, flower beds, and grass plots made of indestructible steel. Shrubs, bushes and miniature trees are also furnished, all of which greatly enhance the detail. Three reproductions of mountains beautifully decorated, each measuring 36 by 18 inches, form the background, and two panels, representing the skyline, each measuring 36 by 28 inches, complete the scenic effect.

The display is light in weight and can be easily moved. The background scenic effects are so placed that the display can either be condensed or extended to fit the space in which it is to be used.

SPECIFICATIONS

		Price	Wstrn. Price			Price	Wstrn. Price
1 No. 076	Block Signal	$3.15	$3.35	1 No. 132	Corner Grass Plot	$2.50	$2.75
1 No. 077	Crossing Gate	4.00	4.35	2 No. 133	Heartshape Grass Plots, $1.50 each	3.00	3.25
1 No. 069	Warning Signal	3.15	3.35	1 No. 135	Circular Grass Plot	1.00	1.15
1 No. 56	Lamp Post	1.65	1.75	1 No. 506	Compo board painted platform, completely wired (2 sections)	6.50	7.25
1 No. 57	Lamp Post	1.65	1.75				
1 No. 58	Lamp Post	1.25	1.35				
1 No. 89	Flag Staff	.75	.80	3 No. 509	Compo board mountains (each)	1.50	1.65
1 No. 184	Bungalow	1.50	1.65	1 No. 508	Compo board sky background (2 sections)	3.00	3.25
1 No. 191	Villa	3.35	3.50	3 No. 505	Trees (each)	.30	.35
1 No. 189	Villa	2.95	3.25	2 No. 504	Bushes (each)	.20	.25
1 No. 092	Signal Tower	2.10	2.25				
1 No. 130	Tunnel	12.50	13.50				
1 No. 131	Corner Elevation	4.50	5.00				

Train and track not included. Price complete $50.00
Code Word "BEAUTY"   Western Price $54.00

Any of the items comprising this scenic railway can be purchased separately at prices listed above.

NO. 199—FOR "LIONEL STANDARD" TRACK

ON account of its larger size we have been able to incorporate many more scenic details, and to supply a large amount of accessories in this scenic railway for "Lionel Standard" Track. The general construction and appearance are similar to the "O" Gauge Scenic Railway described in the opposite column.

The platform of the "Lionel Standard" Scenic Railway is made in three sections and measures 90 inches long by 60 inches deep. The dimensions of the three mountains and the skyline background are the same as those supplied with "O" Gauge Scenic Railway No. 198.

SPECIFICATIONS

		Price	Wstrn. Price			Price	Wstrn. Price
1 No. 124	Station	$9.00	$10.00	1 No. 136	Elevation (large)	$10.00	$11.00
1 No. 189	Villa	2.95	3.25	1 No. 131	Corner Elevation	4.50	5.00
3 No. 191	Villas, $3.35	10.05	10.50	1 No. 132	Corner Grass Plot	2.50	2.75
3 No. 184	Bungalows, $1.50	4.50	4.95	2 No. 133	Heartshape Grass Plots, $1.50	3.00	3.25
1 No. 092	Signal Tower	2.10	2.25				
5 No. 60	Telegraph Posts, $.65	3.25	3.75	2 No. 135	Circular Grass Plots, $1.00	2.00	2.30
2 No. 59	Lamp Posts, $1.50	3.00	3.30	1 No. 507	Compo board painted platform, completely wired (3 sections)	7.50	8.25
3 No. 58	Lamp Posts, $1.25	3.75	4.05				
1 No. 57	Lamp Post	1.65	1.75				
1 No. 89	Flag Staff	.75	.80	3 No. 509	Compo board mountains (each)	1.50	1.65
1 No. 66	Semaphore	3.75	4.00	1 No. 508	Compo board sky background (2 sections)	3.00	3.25
1 No. 78	Automatic Control	5.00	5.50				
1 No. 77	Crossing Gate	4.25	4.50	16 No. 505	Trees (each)	.30	.35
1 No. 69	Warning Signal	3.35	3.50	8 No. 504	Bushes (each)	.20	.25
1 No. 120	Tunnel	5.85	6.50				

Train and track not included. Price complete $80.00
Code Word "NATURE"   Western Price $90.00

Note: Any of the items comprising this scenic railway can be purchased separately at prices listed above.

DEALERS—DISPLAY A SCENIC RAILWAY IN YOUR WINDOW. NO GREATER AID TO INCREASING YOUR TOY SALES HAS EVER BEEN DEVISED.

1926

THE LIONEL CORPORATION

Display Rooms, Offices and Service Station
15-17-19 EAST 26th STREET
(Madison Square North)
NEW YORK CITY

THE HOME OF
Lionel ELECTRIC TRAINS
MODEL RAILROAD ACCESSORIES
"MULTIVOLT" TRANSFORMERS

Factories and Service Departments
SOUTH 21st STREET, IRVINGTON, N. J.
Warehouses
24 NESBITT STREET, NEWARK, N. J.

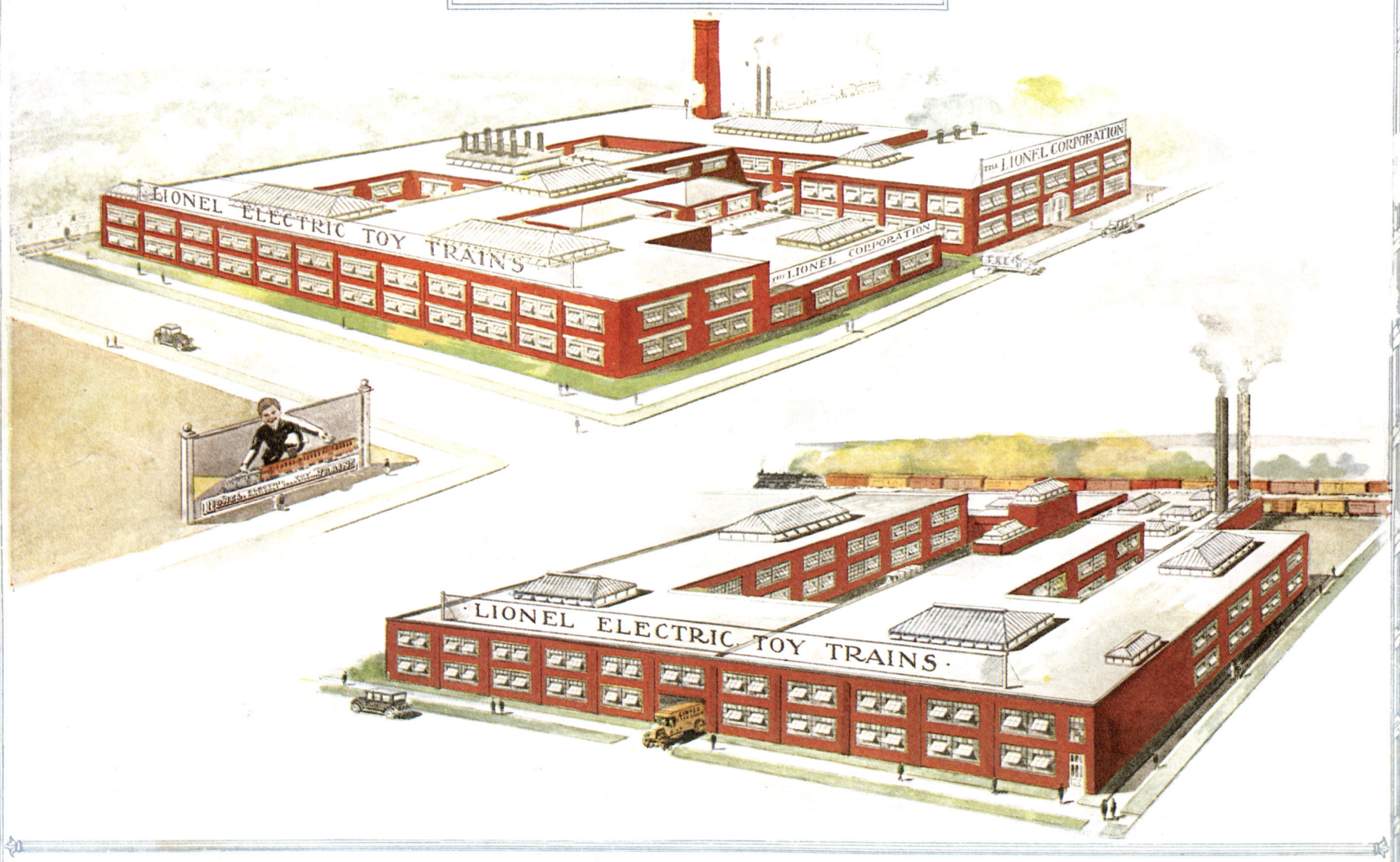

THE LARGEST AMERICAN FACTORIES EXCLUSIVELY PRODUCING MODEL ELECTRIC TRAINS AND RAILROAD EQUIPMENT

LIONEL ELECTRIC TRAINS
MODEL RAILROAD ACCESSORIES
"MULTIVOLT" TRANSFORMERS

The Thrill of Lionel Railroading

BOYS—Lionel will give you all the thrill and fascination of operating a real railroad. You can either play the part of locomotive engineer, train dispatcher, switchman or station master, and perform all the duties of real railroad men with your Lionel Model Electric Railroads, for they are real in everything but size.

In addition to providing unlimited fun and excitement, Lionel will aid you in obtaining a valuable knowledge of electricity and the principles of modern electric railroading. All the latest devices for safeguarding present-day railroad travel, all the most up-to-date equipment, have been faithfully reproduced by Lionel in model form—all built to last, handsomely finished, and inexpensively priced.

Ready? Let's go! All aboard!! You switch on the current from your "Multivolt" Transformer, and the Lionel Limited with its powerful headlight shining and cars brilliantly illuminated, gracefully glides away—smooth and silent, just like a big all-steel Pullman Train.

You advance the transformer switch, and immediately the massive motor responds—increasing its speed and hauling the big train with perfect ease. Down the straightaway stretch we go—cars gently swaying, as real railroad cars do—past the steel telegraph posts, semaphores and block signals.

We hear the realistic sound of the electric bell warning-signal, and whizz!—like a flash we go over the grade crossing, catching a glimpse of the electric crossing-gates as they go down to bar the way to highway traffic until the train has passed.

Now we go dashing over "Lionel Bridge"—a beautiful structure built of steel throughout—and on to the level roadbed again.

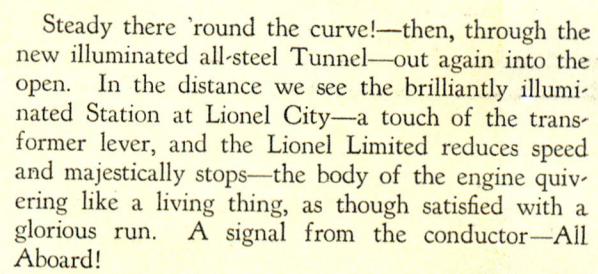

Steady there 'round the curve!—then, through the new illuminated all-steel Tunnel—out again into the open. In the distance we see the brilliantly illuminated Station at Lionel City—a touch of the transformer lever, and the Lionel Limited reduces speed and majestically stops—the body of the engine quivering like a living thing, as though satisfied with a glorious run. A signal from the conductor—All Aboard!

Now we are on our way again, running at full speed, but gradually our train begins to slow down and comes to a dead stop. We look out of the cab window and see another signal directly ahead of us—it is Lionel's marvelous new Automatic Semaphore Train-Control. Its red light says "Danger Ahead," and the red arm, set straight out, gives the same warning. Presently the red light changes to green—the red arm slowly rises to an upright position, and our train again resumes speed. All this has been done without even touching the train, for the Lionel Semaphore Train-Control is absolutely automatic in its action.

Can you think of anything that will hold your interest as intensely as a Lionel Railroad? You cannot find anything more real. On the next page we tell you all about the Lionel 100% Electrically-Controlled Railroads for "O" Gauge and "Lionel Standard" Track. Read every word—you will be thrilled.

Millions of Lionel Outfits are in use, many of them for a decade or more. They are handed down from father to son, which is a striking tribute to the built-in excellence of every part we manufacture.

Start to build your Electric Railroads with Lionel Models, the world's finest product—unequalled anywhere for beauty of design—mechanical detail and precision—electrical perfection and efficiency—handsome and lasting enamel finish.

Say "Lionel" to your dealer and accept no other.

THE LIONEL CORPORATION
15-17-19 East 26th Street
(Madison Square North)
New York, N. Y.

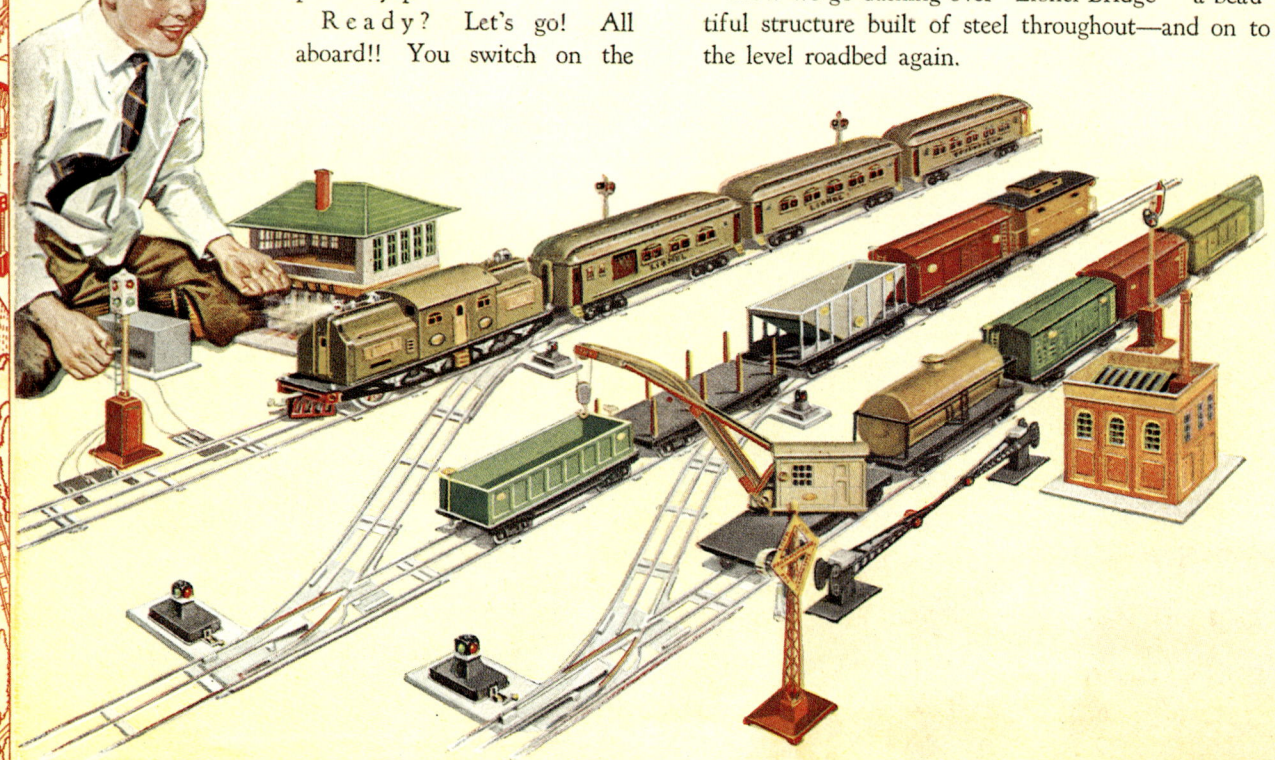

The New Lionel 100% Electrically-Controlled Railroads

BOYS—the thrill of your life awaits you! After reading the previous page you must be all excited about Lionel Model Trains, but we didn't tell you about the new 100% Electrically-Controlled Locomotives and Train Outfits to operate on "O" Gauge as well as "Lionel Standard" Track.

Heretofore, you had to reverse your locomotive by hand or affix a mechanical appliance to the track that would reverse the locomotive at only one spot, but now the wonderful Lionel Electrically-Controlled mechanism enables you to operate your trains at various speeds, stop them, start them or reverse them *at any distance from the track*. Just think of the great fun of operating them like real trains! It seems uncanny, but it is a fact nevertheless.

The illustration on the previous page shows one of the many thousands of Lionel boys operating his Electrically-Controlled Lionel Train. You will notice that his hand is on a little lever. When the lever is moved from side to side it increases or decreases the speed of the train. When the lever is raised, the train comes to a stop. When it is lowered, the train starts off again in the opposite direction, but, boys—the mechanism is so perfect that when the lever is rapidly lowered and raised twice, the train will resume speed in the direction in which it was going before being stopped.

Picture the thrill of reversing your train without even touching it. It's marvelous!

At times, Mr. Engineer, you back up your train to couple on another Pullman or Freight Car. Just think how simply this is done. By one slight movement of the lever, as if by magic, your locomotive will reverse itself.

By sliding the lever to one side the train will gradually reduce speed, and by lowering the same lever the train will stop right up against the car that is to be coupled to it.

Then again, as a real railroad engineer following instructions, you must switch your train from one track to another. This operation is decidedly interesting and clearly exemplifies the realism of Lionel Electrically-Controlled Railroads. Not only can you reverse your Lionel Electric Train by moving a small lever placed *at any distance from the track*, but you can also operate your Electrically-Controlled Switches *at any distance from the track* by means of another small lever.

Other interesting details about Lionel Electrically-Controlled Locomotives are given on page 10. Lionel Electrically-Controlled Locomotives are made in various up-to-date types, the same as used on all the great electrified railroad systems of America.

All Lionel Electrically-Controlled Railroad Accessories, such as Semaphores, Crossing-Gates, Block Signals, Warning-Bell Signals and Train-Controls are automatically operated by the movement of the train, or they can be operated *at any distance from the track* by connecting them to the controlling levers in the new Lionel Switch Tower illustrated on Page 39.

So you see, boys, that Lionel has perfected a distant-control that marks a new epoch in Model Railroading. It is the culmination of twenty-seven years devoted exclusively to the manufacture of Lionel Electric Trains and Model Railroad Accessories—all fully guaranteed—all built to last—all embodying that skilled craftsmanship that has earned unqualified recognition for Lionel as

"STANDARD
of the
WORLD"
Since
1900

Construction of Lionel "O" Gauge Motors

DRIVING GEARS ("A") — They are made of heavy steel blanks, machine-cut. They mesh without friction and are far superior to gears with punched teeth.

Field ("B") — The field is made of a number of specially prepared transformer steel laminations. This construction represents a much stronger field than if a single piece of steel were used.

Third Rail Shoe Support ("C") — Made of heavy fibre to which the third rail contact rollers are attached. Our construction protects rollers from injury, for the brackets can be bent against the fibre without disturbing the arc of the spring that gives them the correct tension against the third rail.

Wheels ("D") — Lionel was first to introduce die-cast wheels. They are absolutely balanced. A nickel-plated steel rim is forced over the tread of the wheel to insure long wear.

Collecting Shoes ("E") — They collect current from the third rail. Made of solid brass turnings and revolve on steel shafts which pass through phosphor bronze supports. They insure perfect contact with the third rail at all times so that locomotives will run at uniform speed.

Frame ("F") — Made of very heavy steel punchings, embodying great detail. Will withstand more than the ordinary amount of wear and tear.

Journals ("G") — Made of heavy brass, nickel-plated. Attached to the frames by mechanical means. They add greatly to the appearance of the structure.

Cowcatchers ("H") — The construction of the cowcatchers varies with the type of locomotive on which they are used. Many of them are part of the steel frame which is made in one piece, and others are heavy castings rigidly attached to the frame.

Flag Posts ("J") — All our locomotives are equipped with four flag posts, two at each end of the frame; a very realistic detail.

Tanks ("K") — These tanks are made of brass, nickel-plated, and are separable pieces attached to the frame, which further accentuates the great detail.

Lionel Automatic Couplers ("L") — Made of heavy steel, nickel-plated and polished. They are scientifically constructed so that cars cannot become detached when in motion, but are easily taken apart when desired. The new improved Lionel Coupler with invisible spring arrangement is a great advance over any similar device ever made.

Illustration shows the type of motor used in "O" Gauge Locomotives Nos. 248, 252 and 253.

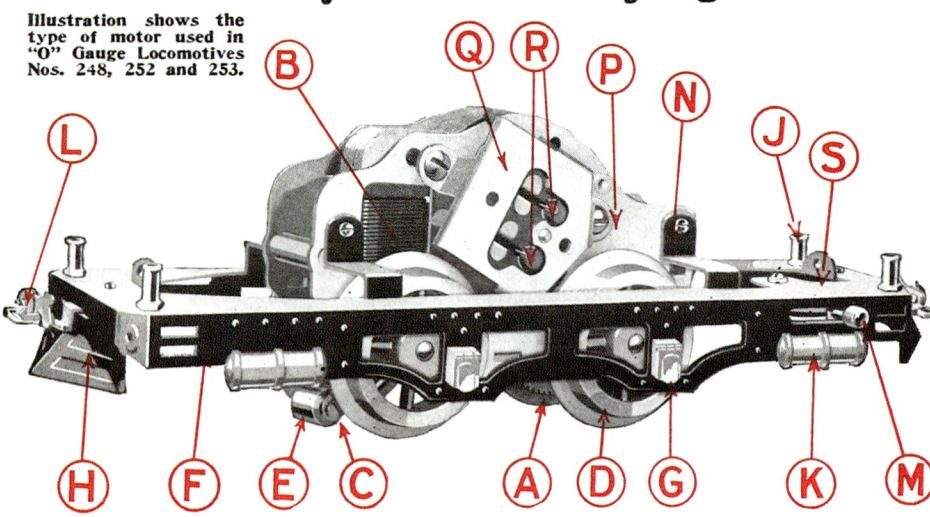

THE NEW LIONEL "O" GAUGE ELECTRICALLY-CONTROLLED SUPER-MOTOR

This marvelous new motor will haul twice as many cars as any other "O" Gauge Motor now on sale. The illustration below shows some of the remarkable features that make this possible. Notice the new system of gearing which gives maximum hauling power with minimum current consumption.

The electric-controlling mechanism is built right into the motor, and is completely protected against injury. This new "O" Gauge Super-Motor, a triumph of engineering skill, is one of Lionel's greatest achievements.

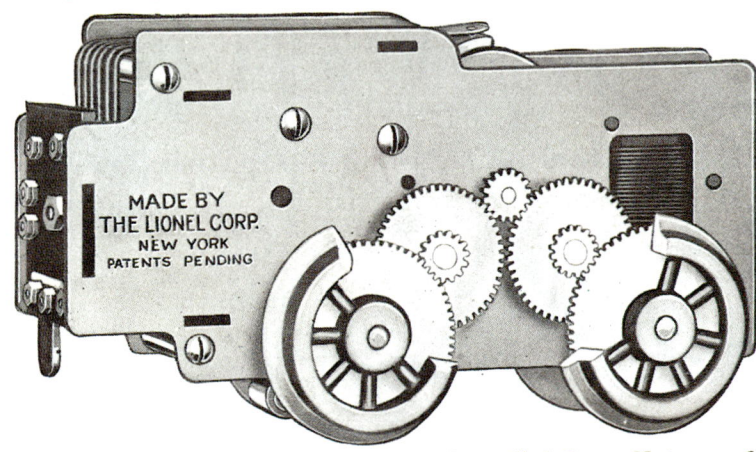

Illustration above shows Electrically-Controlled Super-Motor used in "O" Gauge Locomotives Nos. 254E and 251E.

The same Super-Motor with hand reversing mechanism is used in "O" Gauge Locomotives Nos. 254, 251 and in Twin-Super-Motor No. 256.

Reversing Controllers ("M") — Lionel Reversing Controllers have been in use for many years during which time they have given thorough satisfaction. They are the only controllers in use that cannot get out of order. They operate very easily and due to the brass cups and spring tension, the electrical contact is always permanent.

Frame Support ("N") — The frame is supported to the motor with only four screws. This simple method of construction was originally introduced by us in 1913. All parts of Lionel Locomotives can be easily reached for cleaning.

Side Plates ("P") — Made of heavy gauge steel and support all working parts. All bearing holes are reinforced with phosphor bronze bushings. The alignment of these holes is absolutely perfect so that gears work with minimum friction. All holes are drilled and reamed to proper diameter. The accuracy of these plates compares with the frame work of a very fine clock.

Brush Plate ("Q") — The unique construction permits rapid change of brushes after motor has been in use for a considerable period. The brushes fit in brass cups. Two properly tempered steel springs give the correct pressure of the brush on the commutator until brushes are worn down to the end. Brushes are replaced by simply raising the springs, lifting up worn-out brushes and dropping in new ones.

Brushes ("R") — We were the first manufacturers of model trains to equip our motors with combination gauze and graphite brushes that wear long and are self-lubricating.

Removable Locomotive Body ("S") — The bodies of all Lionel Locomotives are held in place on the frame with only two screws, one at each end of the locomotive. Supporting members are placed at several points of the frame that rigidly hold the body in place.

Commutator — Made of bronze, and perfectly turned when connected to armature so that it is absolutely parallel with brushes. Commutator surface is polished so as to reduce all friction when in contact with brushes.

Armature — Made of specially prepared electrical sheets mounted on a drill rod shaft. It is perfectly insulated and wound with the correct amount of triple insulated wire.

Construction of "Lionel Standard" Super-Motors

Removable Brush Holder (1)—This is one of the most unique features of the Lionel Super-Motor. By simply unscrewing one screw the entire brush holder can be removed from the motor. Change of brushes requires but an instant and the assembled part is replaced without the use of any tools.

Brushes (2)—The brushes are made of bronze and graphite which are self-lubricating. They insure long life to the commutator. They are contained in brass tubes and held in place by a simple spring arrangement which feeds brushes to commutator at the same pressure until the brush is entirely used up. Replacement of brushes is a very simple operation.

Revolving Double Contact Shoes (3)—This method of collecting current from the third rail, so successfully used for many years past on our "O" Gauge Locomotives, has been applied with equal success to the new Super-Motors. The shoes are heavy bronze rollers, securely affixed to the flexible phosphor bronze plate, which insures the proper tension on the third rail and gives a steady flow of current to the motors. This complete shoe assembly is mounted on a heavy fibre plate and is rigidly attached to the motor frame.

New Gear Arrangement (4)—This new method of gearing is embodied only in Lionel Super-Motors. The seven gears in this new layout give the motor greater tractive power, and are almost frictionless. The gears are made of very heavy steel, and teeth are machine cut, not stamped. Special attention is directed to the plate supporting the gear studs, which also acts as an additional bearing for the armature shaft, as described in the following paragraph.

THE New Lionel Super-Motor is so vastly superior in efficiency and design to any motor ever before offered to the public that notwithstanding our enviable reputation as leaders in miniature motor construction, the new and improved Super-Motor is supremely the finest piece of electrical mechanism our factories have ever produced. It is quite fitting that we, as pioneer builders of model locomotives to operate on "Lionel Standard" track, should retain our leadership with the Super-Motor which is the acme of perfection.

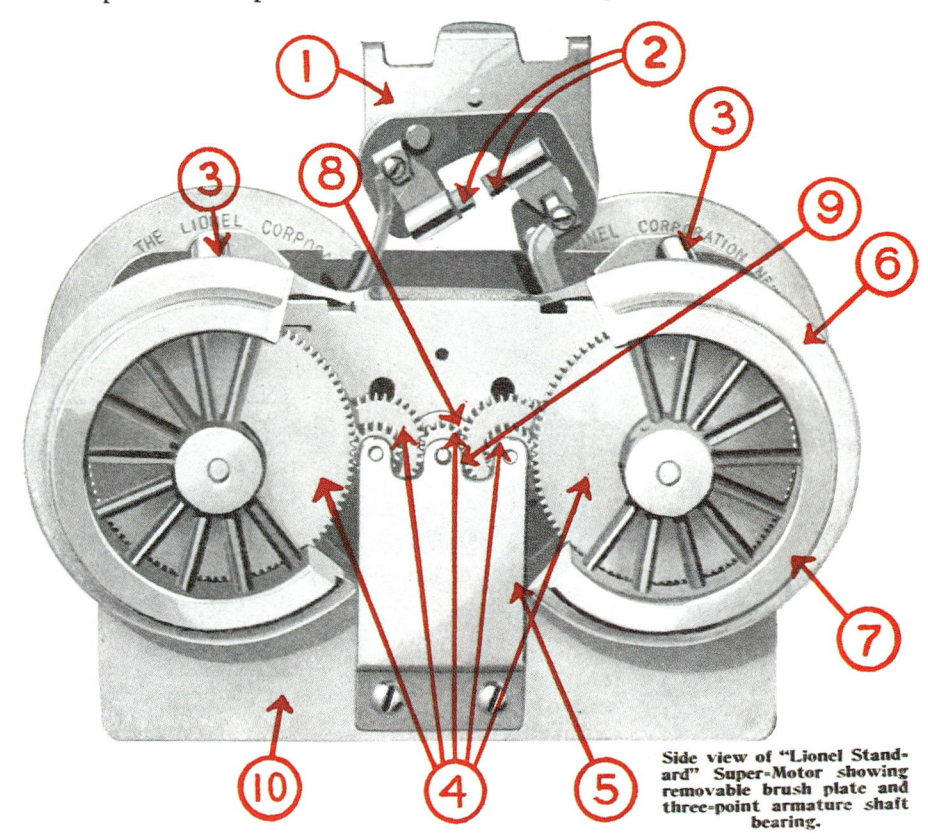

Side view of "Lionel Standard" Super-Motor showing removable brush plate and three-point armature shaft bearing.

Driving Wheels (6)—Particular attention is directed to the driving wheels, which are massive in construction and are accurately die-cast. Their weight adds great tractive power to the motors. All driving wheels are directly geared to the motor, eliminating the use of connecting rods between the wheels, which insures better alignment with less friction.

Steel Tread on Wheels (7)—A steel tread beautifully nickel plated and polished is forced over the rim, insuring longer wear and a smooth, even riding surface. Lionel originated this method of wheel construction. See illustration on Page 7.

Reinforced Bearings (8)—Six phosphor bronze bearings are contained in the side plates of the motor. They add to the life of the motor and insure accurate alignment of the armature shaft and axles.

Armature—The armature is made of laminated electrical steel punchings. It is automatically drum wound with triple-covered magnet wire, dipped in shellac and baked. The armature shaft (9) is made of the best quality drill rod.

Side Plates (10)—Made of heavy steel, with bronze bushings inserted for shaft and axles.

Field—Made of the highest grade electrical steel correctly wound and scientifically designed.

Commutator—Made of heavy copper. The segments are perfectly insulated, making short circuits impossible.

Tractive Power—The tractive power of these motors is remarkable. They will haul from 12 to 20 of our largest size freight or Pullman cars with the greatest ease. The weight of the wheels and motor is close to the track, insuring low centre of gravity, with the result that the locomotive is not top-heavy and slippage of the wheels is therefore unknown. This construction is infinitely superior to the method of loading down the superstructure with useless weight so as to obtain tractive power. This unnecessary weight rapidly wears down all working parts and causes the locomotive to jump the track.

Minimum Current Consumption—The new Lionel Super-Motor is not only more powerful than any motor of its size, but it consumes less than half the current of any motor developing the same power.

Three-Point Armature Shaft Bearing (5)—For the first time in the development of miniature motors it has been possible to perfect an arrangement whereby the armature shaft revolves in three bearings—two of them are contained in the side plates of the motor and the third one in the plate that holds the gearing studs. This three-point-bearing eliminates all vibration of the armature shaft, with the result that the commutator and brushes wear long and evenly. Considering the fact that the commutator and brushes are the life of the motor, this improvement is of great importance.

Construction of "Lionel Standard" and "O" Gauge Twin-Super-Motors

LIONEL TWIN-SUPER-MOTOR LOCOMOTIVES WILL HAUL TWENTY LARGE FREIGHT CARS WITH PERFECT EASE.

ON the previous page we illustrate and describe the new Lionel Super-Motor. In order to develop locomotives of exceptional hauling power, we have introduced two types equipped with two of these powerful Super-Motors. Their great tractive power is obtained by the weight and great efficiency of the Super-Motors, which consume a minimum amount of current. Useless weight is not added to the locomotive in order to obtain tractive power. This added weight only wears down the working parts. In our Twin-Super-Motor Locomotives the powerful motors which are close to the track where they belong, prevents derailing even on sharp curves when traveling at high speed. Both motors work in absolute unison, and are either reversed by a hand lever or are Electrically-Controlled. They are the only Twin-Super-Motor Locomotives made.

WE have modeled the Lionel Twin-Super-Motor Locomotives after the powerful electric engines which great American engineers have designed for prominent electrified railroads. In proportion, Lionel Twin-Super-Motor Locomotives are just as powerful as real ones. Engineers have favored twin-motors in their designs because they give the greatest hauling power—so it is with the new Lionel Twin-Super-Motors. We have just introduced a superb new Electrically-Controlled Twin-Super-Motor Locomotive—the De-Luxe Model No. 408E. Be sure to read about it on Page 17.

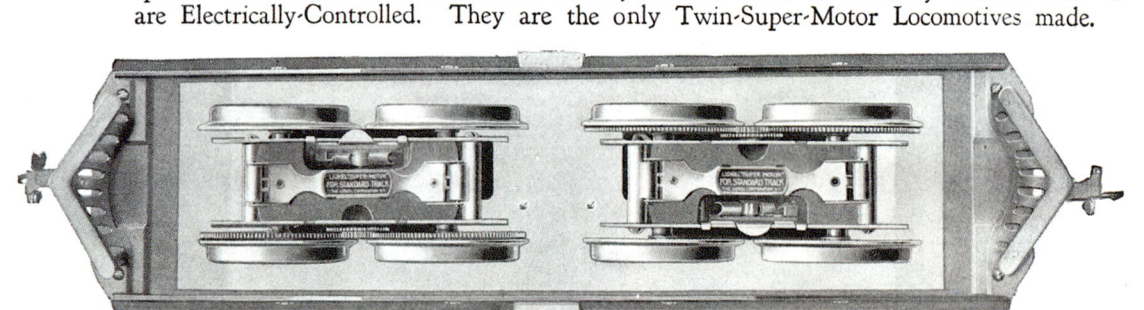

Illustration above is a bottom view of chassis of "Lionel Standard" and "O" Gauge Twin-Super-Motors.

Reversing Controllers and Motor Frame—The illustration below shows the unique construction of the reversing controllers which operate the twin-super-motors. Both controllers function simultaneously by means of a lever conveniently placed on the side of the locomotive body. The slightest touch of the finger sends the locomotive forward or backward or causes it to stop when the lever is placed at "OFF." Accuracy of construction insures positive action of the reversing controller at all times. Our reversing controllers are absolutely dependable—they are free from complicated mechanism.

Electrically-Controlled Twin-Super-Motors.

In addition to the hand-controlled models, Locomotives Nos. 402E and 408E are equipped with the famous electrically-controlled mechanism described on Page 10. These mighty Twin-Super-Motor Locomotives can be started, stopped, reversed and operated at any speed at any distance from the track.

Attention is directed to the heavy steel one-piece frame to which the motors are attached. Great detail is embodied in this frame. The springs and journals are separate brass pieces, heavily nickeled, and are securely fastened to it. Brass steps and flag supports are also attached, while the heavy steel cow-catchers are riveted to both ends, from which protrude the patented Lionel Automatic Couplers. The whole chassis represents a power unit that will give years of service.

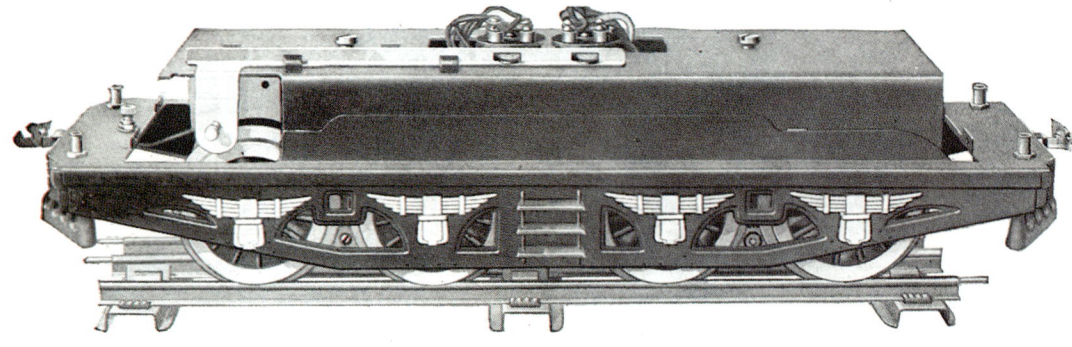

Side View of Twin-Super-Motor Chassis, Showing Heavy Frame and Construction of Reversing Controllers

Lionel Always Leads!

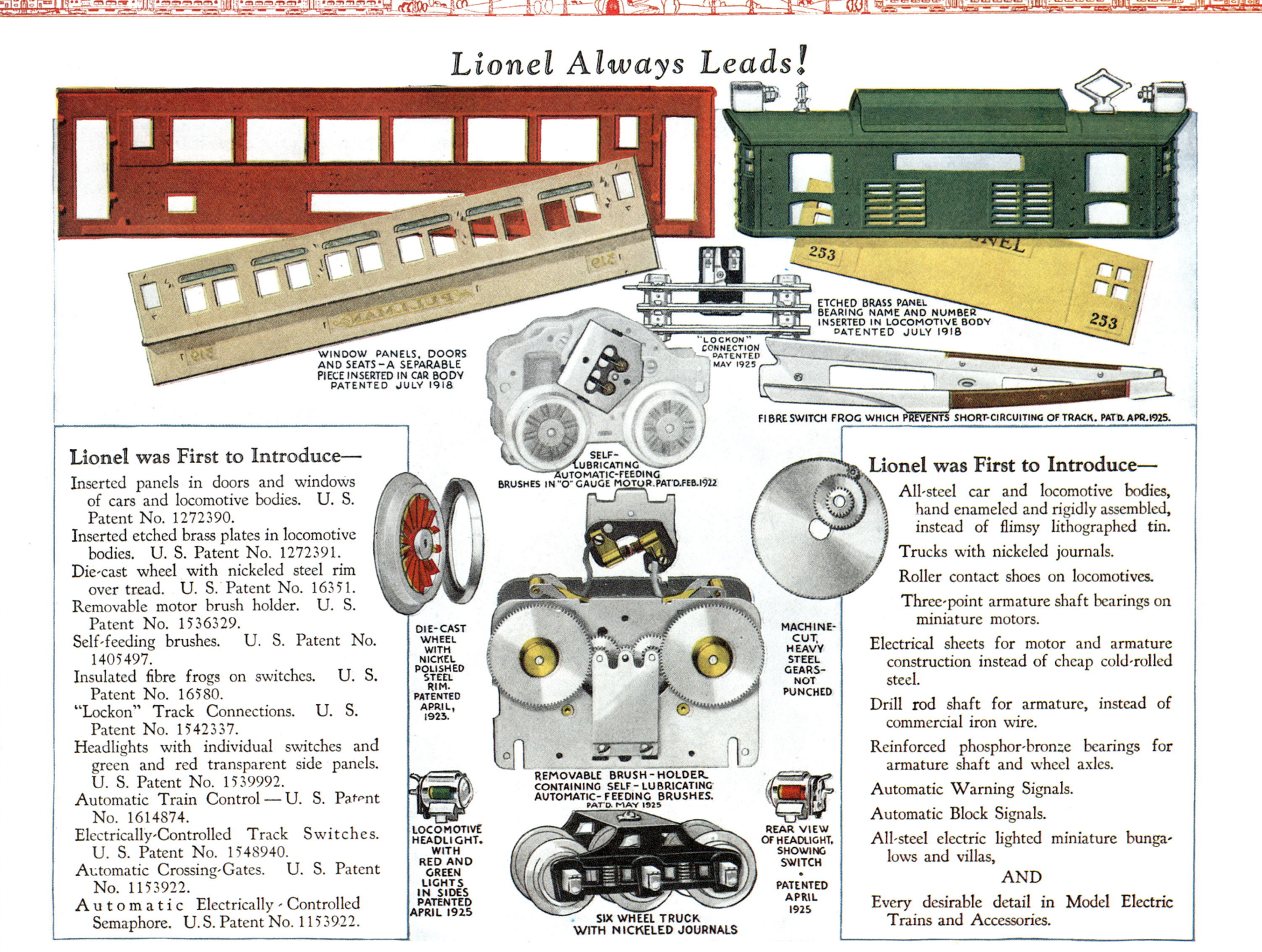

WINDOW PANELS, DOORS AND SEATS – A SEPARABLE PIECE INSERTED IN CAR BODY PATENTED JULY 1918

ETCHED BRASS PANEL BEARING NAME AND NUMBER INSERTED IN LOCOMOTIVE BODY PATENTED JULY 1918

"LOCKON" CONNECTION PATENTED MAY 1925

FIBRE SWITCH FROG WHICH PREVENTS SHORT-CIRCUITING OF TRACK. PAT'D. APR. 1925.

SELF-LUBRICATING AUTOMATIC-FEEDING BRUSHES IN "O" GAUGE MOTOR. PAT'D. FEB. 1922

DIE-CAST WHEEL WITH NICKEL POLISHED STEEL RIM. PATENTED APRIL, 1923.

REMOVABLE BRUSH-HOLDER CONTAINING SELF-LUBRICATING AUTOMATIC-FEEDING BRUSHES. PAT'D. MAY 1925

MACHINE-CUT, HEAVY STEEL GEARS – NOT PUNCHED

LOCOMOTIVE HEADLIGHT. WITH RED AND GREEN LIGHTS IN SIDES PATENTED APRIL 1925

REAR VIEW OF HEADLIGHT, SHOWING SWITCH. PATENTED APRIL 1925

SIX WHEEL TRUCK WITH NICKELED JOURNALS

Lionel was First to Introduce—

Inserted panels in doors and windows of cars and locomotive bodies. U. S. Patent No. 1272390.

Inserted etched brass plates in locomotive bodies. U. S. Patent No. 1272391.

Die-cast wheel with nickeled steel rim over tread. U. S. Patent No. 16351.

Removable motor brush holder. U. S. Patent No. 1536329.

Self-feeding brushes. U. S. Patent No. 1405497.

Insulated fibre frogs on switches. U. S. Patent No. 16580.

"Lockon" Track Connections. U. S. Patent No. 1542337.

Headlights with individual switches and green and red transparent side panels. U. S. Patent No. 1539992.

Automatic Train Control — U. S. Patent No. 1614874.

Electrically-Controlled Track Switches. U. S. Patent No. 1548940.

Automatic Crossing-Gates. U. S. Patent No. 1153922.

Automatic Electrically-Controlled Semaphore. U. S. Patent No. 1153922.

Lionel was First to Introduce—

All-steel car and locomotive bodies, hand enameled and rigidly assembled, instead of flimsy lithographed tin.

Trucks with nickeled journals.

Roller contact shoes on locomotives.

Three-point armature shaft bearings on miniature motors.

Electrical sheets for motor and armature construction instead of cheap cold-rolled steel.

Drill rod shaft for armature, instead of commercial iron wire.

Reinforced phosphor-bronze bearings for armature shaft and wheel axles.

Automatic Warning Signals.

Automatic Block Signals.

All-steel electric lighted miniature bungalows and villas,

AND

Every desirable detail in Model Electric Trains and Accessories.

7

1927

Construction of Lionel Locomotives

LIONEL leadership has been attained by specialization in the manufacture of one product for 27 years. Our entire resources and unsurpassed manufacturing facilities are exclusively devoted to the production of Model Electric Trains, Railroad Accessories and "Multivolt" Transformers.

Reference to the descriptive matter and illustrations on these pages will prove the supremely high quality of Lionel Products. Not only are the raw materials used the best obtainable, but all Locomotives, Pullman and Freight Cars as well as Railroad Accessories, are actually built to scale. Every detail found in real railroad equipment is faithfully reproduced in our models. Space does not permit us to dwell at length on the many improvements incorporated in our goods, but on Page 7 we specify a few of the leading features introduced and patented by us.

All Lionel Cars and Locomotive Bodies are enameled in a variety of attractive colors, and baked at high temperature, which insures a permanent finish that can always be kept bright by any ordinary cleaning process.

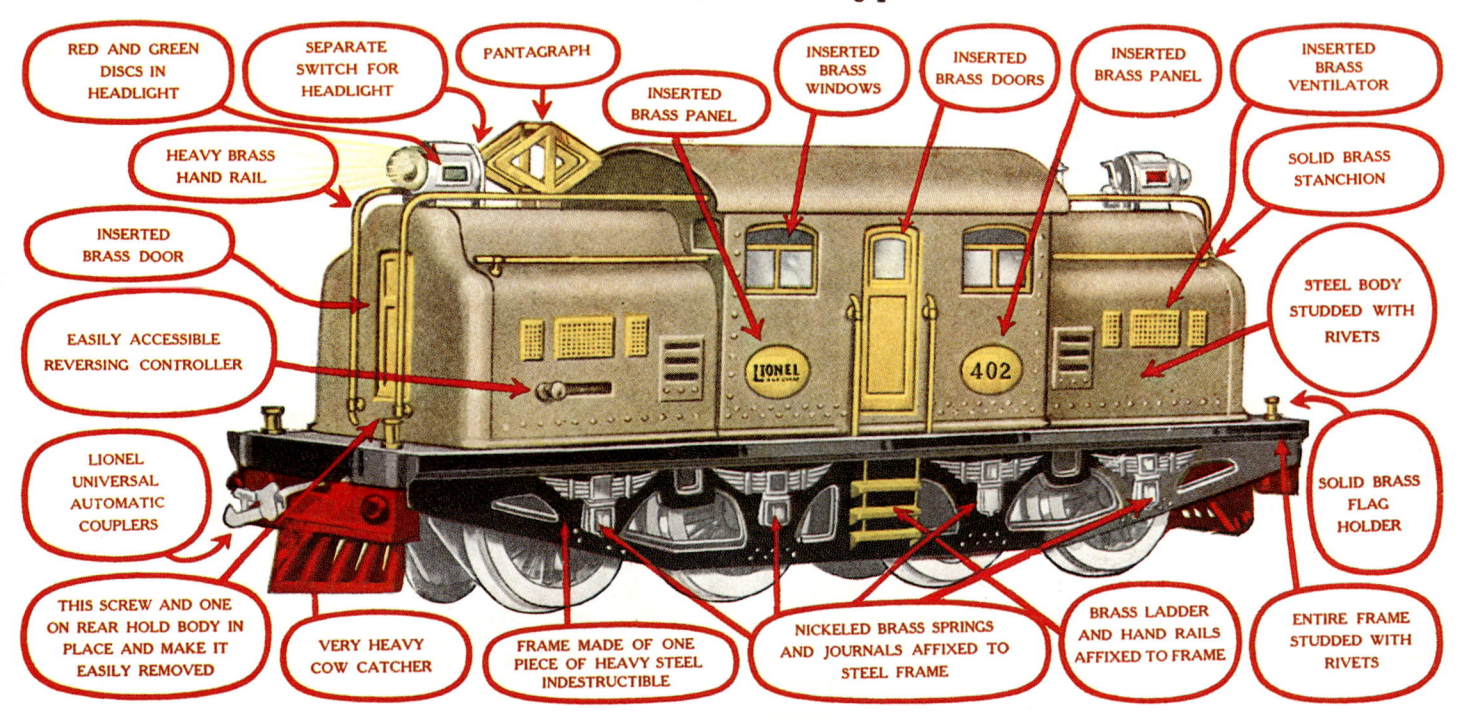

[Diagram labels:] RED AND GREEN DISCS IN HEADLIGHT — SEPARATE SWITCH FOR HEADLIGHT — PANTAGRAPH — INSERTED BRASS PANEL — INSERTED BRASS WINDOWS — INSERTED BRASS DOORS — INSERTED BRASS PANEL — INSERTED BRASS VENTILATOR — HEAVY BRASS HAND RAIL — SOLID BRASS STANCHION — INSERTED BRASS DOOR — STEEL BODY STUDDED WITH RIVETS — EASILY ACCESSIBLE REVERSING CONTROLLER — LIONEL UNIVERSAL AUTOMATIC COUPLERS — SOLID BRASS FLAG HOLDER — THIS SCREW AND ONE ON REAR HOLD BODY IN PLACE AND MAKE IT EASILY REMOVED — VERY HEAVY COW CATCHER — FRAME MADE OF ONE PIECE OF HEAVY STEEL INDESTRUCTIBLE — NICKELED BRASS SPRINGS AND JOURNALS AFFIXED TO STEEL FRAME — BRASS LADDER AND HAND RAILS AFFIXED TO FRAME — ENTIRE FRAME STUDDED WITH RIVETS

The structural details of Lionel Locomotive Bodies are typical of Lionel supreme quality throughout the entire line. Even the lowest priced Lionel Locomotives incorporate many of these features.

We refer with pride to one of our greatest achievements—the Lionel De-Luxe Electrically-Controlled Twin-Super-Motor Locomotive No. 408E illustrated on Page 17. The richness and realism of the details in this new model are far beyond anything hitherto attempted.

Of utmost importance is the fact that cast iron does not enter into the manufacture of any of these bodies—heavy sheet steel is used for every model. Panels and rivets are embossed in the metal which add strength; so that Lionel Locomotives are practically indestructible. Brass and nickeled fittings add further charm to the general appearance of Lionel Locomotives. These fittings are secured to the bodies by a patented process perfected by us.

In all ways Lionel Locomotive Bodies combine sturdy construction and graceful lines, as the indications clearly show.

Construction of Lionel Passenger and Freight Cars

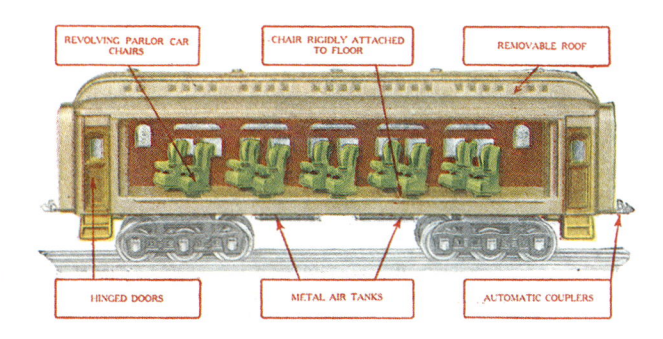

Interior view of Pullman Car showing revolving Parlor-Chairs installed in Cars Nos. 428, 429, 430, 418, 419 and 490, illustrated on Page 31. These chairs are constructed of sheet steel and are rigidly fastened to the floor of car.

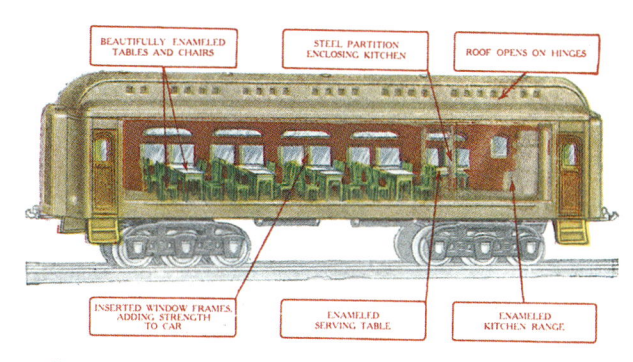

Interior view of No. 431 Dining-Car (same size as Cars Nos. 428, 429, 430, 418, 419 and 490) showing arrangement of tables, chairs and kitchen. This is beyond doubt the most complete car ever made, and is typical of Lionel quality.

ALL Lionel Cars, irrespective of price, are made of sheet steel, and are modeled after the newest designs used on the principal railroads of the country. Great detail is incorporated in them, such as hinged doors, inserted window-frames and seats, metal tanks, etc. Transparencies are placed in the windows and transoms of every Passenger Coach. All roofs are easily removable so that the interior can be reached.

All "Lionel Standard" Observation Cars are equipped with dome light which illuminates red transparent discs in the rear of the observation platform producing a dazzlingly beautiful effect. This rear light is in addition to the centre light found in all Lionel Passenger Cars, excepting Nos. 529, 530, 629 and 630. Cars are finished in a variety of attractive enamel colors, baked at high temperature.

A revolving shoe on one truck collects the current for the interior illumination of the cars. (See illustration on Page 31.) All trucks (excepting those on our 4-wheel "O" Gauge series) are equipped with nickeled journals, which cover the ends of heavy steel nickeled axles. Wheels are made of heavy nickel-plated steel and are perfectly balanced.

Lionel Freight Cars embody great detail and are real in every respect. The arrows indicate the many desirable features incorporated in Lionel Freight Cars that cannot be found in any other make.

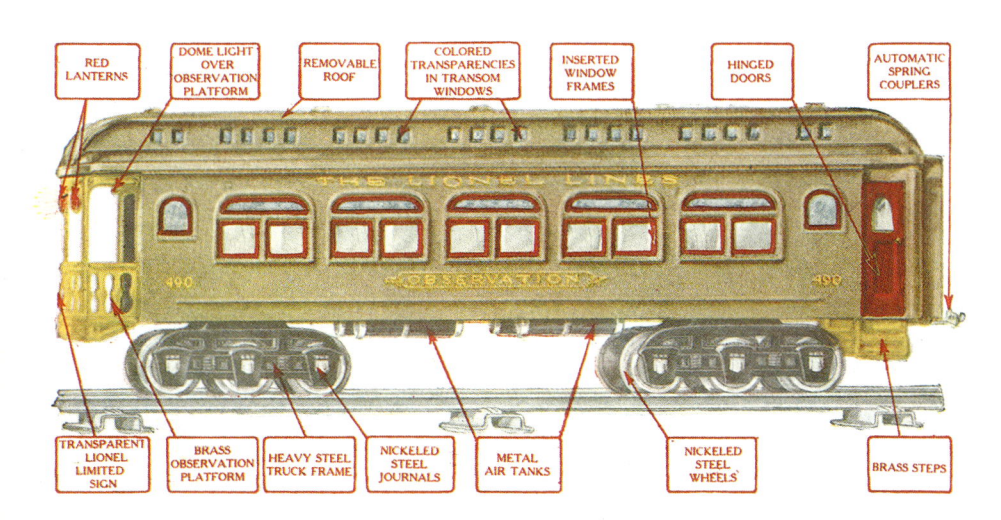

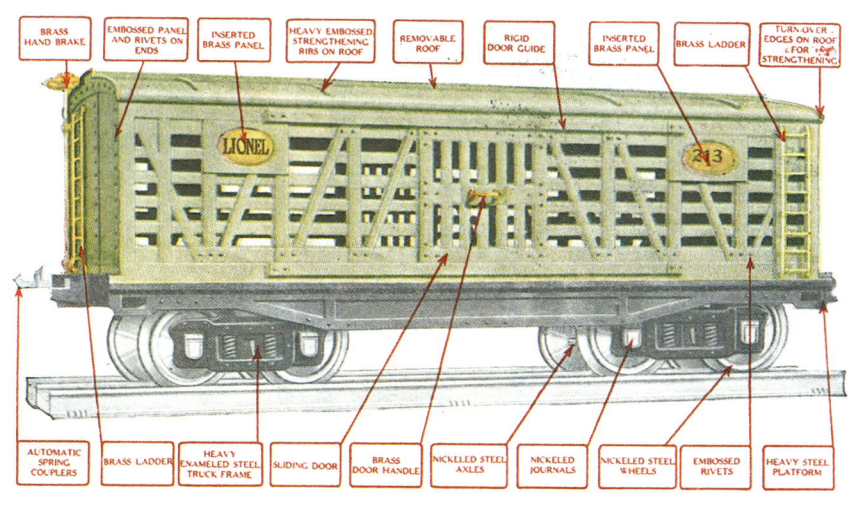

The New Lionel Electrically-Controlled Locomotives

LIONEL engineers after many years of research have developed Electrically-Controlled Locomotives that are in keeping with the other high grade features of Lionel equipment, which means 100% perfection in operation, design, workmanship and efficiency.

Lionel Electrically-Controlled Locomotives shown on the following pages are made in great variety for "O" Gauge as well as for "Lionel Standard" Track. They have withstood the severest tests and carry the usual liberal Lionel guarantee.

One of the outstanding features of Lionel Electrically-Controlled Locomotives is the simplicity of operation. By manipulating a small lever on the controlling rheostat (supplied with each Electrically-Controlled Locomotive and Train Outfit) they may be started, stopped, reversed and operated at any speed at any distance from the track.

The controlling rheostat-lever, when moved from side to side, reduces or increases speed, and when lowered, stops the train. When the lever is raised, train starts in opposite direction. The mechanism is so perfect that when the lever is lowered and raised twice the train will continue in the direction in which it ran before being stopped.

Another desirable feature of Lionel Electrically-Controlled Locomotives is the fact that they can also be reversed by hand, and the controlling unit may be disconnected by moving another small lever.

The two headlights are so connected that when the locomotive is moving forward the front headlight is illuminated, and when the locomotive is reversed, the rear headlight shines, while the other is automatically disconnected.

The Lionel Electrically-Controlled mechanism is built into the motor. Patents are now pending covering this unique construction, as well as the principle that makes it possible to operate Lionel Electrically-Controlled Locomotives without using extra current, with the result that Lionel locomotives are the only ones made that will operate as perfectly on direct current as on alternating current, dry cells or storage batteries.

The construction throughout is dependable, and must not be confused with so-called "Automatic Reversing Locomotives."

Lionel Electrically-Controlled Locomotives are the greatest improvement ever made in model train construction and are worth considerably more than we charge for this very desirable feature.

FOR "LIONEL STANDARD" TRACK 2¼ INCHES WIDE AND LIONEL "O" GAUGE TRACK 1⅜ INCHES WIDE.

Lionel Electrically-Controlled Locomotives and Train Outfits are distinguished by the letter "E" after the catalog number. They are fully described on the following pages.

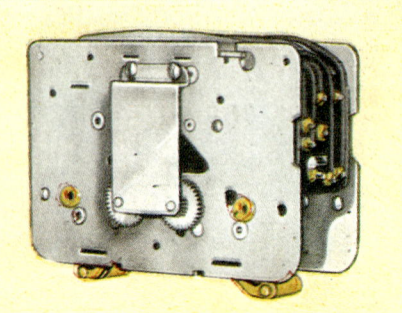

Illustration shows the simplicity and compactness of Lionel Electrically-Controlled Super-Motors. All working parts are mounted between two heavy steel plates. All shaft bearings are reinforced with bronze bushings. All parts are easily accessible, including the removable brush holder, the lever for reversing locomotive by hand and an additional lever for disconnecting the electrically-controlled mechanism.

Locomotives for Lionel "O" Gauge Track—1⅜ Inches Wide

THE new line of Lionel "O" Gauge Locomotives now includes several models equipped with the Lionel Super-Motor that are electrically-controlled, or are equipped with hand-reverse. They are fully described on Page 4. These powerful locomotives haul twice as many cars as any other make.

All Lionel "O" Gauge Locomotives are equipped with automatic couplers.

NOTE:—Length of couplers on locomotives is not included in dimensions given in specifications.

Locomotive No. 248—Equipped with electric headlight. 7½ inches long, 3¾ inches high. Price **$5.75**
Code Word "REGAL"

Locomotive No. 252—Equipped with reversing controller and electric headlight. 8 inches long, 3¾ inches high. Price . . . **$8.00**
Code Word "ELECT"

Locomotive No. 253—Equipped with reversing controller and 2 electric headlights. 9 inches long, 4 inches high. Price . . **$9.75**
Code Word "FINE"

Super-Motor Locomotive No. 254—Equipped with reversing controller and 2 electric headlights. 10 inches long, 4¼ inches high. Price . . **$12.25**
Code Word "MANY"

Electrically-Controlled Super-Motor Locomotive No. 254E—Same as No. 254, but can be started, stopped, reversed and operated at any speed at any distance from the track by means of No. 81 controlling rheostat supplied with it. Price . . **$17.25**
Code Word "GRIT"

Super-Motor Locomotive No. 251—Equipped with reversing controller and 2 electric headlights. 10¼ inches long, 5 inches high. Price . **$15.00**
Code Word "ACME"

Electrically-Controlled Super-Motor Locomotive No. 251E—Same as No. 251, but can be started, stopped, reversed and operated at any speed at any distance from the track by means of No. 81 controlling rheostat supplied with it. Price . **$20.00**
Code Word "GLORY"

Twin-Super-Motor Locomotive No. 256—Equipped with reversing controller and 2 electric headlights. 11½ inches long, 5¼ inches high. Price **$18.25**
Code Word "CHAIN"

Locomotive No. 248—For use with Passenger Cars Nos. 529, 530, 629 and 630.—Freight Cars Nos. 803, 804, 805, 806, 807, 831 and 902.

Locomotive No. 252—For use with Passenger Cars Nos. 529, 530, 629 and 630.—Freight Cars Nos. 803, 804, 805, 806, 807, 831 and 902.

Locomotive No. 253—For use with Passenger Cars Nos. 607, 608, 610 and 612.—Freight Cars Nos. 811, 812, 813, 814, 815, 816 and 817.

Super-Motor Locomotive No. 254 and No. 254E—For use with Passenger Cars Nos. 610 and 612.—Freight Cars Nos. 811, 812, 813, 814, 815, 816 and 817.

Super-Motor Locomotive No. 251 and No. 251E—For use with Passenger Cars Nos. 605 and 606.—Freight Cars Nos. 811, 812, 813, 814, 815, 816 and 817.

Twin-Super-Motor Locomotive No. 256—For use with Passenger Cars Nos. 710 and 712.—Freight Cars Nos. 811, 812, 813, 814, 815, 816 and 817.

Passenger and Freight Train Outfits for Lionel "O" Gauge Track—1⅜ Inches Wide

All Lionel Outfits include electric lamps for headlights, wires for connecting to transformer or batteries, and connecting ties for joining sections of track. Passenger Outfits include electric lamps for interior of cars. All "O" Gauge Train Outfits, excepting No. 290, are equipped with automatic couplers.

No. 290

Outfit No. 290—Comprises 1 No. 152 locomotive with electric headlight, 1 No. 901 gondola car, 1 No. 801 caboose, 8 sections OC curved track, 1 No. 068 warning signal, 1 OTC "Lockon" connection. Track forms a circle 30 inches in diameter. Train is 20½ inches long. Price $5.75
Code Word "RECENT"

Outfit No. 292—Comprises 1 No. 248 locomotive with electric headlight, 1 No. 629 Pullman car, 1 No. 630 observation car, 8 sections OC curved track, 1 No. 068 warning signal, 1 OTC "Lockon" connection. Track forms a circle 30 inches in diameter. Train is 24¼ inches long. Price . . $6.75
Code Word "KEEN"

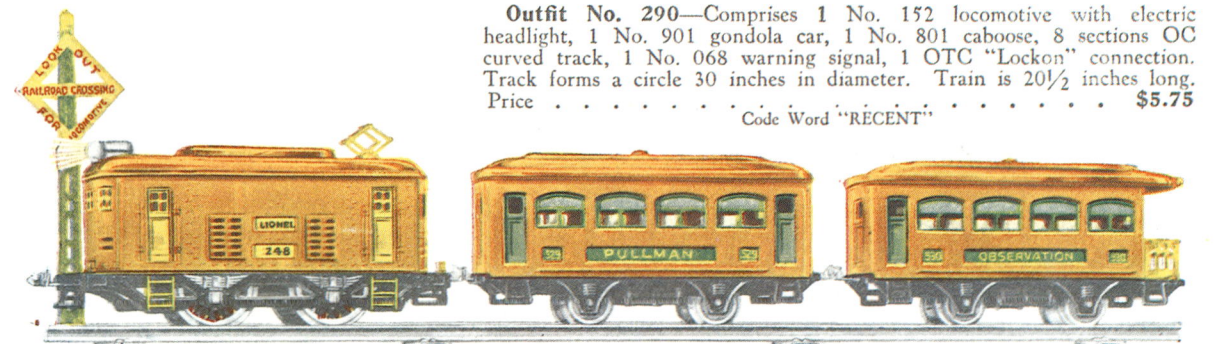

No. 292

Outfit No. 249—Comprises 1 No. 248 locomotive with electric headlight, 1 No. 831 lumber car with load of lumber, 1 No. 807 caboose, 8 sections OC curved track, 1 No. 068 warning signal, 1 OTC "Lockon" connection. Track forms a circle 30 inches in diameter. Train is 24¼ inches long. Price $6.75
Code Word "KATE"

No. 249

Outfit No. 294—Comprises 1 No. 252 reversible locomotive with electric headlight, 2 No. 529 Pullman cars, 1 No. 530 observation car, 8 sections OC curved track, 2 sections OS straight track, 1 No. 88 battery rheostat, 1 No. 068 warning signal, 1 OTC "Lockon" connection. Track forms an oval 40 by 30 inches. Train is 33 inches long. Price . $9.75
Code Word "CORN"

All "O" Gauge Outfits listed on this and the following pages include 1 No. 068 warning signal without extra charge.

No. 294

12

Passenger and Freight Train Outfits for Lionel "O" Gauge Track—1⅜ Inches Wide

Lionel "O" Gauge Illuminated Passenger Trains shown on this page, irrespective of price, are the finest of their kind produced anywhere.
Lionel "Multivolt" Transformers, for Alternating Current, are the best and most efficient for operating all trains.

No. 293

Outfit No. 293—Comprises 1 No. 252 reversible locomotive with electric headlight, 1 No. 803 coal car, 1 No. 804 oil car, 1 No. 805 box car, 1 No. 807 caboose, 8 sections OC curved track, 2 sections OS straight track, 1 No. 88 battery rheostat, 1 No. 068 warning signal, 1 OTC "Lockon" connection. Track forms an oval 40 by 30 inches. Train is 40¼ inches long. Price $10.75
Code Word "UPTON"

WARNING SIGNAL IS INCLUDED IN ALL "O" GAUGE OUTFITS WITHOUT CHARGE.

No. 296

Outfit No. 296—Comprises 1 No. 252 reversible locomotive with electric headlight, 2 No. 607 illuminated Pullman cars, 1 No. 608 illuminated observation car, 8 sections OC curved track, 4 sections OS straight track, 1 No. 88 battery rheostat, 1 No. 068 warning signal, 1 OTC "Lockon" connection. Track forms an oval 50 by 30 inches. Train is 35½ inches long. Price . . $12.75
Code Word "DART"

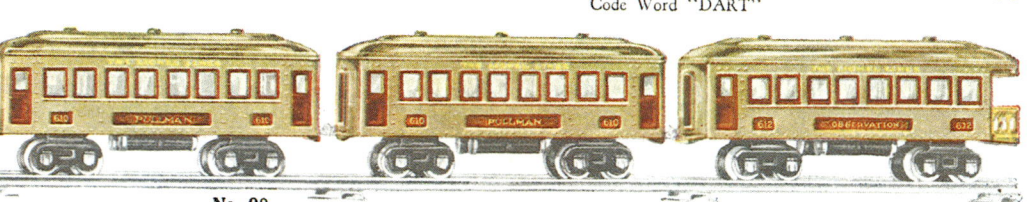

No. 98

Outfit No. 98—Comprises 1 No. 253 reversible locomotive with 2 electric headlights, 2 No. 610 illuminated Pullman cars, 1 No. 612 illuminated observation car, 8 sections OC curved track, 6 sections OS straight track, 1 No. 88 battery rheostat, 1 No. 068 warning signal, 1 OTC "Lockon" connection. Track forms an oval 60 by 30 inches. Train is 39½ inches long. Price . $15.00
Code Word "GOLD"

SEE PAGE 29 FOR SUITABLE FREIGHT CARS TO BE USED WITH THESE TRAINS.

No. 266E Electrically-Controlled Passenger Train Outfit—Same as No. 266 described below, except that it contains No. 254E Electrically-Controlled Super-Motor Locomotive, which can be started, stopped, reversed and operated at any speed at any distance from the track, by means of No. 81 controlling rheostat supplied with it. Price $23.00
Code Word "ILION"

No. 266 and No. 266E

Outfit No. 266—Comprises 1 No. 254 Super-Motor reversible locomotive with 2 electric headlights, 2 No. 610 illuminated Pullman cars, 1 No. 612 illuminated observation car, 8 sections OC curved track, 6 sections OS straight track, 1 No. 88 battery rheostat, 1 No. 068 warning signal, 1 OTC "Lockon" connection. Track forms an oval 60 by 30 inches. Train is 40½ inches long. Price $18.00
Code Word "HEAD"

Passenger and Freight Train Outfits for Lionel "O" Gauge Track—1⅜ Inches Wide

The Electrically-Controlled Passenger and Freight Trains illustrated on this page are among Lionel's greatest achievements. Just think how thrilling it is to be able to start, stop, reverse and operate your train at any speed at any distance from the track!

Nos. 299 and 299E

Outfit No. 299—Comprises 1 No. 254 Super-Motor reversible locomotive with 2 electric headlights, 1 No. 814 box car, 1 No. 813 cattle car, 1 No. 817 caboose, 8 sections OC curved track, 6 sections OS straight track, 1 No. 88 battery rheostat, 1 No. 068 warning signal, 1 OTC "Lockon" connection. Track forms an oval 60 by 30 inches. Train is 40½ inches long. Price $17.00

Code Word "FLORA"

No. 299E Electrically-Controlled Passenger Train Outfit—Same as No. 299, but it contains No. 254E Electrically-Controlled Super-Motor Locomotive, which can be started, stopped, reversed and operated at any speed at any distance from the track by means of No. 81 controlling rheostat supplied with it. Price $21.75

Code Word "QUILL"

Nos. 269 and 269E

Outfit No. 269—Comprises 1 No. 251 Super-Motor reversible locomotive with 2 electric headlights, 1 No. 812 gondola car, 1 No. 813 cattle car, 1 No. 814 box car, 1 No. 815 oil car, 1 No. 817 caboose, 8 sections OC curved track, 6 sections OS straight track, 1 No. 88 battery rheostat, 1 No. 068 warning signal, 1 OTC "Lockon" connection. Track forms an oval 60 by 30 inches. Train is 61 inches long. Price $25.00

Code Word "USHER"

No. 269E Electrically-Controlled Freight Train Outfit—Same as No. 269, but it contains No. 251E Electrically-Controlled Super-Motor Locomotive, which can be started, stopped, reversed and operated at any speed at any distance from the track by means of No. 81 controlling rheostat supplied with it. Price $28.00

Code Word "NECK"

For greatest efficiency always use a Lionel "Multivolt" Transformer to operate your model electric train — fully guaranteed and made completely in Lionel's own factories.

Nos. 97 and 97E

Outfit No. 97—Comprises 1 No. 251 Super-Motor reversible locomotive with 2 electric headlights, 2 No. 605 illuminated Pullman cars, 1 No. 606 illuminated observation car, 8 sections OC curved track, 8 sections OS straight track, 1 No. 88 battery rheostat, 1 No. 068 warning signal, 1 OTC "Lockon" connection. Track forms an oval 70 by 30 inches. Train is 43¼ inches long. Price $22.50

Code Word "EXCEL"

No. 97E Electrically-Controlled Passenger Train Outfit—Same as No. 97, but it contains No. 251E Electrically-Controlled Super-Motor Locomotive, which can be started, stopped, reversed and operated at any speed at any distance from the track by means of No. 81 controlling rheostat supplied with it. Price $25.50

Code Word "JUST"

Passenger Train Outfits for Lionel "O" Gauge Track—1⅜ Inches Wide

No. 268 Twin-Super-Motor "O" Gauge Passenger Train.

Outfit No. 268—Comprises 1 No. 256 Twin-Super-Motor reversible locomotive with 2 electric headlights, 2 No. 710 illuminated Pullman cars, 1 No. 712 illuminated observation car, 8 sections OC curved track, 8 sections OS straight track, 1 No. 88 battery rheostat, 1 No. 068 warning signal, 1 OTC "Lockon" connection. Track forms an oval 70 by 30 inches. Train is 51 inches long. Price $33.00

Code Word "TAKE"

Train Outfit No. 268 with its powerful Super-Motor Locomotive and Illuminated Passenger Cars is the finest "O" Gauge Train in the world. You may use with it our new Freight Cars Nos. 811 to 817, illustrated on Page 29. The locomotive will haul 20 of these Freight Cars with perfect ease.

No. 174 Outfit shown in the accompanying illustration is a complete model railroad to operate on "O" Gauge Track. It includes a large variety of accessories. Every piece is of steel construction and enameled by Lionel's own lustrous and lasting process.

Outfit No. 174—Comprises 1 No. 252 reversible locomotive with electric headlight, 2 No. 607 illuminated Pullman cars, 1 No. 608 illuminated observation car, 10 sections OC curved track, 6 sections OS straight track, 1 OTC "Lockon" connection, 1 No. 88 battery rheostat, 1 pair No. 021 illuminated switches (one right, one left), 1 No. 106 bridge (3 sections), 1 No. 122 illuminated station, 6 No. 60 telegraph posts, 2 No. 62 semaphores, 1 No. 068 warning signal, 1 No. 119 tunnel. Size of track layout 45 by 60 inches. Train is 35½ inches long. Price $37.50

Code Word "DELA"

Super-Motor Locomotives for "Lionel Standard" Track

— 2¼ INCHES WIDE —

Nos. 8 and 8E   Nos. 10 and 10E   Nos. 318 and 318E   Nos. 380 and 380E

No. 8 "Lionel Standard" Super-Motor Reversible Locomotive— with 2 electric headlights. 11 inches long, 4½ inches high. Price **$11.50**
Code Word "POWER"

No. 8E "Lionel Standard" Electrically-Controlled Super-Motor Locomotive— Same as No. 8, but equipped with electrically-controlled mechanism which starts, stops, reverses and operates it at any speed at any distance from the track by means of No. 81 controlling rheostat supplied with it. Price **$17.75**
Code Word "PEPPY"

Above locomotives are for use with Passenger Cars Nos. 332, 337, 338, 339 and 341—Freight Cars Nos. 511 to 517, 218 and 219.

No. 10 "Lionel Standard" Super-Motor Reversible Locomotive— with 2 electric headlights. 11½ inches long, 5¼ inches high. Price **$13.75**
Code Word "PULL"

No. 10E "Lionel Standard" Electrically-Controlled Super-Motor Locomotive— Same as No. 10, but equipped with electrically-controlled mechanism which starts, stops, reverses and operates it at any speed at any distance from the track by means of No. 81 controlling rheostat supplied with it. Price **$20.00**
Code Word "SELF"

Above locomotives are for use with Passenger Cars Nos. 332, 337, 338, 339 and 341—Freight Cars Nos. 511 to 517, 218 and 219.

No. 318 "Lionel Standard" Super-Motor Reversible Locomotive— with 2 electric headlights. 12½ inches long, 5⅜ inches high. Price **$16.50**
Code Word "VERB"

No. 318E "Lionel Standard" Electrically-Controlled Super-Motor Locomotive— Same as No. 318, but equipped with electrically-controlled mechanism which starts, stops, reverses and operates it at any speed at any distance from the track by means of No. 81 controlling rheostat supplied with it. Price **$22.75**
"Code Word "MOVE"

Above locomotives are for use with Passenger Cars Nos. 309, 310 and 312—Freight Cars Nos. 511 to 517, 218 and 219.

No. 380 "Lionel Standard" Super-Motor Reversible Locomotive— with 2 electric headlights. 13½ inches long, 5½ inches high. Price **$18.75**
Code Word "ROCKIES"

No. 380E "Lionel Standard" Electrically-Controlled Super-Motor Locomotive— Same as No. 380, but equipped with electrically-controlled mechanism which starts, stops, reverses and operates it at any speed at any distance from the track by means of No. 81 controlling rheostat supplied with it. Price **$25.50**
Code Word "SAINT"

Above locomotives are for use with Passenger Cars Nos. 428, 429, 430 and 431—Freight Cars Nos. 211 to 219.

All "Lionel Standard" Locomotives are equipped with automatic couplers and 2 electric headlights. Lamps for headlights are included. Details of construction of "Lionel Standard" Super-Motors are given on Page 5. NOTE: Length of couplers on locomotives is not included in dimensions given in specifications.

Twin-Super-Motor Locomotives

FOR "LIONEL STANDARD" TRACK—2¼ INCHES WIDE

AS the American boy expects Lionel to introduce model railroad equipment that is in keeping with electric railroad development, we offer the new Electrically-Controlled Locomotives, made in six different types as illustrated on these pages. They are the result of years of experiment and research by Lionel engineers.

The locomotives shown on this page are for use with Passenger Cars Nos. 428, 429, 430, 431, 418, 419 and 490, illustrated on Page 31; also with Freight Cars Nos. 211 to 219, illustrated on Pages 27 and 28.

The new Electrically-Controlled Locomotives are the only ones made that will operate on direct current as well as on alternating current, dry cells or storage batteries. A patented electrical device makes it possible to operate or reverse these locomotives without using more current than models that are reversed by hand. When the Electrically-Controlled Locomotive is running forward, front headlight is illuminated—when it is reversed, rear one shines brilliantly and forward one is automatically cut out.

All "Lionel Standard" Locomotives are made either with hand reversing controller, or with electrically-controlled reversing mechanism that also can be operated by hand.

We are proud to show the De-Luxe Locomotive No. 408E illustrated on this page. It is one of Lionel's greatest achievements. The illustration clearly shows the great amount of realistic detail incorporated in it. In addition to the details of construction indicated on Page 8, this locomotive includes two operating pantographs, two illuminated signal lanterns on front of locomotive, two flags, and an enormous amount of extra special detail in the superstructure. It is indeed a triumph of model engineering skill.

No. 408E—De-Luxe Twin-Super-Motor Electrically-Controlled Locomotive—the world's finest model.

No. 408E "Lionel Standard" De-Luxe Twin-Super-Motor Electrically-Controlled Locomotive—17 inches long, 8½ inches high to top of pantagraph. This locomotive can be started, stopped, reversed and operated at any speed at any distance from the track by means of No. 81 controlling rheostat supplied with it. Complete with lamps for headlights and front lanterns. Price $44.00
Code Word "FAST"

No. 402 "Lionel Standard" Twin-Super-Motor Reversible Locomotive—17 inches long, 6½ inches high. Complete with 2 lamps for electric headlights. Price $32.25
Code Word "HAVEN"

Nos. 402 and 402E

No. 402E "Lionel Standard" Electrically-Controlled Twin-Super-Motor Locomotive—Same as No. 402, but equipped with electrically-controlled mechanism which starts, stops, reverses and operates it at any speed at any distance from the track by means of No. 81 controlling rheostat supplied with it. Price . . . $40.00
Code Word "YORK"

17

1927

Passenger and Freight Train Outfits for "Lionel Standard" Track — 2¼ Inches Wide

THE "Lionel Standard" Trains on this and the following pages are listed with hand-controlled locomotives as well as with electrically-controlled mechanism.

Outfit No. 347—Comprises 1 No. 8 Super-Motor Reversible Locomotive with 2 electric headlights, 1 No. 337 illuminated Pullman Car, 1 No. 338 illuminated observation car, 8 sections C curved track, 2 sections S straight track, 1 STC "Lockon" connection. Track forms an oval 56 by 42 inches. Train is 38½ inches long. Price . . $20.00
Code Word "ZENA"

Outfit No. 347E—Same as No. 347, except that it contains No. 8E Electrically-Controlled Super-Motor Locomotive which can be started, stopped, reversed and operated at any speed at any distance from the track by means of No. 81 controlling rheostat supplied with it. Price $25.50
Code Word "GLIDE"

Nos. 347 and 347E

All these trains are equipped with automatic couplers, and all Passenger Cars are electrically illuminated.

Outfit No. 353—Comprises 1 No. 8 Super-Motor Reversible Locomotive with 2 electric headlights, 1 No. 511 lumber car with load of lumber, 1 No. 512 gondola car, 1 No. 517 illuminated caboose, 8 sections C curved track, 2 sections S straight track, 1 STC "Lockon" connection. Track forms an oval 56 by 42 inches. Train is 49¼ inches long. Price . . $20.00
Code Word "JACK"

Outfit No. 353E—Same as No. 353, except that it contains No. 8E Electrically-Controlled Super-Motor Locomotive, which can be started, stopped, reversed and operated at any speed at any distance from the track by means of No. 81 controlling rheostat supplied with it. Price . . . $25.50
Code Word "MASK"

Nos. 353 and 353E

Lamps for headlights and cars, wire for connecting to transformer or batteries, and connecting ties for joining sections of track are supplied with every outfit.

Outfit No. 352—Comprises 1 No. 10 Super-Motor Reversible Locomotive with 2 electric headlights, 1 No. 332 illuminated mail and baggage car, 1 No. 339 illuminated pullman car, 1 No. 341 illuminated observation car, 8 sections C curved track, 4 sections S straight track, 1 STC "Lockon" connection. Track forms an oval 69 by 42 inches. Train is 52 inches long. Price . . . $25.00
Code Word "PRINCE"

Outfit No. 352E—Same as No. 352, except that it contains No. 10E Electrically-Controlled Super-Motor Locomotive, which can be started, stopped, reversed and operated at any speed at any distance from the track by means of No. 81 controlling rheostat supplied with it. Price $30.75
Code Word "WIN"

Nos. 352 and 352E

Outfit No. 354—Comprises 1 No. 10 Super-Motor Reversible Locomotive with 2 electric headlights, 1 No. 511 lumber car with load of lumber, 1 No. 512 gondola car, 1 No. 513 cattle car, 1 No. 514 box car, 1 No. 517 illuminated caboose, 8 sections C curved track, 6 sections S straight track, 1 STC "Lockon" connection. Track forms an oval 88 by 42 inches. Train is 75¼ inches long. Price . . . $25.00
Code Word "ZONE"

Outfit No. 354E—Same as No. 354, except that it contains No. 10E Electrically-Controlled Super-Motor Locomotive which can be started, stopped, reversed and operated at any speed at any distance from the track by means of No. 81 controlling rheostat supplied with it. Price $30.75
Code Word "ZEST"

Nos. 354 and 354E

Passenger and Freight Train Outfits for "Lionel Standard" Track—2¼ Inches Wide

Nos. 344 and 344E

AGAIN we refer to the powerful Super-Motors with which all "Lionel Standard" Trains, listed on this and other pages, are equipped. It is amazing to see these wonderful motors haul a large number of Passenger or Freight Cars with perfect ease.

Please remember that all Lionel Train Outfits are complete in every respect. Lamps for headlights and cars are supplied with every outfit, as well as wires for transformer or battery connection, and connecting ties for joining sections of track. All "Lionel Standard" Locomotives, Passenger and Freight Cars are equipped with automatic couplers.

Outfit No. 344—Comprises 1 No. 380 Super-Motor Reversible Locomotive with 2 electric headlights, 1 No. 18 illuminated Pullman Car, 1 No. 190 illuminated observation car, 8 sections C curved track, 4 sections S straight track, 1 STC "Lockon" connection. Track forms an oval 69 by 42 inches. Train is 48 inches long. Price $34.50
Code Word "VERNON"

Outfit No. 344E—Same as No. 344, except that it contains No. 380E Electrically-Controlled Super-Motor Locomotive which can be started, stopped, reversed and operated at any speed at any distance from the track by means of No. 81 controlling rheostat supplied with it. Price $40.25
Code Word "LEVER"

Nos. 355 and 355E

Outfit No. 355—Comprises 1 No. 318 Super-Motor Reversible Locomotive with 2 electric headlights, 1 No. 511 lumber car with load of lumber, 1 No. 512 gondola car, 1 No. 513 cattle car, 1 No. 514 box car, 1 No. 515 oil car, 1 No. 517 illuminated caboose, 8 sections C curved track, 8 sections S straight track, 1 STC "Lockon" connection. Track forms an oval 102 by 42 inches. Train is 90¼ inches long. Price $32.25
Code Word "FRANCE"

Outfit No. 355E—Same as No. 355, except that it contains No. 318E Electrically-Controlled Super-Motor Locomotive which can be started, stopped, reversed and operated at any speed at any distance from the track by means of No. 81 controlling rheostat supplied with it. Price $38.50
Code Word "LORRY"

Nos. 342 and 342E

Outfit No. 342—Comprises 1 No. 318 Super-Motor Reversible Locomotive with 2 electric headlights, 1 No. 310 illuminated mail and baggage car, 1 No. 309 illuminated Pullman car, 1 No. 312 illuminated observation car, 8 sections C curved track, 6 sections S straight track, 1 STC "Lockon" connection. Track forms an oval 88 by 42 inches. Train is 56½ inches long. Price . . $30.75
Code Word "VIEW"

Outfit No. 342E—Same as No. 342, except that it contains No. 318E Electrically-Controlled Super-Motor Locomotive which can be started, stopped, reversed and operated at any speed at any distance from the track by means of No. 81 controlling rheostat supplied with it. Price $37.00
Code Word "FORUM"

Passenger and Freight Train Outfits for "Lionel Standard" Track—2¼ Inches Wide

Nos. 343 and 343E

Outfit No. 343—Comprises 1 No. 380 Super-Motor Reversible Locomotive with 2 electric headlights, 1 No. 320 illuminated mail and baggage car, 2 No. 319 illuminated Pullman cars, 1 No. 322 illuminated observation car, 8 sections C curved track, 8 sections S straight track, 1 STC "Lockon" connection. Track forms an oval 102 by 42 inches. Train is 73 inches long. Price $38.50
Code Word "TIME"

Outfit No. 343E—Same as No. 343, except that it contains No. 380E Electrically-Controlled Super-Motor Locomotive which can be started, stopped, reversed and operated at any speed at any distance from the track by means of No. 81 controlling rheostat supplied with it. Price $48.00
Code Word "QUIRE"

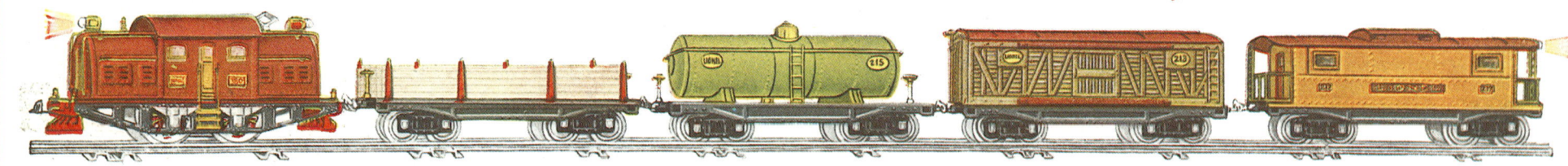

Nos. 356 and 356E

Outfit No. 356—Comprises 1 No. 380 Super-Motor Reversible Locomotive with 2 electric headlights, 1 No. 211 lumber car with load of lumber, 1 No. 213 cattle car, 1 No. 215 oil car, 1 No. 217 illuminated caboose, 8 sections C curved track, 6 sections S straight track, 1 STC "Lockon" connection. Track forms an oval 88 by 42 inches. Train is 69¼ inches long. Price $35.50
Code Word "GROSS"

Outfit No. 356E—Same as No. 356, except that it contains No. 380E Electrically-Controlled Super-Motor Locomotive which can be started, stopped, reversed and operated at any speed at any distance from the track by means of No. 81 controlling rheostat supplied with it. Price $42.25
Code Word "GRAPE"

Nos. 348 and 348E

Outfit No. 348—Comprises 1 No. 380 Super-Motor Reversible Locomotive with 2 electric headlights, 1 No. 428 illuminated Pullman car, 1 No. 429 illuminated Pullman and baggage car, 1 No. 430 illuminated observation car, 8 sections C curved track, 8 sections S straight track, 1 STC "Lockon" connection. Track forms an oval 102 by 42 inches. Train is 70½ inches long. Price $42.25
Code Word "YARD"

Outfit No. 348E—Same as No. 348, except that it contains No. 380E Electrically-Controlled Super-Motor Locomotive which can be started, stopped, reversed and operated at any speed at any distance from the track by means of No. 81 controlling rheostat supplied with it. Price $49.25
Code Word "ONYX"

Twin-Super-Motor Passenger and Freight Trai

Lionel "Multivolt" Transformers—listed as standard by the Underwriters' Laboratories—are the most efficient for operating all trains. Lionel "Multivolt" Transformers are fully described on pages 32 and 33.

Nos. 403 and 403E

COMPLETE details showing the perfect construction of every part that enters into these outfits are given on the following pages:

Twin-Motor construction on Page 6, Locomotive construction on Page 8, and construction of Passenger Coaches on Page 9.

The great hauling power of the locomotives is an outstanding feature. The electrically-controlled mechanism built into Locomotive No. 402E is a source of endless delight. It can be started, stopped, reversed and operated at any speed at any distance from the track. It is wonderful to be able to build a

Nos. 406

A COMPANION number, quite in keeping with the No. 403 Outfit described above, is the new Freight Train No. 406. It is the acme of perfection.

Lionel engineers and car designers have spent considerable time in diligent research to produce the new all-steel freight cars. On Page 28 you will find large illustrations of these cars which will enable you to get a clearer idea of the wonderful detail they embody. Not only are these new cars patterned after the big all-steel cars that carry freight across the country, but they incorporate many original and exclusive features of design that only Lionel can carry out to such perfection.

Attention is drawn to the heavy steel frames upon which the superstructure is mounted, the new steel trucks with nickeled journals, automatic couplers, embossed rivets and other structural details that are so perfectly designed. The car bodies also show a wealth of detail. The Cattle Car and Box Car have sliding doors. The Lumber Car with load of lumber has removable supports inserted in sockets in the platform. The Coal Car has a "Hopper" bottom which operates by turning a wheel on the side. The Caboose is equipped with illuminated lanterns on the rear platform. The powerful Twin-Super-Motor Locomotive No. 402, already described, will easily haul this train, and you can add the new No. 218 Operating Dump Car and No. 219 Operating Derrick Car,

—21—

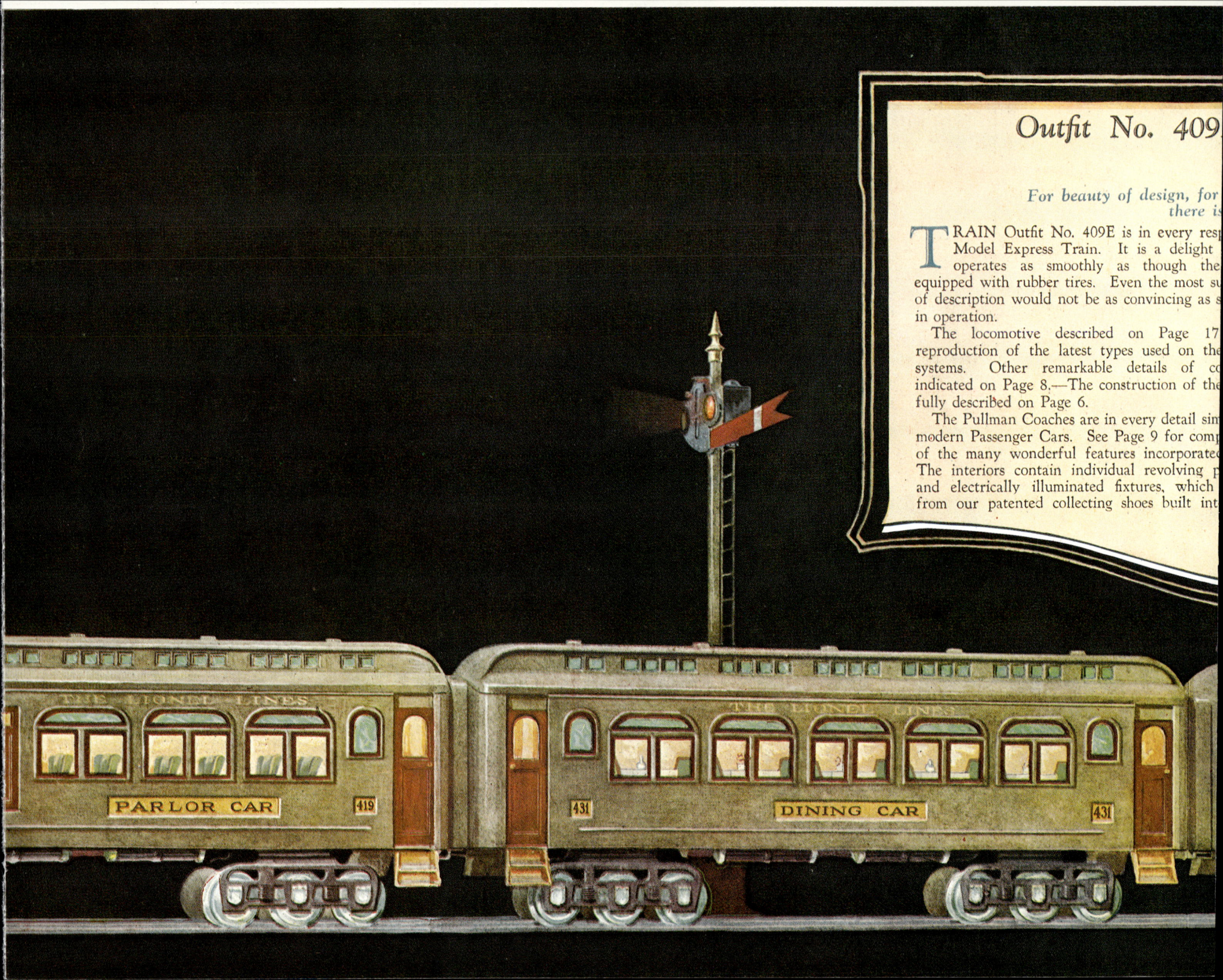

Outfit No. 409E

For beauty of design, for
there is

TRAIN Outfit No. 409E is in every resp
Model Express Train. It is a delight
operates as smoothly as though the
equipped with rubber tires. Even the most s
of description would not be as convincing as s
in operation.

The locomotive described on Page 17
reproduction of the latest types used on the
systems. Other remarkable details of co
indicated on Page 8.—The construction of the
fully described on Page 6.

The Pullman Coaches are in every detail sim
modern Passenger Cars. See Page 9 for comp
of the many wonderful features incorporated
The interiors contain individual revolving p
and electrically illuminated fixtures, which
from our patented collecting shoes built in

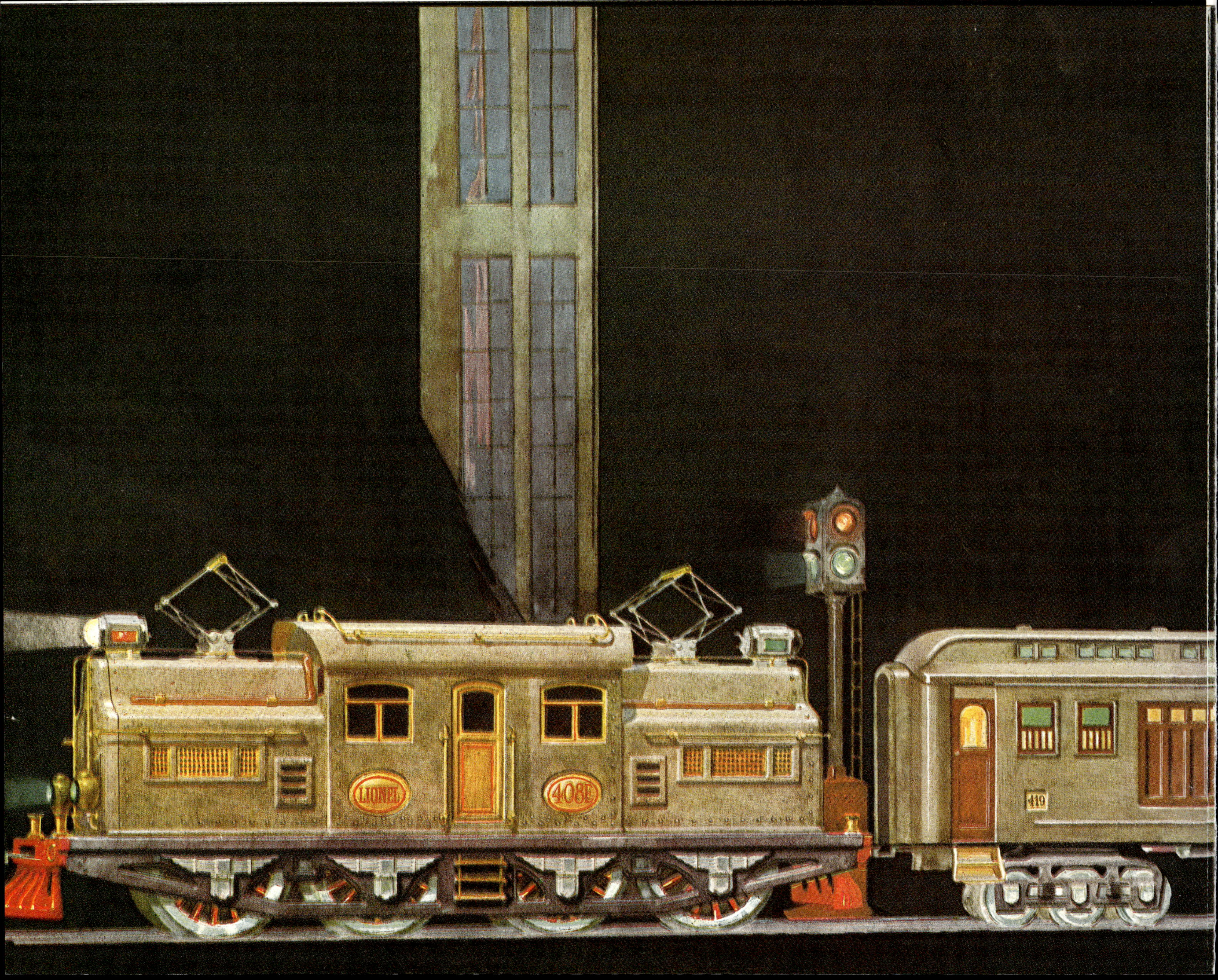
LIONEL
408E
419

Outfits for "Lionel Standard" Track—2¼ inches wide

complete 100% Electrically-Controlled Railroad by using this train with our electrically-controlled accessories, a large variety of which are described in another part of this catalog. They can be added from time to time.

Outfit No. 403—Comprises 1 No. 402 Twin-Super-Motor Reversible Locomotive with 2 electric headlights, 1 No. 418 illuminated pullman car, 1 No. 419 illuminated pullman and baggage car, 1 No. 490 illuminated observation car, 8 sections C curved track, 8 sections S straight track and 1 STC "Lockon" connection. Track forms an oval 102 by 42 inches. Train is 74½ inches long. This train is completely equipped with the new Lionel Automatic Spring Couplers. Outfit also includes lamps for headlights and interior of cars, wires for connecting to source of current, and connecting ties for joining sections of track. Price $60.75
Code Word "PRETTY"

Outfit No. 403E—Same as No 403 described above, except that it contains No. 402E Electrically-Controlled Twin-Super-Motor Locomotive which can be started, stopped, reversed and operated at any speed at any distance from the track by means of No. 81 controlling rheostat supplied with it. Price $67.75
Code Word "DEMY"

illustrated on page 27, with full assurance that you will not be overtaxing this sturdy locomotive. This outfit is truly a remarkable model and one that any boy would be proud to own.

Outfit No. 406—Comprises 1 No. 402 Twin-Super-Motor Reversible Locomotive with 2 electric headlights, 1 No. 211 lumber car with load of lumber, 1 No. 212 gondola car, 1 No. 213 cattle car, 1 No. 214 box car, 1 No. 215 oil car, 1 No. 216 coal car, 1 No. 217 illuminated caboose, 8 sections C curved track, 10 sections S straight track and 1 STC "Lockon" connection. Train is 109¾ inches long. Track forms an oval 116 by 42 inches. This train is completely equipped with the new Lionel Automatic Spring Couplers. Outfit also includes lamps for headlights and caboose, wires for transformer or battery connection and connecting ties for joining sections of track. Code Word "KIRK" Price . $65.50

Outfit No. 406E—Same as No. 406 described in previous column, except that it contains No. 402E Electrically-Controlled Twin-Super-Motor Locomotive which can be started, stopped, reversed and operated at any speed at any distance from the track by means of No. 81 controlling rheostat supplied with it. Price $71.25
Code Word "DIAL"

De Luxe Outfit No. 410E—The world's finest electrically-controlled model freight train. The cars and track equipment in this outfit are the same as No. 406E described above, but it contains the new No. 408E De-Luxe Twin-Super-Motor Locomotive described on Page 17, which can be started, stopped, reversed and operated at any speed at any distance from the track by means of No. 81 controlling rheostat supplied with it. Price $75.00
Code Word "BEST"

Lionel Twin-Super-Motor De-Luxe Special—the World's Finest Electrically-Controlled Model Train

...anical detail and precision, for electrical perfection and efficiency, for handsome and lasting enamel finish, ...a model electric train in the world that compares with this—Lionel's supreme achievement

...De-Luxe ...old, and ...ls were ...ve terms ...he outfit

...n exact ...lectrified ...tion are ...motors is

...the most ...scription ...ese cars. ...r chairs ...current ...six-wheel

trucks. The interior light shining through the colored glass windows produces a very realistic effect.

A feature of the observation car is the dome light on the rear platform (in addition to the interior light) which shows through two red signal lanterns. The transparent "Lionel Limited" sign affixed to the observation railing is another interesting new detail.

The new Dining-Car is real in everything but size. On Page 9 the sectional view of this car shows table, chairs and kitchen completely equipped with range, serving table and a profusion of other details. This is the only completely equipped model Dining-Car made in America.

The Pullman and Baggage Car has two compartments— one is equipped with revolving parlor-car chairs, while the baggage section has sliding doors as used on all cars of this type. All cars are equipped with automatic couplers.

This train is Electrically-Controlled and can be started, stopped, reversed and operated at any speed at any distance from the track.

Outfit No. 409E

Comprises 1 No. 408E Electrically - Controlled Twin - Super - Motor Locomotive with 2 electric headlights
1 No. 418 Illuminated Pullman car
1 No. 419 Illuminated Pullman and baggage car
1 No. 490 Illuminated observation car
1 No. 431 Illuminated dining-car
8 Sections C curved track
10 Sections S straight track
1 No. 81 Controlling rheostat and
1 STC "Lockon" connection

Lamps for headlights, front lanterns and interior of cars are included, as well as wires for connecting to source of current and connecting ties for joining sections of track. Track forms an oval 116 by 42 inches. Complete train is 95 inches long.

Code Word "ETTA"   Price $82.50

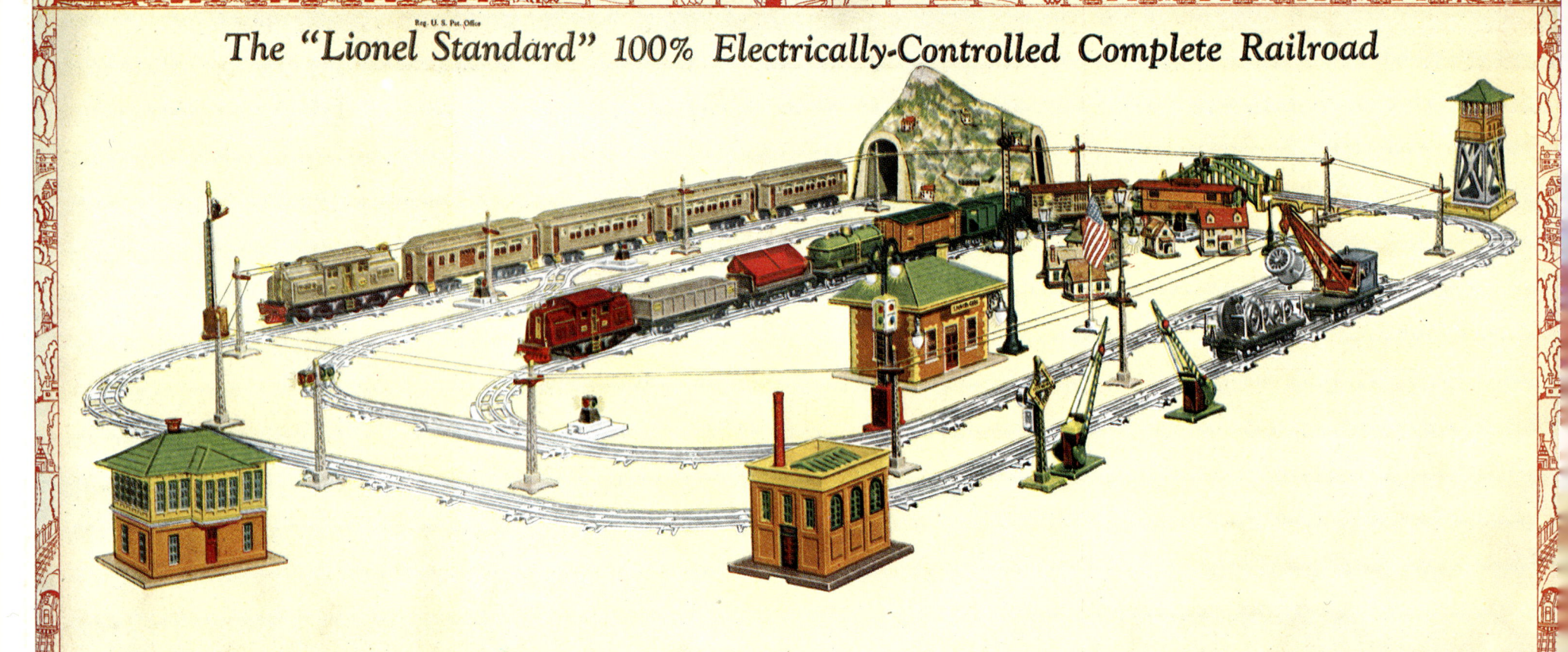

The "Lionel Standard" 100% Electrically-Controlled Complete Railroad

HERE is the finest gift that any boy could wish for—a complete Lionel Electrically-Controlled Railroad, containing not only the best trains we manufacture, but a very large variety of Electrically-Controlled and illuminated Accessories. The Passenger and Freight Trains can be started, stopped, reversed and operated at any speed at any distance from the track. The Switch Signal-Tower, shown in the foreground of the above illustration, enables you to operate all the Electrically-Controlled Accessories at a distance. The specifications of this marvelous model Railroad are given below.

OUTFIT No. 407E—COMPRISES

1 No. 408E Electrically-Controlled Locomotive	1 No. 213 Cattle car	38 S Track
1 No. 380E Electrically-Controlled Locomotive	1 No. 214 Box car	18 C Track
2 No. 81 Controlling rheostats	1 No. 215 Oil car	4 ½S Track
1 No. 418 Pullman car	1 No. 216 Coal car	1 No. 124 Station
1 No. 419 Pullman and baggage car	1 No. 217 Illuminated Caboose	1 No. 189 Villa
1 No. 490 Observation car	1 No. 218 Operating Dump car	1 No. 191 Villa
1 No. 431 Dining-car	1 No. 219 Operating Derrick car	3 No. 184 Bungalows
1 No. 211 Lumber car with load of lumber	1 No. 84 Semaphore	1 No. 438 Signal Tower
1 No. 212 Gondola car	1 Type K Transformer	1 No. 101 Bridge
	3 pr. 222 Switches	1 No. 140L Tunnel
	2 No. 23 Bumpers	12 No. 60 Telegraph Posts

1 No. 78 Train Control	2 No. 59 Lamp posts
1 No. 80 Semaphore	20 STC "Lockon" connections
2 No. 77 Crossing gates	
1 No. 89 Flag Staff	
2 No. 76 Block signals	
1 No. 69 Warning signal	
1 No. 436 Power house	
1 No. 437 Switch tower	
2 No. 67 Lamp posts	
4 No. 56 Lamp posts	
2 No. 57 Lamp posts	

Wires for making electrical connections, connecting ties for joining sections of track, lamps for headlights, interior of cars and all illuminated accessories are supplied with this outfit. Track layout is 12 feet 10 inches long by 6 feet 4 inches wide.

Price complete $300.00
Code Word "ALLY"

"Lionel Standard" Operating Derrick and Dump Cars

FOR USE WITH ALL LOCOMOTIVES OPERATING ON "LIONEL STANDARD" TRACK—2¼ INCHES WIDE

No. 219 Operating Derrick Car

BOYS—here is the most realistic railroad Derrick Car ever built in miniature. Think of the fun you will have operating it just like a real derrick. You can raise or lower the boom, swing it from side to side, and hoist weights with the pulley and tackle. In fact, this Derrick Car will do everything—the same as real ones. All mechanical movements are controlled by levers that operate worm gears. The mechanical arrangement is absolutely similar to that found in large Derrick Cars. By means of the worm gear the position of the boom and location of the housing is not affected by the weights that are lowered or raised. They are always in a rigid position, except when changed by means of the levers. The mechanism is mounted on a solid steel car—11¾ inches long, 5⅜ inches high. The boom is 16 inches long. Car is equipped with automatic couplers. Price $8.50

Code Word "ALUM"

No. 218 Operating Dump Car

Bring up a load of sand or ballast, boys! We must finish that roadbed by to-morrow and run the first Lionel Limited over the new short cut. The new Lionel Operating Dump Car is a marvel of mechanical ingenuity. Not only does it look like the real cars used in the construction of railroads, but it actually dumps the load at any place desired along the track. The mechanical movements that automatically open and tilt the sides of the car are controlled by levers and worm gears. The Lionel Operating Dump Car is 11¾ inches long, 4½ inches high. Entirely constructed of sheet steel and beautifully finished by Lionel's famous enameling process. Equipped with automatic couplers. Price $5.85

Code Word "DEPEW"

New Freight Cars for "Lionel Standard" Track—2¼ Inches Wide

No. 512 Gondola Car—11¼ inches long, 3¼ inches high. Price $2.25
Code Word "EVER"

No. 514 Refrigerator Car—11¼ inches long, 5 inches high. Price $2.95
Code Word "EAST"

No. 211 Lumber Car with load of lumber—11¾ inches long, 3¾ inches high. Price . . $3.35
Code Word "ANT"

No. 213 Cattle Car—11¾ inches long, 5¾ inches high. Price $4.50
Code Word "WAKE"

No. 214 Box Car—11¾ inches long, 5¾ inches high. Price $4.50
Code Word "WOOL"

All "Lionel Standard" Freight Cars are equipped with automatic couplers. Length of couplers on cars is not included in dimensions given in specifications.

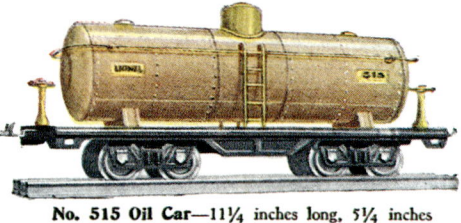

No. 515 Oil Car—11¼ inches long, 5¼ inches high. Price $3.00
Code Word "ELTA"

No. 517 Illuminated Caboose—11¼ inches long, 5½ inches high. Complete with interior lamp. Price $3.35
Code Word "EAGER"

O N Page 9 you will find full details of construction of this marvelous new line of Freight Cars to operate on "Lionel Standard" Track. The illustrations clearly show that every known type of modern car is faithfully reproduced by us. It is great fun to convert your "Lionel Standard" Passenger Train into a big Freighter by adding an assortment of these well-built and handsomely finished cars. Let us repeat that all Lionel Freight Cars are of steel construction throughout. The fittings, such as hand rails, hand brakes, steps, ladders and inserted panels are all made of brass, highly polished. Wheels, journals and axles are of heavy nickeled steel. Beyond doubt, these cars reach the peak of perfection in model railroad rolling stock. The "O" Gauge Cars listed on the opposite page incorporate a great many of the features of these large Freight Cars.

No. 217 Illuminated Caboose—11¾ inches long, 6 inches high. Complete with electric lamp. Price $5.35
Code Word "RAFT"

"Lionel Standard" Freight Cars Nos. 511 to 517 are for use with Locomotives Nos. 8, 8E, 10, 10E, 318 and 318E.

Cars Nos. 211 to 217 can be used with Locomotives Nos. 402, 402E and 408E.

No. 511 Lumber Car with load of lumber—11¼ inches long, 3 inches high. Price . . $2.25
Code Word "EDEN"

No. 513 Cattle Car—11¼ inches long, 5 inches high. Price $2.95
Code Word "EBON"

No. 212 Gondola Car—11¾ inches long, 3½ inches high. Price $3.35
Code Word "ROY"

No. 215 Oil Car—11¾ inches long, 6 inches high. Price $4.50
Code Word "DICE"

No. 216 Coal Car—Has "Hopper" bottom, operated by wheel on side. 11¾ inches long, 4⅞ inches high. Price $4.50
Code Word "ALAMA"

New Freight Cars and Sets for Lionel "O" Gauge Track—1⅜ Inches Wide

No. 805 Box Car—6¾ inches long, 3 inches high.

No. 807 Caboose—6¾ inches long, 3½ inches high.

No. 806 Cattle Car—6¾ inches long, 3 inches high.

No. 803 Coal Car—Has "Hopper" bottom, operated by wheel at side.
Price $.85
Code Word "LOAD"

No. 804 Oil Car
Price $.65
Code Word "FUEL"

No. 805 Box Car
Price $.90
Code Word "VICK"

No. 806 Cattle Car
Price $1.00
Code Word "VEX"

No. 807 Caboose
Price $1.00
Code Word "VAT"

No. 831 Lumber Car with load of lumber
Price $.65
Code Word "VEST"

No. 902 Gondola Car
Price $.65
Code Word "VOTE"

Length of couplers on cars is not included in dimensions given in specifications. Cars Nos. 803, 804, 805, 806, 807, 831 and 902 are for use with Locomotives Nos. 248 and 252.

No. 803 Coal Car—6¾ inches long, 3¼ inches high.

No. 804 Oil Car—6¾ inches long, 3⅞ inches high.

No. 831 Lumber Car—6¾ inches long, 2¼ inches high.

No. 808 "O" Gauge Freight Car Set—Comprises 1 each Nos. 831 Lumber Car, 803 Coal Car, 804 Oil Car, 805 Box Car, 806 Cattle Car, 807 Caboose, described on this page. Very attractively packed. Price $5.00
Code Word "QUORN"

No. 902 Gondola Car—6¾ inches long, 2¼ inches high.

No. 818 "O" Gauge Freight Car Set—Comprises 1 each Nos. 812 Gondola Car, 814 Box Car, 816 Coal Car, 817 Caboose, described on this page. Very attractively packed.
Price $8.75
Code Word "QUEST"

No. 811 Lumber Car with load of lumber
Price $1.75
Code Word "DRUM"

No. 812 Gondola Car
Price $1.75
Code Word "DALE"

No. 813 Cattle Car
Price $2.10
Code Word "YAWL"

No. 814 Box Car
Price $2.10
Code Word "YOKE"

No. 815 Oil Car
Price $2.10
Code Word "YAM"

No. 816 Coal Car—Has "Hopper" bottom, operated by wheel at side.
Price $2.50
Code Word "YOST"

No. 817 Caboose
Price $2.50
Code Word "DEFT"

Length of couplers on cars is not included in dimensions given in specifications. Cars Nos. 811 to 817 are for use with Locomotives Nos. 253, 254, 254E, 251, 251E and 256.

No. 811 Lumber Car—9 inches long, 3 inches high.

No. 814 Box Car—9 inches long, 4 inches high.

No. 812 Gondola Car—9 inches long, 2¾ inches high.

No. 815 Oil Car—9 inches long, 4⅛ inches high.

No. 813 Cattle Car—9 inches long, 4 inches high.

No. 816 Coal Car—9 inches long, 3½ inches high.

No. 817 Caboose—9 inches long, 4½ inches high.

Pullman and Observation Cars for Lionel "O" Gauge Track
1⅜ INCHES WIDE

All Lionel "O" Gauge Passenger Cars (excepting Nos. 529, 530, 629 and 630) have interior lights and are mounted on two 4-wheel trucks. The observation cars have an ornamental brass platform and railing. Lamp is supplied with illuminated cars. Length of couplers on cars is not included in dimensions given in specifications.

THE construction of all Lionel Passenger Cars is worthy of special notice as it represents the highest form of miniature car manufacture. Not only are all bodies made of heavy steel and beautifully embossed with panels, rivets and other details, but they are soldered and rigidly held together by mechanical means. Cross braces and partitions placed inside the cars give still greater strength and makes them almost indestructible. Some outstanding features of Lionel Passenger Cars are hinged doors, inserted window frames and sashes, interior seats, brass steps and handrails and miniature tanks which are affixed to the bottom of the body. The separable inserted pieces are enameled in a variety of colors to harmonize with car body, and accentuate the great detail incorporated in them. All Lionel Cars are handsomely enameled in a variety of attractive colors, and the lasting finish is baked on at high temperature. Roofs are firmly held in place with ornamented screw, easily removable so that interior lamp can be reached.

All cars are equipped with automatic couplers and are mounted on scientifically designed trucks with perfectly aligned nickeled wheels and axles. They operate without friction and are so absolutely true that they will not derail even when traveling at high speed. All the desirable features mentioned here will be seen by referring to the indications on Page 9.

We have incorporated all these features in the "Lionel Standard" Passenger Cars illustrated on the opposite page.

No. 710
No. 710 Illuminated Pullman Car—11½ inches long, 4½ inches high. For use with Locomotive No. 256. Price $3.75
Code Word "HOLLY"

No. 605
No. 605 Illuminated Pullman Car—10⅝ inches long, 4¼ inches high. For use with Locomotives Nos. 251 and 251E. Price $3.25
Code Word "NOVA"

No. 610
No. 610 Illuminated Pullman Car—9 inches long, 3¾ inches high. For use with Locomotives Nos. 253, 254 and 254E. Price $2.95
Code Word "EALING"

No. 607
No. 607 Illuminated Pullman Car—7½ inches long, 3⅜ inches high. For use with Locomotives Nos. 252 and 253. Price $1.65
Code Word "BRAND"

Nos. 529 and 629
No. 529 Pullman Car—6¾ inches long, 3¼ inches high. (Finished in green color.) Price . . . . . . $.75
Code Word "IMPY"

No. 629 Pullman Car—Same as No. 529, but finished in orange yellow color. For use with Locomotives Nos. 248 and 252. Price . . . . $.75
Code Word "FANE"

No. 712
No. 712 Illuminated Observation Car—Same dimensions as No. 710 Pullman Car illustrated above. For use with same locomotive. Price $3.85
Code Word "RISE"

No. 606
No. 606 Illuminated Observation Car—Same dimensions as No. 605 Pullman Car illustrated above. For use with same locomotives. Price . . . $3.50
Code Word "MODE"

No. 612
No. 612 Illuminated Observation Car—Same dimensions as No. 610 Pullman Car illustrated above. For use with same locomotives. Price $3.15
Code Word "WALTON"

No. 608
No. 608 Illuminated Observation Car—Same dimensions as No. 607 Pullman Car illustrated above. For use with same locomotives. Price $1.75
Code Word "TWIG"

Nos. 530 and 630
No. 530 Observation Car—Same dimensions as No. 529 Pullman Car illustrated above. For use with same locomotives. Price . . . . $.80
Code Word "IONA"

No. 630 Observation Car—Same dimensions as No. 629 Pullman Car illustrated above. For use with same locomotives. Price . . . . $.80
Code Word "IDEAL"

Passenger, Baggage and Dining Cars for "Lionel Standard" Track

2¼ INCHES WIDE

No. 338 Illuminated Observation Car — 12 inches long, 4¾ inches high. Price $5.00
Code Word "ORBIT"

No. 337 Illuminated Pullman Car — 12 inches long, 4¾ inches high. Price $4.25
Code Word "PASS"

No. 332 Illuminated Mail and Baggage Car — 12 inches long, 4¾ inches high. Finished in gray or olive green color.
Code Word "WILE"   Price . $4.50

Cars Nos. 332, 337 and 338 are for use with "Lionel Standard" Locomotives Nos. 8, 8E, 10 and 10E.

Cars Nos. 339 and 341 are for use with "Lionel Standard" Locomotives Nos. 318 and 318E.

Cars Nos. 309, 310 and 312 are for use with "Lionel Standard" Locomotives Nos. 380 and 380E.

Illustration shows dome light over platform on "Lionel Standard" Observation Cars — also red lanterns which are illuminated by dome light.

Illustration shows patented revolving shoe which collects current from the third rail for lighting interior of Passenger Coaches.

No. 312 Illuminated Observation Car — 13¼ inches long, 5⅛ inches high. Price . $5.85
Code Word "DOMO"

No. 341 Illuminated Observation Car — 12 inches long, 4¾ inches high. Same in construction and appearance as No. 312 Car. Price $5.45
Code Word "LEO"

No. 309 Illuminated Pullman Car — 13¼ inches long, 5⅛ inches high. Price . $5.00
Code Word "ROAD"

No. 339 Illuminated Pullman Car — 12 inches long, 4¾ inches high. Same in construction and appearance as No. 309 Car. Price $4.50
Code Word "STAR"

No. 310 Illuminated Mail and Baggage Car — 13¼ inches long, 5⅛ inches high. Baggage compartments have sliding doors. Price . $5.35
Code Word "WEC"

No. 490 Illuminated Observation Car — 17½ inches long, 6 inches high. Price $9.50
Code Word "CABIN"

No. 430 Illuminated Observation Car — 17½ inches long, 6 inches high. Price $8.50
Code Word "NERO"

Cars Nos. 418, 419, 490, 428, 429, 430 and 431 are for use with Locomotives Nos. 380, 380E, 402, 402E and 408E.

No. 419 Illuminated Pullman and Baggage Car — 17½ inches long, 6 inches high. Price $8.75
Code Word "COURT"

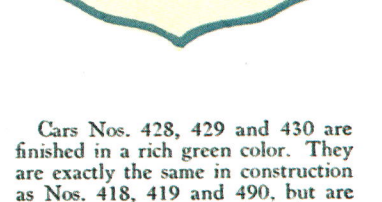

No. 429 Illuminated Pullman and Baggage Car — 17½ inches long, 6 inches high. Price $7.85
Code Word "DORA"

Cars Nos. 428, 429 and 430 are finished in a rich green color. They are exactly the same in construction as Nos. 418, 419 and 490, but are mounted on two 4-wheel trucks.

All "Lionel Standard" Cars are equipped with automatic couplers and interior lighting fixture, complete with electric lamp. Observation cars have ornamental polished brass platform and rails. Roofs are removable so that interior light can easily be reached. Length of couplers on cars is not included in dimensions given in specifications.

No. 418 Illuminated Pullman Car — 17½ inches long, 6 inches high. Price $8.50
Code Word "COMFORT"

No. 428 Illuminated Pullman Car — 17½ inches long, 6 inches high. Price $7.50
Code Word "IRIS"

Illustration shows revolving parlor car chairs installed in Cars Nos. 418, 419, 490, 428, 429 and 430.

To enable you to fully appreciate the fine interior fittings of Cars Nos. 418, 428 and 431, we illustrate them with the side removed, but the outside appearance is the same as Cars Nos. 419, 429, 430 and 490 shown on this page.

No. 431 Dining-Car — 17½ inches long, 6 inches high. Price $10.00
Code Word "FEED"

Illustration shows tables, chairs, kitchen compartment and equipment installed in this car. It can be used with Cars Nos. 418, 419, 490, 428, 429 and 430.

31

1927

Specifications of Lionel "Multivolt" Transformers

Lionel "Multivolt" Transformers are made completely at our own factories. The only parts purchased are the raw materials. We correctly wind and insulate the coils, make the cases, laminations, switch handles, and in fact do every operation. Lionel "Multivolt" Transformers are listed as standard by the Underwriters' Laboratories.

Sub-Base—A metal sub-base resting on four supports is attached to the bottom. The air, circulating between this sub-base and the transformer case, keeps it cool while in operation. Holes in this sub-base provide means for fastening to wall or table.

Separable Plug—All "Multivolt" Transformers are fitted with an approved, separable plug, which is a distinct advantage over the one-piece plug, because the circuit can be immediately broken.

Plug Protecting Device—A unique receptacle for protecting the plug against breakage in shipment. This device consists of a wooden container entirely covering the plug. It is sealed with a conspicuous label which draws attention to the fact that the transformer must be used **only** on **alternating** current of the number of cycles designated. This obviates the possibility of connecting the transformer with wrong current and avoids mishandling.

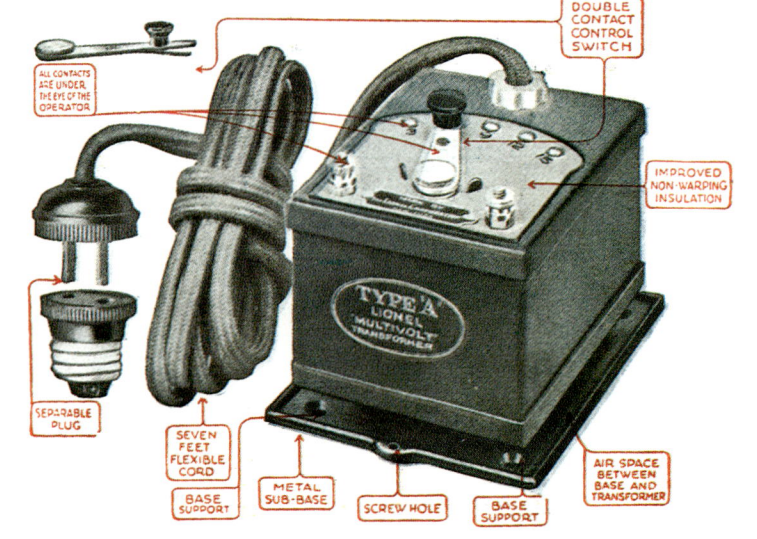

Double Contact Control Switch—This is infinitely superior to the one-piece switch, which is easily bent and does not make positive contact. Our double switch has a flexible, phosphor-bronze contact arm under the rigid switch, so that positive contact with the points is assured. This flexible contact is protected from injury by the rigid brass handle to which it is attached. An exclusive feature of "Multivolt" Transformers.

Laminations—The laminations are made of the best grade of electrical sheets and the windings are perfectly insulated.

Rigid Supports for Coils—The coils and laminations of Lionel "Multivolt" Transformers are rigidly supported inside the case by means of metal bands which prevent these parts from moving and eliminate the possibility of broken lead wires. In addition to these supports, the interior of the case is fitted with an insulating receptacle and the case is air cooled.

Metal Case—The case is beautiful in design and is stamped of heavier steel than is required by the Underwriters' Laboratories.

Finish—"Multivolt" Transformer cases are covered with a rubberoid composition that is applied at 350 degrees Fahrenheit. This is much greater heat than the case is ever subjected to, and the finish cannot be scratched and will not peel off during the entire life of the transformer.

Visible Connections—All contacts and switches are mounted on one piece of heavy insulating material and are at the top of the transformer, right before the user.

Lamp Cord—All "Multivolt" Transformers are fitted with 7 feet of flexible lamp cord which enters the transformer case through an approved porcelain bushing.

It will be seen that "Multivolt" Transformers incorporate every device that will increase their efficiency.

LIONEL DIRECT CURRENT REDUCERS
(Not to Be Used on Alternating Current)

No. 107 Lionel Current Reducer for 110-Volt Circuit—This is constructed of four porcelain tubes wound with best quality of resistance wire. These porcelain tubes are mounted on a substantial base measuring 8 by 10 inches and ¾ inches thick. The porcelain tubes are protected and ventilated by a perforated steel cover lined with heavy asbestos. The sliding lever regulates the voltage so that train will just crawl along or go ahead at express speed. The reducer is connected with the house current by a separable plug with 7 feet of flexible cord. Four porcelain supports with screws are supplied so that the reducer can be screwed to wall or table. Price $10.00

Code Word "KENTUCKY"

No. 170 Lionel Direct Current Reducer for 220-Volt Circuit—This reducer is identical in appearance with No. 107, mentioned above, but is for use on 220 volts. Price $14.50

Code Word "ASBURY"

CONTROLLING RHEOSTATS FOR BATTERIES

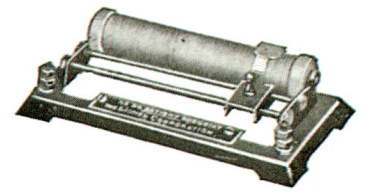

No. 88 Rheostat for Dry Cells or Storage Batteries—It provides a gradual increase or decrease of current. A heat-resisting unit on a porcelain tube is mounted on a steel frame which has a sliding finger that increases or decreases the speed of the train. All parts are of the best quality. The steel base is enameled and other parts are nickel-plated. Size 5 inches long, 2½ inches wide.

Price $1.50

Code Word "BANNER"

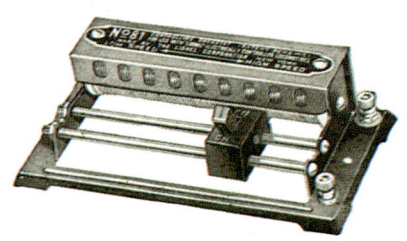

No. 81 Controlling Rheostat—With this rheostat you can operate all Lionel Trains at various speeds as well as start or stop them at any distance from the track. By sliding the finger from side to side, various speeds can be obtained, and by manipulating a small lever up and down, the current is turned on and off, so that the train can be started or stopped at will. The porcelain coil is protected by a perforated steel cover, and air holes prevent overheating. Size 5 inches long, 2½ inches wide.

Code Word "BONE"   Price . . . $2.50

Lionel "Multivolt" Transformers For 110 Volts and 220 Volts—60, 40 and 25 Cycles

LIONEL "MULTIVOLT" TRANSFORMERS are for use only on Alternating Current. Do not use them on Direct Current.

This illustration shows transformer contained within the new Lionel Power Station. They are made in two sizes to accommodate every type of Lionel "Multivolt" Transformer. Full description of this desirable new accessory will be found on Page 39.

The Lionel Power Station is placed over the Transformer, and you can manipulate the controlling switch by simply raising the grating on the roof.

LIONEL "Multivolt" Transformers have been on the market for a great many years and operate all makes of Electric Trains. We justly claim they are best. Don't experiment with other makes of doubtful value. Remember, that all transformers look alike outside, but their imperfections will only be discovered after they are in actual use for a length of time. Lionel "Multivolt" Transformers will last indefinitely and are guaranteed unconditionally as long as they are used on the current for which they are intended. They are absolutely safe and will give steady, even power.

Type "A" Transformer will operate any "O" gauge outfit.

For 110 volts, 60 cycles. 40 watts capacity.

Gives 15 volts in following steps: 4, 7, 10, 13, 15.

Size: 4¼ by 2¾ by 4¼ inches. Sub-base: 3¾ by 4¼ inches.

Price $3.75

Code Word "STRONG"

NOTE: Type "A" Transformer is recommended for use with the train outfits shown on Page 12.

Type "B" Transformer will operate any "O" gauge outfit, and in addition the extra binding posts enable the user to light up lamp-posts, semaphores and other electrically illuminated accessories.

For 110 volts, 60 cycles. 50 watts capacity.

Gives 25 volts in following steps:
Permanent: 7, 8, 15.
Variable: 2, 4, 6, 8, 9, 10, 11, 12, 13, 17, 19, 21, 23, 25.

Size: 4½ by 3¾ by 3 inches. Sub-base: 5 by 4¼ inches.

Price $5.00

Code Word "BRADLEY"

A fully guaranteed transformer at a very popular price.

Type "T" Transformer will operate any "O" gauge or "Lionel Standard" outfit; also has extra binding posts for attaching illuminated electrical accessories.

For 110 volts, 60 cycles. 100 watts capacity.

Gives 25 volts in following steps:
Permanent: 2, 4, 6, 7, 8, 10, 12, 14, 15, 16, 17, 18, 19, 21, 23, 25.
Variable: 2, 6, 8, 10, 12, 14, 16, 17, 18, 19, 21, 23, 25.

Size: 5 by 4 by 3¾ inches. Sub-base 4½ by 5½ inches.

Price $7.50

Code Word "BIRCH"

Type "K" Transformer will operate any outfit as well as illuminated accessories. This transformer has sufficient wattage capacity to operate two trains at once.

Size: 5 by 4 by 4½ inches. Sub-base: 4½ by 5½ inches.

"K"—For 110 volts, 60 cycles. 150 watts capacity. Specifications same as Type "T," but has higher wattage capacity. Price $11.00

Code Word (110 V.) "BINGHAM"

"K"—For 220 volts, 60 cycles. 150 watts capacity. Specifications same as Type "T," but is for use on 220-volt circuit.

Price $14.50

Code Word (220 V.) "BROOK"

Type "C" Transformer will operate any outfit and illuminated accessories on 25 or 40 cycle current.

For 110 volts, 25 to 40 cycles. 75 watts capacity. Specifications same as Type "T," but is for use on 25 or 40 cycle current.

Size: 5 by 4 by 4½ inches. Sub-base: 4½ by 5½ inches.

Price $7.50

Code Word "LAWRENCE"

This transformer is the best obtainable for use on 25 or 40 cycle current.

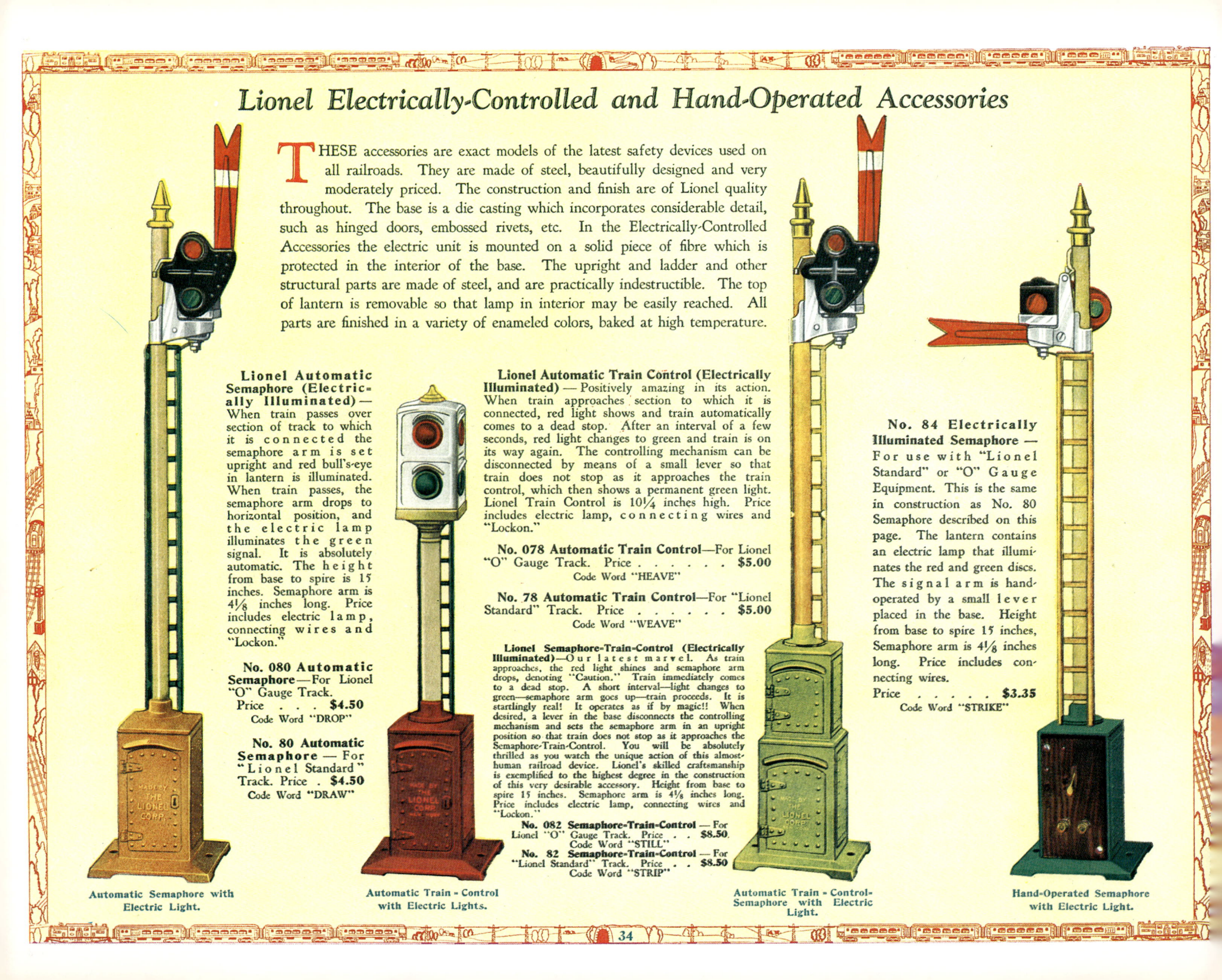

Lionel Electrically-Controlled and Hand-Operated Accessories

THESE accessories are exact models of the latest safety devices used on all railroads. They are made of steel, beautifully designed and very moderately priced. The construction and finish are of Lionel quality throughout. The base is a die casting which incorporates considerable detail, such as hinged doors, embossed rivets, etc. In the Electrically-Controlled Accessories the electric unit is mounted on a solid piece of fibre which is protected in the interior of the base. The upright and ladder and other structural parts are made of steel, and are practically indestructible. The top of lantern is removable so that lamp in interior may be easily reached. All parts are finished in a variety of enameled colors, baked at high temperature.

Lionel Automatic Semaphore (Electrically Illuminated)—When train passes over section of track to which it is connected the semaphore arm is set upright and red bull's-eye in lantern is illuminated. When train passes, the semaphore arm drops to horizontal position, and the electric lamp illuminates the green signal. It is absolutely automatic. The height from base to spire is 15 inches. Semaphore arm is 4⅛ inches long. Price includes electric lamp, connecting wires and "Lockon."

No. 080 Automatic Semaphore—For Lionel "O" Gauge Track.
Price . . . $4.50
Code Word "DROP"

No. 80 Automatic Semaphore—For "Lionel Standard" Track. Price . $4.50
Code Word "DRAW"

Lionel Automatic Train Control (Electrically Illuminated)—Positively amazing in its action. When train approaches section to which it is connected, red light shows and train automatically comes to a dead stop. After an interval of a few seconds, red light changes to green and train is on its way again. The controlling mechanism can be disconnected by means of a small lever so that train does not stop as it approaches the train control, which then shows a permanent green light. Lionel Train Control is 10¼ inches high. Price includes electric lamp, connecting wires and "Lockon."

No. 078 Automatic Train Control—For Lionel "O" Gauge Track. Price $5.00
Code Word "HEAVE"

No. 78 Automatic Train Control—For "Lionel Standard" Track. Price $5.00
Code Word "WEAVE"

Lionel Semaphore-Train-Control (Electrically Illuminated)—Our latest marvel. As train approaches, the red light shines and semaphore arm drops, denoting "Caution." Train immediately comes to a dead stop. A short interval—light changes to green—semaphore arm goes up—train proceeds. It is startlingly real! It operates as if by magic!! When desired, a lever in the base disconnects the controlling mechanism and sets the semaphore arm in an upright position so that train does not stop as it approaches the Semaphore-Train-Control. You will be absolutely thrilled as you watch the unique action of this almost-human railroad device. Lionel's skilled craftsmanship is exemplified to the highest degree in the construction of this very desirable accessory. Height from base to spire 15 inches. Semaphore arm is 4⅛ inches long. Price includes electric lamp, connecting wires and "Lockon."

No. 082 Semaphore-Train-Control — For Lionel "O" Gauge Track. Price . . $8.50
Code Word "STILL"

No. 82 Semaphore-Train-Control — For "Lionel Standard" Track. Price . . $8.50
Code Word "STRIP"

No. 84 Electrically Illuminated Semaphore—For use with "Lionel Standard" or "O" Gauge Equipment. This is the same in construction as No. 80 Semaphore described on this page. The lantern contains an electric lamp that illuminates the red and green discs. The signal arm is hand-operated by a small lever placed in the base. Height from base to spire 15 inches. Semaphore arm is 4⅛ inches long. Price includes connecting wires.
Price $3.35
Code Word "STRIKE"

Automatic Semaphore with Electric Light.

Automatic Train-Control with Electric Lights.

Automatic Train-Control-Semaphore with Electric Light.

Hand-Operated Semaphore with Electric Light.

Lionel Electrically-Controlled Accessories

Lionel Electric Warning Signals—Electric bell with 2 gongs is mounted on an ornamental steel standard, 8¾ inches high, which supports warning sign. Gongs ring while train passes over track section to which it is connected. Bell automatically stops when grade crossing is clear. This realistic accessory is finished in beautiful enameled colors and bell is nickeled steel. Price includes special track, wires and "Lockon."

No. 069 Electric Warning Signal for Lionel "O" Gauge Track. Price $3.15
Code Word "RINGER"

No. 69 Electric Warning Signal for "Lionel Standard" Track. Price $3.35
Code Word "BEWARE"

No. 83 Lionel Traffic and Crossing Signal—An ingenious and up-to-date Lionel accessory. The electric light in the red lantern flashes on and off just like the "blinker" light seen at street intersections. The mechanism is in the base, which also contains binding posts for attaching wires supplied with the signal. This signal is 6¼ inches high. Can be used with "O" Gauge or "Lionel Standard" equipment. A wonderful accessory to use with Lionel bungalows and villas when building model villages. Price . $3.75
Code Word "STAND"

Lionel Automatic Crossing Gates—An exact reproduction of the real ones seen at grade crossings. When train approaches the track section to which it is connected, the gate comes down, and stays in that position. When train passes, gate opens. The action of the gate is just the same as those used on real railroads. It is made of heavy steel. The electric unit is enclosed in the base. Finished in various enameled colors. The Lionel Automatic Crossing Gate is 11 inches long. Price includes special section of track, connecting wires and "Lockon."

No. 077 Automatic Crossing Gate for Lionel "O" Gauge Track. Price $4.00
Code Word "ADVANCE"

No. 77 Automatic Crossing Gate for "Lionel Standard" Track. Price . $4.25
Code Word "TARRY"

No. 87 Lionel Railroad Crossing Signal—Just like those used on many grade crossings. The bright red lantern on white background is illuminated at intervals of a second by means of device placed in the interior. It is thrilling to watch this automatic "blinker" operate continuously without attention, by means of mechanism in the base which also contains terminals for connecting wires. This Crossing Signal is 6¾ inches high. Can be used with "Lionel Standard" or "O" Gauge equipment.
Price $4.75
Code Word "STORE"

Lionel Electric Block Signals—Two electric lanterns showing red and green signals are attached to a steel standard, 8¾ inches high. When train passes over the track section to which it is connected, green lantern lights up, and after it leaves this section the red light shows. This red light goes out as soon as train leaves the second block section. Several of these signals placed around the track carry out real block signaling. Price includes electric lamps, special sections of track, connecting wires and "Lockon."

No. 076 Electric Block Signal for Lionel "O" Gauge Track.
Code Word "FORWARD" Price $3.15

No. 76 Electric Block Signal for "Lionel Standard" Track.
Code Word "ONWARD" Price $3.35

Lionel Accessories and Sets—Electrically-Controlled and Hand Operated

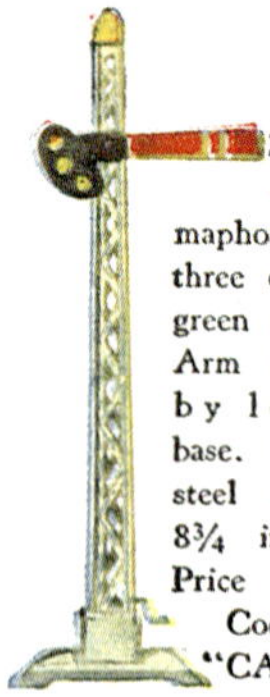

No. 62 Semaphore—The Semaphore arm has three discs — red, green and yellow. Arm is operated by lever near base. Enameled steel standard is 8¾ inches high. Price . . $.80 Code Word "CAUTION"

No. 68 Warning Signal—Enameled steel standard is 8¾ inches high. Brass sign is 2½ inches square. Price . . $.90 Code Word "STOP"

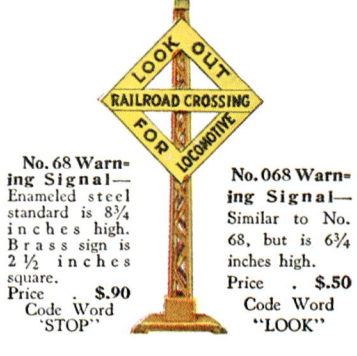

No. 068 Warning Signal—Similar to No. 68, but is 6¾ inches high. Price . . $.50 Code Word "LOOK"

No. 60 Telegraph Post—Arm is equipped with real glass insulators. Enameled steel standard is 8¾ inches high. Price . . $.65 Code Word "WIRE"

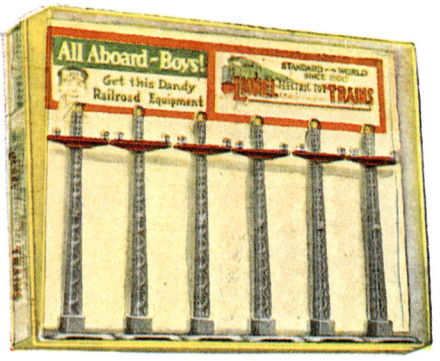

Outfit No. 70—Comprises 2 No. 62 semaphores, 1 No. 59 lamp-post, 1 No. 68 warning sign, 2 extra globes for lamp-post. Very attractively packed. Price . . $4.25
Code Word "HOBART"

Outfit No. 71—Comprises 6 No. 60 steel telegraph posts as described on this page. Very attractively packed. Price $3.75
Code Word "USEFUL"

Automatic Accessory Sets—Lionel Automatic Accessories fully described on the preceding pages are now packed in very attractive sets as illustrated above. It is great fun to add them to your Lionel equipment and build a 100% Electrically-Controlled Railroad.

No. 194 Automatic Accessory Set—For "Lionel Standard" Track—Comprises 1 No. 76 block signal, 1 No. 78 train control, 1 No. 80 semaphore, 1 No. 77 crossing gate, 1 No. 69 warning signal, 5 No. 28 18-volt lamps, 12 fibre pins, connecting wire and 5 sections SS track. Price $21.75
Code Word "OAT"

No. 193 Automatic Accessory Set—For Lionel "O" Gauge Track. This set is the same as No. 194 described above, but is for use with "O" Gauge equipment. Price $21.00
Code Word "OVER"

No. 195 "Lionel Terrace"—Here is a real village in miniature containing bungalow, villas and lamp-posts all electrically illuminated. Just the thing for adding a realistic touch to your train outfit and ideal in connection with sister's doll house. The miniature buildings are artistically arranged in a beautiful landscape setting. Grass plots, bushes, shrubbery, trees and gravel walks add to its beauty.

An American flag majestically waves aloft in the centre of a miniature park. Nothing like it has ever been shown before.

The bungalow and villas are described on Page 37 and the lamp-posts are shown on Page 42.

Size of completely wired platform is 22 inches long, 19 inches wide.

The lamps in the interior of the buildings and lamp-posts are all wired, ready to be connected to the source of current. Only a few dry batteries are necessary to light up the entire village, or our lowest priced "Multivolt" transformer or direct current reducer connected to the house current will do the work.

Code Word "TUFT" Price $17.50

No. 196 Accessory Set—For use with "Lionel Standard" and "O" Gauge equipment. A very desirable assortment of accessories that will add the finishing touches to your Lionel Railroad. Telegraph posts can be placed at intervals around the track—electric lamp-posts can be placed at each side of the illuminated station and the warning signal and semaphore can occupy their proper positions along the railroad. All parts forming this outfit are fully described in this catalog. Outfit comprises 1 No. 127 station, 6 No. 60 telegraph posts, 1 No. 62 semaphore, 1 No. 68 warning signal, 2 No. 58 lamp-posts, 2 No. 39 12-volt lamps, 1 No. 27 12-volt lamp. Price . . $11.50
Code Word "OWL"

Lionel All-Steel Flag-Staffs—Illuminated Bungalows, Villas and Sets

BUILD a model village, boys, with these substantial, handsomely finished illuminated houses. They will greatly enhance the appearance of your Lionel Model Railroad.

No. 89 Flag-Staff and Flag—For use with Lionel model villages or to place in front of a Lionel Station. Flag-staff is 14 inches high. Silk flag may be lowered by cord attached, which can be fastened to hook near the base.
Price . . . . $.75
Code Word "ARTHUR"

No. 191 Illuminated Villa—Beautifully designed. 7⅛ inches long, 5⅛ inches wide and 5¼ inches high. Roof is removable. Complete with interior lighting fixture, lamp and connecting wires. Price $3.35
Code Word "SOLID"

No. 192 Illuminated Villa Set—A handsome assortment of model houses. Comprises 1 No. 191 villa, 1 No. 189 villa and 2 No. 184 bungalows. All complete with interior lights and connecting wires. Very attractively packed.
Price $8.75
Code Word "VILLAGE"

No. 90 Flag-Staff and Flag—The flag-staff (14 inches high) is removable, and fits into an ornamental base mounted on a miniature grass plot with flower border.
Price $1.25
Code Word "PLOT"

No. 186 Illuminated Bungalow Set—Comprises 5 No. 184 bungalows, beautifully finished in assorted colors. Complete with interior lights and connecting wires. Attractively packed.
Price $7.50
Code Word "HAMLET"

No. 184 Illuminated Bungalow—4 inches high, 4¾ inches wide. Beautifully decorated. Complete with interior light and connecting wires. Price $1.50
Code Word "HOME"

No. 189 Illuminated Villa—A model that is architecturally perfect. 5½ inches long, 4⅞ inches wide and 5⅜ inches high. Complete with interior light and connecting wires. Price $2.95
Code Word "MANSE"

Lionel All-Steel Illuminated Stations

No. 124 Illuminated Station—De Luxe Model. There is elegance, grace and architectural dignity to this all-steel station, difficult to show in an illustration. It is an exact reproduction of stations seen in most suburban towns. It is equipped with two corner platform lights and reflectors, all finished in polished nickel. These corner lighting brackets have beautifully designed supporting arms. This station is also fitted with inside light supported on a nickeled fixture. Roof is removable so that interior lamp can be easily reached. A most essential accessory to complete your model railroad. 13½ inches long, 9 inches wide and 13 inches high.
Price, complete with electric lamps and connecting wires $9.00
Code Word "READE"

No. 122 Illuminated Station—This is in every way similar to No. 124 Station described above, but has one inside electric light supported on a nickeled fixture.
Price, complete with electric lamp and connecting wires $6.25
Code Word "CENT"

No. 126 Illuminated Station—This station has been specially designed for use with our smaller train outfits and has many of the architectural and structural features of our larger models. The interior light is supported on a fixture placed beneath the removable roof. A beautifully proportioned model that retails at a low price. 10¼ inches long, 7¼ inches wide and 7 inches high.
Price, complete with electric lamp and connecting wires $4.50
Code Word "ALITE"

No. 127 Illuminated Station—This is particularly adaptable for use with any of our "O" Gauge Trains. Interior light is rigidly fastened to a supporting fixture. Roof is removable so that interior lamp can be easily reached. A better built or lower priced miniature station has never before been offered. 8½ inches long, 4¼ inches wide and 5 inches high.
Price, complete with electric lamp and connecting wires $2.95
Code Word "TONLY"

THE NEW LIONEL ILLUMINATED SWITCH-SIGNAL TOWER—(Illustrated on Next Page)

No. 437 Illuminated Switch-Signal Tower—In keeping with our policy to introduce everything new in model railroading, we are proud to present our new Switch-Signal Tower, which every boy will want to add to his model railroad layout.

It is built absolutely to scale and has a panel board on the rear (see illustration on next page) with six knife-switches which may be used for operating illuminated accessories, such as Stations, Lamp Posts, Bungalows and Villas. The lights in these accessories can be turned on and off by means of these switches, so that it is not necessary to have them illuminated all the time the train is in operation.

One or more controlling levers for "Lionel Standard" or "O" Gauge Electrically-Controlled Switches (illustrated on Page 40) can be attached to the upper part.

The interior of the switch-signal tower is fitted with an electric lamp. The illumination adds realism to this very desirable accessory. The Signal Tower is made of very heavy steel, beautifully enameled in various colors. The windows, doors, sashes and other parts are separable pieces inserted in the main body. The roof is removable so that the interior can easily be reached.

In every way this Switch-Signal Tower is typical of Lionel quality and perfection in model railroad accessories. No railroad layout is complete without one. 10¼ inches long, 9½ inches high, 7¼ inches wide. Price, complete with electric lamp and connecting wires . $8.50
Code Word "ZEV"

Lionel Power Stations. Illuminated Switch-Signal Towers

No. 437 Illuminated Switch Signal-Tower—Front view, showing wonderful detail in the windows, doors and panels, which are separable inserted pieces, beautifully enameled to harmonize with the walls of the structure.

No. 437 Illuminated Switch Signal-Tower—Rear view, showing panel board equipped with six knife-switches. In the upper part of the panel board provision is made for attaching from one to four controlling levers of "Lionel Standard" or "O" Gauge Electrically-Controlled Switches, described on Page 40.

The new Lionel Power Stations—Boys, you see them in every town and on all electrified railroads. Lionel, as usual, is first to reproduce them.

The illustration below shows how simple it is to house a Lionel "Multivolt" Transformer (illustrated and described on Pages 32 and 33) within the Power Station. Transformer is operated by raising the grid in the roof. Lionel Power Stations are made in two sizes to accommodate all types of Lionel "Multivolt" Transformers. In appearance they suggest the massive concrete buildings in which electric current is generated. Notice the beautiful embossing and die work, inserted windows and doors—see how the great chimney stack is reproduced in true proportion.

No. 435 Power Station—For use with Type A or B Transformers. 5¾ inches long, 4½ inches wide, 5⅜ inches high to the roof. Chimney stack rises 4⅜ inches above the roof. Base, which measures 8⅝ inches by 6 inches, is hollow, so that Power Station can be easily placed over transformer. Grid in roof is removable.
Price $2.50
Code Word "JENA"

Illustration above shows transformer housed within the new Lionel Power Station.

No. 436 Power Station—For use with Type T, C or K Transformers. Similar in construction to No. 435 Power Station. Dimensions 7½ inches long, 6 inches wide, 6½ inches high. Chimney stack rises 4½ inches above the roof. Grid in roof is removable. Base measures 9¼ inches by 7¼ inches.
Price $3.35
Code Word "WATTS"

No. 092 Illuminated Signal-Tower—A desirable accessory for "O" Gauge Railroads. Dimensions 5 inches long, 4 inches wide, 5½ inches high. Roof is removable. A handsomely nickeled light fixture is rigidly attached to the base. Price includes electric lamp and connecting wires.
Price . . $2.10
Code Word "CYRIL"

No. 438 Illuminated Signal Tower—The proportions of the Signal-Tower are the same as No. 092 illustrated to the left. We have mounted it on a beautiful structural-steel elevation, embossed with rivets, etc. The base represents reinforced concrete. A brass ladder runs up the entire length of the steel work and the Signal-Tower is surrounded by a brass railing. The illustration clearly shows the wonderful detail and architectural beauty of this desirable new accessory which can be used with all Lionel equipment. Complete height is 10½ inches. Base measures 6x4¾ inches. Price includes electric lamp and connecting wires. Price . . $4.25
Code Word "CARP"

39

1927

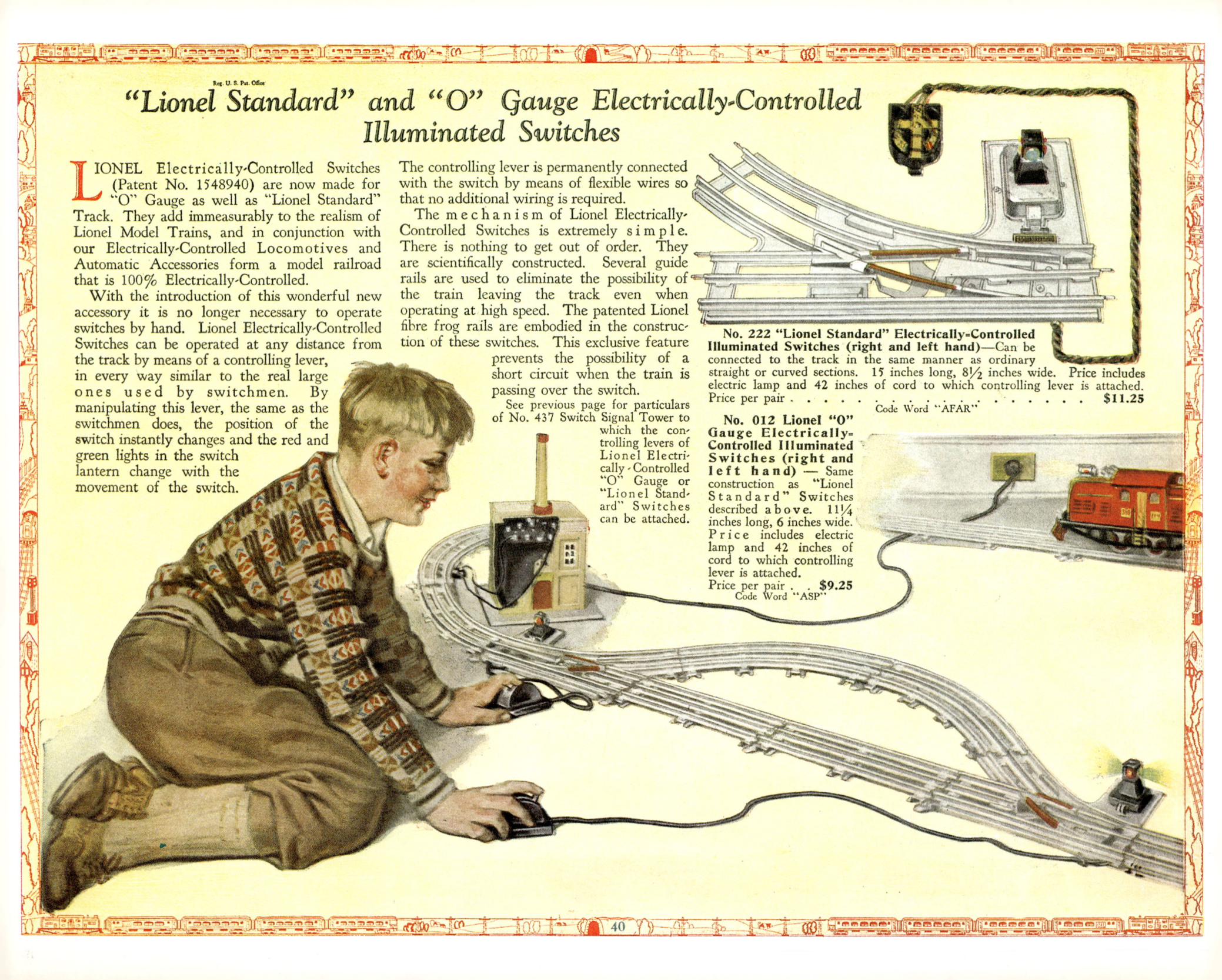

"Lionel Standard" and "O" Gauge Electrically-Controlled Illuminated Switches

LIONEL Electrically-Controlled Switches (Patent No. 1548940) are now made for "O" Gauge as well as "Lionel Standard" Track. They add immeasurably to the realism of Lionel Model Trains, and in conjunction with our Electrically-Controlled Locomotives and Automatic Accessories form a model railroad that is 100% Electrically-Controlled.

With the introduction of this wonderful new accessory it is no longer necessary to operate switches by hand. Lionel Electrically-Controlled Switches can be operated at any distance from the track by means of a controlling lever, in every way similar to the real large ones used by switchmen. By manipulating this lever, the same as the switchmen does, the position of the switch instantly changes and the red and green lights in the switch lantern change with the movement of the switch.

The controlling lever is permanently connected with the switch by means of flexible wires so that no additional wiring is required.

The mechanism of Lionel Electrically-Controlled Switches is extremely simple. There is nothing to get out of order. They are scientifically constructed. Several guide rails are used to eliminate the possibility of the train leaving the track even when operating at high speed. The patented Lionel fibre frog rails are embodied in the construction of these switches. This exclusive feature prevents the possibility of a short circuit when the train is passing over the switch.

See previous page for particulars of No. 437 Switch Signal Tower to which the controlling levers of Lionel Electrically-Controlled "O" Gauge or "Lionel Standard" Switches can be attached.

No. 222 "Lionel Standard" Electrically-Controlled Illuminated Switches (right and left hand)—Can be connected to the track in the same manner as ordinary straight or curved sections. 15 inches long, 8½ inches wide. Price includes electric lamp and 42 inches of cord to which controlling lever is attached.
Price per pair $11.25
Code Word "AFAR"

No. 012 Lionel "O" Gauge Electrically-Controlled Illuminated Switches (right and left hand) — Same construction as "Lionel Standard" Switches described above. 11¼ inches long, 6 inches wide. Price includes electric lamp and 42 inches of cord to which controlling lever is attached.
Price per pair . . $9.25
Code Word "ASP"

"Lionel Standard" and "O" Gauge Track, Switches, Crossings and Bumpers

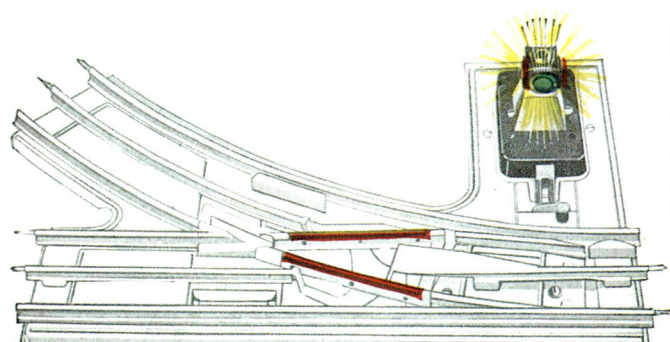

ILLUSTRATION shows the heavy frog rails (Patent No. 16580) inserted in all Lionel Switches at the points where the rails cross. All possibility of short circuit is thus eliminated and headlight does not flicker when train passes over these points. Attention is also directed to the several guide rails attached to Lionel Switches which prevent derailing even when trains are traveling at high speed. Hand lever which moves the rails, sets signals and locks mechanism.

No. 210 "Lionel Standard" Illuminated Switches (right and left hand)—Can be connected to track in same manner as ordinary straight or curved sections. 15 inches long, 8½ inches wide. Price includes electric lamp. Price per pair $6.25
Code Word "NASH"

No. 021 Lionel "O" Gauge Illuminated Switches (right and left hand)—Same construction as No. 210 Switches described above. 11¼ inches long, 6 inches wide. Price includes electric lamp. Price per pair . . $4.50
Code Word "MOSHA"

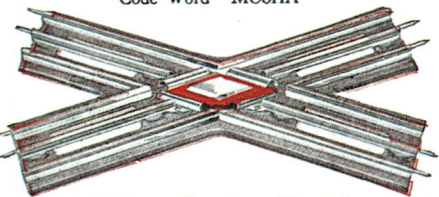

No. 020X Lionel "O" Gauge Crossing—This 45-degree crossing embodies the same high-grade constructional features as our other crossings described on this page. It is largely used when making figure "8" using only curved track. Many other figures can also be formed with it when used in conjunction with "O" Gauge straight or curved track and switches. Size 11¼ inches long, 6 inches wide. Price $1.50
Code Word "CROSS"

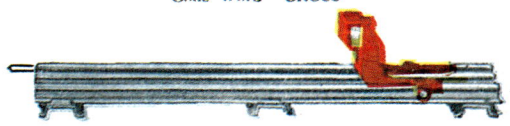

No. 023 Lionel "O" Gauge Bumper—An indispensable accessory for terminals or sidings. Fitted with spring plunger which absorbs shock when car strikes it. The bumper frame is removable. Length 10¼ inches, height 2 inches. Price . . . . $.80
Code Word "DELTO"

No. 23 "Lionel Standard" Bumper—The construction is the same as No. 023 described above. Two spring plungers absorb shock of car. Length 14 inches, height 3 inches. Price $1.25
Code Word "PROVO"

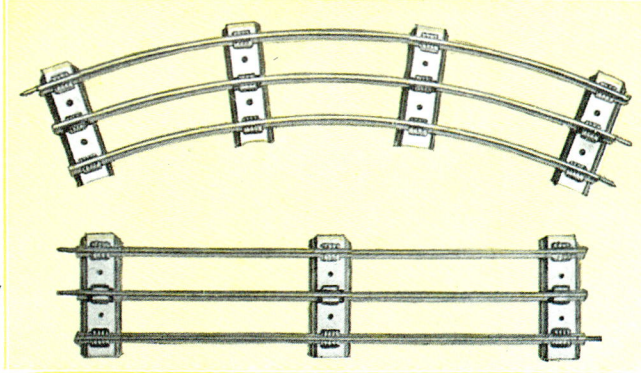

Lionel Track is constructed of heavier metal than any other make. The illustration shows the added strength given to Lionel rails by forming the base outward instead of turning it in. This outward flange gives the track sufficient strength to support the weight of a fully grown person and is made possible by our patented process. Each section of track is tested on 110 volts and therefore will not short-circuit when carrying the low voltage which operates Lionel Trains. The ends of each section have pin terminals which fit in openings in the adjoining sections allowing track to be laid and taken apart without difficulty.

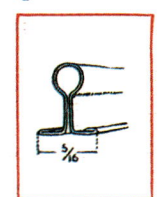

Lionel Track is made in straight and curved sections and the curvature of the track is mechanically correct, allowing trains to run at high speed without derailing.

We illustrate below the improved connecting tie which holds sections of track rigidly together. These connecting ties can be readily inserted and removed.

Lionel "O" Gauge Track—1⅜ inches wide

OC curved track, 11 inches long.
Price per section . . $ .20
Code Word "LEMPS"

OS straight track, 10¼ inches long.
Price per section . . $ .20
Code Word "GLENN"

OSS track, 10¼ inches long. For use with Electrically-Controlled Accessories. Complete with "Lockon" and connecting wires.
Price per section . . $ .40
Code Word "RELAY"

"Lionel Standard" Track—2¼ inches wide

C curved track, 16 inches long. Price per section . . . . . $ .30
Code Word "BUFF"

S straight track, 14 inches long. Price per section . . . . $ .30
Code Word "NYACK"

SS track, 14 inches long. For use with Electrically-Controlled Accessories. Complete with "Lockon" and connecting wires.
Price per section . . . . . $ .60
Code Word "BURT"

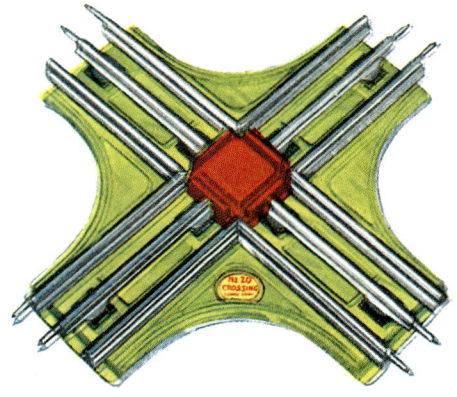

No. 20 "Lionel Standard" Crossing—A great improvement over our former model. The cross rails are mounted on an ornamental steel base, beautifully enameled. A solid molded fibre block placed in the centre where the rails cross, not only prevents short circuit, but is so constructed that the roller contact shoes on the locomotive and cars easily ride over it without derailing. A large variety of figures can be formed when using this crossing in conjunction with switches and track. Size 12 inches square.
Price $1.25
Code Word "BOOST"

No. 020 Lionel "O" Gauge Crossing—The construction of this crossing is exactly the same as No. 20 described above, but is for use with "O" Gauge equipment. Size 10¼ inches square.
Price $1.00
Code Word "ORLA"

"Lockon" Track Connections
(Patent No. 1542337)

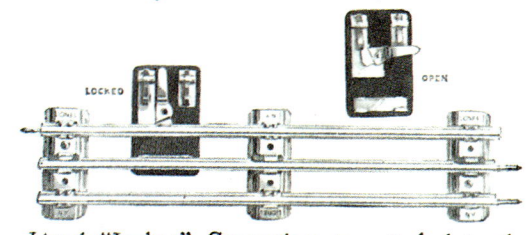

Lionel "Lockon" Connections are attached to the track by simply turning the lever at right angles as shown in the above illustration. The electric connection is as perfect as though the parts were riveted or soldered to the track.

Lionel "Lockon" Connections are free from set screws and binding posts. The fingers that hold the wires in place are made of heavy tempered blue steel and are unbreakable. All other metal parts are nickel-plated and are mounted on a heavy fibre base.

Lionel "Lockon" Connections should be used wherever electric accessories require connection with the track.

OTC "Lockon" for "O" Gauge Track. Price . . . $ .20
Code Word "JOIN"

STC "Lockon" for "Lionel Standard" Track. Price . $ .25
Code Word "JUICE"

Lionel All-Steel Electric Lamp-Posts and Lamp Renewals

NO Model Railroad is complete without the addition of Lionel Lamp-Posts—faithful reproductions of boulevard and street lamp-posts seen everywhere. All Lionel Lamp-Posts are of steel construction, enameled in a variety of beautiful colors. They will not bend or break. The binding posts to which electrical connections are made are conveniently situated, securely fastened and perfectly insulated. There is no chance of short-circuit with Lionel Lamp-Posts, for great care is used in their construction and every one is thoroughly tested. The electric lamps are in exact proportion to the size of the posts. No other make has the dignity and grace of design to be found in the Lionel Lamp-Posts illustrated below.

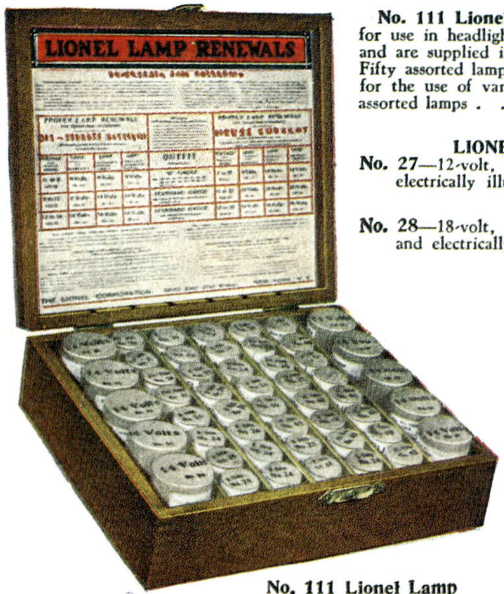

No. 111 Lionel Lamp Assortment—We supply Lionel dealers with a handsome cabinet of lamps for use in headlights and all electrically illuminated accessories. These lamps are of the finest quality and are supplied in 12 volts and 18 volts, suitable for "O" Gauge or "Lionel Standard" equipment. Fifty assorted lamps are packed in each cabinet. The chart on inside of cover gives valuable information for the use of various lamps. Each lamp is packed in a special container. Price per cabinet of 50 assorted lamps $15.00
Code Word "LUX"

LIONEL LAMP RENEWALS—Each lamp packed in special container

No. 27—12-volt, ½-inch round lamp. For use in all "O" Gauge locomotive headlights, cars and electrically illuminated accessories. Price . . . $.30
Code Word "NOSE"

No. 28—18-volt, ½-inch round lamp. For use in all "Lionel Standard" locomotive headlights, cars and electrically illuminated accessories. Price . . . $.30
Code Word "NELA"

No. 39—12-volt, ¾-inch round globe. When operating "O" Gauge equipment use these lamps in Nos. 58, 59, 61 and 67 Lamp-Posts, also in outside fixtures of No. 124 station. Price . . . $.30
Code Word "NICE"

No. 40—18-volt, ¾-inch round globe. This lamp is for use with same accessories as No. 39 lamp, when operating "Lionel Standard" equipment. Price . . . $.30
Code Word "NAVY"

No. 111 Lionel Lamp Assortment

No. 67 Lamp-Post—13 inches high. Complete with two globes. Price . . . $2.95
Code Word "EDMUNDS"

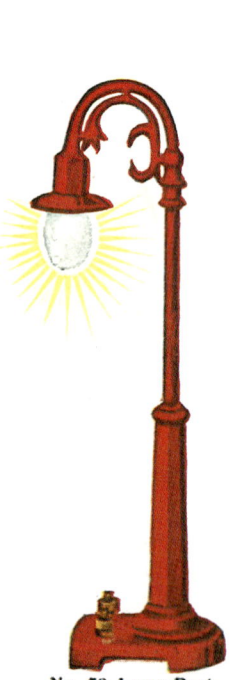

No. 58 Lamp-Post—7⅜ inches high. Complete with globe. Price . . . $1.25
Code Word "JENNY"

No. 57 Lamp-Post—7½ inches high. The top is removable so that the lamp can be easily renewed. Complete with lamp. Price . . . $1.65
Code Word "CHEERY"

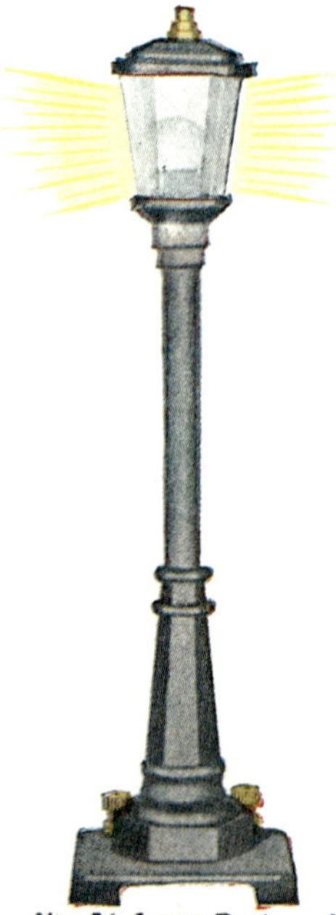

No. 56 Lamp-Post—8¾ inches high. The top is removable so that the lamp can be renewed. Complete with lamp. Price . . . $1.65
Code Word "SHINE"

No. 59 Lamp-Post—Similar in design to No. 61, but is 8¾ inches high. Complete with globe. Price . . $1.50
Code Word "BRIGHT"

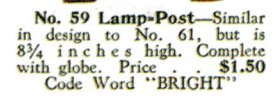

No. 61 Lamp-Post—13 inches high. Complete with globe. Price . . $2.10
Code Word "INDIA"

All-Steel Bridges for "Lionel Standard" and "O" Gauge Track

THE sturdy construction and realistic appearance of Lionel all-steel bridges places them in a class by themselves. They are scale models of the big railroad bridges seen throughout the country. The end piers, bridgework and roadway are exceptionally rigid. The architectural designs are graceful and the embossing work incorporated in them give a dignity and realism that cannot be equalled. Special slots in the roadway hold the track in place, and the spans as well as the bridges are provided with sections of either "O" Gauge or "Lionel Standard" Track. Lionel Bridges can be extended to any length by adding spans shown in the illustrations.

No. 106 Bridge (three sections)—For "O" Gauge track. Complete structure is 31½ inches long, 5½ inches wide, 4 inches high. Price, complete with track $3.35
Code Word "CONN"

No. 108 Bridge (four sections)—For "O" Gauge track. Complete structure is 42 inches long, 5½ inches wide, 4 inches high. Price, complete with track $5.50
Code Word "HOUSA"

No. 109 Bridge (five sections)—For "O" Gauge track. Complete structure is 52½ inches long, 5½ inches wide, 4 inches high. Price, complete with track $7.50
Code Word "MISS"

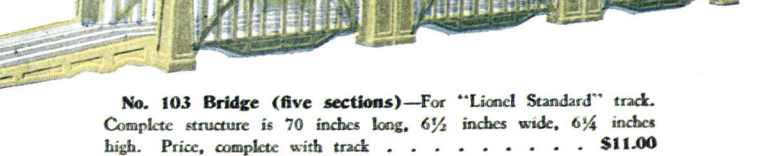

No. 101 Bridge (three sections)—For "Lionel Standard" track. Complete structure is 42 inches long, 6½ inches wide, 6¼ inches high. Price, complete with track $5.85
Code Word "QUEENS"

No. 102 Bridge (four sections)—For "Lionel Standard" track. Complete structure is 56 inches long, 6½ wide, 6¼ inches high. Price, complete with track $8.50
Code Word "KEEPSIE"

No. 103 Bridge (five sections)—For "Lionel Standard" track. Complete structure is 70 inches long, 6½ wide, 6¼ inches high. Price, complete with track $11.00
Code Word "LONDON"

No. 110 Span—For "O" Gauge Track. 10½ inches long, 5½ inches wide, 4 inches high. Price, complete with track $2.50
Code Word "WILLY"

No. 105 Approaches (two sections)—For "O" Gauge Track. Made in reproduction of reinforced concrete. Complete length 21 inches, height 2 inches at centre, width 4¼ inches. Price, complete with track $1.65
Code Word "PARIS"

No. 100 Approaches (two sections)—For "Lionel Standard" Track. Construction is the same as No. 105 described in next column. Complete length 28 inches, height 2 inches at centre, width 5½ inches. Price, complete with track . $2.50
Code Word "BROOKLYN"

No. 104 Span—For "Lionel Standard" Track. 14 inches long, 6½ inches wide, 6¼ inches high. Price, complete with track . . . $3.35
Code Word, "MANN"

Boys — add a new Lionel all-steel illuminated Tunnel to your model railroad. The light shining through the portals produces a brilliant and beautiful effect.

All-Steel Tunnels for "Lionel Standard" and "O" Gauge Track

IN keeping with the supreme quality of Lionel Trains, we are pleased to introduce this wonderful new line of Lionel All-Steel Tunnels, with and without interior electric illumination. They are made of sheet steel, beautifully designed and accurately formed in our special machinery. They stand evenly on the floor without bending. The front and rear entrances are embossed in exact reproduction of heavy stone masonry, having a keystone at the top. The bodies of the tunnels represent mountainsides in miniature and the coloring is rich and harmonious. We draw particular attention to the details on the large-size tunnels on which the mountain roadsides and bridge are wonderfully reproduced, as well as miniature metal "chalets," all in perfect proportion to the size of the tunnels. The windows of the "chalets" are perforated and the lights shining through them make a beautiful picture. The illuminating fixtures for the electrically lighted tunnels are firmly secured to the inside of the entrances. Binding posts for connecting to the source of current are conveniently placed near the base.

No. 140L Illuminated Tunnel—Can be used with any "Lionel Standard" or "O" Gauge Train. This tunnel is made to set on the curve of the track layout. Lights are placed over the forward and rear entrances. Length 37 inches, width 24½ inches, height 20 inches. Portals are 8 inches wide, 8 inches high. . . . . **Price $16.65**
Code Word "SEVA"

No. 130L Illuminated Tunnel—This is for use with all "O" Gauge Trains. The general design and appearance are the same as No. 140L Tunnel described above. Length 26 inches, width 23 inches, height 14½ inches. Portals are 4½ inches wide, 5½ inches high. . . . . **Price $13.75**
Code Word "SOAK"

No. 120 Tunnel—For all Lionel Trains. This splendid model is the very best produced for beauty, grace of design and substantial construction. All Lionel Tunnels are hand-painted in attractive, durable colors. They can be easily cleaned with a damp cloth or chamois. Tunnel is 17 inches long, 12 inches wide and 11 inches high. Portals are 6½ inches wide and 8 inches high . . . **Price $5.85**
Code Word "HUDSON"

No. 120L Illuminated Tunnel—Same construction and size as No. 120 described above, but is equipped with interior light . . . . **Price $6.65**
Code Word "HOPE"

No. 119 Tunnel—For all "O" Gauge Trains and the medium size "Lionel Standard" Trains. Tunnel is 12 inches long, 9 inches wide and 10 inches high. Portals are 5 inches wide and 6½ inches high.
Price $3.35
Code Word "HOSA"

No. 119L Illuminated Tunnel—Same construction and size as No. 119 described above, but is equipped with interior light.
Price $4.25
Code Word "HARP"

No. 118 Tunnel—For "O" Gauge Trains. Tunnel is 8 inches long, 7 inches wide and 7½ inches high. Portals are 4 inches wide and 5½ inches high . . **Price $2.10**
Code Word "SIMPLON"

No. 118L Illuminated Tunnel—Same construction and size as No. 118 described above, but is equipped with interior light.
Price $2.95
Code Word "SUEZ"

"Lionel Standard" and "O" Gauge Scenic Railways

No. 198—FOR "O" GAUGE TRACK

THE platform is made of composition board in two sections, mounted in a rigid wooden frame. The dimensions are 60 by 42 inches. The top of the platform is decorated in colors representing grass plots, roads, etc. Indicating marks show the points at which the accessories are to be placed. The platform is electrically wired so that accessories and track can be connected in a few moments. A large metal tunnel is supplied, realistically painted and embellished with miniature houses. Mountainous sections, flower beds, and grass plots are made of indestructible steel. Shrubs, bushes and miniature trees are also furnished, all of which greatly enhance the detail. Three reproductions of mountains beautifully decorated, each measuring 36 by 18 inches, form the background, and two panels, representing the skyline, each measuring 36 by 28 inches, complete the scenic effect.

The display is light in weight and can be easily moved. The background scenic effects can either be condensed or extended to fit the space in which the Scenic Railway is to be used.

No. 199—FOR "LIONEL STANDARD" TRACK

ON account of its larger size we have been able to incorporate many more scenic details, and to supply a larger amount of accessories in this scenic railway for "Lionel Standard" Track. The general construction and appearance are similar to the "O" Gauge Scenic Railway described in the opposite column.

The platform of the "Lionel Standard" Scenic Railway is made in three sections and measures 90 inches long by 60 inches deep. The dimensions of the three mountains and the skyline background are the same as those supplied with "O" Gauge Scenic Railway No. 198. Specifications are given below.

Dealers — display a Lionel Scenic Railway in your window. No greater aid to increasing your toy sales has ever been devised.

The scenic effects and accessories supplied with Lionel Scenic Railways can be purchased separately if desired, at prices listed in the specifications.

No. 198 "O" Gauge Scenic Railway. Comprises:

1 No. 076 Block signal	$3.15	
1 No. 077 Crossing gate	4.00	
1 No. 069 Warning signal	3.15	
1 No. 56 Lamp post	1.65	
1 No. 57 Lamp post	1.65	
1 No. 58 Lamp post	1.25	
1 No. 89 Flag staff	.75	
1 No. 184 Bungalow	1.50	
1 No. 189 Villa	2.95	
1 No. 191 Villa	3.35	
1 No. 092 Signal tower	2.10	
1 No. 130L Tunnel	13.75	
1 No. 131 Corner elevation	4.50	
1 No. 132 Corner grass plot	2.50	
2 No. 133 Heartshape grass plots	$1.50	3.00
1 No. 134 Circular grass plot (large)		3.00
1 No. 506 Compo board painted platform, completely wired (2 sections)		6.50
3 No. 509 Compo board mountains		1.50
1 No. 508 Compo board sky background (2 sections)		3.00
4 No. 500 Pine bushes	.20	.80
2 No. 501 Small pine trees	.20	.40
3 No. 502 Medium pine trees	.25	.75
3 No. 503 Large pine trees	.30	.90
4 No. 504 Rose bushes	.20	.80
3 No. 505 Oak trees	.30	.90
4 No. 510 Canna bushes	.20	.80

Train and track not included. **Price complete** $50.00

Code Word "BEAUTY"

No. 199 "Lionel Standard" Scenic Railway. Comprises:

1 No. 124 Station	$9.00	
1 No. 189 Villa	2.95	
3 No. 191 Villas	3.35	10.05
3 No. 184 Bungalows	1.50	4.50
1 No. 092 Signal tower		2.10
5 No. 60 Telegraph posts	.65	3.25
2 No. 59 Lamp posts	1.50	3.00
3 No. 58 Lamp posts	1.25	3.75
1 No. 57 Lamp post		1.65
1 No. 89 Flag staff		.75
1 No. 84 Semaphore		3.35
1 No. 78 Automatic train control		5.00
1 No. 77 Crossing gate		4.25
1 No. 69 Warning signal		3.35
1 No. 120 Tunnel		5.85
1 No. 136 Elevation		10.00
1 No. 131 Corner elevation		4.50
1 No. 132 Corner grass plot		$2.50
2 No. 133 Heartshape grass plots	1.50	3.00
1 No. 134 Circular grass plot, large		3.00
1 No. 135 Circular grass plot, small		1.00
1 No. 507 Compo board painted platform, completely wired (3 sections)		7.50
3 No. 509 Compo board mountains	1.50	4.50
1 No. 508 Compo board sky backgr'd (2 sections)		3.00
4 No. 500 Pine bushes	.20	.80
4 No. 501 Small pine trees	.20	.80
4 No. 502 Medium pine trees	.25	1.00
4 No. 503 Large pine trees	.30	1.20
4 No. 504 Rose bushes	.20	.80
8 No. 505 Oak trees	.30	2.40
4 No. 510 Canna bushes	.20	.80

Train and track not included. **Price complete** $80.00

Code Word "NATURE"

Factories of the Lionel Corporation

THE HOME OF

Lionel Electric Trains
MODEL RAILROAD ACCESSORIES
MULTIVOLT" TRANSFORMERS

Display Rooms, Offices and Service Station
15-17-19 EAST 26th STREET
(Madison Square North)
NEW YORK CITY

Factories and Service Departments
SOUTH 21st STREET, IRVINGTON, N. J.
Warehouses
24 NESBITT STREET, NEWARK, N. J.

THE LARGEST AMERICAN FACTORIES EXCLUSIVELY PRODUCING MODEL ELECTRIC TRAINS AND RAILROAD EQUIPMENT

Printed in U.S.A.   The entire contents of this catalog copyrighted 1927 by the Lionel Corporation, New York, N. Y.

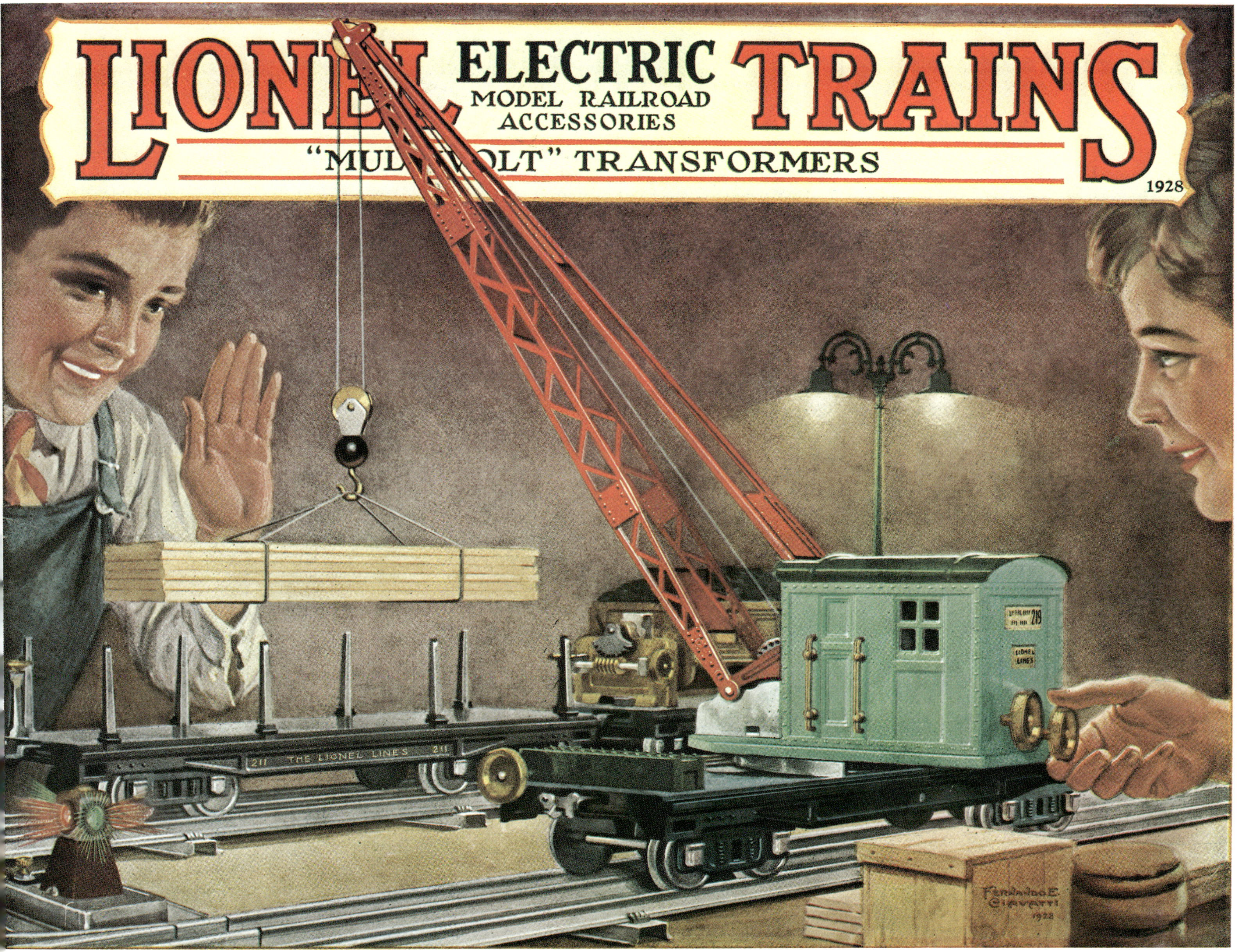
LIONEL
ELECTRIC
MODEL RAILROAD
ACCESSORIES
TRAINS
TRANSFORMERS
1928
211 THE LIONEL LINES 211
219
LIONEL LINES
FERNANDO E. CIAVATTI 1928

Lionel Railroading!
IS AN EXCITING GAME.

BECAUSE it's so real! You boys who are baseball and football fans will get more fun out of Lionel railroading than out of any other sport in the world.

A man with an understanding heart created Lionel Trains—because he loved boys and knew just the kind of excitement that all boys want.

There's action all the time with a Lionel.

There's realism—and the thrill that comes from the personal operation and direction of a great railroad system. There's knowledge to be gained from the study of Lionel Railroad operation — knowledge of electricity, of railroad control, and of transportation that will be valuable to you when you grow up to manhood.

Hundreds of boys who were Lionel fans years ago are today occupying positions of trust on the great railroad systems of the country—helped forward by what they learned as boys through the operation of their Lionel Trains.

You see, Lionel Trains are life-like copies of the great Transcontinental Flyers. Handsome trains in glistening colors. Miniature copies of the best that the world of railroading affords.

Every modern safety device—the signaling and switching systems that you see on every railroad, are to be found in the Lionel Line.

Look at the Locomotives! Big, powerful—STRONG! Able to pull with ease, and at great speed, long lines of Freight or Passenger Cars. The heart of the Locomotive is the famous Lionel Super-Motor.

Compare Lionel Locomotives with others, and note the difference. Compare the Motor of your Lionel. Compare the finish, the strength, the outward appearance, and the many details that make Lionel the finest in quality that it is possible to buy.

THE TREMENDOUS FACTORIES AT IRVINGTON, N. J., WHERE LIONEL TRAINS ARE MADE

How handsome the Pullman Cars are. How brilliantly lighted. Finished to a velvet smoothness in different colors of enamel. Appointed in every respect to look like actual cars on modern railroads.

That's Lionel quality. It is never equaled.

We don't want to tell you too much about Lionel Railroading. We don't want to spoil the surprise and excitement that you will experience when you throw the switch for the first time on your own Lionel Railroad.

But—imagine—your Lionel Railroad!

A marvelous system! With crossovers, switches, illuminated bumpers at the freight sidings — magnificent Lionel steel bridges and illuminated tunnels — a handsome station at Lionel City, its lights gleaming a welcome to the oncoming train.

Passenger trains, freight trains, work trains, moving about at the will of yourself—the young engineer — operated by you from the Switch Tower, and absolutely under your control at any distance from the track because of the perfection of Lionel's 100% "Distant-Control" System (described in more detail on the opposite page).

Semaphores bobbing up and down, automatically controlling your train, signal lights blinking red and green, crossing gates automatically raising and lowering as your train speeds by.

Wouldn't you like to own such a railroad? Of course, and you know Lionel is the only model railroad that gives you all these remarkable features. Here's a surprise!

Lionel now offers the wonderful new "Bild-a-Loco"—the engine with the powerful Super-Motor that you can take out, TAKE APART, and put together again.

Also you can transform the "Bild-a-Loco" into the "Bild-a-Motor," and so have a separate electric motor that will lift twenty times its own weight. And no boy needs to be told what he can do with a motor of this sort. INSIST on Lionel Trains, because they are better and because they cost NO MORE. See the Lionel Model Railroad Display at your local dealers.

The Lionel Corporation
15-17-19 EAST 26th STREET
(Madison Square North)
NEW YORK, N. Y.

The Electrical Brain of Your Lionel
In Lionel's 100% "Distant-Control" Railroads

It humanizes the operation of your train. For the electrical brain of your locomotive responds instantly to your will, although you may be operating your train from the next room.

Lionel's new 100% "Distant-Control" Railroad system designed for "O" gauge as well as for "Lionel Standard" track makes it unnecessary for you to have to reverse your locomotive by hand.

By manipulating the small lever on the controlling rheostat, as the boy is doing in the picture, you can start, stop, switch, reverse and run your train without going near it.

You are, thereby, the master of your train.

And not only that, but while Lionel Semaphores, Crossing Gates, Block Signals, Warning Bells and Train Controls are automatically operated by the movement of the train, they can be controlled by you at any distance from the track, by connecting them with the controlling levers in the new Lionel Switch Towers, Power Station and Panel Board.

It is also interesting to note that the locomotive headlights are so connected that when the train moves forward the front headlight is illuminated, and when in reverse the rear headlight flashes on while the other is disconnected.

Thus the Lionel "Distant-Control" System of electrical operation puts genuine excitement into model railroading—and it is a thrill you can experience only if your train is a Lionel. Boys, don't forget that!

Boys!—here's the proof—

Go to your dealers, and take a Lionel Train in your hands. Feel the weight of it. That's sturdiness, strength! Note the glossy, brilliant smoothness of its enameled finish. Mark the fittings on the engine and cars, and how every detail simulates the perfection of a real railroad train. Rugged strength, beauty and quality is built into every train with typical Lionel thoroughness.

Is there any wonder why Lionel has been "Standard of the World" since 1900!

LIONEL "DISTANT-CONTROL" LOCOMOTIVES AND TRAINS FOR "O" GAUGE AND "LIONEL STANDARD" TRACK ARE LISTED IN GREAT VARIETY IN OTHER PARTS OF THIS CATALOG.

Lionel "Distant-Control" Locomotives and Train Outfits listed on the following pages are distinguished by the letter "E" after the catalog number.

THE LIONEL "DISTANT-CONTROL" SUPER-MOTOR

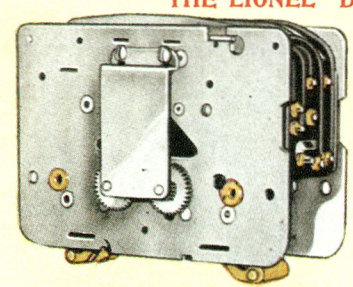

Illustration shows the simplicity and compactness of Lionel "Distant-Control" Super-Motors. All working parts are mounted between two heavy steel plates. All shaft bearings are reinforced with bronze bushings. All parts are easily accessible, including the removable brush holder, lever for reversing the locomotive by hand and an additional lever for disconnecting the "distant-control" mechanism.

1928

Construction of Lionel "O" Gauge Motors

DRIVING GEARS ("A")—They are made of heavy steel blanks, machine-cut. They mesh without friction and are far superior to gears with punched teeth.

Field ("B")—The field is made of a number of specially prepared transformer steel laminations. This construction represents a much stronger field than if a single piece of steel were used.

Third Rail Shoe Support ("C")—Made of heavy fibre to which the third rail contact rollers are attached. Our construction protects rollers from injury, for the brackets can be bent against the fibre without disturbing the arc of the spring that gives them the correct tension against the third rail.

Wheels ("D")—Lionel was first to introduce die-cast wheels. They are absolutely balanced. A nickeled-plated steel rim is forced over the tread of the wheel to insure long wear.

Collecting Shoes ("E")—They collect current from the third rail. Made of solid brass turnings and revolve on steel shafts which pass through phosphor bronze supports. They insure perfect contact with the third rail at all times so that locomotives will run at uniform speed.

Frame ("F")—Made of very heavy steel punchings, embodying great detail. Will withstand more than the ordinary amount of wear and tear.

Journals ("G")—Made of heavy brass, nickel-plated. Attached to the frames by mechanical means. They add greatly to the appearance of the structure.

Cowcatchers ("H")—The construction of the cowcatchers varies with the type of locomotive on which they are used. Many of them are part of the steel frame which is made in one piece, and others are heavy castings rigidly attached to the frame.

Flag Posts ("J")—All our locomotives are equipped with four flag posts, two at each end of the frame; a very realistic detail.

Tanks ("K")—These tanks are made of brass, nickel-plated, and are separable pieces attached to the frame, which further accentuates the great detail.

Lionel Automatic Couplers ("L")—Made of heavy steel, nickel-plated and polished. They are scientifically constructed so that cars cannot become detached when in motion, but are easily taken apart when desired. The new improved Lionel Coupler with invisible spring arrangement is a great advance over any similar device ever made.

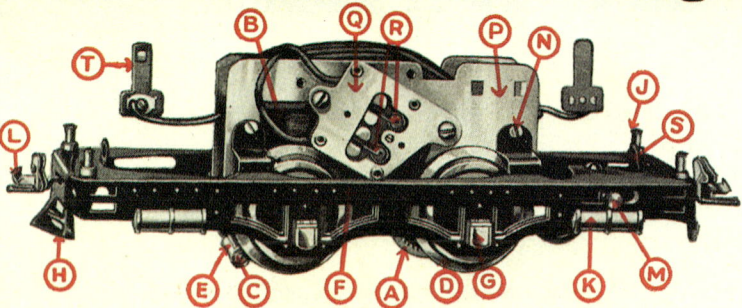

Illustration above shows the type of motor used in "O" Gauge Locomotives Nos. 248, 252 and 253.

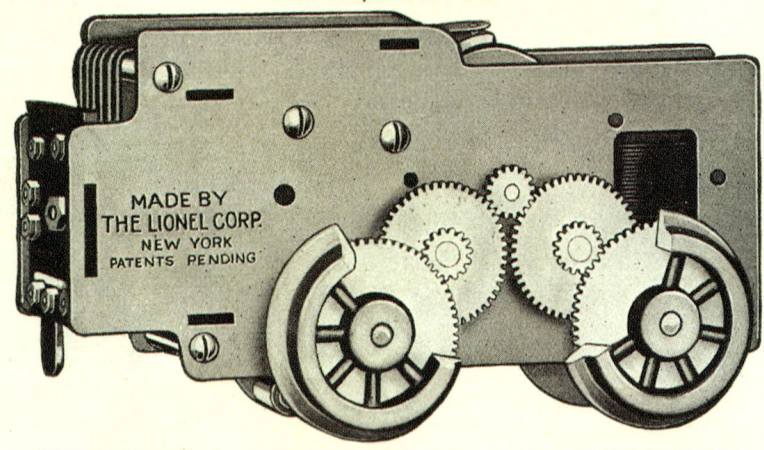

THE NEW "O" GAUGE "DISTANT-CONTROL" SUPER-MOTOR

This marvelous new motor will haul twice as many cars as any other "O" Gauge Motor now on sale. The illustration above shows some of the remarkable features that make this possible. Notice the new system of gearing which gives maximum hauling power with minimum current consumption.

The electric-controlling mechanism is built right into the motor, and is completely protected against injury. This new "O" Gauge Super-Motor, a triumph of engineering skill, is one of Lionel's greatest achievements.

This "Distant-Control" Super-Motor is used in "O" Gauge Locomotives Nos. 254E and 251E.

The same Super-Motor with hand reversing mechanism is used in "O" Gauge Locomotives Nos. 254, 251 and in Twin-Super-Motor No. 256.

Above illustration shows a complete "O" Gauge Twin-Motor Chassis used in Locomotive No. 256. These Twin-Motors develop great hauling power and will pull a long train of cars with perfect ease.

Reversing Controllers ("M")—Lionel Reversing Controllers have been in use for many years during which time they have given thorough satisfaction. They are the only controllers in use that cannot get out of order. They operate very easily, and due to the brass cups and spring tension, the electrical contact is always permanent.

Frame Support ("N")—The frame is supported to the motor with only four screws. This simple method of construction was originally introduced by us in 1913. All parts of Lionel Locomotives can be easily reached for cleaning.

Side Plates ("P")—Made of heavy gauge steel and support all working parts. All bearing holes are reinforced with phosphor bronze bushings. The alignment of these holes is absolutely perfect so that gears work with minimum friction. All holes are drilled and reamed to proper diameter. The accuracy of these plates compares with the frame work of a very fine clock.

Brush Plate ("Q")—The unique construction permits rapid change of brushes after motor has been in use for a considerable period. The brushes fit in brass cups. Two properly tempered steel springs give the correct pressure of the brush on the commutator until brushes are worn down to the end. Brushes are replaced by simply raising the springs, lifting up worn-out brushes and dropping in new ones.

Brushes ("R")—We were the first manufacturers of model trains to equip our motors with combination gauze and graphite brushes that wear long and are self-lubricating.

Removable Locomotive Body ("S")—The bodies of all Lionel Locomotives are held in place on the frame with only two screws, one at each end of the locomotive. Supporting members are placed at several points of the frame that rigidly hold the body in place.

Headlight Connection ("T")—A new method originated by us. The fibre contact makes a permanent electrical connection and eliminates the possibility of broken wires.

Commutator—Made of bronze, and perfectly turned when connected to armature so that it is absolutely parallel with brushes. Commutator surface is polished so as to reduce all friction when in contact with brushes.

Armature—Made of specially prepared electrical sheets mounted on a drill rod shaft. It is perfectly insulated and wound with the correct amount of triple insulated wire.

Construction of "Lionel Standard" Super-Motors
Reg. U.S. Pat. Office

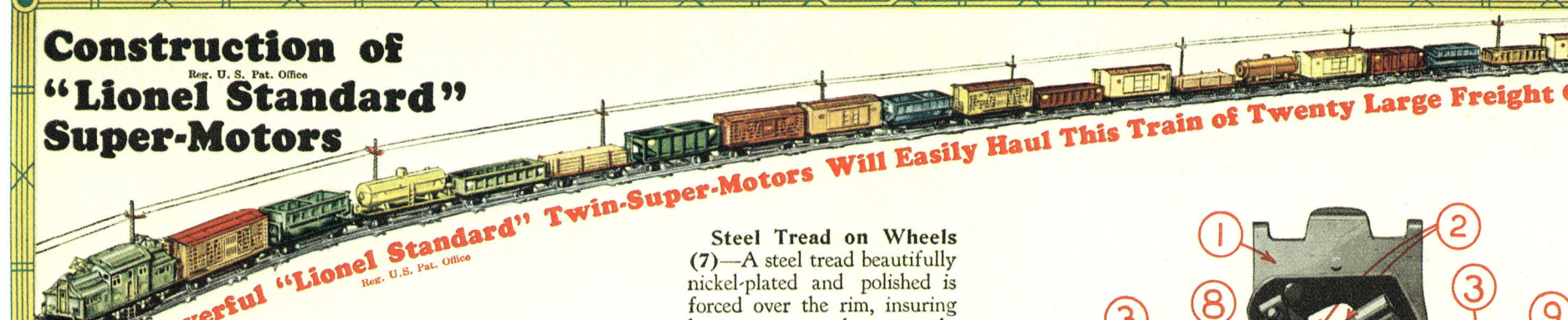

The Powerful "Lionel Standard" Twin-Super-Motors Will Easily Haul This Train of Twenty Large Freight Cars
Reg. U.S. Pat. Office

REMOVABLE BRUSH HOLDER (1) — By simply unscrewing one screw the entire brush holder can be removed from the motor. Change of brushes requires but an instant and the assembled part is replaced without the use of any tools.

Brushes (2) — Made of bronze and graphite which are self-lubricating. They insure long life to the commutator. They are contained in brass tubes and held in place by a simple spring arrangement which feeds brushes to commutator at the same pressure until used up.

Revolving Double Contact Shoes (3) — Are heavy bronze rollers, securely affixed to the flexible phosphor bronze plate, which insures the proper tension on the third rail and gives a steady flow of current to the motors. Complete shoe assembly is mounted on a heavy fibre plate and is rigidly attached to the motor frame.

New Gear Arrangement (4) — This new method of gearing is embodied only in Lionel Super-Motors. The seven gears in this new layout gives the motor greater tractive power, and are almost frictionless. The gears are made of very heavy steel, and teeth are machine cut, not stamped.

Three-Point Armature Shaft Bearing (5) — The armature shaft revolves in three bearings — two of them are contained in the side plates of the motor and the third one in the plate that holds the gearing studs. This three-point-bearing eliminates all vibration of the armature shaft, with the result that the commutator and brushes wear long and evenly.

Driving Wheels (6) — Are massive in construction and accurately die-cast. Their weight adds great tractive power to the motors.

Steel Tread on Wheels (7) — A steel tread beautifully nickel-plated and polished is forced over the rim, insuring longer wear and a smooth, even riding surface. Lionel originated this method of wheel construction. See illustration on Page 7.

Reinforced Bearings (8) — Six phosphor bronze bearings are contained in the side plates of the motor, insuring accurate alignment of the armature shaft and axles.

Armature — Made of laminated electrical steel punchings. It is automatically drum wound with triple-covered magnet wire, dipped in shellac and baked. The armature shaft (9) is made of the best quality drill rod.

Side Plates (10) — Made of heavy steel, with bronze bushings inserted for shaft and axles.

Field — Made of the highest grade electrical steel, correctly wound and scientifically designed.

Commutator — Made of heavy copper. The segments are perfectly insulated, making short-circuits impossible.

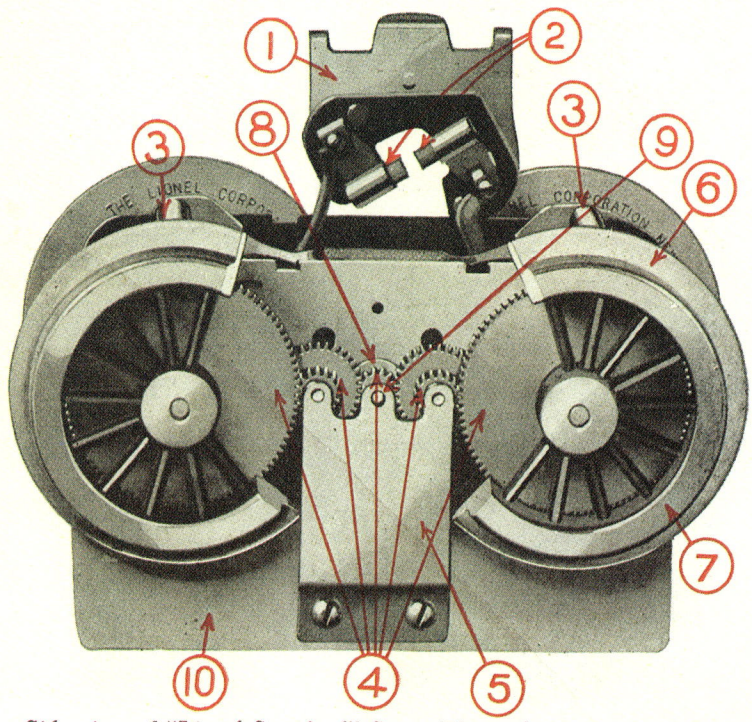

Side view of "Lionel Standard" Super-Motor showing removable brush plate and three-point armature shaft bearing.

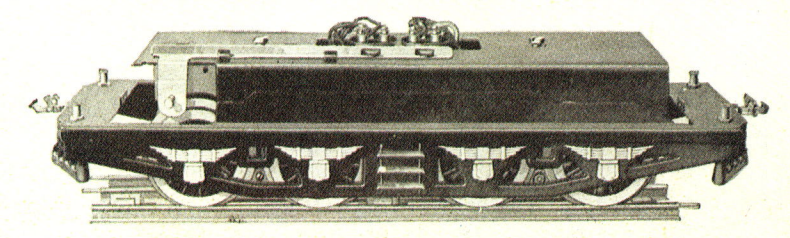

"Lionel Standard" Twin-Super-Motors (with "Distant-Control")

Above illustration shows "Lionel Standard" Twin-Super-Motors fitted to chassis which is entirely constructed of heavy sheet steel. Twin-Super-Motor Locomotives Nos. 402E and 408E are equipped with the famous "Distant-Control" mechanism described on Page 3. They can be started, stopped, reversed and operated at any speed at any distance from the track.

Tractive Power — The tractive power of "Lionel Standard" Super-Motors is remarkable. They will haul from 12 to 20 of our largest size freight or Pullman cars with the greatest ease. The weight of the wheels and motor is close to the track, insuring low centre of gravity, with the result that the locomotive is not top-heavy and slippage of the wheels is therefore unknown. This construction is infinitely superior to the method of loading down the superstructure with useless weight so as to obtain tractive power. This unnecessary weight rapidly wears down all working parts and causes the locomotive to jump the track.

Construction of Lionel Locomotives, Passenger and Freight Cars

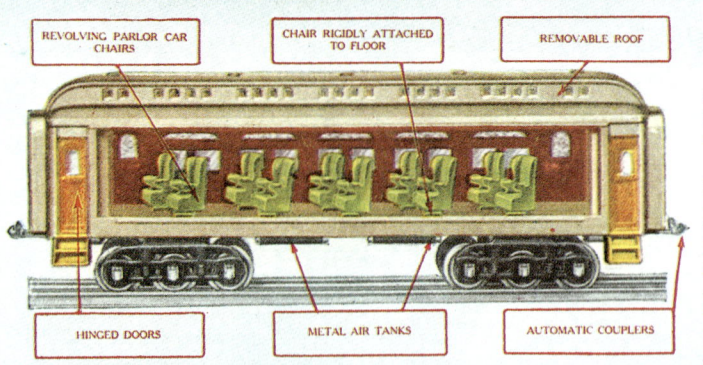

LIONEL leadership has been attained by specialization in the manufacture of one product for 28 years. Our entire resources and unsurpassed manufacturing facilities are exclusively devoted to the production of Model Electric Trains, Railroad Accessories and "Multivolt" Transformers.

Reference to the descriptive matter and illustrations on this page will prove the supremely high quality of Lionel Products. Not only are the raw materials used the best obtainable, but all Locomotives, Pullman and Freight Cars, as well as Railroad Accessories, are actually built to scale. Every detail found in real railroad equipment is faithfully reproduced in our models. Space does not permit us to dwell at length on the many improvements incorporated in our goods, but on Page 7 we specify a few of the leading features introduced and patented by us.

ALL Lionel Cars and Locomotive Bodies are enameled in a variety of attractive colors, and baked at high temperature, which insures a permanent finish that can always be kept bright by any ordinary cleaning process.

The structural details of Lionel Locomotive Bodies are typical of Lionel supreme quality throughout the entire line. Even the lowest priced Lionel Locomotives incorporate many of these features.

We refer with pride to one of our greatest achievements—the Lionel De-Luxe Electrically-Controlled Twin-Super-Motor Locomotive No. 408E illustrated here. The richness and realism of the details in this new model are far beyond anything hitherto attempted.

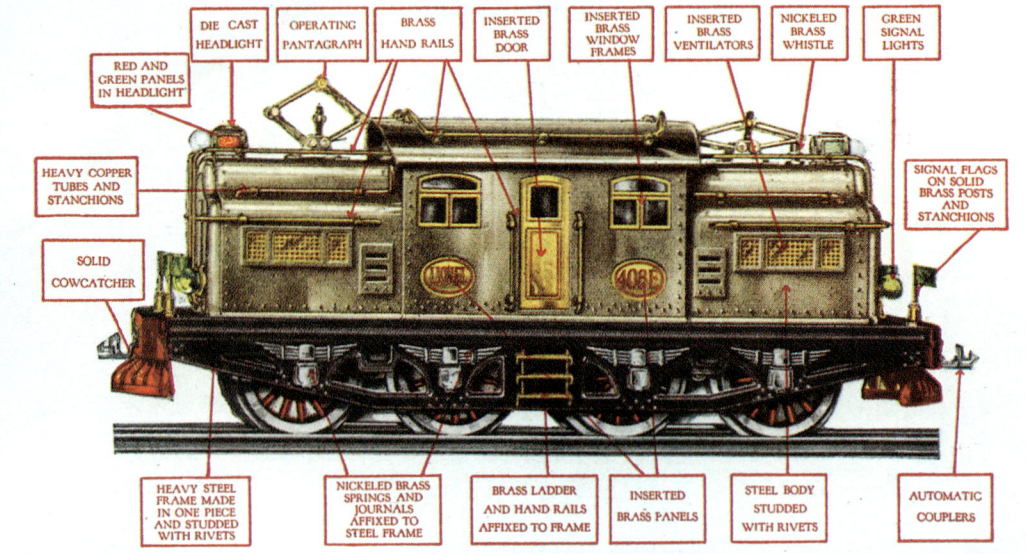

OF utmost importance is the fact that cast iron does not enter into the manufacture of any of these bodies—heavy sheet steel is used for every model. Panels and rivets are embossed in the metal which add strength; so that Lionel Locomotives are practically indestructible. Brass and nickeled fittings add further charm to the general appearance of Lionel Locomotives. These fittings are secured to the bodies by a patented process perfected by us.

In all ways Lionel Locomotive Bodies combine sturdy construction and graceful lines, as the indications clearly show.

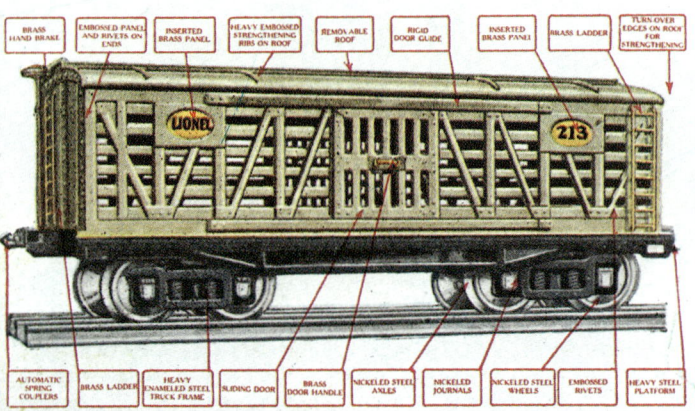

ALL Lionel Cars are made of steel, and are modeled after the newest designs. Great detail is incorporated in them, such as hinged doors, inserted window frames and seats, metal tanks, etc. Transparencies are placed in the windows and transoms of every Passenger Coach. Roofs are removable so that the interior can be reached.

All "Lionel Standard" Observation Cars have a dome light which illuminates red transparent discs in the rear. This rear light is in addition to the centre light found in all 8-wheel Lionel Passenger Cars. Cars are finished in a variety of attractive enamel colors, baked at high temperature.

A revolving shoe collects the current for the interior illumination of the cars. (See illustration on Page 31.) All trucks have nickeled journals, which cover the ends of heavy steel nickeled axles. Wheels are made of nickel-plated steel.

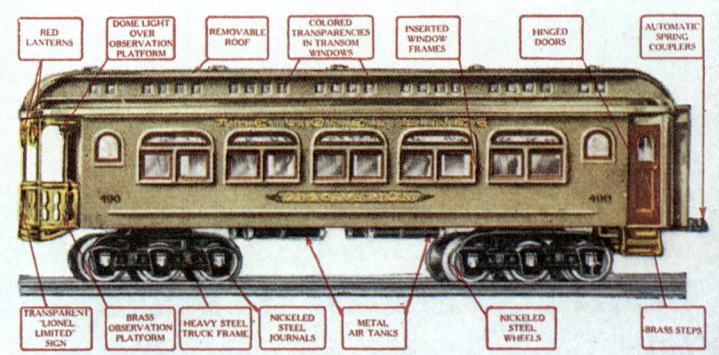

LIONEL ALWAYS LEADS

WINDOW PANELS, DOORS AND SEATS — A SEPARABLE PIECE INSERTED IN CAR BODY
U.S. PATENTS NO. 1272390 AND 1272391 — JULY 16, 1918

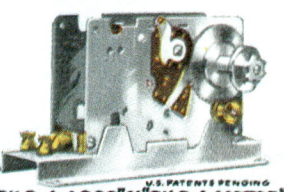

"BILD-A-LOCO" & "BILD-A-MOTOR" ASSEMBLED AND TAKEN APART IN A FEW MOMENTS
U.S. PATENTS PENDING

OPERATING PANTAGRAPHS

CONTROLLING UNITS FOR ELECTRICALLY OPERATED TRACK SWITCHES PATENT PENDING

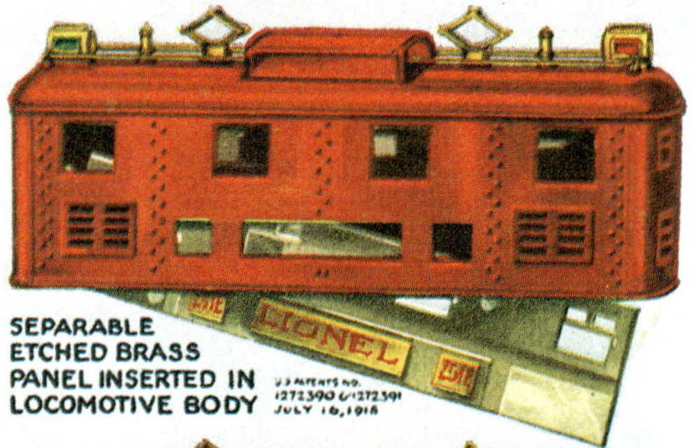

SEPARABLE ETCHED BRASS PANEL INSERTED IN LOCOMOTIVE BODY
U.S. PATENTS NO. 1272390 & 1272391 JULY 16, 1918

FINISHED CAR BODY SHOWING SEPARABLE PANEL INSERTED U.S. PATENTS NO. 1272390 & 1272391 JULY 16, 1918

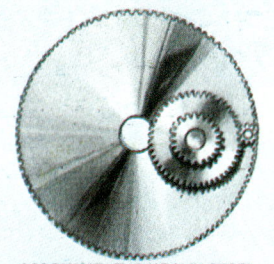

LIONEL WAS FIRST TO INTRODUCE—

Inserted window panels and seats in car bodies. U. S. Patent Nos. 1272390 and 1272391, July 16, 1918.

Inserted etched brass panels in locomotive bodies. U. S. Patent Nos. 1272390 and 1272391, July 16, 1918.

Die-cast wheels with nickeled steel rims. U. S. Reissued Patent No. 16351, May 18, 1926.

Removable brush holder containing self-lubricating automatic-feeding brushes. U. S. Patent No. 1405497, Feb. 7, 1922, and U. S. Patent No. 1536329, May 5, 1925.

"Lockon" Connection. U. S. Patent No. 1542337, June 16, 1925.

Fibre switch point, which prevents short-circuiting of track. U. S. Reissued Patent No. 16580, March 29, 1927.

Automatic Train Control. U. S. Patent No. 1614874, Jan. 18, 1927.

Automatic Warning Signal. Automatic Block Signal.

Automatic Crossing Gate. U. S. Patent No. 1153922, Sept. 21, 1915.

Electrically-Controlled Semaphore. U. S. Patent No. 1153922, Sept. 21, 1915.

Die-cast headlight with electrical connection. U. S. Patent No. 1672871, June 12, 1928.

"Bild-a-Loco" and "Bild-a-Motor." Assembled and taken apart in a few moments. Patents pending.

Electrically-Controlled Track Switches. Patent pending.

Headlight connection. Patent pending.

Operating Pantagraphs. Machine cut, heavy steel gears—not punched.

Trucks (4-wheel and 6-wheel) with nickeled journals.

Self-lubricating automatic-feeding brushes in "O" Gauge Motors.

Hand-enameled Car and Locomotive bodies built of sheet steel instead of flimsy lithographed tin.

Roller contact shoes. Three-point armature shaft bearings on motors.

Electrical sheets for motor and armature construction instead of cheap cold-rolled steel.

Drill rod shaft for armature, instead of commercial iron wire.

Reinforced phosphor-bronze bearings for armature shaft and wheel axles.

All-steel electric miniature bungalows and villas, AND

Every desirable feature in Model Electric Trains and Accessories.

DIE-CAST HEADLIGHT SHOWING RED PANEL AND ELECTRICAL CONNECTION. U.S. PATENT NO. 1672871 JUNE 12, 1928

MACHINE-CUT HEAVY STEEL GEARS — NOT PUNCHED

VIEW OF HEADLIGHT SHOWING GREEN PANEL U.S. PATENT NO. 1672871 JUNE 12, 1928

FINISHED LOCOMOTIVE BODY SHOWING SEPARABLE PANEL INSERTED U.S. PATENTS NO. 1272390 & 1272391 JULY 16, 1918

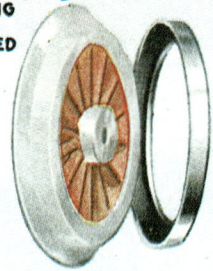

DIE-CAST WHEEL WITH NICKELED STEEL RIM U.S. RE-ISSUED PATENT NO. 16351 - MAY 18, 1926

SIX-WHEEL TRUCK WITH NICKELED JOURNALS

REMOVABLE BRUSH HOLDER CONTAINING SELF-LUBRICATING AUTOMATIC-FEEDING BRUSHES

"LOCKON" CONNECTION U.S. PATENT NO. 1542337 - JUNE 16, 1925

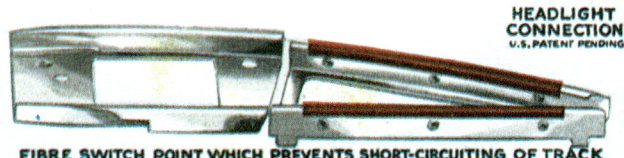

FIBRE SWITCH POINT WHICH PREVENTS SHORT-CIRCUITING OF TRACK U.S. RE-ISSUED PATENT NO. 16580 - MARCH 29, 1927

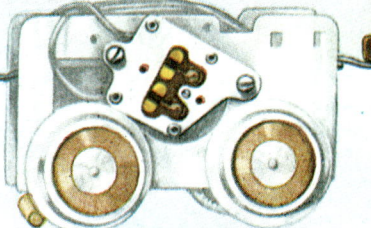

HEADLIGHT CONNECTION U.S. PATENT PENDING

SELF-LUBRICATING AUTOMATIC-FEEDING BRUSHES IN "O" GAUGE MOTOR

LOCOMOTIVES
For "O" Gauge Track 1⅝ Inches Wide

THE new line of Lionel "O" Gauge Locomotives now includes several models equipped with the Lionel "Distant-Control" Super-Motor. Others are equipped with hand-reverse. They are fully described on Page 4. These powerful locomotives haul twice as many cars as any other make.

All Lionel "O" Gauge Locomotives are equipped with automatic couplers.

Note:—Length of couplers on locomotives is not included in dimensions given in specifications.

See Pages 29 and 30 for the correct Passenger and Freight Cars to be used with these locomotives.

Locomotive No. 252—Equipped with reversing controller and electric headlight. 8 inches long, 3¾ inches high. Price . . . $8.00
Code Word "ELECT"

Locomotive No. 248—Equipped with electric headlight. 7½ inches long, 3¾ inches high. Price . . . $5.75
Code Word "REGAL"

Locomotive No. 253—Equipped with reversing controller and 2 electric headlights. 9 inches long, 4 inches high. Price . . . $9.75
Code Word "FINE"

Super-Motor Locomotive No. 251—Equipped with reversing controller and 2 electric headlights. 10¼ inches long, 5 inches high. Price . . . $15.00
Code Word "ACME"

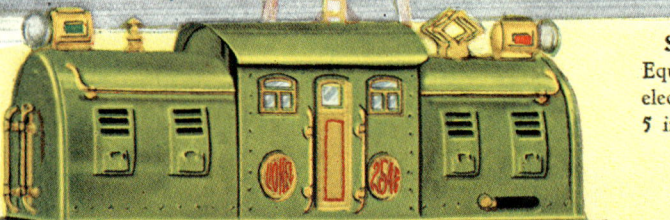

"Distant-Control" Super-Motor Locomotive No. 251E—Same as No. 251, but can be started, stopped, reversed and operated at any speed at any distance from the track. No. 81 controlling rheostat supplied with it. Price . $20.00
Code Word "GLORY"

Super-Motor Locomotive No. 254—Equipped with reversing controller and 2 electric headlights. 10 inches long, 4¼ inches high. Code Word "MANY" Price $12.25

"Distant-Control" Super-Motor Locomotive No. 254E—Same as No. 254, but can be started, stopped, reversed and operated at any speed at any distance from the track. No. 81 controlling rheostat supplied with it. Price . . . $17.25
Code Word "GRIT"

Twin-Super-Motor Locomotive No. 256—A new and improved model. Equipped with reversing controller and 2 electric headlights, operating pantagraphs, flags and many other realistic details. A powerful, sturdy locomotive. 11½ inches long, 5¼ inches high. Price . . . $18.25
Code Word "CHAIN"

8

Passenger and Freight Train Outfits

FOR "O" GAUGE TRACK—1⅜ INCHES WIDE.

ALL Lionel Train Outfits include electric lamps for headlights, wires for connecting to transformer or batteries, and connecting ties for joining sections of track. Locomotives and Cars are equipped with automatic couplers.

See Pages 32 and 33 for suitable Transformers and Reducers with which to operate these outfits from house current.

Warning Signal is included without charge in all "O" Gauge Train Outfits.

No. 249

Outfit No. 249—Comprises 1 No. 248 locomotive with electric headlight, 1 No. 831 lumber car with load of lumber, 1 No. 807 caboose, 8 sections OC curved track, 1 No. 068 warning signal, 1 OTC "Lockon" connection. Track forms a circle 30 inches in diameter. Train is 24¼ inches long.
Price $6.75
Code Word "KATE"

Outfit No. 292—Comprises 1 No. 248 locomotive with electric headlight, 1 No. 629 Pullman car, 1 No. 630 observation car, 8 sections OC curved track, 1 No. 068 warning signal, 1 OTC "Lockon" connection. Track forms a circle 30 inches in diameter. Train is 24¼ inches long. Price . $6.75
Code Word "KEEN"

No. 292

MANY WONDERFUL ACCESSORIES FOR USE WITH THESE TRAINS ARE LISTED THROUGHOUT THIS CATALOG

No. 293

Outfit No. 294—Comprises 1 No. 252 reversible locomotive with electric headlight, 2 No. 529 Pullman cars, 1 No. 530 observation car, 8 sections OC curved track, 2 sections OS straight track, 1 controlling rheostat, 1 No. 068 warning signal, 1 OTC "Lockon" connection. Track forms an oval 40 by 30 inches. Train is 33 inches long.
Price $9.75
Code Word "CORN"

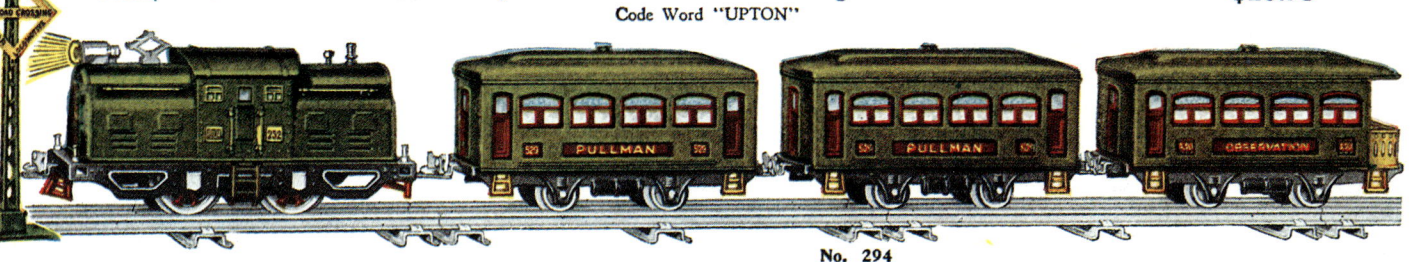

Outfit No. 293—Comprises 1 No. 252 reversible locomotive with electric headlight, 1 No. 803 coal car, 1 No. 804 oil car, 1 No. 805 box car, 1 No. 807 caboose, 8 sections OC curved track, 2 sections OS straight track, 1 controlling rheostat, 1 No. 068 warning signal, 1 OTC "Lockon" connection. Track forms an oval 40 by 30 inches. Train is 40¼ inches long. Price $10.75
Code Word "UPTON"

No. 294

Passenger and Freight Train Outfits for "O" Gauge Track

1⅜ INCHES WIDE

No. 296

BOYS—see the amount of realistic detail embodied in these splendid "O" Gauge Trains. Locomotives have two electric headlights, the passenger cars are all fitted with interior electric lights—the freight cars have sliding doors. Locomotives and Cars are equipped with the Lionel automatic spring couplers. Warning Signals are included with all "O" Gauge Outfits, without charge.
Remember — Lionel "Multivolt" Transformers are specially made to operate Lionel Trains and are therefore the best.

Outfit No. 296—This attractive outfit has always been one of our best numbers. It will be even more popular now as it contains a No. 253 locomotive, which is larger and more powerful than the No. 252, which heretofore was packed with this outfit.

Outfit comprises 1 No. 253 reversible locomotive with 2 electric headlights, 2 No. 607 illuminated Pullman cars, 1 No. 608 illuminated observation car, 8 sections OC curved track, 4 sections OS straight track, 1 controlling rheostat, 1 No. 068 warning signal, 1 OTC "Lockon" connection. Track forms an oval 50 by 30 inches. Train is 36½ inches long. Price $13.25

Code Word "DART"

Nos. 299 and 299E

Outfit No. 299—Comprises 1 No. 254 Super-Motor reversible locomotive with 2 electric headlights, 1 No. 814 box car, 1 No. 813 cattle car, 1 No. 817 caboose, 8 sections OC curved track, 6 sections OS straight track, 1 controlling rheostat, 1 No. 068 warning signal, 1 OTC "Lockon" connection. Track forms an oval 60 by 30 inches. Train is 40½ inches long. Price $17.00

Code Word "FLORA"

No. 299E Electrically-Controlled Freight Train Outfit—Same as No. 299, but it contains No. 254E Electrically-Controlled Super-Motor Locomotive, which can be started, stopped, reversed and operated at any speed, at any distance from the track, by means of No. 81 controlling rheostat supplied with it. Price $21.50

Code Word "QUILL"

Nos. 266 and 266E

Outfit No. 266—Comprises 1 No. 254 Super-Motor reversible locomotive with 2 electric headlights, 2 No. 610 illuminated Pullman cars, 1 No. 612 illuminated observation car, 8 sections OC curved track, 6 sections OS straight track, 1 controlling rheostat, 1 No. 068 warning signal, 1 OTC "Lockon" connection. Track forms an oval 60 by 30 inches. Train is 40½ inches long. Price $17.00

Code Word "HEAD"

No. 266E Electrically-Controlled Passenger Train Outfit—Same as No. 266 except that it contains No. 254E Electrically-Controlled Super-Motor Locomotive, which can be started, stopped, reversed and operated at any speed, at any distance from the track, by means of No. 81 controlling rheostat supplied with it. Price $21.50

Code Word "ILION"

Passenger and Freight Train Outfits
FOR "O" GAUGE TRACK—1 3/8 INCHES WIDE

Nos. 97 and 97E

Outfit No. 97—Comprises 1 No. 251 Super-Motor Reversible Locomotive with 2 electric headlights, 2 No. 605 illuminated Pullman cars, 1 No. 606 illuminated observation car, 8 sections OC curved track, 8 sections OS straight track, 1 controlling rheostat, 1 No. 068 warning signal, 1 OTC "Lockon" connection. Track forms an oval 70 by 30 inches. Train is 43¼ inches long. Price $22.50

Code Word "EXCEL"

No. 97E "Distant-Control" Passenger Train Outfit—Same as No. 97, but it contains No. 251E "Distant-Control" Super-Motor Locomotive, which can be started, stopped, reversed and operated at any speed at any distance from the track by means of No. 81 controlling rheostat supplied with it. Price $25.50

Code Word "JUST"

Nos. 269 and 269E

Outfit No. 269—Comprises 1 No. 251 Super-Motor Reversible Locomotive with 2 electric headlights, 1 No. 812 gondola car, 1 No. 813 cattle car, 1 No. 814 box car, 1 No. 815 oil car, 1 No. 817 caboose, 8 sections OC curved track, 6 sections OS straight track, 1 controlling rheostat, 1 No. 068 warning signal, 1 OTC "Lockon" connection. Track forms an oval 60 by 30 inches. Train is 61 inches long. Price $25.00

Code Word "USHER"

No. 269E "Distant-Control" Freight Train Outfit—Same as No. 269, but it contains No. 251E "Distant-Control" Super-Motor Locomotive, which can be started, stopped, reversed and operated at any speed at any distance from the track by means of No. 81 controlling rheostat supplied with it. Price $28.00

Code Word "NECK"

THE BIG MOGUL OF THE "O" GAUGE LINE
POWERFUL TWIN-MOTORS! OPERATING PANTAGRAPHS! FLAGS!

No. 268

Outfit No. 268—Comprises 1 No. 256 Twin-Super-Motor Reversible Locomotive with 2 electric headlights, 2 No. 710 illuminated Pullman cars, 1 No. 712 illuminated observation car, 8 sections OC curved track, 8 sections OS straight track, 1 controlling rheostat, 1 No. 068 warning signal, 1 OTC "Lockon" connection. Track forms an oval 70 by 30 inches. Train is 51 inches long. Price $33.00

Code Word "TAKE"

Train Outfit No. 268 with its powerful Super-Motor Locomotive and Illuminated Passenger Cars is the finest "O" Gauge Train in the world. You may use with it our new Freight Cars Nos. 811 to 817, illustrated on Page 29. The locomotive will haul 20 of these Freight Cars with perfect ease.

Complete Railroads

For "O" Gauge Track
1⅜ INCHES WIDE

BOYS—here are two wonderful complete railroads that can be set up in very small space. Operate them from the alternating house current with a Lionel "Multivolt" Transformer.

No. 174

NO. 174 Outfit shown above is a complete model railroad to operate on "O" Gauge Track. It includes a large variety of accessories. Every piece is of steel construction and enameled by Lionel's own lustrous and lasting process.

Outfit No. 174 comprises 1 No. 252 reversible locomotive with electric headlight, 2 No. 607 illuminated Pullman cars, 1 No. 608 illuminated observation car, 10 sections OC curved track, 6 sections OS straight track, 1 OTC "Lockon" connection, 1 controlling rheostat, 1 pair No. 021 illuminated switches (one right, one left), 1 No. 106 bridge (3 sections), 1 No. 122 illuminated station, 6 No. 60 telegraph posts, 2 No. 62 semaphores, 1 No. 068 warning signal, 1 No. 119 tunnel. Size of track layout 45 by 60 inches. Train is 35½ inches long. Price **$37.50**

Code Word "DELA"

No. 175E

A NEW COMPLETE "O" GAUGE "DISTANT-CONTROL" RAILROAD

NO. 175E—Introduced to fill the demand for a complete 100% "Distant-Control" "O" Gauge Railroad at a moderate price. The train can be started, stopped, reversed and operated at any speed at any distance from the track. The electric switches can also be controlled at any distance from the track. The No. 437 Switch Tower contains levers by which the Railroad can be operated, and lamp posts illuminated. This is an ideal Lionel Railroad to fit into a small space.

Outfit comprises 1 No. 254E "Distant-Control" locomotive, 2 No. 610 illuminated Pullman cars, 1 No. 612 illuminated observation car, 1 No. 080 semaphore, 1 No. 069 warning signal, 1 No. 90 flag staff, 1 No. 106 bridge, 1 pair No. 012 electrically-controlled switches, 1 No. 437 signal tower, 1 No. 119L illuminated tunnel, 2 No. 56 lamp posts, 8 No. 60 telegraph posts, 1 No. 81 controlling rheostat, 1 OTC "Lockon" connection, 10 sections OC curved track, 16 sections OS straight track. Complete with wires for connecting to source of current, "Lockon" connections, track on bridge, and special track for electric accessories. Track layout is 100 inches by 40 inches. Train is 40½ inches long. Price **$65.00**

Code Word "DAWN"

This Is How Bild-a-Loco Is Assembled

Bild-a-Loco
TRADE-MARK. PATENTS PENDING

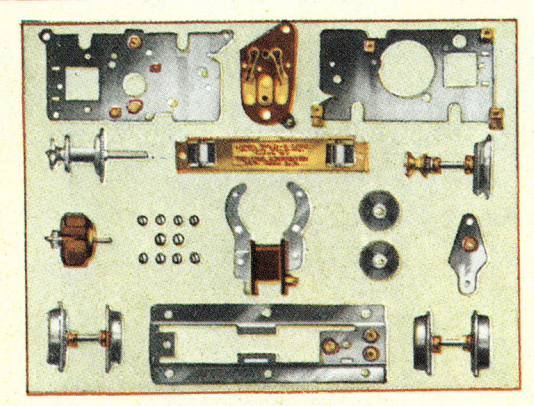

LIONEL'S LATEST TRIUMPH!

LIONEL "BILD-A-LOCO" is a supreme achievement in the development of an interesting and educational form of model railroad engineering for every boy. It is the world's premier construction set. Unlike all other construction sets, when "Bild-a-Loco" is assembled it has a definite purpose—it is the beginning of a Lionel Complete Railroad. The parts are so accurately made that even the youngest boy can assemble them within a few minutes, and when put together they make the most powerful and efficient miniature motor that has ever been designed. It is installed in the locomotive body in a fraction of a minute, and is all ready to operate on Lionel Track that is part of the outfit. Imagine what fun it is to add Pullman and Freight Cars as well as the most realistic and up-to-date railroad accessories that only Lionel can make. By simply removing the driving wheels and replacing them with heavy steel shafts containing pulleys, drums, sprockets, etc., a powerful three-speed reversible motor can be constructed that will raise more than 20 times its own weight, and can be used for innumerable purposes.

The illustrations show the simple method of constructing a "Bild-a-Loco" as well as a Power Motor.

One of the oustanding features of Lionel "Bild-a-Loco" is the fact that there is not a single wire to connect. All connections are automatically made. Lionel "Bild-a-Loco" was first introduced and advertised in 1919, but was ahead of its time. Then the boy was content with just toys—now he demands educational models. No boy can build a "Bild-a-Loco" without getting a better understanding of electricity and mechanics.

On the following pages we illustrate the perfect packing of all the parts that form Lionel "Bild-a-Loco" so none of them can be lost. Each part has a nest of its own in a very heavy steel tray. Clamps securely hold each piece in position. All parts are heavily nickeled and polished and will retain their brightness and lustre forever.

See following pages for "Bild-a-Loco" Outfits and Assembled "Bild-a-Loco" Locomotives

With these parts of precision—

You make this motor in a few moments—

By adding this frame—

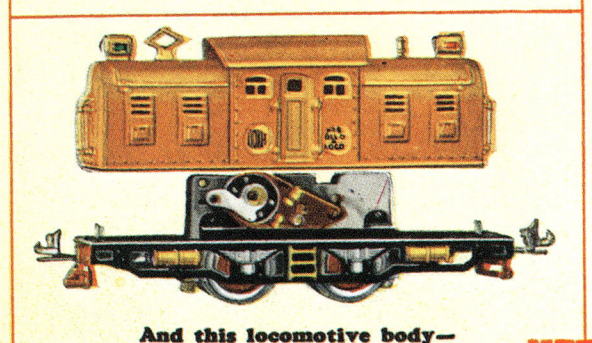

And this locomotive body—

You have a complete Super-Motor Locomotive.

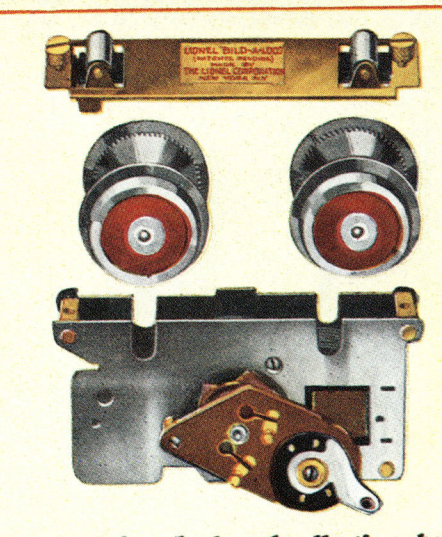

Remove the wheels and collecting shoe—

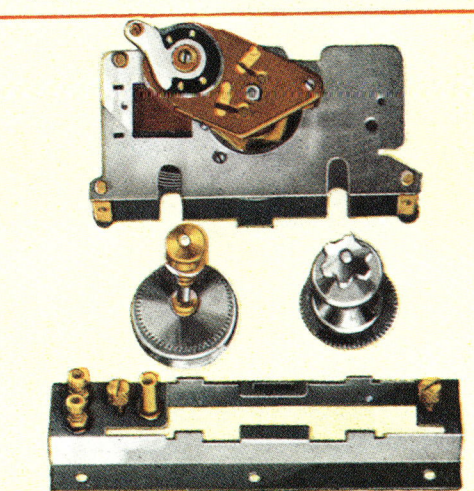

Add these gears, pulley, drum, sprocket and base—

And behold—you have a powerful three-speed reversible Power Motor

13

1928

Bild-a-Loco AND "BILD-A-MOTOR" OUTFITS
TRADE-MARK. PATENTS PENDING   TRADE-MARK. PATENTS PENDING

No. 4U Lionel "O" Gauge "Bild-a-Loco" Outfit—This outfit contains all parts for making No. 4 "Bild-a-Loco" Locomotive illustrated on Page 16, together with 8 sections OC curved track and 1 OTC "Lockon" connection. In addition to the motor parts, special gearing, pulleys, drum, sprocket and base are supplied for constructing Lionel No. 1 "Bild-a-Motor." This motor is reversible, and by means of the various gears three different speeds can be obtained at the same time. The outfit is very attractively and substantially packed. Simple directions for assembling are included. Size of assembled locomotive is given on Page 16.
Price $20.00
Code Word "GRAIL"

No. 9U "Lionel Standard" "Bild-a-Loco" Outfit—This outfit contains all the parts for making No. 9 "Bild-a-Loco" Locomotive illustrated on Page 16. Particular attention is drawn to the body of this locomotive which contains an enormous amount of realistic detail. Included with this outfit are 8 sections C curved track and 1 STC "Lockon" connection, together with gears, pulleys, drum, sprocket and base required for making Lionel No. 2 "Bild-a-Motor." This motor is reversible, and by means of the pulleys three different speeds can be obtained at the same time. All motor parts are numbered and it is an extremely simple matter to assemble the motor in a few moments. Size of assembled locomotive is given on Page 16.
Price $27.50
Code Word "GILT"

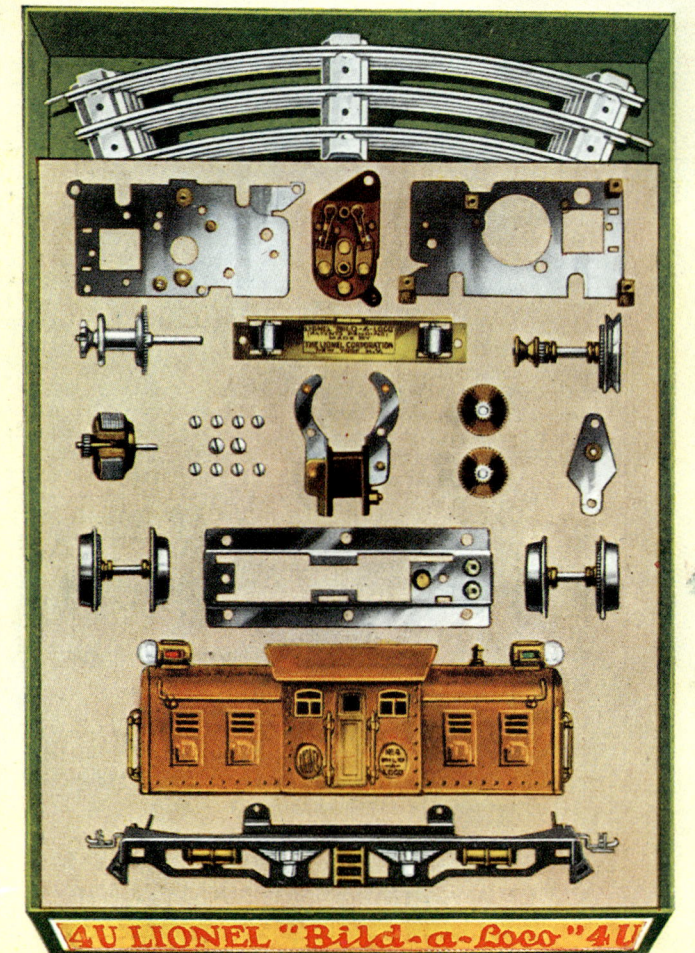

4U LIONEL "Bild-a-Loco" 4U

With this "Bild-a-Loco" Outfit You Can Build

This Powerful Super-Motor Reversible Locomotive

And This Three-Speed Reversible Power-Motor

9U LIONEL "Bild-a-Loco" 9U

With This "Bild-a-Loco" Outfit You Can Build

This Powerful Super-Motor Reversible Locomotive—

And This Three-Speed Reversible Power-Motor

Bild-a-Loco and "Bild-A-Motor" Outfits

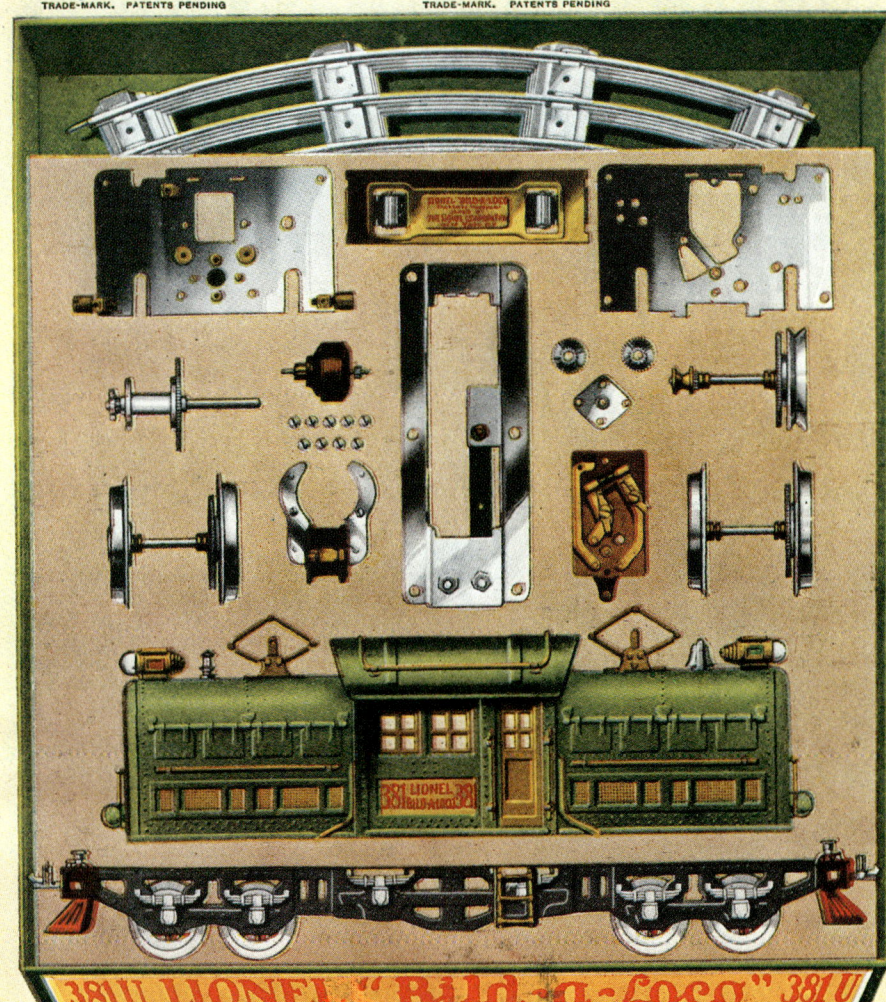

TRADE-MARK. PATENTS PENDING.

381U LIONEL "Bild-a-Loco" 381U

With this "Bild-a-Loco" Outfit You Can Build

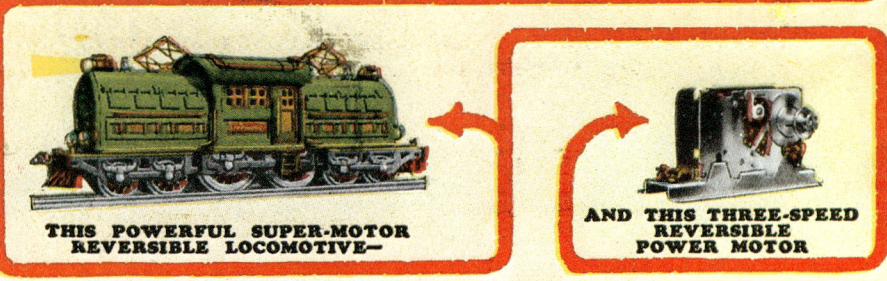

THIS POWERFUL SUPER-MOTOR REVERSIBLE LOCOMOTIVE—

AND THIS THREE-SPEED REVERSIBLE POWER MOTOR

No. 381U "Lionel Standard" "Bild-a-Loco" Outfit (Patents Pending)—This outfit contains all the parts for making No. 381 "Bild-a-Loco" Locomotive illustrated on Page 16. This locomotive is the largest in the Lionel line. In addition to the many features contained in all Lionel Locomotives this model is equipped with two massive pilot trucks containing 4 wheels each. These trucks are so scientifically designed that they will not leave the track irrespective of the speed of the locomotive. Included with the outfit are 8 sections C curved track and 1 STC "Lockon" connection, as well as gears, pulleys, drum sprocket and base required for making Lionel No. 2 "Bild-a-Loco." This motor is reversible and by means of the pulleys three different speeds can be obtained at the same time. Size of assembled locomotive is given on Page 16.
Price $42.50
Code Word "COPE"

"BILD-A-MOTOR"
TRADE-MARK. PATENTS PENDING.

No. 1 Lionel Three-Speed Reversible "Bild-a-Motor"—This motor is the most powerful of its size ever made. Various speeds can be had by using the different gears, pulleys, drum and sprocket. This motor is made in units so that it can be taken down within a minute, but when assembled is so powerful and rigid that it will lift at least 20 times its own weight. By means of a controlling lever, motor can be started, stopped and reversed.
Price $10.00
Code Word "LIFT"

No. 2 Lionel Three-Speed Reversible "Bild-a-Motor" — This motor is similar to the No. 1 in construction, but is larger and more powerful. It can be used for a great many purposes and will develop great power, while at the same time it uses a minimum amount of current. This motor is instructive as well as useful, as all parts can be easily assembled. Can be operated on dry or storage batteries, as well as on reduced alternating or direct current. Price . $15.00
Code Word "HOIST"

Bild-a-Loco AND "BILD-A-MOTOR"
TRADE-MARK. PATENTS PENDING.

Are Invaluable Aids To A Thorough Knowledge Of Electricity

No. 1 "Bild-a-Motor"—Size of the motor is 5½ inches long, 3 inches high, 3 inches wide. Will operate on dry or storage batteries, or on reduced alternating or direct current.

No. 2 "Bild-a-Motor"—Dimensions are 7 inches long, 3⅜ inches high, 4 inches wide. Will operate on dry or storage batteries, or on reduced alternating or direct current.

Assembled Bild-a-Loco Locomotives
TRADE-MARK. PATENTS PENDING

No. 4 "Bild-A-Loco" Locomotive
For "O" Gauge Track

This locomotive is completely assembled and contains the "Bild-a-Loco" Motor described on the previous page. Not only is this locomotive beautiful in appearance and extremely powerful, but the boy will obtain a great amount of education and amusement by being able to remove the motor from the body and take down and assemble all of the motor parts in a jiffy. The body of this locomotive is similar to the No. 254 and No. 254E described on page 8, and is equipped with automatic couplers and 2 electric headlights. All Lionel "Bild-a-Loco" locomotives are in a class by themselves—there is nothing in the world like them. Size—10 inches long—4¼ inches high. Price $15.00

Code Word "URGE"

BOYS! You'll Double Your Fun By Adding a New "Bild-A-Loco" Model Locomotive To Your Railroad Layout

"BILD-A-LOCO" Locomotives Nos. 9E and 381E for "Lionel Standard" Track have the Lionel "Distant-Control" unit incorporated in them. Not only can you take them apart and assemble them in a few moments, but you can also stop, start, reverse or operate them at any speed at any distance from the track.

No. 9 E "Distant-Control" "Bild-A-Loco" Locomotive
For "Lionel Standard" Track

In addition to the interesting design of the "Bild-a-Loco" Motor, this locomotive also contains our electric controlling unit which makes it possible to start, stop and reverse the locomotive at any distance from the track. The body is beautifully designed and contains many features that are typically Lionel. Locomotive contains two electric headlights so arranged that the front one is always illuminated irrespective of the direction in which the locomotive is traveling. This locomotive is equipped with automatic couplers. It measures 14⅝ inches long, 6¼ inches high. No. 81 controlling rheostat is included. Price $27.50

Code Word "UTTER"

No. 381E "Distant-Control" "Bild-A-Loco" Locomotive
For "Lionel Standard" Track

This locomotive is the most elaborate in the Lionel Line. The illustration shows the great detail incorporated in it, and special mention is made of the construction of the two 4-wheel pilot trucks which will not derail even when the locomotive is traveling at a high rate of speed. The "Bild-a-Loco" Motor and electric-controlling mechanism can be removed from the body in a jiffy, and the illustration on the previous page shows the accessibility to all parts. The boy can at will take down and rebuild this motor within a few minutes. It is not amiss to repeat that all parts are so accurately made that no difficulty will be experienced in setting it up, and there is not a single wire to be connected, as all electrical contacts are automatically made. It is extremely efficient, and powerful enough to haul a dozen or more of the largest Pullman or Freight Cars with the greatest ease. Nothing in the way of a model electric locomotive has ever been made here or abroad to compare with this supreme model.

Size—18½ inches long, 8½ inches high.
Price, including No. 81 controlling rheostat $42.50

Code Word "ULTI"

16

Super-Motor Locomotives for "Lionel Standard" Track

— 2¼ INCHES WIDE —

Nos. 8 and 8E

No. 8 "Lionel Standard" Super-Motor Reversible Locomotive — with 2 electric headlights. 11 inches long, 4½ inches high. Price **$11.50**
Code Word "POWER"

No. 8E "Lionel Standard" "Distant-Control" Super-Motor Locomotive — Same as No. 8, but equipped with electrically-controlled mechanism which starts, stops, reverses and operates it at any speed at any distance from the track by means of No. 81 controlling rheostat supplied with it. Price **$17.75**
Code Word "PEPPY"

Above locomotives are for use with Passenger Cars Nos. 332, 337, 338, 339 and 341—Freight Cars Nos. 511 to 517, 218 and 219.

Nos. 10 and 10E

No. 10 "Lionel Standard" Super-Motor Reversible Locomotive — with 2 electric headlights. 11½ inches long, 5¼ inches high. Price **$13.75**
Code Word "PULL"

No. 10E "Lionel Standard" "Distant-Control" Super-Motor Locomotive — Same as No. 10, but equipped with electrically-controlled mechanism which starts, stops, reverses and operates it at any speed at any distance from the track by means of No. 81 controlling rheostat supplied with it. Price **$20.00**
Code Word "SELF"

Above locomotives are for use with Passenger Cars Nos. 332, 337, 338, 339 and 341—Freight Cars Nos. 511 to 517, 218 and 219.

Nos. 318 and 318E

No. 318 "Lionel Standard" Super-Motor Reversible Locomotive — with 2 electric headlights. 12½ inches long, 5⅜ inches high. Price **$16.50**
Code Word "VERB"

No. 318E "Lionel Standard" "Distant-Control" Super-Motor Locomotive — Same as No. 318, but equipped with electrically-controlled mechanism which starts, stops, reverses and operates it at any speed at any distance from the track by means of No. 81 controlling rheostat supplied with it. Price **$22.75**
Code Word "MOVE"

Above locomotives are for use with Passenger Cars Nos. 309, 310 and 312—Freight Cars Nos. 511 to 517, 218 and 219.

No. 380E

No. 380E "Lionel Standard" "Distant-Control" Super-Motor Locomotive — with 2 electric headlights. 13½ inches long, 5½ inches high. This locomotive is equipped with electrically-controlled mechanism which starts, stops, reverses and operates it at any speed at any distance from the track by means of No. 81 controlling rheostat supplied with it. Price **$25.50**
Code Word "SAINT"

Above locomotive is for use with Passenger Cars Nos. 428, 429, 430 and 431—Freight Cars Nos. 211 to 219.

All "Lionel Standard" Locomotives are equipped with automatic couplers and 2 electric headlights. Lamps for headlights are included. Details of construction of "Lionel Standard" Super-Motors are given on Page 5. NOTE: Length of couplers on locomotives is not included in dimensions given in specifications.

Twin-Super-Motor "Distant-Control" Locomotives for "Lionel Standard" Track
2¼ INCHES WIDE

THE new Twin-Super-Motor "Distant-Control" Locomotives shown on this page are the only ones made that will operate on direct current as well as on alternating current, dry cells or storage batteries. This is also true of all Lionel single motor "Distant-Control" locomotives described throughout the catalog. A patented electrical device makes it possible to operate or reverse these locomotives without using more current than models that are reversed by hand. When the "Distant-Control" Locomotive is running forward, front headlight is illuminated—when it is reversed, rear one shines brilliantly and forward one is automatically cut out.

All Lionel Locomotives with "Distant-Control" mechanism incorporate an exclusive device which also enables them to be reversed by hand.

No. 408E "Lionel Standard" De-Luxe Twin-Super-Motor "Distant-Control" Locomotive—One of Lionel's greatest achievements. The illustration clearly shows the great amount of realistic detail incorporated in it. In addition to the details of construction indicated on Page 6, this locomotive includes two operating pantographs, two illuminated signal lanterns on front and rear of locomotive, four flags, and an enormous amount of extra special detail in the superstructure. It is indeed a triumph of model engineering skill.

This locomotive is 17 inches long, and 8½ inches high to top of pantograph. It can be started, stopped, reversed and operated at any speed at any distance from the track by means of No. 81 controlling rheostat supplied with it. Complete with flags, lamps for headlights, also for front and rear lanterns.

Price $44.00
Code Word "FAST"

No. 408E

No. 402E "Lionel Standard" "Distant-Control" Twin-Super-Motor Locomotive—Many of the structural features found in No. 408E are incorporated in this beautiful and powerful model. It will haul a large number of our big passenger or freight cars with perfect ease.

This locomotive is equipped with "Distant-Control" mechanism which starts, stops, reverses and operates it at any speed at any distance from the track by means of No. 81 controlling rheostat supplied with it. Size, 17 inches long, 6½ inches high. Complete with two electric lamps for headlights. Price $40.00
Code Word "YORK"

The locomotives shown on this page are for use with Passenger Cars Nos. 428, 429, 430, 431, 418, 419 and 490, illustrated on Page 31; also with Freight Cars Nos. 211 to 219, illustrated on Pages 27 and 28.

Train Outfits for "Lionel Standard" Track—2¼ Inches Wide

Reg. U.S. Pat. Office

LIONEL Train Outfits are complete in every respect. Lamps for headlights and passenger cars are supplied with every outfit, wires for transformer or battery connection, and connecting ties for joining sections of track. All "Lionel Standard" Trains are equipped with automatic couplers.

Nos. 347 and 347E

Outfit No. 347—Comprises 1 No. 8 Super-Motor reversible locomotive with 2 electric headlights, 1 No. 337 illuminated Pullman car, 1 No. 338 illuminated observation car, 8 sections C curved track, 2 sections S straight track, 1 STC "Lockon" connection. Track forms an oval 56 by 42 inches. Train is 38½ inches long. Price $18.00
Code Word "ZENA"

Outfit No. 347E—Same as No. 347, except that it contains No. 8E "Distant-Control" Super-Motor locomotive, which can be started, stopped, reversed and operated at any speed at any distance from the track by means of No. 81 controlling rheostat supplied with it. Price . . . $22.75
Code Word "GLIDE"

Nos. 353 and 353E

Outfit No. 353—Comprises 1 No. 8 Super-Motor reversible locomotive with 2 electric headlights, 1 No. 511 lumber car with load of lumber, 1 No. 512 gondola car, 1 No. 517 illuminated caboose, 8 sections C curved track, 2 sections S straight track, 1 STC "Lockon" connection. Track forms an oval 56 by 42 inches. Train is 49¼ inches long. Price $20.00
Code Word "JACK"

Outfit No. 353E—Same as No. 353, except that it contains No. 8E "Distant-Control" Super-Motor locomotive, which can be started, stopped, reversed and operated at any speed at any distance from the track by means of No. 81 controlling rheostat supplied with it. Price . . . $25.50
Code Word "MASK"

Nos. 352 and 352E

Outfit No. 352—Comprises 1 No. 10 Super-Motor reversible locomotive with 2 electric headlights, 1 No. 332 illuminated mail and baggage car, 1 No. 339 illuminated Pullman car, 1 No. 341 illuminated observation car, 8 sections C curved track, 4 sections S straight track, 1 STC "Lockon" connection. Track forms an oval 69 by 42 inches. Train is 52 inches long. Price $25.00
Code Word "PRINCE"

Outfit No. 352E—Same as No. 352, except that it contains No. 10E "Distant-Control" Super-Motor locomotive, which can be started, stopped, reversed and operated at any speed at any distance from the track by means of No. 81 controlling rheostat supplied with it. Price . . . $30.75
Code Word "WIN"

Nos. 354 and 354E

Outfit No. 354—Comprises 1 No. 10 Super-Motor Reversible locomotive with 2 electric headlights, 1 No. 511 lumber car with load of lumber, 1 No. 512 gondola car, 1 No. 513 cattle car, 1 No. 514 box car, 1 No. 517 illuminated caboose, 8 sections C curved track, 6 sections S straight track, 1 STC "Lockon" connection. Track forms an oval 88 by 42 inches. Train is 75¼ inches long. Price $25.00
Code Word "ZONE"

Outfit No. 354E—Same as No. 354, except that it contains No. 10E "Distant-Control" Super-Motor locomotive, which can be started, stopped, reversed and operated at any speed at any distance from the track by means of No. 81 controlling rheostat supplied with it. Price . . . $30.75
Code Word "ZEST"

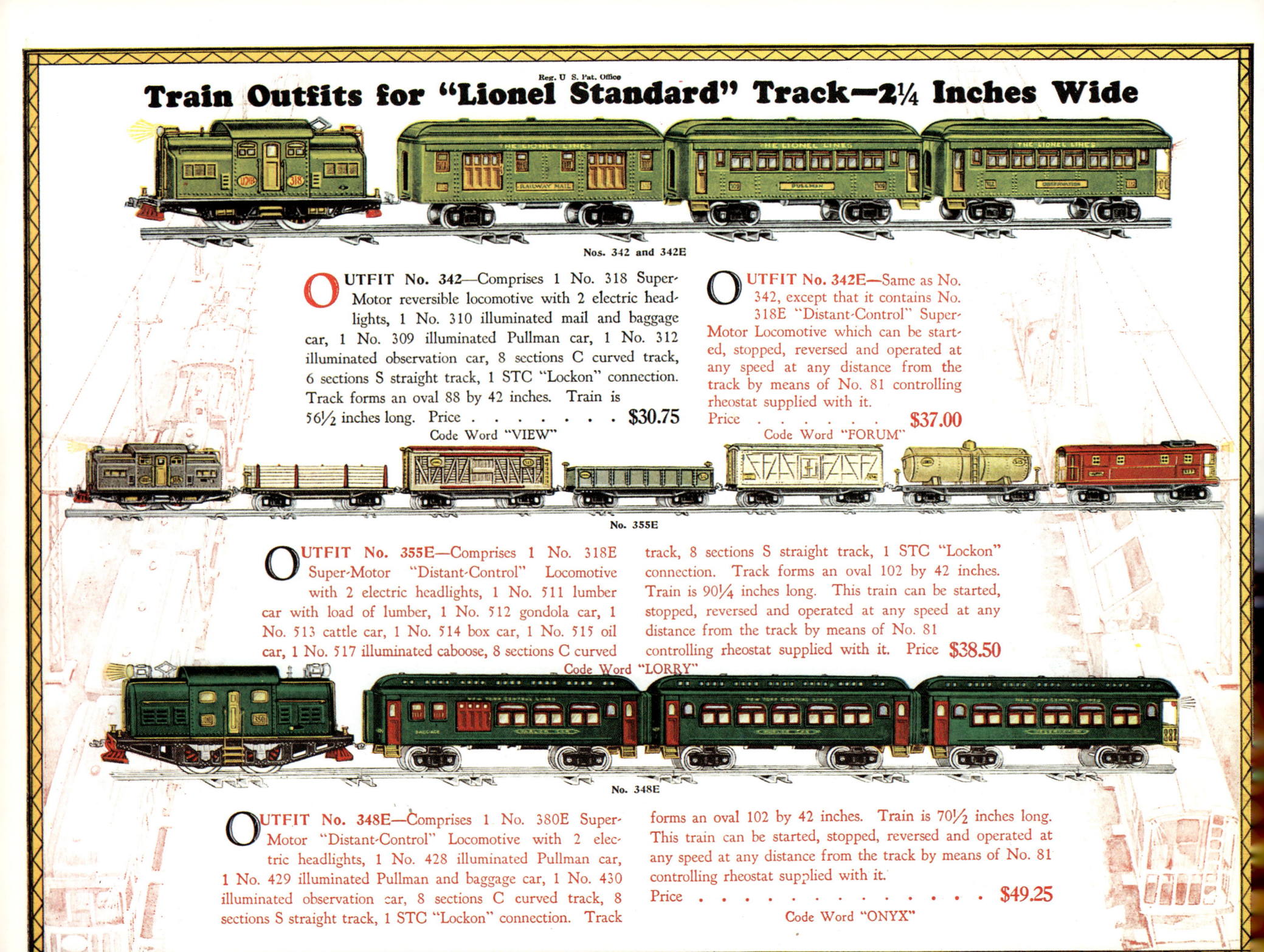

Train Outfits for "Lionel Standard" Track—2¼ Inches Wide

Reg. U S. Pat. Office

Nos. 342 and 342E

OUTFIT No. 342—Comprises 1 No. 318 Super-Motor reversible locomotive with 2 electric headlights, 1 No. 310 illuminated mail and baggage car, 1 No. 309 illuminated Pullman car, 1 No. 312 illuminated observation car, 8 sections C curved track, 6 sections S straight track, 1 STC "Lockon" connection. Track forms an oval 88 by 42 inches. Train is 56½ inches long. Price $30.75

Code Word "VIEW"

OUTFIT No. 342E—Same as No. 342, except that it contains No. 318E "Distant-Control" Super-Motor Locomotive which can be started, stopped, reversed and operated at any speed at any distance from the track by means of No. 81 controlling rheostat supplied with it.
Price $37.00

Code Word "FORUM"

No. 355E

OUTFIT No. 355E—Comprises 1 No. 318E Super-Motor "Distant-Control" Locomotive with 2 electric headlights, 1 No. 511 lumber car with load of lumber, 1 No. 512 gondola car, 1 No. 513 cattle car, 1 No. 514 box car, 1 No. 515 oil car, 1 No. 517 illuminated caboose, 8 sections C curved track, 8 sections S straight track, 1 STC "Lockon" connection. Track forms an oval 102 by 42 inches. Train is 90¼ inches long. This train can be started, stopped, reversed and operated at any speed at any distance from the track by means of No. 81 controlling rheostat supplied with it. Price $38.50

Code Word "LORRY"

No. 348E

OUTFIT No. 348E—Comprises 1 No. 380E Super-Motor "Distant-Control" Locomotive with 2 electric headlights, 1 No. 428 illuminated Pullman car, 1 No. 429 illuminated Pullman and baggage car, 1 No. 430 illuminated observation car, 8 sections C curved track, 8 sections S straight track, 1 STC "Lockon" connection. Track forms an oval 102 by 42 inches. Train is 70½ inches long. This train can be started, stopped, reversed and operated at any speed at any distance from the track by means of No. 81 controlling rheostat supplied with it.
Price $49.25

Code Word "ONYX"

Passenger, Freight and Work Trains for

No. 357 E—"Distant-Control" Work Train

HERE is a new outfit to operate on "Lionel Standard" Track, that will greatly increase the play value of Lionel Trains. It is a work train in every sense of the word. The Derrick car actually operates, and the Dump Car can be tilted by means of the gears at one end. The Gondola contains working implements, barrels, etc., and the realism of the entire train is heightened by the illuminated Caboose at the rear end. Nothing so perfect has ever been shown in the way of a model train outfit.

This Outfit includes No. 380E "Distant-Control" locomotive, 1 No. 81 controlling rheostat, 1 No. 212 gondola car, 1 No. 218 dump car, 1 No. 219 derrick car, 1 No. 217 illuminated caboose, 8 sections C curved track, 8 sections S straight track, and 1 STC "Lockon" connection. Track forms an oval 102 by 42 inches. Train is 69 inches long.
Price . . . . (Code Word "ZEAL") $50.00

ALL THESE TRAINS HAVE THE FA STOPPED, REVERSED AND

No. 403 E—Twin-Super-Motor "Distant-Control" Passenger Train—A Perfect Model

COMPLETE details showing the perfect construction of every part that enters into this outfit are given on the following pages: Twin-Motor construction on Page 5, Locomotive construction and construction of Passenger Coaches on Page 6.

The great hauling power of the locomotive is an outstanding feature. The "Distant-Control" mechanism built into it is a source of end-less delight. It can be started, sto speed at any distance from the build a complete 100% "Distant train with our "Distant-Control" a are described in other parts of this time to time.

No. 410 E—Twin-Super-Motor "Distant-Control" Freight Train—A Powerful De-Luxe Freighter

THIS new De-Luxe "Distant-Control" Freight Train is the acme of perfection. The illustrations give you a clear idea of the wonderful detail in the new freight cars which incorporate many original and exclusive features that only Lionel can carry out to such perfection.

Attention is drawn to the heavy steel frames upon which the super-structure is mounted, the new steel trucks with nickeled journals, automatic couplers, embossed rivets and other structural det car bodies also show a wealth of deta sliding doors. The Lumber Car with inserted in sockets in the platform. which operates by turning a wheel o with illuminated lanterns on the rear

"Lionel Standard" Track—2¼ Inches Wide

LIONEL TRAINS AND REAL TRAINS DIFFER ONLY IN SIZE

...MOUS LIONEL "DISTANT-CONTROL" MECHANISM. THEY CAN BE STARTED, ...OPERATED AT ANY SPEED, AT ANY DISTANCE FROM THE TRACK

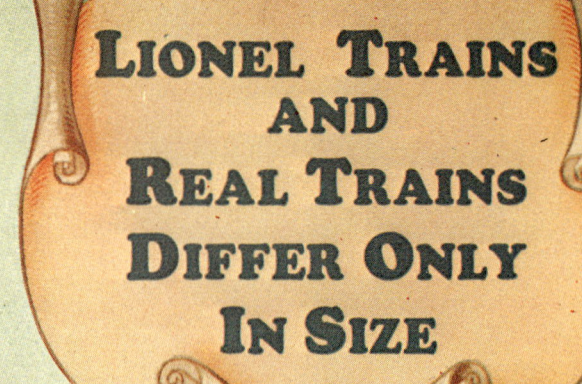

...ped, reversed and operated at any ...k. It is wonderful to be able to ...Control" Railroad by using this ...cessories, a large variety of which ...catalog. They can be added from

Outfit No. 403E—Comprises 1 No. 402E Twin-Super-Motor "Distant-Control" locomotive with 2 electric headlights, 1 No. 418 illuminated Pullman car, 1 No. 419 illuminated Pullman and baggage car, 1 No. 490 illuminated observation car, 8 sections C curved track, 8 sections S straight track and 1 STC "Lockon" connection, 1 No. 81 controlling rheostat. Track forms an oval 102 by 42 inches. Train

is 74½ inches long. This train is completely equipped with the new Lionel Automatic Spring Couplers. Outfit also includes lamps for headlights and interiors of cars, wires for connecting to source of current, and connecting ties for joining sections of track.
Price **$67.75**

Code Word "DEMY"

...ils that are so perfectly designed. The ... The Cattle Car and Box Car have ...load of lumber has removable supports ...he Coal Car has a "Hopper" bottom ... the top. The Caboose is equipped ... platform. The powerful Twin-Super-

Motor "Distant-Control" locomotive No. 408E described on Page 18 will easily haul this train and it can be started, stopped, reversed and operated at any speed at any distance from the track.
Outfit No. 410E—Comprises 1 No. 408E Twin-Super-Motor "Distant-Control" locomotive with 2 electric headlights, 1 No. 211 lumber car with load of lumber, 1 No. 212 gondola car, 1 No. 213 cattle car, 1 No. 214 box car, 1 No.

215 oil car, 1 No. 216 coal car, 1 No. 217 illuminated caboose, 8 sections C curved track, 10 sections S straight track, 1 STC "Lockon" connection and 1 No. 81 controlling rheostat. Train is 109¾ inches long. Track forms an oval 116 by 42 inches. Outfit also includes lamps for headlights, locomotive lanterns and caboose, wires for transformer or battery connection and connecting ties for joining section of track. Price . . (Code Word "BEST") **$75.00**

Passenger, Freight and Work Trains for

No. 357 E—"Distant-Control" Work Train

HERE is a new outfit to operate on "Lionel Standard" Track, that will greatly increase the play value of Lionel Trains. It is a work train in every sense of the word. The Derrick car actually operates, and the Dump Car can be tilted by means of the gears at one end. The Gondola contains working implements, barrels, etc., and the realism of the entire train is heightened by the illuminated Caboose at the rear end. Nothing so perfect has ever been shown in the way of a model train outfit.

This Outfit includes No. 380E "Distant-Control" locomotive, 1 No. 81 controlling rheostat, 1 No. 212 gondola car, 1 No. 218 dump car, 1 No. 219 derrick car, 1 No. 217 illuminated caboose, 8 sections C curved track, 8 sections S straight track, and 1 STC "Lockon" connection. Track forms an oval 102 by 42 inches. Train is 69 inches long.
Price . . . . (Code Word "ZEAL") $50.00

ALL THESE TRAINS HAVE THE FA
STOPPED, REVERSED AND

No. 403 E—Twin-Super-Motor "Distant-Control" Passenger Train— A Perfect Model

COMPLETE details showing the perfect construction of every part that enters into this outfit are given on the following pages: Twin-Motor construction on Page 5, Locomotive construction and construction of Passenger Coaches on Page 6.

The great hauling power of the locomotive is an outstanding feature. The "Distant-Control" mechanism built into it is a source of end- less delight. It can be started, stop speed at any distance from the tra build a complete 100% "Distant train with our "Distant-Control" are described in other parts of this time to time.

No. 410 E—Twin-Super-Motor "Distant-Control" Freight Train — A Powerful De-Luxe Freighter

THIS new De-Luxe "Distant-Control" Freight Train is the acme of per- fection. The illustrations give you a clear idea of the wonderful detail in the new freight cars which incorporate many original and exclusive features that only Lionel can carry out to such perfection.
Attention is drawn to the heavy steel frames upon which the super-structure is mounted, the new steel trucks with nickeled journals, automatic couplers, embossed rivets and other structural det car bodies also show a wealth of deta sliding doors. The Lumber Car with inserted in sockets in the platform. which operates by turning a wheel o with illuminated lanterns on the rear

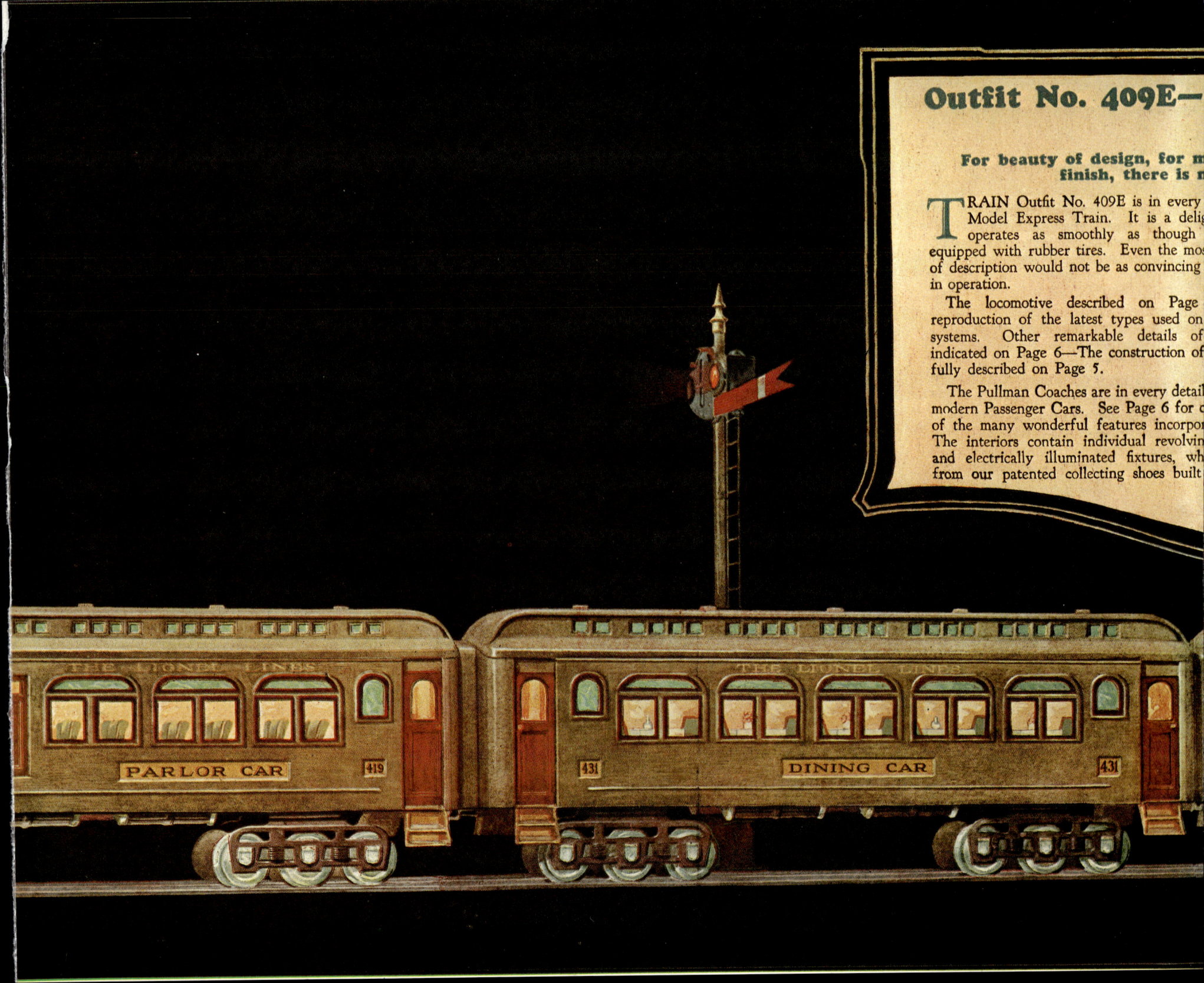

Outfit No. 409E—

**For beauty of design, for m...
finish, there is n...**

TRAIN Outfit No. 409E is in every...
Model Express Train. It is a delig...
operates as smoothly as though...
equipped with rubber tires. Even the mos...
of description would not be as convincing...
in operation.

The locomotive described on Page...
reproduction of the latest types used on...
systems. Other remarkable details of...
indicated on Page 6—The construction of...
fully described on Page 5.

The Pullman Coaches are in every detail...
modern Passenger Cars. See Page 6 for c...
of the many wonderful features incorpor...
The interiors contain individual revolvin...
and electrically illuminated fixtures, wh...
from our patented collecting shoes built...

PARLOR CAR 419

DINING CAR 431

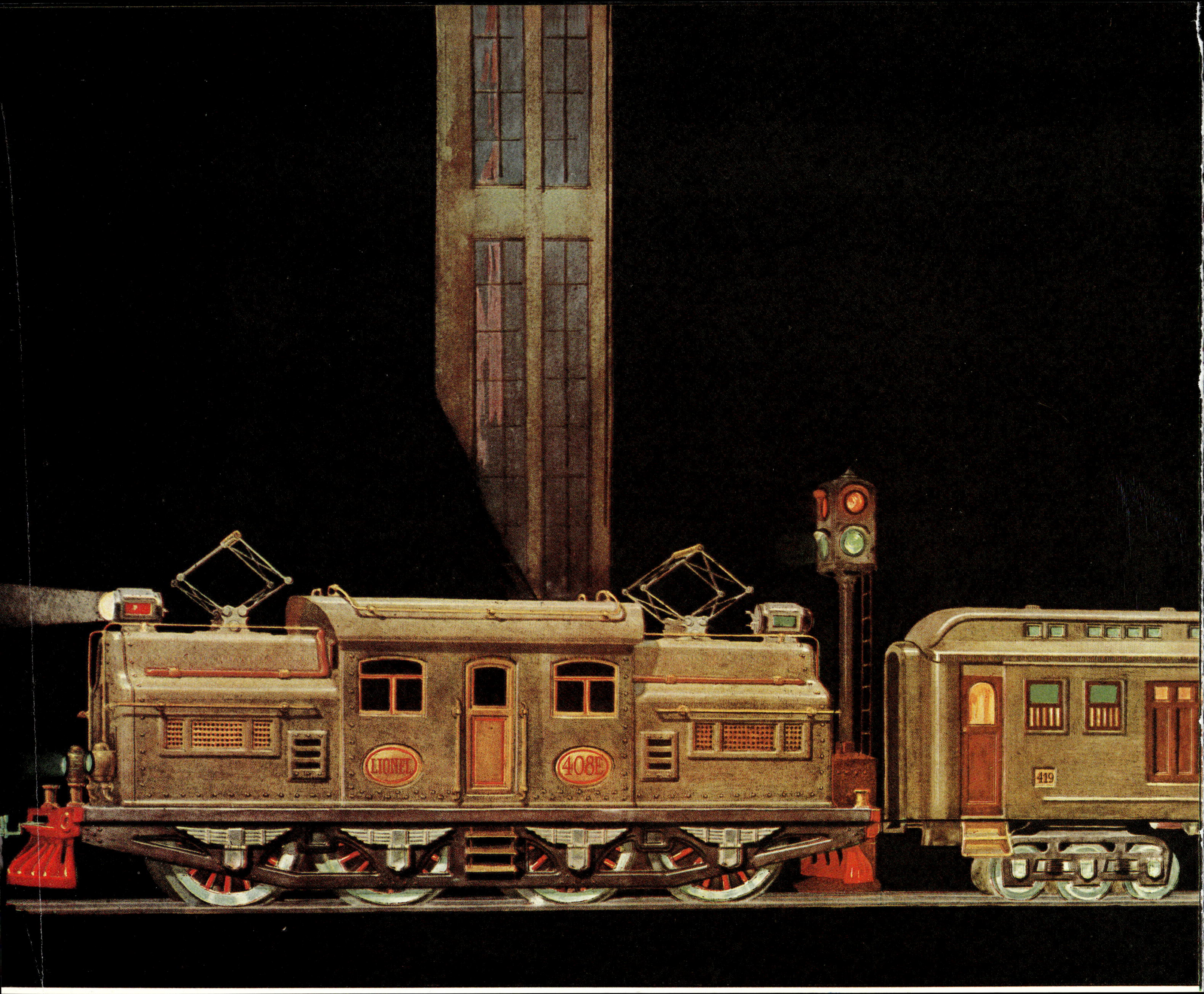
LIONEL
408E
419

"Lionel Standard" Track—2¼ Inches Wide

LIONEL TRAINS AND REAL TRAINS DIFFER ONLY IN SIZE

...MOUS LIONEL "DISTANT-CONTROL" MECHANISM. THEY CAN BE STARTED, ...OPERATED AT ANY SPEED, AT ANY DISTANCE FROM THE TRACK

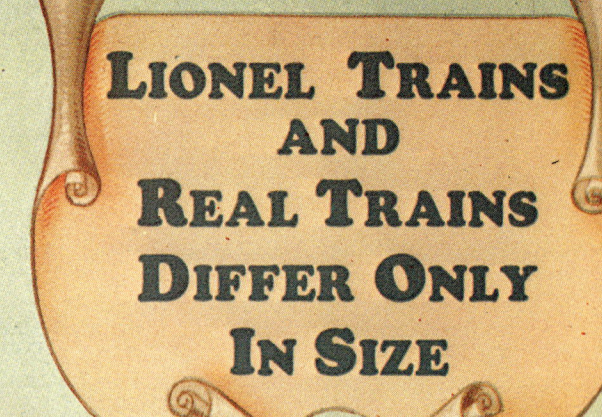

...ped, reversed and operated at any ...k. It is wonderful to be able to ...Control" Railroad by using this ...cessories, a large variety of which ...catalog. They can be added from

Outfit No. 403E—Comprises 1 No. 402E Twin-Super-Motor "Distant-Control" locomotive with 2 electric headlights, 1 No. 418 illuminated Pullman car, 1 No. 419 illuminated Pullman and baggage car, 1 No. 490 illuminated observation car, 8 sections C curved track, 8 sections S straight track and 1 STC "Lockon" connection, 1 No. 81 controlling rheostat. Track forms an oval 102 by 42 inches. Train is 74½ inches long. This train is completely equipped with the new Lionel Automatic Spring Couplers. Outfit also includes lamps for headlights and interiors of cars, wires for connecting to source of current, and connecting ties for joining sections of track. Price **$67.75**

Code Word "DEMY"

...ils that are so perfectly designed. The ...The Cattle Car and Box Car have ...oad of lumber has removable supports ...he Coal Car has a "Hopper" bottom ...the top. The Caboose is equipped ...platform. The powerful Twin-Super-Motor "Distant-Control" locomotive No. 408E described on Page 18 will easily haul this train and it can be started, stopped, reversed and operated at any speed at any distance from the track.

Outfit No. 410E—Comprises 1 No. 408E Twin-Super-Motor "Distant-Control" locomotive with 2 electric headlights, 1 No. 211 lumber car with load of lumber, 1 No. 212 gondola car, 1 No. 213 cattle car, 1 No. 214 box car, 1 No. 215 oil car, 1 No. 216 coal car, 1 No. 217 illuminated caboose, 8 sections C curved track, 10 sections S straight track. 1 STC "Lockon" connection and 1 No. 81 controlling rheostat. Train is 109¾ inches long. Track forms an oval 116 by 42 inches. Outfit also includes lamps for headlights, locomotive lanterns and caboose, wires for transformer or battery connection and connecting ties for joining section of track. Price . . (Code Word "BEST") **$75.00**

...onel Twin-Super-Motor De-Luxe Special—the World's Finest "Distant-Control" Model Train

...nical detail and precision, for electrical perfection and efficiency, for handsome and lasting enamel
...model electric train in the world that compares with this—Lionel's supreme achievement

a De-Luxe
behold, and
...heels were
...lative terms
...g the outfit

an exact
...g electrified
...ruction are
...in-motors is

to the most
description
these cars.
...-car chairs
...ain current
...e six-wheel

trucks. The interior light shining through the colored glass windows produces a very realistic effect.

A feature of the observation car is the dome light on the rear platform (in addition to the interior light) which shows through two red signal lanterns. The transparent "Lionel Limited" sign affixed to the observation railing is another interesting new detail.

The new Dining-Car is real in everything but size. On Page 6 the sectional view of this car shows tables, chairs and kitchen completely equipped with range, serving table and a profusion of other details. This is the only completely equipped model Dining-Car made in America.

The Pullman and Baggage Car has two compartments—one is equipped with revolving parlor-car chairs, while the baggage section has sliding doors as used on all cars of this type. All cars are equipped with automatic couplers.

This train is Electrically-Controlled and can be started, stopped, reversed and operated at any speed at any distance from the track.

Outfit No. 409E Comprises

1 No. 408E "Distant-Control" Twin-Super-Motor Locomotive with 2 electric headlights and front and rear green lanterns, 1 No. 418 Illuminated Pullman car, 1 No. 419 Illuminated Pullman and baggage car, 1 No. 490 Illuminated observation car, 1 No. 431 Illuminated dining-car, 8 Sections C curved track, 10 Sections S straight track, 1 No. 81 Controlling rheostat and 1 STC "Lockon" connection.

Lamps for headlights, front and rear lanterns and interior of cars are included, as well as flags, wires for connecting to source of current and connecting ties for joining sections of track. Track forms an oval 116 by 42 inches. Complete train is 95 inches long. Price **$85.00**

Code Word "ETTA"

The "Lionel Standard" 100% "Distant-Control" Complete Railroad

HERE is the finest gift that any boy could wish for—a complete Lionel "Distant-Control" Railroad, containing not only the best trains we manufacture, but a very large variety of Electrically-Controlled and illuminated Accessories. The Passenger and Freight Trains can be started, stopped, reversed and operated at any speed at any distance from the track. The Switch Signal Tower, shown in the foreground, and the elevated Tower in the rear, enable you to operate all the Electrically-Controlled Accessories at a distance. The specifications of this marvelous model Railroad are given below.

OUTFIT No. 407E—COMPRISES

1 No. 408E "Distant-Control" Locomotive	1 No. 213 Cattle car	38 S Track
1 No. 380E "Distant-Control" Locomotive	1 No. 214 Box car	18 C Track
2 No. 81 Controlling rheostats	1 No. 215 Oil car	4 ½S Track
1 No. 418 Pullman car	1 No. 216 Coal car	1 No. 124 Station
1 No. 419 Pullman and baggage car	1 No. 217 Illuminated Caboose	1 No. 189 Villa
1 No. 490 Observation car	1 No. 218 Operating Dump car	1 No. 191 Villa
1 No. 431 Dining car	1 No. 219 Operating Derrick car	3 No. 184 Bungalows
1 No. 211 Lumber car with load of lumber	1 No. 84 Semaphore	1 No. 438 Signal Tower
1 No. 212 Gondola car	1 Type K Transformer	1 No. 101 Bridge
	3 pr. 222 Switches	1 No. 140L Tunnel
	2 No. 23 Bumpers	12 No. 60 Telegraph Posts

1 No. 78 Train Control	2 No. 59 Lamp posts
1 No. 80 Semaphore	20 STC "Lockon" connections
2 No. 77 Crossing gates	
1 No. 89 Flag Staff	
2 No. 76 Block signals	
1 No. 69 Warning signal	
1 No. 436 Power house	
1 No. 437 Switch tower	
2 No. 67 Lamp posts	
4 No. 56 Lamp posts	
2 No. 57 Lamp posts	

Wires for making electrical connections, connecting ties for joining sections of track, lamps for headlights, interior of cars and all illuminated accessories are supplied with this outfit. Track layout is 12 feet 10 inches long by 6 feet 4 inches wide. Price complete **$300.00**

Code Word "ALLY"

"Lionel Standard" Operating Derrick and Dump Cars

FOR USE WITH ALL LOCOMOTIVES OPERATING ON "LIONEL STANDARD" TRACK—2¼ INCHES WIDE

No. 219 Operating Derrick Car

BOYS—here is the most realistic railroad Derrick Car ever built in miniature. Think of the fun you will have operating it just like a real derrick. You can raise or lower the boom, swing it from side to side, and hoist weights with the pulley and tackle. In fact, this Derrick Car will do everything—the same as real ones. All mechanical movements are controlled by wheels that operate worm gears. The mechanical arrangement is absolutely similar to that found in large Derrick Cars. By means of the worm gears the position of the boom and location of the housing are not affected by the weights that are lowered or raised. They are always in a rigid position, except when changed by means of the levers. The mechanism is mounted on a solid steel car—11¾ inches long, 5⅝ inches high. The boom is 16 inches long. Car is equipped with automatic couplers. Price . $8.50

Code Word "ALUM"

No. 218 Operating Dump Car

Bring up a load of sand or ballast, boys! We must finish that roadbed by to-morrow and run the first Lionel Limited over the new short cut. The new Lionel Operating Dump Car is a marvel of mechanical ingenuity. Not only does it look like the real cars used in the construction of railroads, but it actually dumps the load at any place desired along the track. The mechanical movements that automatically open and tilt the sides of the car are controlled by wheels and worm gears. The Lionel Operating Dump Car is 11¾ inches long, 4½ inches high. Entirely constructed of sheet steel and beautifully finished by Lionel's famous enameling process. Equipped with automatic couplers. Price $5.85

Code Word "DEPEW"

New Freight Cars for "Lionel Standard" Track—2¼ Inches Wide

Reg. U. S. Pat. Office

No. 512 Gondola Car—11¼ inches long, 3¼ inches high. Price $2.25
Code Word "EVER"

No. 515 Oil Car—11¼ inches long, 5¼ inches high. Price $3.00
Code Word "ELTA"

No. 516 Coal Car—11¼ inches long, 4½ inches high. Has "Hopper" bottom, operated by wheel. Price $3.35
Code Word "EPIC"

No. 511 Lumber Car with load of lumber—11¼ inches long, 3 inches high. Price . $2.25
Code Word "EDEN"

No. 514 Refrigerator Car—11¼ inches long, 5 inches high. Price $2.95
Code Word "EAST"

All "Lionel Standard" Freight Cars are equipped with automatic couplers. Length of couplers on cars is not included in dimensions given in specifications.

No. 517 Illuminated Caboose—11¼ inches long, 5½ inches high. Complete with interior lamp. Price $3.35
Code Word "EAGER"

"Lionel Standard" Freight Cars Nos. 511 to 517 are for use with Locomotives Nos. 8, 8E, 9E, 10, 10E, 318 and 318E. Cars Nos. 211 to 217 can be used with Locomotives Nos. 380E, 381E, 402E and 408E.

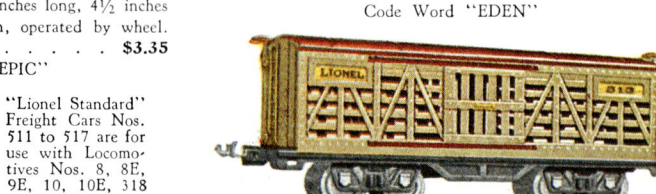

No. 513 Cattle Car—11¼ inches long, 5 inches high. Price $2.95
Code Word "EBON"

No. 211 Lumber Car with load of lumber—11¾ inches long, 3¾ inches high. Price . $3.35
Code Word "ANT"

No. 213 Cattle Car—11¾ inches long, 5¾ inches high. Price $4.50
Code Word "WAKE"

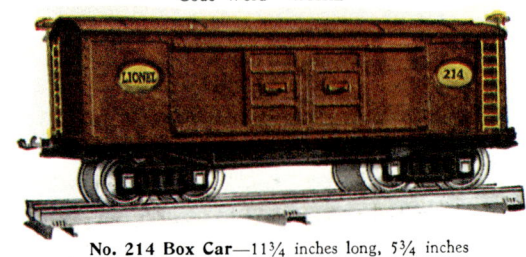

No. 214 Box Car—11¾ inches long, 5¾ inches high. Price $4.50
Code Word "WOOL"

ON Page 6 you will find full details of construction of this marvelous new line of Freight Cars to operate on "Lionel Standard" Track. The illustrations clearly show that every known type of modern car is faithfully reproduced by us. It is great fun to convert your "Lionel Standard" Passenger Train into a big Freighter by adding an assortment of these well-built and handsomely finished cars. Let us repeat that all Lionel Freight Cars are of steel construction throughout. The fittings, such as hand rails, hand brakes, steps, ladders and inserted panels are all made of brass, highly polished. Wheels, journals and axles are of heavy nickeled steel. Beyond doubt, these cars reach the peak of perfection in model railroad rolling stock. The "O" Gauge Cars listed on the opposite page incorporate a great many of the features of these large Freight Cars.

No. 217 Illuminated Caboose—11¾ inches long, 6 inches high. Complete with electric lamp. Price $5.35
Code Word "RAFT"

No. 212 Gondola Car—11¾ inches long, 3½ inches high. Price $3.35
Code Word "ROY"

No. 215 Oil Car—11¾ inches long, 6 inches high. Price $4.50
Code Word "DICE"

No. 216 Coal Car—Has "Hopper" bottom, operated by wheel on side. 11¾ inches long, 4⅞ inches high. Price $4.50
Code Word "ALAMA"

28

New Freight Cars and Sets for Lionel "O" Gauge Track—1⅜ Inches Wide

No. 805 Box Car—6¾ inches long, 3 inches high.

No. 807 Caboose—6¾ inches long, 3½ inches high.

No. 806 Cattle Car—6¾ inches long, 3 inches high.

No. 803 Coal Car—Has "Hopper" bottom, operated by wheel at side.
Price $.85
Code Word "LOAD"

No. 804 Oil Car
Price $.65
Code Word "FUEL"

No. 805 Box Car
Price $.90
Code Word "VICK"

No. 806 Cattle Car
Price $1.00
Code Word "VEX"

No. 807 Caboose
Price $1.00
Code Word "VAT"

No. 831 Lumber Car with load of lumber
Price $.65
Code Word "VEST"

No. 902 Gondola Car
Price $.65
Code Word "VOTE"

Length of couplers on cars is not included in dimensions given in specifications. Cars Nos. 803, 804, 805, 806, 807, 831 and 902 are for use with Locomotives Nos. 248 and 252.

No. 803 Coal Car—6¾ inches long, 3¼ inches high.

No. 804 Oil Car—6¾ inches long, 3⅝ inches high.

No. 831 Lumber Car—6¾ inches long, 2¼ inches high.

No. 808 "O" Gauge Freight Car Set—Comprises 1 each Nos. 831 Lumber Car, 803 Coal Car, 804 Oil Car, 805 Box Car, 806 Cattle Car, 807 Caboose, described on this page. Very attractively packed. Price $5.00
Code Word "QUORN"

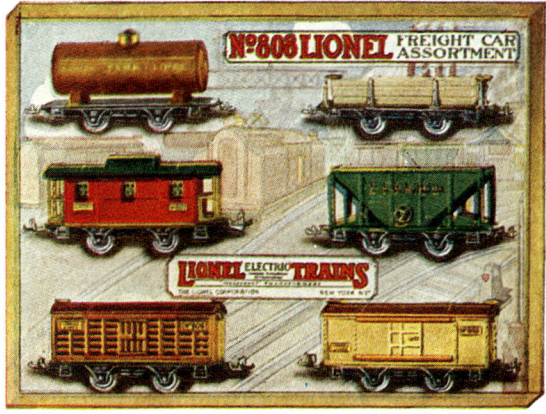

No. 902 Gondola Car—6¾ inches long, 2¼ inches high.

No. 818 "O" Gauge Freight Car Set—Comprises 1 each Nos. 812 Gondola Car, 814 Box Car, 816 Coal Car, 817 Caboose, described on this page. Very attractively packed. Price $8.75
Code Word "QUEST"

No. 811 Lumber Car with load of lumber
Price $1.75
Code Word "DRUM"

No. 812 Gondola Car
Price $1.75
Code Word "DALE"

No. 813 Cattle Car
Price $2.10
Code Word "YAWL"

No. 814 Box Car
Price $2.10
Code Word "YOKE"

No. 815 Oil Car
Price $2.10
Code Word "YAM"

No. 816 Coal Car—Has "Hopper" bottom, operated by wheel at side.
Price $2.50
Code Word "YOST"

No. 817 Caboose
Price $2.50
Code Word "DEFT"

Length of couplers on cars is not included in dimensions given in specifications. Cars Nos. 811 to 817 are for use with Locomotives Nos. 4, 4U, 253, 254, 254E, 251, 251E and 256.

No. 811 Lumber Car—9 inches long, 3 inches high.

No. 814 Box Car—9 inches long, 4 inches high.

No. 812 Gondola Car—9 inches long, 2¾ inches high.

No. 815 Oil Car—9 inches long, 4⅛ inches high.

No. 813 Cattle Car—9 inches long, 4 inches high.

No. 816 Coal Car—9 inches long, 3½ inches high.

No. 817 Caboose—9 inches long, 4½ inches high.

Passenger Cars for Lionel "O" Gauge Track—1⅜ Inches Wide

ALL Lionel "O" Gauge Passenger Cars (excepting Nos. 529, 530, 629 and 630) have interior lights and are mounted on two 4-wheel trucks. The observation cars have an ornamental brass platform and railing. Lamp is supplied with illuminated cars. Length of couplers on cars is not included in dimensions given in specifications.

THE construction of all Lionel Passenger Cars is worthy of special notice as it represents the highest form of miniature car manufacture. Not only are all bodies made of heavy steel and beautifully embossed with panels, rivets and other details, but they are soldered and rigidly held together by mechanical means. Cross braces and partitions placed inside the cars give still greater strength and make them almost indestructible. Some outstanding features of Lionel Passenger Cars are hinged doors, inserted window frames and sashes, interior seats, brass steps and handrails and miniature tanks which are affixed to the bottom of the body. The separable inserted pieces are enameled in a variety of colors to harmonize with car body, and accentuate the great detail incorporated in them. All Lionel Cars are handsomely enameled in a variety of attractive colors, and the lasting finish is baked on at high temperature. Roofs are firmly held in place with ornamental screw, easily removable so that interior lamp can be reached.

All cars are equipped with automatic couplers and are mounted on scientifically designed trucks with perfectly aligned nickeled wheels and axles. They operate without friction and are so absolutely true that they will not derail even when traveling at high speed. All the desirable features mentioned here will be seen by referring to the indications on page 6.

We have incorporated all these features in the "Lionel Standard" Passenger Cars illustrated on the opposite page.

No. 710

No. 710 Illuminated Pullman Car—11½ inches long, 4½ inches high. For use with Locomotive No. 256. Price $3.75
Code Word "HOLLY"

No. 605

No. 605 Illuminated Pullman Car—10⅜ inches long, 4¼ inches high. For use with Locomotives Nos. 251 and 251E. Price $3.25
Code Word "NOVA"

No. 610

No. 610 Illuminated Pullman Car—9 inches long, 3¾ inches high. For use with Locomotives Nos. 4, 4U, 253, 254 and 254E. Price $2.95
Code Word "EALING"

No. 607

No. 607 Illuminated Pullman Car—7½ inches long, 3⅜ inches high. For use with Locomotives Nos. 252 and 253. Price $1.65
Code Word "BRAND"

Nos. 529 and 629

No. 529 Pullman Car—6¾ inches long, 3¼ inches high. (Finished in green color.) Price . . . . $.75
Code Word "IMPY"

No. 629 Pullman Car—Same as No. 529, but finished in orange yellow color. For use with Locomotives Nos. 248 and 252. Price . . $.75
Code Word "FANE"

No. 712

No. 712 Illuminated Observation Car—Same dimensions as No. 710 Pullman Car illustrated above. For use with same locomotive. Price $3.85
Code Word "RISE"

No. 606

No. 606 Illuminated Observation Car—Same dimensions as No. 605 Pullman Car illustrated above. For use with same locomotives. Price $3.50
Code Word "MODE"

No. 612

No. 612 Illuminated Observation Car—Same dimensions as No. 610 Pullman Car illustrated above. For use with same locomotives. Price $3.15
Code Word "WALTON"

No. 608

No. 608 Illuminated Observation Car—Same dimensions as No. 607 Pullman Car illustrated above. For use with same locomotives. Price $1.75
Code Word "TWIG"

Nos. 530 and 630

No. 530 Observation Car—Same dimensions as No. 529 Pullman Car illustrated above. For use with same locomotives. Price . . . . $.80
Code Word "IONA"

No. 630 Observation Car—Same dimensions as No. 629 Pullman Car illustrated above. For use with same locomotives. Price . . . . $.80
Code Word "IDEAL"

Passenger, Baggage, Dining and Mail Cars for "Lionel Standard" Track
— 2¼ INCHES WIDE —

No. 338 Illuminated Observation Car — 12 inches long, 4¾ inches high.
Price . . . $5.00
Code Word "ORBIT"

No. 337 Illuminated Pullman Car — 12 inches long, 4¾ inches high.
Price . . . $4.25
Code Word "PASS"

No. 332 Illuminated Mail and Baggage Car — 12 inches long, 4¾ inches high. Finished in blue or olive green color.
Code Word "WILE"   Price . . $4.50

Cars Nos. 332, 337 and 338 are for use with "Lionel Standard" Locomotives Nos. 8, 8E, 9E, 10 and 10E.

Cars Nos. 339 and 341 are for use with "Lionel Standard" Locomotives Nos. 318 and 318E.

Cars Nos. 309, 310 and 312 are for use with "Lionel Standard" Locomotives Nos. 318, 318E and 380E.

Illustration shows dome light over platform on "Lionel Standard" Observation Cars — also red lanterns which are illuminated by dome light.

No. 312 Illuminated Observation Car — 13¼ inches long, 5⅛ inches high. Price . $5.85
Code Word "DOMO"
No. 341 Illuminated Observation Car — 12 inches long, 4¾ inches high. Same in construction and appearance as No. 312 Car.
Price . . . $5.50
Code Word "LEO"

No. 309 Illuminated Pullman Car — 13¼ inches long, 5⅛ inches high. Price . $5.00
Code Word "ROAD"
No. 339 Illuminated Pullman Car — 12 inches long, 4¾ inches high. Same in construction and appearance as No. 309 Car.
Price . . . $4.50
Code Word "STAR"

No. 310 Illuminated Mail and Baggage Car — 13¼ inches long, 5⅛ inches high. Baggage compartments have sliding doors. Price . $5.35
Code Word "WEC"

Illustration shows patented revolving shoe which collects current from the third rail for lighting interior of Passenger Coaches.

No. 490 Illuminated Observation Car — 17½ inches long, 6 inches high. Price . . . $9.50
Code Word "CABIN"
No. 430 Illuminated Observation Car — 17½ inches long, 6 inches high. Price . . . $8.50
Code Word "NERO"

Cars Nos. 418, 419, 490, 428, 429, 430 and 431 are for use with Locomotives Nos. 380E, 381E, 402E and 408E.

No. 419 Illuminated Pullman and Baggage Car — 17½ inches long, 6 inches high. Price . . . $8.75
Code Word "COURT"
No. 429 Illuminated Pullman and Baggage Car — 17½ inches long, 6 inches high. Price . . . $7.85
Code Word "DORA"

Cars Nos. 428, 429 and 430 are finished in a rich green color. They are exactly the same in construction as Nos. 418, 419 and 490, but are mounted on two 4-wheel trucks. These cars are illustrated on Page 20, in conjunction with outfit No. 348E.

ALL "Lionel Standard" cars are equipped with automatic couplers and interior lighting fixture, complete with electric lamp. Observation cars have ornamental polished brass platform and rails. Roofs are removable so that interior light can easily be reached. Length of couplers on cars is not included in dimensions given in specifications.

No. 418 Illuminated Pullman Car — 17½ inches long, 6 inches high. Price . . . $8.50
Code Word "COMFORT"
No. 428 Illuminated Pullman Car — 17½ inches long, 6 inches high. Price . . . $7.50
Code Word "IRIS"
Illustration shows revolving parlor car chairs installed in Cars Nos. 418, 419, 490, 428, 429 and 430.

To enable you to fully appreciate the fine interior fittings of Cars Nos. 418, 428 and 431, we illustrate them with the side removed, but the outside appearance is the same as Cars Nos. 419, 429, 430 and 490 shown on this page.

No. 431 Dining-Car — 17½ inches long, 6 inches high.
Price . . . $10.00
Code Word "FEED"
Illustration shows tables, chairs, kitchen compartment and equipment installed in this car. It can be used with Cars Nos. 418, 419, 490, 428, 429 and 430.

Specifications of Lionel "Multivolt" Transformers

LIONEL "Multivolt" Transformers are made completely at our own factories. Our Transformer department is the largest in the country devoted exclusively to the manufacture of low-voltage transformers. The only parts purchased are the raw materials. We correctly wind and insulate the coils, make the cases, laminations, switch handles, and in fact do every operation. Lionel "Multivolt" Transformers are listed as standard by the Underwriters' Laboratories.

SUB=BASE—A metal sub-base resting on four supports is attached to the bottom. The air, circulating between this sub-base and the transformer case, keeps it cool while in operation. Holes in this sub-base provide means for fastening to wall or table.

Separable Plug—All "Multivolt" Transformers are fitted with an approved, separable plug, which is a distinct advantage over the one-piece plug, because the circuit can be immediately broken.

Plug Protecting Device—A unique receptacle for protecting the plug against breakage in shipment. This device consists of a wooden container entirely covering the plug. It is sealed with a conspicuous label which draws attention to the fact that the transformer must be used *only* on *alternating* current of the number of cycles designated. This obviates the possibility of connecting the transformer with wrong current and avoids mishandling.

Double Contact Control Switch—This is infinitely superior to the one-piece switch, which is easily bent and does not make positive contact. Our double switch has a flexible, phosphor-bronze, contact arm under the rigid switch, so that positive contact with the points is assured. This flexible contact is protected from injury by the rigid brass handle to which it is attached. An exclusive feature of "Multivolt" Transformers.

Laminations—The laminations are made of the best grade of electrical sheets and the windings are perfectly insulated.

Rigid Supports for Coils—The coils and laminations of Lionel "Multivolt" Transformers are rigidly supported inside the case by means of metal bands which prevent these parts from moving and eliminate the possibility of broken lead wires. In addition to these supports, the interior of the case is fitted with an insulating receptacle and the case is air cooled.

Metal Case—The case is beautiful in design and is stamped of heavier steel than is required by the Underwriters laboratories.

Finish—"Multivolt" Transformer cases are covered with a rubberoid composition that is applied at 350 degrees Fahrenheit. This is much greater heat than the case is ever subjected to, and the finish cannot be scratched and will not peel off during the entire life of the transformer.

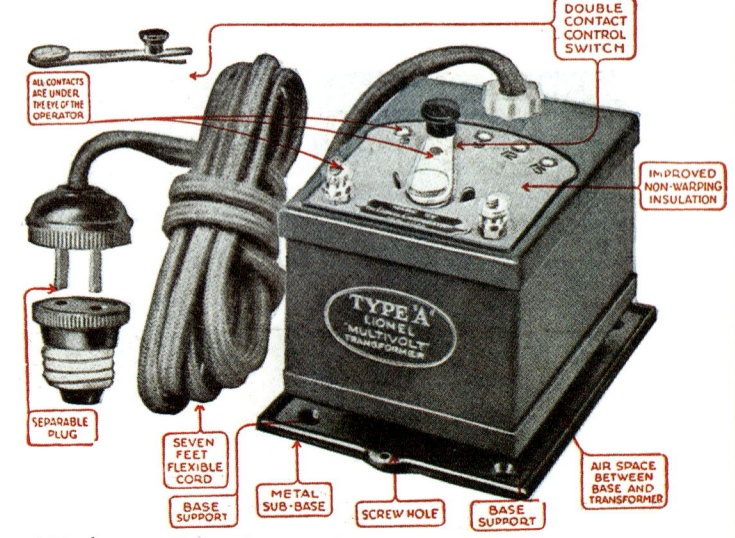

Visible Connections—All contacts and switches are mounted on one piece of heavy insulating material and are at the top of the transformer, right before the user.

Lamp Cord—All "Multivolt" Transformers are fitted with 7 feet of flexible lamp cord which enters the transformer case through an approved porcelain bushing.

It will be seen that "Multivolt" Transformers incorporate every device that will increase their efficiency.

LIONEL DIRECT CURRENT REDUCERS
[NOT TO BE USED ON ALTERNATING CURRENT]

NO. 107 Lionel Direct Current Reducer for 110=Volt Circuit—This is constructed of four porcelain tubes wound with best quality of resistance wire. These porcelain tubes are mounted on a substantial base measuring 8 by 10 inches and ¾ inches thick. The porcelain tubes are protected and ventilated by a perforated steel cover lined with heavy asbestos. The sliding lever regulates the voltage so that train will just crawl along or go ahead at express speed. The reducer is connected with the house current by a separable plug with 7 feet of flexible cord. Four porcelain supports with screws are supplied so that the reducer can be screwed to wall or table. Price . . . **$10.00**
Code Word "KENTUCKY"

No. 170 Lionel Direct Current Reducer for 220=Volt Circuit—This reducer is identical in appearance with No. 107, mentioned above, but is for use on 220 volts. Price . . . **$14.50**
Code Word "ASBURY"

CONTROLLING RHEOSTAT No. 81
[FOR BATTERIES]

NO. 81 Controlling Rheostat—With this rheostat you can, when using dry or storage batteries, operate all Lionel Trains at various speeds as well as start or stop them at any distance from the track. By sliding the finger from side to side, various speeds can be obtained, and by manipulating a small lever up and down, the current is turned on and off, so that the train can be started or stopped at will. The porcelain coil is protected by a perforated steel cover, and air holes prevent overheating. Size 5 inches long, 2½ inches wide. Price . **$2.50**
Code Word "BONE"

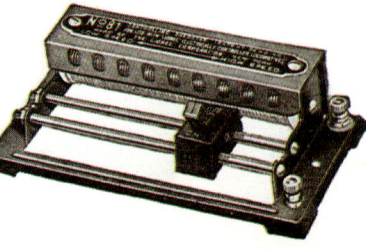

Lionel "Multivolt" Transformers—For 110 and 220 Volts—60, 40 and 25 Cycles

Power Houses for Transformers

THIS illustration shows transformer contained within the new Lionel Power Station, made in two sizes to accommodate every type of Lionel "Multivolt" Transformer. Full description of this desirable new accessory will be found on Page 39.

The Lionel Power Station is placed over the Transformer, and you can manipulate the controlling switch by simply raising the grating on the roof.

LIONEL "Multivolt" Transformers have been on the market for a great many years and operate all makes of Electric Trains. We justly claim they are best. Don't experiment with other makes of doubtful value. Remember, that all transformers look alike outside, but their imperfections will only be discovered after they are in actual use for a length of time. Lionel "Multivolt" Transformers will last indefinitely and are guaranteed unconditionally as long as they are used on the current for which they are intended. They are absolutely safe and will give steady, even power.

For Greatest Efficiency Always Use a Lionel "Multivolt" Transformer with a Lionel Train

Lionel "Multivolt" Transformers Are For Use Only on Alternating Current. Do Not Use Them on Direct Current.

Type "A" Transformer will operate any "O" gauge outfit.

For 110 volts, 60 cycles. 40 watts capacity.

Gives 15 volts in following steps: 4, 7, 10, 13, 15.

Size: 4¼ by 2¾ by 4¼ inches. Sub-base: 3¾ by 4¾ inches.

Price **$3.75**

Code Word "STRONG"

NOTE: Type "A" Transformer is recommended for use with the train outfits shown on Page 12.

Type "B" Transformer will operate any "O" gauge outfit, and in addition the extra binding posts enable the user to light up lamp-posts, semaphores and other electrically illuminated accessories.

For 110 volts, 60 cycles. 50 watts capacity.

Gives 25 volts in following steps:

Permanent: 7, 8, 15.

Variable: 2, 4, 6, 8, 9, 10, 11, 12, 13, 17, 19, 21, 23, 25.

Size: 4½ by 3¾ by 3 inches. Sub-base: 5 by 4¼ inches.

Price **$5.00**

Code Word "BRADLEY"

A fully guaranteed transformer at a very popular price.

Type "T" Transformer will operate any "O" gauge or "Lionel Standard" outfit; also has extra binding posts for attaching illuminated electrical accessories.

For 110 volts, 60 cycles. 100 watts capacity.

Gives 25 volts in following steps:

Permanent: 2, 4, 6, 7, 8, 10, 12, 14, 15, 16, 17, 18, 19, 21, 23, 25.

Variable: 2, 6, 8, 10, 12, 14, 16, 17, 18, 19, 21, 23, 25.

Size: 5 by 4 by 3¾ inches. Sub-base: 4½ by 5½ inches.

Price **$7.50**

Code Word "BIRCH"

Type "K" Transformer will operate any outfit as well as illuminated accessories. This transformer has sufficient wattage capacity to operate two trains at once.

Size: 5 by 4 by 4½ inches. Sub-base 4½ by 5½ inches.

"K"—For 110 volts, 60 cycles. 150 watts capacity. Specifications same as Type "T," but has higher wattage capacity. Price . . **$11.00**

Code Word (110 V.) "BINGHAM"

"K"—For 220 volts, 60 cycles. 150 watts capacity. Specifications same as Type "T," but is for use on 220-volt circuit.

Price **$14.50**

Code Word (220 V.) "BROOK"

Type "C" Transformer will operate any outfit and illuminated accessories on 25 or 40 cycle current.

For 110 volts, 25 to 40 cycles. 75 watts capacity. Specifications same as Type "T," but is for use on 25 or 40 cycle current.

Size: 5 by 4 by 4½ inches. Sub-base: 4½ by 5½ inches.

Price **$7.50**

Code Word "LAWRENCE"

This transformer is the best obtainable for use on 25 or 40 cycle current.

Lionel Electrically-Controlled Accessories

THESE accessories are exact models of the latest safety devices used on all railroads. They are made of steel, beautifully designed and very moderately priced. The construction is of Lionel quality throughout. The base is a die casting which incorporates considerable detail, such as hinged doors, embossed rivets, etc. The upright and ladder and other structural parts are made of steel, and are practically indestructible. The top of lantern is removable so that lamp in interior may be easily reached. Finished in a variety of beautiful enamels baked at high temperature.

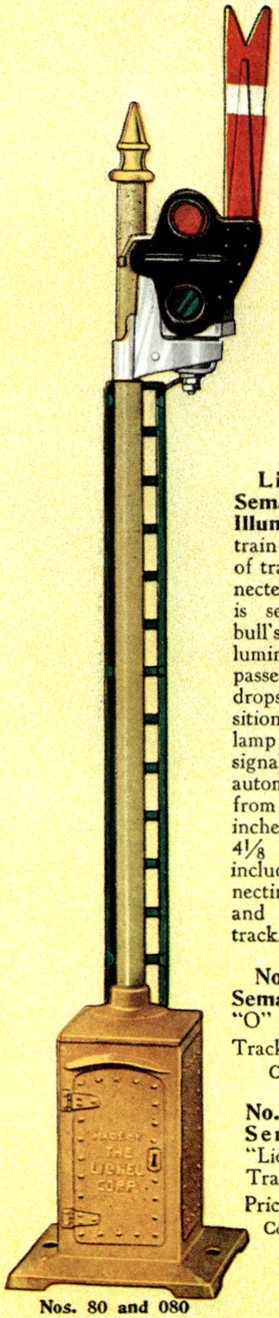

Lionel Automatic Semaphore (Electrically Illuminated) — When train passes over section of track to which it is connected the semaphore arm is set upright and red bull's-eye in lantern is illuminated. When train passes, the semaphore arm drops to horizontal position, and the electric lamp illuminates the green signal. It is absolutely automatic. The height from base to spire is 15 inches. Semaphore arm is 4 1/8 inches long. Price includes electric lamp, connecting wires, "Lockon" and special section of track.

No. 080 Automatic Semaphore—For Lionel "O" Gauge Track. Price . . $4.50
Code Word "DROP"

No. 80 Automatic Semaphore — For "Lionel Standard" Track. Price . . . $4.50
Code Word "DRAW"

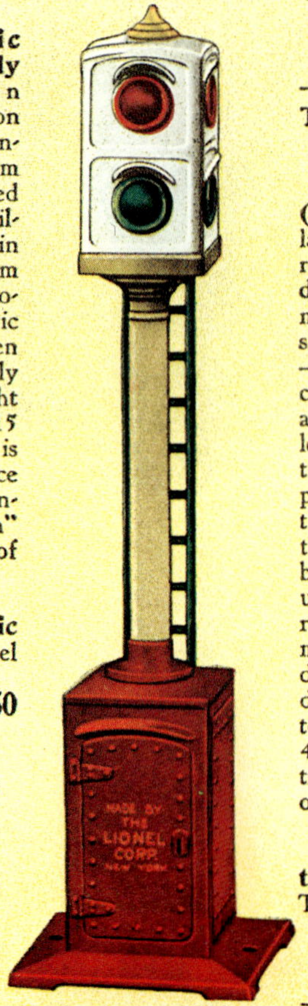

Lionel Automatic Train Control (Electrically Illuminated) — Positively amazing in its action. When train approaches section to which it is connected, red light shows and train automatically comes to a dead stop. After an interval of a few seconds, red light changes to green and train is on its way again. The controlling mechanism can be disconnected by means of a small lever so that train does not stop as it approaches the train control, which then shows a permanent green light. Lionel Train Control is 10 1/4 inches high. Price includes electric lamp, connecting wires and "Lockon."

No. 078 Automatic Train Control—For Lionel "O" Gauge Track. Price . . . $5.00
Code Word "HEAVE"

No. 78 Automatic Train Control—For "Lionel Standard" Track. Price $5.00
Code Word "WEAVE"

Lionel Semaphore-Train-Control (Electrically Illuminated) — Our latest marvel. As train approaches, the red light shines and semaphore arm drops, denoting "Caution." Train immediately comes to a dead stop. A short interval—light changes to green—semaphore arm goes up—train proceeds. It is startlingly real! It operates as if by magic! When desired, a lever in the base disconnects the controlling mechanism and sets the semaphore arm in an upright position so that train does not stop as it approaches the Semaphore-Train-Control. You will be absolutely thrilled as you watch the unique action of this almost-human railroad device. Lionel's skilled craftsmanship is exemplified to the highest degree in the construction of this very desirable accessory. Height from base to spire 15 inches. Semaphore arm is 4 1/8 inches long. Price includes electric lamp, connecting wires and "Lockon."

No. 082 Semaphore-Train-Control—For Lionel "O" Gauge Track. Price $8.50
Code Word "STILL"

No. 82 Semaphore-Train-Control—For "Lionel Standard" Track. Price $8.50
Code Word "STRIP"

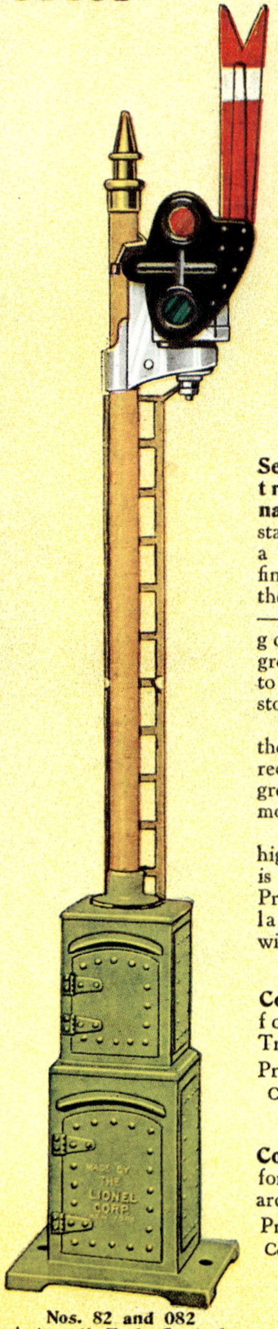

IN all Lionel Electrically-Controlled Accessories the electric unit is mounted on a solid piece of fibre which is protected in the interior of the base.

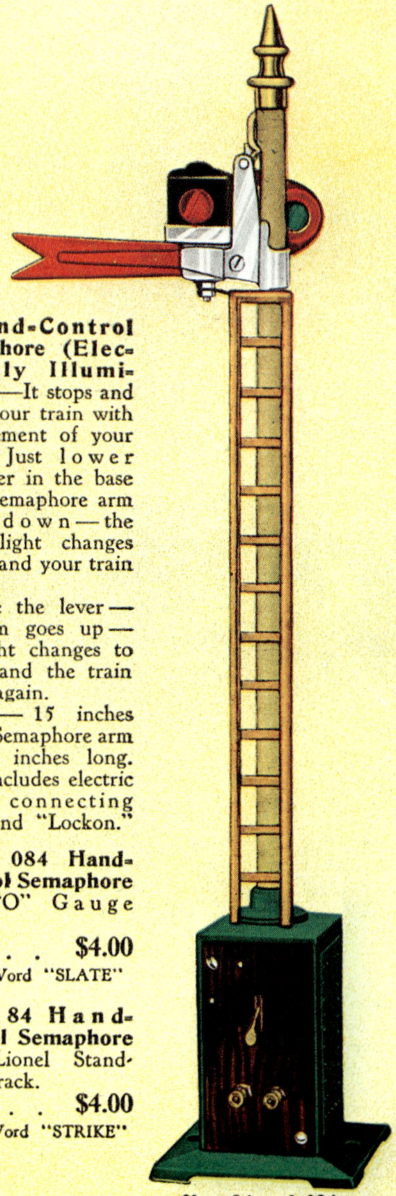

Hand-Control Semaphore (Electrically Illuminated)—It stops and starts your train with a movement of your finger. Just lower the lever in the base—the semaphore arm goes down—the green light changes to red, and your train stops!

Raise the lever—the arm goes up—red light changes to green, and the train moves again.

Size — 15 inches high. Semaphore arm is 4 1/8 inches long. Price includes electric lamp, connecting wires and "Lockon."

No. 084 Hand-Control Semaphore for "O" Gauge Track.
Price . . $4.00
Code Word "SLATE"

No. 84 Hand-Control Semaphore for "Lionel Standard" Track.
Price . . $4.00
Code Word "STRIKE"

Nos. 80 and 080 Automatic Semaphore with Electric Light.

Nos. 78 and 078 Automatic Train Control with Electric Lights.

Nos. 82 and 082 Automatic Train-Control-Semaphore with Electric Light.

Nos. 84 and 084 Hand-Control-Semaphore with Electric Light.

Lionel Electrically-Controlled Accessories

BOYS! See the lights flash on and off — see the gates go up and down — — hear the warning bells ring! The Action is Automatic!

No. 79

No. 79 Flashing Railroad Signal—This is a true reproduction of the very latest type of Crossing Signal used on electrified railroads. A Lionel patented thermostat is mounted in the base which flashes the red lights on and off alternately and continues to do so as long as the current is applied. An electric lamp can be used on "O" Gauge and "Lionel Standard" Track.

Price **$5.00**
Code Word "ROOM"

Nos. 69 and 069

Lionel Electric Warning Signals—Electric bell with 2 gongs is mounted on an ornamental steel standard, 8¾ inches high, which supports warning sign. Gongs ring while train passes over track section to which it is connected. Bell automatically stops when grade crossing is clear. This realistic accessory is finished in beautiful enameled colors, and bell is nickeled steel. Price includes special track, wires and "Lockon."

No. 069 Electric Warning Signal for Lionel "O" Gauge Track.
Price **$3.15**
Code Word "RINGER"

No. 69 Electric Warning Signal for "Lionel Standard" Track.
Price **$3.35**
Code Word "BEWARE"

No. 83

No. 83 Lionel Traffic and Crossing Signal—An ingenious and up-to-date Lionel accessory. The electric light in the red lantern flashes on and off just like the "blinker" light seen at street intersections. The mechanism is in the base, which also contains binding posts for attaching wires supplied with the signal. This signal is 6¼ inches high. Can be used with "O" Gauge or "Lionel Standard" equipment. A wonderful accessory to use with Lionel bungalows and villas when building model villages. Price **$3.75**
Code Word "STAND"

No. 87

No. 87 Lionel Railroad Crossing Signal—Just like those used on many grade crossings. The bright red lantern on white background is illuminated at intervals of a second by means of device placed in the interior. It is thrilling to watch this automatic "blinker" operate continuously without attention, by means of mechanism in the base which also contains terminals for connecting wires. This Crossing Signal is 6¾ inches high. Can be used with "Lionel Standard" or "O" Gauge equipment.
Price **$4.75**
Code Word "STORE"

Nos. 77 and 077

Lionel Automatic Crossing Gates—An exact reproduction of the real ones seen at grade crossings. When train approaches the track section to which it is connected, the gate comes down, and stays in that position. When train passes, gate opens. The action of the gate is just the same as those used on real railroads. It is made of heavy steel. The electric unit is enclosed in the base. Finished in various enameled colors. The Lionel Automatic Crossing Gate is 11 inches long. Price includes special section of track, connecting wires and "Lockon."

No. 077 Automatic Crossing Gate for Lionel "O" Gauge Track.
Price **$4.00**
Code Word "ADVANCE"

No. 77 Automatic Crossing Gate for "Lionel Standard" Track.
Price **$4.25**
Code Word "TARRY"

Nos. 76 and 076

Lionel Electric Block Signals—Two electric lanterns showing red and green signal are attached to a steel standard, 8¾ inches high. When train passes over the track section to which it is connected, green lantern lights up and after it leaves this section the red light shows. This red light goes out as soon as train leaves the second block section. Several of these signals placed around the track carry out real block signaling. Price includes electric lamps, special sections of track, connecting wires and "Lockon."

No. 076 Electric Block Signal for Lionel "O" Gauge Track. Price **$3.15**
Code Word "FORWARD"

No. 76 Electric Block Signal for "Lionel Standard" Track. Price **$3.35**
Code Word "ONWARD"

Lionel Accessories and Accessory Sets

A Model Village! Completely Illuminated!

No. 60    **No. 62**

No. 60 Telegraph Post—Arm is equipped with real glass insulators. Enameled steel standard is 8¾ inches high. Price . . . . **$.65**
Code Word "WIRE"

No. 62 Semaphore—The semaphore arm has three discs—red, green and yellow. Arm is operated by lever near base. Enameled steel standard is 8¾ inches high. Price . . . **$.80**
Code Word "CAUTION"

No. 195 "Lionel Terrace"—A real village in miniature, containing houses and lamp posts all electrically illuminated. Adds realism to your train outfit and ideal in connection with sister's doll house. The buildings are arranged in a beautiful landscape setting. Grass plots, bushes, shrubbery, trees and gravel walks add to its beauty. An American flag majestically waves aloft in the centre. The bungalow and villas are described on Page 37 and the lamp posts are shown on Page 44. Completely wired platform is 22 inches long, 19 inches wide. The lamps in the interior of the building and lamp posts are all wired, ready to be connected to the source of current. Our lowest priced "Multivolt" transformer or direct current reducer connected to the house current, or a few dry batteries will light up the entire village.   (Code Word "TUFT")   Price **$17.50**

No. 068   **No. 68**

No. 68 Warning Signal—Enameled steel standard is 8¾ inches high. Brass sign is 2½ inches square. Price . . . . **$.90**
Code Word "STOP"

No. 068 Warning Signal—Similar to No. 68, but is 6¾ inches high. Price . . . . **$.50**
Code Word "LOOK"

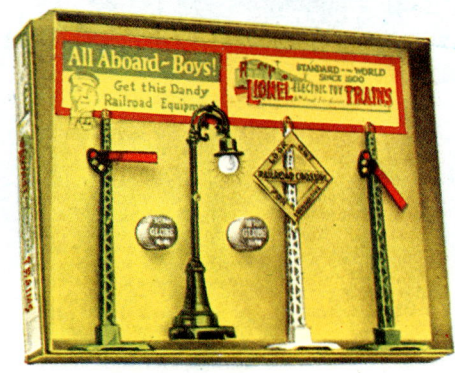

No. 70

Outfit No. 70—Comprises 2 No. 62 semaphores, 1 No. 59 lamp post, 1 No. 68 warning sign, 2 extra globes for lamp post. Very attractively packed. Price . **$4.25**
Code Word "HOBART"

Nos. 193 and 194

Automatic Accessory Sets—Lionel Automatic Accessories fully described on preceding pages are now packed in very attractive sets as illustrated above. It is great fun to add them to your Lionel equipment and build a 100% Electrically-Controlled Railroad.

No. 194 Automatic Accessory Set—For "Lionel Standard" Track—Comprises 1 No. 76 block signal, 1 No. 78 train control, 1 No. 80 semaphore, 1 No. 77 crossing gate and 1 No. 69 warning signal. Price . . . . **$21.75** Code Word "OAT"

No. 193 Automatic Accessory Set—For Lionel "O" Gauge Track. This set is the same as No. 194 described above, but is for use with "O" Gauge equipment. Price . . . . **$21.00** Code Word "OVER"

No. 71

Outfit No. 71—Comprises 6 No. 60 steel telegraph posts as described on this page. Very attractively packed. Price **$3.75**
Code Word "USEFUL"

36

BUILD a model village, boys, with these substantial, handsomely finished illuminated houses. Steel construction throughout. Roofs are removable, so that interior light may be easily reached. Lionel Bungalows and Villas will greatly enhance the appearance of your Model Railroad.

No. 186 Illuminated Bungalow Set—Comprises 5 No. 184 bungalows, beautifully finished in assorted colors. Complete with interior lights and connecting wires. Attractively packed.
Price $7.50
Code Word "HAMLET"

No. 192 Illuminated Villa Set—A handsome assortment of model houses. Comprises 1 No. 191 villa, 1 No. 189 villa, and 2 No. 184 bungalows. All complete with interior lights and connecting wires. Very attractively packed.
Price $8.75
Code Word "VILLAGE"

No. 184 Illuminated Bungalow—4 inches high, 4¾ inches wide. Beautifully decorated. Complete with interior light and connecting wires. Price $1.50
Code Word "HOME"

No. 191 Illuminated Villa—Beautifully designed. 7⅛ inches long, 5⅛ inches wide and 5¼ inches high. Roof is removable. Complete with interior lighting fixture, lamp and connecting wires. Price $3.35
Code Word "SOLID"

No. 189 Illuminated Villa—A model that is architecturally perfect. 5½ inches long, 4⅞ inches high. Complete with interior light and connecting wires.
Price $2.95
Code Word "MANSE"

No. 89 Flag-Staff and Flag—For use with Lionel model villages or to place in front of a Lionel Station. Flag-staff is 14 inches high. Silk flag may be lowered by cord attached, which can be fastened to hook near the base. Price . . $.75
Code Word "ARTHUR"

No. 90 Flag-Staff and Flag—The flag-staff (14 inches high) is removable, and fits into an ornamental base mounted on a miniature grass plot with flower border. Price . . $1.25
Code Word "PLOT"

1928

A BEAUTIFUL NEW LIONEL STATION—COMPLETELY ILLUMINATED

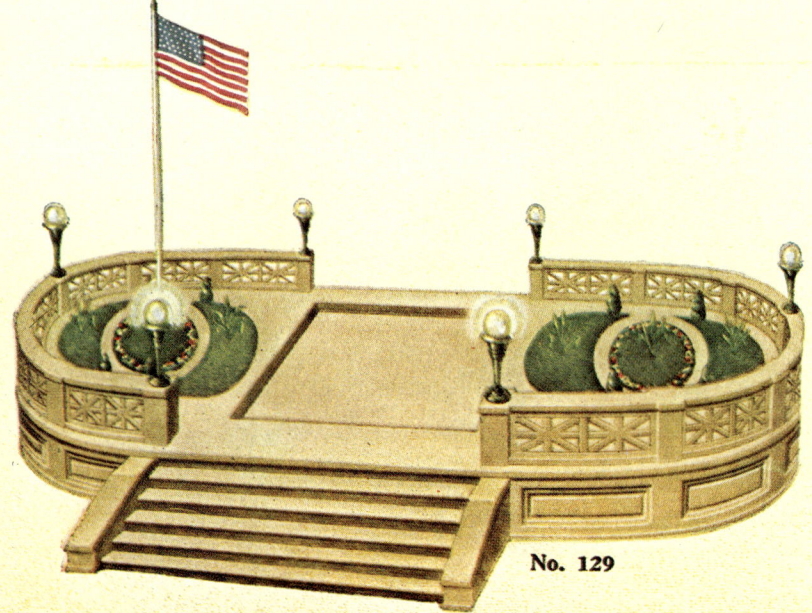

No. 128

No. 129

An Attractive Addition to a Lionel Railroad

NO. 128—This elaborate new station is just what Lionel users have long desired. It is up to date in every detail. The station is mounted on a terrace which contains beautifully landscaped flower beds. In the center bravely floats an American flag mounted on a tall flagstaff. A beautifully designed stairway leads from the ground to the terrace. The retaining wall surrounding the structure represents ornamental masonry. The ticket station is illuminated inside and out by electric bulbs, and several beautifully designed torches illuminate the terrace. The building is equipped with swinging doors and other characteristic Lionel features. The roof is removable so that the electric fixture in the interior can easily be reached. This elaborate station is made entirely of heavy steel, beautifully enameled and decorated. It is 31½ inches long, 18 inches deep and 12 inches high. Price $25.00

Code Word "YEN"

No. 129 Station Platform

THIS platform is the same as the one described above, and is listed separately so that owners of Lionel Stations Nos. 124, 122 and 121 can make use of them in this most elaborate setting, which so greatly adds to the appearance of the entire railroad layout. Price $16.00

Code Word "YIELD"

All-Steel Stations
Power Houses, Switch-Signal Towers and Panel Board

No. 124 Illuminated Station—Equipped with two corner platform lights and reflectors, finished in polished nickel. These lighting brackets have beautifully designed supporting arms. Also fitted with inside light supported on a nickeled fixture. Roof is removable so that interior lamp can be easily reached. 13½ inches long, 9 inches wide and 13 inches high. Price, complete with electric lamps and connecting wires. Code Word "READE" **$9.00**

No. 122 Illuminated Station—This is in every way similar to No. 124 Station described above, but has one inside electric light supported on a nickeled fixture. Price, complete with electric lamp and connecting wires. Code Word "CENT" **$6.25**

No. 126 Illuminated Station—Specially designed for use with our smaller train outfits and has many of the architectural features of our larger models. The interior light is supported on a fixture placed beneath the removable roof. 10¼ inches long, 7¼ inches wide and 7 inches high. Price, complete with electric lamp and connecting wires. Code Word "ALITE" **$4.50**

No. 127 Illuminated Station—For use with any "O" Gauge Train. Interior light is fastened to a supporting fixture. Roof is removable so that lamp can be easily reached. 8½ inches long, 4¼ inches wide and 5 inches high. Price, complete with electric lamp and connecting wires. Code Word "TONLY" **$2.95**

No. 437 Illuminated Switch Signal Tower—for operating Electrically-Controlled Train and Accessories at any distance from the track. Rear view below shows six knife switches attached to panel board, also provision for attaching controlling levers of electrically-controlled track switches described on Page 40. Note the wonderful detail in the windows, doors and panels, which are separable inserted pieces, beautifully enameled to harmonize with the walls of the structure. Size 10¼ inches long, 9½ inches high, 7¼ inches wide. Price, complete with electric lamp and connecting wires. Code Word "ZEV" **$8.50**

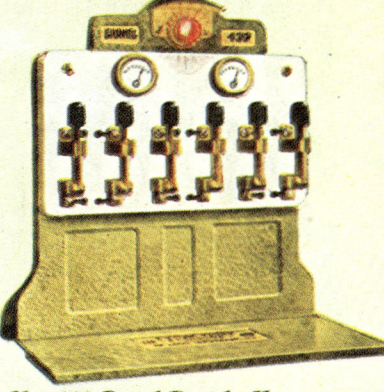

No. 439 Panel Board—You can operate your trains and accessories from one or more of the six knife switches mounted on the marble Panel Board. Provision is made for holding two levers of Lionel Electrically-Controlled Switches, shown in illustration below. Electric lamp at top illuminates small dummy meters. Made of heavy steel beautifully enameled, and the knife switches are mounted on a composition marble slab. Size 8-3/16 inches high and 7-3/16 inches wide. Price. **$5.00** Code Word "FLOW"

Lionel Power Stations—Made in 2 sizes to fit all types of Lionel "Multivolt" Transformers. Base is hollow, so that transformer easily sets within.

No. 435—Grid in roof is removable. Size 5¾ by 4½ inches. 9¾ inches high to chimney. For use with Types A or B Transformers. Price **$2.50** Code Word "JENA"

No. 436—Size 7½ by 6 inches, 11 inches high to chimney. For use with Types T, C and K Transformers. Price **$3.35** Code Word "WATTS"

No. 438 Illuminated Signal Tower—Equipped with 2 knife switches from which "Distant-Control" Trains and Accessories can be operated. Roof is removable so that interior light can be reached. Mounted on a beautiful steel elevation, embossed with rivets, etc. Base represents concrete. A brass ladder runs up the entire length of the steel work. Height is 10½ inches. Base measures 6 by 4¾ inches. Electric lamp and connecting wires included. Price **$4.75** Code Word "CARP"

39

1928

"Distant-Control" and Hand-Operated Switches. New Turntable

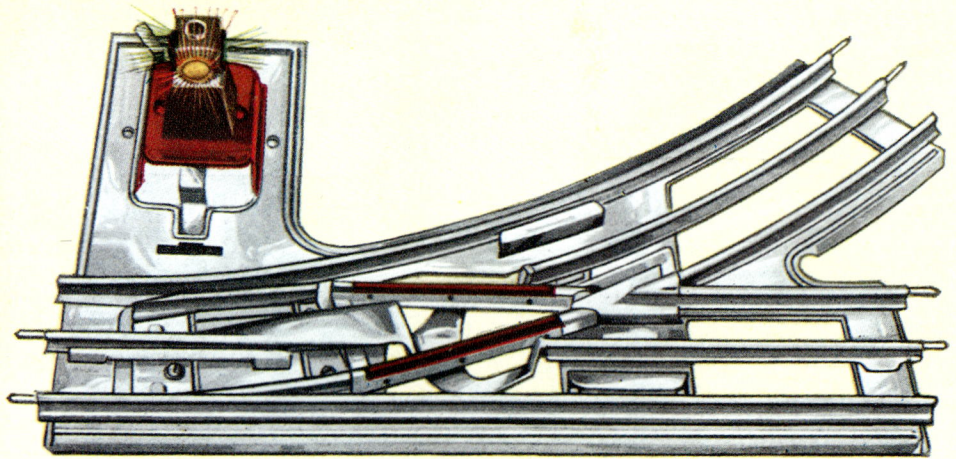

Nos. 210 and 021

Nos. 222 and 012

LIONEL Hand-operated Switches, shown in the above illustration, are equipped with heavy fibre rails (Patents Re. 16580 and 1671236) at the points where the rails cross. All possibility of short circuit is thus eliminated and headlight does not flicker when train passes over these points. Attention is also directed to the several guard rails attached to Lionel Switches which prevent derailing even when trains are traveling at high speed. Hand-lever which moves the rails, sets the signals, changes the lights and locks mechanism. All Lionel Switches are radically different from any others in the market. They are of steel construction throughout and will bear the weight of the heaviest trains without bending or breaking.

No. 210 "Lionel Standard" Illuminated Switches (right and left hand)—15 inches long, 8½ inches wide. Price includes electric lamp. Price per pair . . $6.25
Code Word "NASH"

No. 021 Lionel "O" Gauge Illuminated Switches (right and left hand)—11¼ inches long, 6 inches wide. Price includes electric lamp. Price per pair . . $4.50
Code Word "MOSHA"

LIONEL "Distant-Control" Switches (Patents No. 1548940 and 1671236) can be operated at any distance from the track by means of a controlling lever. By manipulating this lever, the same as switchmen do, the position of the switch instantly changes and the red and green lights change with the movement of the switch. The controlling lever is connected to the switch by means of flexible wires so that no additional wiring is required. The mechanism of Lionel "Distant-Control" Switches is extremely simple. They are scientifically constructed. The guard rails prevent the train leaving the track even when operating at high speed. The patented Lionel fibre rails are embodied in the construction of these switches. This exclusive feature prevents a short circuit when the train is passing over the switch points. See previous page for particulars of Nos. 437 Switch Signal-Tower and 439 Panel Board, to which the controlling levers of these switches can be attached.

No. 222 "Lionel Standard" "Distant-Control" Illuminated Switches (right and left hand)—15 inches long, 8½ inches wide. Price includes electric lamp and 42 inches of cord to which controlling lever is attached. Price per pair $11.25
Code Word "AFAR"

No. 012 Lionel "O" Gauge "Distant-Control" Illuminated Switches (right and left hand)—11¼ inches long, 6 inches wide. Price includes electric lamp and 42 inches of cord to which controlling lever is attached. Price per pair $9.25
Code Word "ASP"

LIONEL Switches and Turntable can be connected to the track in the same manner as ordinary straight or curved sections.

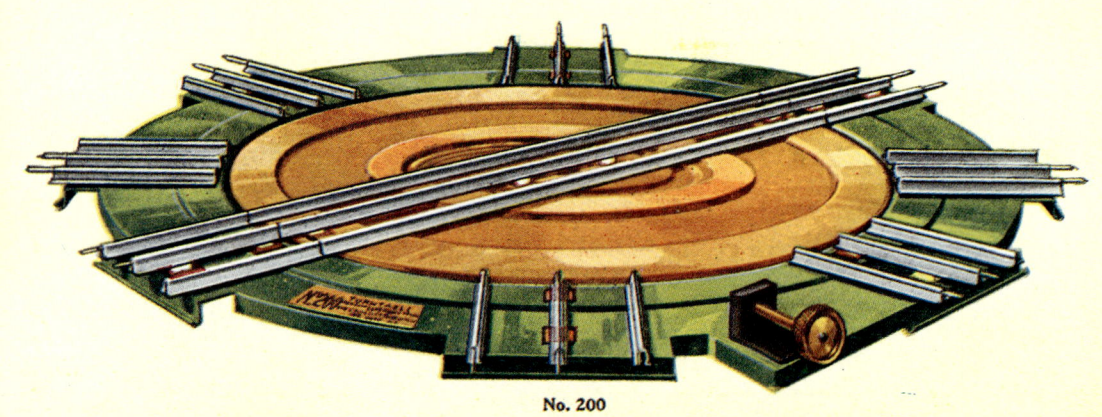

No. 200

No. 200 Turntable
for "Lionel Standard" Track

THIS is an exclusive Lionel Accessory that every boy should have in order to make a complete Lionel Train layout. It is used for switching locomotives to various tracks in the smallest possible space. Every boy is familiar with the use of a Turntable, so it is not necessary to describe its purpose. This Turntable is so perfectly balanced that even when the heaviest locomotive is upon it, it can be easily moved in every direction by means of the worm gear and hand wheel that operate it. Diameter of Turntable is 17 inches. Price $7.50
Code Word "TURK"

"Lionel Standard" and "O" Gauge Track. Lionel Track Accessories

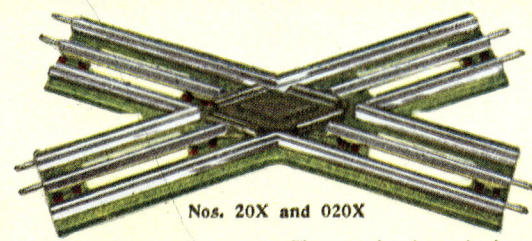

Nos. 20X and 020X

Lionel 45 Degree Crossings. These are largely used when making a figure "8," using all curved track, but a great variety of other track layouts can be formed with them. Steel construction throughout. Rails are mounted on heavy steel ornamental base. A heavy fibre block in centre where rails cross prevents all possibility of short circuit, or cars jumping the track.

No. 020X Crossing for "O" Gauge Track. Size 11¼ inches long. 6 inches wide. Price $1.50
Code Word "CROSS"

No. 20X Crossing for "Lionel Standard" Track. Size 16⅞ inches long, 8 inches wide. Price $1.75
Code Word "BOSS"

Lionel Illuminated Bumpers

Nos. 25 and 025

This bumper is die cast and is surmounted by a red electric light encased in a nickeled steel guard. Electrical contact is automatically made and bumper can be placed at any part of track layout.

No. 025 Bumper for "O" Gauge Track. Length 10¼ inches, height 2¼ inches. Price $1.75
Code Word "HIT"

No. 25 Bumper for "Lionel Standard" Track. Length 16 inches, height 3¼ inches. Price $2.25
Code Word "CAT"

Lionel Spring Bumpers

No. 023 Lionel "O" Gauge Bumper—An indispensable accessory for terminals or sidings. Fitted with spring plunger which absorbs shock when car strikes it. The bumper frame is removable. Length 10¼ inches, height 2 inches. Price . . . . $ .80
Code Word "DELTO"

No. 23 "Lionel Standard" Bumper—The construction is the same as No. 023 described above. Two spring plungers absorb shock of car. Length 14 inches, height 3 inches. Price . $1.25
Code Word "PROVO"

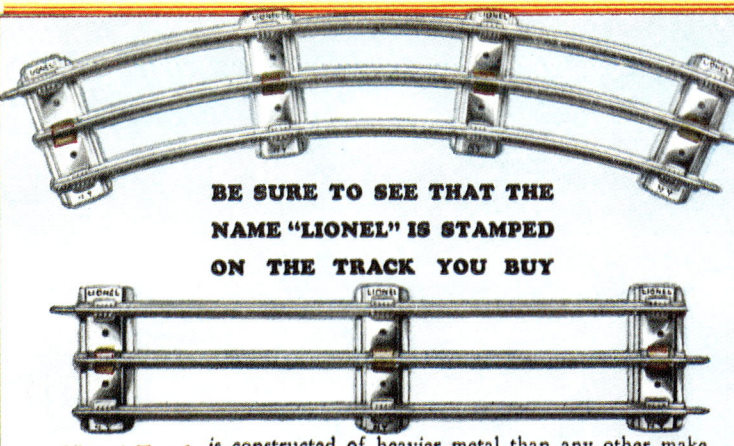

BE SURE TO SEE THAT THE NAME "LIONEL" IS STAMPED ON THE TRACK YOU BUY

Lionel Track is constructed of heavier metal than any other make. The illustration shows the added strength given to Lionel rails by forming the base outward instead of turning it in. This outward flange gives the track sufficient strength to support the weight of a fully grown person and is made possible by our patented process. Each section of track is tested on 110 volts and therefore will not short-circuit when carrying the low voltage which operates Lionel Trains. The ends of each section have pin terminals which fit in openings in the adjoining sections allowing track to be laid and taken apart without difficulty.

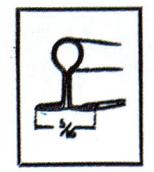

Lionel Track is made in straight and curved sections and the curvature of the track is mechanically correct, allowing trains to run at high speed without derailing.

We illustrate below the improved connecting tie which holds sections of track rigidly together. These connecting ties can be readily inserted and removed.

Lionel "O" Gauge Track—1⅜ inches wide

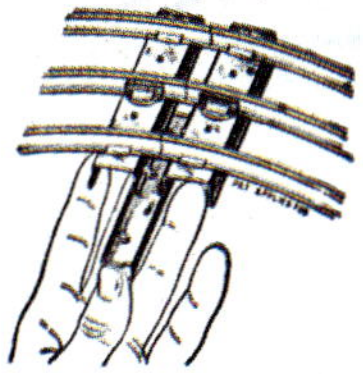

OC curved track, 11 inches long.
Price per section . . . . . $ .20
Code Word "LEMPS"

OS straight track, 10¼ inches long.
Price per section . . . . . $ .20
Code Word "GLENN"

OSS track, 10¼ inches long. For use with Electrically-Controlled Accessories. Complete with "Lockon" and connecting wires. Price per section . . . . $ .40
Code Word "RELAY"

"Lionel Standard" Track—2⅛ inches wide

C curved track, 16 inches long. Price per section . . . . $ .30
Code Word "BUFF"

S straight track, 14 inches long. Price per section . . . . $ .30
Code Word "NYACK"

SS track, 14 inches long. For use with Electrically-Controlled Accessories. Complete with "Lockon" and connecting wires. Price per section . . $ .60
Code Word "BURT"

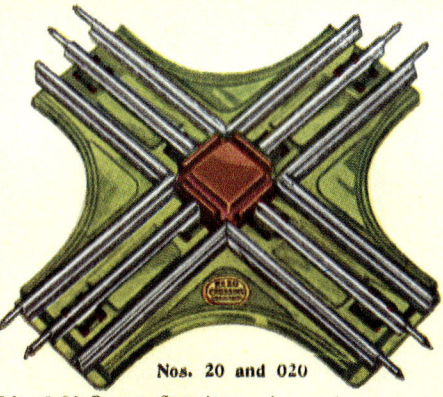

Nos. 20 and 020

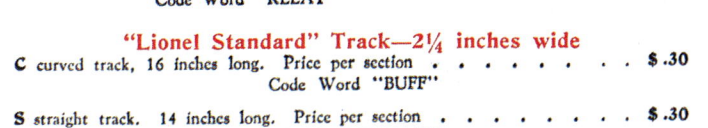

Lionel 90 Degree Crossings. A great improvement over our former models. The cross rails are mounted on an ornamental steel base, beautifully enameled. A solid molded fibre block placed in the centre where the rails cross, not only prevents short circuit, but is so constructed that the roller contact shoes on the locomotive and cars easily ride over it without derailing. A large variety of figures can be formed when using these crossings in conjunction with switches and track.

No. 020 Crossing for "O" Gauge Track. Size 10¼ inches square. Price $1.00
Code Word "ORLA"

No. 20 Crossing for "Lionel Standard" Track. Size 12 inches square. Price $1.25
Code Word "BOOST"

"Lockon" Track Connections
(Patent No. 1542337)

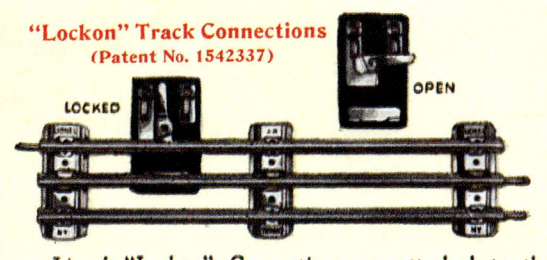

Lionel "Lockon" Connections are attached to the track by simply turning the lever at right angles as shown in the above illustration. The electric connection is as perfect as though the parts were riveted or soldered to the track.

Lionel "Lockon" Connections are free from set screws and binding posts. The fingers that hold the wires in place are made of heavy tempered blue steel and are unbreakable. All other metal parts are nickel-plated and are mounted on a heavy fibre base.

Lionel "Lockon" Connections should be used wherever electric accessories require connection with the track.

OTC "Lockon" for "O" Gauge Track. Price . . $ .20
Code Word "JOIN"

STC "Lockon" for "Lionel Standard" Track. Price . $ .25
Code Word "JUICE"

No. 300 Steel Bridge

For "Lionel Standard" Track—2¼ Inches Wide

NOTHING so elaborate or architecturally perfect as this bridge has ever been made for use with a model electric train. It is faithfully modeled after the famous "Hell-gate" Bridge which spans the East River in New York. The piers, center span and structural features are correct to the minutest detail. It is made entirely of sheet steel, and is substantially constructed throughout. It measures 28¾ inches in length, 11 inches in height and is 10½ inches wide. It is so skillfully designed that it is not necessary for a train to travel up or down grade when passing over it. It is finished in lasting enamel colors, and will greatly add to every boy's "Lionel Standard" Railroad Equipment. Price $15.00

Code Word "HELGA"

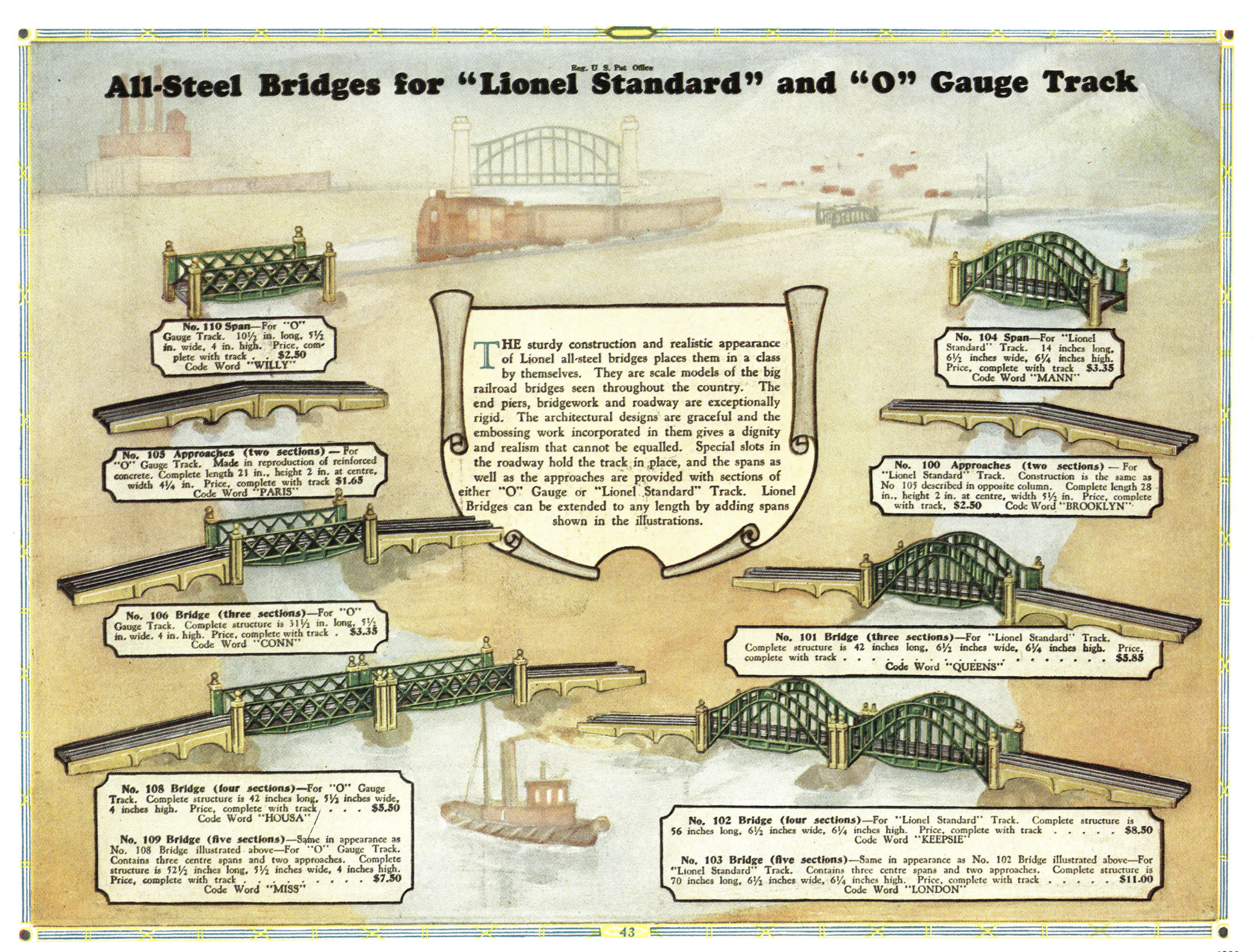

All-Steel Bridges for "Lionel Standard" and "O" Gauge Track

No. 110 Span—For "O" Gauge Track. 10½ in. long, 5½ in. wide, 4 in. high. Price, complete with track . . . $2.50
Code Word "WILLY"

No. 105 Approaches (two sections)—For "O" Gauge Track. Made in reproduction of reinforced concrete. Complete length 21 in., height 2 in. at centre, width 4¼ in. Price, complete with track $1.65
Code Word "PARIS"

No. 106 Bridge (three sections)—For "O" Gauge Track. Complete structure is 31½ in. long, 5½ in. wide, 4 in. high. Price, complete with track . . . $3.35
Code Word "CONN"

No. 108 Bridge (four sections)—For "O" Gauge Track. Complete structure is 42 inches long, 5½ inches wide, 4 inches high. Price, complete with track . . . $5.50
Code Word "HOUSA"

No. 109 Bridge (five sections)—Same in appearance as No. 108 Bridge illustrated above—For "O" Gauge Track. Contains three centre spans and two approaches. Complete structure is 52½ inches long, 5½ inches wide, 4 inches high. Price, complete with track . . . $7.50
Code Word "MISS"

THE sturdy construction and realistic appearance of Lionel all-steel bridges places them in a class by themselves. They are scale models of the big railroad bridges seen throughout the country. The end piers, bridgework and roadway are exceptionally rigid. The architectural designs are graceful and the embossing work incorporated in them gives a dignity and realism that cannot be equalled. Special slots in the roadway hold the track in place, and the spans as well as the approaches are provided with sections of either "O" Gauge or "Lionel Standard" Track. Lionel Bridges can be extended to any length by adding spans shown in the illustrations.

No. 104 Span—For "Lionel Standard" Track. 14 inches long, 6½ inches wide, 6¼ inches high. Price, complete with track $3.35
Code Word "MANN"

No. 100 Approaches (two sections)—For "Lionel Standard" Track. Construction is the same as No. 105 described in opposite column. Complete length 28 in., height 2 in. at centre, width 5½ in. Price, complete with track, $2.50   Code Word "BROOKLYN"

No. 101 Bridge (three sections)—For "Lionel Standard" Track. Complete structure is 42 inches long, 6½ inches wide, 6¼ inches high. Price, complete with track . . . $5.85
Code Word "QUEENS"

No. 102 Bridge (four sections)—For "Lionel Standard" Track. Complete structure is 56 inches long, 6½ inches wide, 6¼ inches high. Price, complete with track . . . $8.50
Code Word "KEEPSIE"

No. 103 Bridge (five sections)—Same in appearance as No. 102 Bridge illustrated above—For "Lionel Standard" Track. Contains three centre spans and two approaches. Complete structure is 70 inches long, 6½ inches wide, 6¼ inches high. Price, complete with track . . . $11.00
Code Word "LONDON"

Lionel All-Steel Lamp Posts

NO Model Railroad is complete without the addition of Lionel Lamp Posts — faithful reproductions of boulevard and street lamp posts seen everywhere. All Lionel Lamp Posts are of steel construction, enameled in a variety of beautiful colors. They will not bend or break. The binding posts to which electrical connections are made are conveniently situated, securely fastened and perfectly insulated. There is no chance of short circuit, for great care is used in their construction and every one is thoroughly tested. The electric lamps are in exact proportion to the size of the posts. No other make has the dignity and grace of design to be found in Lionel Lamp Posts.

No. 67 Lamp Post — 13 inches high. Complete with two globes. Price $2.95
Code Word "EDMUNDS"

No. 58 Lamp Post — 7⅜ inches high. Complete with globe. Price $1.25
Code Word "JENNY"

No. 56 Lamp Post — 8¾ inches high. The top is removable so that the lamp can be renewed. Complete with lamp. Price $1.65
Code Word "SHINE"

No. 57 Lamp Post — 7½ inches high. The top is removable so that the lamp can be renewed. Complete with lamp. Price $1.65
Code Word "CHEERY"

No. 59 Lamp Post — Similar in design to No. 61, but is 8¾ inches high. Complete with globe. Price $1.50
Code Word "BRIGHT"

No. 61 Lamp Post — 13 inches high. Complete with globe. Price $2.10
Code Word "INDIA"

LIONEL LAMP CABINET

No. 111 Lionel Lamp Cabinet — We supply Lionel dealers with a handsome cabinet of lamps for use in headlights and all electrically illuminated accessories. These lamps are of the finest quality and are supplied in 12 volts and 18 volts, suitable for "O" Gauge or "Lionel Standard" equipment. Fifty assorted lamps are packed in each cabinet. The chart on inside of cover gives valuable information for the use of various lamps. Each lamp is packed in a special container. Price per cabinet of 50 assorted lamps $15.00
Code Word "LUX"

LIONEL LAMP RENEWALS
Each Lamp Packed in Special Container

No. 27 — 12 volt, ½-inch round lamp. For use in all "O" Gauge equipment. Price . . . . $.30
Code Word "NOSE"

No. 28 — 18 volt, ½-inch round lamp. For use in all "Lionel Standard" equipment. Price . . . . $.30
Code Word "NELA"

No. 39 — 12 volt, ⅝-inch round globe.

For "O" Gauge Railroads use this lamp on Nos. 58, 59, 61 and 67 Lamp Posts and No. 124 station.
Price . . . . $.30   Code Word "NICE"

No. 40 — 18 volt, ⅝-inch round globe. Same uses as No. 39 lamp, when operating "Lionel Standard" equipment.
Price . . . . $.30
Code Word "NAVY"

The image on the 1928 miniature (upper left) illustrates Lionel's earlier theme, "I jumped for joy." The thirteen boys are having a great time, possibly neglecting the trains themselves. In the final large consumer version, there are only two boys and the focus is on the pleasure of operating the 219 crane. The 1929 miniature image (lower right) is the most faithful to the full-sized version of the seven miniature catalogues illustrated. The major difference is that the enormous power of the headlights appears restrained in the final version.

For the 1930 miniature (upper right), Lionel adopted a vertical format. The head-on image of the 390 steam locomotive on the miniature was replaced by a surrealistic painting on the full-sized version of a layout of several Lionel sets and accessories. Lionel continued the vertical format for the 1931 miniature catalogue (lower left) with a three-color brochure. However, the image chosen for the full-sized catalogue of two boys standing with engineer Bob Butterfield in front of his locomotive and uttering the famous "Just Like Mine," was much more effective.

Lionel's Miniature Catalogues

Lionel produced a series of small consumer catalogues in the 1920s and 1930s. Their full-sized consumer catalogues were the most elaborate toy catalogues ever produced, but the cost of the large four-color format was very significant. Lionel needed a much less expensive sales format so that dealers could freely give something to any boy. Hence we have the miniature catalogue.

The front covers of these catalogues generally resembled those of the full-sized versions and the catalogues illustrated most of the year's line in a reduced size. Generally these catalogues were printed in two colors rather than the full-color printing of the larger catalogues; however, skillful blending of shades of the two colors produced very attractive images at a much lower cost.

The first known miniature catalogue is from 1924. Its front cover bears a striking resemblance to the full-sized catalogue of that year, although it shows more action then does the larger catalogue. The image on the full-sized catalogue ends on the left just beyond the dog and the 78 traffic signal, lending credence to the thought that the large catalogue may have been published later in the year. Missing on that catalogue, but shown on the miniature, is the third boy and the 402 engine in the lower left-hand corner headed on a collision course with the 402 set shown on the right. The additional image lends new meaning to the boys' excitement — a major wreck may be imminent.

The 1927 miniature (left) and the 1926 miniature (right) are just below the 1924. Both miniatures show more than do the full-sized catalogues. The 1926 miniature has a boy operating his 402 set on the living room floor in front of the fireplace. The setting is framed by real world images of the 78 signal and 80 semaphore. Possibly these were intended to show how the youthful Lionel operator could imagine his trains; however, this framing weakens the central image. The artwork was simplified for the 1926 large consumer catalogue.

The 1927 catalogue, which features the new 408 locomotive with its many lights (six) and elaborate trim, is flanked by the 78 signal on the left and an 82 semaphore on the right. The full-sized 1927 has a more effective image — the very powerful 408 is highlighted by being separated out of the realistic landscape shown in the miniature catalogue.

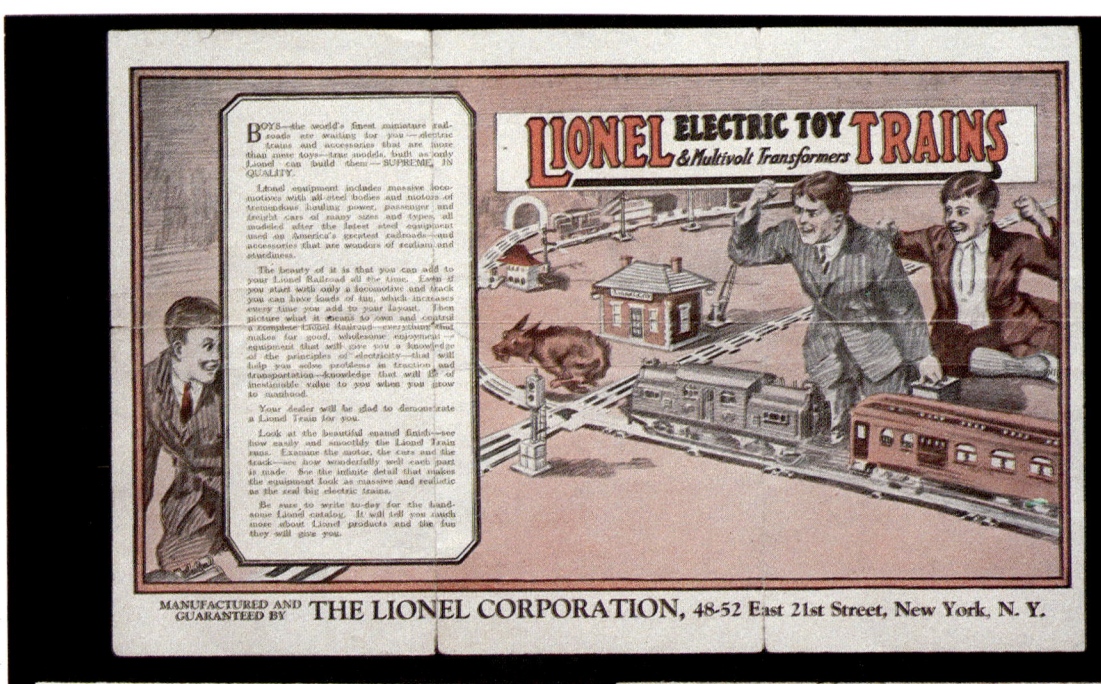

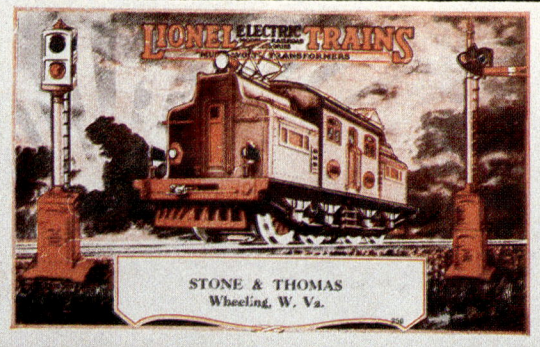

No. 840 Lionel Power Station

There is no accessory more desirable or fitting to be used with Lionel 100% Electrically-Controlled Railroads than this attractive new Power Station. It is possible to control and operate the most elaborate model railroad layout from this central station. Original and ornamental in design, it is embellished with wonderful details, such as doors, windows, frames, etc., all actually inserted, not merely represented by lithography. The stone work and masonry are in exact reproduction of a big concrete building. Steel construction throughout, richly enameled in beautiful colors. Length 26 inches, width 21½ inches, height to top of smokestack 18 inches.

Price .... Code Word "LING" $20.00

THE above illustration shows the provision made for accommodating one or two Lionel Transformers. The switches on the transformers can be reached through openings above them. Illustration also shows the Panel Board on one side of the Power House containing six knife switches. Provision is also made for mounting four operating levers for Lionel Electrically-Controlled Track Switches on this Panel Board.

Printed in U. S. A.   The entire contents of this catalog copyrighted 1928 by the Lionel Corporation, New York, N. Y.

LIONEL ALL-STEEL TUNNELS. SCENIC RAILWAYS

No. 140L Illuminated Tunnel—Can be used with any "Lionel Standard" Train. This tunnel is made to set on the curve of the track layout. Lights are placed over the forward and rear entrances. Length 37 inches, width 24½ inches, height 20 inches. Portals are 8 inches wide, 8 inches high. Price **$16.65**
Code Word "SEVA"

No. 130L Illuminated Tunnel—This is for use with all "O" Gauge Trains. The general design is the same as No. 140L described above. Length 26 inches, width 23 inches, height 14½ inches. Portals are 4½ inches wide, 5½ inches high. Price **$13.75**
Code Word "SOAK"

No. 120L Illuminated Tunnel—For all Lionel Trains. Hand-painted, and graceful in design. Equipped with interior light. Length 17 inches, width 12 inches, height 11 inches. Portals are 6½ inches wide and 8 inches high. Price **$6.25**
Code Word "HOPE"

No. 119 Tunnel—For all "O" Gauge Trains and the medium size "Lionel Standard" Trains. 12 inches long, 9 inches wide and 10 inches high. Portals are 5 inches wide and 6½ inches high. Price....... **$3.35**
Code Word "HOSA"

No. 119L Illuminated Tunnel—Same as No. 119, but is equipped with interior light. Price **$4.25**
Code Word "HARP"

No. 118 Tunnel—For "O" Gauge Trains. Tunnel is 8 inches long, 7 inches wide and 7½ inches high. Portals are 4 inches wide and 5½ inches high. Price. **$2.10**
Code Word "SIMPLON"

DEALERS Lionel Scenic Railways for "O" Gauge and "Lionel Standard" track are great show window attractions.

The scenic effects and accessories supplied with Lionel Scenic Railways can be purchased separately if desired, at prices listed in the specifications.

No. 198 "O" Gauge Scenic Railway. Comprises:

1 No. 076 Block signal		$3.15
1 No. 077 Crossing gate		4.00
1 No. 069 Warning signal		3.15
1 No. 56 Lamp post		1.65
1 No. 57 Lamp post		1.65
1 No. 58 Lamp post		1.25
1 No. 89 Flag staff		.75
1 No. 184 Bungalow		1.50
1 No. 189 Villa		2.95
1 No. 191 Villa		3.35
1 No. 092 Signal tower		2.10
1 No. 130L Tunnel		13.75
1 No. 131 Corner elevation		4.50
1 No. 132 Corner grass plot		2.50
2 No. 133 Heartshape grass plots	$1.50	3.00
1 No. 134 Circular grass plot (large) .		3.00
1 No. 506 Compo board painted platform, completely wired (2 sections)		6.50
3 No. 509 Compo board mountains	1.50	4.50
1 No. 508 Compo board sky background (2 sections)		4.50
4 No. 500 Pine bushes	.20	.80
2 No. 501 Small pine trees...........	.20	.40
3 No. 502 Medium pine trees..........	.25	.75
3 No. 503 Large pine trees...........	.30	.90
4 No. 504 Rose bushes	.20	.80
3 No. 505 Oak trees	.30	.90
4 No. 510 Canna bushes	.20	.80

Size of Platform 60 by 42 inches. Train and Track not included. Price complete **$50.00**
Code Word "BEAUTY"

No. 199 "Lionel Standard" Scenic Railway. Comprises:

1 No. 124 Station		$9.00
1 No. 189 Villa		2.95
3 No. 191 Villas	$3.35	10.05
3 No. 184 Bungalows	1.50	4.50
1 No. 092 Signal tower		2.10
5 No. 60 Telegraph posts	.65	3.25
2 No. 59 Lamp posts	1.50	3.00
3 No. 58 Lamp posts	1.25	3.75
1 No. 57 Lamp post		1.65
1 No. 89 Flag staff		.75
1 No. 84 Semaphore		3.35
1 No. 78 Automatic train control		5.00
1 No. 77 Crossing gate		4.25
1 No. 69 Warning signal		3.35
1 No. 120L Tunnel		6.25
1 No. 136 Elevation		10.00
1 No. 131 Corner elevation		$4.50
1 No. 132 Corner grass plot		2.50
2 No. 133 Heartshape grass plots	$1.50	3.00
1 No. 134 Circular grass plot, large.		3.00
1 No. 135 Circular grass plot, small.		1.00
1 No. 507 Compo board painted platform, completely wired (3 sections)		7.50
3 No. 509 Compo board mountains	1.50	4.50
1 No. 508 Compo board sky backgr'd (2 sections)		3.00
4 No. 500 Pine bushes	.20	.80
4 No. 501 Small pine trees...........	.20	.80
4 No. 502 Medium pine trees..........	.25	1.00
4 No. 503 Large pine trees...........	.30	1.20
4 No. 504 Rose bushes	.20	.80
8 No. 505 Oak trees	.30	2.40
4 No. 510 Canna bushes	.20	.80

Size of Platform 90 by 60 inches. Train and Track not included. Price complete **$80.00**
Code Word "NATURE"

OF THE WORLD SINCE 1900"
LIONEL
CTRIC
TRAINS
RAILROAD
SSORIES
"MULT
TRANSFORMERS
1929

1929

LIONEL RAILROADING!

UNLIMITED FUN
For Dad and His Son

A MAN with an understanding heart created **Lionel** Trains because he loves boys and knows just the kind of excitement they want. Pleasure knows no bounds for the boy and his Dad when indulging in that most fascinating of pastimes — **Lionel** Model Railroading.

Lionel Trains and real trains differ only in size. In accuracy of detail—grace of outline—structural excellence and electrical and mechanical perfection—**Lionel** Electric Trains and Model Railroad Accessories surpass all others.

There's action all the time with a **Lionel**. Is there a boy or man who doesn't thrill at the sight of a **Lionel** Passenger or Freight Train—speedy as a comet—life-like in every detail, flashing by crossings, slowing down to a stop as the automatic semaphore or train control is set against it, and gliding away again as the signal shows "Clear." There's knowledge to be gained from the study of **Lionel** Model Railroading and there's realism!—and the thrill that comes from the personal operation and direction of a great railroad system.

For 29 years the supreme **Lionel** Line has kept pace with all that is new in the development of electric traction. Many hundreds of boys who were **Lionel** fans years ago are today occupying positions of importance on the great railroad systems of the country—helped forward by what they learned as boys through the operation of their **Lionel** Trains.

Boys—throughout this catalog you will find many new and up-to-date additions to the **Lionel** Line that will constantly hold your interest—new types of electric locomotives—and the marvelous new Electrically-Driven STEAM TYPE LOCOMOTIVES and TRAIN OUTFITS. All are life-like copies of the great transcontinental flyers — truly remarkable developments in the realm of Model Railroading.

"Bild-a-Loco"—**Lionel's** revolutionary departure in miniature motor construction, is now developed to the highest possible degree of excellence. This type of motor, which can be snapped out of the locomotive body in a jiffy, taken apart and reassembled in a few moments, is now included in several train sets, both for "O" Gauge and **"Lionel Standard"** Track. Full details of how this motor can be converted into a powerful three-speed reversible stationary motor are given on the following pages.

Lionel Locomotives are massive, strong and powerful, able to pull with ease long strings of Freight or Passenger Cars. The secret of this power lies in the precision of every part that goes into the construction of **Lionel** Motors.

The Pullman Cars are handsome and brilliantly lighted! They are decorated in a variety of durable enamel colors—the interiors fitted in every respect like actual cars on real railroads. That's **Lionel** quality—perfection of detail that has never been equaled.

With the large variety of railroad equipment illustrated in this Railroad Planning Book you will be able to build a complete Model Railroad, true in every detail—a marvelous system of crossovers, electrically-controlled switches, illuminated bumpers, magnificent steel bridges, illuminated tunnels—a railroad system that will delight the heart of every boy, and leave nothing to the imagination.

Passenger Trains, Freight Trains, Work Trains, Coal Trains—all controlled at your will from the **Lionel** Switch Tower or Power Station—by **Lionel's** perfect and exclusive system of "Distant-Control," described in more detail on the next page.

Lionel Automatic and Electrically-Controlled Accessories add immeasurably to your fun. Every known type of railroad device, designed to increase the safety of passengers and efficiency of railroad operation, is faithfully reproduced in model form by **Lionel**.

Wouldn't you like to own such a railroad? Of course you would—and you know that *only* **Lionel** can give you all these remarkable features.

Go to your dealer. Ask for a demonstration. We are confident that your choice will be a **Lionel**.

The Tremendous Factories at Irvington, N. J., Where Lionel Trains Are Made

The
Lionel Corporation
15-17-19 EAST 26th STREET
Madison Square North
NEW YORK, N. Y.

THE LIONEL "DISTANT-CONTROL" SYSTEM
AN ELECTRICAL BRAIN IN YOUR TRAIN

WITH this remarkable invention you can now humanize the operation of your train, for the electrical brain of your locomotive responds instantly to your will, although you may be operating your train from the next room.

Lionel's new 100% "Distant-Control" Railroad system designed for "O" Gauge as well as for **"Lionel Standard"** Track makes it unnecessary to reverse your locomotive by hand.

By manipulating the small lever on the controlling rheostat, as the boy is doing in the picture, you can start, stop, reverse, and operate your train at any speed without going near it. You are, thereby, the master of your train.

Lionel Semaphores, Crossing Gates, Flashing Signals, Warning Bells and Train Controls can not only be automatically operated by the movement of the train, but can also be controlled at any distance from the track by the levers in the new **Lionel** Switch Towers, Power Station and Panel Board. And furthermore—you can switch your train from track to track, or back it on to a siding from any distant point, by means of **Lionel** "Distant-Control" Switches described on another page.

The **Lionel** "Distant-Control" System of electrical operation puts genuine excitement into model railroading—a thrill you can only experience with a **Lionel**—and don't forget that!

Boys—remember that the famous **Lionel** "Distant-Control" mechanism is also incorporated in the new **"Lionel Standard" Gauge Steam Type Locomotives and Train Outfits.**

Go to your dealers, and take a **Lionel** Train in your hands. Feel the weight of it. That's sturdiness, strength! Note the glossy, brilliant smoothness of its enameled finish. Note the fittings on the engine and cars, and how every detail simulates the perfection of a real railroad train. Strength, beauty and quality are built into every train with **Lionel** thoroughness.

That's why **Lionel** has been "Standard of the World" since 1900!

The headlights on Lionel "Distant-Control" Locomotives are so connected that when the train moves forward the front headlight is illuminated, and when in reverse the rear headlight flashes on while the other is disconnected.

Lionel "Distant-Control" Locomotives and Train Outfits listed on the following pages are distinguished by the letter "E" after the catalog number.

THE LIONEL "DISTANT-CONTROL" SUPER-MOTOR

Illustration shows the simplicity and compactness of **Lionel** "Distant-Control" Super-Motors. All working parts are mounted between two heavy steel plates. All shaft bearings are reinforced with bronze bushings. All parts are easily accessible, including the removable brush holder, lever for reversing the locomotive by hand and an additional lever for disconnecting the "Distant-Control" mechanism.

CONSTRUCTION OF LIONEL "O" GAUGE MOTORS

Driving Gears ("A")—They are made of heavy steel blanks, machine-cut. They mesh without friction and are far superior to gears with punched teeth.

Field ("B")—The field is made of a number of specially prepared transformer steel laminations. This construction gives a much stronger field than if a single piece of steel were used.

Third Rail Shoe Support ("C")—Made of heavy fibre to which the third rail contact rollers are attached. Our construction protects rollers from injury, for the brackets can be bent against the fibre without disturbing the arc of the spring that gives them the correct tension against the third rail.

Wheels ("D")—Lionel was first to introduce die-cast wheels. They are absolutely balanced. A nickel-plated steel rim is forced over the tread of the wheel to insure long wear.

Collecting Shoes ("E")—They collect current from the third rail. They are made of *stainless steel* turnings and revolve on steel shafts which pass through phosphor bronze supports. They insure perfect contact with the third rail at all times so that locomotive will run at uniform speed.

Frame ("F")—Made of very heavy steel punchings, embodying great detail. Will withstand more than the ordinary amount of wear and tear.

Journals ("G")—Made of heavy brass, nickel-plated. Attached to the frames by mechanical means. They add greatly to the appearance of the structure.

Cowcatchers ("H")—The construction of the cowcatchers varies with the type of locomotive on which they are used. Many of them are part of the steel frame which is made in one piece, and others are heavy castings rigidly attached to the frame.

Flag Posts ("J")—All our locomotives are equipped with four flag posts, two at each end of the frame; a very realistic detail.

Tanks ("K")—These tanks are made of brass, nickel-plated, and are separable pieces attached to the frame, which further accentuates the great detail.

Lionel Automatic Couplers ("L")—Made of heavy steel, nickel-plated and polished. They are scientifically constructed so that cars cannot become detached when in motion, but are easily taken apart when desired. The new improved Lionel Coupler with invisible spring arrangement is a great advance over any similar device ever made.

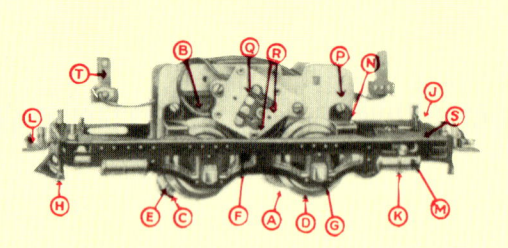

Illustration above shows the type of motor used in "O" Gauge Locomotives Nos. 248, 252 and 253 illustrated on Page 7. Full description of all working parts is given on this page.

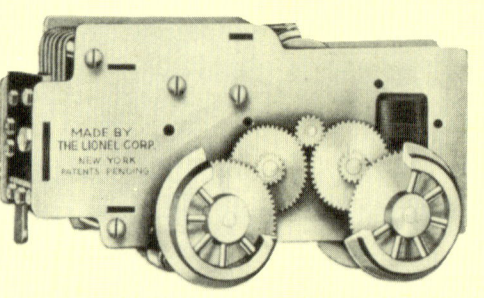

This "Distant-Control" Super-Motor is used in "O" Gauge Locomotives Nos. 254E and 251E. Super-Motor with hand reverse is used in "O" Gauge Locomotives Nos. 254 and 251.

The New "O" Gauge "Distant-Control" Super-Motor

THIS marvelous new motor will haul twice as many cars as any other "O" Gauge Motor now on sale. The illustration shows some of the remarkable features that make this possible. Notice the new system of gearing which gives maximum hauling power with minimum current consumption.

The "Distant-Control" mechanism is built right into the motor, and is completely protected against injury. This new "O" Gauge Super-Motor, a triumph of engineering skill, is one of **Lionel's** greatest achievements.

Above illustration shows the "O" Gauge "Bild-a-Loco" Motor used in Locomotives Nos. 4 and 4U.

Above illustration shows "Bild-a-Loco" converted into "Bild-a-Motor".

The marvelous new "Bild-a-Loco" and "Bild-a-Motor" are fully described on Pages 12 and 13. Be sure to read about this revolutionary new departure in miniature motor construction.

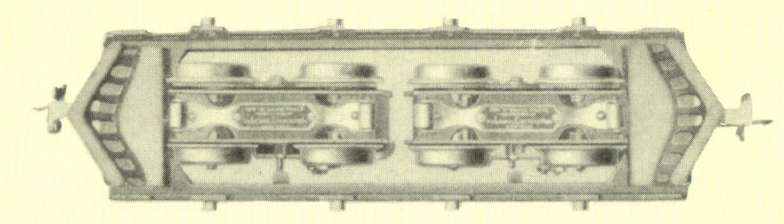

Above illustration shows "O" Gauge Twin-Super-Motor chassis used in Locomotive No. 256. These twin-motors develop great hauling power and will pull a long train of cars with perfect ease. A larger illustration of the "O" Gauge Super-Motor is shown at the top of this page to the right.

Reversing Controllers ("M")—Lionel Reversing Controllers have been in use for many years during which time they have given thorough satisfaction. They are the only controllers in use that cannot get out of order. They operate very easily, and due to the brass cups and spring tension, good electrical contact is always made.

Frame Support ("N")—The frame is supported to the motor with only four screws. This simple method of construction was originally introduced by us in 1913. All parts of Lionel Locomotives can be easily reached for cleaning.

Side Plates ("P")—Made of heavy gauge steel and support all working parts. All bearing holes are reinforced with phosphor bronze bushings. The alignment of these holes is absolutely perfect so that gears work with minimum friction. All holes are drilled and reamed to proper diameter. The accuracy of these plates compares with the frame work of a very fine clock.

Brush Plate ("Q")—The unique construction permits rapid change of brushes after motor has been in use for a considerable period. The brushes fit in brass tubes. Two properly tempered steel springs give the correct pressure of the brush on the commutator until brushes are worn down to the end. Brushes are replaced by simply raising the springs, lifting up worn-out brushes and dropping in new ones.

Brushes ("R")—We were the first manufacturers of model trains to equip our motors with combination gauze and graphite brushes that wear long and are self-lubricating.

Removable Locomotive Body ("S")—The bodies of all Lionel Locomotives are held in place on the frame with only two screws, one at each end of the locomotive. Supporting members are placed at several points of the frame that rigidly hold the body in place.

Headlight Connection ("T")—A new method originated by us. The fibre contact makes a permanent electrical connection and eliminates the possibility of broken wires.

Commutator—Made of bronze, and perfectly turned when connected to armature so that it is absolutely parallel with brushes. Commutator surface is polished so as to reduce all friction when in contact with brushes.

Armature—Made of specially prepared electrical sheets mounted on a drill rod shaft. It is perfectly insulated and wound with the correct amount of triple insulated wire.

CONSTRUCTION OF "LIONEL STANDARD" SUPER-MOTORS

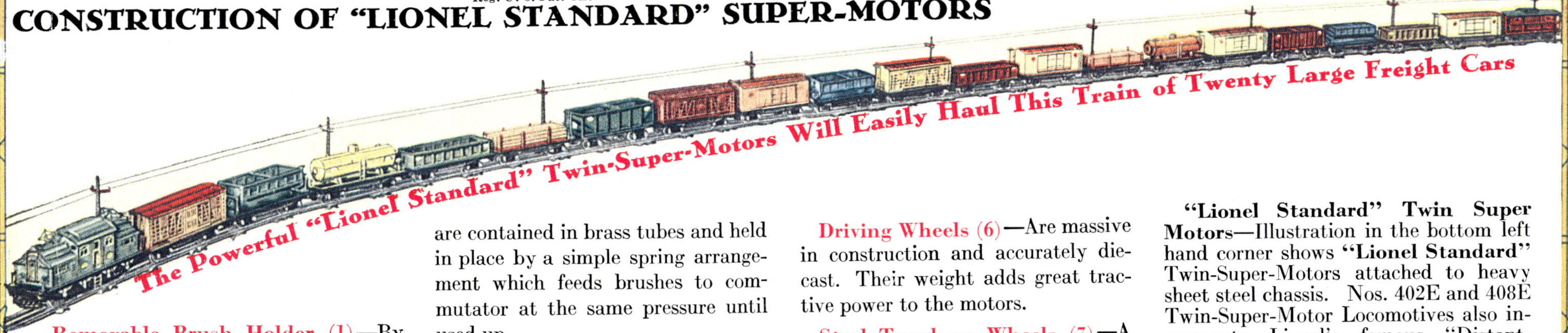

Reg. U. S. Pat. Off.

The Powerful "Lionel Standard" Twin-Super-Motors Will Easily Haul This Train of Twenty Large Freight Cars

Removable Brush Holder (1)—By simply unscrewing one screw the entire brush holder can be removed from the motor. Change of brushes requires but an instant and the assembled part is replaced without the use of any tools.

Brushes (2)—Made of bronze and graphite which are self-lubricating. They insure long life to the commutator. They are contained in brass tubes and held in place by a simple spring arrangement which feeds brushes to commutator at the same pressure until used up.

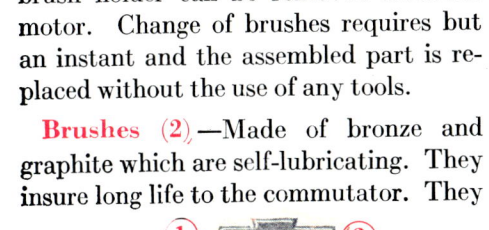

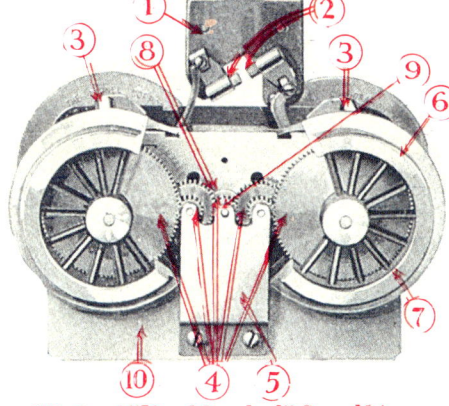

Revolving Double Contact Shoes (3)—Are heavy stainless steel rollers, securely affixed to the flexible phosphor bronze plate, which insures the proper tension on the third rail and gives a steady flow of current to the motors. Complete shoe assembly is mounted on a heavy fibre plate and is rigidly attached to the motor frame.

New Gear Arrangement (4)—This new method of gearing is embodied only in **Lionel** Super-Motors. The seven gears in this new layout give the motor greater tractive power, and are almost frictionless. The gears are made of very heavy steel, and teeth are machine cut, not stamped.

Three-Point Armature Shaft Bearing (5)—The armature shaft revolves in three bearings—two of them are contained in the side plates of the motor and the third one in the plate that holds the gearing studs. This three-point bearing eliminates all vibration of the armature shaft, with the result that the commutator and brushes wear long and evenly.

Driving Wheels (6)—Are massive in construction and accurately die-cast. Their weight adds great tractive power to the motors.

Steel Tread on Wheels (7)—A steel tread beautifully nickel-plated and polished is forced over the rim, insuring longer wear and a smooth even riding surface. **Lionel** originated this method of wheel construction. See illustration on Page 6.

Reinforced Bearings (8) — Six phosphor bronze bearings are contained in the side plates of the motor, insuring accurate alignment of the armature shaft and axles.

Armature—Made of laminated electrical steel punchings. It is automatically drum wound with triple-covered magnet wire, dipped in shellac and baked. The armature shaft is made of the best quality drill rod.

Side Plates (10)—Made of heavy steel, with bronze bushings inserted for shaft and axles.

Field—Made of the highest grade electrical steel, correctly wound and scientifically designed.

Commutator—Made of heavy copper. The segments are perfectly insulated, making short-circuits impossible.

"Lionel Standard" Twin Super Motors—Illustration in the bottom left hand corner shows **"Lionel Standard"** Twin-Super-Motors attached to heavy sheet steel chassis. Nos. 402E and 408E Twin-Super-Motor Locomotives also incorporate Lionel's famous "Distant-Control" unit described on Page 3. These locomotives can be started, stopped, reversed and operated at any speed at any distance from the track.

Side view of "Lionel Standard" Super-Motor. The many remarkable features of this motor are described on this page. This type of motor is installed in Locomotives Nos. 8, 8E, 10, 10E, 318, 318E and 380E.

Above illustration shows "Lionel Standard" Twin-Super-Motors. Locomotive Nos. 402E and 408E are equipped with these powerful motors.

Above illustration shows "Lionel Standard" "Bild-a-Loco" motor installed in Locomotive Nos. 9, 9E, 9U, 381E, 381U, 390 and 390E. See page 12 for full description of Lionel "Bild-a-Loco."

Above illustration shows "Lionel Standard" "Bild-a-Loco" converted into "Bild-a-Motor," an independent three-speed power motor, fully described on page 13.

1929

THESE CONSTRUCTIONAL FEATURES SHOW WHY LIONEL ALWAYS LEADS

WINDOW PANELS, DOORS AND SEATS — A SEPARABLE PIECE INSERTED IN CAR BODY
U.S. PATENTS NO. 1272390 AND 1272391 - JULY 16, 1918

"BILD-A-LOCO" & "BILD-A-MOTOR" ASSEMBLED AND TAKEN APART IN A FEW MOMENTS
U.S. PATENTS PENDING

OPERATING PANTAGRAPHS

CONTROLLING UNITS FOR ELECTRICALLY OPERATED TRACK SWITCHES PATENT PENDING

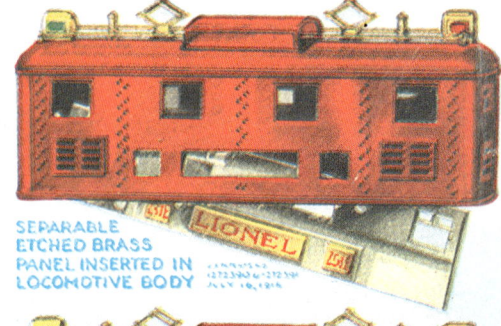

SEPARABLE ETCHED BRASS PANEL INSERTED IN LOCOMOTIVE BODY
U.S. PATENTS NO. 1272390 & 1272391 JULY 16, 1918

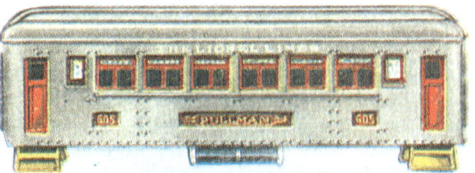

FINISHED CAR BODY SHOWING SEPARABLE PANEL INSERTED
U.S. PATENTS NO. 1272390 & 1272391 JULY 16, 1918

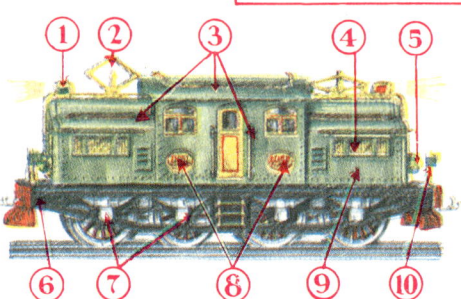

FINISHED LOCOMOTIVE BODY SHOWING SEPARABLE PANEL INSERTED
U.S. PATENTS NO. 1272390 & 1272391 JULY 16, 1918

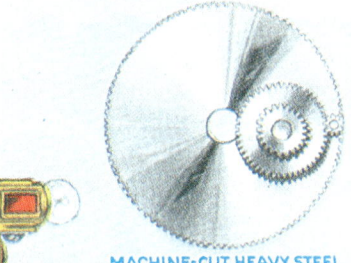

MACHINE-CUT HEAVY STEEL GEARS — NOT PUNCHED

DIE-CAST HEADLIGHT SHOWING RED PANEL AND ELECTRICAL CONNECTION
U.S. PATENT NO. 1672671 JUNE 12, 1928

VIEW OF HEADLIGHT SHOWING GREEN PANEL
U.S. PATENT NO. 1672671 JUNE 12, 1928

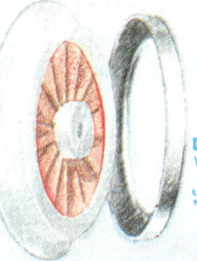

DIE-CAST WHEEL WITH NICKELED STEEL RIM
U.S. RE-ISSUED PATENT NO. 16583 - MAY 18, 1926

Construction of Lionel Cars and Locomotives

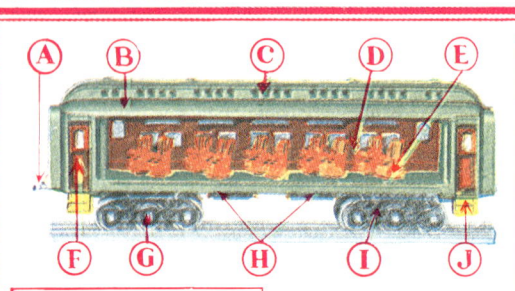

- **A** — Automatic couplers.
- **B** — Removable roof.
- **C** — Colored transparencies in transom windows.
- **D** — Inserted window frames adding strength to car.
- **E** — Revolving parlor car chairs.
- **F** — Hinged doors.
- **G** — Nickeled journals.
- **H** — Metal air tanks.
- **I** — Heavy steel truck frames.
- **J** — Brass steps.

- **1** — Die cast headlights.
- **2** — Operating pantagraphs.
- **3** — Brass hand rails.
- **4** — Inserted brass ventilators.
- **5** — Green signal lights.
- **6** — Heavy steel frame made in one piece.
- **7** — Nickeled journals.
- **8** — Inserted brass panels.
- **9** — Steel body studded with rivets.
- **10** — Signal flags on solid brass posts and stanchions.

REMOVABLE BRUSH HOLDER CONTAINING SELF-LUBRICATING AUTOMATIC-FEEDING BRUSHES
U.S. PATENTS NO. 1636269 - MAY 9, 1922, 1408987 FEB 7, 1922

"LOCKON" CONNECTION
U.S. PATENT NO. 1548337 - JUNE 16, 1925

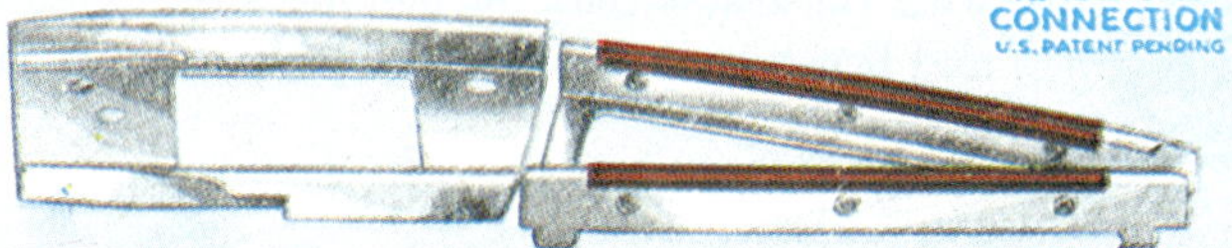

FIBRE SWITCH POINT WHICH PREVENTS SHORT-CIRCUITING OF TRACK
U.S. RE-ISSUED PATENT NO. 16580 - MARCH 29, 1927

SIX-WHEEL TRUCK WITH NICKELED JOURNALS

HEADLIGHT CONNECTION
U.S. PATENT PENDING

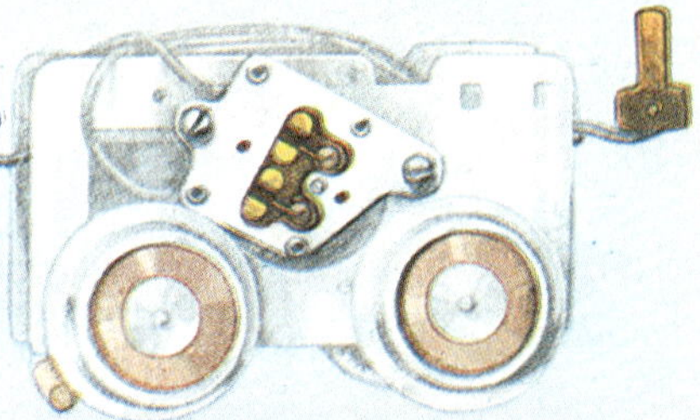

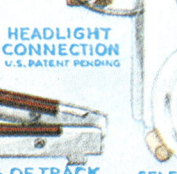

SELF-LUBRICATING AUTOMATIC-FEEDING BRUSHES IN "O" GAUGE MOTOR

LOCOMOTIVES FOR "O" GAUGE TRACK
1⅜ INCHES WIDE

THE new line of Lionel "O" Gauge Locomotives now includes several models equipped with the Lionel "Distant-Control" Super-Motor. Others are equipped with hand-reverse. They are fully described on Page 4. These powerful locomotives haul twice as many cars as any other make.

All Lionel "O" Gauge Locomotives are equipped with automatic couplers.

NOTE—Length of couplers on locomotives is not included in dimensions given in specifications.

See Pages 28 and 29 for the correct Passenger and Freight Cars to be used with these locomotives.

Locomotive No. 248—Equipped with electric headlight. 7⅝ inches long, 4 inches high.
Code Word "REGAL"

Locomotive No. 252—Equipped with reversing controller and electric headlight. 8 inches long, 3⅝ inches high.
Code Word "ELECT"

Locomotive No. 253—Equipped with reversing controller and 2 electric headlights. 9 inches long, 4 inches high.
Code Word "FINE"

Super-Motor Locomotive No. 251—Equipped with reversing controller and 2 electric headlights. 10¼ inches long, 4½ inches high.
Code Word "ACME"

"Distant-Control" Super-Motor Locomotive No. 251E—Same as No. 251, but can be started, stopped, reversed and operated at any speed at any distance from the track. No. 81 controlling rheostat supplied with it.
Code Word "GLORY"

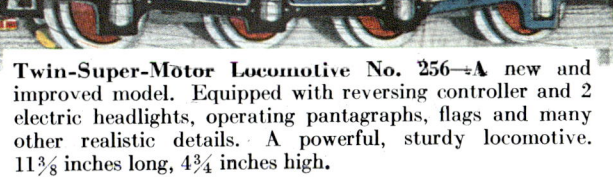

Super-Motor Locomotive No. 254—Equipped with reversing controller and 2 electric headlights. 9½ inches long, 4¼ inches high.
Code Word "MANY"

Twin-Super-Motor Locomotive No. 256—A new and improved model. Equipped with reversing controller and 2 electric headlights, operating pantagraphs, flags and many other realistic details. A powerful, sturdy locomotive. 11⅜ inches long, 4¾ inches high.
Code Word "CHAIN"

Prices are Listed on Page 45

PASSENGER AND FREIGHT TRAIN OUTFITS
For "O" Gauge — Track—1⅜ Inches Wide

ALL Lionel Train Outfits include electric lamps for headlights, wires for connecting to transformer or batteries, and connecting ties for joining sections of track. Locomotives and Cars are equipped with automatic couplers.

See Pages 32 and 33 for suitable Transformers and Reducers with which to operate these outfits from house current.

Warning Signal is included without charge in all "O" Gauge Train Outfits.

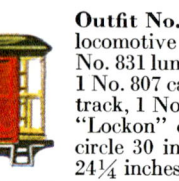

Outfit No. 249—Comprises 1 No. 248 locomotive with electric headlight, 1 No. 831 lumber car with load of lumber, 1 No. 807 caboose, 8 sections OC curved track, 1 No. 068 warning signal, 1 OTC "Lockon" connection. Track forms a circle 30 inches in diameter. Train is 24¼ inches long.

Code Word "KATE"

Outfit No. 292—Comprises 1 No. 248 locomotive with electric headlight, 1 No. 629 Pullman car, 1 No. 630 observation car, 8 sections OC curved track, 1 No. 068 warning signal, 1 OTC "Lockon" connection. Track forms a circle 30 inches in diameter. Train is 24¼ inches long.

Code Word "KEEN"

MANY WONDERFUL ACCESSORIES FOR USE WITH THESE TRAINS ARE LISTED THROUGHOUT THIS CATALOG

Outfit No. 293—Comprises 1 No. 252 reversible locomotive with electric headlight, 1 No. 803 coal car, 1 No. 804 oil car, 1 No. 805 box car, 1 No. 807 caboose, 8 sections OC curved track, 2 sections OS straight track, 1 controlling rheostat, 1 No. 068 warning signal, 1 OTC "Lockon" connection. Track forms an oval 40 by 30 inches. Train is 40¼ inches long.

Code Word "UPTON"

Outfit No. 294—Comprises 1 No. 252 reversible locomotive with electric headlight, 2 No. 529 Pullman cars, 1 No. 530 observation car, 8 sections OC curved track, 2 sections OS straight track, 1 controlling rheostat, 1 No. 068 warning signal, 1 OTC "Lockon" connection. Track forms an oval 40 by 30 inches. Train is 32½ inches long.

Code Word "CORN"

Outfit No. 296—Comprises 1 No. 253 reversible locomotive with 2 electric headlights, 2 No. 607 illuminated Pullman cars, 1 No. 608 illuminated observation car, 8 sections OC curved track, 4 sections OS straight track, 1 controlling rheostat, 1 No. 068 warning signal, 1 OTC "Lockon" connection. Track forms an oval 50 by 30 inches. Train is 36 inches long.

Code Word "DART"

This Train Has Electrically Lighted Cars

Prices are Listed on Page 45

PASSENGER and FREIGHT TRAIN OUTFITS
For "O" Gauge Track—1⅜ Inches Wide

BOYS—see the amount of realistic detail embodied in these splendid "O" Gauge Trains. Locomotives have two electric headlights, the passenger cars are all fitted with interior lights.

LOCOMOTIVES and Cars are equipped with automatic couplers. Warning signals are included with all "O" Gauge Outfits, without charge. Connecting ties for track and wires for electrical connections are also included.

No. 295

Outfit No. 295—Comprises 1 No. 253 reversible locomotive with 2 electric headlights, 1 No. 811 lumber car with load of lumber, 1 No. 812 gondola car, 1 No. 817 caboose, 8 sections OC curved track, 4 sections OS straight track, 1 controlling rheostat, 1 No. 068 warning signal and 1 OTC "Lockon" connection. Track forms an oval 50 by 30 inches. Train is 40¼ inches long.

Code Word "MARCH"

Nos. 266 and 266E

Outfit No. 266—Comprises 1 No. 254 Super-Motor reversible locomotive with 2 electric headlights, 2 No. 610 illuminated Pullman cars, 1 No. 612 illuminated observation car, 8 sections OC curved track, 6 sections OS straight track, 1 controlling rheostat, 1 No. 068 warning signal, 1 OTC "Lockon" connection. Track forms an oval 60 by 30 inches. Train is 40½ inches long.

Code Word "HEAD"

No. 266E "Distant-Control" Passenger Train Outfit—Same as No. 266 except that it contains No. 254E "Distant-Control" Super-Motor Locomotive, which can be started, stopped, reversed and operated at any speed, at any distance from the track, by means of No. 81 controlling rheostat supplied with it.

Code Word "ILION"

No. 299 and 299E

Outfit No. 299—We have greatly enhanced the value of this outfit by adding a No. 812 gondola car. The outfit now comprises 1 No. 254 reversible locomotive with 2 electric headlights, 1 No. 812 gondola car, 1 No. 813 cattle car, 1 No. 814 box car, 1 No. 817 caboose, 8 sections OC curved track, 6 sections OS straight track, 1 controlling rheostat, 1 No. 068 warning signal, 1 OTC "Lockon" connection. Track forms an oval 60 by 30 inches. Train is 52 inches long.

Code Word "FLORA"

No. 299E "Distant-Control" Freight Train Outfit—Same as No. 299 except that it contains No. 254E "Distant-Control" Super-Motor Locomotive, which can be started, stopped, reversed and operated at any speed, at any distance from the track, by means of No. 81 controlling rheostat supplied with it.

Code Word "QUILL"

No. 267

No. 267 "O" Gauge Passenger Outfit with "Bild-a-Loco" Locomotive—All the fun of a Lionel Railroad combined with the added features of a Lionel "Bild-a-Loco" that can be taken apart and reassembled in a few moments. Outfit comprises 1 No. 4 reversible "Bild-a-Loco" with two electric headlights, 2 No. 605 illuminated Pullman Cars, 1 No. 606 illuminated observation car, 8 sections OC curved track, 8 sections OS straight track, 1 controlling rheostat, 1 No. 068 warning signal, 1 OTC "Lockon" connection. Track forms an oval 70 by 30 inches. Train is 45 inches long. Attractively enameled in a rich orange color.

Code Word "GLEAM"

Prices are Listed on Page 45

PASSENGER AND FREIGHT TRAIN OUTFITS for "O" Gauge Track—1⅜ in. wide

Nos. 97 and 97E

Outfit No. 97—Comprises 1 No. 251 Super-Motor Reversible Locomotive with 2 electric headlights, 2 No. 605 illuminated Pullman cars, 1 No. 606 illuminated observation car, 8 sections OC curved track, 8 sections OS straight track, 1 controlling rheostat, 1 No. 068 warning signal, 1 OTC "Lockon" connection. Track forms an oval 70 by 30 inches. Train is 49¼ inches long.
Code Word "EXCEL"

No. 97E "Distant-Control" Passenger Train Outfit—Same as No. 97, but it contains No. 251E "Distant-Control" Super-Motor Locomotive, which can be started, stopped, reversed and operated at any speed at any distance from the track by means of No. 81 controlling rheostat supplied with it.
Code Word "JUST"

Nos. 269 and 269E

Outfit No. 269—Comprises 1 No. 251 Super-Motor Reversible Locomotive with 2 electric headlights, 1 No. 812 gondola car, 1 No. 813 cattle car, 1 No. 814 box car, 1 No. 815 oil car, 1 No. 817 caboose, 8 sections OC curved track, 6 sections OS straight track, 1 controlling rheostat, 1 No. 068 warning signal, 1 OTC "Lockon" connection. Track forms an oval 60 by 30 inches. Train is 62½ inches long.
Code Word "USHER"

No. 269E "Distant-Control" Freight Train Outfit—Same as No. 269, but it contains No. 251E "Distant-Control" Super-Motor Locomotive, which can be started, stopped, reversed and operated at any speed at any distance from the track by means of No. 81 controlling rheostat supplied with it.
Code Word "NECK"

THE BIG MOGUL OF THE "O" GAUGE LINE
POWERFUL TWIN-MOTORS! OPERATING PANTAGRAPHS! FLAGS!

No. 268

Outfit No. 268—Comprises 1 No. 256 Twin-Super-Motor Reversible Locomotive with 2 electric headlights, 2 No. 710 illuminated Pullman cars, 1 No. 712 illuminated observation car, 8 sections OC curved track, 8 sections OS straight track, 1 controlling rheostat, 1 No. 068 warning signal, 1 OTC "Lockon" connection. Track forms an oval 70 by 30 inches. Train is 51 inches long.
Code Word "TAKE"

Train Outfit No. 268 with its powerful Super-Motor Locomotive and Illuminated Passenger Cars is the finest "O" Gauge Train in the world. You may use with it our new Freight Cars Nos. 811 to 817, illustrated on Page 28. The locomotive will haul 20 of these Freight Cars with perfect ease.

Prices are Listed on Page 45

COMPLETE RAILROADS
For "O" Gauge Track
1⅜ INCHES WIDE

BOYS—here are two wonderful complete railroads that can be set up in very small space. Operate them from the alternating house current with a Lionel "Multivolt" Transformer.

No. 174

NO. 174 Outfit shown above is a complete model railroad to operate on "O" Gauge Track. It includes a large variety of accessories. Every piece is of steel construction and enameled by **Lionel's** own lustrous and lasting process.

Outfit No. 174 comprises 1 No. 253 reversible locomotive with two electric headlights, 2 No. 607 illuminated Pullman cars, 1 No. 608 illuminated observation car, 10 sections OC curved track, 6 sections OS straight track, 1 OTC "Lockon" connection, 1 controlling rheostat, 1 pair No. 021 illuminated switches (one right, one left), 1 No. 106 bridge (3 sections), 1 No. 122 illuminated station, 6 No. 060 telegraph posts with extension arms, 1 No. 62 semaphore, 1 No. 89 flag staff, 1 No. 068 warning signal, 1 No. 119 tunnel. Size of track layout 45 by 60 inches. Train is 35½ inches long.

Code Word "DELA"

No. 175E

A NEW COMPLETE "O" GAUGE "DISTANT-CONTROL" RAILROAD

NO. 175E—Introduced to fill the demand for a complete 100% "Distant-Control" "O" Gauge Railroad at a moderate price. The train can be started, stopped, reversed and operated at any speed at any distance from the track. The electric switches can also be controlled at any distance from the track. The No. 437 Switch Tower contains levers by which the Railroad can be operated, and lamp posts illuminated. This is an ideal Lionel Railroad to fit into a small space.

Outfit comprises 1 No. 254E "Distant-Control" locomotive with two electric headlights, 2 No. 610 illuminated Pullman cars, 1 No. 612 illuminated observation car, 1 No. 080 semaphore, 1 No. 069 warning signal, 1 No. 90 flag staff, 1 No. 106 bridge, 1 pair No. 012 electrically-controlled switches, 1 No. 437 signal tower, 1 No. 119L illuminated tunnel, 2 No. 56 lamp posts, 8 No. 060 telegraph posts with extension arms, 1 No. 81 controlling rheostat, 1 OTC "Lockon" connection, 10 sections OC curved track, 16 sections OS straight track. Complete with wires for connecting to source of current, "Lockon" connections, track on bridge, and special track for electric accessories. Track layout is 100 inches by 40 inches. Train is 40½ inches long.

Code Word "DAWN"

Prices are Listed on Page 45

LIONEL "Bild-a-Loco" AND "Bild-a-Motor" OUTFITS

MODEL RAILROAD engineering is made interesting and educational with the new Lionel "Bild-a-Loco" and "Bild-a-Motor"—a revolutionary departure in miniature motor construction. "Bild-a-Loco" is the world's premier construction set. Unlike all other construction sets, however, "Bild-a-Loco" serves a definite purpose—it is the beginning of a complete model railroad. All parts are so accurately made that any boy can assemble them in a few moments, and when put together they make the most powerful and efficient miniature motor ever designed.

All "Bild-a-Loco" motors (with the exception of the No. 4 model) can be instantly snapped in and out of the locomotive body, as the illustrations show. The unique new packing adopted for "Bild-a-Loco" this year gives you the motor completely assembled. Install the motor in the locomotive body, and it is ready to operate on the track provided with the outfit. Imagine what fun it is to add Pullman and

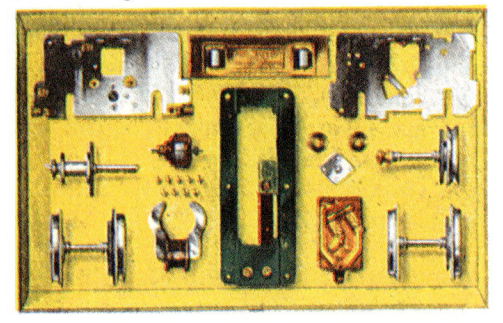

Here are the few simple parts that form Lionel "Bild-a-Loco" and "Bild-a-Motor." Built with the precision of a fine watch. Particular attention is drawn to the entire absence of wires. All electrical connections are automatically made.

Freight Cars, as well as the numerous model railroad accessories shown throughout this catalog.

But that is not all. By simply removing the driving wheels and replacing them with the gears, pulley, drum, sprocket and base included in "Bild-a-Loco" Outfits, a powerful three-speed reversible motor can be constructed in a few moments that will raise 20 times its own weight, and which can be used for innumerable purposes. The illustrations show the simple manner in which this is accomplished.

One of the outstanding features of "Bild-a-Loco" is the fact that there is not a single wire to connect. All connections are automatically made.

"Bild-a-Loco" was first introduced and advertised in 1919, but was then ahead of its time. In the interim it was perfected, and any boy who owns one cannot fail to obtain a better understanding of electricity and mechanics, as well as a vast amount of fun.

"Bild-a-Loco" is perfectly packed; the few simple parts each have a nest of their own, so that they cannot be misplaced.

1. "Bild-a-Loco" Outfit motor is completely assembled, ready to snap in and out of body.
2. "Bild-a-Loco" locomotive with the motor installed in body, ready to operate. 
3. By merely giving a half-turn to two levers, the motor is easily taken out of the body. 
4. "Bild-a-Loco" motor being taken from the body of the locomotive. 
5. To convert "Bild-a-Loco" into "Bild-a-Motor." Turn thumb screws as shown. 
6. The collecting shoe is then lifted from the motor frame. You will note that no tools are required.  
7. The driving wheels are then lifted from the grooves in the side plates of the motor. Every operation is extremely simple.
8. The large gears and shaft supplied with "Bild-a-Loco" Outfits are then inserted in the bearings. 
9. Then the other gear and pulley are dropped into the grooves in the side plates. 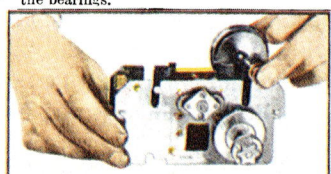
10. The base supplied with "Bild-a-Loco" Outfits is then attached as shown. 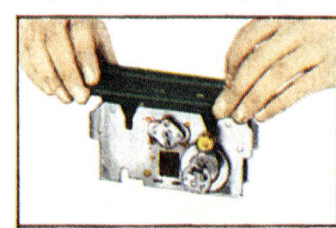
11. All that is now necessary is to tighten the thumb screws in the cross bars of the motor frame. 
12. And you have a three-speed reversible power motor for operating mechanical models or for a thousand other purposes. 

"BILD-A-LOCO" combines two unique models in one—a beautifully designed locomotive and an independent three-speed reversible power motor. "Bild-a-Loco" is good for many years of satisfactory operation, but should parts require replacement they can be installed in a moment. Long delays in the repair shop are not necessary. "Bild-a-Loco" provides a new thrill every minute—it will always hold your interest. Be sure to have your dealer demonstrate these wonderful models for you.

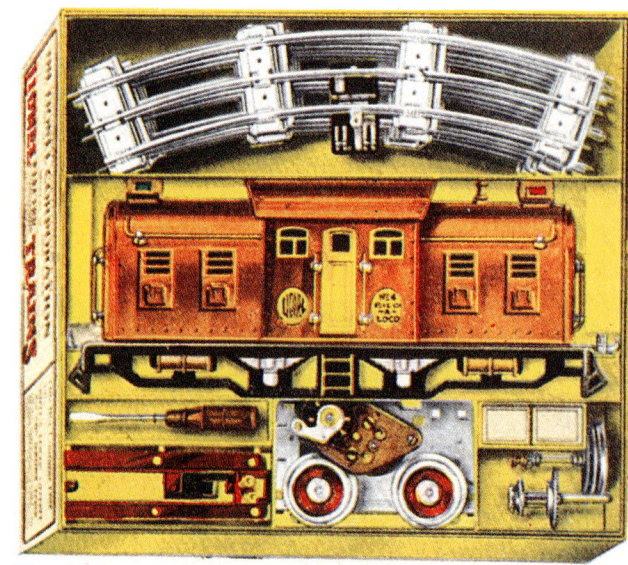

No. 4U Lionel "O" Gauge "Bild-a-Loco" Outfit—Contains all parts for making No. 4 "Bild-a-Loco" locomotive, and No. 1 "Bild-a-Motor" illustrated below, together with 8 sections OC curved track, 1 OTC "Lockon" connection, 1 large gear with pulley and shafting, 1 small gear with shafting, 1 base for motor, 1 screw-driver, and 2 lamps for headlights. The "Bild-a-Motor" is reversible, and three different speeds are obtainable. Very attractively packed. Simple directions for assembling are included. Size of locomotive 9½ inches long, 4¼ inches high. *Code Word* "GRAIL"

With No. 4U Outfit you can construct this powerful "Bild-a-Loco" reversible locomotive and this three-speed reversible "Bild-a-Motor"

Price is Listed on Page 45

LIONEL "Bild-a-Loco" and "Bild-a-Motor" OUTFITS

No. 2 "Bild-a-Motor"

No. 2 Lionel Three-Speed Reversible "Bild-a-Motor"—It can be used for a variety of purposes with construction toys of all kinds. It will develop great power and uses a minimum amount of current. Can be taken down and assembled in a few moments. Operates on dry or storage batteries as well as on reduced alternating or direct current. 7 inches long, 3⅝ inches high, 3 15/16 inches wide.

Code Word "HOIST"

THE gorgeous enameled colors in which all "Bild-a-Loco" models are finished are fully in keeping with the high grade construction of the working parts. Locomotive bodies are embellished with brass and nickeled trim, highly polished. Motor parts and extra gears are heavily nickel plated, and will retain their lustre and brightness forever.

No. 1 Lionel Three-Speed Reversible "Bild-a-Motor"—This powerful motor is similar in construction to the other "Bild-a-Motor" described to the left, but is smaller in size. Made in units so that it can be taken down and reassembled in a few moments. It will lift at least 20 times its own weight. By means of a controlling lever, motor can be started, stopped and reversed. Will operate on dry or storage batteries, or on reduced alternating or direct current. Size 6¼ inches long, 3⅝ inches high, 2¾ inches wide.

Code Word "LIFT"

No. 1 "Bild-a-Motor"

No. 9U "Lionel Standard" "Bild-a-Loco" Outfit—This outfit contains all the parts for making No. 9 "Bild-a-Loco" locomotive illustrated on Page 14, and No. 2 "Bild-a-Motor" illustrated above, together with 8 sections C curved track, 1 STC "Lockon" connection, 1 large gear with pulley and shafting, 1 small gear with shafting, drum and sprocket, 1 base for motor, 1 screw-driver, and 2 lamps for headlights. The "Bild-a-Motor" is reversible, and by means of the various gears three different speeds are obtainable at the same time. Particular attention is drawn to the body of this locomotive which contains an enormous amount of realistic detail. Outfit is very attractively and substantially packed. Simple directions for assembling are included. Size of assembled locomotive is 14½ inches long, 6⅛ inches high.

Code Word "GILT"

With No. 9U Outfit you can construct this powerful "Bild-a-Loco" reversible locomotive and this three-speed reversible "Bild-a-Motor".

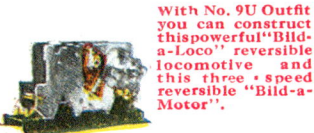

No. 381U "Lionel Standard" "Bild-a-Loco"—This outfit contains all the parts for making No. 381 "Bild-a-Loco" locomotive illustrated on Page 14, and No. 2 "Bild-a-Motor" illustrated above, together with 8 sections C curved track, 1 STC "Lockon" connection, 1 large gear with pulley and shafting, 1 small gear with shafting, drum and sprocket, 1 base for motor, 1 screw-driver and 2 lamps for headlights. This locomotive is the largest in the "Bild-a-Loco" line. In addition to the many features contained in the other "Bild-a-Loco" models, No. 381U is equipped with two massive pilot trucks, each containing 4 wheels. These trucks are so scientifically designed that they will not leave the track, irrespective of the speed of the locomotive. Outfit is very attractively and substantially packed. Simple directions for assembling are included. Size of assembled locomotive is 18 inches long, 6½ inches high.

Code Word "COPE"

With No. 381U Outfit you can construct this powerful "Bild-a-Loco" reversible locomotive and this three-speed reversible "Bild-a-Motor".

Prices are Listed on Page 45

ASSEMBLED "Bild-a-Loco" LOCOMOTIVES
TRADE MARK. PATENTS PENDING

No. 4 Hand Control "Bild-a-Loco" Locomotive for "O" Gauge Track. For complete description of the marvelous new "Bild-a-Loco" motor that can be taken apart and assembled in a jiffy, please refer to Page 12. The body of the No. 4 Locomotive incorporates all the features of Nos. 254 and 254E Locomotives described on Page 7. It is equipped with automatic couplers and two electric headlights. Boys—you will derive a great amount of amusement as well as a keen knowledge of electric motors by being able to study each part as you assemble it or take it apart—the work of a moment. Size 9½ inches long, 4¼ inches high.

Code Word "URGE"

No. 043 "Bild-a-Motor" Set—With these gears and base you can, in a few moments, convert your "O" Gauge "Bild-a-Loco" into a No. 1 reversible three-speed stationary "Bild-a-Motor"—a power motor that will lift 20 times its own weight, as described on Page 12.

Code Word "UNTO"

No. 4

BOYS—the new "Bild-a-Loco" Locomotives shown on this page are completely assembled, ready to operate. You will double your fun by adding "Bild-a-Loco" to your Model Railroad. Nos. 9E and 381E for "Lionel Standard" Track have the famous "Distant-Control" unit incorporated in them. Not only can you take them apart and assemble them in a few moments, but you can also stop, start, reverse or operate them at any speed at any distance from the track.

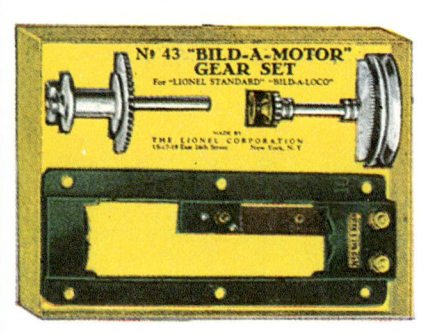

No. 9E "Distant-Control" "Bild-a-Loco" Locomotive for "Lionel Standard" Track. In addition to the interesting design of the "Bild-a-Loco", this locomotive also contains our "Distant-Control" unit which makes it possible to start, stop and reverse the locomotive at any distance from the track. The body is beautifully designed and incorporates many features that are typically Lionel. Locomotive contains two electric headlights so arranged that the front one is always illuminated irrespective of the direction in which the locomotive is traveling. This locomotive is equipped with automatic couplers. It measures 11 inches long, 4¾ inches high. No. 81 controlling rheostat is included.

Code Word "UTTER"

No. 9 Hand Control "Bild-a-Loco" Locomotive for "Lionel Standard" Track. This is in every way similar to No 9E described above, but instead of the electric reversing unit, it is equipped with a hand reversing controller. Complete with two headlights.

Code Word "UMBER"

Nos. 9 and 9E

No. 43 "Bild-a-Motor" Set—With these gears and base you can in a few moments convert your "Lionel Standard" "Bild-a-Loco" into a No. 2 reversible three-speed stationary "Bild-a-Motor"—a power motor that will lift 20 times its own weight, as described on Page 12.

Code Word "EDGE"

No. 43

No. 381E "Distant-Control" "Bild-a-Loco" Locomotive for "Lionel Standard" Track. This locomotive is the most elaborate in the Lionel Line. The illustration shows the great detail incorporated in it, and special mention is made of the construction of the two-4-wheel pilot trucks which will not derail even when the locomotive is traveling at a high rate of speed. The "Bild-a-Loco" motor and "Distant-Control" mechanism can be removed from the body in a jiffy, and the illustrations on the previous page show the accessibility to all parts. The boy can at will take down and rebuild this motor within a few minutes. It is not amiss to repeat that all parts are so accurately made that no difficulty will be experienced in setting it up, and there is not a single wire to be connected, as all electrical contacts are automatically made. It is extremely efficient and powerful enough to haul a dozen or more of the largest Pullman or freight cars with the greatest ease. This supreme model can be seen in conjunction with our finest Pullman cars on Pages 23, 24 and 25. Size 18 inches long, 6½ inches high. Includes No. 81 controlling rheostat and two electric headlights.

Code Word "ULTI"

No. 381 Hand Control "Bild-a-Loco" Locomotive for "Lionel Standard" Track. This is in every way similar to the No. 381E described above, but instead of the electric reversing unit, it is equipped with hand reversing controller. Complete with two electric headlights.

Code Word "SHAKE"

Nos. 381 and 381E

See Pages 28 and 29 for the correct passenger and freight cars to be used with No. 4 "O" Gauge Locomotive.

Prices are Listed on Page 45

See Pages 26, 27 and 29 for the correct passenger and freight cars to be used with Nos. 9, 9E, 381 and 381E "Lionel Standard" Locomotives.

"LIONEL STANDARD" SUPER-MOTOR AND TWIN-SUPER-MOTOR LOCOMOTIVES

No. 408E "Lionel Standard" Twin-Super-Motor "Distant-Control" Locomotive. The illustration clearly shows the great amount of realistic details incorporated in it. Many of the constructional features are indicated on Page 6. Attention is directed to the operating pantographs, illuminated signal lanterns, front and rear flags, brass hand rails, copper exhaust pipes, etc. This locomotive is equipped with "Distant-Control" mechanism, which enables the user to start, stop, reverse and operate it at any speed at any distance from the track by means of No. 81 controlling rheostat supplied with it. Size 17 inches long, 6½ inches high to top of pantograph. Complete with flags, headlight lamps and lamps for front and rear lanterns.
Code Word "FAST"

No. 402E "Lionel Standard" Twin-Super-Motor "Distant-Control" Locomotive. Many of the realistic details found in the No. 408E Locomotive, described above, are incorporated in this beautiful and powerful model. It will haul a large number of our big passenger or freight cars with perfect ease. Equipped with "Distant-Control" mechanism described above. Size 17 inches long, 6½ inches high. Complete with lamps for headlights and No. 81 controlling rheostat.
Code Word "YORK"

FOR "LIONEL STANDARD" TRACK 2¼ INCHES WIDE

See Pages 26, 27 and 29 for correct Freight and Passenger Cars to be used with the Locomotives described on this page.

No. 402E 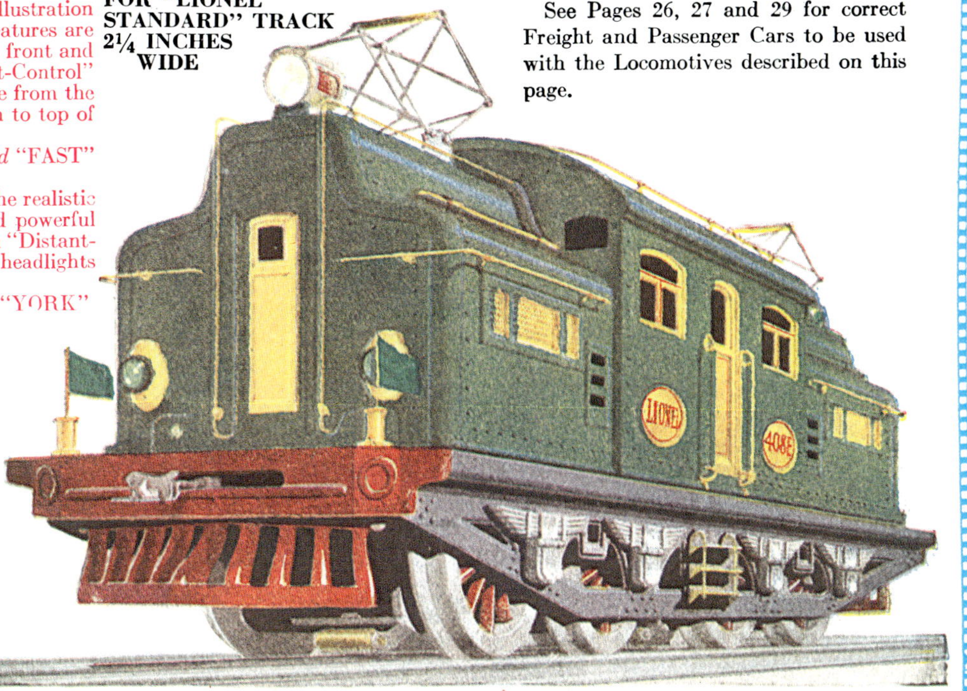   No. 408E

Nos. 8 and 8E   Nos. 10 and 10E   Nos. 318 and 318E

No. 8 "Lionel Standard" Super-Motor Reversible Locomotive—With 2 electric headlights. 11 inches long, 4¾ inches high.
Code Word "POWER"

No. 8E "Lionel Standard" "Distant-Control" Super-Motor Locomotive—Same as No. 8, but equipped with electrically-controlled mechanism which starts, stops, reverses and operates it at any speed at any distance from the track by means of No. 81 controlling rheostat supplied with it.
Code Word "PEPPY"

No. 10 "Lionel Standard" Super-Motor Reversible Locomotive—With 2 electric headlights. 11⅜ inches long, 5 inches high.
Code Word "PULL"

No. 10E "Lionel Standard" "Distant-Control" Super-Motor Locomotive—Same as No. 10, but equipped with electrically-controlled mechanism which starts, stops, reverses and operates it at any speed at any distance from the track by means of No. 81 controlling rheostat supplied with it.
Code Word "SELF"

No. 318 "Lionel Standard" Super-Motor Reversible Locomotive—With 2 electric headlights. 12⅛ inches long, 5⅛ inches high.
Code Word "VERB"

No. 318E "Lionel Standard" "Distant-Control" Super-Motor Locomotive. Same as No. 318, but equipped with electrically-controlled mechanism which starts, stops, reverses and operates it at any speed at any distance from the track by means of No. 81 controlling rheostat supplied with it.
Code Word "MOVE"

No. 380E "Lionel Standard" "Distant-Control" Super-Motor Locomotive. With 2 electric headlights, 13⅜ inches long, 5¼ inches high This locomotive is equipped with electrically-controlled mechanism which starts, stops, reverses and operates it at any speed at any distance from the track by means of No. 81 controlling rheostat supplied with it.
Code Word "SAINT"

All "Lionel Standard" Locomotives are equipped with automatic couplers, and 2 electric headlights. Lamps for headlights are included.   **Prices are Listed on Page 45**   See Page 5 for details of construction of "Lionel Standard" Super-Motors and Twin-Super-Motors.

TRAIN OUTFITS FOR "LIONEL STANDARD" TRACK—2¼ INCHES WIDE

Reg. U. S. Pat. Off.

LIONEL Train Outfits are complete in every respect. Lamps for headlights and passenger cars are supplied with every outfit; also wires for transformer or battery connection and connecting ties for joining sections of track.

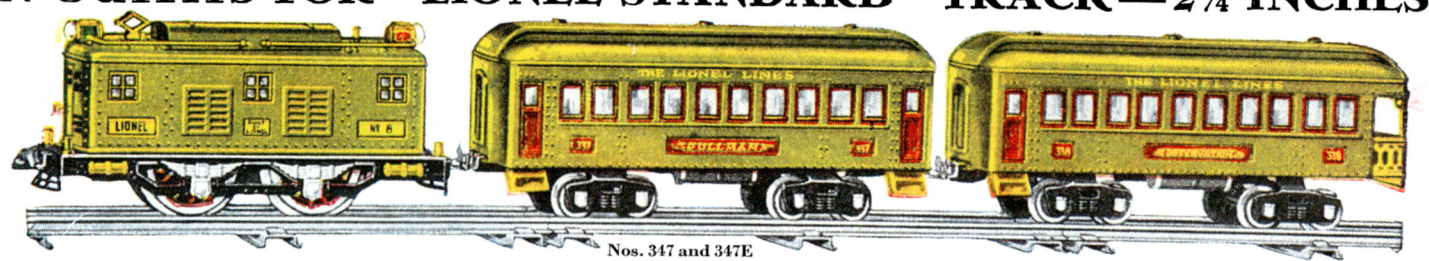

Nos. 347 and 347E

Outfit No. 347—Comprises 1 No. 8 Super-Motor reversible locomotive with 2 electric headlights, 1 No. 337 illuminated Pullman car, 1 No. 338 illuminated observation car, 8 sections C curved track, 2 sections S straight track, 1 STC "Lockon" connection. Track forms an oval 56 by 42 inches. Train is 38½ inches long.
Code Word "ZENA"

Outfit No. 347E—Same as No. 347, except that it contains No. 8E "Distant-Control" Super-Motor locomotive, which can be started, stopped, reversed and operated at any speed at any distance from the track by means of No. 81 controlling rheostat supplied with it.
Code Word "GLIDE"

ALL "Lionel Standard" Trains are equipped with automatic couplers.

It is best to use a Lionel "Multivolt" transformer for operating all Lionel Trains on reduced alternating current. See page 33.

Nos. 353 and 353E

Outfit No. 353—Comprises 1 No. 8 Super-Motor reversible locomotive with 2 electric headlights, 1 No. 511 lumber car with load of lumber, 1 No. 512 gondola car, 1 No. 517 illuminated caboose, 8 sections C curved track, 2 sections S straight track, 1 STC "Lockon" connection. Track forms an oval 56 by 42 inches. Train is 50¼ inches long.
Code Word "JACK"

Outfit No. 353E—Same as No. 353, except that it contains No. 8E "Distant-Control" Super-Motor locomotive, which can be started, stopped, reversed and operated at any speed at any distance from the track by means of No. 81 controlling rheostat supplied with it.
Code Word "MASK"

Nos. 352 and 352E

Outfit No. 352—Comprises 1 No. 10 Super-Motor reversible locomotive with 2 electric headlights, 1 No. 332 illuminated mail and baggage car, 1 No. 339 illuminated Pullman car, 1 No. 341 illuminated observation car, 8 sections C curved track, 4 sections S straight track, 1 STC "Lockon" connection. Track forms an oval 69 by 42 inches. Train is 52 inches long.
Code Word "PRINCE"

Outfit No. 352E—Same as No. 352, except that it contains No. 10E "Distant-Control" Super-Motor locomotive, which can be started, stopped, reversed and operated at any speed at any distance from the track by means of No. 81 controlling rheostat supplied with it.
Code Word "WIN"

Nos. 354 and 354E

Outfit No. 354—Comprises 1 No. 10 Super-Motor Reversible locomotive with 2 electric headlights, 1 No. 511 lumber car with load of lumber, 1 No. 512 gondola car, 1 No. 513 cattle car, 1 No. 514 box car, 1 No. 517 illuminated caboose, 8 sections C curved track, 6 sections S straight track, 1 STC "Lockon" connection. Track forms an oval 88 by 42 inches. Train is 77 inches long.
Code Word "ZONE"

Outfit No. 354E—Same as No. 354, except that it contains No. 10E "Distant-Control" Super-Motor locomotive, which can be started, stopped, reversed and operated at any speed at any distance from the track by means of No. 81 controlling rheostat supplied with it.
Code Word "ZEST"

Prices are Listed on Page 45

TRAIN OUTFITS FOR "LIONEL STANDARD" TRACK 2¼ INCHES WIDE

Reg. U. S. Pat. Off.

Nos. 342 and 342E

Outfit No. 342—Comprises 1 No. 318 Super-Motor reversible locomotive with 2 electric headlights, 1 No. 310 illuminated mail and baggage car, 1 No. 309 illuminated Pullman car, 1 No. 312 illuminated observation car, 8 sections C curved track, 6 sections S straight track, 1 STC "Lockon" connection. Track forms an oval 88 by 42 inches. Train is 57½ inches long.
Code Word "VIEW"

No. 342E "Distant Control" Passenger Train Outfit—Same as No. 342, except that it contains No. 318E "Distant Control" Super-Motor Locomotive, which can be started, stopped, reversed and operated at any speed at any distance from the track by means of No. 81 controlling rheostat supplied with it.
Code Word "FORUM"

No. 340E

No. 340E "Distant Control" Coal Train—A new and welcome addition to the **Lionel** Line. Comprises 1 No. 318E "Distant Control" Super-Motor locomotive with 2 electric headlights, 3 No. 516 coal cars with load of coal in each car, 1 No. 517 illuminated caboose, 8 sections C curved track, 6 sections S straight track, 1 STC "Lockon" connection and 1 No. 81 controlling rheostat. Track forms an oval 88 by 42 inches. Complete train is 66 inches long. This train can be started, stopped, reversed and operated at any speed at any distance from the track.
Code Word "ILK"

No. 355E

No. 355E "Distant Control" Freight Train Outfit—Comprises 1 No. 318E "Distant Control" Super-Motor locomotive with 2 electric headlights, 1 No. 511 lumber car with load of lumber, 1 No. 512 gondola car, 1 No. 513 cattle car, 1 No. 514 box car, 1 No. 515 oil car, 1 No. 517 illuminated caboose, 8 sections C curved track, 8 sections S straight track, 1 STC "Lockon" connection. Track forms an oval 102 by 42 inches. Train is 92 inches long. This train can be started, stopped, reversed and operated at any speed at any distance from the track by means of No. 81 controlling rheostat supplied with it.
Code Word "LORRY"

NEW "LIONEL STANDARD" "BILD-A-LOCO" TRAIN OUTFITS

Nos. 349 and 349E

Outfit No. 349 with "Bild-a-Loco" Locomotive—A handsome new train that will provide unlimited fun for the user. The famous "Bild-a-Loco" locomotive can be taken apart and reassembled in a few moments—Outfit comprises 1 No. 9 reversible "Bild-a-Loco" locomotive with 2 electric headlights, 1 No. 428 illuminated Pullman car, 1 No. 429 illuminated Pullman and baggage car, 1 No. 430 illuminated observation car, 8 sections C curved track, 8 sections S straight track, 1 STC "Lockon" connection. Track forms an oval 102 by 42 inches. Complete train is 73 inches long.
Code Word "PANT"

No. 349E "Distant Control" "Bild-a-Loco" Passenger Train Outfit—Same as No. 349, but in addition the "Bild-a-Loco" locomotive incorporates the famous "Distant-Control" unit, by means of which this train can be started, stopped, reversed and operated at any speed at any distance from the track. No. 81 controlling rheostat included.
Code Word "PERT"

Prices are Listed on Page 45

NEW LIONEL ELECTRICALLY DRIVEN STEAM TYPE LOCOMOTIVES

for "Lionel Standard" Track—2¼ Inches Wide. Equipped with the Famous Lionel "Bild-a-Loco" Motor.

JUST as **Lionel** Electric Locomotives are recognized throughout the world as the last word in Model Electric Railroad construction—so **Lionel** Steam-Type Locomotives are, by far, the most magnificent and perfect of their type that have ever been offered to the boys of America. You have never before seen a Steam-Type Locomotive that is so perfect, so realistic, so striking a piece of mechanism as the New **Lionel**. It transcends in beauty of design, in excellence of construction, and in electrical and mechanical perfection, any model Steam-Type Loco that has ever been made. The new **Lionel** Steam-Type Locomotive is electrically driven by the famous **Lionel** "Bild-a-Loco" Motor (the motor that snaps out in a jiffy—then can be taken apart and quickly reassembled by any boy). The new **Lionel** Steam-Type vibrates with realism and tremendous power. There's a thrill in its grace—power in its heavy steel construction—a suggestion of tremendous speed in its greyhound length. The movement of its pistons and driving rods is so natural in action that you see before you a miniature of a great "Giant of the Rails."

Lionel perfection—**Lionel** attention to minute details—those outstanding **Lionel** characteristics make the new Steam-Type Locomotive a most unusual achievement.

DETAILS OF CONSTRUCTION

Locomotives 14 inches long, 5 inches high. Tender 8¼ inches long, 4½ inches high. Length over all—22¼ inches.

Locomotive has 4 driving wheels—and front and rear pilot trucks. Copper exhaust and steam pipes suggest realism—while brass hand rails add another elaborate touch.

The finish is a beautiful black enamel—with brass and nickel trim.

Headlight on the boiler front—two flags in position—warning bell—lanterns mounted on forward platform above cow-catchers, all located in accordance with construction of modern locomotives.

The tender has 8 wheels and harmonizes with locomotive. Embossed rivets and nickeled journal boxes present the correct touch of realism. The load of coal in the tender is another instance of **Lionel's** attention to details.

The **Lionel** Steam-Type Locomotive is made in two models—with hand reverse—or **Lionel** "Distant-Control," enabling the user to start, stop, reverse and operate train at any speed at any distance from track.

No. 390 and 390E Head-on View

No. 390 and 390E SIDE VIEW

These illustrations are reproduced from actual photographs and are not exaggerated in any way.

No. 390 Hand Control Steam-Type Locomotive and Tender for "Lionel Standard" Track. Locomotive is 14 inches long, 5 inches high. Tender is 8¼ inches long, 4½ inches high. Total length of locomotive and tender is 22¼ inches. Complete with headlight and flags.

Code Word "TRUE."

No. 390E "Distant-Control" Steam-Type Locomotive and Tender for "Lionel Standard" Track. Similar in every way to No. 390, but is equipped with "Distant-Control" mechanism, by which the locomotive can be started, stopped, reversed and operated at any speed at any distance from the track. Complete with No. 81 controlling rheostat, headlight and flags.

Code Word "TONE."

No. 395 and 395E

No. 395 Hand Control Freight Train Outfit for "Lionel Standard" Track. Comprises 1 No. 390 Steam-Type Locomotive and Tender, 1 No. 511 lumber car with load of lumber, 1 No. 512 gondola car, 1 No. 513 cattle car, 1 No. 514 box car, 1 No. 515 oil car, 1 No. 517 illuminated caboose, 8 sections C curved track, 10 sections S straight track and 1 STC "Lockon" connection. Track forms an oval 116 by 42 inches. The entire train is 100 inches long. Complete with headlight, lamp in caboose and flags.

Code Word "TRILL."

No. 395E "Distant-Control" Freight Train Outfit for "Lionel Standard" Track. This is in every way similar to No. 395 Outfit, but locomotive is equipped with "Distant-Control" mechanism, enabling the user to start, stop, reverse or operate train at any speed at any distance from the track. Complete with No. 81 controlling rheostat, headlight, lamp in caboose and flags.

Code Word "TOBY."

Prices are Listed on Page 45

STEAM TYPE PASSENGER AND FREIGHT TRAIN OUTFITS

for "Lionel Standard" Track—2¼ Inches Wide.

No. 391 and 391E OUTFITS

No. 391 Hand Control Freight Train Outfit for "Lionel Standard" Track. Comprises 1 No. 390 Steam-Type Locomotive and Tender, 1 No. 511 lumber car with load of lumber, 1 No. 512 gondola car. 1 No. 517 illuminated caboose, 8 sections C curved track, 4 sections S straight track, 1 STC "Lockon" connection. Track forms an oval 69 by 42 inches. The entire train is 62 inches long. Complete with headlight, lamp for caboose, and flags.

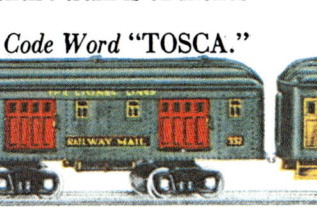

Code Word "TOSCA."

No. 391E "Distant-Control" Freight Train Outfit for "Lionel Standard" Track. This is in every way similar to No. 391 outfit described in the opposite column, but locomotive is equipped with "Distant-Control" mechanism, enabling the user to start, stop, reverse or operate train at any speed at any distance from the track. Complete with No. 81 controlling rheostat, headlight, lamp for caboose, and flags.

Code Word "TOAST."

No. 392 and 392E OUTFITS

No. 392 Hand Control Passenger Train Outfit for "Lionel Standard" Track. Comprises 1 No. 390 Steam-Type Locomotive and Tender, 1 No. 332 illuminated baggage car, 1 No. 339 illuminated Pullman car, 1 No. 341 illuminated observation car, 8 sections C curved track, 6 sections S straight track and 1 STC "Lockon" connection. Track forms an oval 88 by 42 inches. The entire train is 63 inches long. Complete with headlight, lamps for cars, and flags.

Code Word "TWINE."

No. 392E "Distant-Control" Passenger Train Outfit for "Lionel Standard" Track. This is in every way similar to No. 392 outfit described in the opposite column, but locomotive is equipped with "Distant-Control" mechanism, enabling the user to start, stop, reverse or operate train at any speed at any distance from the track. Complete with No. 81 controlling rheostat, headlight, lamps for cars, and flags.

Code Word "TROT."

No. 393 and 393E OUTFITS

No. 393 Hand Control Coal Train Outfit for "Lionel Standard" Track. Comprises 1 No. 390 Steam-Type Locomotive and Tender, 3 No. 516 coal cars, 1 No. 517 illuminated caboose, 8 sections C curved track, 6 sections S straight track, 1 STC "Lockon" connection. Track forms an oval 88 by 42 inches. The entire train is 74 inches long. Complete with headlight, lamp for caboose, and flags.

Code Word "TROOP."

No. 393E "Distant-Control" Coal Train Outfit for "Lionel Standard" Track. This is in every way similar to No. 393 outfit described in the opposite column, but locomotive is equipped with "Distant-Control" mechanism, enabling the user to start, stop, reverse or operate train at any speed at any distance from the track. Complete with No. 81 controlling rheostat, headlight, lamp in caboose, and flags.

Code Word "TWIST."

No. 394E OUTFIT

No. 394E "Distant-Control" Passenger Train Outfit for "Lionel Standard" Track. Comprises 1 No. 390E "Distant-Control" Steam-Type Locomotive and Tender, 1 No. 310 illuminated baggage car, 2 No. 309 illuminated Pullman Cars, 1 No. 312 illuminated observation car, 8 sections C curved track, 8 sections S straight track, 1 STC "Lockon" connection and 1 No. 81 controlling rheostat. This train can be started, stopped, reversed or operated at any speed at any distance from the track. Track forms an oval 102 by 42 inches. The entire train is 81 inches long. Complete with headlight, lamps in cars, and flags.

Code Word "TALE."

Prices are Listed on Page 45

No. 407E "LIONEL STANDARD" 100% "DISTANT-CONTROL" COMPLETE RAILROAD

HERE is the finest gift that any boy could wish for—a complete **Lionel** "Distant-Control" Railroad, containing not only the best trains we manufacture, but a very large variety of Electrically-Controlled and illuminated Accessories. The Passenger and Freight Trains can be started, stopped, reversed and operated at any speed at any distance from the track. The Switch Signal-Tower, shown in the foreground, and the elevated Tower in the rear, enable you to operate all the Electrically-Controlled Accessories at a distance. The specifications of this marvelous model Railroad are given below.

OUTFIT No. 407E—COMPRISES

1 No. 408E "Distant-Control" Locomotive	1 No. 212 Gondola car	38 S Track	1 No. 80 Semaphore	20 STC "Lockon" connections
1 No. 380E "Distant-Control" Locomotive	1 No. 213 Cattle car	18 C Track	2 No. 77 Crossing gates	Wires for making electrical connections, connecting ties for joining sections of track, lamps for headlights, interior of cars and all illuminated accessories are supplied with this outfit. Track layout is 12 feet 10 inches long by 6 feet 4 inches wide.
2 No. 81 Controlling rheostats	1 No. 214 Box car	4 ½S Track	1 No. 89 Flagstaff	
1 No. 418 Pullman car	1 No. 215 Oil car	1 No. 124 Station	2 No. 76 Block signals	
1 No. 419 Pullman and baggage car	1 No. 216 Coal car	1 No. 189 Villa	1 No. 69 Warning signal	
1 No. 490 Observation car	1 No. 217 Illuminated Caboose	1 No. 191 Villa	1 No. 436 Power house	
1 No. 431 Dining-car	1 No. 218 Operating Dump car	3 No. 184 Bungalows	1 No. 437 Switch tower	
1 No. 211 Lumber car with load of lumber	1 No. 219 Operating Derrick car	1 No. 438 Signal Tower	2 No. 67 Lamp posts	
	1 No. 84 Semaphore	1 No. 101 Bridge	4 No. 56 Lamp posts	
	1 Type K Transformer	1 No. 140L Tunnel	2 No. 57 Lamp posts	
	3 pr. 222 Switches	12 No. 60 Telegraph Posts	2 No. 59 Lamp posts	
	2 No. 23 Bumpers	1 No. 78 Train Control		

Code Word "ALLY"

Price is Listed on Page 45

PASSENGER, FREIGHT AND WORK TRAINS

No. 357 E—"Distant-Control" Work Train

HERE is a new outfit to operate on "Lionel Standard" Track, that will greatly increase the play value of Lionel Trains. It is a work train in every sense of the word. The Derrick car actually operates, and the Dump Car can be tilted by means of the gears at one end. The Gondola contains working implements, barrels, etc., and the realism of the entire train is heightened by the illuminated Caboose at the rear end. Nothing so perfect has ever been shown in the way of a model train outfit.

This Outfit includes No. 380E "Distant-Control" locomotive, with two electric headlights, 1 No. 81 controlling rheostat, 1 No. 212 gondola car, 1 No. 218 dump car, 1 No. 219 derrick car, 1 No. 217 illuminated caboose, 8 sections C curved track, 8 sections S straight track, and 1 STC "Lockon" connection. Track forms an oval 102 by 42 inches. Train is 72 inches long. *Code Word "ZEAL."*

**ALL THESE TRAINS HAVE THE FA...
STOPPED, REVERSED AN...**

No. 403 E—Twin-Super-Motor "Distant-Control" Passenger Train — A Perfect Model

COMPLETE details showing the perfect construction of every part that enters into this outfit are given on the following pages: Twin-Motor construction on Page 5, Locomotive construction and construction of Passenger Coaches on Page 6.

The great hauling power of the locomotive is an outstanding feature. The "Distant-Control" mechanism built into it is a source of endless delight. It can be sta... any speed at any distance from th... build a complete 100% "Dista... train with our "Distant-Contr... which are described in other p... added from time to time.

No. 410 E—Twin-Super-Motor "Distant-Control" Freight Train — A Powerful De-Luxe Freighter

THIS new De-Luxe "Distant-Control" Freight Train is the acme of perfection. The illustrations give you a clear idea of the wonderful detail in the new freight cars which incorporate many original and exclusive features that only Lionel can carry out to such perfection.

Attention is drawn to the heavy steel frames upon which the super-structure is mounted, the new steel trucks with nickeled journals, automatic couplers, embossed rivets and other structural details that are so perfectly designed. The car bodies also show a wealth of detail.

The Cattle Car and Box Car have sliding door... able supports inserted in sockets in the platfo... operates by turning a wheel on the top.

Prices are Li...

PASSENGER TRAIN OUTFITS FOR "LIONEL STANDARD" TRACK
2¼ INCHES WIDE

No. 409E

and electrically illuminated fixtures, which obtain current from our patented collecting shoes built into the six-wheel trucks. The interior light shining through the colored glass windows produces a very realistic effect.

A feature of the observation car is the dome light on the rear platform (in addition to the interior light) which shows through two red signal lanterns. The transparent "Lionel Limited" sign affixed to the observation railing is another interesting new detail.

The new Dining-Car is real in everything but size. On Page 29 the sectional view of this car shows tables, chairs and kitchen completely equipped with range, serving table and a profusion of other details. This is the only completely equipped model Dining-Car made in America.

The Pullman and Baggage Car has two compartments—one is equipped with revolving parlor-car chairs, while the baggage section has sliding doors as used on all cars of this type. All cars are equipped with automatic couplers.

No. 411E

ical detail and precision, for for handsome and lasting ectric Train in the world that achievement. Even the most not be as convincing as seeing

TIVE

he "Bild-a-Loco" engine are given well as the front and rear 4-wheel wer. Attention is directed to the ed lanterns, operating pantagraphs, comotive which make it stand out

This illustration shows detail of the lavatory and wash-room compartments, an exact reproduction of the most modern types of all-steel Pullman Cars.

THE PULLMANS
Never before has such a wealth of realistic detail been embodied in a model railroad car. The illustrations show the unique fittings, such as lavatory compartments and wash-rooms, revolving arm chairs, two interior lights, hinged doors, and ventilators in the roof. The roofs are hinged, and when closed are securely locked by means of two steel catches. By merely pressing two plungers in the transom, the roof can be opened instantly.

THE OBSERVATION CAR
Viewing this splendid train from the rear end you can easily imagine yourself looking at a real observation platform. The large clear observation window is free from obstruction. The glass door also adds to the realism. The observation platform is enclosed in an ornamental polished brass railing, while the electric dome light (in addition to the two interior lights) adds brilliance to the general

Showing the detail on the observation platform. Note the large glass observation window, brass hand rail, brass observation rail, swinging glass door, dome LIGHT, and rear end red LANTERNS

effect. This dome light shine over the observation platform

The bodies of the locomoti embossed rivets present an railroad rolling stock. Pullma inserted pieces giving added lettering are of etched brass. rails are of polished brass. Jo

Lionel has produced a and cars comprising this The baked-on finish will always be kept bright and cl

Prices are Listed on Page 45

LIONEL PRESENTS TWO OF THE WORLD'S FINEST MODEL ELECTRIC TRAINS. ANY BOY WOULD BE PROUD TO OWN THEM.

No. 409-E. "DE LUXE EXPRESS" POWERED BY THE FAMOUS LIONEL "DISTANT-CONTROL" TWIN-SUPER-MOTOR LOCOMOTIVE.

THE locomotive described on **Page 15** is an exact reproduction of the latest ty[pe] used on the big electrified systems. Other remarkable details of construct[ion] are indicated on Page 6. The construction of the twin-motors is fully describ[ed] on Page 5.

The Pullman Coaches are in every detail similar to the most modern Passeng[er] Cars. See Page 29 for complete description of the many wonderful features inc[or]porated in these cars. The interiors contain individual revolving parlor-car cha[irs]

No. 411-E. "TRANSCONTINENTAL LIMITED" INCORPORATING THE MARVELOUS "BILD-A-LOCO" "DISTANT CONTROL" TWELVE-WHEEL LOCOMOTIVE.

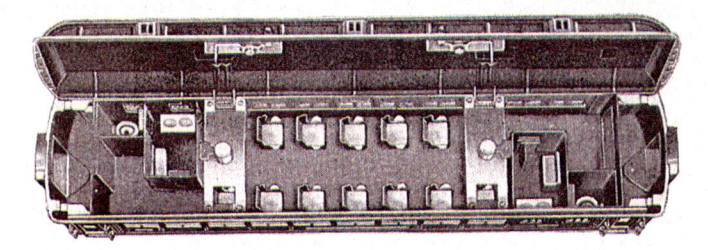

A view of Nos. 412, 413 and 414 Pullman Cars showing hinged roof interior lighting system, rigid interior construction, revolving arm chairs and 2 lavatory and wash-room compartments.

FOR beauty of design, for mecha[nical] electrical perfection and efficien[cy,] enamel finish, there is not a Model E[lectric] compares with this—Lionel's supreme[...] superlative terms of description would [...] this wonderful train in operation.

THE LOCOMO[TIVE]
Full details of the remarkable features of [...] on Page 14. The massive driving wheels as [...] pilot trucks provide tremendous hauling po[wer,] front and rear headlights, front and rear colo[red...] and many other details in the body of this lo[comotive] as a masterpiece.

23

R "LIONEL STANDARD" TRACK—2¼ INCHES WIDE

LIONEL TRAINS AND REAL TRAINS DIFFER ONLY IN SIZE

MOUS LIONEL "DISTANT-CONTROL" MECHANISM. THEY CAN BE STARTED, O OPERATED AT ANY SPEED, AT ANY DISTANCE FROM THE TRACK

stopped, reversed and operated at track. It is wonderful to be able to Control" Railroad by using this accessories, a large variety of rts of this catalog. They can be

Outfit No. 403E—Comprises 1 No. 402E Twin-Super-Motor "Distant-Control" locomotive with 2 electric headlights, 1 No. 418 illuminated Pullman car, 1 No. 419 illuminated Pullman and baggage car, 1 No. 490 illuminated observation car, 8 sections C curved track, 8 sections S straight track, 1 STC "Lockon" connection and 1 No. 81 controlling rheostat. Track forms an oval 102 by 42 inches.

Train is 76 inches long. This train is completely equipped with the new Lionel Automatic Spring Couplers. Outfit also includes lamps for headlights and interiors of cars, wires for connecting to source of current, and connecting ties for joining sections of track.

Code Word "DEMY."

The Lumber Car with load of lumber has removm. The Coal Car has a "Hopper" bottom which boose is equipped with illuminated lanterns on the rear platform. The powerful Twin-Super-Motor "Distant-Control" locomotive No. 408E described on Page 15 will easily haul this train and it can be started, stopped, reversed and operated at any speed at any distance from the track.

Outfit No. 410E—Comprises 1 No. 408E Twin-Super-Motor "Distant-Control" locomotive with 2 electric headlights, 1 No. 211 lumber car with load of Lumber, 1 No. 212 gondola car, 1 No. 213 cattle car, 1 No. 214 box car, 1 No. 215 oil car, 1 No. 216 coal car, 1 No. 217 illuminated

caboose, 8 sections C curved track, 10 sections S straight track, 1 STC "Lockon" connection and 1 No. 81 controlling rheostat. Train is 118 inches long. Track forms an oval 116 by 42 inches. Outfit also includes lamps for headlights, locomotive lanterns and caboose, wires for transformer or battery connection and connecting ties for joining sections of track.

Code Word "BEST."

ted on Page 45

Lionel's famous "Distant-Control" unit enables you to start, stop, reverse and ate this train at any speed, at any distance from the track.

comprises 1 No. 408E "Distant-Control" Twin-Super-Motor Locove with 2 electric headlights and front and rear green lanterns, 1 No. 418 illuted Pullman Car, 1 No. 419 illuminated Pullman and Baggage Car, 1 No. 490 inated Observation Car, 1 No. 431 illuminated Dining-Car, 8 sections C curved track, 10 sections S straight track, 1 No. 81 controlling rheostat and 1 STC "Lockon" connection.

Lamps for headlights, front and rear lanterns and interior of cars are included, as well as flags, wires for connecting to source of current and connecting ties for joining sections of track. Track forms an oval 116 by 42 inches. Complete train is 95½ inches long.

Code Word "ETTA"

the two red lanterns attached to the roof

RUCTION
rs are made of heavy sheet steel, and the gged strength, just the same as on real are hinged, window frames are separable s well as realism. Panels containing the nickeled and polished. Steps and hand rucks are solid brass castings.

FINISH
one effect in the finish of the locomotive t durable enamels harmonize beautifully. peel off, and the locomotive and cars can ely polishing with an ordinary cloth.

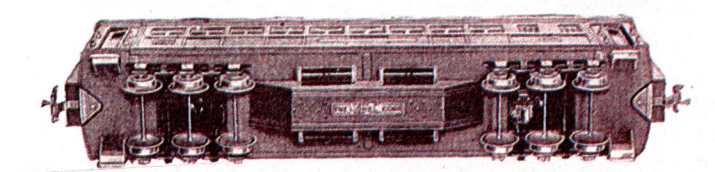

A bottom view of Nos. 412, 413 and 414 Pullman Cars showing the steel underslinging, air tanks, 6-wheel trucks, revolving shoe for conveying current for interior lighting of cars, solid brass journals, steps and automatic couplers.

Outfit No. 411E comprises 1 No. 381E "Distant-Control" "Bild-a-Loco" Locomotive with 2 electric headlights, 2 front lanterns and 2 rear lanterns, 1 No. 412 Pullman Car lettered "California," 1 No. 413 Pullman Car lettered "Colorado," 1 No. 414 Pullman Car lettered "Illinois," 1 No. 416 Observation Car lettered "New York," together with 8 sections C curved track, 16 sections S straight track, 1 No. 81 controlling rheostat and 1 STC "Lockon" connection. Lamps for headlights, front and rear lanterns and interior of cars are included, as well as flags for locomotive, connecting ties and wires for connecting to source of current. Track forms an oval 74 x 128 inches. Complete train is 108½ inches long.

Code Word "SUPERB"

25

"LIONEL STANDARD" OPERATING DERRICK AND DUMP CARS

Reg. U. S. Pat. Off.

For Use with All Locomotives Operating on "LIONEL STANDARD" Track—2¼ Inches Wide

No. 219 Operating Derrick Car

BOYS—here is the most realistic railroad Derrick Car ever built in miniature. Think of the fun you will have operating it just like a real derrick. You can raise or lower the boom, swing it from side to side, and hoist weights with the pulley and tackle. In fact, this Derrick Car will do everything—the same as real ones. All mechanical movements are controlled by wheels that operate worm gears. The mechanical arrangement is absolutely similar to that found in large Derrick Cars. By means of the worm gears the position of the boom and location of the housing are not affected by the weights that are lowered or raised. They are always in a rigid position, except when changed by means of the levers. The mechanism is mounted on a solid steel car—12½ inches long, 6¼ inches high. The boom is 16 inches long. Car is equipped with automatic couplers.

Code Word "ALUM."

No. 218 Operating Dump Car

Bring up a load of sand or ballast, boys! We must finish that roadbed by to-morrow and run the first Lionel Limited over the new short cut. The new Lionel Operating Dump Car is a marvel of mechanical ingenuity. Not only does it look like the real cars used in the construction of railroads, but it actually dumps the load at any place desired along the track. The mechanical movements that automatically open and tilt the sides of the car are controlled by wheels and worm gears. The Lionel Operating Dump Car is 12½ inches long, 4¾ inches high. Entirely constructed of sheet steel and beautifully finished by Lionel's famous enameling process. Equipped with automatic couplers.

Code Word "DEPEW."

Prices are Listed on Page 45

NEW LIONEL ALL STEEL FREIGHT CARS

for "Lionel Standard" Track—2¼ Inches Wide.

BEYOND doubt, the "Lionel Standard" Freight Cars shown on this page reach the peak of perfection in model railroad rolling stock. These freight cars are of steel construction throughout. The fittings, such as hand rails, hand brakes, steps, ladders and inserted panels are all made of brass, highly polished. Wheels, journals, axles and automatic couplers are of heavy

The illustrations clearly show that every known type of modern freight car is faithfully reproduced by us.
It is great fun to convert your passenger train into a big freighter by adding an assortment of these well-built cars, which are handsomely finished in a variety of durable enameled colors.

Freight Cars Nos. 511 to 517 are for use with Locomotives Nos. 8, 8E, 9, 9E, 9U, 10, 10E, 318, 318E, 390, 390E.

No. 511 Lumber Car with load of lumber—11½ inches long, 3¼ inches high.
Code Word "EDEN."

No. 512 Gondola Car—11½ inches long, 3⅜ inches high.
Code Word "EVER."

No. 513 Cattle Car—11½ inches long, 4¾ inches high. Has sliding door.
Code Word "EBON."

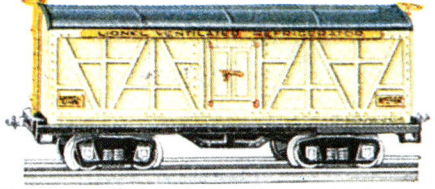

No. 514R Refrigerator Car—11½ inches long, 4¾ inches high. Has double swing doors.
Code Word "EAST."

No. 514 Box Car—11½ inches long, 4¾ inches high. Has sliding door.
Code Word "EGG."

No. 515 Oil Car—11½ inches long, 5⅛ inches high.
Code Word "ELTA."

No. 516 Coal Car—11½ inches long, 4⅛ inches high. Has "Hopper" bottom, operated by wheel.
Code Word "EPIC."

No. 517 Illuminated Caboose—11½ inches long, 5⅜ inches high. Complete with rear platform lamp.
Code Word "EAGER."

Freight Cars Nos. 211 to 217 are for use with Locomotives Nos. 380E, 381, 381E, 381U, 402E and 408E

No. 211 Lumber Car with load of lumber—12½ inches long, 4⅛ inches high.
Code Word "ANT."

No. 212 Gondola Car—12½ inches long, 3¾ inches high.
Code Word "ROY."

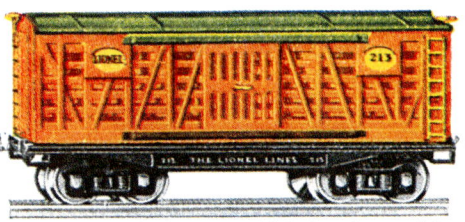

No. 213 Cattle Car—12½ inches long, 5½ inches high. Has sliding door.
Code Word "WAKE."

No. 214 Box Car—12½ inches long, 5½ inches high. Has double sliding doors.
Code Word "WOOL."

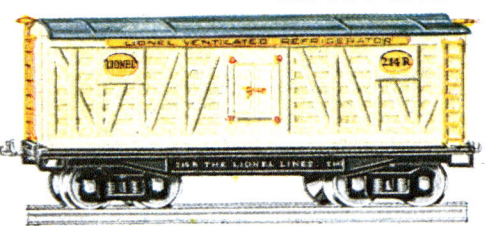

No. 214R Refrigerator Car—12½ inches long, 5½ inches high. Has double swing doors.
Code Word "GONE."

No. 215 Oil Car—12½ inches long, 5½ inches high.
Code Word "DICE."

No. 216 Coal Car—12½ inches long, 5 inches high. Has "Hopper" bottom, operated by wheel.
Code Word "ALAMA."

No. 217 Illuminated Caboose—12½ inches long, 5½ inches high. Complete with Rear platform lamp.
Code Word "RAFT."

Prices are Listed on Page 45

LIONEL "O" GAUGE FREIGHT CARS AND SETS

No. 831 Lumber Car—With load of lumber, 6¾ inches long, 2⅛ inches high.
Code Word "VEST"

No. 803 Coal Car—Has "Hopper" Bottom operated by wheel. 6¾ inches long, 3¼ inches high.
Code Word "LOAD"

No. 805 Box Car—Has sliding door. 6¾ inches long, 3¼ inches high.
Code Word "VICK"

No. 806 Cattle Car—Has sliding door. 6¾ inches long, 3¼ inches high.
Code Word "VEX"

No. 902 Gondola Car—6¾ inches long, 2⅛ inches high.
Code Word "VOTE"

No. 804 Oil Car—6¾ inches long, 3½ inches high.
Code Word "FUEL"

Cars Nos. 803, 804, 805, 806, 807, 831 and 902 are for use with Locomotives Nos. 248 and 252.
Cars Nos. 811 to 817 are for use with Locomotives Nos. 4, 4U, 253, 254, 254E, 251, 251E, and 256.

No. 808 Freight Car Set—Comprises 1 each Nos. 831 Lumber Car, 803 Coal Car, 804 Oil Car, 805 Box Car, 806 Cattle Car, 807 Caboose, described on this page. Very attractively packed.
Code Word "QUORN"

No. 818 Freight Car Set—Comprises 1 each Nos. 812 Gondola Car, 814 Box Car, 816 Coal Car, 817 Caboose, described on this page. Very attractively packed.
Code Word "QUEST"

All **Lionel** Freight Cars are equipped with automatic couplers, nickeled journals and wheels, brass hand rails, steps, and brake wheels.

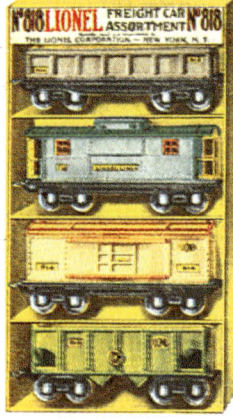

NO. 808 SET

NO. 818 SET

No. 807 Caboose—Has front and rear brass platforms and ladder to roof. 6¾ inches long, 3½ inches high. *Code Word "VAT"*

Cars Nos. 803, 804, 805, 806, 807, 831 and 902 are mounted on 4 wheel trucks.
Cars Nos. 811 to 817 are mounted on two 4-wheel trucks.

No. 811 Lumber Car—With load of lumber. 8⅞ inches long, 2½ inches high.
Code Word "DRUM"

No. 815 Oil Car—8⅞ inches long, 3¾ inches high.
Code Word "YAM"

No. 816 Coal Car—Has "Hopper" bottom operated by wheel. 8⅞ inches long, 3¼ inches high.
Code Word "YOST"

No. 812 Gondola Car—8⅞ inches long, 2⅝ inches high.
Code Word "DALE"

No. 814 Box Car—Has sliding door. 8⅞ inches long, 3¾ inches high.
Code Word "YOKE"

No. 814R Refrigerator Car—Has double swing doors. 8⅞ inches long, 3¾ inches high.
Code Word "DOFF"

No. 813 Cattle Car—Has sliding door. 8⅞ inches long, 3¾ inches high.
Code Word "YAWL"

No. 817 Caboose—Has front and rear brass platforms and ladder to roof. 8⅞ inches long, 4 inches high.
Code Word "DEFT"

Prices are Listed on Page 45

Pullman, Observation, Mail, Baggage and Dining Cars

Illustration shows patented revolving shoe made of stainless steel which collects current for lighting interior of cars.

Lionel "O" Gauge Cars Nos. 710 and 712 are obtainable in red or orange color and are for use with Locomotives Nos. 256, 251 and 251E.

Lionel "O" Gauge Cars Nos. 605 and 606 are for use with Locomotives Nos. 4, 4U, 251 and 251E.

Lionel "O" Gauge Cars Nos. 610 and 612 are for use with Locomotives Nos. 4, 4U, 253, 254 and 254E.

Lionel "O" Gauge Cars Nos. 607 and 608 are for use with Locomotives Nos. 252 and 253.

Lionel "O" Gauge Cars Nos. 529, 530, 629 and 630 are for use with Locomotives Nos. 248 and 252.

Illustration shows dome light and rear end lanterns over platform of "Lionel Standard" Observation Cars.

No. 710 Lionel "O" Gauge Illuminated Pullman Car—11⅜ inches long. 4¾ inches high. *Code Word* "HOLLY"

No. 712 Lionel "O" Gauge Illuminated Observation Car—Same as above, but with brass observation platform. *Code Word* "RISE"

"O" GAUGE
Nos. 710 and 712

"O" GAUGE
Nos. 605 and 606

No. 605 Lionel "O" Gauge Illuminated Pullman Car—10¼ inches long, 4 inches high. *Code Word* "NOVA"

No. 606 Lionel "O" Gauge Illuminated Observation Car—Same as above, but with brass observation platform. *Code Word* "MODE"

"O" GAUGE
Nos. 610 and 612

No. 610 Lionel "O" Gauge Illuminated Pullman Car—8¾ inches long, 3¾ inches high. *Code Word* "EALING"

No. 612 Lionel "O" Gauge Illuminated Observation Car—Same as above, but with brass observation platform. *Code Word* "WALTON"

"O" GAUGE
Nos. 607 and 608

No. 607 Lionel "O" Gauge Illuminated Pullman Car—7½ inches long, 3½ inches high. *Code Word* "BRAND"

No. 608 Lionel "O" Gauge Illuminated Observation Car—Same as above, but with brass observation platform. *Code Word* "TWIG"

"O" GAUGE
Nos. 529, 530, 629 and 630

No. 529 Lionel "O" Gauge Pullman Car—6¾ inches long, 3¼ inches high. *Code Word* "IMPY"

No. 530 Lionel "O" Gauge Observation Car—Same as above, but with brass observation platform. *Code Word* "IONA"

These two cars are finished in green color.

No. 629 Lionel "O" Gauge Pullman Car—6¾ inches long, 3¼ inches high. *Code Word* "FANE"

No. 630 Lionel "O" Gauge Observation Car—Same as above, but with brass observation platform. *Code Word* "IDEAL"

These two cars are finished in red color.

No. 338

No. 338 "Lionel Standard" Illuminated Observation Car—12 inches long, 4¾ inches high. *Code Word* "ORBIT"

No. 332

No. 332 "Lionel Standard" Illuminated Mail and Baggage Car—12 inches long, 4¾ inches high. Finished in blue or red color. *Code Word* "WILE"

No. 337

No. 337 "Lionel Standard" Illuminated Pullman Car—12 inches long, 4¾ inches high. *Code Word* "PASS"

CARS LISTED BELOW ARE FOR "LIONEL STANDARD" TRACK—2¼ INCHES WIDE

All Lionel Passenger Cars are made of heavy steel and are beautifully embossed with rivets and other realistic details. They are finished in a variety of attractive colors.

"Lionel Standard" Cars Nos. 332, 337, 338, 339 and 341 are for use with "Lionel Standard" Locomotives Nos. 8, 8E, 10 and 10E.

"Lionel Standard" Cars Nos. 309, 310 and 312 are for use with "Lionel Standard" Locomotives Nos. 318, 318E, 9, 9E, 9U and 380E.

Nos. 341 and 312

No. 341 "Lionel Standard" Illuminated Observation Car—12 inches long, 4¾ inches high. *Code Word* "LEO"

No. 312 "Lionel Standard" Illuminated Observation Car—Same construction as No. 341, but larger. 13¼ inches long, 5¼ inches high. *Code Word* "DOMO"

Nos. 339 and 309

No. 339 "Lionel Standard" Illuminated Pullman Car—12 inches long, 4¾ inches high. *Code Word* "STAR"

No. 309 "Lionel Standard" Illuminated Pullman Car—Same construction as No. 339, but larger, 13¼ inches long, 5¼ inches high. *Code Word* "ROAD"

No. 310

No. 310 "Lionel Standard" Illuminated Mail and Baggage Car—13¼ inches long, 5¼ inches high. *Code Word* "WEC"

CARS NOS. 428, 429, AND 430 ARE FOR USE WITH LOCOMOTIVES NOS. 9, 9E, 9U, 381, 381E, 381U, 408E AND 402E

CARS NOS. 418, 419, 490 AND 431 ARE FOR USE WITH LOCOMOTIVES NOS. 381, 381E, 381U, 408E AND 402E

No. 490

No. 490 "Lionel Standard" Illuminated Observation Car—17⅝ inches long, 6⅛ inches high. *Code Word* "CABIN"

No. 430 "Lionel Standard" Illuminated Observation Car—Same as above but mounted on 4-wheel trucks. *Code Word* "NERO"

No. 430 Car is shown in Outfit Nos. 349 and 349E on Page 17.

No. 418

No. 418 "Lionel Standard" Illuminated Pullman Car 18¼ inches long, 6⅛ inches high. *Code Word* "COMFORT"

No. 428 "Lionel Standard" Illuminated Pullman Car—Same as No. 418 but mounted on 4-wheel trucks. *Code Word* "IRIS"

No. 418 Car is illustrated with side removed to show interior seating arrangement. No. 428 Car is shown in Outfit Nos. 349 and 349E on Page 17.

No. 419

No. 419 "Lionel Standard" Illuminated Pullman and Baggage Car—18¼ inches long, 6⅛ inches high. *Code Word* "COURT"

No. 429 "Lionel Standard" Illuminated Pullman and Baggage Car—Same as No. 419 but mounted on 4-wheel trucks. *Code Word* "DORA"

No. 429 Car is shown in Outfit Nos. 349 and 349E on Page 17.

No. 431

No. 431 "Lionel Standard" Illuminated Dining Car—18¼ inches long, 6⅛ inches high. *Code Word* "FEED"

Illustration shows tables, chairs, kitchen compartment and equipment installed in this car. It can be used with "Lionel Standard" Cars Nos. 418, 419, 490, 428, 429 and 430.

Nos. 412, 413, 414

No. 412 "Lionel Standard" Illuminated Pullman Car—21½ inches long. 6⅝ inches high. This car is lettered "California." *Code Word* "ROMP"

No. 413 "Lionel Standard" Illuminated Pullman Car—Same as above but lettered "Colorado." *Code Word* "ROPE"

No. 414 "Lionel Standard" Illuminated Pullman Car—Same as above but lettered "Illinois." *Code Word* "REEF"

SEE PAGES 23, 24 & 25 FOR DETAILS OF THESE WONDERFUL NEW PASSENGER CARS

INTERIOR VIEW

Above illustration shows the unique construction of Cars Nos. 412, 413, 414 and 416. The roof is hinged and when closed is securely locked by means of two steel catches which are rigidly fastened to the roof. By merely pressing two plungers in the transom, car can be opened instantly. Interior of car is equipped with 2 electric lights, 2 wash-room and lavatory compartments, as well as revolving seats. These cars are finished in beautiful duo-tone enamel colors.

Prices are Listed on Page 45

CARS NOS. 412 413, 414, 416 ARE FOR USE WITH LOCOMOTIVES NOS. 381 381E 381U 408E 402E

No. 416

No. 416 "Lionel Standard" Illuminated Observation Car, lettered "New York"—This car conforms in size to Nos. 412, 413 and 414 illustrated to the left. The brass observation platform is surrounded by a dome light which shines through 2 red rear end lanterns. In addition, this car is equipped with 2 interior lights. An enlarged illustration of the details in the observation platform of this car will be found on Pages 23, 24 and 25. This car is 21 inches long, 6⅝ inches high. *Code Word* "REST"

LIONEL ELECTRICALLY-CONTROLLED ACCESSORIES

THESE accessories are exact models of the latest safety devices used on all railroads. They are made of steel, beautifully designed and very moderately priced. The construction is of Lionel quality throughout. The base is a die casting which incorporates considerable detail, such as hinged doors, embossed rivets, etc. The upright and ladder and other structural parts are made of steel, and are practically indestructible. The top of lantern is removable so that lamp in interior may be easily reached. Finished in a variety of beautiful enamels baked at high temperature.

Lionel Automatic Semaphore (Electrically Illuminated)—When train passes over section of track to which it is connected the semaphore arm is set upright and red bull's-eye in lantern is illuminated. When train passes, the semaphore arm drops to horizontal position, and the electric lamp illuminates the green signal. It is absolutely automatic. The height from base to spire is 15 inches. Semaphore arm is 4⅛ inches long. Price includes electric lamp, connecting wires, "Lockon" and special section of track.

No. 080 Automatic Semaphore—For Lionel "O" Gauge Track.

Code Word "DROP."

No. 80 Automatic Semaphore—For "Lionel Standard" Track.

Code Word "DRAW."

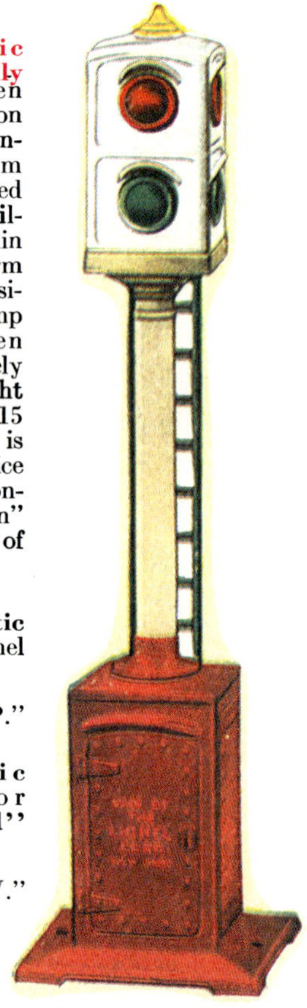

Lionel Automatic Train Control (Electrically Illuminated)—Positively amazing in its action. When train approaches section to which it is connected, red light shows and train automatically comes to a dead stop. After an interval of a few seconds, red light changes to green and train is on its way again. The controlling mechanism can be disconnected by means of a small lever so that train does not stop as it approaches the train control, which then shows a permanent green light. Lionel Train Control is 10¼ inches high. Price includes electric lamp, connecting wires and "Lockon."

No. 078 Automatic Train Control—For Lionel "O" Gauge Track.

Code Word "HEAVE."

No. 78 Automatic Train Control—For "Lionel Standard" Track.

Code Word "WEAVE."

Lionel Semaphore-Train-Control (Electrically Illuminated) — Our latest marvel. As train approaches, the red light shines and semaphore arm drops, denoting "Caution." Train immediately comes to a dead stop. A short interval—light changes to green —semaphore arm goes up—train proceeds. It is startlingly real! It operates as if by magic! When desired, a lever in the base disconnects the controlling mechanism and sets the semaphore arm in an upright position so that train does not stop as it approaches the Semaphore-Train-Control. You will be absolutely thrilled as you watch the unique action of this almost-human railroad device. Lionel's skilled craftsmanship is exemplified to the highest degree in the construction of this very desirable accessory. Height from base to spire 14¾ inches. Semaphore arm is 4⅛ inches long. Price includes electric lamp, connecting wires and "Lockon."

No. 082 Semaphore-Train-Control—For Lionel "O" Gauge Track.

Code Word "STILL."

No. 82 Semaphore-Train-Control—For "Lionel Standard" Track.

Cod Word "STRIP."

IN all Lionel Electrically-Controlled Accessories the electric unit is mounted on a solid piece of fibre which is protected in the interior of the base.

Hand-Control Semaphore (Electrically Illuminated)—It stops and starts your train with a movement of your finger. Just lower the lever in the base —the semaphore arm goes down— the green light changes to red, and your train stops!

Raise the lever— the arm goes up— red light changes to green, and the train moves again.

Size — 15 inches high. Semaphore arm is 4⅛ inches long. Price includes electric lamp, connecting wires and "Lockon."

No. 084 Hand-Control Semaphore for "O" Gauge Track.

Code Word "SLATE."

No. 84 Hand-Control Semaphore for "Lionel Standard" Track.

Code Word "STRIKE."

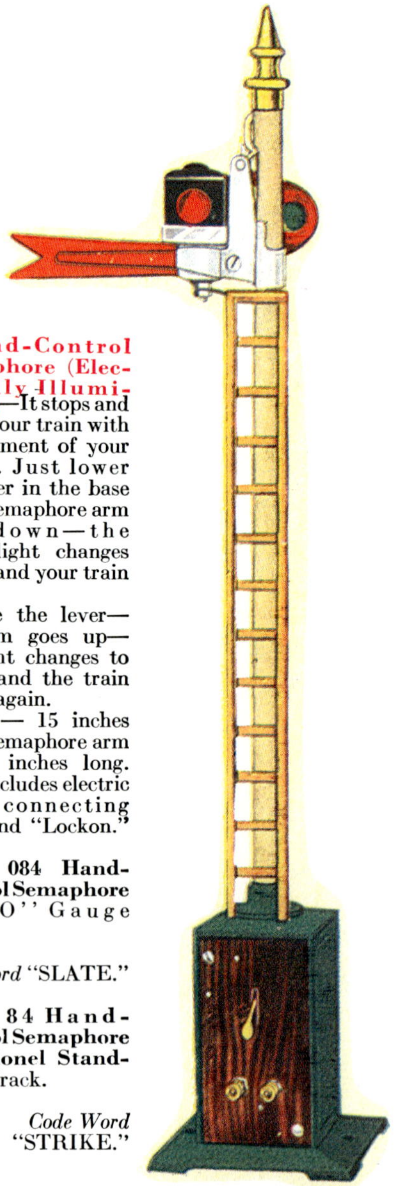

Prices are Listed on Page 45

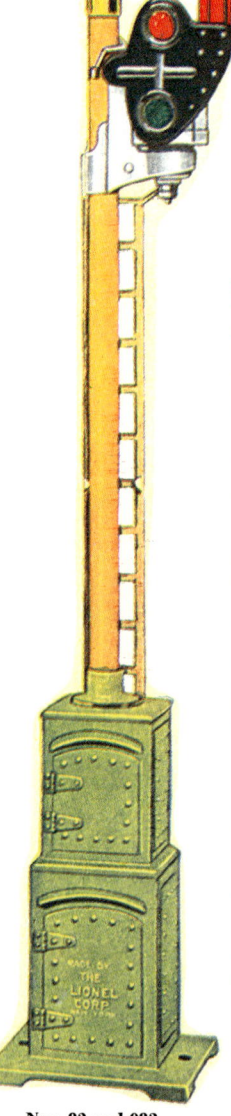

Nos. 80 and 080
Automatic Semaphore
with Electric Light.

Nos. 78 and 078
Automatic Train Control
with Electric Lights.

Nos. 82 and 082
Automatic Train-Control-Semaphore with
Electric Light.

Nos. 84 and 084
Hand-Control-Semaphore
with Electric Light.

LIONEL ELECTRICALLY-CONTROLLED ACCESSORIES

BOYS! See the lights flash on and off — see the gates go up and down — — hear the warning bells ring! The Action is Automatic!

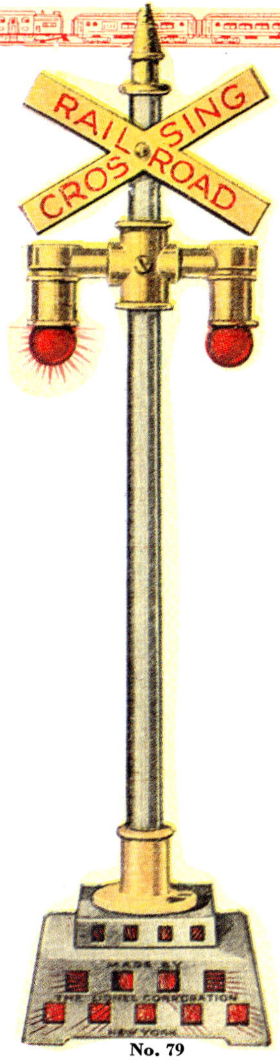

No. 79

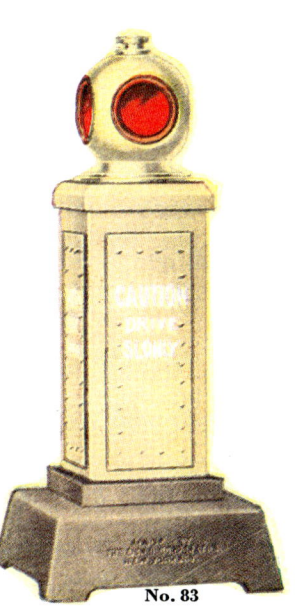

No. 83

No. 87

Nos. 77 and 077

Nos. 69 and 069

No. 79 Flashing Railroad Signal—A true reproduction of the latest type of Crossing Signal used on electrified railroads. The **Lionel** patented thermostat in the base flashes the red lights on and off alternately and continues to do so as long as the current is applied. Electric lamp in base throws a red light through the openings. The base, uprights and arm are made of die castings and steel, beautifully finished. This is a most interesting railroad accessory. Height 11½ inches, base 2¾ inches square. For use with "O" gauge and "Lionel Standard" equipment.
Code Word "ROOM"

No. 83 Lionel Traffic and Crossing Signal—An ingenious and up-to-date **Lionel** accessory. The electric light in the red lantern flashes on and off just like the "blinker" light seen at street intersections. The mechanism is in the base, which also contains binding posts for attaching wires supplied with the signal. This signal is 6¼ inches high. Can be used with "O" Gauge or "Lionel Standard" equipment. A wonderful accessory to use with Lionel bungalows and villas when building model villages.
Code Word "STAND"

No. 87 Lionel Railroad Crossing Signal—Just like those used on many grade crossings. The bright red lantern on white background is illuminated at intervals of a second by means of a device placed in the interior. It is thrilling to watch this automatic "blinker" operate continuously without attention, by means of mechanism in the base which also contains terminals for connecting wires. This Crossing Signal is 6¾ inches high. Can be used with "Lionel Standard" or "O" Gauge equipment.
Code Word "STORE"

Lionel Automatic Crossing Gates—An exact reproduction of the real ones seen at grade crossings. When train approaches the track section to which it is connected, the gate comes down, and stays in that position. When train passes, gate opens. The action of the gate is just the same as those used on real railroads. It is made of heavy steel. The electric unit is enclosed in the base. Finished in various enameled colors. The Lionel Automatic Crossing Gate is 11 inches long. Price includes special section of track, connecting wires and "Lockon."

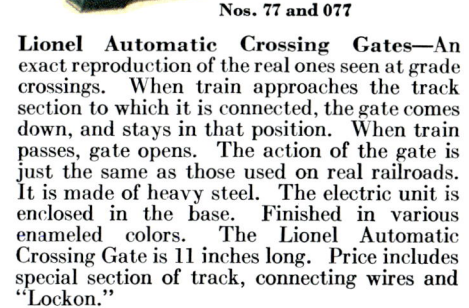

No. 077 Automatic Crossing Gate for Lionel "O" Gauge Track.
Code Word "ADVANCE"

No. 77 Automatic Crossing Gate for "Lionel Standard" Track.
Code Word "TARRY"

Lionel Electric Warning Signals—Electric bell with 2 gongs is mounted on an ornamental steel standard, 8¾ inches high, which supports warning sign. Gongs ring while train passes over track section to which it is connected. Bell automatically stops when grade crossing is clear. This realistic accessory is finished in beautiful enameled colors, and bell is nickeled steel. Price includes special track, wires and "Lockon."

No. 069 Electric Warning Signal for Lionel "O" Gauge Track.
Code Word "RINGER"

No. 69 Electric Warning Signal for "Lionel Standard" Track.
Code Word "BEWARE"

Prices are Listed on Page 45

SPECIFICATIONS OF LIONEL "MULTIVOLT" TRANSFORMERS

LIONEL "Multivolt" Transformers are made completely in our own factories. Our Transformer department is the largest in the country devoted exclusively to the manufacture of low-voltage transformers. The only parts purchased are the raw materials. We correctly wind and insulate the coils, make the cases, laminations, switch handles, and in fact do every operation. Lionel "Multivolt" Transformers are listed as standard by the Underwriters' Laboratories.

SUB-BASE—A metal sub-base resting on four supports is attached to the bottom. The air, circulating between this sub-base and the transformer case, keeps it cool while in operation. Holes in this sub-base provide means for fastening to wall or table.

Separable Plug—All **Lionel** "Multivolt" Transformers are fitted with an approved, separable plug, which is a distinct advantage over the one-piece plug, because the circuit can be immediately broken.

Double Contact Control Switch—This is infinitely superior to the one-piece switch, which is easily bent and does not make positive contact. Our double switch has a flexible, phosphor-bronze, contact arm under the rigid switch, so that positive contact with the points is assured. This flexible contact is protected from injury by the rigid brass handle to which it is attached. An exclusive feature of **Lionel** "Multivolt" Transformers.

Laminations—The laminations are made of the best grade of electrical sheets and the windings are perfectly insulated.

Rigid Supports for Coils—The coils and laminations of **Lionel** "Multivolt" Transformers are rigidly supported inside the case by means of metal bands which prevent these parts from moving and eliminate the possibility of broken lead wires. In addition to these supports, the interior of the case is fitted with an insulating receptacle and the case is air cooled.

Metal Case—The case is beautiful in design and is stamped of heavier steel than is required by the Underwriters laboratories.

Finish—Lionel "Multivolt" Transformer cases are covered with a rubberoid composition that is applied at 350 degrees Fahrenheit. This is much greater heat than the case is ever subjected to, and the finish cannot be scratched and will not peel off during the entire life of the transformer.

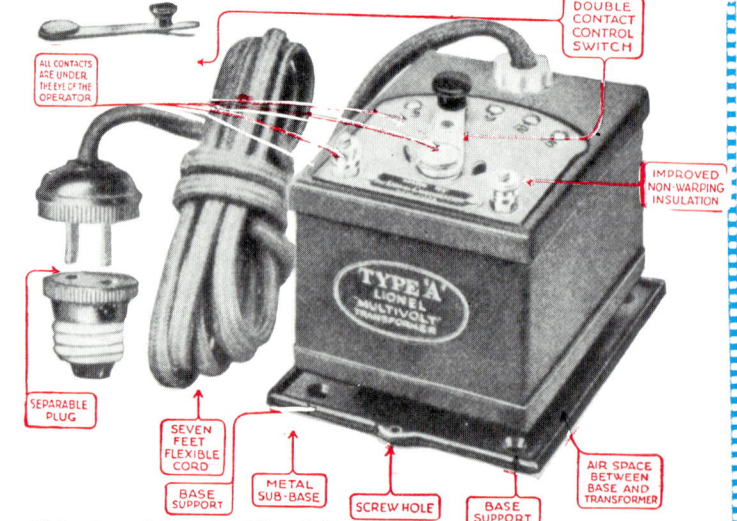

—All contacts and switches are mounted on one piece of heavy insulating material and are at the top of the transformer, right before the user.

—All **Lionel** "Multivolt" Transformers are fitted with 7 feet of flexible lamp cord which enters the transformer case through an approved porcelain bushing.

It will be seen that **Lionel** "Multivolt" Transformers incorporate every device that will increase their efficiency.

LIONEL DIRECT CURRENT REDUCERS
(NOT TO BE USED ON ALTERNATING CURRENT)

NO. 107 Lionel Direct Current Reducer for 110-Volt Circuit—This is constructed of four porcelain tubes wound with best quality of resistance wire. These porcelain tubes are mounted on a substantial base measuring 8 by 11 inches and ¾ inches thick. The porcelain tubes are protected and ventilated by a perforated steel cover lined with heavy asbestos. The sliding lever regulates the voltage so that train will just crawl along or go ahead at express speed. The reducer is connected with the house current by a separable plug with 7 feet of flexible cord. Four porcelain supports with screws are supplied so that the reducer can be screwed to wall or table.

Code Word "KENTUCKY."

No. 170 Lionel Direct Current Reducer for 220-Volt Circuit—This reducer is identical in appearance with No. 107, mentioned above, but is for use on 220 volts.

Code Word "ASBURY."

CONTROLLING RHEOSTAT No. 81
(FOR BATTERIES)

NO. 81 Controlling Rheostat—With this rheostat you can, when using dry or storage batteries, operate **Lionel** Trains at various speeds, or stop and start them at any distance from the track. This is done by sliding the lever from side to side, or manipulating it up and down. This rheostat can also be used with **Lionel** "Multivolt" Transformers when a gradual increase or decrease of current is desired, without touching the lever on the transformer. The porcelain coil of this rheostat is protected by a perforated steel cover, and air holes prevent overheating. Size 4⅞ inches long, 2½ inches wide.

Code Word "BONE."

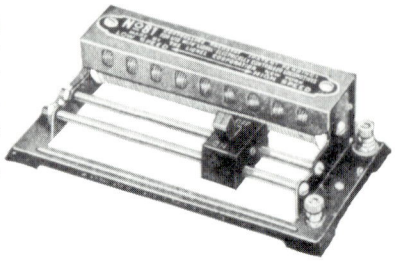

Prices are Listed on Page 45

Lionel "Multivolt" Transformers—For 110 and 220 Volts—60, 40 and 25 Cycles

Power Houses for Transformers

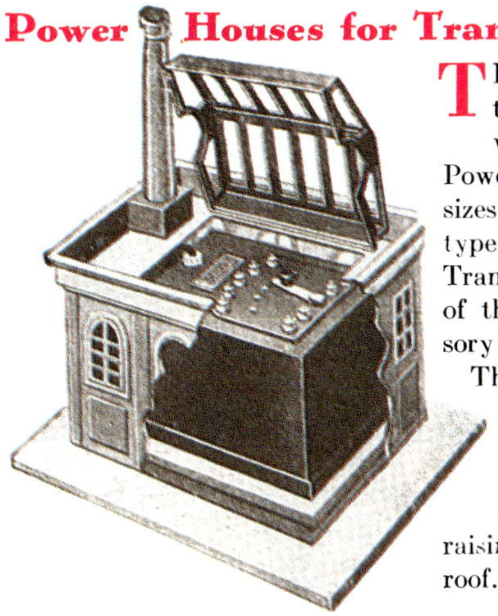

THIS illustration shows transformer contained within the new **Lionel** Power Station, made in two sizes to accommodate every type of **Lionel** "Multivolt" Transformer. Full description of this desirable new accessory will be found on Page 37.

The **Lionel** Power Station is placed over the Transformer, and you can manipulate the controlling switch by simply raising the grating on the roof.

LIONEL "Multivolt" Transformers have been on the market for a great many years and operate all makes of Electric Trains. We justly claim they are best. Don't experiment with other makes of doubtful value.

Remember, that all transformers look alike outside, but their imperfections will only be discovered after they are in actual use for a length of time. **Lionel** "Multivolt" Transformers will last indefinitely and are guaranteed unconditionally as long as they are used on the current for which they are intended. They are absolutely safe and will give steady, even power.

For Greatest Efficiency Always Use a Lionel "Multivolt" Transformer with a Lionel Train

Lionel "Multivolt" Transformers Are For Use Only on Alternating Current. Do Not Use Them on Direct Current.

Type "A" Transformer will operate any "O" gauge outfit.

For 110 volts, 60 cycles. 40 watts capacity.

Gives 15 volts in following steps: 4, 7, 10, 13, 15.

Size: 4⅛ by 3¼ by 3¾ inches. Sub-base: 3¾ by 5 inches.

Code Word "STRONG"

NOTE: Type "A" Transformer is recommended for use with the train outfits shown on Page 8.

Type "B" Transformer will operate any "O" gauge outfit, and in addition the extra binding posts enable the user to light up lamp-posts, semaphores and other electrically illuminated accessories.

For 110 volts, 60 cycles. 50 watts capacity.

Gives 25 volts in following steps:
Permanent: 7, 8, 15.
Variable: 2, 4, 6, 8, 9, 10, 11, 12, 13, 17, 19, 21, 23, 25.

Size: 4¾ by 3⅝ by 4 inches. Sub-base: 5½ by 4⅛ inches.

Code Word "BRADLEY"

A fully guaranteed transformer at a very popular price.

Type "T" Transformer will operate any "O" gauge or "**Lionel Standard**" outfit; also has extra binding posts for attaching illuminated electrical accessories.

For 110 volts, 60 cycles. 100 watts capacity.

Gives 25 volts in following steps:
Permanent: 2, 4, 6, 7, 8, 10, 12, 14, 15, 16, 17, 18, 19, 21, 23, 25.
Variable: 2, 6, 8, 10, 12, 14, 16, 17, 18, 19, 21, 23, 25.

Size: 5 by 4 by 4⅜ inches. Sub-base 6 by 4⅝ inches.

Code Word "BIRCH"

Type "K" Transformer will operate any outfit as well as illuminated accessories. This transformer has sufficient wattage capacity to operate two trains at once.

Size: 5⅛ by 4 by 5 inches. Sub-base 6 by 4⅝ inches.

"K"—For 110 volts, 60 cycles. 150 watts capacity. Specifications same as Type "T," but has higher wattage capacity.

Code Word (110 V.) "BINGHAM"

"K"—For 220 volts, 60 cycles. 150 watts capacity. Specifications same as Type "T," but is for use on 220-volt circuit.

Code Word (220 V.) "BROOK"

Type "C" Transformer will operate any outfit and illuminated accessories on 25 or 40 cycle current.

For 110 volts, 25 to 40 cycles. 75 watts capacity. Specifications same as Type "T," but is for use on 25 or 40 cycle current.

Size: 5⅛ by 4 by 5 inches. Sub-base: 6 by 4⅝ inches.

Code Word "LAWRENCE"

This transformer is the best obtainable for use on 25 or 40 cycle current.

Prices are Listed on Page 45

LIONEL ACCESSORY SETS

A Model Village.   Completely Illuminated.

No. 192

No. 192 Illuminated Villa Set—A handsome assortment of model houses. Comprises 1 No. 191 villa, 1 No. 189 villa, and 2 No. 184 bungalows. All complete with interior lights and connecting wires. Very attractively packed. *Code Word* "VILLAGE"

No. 195

No. 195 "Lionel Terrace"—A real village in miniature, containing houses and lamp posts all electrically illuminated. Adds realism to your train outfit, and ideal in connection with sister's doll house. The buildings are in a beautiful landscape setting complete with grass plots, bushes, shrubbery, trees and gravel walks. An American flag majestically waves aloft in the centre. The bungalow and villas are described on Page 35 and the lamp posts are shown on Page 42. Completely wired platform is 22 inches long, 19 inches wide. The lamps in the buildings and lamp posts are all wired, ready to be connected. Our lowest priced "Multivolt" transformer, or direct current reducer connected to the house current, or a few dry batteries will light up the entire village. *Code Word* "TUFT"

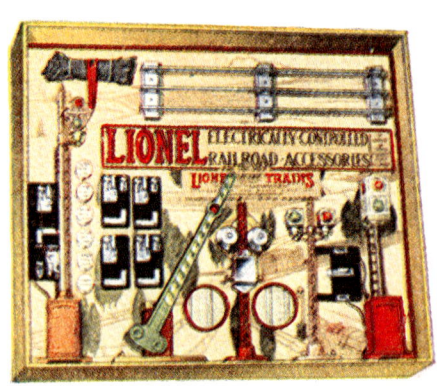

Nos. 193 and 194

Automatic Accessory Sets—Lionel Automatic Accessories fully described on preceding pages are now packed in very attractive sets as illustrated above. Add them to your Lionel equipment.

No. 194 Automatic Accessory Set—For "Lionel Standard" Track—Comprises 1 No. 76 block signal, 1 No. 78 train control, 1 No. 80 semaphore, 1 No. 77 crossing gate and 1 No. 69 warning signal. *Code Word* "OAT"

No. 193 Automatic Accessory Set—For Lionel "O" Gauge Track. This set is the same as No. 194, but is for use with "O" Gauge equipment. *Code Word* "OVER"

No. 186

No. 186 Illuminated Bungalow Set—Comprises 5 No. 184 bungalows, beautifully finished in assorted colors. Complete with interior lights and connecting wires. Attractively packed. *Code Word* "HAMLET"

Outfit No. 70—Illustrated to the right, comprises 2 No. 62 semaphores, 1 No. 59 lamp post, 1 No. 68 warning sign, 2 extra globes for lamp post. Very attractively packed. *Code Word* "HOBART"

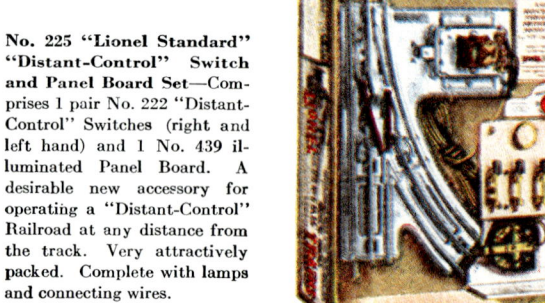

No. 225 "Lionel Standard" "Distant-Control" Switch and Panel Board Set—Comprises 1 pair No. 222 "Distant-Control" Switches (right and left hand) and 1 No. 439 illuminated Panel Board. A desirable new accessory for operating a "Distant-Control" Railroad at any distance from the track. Very attractively packed. Complete with lamps and connecting wires. *Code Word* "OPERA"

Nos. 013 and 225

No. 70

No. 86 "Lionel Standard" Telegraph Post Set—These new telegraph posts incorporate a wonderful new feature, namely: the extension arm attached to the base, by means of which the telegraph posts are rigidly fastened to the track. The set comprises 6 No. 85 telegraph posts, 9 inches high, described on Page 35. Attractively packed. *Code Word* "TENSE"

No. 071 "O" Gauge Telegraph Post Set—Same as above, but for "O" Gauge Track. Comprises 6 No. 060 telegraph posts, 5½ inches high, described on Page 35. *Code Word* "TAUT"

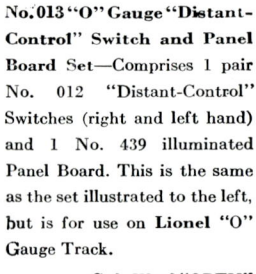

Nos. 071 and 86

No. 013 "O" Gauge "Distant-Control" Switch and Panel Board Set—Comprises 1 pair No. 012 "Distant-Control" Switches (right and left hand) and 1 No. 439 illuminated Panel Board. This is the same as the set illustrated to the left, but is for use on Lionel "O" Gauge Track. *Code Word* "OPEN"

No. 71

Outfit No. 71—Comprises 6 No. 60 steel telegraph posts, as described on Page 35. This set can be used with either "O" Gauge or "Lionel Standard" Railroads. Very attractively packed. *Code Word* "USEFUL"

Add these accessories to your model railroad and add to your fun

Prices are Listed on Page 45

LIONEL ALL-STEEL RAILROAD ACCESSORIES, BUNGALOWS AND VILLAS

The new Telegraph Posts Nos. 85 and 060 for "Lionel Standard" and "O" Gauge Track are fitted with extension arms, by means of which they can be securely fastened to the track layout. These new Telegraph Posts can also be purchased in sets, as illustrated and described on Page 34.

No. 62   **No. 60**

No. 62 Semaphore—The semaphore arm has three discs—red, green and yellow. Arm is operated by lever near base. Enameled steel standard is 8⅞ inches high.
Code Word "CAUTION."

No. 60 Telegraph Post—Arm is equipped with real glass insulators. Enameled steel standard is 8⅞ inches high.
Code Word "WIRE."

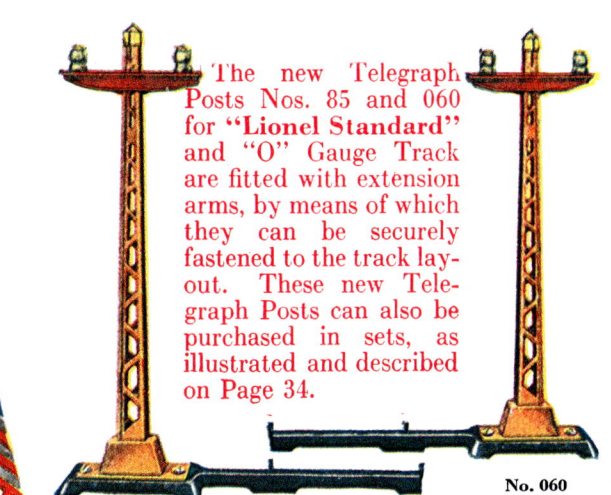

No. 85   **No. 060**

No. 85 Telegraph Post with extension arm. For "Lionel Standard" Track. Equipped with real glass insulators. Beautifully enameled in a variety of colors. Height 9 inches. Length of extension arm over all is 8 inches.
Code Word "QUART."

No. 060 Telegraph Post with extension arm. For "O" Gauge Track. Similar in construction and appearance to No. 85 described above. Height 5½ inches. Length of extension arm over all is 6⅝ inches.
Code Word "QUIET."

No. 068   **No. 68**

No. 68 Warning Signal—For "Lionel Standard" Track. Enameled steel standard is 8⅞ inches high. Brass sign is 3½ inches square.
Code Word "STOP."

No. 068 Warning Signal—For "O" Gauge Track. Similar to No. 68, but is 6⅝ inches high. Brass sign is 2 3/16 inches square.
Code Word "LOOK."

No. 89

No. 89 Flagstaff and Flag—For use with Lionel model villages or to place in front of a Lionel Station. Flagstaff is 14¼ inches high. Silk flag may be lowered by cord attached, which can be fastened to hook near the base.
Code Word "ARTHUR."

No. 90

No. 90 Flagstaff and Flag—The flagstaff (14¾ inches high) is removable, and fits into an ornamental base mounted on a miniature grass plot beautifully ornamented with flower border.
Code Word "PLOT."

No. 191

No. 191 Illuminated Villa—Beautifully designed. 7⅛ inches long, 5 inches wide and 5¼ inches high. Roof is removable. Complete with interior lighting fixture, lamp and connecting wires.
Code Word "SOLID."

No. 184

No. 184 Illuminated Bungalow—4¾ inches long, 4 inches high, 2¾ inches wide. Beautifully decorated. Complete with interior light and connecting wires.
Code Word "HOME."

No. 189

No. 189 Illuminated Villa—A model that is architecturally perfect. Finished in a variety of harmonizing enamel colors. 5½ inches long, 5 inches wide, 5½ inches high. Complete with interior light and connecting wires.
Code Word "MANSE."

Prices are Listed on Page 45

A BEAUTIFUL NEW LIONEL STATION—COMPLETELY ILLUMINATED

No. 128

An Attractive Addition to a Lionel Railroad

NO. 128—This elaborate new station is just what Lionel users have long desired. It is up to date in every detail. The station is mounted on a terrace which contains beautifully landscaped flower beds. In the center bravely floats an American flag mounted on a tall flagstaff. A beautifully designed stairway leads from the ground to the terrace. The retaining wall surrounding the structure represents ornamental masonry. The station is illuminated inside and out by electric bulbs, and beautifully designed torches illuminate the terrace. The building is equipped with swinging doors and other characteristic Lionel features. The roof is removable so that the electric fixture in the interior can easily be reached. This elaborate station is made entirely of heavy steel, beautifully enameled and decorated. It is 31½ inches long, 18 inches deep and 12 inches high.

Code Word "YEN."

No. 129 Station Platform

THIS platform is the same as the one described above, and is listed separately so that owners of Lionel Stations Nos. 124, 122 and 121 can make use of them in this most elaborate setting, which so greatly adds to the appearance of the entire railroad layout.

Code Word "YIELD."

No. 129

Prices are Listed on Page 45

All-Steel Stations
Power Houses, Switch-Signal Towers and Panel Board

No. 124 Illuminated Station—Equipped with two corner platform lights and reflectors, finished in polished nickel. These lighting brackets have beautifully designed supporting arms. Also fitted with inside light supported on a nickeled fixture. Roof is removable so that interior lamp can be easily reached. 13¾ inches long, 9¼ inches wide and 10 inches high. Complete with electric lamps and connecting wires. *Code Word* "READE"

No. 122 Illuminated Station—This is in every way similar to No. 124 Station described above, but has one inside electric light supported on a nickeled fixture. Complete with electric lamp and connecting wires.
Code Word "CENT"

No. 126 Illuminated Station—Specially designed for use with our smaller train outfits and has many of the architectural features of our larger models. The interior light is supported on a fixture placed beneath the removable roof. 10¼ inches long, 7¼ inches wide and 7 inches high. Complete with electric lamp and connecting wires.
Code Word "ALITE"

No. 127 Illuminated Station—For use with any "O" Gauge Train. Interior light is fastened to a supporting fixture. Roof is removable so that lamp can be easily reached. 8½ inches long, 4¼ inches wide and 5 inches high. Complete with electric lamp and connecting wires.
Code Word "TONLY"

No. 437 Illuminated Switch Signal Tower—For operating Electrically-Controlled Train and Accessories at any distance from the track. Rear view below shows six knife switches attached to panel board, also provision for attaching controlling levers of electrically-controlled track switches described on Page 38. Note the wonderful detail in the windows, doors and panels, which are separable inserted pieces, beautifully enameled to harmonize with the walls of the structure. Size 10¼ inches long, 8⅞ inches high, 8⅜ inches wide. Complete with electric lamp and connecting wires.
Code Word "ZEV"

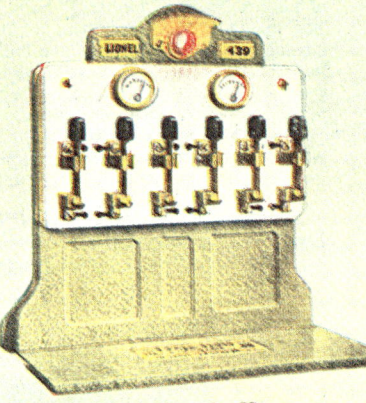

No. 439 Panel Board—You can operate your trains and accessories from one or more of the six knife switches mounted on the marble Panel Board. Provision is made for holding two levers of Lionel Electrically-Controlled Switches, shown in illustration below. Electric lamp at top illuminates small dummy meters. Made of heavy steel beautifully enameled, and the knife switches are mounted on a composition marble slab. Size 8¼ inches high and 7¼ inches wide.
Code Word "FLGW"

Prices are Listed on Page 45

Lionel Power Stations—Made in 2 sizes to fit all types of Lionel "Multivolt" Transformers. Base is hollow, so that transformer easily sets within. Grid in roof is removable.

No. 435—Size 7⅝ by 6 inches. 9½ inches high to chimney. For use with Types A or B Transformers.
Code Word "JENA"

No. 436—Size 9¼ by 7⅝ inches. 10½ inches high to chimney. For use with Types T, C and K Transformers.
Code Word "WATTS"

No. 438 Illuminated Signal Tower—Equipped with 2 knife switches from which "Distant-Control" Trains and Accessories can be operated. Roof is removable so that interior light can be reached. Mounted on a beautiful steel elevation, embossed with rivets, etc. Base represents concrete. A brass ladder runs up the entire length of the steel work. Height is 12 inches. Base measures 6 by 4¾ inches. Electric lamp and connecting wires included.
Code Word "CARP"

37

1929

"DISTANT-CONTROL" AND HAND-OPERATED SWITCHES. NEW TURNTABLE

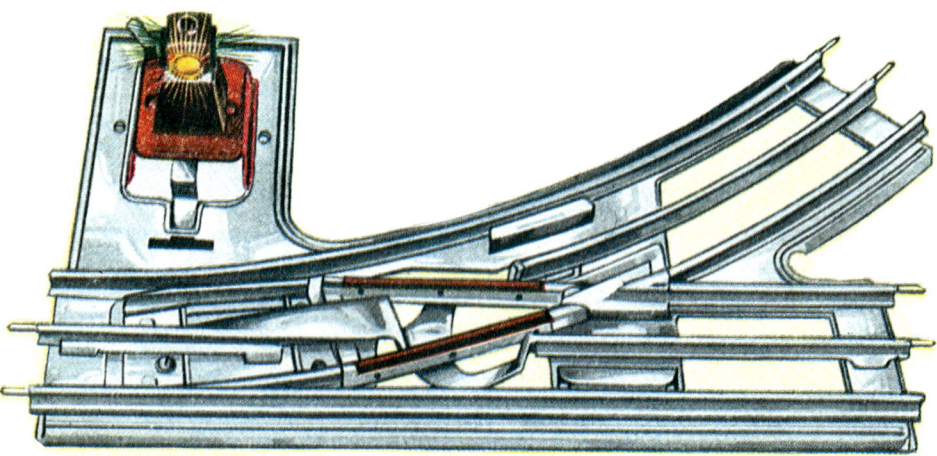

Nos. 210 and 021

Nos. 222 and 012

LIONEL Hand-operated Switches, shown in the above illustration, are equipped with heavy fibre rails (Patents Re. 16580 and 1671236) at the points where the rails cross. All possibility of short circuit is thus eliminated and headlight does not flicker when train passes over these points. Attention is also directed to the several guard rails attached to Lionel Switches which prevent derailing even when trains are traveling at high speed. Hand-lever which moves the rails also sets the signals, changes the lights and locks mechanism. All Lionel Switches are radically different from any others in the market. They are of steel construction throughout and will bear the weight of the heaviest trains without bending or breaking.

No. 210 "Lionel Standard" Illuminated Switches (right and left hand)—15¼ inches long, 8⅝ inches wide. Price per pair includes electric lamps.

Code Word "NASH."

No. 021 Lionel "O" Gauge Illuminated Switches (right and left hand)—10½ inches long, 7¼ inches wide. Price per pair includes electric lamps.

Code Word "MOSHA."

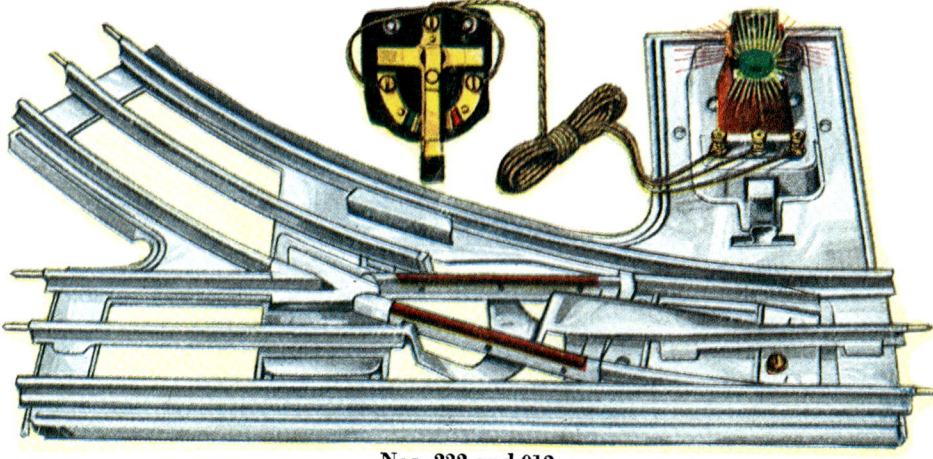

LIONEL "Distant-Control" Switches (Patents Nos. 1548940 and 1671236) can be operated at any distance from the track by means of a controlling lever. By manipulating this lever, the same as switchmen do, the position of the switch instantly changes and the red and green lights change with the movement of the switch. The controlling lever is connected with the switch by means of flexible wires so that no additional wiring is required. The mechanism of Lionel "Distant-Control" Switches is extremely simple. They are scientifically constructed. The guard rails prevent the train leaving the track even when operating at high speed. The patented Lionel fibre rails are embodied in the construction of these switches. This exclusive feature prevents a short circuit when the train is passing over the switch points. See previous page for particulars of Nos. 437 Switch Signal-Tower and 439 Panel Board, to which the controlling levers of these switches can be attached.

No. 222 "Lionel Standard" "Distant-Control" Illuminated Switches (right and left hand)—15¼ inches long, 8⅝ inches wide. Price per pair includes electric lamps and 42 inches of cord to which controlling levers are attached.

Code Word "AFAR"

No. 012 Lionel "O" Gauge "Distant-Control" Illuminated Switches (right and left hand)—10½ inches long, 7¼ inches wide. Price per pair includes electric lamps and 42 inches of cord to which controlling levers are attached.

Code Word "ASP."

LIONEL Switches and Turntable can be connected to the track in the same manner as ordinary straight or curved sections.

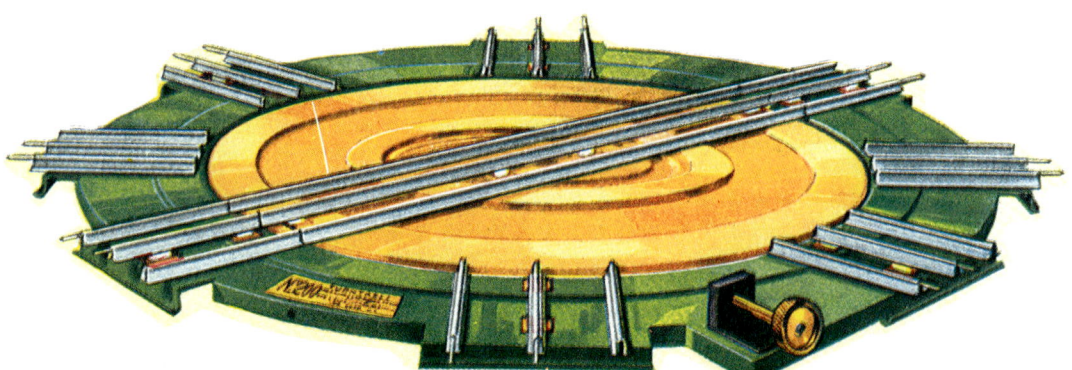

No. 200

No. 200 Turntable
For "Lionel Standard" Track

THIS is an exclusive Lionel Accessory that every boy should have in order to make a complete Lionel Train layout. It is used for switching locomotives to various tracks in the smallest possible space. Every boy is familiar with the use of a Turntable, so it is not necessary to describe its purpose. This Turntable is so perfectly balanced that even when the heaviest locomotive is upon it, it can be easily moved in every direction by means of the worm gear and hand wheel that operate it. Diameter of Turntable is 17 inches.

Code Word "TURK."

Prices are Listed on Page 45

"LIONEL STANDARD" AND "O" GAUGE TRACK. LIONEL TRACK ACCESSORIES

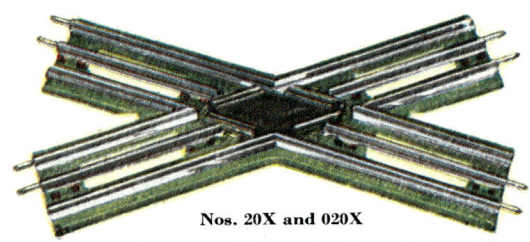

Nos. 20X and 020X

Lionel 45 Degree Crossings—These are largely used when making a figure "8," using all curved track, but a great variety of other track layouts can be formed with them. Steel construction throughout. Rails are mounted on heavy steel ornamental base. A heavy fibre block in centre where rails cross prevents all possibility of short circuit, or cars jumping the track.

No. 020X Crossing for "O" Gauge Track. Size 11½ inches long. 6 inches wide.
Code Word "CROSS."

No. 20X Crossing for "Lionel Standard" Track. Size 16½ inches long, 9 inches wide.
Code Word "BOSS."

Lionel Illuminated Bumpers

Nos. 25 and 025

This bumper is die cast and is surmounted by a red electric light encased in a nickeled steel guard. Electrical contact is automatically made and bumper can be placed at any part of track layout.

No. 025 Bumper for "O" Gauge Track. Length 10¼ inches, height 2⅞ inches.
Code Word "HIT."

No. 25 Bumper for "Lionel Standard" Track. Length 14 inches, height 3¾ inches.
Code Word "CAT."

Lionel Spring Bumpers

No. 023 Lionel "O" Gauge Bumper—An indispensable accessory for terminals or sidings. Fitted with spring plunger which absorbs shock when car strikes it. The bumper frame is removable. Length, 10¼ inches, height 2 inches.
Code Word "DELTO."

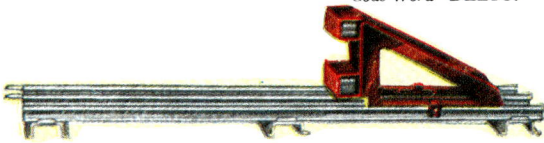

No. 23 "Lionel Standard" Bumper—The construction is the same as No. 023 described above. Two spring plungers absorb shock of car. Length 14 inches, height 3 inches.
Code Word "PROVO."

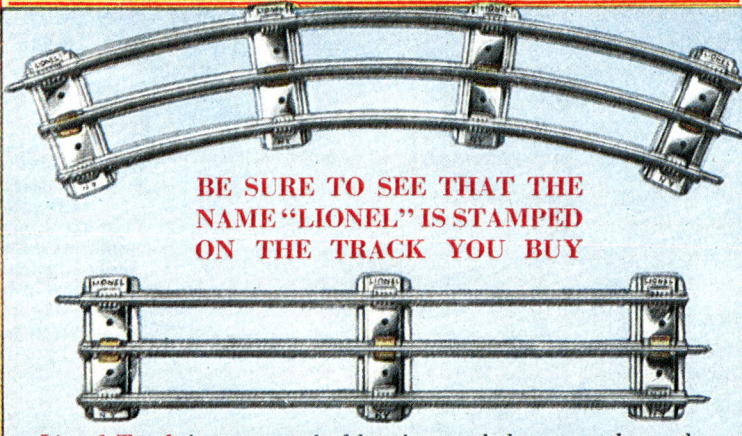

BE SURE TO SEE THAT THE NAME "LIONEL" IS STAMPED ON THE TRACK YOU BUY

Lionel Track is constructed of heavier metal than any other make. The illustration shows the added strength given to Lionel rails by forming the base outward instead of turning it in. This outward flange gives the track sufficient strength to support the weight of a fully grown person and is made possible by our patented process. Each section of track is tested on 110 volts and therefore will not short-circuit when carrying the low voltage which operates Lionel Trains. The ends of each section have pin terminals which fit in openings in the adjoining sections allowing track to be laid and taken apart without difficulty.

Lionel Track is made in straight and curved sections and the curvature of the track is mechanically correct, allowing trains to run at high speed without derailing.

We illustrate below the improved connecting tie which holds sections of track rigidly together. These connecting ties can be readily inserted and removed.

Lionel "O" Gauge Track—1⅜ inches wide

OC curved track, 11 inches long.
Code Word "LEMPS."

OS straight track, 10¼ inches long.
Code Word "GLENN."

OSS track, 10¼ inches long. For use with Electrically-Controlled Accessories. Complete with "Lockon" and connecting wires.
Code Word "RELAY."

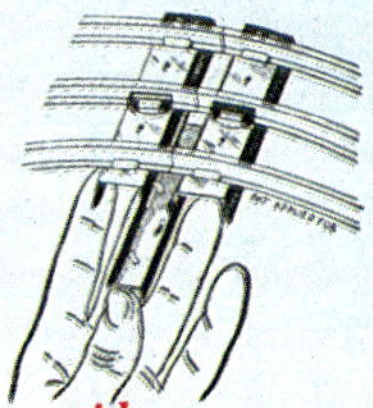

"Lionel Standard" Track—2¼ inches wide

C curved track, 16 inches long.
Code Word "BUFF."

S straight track, 14 inches long.
Code Word "NYACK."

SS track, 14 inches long. For use with Electrically-Controlled Accessories. Complete with "Lockon" and connecting wires.
Code Word "BUBT."

Nos. 20 and 020

Lionel 90 Degree Crossings. A great improvement over our former models. The cross rails are mounted on an ornamental steel base, beautifully enameled. A solid molded fibre block placed in the centre where the rails cross, not only prevents short circuit, but is so constructed that the roller contact shoes on the locomotive and cars easily ride over it without derailing. A large variety of figures can be formed when using these crossings in conjunction with switches and track.

No. 020 Crossing for "O" Gauge Track. Size 8¼ inches square.
Code Word "ORLA."

No. 20 Crossing for "Lionel Standard" Track. Size 11¾ inches square.
Code Word "BOOST."

"Lockon" Track Connections
(Patent No. 1542337)

LOCKED — OPEN

Lionel Lockon Connections are attached to the track by simply turning the lever at right angles as shown in the above illustration. The electric connection is as perfect as though the parts were riveted or soldered to the track.

Lionel "Lockon" Connections are free from set screws and binding posts. The fingers that hold the wires in place are made of heavy tempered blue steel and are unbreakable. All other metal parts are nickel-plated and are mounted on a heavy fibre base.

Lionel "Lockon" Connections should be used wherever electric accessories require connection with the track.

OTC "Lockon" for "O" Gauge Track. *Code Word "JOIN."*
STC "Lockon" for "Lionel Standard" Track.
Code Word "JUICE."

Prices are Listed on Page 45

1929

No. 300 STEEL BRIDGE
Can Be Used With "O" Gauge or "Lionel Standard" Model Railroads

NOTHING so elaborate or architecturally perfect as this bridge has ever been made for use with a model electric train. It is faithfully modeled after the famous "Hell-gate" Bridge which spans the East River in New York. The piers, center span and structural features are correct to the minutest detail. It is made entirely of sheet steel, and is substantially constructed throughout. It measures 28¾ inches in length, 11 inches in height and is 10⅞ inches wide. It is so skillfully designed that it is not necessary for a train to travel up or down grade when passing over it. It is finished in lasting enamel colors, and will greatly add to every boy's Lionel Railroad Equipment.

Code Word "HELGA."

Price is Listed on Page 45

ALL-STEEL BRIDGES for "LIONEL STANDARD" and "O" GAUGE TRACK

Reg. U. S. Pat. Off.

No. 110 Span—For "O" Gauge Track. 10½ in. long, 5½ in. wide, 4⅛ in. high. Complete with track.
Code Word "WILLY"

No. 105 Approaches (two sections)—For "O" Gauge Track. Made in reproduction of reinforced concrete. Complete length 21¼ in., height 2 in. at centre, width 4⅛ in. Complete with track.
Code Word "PARIS"

No. 106 Bridge (three sections)—For "O" Gauge Track. Complete structure is 32½ in. long, 5½ in. wide, 4⅛ in. high. Complete with track.
Code Word "CONN"

No. 108 Bridge (four sections)—For "O" Gauge Track. Complete structure is 43 inches long, 5½ inches wide, 4⅛ inches high. Complete with track.
Code Word "HOUSA"

No. 109 Bridge (five sections) Same in appearance as No. 108 Bridge illustrated above—For "O" Gauge Track. Contains three centre spans and two approaches. Complete structure is 53½ inches long, 5½ inches wide, 4⅛ inches high. Complete with track.
Code Word "MISS"

THE sturdy construction and realistic appearance of Lionel all-steel bridges places them in a class by themselves. They are scale models of the big railroad bridges seen throughout the country. The end piers, bridgework and roadways are exceptionally rigid. The architectural designs are graceful and the embossing work incorporated in them gives a dignity and realism that cannot be equalled. Special slots in the roadway hold the track in place, and the spans as well as the approaches are provided with sections of either "O" Gauge or "Lionel Standard" Track. Lionel Bridges can be extended to any length by adding spans shown in the illustrations.

Prices are Listed on Page 45

No. 104 Span—For "Lionel Standard" Track. 14 inches long, 6½ inches wide, 6¼ inches high. Complete with track.
Code Word "MANN"

No. 100 Approaches (two sections) — For "Lionel Standard" Track. Construction is the same as No. 105 described in opposite column. Complete length 28¼ in., height 2 in. at centre, width 5⅜ in. Complete with track.
Code Word "BROOKLYN"

No. 101 Bridge (three sections)—For "Lionel Standard" Track. Complete structure is 42¼ inches long, 6½ inches wide, 6¼ inches high. Complete with track.
Code Word "QUEENS"

No. 102 Bridge (four sections)—For "Lionel Standard" Track. Complete structure is 56½ inches long, 6½ inches wide, 6¼ inches high. Complete with track.
Code Word "KEEPSIE"

No. 103 Bridge (five sections)—Same in appearance as No. 102 Bridge illustrated above—For "Lionel Standard" Track. Contains three centre spans and two approaches. Complete structure is 70½ inches long, 6½ inches wide, 6¼ inches high. Complete with track.
Code Word "LONDON"

Lionel All-Steel Lamp Posts

NO Model Railroad is complete without the addition of **Lionel Lamp Posts** — faithful reproductions of boulevard and street lamp posts seen everywhere. All Lionel Lamp Posts are of steel construction, enameled in a variety of beautiful colors. They will not bend or break. The binding posts to which electrical connections are made are conveniently situated, securely fastened and perfectly insulated. There is no chance of short circuit, for great care is used in their construction and every one is thoroughly tested. The electric lamps are in exact proportion to the size of the posts. No other make has the dignity and grace of design to be found in Lionel Lamp Posts.

NEW!

No. 54 Lamp Post — 9½ inches high. Complete with two globes. An attractive new double-arm lamp post for use with "O" Gauge Railroads.
Code Word "MOLD."

COLORED LAMPS for Accessories

No. 27R Red Lamp — 12 volts, ½ inch round.
Code Word "NOUN."

No. 28R Red Lamp — 18 volts, ½ inch round.
Code Word "NORTH."

No. 27G Green Lamp — 12 volts, ½ inch round.
Code Word "NAIL."

No. 28G Green Lamp — 18 volts, ½ inch round.
Code Word "NEAT."

The red lamps listed above are for use in the Nos. 025 and 25 Bumpers and No. 79 Flashing Railroad Signal.

The green lamps listed above are for use in the front and rear lanterns of No. 403E Locomotive.

No. 67 Lamp Post — 12⅝ inches high. Complete with two globes.
Code Word "EDMUNDS."

No. 58 Lamp Post — 7½ inches high. Complete with globe.
Code Word "JENNY."

No. 56 Lamp Post — 7¾ inches high. The top is removable so that the lamp can be renewed. Complete with lamp.
Code Word "SHINE."

No. 57 Lamp Post — 7½ inches high. The top is removable so that the lamp can be renewed. Complete with lamp.
Code Word "CHEERY."

No. 59 Lamp Post — Similar in design to No. 61, but is 8⅝ inches high. Complete with globe.
Code Word "BRIGHT."

No. 61 Lamp Post — 12⅝ inches high. Complete with globe.
Code Word "INDIA."

LIONEL LAMP CABINET

No. 111 Lionel Lamp Cabinet — We supply Lionel dealers with a handsome cabinet of lamps for use in headlights and all electrically illuminated accessories. These lamps are of the finest quality and are supplied in 12 volts and 18 volts suitable for "O" Gauge or "Lionel Standard" equipment. Fifty assorted lamps are packed in each cabinet. The chart on inside of cover gives valuable information for the use of various lamps. Each lamp is packed in a special container. Cabinet contains 50 assorted lamps.
Code Word "LUX."

LIONEL LAMP RENEWALS
Each Lamp Packed in Special Container

No. 27 — 12 volt, ½-inch round lamp. For use in all "O" Gauge equipment. *Code Word* "NOSE."

No. 28 — 18 volt, ½-inch round lamp. For use in all "Lionel Standard" equipment. *Code Word* "NELA."

No. 39 — 12 volt, ¾-inch round globe.
For "O" Gauge Railroads use this lamp on Nos. 51, 58, 59, 61 and 67 Lamp Posts and No. 124 station. *Code Word* "NICE."

No. 40 — 18 volt, ¾-inch round globe. Same uses as No. 39 lamp, when operating "Lionel Standard" equipment.
Code Word "NAVY."

Prices are Listed on Page 45

ALL-STEEL TUNNELS FOR "LIONEL STANDARD" AND "O" GAUGE TRACK

LIONEL Tunnels are of steel construction throughout, and are accurately designed and formed in our special machinery. Front and rear entrances are embossed in exact reproduction of heavy stone masonry, having a keystone at the top. The bodies of the tunnels represent mountainsides in miniature, and are hand decorated in beautiful harmonizing colors. We draw particular attention to the details on the large size tunnels illustrated below. Mountain roadsides are realistically reproduced, and the little metal "chalets," bridges, architectural and landscaping details are all in perfect proportion to the size of the tunnel. Several of the tunnels listed below are equipped with interior lights, producing a beautiful effect.

No. 120L

No. 120L Illuminated Tunnel—For use with the large size "Lionel Standard" Trains. Hand painted and graceful in design. Equipped with interior light. Length 17 inches, width 12 inches, height 9⅝ inches. Tunnel openings are 6½ inches wide and 8⅛ inches high.

Code Word "HOPE"

No. 120L Tunnel can be used with all "Lionel Standard" Gauge outfits.

Nos. 119 and 119L Tunnels can be used with outfits Nos. 353, 353E, 347, 347E, 352, 352E, 354, 354E, 340E, 355E, 391, 391E, 392, 392E, 393, 393E, 394E, 395 and 395E, for "Lionel Standard" Track, and all "O" Gauge outfits.

Nos. 119 and 119L

No. 119L Illuminated Tunnel—Suitable for all "O" Gauge Trains and medium size "Lionel Standard" Trains. Equipped with interior light. Length 12 inches, width 9½ inches, height 9¼ inches. Tunnel openings are 5 inches wide and 6½ inches high.

Code Word "HARP"

No. 119 Tunnel—Similar in every way to No. 119L described above, but without interior light.

Code Word "HOSA"

No. 118, A very desirable moderately priced Tunnel may be used with "O" Gauge outfits Nos. 249, 292, 293, 294, 295, and 296.

No. 118

No. 118 Tunnel—For use with small size "O" Gauge Trains. Length 8 inches, width 7¼ inches, height 7 inches. Tunnel openings are 4 inches wide and 5⅜ inches high.

Code Word "SIMPLON"

No. 130L

No. 130L Illuminated Tunnel—A beautiful model suitable for use with large "O" Gauge model railroad layouts. It incorporates a wealth of interesting details. Beautifully hand decorated in gorgeous enamel colors, it presents an imposing appearance as the train glides in and out of it. Lights are placed over the forward and rear entrances. Length 24 inches, width 18½ inches, height 14½ inches. Tunnel openings are 5 inches wide and 6½ inches high.

Code Word "SOAK"

Lionel Tunnels Add Realism To Your Model Railroad

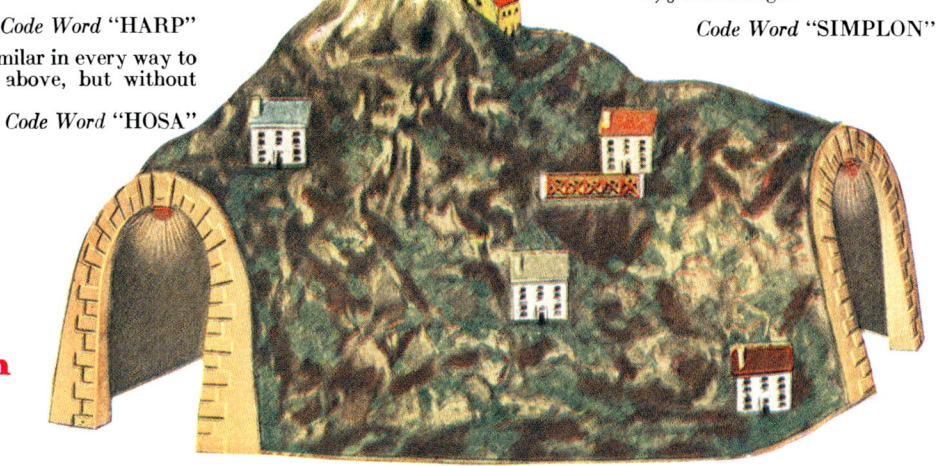

No. 140L

No. 140L Illuminated Tunnel—This is for use with our largest model railroad equipment. No finer accessory for model electric trains has ever been made. This elaborate tunnel is made to fit on the curve of the track, and is so accurately aligned that our largest trains can pass through it easily. The electric lights placed at either end of the tunnel reflect through the windows of the houses on the mountain-side, and present a magnificent vista. Length 35¾ inches, width 23 inches, height 23½ inches. Tunnel openings are 8 inches wide and 8 inches high.

Code Word "SEVA"

Prices are Listed on Page 45

"LIONEL STANDARD" AND "O" GAUGE TRACK FORMATIONS

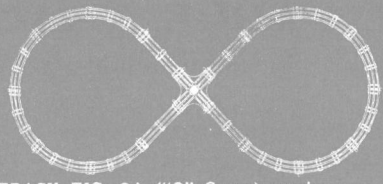

TRACK FIG. OA ("O" Gauge) requires: 12—OC curved track; 4—OS straight track; 1—020, 90 degree crossing. Size over all 70 x 30 in.

TRACK FIG. SA ("Lionel Standard") requires: 12—C curved track; 4—S straight track; 1—20, 90 degree crossing. Size over all 97 x 43 in.

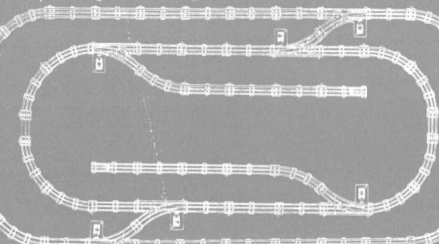

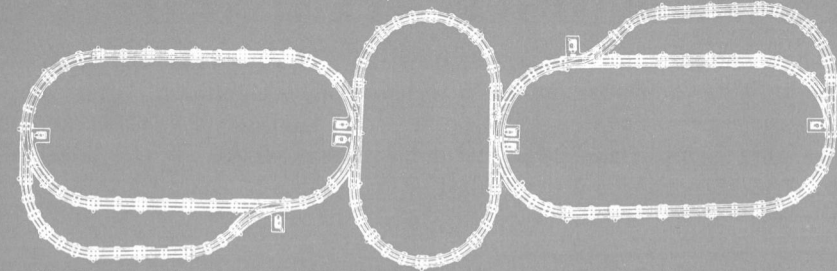

TRACK FIG. OB ("O" Gauge) requires: 24—OC curved track; 18—OS straight track; 2—right hand No. 021 switches; 6—left hand No. 021 switches. Size over all 173 x 53 in.

TRACK FIG. SB ("Lionel Std.") requires: 24—C curved track; 18—S straight track; 2—right hand No. 210 switches; 6—left hand No. 210 switches. Size over all 241 x 71 in.

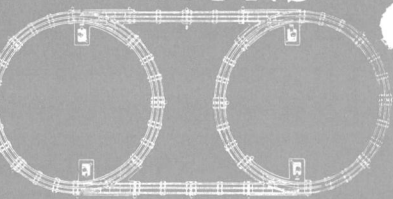

TRACK FIG. OD ("O" Gauge) requires: 12—OC curved track; 4—OS straight track; 2—right hand No. 021 switches; 2—left hand No. 021 switches. Size over all 71 x 30 in.

TRACK FIG. SD ("Lionel Std.") requires: 12—C curved track; 4—S straight track; 2—right hand No. 210 switches; 2—left hand No. 210 switches. Size over all 98 x 42 in.

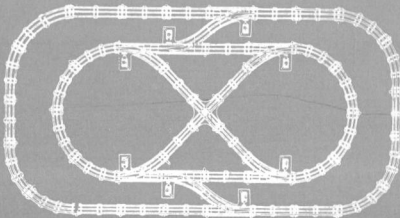

TRACK FIG. OE ("O" Gauge) requires: 32—OS straight track; 18—OC curved track; 2—½ OS straight track; 2—right hand No. 021 switches; 4—left hand No. 021 switches; 2—023 bumpers. Size over all 113 x 52 in.

TRACK FIG. SE ("Lionel Standard") requires: 32—S straight track; 18—C curved track; 2—½ S straight track; 2—right hand No. 210 switches; 4—left hand No. 210 switches; 2—23 bumpers. Size over all 154 x 71 in.

TRACK FIG. OF ("O" Gauge) requires: 16—OC curved track; 4—OS straight track; 2—right hand No. 021 switches; 2—left hand No 021 switches; 1—020, 90 degree crossing. Size over all 90 x 30 in.

TRACK FIG. SF ("Lionel Std.") requires: 16—C curved track; 4—S straight track; 2—right hand No. 210 switches; 2—left hand No. 210 switches; 1—20, 90 degree crossing. Size over all 124 x 43 in.

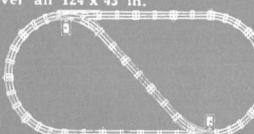

TRACK FIG. OH ("O" Gauge) requires: 8—OC curved track, making a circle 30 in. in diameter.

TRACK FIG. SH ("Lionel Std.") requires: 8—C curved track, making a circle 43 in in diameter.

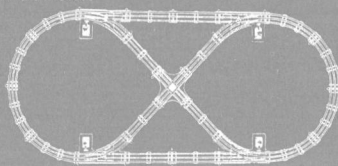

TRACK FIG. OJ ("O" Gauge) requires: 18—OS straight track; 16—OC curved track; 4—right hand No. 021 switches; 4—left hand No. 021 switches; 1—020, 90 degree crossing. Size over all 92 x 41 in.

TRACK FIG. SJ ("Lionel Standard") requires: 18—S straight track; 16—C curved track; 4—right hand No. 210 switches; 4—left hand No. 210 switches; 1—20, 90 degree crossing. Size over all 126 x 57 in.

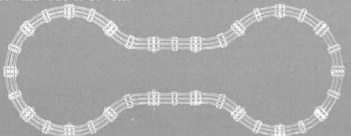

TRACK FIG. OK ("O" Gauge) requires: 14—OC curved track; 1—020X, 45 degree crossing. Size over all 61 x 30 in.

TRACK FIG. SK ("Lionel Standard") requires: 14—C curved track; 1—20X, 45 degree crossing. Size over all 88 x 43 in.

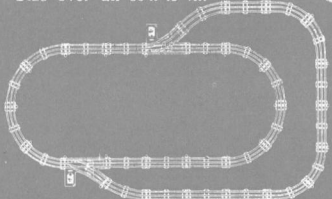

TRACK FIG. OL ("O" Gauge) requires: 8—OC curved track; 9—OS straight track; 2—right hand No. 021 switches. Size over all 71 x 30 in.

TRACK FIG. SL ("Lionel Std.") requires: 8—C curved track; 9—S straight track; 2—right hand No. 210 switches. Size over all 98 x 43 in.

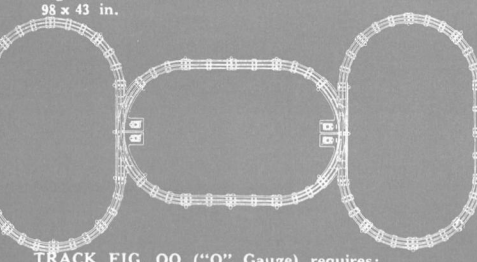

TRACK FIG. OM ("O" Gauge) requires: 8—OC curved track; 8—OS straight track; 2—right hand No. 021 switches; 2—left hand No. 021 switches; 1—020, 90 degree crossing. Size over all 71 x 30 in.

TRACK FIG. SM ("Lionel Std.") requires: 8—C curved track; 8—S straight track; 2—right hand No. 210 switches; 2—left hand No. 210 switches; 1—20, 90 degree crossing. Size over all 98 x 43 in.

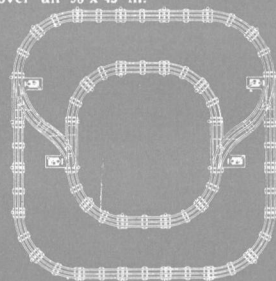

TRACK FIG. ON ("O" Gauge) requires: 16—OC curved track; 2—OS straight track. Size over all 81 x 30 in.

TRACK FIG. SN ("Lionel Standard") requires: 16—C curved track; 2—S straight track. Size over all 117 x 43 in.

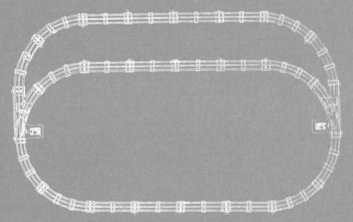

TRACK FIG. OP ("O" Gauge) requires: 14—OC curved track; 12—OS straight track; 1—right hand No. 021 switch; 1—left hand No. 021 switch. Size over all 82 x 51 in.

TRACK FIG. SP ("Lionel Standard") requires: 14—C curved track; 12—S straight track; 1—right hand No. 210 switch; 1—left hand No. 210 switch. Size over all 112 x 71 in.

TRACK FIG. OQ ("O" Gauge) requires: 20—OC curved track; 8—OS straight track; 2—right hand No. 021 switches; 2—left hand No. 021 switches. Size over all 110 x 50 in.

TRACK FIG. SQ ("Lionel Std.") requires: 20—C curved track; 8—S straight track; 2—right hand No. 210 switches; 2—left hand No. 210 switches. Size over all 154 x 71 in.

TRACK FIG. OR ("O" Gauge) requires: 16—OC curved track; 12—OS straight track; 2—right hand No. 021 switches; 2—left hand No. 021 switches. Size over all 61 x 61 in.

TRACK FIG. SR ("Lionel Std.") requires: 16—C curved track; 12—S straight track; 2—right hand No. 210 switches; 2—left hand No. 210 switches. Size over all 85 x 85 in.

TRACK FIG. OT ("O" Gauge) requires: 10—OC curved track; 12—OS straight track; 1—right hand No. 021 switch; 1—left hand No. 021 switch. Size over all 71 x 40 in.

TRACK FIG. ST ("Lionel Standard") requires: 10—C curved track; 12—S straight track; 1—right hand No. 210 switch; 1—left hand No. 210 switch. Size over all 98 x 57 in.

You may use No. 25 or 025 illuminated bumpers instead of Nos. 23 and 023 spring bumpers if desired. You may use No. 222 or 012 electrically-controlled switches instead of Nos. 210 and 021 hand-controlled switches. REFER TO PAGES 38 AND 39 FOR PRICES OF SEPARATE PARTS USED IN MAKING THESE TRACK FORMATIONS.

Manufactured and Guaranteed by THE LIONEL CORPORATION 15 East 26th Street, New York, N.Y.

LIONEL PRICE LIST—1929

Cat. No.	Description	Price
PAGE 7		
248	Loco	$6.00
252	Loco	8.50
253	Loco	10.25
254	Loco	12.75
254E	Loco	18.00
251	Loco	15.75
251E	Loco	21.00
256	Loco	19.00
PAGE 8		
292	Outfit	7.00
249	Outfit	7.00
293	Outfit	11.25
294	Outfit	10.25
296	Outfit	14.00
PAGE 9		
295	Outfit	14.00
266	Outfit	17.75
266E	Outfit	22.50
299	Outfit	17.75
299E	Outfit	22.50
267	Outfit	21.50
PAGE 10		
97	Outfit	23.50
97E	Outfit	26.75
269	Outfit	26.25
269E	Outfit	29.50
268	Outfit	30.00
PAGE 11		
174	Outfit	40.00
175E	Outfit	67.50
PAGE 12		
4U	"Bild-a-Loco"	18.75
PAGE 13		
1	"Bild-a-Motor"	10.00
2	"Bild-a-Motor"	15.00
9U	"Bild-a-Loco"	28.75
381U	"Bild-a-Loco"	44.50
PAGE 14		
4	"Bild-a-Loco"	15.75
9	"Bild-a-Loco"	24.00
9E	"Bild-a-Loco"	28.75
381E	"Bild-a-Loco"	44.50
381	"Bild-a-Loco"	39.50
43	Gear Set	4.00
043	Gear Set	2.75
PAGE 15		
402E	Loco	42.50
408E	Loco	47.50
8	Loco	12.25
8E	Loco	18.50
10	Loco	14.50
10E	Loco	21.00
318	Loco	17.50
318E	Loco	23.75
380E	Loco	26.75
PAGE 16		
347	Outfit	$19.00
347E	Outfit	23.75
353	Outfit	21.00
353E	Outfit	26.75
352	Outfit	26.25
352E	Outfit	32.25
354	Outfit	26.25
354E	Outfit	32.25
PAGE 17		
342	Outfit	32.25
342E	Outfit	38.75
340E	Outfit	38.75
355E	Outfit	40.50
349	Outfit	47.50
349E	Outfit	52.50
PAGE 18		
390	Steam Type	30.00
390E	Steam Type	35.00
395	Steam Type	47.50
395E	Steam Type	52.50
PAGE 19		
391	Steam Type	39.00
391E	Steam Type	44.00
392	Steam Type	41.75
392E	Steam Type	46.75
393	Steam Type	45.00
393E	Steam Type	50.00
394E	Steam Type	55.00
PAGE 20		
407E	Complete RR	325.00
PAGES 21 and 22		
357E	Outfit	52.50
403E	Outfit	70.00
410E	Outfit	77.50
PAGES 23, 24 and 25		
409E	Outfit	87.50
411E	Outfit	110.00
PAGE 26		
219	Derrick Car	9.00
218	Dump Car	6.25
PAGE 27		
511	Flat Car	2.35
512	Gondola Car	2.35
513	Cattle Car	3.10
514	Box Car	3.10
514R	Refrig. Car	3.10
515	Oil Car	3.10
516	Coal Car	3.50
517	Caboose	3.50
211	Flat Car	3.50
212	Gondola Car	3.50
213	Cattle Car	4.75
214	Box Car	4.75
214R	Refrig. Car	4.75
215	Oil Car	4.75
216	Coal Car	4.75
217	Caboose	5.50
PAGE 28		
803	Coal Car	$0.90
804	Oil Car	.70
805	Box Car	1.00
806	Cattle Car	1.10
807	Caboose	1.10
831	Flat Car	.70
902	Gondola Car	.70
811	Flat Car	1.90
812	Gondola Car	1.90
813	Cattle Car	2.25
814	Box Car	2.25
814R	Refrig. Car	2.25
815	Oil Car	2.25
816	Coal Car	2.65
817	Caboose	2.65
808	Frt. Car Set	5.25
818	Frt. Car Set	9.00
PAGE 29		
710	Pullman Car	3.90
712	Obs. Car	4.00
605	Pullman Car	3.50
606	Obs. Car	3.75
610	Pullman Car	3.10
612	Obs. Car	3.25
607	Pullman Car	1.75
608	Obs. Car	1.90
529	Pullman Car	.80
530	Obs. Car	.85
629	Pullman Car	.80
630	Obs. Car	.85
338	Obs. Car	5.25
332	Mail & Bag.	4.75
337	Pullman Car	4.50
341	Obs. Car	5.75
312	Obs. Car	6.00
339	Pullman Car	4.75
309	Pullman Car	5.25
310	Mail & Bag.	5.50
490	Obs. Car	10.00
430	Obs. Car	9.00
418	Pullman Car	9.00
428	Pullman Car	8.00
419	Pull. & Bag.	9.25
429	Pull. & Bag.	8.25
431	Dining Car	10.50
412	Pullman Car	17.50
413	Pullman Car	17.50
414	Pullman Car	17.50
416	Obs. Car	17.50
PAGE 30		
80	Semaphore	4.75
080	Semaphore	4.75
78	Train Control	5.25
078	Train Control	5.25
82	Tr. Cont. Sem.	9.00
082	Tr. Cont. Sem.	9.00
84	Semaphore	4.25
084	Semaphore	4.25
PAGE 31		
79	Flash. Sig.	$5.25
83	Traffic Sig.	4.00
87	Crossing Signal	5.00
77	Crossing Gate	4.50
077	Crossing Gate	4.25
69	Warning Sig.	3.50
069	Warning Sig.	3.25
PAGE 32		
107	Reducer, 110v.	10.00
170	Reducer 220v.	14.50
81	Rheostat	2.50
A	Transformer	3.75
B	Transformer	5.00
T	Transformer	7.50
K	Trans., 110v.	11.00
K	Trans., 220v.	14.50
C	Transformer	7.50
PAGE 34		
192	Villa Set	9.00
195	Terrace Set	18.00
193	Auto. Acc. Set	22.00
194	Auto. Acc. Set	22.75
186	Bungalow Set	8.00
013	Panel Bd. Set	15.50
225	Panel Bd. Set	17.50
71	Tel. Post Set	3.75
70	Accessory Set	4.50
071	Tel. Post Set	3.75
86	Tel. Post Set	4.50
PAGE 35		
62	Semaphore	.90
60	Telegraph Post	.65
85	Telegraph Post	.80
060	Telegraph Post	.65
068	Warning Sig.	.50
68	Warning Sig.	.90
89	Flag Staff	.80
90	Flag Staff	1.30
191	Villa	3.50
184	Bungalow	1.60
189	Villa	3.10
PAGE 36		
128	Station	26.25
129	Platform	16.75
PAGE 37		
124	Station	9.50
122	Station	6.50
126	Station	4.75
127	Station	3.10
437	Switch Tower	9.00
439	Panel Board	5.75
435	Power House	2.75
436	Power House	3.50
438	Signal Tower	5.00
PAGE 38		
210	Switches....Pair	6.50
021	Switches....Pair	5.00
222	Switches....Pair	$11.75
012	Switches....Pair	9.75
200	Turntable	7.75
PAGE 39		
20X	Crossing	1.85
020X	Crossing	1.60
020	Crossing	1.10
20	Crossing	1.30
025	Bumper	1.85
25	Bumper	2.35
023	Bumper	.85
23	Bumper	1.30
OC	Track	.20
OS	Track	.20
OSS	Special Track	.40
C	Track	.30
S	Track	.30
SS	Special Track	.60
OTC	Lockon	.20
STC	Lockon	.25
PAGE 40		
300	Bridge	16.50
110	Span	2.60
105	Bridge	1.75
106	Bridge	3.50
108	Bridge	5.75
109	Bridge	7.75
104	Span	3.50
100	Bridge	2.60
101	Bridge	6.00
102	Bridge	9.00
103	Bridge	11.50
PAGE 42		
67	Lamp Post	3.00
54	Lamp Post	2.35
58	Lamp Post	1.30
56	Lamp Post	1.75
57	Lamp Post	1.75
59	Lamp Post	1.60
61	Lamp Post	2.25
111	Lamp Ass't	15.00
27	12 V. Clear	.30
28	18 V. Clear	.30
39	12 V. Clear	.30
40	18 V. Clear	.30
27G	12 V. Green	.30
27R	12 V. Red	.30
28G	18 V. Green	.30
28R	18 V. Red	.30
PAGE 43		
120L	Tunnel, Ill.	6.50
119	Tunnel	3.50
119L	Tunnel, Ill.	4.50
118	Tunnel	2.25
130L	Tunnel, Ill.	14.50
140L	Tunnel, Ill.	17.50
PAGE 46		
840	Power House	22.50

1929

No. 840—Lionel Power Station

There is no accessory more desirable or fitting to be used with **Lionel** "Distant Control" Railroads than this attractive new Power Station. It is possible to control and operate the most elaborate model railroad layout from this central station. Original and ornamental in design, it is embellished with wonderful details, such as doors, windows, frames, etc., all actually inserted, not merely represented by lithography. The stone work and masonry are in exact reproduction of a big concrete building. Steel construction throughout, richly enameled in beautiful colors. Length 26 inches, width 21½ inches, height to top of smokestack 18 inches.

Code Word "LING"

THE above illustration shows the provision made for accommodating one or two **Lionel** Transformers. The switches on the transformers can be reached through openings above them. Illustration also shows the Panel Board on one side of the Power House containing six knife switches, from which "Distant Control" trains and illuminated accessories can be operated.

Price is Listed on Page 45

LIONEL ELECTRIC TRAINS
MODEL RAILROAD ACCESSORIES
LIONEL
FERNANDO E·CIAVATTI

1930

LIONEL MODEL RAILROADING
"Standard of the World Since 1900"

The Tremendous Factories at Irvington, N. J., Where Lionel Trains Are Made

LIONEL MODEL RAILROADING — Surely there is magic in these words! Suppose, just suppose a world renowned magician was standing alongside of a famous railroad train, say the Twentieth Century Limited. He waves his wand, and lo and behold, the train grows smaller and smaller, until it is only a hundred inches long, and six inches high. And instead of the crack engineer in the cab, YOU are standing next to the train! And that exactly describes a Lionel Train. Real as a real train except for size.

Lionel's supreme leadership has remained unchallenged since Lionel Trains were first created and built in 1900. In other words, ever since your Dad was a boy. He played with electric trains then, and he probably helps you play with yours now. It is play, yes, but it is more than just that. It is a pleasant, exciting way of learning something about the world, about the world of travel; about the world of railroading; about the mysterious force—Electricity. You must think of the Lionel Corporation as a national institution of learning, whose aim is to help the future engineer.

Boys, the Lionel Corporation's staff of mechanical engineers are absolutely capable of building real railroads, and real trains. But they are tirelessly at work making researches, testing new materials, designing new machinery, organizing production to turn out always better and more realistic Lionel Trains for YOU.

There she goes! You have thrown in the switch in the control tower, and the powerful Transcontinental Limited gathers speed down the line. Look at that train! Powerful motored locomotive with headlight gleaming. Long graceful Pullmans and an observation car with a cheerful electric light on the rear platform, and two brilliant red rear running lights. It *does* seem as if some magician had a hand in this. That train is too realistic to be a mere toy.

But, there is more to Lionel Model Railroading than just seeing the train run. You can switch your train electrically to another track. You can control your station lights, lamp posts, tunnel illumination—all from a central power house, or panel board. You can back your freight pulled by a powerful engine, on to a siding to clear the main track for the Limited!

Yes, you can do all of these things, and in the following pages of this catalog, it tells you how.

Most boys would not operate any electric train at all, if they could not have a LIONEL. They know that only LIONEL keeps pace with the very latest developments of real railroads.

But after all, what good would even a real railroad be without locomotives that perform their tasks faithfully, and above all CONTINUOUSLY. One locomotive on the job is worth a dozen in the shop.

And that, boys, is the reason for the nation-wide success of LIONEL. A LIONEL motor is a masterpiece of mechanical and electrical precision. It is the crowning achievement of our staff of master mechanical engineers. It is built and assembled as carefully as the movement in Dad's watch. Every gear is machined to mesh precisely with its fellow gear. Every bearing is accurately installed so that there is no side play to a shaft or axle. Every armature is wound by patented machinery that cannot make a blunder. And after it is installed in the locomotive body, it is more powerful, and will pull more cars than any other make of train ever produced.

Every modern accessory, whether hand or automatically controlled, is included in the Lionel Line. Each one a masterpiece by itself, and a faithful reproduction of the equipment used on real railroads.

Tell Dad to buy you a Lionel Train. You may just as well have the best. They don't cost any more. Go to your dealer. Ask him to run a Lionel Train for you. Be an engineer—a real engineer—a LIONEL ENGINEER.

THE LIONEL CORPORATION
15-17-19 East 26th Street, New York, N. Y.

[Page Two]

IHP REPRODUCTION, 1974

THE LIONEL "DISTANT-CONTROL" SYSTEM

An Electrical Brain In Your Train

THE LIONEL "DISTANT-CONTROL" SUPER-MOTOR

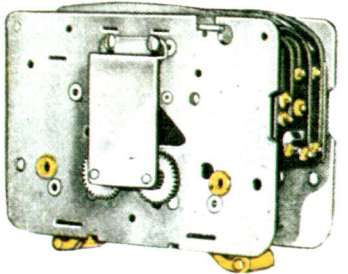

Illustration shows the simplicity and compactness of **Lionel** "Distant-Control" Super-Motors. All working parts are mounted between two heavy steel plates. All shaft bearings are reinforced with bronze bushings. All parts are easily accessible, including the removable brush holder, lever for reversing the locomotive by hand and an additional lever for disconnecting the "Distant-Control" mechanism.

Lionel has pioneered every outstanding improvement in Model Electric Trains.

IHP REPRODUCTION, 1974

OPERATING a Lionel Train by means of Lionel's 100% "Distant-Control" System is the most interesting and most thrilling experience an intelligent boy can have. Nothing equals its perfect operation, its quick as lightning response to the young engineer's commands. Designed for both "O" Gauge and "Lionel Standard" track it makes it unnecessary to reverse your locomotive by hand. All the movements of the railroad can be controlled from *any distant point* by means of a small controlling rheostat just as from a real switch tower. Precisely as the boy is doing in the picture, you can start, stop, reverse and operate your train at any speed without touching your locomotive. You are thereby the chief operator of a railway system. Your locomotive obeys your will. The commands of the young engineer are executed instantly.

This "Distant-Control" System, plus the Lionel "Distant-Control" Electrical Switches, described on another page, makes it possible for you, by manipulating a small lever, to switch your freight on to a siding while the "Limited" roars past, or you can switch your train from one track to another, entirely by remote control.

Furthermore, in addition to their automatic operation by the passing of the train, Lionel Semaphores, Crossing Gates, Warning Bells and Train Controls can be operated from a switch tower at any distance from the track. Just think what this means! Picture the thrill of knowing that at your finger-tips you have the complete control of a railroad system. It is a thrill you can only experience with a Lionel. Remember that!

Lionel "Distant-Control" Locomotives and Train Outfits listed on the following pages are distinguished by the letter "E" after the catalog number.

Many of these wonderful "E" motors are of the Lionel "Bild-a-Loco" type. This "Bild-a-Loco" motor can be snapped out of the locomotive in a jiffy and taken down by the young engineer in a very few seconds. It means that you can oil and clean your entire motor, examine the construction, and learn more about electricity. The Lionel "Bild-a-Motor" is an engineering triumph. There are absolutely no wires to disconnect in taking it apart. The electrical contacts are automatic. It is only necessary to follow the simple instructions that go with each "Bild-a-Loco."

The illustrations in this catalog cannot give you a true idea of Lionel quality. Go to your dealer and examine every part of a Lionel Train. Feel the solidity of it. That means sturdiness, strength! Note the glossy, brilliant smoothness of its enameled finish. Examine the details on the engine and cars, and you will find how thoroughly every particular is carried out. They are real trains in miniature. Strength, beauty and quality are built into every train with Lionel thoroughness.

That's why Lionel has been "Standard of the World" since 1900!

[Page Three]

1930

CONSTRUCTION OF LIONEL "O" GAUGE MOTORS

DRIVING GEARS ("A")—They are made of heavy steel blanks, machine-cut. They mesh without friction and are far superior to gears with punched teeth.

Field ("B")—The field is made of a number of specially prepared transformer steel laminations. This construction gives a much stronger field than if a single piece of steel were used.

Third Rail Shoe Support ("C")—Made of heavy fibre to which the third rail contact rollers are attached. Our construction protects rollers from injury, for the brackets can be bent against the fibre without disturbing the arc of the spring that gives them the correct tension against the third rail.

Wheels ("D")—Lionel was first to introduce die-cast wheels. They are absolutely balanced. A nickel-plated steel rim is forced over the tread of the wheel to insure long wear.

Collecting Shoes ("E")—They collect current from the third rail. They are made of *stainless steel* turnings and revolve on steel shafts which pass through phosphor bronze supports. They insure perfect contact with the third rail at all times so that locomotive will run at uniform speed.

Frame ("F")—Made of very heavy steel punchings, embodying great detail. Will withstand more than the ordinary amount of wear and tear.

Journals ("G")—Made of heavy brass, nickel-plated. Attached to the frames by mechanical means. They add greatly to the appearance of the structure.

Cowcatchers ("H")—The construction of the cowcatchers varies with the type of locomotive on which they are used. Many of them are part of the steel frame which is made in one piece, and others are heavy castings rigidly attached to the frame.

Flag Posts ("J")—All our locomotives are equipped with four flag posts, two at each end of the frame; a very realistic detail.

Tanks ("K")—These tanks are made of brass, nickel-plated, and are separable pieces attached to the frame, which further accentuates the great detail.

Lionel Automatic Couplers ("L")—Made of heavy steel, nickel-plated and polished. They are scientifically constructed so that cars cannot become detached when in motion, but are easily taken apart when desired. The new improved **Lionel** Coupler with invisible spring arrangement is a great advance over any similar device ever made.

[Page Four]

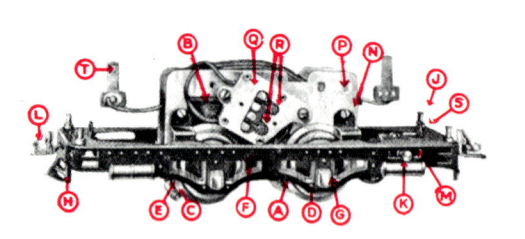

Illustration above shows the type of motor used in "O" Gauge Locomotives Nos. 248, 252 and 253 illustrated on Page 7. Full description of all working parts is given on this page.

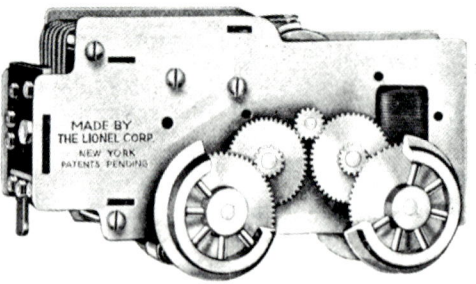

This "Distant-Control" Super-Motor is used in "O" Gauge Locomotives Nos. 254E and 251E. Super-Motor with hand reverse is used in "O" Gauge Locomotives Nos. 254 and 251.

THE NEW "O" GAUGE "DISTANT-CONTROL" SUPER-MOTOR
(Illustrated above, on the right hand side)

THIS marvelous new motor will haul twice as many cars as any other "O" Gauge Motor now on sale. The illustration shows some of the remarkable features that make this possible. Notice the new system of gearing which gives maximum hauling power with minimum current consumption.

The "Distant-Control" mechanism is built right into the motor, and is completely protected against injury. This new "O" Gauge Super-Motor, a triumph of engineering skill, is one of **Lionel's** greatest achievements.

Above illustration shows the "O" Gauge "Bild-a-Loco" Motor used in Locomotives Nos. 4, 257, 258 and 260E.

Above illustration shows "Bild-a-Loco" converted into "Bild-a-Motor".

The marvelous new "Bild-a-Loco" and "Bild-a-Motor" are described on Page 3. Be sure to read about this revolutionary new departure in miniature motor construction.

Above illustration shows "O" Gauge Twin-Super-Motor chassis used in Locomotive No. 256. These twin-motors develop great hauling power and will pull a long train of cars with perfect ease. A larger illustration of the "O" Gauge Super-Motor is shown at the top of this page to the right.

Reversing Controllers ("M")—Lionel Reversing Controllers have been in use for many years during which time they have given thorough satisfaction. They are the only controllers in use that cannot get out of order. They operate very easily, and due to the brass cups and spring tension, good electrical contact is always made.

Frame Support ("N")—The frame is supported to the motor with only four screws. This simple method of construction was originally introduced by us in 1913. All parts of **Lionel** Locomotives can be easily reached for cleaning.

Side Plates ("P")—Made of heavy gauge steel and support all working parts. All bearing holes are reinforced with phosphor bronze bushings. The alignment of these holes is absolutely perfect so that gears work with minimum friction. All holes are drilled and reamed to proper diameter. The accuracy of these plates compares with the frame work of a very fine clock.

Brush Plate ("Q")—The unique construction permits rapid change of brushes after motor has been in use for a considerable period. The brushes fit in brass tubes. Two properly tempered steel springs give the correct pressure of the brush on the commutator until brushes are worn down to the end. Brushes are replaced by simply raising the springs, lifting up worn-out brushes and dropping in new ones.

Brushes ("R")—We were the first manufacturers of model trains to equip our motors with combination gauze and graphite brushes that wear long and are self-lubricating.

Removable Locomotive Body ("S")—The bodies of all Lionel Locomotives are held in place on the frame with only two screws, one at each end of the locomotive. Supporting members are placed at several points of the frame that rigidly hold the body in place.

Headlight Connection ("T")—A new method originated by us. The fibre contact makes a permanent electrical connection and eliminates the possibility of broken wires.

Commutator—Made of bronze, and perfectly turned when connected to armature so that it is absolutely parallel with brushes. Commutator surface is polished so as to reduce all friction when in contact with brushes.

Armature—Made of specially prepared electrical sheets mounted on a drill rod shaft. It is perfectly insulated and wound with the correct amount of triple insulated wire.

CONSTRUCTION OF "LIONEL STANDARD" SUPER-MOTORS

The Powerful "Lionel Standard" Twin-Super-Motors Will Easily Haul This Train of Twenty Large Freight Cars

Reg. U. S. Pat. Off.

Removable Brush Holder (1)—By simply unscrewing one screw the entire brush holder can be removed from the motor. Change of brushes requires but an instant and the assembled part is replaced without the use of any tools.

Brushes (2)—Made of bronze and graphite which are self-lubricating. They insure long life to the commutator. They are contained in brass tubes and held in place by a simple spring arrangement which feeds brushes to commutator at the same pressure until used up.

Revolving Double Contact Shoes (3)—Are heavy stainless steel rollers, securely affixed to the flexible phosphor bronze plate, which insures the proper tension on the third rail and gives a steady flow of current to the motors. Complete shoe assembly is mounted on a heavy fibre plate and is rigidly attached to the motor frame.

New Gear Arrangement (4)—This new method of gearing is embodied only in **Lionel** Super-Motors. The seven gears in this new layout give the motor greater tractive power, and are almost frictionless. The gears are made of very heavy steel, and teeth are machine cut, not stamped.

Three-Point Armature Shaft Bearing (5)—The armature shaft revolves in three bearings—two of them are contained in the side plates of the motor and the third one in the plate that holds the gearing studs. This three-point bearing eliminates all vibration of the armature shaft, with the result that the commutator and brushes wear long and evenly.

Driving Wheels (6)—Are massive in construction and accurately die-cast. Their weight adds great tractive power to the motors.

Steel Tread on Wheels (7)—A steel tread beautifully nickel-plated and polished is forced over the rim, insuring longer wear and a smooth, even riding surface. **Lionel** originated this method of wheel construction. See illustration on Page 6.

Reinforced Bearings (8)—Six phosphor bronze bearings are contained in the side plates of the motor, insuring accurate alignment of the armature shaft and axles.

Armature—Made of laminated electrical steel punchings. It is automatically drum wound with triple-covered magnet wire, dipped in shellac and baked. The armature shaft (9) is made of the best quality drill rod.

Side Plates (10)—Made of heavy steel, with bronze bushings inserted for shaft and axles.

Field—Made of the highest grade electrical steel, correctly wound and scientifically designed.

Commutator—Made of heavy copper. The segments are perfectly insulated, making short-circuits impossible.

"Lionel Standard" Twin-Super-Motors—Illustration in the left hand column shows "Lionel Standard" Twin-Super-Motors attached to a heavy sheet steel chassis. No. 408E Twin-Super-Motor Locomotive also incorporates Lionel's famous "Distant-Control" unit described on Page 3. This locomotive can be started, stopped, reversed and operated at any speed at any distance from the track.

Above illustration shows "Lionel Standard" Twin-Super-Motors. Locomotive No. 408E is equipped with these powerful motors.

Side view of "Lionel Standard" Super-Motor. The many remarkable features of this motor are described on this page. This type of motor is installed in Locomotive Nos. 8, 8E, 10E and 318E.

Above illustration shows "Lionel Standard" "Bild-a-Loco" motor installed in Locomotive Nos. 9E, 384, 384E, 381E and 390E. See page 3 for description of Lionel "Bild-a-Loco."

Above illustration shows "Lionel Standard" "Bild-a-Loco" converted into "Bild-a-Motor," an independent three-speed power motor described on page 3.

[Page Five]

1930

THESE CONSTRUCTIONAL FEATURES SHOW WHY LIONEL ALWAYS LEADS

WINDOW PANELS, DOORS AND SEATS — A SEPARABLE PIECE INSERTED IN CAR BODY
U.S. PATENTS NO. 1272390 AND 1272391 — JULY 16, 1918

FINISHED CAR BODY SHOWING SEPARABLE PANEL INSERTED
U.S. PATENTS NO. 1272390 & 1272391 JULY 16, 1918

"BILD-A-LOCO" & "BILD-A-MOTOR" ASSEMBLED AND TAKEN APART IN A FEW MOMENTS
U.S. PATENTS PENDING

OPERATING PANTAGRAPHS

CONTROLLING UNITS FOR ELECTRICALLY OPERATED TRACK SWITCHES PATENT PENDING

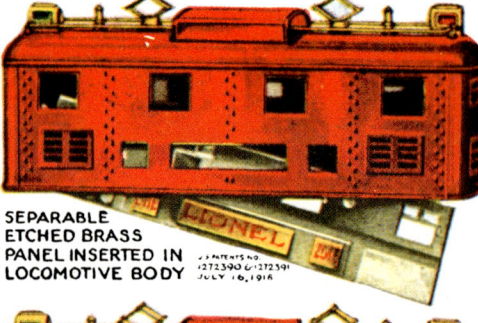

SEPARABLE ETCHED BRASS PANEL INSERTED IN LOCOMOTIVE BODY
U.S. PATENTS NO. 1272390 & 1272391 JULY 16, 1918

FINISHED LOCOMOTIVE BODY SHOWING SEPARABLE PANEL INSERTED
U.S. PATENTS NO. 1272390 & 1272391 JULY 16, 1918

DIE-CAST HEADLIGHT SHOWING RED PANEL AND ELECTRICAL CONNECTION.
U.S. PATENT NO. 1672671 JUNE 12, 1928

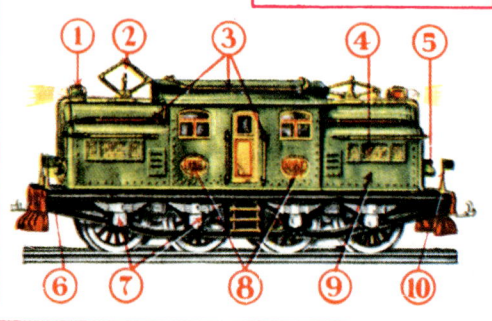

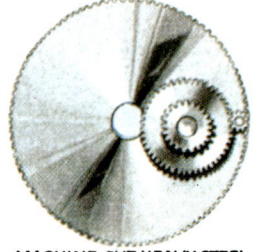

MACHINE-CUT HEAVY STEEL GEARS — NOT PUNCHED

VIEW OF HEADLIGHT SHOWING GREEN PANEL
U.S. PATENT NO. 1672671 JUNE 12, 1928

Construction of Lionel Cars and Locomotives

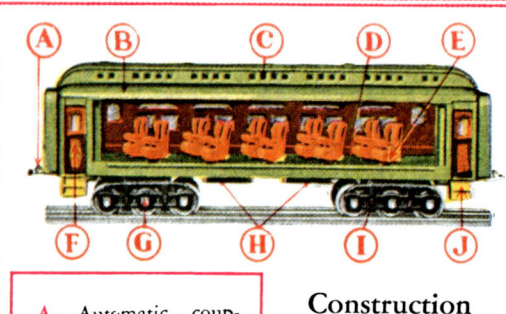

A — Automatic couplers.
B — Removable roof.
C — Colored transparencies in transom windows.
D — Inserted window frames adding strength to car.
E — Revolving parlor car chairs.
F — Hinged doors.
G — Nickeled journals.
H — Metal air tanks.
I — Heavy steel truck frames.
J — Brass steps.

1 — Die cast headlights.
2 — Operating pantagraphs.
3 — Brass hand rails.
4 — Inserted brass ventilators.
5 — Green signal lights.
6 — Heavy steel frame made in one piece.
7 — Nickeled journals.
8 — Inserted brass panels.
9 — Steel body studded with rivets.
10 — Signal flags on solid brass posts and stanchions.

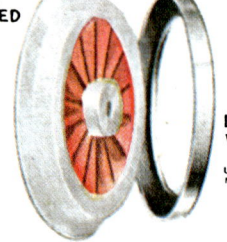

DIE-CAST WHEEL WITH NICKELED STEEL RIM
U.S. RE-ISSUED PATENT NO. 16351 — MAY 18, 1926

SIX-WHEEL TRUCK WITH NICKELED JOURNALS

HEADLIGHT CONNECTION U.S. PATENT PENDING

REMOVABLE BRUSH HOLDER CONTAINING SELF-LUBRICATING AUTOMATIC-FEEDING BRUSHES U.S. PATENTS NO. 1516329 — MAY 5, 1925 1495497 — FEB. 7, 1925

"LOCKON" CONNECTION
U.S. PATENT NO. 1542337 — JUNE 16, 1925

FIBRE SWITCH POINT WHICH PREVENTS SHORT-CIRCUITING OF TRACK
U.S. RE-ISSUED PATENT NO. 16580 — MARCH 29, 1927

SELF-LUBRICATING AUTOMATIC-FEEDING BRUSHES IN "O" GAUGE MOTOR

[Page Six]

LOCOMOTIVES FOR "O" GAUGE TRACK—1⅜ INCHES WIDE

No. 248—Beautifully finished by Lionel's permanent enameling process. A sturdy, electric locomotive, complete with electric headlight and pantagraph. Brass trim throughout with etched name plate. 7⅝ inches long, 4 inches high. Can be used with Cars Nos. 529, 530, 629, 630, 803, 804, 805, 806, 807, 831 and 902.

Code Word "REGAL."   Price, $6.00

No. 253—A splendid New York Central type of locomotive. Equipped with reversing controller, and two electric headlights. Brass trimming. A beautiful, graceful type of locomotive. 9 inches long, 4 inches high. Can be used with Cars Nos. 607, 608, 803, 804, 805, 806, 807, 831 and 902.

Code Word "Fine."   Price, $9.50

LIONEL Locomotives, whether the smallest or the largest, whether electric type or steam type, are designed with one thought in mind — to develop as much hauling power as size permits, and to be absolutely free of operating difficulties. Machine cut gears in the motors, bronze bushings, and other refinements make the **Lionel** motor the best designed and longest lasting in the world. Each locomotive is an accurate copy of a real locomotive. All brass trimmings are genuine brass, and are not dipped. Many basic patents protect important exclusive **Lionel** features that will be found in no other trains.

No. 4 "Bild-a-Loco" Locomotive—Same in appearance and size as No. 254 described to the right, but equipped with the famous Lionel "Bild-a-Loco" motor —the motor that can be taken apart and reassembled in a few moments, or can be converted into a powerful "Bild-a-Motor" that can be used to operate many toys.

Code Word "URGE"   Price, $15.75

No. 252—A reversing locomotive equipped with hand reversing lever and electric headlight. Permanent enamel finish and striped brass trim. 8 inches long, 3⅝ inches high. Can be used with same cars as No. 248 locomotive.

Code Word "ELECT."   Price, $8.50

No. 254—Super-Motor Locomotive, equipped with reversing control and two electric headlights. 9½ inches long, 4¼ inches high. Can be used with Cars Nos. 610, 612, and 810 to 817.

Code Word "MANY."   Price, $12.00

No. 254E "Distant-Control" Super-Motor Locomotive—Same as No. 254, but can be started, stopped, reversed and operated at any speed at any distance from the track. No. 81 controlling rheostat supplied with it.

Code Word "GRIT."   Price, $16.50

STEAM TYPE *and* ELECTRIC TYPE LOCOMOTIVES *for* "O" GAUGE TRACK—1⅜ INCHES WIDE

Nos. 257 and 258

BOYS—HERE IS THE WORLD'S FINEST AND BEST DESIGNED LOW-PRICED STEAM TYPE LOCOMOTIVE.

No. 258—A beautifully designed new "O" Gauge Steam Type Locomotive and Tender—With hand reversing lever. Equipped with pilot trucks, headlight, flags, brass hand rail, copper piping and double-action piston and driving rods. Locomotive is 8 inches long, 3¼ inches high. Tender is 6 inches long, 3¼ inches high. Complete length of locomotive and tender is 14½ inches.
Code Word "HINDU." Price, $11.50

No. 258-T Tender—Exactly as illustrated above, but with double trucks. This tender is supplied with Train Outfit No. 236 illustrated on Page 13, but may be purchased separately if desired.
Code Word "DOCKET."
Price, $1.65

No. 257 "O" Gauge Steam Type Locomotive and Tender—Identical in every respect with No. 258, but is *non-reversible*. These locomotives are designed with a care and attention to detail that is usually not found in a locomotive of this price. Lionel leads the field in Steam Type Locomotives.
Code Word "DIVINE." Price, $10.00

No. 251E—A Super-Motor Locomotive, equipped with "Distant-Control," which enables complete operation, forward or reverse at any distance from the track. Complete with No. 81 controlling rheostat. A splendid model of an electric type locomotive, with great hauling power. Expertly designed with a wealth of detail. Complete with two electric headlights and automatic couplers. 10¼ inches long, 4½ inches high.
Code Word "GLORY." Price, $20.00

No. 256 Twin-Super-Motor Locomotive—Improved model with operating pantographs, reversing control, two electric headlights and flags, and two motors—which means twice the hauling power. A powerful, sturdy brute of a locomotive. 11⅜ inches long, 4¾ inches high.
Code Word "CHAIN." Price, $19.00

No. 251E

No. 256

[Page Eight]

NEW LIONEL "O" GAUGE STEAM TYPE LOCOMOTIVE
(ELECTRICALLY OPERATED)

BOYS—here is the most remarkable "O" Gauge Steam Type Locomotive that has ever been produced. Dozens of blue prints and photographs of famous new locomotives from railroads all over the country were examined, and the best features of each were utilized by Lionel's Engineering Department in designing this locomotive. It is built for speed and power. It is low, long, graceful and sturdy. Complete with its Pacific type oil-burning tender it represents a miracle of model railroad engineering. This New Lionel "O" Gauge Steam Type Locomotive is electrically-driven by the famous Lionel "Bild-a-Loco" motor—the motor that snaps out in a jiffy, and then can be taken apart and quickly reassembled by any boy. It has an "E" type of remote control which enables the operator to start, stop and reverse the locomotive at any distance from the track by operating the control lever.

The rhythm of its double action pistons and driving rods is characteristic of a great "Mogul of the Rails". It will be the pride of every boy who owns one.

DETAILS OF CONSTRUCTION OF NO. 260E LOCOMOTIVE

Locomotive is 11 inches long 3¾ inches high. Tender is 7½ inches long, 3¾ inches high. Length over all 19 inches.

Locomotive has four driving wheels, and front and rear pilot trucks. Copper exhaust and steam pipes are most realistic. Brass hand rails add another elaborate touch. It is finished in beautiful black lustrous enamel. Headlight on the boiler front, two flags in position, warning bell, lanterns mounted on forward platform above cowcatcher, all properly located in accordance with the most modern railroad construction. The tender has 8 wheels and is Pacific oil-burning type. Embossed rivets and nickel journal boxes are characteristic of Lionel's attention to the smallest details. Locomotive and tender are equipped with automatic couplers.
Code Word "PAUL."   Price, $21.50

No. 260E

PASSENGER AND FREIGHT TRAIN OUTFITS

for "O" Gauge Track — 1⅜ Inches Wide

ALL LIONEL Train Outfits are complete with electric lamps for headlights, wires for connecting to transformer or batteries, sufficient track for complete layout and connecting ties for joining sections of track. The locomotive and cars are equipped with automatic couplers. A complete direction book is included in each outfit. Read the directions carefully. You will find them interesting, and they will help you to obtain the fullest enjoyment of your Lionel Train. Types A and B Transformers for alternating current are recommended for "O" Gauge Trains. No. 107 D.C. reducer is recommended for direct current. These are illustrated on Pages 36 and 37. A warning signal is included with all "O" Gauge Train Outfits. Remember, the smallest Lionel Train is manufactured with the same care and attention to detail as the largest and most expensive outfit. Many wonderful accessories for use with these trains are illustrated throughout the catalog. Add accessories and extra track, and your Lionel Train will be more realistic.

No. 249

Outfit No. 249—Comprises 1 No. 248 locomotive with electric headlight, 1 No. 831 lumber car with load of lumber, 1 No. 807 caboose, 8 sections OC curved track, 1 No. 068 warning signal, 1 OTC "Lockon" connection. Track forms a circle 30 inches in diameter. Train is 24¼ inches long.
Code Word "KATE." Price, $7.00

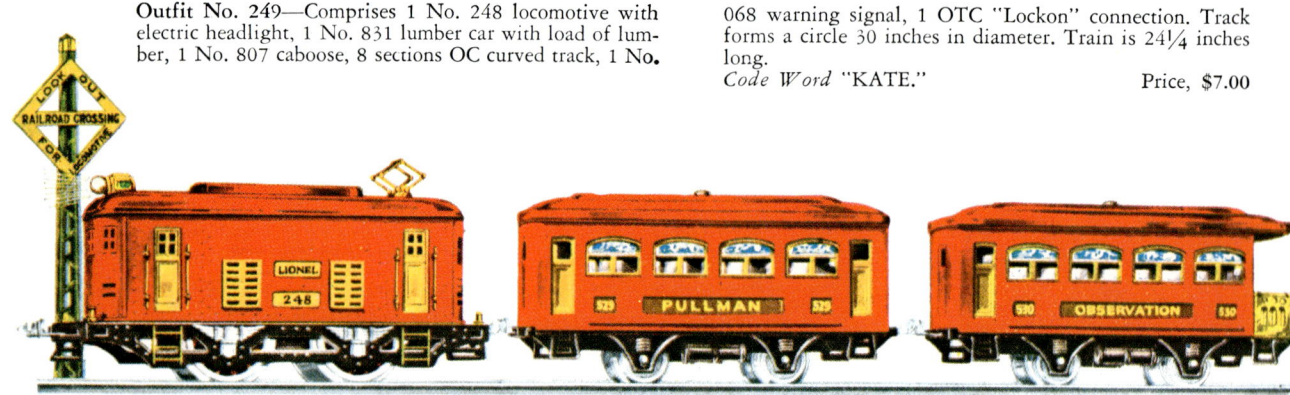

No. 292

Outfit No. 292—Comprises 1 No. 248 locomotive with electric headlight, 1 No. 629 Pullman car, 1 No. 630 observation car, 8 sections OC curved track, 1 No. 068 warning signal, 1 OTC "Lockon" connection. Track forms a circle 30 inches in diameter. Train is 24¼ inches long.
Code Word "KEEN." Price, $7.00

No. 229

Outfit No. 229—Comprises 1 No. 257 Steam Type Locomotive and Tender, 1 No. 831 lumber car with load of lumber, 1 No. 807 caboose, 8 sections OC curved track, 2 sections OS straight track, 1 No. 068 warning signal, 1 OTC "Lockon" connection. Track forms an oval 40 x 30 inches. Train is 30½ inches long.
Code Word "SARA." Price, $11.25

[Page Ten]

PASSENGER AND FREIGHT TRAIN OUTFITS

for "O" Gauge Track—1⅜ Inches Wide

BOYS, you may now have a Steam Type Electrically-driven "O" Gauge Locomotive Outfit, as well as an "O" Gauge Train equipped with an electric type locomotive. Both types are true models of real locomotives.

No. 232

Outfit No. 232. "O" Gauge Passenger Outfit. Comprises 1 No. 257 Steam Type Locomotive and Tender, 1 No. 629 Pullman car, 1 No. 630 observation car, 8 sections OC curved track, 2 sections OS straight track, 1 No. 068 warning signal, 1 OTC "Lockon" connection. Track forms an oval 40 x 30 inches. Train is 30½ inches long.
Code Word "LONG." Price, $11.25

No. 294

Outfit No. 294.—Comprises 1 No. 252 reversible locomotive with electric headlight, 2 No. 529 Pullman cars, 1 No. 530 observation car, 8 sections OC curved track, 2 sections OS straight track, 1 No. 068 warning signal, 1 OTC "Lockon" connection. Track forms an oval 40 by 30 inches. Train is 32½ inches long.
Code Word "CORN." Price, $10.25

No. 234

Outfit No. 234. "O" Gauge Passenger Outfit. Comprises 1 No. 258 reversible Steam Type Locomotive and Tender, 2 No. 529 Pullman cars, 1 No. 530 observation car, 8 sections OC curved track, 4 sections OS straight track, 1 No. 068 warning signal, 1 OTC "Lockon" connection. Track forms an oval 50 x 30 inches. Train is 38½ inches long.
Code Word "RACE." Price, $12.75

[Page Eleven]

PASSENGER AND FREIGHT TRAIN OUTFITS

for "O" Gauge Track—1⅜ Inches Wide

ALL Passenger Cars, from this page forward, are electrically lighted. This is, of course, a realistic touch, but most important to make your train layout real is to add accessories, such as, crossing gates, warning signals, semaphores, additional track, switches, stations, lamp posts, etc. All these are found on a real railroad, and you want your own railroad to be real.

Outfit No. 296—Comprises 1 No. 253 reversible locomotive with 2 electric headlights, 2 No. 607 illuminated Pullman cars, 1 No. 608 illuminated observation car, 8 sections OC curved track, 4 sections OS straight track, 1 No. 068 warning signal, 1 OTC "Lockon" connection. Track forms an oval 50 by 30 inches. Train is 36 inches long.
Code Word "DART."   Price, $12.75

Outfit No. 293—Comprises 1 No. 252 reversible locomotive with electric headlight, 1 No. 803 coal car, 1 No. 804 oil car, 1 No. 805 box car, 1 No. 807 caboose, 8 sections OC curved track, 2 sections OS straight track, 1 No. 068 warning signal, 1 OTC "Lockon" connection. Track forms an oval 40 by 30 inches. Train is 40¼ inches long.
Code Word "UPTON."   Price, $11.25

No. 233. "O" Gauge Freight Outfit. Comprises 1 No. 258 reversible steam type locomotive and tender, 1 No. 902 gondola car, 1 No. 803 coal car, 1 No. 804 oil car, 1 No. 806 cattle car, 1 No. 807 caboose, 8 sections OC curved track, 4 sections OS straight track, 1 OTC "Lockon" connection, 1 No. 068 warning signal. Track forms an oval 50 x 30 inches. Train is 55 inches long.
Code Word "TONY."   Price, $15.50

[Page Twelve]

PASSENGER AND FREIGHT TRAIN OUTFITS

for "O" Gauge Track—1⅜ Inches Wide

EVERY Lionel Electric Train that you buy can be made into a most elaborate complete railroad. As you add extra track, switches, signals, stations, etc., you will find your electric train growing under your eyes into a railroad system. On Page 47 of this catalog you will find several suggestions for intricate track layouts. Be guided by this and use your own ingenuity, and you will be able to obtain so much more educational pleasure out of your Lionel Electric Train.

Nos. 266 and 266E

Outfit No. 266—Comprises 1 No. 254 Super-Motor reversible locomotive with 2 electric headlights, 2 No. 610 illuminated Pullman cars, 1 No. 612 illuminated observation car, 8 sections OC curved track, 6 sections OS straight track, 1 No. 068 warning signal, 1 OTC "Lockon" connection. Track forms an oval 60 by 30 inches. Train is 40½ inches long.
Code Word "HEAD." Price, $16.50

No. 266E "Distant-Control" Passenger Train Outfit—Same as No. 266 except that it contains No. 254E "Distant-Control" Super-Motor Locomotive which can be started, stopped reversed and operated at any speed at any distance from the track by means of No. 81 controlling rheostat supplied with it.
Code Word "ILION." Price, $20.00

Nos. 295 and 295E

Outfit No. 295—Comprises 1 No. 254 reversible locomotive with 2 electric headlights, 1 No. 811 lumber car with load of lumber, 1 No. 812 gondola car, 1 No. 817 caboose, 8 sections OC curved track, 4 sections OS straight track, 1 No. 068 warning signal, 1 OTC "Lockon" connection. Track forms an oval 50 by 30 inches. Train is 41 inches long.
Code Word "MANDEL." Price $15.00

Outfit No. 295E—Same as No. 295, except that it contains No. 254E "Distant-Control" locomotive, which can be started, stopped, reversed and operated at any speed at any distance from the track, by means of No. 81 controlling rheostat supplied with it.
Code Word "FRANKEL." Price, $18.50

No. 236

Outfit No. 236—Comprises 1 No. 258 reversible Steam Type Locomotive and Tender, 2 No. 607 illuminated Pullman cars, 1 No. 608 illuminated observation car, 8 sections OC curved track, 4 sections OS straight track, 1 OTC "Lockon" connection, 1 No. 068 warning signal. Track forms an oval 50 by 30 inches. Train is 42 inches long.
Code Word "CYRIL." Price, $16.50

[Page Thirteen]

1930

PASSENGER AND FREIGHT TRAIN OUTFITS

for "O" Gauge Track—1⅜ Inches Wide

EVERY real railroad has stations, telegraph poles, automatic signals, switches and various other equipment. Make your Lionel Train as realistic as possible. Continually add to your set. Make your layout large. Make it more interesting. It is only by doing these things that you can obtain the full enjoyment with your Lionel Train.

Nos. 97 and 97E

Outfit No. 97—Comprises 1 No. 251 Super-Motor Reversible Locomotive with 2 electric headlights, 2 No. 605 illuminated Pullman cars, 1 No. 606 illuminated observation car, 8 sections OC curved track, 8 sections OS straight track, 1 No. 068 warning signal, 1 OTC "Lockon" connection. Track forms an oval 70 by 30 inches. Train is 49¼ inches long.

Code Word "EXCEL."   Price, $18.50

No. 97E—"Distant-Control" Passenger Train Outfit—Same as No. 97, but it contains No. 251E "Distant-Control" Super-Motor Locomotive, which can be started, stopped, reversed and operated at any speed at any distance from the track by means of No. 81 controlling rheostat supplied with it.

Code Word "JUST."   Price, $22.50

Nos. 299 and 299E

Outfit No. 299—Comprises 1 No. 251 locomotive, 1 No. 812 gondola car, 1 No. 813 cattle car, 1 No. 814 box car, 1 No. 817 caboose, 8 sections OC curved track, 6 sections OS straight track, 1 No. 068 warning signal, 1 OTC "Lockon" connection. Track forms an oval 60 x 30 inches. Train is 52¾ inches long.

Code Word "FLORA."   Price, $18.50

Outfit No. 299E—"O" Gauge Freight Outfit—Same as No. 299, except that it contains No. 251E "Distant-Control" locomotive, which can be started, stopped, reversed and operated at any speed at any distance from the track, by means of No. 81 controlling rheostat supplied with it.

Code Word "QUILL."   Price, $22.50

No. 239E

Outfit No. 239E—"O" Gauge "Distant-Control" Freight Outfit—An outstanding outfit with an exceptionally powerful and realistic new locomotive. Comprises 1 No. 260E "Distant-Control" Steam Type Locomotive and Tender, 1 No. 812 gondola car, 1 No. 813 cattle car, 1 No. 814 box car, 1 No. 815 oil car, 1 No. 817 caboose, 8 sections OC curved track, 8 sections OS straight track, 1 OTC "Lockon" connection, 1 No. 068 warning signal, 1 No. 81 controlling rheostat. Track forms an oval 70 x 30 inches. Train is 70 inches long.

Code Word "JURY."   Price, $25.00

[Page Fourteen]

PASSENGER AND FREIGHT TRAIN OUTFITS
for "O" Gauge Track—1⅜ Inches Wide

LIONEL Trains are real Trains in miniature. Every practical feature that would aid in the operation and realistic appearance of Lionel Trains has been incorporated by our engineers. If you want realism then you surely must have a Lionel Train.

No. 267

Outfit No. 267—"O" Gauge Passenger Outfit with "Bild-a-Loco" Locomotive—Complete with extra gears and base. All the fun of a Lionel Railroad combined with the added features of a Lionel "Bild-a-Loco," that can be taken apart and reassembled in a few moments. With the additional gears and base you can take your motor out of the frame and assemble it into a stationary power motor for operating a derrick or shafting. Outfit comprises 1 No. 4 reversible "Bild-a-Loco" with 2 electric headlights, 1 No. 043 gear set, 2 No. 605 illuminated Pullman cars, 1 No. 606 illuminated observation car, 8 sections OC curved track, 8 sections OS straight track, 1 No. 068 warning signal, 1 OTC "Lockon" connection. Track forms an oval 70 by 30 inches. Train is 45 inches long. Attractively enameled in a rich orange color.
Code Word "GLEAM." Price, $21.50

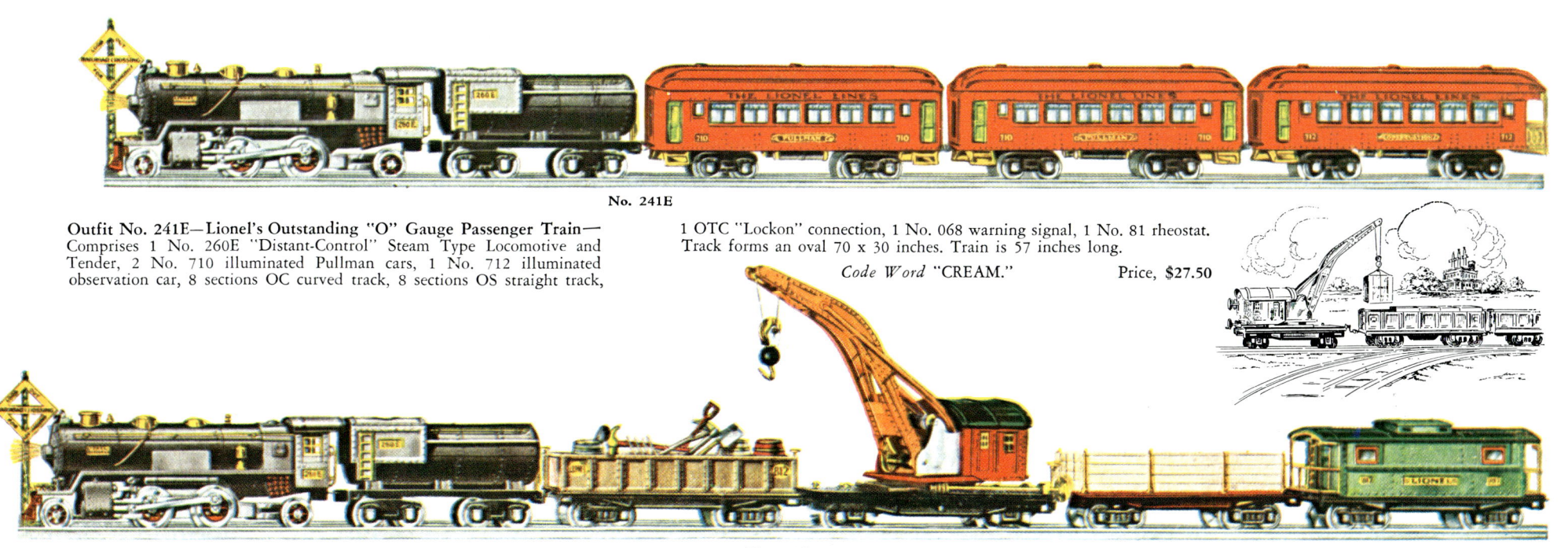

No. 241E

Outfit No. 241E—Lionel's Outstanding "O" Gauge Passenger Train—Comprises 1 No. 260E "Distant-Control" Steam Type Locomotive and Tender, 2 No. 710 illuminated Pullman cars, 1 No. 712 illuminated observation car, 8 sections OC curved track, 8 sections OS straight track, 1 OTC "Lockon" connection, 1 No. 068 warning signal, 1 No. 81 rheostat. Track forms an oval 70 x 30 inches. Train is 57 inches long.
Code Word "CREAM." Price, $27.50

No. 240E

Outfit No. 240E—"O" Gauge Work Train—Outfit includes new "O" Gauge Derrick Car. Comprises 1 No. 260E "Distant-Control" Steam Type Locomotive and Tender, 1 No. 811 lumber car with load of lumber, 1 No. 810 operating derrick car, 1 No. 812 gondola car with tools, 1 No. 817 caboose, 8 sections OC curved track, 8 sections OS straight track, 1 OTC "Lockon" connection, 1 No. 068 warning signal, 1 No. 81 controlling rheostat. Track forms an oval 70 x 30 inches. Train is 60 inches long.
Code Word "SWEET." Price, $30.00

[Page Fifteen]

COMPLETE RAILROADS FOR "O" GAUGE TRACK. 1⅜ INCHES WIDE

No. 174

NO. 174 Outfit shown above is a complete model railroad to operate on "O" Gauge Track. It includes a large variety of accessories. Every piece is of steel construction and enameled by **Lionel's** own lustrous and lasting process.

Outfit No. 174 comprises 1 No. 253 reversible locomotive with two electric headlights, 2 No. 607 Illuminated Pullman cars, 1 No. 608 illuminated observation car, 10 sections OC curved track, 6 sections OS straight track, 1 OTC "Lockon" connection, 1 pair No. 021 illuminated switches (one right, one left), 1 No. 106 bridge (3 sections), 1 No. 122 illuminated station, 6 No. 060 telegraph posts with extension arms, 1 No. 62 semaphore, 1 No. 89 flag staff, 1 No. 068 warning signal, 1 No. 119 tunnel. Size of track layout 45 by 60 inches. Train is 35½ inches long.

Code Word "DELA." Price, $40.00

No. 176E

A NEW COMPLETE "O" GAUGE "DISTANT-CONTROL" RAILROAD

NO. 176E—Introduced to fill the demand for a complete 100% "Distant-Control" "O" Gauge Railroad at a moderate price. The train can be started, stopped, reversed and operated at any speed at any distance from the track. The electric switches can also be controlled at any distance from the track. The No. 437 Switch Tower contains levers by which the Railroad can be operated, and lamp posts illuminated. This is an ideal Lionel Railroad to fit into a small space.

Outfit comprises 1 No. 260E "Distant-Control" steam type locomotive with electric headlight, 2 No. 710 illuminated Pullman cars, 1 No. 712 illuminated observation car, 1 No. 080 semaphore, 1 No. 069 warning signal, 1 No. 90 flag staff, 1 No. 106 bridge, 1 pair No. 012 electrically-controlled switches, 1 No. 437 signal tower, 1 No. 119L illuminated tunnel, 2 No. 56 lamp posts, 8 No. 060 telegraph posts with extension arms, 1 No. 81 controlling rheostat, 1 OTC "Lockon" connection, 10 sections OC curved track, 16 sections OS straight track. Complete with wires for connecting to source of current, "Lockon" connections, track on bridge, and special track for electric accessories. Track layout is 100 inches by 40 inches. Train is 57 inches long.

Code Word "JANE." Price, $72.50

[Page Sixteen]

STEAM TYPE LOCOMOTIVES
(Electrically Driven)
For "Lionel Standard" Track—2¼ Inches Wide

LIONEL Steam Type Locomotives are by far the most perfect of their type ever offered to the boys of America. They transcend in beauty of design, and in electrical and mechanical perfection any model Steam Type Locomotives that have ever been made. Powered by the famous Lionel "Bild-a-Loco" motors—vibrating with realism and tremendous power,—they are miniatures of the great "Giants of the Rails"!

Lionel perfection—attention to minute details—those outstanding Lionel characteristics make the new Steam Type Locomotives a real achievement.

No. 390E STEAM TYPE LOCOMOTIVE

Locomotive—14 inches long, 5 inches high. Tender—8¼ inches long, 4½ inches high. Length over all 22¼ inches.

Locomotive has four driving wheels and front and rear pilot trucks. Copper exhaust and steam pipes, brass hand rails, and headlight mounted on front boiler suggest realism.

The finish is a beautiful black enamel baked on at high temperature.

Locomotive is equipped with "Distant Control" unit so that it can be started, stopped, reversed and operated at any speed at any distance from the track. Complete with No. 81 Controlling Rheostat, headlight bulb and flags.

Code Word "TONE." Price, $35.00

[Page Seventeen]

Reg. U. S. Pat. Off.
"LIONEL STANDARD" LOCOMOTIVES—DISTINCTIVE! SPEEDY! POWERFUL!
For "Lionel Standard" Track—2¼ inches wide

A junior rival of Lionel's Larger Steam Type Locomotive. Powerful, beautifully constructed and designed, it is intended for use with Lionel's medium size "Lionel Standard" Passenger and Freight Cars. It is a real locomotive in all but size. Powered by the famous Lionel "Bild-a-Loco" motor, the motor that can be snapped out in a jiffy without the use of any tools.
Trimmings are of heavy brass and copper. Complete with flags and headlight.

No. 384. "Lionel Standard" Hand Control Steam Type Locomotive and Tender. Locomotive is 12 inches long, 4½ inches high. Tender is 8¼ inches long, 4½ inches high. Complete length of locomotive and tender is 20¼ inches.
Code Word "PUFF." Price, $22.50
No. 384E. "Lionel Standard" "Distant-Control" Steam Type Locomotive and Tender. Similar to No. 384 but equipped with the "Distant-Control" mechanism. Complete with No. 81 Controlling Rheostat, by means of which "Distant-Control" mechanism is operated.
Code Word "PURSE." Price, $27.50

No. 8 "Lionel Standard" Super-Motor Reversible Locomotive—11 inches long, 4¾ inches high.
Code Word "POWER." Price, $12.25
No. 8E. "Lionel Standard" "Distant-Control" Super-Motor Locomotive. Similar to No. 8 but equipped with the "Distant-Control" mechanism. Complete with No. 81 Controlling Rheostat, by means of which "Distant-Control" mechanism is operated.
Code Word "PEPPY." Price, $18.50

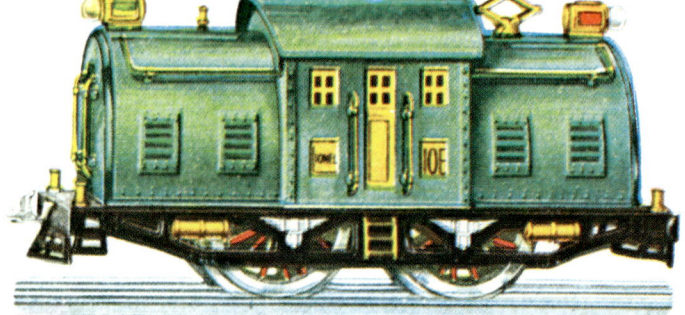

No. 10E "Lionel Standard" "Distant-Control" Super-Motor Locomotive— A splendid Chicago, Milwaukee and St. Paul type of locomotive. All trimmings are of genuine heavy gauge brass. Locomotive is complete with automatic couplers and two headlights. 11⅜ inches long, 5 inches high. Equipped with "Distant-Control" mechanism. Complete with No. 81 Controlling Rheostat, by means of which "Distant-Control" mechanism is operated.
Code Word "SELF." Price, $21.00

No. 318E "Lionel Standard" "Distant-Control" Super-Motor Locomotive— This is a powerful locomotive and will pull many more cars than its standard equipment. Finished in a marvelous new two-tone enamel. Complete with two headlights. 12⅛ inches long, 5⅛ inches high. Equipped with "Distant-Control" mechanism. Complete with No. 81 Controlling Rheostat, by means of which "Distant-Control" mechanism is operated.
Code Word "MOVE." Price, $23.75

[Page Eighteen]

Reg. U. S. Pat. Off.
"LIONEL STANDARD" "BILD-A-LOCO" AND TWIN SUPER-MOTOR LOCOMOTIVES
For "Lionel Standard" Track—2¼ inches wide

All "Lionel Standard" Locomotives are equipped with automatic couplers and two electric headlights. Lamps for headlights are included.

See pages 28, 29 and 30 for correct freight and passenger cars to be used with the locomotives described on these pages.
See page 5 for details of construction of "Lionel Standard" Super-Motors and Twin Super-Motors.

No. 381E "Distant-Control" "Bild-a-Loco" Locomotive for "Lionel Standard" Track. This locomotive is the most elaborate in the Lionel Line. The illustration shows the great detail incorporated in it, and special mention is made of the construction of the two-4-wheel pilot trucks which will not derail even when the locomotive is traveling at a high rate of speed. The "Bild-a-Loco" motor and "Distant-Control" mechanism can be removed from the body in a jiffy. The boy can at will take down and rebuild this motor within a few minutes. It is not amiss to repeat that all parts are so accurately made that no difficulty will be experienced in setting it up, and there is not a single wire to be connected, as all electrical contacts are automatically made. It is extremely efficient and powerful enough to haul many of the largest Pullman or freight cars with the greatest ease. This supreme model can be seen in conjunction with our finest Pullman cars on Pages 24 and 25. Size 18 inches long, 6½ inches high. Includes No. 81 Controlling Rheostat and two electric headlights.
Code Word "ULTI." Price, $44.50

No. 9E "Distant-Control" "Bild-a-Loco" Locomotive for "Lionel Standard" Track. In addition to the interesting design of the "Bild-a-Loco" motor, this locomotive also contains our "Distant-Control" unit which makes it possible to start, stop and reverse the locomotive at any distance from the track. The body is beautifully designed and incorporates many features that are typically Lionel. Locomotive contains two electric headlights so arranged that the front one is always illuminated irrespective of the direction in which the locomotive is traveling. This locomotive is equipped with automatic couplers. It measures 14½ inches long, 6¼ inches high. No. 81 controlling rheostat is included.
Code Word "UTTER." Price, $28.75

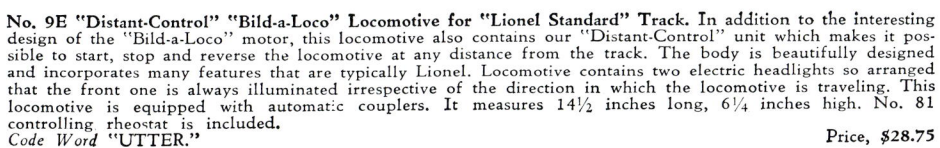

No. 408E "Lionel Standard" Twin-Super-Motor "Distant-Control" Locomotive. The illustration clearly shows the great amount of realistic details incorporated in it. Many of the constructional features are indicated on Page 6. Attention is directed to the operating pantagraphs, illuminated signal lanterns, front and rear flags, brass hand rails, copper exhaust pipes, etc. This locomotive is equipped with "Distant-Control" mechanism, which enables the user to start, stop, reverse and operate it at any speed at any distance from the track by means of No. 81 controlling rheostat supplied with it. Size 17 inches long, 6½ inches high to top of pantagraph. Complete with flags, headlight lamps and lamps for front and rear lanterns.
Code Word "FAST." Price, $47.50

[Page Nineteen]

1930

PASSENGER AND FREIGHT TRAIN OUTFITS

for "Lionel Standard" Track—2¼ Inches Wide

LIONEL Train Outfits are complete in every respect. Lamps for headlights and passenger cars are supplied with every outfit; also wires for transformer or battery connection and connecting ties for joining sections of track.

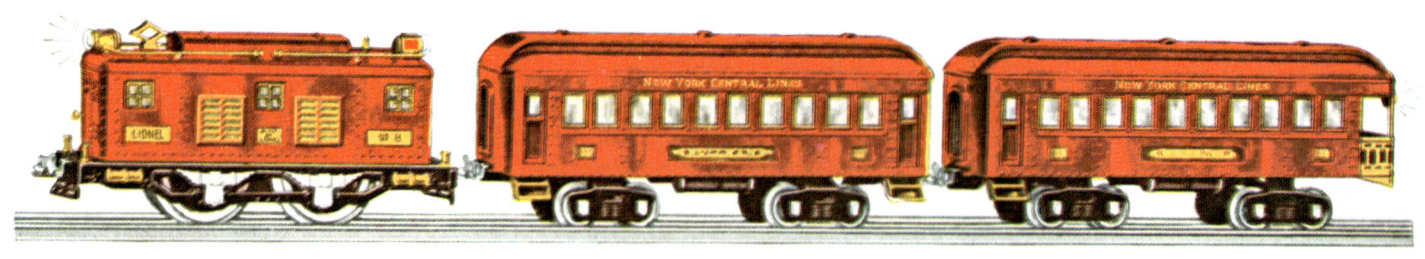

Nos. 347 and 347E

Outfit No. 347—Comprises 1 No. 8 Super-Motor reversible locomotive with 2 electric headlights, 1 No. 337 illuminated Pullman car, 1 No. 338 illuminated observation car, 8 sections C curved track, 2 sections S straight track, 1 STC "Lockon" connection. Track forms an oval 56 by 42 inches. Train is 38½ inches long.
Code Word "ZENA." Price, $19.00

Outfit No. 347E—Same as No. 347, except that it contains No. 8E "Distant-Control" Super-Motor locomotive, which can be started, stopped, reversed and operated at any speed at any distance from the track by means of No. 81 controlling rheostat supplied with it.
Code Word "GLIDE." Price, $23.75

Nos. 385 and 385E

Outfit No. 385. "Lionel Standard" Passenger Outfit. Greatest value ever shown in a steam type outfit. Comprises 1 No. 384 locomotive and tender, 1 No. 337 illuminated Pullman car, 1 No. 338 illuminated observation car, 8 sections C curved track, 2 sections S straight track, 1 STC "Lockon" connection. Track forms an oval 56 x 42 inches. Train is 47½ inches long.
Code Word "HENRY." Price, $27.50

Outfit No. 385E. "Lionel Standard" "Distant-Control" Passenger Outfit. Similar to No. 385, except that it contains No. 384E locomotive, which can be started, stopped, reversed and operated at any speed at any distance from the track by means of No. 81 controlling rheostat supplied with it.
Code Word "LEE." Price, $32.50

Nos. 353 and 353E

Outfit No. 353—Comprises 1 No. 8 Super-Motor reversible locomotive with 2 electric headlights, 1 No. 511 lumber car with load of lumber, 1 No. 512 gondola car, 1 No. 517 illuminated caboose, 8 sections C curved track, 2 sections S straight track, 1 STC "Lockon" connection. Track forms an oval 56 by 42 inches. Train is 50¼ inches long.
Code Word "JACK." Price, $20.00

Outfit No. 353E—Same as No. 353, except that it contains No. 8E "Distant-Control" Super-Motor locomotive, which can be started, stopped, reversed and operated at any speed at any distance from the track by means of No. 81 controlling rheostat supplied with it.
Code Word "MASK." Price, $25.00

PASSENGER AND FREIGHT TRAIN OUTFITS

for "Lionel Standard" Track — 2¼ Inches Wide

ALL "Lionel Standard" Trains are equipped with automatic couplers.

It is best to use a Lionel "Multivolt" transformer for operating all Lionel Trains on reduced alternating current. See page 37.

No. 352E

Outfit No. 352E—Comprises 1 No. 10E "Distant-Control" Super-Motor locomotive with 2 electric headlights, 1 No. 332 illuminated mail and baggage car, 1 No. 339 illuminated Pullman car, 1 No. 341 illuminated observation car, 8 sections C curved track, 4 sections S straight track, 1 STC "Lockon" connection and 1 No. 81 controlling rheostat. Track forms an oval 69 by 42 inches. Train is 52 inches long. This train can be started, stopped, reversed and operated at any speed at any distance from the track. *Code Word* "WIN." Price, $30.00

Nos. 386 and 386E

Outfit No. 386. Comprises 1 No. 384 Steam Type Locomotive and Tender, 1 No. 512 gondola car, 1 No. 513 cattle car, 1 No. 517 caboose, 8 sections C curved track, 4 sections S straight track, 1 STC "Lockon" connection. Track forms an oval 69 x 42 inches. Train is 59½ inches long.
Code Word "MIKE." Price, $27.50

Outfit No. 386E. "Distant-Control" Freight Outfit. Similar to No. 386, except that it contains No. 384E "Distant-Control" locomotive, which can be started, stopped, reversed and operated at any speed at any distance from the track by means of No. 81 controlling rheostat supplied with it.
Code Word "PAT." Price, $32.50

No. 354E

Outfit No. 354E—Comprises 1 No. 10E "Distant-Control" Super-Motor locomotive with 2 electric headlights, 1 No. 511 lumber car with load of lumber, 1 No. 512 gondola car, 1 No. 513 cattle car, 1 No. 514 box car, 1 No. 517 illuminated caboose, 8 sections C curved track, 6 sections S straight track, 1 STC "Lockon" connection and 1 No. 81 controlling rheostat. Track forms an oval 88 by 42 inches. Train is 77 inches long. This train can be started, stopped, reversed and operated at any speed at any distance from the track.
Code Word "ZEST." Price, $30.00

[Page Twenty-One]

PASSENGER TRAIN OUTFITS

for "Lionel Standard" Track—2¼ Inches Wide

No. 342E

No. 342E. "Distant-Control" Passenger Train Outfit—Comprises 1 No. 318E "Distant-Control" Super-Motor locomotive with 2 electric headlights, 1 No. 310 illuminated mail and baggage car, 1 No. 309 illuminated Pullman car, 1 No. 312 illuminated observation car, 8 sections C curved track, 6 sections S straight track, 1 STC "Lockon" connection. Track forms an oval 88 by 42 inches. Train is 57½ inches long. Train may be started, stopped, reversed or operated at any speed at any distance from the track by means of No. 81 controlling rheostat supplied with it.
Code Word "FORUM."   Price, $38.75

Nos. 387 and 387E

No. 387. "Lionel Standard" Hand Control Passenger Train Outfit—Exceptional value with Lionel's newest and most popular-priced steam type locomotive. Comprises 1 No. 384 Steam Type Locomotive and Tender, 1 No. 332 illuminated mail and baggage car, 1 No. 339 illuminated Pullman car, 1 No. 341 illuminated observation car, 8 sections C curved track, 4 sections S straight track, 1 STC "Lockon" connection. Track forms an oval 69 x 42 inches. Train is 61 inches long.
Code Word "DORSET."   Price, $35.00

No. 387E. "Lionel Standard" "Distant-Control" Passenger Outfit—Similar to No. 387, except that it contains No. 384E "Distant-Control" locomotive, which can be started, stopped, reversed and operated at any speed at any distance from the track by means of No. 81 controlling rheostat supplied with it.
Code Word "ISABEL."   Price, $40.00

No. 394E

No. 394E. "Lionel Standard" "Distant-Control" Passenger Outfit—Comprises 1 No. 390E "Distant-Control" Steam Type Locomotive and Tender, 1 No. 310 illuminated baggage car, 1 No. 309 illuminated Pullman car, 1 No. 312 illuminated observation car, 8 sections C curved track, 8 sections S straight track, 1 STC "Lockon" connection, 1 No. 81 controlling rheostat. Train can be started, stopped, reversed and operated at any speed at any distance from the track by means of No. 81 controlling rheostat. Track forms an oval 102 x 42 inches. Train is 67 inches long.
Code Word "JOURNEY."   Price, $50.00

PASSENGER AND FREIGHT TRAIN OUTFITS

for "Lionel Standard" Track—2¼ Inches Wide

No. 393E

No. 393E. "Distant-Control" Coal Train Outfit—Comprises 1 No. 390E Steam Type Locomotive and Tender, 3 No. 516 coal cars, 1 No. 517 illuminated caboose, 8 sections C curved track, 6 sections S straight track, 1 STC "Lockon" connection. Train may be started, stopped, reversed or operated at any speed at any distance from the track by means of No. 81 controlling rheostat supplied with it. The entire train is 74 inches long. Track forms an oval 88 by 42 inches. Complete with headlight, lamp for caboose and flags.

Code Word "TWIST." Price, $50.00

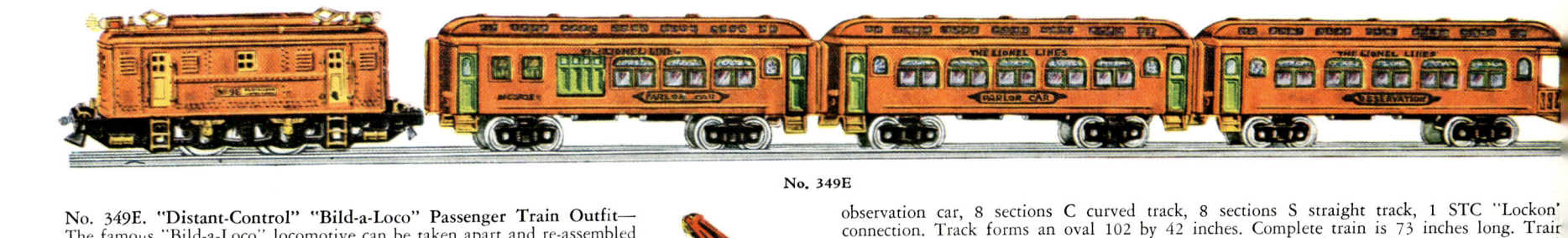

No. 349E

No. 349E. "Distant-Control" "Bild-a-Loco" Passenger Train Outfit—The famous "Bild-a-Loco" locomotive can be taken apart and re-assembled in a few moments. Outfit comprises 1 No. 9E "Distant-Control" "Bild-a-Loco" locomotive with 2 electric headlights, 1 No. 428 illuminated Pullman car, 1 No. 429 illuminated Pullman and baggage car, 1 No. 430 illuminated observation car, 8 sections C curved track, 8 sections S straight track, 1 STC "Lockon" connection. Track forms an oval 102 by 42 inches. Complete train is 73 inches long. Train may be started, stopped, reversed or operated at any speed at any distance from the track by means of No. 81 controlling rheostat supplied with it.

Code Word "PERT." Price, $52.50

No. 358E

No. 358E. "Lionel Standard" "Distant-Control" Work Train—Comprises 1 No. 390E "Distant-Control" Steam Type Locomotive and Tender, 1 No. 212 gondola car complete with tools, 1 No. 218 operating dump car, 1 No. 219 operating derrick car, 1 No. 217 illuminated caboose, 8 sections C curved track, 8 sections S straight track, 1 STC "Lockon" connection, 1 No. 81 controlling rheostat. Train can be started, stopped, reversed and operated at any speed at any distance from the track by means of No. 81 controlling rheostat. Track forms an oval 102 x 42 inches. Train is 79½ inches long.

Code Word "CLARENCE." Price, $55.00

SUPER "LIONEL STANDARD" PASSENGER OUTFIT WITH NEWEST 21 INCH CARS...

No. 409E. "Lionel Standard" Passenger Outfit. Comprises 1 No. 381E "Distant-Control" "Bild-a-Loco" locomotive with two electric headlights, 2 front lanterns and 2 rear lanterns, 1 No. 412 Pullman car (lettered California), 1 No. 413 Pullman car (lettered Colorado), 1 No. 416 observation car (lettered New York), 8 sections C curved track, 10 sections S straight track, 1 No. 81 controlling rheostat, 1 STC "Lockon" connection. Train can be started, stopped, reversed and operated at any speed at any distance from the track by means of No. 81 controlling rheostat. Track forms an oval 116 x 42 inches. Train is 85½ inches long.
Code Word "ETTA." Price, $85.00

THE "TRANSCONTINENTAL" LIMITED

No. 411E. "Lionel Standard" De Luxe FOUR 21 INCH CAR OUTFIT NOW POWERED WITH THE FAMOUS SUPER-TWIN MOTOR LOCOMOTIVE—OUTSTANDING VALUE. Comprises 1 No. 408E "Distant-Control" Twin-Super-Motor locomotive with two electric headlights, 1 No. 412 Pullman car (lettered California), 1 No. 413 Pullman car (lettered Colorado), 1 No. 414 Pullman car (lettered Illinois), 1 No. 416 observation car (lettered New York), 8 sections C curved track, 16 sections S straight track, 1 STC "Lockon" connection, 1 No. 81 controlling rheostat. Train can be started, stopped, reversed and operated at any speed at any distance from the track by means of No. 81 controlling rheostat. Track forms an oval 74 x 128 inches. Train is 107 inches long.
Code Word "SUPERB." Price $97.50

NEW DE-LUXE "LIONEL STANDARD" "DISTANT-CONTROL" STEAM TYPE FREIGHT TRAIN..

No. 423E. "Lionel Standard" Freight Train. Comprises 1 No. 390E "Distant-Control" Steam Type Locomotive and Tender, 1 No. 211 lumber car with load of lumber, 1 No. 212 gondola car, 1 No. 213 cattle car, 1 No. 214 box car, 1 No. 215 oil car, 1 No. 216 coal car, 1 No. 217 illuminated caboose, 8 sections C curved track, 10 sections S straight track, 1 STC "Lockon" connection, 1 No. 81 controlling rheostat. Train can be started, stopped, reversed and operated at any speed at any distance from the track by means of No. 81 controlling rheostat. Track forms an oval 116 x 42 inches. Train is 121½ inches long.
Code Word "SAM." Price $67.50

THE BIG THREE—ARISTOCRATS OF THE LIONEL FLEET OF SUPER TRAINS
for "Lionel Standard" Track—2¼ Inches Wide

No. 409E

No. 408E

No. 411E

No. 423E

[Page Twenty-Five]

FREIGHT TRAIN OUTFITS AND "THE BLUE COMET"

for "Lionel Standard" Track — 2¼ Inches Wide

No. 395E

No. 395E "Distant-Control" Freight Train Outfit—Comprises 1 No. 390E "Distant-Control" Steam Type Locomotive and Tender, 1 No. 511 lumber car with load of lumber, 1 No. 512 gondola car, 1 No. 513 cattle car, 1 No. 514 box car, 1 No. 515 oil car, 1 No. 517 illuminated caboose, 8 sections C curved track, 10 sections S straight track, and 1 STC "Lockon" connection. Track forms an oval 116x42 inches. The entire train is 100 inches long. Complete with headlight, lamp in caboose and flags. This train may be started, stopped, reversed and operated at any speed at any distance from the track by means of the No. 81 Controlling Rheostat supplied with it.
Code Word "TOBY." Price, $52.50

No. 396E

No. 396E—Designed in conjunction with the Central Railroad of New Jersey engineers as a replica of their famous Flyer to Atlantic City, described in the booklet accompanying each train. Comprises 1 No. 390E "Distant-Control" Steam Type Locomotive and Tender, 1 No. 420 Illuminated Pullman car lettered "FAYE," 1 No. 421 Illuminated Pullman car lettered "WESTPHAL," 1 No. 422 illuminated observation car lettered "TEMPEL," 8 sections C curved track, 8 sections S straight track, 1 STC "Lockon" connection, 1 No. 81 controlling rheostat. Train can be started, stopped, reversed and operated at any speed at any distance from the track by means of No. 81 controlling rheostat. Track forms an oval 102x42 inches. Train is 78 inches long. Complete outfit finished in Royal Blue.
Code Word "COMET." Price, $65.00

No. 410E

No. 410E "Lionel Standard" "Distant-Control" Freight Outfit—Comprises 1 No. 408E Twin-Super-Motor "Distant-Control" Locomotive with 2 electric headlights, 1 No. 211 lumber car with load of lumber, 1 No. 212 gondola car, 1 No. 213 cattle car, 1 No. 214 box car, 1 No. 215 oil car, 1 No. 216 coal car, 1 No. 217 illuminated caboose, 8 sections C curved track, 10 sections S straight track, 1 STC "Lockon" connection and 1 No. 81 controlling rheostat. Train is 118 inches long. Track forms an oval 116x42 inches. Outfit also includes lamps for headlights, locomotive lanterns and caboose, wires for transformer or battery connection and connecting ties for joining sections of track. This train can be started, stopped, reversed and operated at any speed at any distance from the track by means of No. 81 controlling rheostat.
Code Word "BEST." Price, $77.50

[Page Twenty-Six]

No. 407E "LIONEL STANDARD" 100% "DISTANT-CONTROL" COMPLETE RAILROAD

Reg. U. S. Pat. Off.

HERE is a real railroad. The finest gift that any boy can possibly receive. This is a complete **Lionel** "Distant-Control" Railroad including our two finest trains—work train with Steam Type Locomotive, and a gigantic twin-motor passenger train, as well as a large variety of electrically-controlled and illuminated accessories. Both of the trains have "Distant-Control" and can be started, stopped, reversed and operated at any speed at any distance from the track. The large power house is a central operating station from which you can control everything. This is a marvelous model railroad. Specifications are given below.

OUTFIT NO. 407E—Comprises:

1 No. 408E "Distant-Control" Locomotive	1 No. 218 Operating Dump Car	20 C Track	2 No. 77 Crossing Gates
1 No. 390E "Distant-Control" Locomotive	1 No. 219 Operating Derrick Car	2 ½S Track	1 No. 69 Warning Signal
2 No. 81 Controlling Rheostats	1 Type K Transformer	1 No. 128 Station	1 No. 840 Power House
1 No. 412 Pullman Car	4 pr. 222 Switches	1 No. 300 Bridge	2 No. 67 Lamp Posts
1 No. 413 Pullman Car	2 No. 23 Bumpers	1 No. 140L Tunnel	4 No. 56 Lamp Posts
1 No. 414 Pullman Car	1 Set 208 Tools	12 No. 85 Telegraph Posts	1 No. 87 Signal
1 No. 416 Observation Car	1 Set 209 Barrels	1 No. 78 Train Control	1 No. 79 Flashing Signal
1 No. 212 Gondola Car	47 S Track	1 No. 80 Semaphore	1 No. 195 Terrace
1 No. 217 Illuminated Caboose			16 STC "Lockon" Connections

Wires for making electrical connections, connecting ties for joining sections of track, lamps for headlights, interior of cars and all illuminated accessories are supplied with this outfit. Track layout is 12 feet long by 11 feet wide.
Code Word "ALLY."

Price $350.00

This is a plan of the track layout for the Lionel complete railroad.

[*Page Twenty-Seven*]

1930

PASSENGER CARS FOR "LIONEL STANDARD" TRACK—2¼ INCHES WIDE

ALL Lionel Passenger Cars are made of heavy steel and are beautifully embossed with rivets and other realistic details. They are finished in a variety of attractive colors.

"Lionel Standard" Cars Nos. 332, 337, 338, 339 and 341 are for use with "Lionel Standard" Locomotives Nos. 8, 8E, 10E, 384 and 384E.

"Lionel Standard" Cars Nos. 309, 310 and 312 are for use with "Lionel Standard" Locomotives Nos. 318E, 9E and 390E.

No. 338 "Lionel Standard" Illuminated Observation Car—12 inches long, 4¾ inches high.
Code Word "ORBIT."
Price $5.25

No. 332 "Lionel Standard" Illuminated Mail and Baggage Car—12 inches long, 4¾ inches high. Finished in blue or red color.
Code Word "WILE."
Price $4.75

No. 337 "Lionel Standard" Illuminated Pullman Car—12 inches long, 4¾ inches high.
Code Word "PASS."
Price $4.50

No. 341 "Lionel Standard" Illuminated Observation Car—12 inches long, 4¾ inches high.
Code Word "LEO."
Price $5.75

No. 312 "Lionel Standard" Illuminated Observation Car—Same construction as No. 341, but larger. 13¼ inches long, 5¼ inches high.
Code Word "DOMO."
Price $6.00

No. 339 "Lionel Standard" Illuminated Pullman Car—12 inches long, 4¾ inches high.
Code Word "STAR."
Price $4.75

No. 309 "Lionel Standard" Illuminated Pullman Car—Same construction as No. 339, but larger. 13¼ inches long, 5¼ inches high.
Code Word "ROAD."
Price $5.25

No. 310 "Lionel Standard" Illuminated Mail and Baggage Car—13¼ inches long, 5¼ inches high.
Code Word "WEC."
Price $5.50

Cars Nos. 427, 428, 429 and 430 are for use with locomotives Nos. 9E, 381E and 408E. Cars Nos. 418, 419, 490 and 431 are for use with Locomotives Nos. 381E and 408E.

No. 490 "Lionel Standard" Illuminated Observation Car—17⅝ inches long, 6⅛ inches high.
Code Word "CABIN."
Price $10.00

No. 430 "Lionel Standard" Illuminated Observation Car—Same as above, but mounted on 4-wheel trucks.
Code Word "NERO."
Price $9.00

No. 418 "Lionel Standard" Illuminated Pullman Car—18¼ inches long, 6⅛ inches high.
Code Word "COMFORT."
Price $9.00

No. 428 "Lionel Standard" Illuminated Pullman Car—Same as No. 418 but mounted on 4-wheel trucks.
Code Word "IRIS."
Price $8.00

No. 418 Car is illustrated with side removed to show interior seating arrangement.

No. 419 "Lionel Standard" Illuminated Pullman and Baggage Car—18¼ inches long, 6⅛ inches high.
Code Word "COURT."
Price $9.25

No. 429 "Lionel Standard" Illuminated Pullman and Baggage Car—Same as No. 419 but mounted on 4-wheel trucks.
Code Word "DORA."
Price $8.25

Cars Nos. 420, 421 and 422 are for use with Locomotive No. 390E. Cars Nos. 412, 413, 414 and 416 are for use with Locomotives Nos. 381E and 408E.

No. 431 "Lionel Standard" Illuminated Dining Car—18¼ inches long, 6⅛ inches high.
Code Word "FEED."
Price $10.50

No. 427 "Lionel Standard" Illuminated Dining Car. Same as No. 431 but mounted on four-wheel trucks.
Code Word "FRANCES."
Price $9.50

Illustration shows tables, chairs, kitchen compartment and equipment installed in these cars.

No. 420 "Lionel Standard" Illuminated Pullman Car, 18 inches long, 5 inches high. This car is lettered "Faye."
Code Word "FAYE."
Price $12.00

No. 421 "Lionel Standard" Illuminated Pullman Car. Same as above but lettered "Westphal."
Code Word "WESTPHAL."
Price $12.00

Illustration shows patented revolving shoe made of stainless steel which collects current for lighting interior of cars.

Illustration shows dome light and rear end lanterns over platform of "Lionel Standard" Observation Cars.

No. 422 "Lionel Standard" Illuminated Observation Car. 18 inches long, 5 inches high. This car is lettered "Tempel."
Code Word "TEMPEL."
Price $12.50

No. 412 "Lionel Standard" Illuminated Pullman Car—21½ inches long, 6⅝ inches high. This car is lettered "California."
Code Word "ROMP."
Price $15.00

No. 413 "Lionel Standard" Illuminated Pullman Car—Same as above but lettered "Colorado."
Code Word "ROPE."
Price $15.00

No. 414 "Lionel Standard" Illuminated Pullman Car—Same as above but lettered "Illinois."
Code Word "REEF."
Price $15.00

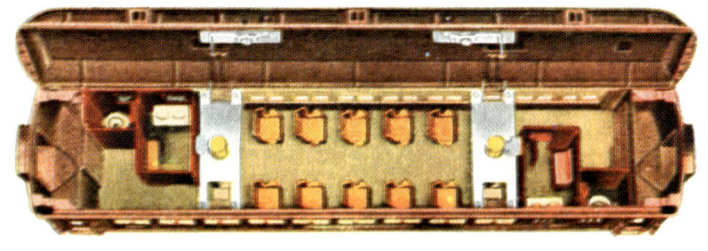

Above illustration shows the unique construction of Cars Nos. 412, 413, 414 and 416. The roof is hinged and when closed is securely locked by means of two steel catches which are rigidly fastened to the roof. By merely pressing two plungers in the transom, car can be opened instantly. Interior of car is equipped with 2 electric lights, 2 wash-room and lavatory compartments, as well as revolving seats. These cars are finished in beautiful duo-tone enamel colors.

No. 416 "Lionel Standard" Illuminated Observation Car, lettered "New York." This car conforms in size to Nos. 412, 413 and 414 illustrated to the left. The brass observation platform is surmounted by a dome light which shines through 2 red rear end lanterns. In addition, this car is equipped with 2 interior lights. This car is 21 inches long, 6⅝ inches high.
Code Word "REST."
Price $15.00

[Page Twenty-Eight]

NEW LIONEL ALL STEEL FREIGHT CARS

for "Lionel Standard" Track—2¼ Inches Wide

BEYOND doubt, the "Lionel Standard" Freight Cars shown on this page reach the peak of perfection in model railroad rolling stock. These freight cars are of steel construction throughout. The fittings, such as hand rails, hand brakes, steps, ladders and inserted panels are all made of brass, highly polished. Wheels, journals, axles and automatic couplers are of heavy nickeled steel.

The illustrations clearly show that every known type of modern freight car is faithfully reproduced by us.

It is great fun to convert your passenger train into a big freighter by adding an assortment of these well-built cars, which are handsomely finished in a variety of durable enameled colors.

Freight Cars Nos. 511 to 517 are for use with Locomotives Nos. 8, 8E, 9E, 10E, 318E, 384, 384E and 390E.

No. 511 Lumber Car with load of lumber—11½ inches long, 3¼ inches high.
Code Word "EDEN." Price, $2.35

No. 512 Gondola Car—11½ inches long, 3⅜ inches high.
Code Word "EVER." Price, $2.35

No. 513 Cattle Car—11½ inches long, 4¾ inches high. Has sliding door.
Code Word "EBON." Price, $3.10

No. 514R Refrigerator Car—11½ inches long, 4¾ inches high. Has double swing doors.
Code Word "EAST." Price, $3.10

No. 514 Box Car—11½ inches long, 4¾ inches high. Has sliding door.
Code Word "EGG." Price, $3.10

No. 515 Oil Car—11½ inches long, 5⅛ inches high.
Code Word "ELTA." Price, $3.10

No. 516 Coal Car—11½ inches long, 4⅛ inches high. Has "Hopper" bottom, operated by wheel.
Code Word "EPIC." Price, $3.50

No. 517 Illuminated Caboose—11½ inches long, 5⅜ inches high. Complete with rear platform lamp.
Code Word "EAGER." Price, $3.50

Freight Cars Nos. 211 to 217 are for use with Locomotives Nos. 381E and 408E.

No. 211 Lumber Car with load of lumber—12½ inches long, 4⅛ inches high.
Code Word "ANT." Price, $3.50

No. 212 Gondola Car—12½ inches long, 3¾ inches high.
Code Word "ROY." Price, $3.50

No. 213 Cattle Car—12½ inches long, 5½ inches high. Has sliding door.
Code Word "WAKE." Price, $4.75

No. 214 Box Car—12½ inches long, 5½ inches high. Has double sliding doors.
Code Word "WOOL." Price, $4.75

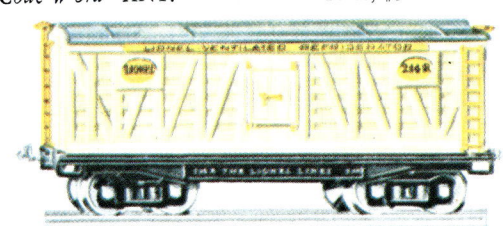

No. 214R Refrigerator Car—12½ inches long, 5½ inches high. Has double swing doors.
Code Word "GONE." Price, $4.75

No. 215 Oil Car—12½ inches long, 5½ inches high.
Code Word "DICE." Price, $4.75

No. 216 Coal Car—12½ inches long, 5 inches high. Has "Hopper" bottom, operated by wheel.
Code Word "ALAMA." Price, $4.75

No. 217 Illuminated Caboose—12½ inches long, 5½ inches high. Complete with rear platform lamp.
Code Word "RAFT." Price, $5.50

[Page Twenty-nine]

OPERATING DERRICK AND DUMP CARS AND MERCHANDISE CONTAINERS FOR "LIONEL STANDARD" TRACK—2¼ INCHES WIDE. FREIGHT SHED FOR ALL LIONEL OUTFITS

No. 219

No. 219 Derrick Car—Lionel's famous realistic railroad derrick car. Operating exactly like a real derrick. The boom may be raised or lowered. The entire cab may be swung around in a complete circle, and pulley and tackle may be operated separately. All mechanical movements are controlled by wheels operating worm gears. Self-locking. The boom or cab may be operated from any position. It is mounted on a solid steel car 12½ inches long, 6¼ inches high. The boom is 16 inches long. Car is equipped with automatic couplers.

Code Word "ALUM." Price, $9.00

No. 205

No. 205—A set of three L. C. L. (less than carload lots) Steel Merchandise Containers—Complete with one set of chains. A realistic railroad accessory, patterned exactly after the originals, a photograph of which is shown above. This set of containers may be used in either the Nos. 512 or 212 Gondola Cars. They are made of heavy gauge sheet steel, beautifully embossed and brass trimmed. Complete with hinged door and fastener. Finished in Lionel's permanent enamel. Dimensions 3¼ inches long, 3 inches wide, 4 inches high.

Code Word "CHARLES." Price, per set of 3, $3.00

No. 155

No. 155 Freight Shed—A new illuminated all-steel beautifully enameled Freight Shed. Solidly constructed of heavy gauge sheet steel. Complete with terminals for wires and two electric bulbs. Used in conjunction with Lionel Freight Cars. Plenty of room on the platform for all sorts of merchandise and baggage. 18 inches long, 11 inches high, 8 inches wide.

Code Word "JOCKEY." Price, $7.50

No. 218

No. 218 Operating Dump Car—Lionel's operating dump car is a marvel of mechanical ingenuity. A true model of the real cars used in the construction of railroads. It actually dumps a load at any place desired along the track. Wheels and worm gears control the mechanism that automatically opens and tilts the sides of the car. Size 12½ inches long, 4¾ inches high. Entirely constructed of sheet steel and beautifully finished by Lionel's famous enameling process. Equipped with automatic couplers.

Code Word "DEPEW." Price, $6.25

[Page Thirty]

NEW "O" GAUGE DERRICK CAR—NEW FREIGHT ACCESSORIES

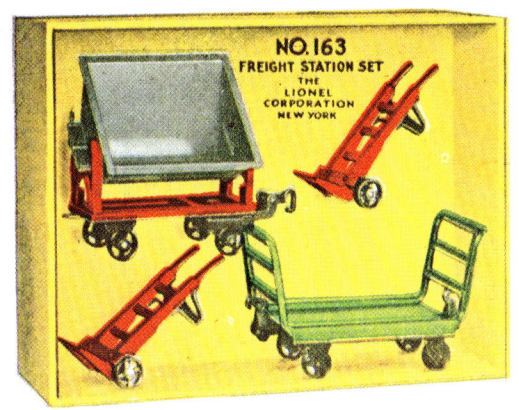

No. 163 Freight Station Set—Comprises 2 No. 157 Hand Trucks, 1 No. 162 Dump Truck, and 1 No. 160 Baggage Truck. They are exact reproductions of the trucks seen on all freight stations. They are of very substantial construction and are beautifully enameled in brilliant colors.
Code Word "DROME." Price per set $3.00

No. 161 Baggage Truck—4½ inches long, 2 inches wide, 2⅜ inches high.
Code Word "FLEET." Price 75c

No. 162 Dump Truck—By raising the levers attached to the supports, body may be tilted and the contents dumped at the side of the truck. The body automatically swings back and locks into position. 4¼ inches long, 2¾ inches wide, 2½ inches high.
Code Word "LOUVER." Price $1.25

No. 157 Hand Truck—3¼ inches long, 1⅝ inches wide.
Code Word "RIGID." Price 50c

No. 2 Lionel Three-Speed Reversible "Bild-a-Motor"—It can be used for a variety of purposes with construction toys of all kinds. It will develop great power and uses a minimum amount of current. Can be taken down and reassembled in a few moments. Operates on dry or storage batteries as well as on reduced alternating or direct current. 7 inches long, 3⅝ inches high, 3-15/16 inches wide.
Code Word "HOIST." Price $7.50

No. 1 Lionel Three-Speed Reversible "Bild-a-Motor"—This powerful motor is similar in construction to the other "Bild-a-Motor" described above, but is smaller in size. Made in units so that it can be taken down and reassembled in a few moments. It will lift at least 20 times its own weight. By means of a controlling lever, motor can be started, stopped, and reversed. Will operate on dry or storage batteries, or on reduced alternating or direct current. Size 6⅛ inches long, 3⅛ inches high, 2¾ inches wide.
Code Word "LIFT." Price $5.00

A most faithful reproduction of the derrick cars in use on all the big railroads throughout the country. You can raise or lower the boom, swing it from side to side, and hoist weights with the pulley and tackle. The gears are actually machine cut, and operate so easily that the heaviest weight the car is built to lift can be handled without noticeable effort. It is of very substantial construction and is beautifully enameled in brilliant colors. Length of Car 9¼ inches. Height of Car 4½ inches. Length of Boom 9¼ inches.

Code Word "CHASER." Price $7.50

LIONEL "O" GAUGE FREIGHT CARS AND SETS

No. 831 Lumber Car—With load of lumber, 6¾ inches long, 2⅛ inches high.
Code Word "VEST." Price, 70¢.

No. 803 Coal Car—Has "Hopper" bottom operated by wheel. 6¾ inches long, 3¼ inches high.
Code Word "LOAD." Price, $1.00.

No. 805 Box Car—Has sliding door. 6¾ inches long, 3¼ inches high.
Code Word "VICK." Price, $1.00.

No. 806 Cattle Car—Has sliding door. 6¾ inches long, 3¼ inches high.
Code Word "VEX." Price, $1.10.

No. 902 Gondola Car—6¾ inches long, 2⅛ inches high.
Code Word "VOTE." Price, 70¢.

No. 804 Oil Car—6¾ inches long, 3½ inches high.
Code Word "FUEL." Price, 90¢.

Cars Nos. 803, 804, 805, 806, 807, 831 and 902 are for use with Locomotives Nos. 248, 252, 257 and 258.
Cars Nos. 811 to 817 are for use with Locomotives Nos. 4, 253, 254, 254E, 251, 251E, 256 and 260E.

No. 808 Freight Car Set—Comprises 1 each Nos. 831 Lumber Car, 803 Coal Car, 804 Oil Car, 805 Box Car, 806 Cattle Car, 807 Caboose, described on this page. Very attractively packed.
Code Word "QUORN." Price, $5.25.

No. 818 Freight Car Set—Comprises 1 each Nos. 812 Gondola Car, 814 Box Car, 816 Coal Car, 817 Caboose, described on this page. Very attractively packed.
Code Word "QUEST." Price, $9.00.

All Lionel Freight Cars are equipped with automatic couplers, nickeled journals and wheels, brass hand rails, steps, and brake wheels.

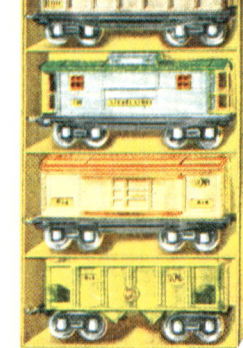

No. 808 SET

No. 818 SET

No. 807 Caboose—Has front and rear brass platforms and ladder to roof. 6¾ inches long, 3½ inches high.
Code Word "VAT." Price, $1.10.

Cars Nos. 803, 804, 805, 806, 807, 831 and 902 are mounted on 4 wheel trucks.
Cars Nos. 811 to 817 are mounted on two 4-wheel trucks.

No. 811 Lumber Car—With load of lumber. 8⅞ inches long, 2½ inches high.
Code Word "DRUM." Price, $1.90.

No. 815 Oil Car—8⅞ inches long, 3¾ inches high.
Code Word "YAM." Price, $2.25.

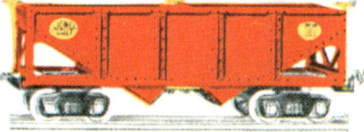

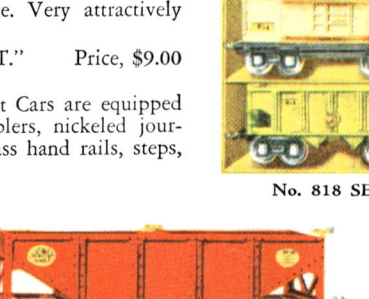

No. 816 Coal Car—Has "Hopper" bottom operated by wheel. 8⅞ inches long, 3¼ inches high.
Code Word "YOST." Price, $2.65.

No. 812 Gondola Car—8⅞ inches long, 2⅝ inches high.
Code Word "DALE." Price, $1.90.

No. 814 Box Car—Has sliding door. 8⅞ inches long, 3¾ inches high.
Code Word "YOKE." Price, $2.25.

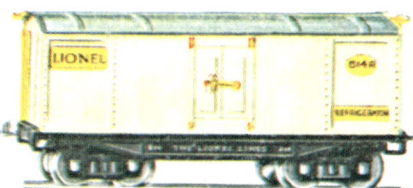

No. 814R Refrigerator Car—Has double swing doors. 8⅞ inches long, 3¾ inches high.
Code Word "DOFF." Price, $2.25.

No. 813 Cattle Car—Has sliding door. 8⅞ inches long, 3¾ inches high.
Code Word "YAWL." Price, $2.25.

No. 817 Caboose—Has front and rear brass platforms and ladder to roof. 8⅞ inches long, 4 inches high.
Code Word "DEFT." Price, $2.65.

[Page Thirty-two]

PASSENGER CARS FOR "O" GAUGE TRACK—1⅜ INCHES WIDE

Lionel "O" Gauge Cars Nos. 607 and 608 are for use with Locomotives Nos. 252, 253, 257 and 258.

No. 630 Lionel "O" Gauge Observation Car—6¾ inches long, 3¼ inches high. *Code Word* "IDEAL." Price, $0.85
No. 530 Lionel "O" Gauge Observation Car—Same as No. 630 illustrated, but may be obtained finished in green or terra cotta. *Code Word* "IONA." Price, $0.85

No. 608 Lionel "O" Gauge Illuminated Observation Car—7½ inches long, 3½ inches high. *Code Word* "TWIG." Price, $1.75

No. 612 Lionel "O" Gauge Illuminated Observation Car—8¾ inches long, 3¾ inches high. *Code Word* "WALTON." Price, $3.00

Lionel "O" Gauge Cars Nos. 710 and 712 are obtainable in red or orange color, and are for use with Locomotives Nos. 251, 251E, 256 and 260E.

No. 712 Lionel "O" Gauge Illuminated Observation Car—11⅜ inches long, 4¼ inches high. *Code Word* "RISE." Price, $4.00

No. 606 Lionel "O" Gauge Illuminated Observation Car—10¼ inches long, 4 inches high. *Code Word* "MODE." Price, $3.75

No. 710 Lionel "O" Gauge Illuminated Pullman Car—11⅜ inches long, 4¼ inches high. *Code Word* "HOLLY." Price, $3.90

ALL Lionel "O" Gauge Passenger Cars are made of heavy steel and are beautifully embossed with rivets and other realistic details. They are finished in a variety of attractive colors. Except for Nos. 529, 530, 629 and 630 Cars, all Lionel Passenger Cars are illuminated.

The No. 840 Power Station shown in the above illustration is fully described on Page 44.

No. 605 Lionel "O" Gauge Illuminated Pullman Car—10¼ inches long, 4 inches high. *Code Word* "NOVA." Price, $3.50

Lionel "O" Gauge Cars Nos. 605 and 606 are for use with Locomotives Nos. 4, 251, 251E and 260E.

Lionel "O" Gauge Cars Nos. 610 and 612 are for use with Locomotives Nos. 4, 253, 254 and 254E.

No. 529 Lionel "O" Gauge Pullman Car—Same as No. 629 illustrated, but may be obtained finished in green or terra cotta. *Code Word* "IMPY." Price, $0.80
No. 629 Lionel "O" Gauge Pullman Car—6¾ inches long, 3¼ inches high. *Code Word* "FANE." Price, $0.80

No. 607 Lionel "O" Gauge Illuminated Pullman Car—7½ inches long, 3½ inches high. *Code Word* "BRAND." Price, $1.65

No. 610 Lionel "O" Gauge Illuminated Pullman Car—8¾ inches long, 3¾ inches high. *Code Word* "EALING." Price, $2.95

Lionel "O" Gauge Cars Nos. 529 and 530, 629 and 630 are for use with Locomotives Nos. 248, 252, 257 and 258.

[Page Thirty-Three]

1930

LIONEL ELECTRICALLY-CONTROLLED ACCESSORIES

IN all Lionel Electrically-Controlled Accessories the electric unit is mounted on a solid piece of fibre which is protected in the interior of the base.

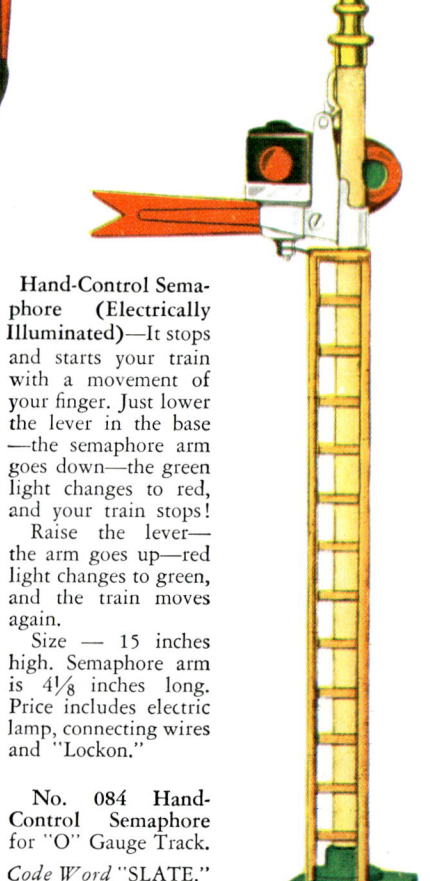

THESE accessories are exact models of the latest safety devices used on all railroads. They are made of steel, beautifully designed and very moderately priced. The construction is of Lionel quality throughout. The base is a die casting which incorporates considerable detail, such as hinged doors, embossed rivets, etc. The upright and ladder and other structural parts are made of steel, and are practically indestructible. The top of lantern is removable so that lamp in interior may be easily reached. Finished in a variety of beautiful enamels baked at high temperature.

Lionel Automatic Semaphore (Electrically Illuminated) — When train passes over section of track to which it is connected the semaphore arm is set upright and green bull's-eye in lantern is illuminated. When train passes, the semaphore arm drops to horizontal position, and the electric lamp illuminates the red signal. It is absolutely automatic. The height from base to spire is 15 inches. Semaphore arm is 4⅛ inches long. Price includes electric lamp, connecting wires, "Lockon" and special section of track.

No. 080 Automatic Semaphore — For Lionel "O" Gauge Track.
Code Word "DROP."   Price, $4.75

No. 80 Automatic Semaphore — For "Lionel Standard" Track.
Code Word "DRAW."   Price, $4.75

Lionel Automatic Train Control (Electrically Illuminated) — Positively amazing in its action. When train approaches section to which it is connected, red light shows and train automatically comes to a dead stop. After an interval of a few seconds, red light changes to green and train is on its way again. The controlling mechanism can be disconnected by means of a small lever so that train does not stop as it approaches the train control, which then shows a permanent green light. Lionel Train Control is 10¼ inches high. Price includes electric lamp, connecting wires and "Lockon."

No. 078 Automatic Train Control — For Lionel "O" Gauge Track.
Code Word "HEAVE."   Price, $5.25

No. 78 Automatic Train Control — For "Lionel Standard" Track.
Code Word "WEAVE."   Price, $5.25

Lionel Semaphore - Train - Control (Electrically Illuminated) — Our latest marvel. As train approaches, the red light shines and semaphore arm drops, denoting "Caution." Train immediately comes to a dead stop. A short interval —light changes to green—semaphore arm goes up—train proceeds. It is startlingly real! It operates as if by magic! When desired, a lever in the base disconnects the controlling mechanism and sets the semaphore arm in an upright position so that train does not stop as it approaches the Semaphore-Train-Control. You will be absolutely thrilled as you watch the unique action of this almost-human railroad device. Lionel's skilled craftsmanship is exemplified to the highest degree in the construction of this very desirable accessory. Height from base to spire 14¾ inches. Semaphore arm is 4⅛ inches long. Price includes electric lamp, connecting wires and "Lockon."

No. 082 Semaphore-Train-Control — For Lionel "O" Gauge Track.
Code Word "STILL."   Price, $7.50

No. 82 Semaphore-Train-Control — For "Lionel Standard" Track.
Code Word "STRIP."   Price, $7.50

Hand-Control Semaphore (Electrically Illuminated) — It stops and starts your train with a movement of your finger. Just lower the lever in the base —the semaphore arm goes down—the green light changes to red, and your train stops!
Raise the lever— the arm goes up—red light changes to green, and the train moves again.
Size — 15 inches high. Semaphore arm is 4⅛ inches long. Price includes electric lamp, connecting wires and "Lockon."

No. 084 Hand-Control Semaphore for "O" Gauge Track.
Code Word "SLATE."   Price, $4.25

No. 84 Hand-Control Semaphore for "Lionel Standard" Track.
Code Word "STRIKE"   Price, $4.25

Nos. 80 and 080
Automatic Semaphore
with Electric Light

Nos. 78 and 078
Automatic Train Control
with Electric Lights.

Nos. 82 and 082
Automatic Train-Control-Semaphore with
Electric Light.

Nos. 84 and 084
Hand-Control-Semaphore
with Electric Light.

[Page Thirty-Four]

LIONEL ELECTRICALLY-CONTROLLED ACCESSORIES

BOYS! See the lights flash on and off — see the gates go up and down — — hear the warning bells ring! The Action is Automatic!

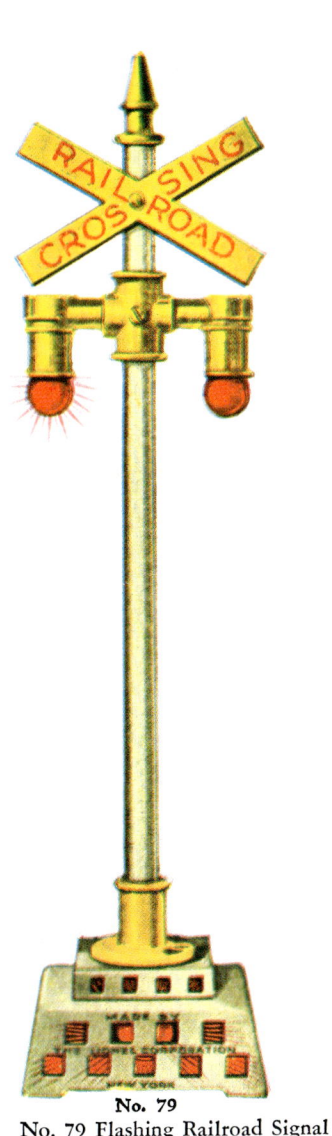

No. 79

No. 79 Flashing Railroad Signal—A true reproduction of the latest type of Crossing Signal used on electrified railroads. The Lionel patented thermostat in the base flashes the red lights on and off alternately and continues to do so as long as the current is applied. Electric lamp in base throws a red light through the openings. The base, uprights and arm are made of die castings and steel, beautifully finished. Height 11½ inches, base 2¾ inches square. For use with "O" gauge and "Lionel Standard" equipment.
Code Word "ROOM." Price, $5.25

No. 83

No. 83 Lionel Traffic and Crossing Signal—An ingenious Lionel accessory. The light in the red lantern flashes on and off like the "blinker" light seen at street intersections. The mechanism is in the base, which also contains binding posts for attaching wires supplied with the signal. This signal is 6¼ inches high. Can be used with "O" Gauge or "Lionel Standard" equipment. A wonderful accessory to use when building model villages.
Code Word "STAND."
Price, $4.00

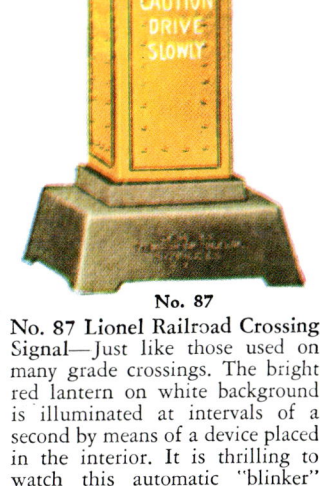

No. 87

No. 87 Lionel Railroad Crossing Signal—Just like those used on many grade crossings. The bright red lantern on white background is illuminated at intervals of a second by means of a device placed in the interior. It is thrilling to watch this automatic "blinker" operate continuously without attention. The base contains terminals for connecting wires. This Crossing Signal is 6¾ inches high. Can be used with "Lionel Standard" or "O" Gauge equipment.
Code Word "STORE."
Price, $4.50

Nos. 77 and 077

Lionel Illuminated Automatic Crossing Gates—An exact reproduction of the real ones seen at grade crossings. When train approaches the track section to which it is connected, a red light illuminates and the gate comes down and stays in that position. When train passes, gate opens and the light goes out. The action is the same as on real railroads. Gate is made of heavy steel. The electric unit is in the base. Finished in enameled colors. Gate is 11 inches long. Price includes special section of track, connecting wires and "Lockon".
No. 077 Automatic Crossing Gate for Lionel "O" Gauge Track.
Code Word "ADVANCE." Price, $4.25
No. 77 Automatic Crossing Gate for "Lionel Standard" Track.
Code Word "TARRY." Price, $4.50

Nos. 69 and 069

Lionel Electric Warning Signals—Electric bell with 2 gongs is mounted on steel standard, 8¾ inches high which supports warning sign. Gongs ring while train passes over track section to which it is connected. Bell automatically stops when grade crossing is clear. This accessory is finished in beautiful enameled colors, and bell is nickeled steel. Price includes special track, wires and "Lockon."
No. 069 Electric Warning Signal for Lionel "O" Gauge Track.
Code Word "RINGER." Price, $3.25
No. 69 Electric Warning Signal for "Lionel Standard" Track.
Code Word "BEWARE." Price, $3.50

[Page Thirty-Five]

NEW LIONEL CIRCUIT BREAKER

No. 91 Circuit Breaker—Should be purchased with every outfit. This circuit breaker is an ingenious device that functions as an automatic and never-failing safety signal in case of any short-circuit on the track or if the train leaves the rails. In case of either of these occurrences, the current is immediately shut off from the transformer, which prevents it overheating and the red light becomes illuminated and stays that way until the train is put back on the track or the short-circuit is discovered. It is an invaluable accessory to your outfit and we highly recommend its use. The mechanism is enclosed in a die cast case, beautifully enameled. The bulb is surmounted by a polished brass guard.

Size—2¾ inches square—4¼ inches high.

Code Word "SAFETY."   Price, $3.25

[Page Thirty-Six]

LIONEL DIRECT CURRENT REDUCERS
(NOT TO BE USED ON ALTERNATING CURRENT)

No. 107 Lionel Direct Current Reducer for 110-Volt Circuit—This is constructed of four porcelain tubes wound with best quality of resistance wire. These porcelain tubes are mounted on a substantial base measuring 8 by 11 inches and ¾ inches thick. The porcelain tubes are protected and ventilated by a perforated steel cover lined with heavy asbestos. The sliding lever regulates the voltage so that train will just crawl along or go ahead at express speed. The reducer is connected with the house current by a separable plug with 7 feet of flexible cord. Four porcelain supports with screws are supplied so that the reducer can be screwed to wall or table.

Code Word "KENTUCKY."   Price, $10.00

No. 170 Lionel Direct Current Reducer for 220-Volt Circuit—This reducer is identical in appearance with No. 107, mentioned above, but is for use on 220 volts.

Code Word "ASBURY."   Price, $14.50

CONTROLLING RHEOSTAT No. 81
(FCR BATTERIES)

No. 81 Controlling Rheostat—With this rheostat you can, when using dry or storage batteries, operate Lionel Trains at various speeds, or stop and start them at any distance from the track. This is done by sliding the lever from side to side, or manipulating it up and down. This rheostat can also be used with Lionel "Multivolt" Transformers when a gradual increase or decrease of current is desired, without touching the lever on the transformer. The porcelain coil of this rheostat is protected by a perforated steel cover, and air holes prevent over-heating. Size 4⅞ inches long, 2½ inches wide.

Code Word "BONE."   Price, $2.50

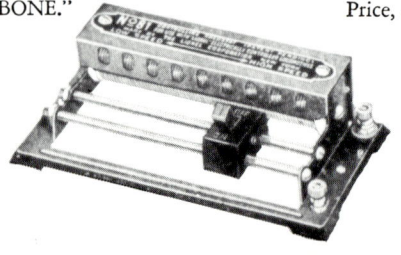

SPECIFICATIONS OF LIONEL "MULTIVOLT" TRANSFORMERS
(DESCRIBED ON PAGE THIRTY-SEVEN)

Sub-Base—A metal sub-base resting on four supports is attached to the bottom. The air, circulating between this sub-base and the transformer case, keeps it cool while in operation.

Separable Plug—All Lionel "Multivolt" Transformers are fitted with an approved separable plug.

Double Contact Control Switch—This is infinitely superior to the one-piece switch, which is easily bent and does not make positive contact. Our double switch has a flexible, phosphor-bronze contact arm under the rigid switch, so that positive contact with the points is assured. The flexible contact is protected from injury by the rigid brass handle to which it is attached. An exclusive feature of Lionel "Multivolt" Transformers.

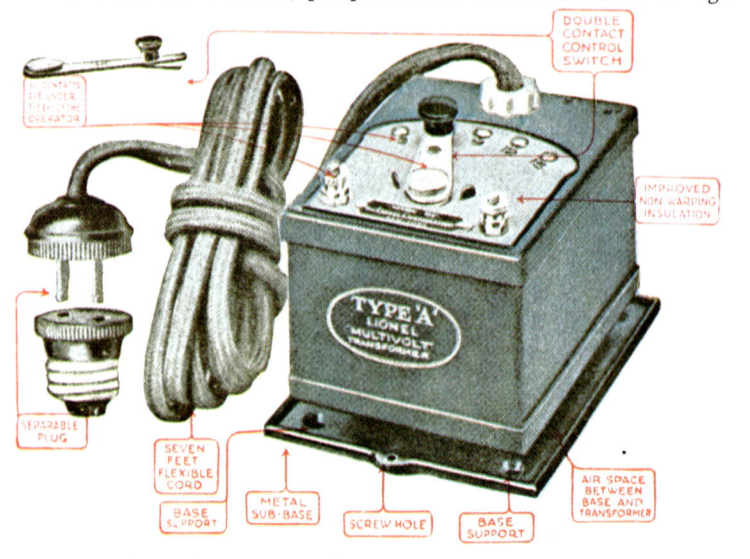

Laminations—The laminations are made of the best grade of electrical sheets and the windings are perfectly insulated.

Rigid Supports for Coils—The coils and laminations of Lionel "Multivolt" Transformers are rigidly supported inside the case by metal bands which prevent these parts from moving and eliminate the possibility of broken lead wires.

Metal Case—The case is beautiful in design and is stamped of heavier steel than is required by the Underwriters Laboratories.

Finish—Lionel "Multivolt" Transformer cases are covered with a rubberoid composition that is applied at 350 degrees Fahrenheit. This is much greater heat than the case is ever subjected to, and the finish cannot be scratched and will not peel off during the entire life of the transformer.

Visible Connections—All contacts and switches are mounted on one piece of heavy insulating material and are at the top of the transformer, right before the user.

Lamp Cord—All Lionel "Multivolt" Transformers are fitted with 7 feet of flexible lamp cord which enters the transformer case through an approved porcelain bushing.

It will be seen that Lionel "Multivolt" Transformers incorporate every device that will increase their efficiency.

LIONEL "MULTIVOLT" TRANSFORMERS—FOR 110 AND 220 VOLTS—60, 40 AND 25 CYCLES

LIONEL "Multivolt" Transformers are made completely in our own factories. Our Transformer department is the largest in the country devoted exclusively to the manufacture of low-voltage transformers. The only parts purchased are the raw materials. We correctly wind and insulate the coils, make the cases, laminations, switch handles, and in fact do every operation. Lionel "Multivolt" Transformers are listed as standard by the Underwriters' Laboratories.

LIONEL "Multivolt" Transformers have been on the market for a great many years and operate all makes of Electric Trains. We justly claim they are best. Don't experiment with other makes of doubtful value. Remember, that all transformers look alike outside, but their imperfections will only be discovered after they are in actual use for a length of time. Lionel "Multivolt" Transformers will last indefinitely and are guaranteed unconditionally as long as they are used on the current for which they are intended. They are absolutely safe and will give steady, even power.

With the introduction of the Type F Transformer, a new low priced highly efficient transformer is available for the operation of small trains on 110 volts, 25 to 40 cycle, alternating current.

The Types A, B and F Transformers are now designed to deliver current in one volt steps. This eliminates the need for the No. 81 rheostat, formerly supplied with the "O" Gauge outfits.

For Greatest Efficiency Always Use a Lionel "Multivolt" Transformer with a Lionel Train

Lionel "Multivolt" Transformers Are for Use Only on Alternating Current. Do Not Use Them on Direct Current.

TYPE A TRANSFORMER will operate any "O" Gauge outfit and in addition the extra binding post will enable the user to light up a few lamp posts or other electrically illuminated accessories. For 110 volts, 60 cycles, 40 watts capacity. Gives 15 volts in following steps: Permanent—5. Variable, 6, 7, 8, 9, 10, 11, 12, 13, 14, 15. Size: 4⅛x3¼x3¾ inches. Sub-base: 3¾ by 5 inches.
Code Word "STRONG." Price $3.75
TYPE F TRANSFORMER—Same specifications as Type A but for 110 volts, 25 to 40 cycle alternating current.
Code Word "HYDRO." Price $3.75

TYPE B TRANSFORMER will operate any "O" Gauge outfit and in addition the extra binding posts enable the user to light up lamp posts, semaphores, and other electrically illuminated accessories. For 110 volts, 60 cycles, 50 watts capacity. Gives 25 volts in following steps: Permanent—6, 7, 13. Variable—8, 9, 10, 11, 12, 14, 15, 16, 17, 18, 21, 22, 23, 24, 25.

Size: 4¾x3⅝x4 inches. Sub-base: 5½x 4⅛ inches.
Code Word "BRADLEY." Price $5.00

TYPE "T" TRANSFORMER will operate any "O" Gauge or "Lionel Standard" outfit; also has extra binding posts for attaching illuminated electrical accessories.
For 110 volts, 60 cycles, 100 watts capacity.
Gives 25 volts in following steps: Permanent—2, 4, 6, 7, 8, 10, 12, 14, 15, 16, 17, 18, 19, 21, 23, 25. Variable—2, 6, 8, 10, 12, 14, 16, 17, 18, 19, 21, 23, 25.
Size: 5 by 4 by 4⅜ inches. Sub-base: 6 by 4⅝ inches.
Code Word "BIRCH." Price $7.50

TYPE "K" TRANSFORMER will operate any outfit as well as illuminated accessories. This transformer has sufficient wattage capacity to operate two trains at once.
Size: 5⅛ by 4 by 5 inches. Sub-base: 6 by 4⅝ inches.
"K"—For 110 volts, 60 cycles, 150 watts capacity. Specifications same as Type "T," but has higher wattage capacity.
Code Word (110 V.) "BINGHAM."
Price $11.00
"K"—For 220 volts, 60 cycles, 150 watts capacity. Specifications same as Type "T," but is for use on 220-volt circuit.
Code Word (220 V.) "BROOK." Price $14.50

TYPE "C" TRANSFORMER will operate any outfit and illuminated accessories on 25 or 40 cycle current.
For 110 volts, 25 to 40 cycles, 75 watts capacity. Specifications same as Type "T," but is for use on 25 or 40 cycle current.
Size: 5⅛ by 4 by 5 inches. Sub-base: 6 by 4⅝ inches.
Code Word "LAWRENCE." Price $7.50
This transformer is the best obtainable for use on 25 or 40 cycle current.

[Page Thirty-Seven]

"DISTANT-CONTROL" AND HAND-OPERATED SWITCHES. NEW TURNTABLE

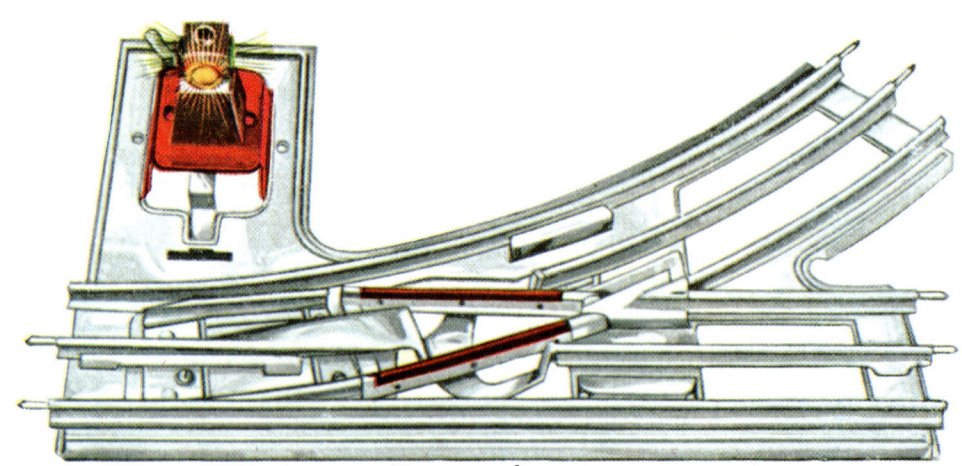

Nos. 210 and 021

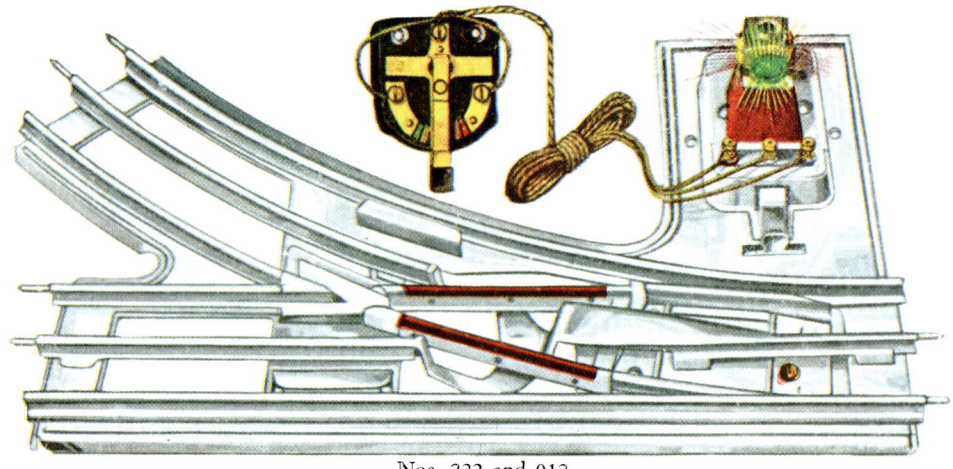

Nos. 222 and 012

LIONEL Hand-operated Switches, shown in the above illustration, are equipped with heavy fibre rails (Patents Re. 16580 and 1671236) at the points where the rails cross. All possibility of short circuit is thus eliminated and headlight does not flicker when train passes over these points. Attention is also directed to the several guard rails attached to Lionel Switches which prevent derailing even when trains are traveling at high speed. Hand-lever which moves the rails also sets the signals, changes the lights and locks mechanism. All Lionel Switches are radically different from any others in the market. They are of steel construction throughout and will bear the weight of the heaviest trains without bending or breaking.

No. 210 "Lionel Standard" Illuminated Switches (right and left hand)—
15¼ inches long, 8⅝ inches wide. Price includes electric lamps.

Code Word "NASH." Price per Pair, $6.50

No. 021 Lionel "O" Gauge Illuminated Switches (right and left hand)—
10½ inches long, 7¼ inches wide. Price includes electric lamps.

Code Word "MOSHA." Price per Pair, $5.00

LIONEL "Distant-Control" Switches (Patents Nos. 1548940 and 1671236) can be operated at any distance from the track by means of a controlling lever. By manipulating this lever, the same as switchmen do, the position of the switch instantly changes and the red and green lights change with the movement of the switch. The controlling lever is connected with the switch by means of flexible wires so that no additional wiring is required. The mechanism of Lionel "Distant-Control" Switches is extremely simple. They are scientifically constructed. The guard rails prevent the train leaving the track even when operating at high speed. The patented Lionel fibre rails are embodied in the construction of these switches. This exclusive feature prevents a short circuit when the train is passing over the switch points. See page 45 for particulars of Nos. 437 Switch Signal-Tower and 439 Panel Board, to which the controlling levers of these switches can be attached.

No. 222 "Lionel Standard" "Distant-Control" Illuminated Switches (right and left hand)—
15¼ inches long, 8⅝ inches wide. Price includes electric lamps and 42 inches of cord to which controlling levers are attached.
Code Word "AFAR." Price per Pair, $11.75

No. 012 Lionel "O" Gauge "Distant-Control" Illuminated Switches (right and left hand)—
10½ inches long, 7¼ inches wide. Price includes electric lamps and 42 inches of cord to which controlling levers are attached.
Code Word "ASP." Price per Pair, $9.75

LIONEL Switches and Turntable can be connected to the track in the same manner as ordinary straight or curved sections.

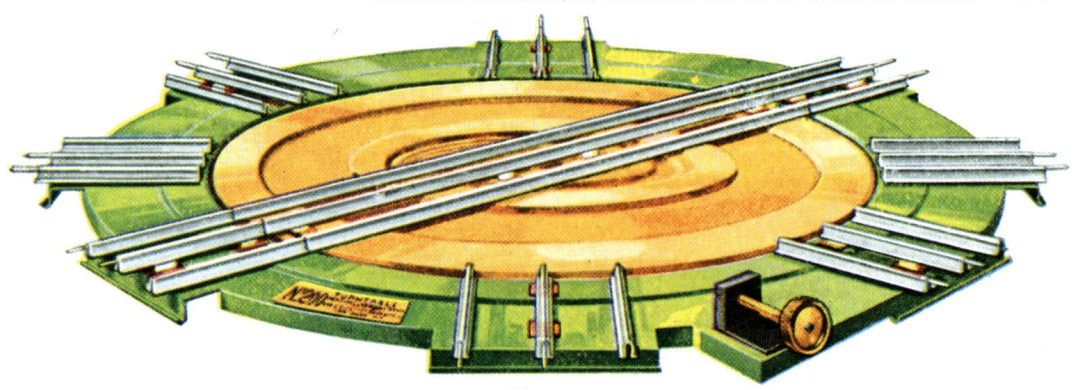

No. 200

NO. 200 TURNTABLE
For "Lionel Standard" Track

THIS is an exclusive Lionel Accessory that every boy should have in order to make a complete Lionel Train layout. It is used for switching locomotives to various tracks in the smallest possible space. Every boy is familiar with the use of a Turntable, so it is not necessary to describe its purpose. This Turntable is so perfectly balanced that even when the heaviest locomotive is upon it, it can be easily moved in every direction by means of the worm gear and hand wheel that operate it. Diameter of Turntable is 17 inches.

Code Word "TURK." Price, $6.00

[Page Thirty-Eight]

Reg. U. S. Pat. Off.
"LIONEL STANDARD" AND "O" GAUGE TRACK. LIONEL TRACK ACCESSORIES

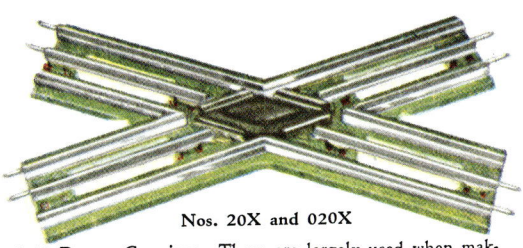

Nos. 20X and 020X

Lionel 45 Degree Crossings—These are largely used when making a figure "8," using all curved track, but a great variety of other track layouts can be formed with them. Steel construction throughout. Rails are mounted on heavy steel ornamental base. A heavy fibre block in centre where rails cross prevents all possibility of short circuit, or cars jumping the track.

No. 020X Crossing for "O" Gauge Track. Size 11½ inches long, 6 inches wide.
Code Word "CROSS." Price, $1.60

No. 20X Crossing for "Lionel Standard" Track. Size 16½ inches long, 9 inches wide.
Code Word "BOSS." Price, $1.85

Lionel Illuminated Bumpers

Nos. 25 and 025

This bumper is die cast and is surmounted by a red electric light encased in a nickeled steel guard. Electrical contact is automatically made and bumper can be placed at any part of track layout.

No. 025 Bumper for "O" Gauge Track. Length 10¼ inches, height 2⅞ inches.
Code Word "HIT." Price, $1.85

No. 25 Bumper for "Lionel Standard" Track. Length 14 inches, height 3¾ inches.
Code Word "CAT." Price, $2.35

Lionel Spring Bumpers

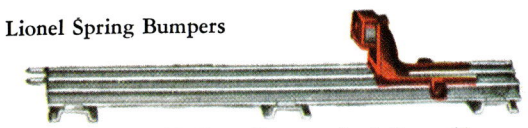

No. 023 Lionel "O" Gauge Bumper—An indispensable accessory for terminals or sidings. Fitted with spring plunger which absorbs shock when car strikes it. The bumper frame is removable. Length, 10¼ inches, height 2 inches.
Code Word "DELTO." Price, 85¢

No. 23 "Lionel Standard" Bumper—The construction is the same as No. 023 described above. Two spring plungers absorb shock of car. Length 14 inches, height 3 inches.
Code Word "PROVO." Price, $1.30

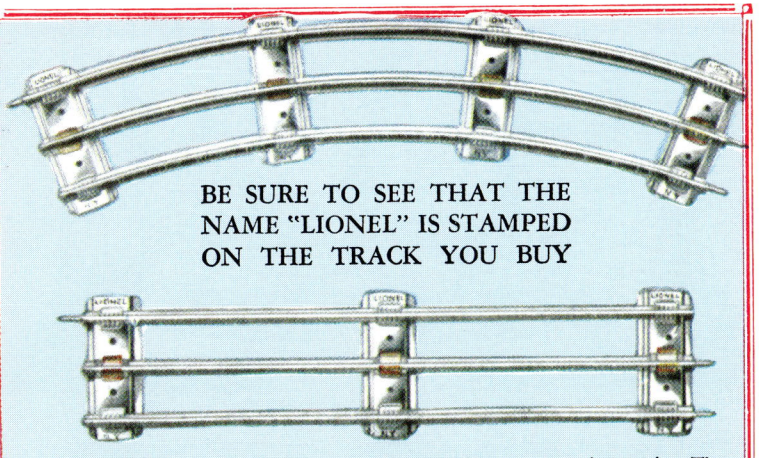

BE SURE TO SEE THAT THE NAME "LIONEL" IS STAMPED ON THE TRACK YOU BUY

Lionel Track is constructed of heavier metal than any other make. The illustration shows the added strength given to **Lionel** rails by forming the base outward instead of turning it in. This outward flange gives the track sufficient strength to support the weight of a fully grown person and is made possible by our patented process. Each section of track is tested on 110 volts and therefore will not short-circuit when carrying the low voltage which operates **Lionel** Trains. The ends of each section have pin terminals which fit in openings in the adjoining sections allowing track to be laid and taken apart without difficulty.

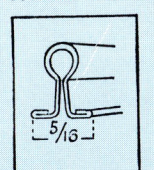

Lionel Track is made in straight and curved sections and the curvature of the track is mechanically correct, allowing trains to run at high speed without derailing.

We illustrate below the improved connecting tie which holds sections of track rigidly together. These connecting ties can be readily inserted and removed.

Lionel "O" Gauge Track—1⅜ inches wide

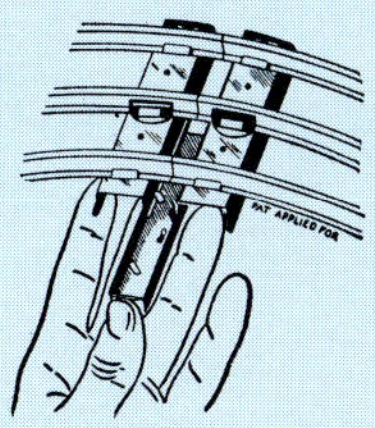

OC curved track, 11 inches long.
Code Word "LEMPS." Price, 20¢

OS straight track, 10¼ inches long.
Code Word "GLENN." Price, 20¢

OSS track, 10¼ inches long. For use with Electrically-Controlled Accessories. Complete with "Lockon" and connecting wires.
Code Word "RELAY." Price, 40¢

"Lionel Standard" Track—2¼ inches wide

C curved track, 16 inches long.
Code Word "BUFF." Price, 30¢

S straight track, 14 inches long.
Code Word "NYACK." Price, 30¢

SS track, 14 inches long. For use with Electrically-Controlled Accessories. Complete with "Lockon" and connecting wires.
Code Word "BURT." Price, 60¢

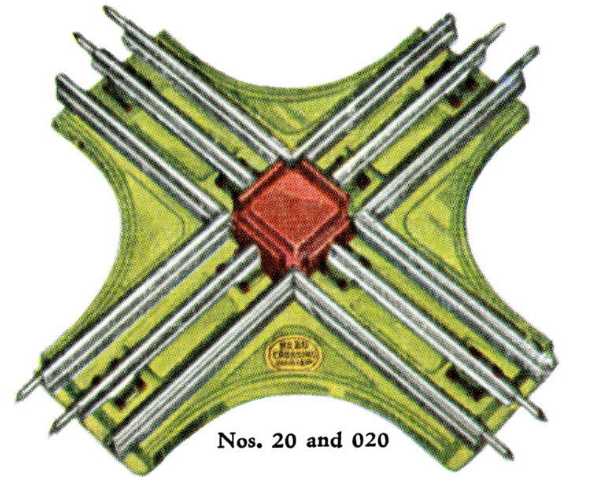

Nos. 20 and 020

Lionel 90 Degree Crossings—A great improvement over our former models. The cross rails are mounted on an ornamental steel base, beautifully enameled. A solid molded fibre block placed in the centre where the rails cross, not only prevents short circuit, but is so constructed that the roller contact shoes on the locomotive and cars easily ride over it without derailing. A large variety of figures can be formed when using these crossings in conjunction with switches and track.

No. 020 Crossing for "O" Gauge Track. Size 8¼ inches square.
Code Word "ORLA." Price, $1.10

No. 20 Crossing for "Lionel Standard" Track. Size 11¾ inches square.
Code Word "BOOST." Price, $1.30

"Lockon" Track Connections
(Patent No. 1542337)

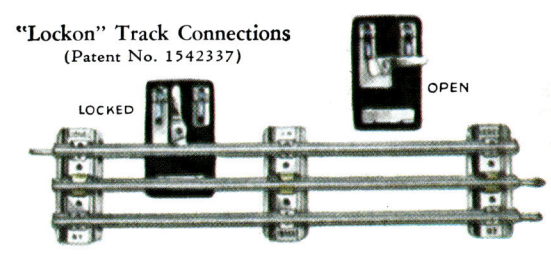

Lionel "Lockon" Connections are attached to the track by simply turning the lever at right angles as shown in the above illustration. The electric connection is as perfect as though the parts were riveted or soldered to the track.

Lionel "Lockon" Connections are free from set screws and binding posts. The fingers that hold the wires in place are made of heavy tempered blue steel and are unbreakable. All other metal parts are nickel-plated and are mounted on a heavy fibre base.

Lionel "Lockon" Connections should be used wherever electric accessories require connection with the track.

OTC "Lockon" for "O" Gauge Track.
Code Word "JOIN." Price, 20¢

STC "Lockon" for "Lionel Standard" Track.
Code Word "JUICE." Price, 25¢

LIONEL ACCESSORY SETS FOR YOUR TRAIN LAYOUT

No. 195
A MODEL VILLAGE. COMPLETELY ILLUMINATED

No. 195 "Lionel Terrace"—A real village in miniature, containing houses and lamp posts all electrically illuminated. Adds realism to your train outfit, and ideal in connection with sister's doll house. The buildings are in a beautiful landscape setting complete with grass plots, bushes, shrubbery, trees and gravel walks. An American flag majestically waves aloft in the centre. The bungalow and villas are described on Page 42 and the lamp posts are shown on Page 43. Completely wired platform is 22 inches long, 19 inches wide. The lamps in the buildings and lamp posts are all wired, ready to be connected. Our lowest priced "Multivolt" transformer, or direct current reducer connected to the house current, or a few dry batteries will light up the entire village.
Code Word "TUFT." Price, $18.00

No. 192
No. 192 Illuminated Villa Set—A handsome assortment of model houses. Comprises 1 No. 191 villa, 1 No. 189 villa, and 2 No. 184 bungalows. All complete with interior lights and connecting wires. Very attractively packed.
Code Word "VILLAGE." Price, $9.00

No. 71
Outfit No. 71—Comprises 6 No. 60 steel telegraph posts, as described on Page 42. This set can be used with either "O" Gauge or "Lionel Standard" Railroads. Very attractively packed.
Code Word "USEFUL." Price, $3.75

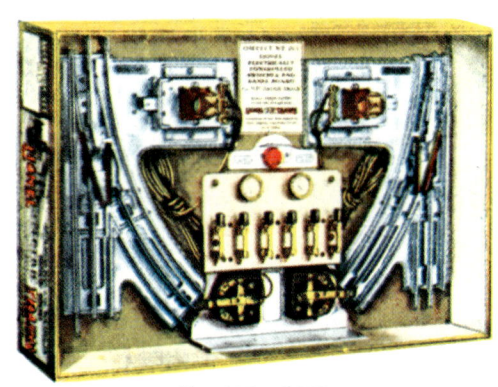

Nos. 013 and 225
No. 225 "Lionel Standard" "Distant-Control" Switch and Panel Board Set—Comprises 1 pair No. 222 "Distant-Control" Switches (right and left hand) and 1 No. 439 illuminated Panel Board. A desirable new accessory for operating a "Distant-Control" Railroad at any distance from the track. Very attractively packed. Complete with lamps and connecting wires.
Code Word "OPERA." Price, $17.50

No. 013 "O" Gauge "Distant-Control" Switch and Panel Board Set—Comprises 1 pair No. 012 "Distant-Control" Switches (right and left hand) and 1 No. 439 illuminated Panel Board. This is the same as the set illustrated above, but is for use on Lionel "O" Gauge Track.
Code Word "OPEN." Price, $15.50

Nos. 071 and 86
No. 86 "Lionel Standard" Telegraph Post Set—These new telegraph posts incorporate a wonderful new feature, namely: the extension arm attached to the base, by means of which the telegraph posts are rigidly fastened to the track. The set comprises 6 No. 85 telegraph posts, 9 inches high, described on Page 42. Attractively packed.
Code Word "TENSE." Price, $4.50

No. 071 "O" Gauge Telegraph Post Set—Same as above, but for "O" Gauge Track. Comprises 6 No. 060 telegraph posts, 5½ inches high, described on Page 42.
Code Word "TAUT." Price, $3.75

No. 186
No. 186 Illuminated Bungalow Set—Comprises 5 No. 184 bungalows, beautifully finished in assorted colors. Complete with interior lights and connecting wires. Attractively packed.
Code Word "HAMLET." Price, $8.00

No. 70
Outfit No. 70—Comprises 2 No. 62 semaphores, 1 No. 59 lamp post, 1 No. 68 warning sign, 2 extra globes for lamp post. Very attractively packed.
Code Word "HOBART." Price, $4.50

[Page Forty]

ALL-STEEL TUNNELS FOR "LIONEL STANDARD" AND "O" GAUGE TRACK

Reg. U. S. Pat. Off.

LIONEL Tunnels are of steel construction throughout, and are accurately designed and formed in our special machinery. Front and rear entrances are embossed in exact reproduction of heavy stone masonry, having a keystone at the top. The bodies of the tunnels represent mountainsides in miniature, and are hand decorated in beautiful harmonizing colors. We draw particular attention to the details on the large size tunnels illustrated below. Mountain roadsides are realistically reproduced, and the little metal "chalets," bridges, architectural and landscaping details are all in perfect proportion to the size of the tunnel. Several of the tunnels listed below are equipped with interior lights, producing a beautiful effect.

No. 120L

No. 120L Tunnel—May be used with all Lionel Outfits.

No. 130L Tunnel—May be used with all "O" Gauge Outfits.

No. 140L Tunnel—May be used with all "Lionel Standard" Outfits.

Nos. 119 and 119L

No. 118—May be used with "O" Gauge Outfits Nos. 249, 292, 232, 234 and 294.

Nos. 119 and 119L Tunnels—May be used with Outfits Nos. 347, 347E, 353, 353E, 385 and 385E for "Lionel Standard" Track, and all "O" Gauge Outfits.

No. 118

No. 120L Illuminated Tunnel—For use with the large size "Lionel Standard" Trains. Hand painted and graceful in design. Equipped with interior light. Length 17 inches, width 12 inches, height 9⅝ inches. Tunnel openings are 6½ inches wide and 8⅛ inches high.
Code Word "HOPE." Price, $6.50

No. 119L Illuminated Tunnel—Suitable for all "O" Gauge Trains and medium size "Lionel Standard" Trains. Equipped with interior light. Length 12 inches, width 9½ inches, height 9¼ inches. Tunnel openings are 5 inches wide and 6½ inches high.
Code Word "HARP." Price, $4.50

No. 119 Tunnel—Similar in every way to No. 119L described above, but without interior light.
Code Word "HOSA." Price, $3.50

No. 118 Tunnel—For use with small size "O" Gauge Trains. Length 8 inches, width 7¼ inches, height 7 inches. Tunnel openings are 4 inches wide and 5⅜ inches high.
Code Word "SIMPLON." Price, $2.25

No. 130L

No. 140L

LIONEL

TUNNELS

ADD REALISM

TO YOUR

MODEL

RAILROAD

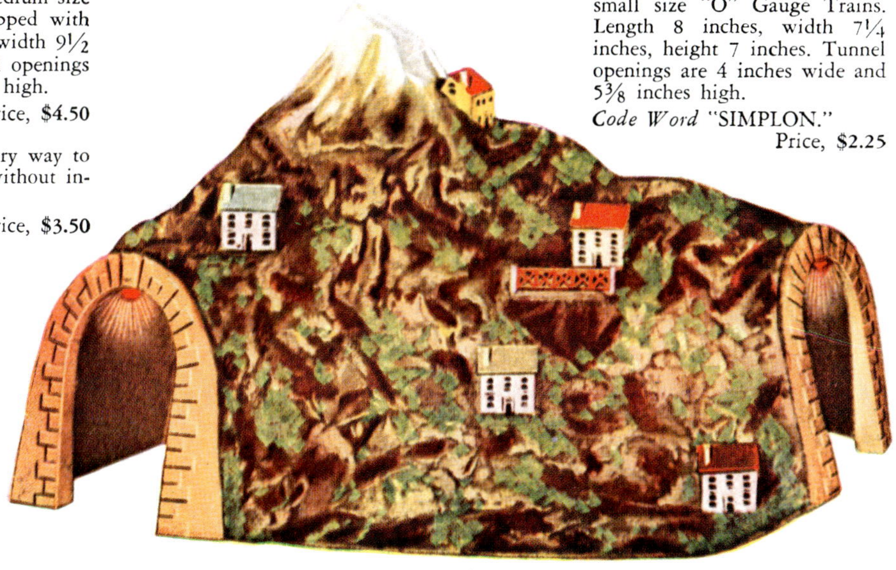

No. 130L Illuminated Tunnel—A beautiful model suitable for use with large "O" Gauge model railroad layouts. It incorporates a wealth of interesting details. Beautifully hand decorated in gorgeous enamel colors, it presents an imposing appearance as the train glides in and out of it. Lights are placed over the forward and rear entrances. Length 24 inches, width 18½ inches, height 14½ inches. Tunnel openings are 5 inches wide and 6½ inches high.
Code Word "SOAK." Price, $14.50

No. 140L Illuminated Tunnel—This is for use with our largest model railroad equipment. No finer accessory for model electric trains has ever been made. This elaborate tunnel is made to fit on the curve of the track, and is so accurately aligned that our largest trains can pass through it easily. The electric lights placed at either end of the tunnel reflect through the windows of the houses on the mountain-side, and present a magnificent vista. Length 35¾ inches, width 23 inches, height 23½ inches. Tunnel openings are 8 inches wide and 8 inches high.
Code Word "SEVA." Price, $17.50

LIONEL ALL-STEEL RAILROAD ACCESSORIES, BUNGALOWS AND VILLAS

No. 62

No. 60

The new Telegraph Posts Nos. 85 and 060 for "Lionel Standard" and "O" Gauge Track are fitted with extension arms, by means of which they can be securely fastened to the track layout. These new Telegraph Posts can also be purchased in sets, as illustrated and described on Page 38.

No. 85

No. 060

No. 068

No. 68

No. 62 Semaphore—The semaphore arm has three discs—red, green and yellow. Arm is operated by lever near base. Enameled steel standard is 8⅞ inches high.

Code Word "CAUTION." Price, 90¢

No. 60 Telegraph Post—Arm is equipped with real glass insulators. Enameled steel standard is 8⅞ inches high.

Code Word "WIRE." Price, 65¢

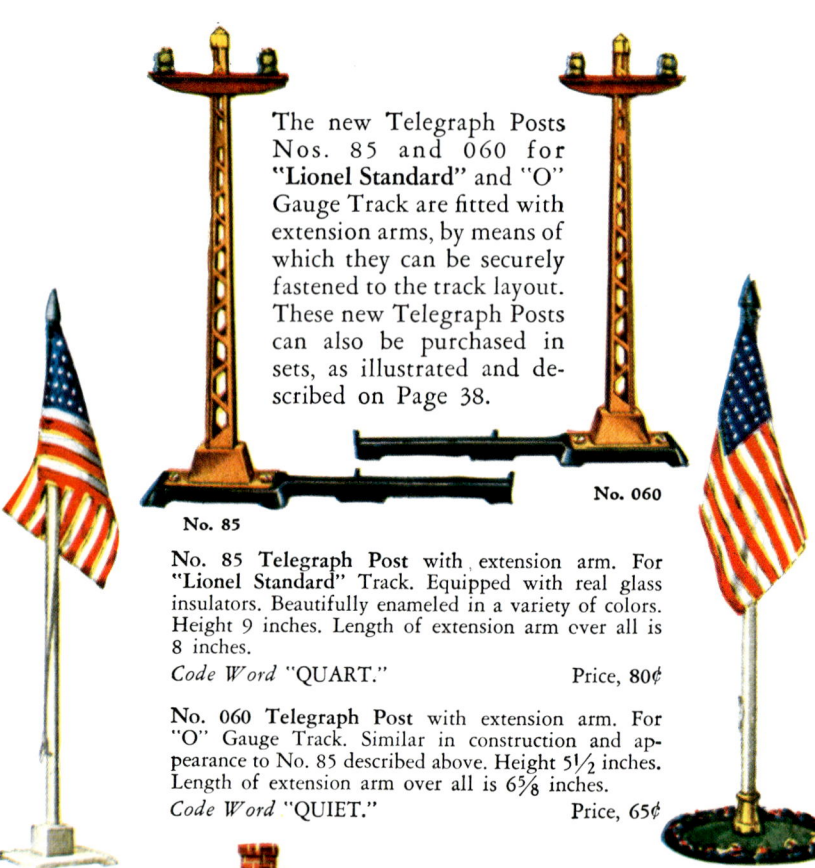

No. 85 Telegraph Post with extension arm. For "Lionel Standard" Track. Equipped with real glass insulators. Beautifully enameled in a variety of colors. Height 9 inches. Length of extension arm over all is 8 inches.

Code Word "QUART." Price, 80¢

No. 060 Telegraph Post with extension arm. For "O" Gauge Track. Similar in construction and appearance to No. 85 described above. Height 5½ inches. Length of extension arm over all is 6⅝ inches.

Code Word "QUIET." Price, 65¢

No. 68 Warning Signal—For "Lionel Standard" Track. Enameled steel standard is 8⅞ inches high. Brass sign is 3½ inches square.

Code Word "STOP." Price, 90¢

No. 068 Warning Signal—For "O" Gauge Track. Similar to No. 68, but is 6⅝ inches high. Brass sign is 2⅞ inches square.

Code Word "LOOK." Price, 50¢

No. 89

No. 90

No. 191

No. 184

No. 189

No. 89 Flagstaff and Flag—For use with Lionel model villages or to place in front of a Lionel Station. Flagstaff is 14¼ inches high. Silk flag may be lowered by cord attached, which can be fastened to hook near the base.

Code Word "ARTHUR." Price, 80¢

No. 90 Flagstaff and Flag—The flagstaff (14¾ inches high) is removable, and fits into an ornamental base mounted on a miniature grass plot beautifully ornamented with flower border.

Code Word "PLOT." Price, $1.30

No. 191 Illuminated Villa—Beautifully designed. 7⅛ inches long, 5 inches wide and 5¼ inches high. Roof is removable. Complete with interior lighting fixture, lamp and connecting wires.

Code Word "SOLID." Price, $3.50

No. 184 Illuminated Bungalow—4¾ inches long, 4 inches high, 2¾ inches wide. Beautifully decorated. Complete with interior light and connecting wires.

Code Word "HOME." Price, $1.60

No. 189 Illuminated Villa—A model that is architecturally perfect. Finished in a variety of harmonizing enamel colors. 5½ inches long, 5 inches wide, 5½ inches high. Complete with interior light and connecting wires.

Code Word "MANSE." Price, $3.10

[Page Forty-two]

LIONEL ALL-STEEL LAMP POSTS

NO Model Railroad is complete without the addition of **Lionel** Lamp Posts—faithful reproductions of boulevard and street lamp posts seen everywhere. All **Lionel** Lamp Posts are of steel construction, enameled in a variety of beautiful colors.

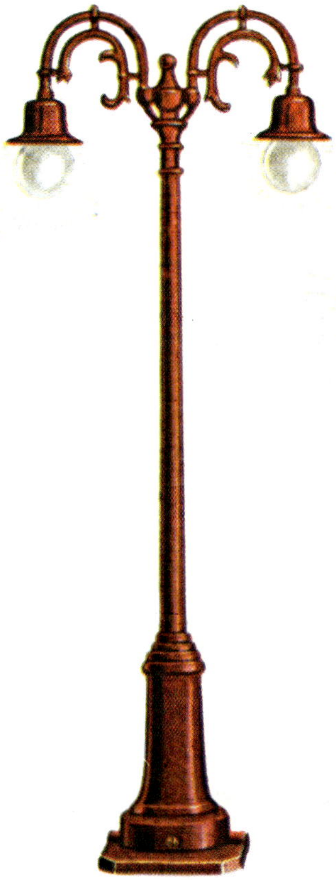

No. 54
No. 54 Lamp Post—9½ inches high. Complete with two globes. An attractive new double-arm lamp post.
Code Word "MOLD."
Price, $2.35

No. 57
No. 57 Lamp Post—7½ inches high. The top is removable so that the lamp can be renewed. Complete with lamp.
Code Word "CHEERY."
Price, $1.75

No. 58
No. 58 Lamp Post—7½ inches high. Complete with globe.
Code Word "JENNY."
Price, $1.30

No. 56
No. 56 Lamp Post—7¾ inches high. The top is removable so that the lamp can be renewed. Complete with lamp.
Code Word "SHINE."
Price, $1.75

No. 59
No. 59 Lamp Post—Similar in design to No. 61, but is 8⅝ inches high. Complete with globe.
Code Word "BRIGHT."
Price, $1.60

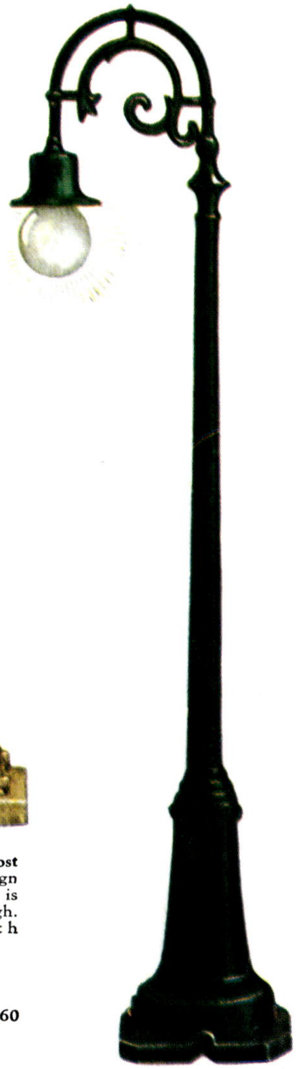

No. 67
No. 67 Lamp Post—12⅝ inches high. Complete with two globes.
Code Word "EDMUNDS."
Price, $3.00

No. 61
No. 61 Lamp Post—12⅝ inches high. Complete with globe.
Code Word "INDIA."
Price, $2.25

LIONEL LAMP CABINET — FOR DEALERS

No. 111 Lionel Lamp Cabinet—We supply Lionel dealers with a handsome cabinet of lamps for use in headlights and all electrically illuminated accessories. These lamps are of the finest quality and are supplied in 12 volts and 18 volts suitable for "O" Gauge or "Lionel Standard" equipment. Fifty assorted lamps are packed in each cabinet. The chart on inside of cover gives valuable information for the use of various lamps. Each lamp is packed in a special container. Cabinet contains 50 assorted lamps.
Code Word "LUX."   Price, $15.00

COLORED LAMPS FOR ACCESSORIES

No. 27R Red Lamp—12 volts, ½" round. *Code Word* "NOUN." Price, 30c
No. 28R Red Lamp—18 volts, ½" round. *Code Word* "NORTH." Price, 30c
No. 27G Green Lamp—12 volts, ½" round. *Code Word* "NAIL." Price, 30c
No. 28G Green Lamp—18 volts, ½" round. *Code Word* "NEAT." Price, 30c

The red lamps listed above are for use in the Nos. 025 and 25 Bumpers, No. 79 Flashing Railroad Signal, and No. 77 and 077 Crossing Gates.
The green lamps listed above are for use in the front and rear lanterns of No. 408E Locomotive.

LIONEL LAMP RENEWALS
Each Lamp Packed in Special Container.

No. 27—12 volt, ½" round lamp. For use in all "O" Gauge equipment. *Code Word* "NOSE." Price, 30c
No. 23—18 volt, ½" round lamp. For use in all "Lionel Standard" equipment. *Code Word* "NELA." Price, 30c
No. 39—12 volt, ¾" round globe. For "O" Gauge Railroads use this lamp on Nos. 54, 58, 59, 61 and 67 Lamp Posts and No. 124 station. *Code Word* "NICE." Price, 30c
No. 40—18 volt, ¾" round globe. Same uses as No. 39 lamp, when operating "Lionel Standard" equipment. *Code Word* "NAVY." Price, 30c

[Page Forty-Three]

ALL STEEL STATIONS AND POWER HOUSE

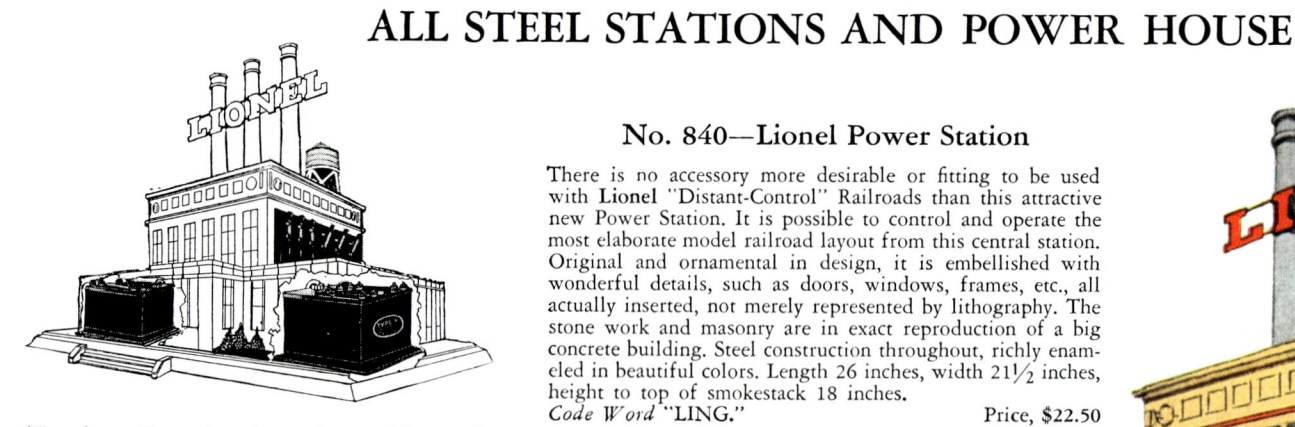

No. 840—Lionel Power Station

There is no accessory more desirable or fitting to be used with Lionel "Distant-Control" Railroads than this attractive new Power Station. It is possible to control and operate the most elaborate model railroad layout from this central station. Original and ornamental in design, it is embellished with wonderful details, such as doors, windows, frames, etc., all actually inserted, not merely represented by lithography. The stone work and masonry are in exact reproduction of a big concrete building. Steel construction throughout, richly enameled in beautiful colors. Length 26 inches, width 21½ inches, height to top of smokestack 18 inches.
Code Word "LING." Price, $22.50

The above illustration shows the provision made for accommodating one or two **Lionel** Transformers. The switches on the transformers can be reached through openings above them. Illustration also shows the Panel Board on one side of the Power House containing six knife switches, from which "Distant-Control" trains and illuminated accessories can be operated.

No. 124 Illuminated Station—Equipped with two corner platform lights and reflectors, finished in polished nickel. These lighting brackets have beautifully designed supporting arms. Also fitted with inside light supported on a nickeled fixture. Roof is removable so that interior lamp can be easily reached. 13¾ inches long, 9¼ inches wide and 10 inches high. Complete with electric lamps and connecting wires.
Code Word "READE." Price, $9.50

No. 122 Illuminated Station—This is in every way similar to No. 124 Station described above, but has one inside electric light supported on a nickeled fixture. Complete with electric lamp and connecting wires.
Code Word "CENT." Price, $6.50

No. 126 Illuminated Station—Specially designed for use with our smaller train outfits and has many of the architectural features of our larger models. The interior light is supported on a fixture placed beneath the removable roof. 10¼ inches long, 7¼ inches wide and 7 inches high. Complete with electric lamp and connecting wires.
Code Word "ALITE." Price, $4.75

No. 127 Illuminated Station—For use with any "O" Gauge Train. Interior light is fastened to a supporting fixture. Roof is removable so that lamp can be easily reached. 8½ inches long, 4¼ inches wide and 5 inches high. Complete with electric lamp and connecting wires.
Code Word "TONLY." Price, $3.10

[*Page Forty-four*]

ALL STEEL STATION, POWER HOUSE, SWITCH SIGNAL TOWERS AND PANEL BOARD

An Attractive Addition to a Lionel Railroad

No. 128—This elaborate new station is up to date in every detail. It is mounted on a terrace which contains landscaped flower beds. In the center bravely floats an American flag mounted on a tall flagstaff. A beautifully designed stairway leads from the ground to the terrace. The retaining wall surrounding the structure represents ornamental masonry. The station is illuminated inside and out by electric bulbs, and beautiful torches illuminate the terrace. The roof is removable so that the electric fixture in the interior can easily be reached. This elaborate station is made entirely of heavy steel, beautifully enameled and decorated. It is 31½ inches long, 18 inches deep and 12 inches high.
Code Word "YEN." Price, $26.25

No. 129 Station Platform

This platform is the same as the one described to the left, and is listed separately so that owners of Lionel Stations Nos. 124, 122 and 121 can make use of them in this most elaborate setting, which so greatly adds to the appearance of the entire railroad layout.
Code Word "YIELD." Price, $16.75

No. 438 Illuminated Signal Tower—Equipped with 2 knife switches from which "Distant-Control" Trains and Accessories can be operated. Roof is removable so that interior light can be reached. Mounted on a beautiful steel elevation, embossed with rivets, etc. Base represents concrete. A brass ladder runs up the entire length of the steel work. Height is 12 inches. Base measures 6 by 4¾ inches. Electric lamp and connecting wires included.
Code Word "CARP." Price, $5.00

Lionel Power Stations—Made in 2 sizes to fit all types of Lionel "Multivolt" Transformers. Base is hollow, so that transformer easily sets within. Grid in roof is removable.

No. 435—Size 7⅞ by 6 inches. 9½ inches high to chimney. For use with Types A, B or F Transformers.
Code Word "JENA." Price, $2.75

No. 436—Size 9¼ by 7⅝ inches. 10½ inches high to chimney. For use with Types T, C and K Transformers.
Code Word "WATTS." Price, $3.50

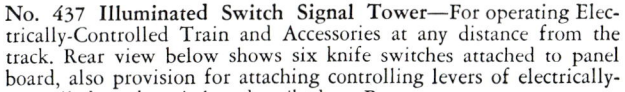

No. 437 Illuminated Switch Signal Tower—For operating Electrically-Controlled Train and Accessories at any distance from the track. Rear view below shows six knife switches attached to panel board, also provision for attaching controlling levers of electrically-controlled track switches described on Page 38. Note the wonderful detail in the windows, doors and panels, which are separable inserted pieces. Size 10¼ inches long, 8⅞ inches high, 8⅜ inches wide. Complete with electric lamp and connecting wires.
Code Word "ZEV." Price, $9.00

No. 439 Panel Board—You can operate your trains and accessories from one or more of the six knife switches mounted on the marble Panel Board. Provision is made for holding two levers of Lionel Electrically-Controlled Switches, shown in illustration below. Electric lamp at top illuminates small dummy meters. Made of heavy steel beautifully enameled, and the knife switches are mounted on a composition marble slab. Size 8¼ inches high and 7¼ inches wide.
Code Word "FLOW." Price, $5.75

[Page Forty-Five]

No. 300 STEEL BRIDGE
For "O" Gauge or "Lionel Standard" Railroads

This is the most realistic bridge that has ever been produced for model railroads. It is a replica of the famous "Hell-Gate" Bridge which spans the East River in New York. It is constructed entirely of sheet steel, and is enameled in beautiful colors. The Bridge is 28¾ inches long, 11 inches high and 10⅞ inches wide. The train passes through the bridge at its own level without the necessity of grade approaches. Any boy should be proud to own this marvelous bridge.
Code Word "HELGA."   Price, $16.50

"LIONEL STANDARD" BRIDGES

No. 104 Span—For "Lionel Standard" Track. 14 inches long, 6½ inches wide, 6¼ inches high. Complete with track.
Code Word "MANN."   Price, $3.50

No. 100 Approaches (two sections)—For "Lionel Standard" Track. Construction is the same as No. 105 described in opposite column. Complete length 28¼ in., height 2 in. at centre, width 5⅜ in. Complete with track.
Code Word "BROOKLYN."   Price, $2.60

No. 101 Bridge (three sections)—For "Lionel Standard" Track. Complete structure is 42¼ inches long, 6½ inches wide, 6¼ inches high. Complete with track.
Code Word "QUEENS."   Price, $6.00

No. 102 Bridge (four sections)—For "Lionel Standard" Track. Complete structure is 56½ inches long, 6½ inches wide, 6¼ inches high. Complete with track.
Code Word "KEEPSIE."   Price, $9.00

No. 103 Bridge (five sections) Same in appearance as No. 102 Bridge—For "Lionel Standard" Track. Contains three centre spans and two approaches. Complete structure is 70½ inches long, 6½ inches wide, 6¼ inches high. Complete with track.
Code Word "LONDON."   Price, $11.50

ALL STEEL BRIDGES

No other model railroad bridges approach Lionel for sturdiness of construction and realism of appearance. They are all designed after famous bridges throughout the country. They are elaborately embossed, and beautifully finished. In addition to the bridges illustrated, a bridge of any desired size may be constructed by adding extra spans. Your railroad system cannot be complete without a Lionel Bridge.

"O" GAUGE BRIDGES

No. 110 Span—For "O" Gauge Track. 10½ in. long, 5½ in. wide, 4⅛ in. high. Complete with track.
Code Word "WILLY."   Price, $2.60

No. 105 Approaches (two sections) For "O" Gauge Track. Made in reproduction of reinforced concrete. Complete length 21¼ in., height 2 in. at centre, width 4⅛ in. Complete with track.
Code Word "PARIS."   Price, $1.75

No. 106 Bridge (three sections)—For "O" Gauge Track. Complete structure is 32½ in. long, 5½ in. wide, 4⅛ in. high. Complete with track.
Code Word "CONN."   Price, $3.50

No. 108 Bridge (four sections)—For "O" Gauge Track. Complete structure is 43 inches long, 5½ inches wide, 4⅛ inches high. Complete with track.
Code Word "HOUSA."   Price, $5.75

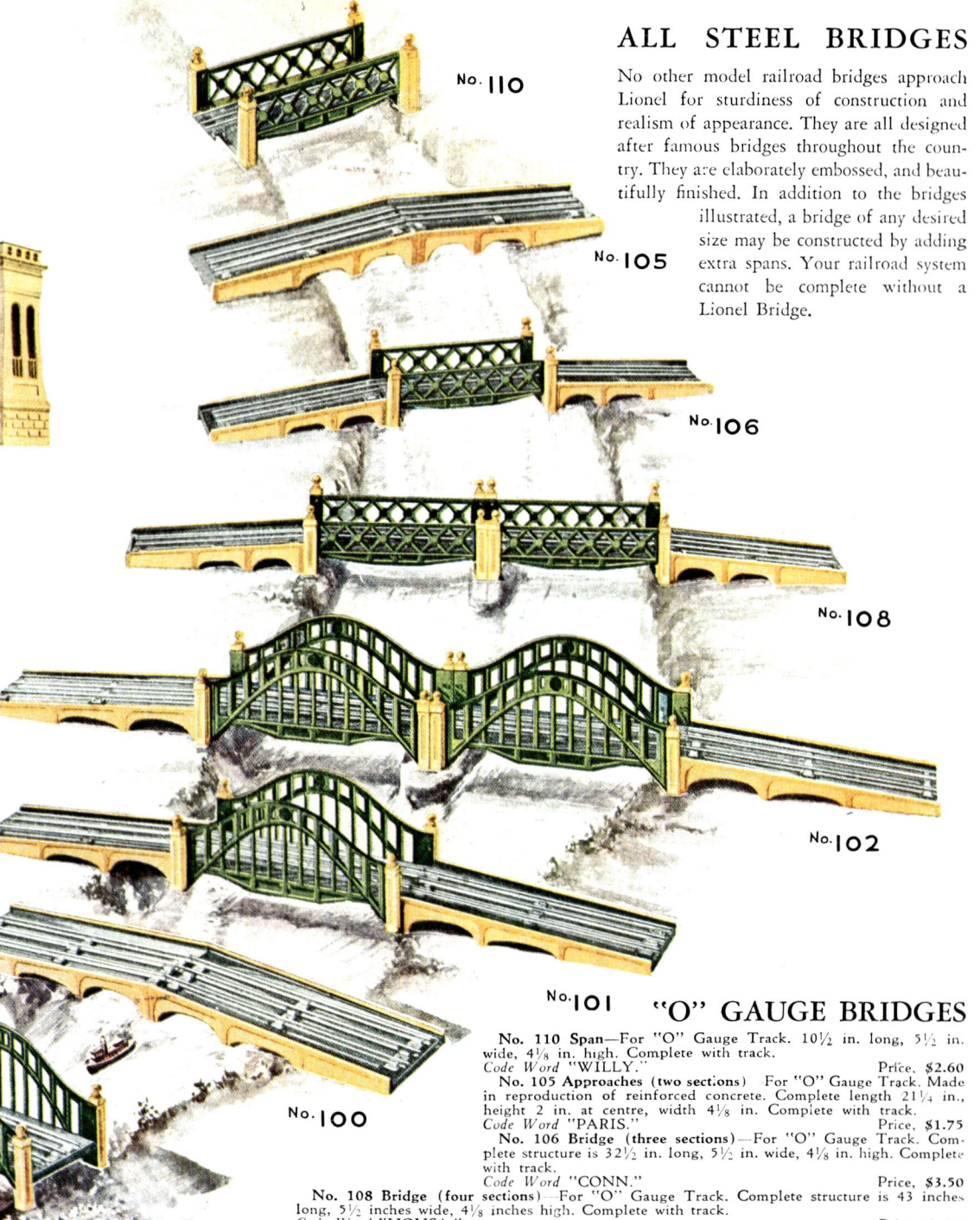

No. 109 Bridge (five sections) Same in appearance as No. 108 Bridge. For "O" Gauge Track. Contains three centre spans and two approaches. Complete structure is 53⅞ inches long, 5½ inches wide, 4⅛ inches high. Complete with track.
Code Word "MISS."   Price, $7.75

"LIONEL STANDARD" AND "O" GAUGE TRACK FORMATIONS

TRACK FIG. OA ("O" Gauge) requires: 12—OC curved track; 4—OS straight track; 1—020, 90 degree crossing. Size over all 70 x 30 in.

TRACK FIG. SA ("Lionel Standard") requires: 12—C curved track; 4—S straight track; 1—20, 90 degree crossing. Size over all 97 x 43 in.

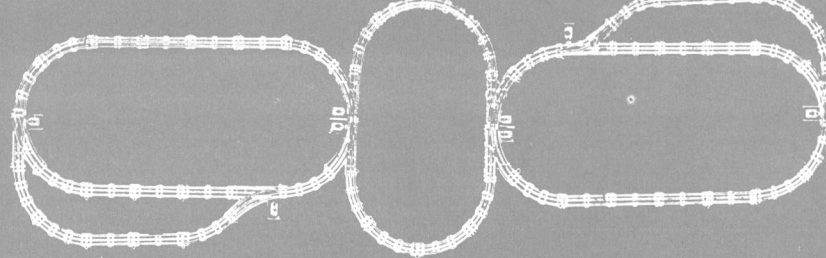

TRACK FIG. OB ("O" Gauge) requires: 24—OC curved track; 18—OS straight track; 2—right hand No. 021 switches; 6—left hand No. 021 switches. Size over all 173 x 53 in.

TRACK FIG. SB ("Lionel Std.") requires: 24—C curved track; 18—S straight track; 2—right hand No. 210 switches; 6—left hand No. 210 switches. Size over all 241 x 71 in.

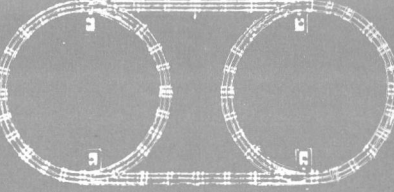

TRACK FIG. OD ("O" Gauge) requires: 12—OC curved track; 4—OS straight track; 2—right hand No. 021 switches; 2—left hand No. 021 switches. Size over all 71 x 30 in.

TRACK FIG. SD ("Lionel Std.") requires: 12—C curved track; 4—S straight track; 2—right hand No. 210 switches; 2—left hand No. 210 switches. Size over all 98 x 42 in.

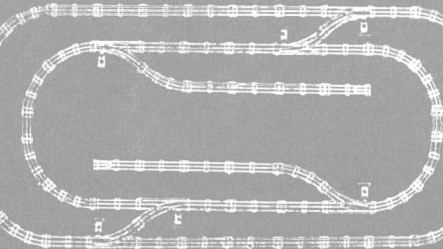

TRACK FIG. OE ("O" Gauge) requires: 32—OS straight track; 18—OC curved track; 2—½ OS straight track; 2—right hand No. 021 switches; 4—left hand No. 021 switches; 2—023 bumpers. Size over all 113 x 52 in.

TRACK FIG. SE ("Lionel Standard") requires: 32—S straight track; 18—C curved track; 2—½ S straight track; 2—right hand No. 210 switches; 4—left hand No. 210 switches; 2—23 bumpers. Size over all 154 x 71 in.

TRACK FIG. OF ("O" Gauge) requires: 16—OC curved track; 4—OS straight track; 2—right hand No. 021 switches; 2—left hand No. 021 switches; 1—020, 90 degree crossing. Size over all 90 x 30 in.

TRACK FIG. SF ("Lionel Std.") requires: 16—C curved track; 4—S straight track; 2—right hand No. 210 switches; 2—left hand No. 210 switches; 1—20, 90 degree crossing. Size over all 124 x 43 in.

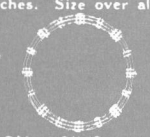

TRACK FIG. OH ("O" Gauge) requires: 8—OC curved track, making a circle 30 in. in diameter.

TRACK FIG. SH ("Lionel Std.") requires: 8—C curved track, making a circle 43 in. in diameter.

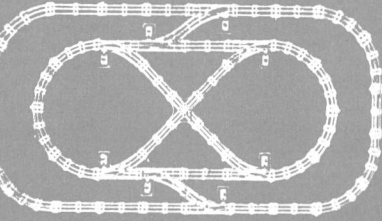

TRACK FIG. OJ ("O" Gauge) requires: 18—OS straight track; 16—OC curved track; 4—right hand No. 021 switches; 4—left hand No. 021 switches; 1—020, 90 degree crossing. Size over all 92 x 41 in.

TRACK FIG. SJ ("Lionel Standard") requires: 18—S straight track; 16—C curved track; 4—right hand No. 210 switches; 4—left hand No. 210 switches; 1—20, 90 degree crossing. Size over all 126 x 57 in.

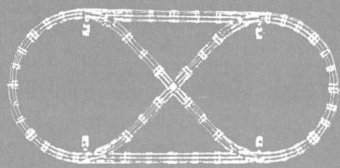

TRACK FIG. OK ("O" Gauge) requires: 14—OC curved track; 1—020X, 45 degree crossing. Size over all 61 x 30 in.

TRACK FIG. SK ("Lionel Standard") requires: 14—C curved track; 1—20X, 45 degree crossing. Size over all 88 x 43 in.

TRACK FIG. OL ("O" Gauge) requires: 8—OC curved track; 9—OS straight track; 2—right hand No. 021 switches. Size over all 71 x 30 in.

TRACK FIG. SL ("Lionel Std.") requires: 8—C curved track; 9—S straight track; 2—right hand No. 210 switches. Size over all 98 x 43 in.

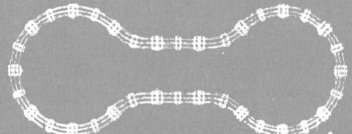

TRACK FIG. OM ("O" Gauge) requires: 8—OC curved track; 8—OS straight track; 2—right hand No. 021 switches; 2—left hand No. 021 switches; 1—020, 90 degree crossing. Size over all 71 x 30 in.

TRACK FIG. SM ("Lionel Std.") requires: 8—C curved track; 8—S straight track; 2—right hand No. 210 switches; 2—left hand No. 210 switches; 1—20, 90 degree crossing. Size over all 98 x 43 in.

TRACK FIG. ON ("O" Gauge) requires: 16—OC curved track; 2—OS straight track. Size over all 81 x 30 in.

TRACK FIG. SN ("Lionel Standard") requires: 16—C curved track; 2—S straight track. Size over all 117 x 43 in.

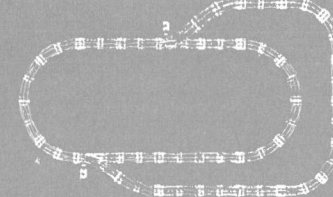

TRACK FIG. OP ("O" Gauge) requires: 14—OC curved track; 12—OS straight track; 1—right hand No. 021 switch; 1—left hand No. 021 switch. Size over all 82 x 51 in.

TRACK FIG. SP ("Lionel Standard") requires: 14—C curved track; 12—S straight track; 1—right hand No. 210 switch; 1—left hand No. 210 switch. Size over all 112 x 71 in.

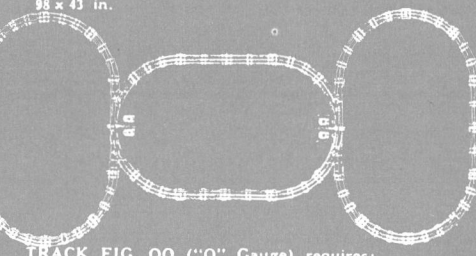

TRACK FIG. OQ ("O" Gauge) requires: 20—OC curved track; 8—OS straight track; 2—right hand No. 021 switches; 2—left hand No. 021 switches. Size over all 110 x 50 in.

TRACK FIG. SQ ("Lionel Std.") requires: 20—C curved track; 8—S straight track; 2—right hand No. 210 switches; 2—left hand No. 210 switches. Size over all 154 x 71 in.

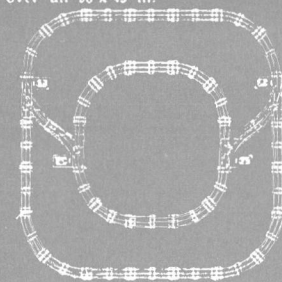

TRACK FIG. OR ("O" Gauge) requires: 16—OC curved track; 12—OS straight track; 2—right hand No. 021 switches; 2—left hand No. 021 switches. Size over all 61 x 61 in.

TRACK FIG. SR ("Lionel Std.") requires: 16—C curved track; 12—S straight track; 2—right hand No. 210 switches; 2—left hand No. 210 switches. Size over all 85 x 85 in.

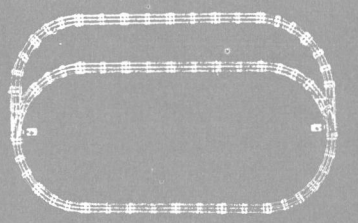

TRACK FIG. OT ("O" Gauge) requires: 10—OC curved track; 12—OS straight track; 1—right hand No. 021 switch; 1—left hand No. 021 switch. Size over all 71 x 40 in.

TRACK FIG. ST ("Lionel Standard") requires: 10—C curved track; 12—S straight track; 1—right hand No. 210 switch; 1—left hand No. 210 switch. Size over all 98 x 57 in.

You may use No. 25 or 025 illuminated bumpers instead of Nos. 23 and 023 spring bumpers if desired. You may use No. 222 or 012 electrically-controlled switches instead of Nos. 210 and 021 hand-controlled switches. REFER TO PAGES 38 AND 39 FOR PRICES OF SEPARATE PARTS USED IN MAKING THESE TRACK FORMATIONS

Manufactured and Guaranteed by THE LIONEL CORPORATION 15 East 26th Street, New York, N.Y.

A REAL ELECTRIC RANGE FOR GIRLS

GIRLS, the new Lionel Electric Range is built absolutely in accordance with specifications of the large ranges used by Mother. It is of the correct size to enable you to cook and bake, the same as Mother does, and yet it is small enough to be used in the playroom.

No range ever produced before is built like the Lionel. It is in a class by itself. It must not be confused with other toy electric ranges. It is real in everything but size. Imagine owning an electric range with a porcelain finish and equipped with genuine practical heating units! It is the only toy range ever built, that is finished in porcelain. You do not have to sit on the floor in order to bake or cook with this range, nor does the range have to be placed on a table. It is just of the right height for you to stand in front of it and start right in cooking.

The Lionel Range can be used in absolute safety by the smallest girl and has the approval of the Underwriters Laboratories.

Feast your eyes on its beautiful contrasting colors! Rub your hand over the glossy, gleaming porcelain! Marvel at the lasting, highly nickeled cooking top! Examine the heat indicator in the oven door! See the gleam of the red pilot light when the current is turned on! All of these details can only be found in the Lionel Range for Girls or in Mother's real electric range.

Specifications and Dimensions of Lionel Range:

THERE are two electric units in the oven, one or both of which can be used by means of the two switches on the panel board. There are also two open burners, both of which can be used at the same time. A toggle switch throws all the current into the oven or into the burners. A pilot light shines red as soon as the current is turned on. The oven door is equipped with a thermometer showing the temperature in the oven. The range is finished in beautiful porcelain colors.

Heating units in oven are 625 watts each, or 1250 watts for both. Heating units for open burners are 625 watts each. They are made of the best grade of nichrome wire.

Height over all   33 inches
Width . . .   26 inches
Depth . . .   12 inches
Height of cooking units from floor . .   25½ inches
Dimensions of oven   9½ inches square

Included with this Range are 5 cooking utensils.

Code Word "COOKERY."

Price, $29.50

LIONEL ELECTRIC TRAINS
THE TRAINS THAT RAILROAD MEN BUY FOR THEIR BOYS

"Just Like Mine", SAYS BOB BUTTERFIELD, ENGINEER OF THE "20TH CENTURY LIMITED" (See Page 3)

MODEL RAILROADING IS A ROMANTIC ADVENTURE

SAMUEL VAUCLAIN, PRESIDENT, BALDWIN LOCOMOTIVE WORKS, AND HIS GRANDCHILDREN WITH THEIR LIONEL ELECTRIC TRAINS

"In my boyhood, railroads seemed more romantic and adventurous than any other calling and they have never ceased to provide that interest to this day. There is great work yet to be done in the further development of railroading, for a railroad and its equipment are never a finished job. The opportunities of the future in transportation call for the exercise of practically unlimited inventive and engineering skill and business ability in the further perfecting of our railroads. Railroading today promises more of romance, adventure and breadth of experience than ever before in the history or transportation."

GENERAL W. W. ATTERBURY,
President, The Pennsylvania Railroad.

Lionel Electric Trains afford the American Boy the thrill and adventure of railroading. They provide him with the means of exercising his mind so that he may grow up to be the type of man who will add his inventiveness and effort to the development of the country's future, as General W. W. Atterbury so vividly testifies.

GENERAL W. W. ATTERBURY—PRES. THE PENNSYLVANIA RAILROAD

[Page Two]

FAMOUS ENGINEERS WHO HAVE CHOSEN LIONEL TRAINS FOR THEIR BOYS

Leading railroad executives and engineers were invited to examine Lionel Model Electric Railroads and to express an opinion concerning them. All agreed that Lionel trains and accessories are extraordinarily accurate copies of actual railroad locomotives, cars and equipment. It was also found in many cases their sons or grandsons were proud possessors of Lionel trains. You can't find better evidence than this! **"Lionel trains are the trains railroad men buy for their boys."**

Read what these famous engineers have to say.

"Boys often come to me at the different railroad stations along the line and ask me questions about my engine, and about railroads. I find that most of them have Lionel trains—and that these fine model electric railroads have taught them a great deal about railroad operation. Lionel railroads are best for every boy, because there is no make-believe about them. They are like real railroads in everything but size. I like their strength—their speed and their beautiful colors.

S. E. Godshall

ENGINEER S. E. GODSHALL
"Pennsylvania Limited,"
Pennsylvania R. R.

"The Lionel 'Blue Comet' model train that my grandsons have, is just like the big 'Blue Comet' that I drive daily between New York and Atlantic City. You can tell the boys of the country for me that Lionel trains are the only real, true-to-life model trains that I know of. They are so sturdy, so beautifully made and so accurate in detail that every boy will enjoy playing with them—and learn as he plays. I call it real railroading in miniature."

W. J. Smith

ENGINEER W. J. SMITH
"Blue Comet"
Jersey Central R. R.

"Of course I buy Lionel Model Electric trains for my boy! They are like real trains in everything but size—they operate like real trains. You can build a complete railroad system with Lionel Trains and Accessories—approximating actual railroad conditions almost to a 'T.' My boy gets real fun out of Lionel railroading, and besides it develops his little mind. I'm for Lionel Electric Trains."

John A. Garlitz

ENGINEER J. A. GARLITZ
Baltimore & Ohio R. R.

"There can only be one answer to the question, 'What railroad trains do I buy for my boys?'—**Lionel Trains!** Why? Because they are true to life, true to detail, mechanically perfect, long-lasting, beautiful copies of the great engines and cars that we have on our great railroad. I teach my grandsons railroading with Lionel equipment. They learn the principles of railroad operation—the switching and movement of trains. They learn something of mechanics, something of electricity, and they have a world of fun besides. Lionel trains are the only trains I would select for boys."

Robert E. Butterfield

ENGINEER R. E. BUTTERFIELD
"20TH CENTURY"
New York Central R. R.

[Page Three]

1931

WHY RAILROAD MEN SELECT LIONEL TRAINS FOR THEIR BOYS

THERE must be a reason why Lionel Trains are "The trains that Railroad men buy for their Boys." For Railroad men know trains and they know what is best for their boys.

They know that Model Railroading with Lionel Electric Trains is not only great fun but it is the means of learning many things. For, as you play with your Lionel train you will find out why and how they operate and the part that electricity plays in operating them.

Perhaps your dad, as well as thousands of other boys' dads, obtained his early training for the job he holds to-day, by playing with a Lionel train.

Lionel trains have been made for over 31 years; each year growing better and better; keeping pace with the modern improvements on the big railroads of the country.

When your dad had his Lionel years ago, it was then a fine copy of the railroads of the day. But now, you can have a train that is superior. You can have a greater choice of the most complete model railroad equipment ever built. When your dad gets you your Lionel Electric Train for Christmas, you can be sure that you will be playing with a real train, real equipment, real signals, real—like the big railroads, except for size.

LIONEL 100% DISTANT CONTROL SYSTEM

Think what you could do with Lionel's Distant Control. You can sit far away from your train, even in another room, if you like, and you can operate your Railroad. You can make the train go forward, stop and reverse without touching the train itself. And that's not all. The gates at the crossing will lower and raise by themselves, their red lanterns glowing brilliantly. Bells will ring their warning, traffic lights will blink. The distant control system, by means of a small lever, makes it possible for you to switch your freight on to a siding while the Lionel Limited roars past. Picture the thrill of knowing that at your finger tips you can have complete control of your whole railroad system. It is a thrill that you can only experience with Lionel Trains.

The Lionel Distant Control Locomotives and train outfits in this Planning Book are distinguished by the letter "E" after the catalog number. Many of the marvelous "E" motors are of the Lionel "Bild-a-Loco" type. This "Bild-a-Loco" motor can be snapped out of the locomotive in a jiffy. This means that you can examine the construction, clean and oil the motor. There are no wires to disconnect, the electrical contacts are automatic.

You cannot realize what all this means until you see for yourself. Go to your nearest dealer—he will be glad to let you examine every part of a Lionel train. Then you can feel its solidity. You can see how powerful the locomotives are. You can see the brilliant, glossy smoothness of their enamel finish. You can see for yourself why Lionel Electric Trains are "The trains that Railroad men buy for their Boys."

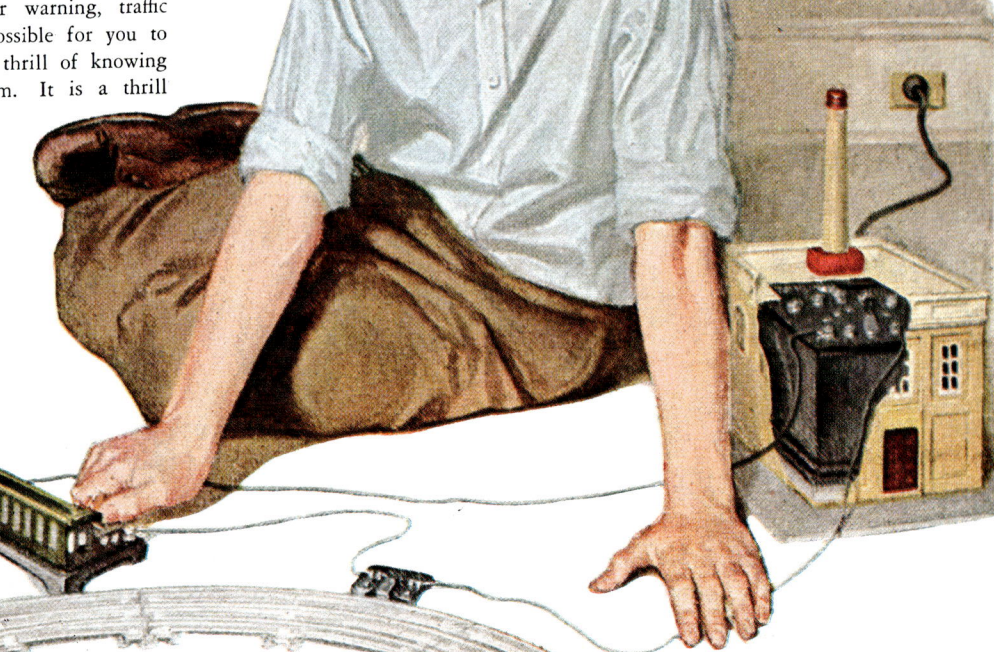

[Page Four]

STERLING SILVER FOR STERLING QUALITY LIONEL TRAINS

Immense Power Presses stamp the heavy steel sheets into Lionel Locomotives and Cars.

Automatic Machines construct Lionel track by the millions.

The real Santa Claus who makes the original models of Lionel Locomotives.

So great is the demand for Lionel Electric Trains that it takes 3 large modern factories to produce enough trains to supply the boys of America.

You can get a better idea of how wonderful Lionel Trains are, when we tell you what materials are used in making them and the tremendous quantities necessary. To be sure that these materials are the best, they are thoroughly tested in our own Laboratories.

You will be amazed to know that in order to produce a year's supply of Lionel Trains, we require 2,375,000 pounds of cold rolled steel. Not just ordinary tin, but real steel which, when stamped under tremendous pressure, becomes locomotives and cars.

Can you picture 97,950,000 feet of copper wire? I guess not. If it were stretched in a continuous line, it would measure 18,660 miles or two-thirds around the world. Now, add to this, 500,000 feet of nickel resistance wire and what total do you get?

There are more than 3,600,000 parts made of copper in a year's supply of Lionel Electric Trains. And, in addition to this, we use 29,000 pounds of brass sheets, which when finished, make 3,840,000 nameplates and other parts.

Of the screw machine parts, there are 30,250,000 of 159 different kinds. We will bet you wouldn't want to sort them out. Neither would we. We started to add the number of machined screws, rivets and bolts and they ran into millions.

Now, you may want to know how we get those beautiful colors which make Lionel Trains so good to look at. Of the best enamels obtainable, we use 5,000 gallons in 34 different colors, which when mixed under the trained eyes of Lionel color experts, become the multicolored spectrum of the Lionel Palette.

And, if you were walking through the factory, you would see an immense stock of kegs and you would want to know what they contained. In these drums we store a thousand gallons of varnish and you will never guess where most of it is used. It is employed to insulate the silk covered wire that's wound around the motor, and to impregnate the core and coils of Lionel "Multivolt" Transformers. You see, we take no chances. No wonder Lionel Motors and Transformers last for years.

Speaking of Motors, do you know that we use the purest sterling silver obtainable? Yes, indeed. There are myriads of sterling silver contact points. We use silver because good silver is the best conductor known and we would use platinum if it would make Lionel Trains any better.

In addition to all these materials, you could never guess what else goes into the manufacture of Lionel Locomotives, Cars and Accessories. Here are a few of them: Bakelite, Fibre, Asbestos, Porcelain, Rubber, Monel Metal, Aluminum, Nickel, Zinc, Solder, Glass, Celluloid, Silk, Cotton, Wood, Linen, and many, many more!

THE LIONEL CORPORATION, 15 East 26th Street, New York

WHAT EVERY BOY SHOULD KNOW ABOUT LIONEL SUPER MOTORS

1.—**LEVER**—that disconnects remote control unit so trains may be reversed by hand if desired.

2.—**FIELD**—made of specially prepared silicon steel laminations and scientifically wound.

3.—**DRIVING WHEELS**—accurately die cast and heavy, to give stability and tractive power to motor. Nickel plated steel rim, brightly polished, gives longer wear and smooth riding surface.

4.—**DRIVING GEARS**—machine cut of heavy steel. The seven gears mesh perfectly, giving greater tractive power and eliminating friction.

5.—**ARMATURE SHAFT BEARINGS**—Armature shaft revolves in three bakelite bearings. This 3 point support eliminates all vibration with the result that brushes wear evenly as well as prolong life of commutator.

6.—**ARMATURE**—of laminated electrical steel, drum wound with triple-covered magnet wire. Supported by best quality drill rod armature shaft. Protected by high grade shellac and baked.

7.—**SIDE PLATES**—support all working parts of motor. Made of heavy gauge steel. Holes are drilled and reamed and are aligned perfectly to overcome friction. Held together with heavy brass spacing bars.

8.—**AXLES**—made of heavy steel drill rod.

9.—**BRUSHES**—self lubricating bronze and graphite, contained in brass tubes and fed to commutator by tempered spring. Are long-wearing.

10.—**COMMUTATOR**—Polished heavy bronze made in segments and perfectly insulated. Lathe turned so as to reduce wear on brushes.

11.—All electrical motor contacts are in a specially designed insulated material—an exclusive Lionel patent.

THE Lionel "O" Gauge and "Lionel Standard" Super Motors by actual laboratory tests, have been proved superior to other motors of similar size.

They have maximum hauling power with minimum current consumption. They operate quietly and keep cool, even under strenuous treatment. They are fool-proof and with proper care will outlast any motor of similar capacity.

The "distant control" mechanism is built right into the motor and is completely protected against injury.

No other motors in model electric trains embody so many marvelous features.

The illustrations and descriptions on this page show some of the unusual features that make Lionel motors "Super Motors."

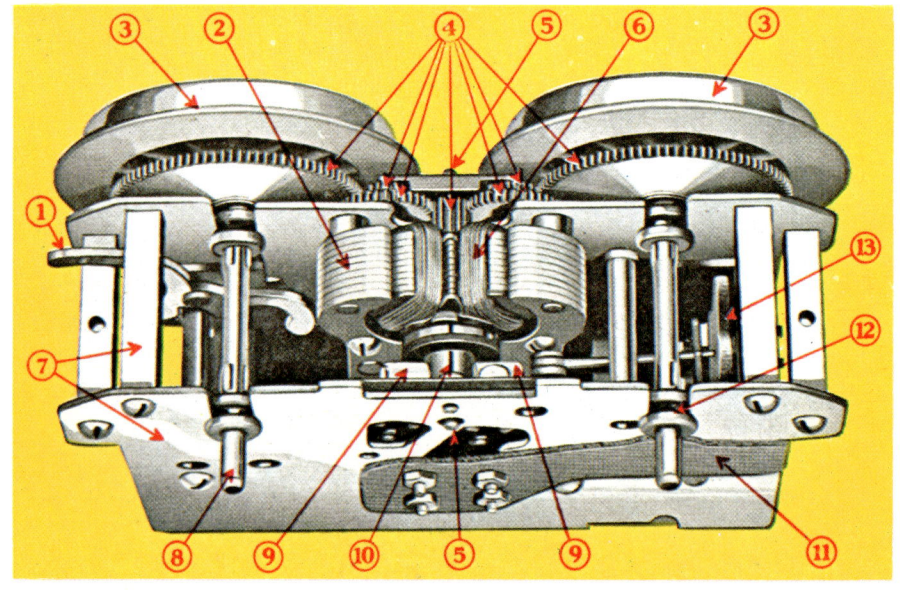

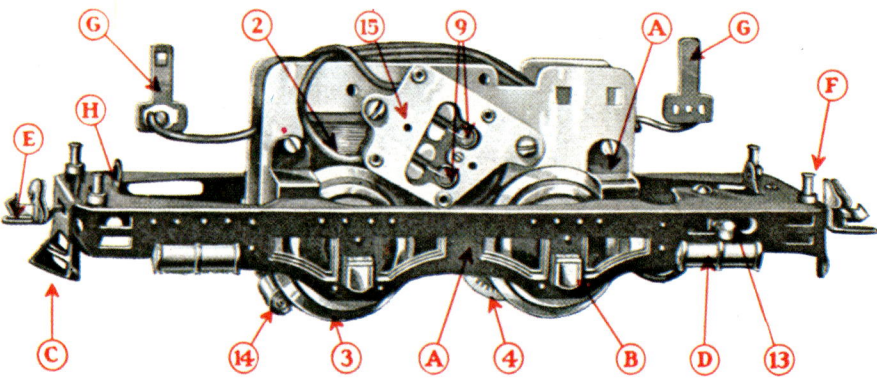

12.—**AXLE BEARINGS**—stainless steel bearings contained in side plates of motor. Will not wear out. Perfect alignment makes axles and gears operate frictionless and noiseless.

13.—**REVERSING CONTROLLER**—This lever controls operation of locomotive either forward, reverse or stop.

14.—**DOUBLE CONTACT SHOES**—collect current from center rail. Made of stainless steel and revolve on steel shafts. They are supported by flexible phosper bronze plates, giving proper tension to insure perfect contact.

15.—**BRUSH HOLDER**—of heavy fibre. Perfectly insulated. Brushes can be changed rapidly.

A.—**SUPPORTING FRAME**—made of heavy steel, faithfully detailed. Will stand extraordinary wear and tear. Motor is attached by four screws, making it easily removable for cleaning and oiling.

B.—**JOURNALS**—of heavy copper add greatly to appearance of locomotive.

C.—**COWCATCHERS**—vary with the type of locomotive. Many of them are part of steel frame. Others are heavy casting securely attached to frame.

D.—**TANKS**—made of brass, nickel plated. They beautify locomotive.

E.—**AUTOMATIC COUPLERS**—scientifically constructed so that cars cannot become detached while in motion, yet easily uncoupled when desired. Made of heavy steel, nickel plated and polished.

F.—**FLAG POSTS**—all locomotives are equipped with four flag posts, a realistic detail.

G.—**HEADLIGHT CONNECTIONS**—an original method giving perfect electrical connection and eliminating the possibility of broken wires.

H.—**CLAMP SUPPORT**—Screw holds body to frame—easily removed.

[Page Six]

FEATURING THE NEW HINGED BOILER FRONT "O" GAUGE LOCOMOTIVES

Patented Hinged Boiler Front with automatic lock ingeniously conceals and protects lamp, yet gives easy access to it. Genuine optical lens projects a powerful beam of light. Pilot lights glow colorfully. Featured on locomotives Nos. 262, 260E, 400E.

262 $10.00

261 $8.50

260E $22.50

No. 262—A new steam type locomotive and tender equipped with hand reversing lever, front and rear pilot trucks, and double-action piston driving rods. The new hinged boiler front makes possible a realistic headlight which throws a real beam of light. Locomotive is copper trimmed throughout. Complete with bulbs and flags, this is a high speed, powerful, graceful locomotive patterned after the most modern locomotives in America. Its wealth of detail and excellent design are not usually found in locomotives at this low price. Locomotive is 9¾ inches long, 3¼ inches high. Tender is 6 inches long, 3¼ inches high. Length over all 16½ inches.

Locomotive and Tender—*Code Word* "BETTER."   Price, $10.00

No. 261 Steam Type Locomotive and Tender—Exactly the same as No. 262 but is non-reversible. *Code Word* "BETTY."   Price, $8.50

No. 260E Steam Type Locomotive and Tender—Modelled after the latest Timken types. Reversible by famous "Distant-Control" unit. It has the new hinged boiler front feature. Red light under fire box adds to realism. Improved electric reverse cut-off in cab.

Locomotive is equipped with 4 driving wheels, a pilot truck and trailer truck. It has copper exhaust pipes and brass hand rails. Complete with flags and warning bell. The oil tank type double truck tender compliments the low, speedy powerful lines of the locomotive.

Specifications: Locomotive 11⅝ inches long, 4⅛ inches high. Tender 7¼ inches long, 4⅛ inches high. Length over-all 19⅝ inches.

Locomotive and Tender
Code Word "PAUL."   Price, $22.50

[*Page Seven*]

THREE SWIFT AND POWERFUL "O" GAUGE LOCOMOTIVES

Lionel Locomotives, regardless of size or type, are designed with one thought in mind—to develop as much hauling power as size permits and to be absolutely free of operating difficulties. Machine cut gears in the motors, bronze bushings and other refinements make the Lionel motor the finest in point of design and durability.

No. 251E—A Super-Motor Locomotive, equipped with "Distant-Control," which enables complete operation, forward or reverse at any distance from the track. A splendid model of an electric type locomotive, with great hauling power. Expertly designed with a wealth of detail. Complete with No. 81 controlling rheostat, two electric headlights and automatic couplers. 10¼ inches long, 4½ inches high. Can be used with cars Nos. 605, 606, 710, 712 and 810 to 817 and 820.

Code Word "GLORY."   Price, $20.00

No. 251—Same as 251E but without "Distant-Control" and Rheostat.
Code Word "FAME."   Price, $15.00

No. 254E Super-Motor Locomotive equipped with "Distant-Control"—At any distance from the track, you can stop, start, reverse or slow-down this locomotive. It is supplied complete with No. 81 controlling rheostat and two electric headlights. Can be used with cars Nos. 605, 606, 613, 614, and 810 to 817 and 820. 9½ inches long, 4¼ inches high.
Code Word "GRIT."   Price, $16.50

No. 254—Same as No. 254E but with hand reverse and without "Distant-Control" and Rheostat.
Code Word "MANY."   Price, $12.00

No. 4—Same as No. 254 but equipped with Bild-A-Loco motor.
Code Word "URGE."   Price, $12.00

No. 252—A colorful locomotive equipped with hand reversing lever and electric headlight. Permanent enamel finish and bright brass trim. 8 inches long, 3⅝ inches high. Can be used with same cars as No. 248 locomotive.
Code Word "ELECT."   Price, $8.50

[Page Eight]

"O" GAUGE LOCOMOTIVES AND 3-SPEED REVERSIBLE BILD-A-MOTORS

The Lionel three speed Reversible Bild-A-Motor is a powerful and versatile power plant. It is unusual in its fun value and can be used for a variety of purposes. A belt can be attached to its shaft and the motor can be made to run construction toys and miniature machine shops.

It will develop great power and is capable of lifting 20 times its own weight. By means of a controlling lever, the motor can be started, reversed and stopped. Will operate on dry or storage batteries or on reduced Direct or Alternating current.

Made in units so that it can be taken down and re-assembled in a few moments.

No. 1 Lionel Three Speed Reversible Bild-A-Motor is 6⅛ inches long, 3⅛ inches high, 2¾ inches wide. *Code Word "LIFT."*   Price, **$5.00**

No. 2 Lionel Three Speed Reversible Bild-A-Motor is 7 inches long, 3⅝ inches high, 4 inches wide. *Code Word "HOIST."*   Price, **$7.50**

No. 248—Beautifully finished by Lionel's permanent enameling process. A sturdy, electric locomotive, complete with electric headlight and pantagraph. Brass trim throughout with etched name plate. 7⅝ inches long, 4 inches high. Can be used with Cars. Nos. 529, 530, 629, 630, 803, 804, 805, 806, 807, 831 and 902.

Code Word "REGAL."   Price, **$5.00**

No. 253—A splendid New York Central type locomotive. Equipped with reversing controller and two electric headlights. Brass trimming. A beautiful, graceful type of locomotive. 9 inches long, 4 inches high. Can be used with Cars Nos. 603, 604, 607, 608, 803, 804, 805, 806, 807, 831 and 902.

Code Word "FINE."   Price, **$9.50**

No. 253E—Same as No. 253 but with "Distant Control" and No. 81 controlling rheostat which can be used at any distance from track to start, stop, slow-down or reverse the locomotive.

Code Word "FUN."   Price, **$13.00**

[*Page Nine*]

THE LARGEST AND MOST POWERFUL MODEL LOCOMOTIVE EVER BUILT

FOR "LIONEL STANDARD" TRACK

Patented Hinged Boiler Front with automatic lock, ingeniously conceals and protects lamp, yet gives easy access to it. Genuine optical lens projects a powerful beam of light. Pilot lights glow colorfully. Featured on locomotives Nos 261, 262, 260E, 400E.

Never before in the history of model train building has such a powerful locomotive been offered the American boy. This new No. 400E with "Distant-Control" is master of them all—a veritable giant of the rails.

In its creation, Lionel engineers have faithfully reproduced in steel, copper, brass and nickel, all of those fine and minute details that are found only in the largest, most modern railroad engines. Its long, low lines, its beauty of color and design and its mechanical precision opens the door for every boy to greater fun and enjoyment.

Powered by the famous "Bild-A-Loco" super motor, it will pull with ease an incredibly long train of cars. It has heavy, double-action piston and driving rods, 4 large drive wheels, 4-wheel pilot truck and 4-wheel trailer truck. The oil tender has two six-wheel trucks.

Green lanterns provide colorful warning lights and the fire box glows realistically. Complete with flags, and No. 81 controlling rheostat. You can use the rheostat at any distance from the track, to start, stop, slow-down or reverse the locomotive.

The **No. 400E** will be found in the following outfits: Nos. 432E, 358E, 396E, 423E and 433E. Select whichever outfit suits your fancy.

Specifications: Length 18½ inches, height 5¾ inches, Tender is 11⅜ inches long and 5¼ inches high. Locomotive and Tender 30½ inches long over-all.

No. 400E complete with Tender — *Code Word "MOGUL."*   Price, $42.50

[Page Ten]

HERE ARE TWO DANDY "LIONEL STANDARD" LOCOMOTIVES

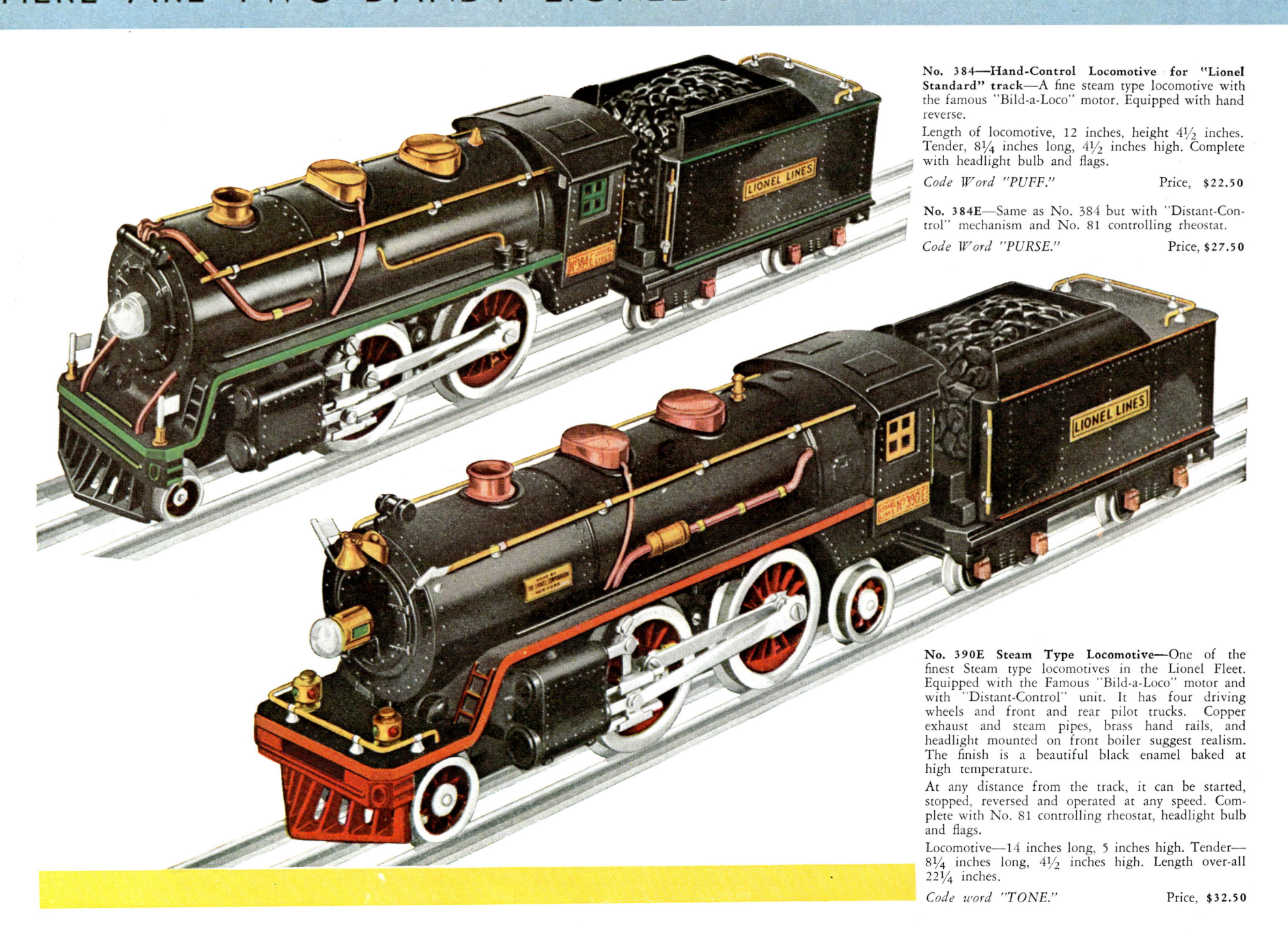

No. 384—Hand-Control Locomotive for "Lionel Standard" track—A fine steam type locomotive with the famous "Bild-a-Loco" motor. Equipped with hand reverse.

Length of locomotive, 12 inches, height 4½ inches. Tender, 8¼ inches long, 4½ inches high. Complete with headlight bulb and flags.

Code Word "PUFF."   Price, $22.50

No. 384E—Same as No. 384 but with "Distant-Control" mechanism and No. 81 controlling rheostat.

Code Word "PURSE."   Price, $27.50

No. 390E Steam Type Locomotive—One of the finest Steam type locomotives in the Lionel Fleet. Equipped with the Famous "Bild-a-Loco" motor and with "Distant-Control" unit. It has four driving wheels and front and rear pilot trucks. Copper exhaust and steam pipes, brass hand rails, and headlight mounted on front boiler suggest realism. The finish is a beautiful black enamel baked at high temperature.

At any distance from the track, it can be started, stopped, reversed and operated at any speed. Complete with No. 81 controlling rheostat, headlight bulb and flags.

Locomotive—14 inches long, 5 inches high. Tender—8¼ inches long, 4½ inches high. Length over-all 22¼ inches.

Code word "TONE."   Price, $32.50

[Page Eleven]

1931

IF YOU PREFER ELECTRIC TYPE LOCOMOTIVES YOU CAN'T BEAT THESE TWO

FOR "LIONEL STANDARD" TRACK

No. 408E "Lionel Standard" Twin-Super-Motor "Distant Control" Locomotive. This powerful locomotive is capable of hauling a long line of cars at any speed desired. It is the only twin motor locomotive on the market. Operating pantographs, illuminated signal lanterns, front and rear flags, brass hand rails, copper exhaust pipes, are a few of its realistic details. This locomotive is equipped with "Distant Control" mechanism, which enables the user to start, stop, reverse and operate it at any speed at any distance from the track by means of No. 81 controlling rheostat supplied with it. Size 17 inches long, 6½ inches high to top of pantagraph. Complete with headlight lamps and lamps for rear lanterns. *Code Word "FAST."* Price, $47.50

See pages 35 and 36 for correct passenger and freight cars to be used with these locomotives.

No. 381E "Distant-Control" "Bild-a-Loco" Locomotive for "Lionel Standard" track. An exact reproduction of the Chicago, Milwaukee and St. Paul locomotive used on the famous Olympian.

The most elaborate electric type locomotive in the Lionel Line. The two 4-wheel pilot trucks will not derail at any speed. Any boy can easily remove and disassemble the Bild-a-Loco motor and re-build it in a jiffy. All parts are so accurately made that no difficulty will be experienced in setting it up. Not a single wire to be connected—all electrical contacts are made automatically. Powerful enough to haul a long line of the largest Pullmans.

Two electric headlights and No. 81 Rheostat are included. You can use the rheostat to start, stop, slow-down or reverse the locomotive at any distance from the track.

Size 18 inches long, 6½ inches high.

Code Word "ULTI." Price, $44.50

Chicago, Milwaukee, St. Paul and Pacific Railroad Company

874 UNION STATION
CHICAGO, ILLINOIS

H. A. SCANDRETT
President

The Lionel Corporation,
15-17-19 East 26th Street,
New York City

Gentlemen:

Recently I have had an opportunity to see some of the Lionel Electric Locomotives modeled after one of the types in service on the Chicago, Milwaukee, St. Paul and Pacific Railroad.

You are to be complimented upon having produced a miniature locomotive so closely resembling, in general appearance and many details, the giant electric motors which haul our "Olympian" and other trains across the mountains in the northwest on our Chicago-Seattle route.

I congratulate the young people who are the fortunate possessors of your interesting and attractive locomotives and trains.

Very truly yours,

H A Scandrett
President

[Page Twelve]

ADD AN ELECTRIC LOCO TO YOUR RAILROAD—THEY ARE BEAUTIES

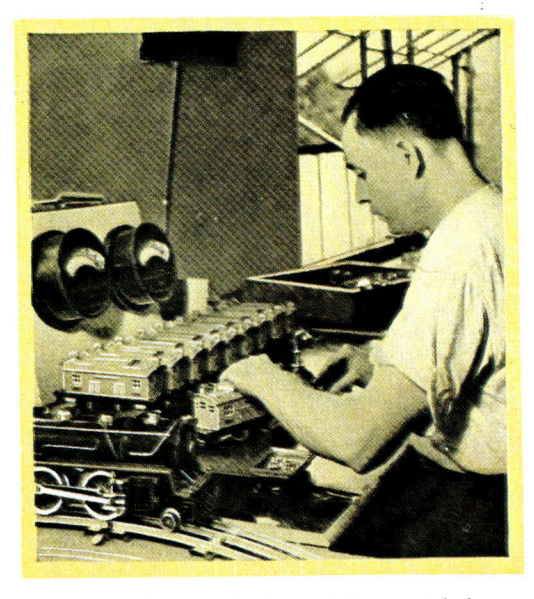

Every Lionel locomotive is carefully tested before it leaves the Lionel factories. It reaches you in perfect condition.

No. 8E "Lionel Standard" "Distant-Control" Super-Motor Locomotive—Equipped with the "Distant-Control" mechanism. Complete with No. 81 Controlling Rheostat, by means of which at any distance from the track, you can start, stop, slow-down or reverse the locomotive.

Code Word "PEPPY."   Price, $15.00

No. 8 "Lionel Standard" Super-Motor Reversible Locomotive—Similar to No. 8E but without "Distant-Control." 11 inches long, 4¾ inches high.

Code Word "POWER."   Price, $11.00

No. 318E "Lionel Standard" "Distant-Control" Super-Motor Locomotive—This is a powerful locomotive and will pull many more cars than its standard equipment. Finished in a marvelous new two-tone enamel. Complete with two headlights and No. 81 Controlling Rheostat, by means of which you can at any distance from the track, start, stop, slow-down or reverse the locomotive. It is 12⅛ inches long, 5⅛ inches high.

Code Word "MOVE."   Price, $20.00

No. 318 "Lionel Standard" Locomotive—Same as No. 318E but with hand reversing lever.

Code Word "VERB."   Price, $16.00

No. 9E "Distant-Control" "Bild-a-Loco" Locomotive for "Lionel Standard" Track—In addition to the interesting design of the "Bild-a-Loco" motor, this locomotive also contains a "Distant-Control" unit which makes it possible to start, stop and reverse the locomotive at any distance from the track. The body is beautifully designed and incorporates many features that are typically Lionel. Locomotive contains two electric headlights so arranged that the front one is always illuminated irrespective of the direction in which the locomotive is traveling. Equipped with automatic couplers. Measures 14½ inches long, 6¼ inches high. No. 81 controlling rheostat is included.

Code Word "UTTER."   Price, $28.75

[Page Thirteen]

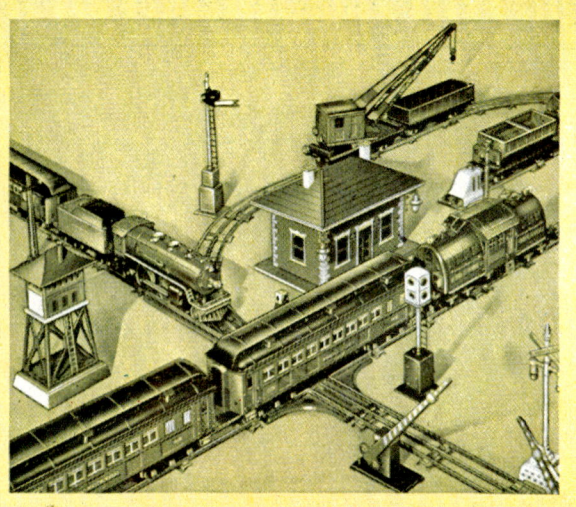

Build Realism into your Railroad......you can do it only with Lionel Accessories..

Model Railroading is the most fascinating and thrilling hobby any boy can have. It may begin with a modest set and a few accessories to which more can be added from time to time until it becomes a complete model railroad. Even then, there can be a lot of fun in rearranging the track formation and accessories.

But it is important that in laying the foundation for a realistic railroad system, you begin with the best, most authentic model Electric Trains and Accessories. There can be no other than Lionel equipment because every piece of Lionel equipment is a faithful copy of the best railroad equipment in the country.

Every boy wants a model railroad that is real in appearance, perfect in construction and dependable in performance. Lionel Trains and Accessories are real, accurate, true to the most minute details.

And too, with Lionel Electric Trains and Accessories, you have the most complete selection of model railroad equipment anywhere in the world. Fine locomotives of every size and type, sleek and trim, powerful and speedy, dependable and beautiful. And cars of every description—Pullmans, Diners, Observations, Mail cars, Lumber cars, Oil cars, Coal cars, Milk cars, Derrick cars, Searchlight cars and every other type of car that can be found on real railroads.

And as for accessories, you have a still greater range from which to choose. Beautiful stations of all descriptions—bridges of sturdy steel construction, power houses, freight sheds, tunnels, villas, crossing gates, traffic signals, bell signals, semaphores, telegraph posts, etc., and such advanced electrical developments as automatic switches and circuit breakers. All Lionel creations are patented against infringements.

No wonder leading railroad executives and engineers all agree that Lionel Electric Trains and Accessories are the most marvelous, most authentic model railroad equipment in the world.

If it is your ambition to have the best, most complete railroad system, you can do it only with Lionel Electric Trains and Accessories.

THE MOST POWERFUL MODEL RAILROAD IN THE WORLD. THE 400E STEAM TYPE LOCOMOTIVE PULLING A TRAIN OF TWENTY CARS

[Page Fourteen]

SEE HOW INEXPENSIVE GOOD OUTFITS CAN BE — YOU CAN AFFORD ONE

FOR "O" GAUGE TRACK

292
$5.95

132
$7.50

131
$7.50

148
$9.95

Outfit No. 292 Comprises:

1—No. 248 locomotive with electric headlight
1—No. 629 Pullman car
1—No. 630 observation car
8—OC curved track
1—OTC "Lockon" connection
1—No. 27 lamp

A train of exceptionally fine appearance, enamelled throughout in lustrous harmonizing colors.

Train is 24½ inches long. Track forms a circle 30 inches in diameter.

Code Word "KEEN."
Price, **$5.95**

Outfit No. 132 Comprises:

1—No. 248 locomotive with electric headlight
1—No. 603 Pullman car
1—No. 604 observation car
8—OC curved track
1—OTC "Lockon" connection
1—No. 068 warning signal
1—No. 27 lamp

A new Passenger Train Outfit closely resembling the large Expresses. Cars are 7½ inches long, equipped with double swivel trucks.

Train is 26¼ inches long. Track forms circle 30 inches in diameter.

Code Word "ICON."
Price, **$7.50**

Outfit No. 131 Comprises:

1—No. 248 locomotive with electric headlight
1—No. 831 flat car with load of lumber
1—No. 804 oil car
1—No. 807 caboose
8—OC curved track
1—OTC "Lockon" connection
1—No. 068 warning signal
1—No. 27 lamp

A new, 3-car freight train outfit of contrasting colors. The variety of cars offers opportunity for a lot of fun.

Train is 33¾ inches long. Track forms circle 30 inches in diameter.

Code Word "IGLOO."
Price, **$7.50**

Outfit No. 148 Comprises:

1—No. 261 steam type locomotive
1—No. 529 Pullman car
1—No. 530 observation car
8—sections OC curved track
2—sections OS straight track
1—OTC "Lockon" connection
1—No. 068 warning signal

The first time that a Lionel steam type passenger train has ever been offered at such an unusually low price.

Locomotive equipped with headlight and front and rear pilot trucks. Length of locomotive and tender 16 inches Length of train 32 inches.

Code Word "ETHEL."
Price, **$9.95**

[Page Fifteen]

THOUSANDS OF BOYS WILL WANT THESE COLORFUL OUTFITS

FOR "O" GAUGE TRACK

139 $9.95

296 $12.50

296E $15.95

134 $10.75

293 $11.25

No. 139 "O" Gauge Freight Outfit Comprises:

1—No. 261 steam type locomotive and tender
1—No. 831 flat car with load of lumber
1—No. 807 caboose
8—sections OC curved track
2—sections OS straight track
1—OTC "Lockon" connection
1—No. 068 warning signal

The powerful No. 261 locomotive is combined with two colorful freight cars. Length of train 32 inches. Track forms an oval 40 x 30 inches.

Code Word "JAMES."
Price, $9.95

Outfit No. 134 Comprises:

1—No. 252 reversible locomotive with electric headlight
2—No. 603 pullman cars
1—No. 604 observation car
8—OC curved track
2—OS straight track
1—OTC "Lockon" connection
1—068 warning signal
1—No. 27 lamp

A new 3-car train with reversible locomotive. Cars are 7½ inches long, each equipped with two 4-wheel swivel trucks and are enameled in beautiful two-tone effects.

Train is 35½ inches long. Track forms an oval 40 x 30 inches.

Code Word "ILEX."
Price, $10.75

Outfit No. 293 Comprises:

1—No. 252 reversible locomotive with electric headlight
1—No. 804 oil car
1—No. 805 box car
1—No. 803 coal car
1—No. 807 caboose
8—OC curved track
2—OS straight track
1—OTC "Lockon" connection
1—No. 068 warning signal
1—No. 27 lamp

A four-car freight set with reversible locomotive. Train is elaborate in detail and alive with color.

Train is 42¼ inches long. Track forms oval 40 x 30 inches.

Code Word "UPTON."
Price, $11.25

Outfit No. 296 Comprises:

1—No. 253 reversible locomotive with 2 electric headlights
2—No. 607 illuminated Pullman cars
1—No. 608 illuminated observation car
8—OC curved track
4—OS straight track
1—OTC "Lockon" connection
1—No. 068 warning signal
5—No. 27 lamps

Train is 36½ inches long. Track forms oval 50 x 30 inches.

Code Word "DART."
Price, $12.50

Outfit No. 296E—Same as No. 296 except that it contains 1 No. 253E "Distant Control" electric type locomotive and 1 No. 81 controlling rheostat, which can be used to start, stop, slow-down or reverse the train at any distance from the track.

Code Word "GRACE."
Price, $15.95

[Page Sixteen]

YOU CAN'T GO WRONG IF YOU CHOOSE A LIONEL SET

FOR "O" GAUGE TRACK

136
$12.75

133
$12.75

138
$14.50

Outfit No. 136 Comprises:

- 1—No. 262 reversible steam type locomotive with concealed headlight
- 1—No. 262T tender
- 1—No. 603 Pullman car
- 1—No. 604 observation car
- 8—OC curved track
- 2—OS straight track
- 1—OTC "Lockon" connection
- 1—No. 068 warning signal
- 1—No. 27 lamp

New, reversible steam type Locomotive with patented hinged front and concealed headlight. Double truck cars of two-tone enamel. A train of exceptional beauty and sturdiness.

Train is 33¼ inches long. Track forms oval 40 x 30 inches.

Code Word "IMAGE." Price, **$12.75**

Outfit No. 133 Comprises:

- 1—No. 262 reversible steam type locomotive with concealed headlight
- 1—No. 262T tender
- 1—No. 902 gondola car with 2 barrels
- 1—No. 804 oil car
- 1—No. 807 caboose
- 8—OC curved track
- 2—OS straight track
- 1—OTC "Lockon" connection
- 1—No. 068 warning signal
- 1—No. 27 lamp

A new freight train with the new larger reversible locomotive. The gondola car is furnished with two barrels.

Train is 40½ inches long. Track forms oval 40 x 30 inches.

Code Word "IMPROVE." Price, **$12.75**

Outfit No. 138 Comprises:

- 1—No. 253 reversible type locomotive with two electric headlights
- 2—No. 613 illuminated Pullman cars
- 1—No. 614 illuminated observation car
- 8—OC curved track
- 4—OS straight track
- 1—OTC "Lockon" connection
- 1—No. 068 warning signal
- 5—No. 27 lamps

This outfit combines an efficient, sturdy New York Central type locomotive, with three brand new 10¼ inch cars.

The cars are enameled in harmonizing two-tone colors and are equipped with patented removable roofs. Illuminated throughout.

Train is 43¾ inches long. Track forms oval 50 x 30 inches.

Code Word "IMPRESS." Price, **$14.50**

[Page Seventeen]

1931

OH BOY! HOW WOULD YOU LIKE TO OWN ONE OF THESE?

FOR "O" GAUGE TRACK

142 $16.50
142E $20.00

236 $15.00

233 $16.00

Outfit No. 233 Comprises:
- 1—No. 262 reversible steam type locomotive with concealed headlight
- 1—No. 262T tender
- 1—No. 902 gondola car with 2 barrels
- 1—No. 806 cattle car
- 1—No. 803 coal car
- 1—No. 804 oil car
- 1—No. 807 caboose
- 8—OC curved track
- 4—OS straight track
- 1—OTC "Lockon" connection
- 1—No. 068 warning signal
- 1—No. 27 lamp

Train is 55 inches long. Track forms an oval 50 x 30 inches.

Code Word "INLAY." Price, $16.00

Outfit No. 236 Comprises:
- 1—No. 262 reversible steam type locomotive with concealed headlight
- 1—No. 262T tender
- 2—No. 607 illuminated Pullman cars
- 1—No. 608 illuminated observation car
- 8—OC curved track
- 4—OS straight track
- 1—OTC "Lockon" connection
- 1—No. 068 warning signal
- 4—No. 27 lamps

Equipped with the new steam type locomotive and tender. The illuminated cars are in beautiful two-tone enamel.

Train is 42¼ inches long. Track forms oval 50 x 30 inches.

Code Word "INCH." Price, $15.00

Outfit No. 142 Comprises:
- 1—No. 4 reversible locomotive with "Bild-a-Loco" motor and 2 electric headlights
- 2—No. 605 illuminated Pullman cars
- 1—No. 606 illuminated observation car
- 8—OC curved track
- 6—OS straight track
- 1—OTC "Lockon" connection
- 1—No. 068 warning signal
- 5—No. 27 lamps

Train is 45 inches long. Track forms oval 60 x 30 inches.

Code Word "INCLINE." Price, $16.50

Outfit No. 142E
Same as No. 142 except that it contains No. 254E "Distant-Control" locomotive and No. 81 controlling rheostat.

Code Word "INDEX." Price, $20.00

[Page Eighteen]

WHAT'S A RAILROAD WITHOUT A FREIGHT TRAIN—YOU SHOULD HAVE ONE

FOR "O" GAUGE TRACK

135 $21.50

144 $18.50

299 18.50

299E 22.50

Outfit No. 144 Comprises:

- 1—No. 262 reversible steam type locomotive with concealed headlight
- 1—No. 262T tender
- 2—No. 613 illuminated Pullman cars
- 1—No. 614 illuminated observation car
- 8—OC curved track
- 6—OS straight track
- 1—OTC "Lockon" connection
- 1—No. 068 warning signal
- 4—No. 27 lamps

The cars in this outfit are handsomely enameled in bright two-tone colors, and are equipped with patented removable roofs.

Train is 49¼ inches long. Track forms oval 60 x 30 inches.

Code Word "INTAKE." Price, $18.50

Outfit No. 135 Comprises:

- 1—No. 262 reversible steam type locomotive with concealed headlight
- 1—No. 262T tender
- 1—No. 812 gondola car with 4 barrels and a set of tools
- 1—No. 810 derrick car
- 1—No. 817 caboose
- 8—OC curved track
- 4—OS straight track
- 1—OTC "Lockon" connection
- 1—No. 068 warning signal
- 1—No. 27 lamp

A new attractive work train. The crane in this outfit is a perfect working model. By means of its worm gears, the entire cab can be swung around and the pulley and tackle can be operated separately.

Train is 47 inches long. Track forms oval 50 x 30 inches.

Code Word "INWARD." Price, $21.50

Outfit No. 299 Comprises:

- 1—No. 251 reversible locomotive with 2 electric headlights
- 1—No. 812 gondola car with 4 barrels
- 1—No. 813 cattle car
- 1—No. 814 box car
- 1—No. 817 caboose
- 8—OC curved track
- 6—OS straight track
- 1—OTC "Lockon" connection
- 1—No. 068 warning signal
- 2—No. 27 lamps

The largest and most powerful electric type locomotive in the "O" Gauge line, combined with four handsome freight cars. Train is 52¾ inches long.

Code Word "FLORA." Price, $18.50

Outfit No. 299E

Same as No. 299, except that it contains No. 251E "Distant-Control" locomotive and No. 81 controlling rheostat. By the use of the rheostat, you can at any distance from the track, start, stop, slow-down or reverse the locomotive.

Code Word "QUILL." Price, $22.50

[Page Nineteen]

HERE ARE THE FINEST OUTFITS IN THE "O" GAUGE LINE

FOR "O" GAUGE TRACK

240E $32.50

241E $30.00

239E $27.50

Outfit No. 240E Comprises:

- 1—No. 260E "Distant-Control" Steam Type locomotive with concealed headlight and amber light under fire box
- 1—No. 260T tender
- 1—No. 812 Gondola car with 4 barrels and a set of tools
- 1—No. 810 derrick car
- 1—No. 811 lumber car
- 1—No. 817 caboose
- 8—OC curved track
- 8—OS straight track
- 1—OTC "Lockon" connection
- 1—No. 81 controlling rheostat
- 2—No. 28 lamps

You have seen real work trains like these. There's a lot of fun in playing with this set, especially the derrick.

By using the rheostat you can start, stop, slow-down or reverse the train at any distance from the track.

Train is 62 inches long. Track forms an oval 70 x 30 inches.

Code Word "SWEET"   Price, $32.50

Outfit No. 241E Comprises:

- 1—No. 260E "Distant-Control" Steam Type locomotive with concealed headlight and amber light under fire box
- 1—No. 260T tender
- 2—No. 710 illuminated pullman cars
- 1—No. 712 illuminated observation car
- 8—OC curved track
- 8—OS straight track
- 1—OTC "Lockon" connection
- 1—No. 81 controlling rheostat
- 2—No. 28 lamps
- 3—No. 27 lamps

The aristocrat of the "O" Gauge Passenger Line. A genuine railroad train in miniature with the largest steam type locomotive in the "O" Gauge series. By using the rheostat you can start, stop, slow-down or reverse the train at any distance from the track.

Train is 58½ inches long. Track forms an oval 70 x 30 inches.

Code Word "CREAM"   Price, $30.00

Outfit No. 239E Comprises:

- 1—No. 260E "Distant-Control" Steam Type locomotive with concealed headlight and amber light under fire box
- 1—No. 260T tender
- 1—No. 812 gondola car with 4 barrels
- 1—No. 814 box car
- 1—No. 815 oil car
- 1—No. 813 cattle car
- 1—No. 817 caboose
- 8—OC curved track
- 8—OS straight track
- 1—OTC "Lockon" connection
- 1—No. 81 controlling rheostat
- 2—No. 28 lamps

A complete freight train set equipped with the latest type of steam locomotive and oil tank tender in the "O" Gauge series. By using the rheostat you can start, stop, slow-down or reverse the train at any distance from the track.

Every modern improvement for the shipping of freight has been incorporated in this set. You will get a lot of real fun out of it.

Train is 72½ inches long. Track forms an oval 70 x 30 inches.

Code Word "JURY"   Price, $27.50

[Page Twenty]

AND HERE ARE THE LOWEST PRICED "LIONEL STANDARD" OUTFITS

FOR "LIONEL STANDARD" TRACK

347 — $17.50

360 — $21.00
360E — $25.00

362 — $28.50
362E — $32.75

Outfit No. 347 Comprises:
- 1—No. 8 reversible locomotive with two electric headlights
- 1—No. 337 illuminated Pullman car
- 1—No. 338 illuminated observation car
- 8—C curved track
- 2—S straight track
- 1—STC "Lockon" connection
- 5—No. 28 lamps

While this is the lowest price "Lionel Standard" Train in the line, it is nevertheless sturdily built and handsomely enameled. You can always add additional cars and other equipment.
Train is 38½ inches long. Track forms an oval 57 x 45 inches.

Code Word "ZENA." Price, **$17.50**

Outfit No. 360 Comprises:
- 1—No. 8 reversible locomotive with two electric headlights
- 1—No. 332 illuminated mail and baggage car
- 1—No. 337 illuminated Pullman car
- 1—No. 338 illuminated observation car
- 8—C curved track
- 4—S straight track
- 1—STC "Lockon" connection
- 6—No. 28 lamps

Train is 52½ inches long. Track forms an oval 71 x 45 inches.

Code Word "RENT." Price, **$21.00**

Outfit No. 360E—Similar to No. 360 except that it contains No. 8E "Distant-Control" locomotive and 1 No. 81 controlling rheostat, which can be used to start, stop, slow-down or reverse the train at any distance from the track.

Code Word "RADIANT."
Price, **$25.00**

Outfit No. 362 Comprises:
- 1—No. 384 reversible steam type locomotive with electric headlight
- 1—No. 384T tender
- 1—No. 309 illuminated Pullman car
- 1—No. 312 illuminated observation car
- 8—C curved track
- 2—S straight track
- 1—STC "Lockon" connection
- 4—No. 28 lamps

This realistic steam type locomotive and tender is combined with large cars, making a splendidly proportioned outfit. Train is 50¼ inches long. Track forms an oval 57 x 45 inches.

Code Word "SONNET." Price, **$28.50**

Outfit No. 362E—Similar to No. 362, except that it contains No. 384E "Distant-Control" locomotive and 1 No. 81 controlling rheostat, which can be used to start, stop, slow-down or reverse the train at any distance from the track.

Code Word "SUBTLE." Price, **$32.75**

WHAT STRIKING COLORS AND WHAT REALISTIC DETAIL!

FOR "LIONEL STANDARD" TRACK

342E $32.50

386 $27.50
386E $32.50

361 $22.50
361E $27.50

Outfit No. 342E Comprises:

1—No. 318E "Distant-Control" locomotive with two electric headlights
1—No. 310 illuminated mail and baggage car
1—No. 309 illuminated Pullman car
1—No. 312 illuminated observation car
8—C curved track
6—S straight track
1—STC "Lockon" connection
1—No. 81 controlling rheostat
6—No. 28 lamps

This is one of the most popular lower-priced outfits in the "Lionel Standard" series. It is highly enamelled in Duo-Tone colors.

By using the rheostat you can start, stop, slow-down or reverse the train at any distance from the track.

Train is 57½ inches long. Track forms an oval 85¼ x 45 inches.

Code Word "FORUM"   Price, $32.50

Outfit No. 386 Comprises:

1—No. 384 reversible steam type locomotive with electric headlight
1—No. 384T tender
1—No. 512 gondola car with 8 barrels
1—No. 513 cattle car
1—No. 517 illuminated caboose
8—C curved track
4—S straight track
1—STC "Lockon" connection
2—No. 28 lamps

A popular freight outfit. Locomotive is powered with the famous Lionel "Bild-a-Loco" motor. Train is well balanced with an interesting variety of cars.

Train is 60½ inches long. Track forms an oval 71 x 45 inches.

Code Word "MIKE"   Price, $27.50

Outfit No. 386E—Similar to No. 386, except that it contains No. 384E "Distant-Control" locomotive and 1 No. 81 controlling rheostat, which can be used to control the train at any distance from the track.

Code Word "PAT"   Price, $32.50

Outfit No. 361 Comprises:

1—No. 318 reversible locomotive with two electric headlights
1—No. 511 flat car with load of lumber
1—No. 512 gondola car with 8 barrels
1—No. 514 box car
1—No. 517 illuminated caboose
8—C curved track
6—S straight track
1—STC "Lockon" connection
3—No. 28 lamps

A new four-car freight train with a larger and more powerful locomotive than ever before. It includes an excellent set of cars with bright color combinations.

Train is 66½ inches long. Track forms an oval 85¼ x 45 inches.

Code Word "NATION"   Price, $22.50

Outfit No. 361E—Similar to No. 361 except that it contains No. 318E "Distant-Control" locomotive and 1 No. 81 Controlling Rheostat, which can be used to control the train at any distance from the track.

Code Word "NAUTICAL"   Price, $27.50

[Page Twenty-two]

THINK OF THE FUN YOU CAN HAVE WITH THESE BEAUTIFUL SETS

FOR "LIONEL STANDARD" TRACK

394E $42.50

364E $40.00

363E $42.50

Outfit No. 394E Comprises:
- 1—No. 390E "Distant-Control" steam type locomotive with electric headlight
- 1—No. 390T tender
- 1—No. 309 illuminated pullman car
- 1—No. 310 illuminated mail and baggage car
- 1—No. 312 illuminated observation car
- 8—C curved track
- 8—S straight track
- 1—STC "Lockon" connection
- 1—No. 81 controlling rheostat
- 5—No. 28 lamps

One of the most popular large steam type Passenger outfits in the line. It includes illuminated two-tone enamel baggage and pullman cars, each 13¼ inches long. By using the rheostat you can start, stop, slow-down or reverse the train at any distance from the track.

Train is 67 inches long. Track forms an oval 99½ x 45 inches.

Code Word "JOURNEY"   Price, $42.50

Outfit No. 364E Comprises:
- 1—No. 9E "Distant-Control" locomotive with two electric headlights
- 2—No. 424 illuminated Pullman cars
- 1—No. 426 illuminated observation car
- 8—C curved track
- 8—S straight track
- 1—STC "Lockon" connection
- 1—No. 81 controlling rheostat
- 6—No. 28 lamps

An entirely new Passenger train with New York Central type locomotive. Beautifully designed new 16 inch, 6-wheel truck pullmans and observation car are included. The cars are equipped with patented removable roofs and are complete in all details.

By using the rheostat you can start, stop, slow-down or reverse the train at any distance from the track.

Train is 68½ inches long. Track forms an oval 99½ x 45 inches.

Code Word "LILY"   Price, $40.00

Outfit No. 363E Comprises:
- 1—No. 390E "Distant-Control" steam type locomotive with electric headlight
- 1—No. 390T tender
- 1—No. 511 flat car with load of lumber
- 1—No. 514R Refrigerator car
- 1—No. 515 oil car
- 1—No. 516 coal car with coal
- 1—No. 517 illuminated caboose
- 8—C curved track
- 6—S straight track
- 1—STC "Lockon" connection
- 1—No. 81 controlling rheostat
- 2—No. 28 lamps

Powerful, large steam type locomotive in a brand new combination with five well modelled and beautifully enamelled freight cars. A realistic train that will give you hours and hours of fun.

By using the rheostat you can start, stop, slow-down or reverse the train at any distance from the track.

Train is 89 inches long. Track forms an oval 85¼ x 45 inches.

Code Word "LAURA"   Price, $42.50

[Page Twenty-three]

EVEN THE BIG ROADS GIVE LIONEL THE STAMP OF APPROVAL

FOR "LIONEL STANDARD" TRACK

409E $85.00

368E $50.00

432E $55.00

Outfit No. 432E Comprises:

1—No. 400E "Distant Control" steam type locomotive with concealed headlight and illuminated fire box
1—No. 400T tender
1—No. 419 illuminated Pullman and Baggage car
1—No. 418 illuminated Pullman
1—No. 490 illuminated observation car
8—C curved track
8—S straight track
1—STC "Lockon" connection
1—No. 81 controlling rheostat
6—No. 28 lamps

A new giant 30½ inch steam type locomotive combined with three illuminated cars, 18¼ inches long. With the No. 81 controlling rheostat you can start, stop, slow-down or reverse the train at any distance from the track.

Train is 88½ inches long. Track forms an oval 99½ x 45 inches.

Code Word "VIKING."   Price, $55.00

Outfit No. 368E Comprises:

1—No. 390E "Distant-Control" steam type locomotive with electric headlight
1—No. 390T tender
2—No. 424 illuminated Pullman cars
1—No. 426 illuminated observation car
8—C curved track
8—S straight track
1—STC "Lockon" connection
1—No. 81 controlling rheostat
5—No. 28 lamps

A new Passenger train modeled after the famous Pennsylvania Limited. The powerful 390E steam type locomotive with streamline Pullmans, forms a majestic combination. The 16 inch cars are equipped with patented removable roofs. By use of the No. 81 controlling rheostat you can start, stop, slow-down or reverse the train at any distance from the track.

Train is 73½ inches long. Track forms an oval 99½ x 45 inches.

Code Word "PENN."   Price, $50.00

Outfit No. 409E Comprises:

1—No. 381E "Distant-Control" electric type locomotive with two electric headlights and four colored signal lights
1—No. 412 illuminated Pullman car, lettered "California"
1—No. 413 illuminated Pullman car, lettered "Colorado"
1—No. 416 illuminated observation car, lettered "New York"
8—C curved track
10—S straight track
1—STC "Lockon" connection
1—No. 81 controlling rheostat
13—No. 28 lamps

A faithful copy of Chicago, Milwaukee and St. Paul's Olympian. Cars are each 21½ inches long and are equipped with hinged roofs showing complete interior detail — washrooms, revolving chairs, compartments, etc. Enameled in beautiful two-toned colors.

By using the 81 rheostat you can start, stop, slow-down or reverse the train at any distance from the track.

Train is 86½ inches long. Track forms an oval 114 x 45 inches.

Code "OLYMPIAN."   Price, $85.00

[Page Twenty-four]

THE CRACK TRAIN OF THE LIONEL FLEET—NAMED FOR A FAMOUS LIMITED

FOR "LIONEL STANDARD" TRACK

358E
$60.00

433E
$85.00

Outfit No. 358E Comprises:

- 1—No. 400E "Distant-Control" steam type locomotive with concealed headlight and illuminated fire box
- 1—No. 400T tender
- 1—No. 212 gondola car complete with 4 barrels and set of tools
- 1—No. 219 derrick car
- 1—No. 220 floodlight car
- 1—No. 217 illuminated caboose
- 8—C curved track
- 8—S straight track
- 1—STC "Lockon" connection
- 1—No. 81 controlling rheostat
- 5—No. 28 lamps

The famous "Lionel Standard" Work Train is now equipped with the new giant No. 400E steam type locomotive and tender and new flood light car. By using the rheostat you can start, stop, slow-down or reverse the train at any distance from the track.

Train is 88 inches long. Track forms an oval 99½ x 45 inches.

Code Word "CLARENCE"   Price, **$60.00**

Outfit No. 433E Comprises:

- 1—No. 400E "Distant-Control" steam type locomotive with concealed headlight and illuminated fire box
- 1—No. 400T tender
- 1—No. 412 illuminated Pullman car, lettered "California"
- 1—No. 413 illuminated Pullman car, lettered "Colorado"
- 1—No. 416 illuminated observation car, lettered "New York"
- 8—C curved track
- 10—S straight track
- 1—STC "Lockon" connection
- 1—No. 81 controlling rheostat
- 9—No. 28 lamps

This is the Twentieth Century Limited, the crack train of the Lionel line. It is 98 inches long. Track forms an oval 114 x 45 inches.

The finest steam type Passenger Train Set ever manufactured. It includes new giant size No. 400E locomotive and tender and the largest passenger cars in the Lionel Line with complete interior detail, such as wash-rooms, revolving chairs, interior lights, etc.

By using the rheostat you can start, stop, slow-down or reverse the train at any distance from the track.

Code Word "CENTURY"   Price, **$85.00**

[Page Twenty-five]

1931

A PRIZE POSSESSION FOR ANY BOY — THE BLU...

Outfit No. 396E—Comprises:

1—No. 400E "Distant-Control" steam type locomotive with concealed headlight and illuminated fire box. 1—No. 400T tender. 1—No. 421 illuminated Pullman car, lettered "Westphal." 1—No. 420 illuminated Pullman car, lettered "Faye." 1—No. 422 illuminated observation car, lettered "Temple." 8—C curved track. 8—S straight track. 1—STC "Lockon" connection. 1—No. 81 controlling rheostat. 6—No. 28 lamps.

Designed in conjunction with the Central Railroad of New Jersey engineers as a replica of their justly famous Flyer to Atlantic City, described in a booklet accompanying each train. The giant No. 400E locomotive and all cars are finished in two beautiful shades of Royal Blue. You can control operation of train at any distance from the track. Train is 91½ inches long. Track forms an oval 99½ x 45 inches.

Code Word "COMET." Price, $70.00

Outfit No. 411E Comprises:

1—408E "Distant Control" electric type twin-motor locomotive with two electric headlights and four colored signal lights. 1—No. 412 illuminated Pullman car, lettered "California." 1—No. 413 illuminated Pullman car, lettered "Colorado." 1—No. 414 illuminated Pullman car, lettered "Illinois." 1—No. 416 illuminated observation car, lettered "New York." 8—C curved track. 16—S straight track. 1—STC "Lockon" connection. 1—No. 81 controlling rheostat. 15—No. 28 lamps.

Train is 107 inches long. Track forms an oval 72 x 128 inches. Without question, the finest miniature electric train in the world. Equipped with powerful 17-inch twin-motor locomotive, and 21½ inch cars. The outfit includes an elaborate lighting system of 15 lamps. The train is nearly 9 feet in length.

Code Word "AMBASSADOR." Price, $97.50

Outfit No. 423E Comprises:

1—No. 400E "Distant-Control" steam type locomotive with concealed headlight and illuminated fire box. 1—No. 400T tender. 1—No. 211 flat car with load of lumber. 1—No. 212 gondola car with 8 barrels. 1—No. 213 cattle car. 1—No. 214 box car. 1—No. 215 oil car. 1—No. 216 coal car. 1—No. 217 illuminated caboose. 8—C curved track. 10—S straight track. 1—STC "Lockon" connection. 1—No. 81 controlling rheostat. 3—No. 28 lamps.

Train is 131 inches long. Track forms an oval 114 x 45 inches. This majestic freight train is equipped with the powerful No. 400E steam type locomotive and 12-wheel oil-tank tender. The train is a "Giant of the Rails" in miniature. It has seven freight cars, each one different, and each one of intense interest to all boys.

Code Word "MASTER." Price, $72.50

[Page Twenty-six]

ARISTOCRATS OF MINIATURE RAILROADING

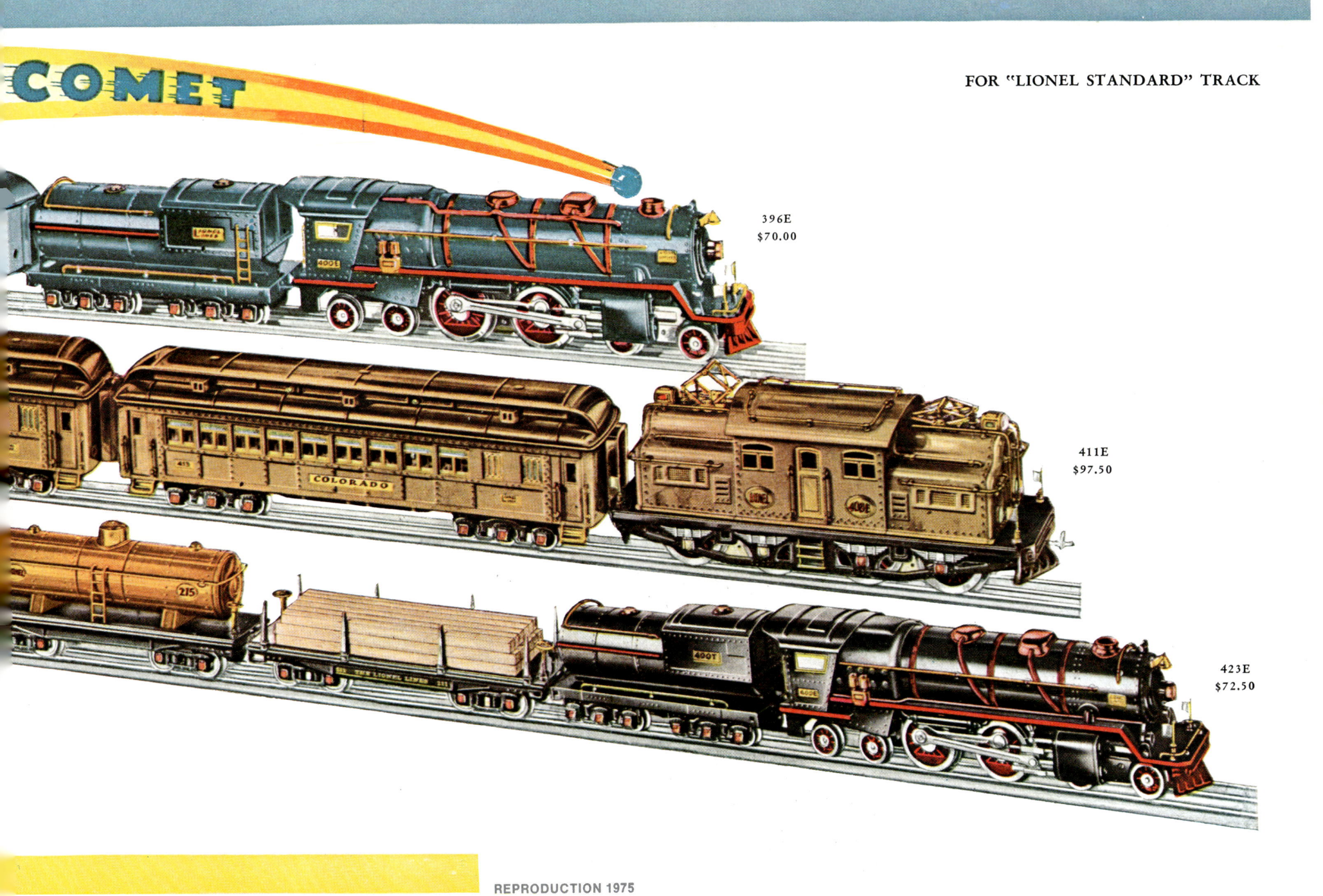

COMET

FOR "LIONEL STANDARD" TRACK

396E $70.00

411E $97.50

423E $72.50

REPRODUCTION 1975

[Page Twenty-seven]

LIONEL CIRCUIT BREAKER AND DIRECT CURRENT REDUCER

SPECIFICATIONS FOR LIONEL "MULTIVOLT" TRANSFORMERS

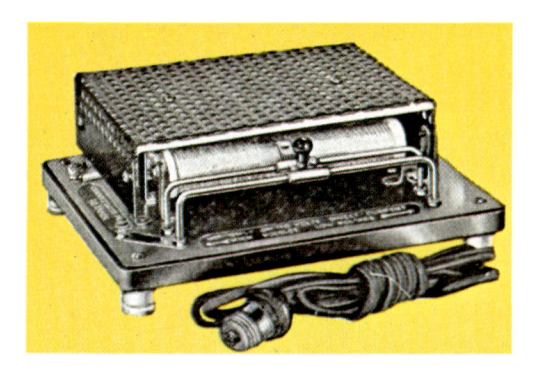

No. 107 DIRECT CURRENT REDUCER for 110 volt circuit, reduces the D. C. house current so that Lionel Trains can be operated. It is constructed of four porcelain tubes wound with best quality enamelled resistance wire. These tubes are protected and ventilated by perforated steel covering lined with heavy asbestos. They are mounted on a substantial base 8" x 11" and ¾ inches thick.

The sliding lever regulates the voltage so that train can crawl or go ahead at express speed. The reducer is connected to the house current by a bakelite plug attached to 7 feet of well insulated cord. 4 porcelain supports make it possible for reducer to be screwed on wall or table.

Code Word "KENTUCKY."   Price, **$10.00**

No. 170 DIRECT CURRENT REDUCER for 220 volt circuit.
Code Word "ASBURY."   Price, **$14.50**

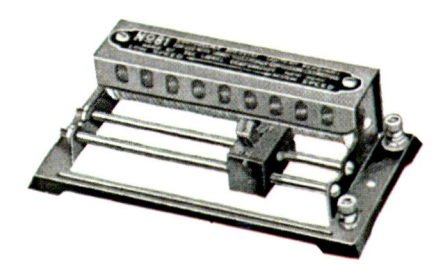

The No. 81 Controlling Rheostat increases or decreases the current supplied through the transformer in steps of less than one volt. This gives you a very delicate control of your set. By manipulating the controlling lever you can start and stop your train at will. If your locomotive is of the E type Distant Control, the No. 81 Controlling Rheostat permits you to start, stop, slow-down or reverse your train from any distance.

The porcelain coil in this rheostat is protected by perforated steel covering and the air holes prevent over-heating. The No. 81 Rheostat can also be used with Dry Batteries.

Size 4⅞ inches long, 2½ inches wide.

Code Word "BONE."   Price, **$2.50**

No. 91 Circuit Breaker—Every Lionel fan should have one. It is an ingenious device that functions as an automatic and never failing safety signal in case of short circuit or if the train leaves the rails.

In case of either of these occurrences, the red light becomes illuminated and the current is immediately shut off from the transformer until the fault is remedied. The Circuit Breaker is an invaluable accessory to your outfit.

The mechanism is enclosed in a die cast case, beautifully enamelled. The bulb is surmounted by highly polished brass guard. You should have one!

Size 2¾ inches square, 4¼ inches high.

Code Word "SAFETY."   Price, **$3.25**

LAMINATIONS—The laminations are made of electrical sheets of silicon steel.

COILS—The primary coils are wound with enamel wire with glasssine paper between layers. The secondary coil is wound with cotton covered enamel wire. Coils are then impregnated in a high grade varnish and baked to exclude moisture.

METAL CASE—The coils are contained in a well designed steel case of a heavier weight than is required by the Underwriters' Laboratories.

SUB-BASE—The sub-base electrically welded to the case permits the circulation of air under the transformer, which keeps it cool while in operation.

DOUBLE CONTACT SWITCH—This switch is infinitely superior to the one piece type which is easily bent and does not make positive contact. Our double switch has a flexible phosphor bronze contact riveted underneath a heavy brass piece which protects it from injury and insures positive contact with the points. An exclusive feature of Lionel "Multivolt" Transformers.

RIGID SUPPORTS FOR COILS—The coils and laminations in Lionel "Multivolt" Transformers are rigidly supported inside the case by metal bands which prevent these parts from moving and eliminates the possibility of broken lead wires.

SEPARABLE PLUG—All Lionel "Multivolt" Transformers are fitted with an improved Bakelite plug.

CONNECTIONS—All binding posts, contact points and switch are mounted on one piece of heavy insulating material, all conveniently located at the top of the transformer—right before the eyes of the user.

LAMP CORD—7 feet of best grade flexible lamp cord are supplied with each transformer.

FINISH—Lionel "Multivolt" Transformers are finished with a rubberoid enamel that is applied at 350 degrees Fahrenheit. This finish can not be scratched nor will it peel off during the life of the transformer.

The above specifications prove conclusively the superiority of Lionel "Multivolt" Transformers.

[Page Twenty-eight]

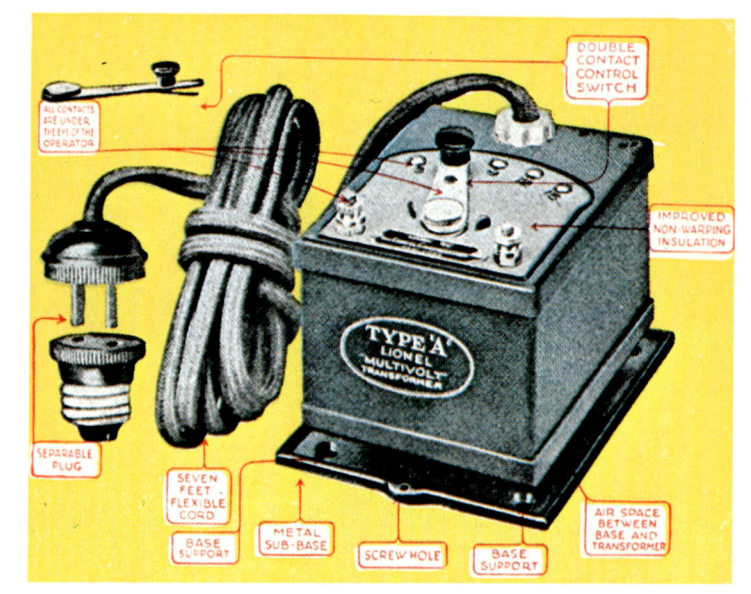

LIONEL "MULTIVOLT" TRANSFORMERS ARE INCOMPARABLE

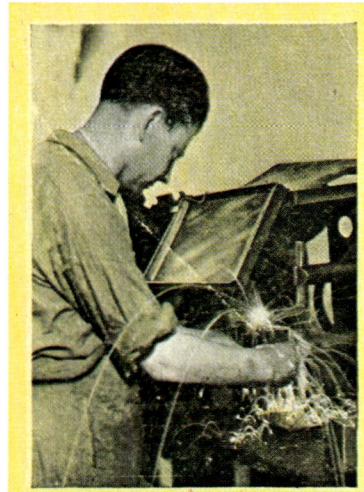

Lionel "Multivolt" Transformers reduce the (A.C.) house current so that Lionel Trains, which require low voltage, can be operated. Three essential parts are contained in the protecting case. These parts are, the Primary coil, the Secondary coil and the core of laminated steel.

From the outside, all transformers are essentially alike. Their life and efficiency depends upon the design of their mechanism and the quality of materials used in their construction. Lionel "Multivolt" Transformers, after extensive laboratory tests by an engineer of great repute, have been found superior to every other toy transformer on the market.* They will run more trains with less heating than any other transformer rated at 50% more wattage.

They are made of the best, most costly materials available. The laminations are made of Silicon steel. The coils are of cotton covered enameled wire—not just ordinary wire such as is found in cheaper transformers. For further efficiency, these coils are dipped in high grade varnish and baked to exclude all moisture as well as to make for solid construction. This painstaking method gives perfect insulation, higher efficiency, less heating and longer life. Lionel "Multivolt" Transformers offer the largest range of fixed voltage at intervals of 1 or 2 volts as against intervals of 5 or 6 volts in a cheaper transformer. Unlike other transformers, they will give as much reduced wattage as is taken in from the house main, with no loss in the "transferring." That's why Lionel "Multivolt" Transformers are economical, in the long run

Each transformer has a high voltage cord insulated by an extra outer wrapper of fabric and equipped with a genuine bakelite plug instead of moulded composition.

They are listed as standard by the National Board of Underwriters and are unconditionally guaranteed as long as they are used on Alternating Current, as specified.

The Lionel Corporation is the largest manufacturer of Toy Transformers. You can be sure that in buying a Lionel "Multivolt" Transformer, you are getting the best Toy Transformer manufactured.

Take no chances with cheaper makes. Be sure to use only a Lionel "Multivolt" Transformer with Lionel Electric Trains.

*Space does not permit the complete report of these tests. It will be issued in pamphlet form and mailed upon request.

Welding a Multivolt Transformer

Types A and F will operate any "O" Gauge outfit and a few accessories. Type B will operate any "O" Gauge outfit and many accessories. Types C and T will operate any "O" Gauge or Standard Gauge outfit and many accessories. Types K and K220 will operate any "O" Gauge or Standard Gauge outfit and all accessories or two trains at the same time.

TYPE	ALTERNATING CURRENT VOLTS	CYCLES	RATED WATTAGE	ACTUAL CAPACITY	VOLTAGES OBTAINED BY USING— SWITCH BINDING POSTS	FIXED BINDING POSTS	SIZE	CODE WORD	PRICE
A	110	60	40	60	Volts 6 to 10 11 to 15	Volts 5	3¾" x 5⅛" x 3¼"	STRONG	3.75
F	110	25 to 40	40	60	6 to 10 11 to 15	5	4¼" x 5½" x 3¾"	HYDRO	3.75
B	110	60	50	75	8 to 12, 14 to 18 21 to 25	6-7-13	4¼" x 5½" x 3¾"	BRADLEY	5.00
C	110	25 to 40	75	100	2 to 10, 10 to 18 17 to 25	2-4-6-7-8-10-12-14-15 16-17-18-19-21-23-25	4¾" x 6" x 4⅝"	LAWRENCE	7.50
T	110	60	100	125	2 to 10, 10 to 18 17 to 25	2-4-6-7-8-10-12-14 15-16-17-18-19-21-23-25	4¾" x 6" x 4⅝"	BIRCH	7.50
K	110	60	150	175	2 to 10, 10 to 18 17 to 25	2-4-6-7-8-10-12-14 15-16-17-18-19-21-23-25	4½" x 6" x 4"	BINGHAM	11.00
K220	220	60	150	175	2 to 10, 10 to 18 17 to 25	2-4-6-7-8-10-12-14 15-16-17-18-19-21-23-25	4¾" x 6" x 4⅝"	BROOK	14.50

[Page Twenty-nine]

THE OPEN TOP CARS DISCLOSE LUXURIOUS INTERIORS

Lionel Pullman and Observation cars are Constructed of Heavy Steel and are exact miniatures of the real cars. Their structural design makes them sturdy and strong. Beautifully embossed heavy gauge steel is used for the body construction and this is further re-enforced by separable panels as shown in the picture below. The top has an extra inner roof and is supported by heavy nickeled arches. The polished brass steps enhance the appearance. All doors swing open like real ones.

No other cars have so many patented features. For instance, note the removable roof feature. By pressing the nickeled roof clips, the top comes off, disclosing luxurious and life-like interiors. See the revolving pullman chairs, the private compartments with porcelain wash basin and closet. Notice the stained glass effect in transoms and transparencies in windows. Each car is brilliantly illuminated and there is a light in the observation platform.

The care and faithfulness of these innumerable details make Lionel cars the finest ever built.

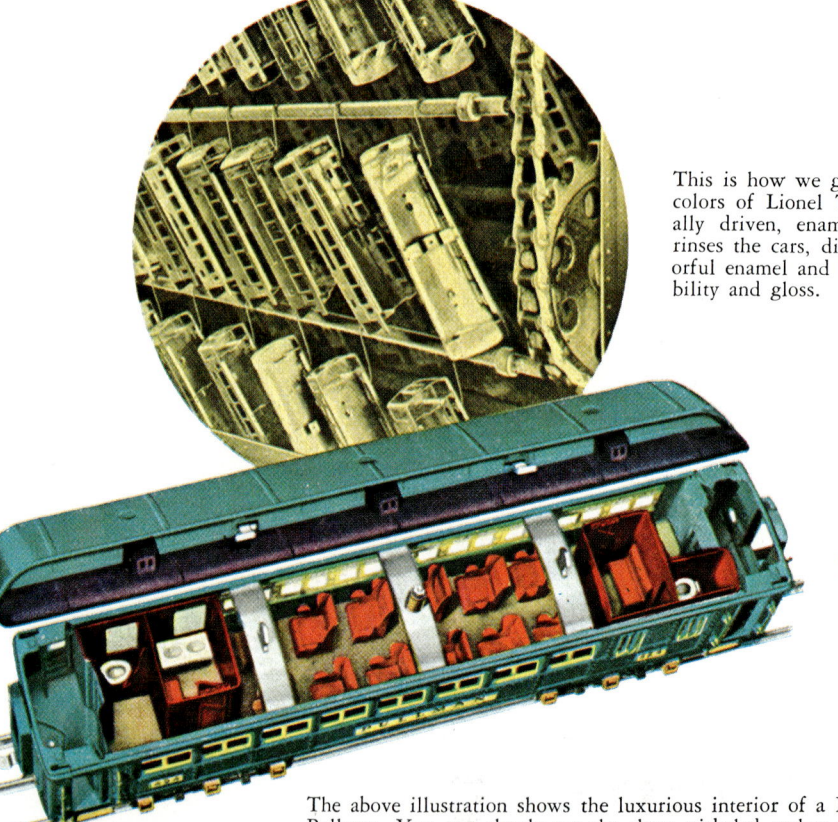

This is how we get the gorgeous colors of Lionel Trains. Electrically driven, enamelling machine rinses the cars, dips them in colorful enamel and bakes for durability and gloss.

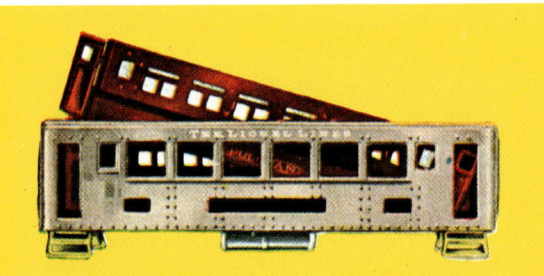

Window panels, doors and seats — a separable piece.

1. Automatic couplers
2. Removable roof
3. Roof lock
4. Stained glass transparency
5. Interior lamps
6. Inserted window frames
7. Air ventilators
8. Observation lamp
9. Transparent lanterns
10. Hinged doors
11. Brass steps
12. Porcelain lavatory
13. Porcelain wash basin
14. Double row revolving parlor chairs
15. Metal air tanks
16. Brass journals
17. 6 wheel heavy steel truck
18. Brass observation platform

Cut-a-way showing the car interior.

The heavy steel trucks of Lionel cars are realistically embossed and embellished with copper Journal boxes. The wheels are heavy steel and nickel.

The above illustration shows the luxurious interior of a Lionel Pullman. You can clearly see the three nickeled arches which support the roof. The center one holds the electric bulb that illuminates the interior. Notice the wash rooms and other details. The pullman chairs revolve just like the real ones. This interior will be found on Cars No. 412-413-414-416-420-421-422.

How beautiful and real-like are the Lionel observation cars. The platform is made of heavy brass. The dome light illuminates the red tail lights and transparent nameplate, giving colorful effects.

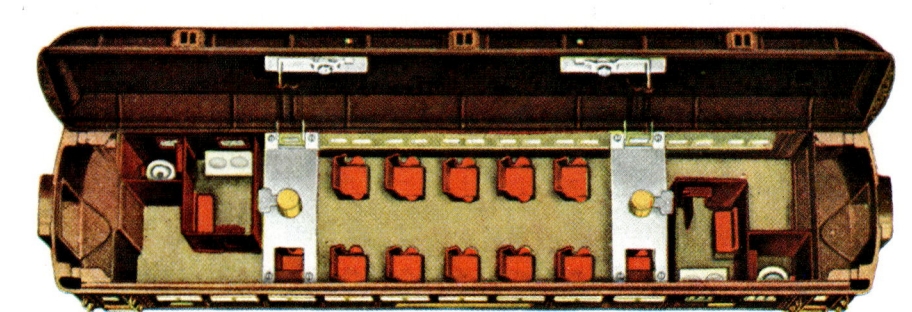

Cars No. 412-413-414 and 416 have the hinged roof feature. Press the two steel roof locks and the roof will swing open.

[Page Thirty]

STURDY PULLMAN AND OBSERVATION CARS FOR "O" GAUGE TRAINS

All Lionel "O" Gauge Passenger Cars are made of heavy steel and are beautifully embossed with rivets and other realistic details. They are finished in a variety of attractive colors.

All Passenger cars except numbers 529-530-629-630-603-604 are illuminated.

Lionel "O" Gauge cars numbers 529-530-629-630 are for use with locomotives No. 248-261-262.

Lionel "O" Gauge cars numbers 603-604-607-608 are for use with locomotives No. 252-253-261-262.

Lionel "O" Gauge cars numbers 605 and 606 are for use with locomotives No. 254-254E-251 and 251E.

Lionel "O" Gauge cars No. 613 and 614 are for use with locomotives No. 253-261-262.

Lionel "O" Gauge cars No. 710 and 712 are obtainable in red or orange and are for use with locomotives No. 251-251E and 260E.

No. 613 Lionel "O" Gauge illuminated Pullman Car—10⅛ inches long, 3¾ inches high.
Code Word "LUXURY." Price, $3.25

No. 614 Lionel "O" Gauge illuminated Observation Car—10⅛ inches long, 3¾ inches high.
Code Word "CINCH." Price, $3.50

No. 607 Lionel "O" Gauge illuminated Pullman Car—7½ inches long, 3½ inches high.
Code Word "BRAND" Price, $1.65

No. 603—Similar to No. 607, but without interior illumination.
Code Word "SAND." Price, $1.25

No. 710 Lionel "O" Gauge illuminated Pullman Car—11⅜ inches long, 4¼ inches high.
Code Word "HOLLY." Price, $3.90

No. 605 Lionel "O" Gauge illuminated Pullman Car—10¼ inches long, 4 inches high.
Code Word "NOVA." Price, $3.50

No. 629 "O" Gauge Pullman Car—6¾ inches long, 3¼ inches high. Enameled in red.
Code Word "FANE." Price, $0.80

No. 529 Lionel "O" Gauge Pullman Car—Same as No. 629 illustrated, but may be obtained finished in green or terra cotta.
Code Word "IMPY." Price, $0.80

No. 608 Lionel "O" Gauge illuminated Observation Car—7½ inches long, 3½ inches high.
Code Word "TWIG." Price, $1.75

No. 604—Similar to No. 608, but without interior illumination.
Code Word "SWIG." Price, $1.25

No. 712 Lionel "O" Gauge illuminated Observation Car—11⅜ inches long, 4¼ inches high.
Code Word "RISE." Price, $4.00

No. 606 Lionel "O" Gauge illuminated Observation Car—10¼ inches long, 4 inches high.
Code Word "MODE." Price, $3.75

No. 630 Lionel "O" Gauge Observation Car—6¾ inches long, 3¼ inches high. Enameled in red.
Code Word "IDEAL." Price, $0.85

No. 530 Lionel "O" Gauge Observation Car—Same as No. 630 illustrated, but may be obtained finished in green or terra cotta.
Code Word "IONA." Price, $0.85

[Page Thirty-one]

CONVERT YOUR TRAIN INTO A FREIGHT WITH THESE REALISTIC CARS

No. 809 Operating Dump Car—Length 6¾ inches.
Code Word "CASCADE." Price, **$1.25**

No. 902 Gondola Car with 2 barrels—6¾ inches long, 2⅛ inches high.
Code Word "VOTE." Price, **75c.**

No. 811 Lumber Car—With load of lumber. 8⅞ inches long, 2½ inches high.
Code Word "DRUM." Price, **$1.90**

No. 812 Gondola Car with 4 barrels—8⅞ inches long, 2⅝ inches high.
Code Word "DALE." Price, **$2.00**

No. 804 Oil Car—6¾ inches long, 3½ inches high.
Code Word "FUEL." Price, **$1.00**

No. 831 Lumber Car—With load of lumber, 6¾ inches long, 2⅛ inches high.
Code Word "VEST." Price, **70c.**

No. 816 Coal Car—Has "Hopper" bottom operated by wheel. 8⅞ inches long, 3¼ inch high.
Code Word "YOST." Price, **$2.65**

No. 815 Oil Car—8⅞ inches long, 3¾ inches high.
Code Word "YAM." Price, **$2.25**

No. 803 Coal Car—Has "Hopper" bottom operated by wheel. 6¾ inches long, 3¼ inches high.
Code Word "LOAD." Price, **$1.00**

No. 806 Cattle Car—Has sliding door. 6¾ inches long, 3¼ inches high.
Code Word "VEX." Price, **$1.10**

No. 814 Box Car—Has sliding door. 8⅞ inch long, 3¾ inches high.
Code Word "YOKE." Price, **$2.25**

No. 814R Refrigerator Car—Has double swing doors. 8⅞ inches long, 3¾ inches high.
Code Word "DOFF." Price, **$2.25**

No. 805 Box Car—Has sliding door. 6¾ inches long, 3¼ inches high.
Code Word "VICK." Price, **$1.00**

No. 807 Caboose—Has front and rear brass platforms and ladder to roof. 6¾ inches long, 3½ high.
Code Word "VAT." Price, **$1.10**

No. 813 Cattle Car—Has sliding door 8⅞ inches long, 3¾ high.
Code Word "YAWL." Price, **$2.25**

No. 817 Caboose—Has front and rear brass platforms and ladder to roof. 8⅞ inches long, 4 inches high.
Code Word "DEFT." Price, **$2.65**

Above single truck cars may be used with locomotives Nos. 248, 252, 261, 262.

Above double truck cars may be used with locomotives Nos. 4, 253, 254, 254E, 251, 251E, 261, 262, 260E.

[Page Thirty-two]

LOADS OF FUN FOR YOU WITH LIONEL ACCESSORIES

162 $1.25

157 $0.50

161 $0.75

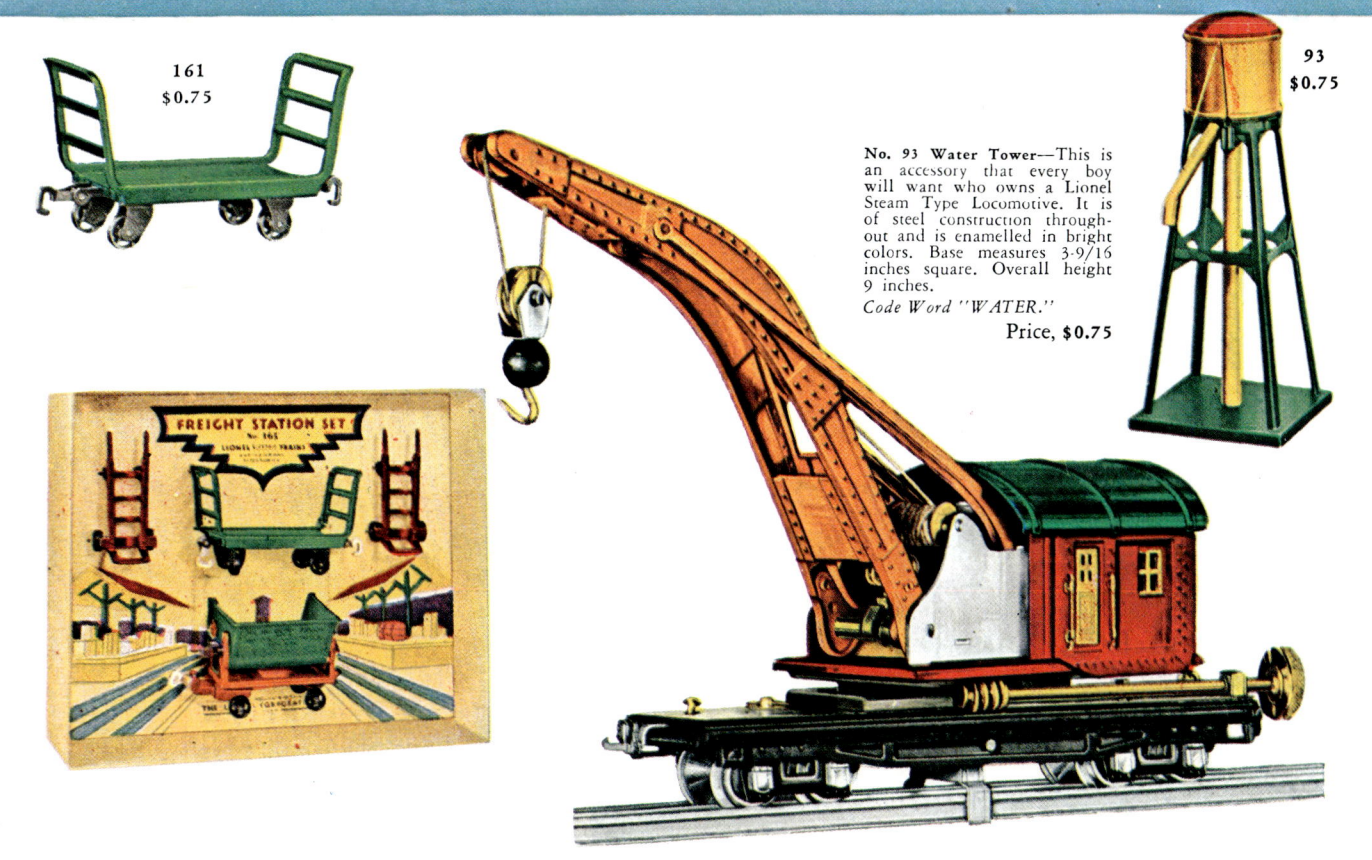

93 $0.75

No. 93 Water Tower—This is an accessory that every boy will want who owns a Lionel Steam Type Locomotive. It is of steel construction throughout and is enamelled in bright colors. Base measures 3-9/16 inches square. Overall height 9 inches.

Code Word "WATER."

Price, $0.75

No. 162 Operating Dump Truck can be tilted for dumping contents. 4¼ inches long, 2¾ inches wide, 2½ inches high.

Code Word "LOUVER." Price, $1.25

No. 157 Hand Truck—3¼ inches long, 1⅝ inches wide.

Code Word "RIGID." Price, $0.50

No. 161 Baggage Truck—4½ inches long, 2 inches wide, 2⅝ inches high.

Code Word "FLEET." Price, $0.75

No. 163 Freight Station Set (right)—Comprises 2 No. 157 Hand Trucks, 1 No. 162 Dump Truck, and 1 No. 160 Baggage Truck. They are exact reproductions of the trucks seen on all freight stations.

Code Word "DROME." Price, per set, $3.00

No. 810 Derrick Car—A most faithful reproduction of the derrick cars in use on all the big railroads throughout the country. You can raise or lower the boom, swing it from side to side, and hoist weights with the pulley and tackle. The gears are actually machine cut, and operate so easily that heavy weights can be lifted without noticeable effort. It is of very substantial construction and is beautifully enamelled in brilliant colors. Length of car 9¼ inches. Height of car 4½ inches. Length of Boom 9¼ inches.

Code Word "CHASER." Price, $7.50

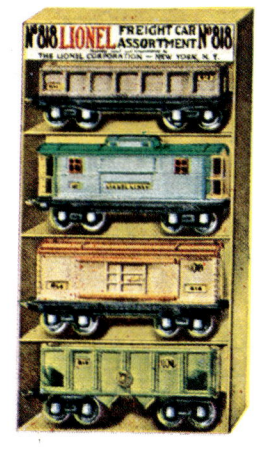

No. 808 Freight Car Set (right) Comprises Nos. 831 Lumber car, 803 Coal car, 804 Oil car, 805 Box car, 806 Cattle car, 807 Caboose, described on page 32. Very attractively packed.

Code Word "QUORN."

Price, $5.25

No. 818 Freight Car Set (left)—Comprises Nos. 812 Gondola car, 814 Box car, 816 Coal car, 817 Caboose, described on page 32. Very attractively packed.

Code Word "QUEST."

Price, $9.00

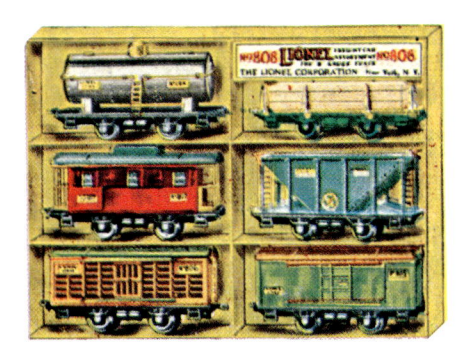

Here is the last word in model railroad building—a floodlight car with two powerful lights and revolving reflectors which can be adjusted to any angle. They are equipped with genuine optical lenses and fitted with No. 28 Mazda lamps. Reflectors, stanchions and hand rails are made of highly polished brass. A universal switch on the platform of the car makes it possible to illuminate each lamp separately or both at one time. Lights can also be cut off with the same switch. 8⅞ inches long, 3¾ inches high.

No. 820 Floodlight Car for "O" Gauge track.

Code Word "ARC." Price, $4.00

[Page Thirty-three]

OPERATE YOUR FREIGHT — ILLUMINATE THE YARD

FOR "LIONEL STANDARD" TRACK

No. 219 Derrick Car—Lionel's famous realistic railroad derrick car. Operating exactly like a real derrick. The boom may be raised or lowered. The entire cab may be swung around in a complete circle, and pulley and tackle may be operated separately. All mechanical movements are controlled by wheels operating worm gears. Self-locking. The boom or cab may be operated from any position. It is mounted on a solid steel car 12½ inches long. 6¼ inches high. The boom is 16 inches long. Car is equipped with automatic couplers.

Code Word "ALUM."   Price, $9.00

Just think of the fun you can have by making your room dark then starting this floodlight car around the track, with its powerful lights that can be swung to any angle. The cases for lights are made of polished brass. Lenses are of optical crystal.

No. 520 Floodlight Car for "Lionel Standard" track. Size 11½ inches long, 4 inches high. Complete with 2 No. 28 lamps.

Code Word "LIGHT."   Price, $5.00

No. 220 Floodlight Car—Similar to No. 520 but 12½ inches long, 4½ inches high. Complete with 2 No. 28 lamps.

Code Word "FLOOD."   Price, $6.00

No. 205—Steel Merchandise Containers (Manufactured under license granted by the L. C. L. Corp.)—Set comprises 3 containers and one set of brass lifting chains. A realistic railroad accessory, patterned exactly after the originals. This set may be used in either the Nos. 512 or 212 Gondola cars. They are made of heavy gauge sheet steel, beautifully embossed and brass trimmed. Equipped with hinged door and fastener. Finished in Lionel's permanent enamel.

Dimensions 3¼ inches long, 3 inches wide, 4 inches high.

Code Word "CHARLES."   Price, per set of 3, $3.00

No. 155 Freight Shed—A new illuminated all-steel beautifully enameled Freight Shed. Solidly constructed of heavy gauge sheet steel. Complete with terminals for wires and two electric bulbs. Used in conjunction with Lionel Freight Cars. Plenty of room on the platform for Lionel hand trucks, baggage trucks and operating dump trucks described on preceding page. 18 inches long. 11 inches high. 8 inches wide.

Code Word "JOCKEY."   Price, $7.50

No. 218 Operating Dump Car—Lionel's operating dump car is a marvel of mechanical ingenuity. A true model of the real cars used in the construction of railroads. It actually dumps a load at any place desired along the track. Wheels and worm gears control the mechanism that automatically opens and tilts the sides of the car. Entirely constructed of sheet steel and beautifully finished by Lionel's famous enameling process. Equipped with automatic couplers. Size 12½ inches long, 4¾ inches high.

Code Word "DEPEW."   Price, $6.25

[Page Thirty-four]

ADD NEW FREIGHT CARS TO YOUR "LIONEL STANDARD" OUTFIT

THE peak of perfection in model railroad rolling stock. These freight cars are made of steel. The fittings, such as hand rails, hand brakes, steps, ladders and inserted panels are highly polished brass. Wheels, axles and automatic couplers are heavy nickelled steel. Journals are copper.

It is great fun to convert your passenger train into a freighter. Here are some good ones to choose from.

No. 511 Lumber Car with load of lumber—11½ inches long, 3¼ inches high.
Code Word "EDEN."   Price, $2.35

No. 512 Gondola Car—11½ inches long, 3⅜ inches high. Complete with 8 barrels.
Code Word "EVER."   Price, $2.60

No. 513 Cattle Car—11½ inches long, 4¾ inches high. Has sliding door.
Code Word "EBON."   Price, $3.10

No. 514R Refrigerator Car—11½ inches long, 4¾ inches high. Has double swing doors.
Code Word "EAST."   Price, $3.10

No. 514 Box Car—11½ inches long, 4¾ inches high. Has sliding door.
Code Word "EGG."   Price, $3.10

No. 515 Oil Car—11½ inches long, 5⅛ inches high.
Code Word "ELTA."   Price, $3.10

No. 516 Coal Car—11½ inches long, 4⅛ inches high. Has "Hopper" bottom, operated by wheel.
Code Word "EPIC."   Price, $3.50

No. 517 Illuminated Caboose—11½ inches long, 5⅜ inches high. Complete with rear platform lamp.
Code Word "EAGER."   Price, $3.50

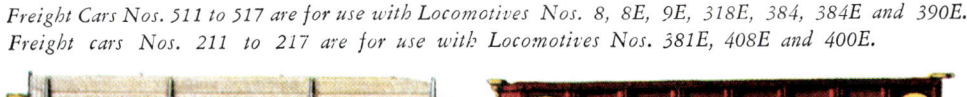

Freight Cars Nos. 511 to 517 are for use with Locomotives Nos. 8, 8E, 9E, 318E, 384, 384E and 390E.
Freight cars Nos. 211 to 217 are for use with Locomotives Nos. 381E, 408E and 400E.

No. 211 Lumber Car with load of lumber—12½ inches long, 4⅛ inches high.
Code Word "ANT."   Price, $3.50

No. 212 Gondola Car—12½ inches long, 3¾ inches high. Complete with 8 barrels.
Code Word "ROY."   Price, $3.75

No. 213 Cattle Car—12½ inches long, 5½ inches high. Has sliding door.
Code Word "WAKE."   Price, $4.75

No. 214 Box Car—12½ inches long, 5½ inches high. Has double sliding doors.
Code Word "WOOL."   Price, $4.75

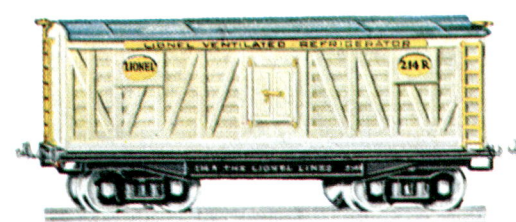

No. 214R Refrigerator Car—12½ inches long, 5½ inches high. Has double swing doors.
Code Word "GONE."   Price, $4.75

No. 215 Oil Car—12½ inches long, 5½ inches high.
Code Word "DICE."   Price, $4.75

No. 216 Coal Car—12½ inches long, 5 inches high. Has "Hopper" bottom operated by wheel.
Code Word "ALAMA."   Price, $4.75

No. 217 Illuminated Caboose—12½ inches long, 5½ inches high. Complete with rear platform lamp.
Code Word "RAFT."   Price, $5.50

[Page Thirty-five]

YOU SHOULD HAVE SOME NEW "LIONEL STANDARD" PULLMANS

All Lionel Passenger Cars are made of heavy steel and are beautifully embossed with rivets and other realistic details. They are finished in a variety of attractive colors.

"Lionel Standard" Cars Nos. 332, 337 and 338 are for use with Locomotives Nos. 8, 8E, 384 and 384E.

"Lionel Standard" Cars Nos. 309, 310 and 312 may be used with Locomotives Nos. 384, 384E, 318 and 318E.

"Lionel Standard" Cars Nos. 424 and 426 may be used with Locomotives Nos. 9E and 390E.

"Lionel Standard" Cars Nos. 420, 421 and 422 may be used with Locomotives Nos. 390E and 400E.

"Lionel Standard" Cars Nos. 412, 413, 414 and 416 may be used with Locomotives Nos. 381E, 400E and 408E.

"Lionel Standard" Cars Nos. 418, 419, 431 and 490 may be used with Locomotives Nos. 400E and 408E.

No. 490 "Lionel Standard" illuminated Observation Car—$17\frac{5}{8}$ inches long, $6\frac{1}{8}$ inches high.
Code Word "CABIN." Price, **$10.00**

No. 431 "Lionel Standard" illuminated Dining Car—$18\frac{1}{4}$ inches long, $6\frac{1}{8}$ inches high.
Code Word "FEED." Price, **$10.50**

No. 418 "Lionel Standard" illuminated Pullman Car—$18\frac{1}{4}$ inches long, $6\frac{1}{8}$ inches high.
Code Word "COMFORT." Price, **$9.00**

No. 419 "Lionel Standard" illuminated Pullman Baggage Car—$18\frac{1}{4}$ inches long, $6\frac{1}{8}$ inches high.
Code Word "COURT." Price, **$9.25**

No. 312 "Lionel Standard" illuminated Observation Car—$13\frac{1}{4}$ inches long, $5\frac{1}{4}$ inches high. *Code Word "DOMO."* Price, **$5.50**

No. 309 "Lionel Standard" illuminated Pullman Car—$13\frac{1}{4}$ inches long, $5\frac{1}{4}$ inches high. *Code Word "ROAD."* Price, **$4.75**

No. 310 "Lionel Standard" illuminated Mail and Baggage Car—$13\frac{1}{4}$ inches long, $5\frac{1}{4}$ inches high. *Code Word "WEC."* Price, **$4.75**

No. 332 "Lionel Standard" illuminated Mail and Baggage Car—12 inches long, $4\frac{3}{4}$ inches high. Finished in blue or red color. *Code Word "WILE."* Price, **$4.75**

No. 338 "Lionel Standard" illuminated Observation Car—12 inches long, $4\frac{3}{4}$ inches high.
Code Word "ORBIT." Price, **$5.25**

No. 337 "Lionel Standard" illuminated Pullman Car—12 inches long, $4\frac{3}{4}$ inches high.
Code Word "PASS." Price, **$4.50**

No. 420 "Lionel Standard" illuminated Pullman Car. 18 inches long, 5 inches high. This car is lettered "Faye."
Code Word "FAYE." Price, **$12.00**

No. 421 "Lionel Standard" illuminated Pullman Car. Same as above, but lettered "Westphal."
Code Word "WESTPHAL." Price, **$12.00**

No. 424 "Lionel Standard" Pullman Car. 16 inches long. $5\frac{1}{2}$ inches high.
Code Word "IRVINGTON." Price, **$9.50**

No. 412 Lionel Standard" illuminated Pullman Car—$21\frac{1}{2}$ inches long. $6\frac{5}{8}$ inches high. This car is lettered "California."
Code Word "ROMP." Price, **$15.00**

No. 413 "Lionel Standard" illuminated Pullman Car—Same as above but lettered "Colorado."
Code Word "ROPE." Price, **$15.00**

No. 414 "Lionel Standard" illuminated Pullman Car—Same as above but lettered "Illinois."
Code Word "REEF." Price, **$15.00**

No. 422 "Lionel Standard" illuminated Observation Car. 18 inches long, 5 inches high. This car is lettered "Tempel."
Code Word "TEMPEL." Price, **$12.50**

No. 426 "Lionel Standard" Observation Car. 16 inches long, $5\frac{1}{2}$ inches high.
Code Word "HILLSIDE." Price, **$9.50**

No. 416 "Lionel Standard" illuminated Observation Car, lettered "New York." This car conforms in size to Nos. 412, 413 and 414 illustrated above. The brass observation platform is surmounted by a dome light which shines through 2 red rear end lanterns. In addition, this car is equipped with 2 interior lights. This car is 21 inches long, $6\frac{5}{8}$ inches high.
Code Word "REST." Price, **$15.00**

ILLUMINATE YOUR LIONEL VILLAGE WITH THESE BRILLIANT LAMP POSTS

No. 67 Lamp Post — 12⅝ inches high. Complete with two globes.
Code Word "EDMUNDS."
Price, $3.00

No. 58 Lamp Post — 7½ inches high. Complete with globe.
Code Word "JENNY."
Price, $1.30

No. 54 Lamp Post — 9½ inches high. Complete with two globes. An attractive new double-arm lamp post.
Code Word "MOLD."
Price, $2.35

No. 57 Lamp Post — 7½ inches high. The top is removable so that the lamp can be renewed. Complete with lamp.
Code "CHERRY."
Price, $1.75

No. 53 Lamp Post — An extremely attractive lamp post. Height to top of bulb 8½ inches. Price includes bulb.
Code "POST."
Price, $1.35

No. 56 Lamp Post — 7¾ inches high. The top is removable so that the lamp can be renewed. Complete with lamp.
Code "SHINE."
Price, $1.75

No. 59 Lamp Post — Similar in design to No. 61, but is 8⅝ inches high. Complete with globe.
Code Word "BRIGHT."
Price, $1.60

No. 61 Lamp Post — 12⅝ inches high. Complete with globe.
Code Word "INDIA."
Price, $2.25

No. 111 Lionel Lamp Cabinet — This is the lamp cabinet you will see at your dealer's. Each cabinet contains 50 assorted lamps in 12 and 18 volts, suitable for "O" Gauge and "Lionel Standard" equipment. Each lamp is individually packed.
Code Word "LUX."
Price, $15.00

COLORED LAMPS FOR ACCESSORIES

No. 27R Red Lamp—12 volts, ½" round, *Code "NOUN."* Price, $0.30
No. 28R Red Lamp—18 volts, ½" round, *Code "NORTH."* Price, $0.30
No. 27G Green Lamp—12 volts, ½" round, *Code "NAIL."* Price, $0.30
No. 28G Green Lamp—18 volts, ½" round, *Code "NEAT."* Price, $0.30

The red lamps listed above are for use in the Nos. 025 and 25 Bumpers, No. 70, Flashing Railroad Signal, and No. 77 and 077 Crossing Gates.

The green lamps listed above are for use in the front and rear lanterns of No. 408E locomotive.

LIONEL LAMP RENEWALS

No. 27—12 volt, ½" round lamp. For use in all "O" Gauge equipment. *Code "NOSE."* Price, $0.30
No. 28—18 volt, ½" round lamp. For use in all "Lionel Standard" equipment. *Code "NELA."* Price, $0.30
No. 39—12 volt, ¾" round globe. For "O" Gauge Railroads use this lamp on Nos. 54, 58, 59, 61 and 67 Lamp Posts and No. 124 station. *Code "NICE."* Price, $0.30
No. 40—18 volt, ¾" round globe. Same uses as No. 39 lamp, when operating "Lionel Standard" equipment. *Code "NAVY."* Price, $0.30

[*Page Thirty-seven*]

1931

NO RAILROAD IS COMPLETE WITHOUT AUTOMATIC ACCESSORIES

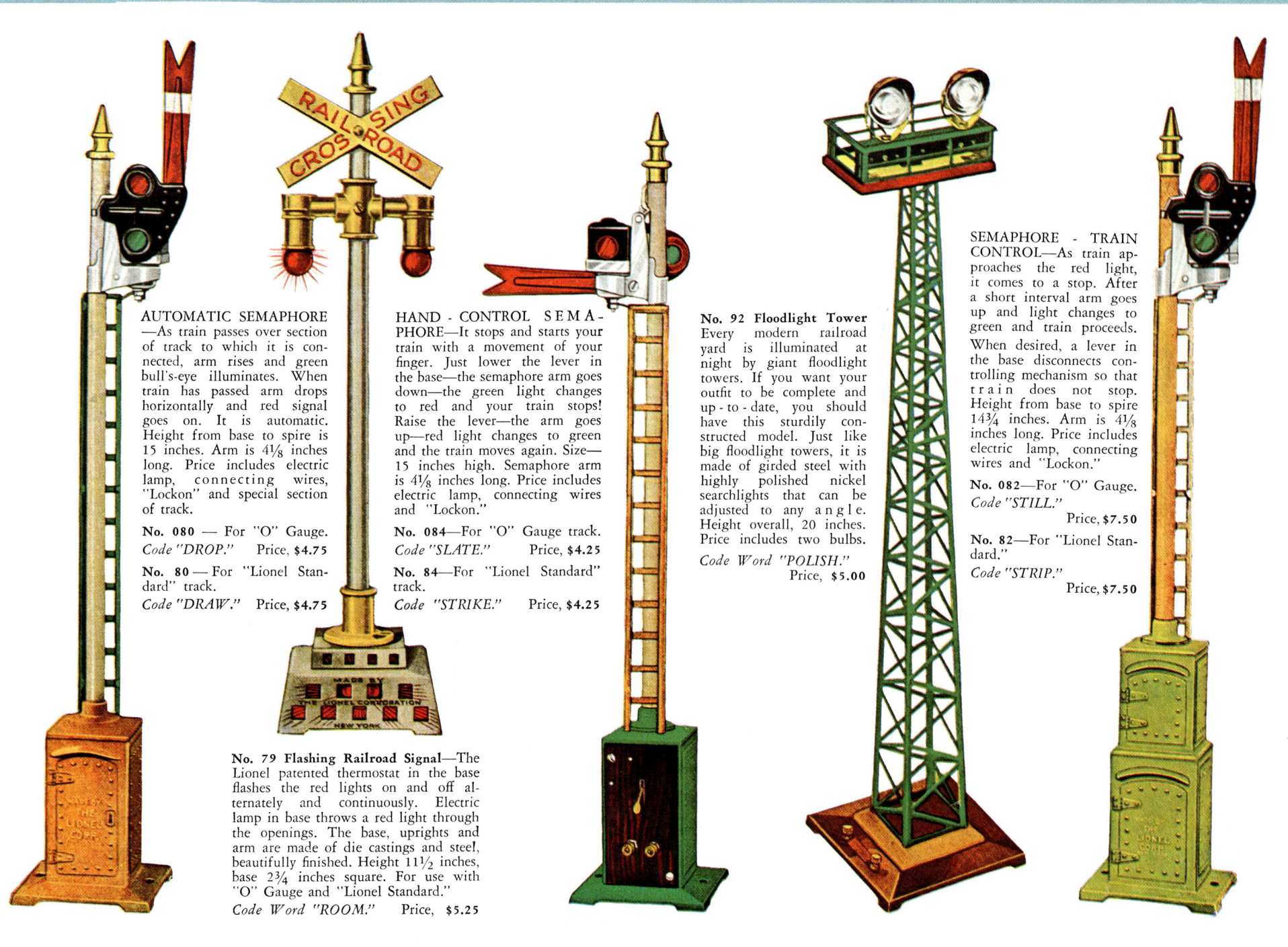

AUTOMATIC SEMAPHORE—As train passes over section of track to which it is connected, arm rises and green bull's-eye illuminates. When train has passed arm drops horizontally and red signal goes on. It is automatic. Height from base to spire is 15 inches. Arm is 4 1/8 inches long. Price includes electric lamp, connecting wires, "Lockon" and special section of track.

No. 080 — For "O" Gauge.
Code "DROP." Price, **$4.75**

No. 80 — For "Lionel Standard" track.
Code "DRAW." Price, **$4.75**

HAND-CONTROL SEMAPHORE—It stops and starts your train with a movement of your finger. Just lower the lever in the base—the semaphore arm goes down—the green light changes to red and your train stops! Raise the lever—the arm goes up—red light changes to green and the train moves again. Size—15 inches high. Semaphore arm is 4 1/8 inches long. Price includes electric lamp, connecting wires and "Lockon."

No. 084—For "O" Gauge track.
Code "SLATE." Price, **$4.25**

No. 84—For "Lionel Standard" track.
Code "STRIKE." Price, **$4.25**

No. 79 Flashing Railroad Signal—The Lionel patented thermostat in the base flashes the red lights on and off alternately and continuously. Electric lamp in base throws a red light through the openings. The base, uprights and arm are made of die castings and steel, beautifully finished. Height 11 1/2 inches, base 2 3/4 inches square. For use with "O" Gauge and "Lionel Standard."
Code Word "ROOM." Price, **$5.25**

No. 92 Floodlight Tower
Every modern railroad yard is illuminated at night by giant floodlight towers. If you want your outfit to be complete and up-to-date, you should have this sturdily constructed model. Just like big floodlight towers, it is made of girded steel with highly polished nickel searchlights that can be adjusted to any angle. Height overall, 20 inches. Price includes two bulbs.

Code Word "POLISH."
Price, **$5.00**

SEMAPHORE - TRAIN CONTROL—As train approaches the red light, it comes to a stop. After a short interval arm goes up and light changes to green and train proceeds. When desired, a lever in the base disconnects controlling mechanism so that train does not stop. Height from base to spire 14 3/4 inches. Arm is 4 1/8 inches long. Price includes electric lamp, connecting wires and "Lockon."

No. 082—For "O" Gauge.
Code "STILL."
Price, **$7.50**

No. 82—For "Lionel Standard."
Code "STRIP."
Price, **$7.50**

[Page Thirty-eight]

BELLS RING, LIGHTS BLINK, GATES LOWER, TRAINS STOP—AUTOMATICALLY

Electric Warning Signal—Electric bell with two gongs is mounted on steel standard 8¾" high. Gongs ring while train passes over track section to which it is connected. Bell stops ringing when crossing is clear. Finished in bright colors. Bell is nickeled steel. Price includes special track, wires and "Lockon."

No. 069 for "O" Gauge track.
Code Word "RINGER"
Price, $3.25

No. 69 for "Lionel Standard" track.
Code Word "BEWARE"
Price, $3.50

No. 87 Railroad Crossing Signal—Just like those used on many grade crossings. The bright red lantern on white background is illuminated at intervals of a second by means of a device placed in the interior. It is thrilling to watch this automatic "blinker" operate continuously without attention. The base contains terminals for connecting wires. This crossing signal is 6¾ inches high. Can be used with "Lionel Standard" or "O" Gauge equipment.
Code Word "STORE"
Price, $3.50

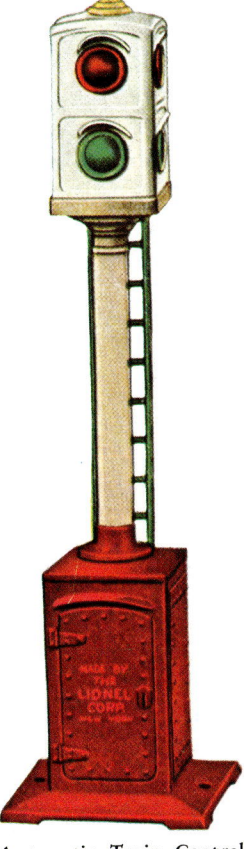

Automatic Train Control—When train approaches, red light glows and train automatically stops. After an interval, red light changes to green and train proceeds. Can be disconnected so that train will not stop. 10¼ inches high. Price includes lamp, connecting wires and "Lockon."

No. 078—For "O" Gauge track. *Code* "HEAVE."
Price, $5.25

No. 78— For "Lionel Standard" Track. *Code* "WEAVE." Price, $5.25

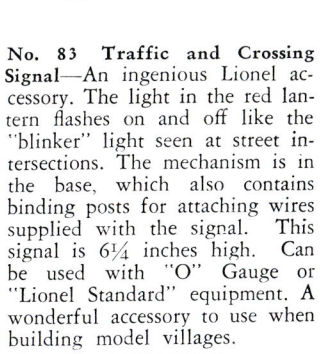

No. 83 Traffic and Crossing Signal—An ingenious Lionel accessory. The light in the red lantern flashes on and off like the "blinker" light seen at street intersections. The mechanism is in the base, which also contains binding posts for attaching wires supplied with the signal. This signal is 6¼ inches high. Can be used with "O" Gauge or "Lionel Standard" equipment. A wonderful accessory to use when building model villages.
Code Word "STAND"
Price, $3.00

Nos. 77 and 077 Illuminated Automatic Crossing Gates—An exact reproduction of the real ones seen at grade crossings. When train approaches the track section to which it is connected, the red light illuminates and the gate comes down. When train passes, gate rises, and the light goes out. Gate is made of heavy steel. The electric unit is in the base. Finished in enameled colors. Gate is 11 inches long. Price includes special section of track, connecting wires and "Lockon."

No. 077—for "O" Gauge track.
Code Word "ADVANCE"
Price, $4.25

No. 77—for "Lionel Standard" track.
Code Word "TARRY"
Price, $4.50

[Page Thirty-nine]

1931

TELEGRAPH POSTS, FLAG POSTS – A FINAL TOUCH OF RAILROAD REALISM

This isn't a picture of an actual railroad—merely the No. 262 locomotive and a set of No. 60 telegraph posts. Build this realism into your model railroad with Lionel accessories.

No. 60 Telegraph Post—Arm is equipped with real glass insulators. Enamelled steel standard is 8⅞ inches high.
Code Word "WIRE." Price, $0.65

No. 85 Telegraph Post with extension arm. For "Lionel Standard" Track. Equipped with real glass insulators. Beautifully enamelled in a variety of colors. Height 9 inches. Length of extension arm overall is 8 inches.
Code Word "QUART." Price, $0.80

No. 060 Telegraph Post with extension arm. For "O" Gauge track. Similar in construction and appearance to No. 85 described above. Height 5½ inches. Length of extension arm over-all is 6⅝ inches.
Code Word "QUIET." Price, $0.65

No. 90 Flagstaff and Flag — The flagstaff (14¾ inches high) is removable, and fits into an ornamental base mounted on a miniature grass plot beautifully ornamented with flower border.
Code Word "PLOT." Price, $1.00

No. 89 Flagstaff and Flag—For use with Lionel model villages or to place in front of a Lionel Station. Flagstaff is 14¼ inches high. Silk flag may be lowered by cord attached, which can be fastened to hook near the base.
Code Word "ARTHUR." Price, $0.75

No. 86 "Lionel Standard" Telegraph Post Set—These new telegraph posts incorporate a wonderful new feature, namely: the extension arm attached to the base, by means of which the telegraph posts are rigidly fastened to the track. The set comprises 6 No. 85 telegraph posts, 9 inches high, described on this page. Attractively packed.
Code Word "TENSE." Price, $4.50

No. 071 "O" Gauge Telegraph Post Set—Same as above, but for "O" Gauge track. Comprises 6 No. 060 telegraph posts, 5½ inches high, described on this page.
Code Word "TAUT." Price, $3.75

No. 62 Semaphore — The semaphore arm has three discs—red, green and yellow. Arm is operated by lever near base. Enamelled steel standard is 8⅞ inches high.
Code Word "CAUTION." Price, $0.90

No. 68 Warning Signal—For "Lionel Standard" track. Enameled steel standard is 8⅞ inches high. Brass sign is 3½ inches square.
Code Word "STOP." Price, $0.90

No. 068 Warning Signal—For "O" Gauge track. Similar to No. 68, but is 6⅝ inches high. Brass sign is 2 3/16 inches square.
Code Word "LOOK." Price, $0.50

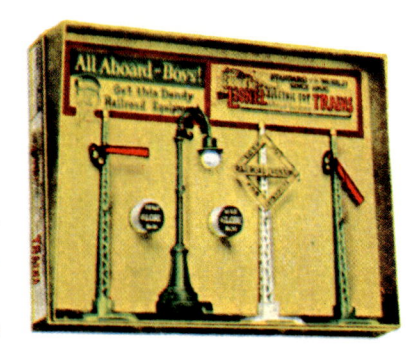

Outfit No. 70—Comprises 2 No. 62 semaphores, 1 No. 59 lamp post, 1 No. 68 warning sign, 2 extra globes for lamp post. Very attractively packed.
Code Word "HOBART." Price, $4.50

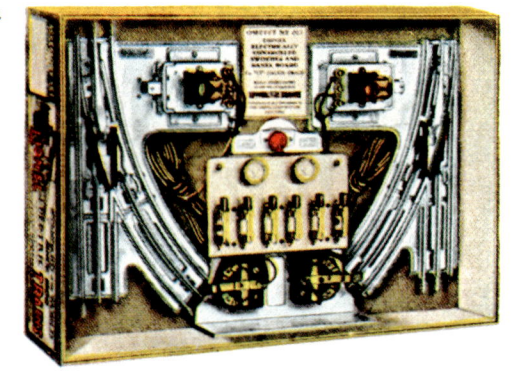

No. 225 "Lionel Standard" "Distant-Control" Switch and Panel Board Set—Comprises 1 pair No. 222 "Distant-Control" Switches (right and left hand) and 1 No. 439 illuminated Panel Board. A desirable accessory for operating a "Distant-Control" Railroad at any distance from the track. Very attractively packed. Complete with lamps and connecting wires.
Code Word "OPERA." Price, $17.50

No. 013 "O" Gauge "Distant-Control" Switch and Panel Board Set—Comprises 1 pair No. 012 "Distant-Control" Switches (right and left hand) and 1 No. 439 illuminated Panel Board. This is the same as the set illustrated above, but is for use on Lionel "O" Gauge track.
Code Word "OPEN." Price, $15.50

Outfit No. 71—Comprises 6 No. 60 steel telegraph posts, as described on this page. This set can be used with either "O" Gauge or "Lionel Standard" Railroads. Very attractively packed.
Code Word "USEFUL." Price, $3.75

[Page Forty]

ALL STEEL TUNNELS AND BEAUTIFUL TRUE-TO-LIFE VILLAS

No. 118 Tunnel—For use with small size "O" Gauge trains. Length 8 inches, width 7¼ inches, height 7 inches. Tunnel openings are 4 inches wide by 5⅜ inches high.

Code Word "SIMPLON." Price, $2.25

No. 119L Illuminated Tunnel—Suitable for all "O" Gauge trains and medium size "Lionel Standard" trains. Equipped with interior light. Length 12 inches, width 9½ inches, height 9¼ inches. Tunnel openings are 5 inches wide and 6½ inches high.

Code Word "HARP." Price, $4.50

No. 119 Tunnel—Similar in every way to No. 119L described above, but without interior light.

Code Word "HOSA." Price, $3.50

No. 140L Illuminated Tunnel—No finer accessory than this highly decorative all steel tunnel has ever been made for model electric trains. It is made for use with our largest model railroad equipment. The electric lights which are placed at both ends of the tunnel reflect through the windows of the houses on the mountain side, presenting a magnificent view. Length 35¾ inches, width 23 inches, height 23½ inches. Tunnel openings are 8 inches square.

Code Word "SEVA." Price, $17.50

No. 130L Illuminated Tunnel—Similar to No. 140L except for use with "O" Gauge equipment. Length 24 inches, width 18½ inches, height 14½ inches. Tunnel openings are 5 inches wide and 6½ inches high.

Code Word "SOAK." Price, $14.50

No. 184 Illuminated Bungalow—4¾ inches long, 4 inches high, 2¾ inches wide. Beautifully decorated. Complete with interior light and connecting wires.

Code Word "HOME." Price, $1.25

No. 120L Illuminated Tunnel—For use with the large size "Lionel Standard" Trains. Hand painted and graceful in design. Equipped with interior light. Length 17 inches, width 12 inches, height 9⅝ inches. Tunnel openings are 6½ inches wide and 8⅛ inches high.

Code Word "HOPE." Price, $6.50

No. 192 Illuminated Villa Set—An attractive assortment of model houses. Comprises 1 No. 191 villa, 1 No. 189 villa and 2 No. 184 bungalows. Each is complete with interior lights and connecting wires.

Code Word "VILLAGE." Price, $7.00

No. 186 Illuminated Bungalow Set—Comprises 5 No. 184 bungalows, beautifully finished in assorted colors. Complete with interior lights and connecting wires. Attractively packed.

Code Word "HAMLET." Price, $6.25

No. 191 Illuminated Villa—Beautifully designed. 7⅛ inches long, 5 inches wide and 5¼ inches high. Roof is removable. Complete with interior lighting fixture, lamp and connecting wires.

Code Word "SOLID." Price, $2.50

No. 189 Illuminated Villa—A model that is architecturally perfect. Finished in a variety of harmonizing enamel colors. 5½ inches long, 5 inches wide, 5½ inches high. Complete with interior light and connecting wires.

Code Word "MANSE." Price, $2.00

[Page Forty-one]

ARCHITECTURAL GEMS – JUST LIKE THE REAL STATIONS

No. 114 Station—A new beautifully designed 19¾ inch railroad station that is a replica of the terminal stations built in recent years by the leading railroads of America. The walls are embossed to represent limestone construction. It is equipped with swinging doors, two ornamental outside lighting brackets and two interior lights. The interior bulbs, when illuminated, light up the grilled windows and give a most pleasing and realistic effect. The roof has a grilled skylight through which access to the interior of the station is made possible. This station is the most beautiful and the largest ever produced by Lionel, and is a handsome adjunct to any model railroad. Complete with 4 bulbs.

Code Word "SUPREME."   Price, $15.00

No. 127 Illuminated Station—For use with any "O" Gauge train. Interior light is fastened to a supporting fixture. Roof is removable so that lamp can be easily reached. 8½ inches long, 4¼ inches wide and 5 inches high. Complete with electric lamp and connecting wires.
Code Word "TONLY."   Price, $3.10

No. 126 Illuminated Station—Specially designed for use with our smaller train outfits and has many of the architectural features of our larger models. The interior light is supported on a fixture placed beneath the removable roof. 10¼ inches long, 7¼ inches wide and 7 inches high. Complete with electric lamp and connecting wires.
Code Word "ALITE."   Price, $4.75

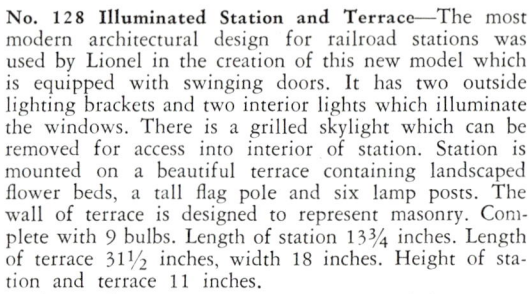

No. 128 Illuminated Station and Terrace—The most modern architectural design for railroad stations was used by Lionel in the creation of this new model which is equipped with swinging doors. It has two outside lighting brackets and two interior lights which illuminate the windows. There is a grilled skylight which can be removed for access into interior of station. Station is mounted on a beautiful terrace containing landscaped flower beds, a tall flag pole and six lamp posts. The wall of terrace is designed to represent masonry. Complete with 9 bulbs. Length of station 13¾ inches. Length of terrace 31½ inches, width 18 inches. Height of station and terrace 11 inches.
Code Word "UKASE."   Price, $26.25

No. 129 Station Platform—Same as the terrace described above. For use with stations that have no platform.
Code Word "YIELD."   Price, $16.75

No. 113 Illuminated Station—Same as No. 128 but without terrace. Complete with 3 bulbs.
Code Word "UPAS."   Price, $10.00

No. 112 Station—Same as No. 113 but without outside lighting brackets.
Code Word "UNRID."   Price, $7.50

[Page Forty-two]

IT'S A THRILL TO CONTROL THE SWITCHES OF THESE POWER HOUSES

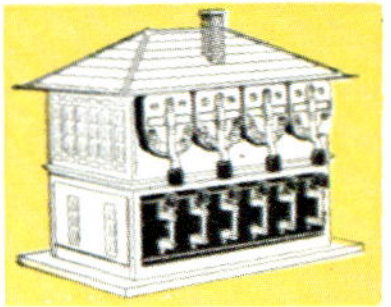

No. 437 Illuminated Switch Signal Tower—For operating Electrically-Controlled Train and Accessories at any distance from the track. Rear view right shows six knife switches attached to panel board, also provision for attaching controlling levers of electrically-controlled track switches. Note the wonderful detail in the windows, doors and panels, which are separable inserted pieces. Complete with electric lamp and connecting wire. Size 10¼ inches long, 8⅞ inches high, 8⅜ inches wide.

Code Word "ZEV." Price, $7.50

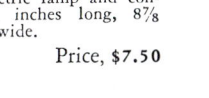

Lionel Power Stations—Made in 2 sizes to fit all types of Lionel "Multivolt" Transformers. Base is hollow, so that transformer can be set inside easily. Grid in roof is removable.
No. 435—Size 7⅝ by 6 inches, 9½ inches high to chimney. For use with Types A, B or F Transformers.
Code Word "JENA." Price, $2.00
No. 436—Size 9¼ by 7⅝ inches, 10½ inches high to chimney. For use with Types T, C and K Transformers.
Code Word "WATTS." Price, $3.00

No. 840 Power Station—There is no accessory more desirable or fitting to be used with Lionel "Distant-Control" Railroads than this attractive new Power Station. It is possible to control and operate the most elaborate model railroad layout from this central station. The stone work and masonry are in exact reproduction of a big concrete building. Actual doors and windows. Steel construction throughout, richly enamelled in beautiful colors. Length 26 inches, width 21½ inches, height to top of smokestack 18 inches.

Code Word "LING." Price, $22.50

The illustration at right shows the provision made for accommodating one or two Lionel Transformers. The switches on the transformers can be reached through openings above them. Illustration also shows the Panel Board on one side of the Power House containing six knife switches, from which "Distant-Control" trains and illuminated accessories can be operated.

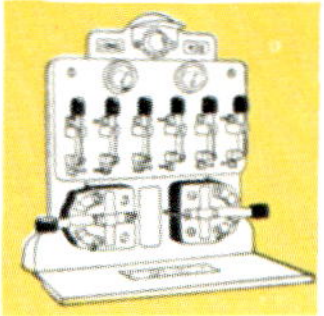

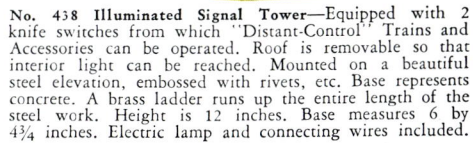

No. 439 Panel Board—You can operate your trains and accessories from one or more of the six knife switches mounted on the marble Panel Board. Provision is made for holding two levers of Lionel Electrically-Controlled Switches, shown in illustration at left. Electric lamp at top illuminates small dummy meters. The knife switches are mounted on a composition marble slab. Made of heavy steel beautifully enamelled. Size 8¼ inches high and 7¼ inches wide.

Code Word "FLOW." Price, $4.50

No. 438 Illuminated Signal Tower—Equipped with 2 knife switches from which "Distant-Control" Trains and Accessories can be operated. Roof is removable so that interior light can be reached. Mounted on a beautiful steel elevation, embossed with rivets, etc. Base represents concrete. A brass ladder runs up the entire length of the steel work. Height is 12 inches. Base measures 6 by 4¾ inches. Electric lamp and connecting wires included.

Code Word "CARP." Price, $5.00

[Page Forty-three]

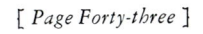

1931

EVERY RAILROAD MUST HAVE A BRIDGE — CHOOSE ONE FOR YOURS

271
$3.00

270
$1.50

IT WILL ADD REALISM AND INCREASE YOUR FUN

The designs for the new Lionel Bridges, illustrated on this page, were taken from the great railroad bridges in America. They are realistically built to represent heavy steel girder construction. Track bed is designed to hold track rigidly. The train passes through them at its own level without the necessity of grade approaches. Each bridge embodies a foot path on each side with a handsome portal at either end of the path. The bridges are made entirely of sheet steel and are enamelled in attractive colors. Any boy will be proud to own one of them.

No. 270 Single Span Railroad Bridge for "O" Gauge—10¼ inches in length. Complete with one section of track.
Code Word "ZAFFER."   Price, $1.50

No. 271 Two-Span Railroad Bridge for "O" Gauge—20½ inches in length. Complete with two sections of track.
Code Word "ZEBRA."   Price, $3.00

No. 272 Three-Span Railroad Bridge for "O" Gauge—Same as No. 271 except that it has three spans. 30¾ inches in length. Complete with three sections of track.
Code Word "ZINC."   Price, $4.50

282
$7.50

280
$2.50

No. 280 Single Span Railroad Bridge for "Lionel Standard"—14 inches in length. Complete with one section of track.
Code Word "ZONE."   Price, $2.50

No. 281 Two-Span Railroad Bridge for "Lionel Standard"—Same as No. 282 except that it has two spans. 28 inches in length. Complete with two sections of track.
Code Word "ZYME."   Price, $5.00

No. 282 Three-Span Railroad Bridge for "Lionel Standard"—42 inches in length. Complete with three sections of track.
Code Word "ZENITH."   Price, $7.50

ALL TRUE MODELS OF STURDY STEEL CONSTRUCTION

Lionel's Famous "Hell Gate Bridge" for "O" Gauge and "Lionel Standard"

No. 300 Steel Bridge—This is the most realistic bridge that has ever been produced for model railroads. It is constructed entirely of sheet steel, and is enameled in beautiful colors. The train passes through the bridge at its own level without the necessity of grade approaches. Any boy should be proud to own this marvelous bridge. It is 28¾ inches long, 11 inches high and 10⅞ inches wide.

Code Word "HELGA."   Price, $16.50

Colonel Lindbergh in his trans-Pacific plane flying over Hell Gate Bridge which spans the East River in New York. Notice how true to the original is the Lionel model.

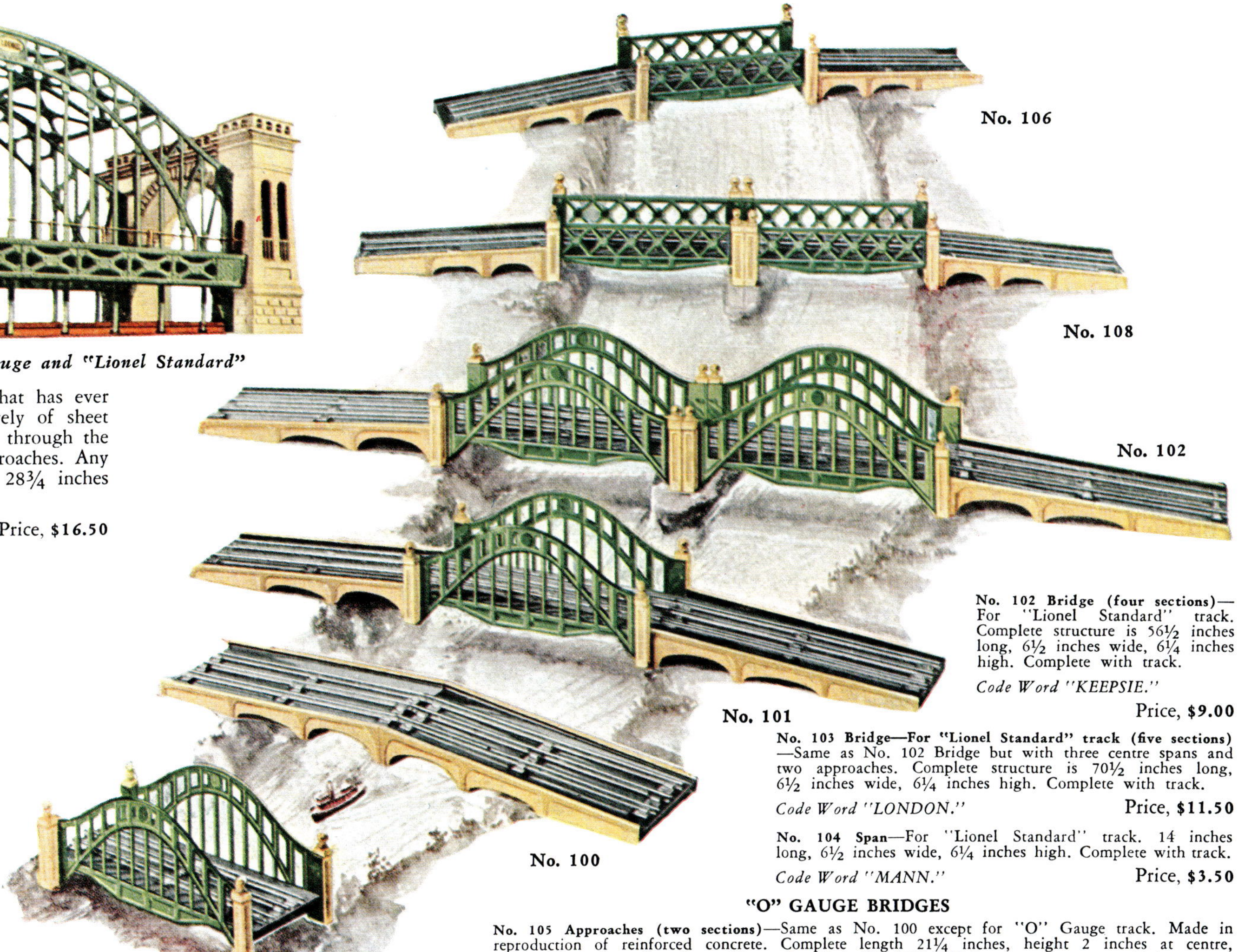

"LIONEL STANDARD" BRIDGES

No. 100 Approaches (two sections)—For "Lionel Standard" track. Complete length 28¼ inches, height 2 inches at center, width 5⅜ inches. Complete with track.
Code Word "BROOKLYN."   Price, $2.60

No. 101 Bridge (three sections)—For "Lionel Standard" track. Complete structure is 42½ inches long, 6½ inches wide, 6¼ inches high. Complete with track.
Code Word "QUEENS."   Price, $6.00

No. 102 Bridge (four sections)—For "Lionel Standard" track. Complete structure is 56½ inches long, 6½ inches wide, 6¼ inches high. Complete with track.
Code Word "KEEPSIE."   Price, $9.00

No. 103 Bridge—For "Lionel Standard" track (five sections)—Same as No. 102 Bridge but with three centre spans and two approaches. Complete structure is 70½ inches long, 6½ inches wide, 6¼ inches high. Complete with track.
Code Word "LONDON."   Price, $11.50

No. 104 Span—For "Lionel Standard" track. 14 inches long, 6½ inches wide, 6¼ inches high. Complete with track.
Code Word "MANN."   Price, $3.50

"O" GAUGE BRIDGES

No. 105 Approaches (two sections)—Same as No. 100 except for "O" Gauge track. Made in reproduction of reinforced concrete. Complete length 21¼ inches, height 2 inches at centre, width 4⅛ inches. Complete with track. *Code Word "PARIS."*   Price, $1.75

No. 106 Bridge (three sections)—For "O" Gauge track. Complete structure is 32½ inches long, 5½ inches wide, 4⅛ inches high. Complete with track.
Code Word "CONN."   Price, $3.50

No. 108 Bridge (four sections)—For "O" Gauge track. Complete structure is 43 inches long, 5½ inches wide, 4⅛ inches high. Complete with track.
Code Word "HOUSA."   Price, $5.75

No. 109 Bridge—For "O" Gauge track (five sections)—Same in appearance as No. 108 Bridge, but with three centre spans and two approaches. Complete structure is 53⅞ inches long, 5½ inches wide, 4⅛ inches high. Complete with track.
Code Word "MISS."   Price, $7.75

No. 110 Span—For "O" Gauge track. Like No. 106 without the approaches. 10½ inches long, 5½ inches wide, 4⅛ inches high. Complete with track. *Code Word "WILLY."*   Price, $2.60

[Page Forty-five]

A NEW IMPROVED ELECTRICALLY CONTROLLED SWITCH

NO. 210 AND 021 LIONEL HAND OPERATED SWITCH (LEFT)

Lionel Hand-operated Switches, shown in the above illustration, are equipped with heavy fibre rails (Patents Re. 16580 and 1671236) at the points where the rails cross. All possibility of short circuit is thus eliminated and headlight does not flicker when train passes over these points. Attention is also directed to the several guard rails attached to Lionel Switches which prevent derailing even when trains are traveling at high speed. Hand-lever which moves the rails also sets the signals, changes the lights and locks mechanism. All Lionel Switches are radically different from any others on the market. They are of steel construction throughout and will bear the weight of the heaviest trains without bending or breaking.

No. 210 "Lionel Standard" illuminated Switches (right and left hand)—15¼ inches long, 8⅝ inches wide. Price includes electric lamps.
Code Word "NASH."   Price, Per Pair, **$6.50**

No. 210 Left Hand Switch.
Code Word "FORE."   Price, **$3.50**

No. 210 Right Hand Switch.
Code Word "AFT."   Price, **$3.50**

No. 021 Lionel "O" Gauge illuminated Switches (right and left hand)—10½ inches long, 7¼ inches wide. Price includes electric lamps.
Code Word "MOSHA."   Price, Per Pair, **$5.00**

No. 021 Left Hand Switch.
Code Word "POINT."   Price, **$2.75**

No. 021 Right Hand Switch.
Code Word "PUNT."   Price, **$2.75**

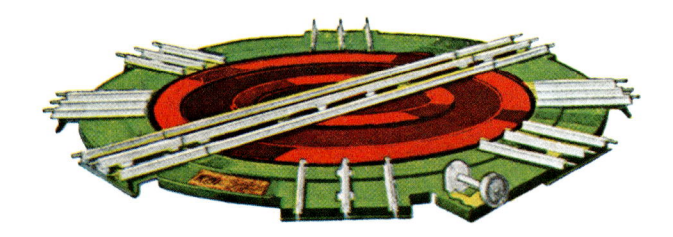

AUTOMATICALLY CLEARS TRACKS
MAKING DERAILMENT IMPOSSIBLE

Lionel "Distant-Control" Switches can be operated at any distance from the track by manipulating the small lever which is connected to the switch by flexible cord. The slightest movement of the lever changes the position of the switch as well as the red and green signal lights. Now, we have developed a new automatic attachment to these "Lionel Standard" gauge switches which absolutely prevents the derailment of trains. Should a train approach an open switch, which would ordinarily derail it, the new automatic device instantly sets the track in a clear position so that train can go on its way without derailing.

When using two of these Electrically controlled switches, should one be set at clear and the next one set against the train, the automatic device will correct the error. The mechanism is all contained in the switch and no additional wiring is required. Guard rails prevent the train leaving track even at high speeds. The Patented Lionel fibre rails prevent short circuits when the train passes over switch points.

UNUSUAL FEATURES OF No. 222 SWITCH

1. Derailment impossible.
2. One control switch need only be thrown to change route of train.
3. Switch is either clear or becomes clear when the train approaches from either direction.
4. Lights in signals do not become dim nor does train slow down when switch automatically corrects its position.
5. It is impossible to destroy actuating unit.
6. No wires, clips, special rails or other attachments are required for installation. The switch is entirely self-contained.
7. Switch is adaptable to many automatic self-switching arrangements, which are ideal for large track formations.

No. 222 "Lionel Standard" "Distant-Control" illuminated Switches (right and left hand)—15¼ inches long, 8⅝ inches wide. Price includes electric lamps and 42 inches of cord to which controlling levers are attached.
Code Word "AFAR."   Price, Per Pair, **$12.00**

No. 222 Left Hand Switch.
Code Word "LEFT."   Price, **$6.25**

No. 222 Right Hand Switch.
Code Word "RIGHT."   Price, **$6.25**

No. 012 "Lionel 'O' Gauge" "Distant-Control" illuminated Switches (right and left hand)—10½ inches long, 7¼ inches wide. Price includes electric lamps and 42 inches of cord to which controlling levers are attached.
Code Word "ASP."   Price, Per Pair, **$9.75**

No. 012 Left Hand Switch.
Code Word "WEST."   Price, **$5.00**

No. 012 Right Hand Switch.
Code Word "SOUTH."   Price, **$5.00**

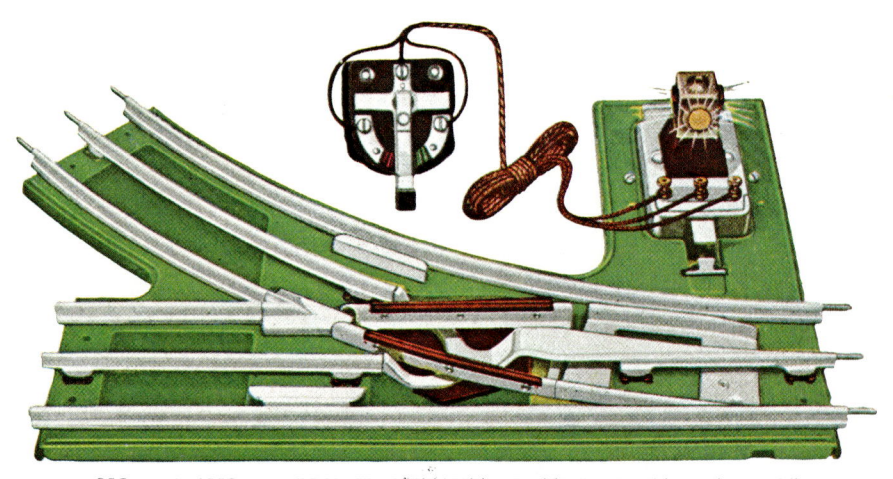

No. 200 TURNTABLE for "Lionel Standard" track. This is an exclusive Lionel Accessory that every boy should have in order to make a complete Lionel Train layout. It is used for switching locomotives to various tracks in the smallest possible space. Every boy is familiar with the use of a Turntable, so it is not necessary to describe its purpose. This Turntable is so perfectly balanced that even when the heaviest locomotive is upon it, it can be easily moved in every direction by means of the worm gear and hand wheel that operate it. Diameter of Turntable is 17 inches.

Code Work "TURK."   Price, **$5.00**

NO. 222 AND 012 LIONEL DISTANT CONTROL SWITCH (RIGHT)

[Page Forty-six]

GET MORE TRACK AND CROSSINGS FOR LARGER RAILROADS

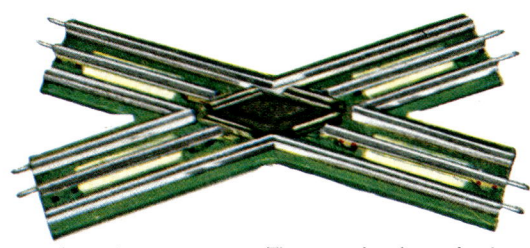

Lionel 45 degree Crossings—These are largely used when making a figure "8," using all curved track, but a great variety of other track layouts can be formed with them. Steel construction throughout. Rails are mounted on heavy steel ornamental base. A heavy fibre block in centre where rails cross, prevents all possibility of short circuit, or cars jumping the track.

No. 020X Crossing for "O" Gauge track. Size 11½ inches long, 6 inches wide.
Code Word "CROSS." Price, $1.60

No. 20X Crossing for "Lionel Standard" track. Size 16½ inches long, 9 inches wide.
Code Word "BOSS." Price, $1.85

This bumper is die cast and is surmounted by a red electric light encased in a nickeled steel guard. Electrical contact is automatically made and bumper can be placed at any part of track layout. Price includes section of track.

No. 025 Bumper for "O" Gauge track. Length 10¼ inches, height 2⅞ inches.
Code Word "HIT." Price, $1.85

No. 25 Bumper for "Lionel Standard" track. Length 14 inches, height 3¾ inches.
Code Word "CAT." Price, $2.35

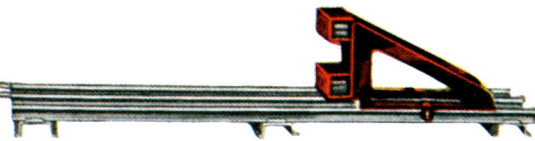

No. 23 "Lionel Standard" Bumper—The construction is the same as No. 023 described below. Two spring plungers absorb shock of car. Length 14 inches, height 3 inches.
Code Word "PROVO." Price, $1.30

No. 023 Lionel "O" Gauge Bumper—An indispensable accessory for terminals or sidings. Fitted with spring plunger which absorbs shock when car strikes it. The bumper frame is removable. Length 10¼ inches, height 2 inches. Price includes section of track.
Code Word "DELTO." Price, $0.85

Lionel "Lockon" Connections are attached to the track by simply turning the lever at right angles as shown in the illustration below. The electric connection is as perfect as though the parts are riveted or soldered to the track.

Lionel "Lockon" Connections are free from set screws and binding posts. The fingers that hold the wires in place are made of heavy tempered blue steel and are unbreakable. All other metal parts are nickel-plated and are mounted on a heavy fibre base.

Lionel "Lockon" Connections should be used wherever electric accessories require connection with the track.

OTC "Lockon" for "O" Gauge track.
Code Word "JOIN." Price, $0.20

STC "Lockon" for "Lionel Standard" track.
Code Word "JUICE." Price, $0.25

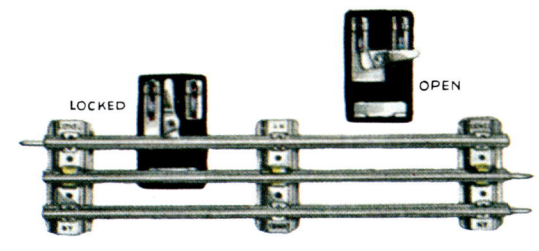

Lionel 90 degree Crossings—A great improvement over former models. The cross rails are mounted on an ornamental steel base, beautifully enameled. A solid molded fibre block placed in the centre where the rails cross, not only prevents short circuit, but is so constructed that the roller contact shoes on the locomotive and cars easily ride over it without derailing. A large variety of figures can be formed when using these crossings in conjunction with switches and track.

No. 020 Crossing for "O" Gauge track. Size 8¼ inches square.
Code Word "ORLA." Price, $1.10

No. 20 Crossing for "Lionel Standard" track. Size 11¾ inches square.
Code Word "BOOST." Price, $1.30

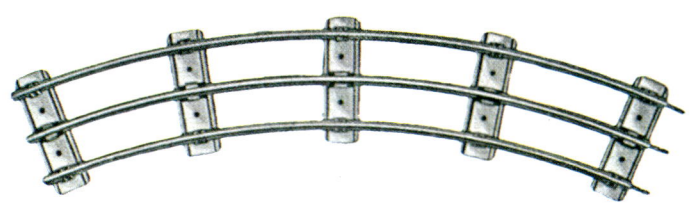

WHEN YOU BUY ADDITIONAL TRACK FOR YOUR RAILROAD BE SURE IT IS LIONEL.

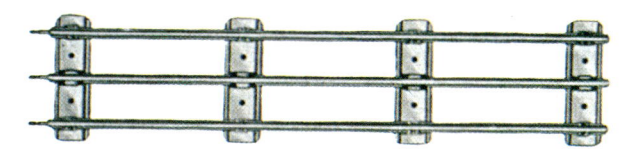

Lionel Track is constructed of heavier metal than any other make. The illustration shows the added strength given to Lionel rails by forming the base outward instead of turning it in. This outward flange gives the track sufficient strength to support the weight of a fully grown person and is made possible by our patented process. Five cross ties are used on curved track and four on straight track in "Lionel Standard" Gauge. Each section of track is tested on 110 volts and therefore, will not short-circuit when carrying the low voltage which operates Lionel Trains. The ends of each section have pin terminals which fit in openings in the adjoining sections allowing track to be laid and taken apart without difficulty.

Lionel Track is made in straight and curved sections and the curvature of the track is mechanically correct, allowing trains to run at high speed without derailing.

We illustrate below the improved connecting tie which holds sections of track rigidly together. These connecting ties can be readily inserted and removed. You get one with each section of track.

Lionel "O" Gauge Track—1⅜ inches wide

OC curved track, 11 inches long.
Code Word "LEMPS." Price, $0.20

OS straight track, 10¼ inches long.
Code Word "GLENN." Price, $0.20

OSS track, 10¼ inches long. For use with Electrically-Controlled accessories. Complete with "Lockon" and connecting wires.
Code Word "RELAY." Price, $0.40

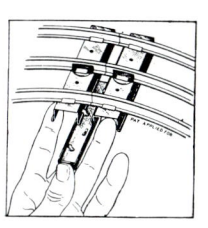

"Lionel Standard" Track—2¼ inches wide

C curved track, 16 inches long.
Code Word "BUFF." Price, $0.30

S straight track, 14 inches long.
Code Word "NYACK." Price, $0.30

SS track, 14 inches long. For use with Electrically-Controlled accessories. Complete with "Lockon" and connecting wires.
Code Word "BURT." Price, $0.60

[Page Forty-seven]

SOMETHING NEW — "SILENT TRACK" BED FOR BOTH GAUGES

HOLDS TRACK RIGIDLY WITHOUT FASTENING — SILENCES OPERATION — RESEMBLES A REAL ROCK-BALLASTED ROADBED

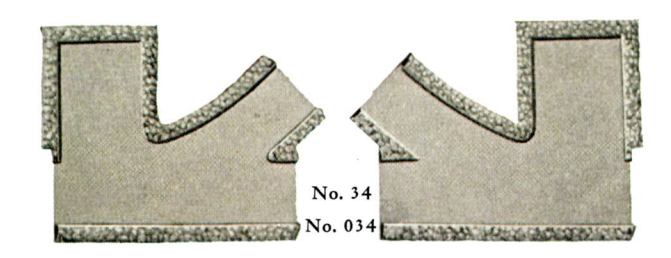

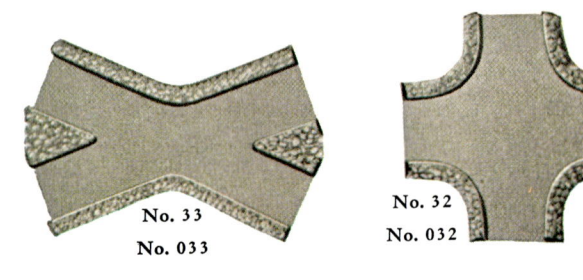

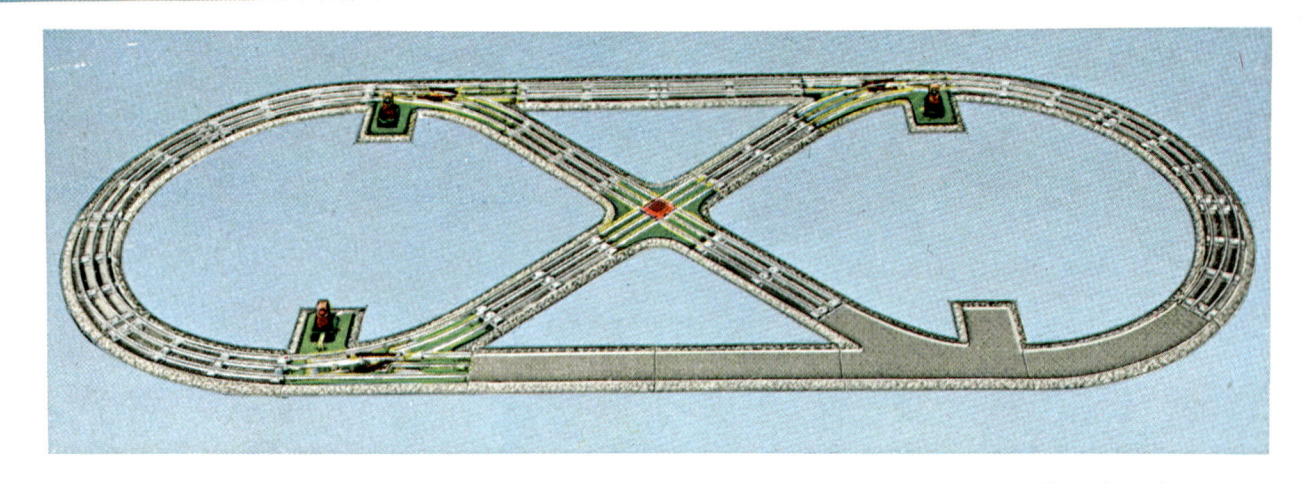

Lionel's "Silent Track Bed" is the most important contribution in years to realism in miniature railroads. It is made of sponge rubber, with moulded edges to represent rock ballast. Lay your tracks on "Silent Track Bed" and your electric train layout will become a railroad system in miniature. Furthermore, the "Silent Track Bed" deadens the noise of a moving train and protects polished floors.

Sections of track bed are obtainable for straight and curved track, switches and crossings, in both gauges. Length of "Silent Track Bed" sections is equivalent to the length of a section of track.

No. 030 for "O" Gauge curved track.
Code Word "RANCH." Price, $0.25

No. 031 for "O" Gauge straight track.
Code Word "RAID." Price, $0.25

No. 032 for "O" Gauge 90 degree crossing.
Code Word "REDRAW." Price, $0.50

No. 033 for "O" Gauge 45 degree crossing.
Code Word "RECTOR." Price, $0.50

No. 034 for "O" Gauge Switches.
Code Word "RELUME." Price, Per Pair, $1.25

No. 30 for "Lionel Standard" curved track.
Code Word "RASP." Price, $0.35

No. 31 for "Lionel Standard" straight track.
Code Word "RAVEL." Price, $0.35

No. 32 for "Lionel Standard" 90 degree crossing.
Code Word "RAMBLE." Price, $0.75

No. 33 for "Lionel Standard" 45 degree crossing.
Code Word "RAPID." Price, $0.75

No. 34 for "Lionel Standard" Switches.
Code Word "RESEND." Price, Per Pair, $1.75

THE LAYOUT IS HALF OF THE FUN — BUILD SOME OF THESE

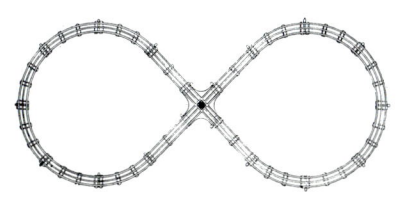

12—curved track
4—straight track
1—90-degree crossing

"O" Gauge Layout, 70 x 30 inches
"Standard" Gauge Layout, 97 x 43 inches

16—curved track
2—straight track

"O" Gauge Layout, 81 x 30 inches
"Standard" Gauge Layout, 117 x 43 inches

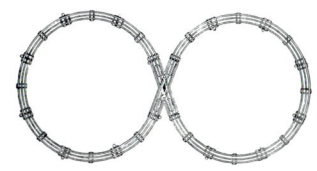

14—curved track
1—45-degree crossing

"O" Gauge Layout, 61 x 30 inches
"Standard" Gauge Layout, 88 x 43 inches

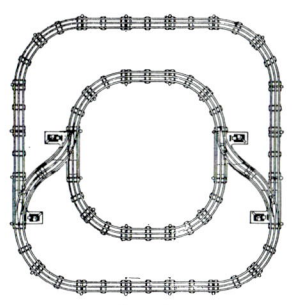

16—curved track
12—straight track
2—pair switches

"O" Gauge Layout, 61 x 61 inches
"Standard" Gauge Layout, 85 x 85 inches

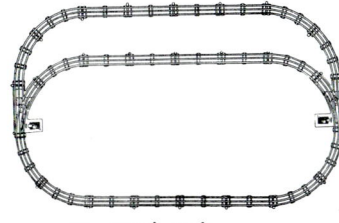

10—curved track
12—straight track
1—pair switches

"O" Gauge Layout, 71 x 40 inches
"Standard" Gauge Layout, 98 x 57 inches

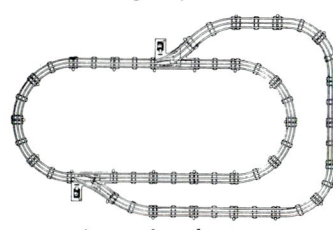

14—curved track
12—straight track
1—pair switches

"O" Gauge Layout, 82 x 51 inches
"Standard" Gauge Layout, 112 x 71 inches

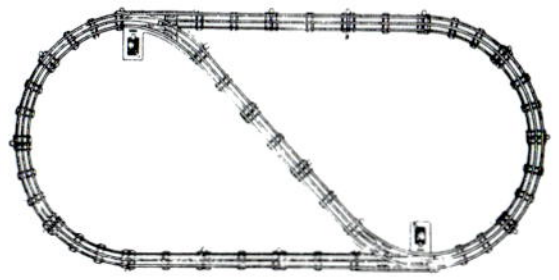

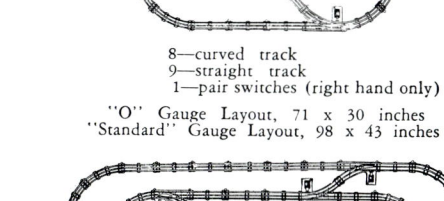

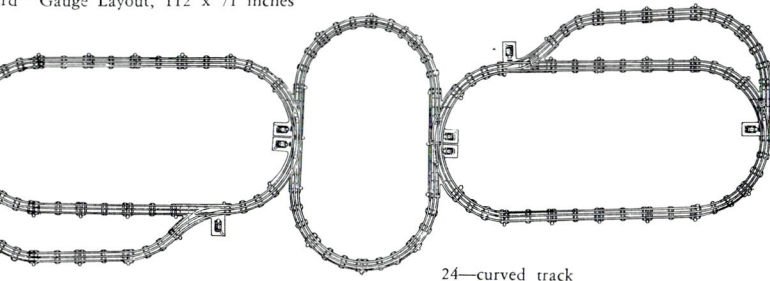

"O" Gauge Layout, 173 x 53 inches
"Standard" Gauge Layout, 241 x 71 inches

8—curved track
9—straight track
1—pair switches (right hand only)

"O" Gauge Layout, 71 x 30 inches
"Standard" Gauge Layout, 98 x 43 inches

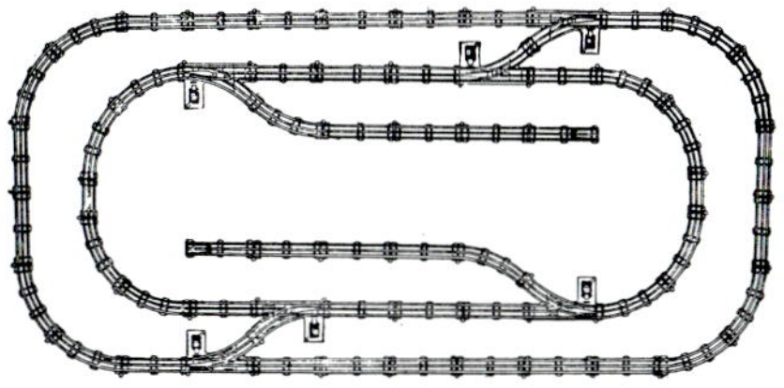

18—curved track
32—straight track
2—1/2 straight track
3—pair switches (2 prs. Left Hand & 1 pr. Right Hand)
2—bumpers

"O" Gauge Layout, 113 x 52 inches
"Standard" Gauge Layout, 154 x 71 inches

24—curved track
18—straight track
4—pair switches (3 prs. Left Hand & 1 pr. Right Hand)

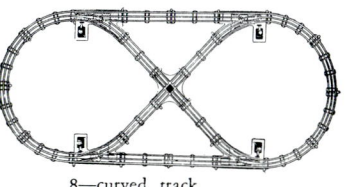

8—curved track
8—straight track
2—pair switches
1—90-degree crossing

"O" Gauge Layout, 71 x 30 inches
"Standard" Gauge Layout, 98 x 43 inches

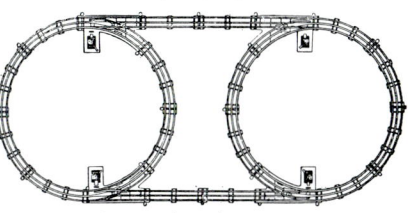

12—curved track
4—straight track
2—pair switches

"O" Gauge Layout, 71 x 30 inches
"Standard" Gauge Layout, 98 x 42 inches

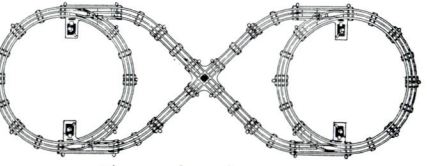

16—curved track
4—straight track
2—pair switches
1—90-degree crossing

"O" Gauge Layout, 90 x 30 inches
"Standard" Gauge Layout, 124 x 43 inches

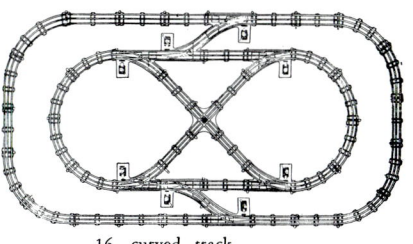

16—curved track
18—straight track
4—pair switches
1—90-degree crossing

"O" Gauge Layout, 92 x 41 inches
"Standard" Gauge Layout, 126 x 57 inches

The above track lay-outs can be made with either "O" gauge or "Lionel Standard" track. When ordering be sure to give Catalog Number and Letters as listed below.

Standard Gauge—2¼" Wide		"O" Gauge—1⅜" Wide	
C —curved track	.30 each	OC —curved track	.20 each
S —straight track	.30 each	OS —straight track	.20 each
½S —straight track	.30 each		
210 —hand operated switches	6.50 (pair)	021 —hand operated switches	5.00 (pair)
222 —electrically operated switches	12.00 (pair)	012 —electrically operated switches	9.75 (pair)
20 —90 degree crossing	1.30 each	020 —90 degree crossing	1.10 each
20X—45 degree crossing	1.85 each	020X—45 degree crossing	1.60 each
23 —Spring bumper	1.30 each	023 —Spring bumper	.85 each
25 —Illuminated Bumper	2.35 each	025 —Illuminated bumper	1.85 each

[Page Forty-nine]

ALL READY FOR YOU — COMPLETE "O" GAUGE RAILROADS

No. 176E—Introduced to fill the demand for a complete 100% "Distant-Control" "O" Gauge Railroad at a moderate price. The train can be started, stopped, reversed and operated at any speed at any distance from the track. The electric switches can also be controlled at any distance from the track. The No. 437 Switch Tower contains levers by which the Railroad can be operated, and lamp posts illuminated. This is an ideal Lionel Railroad to fit into a small space.

Outfit comprises 1 No. 260E "Distant-Control" steam type locomotive with electric headlight, 2 No. 710 illuminated Pullman Cars, 1 No. 712 illuminated observation car, 1 No. 080 semaphore, 1 No. 069 warning signal, 1 No. 90 flag staff, 1 No. 106 bridge, 1 pair No. 012 electrically-controlled switches, 1 No. 437 signal tower, 1 No. 119L illuminated tunnel, 2 No. 56 lamp posts, 8 No. 060 telegraph posts with extension arms, 1 No. 81 controlling rheostat, 1 OTC "Lockon" connection, 10 sections OC curved track, 16 sections OS straight track. Complete with special track for automatic accessories and necessary wire. Track layout is 100 inches by 40 inches. Train is 57 inches long.

Code Word "JANE." Price, $75.00

No. 174—A complete model railroad to operate on "O" Gauge Track. It includes a large variety of accessories. Every piece is of steel construction and enameled by Lionel's own lustrous, durable process.

Outfit No. 174 comprises 1 No. 253 reversible locomotive with two electric headlights, 2 No. 607 illuminated Pullman cars, 1 No. 608 illuminated observation car, 10 sections OC curved track, 6 sections OS straight track, 1 OTC "Lockon" connection, 1 pair No. 021 illuminated switches (one right, one left), 1 No. 106 bridge, 1 No. 122 illuminated station, 6 No. 060 telegraph posts with extension arms, 1 No. 62 semaphore, 1 No. 89 flag staff, 1 No. 068 warning signal, 1 No. 119 tunnel. Size of track layout 45 by 60 inches. Train is 35½ inches long.

Code Word "DELA." Price, $40.00

[Page Fifty]

WHAT A GIFT! A COMPLETE "LIONEL STANDARD" RAILROAD

HERE is a real railroad. The finest gift that any boy can possibly receive. This is a complete Lionel "Distant-Control" Railroad including our two finest trains—work train with giant size Steam Type Locomotive, and a powerful twin-motor passenger train, as well as a large variety of electrically-controlled and illuminated accessories. Both of the trains have "Distant-Control" and can be started, stopped, reversed and operated at any speed at any distance from the track. The large power house is a central operating station from which you can control everything. This is a marvelous model railroad. Specifications are given below.

OUTFIT NO. 407E—Comprises:

1 No. 400E "Distant-Control" Locomotive	1 No. 220 Floodlight Car	20 C Track	2 No. 77 Crossing Gates
1 No. 408E "Distant-Control" Locomotive	1 No. 219 Operating Derrick Car	2 ½S Track	1 No. 69 Warning Signal
2 No. 81 Controlling Rheostats	1 Type K Transformer	1 No. 128 Station	1 No. 840 Power House
1 No. 412 Pullman Car	4 pr. 222 Switches	1 No. 300 Bridge	2 No. 67 Lamp Posts
1 No. 413 Pullman Car	2 No. 23 Bumpers	1 No. 140L Tunnel	4 No. 56 Lamp Posts
1 No. 414 Pullman Car	1 Set 208 Tools	12 No. 85 Telegraph Posts	1 No. 87 Signal
1 No. 416 Observation Car	1 Set 209 Barrels	1 No. 78 Train Control	1 No. 79 Flashing Signal
1 No. 212 Gondola Car	47 S Track	1 No. 80 Semaphore	1 No. 195 Terrace
1 No. 217 Illuminated Caboose			16 STC "Lockon" Connections

Wires for making electrical connections, connecting ties for joining sections of track, lamps for headlights, interior of cars and all illuminated accessories are supplied with this outfit. Track layout is 12 feet long by 11 feet wide.   *Code Word "ALLY."*   Price, $350.00

This is a plan of the track layout for the Lionel 407E complete railroad.

© The Lionel Corporation. Printed in U.S.A.

1931

IF MODEL RAILROADING IS YOUR HOBBY—

IF YOU LIKE RAILROAD STORIES—
IF YOU HAVE A LIONEL TRAIN—

YOU SHOULD READ THE LIONEL MAGAZINE

THOUSANDS of boys have made Model Railroading their hobby. Wouldn't it be fun to keep in touch with them, to exchange ideas, to discuss railroad problems, to show them your track layout, to see what they have been able to do with theirs?

You can do this through the Lionel Magazine for Boys. It is an educational magazine full of valuable information, stories of railroad adventure and articles about Railroading and famous Railroad men. It is full of suggestions that will increase the fun you can get out of your Lionel Electric Trains and model railroading.

There are many beautiful illustrations, clever cartoons, puzzles, prize contests, questions and answers and other interesting features.

The Lionel Magazine is published every other month. A year's subscription costs only 50c. By subscribing now, you will become a member of the Lionel Engineers Club and a handsome certificate of membership will be sent to you. If you prefer, send 10c. for a sample copy.

THE LIONEL CORPORATION
15 EAST 26th STREET   NEW YORK, N. Y.

Size of Magazine Page 9 x 12 inches

LIONEL ELECTRIC TRAINS
THE TRAINS THAT RAILROAD MEN BUY FOR THEIR BOYS

10¢ A COPY

1932

"A Boy's Dream Come True"

"THE TRAINS THAT RAILROAD MEN BUY FOR THEIR BOYS"

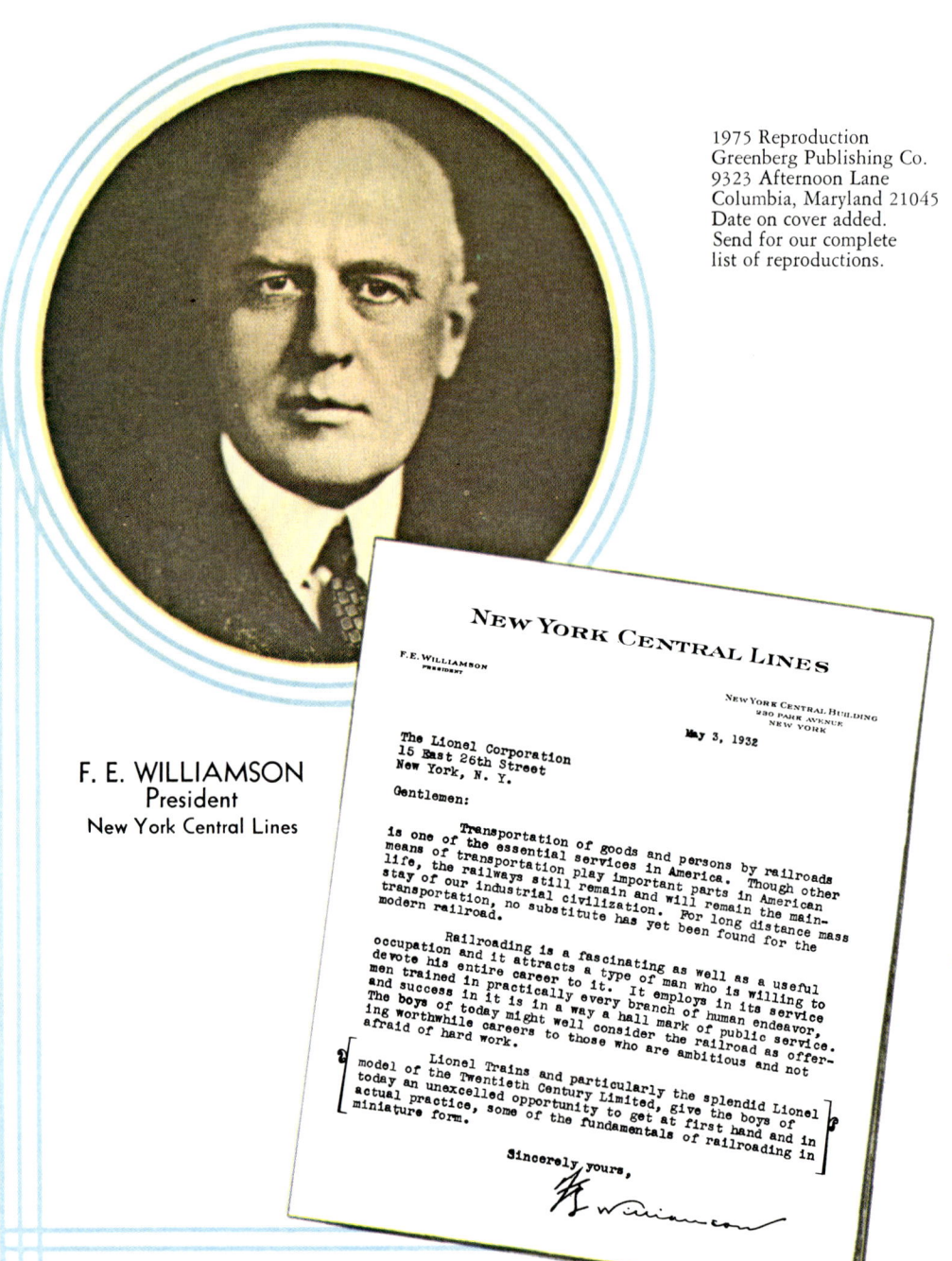

1975 Reproduction
Greenberg Publishing Co.
9323 Afternoon Lane
Columbia, Maryland 21045
Date on cover added.
Send for our complete
list of reproductions.

F. E. WILLIAMSON
President
New York Central Lines

NEW YORK CENTRAL LINES

F. E. WILLIAMSON
PRESIDENT

NEW YORK CENTRAL BUILDING
230 PARK AVENUE
NEW YORK

May 3, 1932

The Lionel Corporation
15 East 26th Street
New York, N.Y.

Gentlemen:

Transportation of goods and persons by railroads is one of the essential services in America. Though other means of transportation play important parts in American life, the railways still remain and will remain the mainstay of our industrial civilization. For long distance mass transportation, no substitute has yet been found for the modern railroad.

Railroading is a fascinating as well as a useful occupation and it attracts a type of man who is willing to devote his entire career to it. It employs in its service men trained in practically every branch of human endeavor, and success in it is in a way a hall mark of public service. The boys of today might well consider the railroad as offering worthwhile careers to those who are ambitious and not afraid of hard work.

Lionel Trains and particularly the splendid Lionel model of the Twentieth Century Limited, give the boys of today an unexcelled opportunity to get at first hand and in actual practice, some of the fundamentals of railroading in miniature form.

Sincerely yours,

F E Williamson

"Every railroad man has a warm spot for Lionel Trains. They are not only beautiful but mechanically perfect. I have all the more reason to be proud of them, having seen the Lionel replica of the 'Olympian,' the crack train of the Chicago, Milwaukee, St. Paul & Pacific which I drive daily."

Otto J Christensen
Chicago, Milwaukee, St. Paul & Pacific Railroad

"I was particularly thrilled to see Lionel's model of the 'Pennsylvania Limited.' Naturally, I who drive the 'Pennsylvania Limited' nearly every day would be, but I can understand what a thrill it must be for the lucky boys who are privileged to play with Lionel's replica of this famous train."

E. H. Earhart
The Pennsylvania Railroad

"I have watched my grandsons, Austin and Robert, enjoy the thrills of model railroading as they play with their Lionel model of the 'Blue Comet.' It seems as fascinating to them as it is for me to drive the real 'Blue Comet.' Judging from the questions which they ask, they are learning as they play."

W. J. Smith
The Central Railroad of New Jersey

"Boys of to-day are living in a marvelous age. Lionel Trains have made possible the transfer to the home of whole railroad systems in miniature. As he plays, the boy learns the principles of modern railroading—just as we apply them in operating the North Coast Limited of the Northern Pacific Railway."

W. F. Broughshott
Northern Pacific Railway

"It is natural for Railroad Men to buy Lionel Trains for their boys. They are the most realistic model trains made. They are sturdily built and powerful. They are also beautiful to look at, not only for their color but for their stream line proportions. More power to Lionel Electric Trains! I heartily endorse them."

J. P. McAfee
Atchison, Topeka & Santa Fe Railroad

© The Lionel Corporation. Printed in U.S.A.

TAKE YOUR DAD INTO PARTNERSHIP ··· MAKE HIM YOUR PAL

THAT Dad of yours can be a mighty good pal. Take him into partnership and let him help you build a real railroad system with Lionel Trains and Accessories.

Dad knows nearly everything. But he also wants you to know the things he has learned through the school of experience. He realizes how a Lionel Train will help you to learn the principles of Electricity and Mechanics and knows it will be helpful to you in years to come. He realizes how important it is for you to acquire a working knowledge of railroad problems and the various meanings of signals and train controls. He knows that a Lionel Train will develop in you the instinct to think and act quickly.

All this you can get in the most practical way—by actually laying out track, setting up a signal system and operating the train itself.

Tell your Dad why you want a Lionel Train and how much it will mean to you and to him. Get him to help you work out your railroad system and you'll soon realize, as you never did before, what a regular fellow he is.

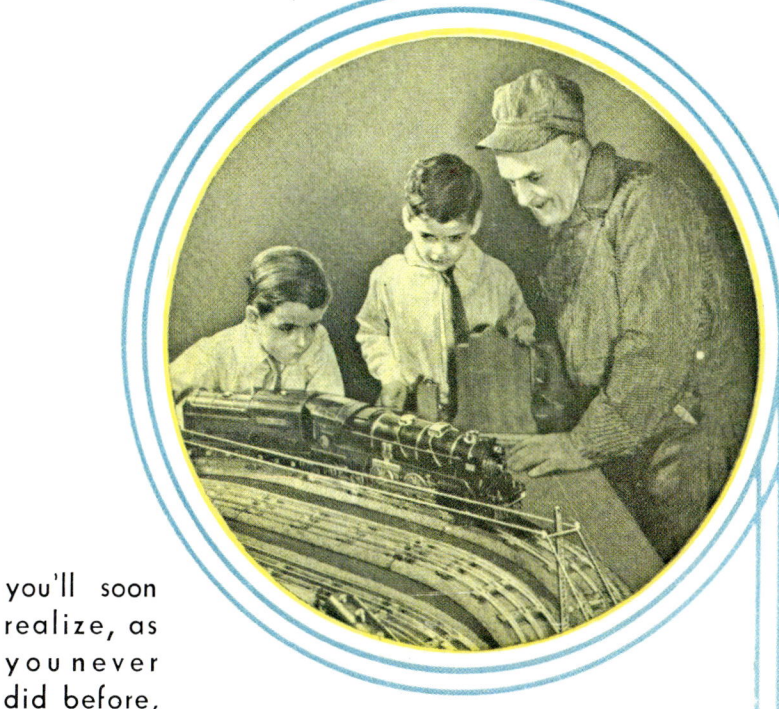

Bob Butterfield—Famous Engineer of the "Twentieth Century Limited," running Lionel's "Twentieth Century" for his grandchildren, Richard and Bob Butterfield 3rd. (See page 25.)

You'll realize that no buddy of yours, no one except your Mother, has your interest and your happiness so at heart as your Dad. And that's another reason why you should take him into partnership with you in building a model railroad. For Lionel Trains have a way of making a lifelong comradeship between a boy and his Dad.

Go to your Dad now. Ask him to go into partnership with you in selecting and operating your Lionel Train.

THE LIONEL CORPORATION
15 EAST 26TH STREET   NEW YORK, N. Y.

[Page Three]

1932

POWERFUL "O" GAUGE LOCOMOTIVES WITH HINGED BOILER FRONTS

FOR "O" GAUGE TRACK

Patented Hinged Boiler Front, with automatic lock. Conceals and protects lamp and makes renewal easy. Genuine optical lens projects a powerful beam of light. Pilot lights glow colorfully. Featured on locomotives Nos. 262, 260E, 392E and 400E.

262 $10.00

260E $19.75

No. 260E Steam Type Locomotive and Tender—Modelled after the latest Timken types. Reversible by the famous Lionel "Distant Control" unit. Has the new hinged boiler front feature. Red light under fire box adds to realism. Improved electric reverse cut-off in cab. Equipped with four driving wheels, a pilot truck and trailer truck. It has copper exhaust pipes and brass hand rails. Complete with flags and warning bell. The oil type double truck tender conforms with the low, speedy powerful lines of the locomotive. Locomotive, 11⅝ inches long, 4⅛ inches high. Tender, 7¼ inches long, 4⅛ inches high. Length overall 19⅝ inches.

Locomotive and Tender— Price, $19.75

No. 262 Steam Type Locomotive and Tender—This is a high-speed, graceful locomotive patterned after the most modern locomotives in America. Its wealth of detail and excellent design are not usually found in locomotives at this low price. Equipped with hand reversing lever, front and rear pilot trucks and double-action piston driving rods. The new, hinged boiler-front contains realistic headlight which throws a real beam of light. Copper trimmings throughout. Complete with bulb and flags. Locomotive, 9¾ inches long, 3¼ inches high. Tender, 6 inches long, 3¼ inches high. Length overall 16½ inches.

Locomotive and Tender— Price, $10.00

[Page Four]

SPEEDY AND GRACEFUL LOCOMOTIVES AT NEW LOW PRICES

FOR "O" GAUGE TRACK

No. 253E Electric Type "Distant Control" Locomotive.—A splendid New York Central type. It is beautifully trimmed in brass and has two headlights and a pantagraph. Flags are included for front and rear platforms. Furnished with No. 81 Controlling Rheostat which can be used to start, stop, slow down or reverse the locomotive at any distance from the track. For use with Cars Nos. 603, 604, 607, 608, 613, 614, 803, 804, 805, 806, 807, 809, 831 and 902. Locomotive 9 inches long, 4 inches high. **Price, $10.75**

No. 253 Electric Type Locomotive—Same as No. 253E but with hand reverse instead of "Distant Control." **Price, $7.75**

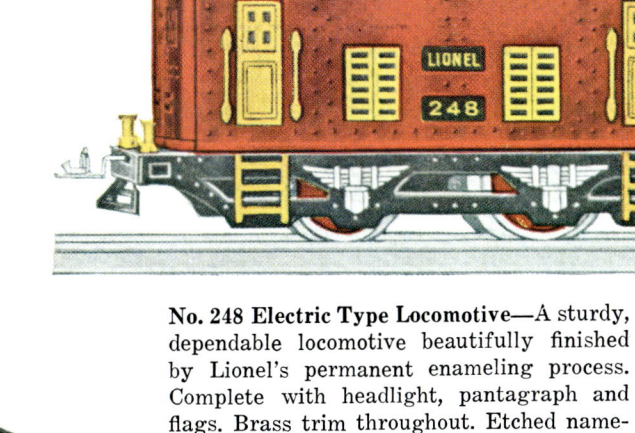

No. 248 Electric Type Locomotive—A sturdy, dependable locomotive beautifully finished by Lionel's permanent enameling process. Complete with headlight, pantagraph and flags. Brass trim throughout. Etched nameplates. Can be used with Cars Nos. 529, 530, 629, 630, 803, 804, 805, 806, 807, 809, 831 and 902. Locomotive 7⅝ inches long, 4 inches high. **Price, $5.00**

No. 259 New Steam Type Reversible Locomotive and Tender—The most important addition to the "O" Gauge line. Constructed of steel stampings, not cast. Beautifully detailed with brass and copper trimmings. Double action connecting rods are fascinating in their movement. Pilot and trailer trucks add to its realism. Boiler front contains new and realistic feature. In the center is concealed headlight which projects a powerful ray. There are also two colored pilot lights and an illuminated number plate. Never before has a locomotive in this low price range exceeded the beauty, workmanship and detail of this model. Included in the outfits Nos. 177, 178, 180. Locomotive, 9½ inches long, 3¼ inches high. Tender, 6 inches long, 3¼ inches high. Length overall 15½ inches. **Locomotive and Tender—Price, $7.50**

MODERNIZE YOUR RAILROAD • ADD AN ELECTRIC TYPE LOCOMOTIVE

FOR "O" GAUGE TRACK

No. 251E Electric Type "Distant Control" Locomotive with Super-Motor—A splendid model with great hauling power. Fashioned after the types now extensively used by leading railroads to pull their expresses out of terminals. Has a wealth of detail, two electric headlights, two pantagraphs and automatic couplers. Furnished with No. 81 controlling rheostat which can be used at any distance from the track to start, stop, slow down or reverse the locomotive. Can be used with cars Nos. 605, 606, 710, 712, 810 to 817, 820. Locomotive 10¼ inches long, 4½ inches high. **Price, $12.75**

No. 251 Electric Type Locomotive—Same as No. 251E but with hand reverse instead of "Distant Control." **Price, $9.75**

No. 254E Electric Type "Distant Control" Locomotive with Super-Motor.—An ideal locomotive, beautifully enameled. Has embossed ventilators and is trimmed with brass. Equipped with two headlights and pantagraph. Furnished with No. 81 controlling rheostat which can be used at any distance from the track to start, stop, slow down or reverse the locomotive. Can be used with Cars Nos. 605, 606, 613, 614, 810 to 817, 820. Locomotive 9½ inches long, 4¼ inches high. **Price, $11.75**

No. 254 Super-Motor Electric Type Locomotive—Same as No. 254E but with hand reverse instead of "Distant Control." **Price, $8.75**

No. 4 Electric Type Locomotive—Same as No. 254 but with the powerful Bild-A-Loco motor. **Price, $8.75**

THE LIONEL POLICY

Lionel locomotives, regardless of size or type, are designed with one thought in mind—to develop as much hauling power as size permits, to be silent and smooth-running and to last indefinitely with proper care. The motors are built of special steel, the gears are accurately machine cut with bronze bushings throughout. Every locomotive is beautifully enameled through Lionel's exclusive permanent enameling process. Other refinements make Lionel locomotives the finest in design and performance. You can't go wrong no matter which you choose. Get a spare locomotive for extra fun!

No. 252 Electric Type Locomotive—A graceful model realistically embossed. Equipped with electric headlight and pantagraph. Flags decorate front and rear platforms. Finished by Lionel's permanent enameling process and trimmed in polished brass. Has hand reversing lever. Can be used with Cars Nos. 529, 530, 629, 630, 803, 804, 805, 806, 807, 809, 831 and 902. Locomotive 8 inches long, 3⅝ inches high. **Price, $6.00**

{ *Page Six* }

START, STOP OR REVERSE YOUR TRAIN ... FROM ANY DISTANCE!

LIONEL'S FAMOUS "DISTANT CONTROL" SYSTEM

JUST imagine the thrill of sitting at the controls of your Lionel Railroad at any distance from the track and operating your train without actually touching it. This is accomplished by means of the rheostat included with every "E" type locomotive. Place it anywhere. A touch of the lever—and you can start your train or stop it, make it go forward or backward, fast or slow—just as you desire.

The "Distant Control" unit is built right into the motor of all "E" type locomotives. It is the never failing mechanism that obeys your will. See how it responds to your slightest wish!

If you have a system of many tracks, as every railroad should have, the lever of your electrically controlled switches will route your trains. It's so much fun to switch your freight to a siding, permitting the Lionel Express to roar by! And all this, from any distance!

Space has been provided on the 437 Signal Tower and the 439 Panel Board to attach the control levers of your track switches. Like the 840 Power Station and the 438 Signal Tower, the knife switches on the panel board will control the illumination of your stations, bungalows, lamp posts, and other accessories as well as connect the power to any of the tracks you wish to operate. This will centralize the control of your road.

And that's not all! By means of Lionel's exclusive patented insulated track, the gates at the crossings will lower automatically—their red lanterns glowing brilliantly. Bells will ring their warning! Signal lights blink—semaphores operate—all by themselves. It's almost like magic!

You cannot realize what all this means until you see for yourself. Go to the nearest dealer. He will be glad to demonstrate to you the marvels of Lionel "Distant Control." He will show you the latest developments in Lionel Trains and Accessories. But remember, when you select your Lionel train, only an "E" type locomotive can give you the fun and thrill that come with Lionel "Distant Control."

[Page Seven]

LARGEST AND MOST POWERFUL MODEL LOCOMOTIVE EVER BUILT

FOR "LIONEL STANDARD" TRACK

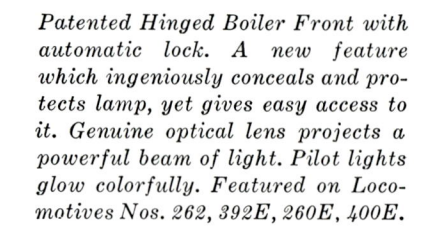

Patented Hinged Boiler Front with automatic lock. A new feature which ingeniously conceals and protects lamp, yet gives easy access to it. Genuine optical lens projects a powerful beam of light. Pilot lights glow colorfully. Featured on Locomotives Nos. 262, 392E, 260E, 400E.

NO. 400E "DISTANT CONTROL" STEAM TYPE LOCOMOTIVE AND TENDER

NEVER before in the history of Model Railroad construction has such a powerful locomotive been offered to the American boy.

In its creation, Lionel engineers have faithfully reproduced in steel, copper, brass and nickel, all of those fine and minute details that are found in the largest, most modern railroad engines. Its long, low lines, its beauty of design, its faithful details and its mechanical precision make LIONEL'S 400E the master of them all.

Powered by the famous "Bild-A-Loco" Super Motor, it will pull with ease an incredibly long train of cars. It has heavy, double-action piston and driving rods, four large drive wheels, 4-wheel pilot truck and 4-wheel trailer truck. The 400T oil tender is heavily embossed and has two 6-wheel trucks with copper journals.

Green lanterns provide colorful warning lights and the fire box glows realistically. Name plates are illuminated. Complete with flags, and No. 81 controlling rheostat, which can be used at any distance from the track to start, stop, slow down or reverse the locomotive. Included in outfits Nos. 432E, 358E, 433E, 396E, 423E. Locomotive, 18½ inches long, 5¾ inches high. Tender, 11⅜ inches long, 5¼ inches high. Length over all 30½ inches.

Locomotive and Tender— **Price, $45.00**

[*Page Eight*]

POWERFUL • SPEEDY • MAJESTIC • • JUST RARIN' TO GO!

FOR "LIONEL STANDARD" TRACK

No. 392E Steam Type "Distant Control" Locomotive and Tender—The latest "Lionel Standard" model, fashioned after the famous Timken types. Equipped with double pilot trucks, heavy trailer trucks and double action piston rods. Powerful concealed headlight is contained within a patented hinged boiler front. Red and green pilot lights provide colorful warning signals. The number plate on boiler front is illuminated. Splendidly detailed and trimmed with brass and copper. Fire box glows realistically. Powered by the famous "Bild-A-Loco" motor which provides great pulling power. Furnished with No. 81 controlling rheostat which can be used at any distance from the track to start, stop, slow down or reverse the locomotive. Locomotive is 16½ inches long, 5 inches high. Tender 8½ inches long, 5 inches high. Overall length 25 inches. Included in outfits Nos. 370E, 371E, 372E.

Locomotive and Tender—Price, $35.00

No. 384E Steam Type "Distant Control" Locomotive and Tender—A dependable engine with the powerful "Bild-A-Loco" motor. Complete with headlight bulb and flags. Furnished with No. 81 controlling rheostat which can be used at any distance from the track to start, stop, slow down or reverse the locomotive. Locomotive, 12 inches long, 4½ inches high. Coal tender, 8¼ inches long, 4½ inches high. Overall length 21 inches. Included in outfit Nos. 362E and 386E.   Price, $23.50

No. 384 Steam Type Locomotive and Tender—Same as No. 384E but with hand reverse instead of "Distant Control." Included in outfit Nos. 362 and 386.

Price, $19.75

NO WONDER ELECTRIC TYPE LOCOMOTIVES ARE SO POPULAR!

FOR "LIONEL STANDARD" TRACK

ELECTRIFICATION OF ROADS

ELECTRIC Locomotives are now more popular than ever because of the modernization and electrification of many railroads. The Chicago, Milwaukee, St. Paul and Pacific Railroad now has 656 miles of electrified road. The New York Central Railroad has more than 438 miles of electrified track and has recently added ten new powerful electric locomotives to its service.

The Pennsylvania Railroad is now completing a project to electrify its line between New York and Washington, a distance of 226 miles with nearly 2,000 miles of trackage.

No wonder that Lionel Electric Type Locomotives have become so popular with the boys all over the country.

The famous "Olympian" of the Chicago, Milwaukee, St. Paul and Pacific Railroad. From the Great Lakes to Puget Sound these fine trains speed across plains, through valleys and over mountains. For more than 656 miles the "Olympian" is hauled by the electric type here illustrated. Lionel's model No. 381E is a faithful replica of this powerful locomotive. On page 24 you will find Lionel's model of the "Olympian."

No. 318E Super Motor Electric Type Locomotive with "Distant Control"—This beautiful model is finished in two-tone enamel and handsomely trimmed. Its powerful motor is capable of hauling a long line of cars. Complete with two headlights and pantagraph. Furnished with No. 81 controlling rheostat which can be used at any distance from the track to start, stop, slow down or reverse the locomotive. 12⅛ inches long, 5⅛ inches high. **Price, $14.50**

No. 318 Electric Type Locomotive—Same as No. 318E, but with hand reverse instead of "Distant Control." **Price, $10.75**

No. 381E Electric Type "Bild-A-Loco" Locomotive with "Distant Control"—An exact reproduction of the Electric Locomotives used by the Chicago, Milwaukee, St. Paul and Pacific Railroad to haul the famous "Olympian." The most elaborate electric type locomotive in the Lionel line. Will haul a long line of the largest Pullmans.

Heavily embossed and minutely detailed. Enameled by the Lionel permanent process and richly trimmed in brass. Any boy can easily remove and dismantle the "Bild-A-Loco" motor and rebuild it, in a jiffy. All electric contacts are made automatically—not a single wire to connect.

Locomotive is complete with two electric headlights, operating pantagraphs and four pilot lights. Furnished with No. 81 controlling rheostat which can be used at any distance from the track to start, stop, slow down or reverse the locomotive. Locomotive 18 inches long, 6½ inches high.

Price, $32.50

NOW EVERY BOY CAN HAVE A SPARE "ELECTRIC" LOCOMOTIVE

FOR "LIONEL STANDARD" TRACK

No. 8E Electric Type "Distant Control" Locomotive—Powered by Lionel Super-Motor. Beautifully detailed with brass trimmings, inset windows and embossed ventilators. Enameled in bright red. Complete with 2 headlights, pantagraph and flags. Furnished with No. 81 controlling rheostat which can be used at any distance from the track to start, stop, slow down or reverse the locomotive. Locomotive 11 inches long, 4¾ inches high.
Price, $13.50

No. 8 Electric Type Locomotive—Same as No. 8E, but with hand reverse instead of "Distant Control."
Price, $9.75

Now every boy can afford an Electric type locomotive. These models have been greatly reduced. Get a spare locomotive for your Railroad.

No. 9E Electric Type "Bild-A-Loco" "Distant Control" Locomotive—The body is gracefully proportioned and enameled in Duo Tone. The brass trimmings complement the color scheme. Equipped with 2 headlights. Warning lanterns on front and rear platform. Brass pantagraphs give realism. The "Bild-A-Loco" Motor is powerful and swift. Furnished with No. 81 controlling rheostat which can be used at any distance from the track to start, stop, slow down or reverse the locomotive. 14½ inches long, 6¼ inches high.
Price, $19.50

Note: See pages 43 and 44 for correct Passenger and Freight cars to be used with each locomotive.

The Only Model Locomotive Built With Twin Motors

No. 408E Twin Super-Motor Electric Type Locomotive with "Distant Control"—The only model locomotive on the market with a twin motor. It has an abundance of power and is capable of hauling a long line of cars with remarkable speed. Pantagraphs can be raised or lowered. Illuminated signal lights and headlights, front and rear flags, brass hand rails, inset windows and doors are only a few of its many realistic details. Furnished with No. 81 controlling rheostat which can be used at any distance from the track to start, stop, slow down or reverse the locomotive. 17 inches long, 6½ inches high to top of pantagraph. Includes lamps.
Price, $39.50

SUCH CAREFUL CONSTRUCTION • SUCH FAITHFUL REALISM!

How gorgeous colors are obtained on Lionel Cars

A PARTIAL view of the gigantic electrically operated baking ovens that make possible the beautiful enamel finish on Lionel Trains. The cars enter an enormous oven measuring more than 70 feet in length and, in a series of continuous operations, pass through a heated bath of cleansing solution, through the enameling vats and then are baked at a temperature of 350 degrees Fahrenheit. Endless chains bring them out at the extreme end of the oven, and lo and behold, the plain steel bodies have been transformed into gorgeously enameled masterpieces! The glossy, lasting finish on Lionel cars has never been duplicated.

The heavy steel trucks of Lionel cars are realistically embossed and embellished with copper journal boxes. They are designed for high speed so that they will follow the track smoothly without derailing. The wheels are made of heavy steel and nickeled for beauty and long wear.

How beautiful and life-like are the Lionel observation cars. The platform is made of heavy brass. The dome light illuminates the red tail light and transparent nameplate, giving a colorful effect.

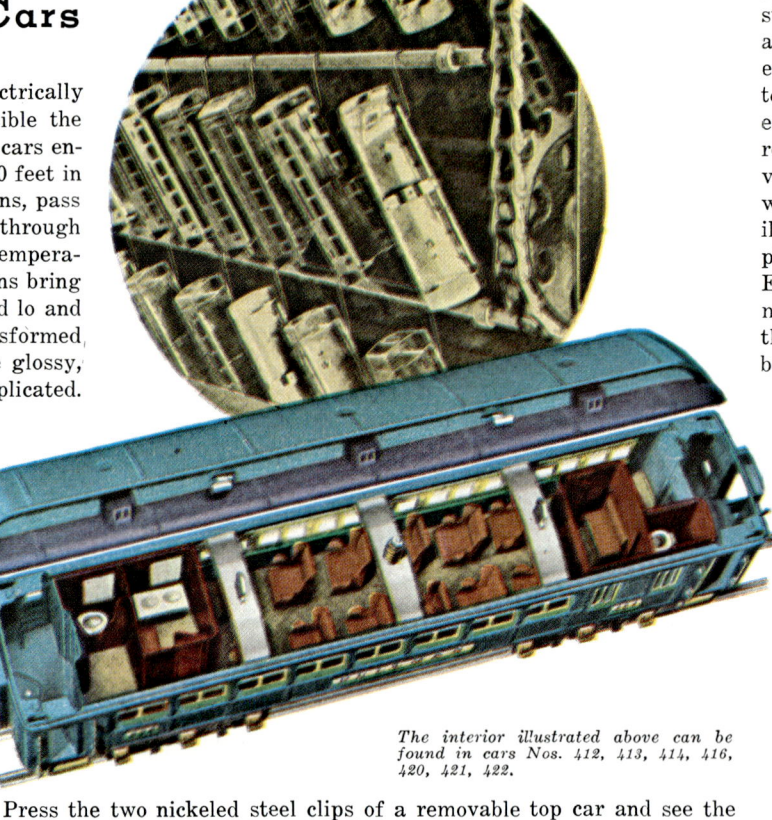

The interior illustrated above can be found in cars Nos. 412, 413, 414, 416, 420, 421, 422.

Press the two nickeled steel clips of a removable top car and see the luxurious interior of a Lionel Pullman. Study the sturdy construction and the arches which support the roof. Electric lamps illuminate the interior. The doors swing open and disclose porcelain wash basin and closet. The Pullman chairs revolve just like real ones. A couch can be seen in one of the compartments.

Cars No. 412, 413, 414 and 416 have the hinged roof feature as illustrated below. Press the two steel locks and the roof will swing open.

LIONEL Pullman and Observation cars are exact miniatures of real ones. They are made entirely of sheet steel, heavily embossed and **carefully detailed**. Inset panels and windows add to their structural strength. Transparencies in windows and stained glass effect in transoms add to their realism. Many of the large cars feature the patented removable roof. By pressing the nickeled clips, the roof is easily removed, disclosing luxurious interiors—revolving Pullman chairs, private compartments, porcelain wash basins, life-like furnishings. The interior is brilliantly illuminated and lights glow cheerfully on the observation platform.

Every car is beautifully enameled by Lionel's exclusive permanent enameling process. The care and faithfulness of these innumerable details make Lionel cars the finest ever built.

DETAILS OF CAR CONSTRUCTION

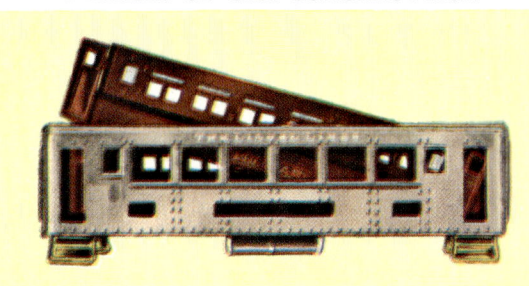

Window panels, doors and seats—a separable piece.

1. Automatic couplers
2. Removable roof
3. Roof lock
4. Stained glass transparency
5. Interior lamps
6. Inserted window frames
7. Air ventilators
8. Observation lamp
9. Transparent lanterns
10. Hinged doors
11. Brass steps
12. Porcelain lavatory
13. Porcelain wash basin
14. Double row revolving parlor chairs
15. Metal air tanks
16. Brass journals
17. 6 wheel heavy steel truck
18. Brass observation platform

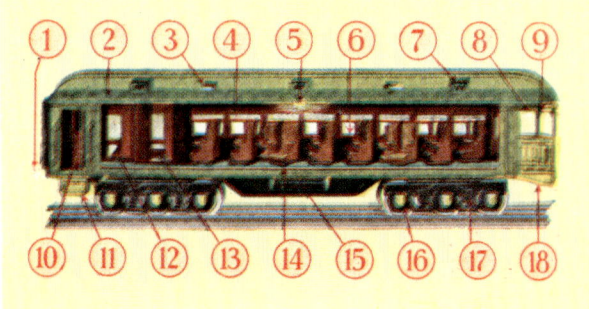

[Page Twelve]

POINT BY POINT LIONEL MOTORS OUTCLASS ALL OTHERS

1. **LEVER**—That disconnects remote control unit so trains may be reversed by hand if desired.

2. **FIELD**—Made of specially prepared electrical steel laminations and scientifically wound.

3. **DRIVING WHEELS**—Accurately die cast and heavy, to give stability and tractive power to motor. Nickel plated steel rim, brightly polished, gives longer wear and smooth riding surface.

4. **DRIVING GEARS**—Machine cut of heavy steel. The precision gears mesh perfectly, giving greater tractive power and eliminating friction.

5. **ARMATURE SHAFT BEARINGS**—Armature shaft revolves in special long-wearing bakelite bearings. Friction is reduced to a minimum, thus eliminating the necessity for constant lubrication.

6. **ARMATURE**—Of laminated electrical steel, drum wound with double silk covered magnet wire. Supported by best quality drill rod armature shaft. Protected by high grade varnish and baked.

7. **SIDE PLATES**—Support all working parts of motor. Made of heavy gauge steel. Holes are drilled and reamed and are aligned perfectly to overcome friction. Held together with heavy brass spacing bars.

8. **AXLES**—Made of heavy steel drill rod.

9. **BRUSHES**—Self-lubricating bronze and graphite, contained in brass tubes and fed to commutator by tempered spring. Are long-wearing.

10. **COMMUTATOR**—Polished hard copper segments rigidly mounted and perfectly insulated. Lathe turned so as to reduce wear on brushes.

11. All electrical motor contacts are in a specially designed insulating material—an exclusive Lionel patent.

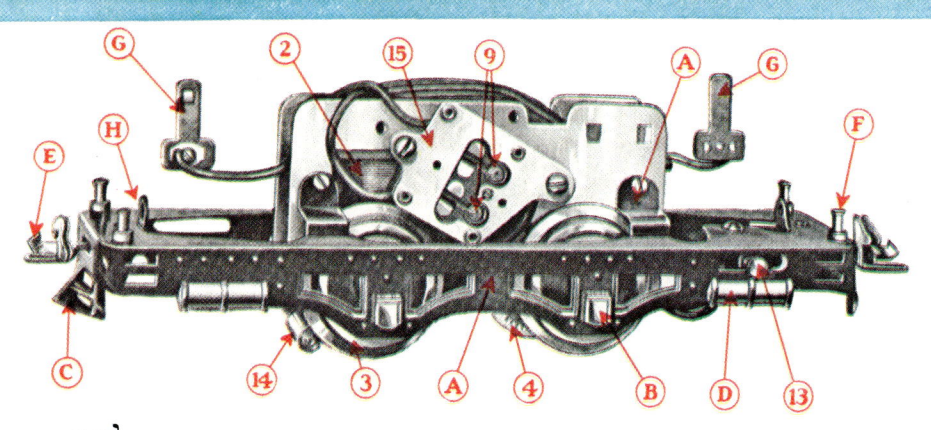

*T*HERE is more to a Lionel Electric Train than its beauty of line, its realistic details, its dashing color. For Lionel Trains unquestionably are marvels of mechanical and electrical efficiency.

The Lionel "O" Gauge and "Standard" Gauge Super Motors are the result of the highest engineering skill. By actual laboratory tests, they are far superior to any other motor of similar size and purpose. They operate quietly, smoothly and keep cool even under strenuous treatment. Their maximum hauling power is achieved with surprisingly small current consumption. And what's more, they are fool-proof and with proper care will last indefinitely.

The famous Lionel "E" "Distant Control" mechanism is built right into the motor and is completely protected against injury. No other motors have so many original and marvelous features. See for yourself. Study the description on this page, and you will realize why Lionel motors are "Super Motors."

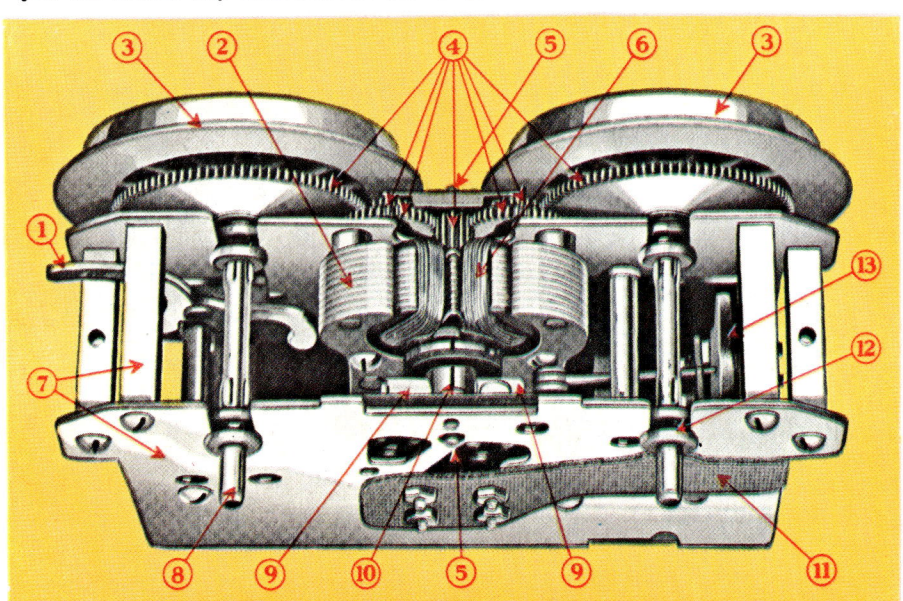

12. **AXLE BEARINGS**—Stainless steel bearings contained in side plates of motor. Will not wear out. Perfect alignment makes axles and gears operate frictionless and noiseless.

13. **REVERSING CONTROLLER**—This lever controls operation of locomotive either forward, reverse or stop.

14. **DOUBLE CONTACT SHOES**—Collect current from center rail. Made of stainless steel and revolve on steel shafts. They are supported by flexible phosphor bronze plates, giving proper tension to insure perfect contact.

15. **BRUSH HOLDER**—Of bakelite. Perfectly insulated. Brushes can be changed rapidly.

A. **SUPPORTING FRAME**—Made of heavy steel, faithfully detailed. Will stand extraordinary wear and tear. Motor is attached by four screws, making it easily removable for cleaning and oiling.

B. **JOURNALS**—Of heavy copper. Add greatly to appearance of locomotive.

C. **COWCATCHERS**—Vary with the type of locomotive. Many of them are part of steel frame. Others are heavy castings securely attached to frame.

D. **TANKS**—Made of lacquered brass. They beautify the locomotive.

E. **AUTOMATIC COUPLERS**—Scientifically constructed so that cars cannot become detached while in motion, yet easily uncoupled when desired. Made of heavy steel, nickel plated and polished.

F. **FLAG POSTS**—Many locomotives are equipped with two or four flag posts, a realistic detail.

G. **HEADLIGHT CONNECTIONS**—An original method giving perfect electrical connection and eliminating the possibility of broken wires.

H. **CLAMP SUPPORT**—Screw holds body to frame—easily removed.

[*Page Thirteen*]

THE LOWEST PRICED LIONEL TRAINS—WONDERFUL VALUES

FOR "O" GAUGE TRACK

No. 179
$7.95

No. 173 "O" Gauge Complete Railroad consists of:

- No. 248 Electric Type Locomotive with Headlight—beautifully enameled in red with brass trimmings.
- 2—No. 629 Pullman Cars—Carefully detailed. Realistically proportioned.
- 1—No. 630 Observation Car—With brass platform.
- 1—No. 435 Power Station—With skylight permitting access to transformer.
- 1—Type "Y" Transformer—110 volts, 60 cycles, capacity 50 watts.
- 1—pair No. 021 Manual Control Switches—Gleaming signal lights.
- 10—sections OC curved track.
- 3—sections OS straight track.
- 1—OTC "Lockon" Connection.
- 2—No. 184 Bungalows—With interior illumination.
- 1—No. 1012X Station—Beautifully lithographed.
- 1—Hand Made Tunnel—Constructed of felt composition. Beautifully decorated with trees, shrubbery and small houses.
- 4—No. 060 Telegraph Posts—5½ inches high.
- 3—No. 27 Lamps.
- Table—Measures 42 by 48 inches and has 18-inch folding legs. Decorated with imitation grass, shrubs and flower plot.

This is the only complete table outfit on the market. Another evidence of Lionel leadership. Table is of convenient height. Best of all, it has folding legs. When you are through playing, fold it up and put it away. Train is 31¼ inches long. **Price, $29.75**

No. 173S—Same as No. 173, but with Steam Type Locomotive outfit No. 178 instead of Electric Type train.
Price, $32.50

Outfit No. 292 consists of:

- 1—No. 248 Electric Type Locomotive with Headlight—Sturdily constructed. Beautifully enameled. Minutely detailed. Brass fittings.
- 1—No. 629 Pullman Car—Inset transparent windows. Made of steel stampings.
- 1—No. 630 Observation Car—Like No. 629, but with rear platform.
- 8—sections of OC curved track.
- 1—OTC "Lockon" Connection—By which contact is made from transformer to track.
- 1—No. 27 Lamp.

The finest train ever made to sell at so low a price. Cars are beautifuly enameled through Lionel's permanent process, and are 6¾ inches long. Train is 24½ inches long. Track forms circle 30 inches in diameter.

Price, $5.95

Outfit No. 179 consists of:

- 1—No. 252 Reversible Electric Type Locomotive—A modern design. Electric headlight and hand reversing lever. Ladders, flag holders, pantagraph, doors, windows and hand rails are made of brass.
- 1—No. 831 Flat Car—With load of real lumber which can be removed. Nickeled stakes hold lumber in place.
- 1—No. 804 Oil Car—Silver finish, with brass details.
- 1—No. 807 Caboose—Inset transparent windows. Beautifully enameled.
- 8—sections of OC curved track.
- 2—sections of OS straight track.
- 1—OTC "Lockon" Connection—By which contact is made from transformer to track.
- 1—No. 068 Warning Signal.
- 1—No. 27 Lamp.

Here's a new freight outfit with a powerful locomotive and three handsome cars. 33½ inches long. Track forms oval 40 by 30 inches.

Price, $7.95

No. 173
$29.75

[Page Fourteen]

NEVER BEFORE SO FINE A LOCOMOTIVE IN THIS PRICE CLASS

FOR "O" GAUGE TRACK

178 — $9.50

177 — $9.50

180 — $11.95

No one would have dreamed that outfits at these prices could have such a locomotive. It has a steel stamped body of graceful lines and elaborately detailed. The new concealed headlight throws a strong beam. Lamp can be easily removed. Coal type tender of embossed steel durably enameled and detailed with brass name plate, ladder, hand rails and copper journals. As for the motor, it's a LIONEL and that is the best anyone can say about a motor.

Outfit No. 178 consists of:

- 1—No. 259 Steam Type Reversible Locomotive.
- 1—No. 259T Coal Tender.
- 1—No. 529 Pullman Car—Beautifully enameled in durable colors. Copper journal boxes.
- 1—No. 530 Observation Car—Similar to No. 529, but with rear platform. Richly decorated with brass trimmings.
- 8—sections of OC curved track.
- 2—sections of OS straight track.
- 1—OTC "Lockon" Connection—By means of which contact is made from transformer to track.
- 1—No. 068 Warning Signal.
- 1—No. 27 Lamp.

Accuracy of detail is an important consideration in the selection of an electric train, for realism adds zest to the fun of model railroading. Lionel gives you realism in this splendid model. 31 inches long. Track forms oval 40 by 30 inches.

Price, $9.50

Outfit No. 177 consists of:

- 1—No. 259 Steam Type Reversible Locomotive.
- 1—No. 259T Coal Tender.
- 1—No. 831 Flat Car—With real lumber. Nickeled stakes hold lumber in place. Brass hand brakes. Copper journal boxes.
- 1—No. 807 Caboose—With front and rear platforms, brass ladders and hand rails. Embossed doors and windows. Copper journal boxes.
- 8—sections of OC curved track.
- 2—sections of OS straight track.
- 1—OTC "Lockon" Connection—By means of which contact is made from transformer to track.
- 1—No. 068 Warning Signal.
- 1—No. 27 Lamp.

You'll never know how much real fun there is in a freight outfit until you have owned one. It is great sport. This outfit, with its No. 259 steam type locomotive, is one of the finest in the low price field. 31 inches long. Track forms oval 40 by 30 inches.

Price, $9.50

Outfit No. 180 consists of:

- 1—No. 259 Steam Type Reversible Locomotive.
- 1—No. 259T Coal Tender.
- 2—No. 603 Pullman Cars—Durably enameled by Lionel's permanent process. Four wheel trucks. Realistic details.
- 1—No. 604 Observation Car—Similar to No. 603, but with rear platform accurately detailed with brass railings. Copper journal boxes. Inset windows. Stained glass transoms.
- 8—sections of OC curved track.
- 2—sections of OS straight track.
- 1—OTC "Lockon" Connection—By means of which contact is made from transformer to track.
- 1—No. 068 Warning Signal.
- 1—No. 27 Lamp.

The lowest priced Lionel steam type train with cars having four wheel trucks. Cars are excellently proportioned. With the new, sleek 259 locomotive they form an outfit of unrivaled value. 41 inches long. Track forms oval 40 by 30 inches.

Price, $11.95

OH BOY! HOW WOULD YOU LIKE TO OWN ONE OF THESE?

FOR "O" GAUGE TRACK

296 .. $10.95
296E .. $14.50

133 .. $12.75

138 .. $14.50
138E .. $17.50

THE No. 253 Electric Type Locomotive on this page is a splendid New York Central type. It has a powerful motor and can pull many more cars than pictured here. It's great to know that you can always add extra cars to your set and have plenty of reserve power in your locomotive. You will like the 253 Locomotive, with its heavily embossed ventilators and other details. It's trim and slick and beautifully enameled.

Outfit No. 296E consists of:
- 1—No. 253E Electric Type "Distant Control" Locomotive.
- 2—No. 607 Pullman Cars—With interior lights. Four wheel trucks. Brightly enameled in harmonizing colors. Inset transparent windows.
- 1—No. 608 Observation Car—Similar to No. 607, but with rear platform richly decorated with brass trimmings. Interior light. Carefully designed after real cars. Deeply embossed.
- 8—sections of OC curved track.
- 4—sections of OS straight track.
- 1—OTC "Lockon" Connection—By means of which contact is made from transformer to track.
- 1—No. 068 Warning Signal.
- 5—No. 27 Lamps. 1—No. 81 Rheostat.

This splendid outfit has always been one of the most popular electric types. Now reduced in price, so that more boys may own one! 36½ inches long. Track forms an oval 50 by 30 inches.
Price, $14.50

Outfit No. 296:
Same as No. 296E, but with hand reverse instead of "Distant Control."
Price, $10.95

Outfit No. 133 consists of:
- 1—No. 262 Steam Type Reversible Locomotive—With concealed headlight and open boiler front. Double piston action. Front and rear pilot trucks. Brass and copper tubing. Realistic cab windows. Two pilot lights.
- 1—No. 902 Gondola Car—With two barrels. Deeply embossed, accurately detailed. Barrels may be opened and filled.
- 1—No. 804 Oil Car—Silver finish and detailed in brass.
- 1—No. 807 Caboose.
- 8—sections of OC curved track.
- 2—sections of OS straight track.
- 1—No. 068 Warning Signal.
- 1—OTC "Lockon" Connection—By means of which contact is made from transformer to track.
- 1—No. 27 Lamp.

A lot of fun is in store for the boy who owns this outfit. It looks just like a real train—and it is, except for size. 40½ inches long. Track forms oval 40 by 30 inches.
Price, $12.75

Outfit No. 138E consists of:
- 1—No. 253E Electric Type "Distant Control" Locomotive.
- 2—No. 613 Illuminated Pullman Cars—Removable roofs. Four-wheel trucks. Brass steps. Copper journal boxes. Stained glass transoms. 10¼ inches long.
- 1—No. 614 Illuminated Observation Car—Same as No. 613, but with rear platform.
- 8—sections of OC curved track.
- 4—sections of OS straight track.
- 1—OTC "Lockon" Connection—By which contact is made from transformer to track.
- 1—No. 068 Warning Signal.
- 5—No. 27 Lamps.
- 1—No. 81 Rheostat.

We didn't stop at making this model train beautiful in color and detail. But we powered it with an exceptionally efficient motor. We included "Distant Control" operation. And then gave it a price which will appeal to every thoughtful boy. Outfit is 43¾ inches long. Track forms oval 50 by 30 inches.
Price, $17.50

Outfit No. 138:
Same as No. 138E, but with hand reverse instead of "Distant Control."
Price, $14.50

[Page Sixteen]

WHICHEVER OUTFIT YOU CHOOSE YOU CAN'T GO WRONG

FOR "O" GAUGE TRACK

183 . . $15.00
183E . . $18.00

236 $15.00

142 . . $16.50
142E . . $19.50

YOU won't go wrong with any of these outfits. The locomotives are speedy and powerful. The No. 254E model is copied after a type that is very popular on modern electrified roads. You can see more of them every day. It is gracefully designed and nicely trimmed. The No. 4 is exactly the same in appearance, but has the famous Bild-A-Loco motor, which is not only powerful but can be easily removed and used as a power plant to run other toys or miniature machine shops.

Outfit No. 236 consists of:

1—No. 262 Steam Type Reversible Locomotive—With concealed headlight and Lionel's exclusive open boiler front feature. Includes flag holders and flags. Brass and copper tubing. Front and rear pilot trucks.
1—No. 262T Coal Tender.
2—No. 607 Illuminated Pullman Cars—Inset transparent windows. Copper journal boxes. Four wheel trucks. 7½ inches long, 3½ inches high.
1—No. 608 Illuminated Observation Car—With rear platform embellished with brass trimmings.
8—sections of OC curved track.
4—sections of OS straight track.
1—OTC "Lockon" Connection—By means of which contact is made from transformer to track.
1—No. 068 Warning Signal.
4—No. 27 Lamps.

Be a popular boy! Every boy owning one of these sets is. Chums of yours will come to watch you operate it. It's one of the finest, low-priced models ever made. 42¼ inches long. Track forms oval 50 by 30 inches.

Price, $15.00

Outfit No. 142E consists of:

1—No. 254E "Distant Control" Locomotive—With two electric headlights.
2—No. 605 Illuminated Pullman Cars—Exceptionally long. Doors open and shut. Brass steps. Inset windows and brass nameplates.
1—No. 606 Illuminated Observation Car—Brass platform. Like its companion Pullmans, it is stamped out of steel and enameled by Lionel's permanent process.
8—sections of OC curved track.
6—sections of OS straight track.
1—OTC "Lockon" Connection—To make contact from transformer to track.
1—No 068 Warning Signal.
1—No. 81 Controlling Rheostat.
5—No. 27 Lamps.
1—No. 81 Rheostat.

More and more railroads are turning to electric type locomotives for passenger as well as freight traffic. Here is an excellent model, beautifully colored and expertly proportioned. 45 inches long. Track forms oval 60 by 30 inches.

Price, $19.50

Outfit No. 142:
Same as No. 142E, but has No. 4 Locomotive with hand reverse instead of "Distant Control."

Price, $16.50

Outfit No. 183E consists of:

1—No. 254E "Distant Control" Locomotive—With two electric headlights.
1—No. 812 Gondola Car—With four barrels. You can open and fill them with cargo.
1—No. 820 Floodlight Car—Projects powerful beams. Each light can be tilted to any angle, illuminated separately or in combination. Polished reflectors. Crystal lens.
1—No. 817 Caboose—A perfect copy. Brass ladders and platform details. Inset windows. Durably enameled finish.
8—sections of OC curved track.
4—sections of OS straight track.
1—OTC "Lockon" Connection—To make contact from transformer to track.
1—No. 068 Warning Signal.
4—No. 27 Lamps.
1—No. 81 Controlling Rheostat.

Never before has so much value been packed into an outfit priced so low. You will enjoy many happy hours in playing with this amusing, colorful train. All cars have double trucks with copper journal boxes. 42¼ inches long. Track forms oval 50 by 30 inches.

Price, $18.00

Outfit No. 183:
Same as No. 183E, but with hand reverse instead of "Distant Control."

Price, $15.00

Reproduction, Greenberg Publishing Co.

YOU WILL BE PROUD TO OWN ANY ONE OF THESE FINE SETS

FOR "O" GAUGE TRACK

135 $21.50

144 $18.50

181 $17.00

HERE is a dandy locomotive. Plenty of pep and speed. It's nice to see the double action piston rods work back and forth with speed and smoothness. Did you ever stop to think that in proportion to the size of real trains Lionel Locomotives travel between 60 and 80 miles an hour? Some speed, eh? And some Locomotives!

Outfit No. 135 consists of:

1—No. 262 Steam Type Reversible Locomotive—With concealed headlight.
1—No. 262T Coal Tender.
1—No. 812 Gondola Car—With four barrels which you can open and fill. All real work trains carry them filled with nails, spikes, etc. A box of miniature tools with spade, pick and shovel is included with this car.
1—No. 810 Derrick Car—Has many uses. You can operate the boom, raise the hook and tackle or swing the entire cab around by means of worm gears.
1—No. 817 Caboose—Every detail, down to the little rivets and the number plates, was faithfully copied from an actual railroad caboose.
8—sections of OC curved track.
4—sections of OS straight track.
1—OTC "Lockon" Connection—To make contact from transformer to track.
1—No. 068 Warning Signal
1—No. 27 Lamp.

You will have more amusement, pleasure and interest in operating a model railroad than in any other game. Here is a set that delivers the maximum fun —at an exceptionally low price. 47 inches long. Track forms oval 50 by 30 inches.   **Price, $21.50**

Outfit No. 144 consists of:

1—No. 262 Steam Type Reversible Locomotive—With concealed headlight.
1—No. 262T Coal Tender.
2—No. 613 Illuminated Pullman Cars—Long and sleek. Just like the big De Luxe cars of famous express trains. Interior lights illuminate the stained glass transoms and cast a diffused ray through the transparent windows. An expertly designed model, with patented removable roofs.
1—No. 614 Illuminated Observation Car—Similar to No. 613, but with minutely detailed rear platform. Brass railings. Swinging doors. Attractive nameplates. Copper journal boxes. 10⅛ inches long.
8—sections of OC curved track.
6—sections of OS straight track.
1—OTC "Lockon" Connection—By means of which contact is made from transformers to track.
1—No. 068 Warning Signal
4—No. 27 Lamps.

Push in a clip and . . . presto! Off come the tops of these beautiful two-tone cars. Notice the construction—the low undercarriage. See how compact and real the whole train appears. Then just try to deny yourself the excitement and the thrill of owning this fast, luxurious express. 49¼ inches long. Track forms oval 60 by 30 inches.

Price, $18.50

Outfit No. 181 consists of:

1—No. 262 Steam Type Reversible Locomotive—With concealed headlight.
1—No. 262T Coal Tender.
1—No. 812 Gondola Car—With barrels. Take off the barrel tops and you can use the barrels to carry cargo. Or remove the barrels entirely and you can use gondola for loads of sand, pebbles or dozens of small articles. A deeply embossed, true-to-life model.
1—No. 814 Box Car—Another car that you can use to carry freight. Sliding doors. Brass hand brakes and ladders.
1—No. 817 Caboose—A vivid example of Lionel craftsmanship. Even the windows are stamped separately out of brass and inserted in position.
8—sections of OC curved track.
4—sections of OS straight track.
1—OTC "Lockon" Connection—By means of which contact is made from transformer to track.
1—No. 068 Warning Signal.
1—No. 27 Lamp.

Start your complete railroad with this excellent freight model. Set it up permanently in attic or cellar. Then get Dad to help you add accessories and cars from time to time. 48 inches long. Track forms oval 50 by 30 inches.

Price, $17.00

[Page Eighteen]

CRACK TRAINS OF THE "O" GAUGE LINE • BE SURE TO SEE THEM

FOR "O" GAUGE TRACK

240E
$32.50

241E
$30.00

239E
$27.50

SELECT any of these outfits and you will have chosen the finest "O" Gauge locomotive ever built. And built like all real locomotives—of steel stampings, not ordinary castings. Cast locomotives are top-heavy and crack when they fall. Lionel locomotives, because of their steel bodies, have low centers of gravity and can take curves at high speed without going off the track. For complete description of 260E locomotive see page 4.

Outfit No. 240E consists of:

- 1—No. 260E Steam Type "Distant Control" Locomotive—With concealed headlight and illuminated firebox.
- 1—No. 260T Oil Tender.
- 1—No. 812 Gondola Car—With four barrels and set of tools. You will have fun galore with this car and its equipment.
- 1—No. 810 Derrick Car—By means of worm gears you can raise or lower boom and tackle and swing cab around to any position.
- 1—No. 820 Floodlight Car—With two powerful searchlights which may be tilted to any angle. You can light one at a time or both. Brass trimmings. Realistic details.
- 1—No. 817 Caboose.
- 8—sections of OC curved track.
- 8—sections of OS straight track.
- 1—OTC "Lockon" Connection—By means of which contact is made from transformer to track.
- 1—No. 81 Controlling Rheostat.
- 1—No. 28, 1 No. 28A and 2 No. 27 Lamps.

Here's a train that's just chock full of fun and entertainment. Powerful floodlights project brilliant beams of light as they circle the track. You must have a work train if you hope to have a complete railroad. 62 inches long. Track forms oval 70 by 30 inches.

Price, $32.50

Outfit No. 241E consists of:

- 1—No. 260E Steam Type "Distant Control" Locomotive—With concealed headlight and illuminated firebox.
- 1—No. 260T Oil Tender.
- 2—No. 710 Illuminated Pullman Cars—The most beautiful ever constructed for "O" Gauge. Swinging doors. Brass steps. Stained glass effect in transoms, transparent windows. Durably enameled by Lionel's patented process.
- 1—No. 712 Illuminated Observation Car—Similar to No. 710, but with rear platform, finely detailed in brass.
- 8—sections of OC curved track.
- 8—sections of OS straight track.
- 1—OTC "Lockon" Connection—By means of which contact is made from transformer to track.
- 1—No. 81 Controlling Rheostat.
- 1—No. 28, 1 No. 28A and 3 No. 27 Lamps.

Aristocrat of "O" Gauge trains. Enchanting is the only word that fully describes the joy you will have in owning and playing with this extremely realistic, modern outfit. 58½ inches long. Track forms oval 70 by 30 inches.

Price, $30.00

Outfit No. 239E consists of:

- 1—No. 260E Steam Type "Distant Control" Locomotive—With concealed headlight and illuminated firebox.
- 1—No. 260T Oil Tender.
- 1—No. 812 Gondola Car—With four barrels. You can remove barrels, open and fill them with cargo. Car is minutely detailed with embossed rivets, brass number plates and hand brakes.
- 1—No. 814 Box Car—With sliding doors. Beautifully enameled. Front and rear hand brakes and ladders.
- 1—No. 815 Oil Car—A duplicate of those picturesque cars used to transport oil. Accurately proportioned.
- 1—No. 813 Cattle Car—Slatted sides. Sliding doors.
- 1—No. 817 Caboose—Inset windows. Complete with every detail. This car, like all others in the outfit, has copper journal boxes.
- 8—sections of OC curved track.
- 8—sections of OS straight track.
- 1—OTC "Lockon" Connection—By means of which contact is made from transformer to track.
- 1—No. 81 Controlling Rheostat.
- 1—No. 28 and 1 No. 28A Lamps.

Every modern improvement for the shipment of freight has been incorporated in this long set. You will be kept busy continually in making up and dispatching this complete train. 72½ inches long. Track forms oval 70 by 30 inches.

Price, $27.50

A COMPLETE "LIONEL STANDARD" RAILROAD FOR A LUCKY BOY

▲▲▲ JUST imagine the hours of endless fun and pleasure that are packed into this outfit! Put yourself at the controls. On one side you have levers for manipulating switches. On another side the panel board which operates your modern signal bridge. And then, of course, there is the rheostat and the semaphore control. ¶Pull a lever, and you set in motion a great railroad system. ¶In the distance is a mountain peak, bored with a railroad tunnel. As your train shoots out of it, a semaphore arm bobs automatically. The switch lantern changes color. Your sleek Pullman Express flies past suburban homes with lighted windows. Then past a city park. Three lights blink on, in a signal bridge overhead. The speed slackens. After its fast journey, the train gracefully comes to a stop in front of a station with dazzling lights. ¶On the platform, passengers are scurrying about. A red cap carries a load of baggage. Our friend, the Pullman porter, is smiling to everyone and offering his assistance. The conductor gazes at his watch, his arm raised for the signal. The engineer hurries around his locomotive, an oil can in his hand. ¶A scheduled minute passes. Then the train moves off. 'Round a curve with increasing speed. Past a power house. Out into the open country. ¶Far away looms a mountain. It is dotted with trees and houses that look tiny in the distance. The train thunders toward it . . . breaking records in speed and endurance. Now a valley appears between the mountain ranges. Then a freight depot, loaded with trucks and cargo. At last the tunneled mountain again, bulking large and black against the night. And then the trip is over.

This complete railroad set was made for boys with vision and ambition. The track and accessories may be arranged and re-arranged in dozens of different ways, each one offering new thrill and excitement.

This railroad will make you the most popular boy in town. And prouder than any other. Just wait and see!

No. 405E Complete Railroad consists of:

No. 364E "Lionel Standard" Outfit—No. 9E Locomotive enameled in two-tone green. Two pantagraphs. Two headlights. Eight wheels. Powered by the famous "Bild-A-Loco" motor. Accompanied by three 16 inch, twelve wheel Pullman and observation cars. Interior illumination. Removable roofs. Complete with No. 81 Rheostat and STC "Lockon."
No. 921 Park—Forming the attractive centerpiece.
No. 917 Mountain—Made of a durable felt composition.
No. 155 Freight Shed and No. 163 Set of Freight Trucks.
No. 915 Tunnel Mountain—Similar in construction to No. 917.
No. 80 Automatic Semaphore.
Pair No. 223 "Distant Control" Non-derailing Switches.
No. 114 Station—A close copy of a real station.
No. 550 Set of Figures—Real people in miniature.
No. 90 Flagstaff and Flag—With ornamental base.
No. 438 Illuminated Signal Tower—With knife switches.
No. 436 Power House to enclose your transformer.
No. 440 Position Light Signal Bridge—A new, important addition to model railroading, complete with panel board.
Type "T" Transformer—Capable of supplying 2 to 25 volts.
10 sections of C curved track.
18 sections of S straight track.
2 sections of ½ S straight track.
Track forms layout 11 feet, 6 inches long, 7 feet wide.

Read about the special features of these accessories on other pages of this catalog.   **Price, $150.00**

[Page Twenty]

FORERUNNERS OF THE "LIONEL STANDARD" GAUGE LINE

FOR "LIONEL STANDARD" TRACK

347
$15.00

360E
$21.75

62 . . $25.00
62E . . $28.75

THE 8 and 8E Electric Type Locomotives are powered by the Lionel "Super Motor," which means abundance of power and arrow-like speed. Minutely detailed even to the smallest rivets. Brass trimmed with hand rails, pantagraph and flagholders. Realistically embossed ventilators. And two sparkling headlights to brighten the way.

Outfit No. 347 consists of:
- 1—No. 8 Electric Type Reversible Locomotive—With two electric headlights.
- 1—No. 337 Illuminated Pullman Car—12 inches long. Transparent, inset windows. Brass steps. Swinging doors. Bright, durable enamel finish.
- 1—No. 338 Illuminated Observation Car—Similar to No. 337, but with rear illuminated platform richly decorated with brass.
- 8—sections of C curved track.
- 2—sections of S straight track.
- 1—STC "Lockon" Connection—By means of which contact is made from transformer to track.
- 5—No. 28 Lamps.

A modern passenger train. Sturdily built locomotive with two brilliantly enameled cars. Brass trimmings and copper journal boxes. An attractive outfit and the lowest priced in the "Lionel Standard" line. 38½ inches long. Track forms oval 57 by 45 inches. **Price, $15.00**

Outfit No. 360E consists of:
- 1—No. 8E Electric Type "Distant Control" Locomotive—With two electric headlights.
- 1—No. 332 Illuminated Mail and Baggage Car—With doors that slide open. Like its companion cars, it is 12 inches long.
- 1—No. 337 Illuminated Pullman Car—Stained glass effect in transoms and inset transparent windows.
- 1—No. 338 Illuminated Observation Car—Carefully detailed illuminated rear platform.
- 8—sections of C curved track.
- 4—sections of S straight track.
- 1—STC "Lockon" Connection—By means of which contact is made from transformer to track.
- 1—No. 81 Controlling Rheostat.
- 6—No. 28 Lamps.

Start your Standard Gauge railroad with this beautifully enameled outfit. Cars are elaborately trimmed and in keeping with proportions and details of the country's finest express trains. 52½ inches long. Track forms oval 71 by 45 inches. **Price, $21.75**

Outfit No. 362E consists of:
- 1—No. 384E Steam Type "Distant Control" Locomotive—With headlight, pilot flags, brass and copper tubing. Powerful motor.
- 1—No. 384T Coal Tender.
- 1—No. 309 Illuminated Pullman Car—Deeply embossed details. Stained glass effect in transoms. Inset transparent windows. Durably enameled.
- 1—No. 312 Illuminated Observation Car—Similar to No. 309, but with illuminated rear platform decorated in brass.
- 8—sections of C curved track.
- 2—sections of S straight track.
- 1—STC "Lockon" Connection—By means of which contact is made from transformer to track.
- 1—No. 81 Controlling Rheostat.
- 4—No. 28 Lamps.

This powerful steam type locomotive is combined with 13¼ inches illuminated cars, making it a splendidly proportioned outfit. 50¼ inches long. Track forms oval 57 by 45 inches. **Price, $28.75**

Outfit No. 362—Same as No. 362E, but with hand reverse instead of "Distant Control." **Price, $25.00**

[Page Twenty-one]

NOW ANY BOY CAN AFFORD A STANDARD GAUGE TRAIN

FOR "LIONEL STANDARD" TRACK

361E
$27.50

THE Lionel "Distant Control" train outfits on this page and throughout the book are distinguished by the letter "E." With each "E" type outfit and locomotive you get the No. 81 rheostat. By means of the controlling lever you can make the train go forward or backward, slow up or speed ahead, without touching the train itself. Get an "E" type outfit and enjoy the thrill of a 100% DISTANT CONTROL TRAIN.

Outfit No. 361E consists of:
- 1—No. 318E Electric Type "Distant Control" Locomotive—With two headlights. Finished in beautiful two-tone enamel. Powered by Lionel's famous super-motor.
- 1—No. 511 Flat Car—With load of lumber. Brass stakes hold lumber in place. Polished metal hand brakes. Four wheel trucks.
- 1—No. 514 Box Car—Brass ladders. Realistic slats. Sliding doors.
- 1—No. 520 Floodlight Car—Two powerful lights. Revolving reflectors. Brass stanchions and hand rails.
- 1—No. 517 Illuminated Caboose—Carefully detailed platforms. Striking colors in Lionel's permanent enamel. Deep embossing.
- 8—sections of C curved track.
- 6—sections of S straight track.
- 1—STC "Lockon" Connection—By means of which contact is made from transformer to track.
- 1—No. 81 Controlling Rheostat.
- 5—No. 28 Lamps.

A large, modern freight outfit that includes four very interesting cars. An extremely popular locomotive, a floodlight car and a generous quantity of track make this outfit outstanding among lower priced Standard Gauge Sets. You will enoy the thrill of power and mastery in directing its course around the track. 66½ inches long. Track forms oval 85¼ by 45 inches.
Price, $27.50

Outfit No. 386E consists of:
- 1—No. 384E Steam Type Reversible Locomotive—With electric headlight. Pilot flags. Realistic piston action. Brass and copper tubing. Inset cab window. Powered by the famous Bild-A-Loco.
- 1—No. 384T Coal Tender. Deeply embossed, accurately copied.
- 1—No. 512 Gondola Car—With eight barrels, which can be opened and filled with miniature cargo.
- 1—No. 513 Cattle Car—Actual slats in sides, and sliding doors. Beautifully colored. Copper journal boxes. Brass ladders and brakes.
- 1—No. 517 Illuminated Caboose—Carefully detailed front and rear platforms with brass railings and ladders.
- 8—sections of C curved track.
- 4—sections of S straight track.
- 1—STC "Lockon" Connection—By means of which contact is made from transformer to track.
- 1—No. 81 Controlling Rheostat.
- 2—No. 28 Lamps.

A speedy freight outfit. Brilliantly colored and truly authentic. You will spend many happy hours with this highly amusing outfit. 60½ inches long. Track forms oval 71 by 45 inches. **Price, $31.50**

Outfit No. 386—Same as No. 386E, but with hand reverse instead of "Distant Control." **Price, $27.50**

Outfit No. 364E consists of:
- 1—No. 9E Electric Type "Distant Control" Locomotive—With two electric headlights. Powered by the Bild-A-Loco motor. Front and rear pilot trucks. Colored pilot lamps and flag holders. Brass pantagraphs. Inset windows. Beautiful two-tone enamel finish.
- 1—No. 424 Illuminated Pullman Car—Six wheel trucks, swinging doors, brass steps. Transparent windows, stained glass transoms, removable roof. Lettered "Liberty Bell."
- 1—No. 425 Illuminated Pullman Car—Lettered "Stephen Girard." Like its companion cars, it is 16 inches long.
- 1—No. 426 Illuminated Observation Car—Similar to No. 424, but with rear platform. Brass railings. Lettered "Coral Isle."
- 8—sections of C curved track.
- 8—sections of S straight track.
- 1—STC "Lockon" Connection—By means of which contact is made from transformer to track.
- 1—No. 81 Controlling Rheostat.
- 6—No. 28 Lamps.

An entirely new passenger train with our famous New York Central type locomotive. Accurately copied after the trains on this famous road. Beautifully designed, artistically colored. Pullman and observation cars have six wheel trucks. Train is 68½ inches long. Track forms oval 99½ by 45 inches. **Price, $40.00**

[*Page Twenty-two*]

THE NEWEST LOCOMOTIVE IN THREE DANDY COMBINATIONS

FOR "LIONEL STANDARD" TRACK

370E $45.00

Pennsylvania Limited

372E $55.00

371E $47.50

THE three outfits on this page feature the 392E Steam Type "Distant Control" Locomotive. It embodies the patented hinged boiler front with concealed headlight, permitting easy access to lamp. Throws a powerful beam. The fire box is illuminated by an amber light which gives a realistic fire reflection. Sand domes are in copper. A beautiful stream line engine with real piston action. With it is furnished the No. 81 rheostat, which permits you to start, stop, slow down or reverse the locomotive at any distance from the track.

Outfit No. 370E consists of:

1—No. 392E Steam Type "Distant Control" Locomotive—With concealed headlight.
1—No. 384T Coal Tender.
1—No. 310 Illuminated Mail and Baggage Car—Doors slide open so that car can be loaded. Designed after the latest types.
1—No. 309 Illuminated Pullman Car—13¼ inches long, 5¼ inches high.
1—No. 312 Illuminated Observation Car—Has brass rail and illuminated platform.
8—sections of C curved track.
8—sections of S straight track.
1—STC "Lockon" Connection—By means of which contact is made from transformer to track.
1—No. 81 Controlling Rheostat.
5—No. 28 and 1 No. 28A Lamps.

The lowest priced outfit with the new 392E locomotive. Very attractive and realistic in appearance. Cars are beautifully enameled in three harmonizing colors. The baggage car provides loads of fun. Load it with mail and start it off on its route. 69¾ inches long. Track forms oval 99½ by 45 inches.

Price, $45.00

Outfit No. 372E consists of:

1—No. 392E Steam Type "Distant Control" Locomotive—With concealed headlight.
1—No. 384T Coal Tender.
1—No. 424 Illuminated Pullman Car—16 inches long, 5½ inches high. Has six-wheel trucks and copper journal boxes.
1—No. 425 Illuminated Pullman Car—Like its companion cars, it has removable roof feature, and doors that actually open.
1—No. 426 Illuminated Observation Car—Long and graceful. Two-tone enamel. Brass illuminated platform.
8—sections of C curved track.
8—sections of S straight track.
1—STC "Lockon" Connection—By means of which contact is made from transformer to track.
1—No. 81 Controlling Rheostat.
5—No. 28 and 1 No. 28A Lamps.

You boys who have ridden on De Luxe express trains will know at a glance how realistic this De Luxe model is. Perfect proportions. Beautiful colors. Interior lights. Removable roofs. And speed—in proportion to its size, it can do 70 miles an hour! 76½ inches long. Track forms oval 99½ by 45 inches.

Price, $55.00

Outfit No. 371E consists of:

1—No. 392E Steam Type "Distant Control" Locomotive—With concealed headlight.
1—No. 384T Coal Tender.
1—No. 511 Flat Car—With load of lumber. Brass stakes and hand brake wheels.
1—No. 514R Refrigerator Car—With hinged doors.
1—No. 515 Oil Car—Trimmed in brass.
1—No. 516 Coal Car—With hopper bottom. You can remove the imitation coal and load it with your own cargo.
1—No. 517 Illuminated Caboose—Typical railroad rolling stock.
8—sections of C curved track.
6—sections of S straight track.
1—STC "Lockon" Connection—By means of which contact is made from transformer to track.
1—No. 81 Controlling Rheostat.
2—No. 28 and 1 No. 28A Lamps.

Actual railroad specifications were used as guides in the construction of the locomotive and cars of this train. See it. Then you will never be satisfied until you own it. 91¾ inches long. Track forms oval 85¼ by 45 inches.

Price, $47.50

[Page Twenty-three]

1932

LIONEL'S MODEL OF THE "OLYMPIAN" AND A SPEEDY MATE

FOR "LIONEL STANDARD" TRACK

409E
$65.00

432E
$55.00

THE Lionel "Distant Control" train outfits on this page and throughout the book are distinguished by the letter "E." With each "E" type outfit and locomotive you get the No. 81 rheostat. By means of the controlling lever you can make the train go forward or backward, slow up or speed ahead, without touching the train itself. Get an "E" type outfit and enjoy the thrill of a 100% DISTANT CONTROL TRAIN.

Outfit No. 409E consists of:

- 1—No. 381E Electric Type "Distant Control" Locomotive—Designed after the powerful types that haul the famous "Olympian." Has two electric headlights, flags and adjustable pantagraphs. Richly embossed and handsomely trimmed. Copper journal boxes.
- 1—No. 412 Illuminated Pullman Car—With hinged roof. Press the clips and the top opens.
- 1—No. 413 Illuminated Pullman Car—Enameled in permanent colors. Inset windows and embossed details.
- 1—No. 416 Illuminated Observation Car—Like the other cars in this set, it is 21½ inches long, 6⅞ inches high. Illuminated brass platform.
- 8—sections of C curved track.
- 10—sections of S straight track.
- 1—STC "Lockon" Connection—By means of which contact is made from transformer to track.
- 1—No. 81 Controlling Rheostat.
- 13—No. 28 Lamps.

A faithful copy of the "Olympian" that runs on the Chicago, Milwaukee, St. Paul and Pacific Railroad. A speedy and powerful locomotive—just raring to go! The cars are solidly built with inset panels. When the roof is opened, luxurious interior details are disclosed. Just think of it—revolving chairs, porcelain basins, private compartments and doors that actually swing open. Only Lionel can build such cars. Get the "Olympian" and have the thrill of your life; 86½ inches long. Track forms oval 114 by 45 inches.

Price, $65.00

Outfit No. 432E consists of:

- 1—No. 400E Steam Type "Distant Control" Locomotive—With concealed headlight and illuminated fire box.
- 1—No. 400T Oil Tender—With six-wheel trucks and copper journal boxes. Realistically embossed and beautifully proportioned.
- 1—No. 419 Illuminated Pullman and Baggage Car—The doors slide open and you can have lots of fun loading baggage.
- 1—No. 418 Illuminated Pullman Car—18¼ inches long. This series embodies great structural strength.
- 1—No. 490 Illuminated Observation Car—Colored tail lights and a transparent nameplate make a cheerful sight.
- 8—sections of C curved track.
- 8—sections of S straight track.
- 1—STC "Lockon" Connection—By means of which contact is made from transformer to track.
- 1—No. 81 Controlling Rheostat.
- 5—No. 28 and 1 No. 28A Lamps.

There is no fun, no thrill, no pleasure in the world to compare with the downright joy you will get out of the hobby of building railroads—in miniature. Start right—with Standard Gauge and with an outfit such as this. 88½ inches long. Track forms oval 99½ by 45 inches.

Price, $55.00

[Page Twenty-four]

CRACK TRAIN OF THE LIONEL LINE—COPY OF A FAMOUS LIMITED

FOR "LIONEL STANDARD" TRACK

358E $60.00

433E $85.00

THE 400E Locomotive which pulls these two outfits is unquestionably the masterpiece of all model railroads. It is far ahead of its time and far ahead of any competition. Lionel engineers spent two years in studying, designing and constructing it. And you can spend years in enjoying its masterful appearance and powerful performance.

Outfit No. 358E consists of:

- 1—No. 400E Steam Type "Distant Control" Locomotive—With concealed headlight and illuminated firebox.
- 1—No. 400T Oil Tender—An exclusive Lionel model.
- 1—No. 212 Gondola Car—With eight barrels and set of tools.
- 1—No. 219 Derrick Car—With worm gear control.
- 1—No. 220 Floodlight Car—With adjustable reflectors. Throws powerful beams of light.
- 1—No. 217 Illuminated Caboose—Gives true railroad atmosphere.
- 8—sections of C curved track.
- 8—sections of S straight track.
- 1—STC "Lockon" Connection—By means of which contact is made from transformer to track.
- 1—No. 81 Controlling Rheostat.
- 4—No. 28 and 1 No. 28A Lamps.

Loads of fun in this famous work train. Fill the barrels with a cargo of pebbles. Lift them with the derrick. Swing them on to the gondola. And away you go across the country with full speed ahead! When you consider the quality of workmanship, the painstaking details, and the fun in store for you, this De Luxe outfit is a real value. 88 inches long. Track forms oval 99½ by 45 inches. **Price, $60.00**

Outfit No. 433E consists of:

- 1—No. 400E Steam Type "Distant Control" Locomotive—With concealed headlight and illuminated fire box.
- 1—No. 400T Oil Tender.
- 1—No. 412 Illuminated Pullman Car—21½ inches long, 6⅝ inches high. Has two six-wheel trucks with copper journal boxes.
- 1—No. 413 Illuminated Pullman Car—Like the other cars in this outfit, it has a patented hinged roof. Just press the nickeled clip and it's open!
- 1—No. 416 Illuminated Observation Car—The light on brass platform illuminates the tail lights and the transparent nameplate.
- 8—sections of C curved track.
- 10—sections of S straight track.
- 1—STC "Lockon" Connection—By means of which contact is made from transformer to track.
- 1—No. 81 Controlling Rheostat.
- 8—No. 28 and 1 No. 28A Lamps.

Copied after the famous "Twentieth Century Limited," this prize outfit is one of the finest ever built. Cars are illuminated and have removable roofs, disclosing completely detailed interiors. They are long and graceful and enameled by the famous Lionel baked process. The doors swing open. The windows are transparent, with stained glass effect in transoms. Never before have you seen such luxury. The boy who gets this outfit will be lucky. And may that boy be you! 98 inches long. Track forms oval 114 by 45 inches. **Price, $85.00**

[Page Twenty-five]

··THE ARISTOCRATS OF MODEL RAILROADING·· NO

THE BLU

Outfit No. 411E consists of:

1—No. 408E Electric Type "Distant Control" Locomotive—With twin motors, two electric headlights and four colored signal lights. The most powerful locomotive in the Lionel line. And a beauty, too! Designed for speed and built like a dreadnaught. Pantagraphs can be raised or lowered.
1—No. 412 Illuminated Pullman Car.
1—No. 413 Illuminated Pullman Car.
1—No. 414 Illuminated Pullman Car.
1—No. 416 Illuminated Observation Car. The largest series in the Lionel line. 21 inches long, 6⅝ inches high. Heavily embossed and minutely detailed even to the smallest rivet. Hinged roofs easily opened, disclosing luxurious interiors.
8—sections of C curved track.
16—sections of S straight track.
1—STC "Lockon" Connection—By means of which contact is made from transformer to track.
1—No. 81 Controlling Rheostat.
11—No. 28 and 4 No. 28 G Lamps.

Finest, largest, most complete passenger train ever produced. Twin-motor locomotive provides an abundance of power. Add as many cars as you like. The locomotive will run away with them. The four 21½ inch De Luxe Pullman cars with double lighting make this train an impressive sight. Years ahead of any other on the market. Built for those who want the best and know the best when they see it. Train is 107 inches long. Track forms oval 72 by 128 inches.

Price, $97.50

[*Page Twenty-six*]

Outfit No. 396E consists of:

1—No. 400E Steam Type "Distant Control" Locomotive—With concealed headlight and illuminated fire box. Built exactly like the real locomotives, of steel stampings and not cast.
1—No. 400T Oil Tender.
1—No. 421 Illuminated Pullman Car—With six-wheel trucks and copper journals.
1—No. 420 Illuminated Pullman Car.
1—No. 422 Illuminated Observation Car—When the room is darkened, the tail lights and transparent nameplate make a thrilling sight. Like its companion cars, it is 18 inches long, 5 inches high.
8—sections C curved track.
8—sections S straight track.
1—STC "Lockon" Connection—By means of which contact is made from transformer to track.
1—No. 81 Controlling Rheostat.
5—No. 28 and 1 No. 28A Lamps.

An exact replica of the "Blue Comet," the most famous train to Atlantic City. Like the original train, it is enameled in royal blue with two-tone effects. Truly the most graceful model ever produced. Cars are low and long—accurately proportioned. They have interior illumination and removable roofs. Richly detailed in brass. It's fascinating to watch the piston action as the train speeds along the track. 91½ inches long. Track forms oval 99½ by 45 inches.

Price, $70.00

Outfit No. 423E consists of:

1—No. 400E Steam Type "Distant Control" Locomotive—Concealed headlight and illuminated fire box. A real miniature of a stream line Timken. You have never seen anything like it. The No. 400T Oil Tender is the most modern type used. Steel stamped throughout and beautifully proportioned. A fit companion to the 400E.
No. 211 Flat Car—With load of real lumber. The nickeled stakes and brake wheels make it most interesting.
No. 212 Gondola Car—With eight barrels. Fill the barrels with cargo. It's lots of fun.
No. 213 Cattle Car—With actual slats same as real ones. The doors slide open to permit loading.
No. 214 Box Car—Carefully embossed and with sliding doors. Brass ladders and brake wheels.
No. 215 Oil Car—Just like the kind that brings in the oil from the refineries.
No. 216 Coal Car—Always a fascinating number. A wheel in the center controls the hoppers which open for unloading.

ETTER, MORE BEAUTIFUL TRAINS WERE EVER MADE ..

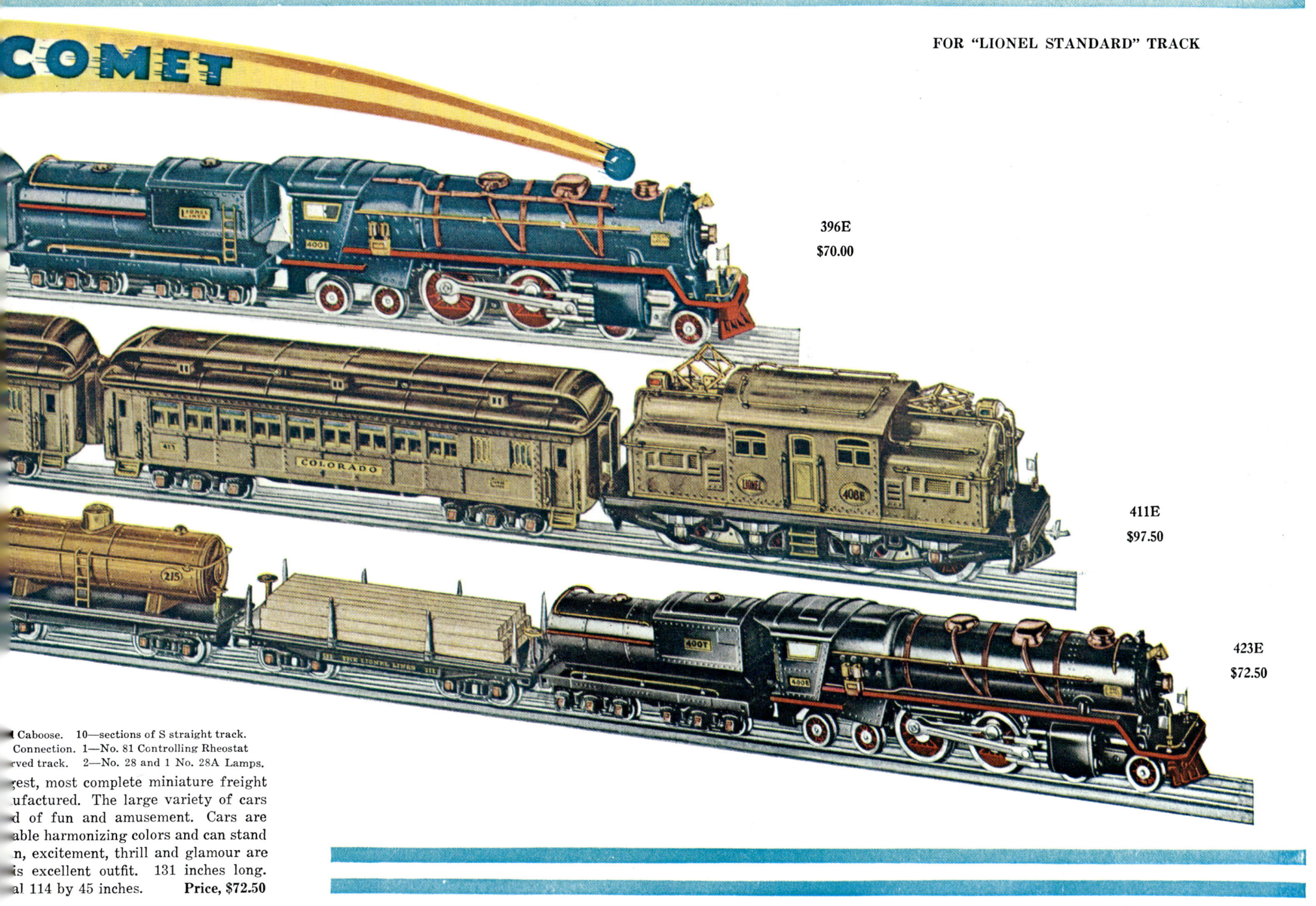

FOR "LIONEL STANDARD" TRACK

COMET

396E
$70.00

411E
$97.50

423E
$72.50

Caboose.   10—sections of S straight track.
Connection. 1—No. 81 Controlling Rheostat
rved track.   2—No. 28 and 1 No. 28A Lamps.

gest, most complete miniature freight
ufactured. The large variety of cars
d of fun and amusement. Cars are
able harmonizing colors and can stand
n, excitement, thrill and glamour are
is excellent outfit.   131 inches long.
al 114 by 45 inches.   **Price, $72.50**

[Page Twenty-seven]

1932

LIONEL "MULTIVOLT" TRANSFORMERS ARE DEPENDABLE

Lionel "Multivolt" Transformers reduce alternating current to the low voltage required for operating Lionel Trains. From exterior appearances all transformers are essentially alike. Their life and efficiency depend upon the design of the component parts and the quality of materials used. Three essential parts are contained in a heavy steel case. These parts are, the Primary coil, the Secondary coil and the core of laminated steel.

Lionel "Multivolt" Transformers, after extensive laboratory tests by capable engineers, have been found superior to every toy transformer on the market. They are made of the best materials obtainable. The laminations are made of Silicon steel. The coils are wound with enameled wire with insulated covering—not ordinary enameled wire such as is found in cheaper transformers. The insulation is the finest procurable.

For greater efficiency, these coils are dipped in a high grade varnish and baked to exclude all moisture as well as to make for solid construction. Lionel "Multivolt" Transformers offer the largest range of fixed voltages at intervals of one or two volts as against intervals of five or six volts in cheaper transformers. They will run more trains with less heating than other transformers rated at considerably more wattage.

Because of their scientific design, Lionel Transformers can withstand continuous overloads and even temporary short circuits with less danger of burning out than any other transformer manufactured.

They are listed as standard by the National Board of Underwriters and are unconditionally guaranteed as long as they are used as specified. The National Board of Underwriters has even approved Lionel's 100 watt transformer which is the only transformer of this wattage to receive such an endorsement.

Lionel "Multivolt" Transformers operate only on (A.C.) Alternating current. Before selecting your transformer ask your light company to advise you what type of current you have, the voltage and the cycle. The chart below will help you in selecting your transformer.

> Types "A" and "F" will operate any "O" Gauge outfit and a few accessories. Type "B" will operate any "O" Gauge outfit and many accessories. Types "C" and "T" will operate any "O" Gauge or Standard Gauge outfit and many accessories. Type "K" will operate any "O" Gauge or Standard Gauge outfit and all accessories or two trains at the same time.

Capacity Chart of Lionel "Multivolt" Transformers

TYPE	ALTERNATING CURRENT VOLTS	CYCLES	RATED WATTAGE	ACTUAL CAPACITY	VOLTAGES OBTAINED BY USING— SWITCH BINDING POSTS	FIXED BINDING POSTS	SIZE	PRICE
A	110	60	60	60	Volts 6 to 10, 11 to 15	Volts 5	3¾" x 5⅛" x 3¼"	$3.75
F	110	25 to 40	40	50	6 to 10, 11 to 15	5	4¼" x 5½" x 3¾"	3.75
B	110	60	75	75	8 to 12, 14 to 18, 21 to 25	6-7-13	4¼" x 5½" x 3¾"	5.00
C	110	25 to 40	75	100	2 to 10, 10 to 18, 17 to 25	2-4-6-7-8-10-12-14-15 16-17-18-19-21-23-25	4¾" x 6" x 4⅝"	7.50
T	110	60	100	125	2 to 10, 10 to 18, 17 to 25	2-4-6-7-8-10-12-14 15-16-17-18-19-21-23-25	4¾" x 6" x 4⅝"	7.50
K	110	60	150	175	2 to 10, 10 to 18, 17 to 25	2-4-6-7-8-10-12-14 15-16-17-18-19-21-23-25	4½" x 6" x 4"	11.00

A-B-T and K Transformers Can Now Be Had for 220 Volts. Specifications and Prices Same as 110-Volt Types Listed Above.

[Page Twenty-eight]

ESSENTIALS IN THE OPERATION OF LIONEL ELECTRIC TRAINS

Details and Construction of Lionel "Multivolt" Transformers

Laminations—The laminations are made of sheets of silicon steel of excellent magnetic quality.

Coils—The primary coil is wound with enamel wire with glassine paper between layers. The secondary coil is wound with cotton-covered enamel wire. Coils are then impregnated in a high grade varnish and baked to exclude moisture.

Metal Case—The coils are contained in a well designed steel case of a heavier weight than is required by the Underwriters' Laboratories.

Sub-Base—The sub-base electrically welded to the case permits the circulation of air under the transformer, which keeps it cool while in operation.

Double Contact Switch—This switch is infinitely superior to the one-piece type which is easily bent and does not make positive contact. Our double switch has a flexible phosphor bronze contact riveted underneath a heavy brass piece which protects it from injury and insures positive contact with the points. An exclusive feature of Lionel "Multivolt" Transformers.

Rigid Supports for Coils—The coils and laminations in Lionel "Multivolt" Transformers are rigidly supported inside the case by metal clamps which prevent these parts from moving and eliminates the possibility of broken lead wires.

Separable Plug—All Lionel "Multivolt" Transformers are fitted with an improved Bakelite plug.

Connections—All binding posts, contact points and switch are mounted on one piece of heavy insulating material, all conveniently located at the top of the transformer—right before the eyes of the user.

Lamp Cord—Seven feet of best grade flexible lamp cord are supplied with each transformer.

Finish—Lionel "Multivolt" Transformers are finished with a rubberoid enamel that is applied at 350 degrees Fahrenheit. This finish cannot be scratched nor will it peel off during the life of the transformer.

The above specifications prove conclusively the superiority of Lionel "Multivolt" Transformers.

No. 107 Direct Current Reducer for 110 Volt Circuit—Reduces the direct current to the low voltage required for operating Lionel Electric Trains. Used in place of a transformer when house current is "D. C." The very highest grade of resistance wire is wound on four porcelain tubes. These tubes are protected and ventilated by perforated steel covering lined with heavy asbestos. They are mounted on an 8 by 11 inch unbreakable base, made of insulated composition.

The sliding lever regulates the voltage so that you can operate your train at very slow pace or make it fly at express speed.

The direct current reducer is equipped with a heavy lamp cord insulated by an extra outer wrapper of fabric and a genuine bakelite plug instead of one made of moulded material. Price, $7.50

No. 170 Direct Current Reducer for 220 Volt Circuit. Price, $7.50

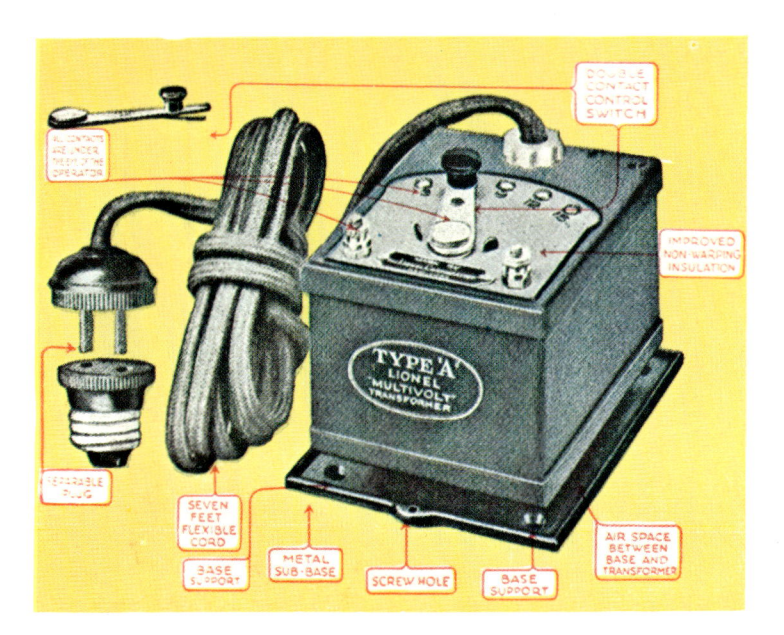

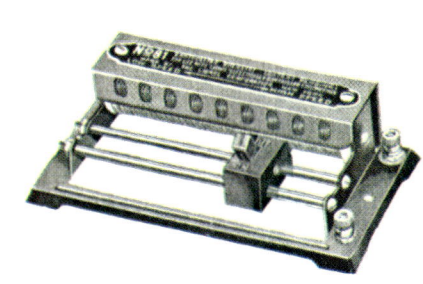

No. 91 Circuit Breaker—Every Lionel fan should have one. It is an ingenious device that functions as an automatic and never failing safety signal in case of short circuit or if the train leaves the rails.

In case of either of these occurrences, the red light becomes illuminated and the current is immediately shut off from the transformer until the fault is remedied. The Circuit Breaker is an invaluable accessory to your outfit.

The mechanism is enclosed in a die cast case, durably enameled. The bulb is surmounted by a highly polished brass guard. You should have one! 2¾ inches square, 4¼ inches high. Price, $3.25

No. 81 Controlling Rheostat—Used for increasing or decreasing the current delivered through the transformer, in steps of less than one volt. This gives you a very delicate control of your train set. By manipulating the small lever you can start and stop your train at will. If your locomotive is of the "E" type Distant Control, this rheostat will, at any distance from the track, start, stop, slow down or reverse your train. The resistance coil is protected by a perforated steel covering which is air cooled.

This rheostat can also be used when trains are operated on dry or storage batteries. 4⅞ inches long, 2½ inches wide. Price, $2.50

NEWEST AUTOMATIC SIGNALS—JUST LIKE THE REAL ONES!

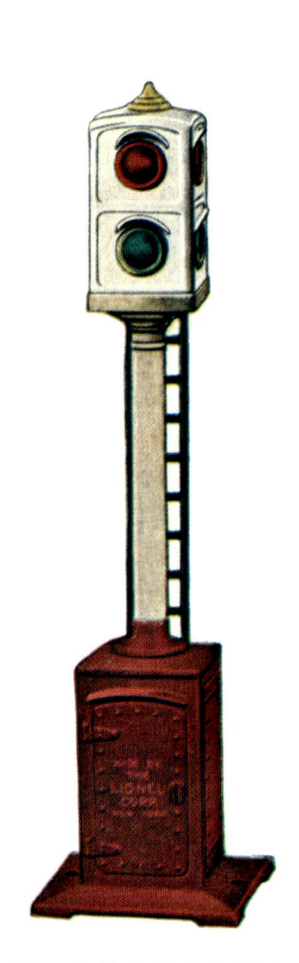

Position Light Signal Bridge

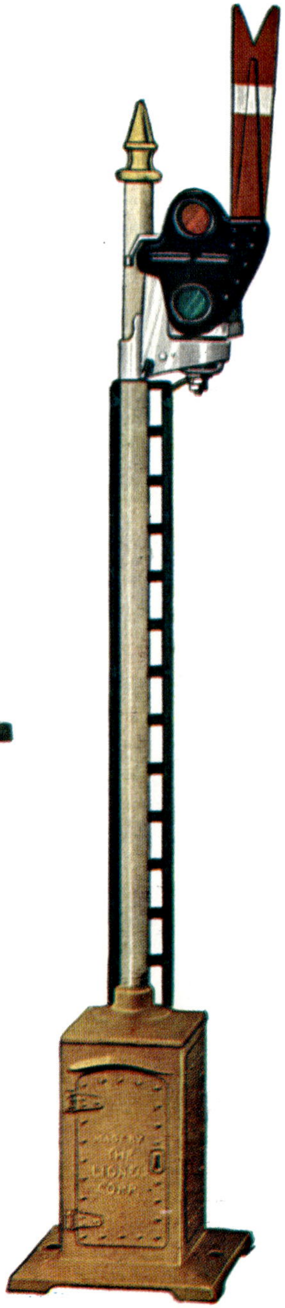

THIS new accessory is an accurate reproduction of those used on modern railroads. Instead of using colored lights as signals, the position of clear lights determines the movement of the train.

When the three lights are in a horizontal position, train stops and remains stationary until the light changes to vertical position. The position of lights is controlled by means of illuminated panel board supplied. Through the two control levers in the center of panel, one for each set of lamps, you can control the movement of two trains. The light housing can be reversed to illuminate in opposite directions. The four knife switches on the panel can be used to control other accessories.

Provision is also made on panel board for attaching control levers of electrically operated switches. (See illustration on page 46.)

Complete with fibre pins, two "Lockons" and connecting wires. 20 inches wide, 14½ inches high, 3¾ inches deep.

No. 0440 for "O" Gauge Track. Price, $12.50
No. 440 for "Lionel Standard." Price, $12.50

Automatic Train Control—When train approaches, red light glows and train automatically stops. After an interval, red light changes to green and train proceeds. Can be set so that train will not stop and light remains at green. Includes lamp, connecting wires and "Lockon." 10¼ inches high.

No. 078—For "O" Gauge. Price, $4.50
No. 78—For "Lionel Standard." Price, $4.50

Color Light Train Control—As train passes over track to which control is connected, yellow caution light goes off, red light shines and train stops. After an interval, red light goes off, green light shines and train proceeds. When the last car leaves block, light changes to yellow. This action goes on indefinitely with remarkable precision. By means of a small lever at the base, you can control the intervals between light changes, or you can cut out the control so that the train proceeds without stopping. Includes special section of SS track, two No. 28 clear lamps, one No. 29 special yellow lamp, two "Lockons" and four fibre pins. 11¼ inches high.

No. 099 Color Light Train Control for "O" Gauge. Price, $5.50
No. 99 Color Light Train Control for "Lionel Standard." Price, $5.50

Automatic Semaphore—As train passes over special patented section of track, arm rises and green bull's-eye is illuminated. When train has passed, arm drops horizontally and red bull's-eye is illuminated. Automatic in operation. From base to spire, 15 inches high. Includes lamp, connecting wires, "Lockon" and special track.

No. 080—For "O" Gauge Track. Price, $4.75
No. 80—For "Lionel Standard." Price, $4.75

Nos. 80 and 080

[Page Thirty]

NO RAILROAD IS COMPLETE WITHOUT THESE ACCESSORIES

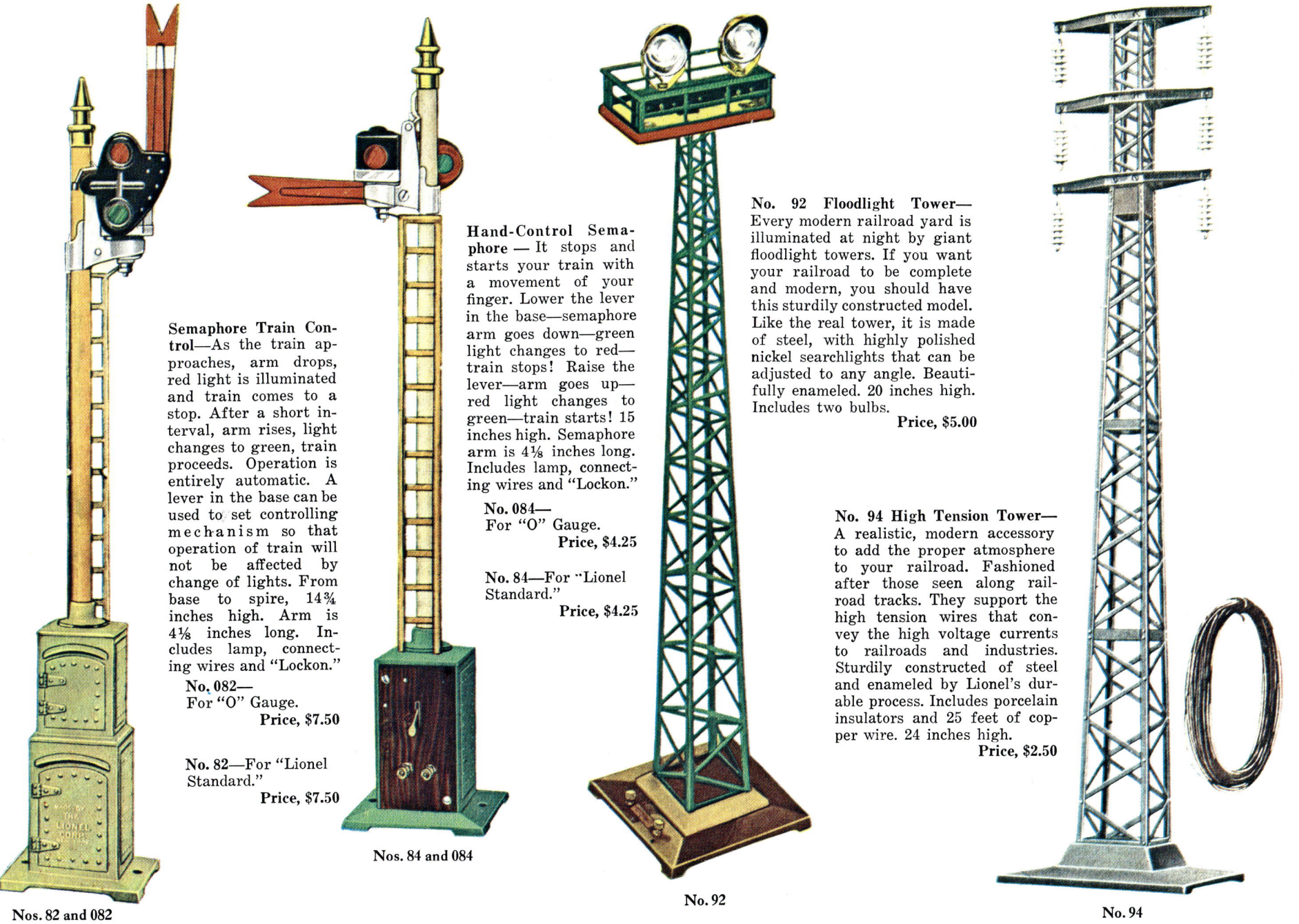

Semaphore Train Control—As the train approaches, arm drops, red light is illuminated and train comes to a stop. After a short interval, arm rises, light changes to green, train proceeds. Operation is entirely automatic. A lever in the base can be used to set controlling mechanism so that operation of train will not be affected by change of lights. From base to spire, 14¾ inches high. Arm is 4⅛ inches long. Includes lamp, connecting wires and "Lockon."

No. 082—
For "O" Gauge.
Price, $7.50

No. 82—For "Lionel Standard."
Price, $7.50

Hand-Control Semaphore—It stops and starts your train with a movement of your finger. Lower the lever in the base—semaphore arm goes down—green light changes to red—train stops! Raise the lever—arm goes up—red light changes to green—train starts! 15 inches high. Semaphore arm is 4⅛ inches long. Includes lamp, connecting wires and "Lockon."

No. 084—
For "O" Gauge.
Price, $4.25

No. 84—For "Lionel Standard."
Price, $4.25

No. 92 Floodlight Tower—Every modern railroad yard is illuminated at night by giant floodlight towers. If you want your railroad to be complete and modern, you should have this sturdily constructed model. Like the real tower, it is made of steel, with highly polished nickel searchlights that can be adjusted to any angle. Beautifully enameled. 20 inches high. Includes two bulbs.
Price, $5.00

No. 94 High Tension Tower—A realistic, modern accessory to add the proper atmosphere to your railroad. Fashioned after those seen along railroad tracks. They support the high tension wires that convey the high voltage currents to railroads and industries. Sturdily constructed of steel and enameled by Lionel's durable process. Includes porcelain insulators and 25 feet of copper wire. 24 inches high.
Price, $2.50

Nos. 82 and 082

Nos. 84 and 084

No. 92

No. 94

[Page Thirty-one]
1932

EVERY RAILROAD HAS WARNING SIGNALS • YOURS SHOULD TOO!

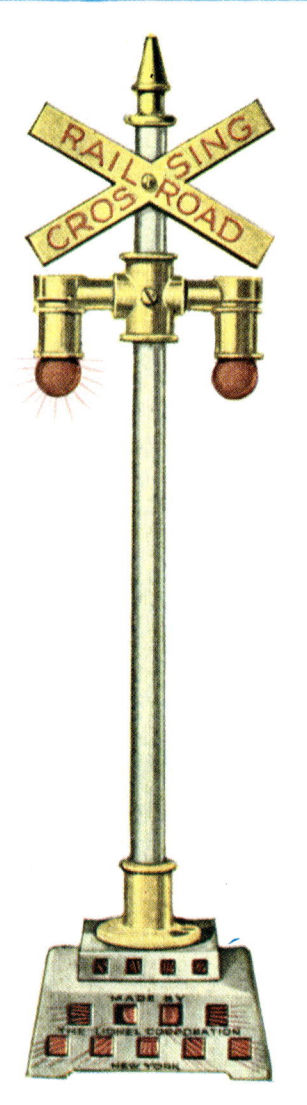

SPECIAL NOTICE
Nos. 69, 069, 77 and 077 on this page as well as Nos. 80 and 080 on page 30 are operated through Lionel's OSS or SS track. This track is an exclusive Lionel patent, No. 1636416. Beware of infringements and substitutes.

No. 83 Traffic and Crossing Signal—An ingenious device constructed for use in your Lionel village. Closely resembles traffic blinkers of real boulevards and highways. The light flashes on and off continuously. Controlling mechanism is contained in the base. Includes connecting wires. 6¼ inches high. Price, $3.00

No. 79 Flashing Crossing Signal—Red lights flash on and off alternately and continuously, by means of patented thermostat in the base. Red light glows through openings in base. Upright, arm and base are made of die castings and steel and are beautifully enameled. 11½ inches high. Base 2¾ inches square. For use with "O" Gauge and "Lionel Standard." Price, $5.25

Electric Warning Signal—Gongs ring automatically when train passes over patented special section of track to which this signal is connected. Bell stops ringing when crossing is clear. Finished in bright colors. Gongs are made of nickeled steel. Includes section of special patented track, connecting wires and "Lockon."
No. 069—For "O" Gauge. Price, $3.25
No. 69—For "Lionel Standard." Price, $3.50

No. 87—Railroad Crossing Signal—An accurately detailed model of those used on grade crossings throughout the country. Bright red lantern is mounted on a white background. Flashes at one second intervals by means of a self-contained patented device. Base contains terminals for connecting wires. 6¾ inches high. For use with "O" Gauge and "Lionel Standard." Price, $3.50

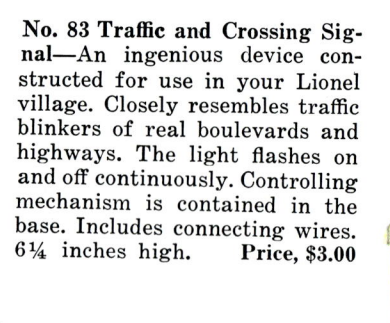

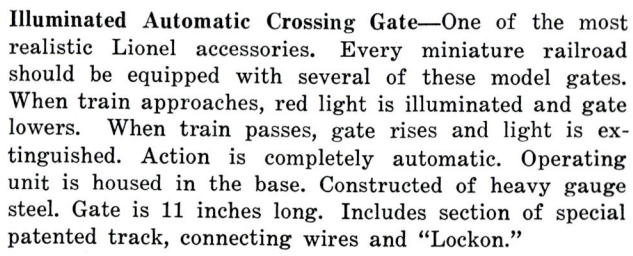

Illuminated Automatic Crossing Gate—One of the most realistic Lionel accessories. Every miniature railroad should be equipped with several of these model gates. When train approaches, red light is illuminated and gate lowers. When train passes, gate rises and light is extinguished. Action is completely automatic. Operating unit is housed in the base. Constructed of heavy gauge steel. Gate is 11 inches long. Includes section of special patented track, connecting wires and "Lockon."
No. 077—For "O" Gauge. Price, $4.25
No. 77—For "Lionel Standard." Price, $4.50

[Page Thirty-two]

Reproduction, Greenberg Publishing Co.

ADD LIGHT, COLOR AND REALISM WITH THESE LAMP POSTS

No. 67 Lamp Post—Just like those seen in big cities. Complete with two globes. 12⅝ inches high.
Price, $3.00

No. 58 Lamp Post—A true copy of the real ones. Complete with globe. 7½ inches high.
Price, $1.30

No. 54 Lamp Post—An attractive, graceful, double arm lamp post. Complete with two globes. 9½ inches high.
Price, $2.35

No. 57 Lamp Post—Top is removable so that lamp can be renewed. Complete with lamp. 7½ inches high.
Price, $1.75

No. 53 Lamp Post—New and very popular model. Complete with globe. 8½ inches high.
Price, $1.35

No. 56 Lamp Post—Top can be removed so that lamp can be renewed. Complete with lamp. 7¾ inches high.
Price, $1.75

No. 59 Lamp Post—Very graceful. Complete with globe. 8⅝ inches high.
Price, $1.60

No. 61 Lamp Post—Popular along the boulevards. Complete with globe. 12⅝ inches high.
Price, $2.25

Renewal Lamps for Lionel Electric Trains and Accessories

No. 29 Yellow Lamp—18 volts, ½" round. Price, $.30
No. 27R Red Lamp—12 volts, ⅝" round. Price, $.30
No. 27G Green Lamp—12 volts, ⅝" round. Price, $.30
No. 28R Red Lamp—18 volts, ⅝" round. Price, $.30
No. 28A Amber Lamp—18 volts, ⅝" round. Price, $.30
No. 28G Green Lamp—18 volts, ⅝" round. Price, $.30

The red lamps listed are for use in Nos. 025 and 25 Bumpers, in No. 79, Flashing Railroad Signals, and in Nos. 77 and 077 Automatic Crossing Gates.

Green lamps are for use in front and rear lanterns of 408E Electric Type Locomotive.

Yellow lamps for use in 99 and 099 train controls.

No. 27—12 volt, ½" round lamp. For use in all "O" Gauge equipment. Price, $.25
No. 28—18 volt, ½" round lamp. For use in all "Lionel Standard" equipment. Price, $.25
No. 39—12 volt, ¾" heart shaped globe. For use with Nos. 54 and 58 lamp posts. Price, $.30
No. 40—18 volt, ¾" heart shaped globe. For use with Nos. 61 and 67 lamp posts and all trains. Price, $.30
No. 53-8—18 volt, 1" heart shaped globe. For use with No. 53 lamp post. Price, $.30

Reproduction, Greenberg Publishing Co.

[Page Thirty-three]
1932

JUST LIKE THE REAL RAILROAD STATIONS IN YOUR TOWN

No. 127 Station—Designed for use with "O" Gauge outfits. Artistically enameled. Interior is illuminated. Roof is removable. Complete with electric lamp and connecting wires. 8½ inches long, 4¼ inches wide, 5 inches high.
Price, $2.95

No. 128
$26.25

No. 114 Station—This beautifully designed model closely resembles terminals erected by leading railroads in recent years. Constructed of steel and embossed to represent limestone construction. Equipped with swinging doors, two ornamental outside lighting brackets and two interior lights. When illuminated, the grill work above the windows and doors gives the most realistic effect. The roof has a removable grilled skylight. Complete with two globes and two lamps. 19¾ inches long, 9 inches high, 9½ inches wide.
Price, $15.00

No. 129 Station Terrace—As illustrated above but without station. Embossed steel, enameled to represent limestone construction. Six wide steps lead to platform containing flower beds, grass plots, flagstaff and flag. Six stately illuminated lamp posts on railing. For use with stations Nos. 126, 112 and 113. It is 31½ inches long, 18 inches wide.
Price, $16.75

No. 113 Station—Constructed of steel and embossed to represent limestone construction. Realistically grilled windows. Two outside lighting brackets, one interior lamp. Swinging doors. skylights. 13¾ inches long, 9¼ inches wide, 9 inches high.
Price, $10.00

No. 112 Station—Same as No. 113, but without outside lighting brackets and globes. Price, $7.50

No. 126 Station—Designed for use with smaller train outfits. Made of stamped steel with a beautiful crackle finish. Roof is removable and interior is illuminated. Complete with electric lamp and connecting wires. 10¼ inches long, 7¼ inches wide, 7 inches high. Price, $4.75

No. 128 Station and Terrace—A combination of No. 113 Station and No. 129 Terrace. It makes an impressive sight and gives majesty to your Railroad.
Price, $26.25

No. 113
$10.00

[*Page Thirty-four*]

LIONEL'S NEW TRUE-TO-LIFE FIGURES FOR YOUR RAILROAD

No. 550 Lionel Miniature Railroad Figures

Your wish has come true! What could be more lifelike than these beautiful Lionel three-inch figures. They will add life to your railroad station. The engineer with his blue overalls can be placed beside the engine as though he were oiling it. The man with the bag is ready to climb on. The porter with his removable stool is waiting for the passengers. The woman with arm raised seems to say "Wait for me" and the Red Cap loaded with bags is following her. He will be glad when you remove his heavy load of bags. Watch in hand, the conductor is ready to give the signal. All aboard! The train is ready to start. **Price per set, $1.75**

Individual Figures Can Be Purchased Separately

No. 551—Engineer.	Price, $.25	No. 554—Male Passenger.	Price, $.25
No. 552—Conductor.	Price, $.25	No. 555—Female Passenger.	Price, $.25
No. 553—Porter with removable footstool.	Price, $.25	No. 556—Red Cap with removable luggage.	Price, $.50

No. 90 Flagstaff and Flag — Flagstaff fits into an ornamental base mounted on a miniature grass plot with flowered border. 14¾ inches high. **Price, $1.00**

No. 89 Flagstaff and Flag — Same as No. 90 but with square metal base. **Price, $.75**

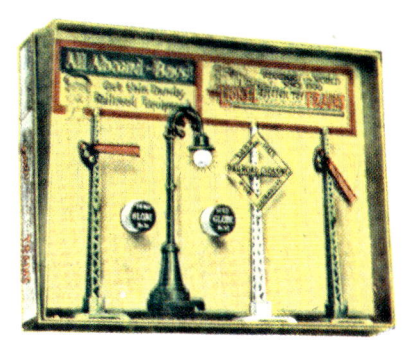

No. 70 Accessory Outfit — Consists of 2 No. 62 semaphores, 1 No. 59 lamp post, 1 No. 68 warning signal, 2 extra globes. These accessories will add much to the realism of your railroad. **Price, $4.50**

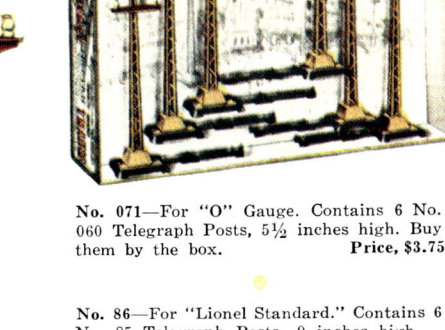

No. 192 Illuminated Villa Set — An attractive assortment of model houses. Comprises 1 No. 191 villa, 1 No. 189 villa and 2 No. 184 bungalows. Each is complete with interior lights and connecting wires. **Price, $7.00**

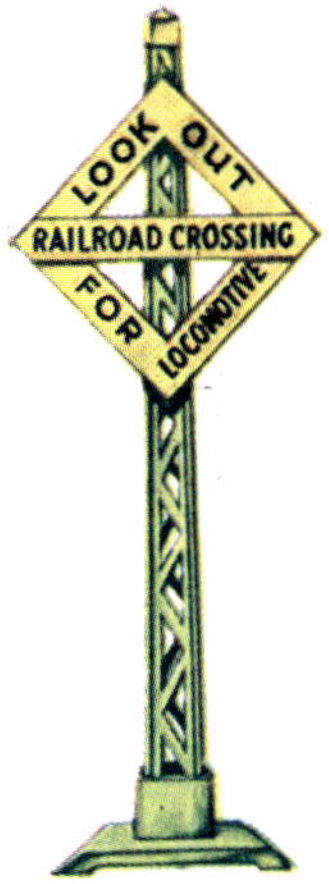

No. 62 Semaphore — Brightly colored arm has 3 discs—red, green, yellow—and is operated by lever near base. Enameled by Lionel's patented permanent process. 8⅞ inches high. **Price, $.90**

Warning Signal — Brass cross arms mounted on enameled structural steel standard. Brightly colored, realistically detailed.
No. 068 — For "O" Gauge. 6⅝ inches high. **Price, $.50**
No. 68 — For "Lionel Standard." 8⅞ inches high. **Price, $.90**

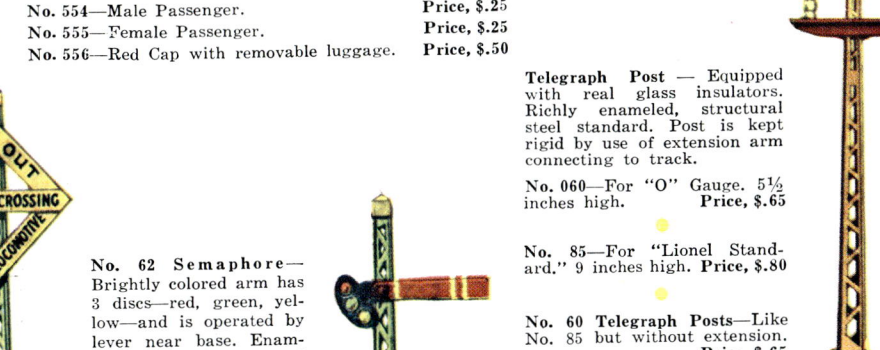

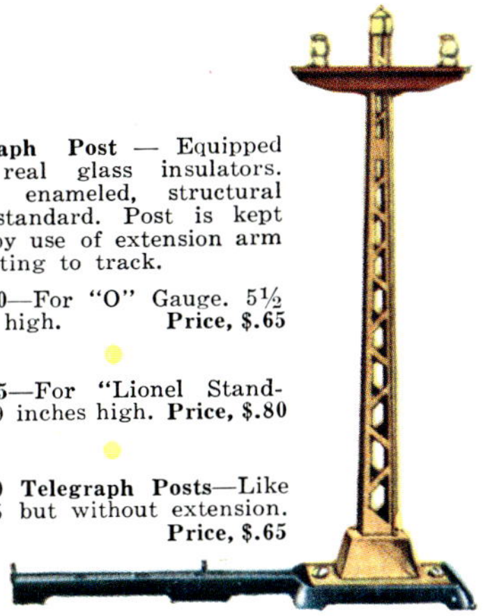

Telegraph Post — Equipped with real glass insulators. Richly enameled, structural steel standard. Post is kept rigid by use of extension arm connecting to track.
No. 060 — For "O" Gauge. 5½ inches high. **Price, $.65**
No. 85 — For "Lionel Standard." 9 inches high. **Price, $.80**
No. 60 Telegraph Posts — Like No. 85 but without extension. **Price, $.65**

No. 071 — For "O" Gauge. Contains 6 No. 060 Telegraph Posts, 5½ inches high. Buy them by the box. **Price, $3.75**

No. 86 — For "Lionel Standard." Contains 6 No. 85 Telegraph Posts, 9 inches high. **Price, $4.50**

No. 186 Illuminated Bungalow Set — Comprises 5 No. 184 bungalows, beautifully finished in assorted colors. Complete with interior lights and connecting wires. Attractively packed. **Price, $6.25**

[Page Thirty-five]

AND NOW YOU CAN HAVE REAL VILLAGES AND COUNTRYSIDES

No. 920
$25.00

ONE of the most fascinating elements of Model Railroading is the creation of naturalistic effects such as Villages and Countrysides. To add the spirit of realism to your railroad, Lionel artisans have created the NEW LIONEL PARKS. Without any effort on your part you can quickly transform your layout into a realistic miniature landscape.

No. 921 Lionel Scenic Park is a miniature piazza with grass plots and flowering shrubs. Steps rise along the terrace to the landscaped homes and bungalows. A real suburban effect is created. Shade trees and hedges make the scene more colorful. The grass is almost real.

Six illuminated all-steel villas and three illuminated bungalows complete the community.

The park is solidly constructed of plywood and strong felt composition and is hand painted. It comes in three sections to which others can be added. Each section is completely wired and ready to plug in. Run your tracks around the Lionel Park and see an enchanted scene. 85 inches long, 31½ inches wide, 10 inches high. **Price, $35.00**

No. 921C—The Center Section of No. 921—Can be purchased separately to be added to No. 920 or to further enlarge No. 921. With little effort on your part, the center plot can be removed and remodeled after your own wishes. You may wish to build a lake or a center park with the use of No. 910 grove of trees or No. 922 illuminated lamp terrace. (See page 38.) This section is completely wired and ready for use. 28 inches long, 31½ inches wide, 10 inches high. **Price, $10.00**

IT seems as though a fairy godmother had waved her wand over a beautiful countryside and transformed it into miniature form. By placing this park in the center of your layout, you will add that touch of life so necessary to the enjoyment of model railroading.

The plaza can be further enlivened with miniature automobiles and trucks. Lionel figures can add the human interest.

High up on the bluff nestle four villas and two bungalows surrounded by shade trees and flowering bushes. The homes are constructed of steel and their interiors are illuminated.

The lights filter through the windows and cast homey reflections on the bright green lawn. As soon as you see it you will want it for your very own.

The park is constructed of heavy plywood and durable felt composition. It is built in two sections and can always be enlarged by adding one or more No. 921C center sections. Each section is completely wired and ready for use.

No. 920—57 inches long, 31½ inches wide, 10 inches high. **Price, $25.00**

No. 921, $35.00

AT last you can operate your train through valleys and countrysides! All the charm and beauty of a hillside have been condensed in this beautiful Lionel creation. Nestled on a knoll is a little red roofed house. At the foot of the mountain, stately cedars and shrubs surround a country home.

Made of strong felt composition mounted on a wooden base. Hand painted and decorated. Trees are made by a new process and are the most realistic replicas produced.

No. 917—34 inches long, 9½ inches high, 15 inches wide. **Price, $4.00**

No. 918—30 inches long, 9½ inches high, 10 inches wide. **Price, $3.00**

No. 917, $4.00—No. 918, $3.00

[Page Thirty-six]

MOUNTAINS AND TUNNELS TO ADD REALISM AND COLOR

No. 140L Illuminated Tunnel—Sturdily constructed of heavy steel. Colorful bungalows and decoration make this look like a real mountainside. Electric lights at both arches reflect through the windows of the houses, giving a very realistic effect. For use with the largest Lionel trains. 35¾ inches long, 23 inches wide, 23½ inches high. Tunnel openings measure 8¼ inches high, 8¼ inches wide. **Price, $17.50**

No. 130L Illuminated Tunnel—Similar to above but for "O" Gauge track. 24 inches long, 18½ inches wide, 14½ inches high. Tunnel openings 5 inches wide by 6½ inches high. **Price, $12.50**

No. 120L Illuminated Tunnel—Constructed of sheet steel and permanently enameled in highly decorative colors. Bungalow and bridge stamped of steel and inserted. Footpaths, bridge and waterfalls are hand painted and add realistic effect. Interior illumination. For use with the large size "Lionel Standard" trains. 17 inches long, 12 inches wide, 9⅝ inches high. Tunnel openings measure 8⅛ inches high, 6½ inches wide. **Price, $6.50**

No. 119L Illuminated Tunnel—Constructed of sheet steel and permanently enameled in highly decorative colors. Interior illumination. For use with all "O" Gauge trains and medium size "Lionel Standard" trains. 12 inches long, 9½ inches wide, 9¼ inches high. Tunnel openings measure 6½ inches high, 5 inches wide. **Price, $4.50**

No. 119 Tunnel—Same as No. 119L, but without interior illumination. **Price, $3.50**

No. 118 Tunnel—Constructed of sheet steel and enameled in beautiful colors by Lionel's permanent process. For use with small size "O" Gauge trains. 8 inches long, 7¼ inches wide, 7 inches high. Tunnel openings measure 5⅝ inches high, 4 inches wide. **Price, $2.25**

Nos. 118—119—119L—120L

No. 916 "O" Gauge Curved Tunnel—A most beautiful effect created out of strong felt composition reinforced by a wooden base. Tall oaks and stately cedars enrich the grass covered valley. Little houses with their bright roofs nestle on the hillside. A summer sun seems to have been transfixed to the landscape. You will have joyful moments watching your Lionel Train playing "hide and seek" as it runs through this tunnel. 37 inches long, 30½ inches wide, 13½ inches high. Tunnel openings measure 4¾ inches wide, 5½ inches high. **Price, $5.00**

No. 915 Large Tunnel Mountain—Rising from a wooded valley is this rugged and stately mountain. Along its sides, cheerful little homes nestle comfortably. The color of the great outdoors has been faithfully reproduced in this miniature creation. The imitation grass completes the naturalistic effect. Through the tunnel openings you can lay your track and then watch your train disappear in the heart of the mountain. Solidly constructed of moulded felt and reinforced by a wooden base. Just the thing to lend a romantic atmosphere to your railroad.

65 inches long, 28½ inches wide, 23½ inches high. Tunnel openings measure 6¼ inches wide, 7¾ inches high. **Price, $15.00**

[Page Thirty-seven]

Reproduction, Greenberg Publishing Co.

1932

IT'S EASY TO CREATE LANDSCAPES AND COUNTRY SCENES

No. 910 Grove of Trees—So natural are these trees that when photographed they are difficult to distinguish from real ones, as the picture illustrates. Produced by a special secret Lionel process. The wooden base is covered with imitation grass. By placing several of these groves together or by grouping them with the others on this page, you can create marvelous effects around your railroad. 16 inches long, 8 inches deep.
Price, $1.50

No. 914 Park Landscape—A beautiful centerpiece which can be used in conjunction with other scenic parks shown on this page. Consists of two grass plots with Cedars and flowering bushes. In the center is a garden vase with flowering foliage. Base represents a concrete walk. 16 inches long, 8 inches deep.
Price, $1.50

No. 922 Illuminated Lamp Terrace—Just like those seen in the center of boulevards and parks. Flowering shrubs and green grass surround the No. 56 lamp post, which is 7¾ inches high. This will add realism to your railroad. 13 inches long, 3¾ inches deep.
Price, $2.50

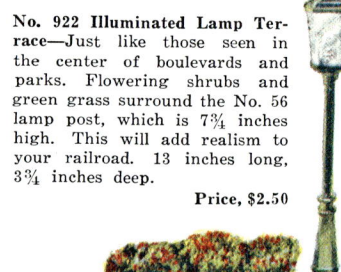

No. 919 Lionel Park Grass—A most practical and ingenious addition to the Lionel line, by means of which you can create beautiful effects around your railroad. It can be spread along the track or used to bank the Villas and Parks on this page. For permanent effects, cover the ground with shellac or glue and pour the grass over it. When dry, shake off or blow away the excess. Illustration suggests how it can be used. 8 oz. to a bag.
Price, $.25

No. 911 Illuminated Country Estate—Composed of the all steel Villa No. 191 with removable roof permitting access to bulb and wire connections, naturalistic shrubbery, hedges and trees. The wooden base is covered with imitation soft green grass. 16 inches long, 8 inches deep.
Price, $3.75
No. 191 Illuminated Villa—Same as in No. 911 but without landscape.
Price, $2.50

No. 913 Illuminated Landscaped Bungalow—A beautiful country bungalow in the midst of a green lawn. Hedges and flowering bushes surround it. Shade trees along the side add a natural setting. Bungalow is made of steel with a removable roof permitting access to bulb and wire connections. 16 inches long, 8 inches deep.
Price, $2.50
No. 184 Illuminated Bungalow—Same as in No. 913 but without landscape.
Price, $1.25

No. 912 Illuminated Suburban Home—A real home-like effect is produced by the No. 189 all steel illuminated Villa with removable roof permitting access to bulb and wire connections. It is surrounded by hedges and flowering shrubbery. Cypress trees and oaks stand majestically on a grass plot. Base is constructed of wood. 16 inches long, 8 inches deep.
Price, $3.25
No. 189 Illuminated Villa—Same as in No. 912 but without landscape.
Price, $2.00

[*Page Thirty-eight*]

THRILLS GALORE—WATCHING TRAINS GO OVER BRIDGES

Lionel's Famous "Hell Gate Bridge" for "O" Gauge and "Lionel Standard"

No. 300 Hell Gate Bridge—This is the most realistic bridge that has ever been produced for model railroads. An exact replica of the famous bridge that spans the East River in New York. Constructed entirely of sheet steel and enameled in beautiful colors through Lionel's permanent process. The train passes through the bridge at its own level without the necessity of grade approaches. This bridge is an excellent addition to any railroad. 28¾ inches long, 11 inches high, 10⅞ inches wide.
Price, $16.50

No. 271 $3.00

No. 270 Single Span for "O" Gauge—Complete with one section of track. 10¼ inches long. **Price, $1.50**

No. 271 Two-Span for "O" Gauge—Complete with two sections of track. 20½ inches long. **Price, $3.00**

No. 272 Three-Span for "O" Gauge—Complete with three sections of track. 30¾ inches long. **Price, $4.50**

No. 282 $7.50

No. 282 Three-Span for "Lionel Standard"—Consists of 3 sections of No. 280 Single Span described below. Complete with 3 sections of track. 42 inches long.
Price, $7.50

No. 281 Two-Span for "Lionel Standard"—Consists of 2 sections of No. 280 Single Span described below. Complete with 2 sections of track. 28 inches long.
Price, $5.00

No. 280 $2.50

No. 280 Single Span for "Lionel Standard"—Built of steel to represent modern heavy girder construction. Footpaths and portals on each side. Handsomely enameled through Lionel's permanent process. Complete with one section of track. 14 inches.
Price, $2.50

AMERICA'S foremost bridge builders supplied the designs for these Lionel all steel bridges. Carefully detailed with embossed rivets. Footpaths and portals add to their realism. Train passes through them at its own level without the necessity of grade approaches. Attractively enameled through Lionel's patented permanent process. Every boy will be proud to own any one of these bridges. And just think of the fun!

[Page Thirty-nine]

1932

ADDITIONAL PASSENGER CARS FOR YOUR "O" GAUGE TRAIN

ALL Lionel "O" Gauge Passenger Cars are made of steel stampings and beautifully embossed with rivets and other realistic details. Most of them, as described, have interior illumination. They are finished in a variety of attractive colors and enameled by Lionel's patented permanent process. They are equipped with automatic couplers. Wheels are constructed of heavy steel with nickeled rims.

All Passenger cars are illuminated with the exception of Nos. 529-530-629-630-603-604.

"O" Gauge cars Nos. 529-530-629-630 are for use with locomotives Nos. 248-252-259-262.

"O" Gauge cars Nos. 603-604-607-608 are for use with locomotives Nos. 252-253-259-262.

"O" Gauge cars Nos. 605 and 606 are for use with locomotives 254-254E-251-251E and No. 4.

"O" Gauge cars Nos. 613-614 are for use with locomotives Nos. 253-262.

"O" Gauge cars Nos. 710-712 are for use with locomotives Nos. 251-251E-260E.

No. 607 "O" Gauge Illuminated Pullman Car—Has inset windows and constructed of heavy steel. Permanently enameled. 2 four wheel trucks. 7½ inches long, 3½ inches high.
Price, $1.65

No. 603 "O" Gauge Pullman Car—Similar to No. 607 but without interior illumination.
Price, $1.25

No. 608 "O" Gauge Illuminated Observation Car—Heavy steel construction. inset windows. Realistic brass observation platform. 2 four wheel trucks, 7½ inches long, 3½ inches high.
Price, $1.75

No. 604 "O" Gauge Observation Car—Similar to No. 608 but without interior illumination.
Price, $1.25

No. 710 "O" Gauge Illuminated Pullman Car—Heavy steel construction, inset windows, doors that actually swing open. Obtainable in red or orange. Transparent windows. Brass steps. 2 four wheel trucks. 11⅜ inches long, 4¼ inches high.
Price, $3.90

No. 605 "O" Gauge Illuminated Pullman Car—Similar to No. 710 but 10¼ inches long, 4 inches high.
Price, $3.50

No. 712 "O" Gauge Illuminated Observation Car—Beautifully enameled by Lionel's permanent enameling process. Obtainable in red or orange. Doors swing open. Transparent windows. Embossed details. Brass platform. 2 four wheel trucks. 11⅜ inches long, 4¼ inches high.
Price, $4.00

No. 606 "O" Gauge Illuminated Observation Car—Similar to No. 712 but 10¼ inches long, 4 inches high.
Price, $3.75

No. 613 "O" Gauge Illuminated Pullman Car—Has removable roof feature. Just press the nickel clips and the roof may be easily removed. Inset windows with transparencies and stained glass effect in transoms. Enameled in duo-tone colors. Brass steps. 2 four wheel trucks with copper journals. 10⅛ inches long, 3¾ inches high.
Price, $3.25

No. 614 "O" Gauge Illuminated Observation Car—Similar to No. 613 but with brass observation platform. 10⅛ inches long, 3¾ inches high.
Price, $3.50

No. 629 "O" Gauge Pullman Car—Made of steel stampings and enameled in red with Lionel's permanent finish. 6¾ inches long, 3¼ inches high.
Price, $.80

No. 529 "O" Gauge Illuminated Pullman Car—Same as No. 629 but enameled only in Green or Terra Cotta.
Price, $.80

No. 630 "O" Gauge Observation Car—Built exactly like No. 629 but has brass observation platform. 6¾ inches long, 3¼ inches high.
Price, $.85

No. 530 "O" Gauge Observation Car—Same as No. 630 but enameled only in Green or Terra Cotta.
Price, $.85

[Page Forty]

Reproduction, Greenberg Publishing Co.

FOR A BIG 'ROAD ADD FREIGHT CARS TO YOUR EQUIPMENT

FOR "O" GAUGE TRACK

No. 809 "O" Gauge Dump Car—Has excellent play value. The hopper can be swung open on either side. Has brass brake wheels and copper journal boxes. 6¾ inches long. **Price, $1.25**

No. 902 "O" Gauge Gondola Car—With two barrels. Deeply embossed and permanently enameled through Lionel's permanent process. Brass brake wheels. Barrels can be opened and filled. 6¾ inches long, 2⅛ inches high. **Price, $.75**

No. 811 "O" Gauge Flat Car—With load of real lumber. Has two four-wheel trucks, copper journals. Nickeled stakes keep lumber in place. Lumber can be removed. Brass brake wheel. 8⅞ inches long, 2½ inches high. **Price, $1.90**

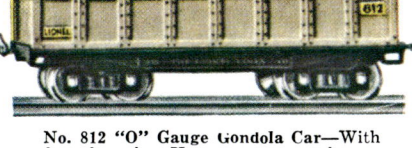

No. 812 "O" Gauge Gondola Car—With four barrels. Heavy gauge steel construction, deeply embossed. Brass hand brakes. Two four-wheel swivel trucks with copper journals. 8⅞ inches long, 2⅝ inches high. **Price, $2.00**

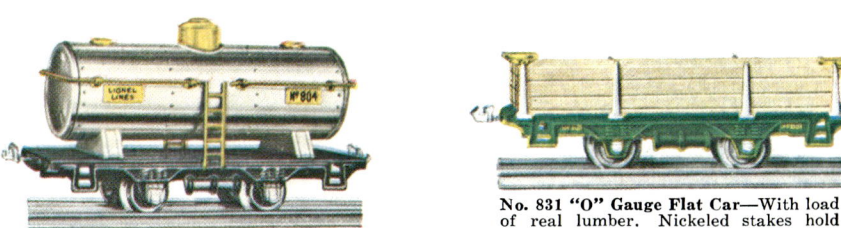

No. 804 "O" Gauge Oil Car—An exact replica of the cars used to haul the oil supply of the country. Bronzed in silver and trimmed in brass. 6¾ inches long, 3½ inches high. **Price, $1.00**

No. 831 "O" Gauge Flat Car—With load of real lumber. Nickeled stakes hold lumber in place. Lumber can be removed. Brass brake wheels. 6¾ inches long, 2⅛ inches high. **Price, $.70**

No. 816 "O" Gauge Coal Car—Accurately embossed even to the smallest rivets. Has hopper bottom operated by wheel in the center. Four-wheel swivel trucks, brass brake wheels. 8⅞ inches long, 3¼ inches high. **Price, $2.65**

No. 815 "O" Gauge Oil Car—Enameled through Lionel's permanent process. Heavily embossed and artistically detailed. Brass trimmings. Two four-wheel swivel trucks. 8⅞ inches long, 3¾ inches high. **Price, $2.25**

No. 803 "O" Gauge Coal Car—Realistically embossed. Has hopper bottom operated by wheel. Brass ladder and brake wheels. 6¾ inches long, 3¼ inches high. **Price, $1.00**

No. 806 "O" Gauge Cattle Car—Slatted like the real ones. Has sliding doors giving easy access to interior. Brass ladder and brake wheels. 6¾ inches long, 3¼ inches high. **Price, $1.10**

No. 814 "O" Gauge Box Car—Handsomely enameled in contrasting colors. Rivets finely embossed. Doors slide open and car can be filled. 8⅞ inches long, 3¾ inches high. **Price, $2.25**

No. 814R "O" Gauge Refrigerator Car—All steel construction and handsomely enameled. Has double swinging doors. 8⅞ inches long, 3¾ inches high. **Price, $2.25**

No. 805 "O" Gauge Box Car—Deeply embossed. Door slides open and car can be filled. 6¾ inches long, 3¼ inches high. **Price, $1.00**

No. 807 "O" Gauge Caboose—A typical railroad accessory. Has front and rear brass platform and ladder to roof. 6¾ inches long, 3½ inches high. **Price, $1.10**

No. 813 "O" Gauge Cattle Car—Slatted sides and enameled in contrasting colors. Doors slide open, permitting loading of car. Two four-wheel swivel trucks. 8⅞ inches long, 3¾ inches high. **Price, $2.25**

No. 817 "O" Gauge Caboose—Heavily embossed and enameled in harmonizing colors. Has front and rear brass platform and ladder to roof. 8⅞ inches long, 4 inches high. **Price, $2.65**

Above single truck cars may be used with Locomotives Nos. 248, 252, 259, 262.

Above double truck cars may be used with Locomotives Nos. 4, 253, 254, 254E, 251, 251E, 262, 260E.

[Page Forty-one]

LOADS OF FUN WITH THIS MODERN FREIGHT EQUIPMENT

No. 163—An excellent companion set to any freight station. Consists of two No. 157 Hand Trucks, one No. 162 Dump Truck, one No. 161 Baggage Truck. These are exact reproductions of freight equipment seen at all railroad depots.
Price, $3.00

No. 161 Baggage Truck—Can be loaded with baggage and barrels. Will give a realistic atmosphere to freight sheds or stations. 4½ inches long, 2 inches wide, 2⅝ inches high.
Price, $.75

No. 157 Hand Truck—Made of steel and enameled with Lionel's permanent finish. 3¼ inches long, 1⅝ inches wide.
Price, $.50

No. 162 Operating Dump Truck—Can be tilted on either side for dumping contents. Like its companion pieces, it is indispensable in freight stations. 4¼ inches long, 2¾ inches wide, 2½ inches high.
Price, $1.25

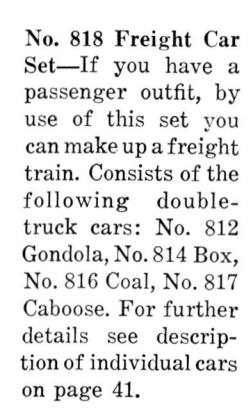

No. 808 Freight Car Set—Six interesting freight cars. Can be used with a spare engine. Consists of the following cars: No. 831 Lumber, No. 803 Coal, No. 804 Oil, No. 805 Box, No. 806 Cattle, No. 807 Caboose. For further details see description of individual cars on page 41.
Price, $5.25

No. 818 Freight Car Set—If you have a passenger outfit, by use of this set you can make up a freight train. Consists of the following double-truck cars: No. 812 Gondola, No. 814 Box, No. 816 Coal, No. 817 Caboose. For further details see description of individual cars on page 41.
Price, $9.00

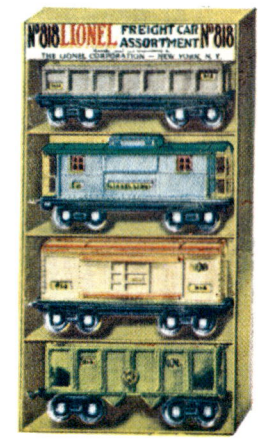

No. 810 "O" Gauge Derrick Car—A faithful reproduction of the derrick cars in use on all the big railroads throughout the country. You can raise or lower the boom, swing it from side to side and hoist weights with the pulley and tackle. The gears are accurately machine cut and operate so easily that heavy weights can be lifted without noticeable effort. A clamping device is hidden under the frame and prevents tipping when heavy weights are lifted. Sturdily constructed and beautifully enameled in bright, permanent colors. 9¼ inches long, 4½ inches high. Boom is 9¼ inches long.
Price, $7.50

No. 820 "O" Gauge Floodlight Car—A wonderful accessory. Full of play value. Two powerful floodlights with revolving reflectors which can be adjusted to any angle. Equipped with genuine crystal lenses and two No. 27 lamps. Reflectors, stanchions and hand rails are made of highly polished brass. A universal switch illuminates each lamp separately or both at one time. Same switch can be used to cut off lights. 8⅞ inches long, 3¾ inches high.
Price, $4.00

[*Page Forty-two*]

ELEGANT "LIONEL STANDARD" PULLMAN AND OBSERVATION CARS

ALL Lionel Passenger Cars are made of heavy steel and are beautifully embossed even to the finest details. They are finished in a variety of attractive colors and enameled by Lionel's patented permanent process. Most of the numbers here illustrated have the patented hinged or removable roof feature. Interiors are luxuriously furnished.

"Lionel Standard" cars Nos. 332, 337, 338 are for use with locomotives Nos. 8, 8E, 384, 384E.

"Lionel Standard" cars Nos. 309, 310, 312 may be used with locomotives Nos. 384, 384E, 318, 318E, 392E.

"Lionel Standard" cars Nos. 424, 426 may be used with locomotives Nos. 9E, 392E.

"Lionel Standard" cars Nos. 420, 421, 422 may be used with locomotives Nos. 392E, 400E.

"Lionel Standard" cars Nos. 412, 413, 414, 416 may be used with locomotives Nos. 381E, 400E, 408E.

"Lionel Standard" cars Nos. 418, 419, 431, 490 may be used with locomotives Nos. 400E, 408E.

No. 490 "Lionel Standard" Illuminated Observation Car—Made of steel. Doors actually open. Realistic brass steps. Inset transparent windows and stained glass transoms. Brilliantly enameled. Six-wheel trucks with copper journals. 17⅝ inches long, 6⅛ inches high. **Price, $10.00**

No. 431 "Lionel Standard" Illuminated Dining Car—Same as No. 490, but 18¼ inches long. 6¼ inches high. **Price, $10.50**

No. 418 "Lionel Standard" Illuminated Pullman Car—18¼ inches long, 6⅛ inches high. **Price, $9.00**

No. 419 "Lionel Standard" Illuminated Pullman and Baggage Car—Has swinging doors and six-wheel trucks. **Price, $9.25**

No. 424 "Lionel Standard" Pullman Car—Sturdily constructed of steel. Has roof which can be removed by pressing nickeled steel clips. Inset transparent windows and stained glass transoms. Doors swing open. Brass hand rails and steps. Six-wheel trucks with copper journal boxes. 16 inches long, 5½ inches high. **Price, $9.50**

No. 425 "Lionel Standard" Pullman Car—Same as No. 424, but lettered "Stephen Gerard." 16 inches long, 5½ inches high. **Price, $9.50**

No. 426 "Lionel Standard" Observation Car—Similar to No. 424, but has brass platform and illuminated tail lights and nameplate. 16 inches long, 5½ inches high. **Price, $9.50**

No. 312 "Lionel Standard" Illuminated Observation Car—Handsomely enameled in duo-tone. Has brass platform, four-wheel trucks and copper journal boxes. 13¼ inches long, 5¼ inches high. **Price, $5.50**

No. 309 "Lionel Standard" Illuminated Pullman Car—Swinging doors, transparent inset windows, stained glass transoms. 13¼ inches long, 5¼ inches high. **Price, $4.75**

No. 310 "Lionel Standard" Illuminated Mail and Baggage Car—Doors slide open and permit loading of car. 13¼ inches long, 5¼ inches high. **Price, $4.75**

No. 332 "Lionel Standard" Illuminated Mail and Baggage Car—Finished in blue or red. 12 inches long, 4¾ inches high. **Price, $4.25**

No. 338 "Lionel Standard" Illuminated Observation Car—Illuminated platform, copper journal boxes. 12 inches long, 4¾ inches high. **Price, $4.50**

No. 337 "Lionel Standard" Illuminated Pullman Car—Beautifully enameled. 12 inches long, 4¾ inches high. **Price, $3.75**

No. 420 "Lionel Standard" Illuminated Pullman Car—Made of heavy steel, handsomely enameled by Lionel's permanent process. Beautifully proportioned. Has six-wheel trucks, inset transparent windows, stained glass transoms. Doors swing open. Roof is removed by pressing nickel clips. Copper journal boxes. Brass steps. 18 inches long, 5 inches high. **Price, $12.00**

No. 421 "Lionel Standard" Illuminated Pullman Car—Same as No. 420, but lettered "Westphal." **Price, $12.00**

No. 422 "Lionel Standard" Illuminated Observation Car—Exactly like No. 420, but has brass illuminated platform. Tail lights and transparent nameplate glow brightly. 18 inches long, 5 inches high. **Price, $12.50**

No. 412 "Lionel Standard" Illuminated Pullman Car—Hinged roof, disclosing luxurious furnishings and revolving chairs. Lettered "California." For further details see page 12. 21½ inches long, 6⅝ inches high. **Price, $15.00**

No. 413 "Lionel Standard" Illuminated Pullman Car—Same as No. 412, but lettered "Colorado." **Price, $15.00**

No. 414 "Lionel Standard" Illuminated Pullman Car—Same as No. 413, but lettered "Illinois." **Price, $15.00**

No. 416 "Lionel Standard" Illuminated Observation Car—Similar to Nos. 412, 413, 414, except that it has brass platform surmounted by a dome light which shines through tail lights and transparent nameplate. Lettered "New York." Has two interior lights. 21 inches long, 6⅝ inches high. **Price, $15.00**

[Page Forty-three]

1932

LOAD YOUR FREIGHT ON THESE FASCINATING CARS

THE peak of perfection in model railroad rolling stock. These freight cars are made of steel. The fittings, such as hand rails, brakes, and ladders are highly polished brass. Wheels, axles and automatic couplers are heavy nickeled steel. Journals are copper. It is great fun to convert your passenger train into a freighter. You can do so by getting extra cars. Here are some good ones to choose from:

FOR "LIONEL STANDARD" TRACK

No. 511 Flat Car—With load of real lumber which can be loaded and unloaded. Brass stakes hold lumber in place. Brass hand brakes. Copper journal boxes. 11½ inches long, 3¼ inches high.
Price, $2.35

No. 512 Gondola Car—Colorfully enameled by Lionel's permanent process. Solidly constructed of sheet steel. Brass hand brakes and nameplates. Complete with eight barrels. 11½ inches long, 3⅜ inches high.
Price, $2.60

No. 513 Cattle Car—Slatted like the real ones. Sliding doors permit you to load it with freight. Brass hand brakes and nameplates. Colorfully enameled in duo-tone. 11½ inches long, 4¾ inches high.
Price, $3.10

No. 514R Refrigerator Car—Just like the cars used on all big railroads to transport vegetables and fruits. Swinging doors with brass locks. 11½ inches long, 4¾ inches high.
Price, $3.10

No. 514 Box Car—Sliding doors. Deeply embossed sides. Brass hand brakes and nameplates. 11½ inches long, 4¾ inches high.
Price, $3.10

No. 515 Oil Car—Duplicate of the cars used to transport crude oil over the railroads. 11½ inches long, 5⅛ inches high.
Price, $3.10

No. 516 Coal Car—Operating hopper bottoms for removal of contents of car. 11½ inches long, 4⅛ inches high.
Price, $3.50

No. 517 Illuminated Caboose—Complete with rear platform lamp. Inset windows, brass decorated platforms. 11½ inches long, 5⅜ inches high.
Price, $3.50

Freight Cars Nos. 211 to 217 are for use with locomotives 408E and 400E
Nos. 511 to 517 are for use with locomotives Nos. 8, 8E, 9E, 318E, 384, 384E, 392E

No. 211 Flat Car—With load of lumber, which can be removed. Nickeled stakes hold lumber in place. 12½ inches long, 4⅛ inches high.
Price, $3.50

No. 212 Gondola Car—Brass number plates. Deeply embossed sides. Complete with eight barrels. 12½ inches long, 3¾ inches high.
Price, $3.75

No. 213 Cattle Car—Sliding doors. Real slatted sides. 12½ inches long, 5½ inches high.
Price, $4.75

No. 214 Box Car—Four sliding doors. Brass ladder and number plates. 12½ inches long, 5½ inches high.
Price, $4.75

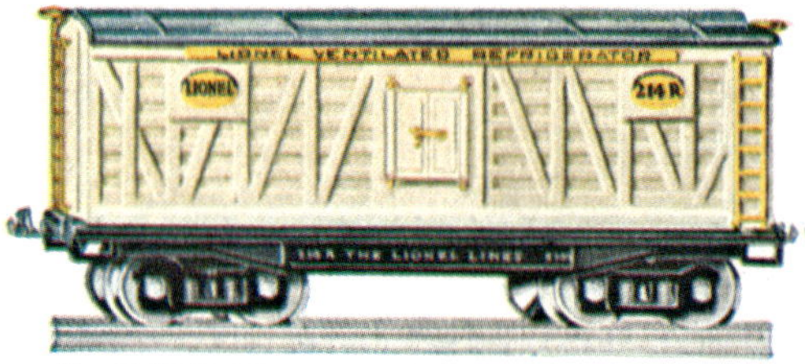

No. 214R Refrigerator Car—Double swinging doors with brass lock. 12½ inches long, 5½ inches high.
Price, $4.75

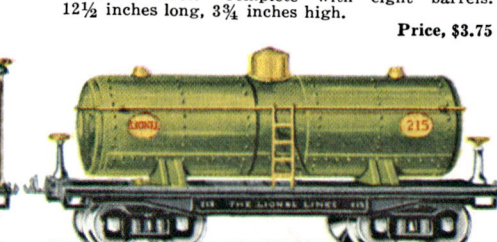

No. 215 Oil Car—Richly enameled and decorated in brass and nickel. 12½ inches long, 5½ inches high.
Price, $4.75

No. 216 Coal Car—Hopper bottoms can be operated by wheel in center of car for dumping contents. 12½ inches long, 5 inches high.
Price, $4.75

No. 217 Illuminated Caboose—Has two brass platforms with rear illumination. Colorfully enameled. 12½ inches long, 5½ inches high.
Price, $5.50

[Page Forty-four]

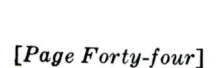

NECESSARY EQUIPMENT FOR YOUR FREIGHT TERMINALS

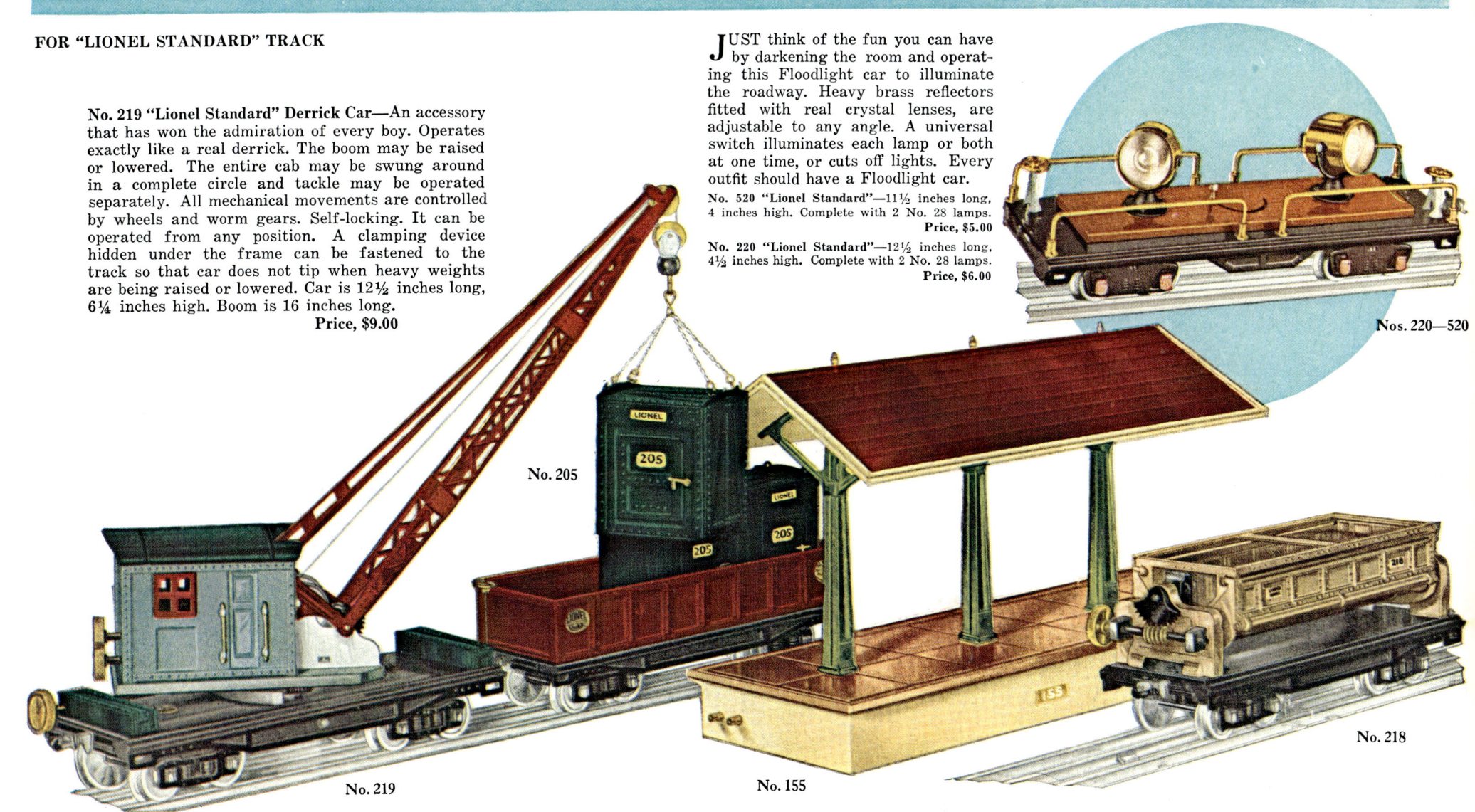

FOR "LIONEL STANDARD" TRACK

No. 219 "Lionel Standard" Derrick Car—An accessory that has won the admiration of every boy. Operates exactly like a real derrick. The boom may be raised or lowered. The entire cab may be swung around in a complete circle and tackle may be operated separately. All mechanical movements are controlled by wheels and worm gears. Self-locking. It can be operated from any position. A clamping device hidden under the frame can be fastened to the track so that car does not tip when heavy weights are being raised or lowered. Car is 12½ inches long, 6¼ inches high. Boom is 16 inches long.
Price, $9.00

JUST think of the fun you can have by darkening the room and operating this Floodlight car to illuminate the roadway. Heavy brass reflectors fitted with real crystal lenses, are adjustable to any angle. A universal switch illuminates each lamp or both at one time, or cuts off lights. Every outfit should have a Floodlight car.

No. 520 "Lionel Standard"—11½ inches long, 4 inches high. Complete with 2 No. 28 lamps.
Price, $5.00

No. 220 "Lionel Standard"—12½ inches long, 4½ inches high. Complete with 2 No. 28 lamps.
Price, $6.00

Nos. 220—520

No. 205

No. 219

No. 155

No. 218

No. 205 Steel Merchandise Containers (manufactured under license granted by L. C. L. Corporation)—A realistic railroad accessory patterned after the real ones that are used throughout the country to transport special freight. They are made of heavy gauge sheet steel, heavily embossed and trimmed in brass. The doors are hinged and have a locking device. This set may be used with No. 512 and No. 212 Gondola Cars. 3¼ inches long, 3 inches wide, 4 inches high.
Price per set of three, $3.00

No. 155 Freight Shed—A beautifully designed all steel railroad accessory. Just the thing for completing a railroad freight siding, and to lend the right atmosphere to your freight train. The platform has ample space for accommodating Lionel Hand Trucks, Baggage Trucks and Dump Trucks described on page 42. It is colorfully enameled by Lionel's permanent process and is illuminated by two lamps under the roof. 18 inches long, 11 inches high, 8 inches wide.
Price, $7.50

No. 218 "Lionel Standard' Operating Dump Car—A marvel of mechanical ingenuity. A true replica of the real dump cars used in the construction of railroads. Wheels and worm gears control the mechanism which automatically tilts the car and opens the sides for dumping. Entirely constructed of sheet steel and beautifully embossed. Finished by Lionel's permanent enameling process. Fill the car with sand or pebbles and then dump along the road. You have never had such fun. 12½ inches long, 4¾ inches high.
Price, $5.00

[Page Forty-five]

CENTRAL OPERATING STATIONS, TOWERS AND POWER HOUSES

No. 437 Illuminated Switch Signal Tower—For operating "Distant Control" trains and accessories at any distance from the track. May be used with "O" Gauge or "Lionel Standard" equipment. Rear view, illustrated in inset, shows the six knife switches attached to panel board and illustrates how switch control levers can be attached. In this way, you can operate your railroad from one central point. Beautifully embossed with many details. Windows, doors and panels are separate pieces. It is illuminated and includes electric lamp and connecting wires. 10¼ inches long, 8⅞ inches high, 8⅜ inches wide. **Price, $7.50**

No. 439 Panel Board—A very practical accessory by which you can operate your "Distant Control" trains and accessories. Six knife switches mounted on a marble composition panel board, make this possible. Provision is made for mounting two switch controls, thus enabling you to operate your switches and accessories from one central point. Electric lamp at top illuminates small dummy meters. Made of heavy steel and beautifully enameled by Lionel's permanent process. Can be used for "O" Gauge or "Lionel Standard." 8¼ inches high, 7¼ inches wide. **Price, $3.75**

No. 840 Power Station—No other accessory will add as much atmosphere and romance to your Lionel "Distant Control" Railroad. It is an exact replica of the big power stations throughout the country. Constructed entirely of sheet steel and artistically embossed to imitate concrete. All windows are inset. Three stately smoke stacks and a water tank lend a touch of industrial atmosphere. It is built to accommodate one or two Lionel Transformers. The interior is beautifully illuminated. The grid roofs can be opened so that transformer switches can be operated. A panel board on one side contains six knife switches from which "Distant Control" Trains and illuminated accessories can be operated. The station can be lifted off the platform and two transformers can be fitted into the hollows planned for them. Colorfully enameled through Lionel's permanent process. Truly a marvelous accessory that any boy will be proud to own. 26 inches long, 21½ inches wide, 18 inches to top of smokestack. **Price, $17.50**

No. 436 Power Station—Can be used for either "O" Gauge or "Lionel Standard." As illustration shows, it will house any size transformer which can be operated through removable skylight. Base is hollow so that transformer can be set inside easily. Constructed of heavy gauge steel and beautifully enameled. 9¼ inches long, 7⅝ inches wide, 10½ inches to top of chimney. **Price, $3.00**

No. 435 Power Station—Same as No. 436 but will house only Types A, B and F transformers. 7⅝ inches long, 6 inches wide, 9½ inches to top of chimney. **Price, $2.00**

The illustration at right shows the provision made for accommodating one or two Lionel Transformers. The switches on the transformers can be reached through openings above them. Illustration also shows the Panel Board on one side of the Power House containing six knife switches, from which "Distant Control" trains and illuminated accessories can be operated.

No. 438 Illuminated Signal Tower—Just like the ones you see on all big railroads. Equipped with two knife switches from which "Distant Control" Trains and Accessories can be operated. Roof is constructed of sheet steel and handsomely enameled. It is removable so that interior light can be reached. Supports are embossed to imitate steel girder construction and detailed with rivets. Base represents concrete. A brass ladder leads to the switches. Electric lamp and connecting wires included. 12 inches high. Base measures 6 inches by 4¾ inches. **Price, $5.00**

[Page Forty-six]

WHAT EVERY BOY NEEDS ·· A ROUNDHOUSE AND WEIGHING SCALE

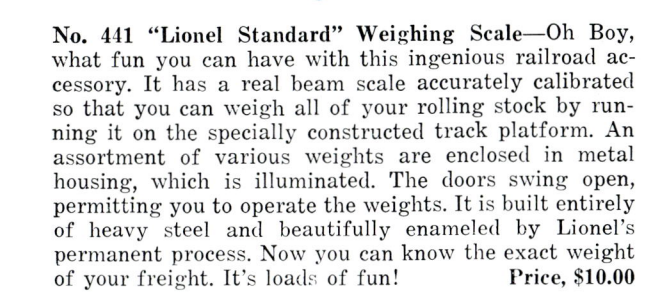

No. 441 "Lionel Standard" Weighing Scale—Oh Boy, what fun you can have with this ingenious railroad accessory. It has a real beam scale accurately calibrated so that you can weigh all of your rolling stock by running it on the specially constructed track platform. An assortment of various weights are enclosed in metal housing, which is illuminated. The doors swing open, permitting you to operate the weights. It is built entirely of heavy steel and beautifully enameled by Lionel's permanent process. Now you can know the exact weight of your freight. It's loads of fun! **Price, $10.00**

The Lionel 444 Roundhouse can be used in one or more sections, which you can add from time to time. 4 sections make a complete roundhouse and lend a real railroad appearance to your layout. When placed together, the inner walls can be easily removed to give the appearance of a complete roundhouse. By use of the No. 200 "Lionel Standard" Turntable you can lead all tracks to the roundhouse.

No. 93 Water Tower—Place it anywhere on your Lionel layout and it will lend a realistic touch. It's fun to run your locomotive under its spout and make believe you are replenishing the water supply. Made entirely of sheet steel and enameled in bright colors through Lionel's permanent process. 9 inches high. Base is 3 9/16 inches square. **Price, $.75**

No. 444 Lionel Roundhouse—Every railroad has a roundhouse and every Lionel fan should have one for his railroad. This is one of the most important and practical accessories ever designed. Constructed of steel and heavily reinforced by girder effect. The interior is illuminated and equipped with bumper. You can house the largest Lionel locomotive by running a standard track to the bumper inside, as illustrated. By using a No. 020X "O" Gauge 45 degree crossing across the opening, you can house 2 "O" Gauge locomotives. 26 windows and 4 doors enhance the appearance and demonstrate Lionel's painstaking methods of construction. The doors actually swing open. Grilled skylights can be removed to permit lamp renewals. Finished in harmonious durable enamels.
Back 24 inches wide   Front 8¾ inches wide
Opening 8 inches high Overall height 14½ inches
Price, $12.50

No. 200 Turntable for "Lionel Standard"—Especially adaptable for use with No. 444 Roundhouse, as illustrated. Perfectly balanced so that the heaviest locomotives can be easily turned in any direction by means of the worm gear and hand wheel on the turntable. Heavily constructed of steel and artistically enameled. 17 inches in diameter. **Price, $5.00**

[*Page Forty-seven*]

HERE ARE A FEW EXAMPLES TO HELP YOU PLAN YOUR LAYOUT

IT'S fun to build your own railroad and it's easy with Lionel accessories. But first, you must plan the track layout. This you can do by means of Lionel straight and curved track as well as switches and crossings. The more switches—the more fun.

On this page we have given you several simple, yet interesting suggestions to illustrate the principles involved in making a workable layout. They can be formed for "Standard" or "O" Gauge track. The amount of materials required is shown under each illustration. But perhaps you will want to invent your own system, depending upon the size of the space you have available as well as the amount of accessories that you have.

After your layout is made, you can create natural effects by means of the scenic parks, mountains and tunnels such as you will find on pages 36, 37, 38.

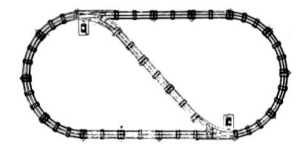

1. This is formed with:
   8 sections of curved track
   9 sections of straight track
   1 pair of switches (right hand only)
   "O" Gauge layout, 71 x 30 inches
   "Standard" Gauge layout, 98 x 43 inches

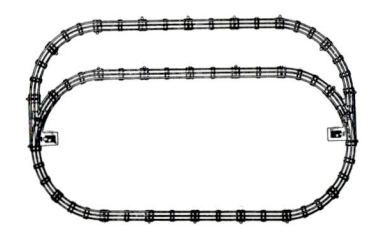

2. This is formed with:
   10 sections of curved track
   12 sections of straight track
   1 pair of switches
   "O" Gauge layout, 71 x 40 inches
   "Standard" Gauge layout, 98 x 57 inches

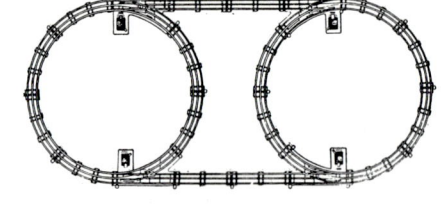

3. This is formed with:
   12 sections of curved track
   4 sections of straight track
   2 pairs of switches
   "O" Gauge layout, 71 x 30 inches
   "Standard" Gauge layout, 98 x 42 inches

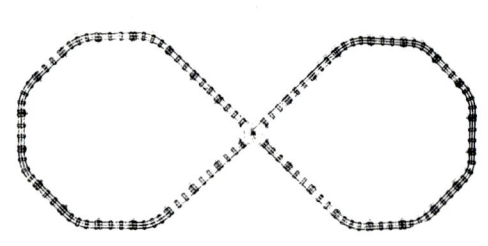

4. This is formed with:
   22 sections of straight track
   12 sections of curved track
   1 90° crossing
   "O" Gauge layout, 11 ft. 2 in. x 4 ft. 5 inches
   "Standard" Gauge layout, 16 ft. x 6 ft. 8 inches

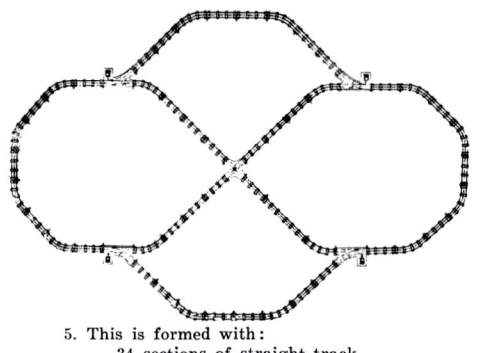

5. This is formed with:
   34 sections of straight track
   16 sections of curved track
   1 90° crossing
   2 pairs of switches
   "O" Gauge layout, 12 ft. 9 in. x 8 ft. 5 inches
   "Standard" Gauge layout, 18 ft. x 12 ft.

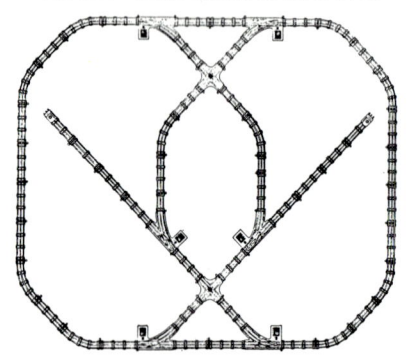

6. This is formed with:
   36 sections of straight track
   10 sections of curved track
   2 half sections of straight track
   3 pairs of switches
   2 90° crossings
   2 bumpers
   "O" Gauge layout, 10 ft. x 6 ft. 10 in.
   "Standard" Gauge layout, 12 ft. 4 in. x 10 ft. 2 inches

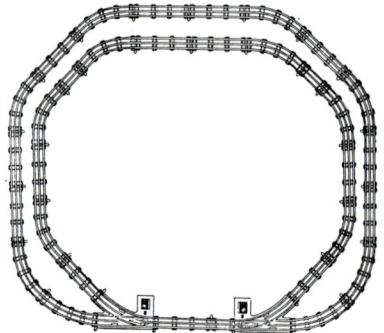

7. This is formed with:
   15 sections of straight track
   14 sections of curved track
   3 half sections of straight track
   1 pair of switches
   "O" Gauge layout, 5 ft. 6 in. x 4 ft. 6 inches
   "Standard" Gauge layout, 8 ft. x 6 ft. 10 inches

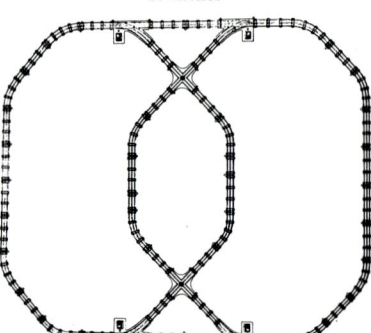

8. This is formed with:
   30 sections of straight track
   12 sections of curved track
   2 half sections of straight track
   2 pairs of switches
   2 90° crossings
   "O" Gauge layout, 10 ft. x 6 ft. 10 in.
   "Standard" Gauge layout, 12 ft. 4 in. x 10 ft. 2 inches

[*Page Forty-eight*]

EXTRA TRACK AND CROSSINGS FOR AN INTERESTING ROAD

Lionel 45 Degree Crossing—By using 14 sections of either "O" Gauge or "Lionel Standard" curved track, you can make a figure "8" layout. It can also be used with straight and curved track to make a variety of interesting layouts. It is of steel construction throughout. The heavy fibre lock in center where rails cross, prevents cars from jumping track and avoids short circuit.

No. 020X—for "O" Gauge. 11½ inches long, 6 inches in its extreme width. **Price, $1.60**

No. 20X—for "Lionel Standard." 16½ inches long, 9 inches in its extreme width. **Price, $1.85**

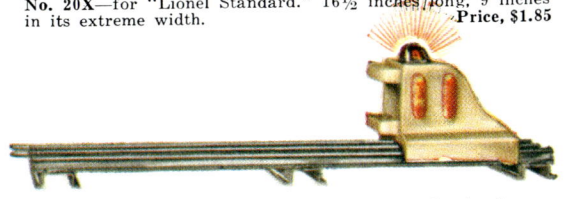

Illuminated Bumper—An important accessory in the formation of railroad sidings. Electrical contact is automatically made. It is die cast, handsomely enamelled and surmounted by red electric light which is protected by nickeled steel guard. Includes section of track.

No. 025—for "O" Gauge. 10¼ inches long, 2⅞ inches high. **Price, $1.85**

No. 25—for "Lionel Standard." 14 inches long, 3¾ inches high. **Price, $2.35**

No. 23 "Lionel Standard" Bumper—An indispensable accessory for terminals or sidings. Fitted with plunger to absorb shocks when car strikes it. The frame is removable. 14 inches long, 3 inches high. Includes section of track. **Price, $1.30**

No. 023 "O" Gauge Bumper—Constructed of heavy steel and fitted with spring plunger to absorb shocks. The frame is removable. Includes section of track. 10¼ inches long, 2 inches high. **Price, $.85**

Fibre Pins for use on special sections of track. **Price, 5c each**
Steel Pins for all track. **Price, 10c a doz.**

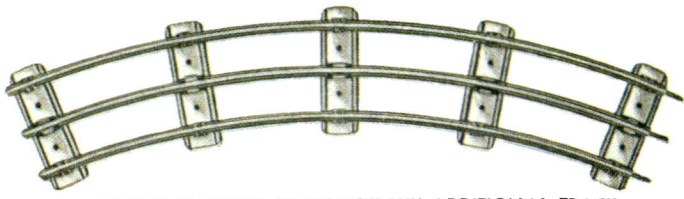

AVOID IMITATIONS. WHEN YOU BUY ADDITIONAL TRACK BE SURE THAT THE NAME "LIONEL" IS STAMPED ON IT

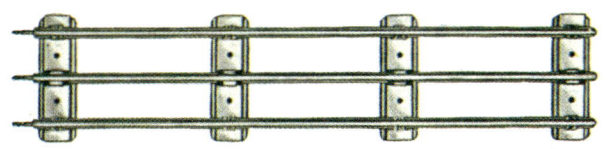

LIONEL track is made in two widths: "O" Gauge which is 1⅜ inches wide and "Lionel Standard" Gauge which is 2¼ inches wide. This explains the difference between "O" Gauge and "Lionel Standard" Gauge trains. Lionel track is constructed with great care. It is made of extremely heavy gauge metal and supported by sturdy cross ties.

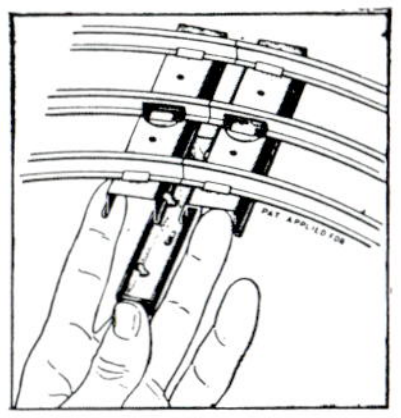

The base of the rail is formed by doubling the flange as illustrated to the left. This is an exclusive Lionel Patent and further strengthens the track so that a full grown person can stand on it without bending it.

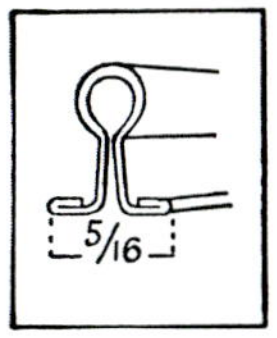

One end of each section of track has three steel pins which fit into the openings of adjoining sections. This makes a perfect connection yet makes it possible to remove sections easily. With each piece of track you get a connecting clip. By inserting this clip between adjoining sections as shown above, the tracks are locked firmly.

Each section of Lionel track is perfectly insulated and carefully tested. The radius of curved track is scientifically determined so that trains going at full speed will not derail.

These facts prove the superiority of Lionel track. Insist on Lionel, the name is stamped on every piece.

Lionel "O" Gauge Track—1⅜ inches wide

OC curved—11 inches long. **Price, $.20**
OS straight—10¼ inches long. **Price, $.20**
½ OS—Half section of straight track—5 inches long. **Price, $.20**
OSS Special Insulated Track (Patent No. 1,636,416)—10¼ inches long. For use with electrically controlled accessories. Complete with "Lockon" and connecting wires. **Price, $.40**

"Lionel Standard" Track—2¼ inches wide.

"C" curved—16 inches long. **Price, $.30**
"S" straight—14 inches long. **Price, $.30**
½ S—Half section of straight track—7 inches long. **Price, $.30**
SS Special Insulated Track (Patent No. 1,636,416)—14 inches long. For use with electrically controlled accessories. Complete with "Lockon" and connecting wires. **Price, $.60**

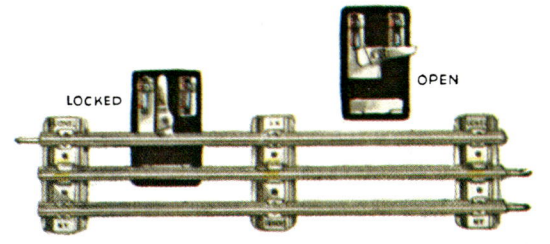

LIONEL "Lockon" connections are necessary to connect wires from transformer or rheostat to the track. They are also used to connect electric accessories which operate through track. Connections are made to the track by simply turning the lever at right angles, fitting it to center and outside rails and then locking it in place as shown in the illustration above. Electric connection is then as perfect as though the parts were riveted or soldered to the track.

Lionel "Lockon" connections are free from set screws and binding posts and simple to insert. The fingers that hold the wires are made of heavy tempered blue steel and are unbreakable. All other metal parts are nickel plated and mounted on a heavy fibre base.

OTC "Lockon" for "O" Gauge. **Price, $.20**
STC "Lockon" for "Lionel Standard." **Price, $.25**

Lionel 90 Degree Crossings—A necessary adjunct to the formation of railroad layouts. The cross rails are mounted on an ornamental steel base, beautifully enamelled. A solid moulded fibre block placed in the center where the rails cross, prevents short circuits and permits locomotives and cars to ride over it without derailing. A large variety of figures can be formed when using these crossings in conjunction with switches and track.

No. 020 "O" Gauge Crossing—8¼ inches square. **Price, $1.10**

No. 20 "Lionel Standard" Crossing—11¾ inches square. **Price, $1.30**

[Page Forty-nine]

REMEMBER, THE MORE SWITCHES YOU HAVE, THE MORE FUN!

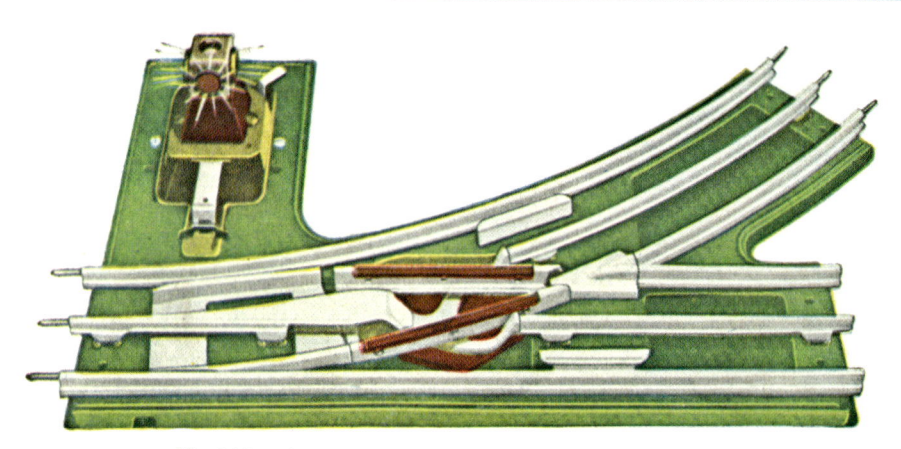

No. 210 and 021 Lionel Hand Operated Switch (Left)

LIONEL HAND OPERATED SWITCHES—All Lionel switches are radically different from others on the market. They are of heavy steel construction throughout and will bear the weight of the heaviest trains without bending or breaking. They are beautifully enameled by Lionel's permanent process. Heavy fibre insulation at the points where the rails cross eliminates all possibility of short circuits and avoids flickering of headlight as train passes over these points. This is an exclusive Lionel feature made under *Patents Re 16580 and 1671236.* Guard rails attached to Lionel switches prevent derailing even when the train is traveling at high speed. Hand lever which moves the rails, also set the signals, changes the lights and locks the mechanism.

"Lionel Standard" Illuminated Switches

No. 210 Right and Left Hand—15¼ inches long, 8⅝ inches wide. Includes electric lamps.
Price Per Pair, $6.50

No. 210 Right Hand Switch—Includes electric lamp.
Price, $3.50

No. 210 Left Hand Switch—Includes electric lamp.
Price, $3.50

"O" Gauge Illuminated Switches

No. 021 Right and Left Hand—10½ inches long, 7¼ inches wide. Includes electric lamps.
Price Per Pair, $5.00

No. 021 Right Hand Switch—Includes electric lamp.
Price, $2.75

No. 021—Left Hand Switch—Includes electric lamp.
Price, $2.75

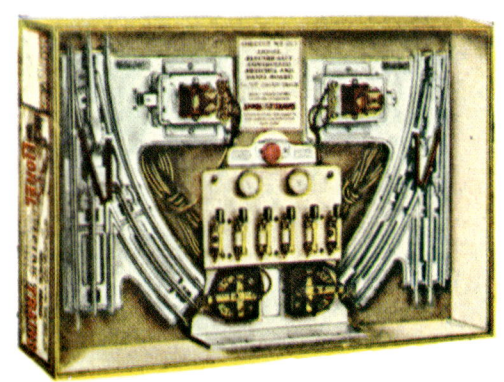

No. 225 "Lionel Standard" "Distant Control" Switch and Panel Board Set—An excellent adjunct to your model railroad. The more switches you have the more interesting layout you can make. Set is comprised of one pair of No. 222 "Distant Control" Switches (right and left hand) and one No. 439 Illuminated Panel Board. By means of the Panel Board, you can operate your "Distant Control" railroad from one central point at any distance from the track. Complete with lamps and connecting wires.
Price, $14.75

No. 223. A new electrically controlled "non-derailing" switch. Automatically clears track

LIONEL "DISTANT CONTROL" SWITCHES can be operated at any distance from the track by use of the control lever attached to connecting cord. By moving this lever, the position of the switch changes, as well as the red and green signal lights. The new switch No. 223 embodies the Lionel patented attachment which absolutely prevents the derailment of trains. Should a train approach an open switch, this automatic device instantly sets the track in a clear position so that the train can go on its way without derailing. When using two of these switches, should one be set open and the other against the train, the automatic device will correct the error. Mechanism is contained within the switch and no extra wiring is required. Guard rails prevent train from leaving track, even at high speed. The patented fibre rails prevent short circuit when train passes over switch points. Remember, the more switches—the more fun!

No. 223 Right and Left Hand—15¼ inches long, 8⅝ inches wide. Includes 42 inches of cord, controlling lever and two lamps.
Price Per Pair, $12.00

No. 223 Right Hand Switch. Price, $6.25

No. 223 Left Hand Switch. Price, $6.25

No. 222 "Lional Standard" "Distant Control" Illuminated Switches (Right and Left Hand)—15¼ inches long, 8⅝ inches wide. Price includes electric lamps and 42 inches of cord to which controlling levers are attached.
Price Per Pair, $11.00

No. 222 Left Hand Switch. Price, $6.00

No. 222 Right Hand Switch. Price, $6.00

No. 012 Lionel "O" GAUGE "Distant Control" Illuminated Switches (Right and Left Hand)—10½ inches long, 7¼ inches wide. Price includes electric lamps and 42 inches of cord to which controlling levers are attached.
Price Per Pair, $9.75

No. 012 Left Hand Switch. Price, $5.00

No. 012 Right Hand Switch. Price, $5.00

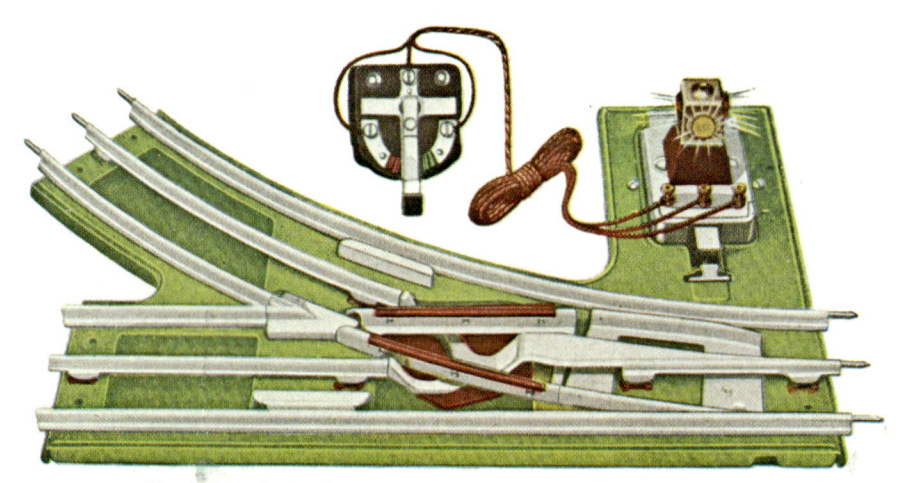

No. 222 and 012 Lionel "Distant Control" Switch (Right)
No. 223, same as above, but with new non-derailing feature

[Page Fifty]

·· AND NOW! A LIONEL ELECTRIC RANGE FOR SISTER ··

Lionel Silent Track Bed

ONE of the most important contributions to Model Railroading. "Silent Track Bed" with its moulded edges resembles a rock ballasted road and adds greatly to the realism of your railroad. It silences the sound of a moving train. It holds the track rigidly in place without fastening, and protects floors. Made of first grade sponge rubber. Can be had in "O" Gauge or "Lionel Standard" for straight or curved track, as well as for all types of switches and crossings.

FOR "O" GAUGE	FOR STANDARD GAUGE
No. 030—For curved track. Price, $.20	No. 30—For curved track. Price, $.30
No. 031—For straight track. Price, $.20	No. 31—For straight track. Price, $.30
No. 032—For 90° crossing. Price, $.50	No. 32—For 90° crossing. Price, $.75
No. 033—For 45° crossing. Price, $.50	No. 33—For 45° crossing. Price, $.75
No. 034—For switches. Price, Per Pair, $1.25	No. 34—For switches. Price, Per Pair, $1.75

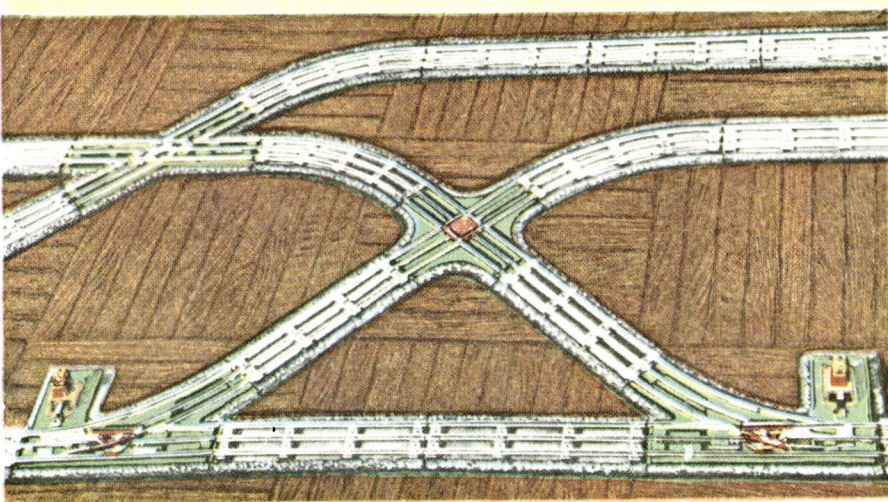

HERE is a real gift for the little girl. The Lionel Electric Range has been built with the same principles of quality—the same painstaking methods of manufacture that have made Lionel Trains "The Standard of the World."

The Lionel Electric Range is an efficient toy range with all the practical features of a large range. Solidly constructed of steel and with a high grade porcelain finish. Oven walls are heavily insulated with asbestos, keeping exterior cool. The cooking surface is of stainless steel and easy to keep clean.

There are two electric units in the oven, one bakes and the other broils, either of which or both can be used by means of the two switches on the left of panel board. The two open burners have a capacity of 625 watts each. They can be operated by the two right switches on the panel board, singly or together. A toggle switch throws all the current into the oven or into the burners. While the current is on, a pilot light shines red. The oven door is equipped with a thermometer showing the temperature in the oven. Included with the range are five cooking utensils.

The Lionel Electric Range will initiate the little girl in the art of cookery. There's lots of fun in playing housewife.

Width, 25 inches.
Depth, 11 inches.
Cooking Surface, 25 inches from floor.
Height overall, 33 inches.
Oven, 9½ inches square, 10 inches deep.

Diameter of Open Burners, 5½ inches.
Cooking Surface, 14¼ inches wide, 11¾ inches.
Heating units in oven are 625 watts each.
Open burners, 625 watts each.

No. 455   Price, $29.50

HOW TO GET MORE FUN AND THRILL OUT OF YOUR LIONEL RAILROAD

...READ HOW TO WIN A MEMBERSHIP IN THE FAMOUS LIONEL ENGINEERS CLUB

THOUSANDS and thousands of boys in every state of the Union are full-fledged members of this famous model railroading club. There are members even in Canada, South America, England, Australia, South Africa, China and Japan. Wherever you go, you will meet boys wearing the Lionel Engineers button. You will see hanging proudly on their walls a framed certificate proving them qualified members of the famous Lionel Engineers Club.

You cannot get the full fun out of model railroading; you cannot get the thrill you are entitled to out of your Lionel Train, unless you, too, become a member of this club. Here is why:

(1) Membership in the Lionel Engineers Club puts you in contact with other boys all over the world with whom you can exchange letters, form friendships and get ideas for operating your Lionel Railroad.

(2) Membership entitles you to a full year's free subscription to the Lionel Magazine—the only model railroading magazine published. Each issue is packed from cover to cover with information you need. It gives you full details on how to make all kinds of new track layouts. Tells you how to use bridges, switches, stations and signaling systems. How to solve actual problems of railroad operation; how to tell the different types of signals and locomotives; how to recognize the insignia of famous railroads, etc. It gives you thrilling stories of the true adventures of famous railroad men, it tells you all the fascinating history and romance of railroading from the early days right down to today. Nobody except a member of the Lionel Engineers Club can get this magazine—and no other magazine at any price gives you all you get in the Lionel Magazine, free of charge.

Apply for your membership today. A year's membership includes full voting privileges, engraved membership certificate, handsome bronze button, and bi-monthly issues of the Lionel Magazine. Only fifty cents. Use the coupon.

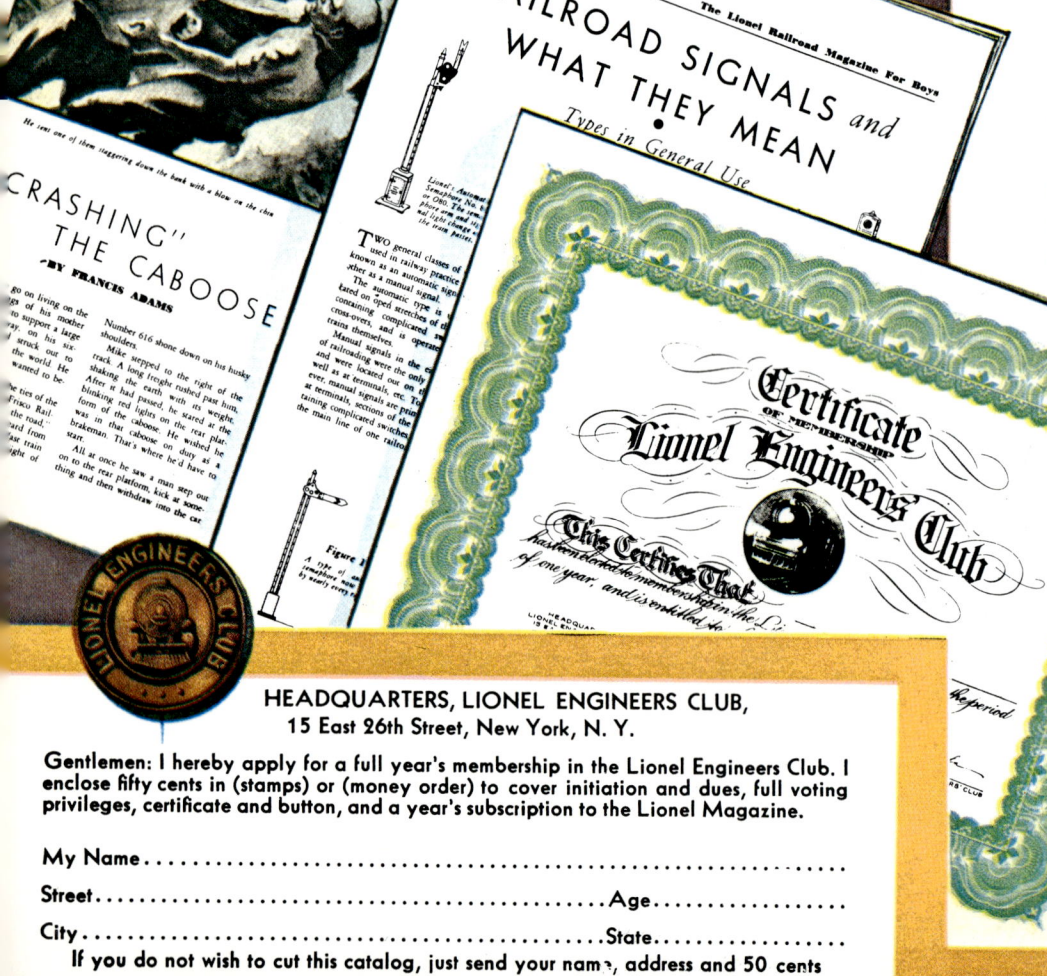

HEADQUARTERS, LIONEL ENGINEERS CLUB,
15 East 26th Street, New York, N. Y.

Gentlemen: I hereby apply for a full year's membership in the Lionel Engineers Club. I enclose fifty cents in (stamps) or (money order) to cover initiation and dues, full voting privileges, certificate and button, and a year's subscription to the Lionel Magazine.

My Name..
Street..Age............
City..State............

If you do not wish to cut this catalog, just send your name, address and 50 cents

R0163909417 bstra

625
.19
L763

LIONEL CATALOGUES
GREENBERG'S LIONEL
CATALOGUES

VOL. II 1923-32

R0163909417